American Slang

American Slang

Edited by
Robert L. Chapman, Ph.D.

Abridged edition of the *New Dictionary of American Slang*

HARPER & ROW, PUBLISHERS, New York
Cambridge, Philadelphia, San Francisco, Washington
London, Mexico City, São Paulo, Singapore, Sydney

This work is an abridgment of the *New Dictionary of American Slang,* published by Harper & Row, Publishers.

 For information address Harper & Row, Publishers, Inc., 10 East 53rd Street, New York, N.Y. 10022. Published simultaneously in Canada by Fitzhenry & Whiteside Limited, Toronto.

First PERENNIAL LIBRARY edition published 1987

Designed by Sidney Feinberg

Library of Congress Cataloging-in-Publication Data

Chapman, Robert L.
American slang.

Abridged ed. of: New dictionary of American slang. c1986.
1. English language—United States—Slang—Dictionaries.
2. English language—Slang—Dictionaries.
3. Americanisms—Dictionaries. I. Title.
PE2846.C46 1987 427'.973 87-45028
ISBN 0-06-096160-0 (pbk.)

---

89 90 91 MPC 10 9 8 7 6 5 4 3

Contents

. . . banish plump Jack, and banish all the world.

Henry IV, Part 1

Considering Language then as some mighty potentate, into the majestic audience-hall of the monarch ever enters a personage like one of Shakespere's clowns, and takes position there, and plays a part even in the stateliest ceremonies. Such is Slang, or indirection, an attempt of common humanity to escape from bald literalism, and express itself illimitably.

Walt Whitman, "Slang in America"

Preface

The editor of a new dictionary of slang owes explanations to people at large and to those who use the book. To the public he should explain *why* such a book is made and deserves to be made. To the users he must explain *how* the book was made and how to use it. Finally, to all these and to himself, he must attempt to explain *what* slang is, anyway. (For a brief working answer to this last question, the reader may look up *slang* in this dictionary; for a more considered account, see below.)

Why This Book Was Made The question will be: Why does a serious scholar devote himself to this uncouth sort of language, and why does he connive, worse yet, in foisting it on us and our innocent youth? Even though to a lexicographer that question is not very relevant, it is far from trivial. Dictionaries are popularly thought to have strong influence. They are thought to give validity and authority to their entries, and therefore to have social and moral impact. A dictionary like this, which specializes in terms not to be lightly used in polite society, is therefore thought of as teaching and advocating these terms, and hence akin to pornography.

The question may be answered in two veins, the theoretical and the historical. Theoretically, in linguistics any corpus or body of vocabulary is worth recording, and all are equally worthy. Linguistics, lexicography, is like a science in that its values have to do with accuracy, completeness, and demonstrability rather than with moral or social good. As a lexicographer I collect and record slang because it is there, and I take as much professional delight in a faithful transcript of all this nasty talk as I do in capturing and recording for our descendants the differing elegancies of standard language.

So, as a lexicographer I answer that I will collect every slang term I can get my hands on, will treat these as carefully and responsibly as I am able, and will leave their use up to others, who will have been warned against the undeliberate wielding of these powerful and provocative words. Yes, children will sneak off into corners with this book, and find the dirty words, and have dirty thoughts. If I believed that our whole culture could be made the least bit more decent, more respectful, more harmonious, happier, and mentally healthier by *not* making a slang dictionary, I might refrain. But I do not believe that and have not refrained.

This line of justification is nicely summed up in a story I heard Elie Wiesel tell: A magisterial historian was challenged with the question, "Why does a scholar like you occupy himself with a silly and contemptible subject like X?" To which the savant replied, "X is, as you say, silly and contemptible; but the *history* of X is scholarship!"

History of Slang Lexicography In historical justification, this book joins itself to an Anglo-American tradition going back just over two hundred years, and of which the high spots may be mentioned.

Credit as founder of general slang lexicography, as distinct from those who dealt in specialized lexicons, goes to the distinguished British antiquarian Francis Grose, who published *A Classical Dictionary of the Vulgar Tongue* in 1785. After two further editions, the book became the basis of an 1811 updating and expansion called *Lexicon Balatronicum: A Dictionary of Buckish Slang, University Wit, and Pickpocket Eloquence,* of about 260 pages, with nearly five thousand defined entries. A half-dozen or so earlier compilations exist from as early as the 1560s, but they deal only in the special vocabularies of thieves and tramps. Grose's book and its successor include the slang of the so-called *balatrones* —"jesters, buffoons, contemptible persons; literally, babblers," who are urban dandies or men-about-town—and of the learned humorists of and from the universities, as well as of thieves.

Grose's work held the field until 1859, when it was superseded by John C. Hotten's *A Dictionary of Modern Slang, Cant, and Vulgar Words*, which had new editions in 1860, 1864, and 1874. The attribution to Hotten is not certain, since the book was anonymous, but it is generally accepted. Henry Bradley of the *Oxford English Dictionary* judged it "a work of considerable merit" and praised its scholarly authority.

In 1887 Albert M. V. Barrere, Professor of French at the Royal Military Academy in Woolwich, published at his own expense *Argot and Slang: A New French and English Dictionary.* Two years later the Ballantyne Press brought out for subscribers only *A Dictionary of Slang, Jargon & Cant*, in two volumes totaling 956 pages. Barrere had as collaborator Charles Godfrey Leland, an American. Leland had been a Philadelphia lawyer, a journalist and editor, a three-day barricades veteran of the 1848 Revolution in Paris, on the whole a rather Hemingwayish character, and was the first American to figure prominently in general slang lexicography. He had made a particular study of British gypsies and their language, and was the first to describe Shelta, a jargon of certain Irish and Welsh gypsies. The dictionary embraces "English, American, and Anglo-Indian slang, Pidgin English, tinkers' jargon and other irregular phraseology."

One year later the first volume of John Stephen Farmer and William Ernest Henley's *Slang and Its Analogues* was published, without Henley's name on the title page. Henley let his name be used on Volume 2 in 1891 and on the subsequent five volumes through 1904. He was a poet and editor, now undervalued as a poet though popularly known for the stirring *Invictus*, set to music as a virile baritone solo and ending "I am the master of my fate; I am the captain of my soul." Contemporary brief biographies of Henley refrain from mentioning the slang dictionary, and indeed his part in it is not well understood. Farmer, probably the originator and major author, was a prodigious scholar and editor, especially of Tudor drama and other texts of that epoch. His production comes to more than twenty volumes in that field alone. He also collected and edited six volumes of songs, especially of the "merry" sort. He wrote three books on spiritualism, a late Victorian craze. More to the point here, in 1888 he published *Americanisms Old and New*, "by J. S. F.," surely written as a preliminary by-product of his work on the seven-volume slang dictionary. An American authority on our national English, Richard H. Thornton, discovered that nine-tenths of the examples in Farmer's 564-page book came from material published in 1888. This indicates very great efficiency and/or a white-hot pace of work. When the Farmer and Henley work was completed in 1904, it amounted to 2736 pages.

A less useful contribution to general slang lexicography was James Maitland's 308-page *The American Slang Dictionary* of 1891. This book is not a jewel in the tradition, perhaps for the reasons that caused an anonymous reviewer in the *Nation* to observe that most of the entries were not American and not slang, and that the philological grounding of the editor was meager indeed. The review concluded, in cruelly measured words that make any slang lexicographer cringe in a nightmare, " . . . it must be said of the present work that it not only has no reason to show for its existence, but furnishes a good many reasons to suggest the desirability of its non-existence."

After Farmer and Henley, good general slang lexicography was not resumed until 1937, when Eric Partridge brought out the first edition of his masterwork, *A Dictionary of Slang and Unconventional English,* which was updated and enlarged in seven editions and numerous reprintings by Partridge himself through 1980 and has recently been posthumously revised and published in an eighth. Eric Partridge—New Zealander, Australian, Englishman, soldier, scholar, university teacher, essayist, novelist—is the lofty star at whose work and book all other slang lexicographers must hopelessly aim. He is also, for the twentieth century, the one who made slang lexicography more or less respectable and enabled us to cease lurking behind pseudonyms or anonyms or initials, or being privately and furtively printed.

The first full-scale dictionary of American slang had to wait until 1960, when Harold Wentworth and Stuart Berg Flexner's *Dictionary of American Slang* was published by Thomas Y. Crowell (a company now incorporated into Harper & Row). Professor Wentworth had previously written an *American Dialect Dictionary*, portions of which were adapted for the slang dictionary. Mr. Flexner added thousands of slang definitions from other sources and wrote an invaluable preface, our best treatment of the sociolinguistics of slang. He also did the immense analytical work reflected in the appendix, which treats the processes of word-formation in slang with unequaled authority and exhaustiveness. Flexner was responsible for final defining and editing of all the entries in the seven-hundred-page volume, which at once became the standard work in its field. Wentworth and Flexner, as it is usually called, was enlarged and updated in 1967 and 1975 and is the basis of the present book.

These are the theoretical and historical justifications of this book, to which a practical note must be added. First, obviously the book has a primary utility for people who find slang terms in their reading, or who overhear them, and need help with their meaning. Finally, it means to serve people who just plain enjoy slang and are curious about it and where it came from.

How This Book Was Made This dictionary came into being in a five-stage process that may be quickly explained but was only slowly carried out.

1. Policies were determined and a "style manual" made that embodied these decisions on the format of the entries, their typefaces, their punctuation, the ordering of information, etc. The basic policies of the book are that it means to be a general dictionary of current American slang, rather than a collection of special vocabularies, a scholarly historical treatment, or a book with regional or other bias.
2. The Wentworth and Flexner *Dictionary of American Slang* was "recycled" and its wealth of material retained, altered, or discarded according to the new policies.
3. A corps of collectors was recruited for the accumulation of new material. At its most numerous this group consisted of fifty or more collectors, these dwindling as the years passed to an indefatigable hard core who are still submitting material as this preface is written. The collectors are listed, gratefully, after the preface.

4. The definitions were written, rewritten, and then were edited and reedited by gimlet-eyed faultfinders whose crucial work is also acknowledged, gratefully, below.
5. Computers were used throughout in many ways. Citations were stored and sorted in computers. Entries were coded and typed directly onto discs, making editing and checking more easy, fast, and reliable. And, the typesetting was computer-generated.

Working by these stages and with this copious help, and having the advantage of standing on the strong shoulders of predecessors, making a dictionary is not the momentous and Olympian task it is popularly thought to be. It is simply an affair of knowing it can be done and knowing the practical steps to take. And working and worrying.

The style and apparatus of this dictionary are explained in the section called "Guide to the Dictionary."

What Is Slang? In linguistics, where definitions at best are often imprecise and leaky, that of slang is especially notorious. The problem is one of complexity, such that a definition satisfying to one person or authority would seem inadequate to another because the prime focus is different. Like the proverbial blind men describing an elephant, all correctly, none sufficiently, we tend to stress one aspect or another of slang. My own stress will be on the individual psychology of slang speakers.

Sociolinguistic Aspects of Slang The external and quantitative aspects of slang, its sociolinguistics, have been very satisfactorily treated, nowhere more so than in Stuart Berg Flexner's masterful preface to the *Dictionary of American Slang.* Readers may also consult Eric Partridge's 1954 book *Slang To-Day and Yesterday*, in particular parts III and IV.

Updating Flexner's discussion of the social milieus from which American slang emerges would involve no real correction of his findings, but only an account of the historical shifts that twenty-five years have brought.

Recorded slang emerged, as the sketch of dictionaries has shown, from the special languages of subcultures, or perhaps we should call the more despised of them "undercultures." The group studied longest and most persistently has been the criminal underworld itself, including the prison population, whose "cant" or "argot" still provides a respectable number of unrespectable terms. Other undercultures contributing heavily are those of hoboes, of gypsies, of soldiers and sailors, of the police, of narcotics users, of gamblers, of cowboys, of all sorts of students, of show-business workers, of jazz musicians and devotees, of athletes and their fans, of railroad and other transportation workers, and of immigrant or ethnic populations cutting across these other subcultures.

In the 1980s, we must note that some of these traditional spawning grounds for slang have lost their productivity, and that other subcultures have emerged to replace them. For example, general adoption of terms from hoboes, from railroad workers, from gypsies, and from cowboys has very nearly ceased, although the contributions of all these persist in the substrata of current slang. Criminals and police (cops and robbers) still make their often identical contributions, and gamblers continue to give us zesty coinages. Teenagers and students can still be counted on for innovation and effrontery. Show business workers, although they have largely shed the raffish image of their roving and carnival past, are still a fertile source of slang. But several centers of gravity have shifted greatly during the past fifty or so years, as reflected in the entries of this book.

For example, the adoption of military, naval, and merchant marine slang has slowed to a relative trickle, not surprisingly. World Wars 1 and 2 probably gave us more general slang than any other events in history but they are now history, and the Korean and Vietnam wars have had in comparison a meager effect. Railroad slang has been replaced, though on a lesser scale, by the usage of airline workers and truck drivers. The jazz world, formerly so richly involved with drug use, prostitution, booze, and gutter life, is no longer so contributory, nor has rock and roll quite made up the loss, but taken as a whole, popular music —rock, blues, funk, rap, reggae, etc.—are making inroads.

Terms from "the drug scene" have multiplied astronomically, and a specialized book this size could easily be made from them alone. The "counterculture" helped disseminate many drug terms that might otherwise have remained part of a special vocabulary. Sports also make a much larger contribution, with football and even basketball not challenging but beginning to match baseball as prime producers. Among the immigrant-ethnic bestowals, the influx from Yiddish continues strong in spite of the sociological shifting of the Jewish population. The old Dutch and German sources have dried up. The Italian carries on in modest proportion. The Hispanic has been surprisingly uninfluential, although a heavier contribution is surely predictable. All these are far outstripped by increased borrowing from black America, and this from the urban ghetto rather than the old Southern heartland. Close analysis would probably show that, what with the prominence of black people in the armed forces, in music, in the entertainment world, and in street and ghetto life, the black influence on American slang has been more pervasive in recent times than that of any other ethnic group in history. This can be conjectured, of course, without any implication that black Americans constitute a homogeneous culture.

Some sources of the slang in this book will be entirely or relatively new. Examples of this are the computer milieu and the hospital-medical-nursing complex. In the first case an exciting technological inundation is at the base, and in the other, as in so many other trends of our era, the reason is television.

In the matter of sex, our period has witnessed a great increase in the number of terms taken over from homosexuals, expecially male homosexuals. And it would be wrong to restrict the range of their contribution to sex terms alone, since the gay population merges with so many others that are educated, witty, observant, acerbic, and modish.

The "growth sector" hardest to characterize just now is in linear descent from the people old Captain Francis Grose, and Ben Jonson and others before him, called "university wits." Today, trying to mark off this most fecund assemblage, I need a clumsy compound like "the Washington-Los Angeles-Houston-Wall Street-Madison Avenue nexus." Our culture occupies these centers, and they occupy the culture through pervasive and unifying communications media. They give us the slang of the brass, of the execs, of middle management, of dwellers in bureaucracies, of yuppies, and of the talk shows and the "people" sort of columns and magazines. Bright, expressive, sophisticated people, moving and prospering with our lively popular culture, and not entirely buying it. They are the trend-setters and source of the slang that seems to come from everywhere and not to be susceptible of labeling. We will need more historical perspective before we can be usefully analytic about them, but they, whoever they are, clearly make up the wave of the present.

This new emphasis in the fortunes of American slang, by the way, points to one of its important distinctions, that between what I call "primary" and "secondary" slang. Primary slang is the pristine speech of subculture members, so very natural to its speakers that it seems they might be mute without it. Of course they would not be, since we know that slang is by definition always an alternative idiom, to be chosen rather than required. Much of teenage talk, and the speech of urban street gangs, would be examples of primary slang. Secondary slang is chosen not so much to fix one in a group as to express one's attitudes and resourcefulness by *pretending*, momentarily, in a little shtick of personal guerilla theater, to be a member of a street gang, or a criminal, or a gambler, or a drug user, or a professional football player, and so forth—and hence to express one's contempt, superiority, and cleverness by borrowing someone else's verbal dress. Secondary slang is a matter of stylistic choice rather than true identification. The increasing currency of the "Washington-Los Angeles-Houston, etc.," sort of slang may mean that in the future secondary or acquired slang will be our major variety. That is, the old disreputable groups will blend gradually into the mass, and slang will become more a matter of individual wit and self-advertisement, with its sources no more apparent than those of, say, a dirty joke. In fact it may be conjectured that even now the strong influence of black slang and gay slang has less to do with those subcultures per se than with the fact that both put a very high premium on verbal skill. Blacks, for example, are particularly given to rhyme and other prosodic features that seem to be increasingly prominent in slang.

Individual Psychology of Slang Obviously an individual in one of the groups or subcultures mentioned above, or any of many others, resorts to slang as a means of attesting membership in the group and of dividing him- or herself off from the mainstream culture. He or she merges both verbally and psychologically into the subculture that preens itself on being different from, in conflict with, and superior to the mainstream culture, and in particular to its assured rectitude and its pomp. Slang is thus an act of bracketing a smaller social group that can be comfortably joined and understood and be a shelter for the self. It is simultaneously an act of featuring and obtruding the self within the subculture—by cleverness, by control, by up-to-dateness, by insolence, by virtuosities of audacious and usually satirical wit, by aggression (phallic, if you wish). All this happens at fairly shallow levels in the psyche and can be readily understood. It explains most of what we know and feel about slang.

But what explains "it"? If, as the authorities agree, slang is a universal human trait and as old as the race itself, and if it came into being in the same human society where language itself was born, can we not seek deeper and more generalized explanations? Authorities also agree, as it happens, that the roots of slang must be sought in the deepest parts of the mind, in the unconscious itself. Although that territory is perilous ground for a working lexicographer, a few conjectures and a few relationships can be proposed for consideration.

It seems to me that the deeper psychodynamics of slang have to do with two things: (1) defense of the ego against the superego, and (2) our simultaneous eagerness and reluctance to be human.

Surely wounded egos are the most common human nonanatomic possession. Slang might be seen as a remedy for them, as a self-administered therapy old as the first family that spoke. The family, like society, entails a hierarchy of power and of right, against which the healthy growing self of the child needs measures to compensate for its weakness and sinfulness. Slang as a remedy denies the weakness and brags about the sinfulness.

In this view, it would not be too much to claim that therapeutic slang is necessary for the development of the self; that society would be impossible without slang. It is curious that a linguistic phenomenon that seems so fleeting and so frivolous, as slang undeniably does, should at the same time be so deep and so vital to human growth and order. This is only one of the paradoxes of slang.

This aspect of slang is "deeper" than the matters mentioned above, like group identification and so on, only because it existed before groups, and it persists as groups themselves chop and change in the flux of history. In this aspect slang is similar to, and perhaps the same as, profanity. Like profanity slang is a surrogate for destructive physical action. Freud once remarked that the founder of civilization was the first man who hurled a curse rather than a rock or spear at his enemy. Slang also has this usefulness, and I suspect that profanity is a subcategory of slang, the more elemental phenomenon.

Hence, slang is language that has little to do with the main aim of language, the connection of sounds with ideas in order to communicate ideas, but is rather an attitude, a feeling, and an act. To pose another paradox: Slang is the most nonlinguistic sort of language.

"Our simultaneous eagerness and reluctance to be human"—what can that have to do with slang? My notion here is that when you try to consider it deeply slang seems to join itself with several other phenomena: with Freud's "dream-work," with comedy, with elements of myth.

It seems to me that slang (I mean the slang impulse of the psyche) shares with all these the salvational and therapeutic function of both divorcing us from and maintaining our connection with genetic animality. Dream-work relieves us of the need to be reasonable and discharges the tension of the great burden with which our angelic rationality charges us. Although we are uncomfortable with paradox in ordinary language, we easily tolerate it in slang, where it seems as much at home as it is in the study of logic.

Slang links itself with comedy in the respect that it exploits and even celebrates human weakness, animality, without working to extirpate it. It makes room for our vileness, but only so much room. The great comic figures of our culture usually come in pairs, each member having its legitimacy, and each limiting the other: Sancho Panza and Don Quixote; Falstaff and Prince Hal; Huck Finn and who?—Tom Sawyer, Aunt Polly, even Jim. To these we may add the Wife of Bath, whose counterfigure was a part of herself, making her more like most of us than Sancho or Falstaff or Huck are. We may add, without too much strain, the comic figure Dante Alighieri over against Beatrice and the lightweight devil Mephistopheles over against Faust. What we seem to have in the comic heroes and in our own slang impulse is a reaching for or clinging to the primal earth, a *nostalgie de la boue*, which helps make tolerable the hard aspiration to be civilized and decent.

As to myth, Sancho, Alice of Bath, and Falstaff are modern myths themselves. For ancient myth we might think of Antaeus, whose strength was valid only while he had his feet on the earth, and of Silenus and the satyrs, and even of the Devil himself, who must, when he is not quoting scripture, speak a great deal of slang. We may also attend to the intriguing "trickster" figure who is so prevalent in world mythology. C. G. Jung reminds me of the slang impulse when he asserts, for example, ". . . [the trickster's] fondness for sly jokes and malicious pranks, his powers as a shape-shifter, his dual nature, half animal, half divine, his exposure to all kinds of tortures, and—last but not least—his approximation to the figure of a saviour." In the same essay, "On the Psychology of the Trickster-Figure," Jung relates the trickster to the medieval Feast of Fools and other manifestations of the comic and slang spirit, especially those that deflate pomp, that prick presumption, that trip up our high horses. Jung believed that the civilizing process began within the framework of the trickster myth, which is a race memory of the human achievement of self-consciousness.

As the literary scholar Wylie Sypher said, "... man is not man without being somehow uneasy about the 'nastiness' of his body, [and] obscenity... is a threshold over which man enters into the human condition." For *obscenity* we might read *slang*, and observe that we are not so far beyond the threshold that we cannot always reach it with our foot, which is of clay.

Slang is also the idiom of the life force. That is, it has roots somewhere near those of sexuality, and it regularly defies death. What I have in mind is partly the "dirty" and taboo constituent of slang, but even more its tendency to kid about being hanged, electrocuted, murdered, or otherwise annihilated. Gallows humor is, from this point of view, more central to slang than may have been thought.

One changing pattern that has obvious connections with both socio- and psycholinguistics is the relation of slang to gender. In these times, and partly because of the feminist movement, women are more and more using the taboo and vulgar slang formerly accounted a male preserve. Sociologically this shows the determination of some women to enter the power structure by taking on this badge, among others, that denotes "maleness," and simultaneously to shed the restrictions of the "ladylike" persona. Psychologically the implications are not that clear, but it may be that some women are determined to replicate at the core of their psyches the aggressive and ordering nature we have usually identified as a part of profound maleness, or else to show that these masculine traits do not lie as deep as we thought.

Apologies Our aim has been to make a dictionary of current general American slang, but even a cursory look will show that we have retained from the *Dictionary of American Slang* many entries that are only dubiously current and not very general. We have done so for two reasons: (1) we felt that these would be helpful to readers baffled by slang found in earlier writings or writings that use earlier slang, and (2) some of these obsolete terms are aids in understanding the derivation of current terms.

In the absence of a litmus test for slang and nonslang we must ask some indulgence. Slang shares misty boundaries with a relaxed register usually called "informal" or "colloquial," and we have inevitably strayed across the boundary. Eric Partridge spared himself the embarrassment of this apology by calling his book the dictionary of "slang and unconventional English." This book should probably have the same title.

Slang also shares a boundary with a stylistic register we might call "figurative idiom," in which inventive and poetic terms, especially metaphors, are used for novelty and spice, and incidentally for self-advertisement and cheekiness, in relief of a standard language that is accurate and clear but not personal and kinetic.

Here again we beg the indulgence of those who disagree with our choices, as we would hope to be indulgent of theirs.

We are interested in getting the book right, and would be grateful for corrections and suggestions. These can be addressed to the publisher.

ROBERT L. CHAPMAN
May 1986

Acknowledgments

Grateful acknowledgment is made to the following collectors, who have provided material for the book.

Palmer Price (Mrs. William Carl) Clark of Fairfax, Virginia
Bernard Kane of Ridley Park, Pennsylvania
Joseph Oleszycki of Philadelphia, Pennsylvania

Bernard Arkules of Scottsdale, Arizona
Jean Billman of Macon, Georgia
Brian A. Court of Vandalia, Ohio
Kendra Crossen of Somerville, Massachusetts
Porter J. Crow of West Palm Beach, Florida
Julie Downs of North Bend, Oregon
Maria Erskine of Pickering, Ontario, Canada
Elizabeth Glick of Whittier, California
Jeanne Goessling of Evanston, Illinois
William J. Griffin of Nashville, Tennessee
Paul Kocak of Dover, New Jersey
Stanley L. Korwin of San Francisco, California
Esther Lafair of Philadelphia, Pennsylvania
Virginia Langlois of Rutland, Vermont
Arlene Larson of Casper, Wyoming
Joyce Mahan of Tuscaloosa, Alabama
Altha Patten of Linden, New Jersey
Robert F. Perkins of Fort Atkinson, Wisconsin
Jane Sarnoff of New York, New York

John Shunny of Albuquerque, New Mexico
Judy Tucker of Elkins Park, Pennsylvania

Leslie R. Axelrod of Highland Park, Illinois
Dorothy M. Barrett of Elyria, Ohio
Nancy Burkhalter of Columbus, Ohio
John Campbell of Columbus, Georgia
Jane Closson of Winnemucca, Nevada
Jane Coil Cole of Madison, New Jersey
Keith Denning of Brooklyn, New York
David De Witt of Glenview, Illinois
Marjorie Glazer of Worcester, Massachusetts
Barry Goldstein of Newton Centre, Massachusetts
Stanley Gutin of Wilkes-Barre, Pennsylvania
Batya Harlow of Leonia, New Jersey
David L. Kent of Austin, Texas
Ruth McGrew of St. Paul, Minnesota
John T. Metcalf of Lake Forest, Illinois
Katherine Noordsij of Madison, New Jersey
Angela Palmisono of Ridgefield, New Jersey
Dorothy Powell of Huntington Beach, California
Lawrence C. Scholz of West Orange, New Jersey
Michael Silvia of Acushnet, Massachusetts
Betti Slack of Boulder, Colorado
Susan Welch of Highland Park, New Jersey
Laura Winters of Totowa, New Jersey

Additional acknowledgment is gratefully made to those below for particular help and advice:

Robert S. Claiborne of New York City for collegial and very sage counsel and miscellaneous contributions
Captain Jack Gill for Army terms
Captain Jack B. Moser of Orlando for airline terms
Norman Roberts of Pearl City, Hawaii, for Hawaiian slang
Eva Witte

And, finally, we acknowledge the important contribution of the group of people at Harper & Row who made this dictionary and its parent book, the *New Dictionary of American Slang,* possible: Carol Cohen, Editorial Director, trade reference division; Helen Moore, Editor; Susan Randol, Assistant Editor; Paul

Heacock, Editor; Scott Prentzas, Editorial Assistant; Eric Wirth, Production Editor; Roz Barrow, Director of Production; Coral Tysliava, Managing Editor; Lucy Adelman O'Brien, Associate Editor; Gail Gavert, Assistant Editor; Beena Kamlani, Assistant Editor; Jean Palmer, Debby Carpenter, and Portia Levine, word processors; Brenda Woodward and Bernie Borok, proofreaders.

Guide to the Dictionary

The editors have tried to make the apparatus of this book clear and self-explanatory, but a few guidelines may help the reader. These are given more or less in the order of the elements in the definition block itself.

The Main Entry The main entry sometimes contains portions that do not appear in boldface and are not taken into account in alphabetization. These include the articles *a, an,* and *the,* when they appear at the beginning of an entry, and the variable pronoun in a phrase, indicated by *someone, someone's, something, one's,* etc. Variant forms following *or* and variants found within parentheses appear in boldface but do not affect alphabetization.

Impact Symbols Main entries considered to have strong social or emotional impact are indicated by delta symbols bracketing the entry itself or the separate definition numbers if the impact symbol does not apply to all senses of the term. The symbols are assigned on a two-level principle, corresponding to what have usually been called "taboo" and "vulgar" levels. Taboo terms are *never* to be used, and vulgar terms are to be used only when one is aware of and desires their strong effect. In this book terms of contempt and derision for racial or other groups have been included among the taboo terms.

Terms of strongest impact are marked with the symbols ◀ ▶ and those of lesser impact with the symbols ◁ ▷. The assignment of these is a matter of editorial judgment, and not everyone will agree with us. In some places it was difficult to assign impact symbols to terms that are acceptable within a group but are considered offensive when used by those outside the group. We have taken account of recent changes in the currency and acceptability of terms previously unspeakable, and some may feel we have gone too far with the trend.

Pronunciations Words are respelled for pronunciation only when "normal" pronunciation cannot be readily ascertained or when pronunciation is crucial to the meaning of the term. The system of respelling is designedly very simple, depending on what we regard as a majority pronunciation of the respelled syllable and showing stressed syllables in capital letters.

Part-of-Speech Labels Parts of speech and a few other grammatical particulars are indicated by rather self-explanatory abbreviations or labels:

n	noun
v	verb
pron	pronoun
adj	adjective
adv	adverb
affirmation	
negation	
conj	conjunction
prep	preposition
interj	interjection
modifier	
infix	
phr	phrase
sentence	
pres part	present participle
past part	past participle
prefix	
suffix	
combining form	
combining word	

Variant Forms Variation is shown in three ways:

1. In the main entry itself, up to three variants are shown, separated by *or*.
2. Where there are more than three variants, or they apply to various parts of the main entry, they are shown in parentheses with the label *Variations*.
3. Where variant forms apply to particular numbered definitions, this is shown by printing the form or forms at the beginning of the numbered sense, introduced by *also*.

Dating Labels Even though this is not meant to be a full-fledged historical dictionary, the time of origin and/or special currency of the terms is shown by a dating phrase. These usually designate the early, middle, or late part of a century, or in more recent times they indicate decades of origin when known. All labels are based upon evidence found in published scholarship or lexicography, and most are of course subject to correction where better evidence is found.

When an entry does not carry a dating label, the inference is either that the date was undiscoverable or that the term is relatively recent and would have to be labeled *1970s* or *1980s.*

Provenience Labels When the social group or milieu from which a term emerged is known, it is indicated by a labeling that is often intermixed with the dating labels; for example, *fr late 1800s cowboys,* or *esp 1960s teenagers.* Two abbreviations are used in provenience labels: *fr* for *from* and *esp* for *especially.* Some attempt at precision has been made in these labels, but they are regrettably sometimes rather vague and general. Nevertheless, no label has been applied without evidence.

Definitions Definitions were written in what most users will accept as a normal form. A few explanations need to be made, however:

1. The usual distinction between transitive and intransitive verbs has not been used, in the belief that the definitions and the examples will make that distinction clear when useful.
2. After the label *sentence,* another sentence has been provided that translates the main entry sentence.
3. Interjections, prefixes and suffixes, and combining forms and words have been explained "objectively," with no attempt made to provide a strictly substitutable version of the form.
4. When a word is defined in one part of speech but is often used in others, it may be "defined by example" in this book. The most common case is the one where a noun is often used as an attributive modifier, which in this book is shown by the label *modifier* followed by a colon and by an example of the use. Definitions by example apply strictly only to part-of-speech shifts from the definition immediately preceding them.
5. Definitions are not always given in chronological order, even when that is known. The order is rather a logical-semantic one that attempts to show how senses have grown from previous senses. Sometimes the order can hardly be anything but arbitrary.

Slang Synonyms Often slang synonyms will be provided at the ends of definitions, after an equal sign. This is meant to be an aid in definition rather than a serious comprehensive collection of synonyms.

Slang synonyms are also used as quick definitions when a full definition is given elsewhere, at a synonymous entry, usually at a more current or frequently used or interesting term. Slang synonyms are not used as cross-references to variant terms, although sometimes this distinction may not be a sharp one.

Editorial Notes When certain information seems useful but does not fit into the normal format of the definition block, it is included as an editorial note. These are introduced by a large black dot.

Examples In this book usage examples are given either when they have been collected from the media or when an invented example seems to help in definition or in showing context and structure. Examples thus have a double function: to illustrate usage and to validate usage and the inclusion of the term.

Examples are attributed to authors, especially when these are well known; when newspapers or magazines are cited, authors are generally not named, even though the articles may have had bylines. Attributions are to be taken essentially as evidence that the material quoted did in fact appear in the place or under the name cited. They are not, of course, to be taken as characterizing the typical style of the source.

Derivations Derivations are given in square brackets at the end of the definition block proper, before the cross-references.

Slang etymology is less certain and precise than standard etymology, for two chief reasons: (1) because of the moral and social dubiousness of slang, relatively little of it was printed over the centuries, yielding less evidence than one needs; and (2) it is an etymology of meaning rather than form, and semantic connections are seldom as public, positive, and knowable as are formal relations. Hence slang etymology must be to an uncomfortable degree a matter of assessing probabilities.

Derivations are not given here when they are deemed to be obvious. When they are accepted and demonstrable, they are stated as fact. When probability, or even possibility, proposes them, they are stated tentatively. The ruling criterion has been common sense and occasionally another sense that in German is called *Sprachgefühl,* a sort of personal linguistic intuition.

In cases where a derivation seems patently necessary, but none can be discovered or surmised, the notation *origin unknown* is used. This must not be taken absolutely, but only to mean that the derivation is not now known to the editor.

A part of the fun of making a slang dictionary is the exercise of ingenuity and insight for derivations, especially those that have not apparently been proposed before. The editor does not apologize for his attempts, although he asks to be enlightened if ignorant and corrected if perverse.

Cross-References An extraordinary attempt has been made to help the user find the term in question by cross-referencing nearly every important term in every phrase (prepositions, particles, articles, and the like are, of course, not cross-referenced). Since this book defines a very great number of phrasal entries, much space has been given to this purpose, and we hope these merely utilitarian features will not get in the way.

A

A *narcotics* **1** *n* Amphetamine **2** *n* LSD; =ACID

abbot *n narcotics* Nembutal (a trade name), a barbiturate; =DOWNER [fr the name of the pharmaceutical company that produces it]

A-bomb **1** *n* An atomic bomb **2** *n hot rodders* A car especially modified for quick acceleration and speed; =HOT ROD **3** *n narcotics* A combination of drugs, typically marijuana plus opium

abortion *n* Something of very poor quality; a messy failure: *That show is a real abortion*

above one's **head** *See* IN OVER one's HEAD

academy *See* LAUGHING ACADEMY

Acapulco gold *n phr narcotics* Marijuana of high quality grown near Acapulco, Mexico, and having leaves with a golden hue

account *See* NO-ACCOUNT

accounting *See* CREATIVE ACCOUNTING

AC-DC (Variations: **AC/DC** or **ac-dc** or **ac/dc**) **1** *adj* Practicing both heterosexual and homosexual sex; bisexual **2** *adv: I think she does it AC-DC* [fr the abbreviations for the two types of electrical current, alternating and direct; an appliance that can operate with either type is marked *AC-DC*]

ace **1** *n* A person of extraordinary skill, usu in a specified activity: *poker ace/ the ace of headwaiters* **2** *modifier: an ace mechanic/ the ace professor* **3** *adv: He did it ace every time*—Richard Merkin **4** *n fr WW1* A combat pilot who has shot down five or more enemy aircraft **5** *n* An unusually pleasant, generous, and decent person, esp a male; =PRINCE **6** *n black & street gang* A very close friend; =BUDDY, PAL **7** *n black* A man who favors flamboyant, up-to-the-minute dress; =DUDE **8** *n narcotics* A marijuana cigarette; =JOINT **9** *n* A dollar bill **10** *n golf* A hole scored in one stroke **11** *n racquet games* An unreturnable serve that scores a quick point **12** *v sports* To score by an ace: *He aced the fifth hole/ She aced him six times in one set* **13** *v* (also **ace out**) *college students* To make a perfect or nearly perfect score: *Ace the test and you go on to the next subject*—Flying **14** *n restaurant* A table for one; also, a single customer [fr the name of the unitary playing card] *See* CASE ACE, CHINESE ACE, COME WITHIN AN ACE, COOL AS A CHRISTIAN WITH ACES WIRED

◁ **ace boon coon** ▷ or **ace boon** or **ace buddy** *n phr black* A very good friend; best friend

ace-high *adj* Of the best; first rate: *His reputation is ace-high*

ace in the hole *n phr* Something held privately in reserve until needed, esp for a winning stroke; a hidden reserve or advantage [fr poker term *in the hole* for a card dealt face down in a stud game]

ace out *See* ACE

aces wired *See* COOL AS A CHRISTIAN WITH ACES WIRED

ace up one's **sleeve** *n phr* A hidden advantage, esp a tricky one [fr a common technique of magicians and cardsharps]

acid *narcotics* **1** *n* The hallucinogen LSD, which is chemically an acid; =A **2** *modifier: an acid party*

See AUGUSTUS OWSLEY, BATTERY ACID

acid freak or **acidhead** *n phr* or *n narcotics* A person who uses LSD, esp one who uses the drug heavily or habitually: *He has suggested that some of our recent Presidents were acidheads*—Saul Bellow

acid pad *n phr narcotics* A place, esp someone's home or apartment, where LSD is taken

acid rock **1** *n phr* A form of very loud rock music featuring electronic sound effects and often accompanied by stroboscopic and other extraordinary lighting to suggest the hallucinatory impact of LSD **2** *modifier: an acid rock disk/ acid-rock guitar*

across the board **1** *adj phr horse-racing* Designating a bet in which the same amount of money is wagered on the horse to win, place, or show **2** *adv phr: $2 across the board on Duck Giggle in the fifth* **3** *adj phr* Designating an equal alteration to each member of a related set, esp an equal raising or lowering of related wages or salaries: *They got an across-the-board increase of 80 cents an hour* **4** *adv phr: The fees were lowered across the board* [fr the *totalizator board* that shows the odds at horse-racing tracks]

act **1** *n* A display of pretended feeling; an affected pretense: *His elaborate grief was just an act* **2** *n* A dramatic mimicking; =SHTICK, TAKE-OFF: *You oughta see my Brando act*

See a CLASS ACT, CLEAN UP one's ACT, DO THE DUTCH, GO INTO one's ACT, SISTER ACT

action **1** *n* Gambling activity; a crap game or other game of chance: *Most people now go to Atlantic City for the action* **2** *n* Activity or entertainment: *looking for the local action* **3** *n* The, or a, sex act: *He was ogling the girls, looking for a little action*

See a PIECE OF THE ACTION, WHERE THE ACTION IS

◁ **act like** one's **shit doesn't stink**▷ *v phr* To behave with self-assured haughtiness; show a sense of superiority

actor *n sports* An athlete who is good at pretending he has been hurt or fouled; esp, a baseball player who very convincingly mimes the pain of being hit by a pitch

Ada from Decatur *See* EIGHTER FROM DECATUR

Adam *See* NOT KNOW someone FROM ADAM

add one's **two cents in** *See* PUT one's TWO CENTS IN

ad lib **1** *v phr* To speak, play, dance, or otherwise perform a passage not in one's prescribed plan, often with an original and spontaneous effect: *The Senator ad libbed for ten minutes waiting for the President to show* **2** *n phr* A passage or comment, etc, given spontaneously: *He forgot his lines and did a stupid ad lib* **3** *modifier: an ad-lib gag/ a quick ad-lib put-down* **4** *adv: They danced ad lib until the conductor found his place again* [fr Latin *ad libitum* "as one wishes"]

advantage *See* HOME-COURT ADVANTAGE

Afro **1** *n* A hair style worn by many blacks and some whites, usu with an exaggerated bouffant style of tightly curled hair **2** *n* A black person **3** *modifier: an Afro social club*

◁ **Afro-Saxon**▷ *n black* A black person who has assumed the behavior and values of the dominant white society; =OREO, TOM

against the wall *See* UP AGAINST THE WALL

age out *v phr narcotics* To reach an age, usu in the 30s or 40s, when drugs no longer have the desired effect, whereupon the user gradually withdraws from them voluntarily

ager *See* GOLDEN-AGER

a-go-go *esp 1960s & 70s* **1** *n* A discotheque or other venue for rock-and-roll dancing **2** *modifier: a couple of a-go-go patrons/ a-go-go music* **3** *adj* Rapid and dizzying tempo: *our crazy a-go-go pace of life* **4** *adj* In the newest style; faddish; = TRENDY: *his a-go-go opinions about sexual freedom* [fr French *à gogo* "galore," used in the name of a Parisian club, *Whisky à Gogo*]

See GO-GO

ah *See* OOH AND AH

ahead *See* STRAIGHT-AHEAD

ahead of the game *adv phr* In a winning or advantageous position: *Hard as I try, I can't seem to get ahead of the game*

-aholic *suffix used to form nouns and adjectives* Addicted to and over-engaging in what is indicated: *fuckaholic/ sleepaholic/ workaholic*

something or someone **ain't** ***negation*** Something or someone emphatically is not • Said as a wry and intensive negator in a comparative statement: *Well, she sings OK, but Joan Sutherland she ain't* [perhaps fr a Yiddish syntactic pattern]

air ***See*** a BEAR IN THE AIR, DANCE ON AIR, FLOATING ON AIR, FULL OF HOT AIR, GET THE AIR, GIVE someone THE AIR, GO UP IN THE AIR, GRAB A HANDFUL OF AIR, HOT AIR, SUCK AIR, UP IN THE AIR

air one's **dirty linen** ***See*** WASH one's DIRTY LINEN

airhead or **airbrain** ***n*** A stupid or silly person; vapid nincompoop; = BUBBLEHEAD, DITZ: *The steel-bellied airheads were in Lonnie's suite*—Dan Jenkins

airheaded or **airbrained** ***adj*** Stupid; silly; vapid; = BUBBLEHEADED, DITZY: *the delightfully airbrained Mickie*—Village Voice

airs ***See*** PUT ON AIRS

aisles ***See*** LAY THEM IN THE AISLES

◁**AK** or **ak**▷ (pronounced as separate letters) **1** ***n*** = ALTER KOCKER **2** ***n*** = ASS-KISSER

aka (pronounced as separate letters) ***prep phr*** Also known as; alias: *He's an asshole, aka a big deal*

Alibi Ike ***n phr*** A person who habitually offers plausible explanations for dubious actions

alike ***See*** LOOK-ALIKE

alky or **alki** (AL kee) **1** ***n*** Alcohol **2** ***n*** *esp 1920s* Inferior or bootleg whiskey **3** ***n*** A chronic alcoholic, esp one who is a homeless drifter or street denizen; = BUM

all bases ***See*** TOUCH ALL BASES

all by one's **lonesome** ***adv phr*** Alone; solo: *She did it all by her lonesome*

all ears ***adj phr*** Very eager to hear; keenly attentive: *Something juicy's coming, and they're all ears*

Alley ***See*** TIN PAN ALLEY

alley cat **1** ***n phr*** A homeless cat; stray cat **2** ***n phr*** A sexually promiscuous person, esp a woman

all get out or **all get up** ***n phr*** *fr late 1800s* The extreme or absolute case of what is indicated: *overwhelmingly white, and affluent as all get-out*—Ebony

all hell broke loose ***sentence*** Things became very turbulent, dangerous, noisy, etc: *All Hell Breaking Loose*—Time

alligator **1** ***n*** *black* An assertively masculine, flashily dressed, and up-to-the-minute male; = DUDE, SPORT **2** ***n*** *esp 1930s jive talk* An active devotee of swing and jive music, dancing, and speech • The salutation "See you later, alligator" was commonly heard **3** ***n*** *black jazz musicians* A white jazz musician or jazz enthusiast

alligators ***See*** UP TO one's ASS IN something

all in ***adj phr*** *fr early 1900s* Tired; exhausted; = BEAT, POOPED

all in one piece or **in one piece** ***adv phr*** Intact; unharmed: *brought us kids through it all in one piece*—Playboy/ *She came out of it in one piece*

all-originals scene ***n phr*** *black* An occasion where only blacks are present: *I dig you holding this all-originals scene at the track*—Malcolm X

all-out **1** ***adj*** Holding nothing back; sparing nothing: *an all-out effort* **2** ***adv:*** *He ran all-out for ten minutes*

all over ***See*** HAVE IT ALL OVER someone or something

all over someone **1** ***adj phr*** Very affectionate; eagerly amorous: *The wife went to get some popcorn and the husband was all over me*—Playgirl **2** ***adj phr*** Aggressively smothering or battering; assaulting: *They broke through the line and were all over the quarterback*

all over the lot (or **the ballpark**) ***adv phr*** Very unfocused and inconsistent; confused: *His answers are all over the lot/ But otherwise...you were all over the ballpark*—Philadelphia

all-pro ***adj*** Of first quality; blue-ribbon; stellar: *an all-pro team of Washington super-lobbyists*—Washingtonian [fr the annual designation of professional football players to the putative team of the best]

all reet (or **reat** or **root**) ***interj*** *esp 1930s jive talk* An exclamation of approval: *"All reat"... is the rug-cutters' way of saying "all right"*—New Yorker

all (or **aw**) **right** (aw RĪT) ***interj*** An exclamation of strong approval, esp of something well done or successful; = WAY TO GO

all-right *adj* Good; commendable; of the proper sort: *all-right guys trying to make a living*—James M Cain

all right already *interj* A comment protesting that one has heard or had enough or a bit too much [fr Yiddish idiom patterns, and translating Yiddish *genuk shoyn*]

all righty *affirmation* (Variations: **rightie** or **rightee** or **rightey** may replace **righty**) A humorous or deliberately cute and childish way of saying "all right"

all she wrote *See* THAT'S ALL SHE WROTE

all shook up or **all shook** *See* SHOOK UP

all one's **switches** *See* NOT HAVE ALL one's SWITCHES ON

all that jazz *n phr* Other such things; etcetera: *baseball, apple pie, Chevrolet, and all that jazz*

all that meat and no potatoes *interj* An exclamation of pleasure and appreciation, by a man, on seeing a well-built woman ● Has the sense of a wolf-whistle; regarded by many women as offensive

all the answers *See* KNOW ALL THE ANSWERS

all the moves *See* HAVE ALL THE MOVES

all there *adj phr* Intelligent; =TOGETHER: *At least Prudence is all there*
See NOT ALL THERE

all the way *adv phr* Without reservation; to the end: *I'll back her all the way*
See GO ALL THE WAY

all thumbs *adj phr* Very awkward; inept: *I'm all thumbs when it comes to drawing*

all together *See* GET IT TOGETHER, HAVE IT ALL TOGETHER

all to hell *See* EXCUSE ME ALL TO HELL, PARDON ME ALL TO HELL

all washed up *See* WASHED UP

all wet *adj phr fr 1920s* Incorrect; wrong: *Your idea is all wet, I'm afraid*

along for the ride *See* GO ALONG FOR THE RIDE

Alps *See* JEWISH ALPS

already **1** *adv* Without further ado; such being the case: *Let's go already* **2** *adv* Right now; at once: *Shut up already* **3** *adv* Very specifically; precisely: *Drop dead already* ● Used chiefly for a humorous exasperated effect and to suggest Yiddish speech patterns

also-ran *n* A person, competitive product, etc, that does not succeed; a person of mediocre talents; =LOSER [fr the term for a race-horse who runs fourth or worse]

◁ **alter kocker** (or **cocker**)▷ (AL tə KAH kər) *n phr* An old man, esp a disgusting and querulous one; =AK: *You young bloods have got it all over us alter cockers*—Bernard Malamud [fr the Yiddish, literally "old shitter"]

the **altogether** *See* IN THE ALTOGETHER

alum (ə LUM) *n* An alumnus or alumna

ambish (am BISH) *n esp theater* Ambition; aggressiveness

ambulance chaser **1** *n phr fr late 1800s* Any unethical lawyer, or one who is too aggressive in getting clients; =SHYSTER **2** *n phr fr early 1900s* A lawyer or lawyer's helper who urges accident victims to sue for damages, negligence, etc

ammo (AM oh) **1** *n fr around 1930* Ammunition: *The platoon is out of ammo* **2** *modifier: The fat ammo barge rocked up and down*—This Week **3** *n* Information and other material that may be used in a debate, campaign, exposé, etc: *Your shabby personal life gives lots of ammo to the opposition*

amp **1** *n* An audio amplifier, esp one used for electronic musical instruments **2** *n narcotics* An ampoule of a narcotic

amscray *v* To leave at once; =BEAT IT, SCRAM [pig Latin for *scram*]

◁ **Amy-John**▷ *n homosexuals* A lesbian, esp one who plays the dominant role; =BUTCH, DIESEL DYKE [origin uncertain; perhaps fr French *ami Jean* "friend John," or fr a corruption of *Amazon* "female warrior"]

anchor man **1** *n phr college students fr 1920s* The student having the lowest academic standing in the class **2** *n phr* (also **anchor**, **anchor person**) A television news broadcaster who has the principal and coordinating role in the program

and how *interj fr early 1900s* An exclamation of emphatic agreement or confirmation: *Are we happy? And how!*

angel **1** *n fr about 1920* A person who contributes to a politician's campaign fund **2** *n* *fr theater fr 1920s* A financial contributor to any enterprise, esp a stage production; =BUTTER-AND-EGG MAN **3** *v: My doctor angeled one of Hansberry's plays* **4** *n underworld* A thief's or confidence man's victim; =MARK, PATSY **5** *n homosexuals fr 1930s* A homosexual male

angel dust *narcotics* **1** *n phr* The powdered form of PCP, a tranquilizer used in veterinary medicine, which as a narcotic is either sniffed or smoked in a tightly rolled cigarette **2** *n phr* A synthetic heroin

Angelino or **Angeleno** (an jə LEE noh) *n* A resident or native of Los Angeles

angle *n* Something one does for profit or advantage, esp a devious action disguised as altruism: *That guy never does anything unless there's an angle*

◁ **Anglo** ▷ *n Hispanics* A white person; =PATTY

ankle *v* To walk: *I ankled over to the bar* [perhaps in part from *angle*, cited fr 1890s in sense of "to walk"]

Ann *See* MARY ANN

Annie *See* BASEBALL ANNIE

Annie Oakley or **Annie** *n phr* or *n fr early 1900s sports & show business* A free ticket or pass to a game or entertainment [fr the name of a 19th-century trick-shot artist who could riddle a playing card tossed into the air so that it looked like an often-punched ticket]

another country (or **county** or **precinct**) **heard from** *sentence* Still another voice makes itself heard • Usu a contemptuous response to a new or unwanted contribution of opinion

answers *See* KNOW ALL THE ANSWERS

ante *See* PENNY ANTE, UP THE ANTE

antifreeze *n narcotics* Heroin

antinuke **1** *adj* Antinuclear; opposed to nuclear energy and nuclear armaments **2** *n: The antinukes assaulted Wall Street, holding hands, singing, and sitting in* —New York Daily News

ants or **ants in** one's **pants** **1** *n* or *n phr* An unrelaxed, disturbed condition; anxiety; acute restlessness: *After two days at sea she began to get ants* **2** *n* or *n phr* Sexual excitement; =the HOTS

antsy **1** *adj* In an anxious, disturbed state; nervous; jittery: *But when things are quiet, I get antsy* —Jackie Friedrich **2** *adj* Sexually aroused; lustful; =HOT

any old *adj phr* Having only ordinary or mediocre quality; of no special distinction: *Any old car will do me*

A-OK or **A-Okay** or **A O-K** *fr astronautics fr 1960s* **1** *adj* Proceeding or functioning properly; giving no cause for worry; =COPACETIC, GO: *Your X rays are A-OK* **2** *adv: The plan's going A-OK*

ape ◀**1**▶ *n* A black person **2** *n beat talk & rock and roll* The best or greatest; the ultimate: *Her paintings are truly ape* **3** *adj* (also **ape-shit**) Stupid and destructive; irrational; berserk: *You acted like you were ape, pounding the wall* **4** *adj* (also **ape-shit**) Very enthusiastic; highly excited; =BANANAS: *He's ape about my new symphony* **5** *n* An especially strong and pugnacious hoodlum; a strong-arm man or muscle man; =GOON, GORILLA

See DRAPE APE, GO APE, HOUSE APE, RUG APE

the **ape** *adv phr beat talk & rock and roll* Very well; best: *Maybe we could dig each other the ape*—S Boal

ape hangers *n phr motorcyclists* High swooping motorcycle handlebars

◁ **ape-shit** ▷ *See* APE, GO APE

apparatchik *n* An aide, staff member, etc, esp of a bureaucratic sort; flunky: *the politicians and their technocratic apparatchiki on both sides*—Philadelphia [fr Russian, "member of the Communist party, or *apparat*"]

apple **1** *n* A man; fellow; =ARTICLE, GUY • Always preceded by an adjective: *He's a real slick apple* **2** *n* A ball, esp a baseball **3** *n esp 1930s jazz musicians* A street or district where excitement may be found **4** *n esp 1930s jazz musicians* Any large town or city ◁**5**▷ *n Native American* A Native American who has taken on the values and behavior of the white community; =UNCLE TOMAHAWK [fr the fact that an *apple* is red on the outside but white on the inside]

See the BIG APPLE, HEN-APPLE, HORSE APPLES, SAD APPLE, SWALLOW THE APPLE, WISE GUY

the **Apple** *See* the BIG APPLE

applejack cap *n phr black* A round, usu knitted and bright-colored cap with a wide peak and a pompom; =BOP CAP

◁ **apple-knocker** ▷ *n* A rural person; unsophisticated rustic; =HICK [fr the practice of *knocking apples* out of trees]

apple-pie order *n phr* A condition of neatness, correctness, and propriety: *MacFarlane finds in this "apple-pie order of oppositeness"... a singular problem*—Toronto Life

apple-polish *v* To flatter and pamper in order to gain personal advantage; curry favor; =BROWN-NOSE, SUCK UP TO someone: *He started apple-polishing the Skipper as soon as he got on board*

apple-polisher *n* A person who apple-polishes [fr the traditional figure of the pupil who brings the teacher a shiny red apple]

applesauce *n fr early 1900s* Nonsense; pretentious talk; =BULLSHIT, BUNK: *"Ideologies"... freely translated into American means "applesauce"* —Max Eastman [fr the fact that relatively cheap, hence worthless, *applesauce* would be copiously served instead of choicer food in boarding houses]

appropriate *v esp WW2 Army* =LIBERATE

Archie Bunker **1** *n phr* A bigoted lower-middle-class American; =HARD HAT, REDNECK **2** *modifier: He has the support of the traditional Republican establishment, and is adding the Archie Bunker vote*—James Reston [fr the name of the leading character of a television comedy series "All in the Family," who exhibited the traits indicated]

-arino *See* -ERINO

Arky or **Arkie** **1** *n* A migratory worker, esp one from Arkansas **2** *n* Any poor Southern farmer, esp a white sharecropper **3** *modifier: the Arky drawl of the CB radio user* **4** *n* =OKIE

arm *n* A police officer [police sense fr *arm of the law*]
See AS LONG AS YOUR ARM, CROOKED ARM, GLASS ARM, HOOK ARM, ONE-ARM BANDIT, RIDE THE ARM, STIFF, TWIST someone's ARM

the **arm** *See* RIDE THE ARM, A SHOT IN THE ARM

an **arm and a leg** *n phr* An exorbitantly high price: *The trip cost an arm and a leg*

armchair general (or **strategist**) *n phr* A person who speaks authoritatively but not convincingly on matters where that person lacks practical experience; =BLOWHARD, KNOW-IT-ALL

armpit *n* A very undesirable place; geographical nadir; =ASSHOLE, the PITS: *My home town is the armpit of the universe*
See PULL TEETH THROUGH THE ARMPIT

Armstrong mower *n phr* A scythe

Armstrong starter *n phr* A crank for starting an engine

arm-waver *n* An excitable or emphatic person

the (or the **old**) **army game** *n phr* Any swindle or confidence game; a dishonest gambling game; =FLIM-FLAM: *It's nothing but... the army game*—James M Cain

-aroo *See* -EROO

-arooney or **-erooney** *suffix used to form nouns* A suffix added to the term indicated to imply familiarity or humor: *This little cararooney's got only 10,000 miles on her*

around the bend **1** *adv phr* With most or the hardest part done; =OVER THE HILL: *Two more days and we'll be around the bend on this project* **2** *adj phr chiefly British* Insane; =BONKERS: *It's a wonder Vanderbilt... isn't totally around the bend herself*—Washington Post

around (or **round**) **the horn** **1** *adj phr* *adj phr baseball* Of throws from third base to second base to first base: *a brilliant round-the-horn double play* [fr the length and circuitousness of a voyage around Cape Horn at the southern tip of South America]

around the world *See* GO AROUND THE WORLD

arrow *See* STRAIGHT ARROW

art *See* STATE OF THE ART, TIT ART

article *n* A person, esp one considered to be clever, cute, or resourceful; =NUMBER • Always preceded by an adjective, or by the locution "Quite an": *He is some slick article/Your little sister's quite an article*

artillery **1** *n underworld fr early 1900s* A weapon or weapons, esp a handgun; =HEATER **2** *n narcotics* A drug user's hypodermic syringe

See HEAVY ARTILLERY

artist *See* BULLSHIT ARTIST, BUNCO ARTIST, GYP, OFF ARTIST, PUT-ON, RIPOFF

artsy-craftsy or **artsy** or **arty** *adj fr 1940s* Pretentiously and self-consciously artistic; straining for esthetic effect: *an artsy-craftsy little boutique*

artsy-fartsy or **artsy-smartsy** *adj* Pompously or blatantly esthetical • The superlative degree of **artsy-craftsy**: *The...pianist veers toward the artsy-fartsy*—Village Voice

asap or **ASAP** (pronounced either as separate letters or as an acronym AY sap) *adv armed forces* Right away; immediately: *Our job is simple—to liberate US POWs from Asia, ASAP* —Washington Post [fr *as soon as possible*]

ash can *See* KNOCK someone or something FOR A LOOP

ashes *See* GET one's ASHES HAULED

◁ **Asiatic** ▷ *adj Navy & Marine Corps fr before WW2* Crazy; wild; violent: *He could wind up some tapped-out old Asiatic rumdum*—Earl Thompson [fr presumed unstable character of those who had served too long in *Asiatic* posts]

ask for it *v phr fr early 1900s* To behave in a way that invites and deserves trouble; provoke: *I'm sorry you had that wreck, but with no brakes you were asking for it*

asleep at the switch *adj phr fr railroad* Not attending to one's duty; unvigilant; inattentive

as long as your arm *adj phr* Very extensive; remarkably long: *The guy's a jailbird, a record as long as your arm*—WT Tyler

as per usual *adv phr* As usual

◁ **ass** ▷ **1** *n* The buttocks; posterior; =BUTT: *a kick in the ass* **2** *n* The anus; =ASSHOLE: *You can take it and shove it up your ass* **3** *n* A person regarded solely as a sex partner or target; =TAIL: *She looks like good ass* **4** *n* Sexual activity; sexual gratification: *He was out looking for ass* **5** *n* The whole self; the person • Used for emphasis and euphony: *Get your ass out of here pronto/ I'm out in Kansas for the first time... eighteen or nineteen, my ass drafted* —WT Tyler
See one's ASS IS DRAGGING, someone's ASS IS ON THE LINE, BARREL ASS, BET YOUR BOOTS, BURN someone's ASS, BUST one's ASS, CANDY ASS, CANDY-ASSED, CHEW someone's ASS, COLD AS HELL, COVER one's ASS, DEADASS, DRAG ASS, DRAG one's TAIL, DUMB-ASS, FALL ON one's ASS, FLAT-ASS, FLAT ON one's ASS, GET one's ASS IN GEAR, GET one's HEAD OUT OF one's ASS, GET OFF one's ASS, GET THE LEAD OUT, GET THE RED ASS, GIVE someone A PAIN, GO POUND SALT, GRIPE one's ASS, one HAS HAD IT, HAUL ASS, HAVE A BUG UP one's ASS, HAVE someone's ASS, HAVE one's ASS IN A SLING, HAVE one's HEAD PULLED, HAVE LEAD IN one's PANTS, one's HEAD IS UP one's ASS, HORSE'S ASS, IN A PIG'S ASS, IT WILL BE someone's ASS, JUMP THROUGH one's ASS, KICK ASS, a KICK IN THE ASS, KISS MY ASS, MAN WITH A PAPER ASS, MY ASS, NO SKIN OFF MY ASS, NOT KNOW one's ASS FROM one's ELBOW, ON one's ASS, OUT ON one's ASS, a PAIN IN THE ASS, PIECE OF ASS, PISSY, PULL something OUT OF one's ASS, PUT one's ASS ON THE LINE, RAGGEDY-ASS, a RAT'S ASS, RATTY, SHAG ASS, SHIT-ASS, a SHOT IN THE ASS, SIT ON one's ASS, SIT THERE WITH one's FINGER UP one's ASS, SMART-ASS, SOFT-ASS, SORRY-ASS, STAND AROUND WITH one's FINGER UP one's ASS, STICK IT, SUCK ASS, TEAR OFF A PIECE, THROW someone OUT ON someone's ASS, TIRED-ASS, UP TO one's ASS IN something, WHAT'S-HIS-NAME, WILD-ASS, WORK one's ASS OFF

◁ **-ass** or **-assed** ▷ **1** ***suffix used to form adjectives*** Having buttocks of the specified sort: *big-ass/ fat-assed* **2** ***suffix used to form adjectives and nouns*** Having a specified character or nature to a high degree: *badass/ wildassed/ silly-ass*

◁ **ass backwards** ▷ **1** *adv phr* In a reversed position or confused manner: *She had it all ass backwards* **2** *adj phr: The whole plan is ass backwards*

◁ **assbite** ▷ *n* A strong rebuke; reprimand: *I took the assbite without looking at him*—Joseph Wambaugh

◁ **assed** ▷ *See* HALF-ASSED, PUCKER-ASSED, RED-ASSED

◀ **assfuck** ▶ **1** *v* To do anal intercourse; =BUGGER, BUNGHOLE **2** *n* An act of anal intercourse

◁ **asshole** or **butthole** ▷ **1** *n* The anus; rectum **2** *n* A fool; idiot: *Oh, Christ, what ass-holes be Americans*—Norman Mailer/ *Better not, you butthole*—Cameron Crowe **3** *n* =ASSHOLE BUDDY **4** *n* The most despised and loathsome part; =ARMPIT: *This town's the asshole of the North*

See BLOW IT OUT, BREAK OUT INTO ASSHOLES, FLAMER, TANGLE ASSHOLES

◁ **asshole** (or **buttfuck**) **buddy**▷ *n phr* A very close friend; best friend; =PAL • Usu with only a humorous connotation of homosexuality: *The big cheese who teaches you butt-fuck buddies how to blow a few of the Baptists away*—Richard Merkin/ *Agnelli discussed his "asshole buddy David Rockefeller"*—Village Voice

◁ **asshole deep**▷ *See* UP TO one's ASS IN something

◁ **ass in a sling**▷ *See* HAVE one's ASS IN A SLING

◁ one's **ass is dragging**▷ *sentence* The subject is very tired; one is exhausted, and hence sluggish

◁ one's **ass is getting light**▷ *sentence Army* The subject has been repeatedly and thoroughly rebuked; one has been severely chastened [fr the concept that when one is thoroughly rebuked one's anus is chewed or reamed out]

◁ one's **ass is grass**▷ *sentence fr 1940s* The subject is in trouble; one will be ruined, undone, etc: *Give me a title, in short, or your ass is grass* —Boston Magazine

◁ someone's **ass is on the line**▷ *sentence* Someone is at risk; someone has taken a perilous responsibility: *A friend's ass is on the line and I promised I'd talk to you*—Lawrence Sanders

◁ **asskicker**▷ *fr Army* **1** *n* An energetic person, esp an officer who harasses subordinates **2** *n* Something that functions very well: *That little motor's a real asskicker* **3** *n* An exhausting experience

◁ **asskicking**▷ *adj Army* Functioning or performing well: *That's an asskicking little heater*

◁ **ass-kisser**▷ *n* (Variations: **licker** or **sucker** may replace **kisser**) A person who flatters and serves obsequiously to gain favor with a superior; sycophant; =AK, BROWN-NOSE, YES-MAN

◁ **ass-kissing**▷ *n* Flattery; currying favor with superiors; =BROWN-NOSING: *It's a short step from lip service to ass-kissing*—Saul Bellow

◁ **ass man**▷ **1** *n phr* A man with an extraordinary and consuming interest in doing the sex act; lecher; satyr; =COCKSMAN **2** *n phr* A man whose favorite part of female anatomy is the buttocks

◁ one's **ass** (or **buns** or **tail**) **off**▷ *adv phr* Very hard; one's best; to one's utmost: *I worked my ass off for that ungrateful jerk/ listen to Oscar Peterson play his buns off*—Down Beat

◁ **ass over tincups** (or **teacups** or **teakettle**)▷ *adv phr* In or into helplessness; head over heels: *She's so beautiful she'll knock you ass over tincups* [a variant of the early-20th-century British *arse over tip* "head over heels"]

◁ **assy**▷ *adj homosexuals* Malicious; nasty; mean; =BITCHY

-ateria *suffix used to form nouns* (Variations: **-teria** or **-eria** or **-eteria**) Place or establishment where the indicated thing is done or sold: *bookateria/ caviarteria*

Atkins *See* TOMMY ATKINS

at liberty *adv phr* Unemployed

-atorium or **-torium** or **-orium** *suffix used to form nouns* Place where an indicated thing is done: *drinkatorium/ lubritorium/ printorium*

attaboy or **attagirl** *interj* An exclamation of approval or encouragement; =WAY TO GO [fr *that's the boy*]

at the double *See* ON THE DOUBLE

attitude *n fr black & prison* A resentful and hostile manner; pugnacity

See HAVE AN ATTITUDE

attrit **1** *v* To dispose of or dispense with gradually; subject to attrition: *Workers never retire, resign, or die... they are attritted*—New York Times **2** *v* To kill: *Well, if we can attrit the population base of the Vietcong, it'll accelerate the process of degrading the VC*—Frances FitzGerald

audible **1** *n football* A play or formation announced at the line of scrimmage and different from the one called in the huddle **2** *n* Any sudden or impromptu change of instructions, esp when issued orally: *The boss said if anything went wrong he'd give us an audible*

Augustus Owsley *n phr narcotics* A high-grade form of LSD [fr the name of the man who first produced this high-grade variety]

aunt or **Aunt** **1** *n* The madame of a brothel **2** *n homosexuals* An elderly male homosexual

Aunt Tom *n phr* A woman who does not support or sympathize with the women's liberation movement [fr the analogy with *Uncle Tom*]

Aussie 1 *n* An Australian **2** *adj: the Aussie movie industry*

avoirdupois (AV ər də poyz) *n* Body weight; fat or fatness: *too much avoirdupois, so I'm dieting*

aw *interj* An exclamation of entreaty, disappointment, disbelief, regret, and various other uncomfortable feelings • Used either alone or before certain fixed expressions like "come on," "hell," "man," "shit," or "shoot"

away 1 *adv baseball* Out: *Two away in the top of the eighth* **2** *adv underworld* In prison

awesome *teenagers adj* Excellent; wonderful; outstanding; = COOL, NEAT

awful *See* GOD-AWFUL

AWOL or **awol** (pronounced either as separate letters or as an acronym AY wawl) *armed forces fr WW1* **1** *adj* Absent without leave **2** *n* A person who is absent without leave

aw right *See* ALL RIGHT

aw shucks 1 *interj* An exclamation of embarrassment, self-abnegation, regret, and various other mildly uncomfortable feelings • Usu used in imitation of rural or extremely naive, boyish males **2** *v phr: good-ole-boy aw shucksing*—Time [a euphemism for *aw shit*]

awshucksness *n phr* Modesty; self-abnegating embarrassment: *Young Crosby displayed all the easygoing awshucksness of his late father*—Time

ax or **axe 1** *v* To dismiss someone from a job, a team, a school, a relationship, etc; = CAN, FIRE: *who suggested to Reagan that Deaver be axed*—Washingtonian **2** *v* To eliminate; cut: *They axed a lot of useless stuff from the budget* **3** *n jazz musicians fr 1950s* Any musical instrument, esp the saxophone: *The piano player noodled on his ax* **4** *n rock and roll* A guitar [sense three originally fr the resemblance in shape between a saxophone and an ax, and possibly fr the rhyme with *sax*; also related to the transferred idea of *chops*, originally related to a musician's embouchure, then thought of as blows with an ax]

the **ax** *See* GIVE someone THE AIR

Aztec two-step *n phr* Diarrhea; = MONTEZUMA'S REVENGE, TURISTA

B

B *narcotics* **1** *n* Benzedrine (a trade name); =BENNY **2** *n* =BEE

babe *n* A girl or woman, esp a sexually desirable one; =CHICK, DOLL • Used almost entirely by men, and considered offensive by many women

baby **1** *n* A wife, girlfriend, or other cherished woman; also, less frequently, a husband, boyfriend, or cherished man: *My baby don't love me no more* **2** *n* Any cherished or putatively cherished person • This expanded use apparently began in and is characteristic of show business **3** *n* A mean and dangerous man; =TOUGH GUY: *I knew there'd be trouble when those babies walked in* **4** *n* Anything regarded with special affection, admiration, pride, or awe: *Those babies'll turn on a dime/ What we had heard was the firing of those big babies a mile and a half from shore*—Time

See BAWL BABY

baby blues *n phr* Blue eyes

babycakes or **honeycakes** *n* A sweetheart or other cherished person • A term of endearment: *I know it's early, Babycakes*—Armistead Maupin/ *"Ain't that right, baby?" "Sure is, honeycakes"*—New Yorker

baby-sit **1** *v* To attend and care for anyone or anything: *He baby-sat his weeping pal/ I had to baby-sit the new printer for the computer, feeding it more paper all day* **2** *v narcotics* To be a guide and companion to someone undergoing a psychedelic drug experience [fr the practice of employing someone to stay with and care for a child or children while the parents are not at home]

bach or **batch** *n* A bachelor

bachelor girl **1** *n phr* An unmarried young woman, usu with a career or a profession **2** *modifier: a bachelor-girl apartment*

bach (or **batch**) **it** *v phr* To live alone as an unmarried man, esp to do so for a brief and often slovenly period while one's wife is away: *He had to bach it a while when his wife went to her mother's*

back **1** *v* To give one's support to some effort or person: *I'll back your application* **2** *v* To bet on: *He backed Green Goo in the eighth* **3** *v* To contribute money for; =BANKROLL: *My cousin backed the rock show in the park*

See BIRDYBACK, FISHYBACK, GET one's or someone's BACK UP, GET OFF someone's BACK, GET THE MONKEY OFF, GIVE someone THE SHIRT OFF one's BACK, KNOCK BACK, LAID-BACK, MOSSBACK, ON someone's BACK, PIGGYBACK, PIN someone's EARS BACK, SCRATCH someone's BACK, YOU SCRATCH MY BACK, I SCRATCH YOURS

backasswards *adv* =ASS BACKWARDS

back-breaker *n* A very difficult job or task; =BALL-BUSTER, BITCH, PISSER

the **back burner** *n phr* The location of an idea, project, suggestion, etc, when it is kept in ready reserve for the time being: *Sounds great, but let's put it on the back burner for a few weeks*

See ON THE BACK BURNER

back-burner **1** *v* To put a project, idea, suggestion, etc, in reserve: *Shall we just back-burner that one?* **2** *modifier: a back-burner crisis*—Elizabeth Drew

back-door *adj* Dishonest; dubious: *a sleazy little back-door business*

back down *v phr fr middle 1800s* To retreat from one's position; surrender; retract: *He wouldn't back down even when they beat him up*

backhouse *n* An outdoor toilet house without plumbing; outhouse

back number *n phr fr late 1800s* Someone or something out of date; =HAS-BEEN: *Mr Stale is a back number*—H McHugh

back off **1** *v phr* To stop annoying or harassing • Often a command or threat **2** *v phr* To soften or moderate; relent: *The President backed off a little from his hardnosed line* **3** *v phr* To slow down; go easier: *Hey, back off a little, I don't get you*

back out *v phr fr middle 1800s* To cancel or renege on an arrangement; =FINK OUT: *We can't back out just because we're scared*

backroom *adj* Having to do with political expediency; from the inner circles of party affairs: *a backroom decision/ backroom motives*

backscratch *See* YOU SCRATCH MY BACK, I SCRATCH YOURS

back seat *See* TAKE A BACK SEAT

backseat driver *n phr* A person who gives unwanted and officious advice; =KIBITZER

back talk *n phr* Impudent response; impertinent comment; =SASS

one's **back teeth are floating** *sentence* One needs very urgently to urinate

back to square one *adv phr* Returned to the starting point, usu having wasted a great deal of effort; no farther ahead: *sends the search back to square one*—Village Voice

back to the salt mines *adv phr* Returned to hard work and unremitting discomfort, after a period of relative ease and pleasure: *I had a week off, then back to the salt mines* [fr the tradition of Russian penal servitude in Siberian *salt mines*]

back-track *See* BOOT

backup **1** *n* A replacement, substitute or something or someone in reserve: *We can't afford to lose her because we've got no backup* **2** *modifier: a backup system/ backup wide receiver* ◁**3**▷ *n* An occasion when several males do the sex act serially with one woman; =GANG BANG

back up **1** *v phr* To support or confirm, esp to verify the statement of: *You explain it, and I'll back up your version* **2** *v phr* To refer to some earlier place: *They couldn't understand, so he backed up and told 'em once more*

back someone **up** **1** *v phr* To confirm what someone says; support what someone does: *If you want to go in to complain, I'll back you up* **2** *v phr* To be ready to substitute for; be in reserve: *We've got three drivers to back him up*

bacon *See* BRING HOME THE BACON

bad *adj esp teenagers fr jazz musicians & black fr early 1950s* Good; excellent; admirable: *real bad licks/ bad nigger* • The use is attested from slavery times, when this sense was marked by a lengthened vowel and a falling tone in pronunciation

◁**badass**▷ *fr black* **1** *n* A belligerent and worthless person; =BUM: *It's the badasses who don't want him back*—Philadelphia Journal/ *He still burned with a desire to show us Mad Dogs what a badass we'd passed up*—Easyriders **2** *adj: sounds as bad-ass as John Denver singing "Macho Man"*—Aquarian

bad books *See* IN someone's BAD BOOKS

bad cop *See* GOOD COP BAD COP

baddie **1** *n* Someone or something that is bad, esp a movie, television, or sports villain **2** *n* A criminal or other habitually reprehensible person; =BAD MAN

bad egg *n phr fr middle 1800s* A villain, criminal, or other deplorable person; =BADDIE

badge *See* SCARE BADGE

badge bandit *n phr hot rodders* A police officer

badger game **1** *n phr* A method of extortion in which a woman entices the victim into a sexually compromising situation, whereupon a male accomplice appears and demands payment for keeping the situation quiet **2** *n phr* Any means of blackmail, extortion, or intimidation

bad man (or **guy**) *n phr fr late 1800s cowboys* A villain, esp a killer, rustler, etc, in a cowboy movie

bad-mouth *fr black* **1** *v phr* To disparage; denigrate: *I won't bad-mouth him, but I don't like him* **2** *n phr: If you can't say anything good, at least don't be a bad mouth* **3** *n* *phr* A person who speaks in a belligerent, provocative way

bad news **1** *n phr* An unpleasant or depressing person, esp a persistently annoying one: *Isn't she bad news since her old man left her?* **2** *n phr* A dangerous person; a menace: *Their big new linebacker is bad news* **3** *n phr* Any unfortunate or regrettable situation or event: *That meeting was strictly bad news* **4** *n phr* The bill for goods or services, esp a restaurant check; =BEEF

bad nigger *black* **1** *n phr* A black person, usu a male, who wins the respect of his own people by resisting the dominant white society: *A bad nigger was a nigger who "didn't take no shit from nobody"*—Claude Brown ◁**2**▷ *n phr* A belligerent black male, esp one who mistreats women

bad paper *n phr* Worthless or counterfeit money, checks, etc: *They passed some bad paper*

bad rap **1** *n phr underworld* An erroneous conviction or sentence; wrongful punishment; =BUM RAP **2** *n phr* Any unjustified condemnation: *Mobil has taken a bad rap from Congress*—Newsweek

bad scene *n phr fr black & 1960s counterculture* Something unpleasant, esp a displeasing and depressing experience or situation

◁**bad shit**▷ **1** *n phr* Something menacing and nasty: *A lot of bad shit goes down at the track, man*—Harry Crews **2** *n phr* Bad luck

bad (or **bum** or **down**) **trip** **1** *n phr narcotics* A frightening or depressing drug experience, esp a nightmarish time with LSD **2** *n phr fr 1960s counterculture* Any unpleasant occasion or experience; =BUMMER, DOWNER: *The party was a real bad trip*

bag ◁**1**▷ *n* The scrotum ◁**2**▷ *n* A condom **3** *n baseball* The cushionlike marker that serves as a base **4** *n narcotics* A portion of narcotics, often wrapped in a paper or glassine envelope: *They found three nickel bags of marijuana on him* ◁**5**▷ *n* A woman's breast **6** *v* To get or capture: *to bag a gold medal/ They bagged the mugger in the next block* **7** *v* To arrest: *You don't have to bag nuns*—Philadelphia Journal **8** *n* An unattractive girl or woman; ugly woman **9** *n* An old woman, esp a repulsive old shrew; =OLD BAT **10** *n esp 1960s counterculture* That which one prefers or is doing currently; =KICK, THING **11** *n* An environment; milieu: *That fox comes out of a very intellectual bag*—WM Kelley **12** *v* To discharge; =CAN, FIRE: *Just say the author was willing to bag an old friend*—Philadelphia Journal **13** *v* To suppress; get rid of; discard: *Let's bag the whole notion, okay?* **14** *v esp students* To avoid; =SKIP: *Like bag this movie, for sure*—Newsweek **15** *v* (also **bag it**) *esp students* To abandon; cease; give up: *I had to bag it...I had to give up all that stuff*—New York

See BROWN-BAG, DIME BAG, DITTY BAG, DOGGY BAG, DOUCHE BAG, FAG BAG, FLEABAG, GRAB-BAG, HALF IN THE BAG, HOLD THE BAG, IN THE BAG, LET THE CAT OUT OF THE BAG, NICKEL BAG, SANDBAG, SLEAZEBAG, SLIMEBAG, STASH BAG, WINDBAG

baggage smasher *n phr fr middle 1800s* A baggage-handler at a railroad station, airport, etc

bagged *adj* Drunk

See HALF-BAGGED

bagger ***See*** BROWN BAGGER, DOUBLE-BAGGER, FOUR-BAGGER, ONE-BAGGER, THREE-BAGGER, TWO-BAGGER

baggies **1** *n* A pair of loose-cut boxer-type men's bathing trunks: *girls in bikinis and boys in "baggies"*—New York Times **2** *n* A pair of full trousers, resembling those of the 1930s: *Then comes a pair of "baggies," very baggy trousers*—New Yorker

bag job *n phr* A theft or burglary: *Someone had done a bag job on his precious files*—C McCrystal/ *The spectators...sure know a bag job when they see one*—Sports Illustrated

bag lady or **shopping-bag lady** or **bag woman** **1** *n phr* A woman who goes about the streets collecting discarded objects and taking them home in shopping bags: *a bag lady whose tiny room was crammed with garbage*—New York Post **2** *n phr* A homeless woman, often elderly, who lives in public places and carries her possessions in shopping bags: *bag ladies, the Big Apple's discarded, homeless women*—New York Post

bagman **1** *n underworld* A person who collects money for bribers, extortionists, mobsters, etc: *The defendant was described... as the "bagman" or collector*—New York Times **2** *n narcotics* A person who peddles drugs; =PUSHER

bag (or **load**) **of wind** *n phr* =WINDBAG

bag of worms *See* CAN OF WORMS

bags **1** *n* Trousers ◁**2**▷ *n* A woman's breasts; =TITS **3** *n* A great quantity: *He's got bags of money*
See MONEYBAGS

bag some rays *v phr* To sunbathe

bag your face *sentence high school students* Conceal your face; you are repulsive • A generalized insult

bag Zs *See* COP ZS

bail *See* JUMP BAIL

bail someone **out** *v phr* To get someone out of a difficult plight; relieve someone of debt, embarrassment, etc: *I'll bail you out this time, but next time bring enough money*

baked *See* HALF-BAKED

the **baker** *n phr underworld* The electric chair

Baker flying *See* HAVE THE RAG ON

baldy or **baldie** **1** *n* A bald man **2** *n* A worn automobile tire

ball ◁**1**▷ *n* A testicle; =NUT ◁**2**▷ *v* To do the sex act; copulate with; =SCREW **3** *v narcotics* To introduce a narcotic, like cocaine, into the body through the genitals **4** *n early 1900s underworld* A dollar, esp a silver dollar **5** *n early 1900s underworld* A prisoner's allowance for making small purchases **6** *n lunch counter* A single scoop of ice cream **7** *n narcotics* A pill or portion of marijuana or some other narcotic **8** *v* To have an especially good time; enjoy oneself in a relaxed and uninhibited way: *A good-time town, where everybody comes to ball*—New York Daily News
See BALL UP, BEANBALL, BILLYBALL, BUTTERFLY BALL, CARRY THE LOAD, EMERY BALL, FIREBALL, FLY COP, FORKBALL, GET ON THE BALL, GO FOR THE LONG BALL, GOOFBALL, GOPHER BALL, GREASEBALL, GREEDBALL, HAVE A BALL, JUNK-BALL, KEEP one's EYE ON THE BALL, MEATBALL, NOT GET one's BALLS IN AN UPROAR, NUTBALL, ODDBALL, ON THE BALL, PLAY BALL, PLAY CATCH-UP, SLEAZEBAG, SLIMEBAG, SLUDGEBALL, SMOKEBALL, SOFTBALL, SOURBALL, THAT'S THE WAY THE BALL BOUNCES

-ball **1** *combining word* A person who is obnoxious or strange because of what is indicated: *oddball/ goofball/ dirtball/ sleazeball* **2** *combining word* Baseball of a specified sort: *Billyball/ greedball*

a **ball** *n phr* An especially good time; an occasion of extraordinary pleasure: *The concert was a ball*

ball-and-chain *n* One's wife; =OLD WOMAN

◁**ball-bearing hostess**▷ *n phr airline* A male cabin attendant on an aircraft

◁**ball-buster**▷ (Variations: **breaker** or **wracker** may replace **buster**) **1** *n* Something that is very difficult to accomplish; a Herculean task; =KILLER **2** *n* Someone who assigns and monitors extremely difficult tasks: *a real ball-buster of a skipper* **3** *n* A woman who saps or negates a man's masculinity; castrating female

◁**ball-busting**▷ **1** *n* The sapping or destruction of masculinity; =NUT-CRUNCHING **2** *adj: his lily-black reputation with that ball-busting wife of his*—Charles Beardsley

balled up *adj phr* In a thoroughly confused and futile condition; erroneous and useless because of perverse incompetence; =BOLLIXED UP, FUCKED UP, SCREWED UP: *Things were totally balled up when the alarm went* [origin uncertain; perhaps, as euphemistically explained, fr the helplessness of a horse on a slippery street when its shoes have accumulated *balls* of ice; somehow the term has come to be associated with the testicles, as the related term *bollixed up* shows]

ball game **1** *n phr* A given set of conditions; complex of circumstances; situation: *What we do and what they do isn't the same ball game* **2** *n phr* A competition; rivalry: *It's NBC ahead in the network ratings ball game, NBC says*—R Doan **3** *n phr* The decisive element or event, esp in a competition or encounter; =the NAME OF THE GAME: *The third ward vote is the ball game in this town*
See LOSE THE BALLGAME, THAT'S THE BALL GAME, a WHOLE NEW BALL GAME, a WHOLE 'NOTHER THING

the **ball is in** someone's **court** *sentence* The next action, decision, response, etc, belongs to the person or persons indicated: *That's my offer. The ball is in your court* [fr tennis]

ball of fire **1** *n phr* A dazzling performer; spectacularly successful striver; overachiever; =GO-GETTER, HOT SHOT **2** *n phr railroad* A very fast train

ball of wax *See* the WHOLE BALL OF WAX

balloon *See* GO OVER LIKE A LEAD BALLOON, TRIAL BALLOON

balloonheaded *adj* Stupid; oafish: *Listen, you balloon-headed fool* —Jerome Weidman

ballot box *See* STUFF THE BALLOT BOX

ballpark *See* ALL OVER THE LOT, IN THE BALLPARK

ballpark figure (or **estimate**) *n phr* A rough numerical approximation: *I'd say forty, but that's a ballpark figure*

balls ◁**1**▷ *n* The testicles ◁**2**▷ *n* Courage; nerve; =GUTS: *They have balls but not soul*—Richard Goldstein/ *I admire a woman with the balls to bare her breasts*—Playboy **3** *interj* An exclamation of incredulity, disappointment, or disgust **4** *n British* Nonsense; =POPPYCOCK: *He was talking high-minded balls. Twaddle!*—Saul Bellow

See BLUE BALLS, BUST one's ASS, the CAT'S MEOW, DOES HOWDY DOODY HAVE WOODEN BALLS, FREEZE THE BALLS OFF A BRASS MONKEY, GRIPE one's ASS, HAVE BRASS (or CAST-IRON) BALLS, HAVE someone BY THE BALLS, HAVE THE WORLD BY THE BALLS, NOT GET one's BALLS IN AN UPROAR, TIGHT AS KELSEY'S NUTS

balls-out *adj car-racing & motorcyclists* Very great; extreme; total: *the balls-out go-power of modern snowmobiles*—Car and Driver

balls to the wall *fr Air Force* **1** *adv phr* At or to the extreme; at full speed; =ALL-OUT, FLAT OUT: *driving balls to the wall* **2** *adj phr: They are not the cigar-chomping "balls to the wall" warmongers of popular perceptions*—Newsweek [fr the thrusting of an aircraft throttle, topped by a ball, to the bulkhead of the cockpit to attain full speed]

◁**ballsy**▷ *adj* Courageous; spunky; =GUTSY: *Valerie Green's a very ballsy lady*—Anne Bernays

ball the jack **1** *v phr* To move or work very rapidly **2** *v phr* To gamble or risk everything on one stroke or try [fr railroad term meaning "to go full speed"; related to the railroad sense of *highball* and of *jack*]

ball up **1** *v phr* To confuse; mix up; lead astray: *This guy has balled me up totally* **2** *v phr* To wreck or ruin by incompetence; botch; =FUCK UP, SCREW UP: *I managed to ball up the whole project* **3** *n: The second concert was a thorough ball-up*

See BALLED UP

ball-wracker *See* BALL-BUSTER

bally *n and v* =BALLYHOO

ballyhoo **1** *n circus & carnival* A short sample of a sideshow, presented with a barker's spiel **2** *n* Advertising or publicity, esp of a raucous and colorful sort; =FLACK, HYPE: *to peddle a product with sheer ballyhoo* **3** *modifier: the ballyhoo department/ a ballyhoo expert* **4** *v: They ballyhooed him right into office* [origin unknown]

baloney or **balony** or **boloney** **1** *n* Nonsense; pretentious talk; bold and deceitful absurdities; =APPLESAUCE, BULLSHIT, HOOEY: *No matter how you slice it, it's still baloney*—Carl Sandburg **2** *v: And don't try to baloney me, either* **3** *n* A stupid person: *You dumb baloney*—Jerome Weidman **4** *n electricians* Insulated cable

bam[1] **1** *v* To strike or hit: *Heads may be biffed or bammed*—M Doolittle **2** *interj* An exclamation imitating a hard blow

See WHAM-BAM THANK YOU MA'AM

bam[2] *n narcotics* A mixture of a depressant with a stimulant drug, esp of a barbiturate with an amphetamine [fr *barbiturate* + *amphetamine*]

bam[3] *n fr WW2* A woman Marine [fr *broad-assed Marine*]

bamboozle *fr early 1700s* *v* To hoax; trick; swindle; =FLIMFLAM: *My worthy opponent thrives by bamboozling the public*

banana **1** *n show business* A comedian, esp in a burlesque show • These performers were ranked as "top banana," "second banana," etc **2** *n black* A sexually attractive light-skinned black woman • Considered offensive by the women to whom this term is applied **3** *n* The nose, esp a big or hooked nose ◁**4**▷ *n* The penis ◁**5**▷ *n* An Oriental sympathetic with and part of the white majority society • Because white on the inside though yellow on the outside **6** *n* An automobile bumper-guard **7** *n* *hospital* A patient with jaundice

See HAVE one's BANANA PEELED, TOP BANANA

bananahead *n* A stupid person

banana oil *n fr 1920s* Nonsense, esp when used to flatter and mislead; =BUNK [perhaps fr the oily smoothness and fruity odor of amyl acetate; when used to tighten the fabric of airplane wings, amyl acetate was called *dope*, perhaps lending the suggestion of a soothing intoxicant]

◁**banana republic**▷ *n phr* A small country, esp Central American, dominated by foreign companies [fr the fact that such places were typically under the control of the United Fruit Company, and grew bananas]

bananas **1** *adj* Crazy; =NUTS: *Others were simply unprincipled and crooked, he was in addition bananas* —Saul Bellow **2** *adj* Very enthusiastic; highly excited; =APE **3** *adj underworld* Homosexual **4** *interj* =BANANA OIL

See GO BANANAS

band ***See*** TO BEAT THE BAND

Band-Aid **1** *n* A temporary or stopgap remedy: *All they did to rectify the problem was to put a Band-Aid on it* —Wall Street Journal **2** *modifier: a Band-Aid expedient* [fr *Band-Aid*, trade name for a brand of small adhesive bandages]

B and D *n phr* Bondage and discipline; sadomasochistic sexual practice

bandit **1** *n armed forces fr WW2* An enemy aircraft **2** *n prison* An aggressive homosexual who often resorts to violence

See BADGE BANDIT, LIKE A BANDIT, MAKE OUT LIKE A BANDIT, ONE-ARM BANDIT

the **bandwagon** **1** *n phr* The strong current popularity and impetus of a person, idea, party, etc: *the Reagan bandwagon/ the antinuke bandwagon* **2** *modifier: the bandwagon phenomenon*

See GET ON THE BANDWAGON

bang **1** *n* A very pleasurable sensation; surge of joy; thrill: *This'll give you a big bang* **2** *n narcotics* An injection of a narcotic, esp an intravenous shot of heroin **3** *v: They banged some horse and got high* ◁**4**▷ *v* To do the sex act with or to; copulate with: *He banged her twice and left happy* ◁**5**▷ *n* The sex act: *The wedding night, you idiot. The first bang. How was it?* —Lawrence Sanders **6** *n underworld* A criminal charge or prison sentence; =RAP **7** *adv* Precisely: *bang on the hour* **8** *n computer* An exclamation point

See GANG BANG, GET A BANG OUT OF someone or something, GO OVER WITH A BANG, WHIZBANG, WITH A BANG

banger **1** *n hot rodders* A cylinder in an automobile engine: *a souped-up four-banger* **2** *n* A car: *this wonderful banger*—Sports Illustrated **3** *n* A boxer who hits hard: *He's a great banger*—Time

See BIBLE-BANGER, BIT BANGER, FOUR-BANGER, WALL BANGER

bang for the buck *n phr* Value for what one pays: *You get the best bang for the buck right here*—Chicago Magazine [fr a frivolous way of referring to the national defense budget and the destructive power it produces]

bang pipes *v phr* To get practical work experience; work in the field rather than in a cloistered office: *We insist that people bang pipes for a while and go out in the field and talk to customers*—Morris County Daily Record

bang the hostess *v phr airline* To ring for the cabin attendant

bang to rights ***See*** DEAD TO RIGHTS

bang-up *adj fr early 1800s* Excellent; superior: *I have some bang-up gin* —Gene Fowler/ *You've done a bang-up job on that report, Smythe*

banjax *v fr Irish fr early 1900s* To defeat utterly; =CLOBBER: *She upped and banjaxed the old man*—New Yorker

bankable *adj* Having a reputation or influence that insures the success of a project: *after a decade when bankable stars have all but monopolized movies*—New York/ *She had established herself as the most bankable female actress in Hollywood*—Philadelphia

bank on *v phr* Depend or rely on: *You can bank on his word*

bankroll *v* To finance; put up the money for, esp for a theatrical production; =ANGEL: *Whoever bankrolled this turkey will go broke*
See PHILADELPHIA BANKROLL

bar *See* HERSHEY BAR, NUTBALL, SIDEBAR, SISSY BAR

barber **1** *n baseball* A talkative baseball player **2** *v* To converse; chat: *I shouldn't ought to barber with you*—Raymond Chandler **3** *n baseball* A pitcher who forces the batter back from the plate by throwing at his head [pitching sense fr association with a close shave, meaning a near miss]

barber chair *n phr astronautics* The adjustable seat used by an astronaut in a space craft

barbershop quartet *n phr* The trick or torment of holding someone's head and rubbing very hard and painfully at a small area of scalp with the fist; =NOOGIE [because a *quartet* of fingers is working on the hair, as it were]

Barbie Doll **1** *n phr* A mindless man or woman; a person lacking any but typical, bland, and neatly attractive traits: *a Barbie Doll...programmed to sing, dance, and fall in love* —Time **2** *modifier: Our Barbie Doll president with his Barbie Doll wife*—Hunter S Thompson [fr the trade name of a very popular blue-eyed blonde teenaged doll for young children]

barbs *n narcotics* Barbiturates

barbwire garter *See* WIN THE PORCELAIN HAIRNET

◁ **bare-ass** or **bare-assed**▷ *adj* Naked; =BUCK NAKED

bareback rider *n phr* A man who does the sex act without using a condom

bare-bones *adj* Unadorned; spare; austere: *a bare-bones prose style*

bare face hanging out *See* STAND THERE WITH one's BARE FACE HANGING OUT

barf **1** *v chiefly students* To vomit [probably echoic] **2** *v computer* To respond strangely or with an error warning after unacceptable input: *The machine barfed when I put in the wrong password*

Barf City *adj phr chiefly students* Disgusting; loathsome; =YUCKY

bar-fly *n* A heavy drinker; =LUSH, SOUSE

barf me out *interj high school students* An exclamation of disgust; =YUCK

bargain *See* NO BARGAIN

bargaining chip *n phr* Something to be offered, conceded, threatened, etc, in negotiations; a "card that one plays" in bargaining: *The prime minister went to the summit meeting without very many strong bargaining chips/ He is using his information like a bargaining chip*—New York Times

barge in **1** *v phr* To enter a place without hesitation or ceremony, esp when not invited: *You can't just barge into the Yale Club* **2** *v phr* To interrupt; esp, to intrude with unwanted counsel; =BUTT IN, KIBITZ

bar-girl *n* =B-GIRL

barhop *v* (also **bar crawl** or **pub crawl**) To go drinking from bar to bar

barn *See* someone CAN'T HIT THE SIDE OF A BARN

barn-burner *n* Anything sensational or exciting: *whether they have a barn burner of a natural gas well or a dry hole*—Newsweek/ *George's Bank has proved to be, in the words of one oil-company executive, "no barn-burner"*—Boston Globe

barnstorm **1** *v fr early 1900s* To travel as an entertainer, making short or one-night appearances in small towns **2** *v fr 1920s* To travel about in an airplane or with an air show, doing aerobatics, giving rides, etc, esp in rural places

barracks bag *See* BLOW IT OUT

barracks lawyer *See* LATRINE LAWYER

barrel or **barrel along** *v* or *v phr* To speed, esp to drive a car very fast; career
See CRACKER-BARREL, LIKE SHOOTING FISH IN A BARREL, OVER A BARREL, SCRAPE THE BOTTOM OF THE BARREL

◁ **barrel ass**▷ *v phr* To barrel: *We're barrel-assing toward Van Nuys* —Esquire

bar the door *See* KATIE BAR THE DOOR

base *See* GET TO FIRST BASE, OFF BASE, TOUCH BASE WITH someone

baseball *See* OLDER THAN GOD

baseball Annie *n phr* A young female baseball fan: *The baseball*

Annies... are a fairly comely lot—Wall Street Journal

bases ***See*** TOUCH ALL BASES

bash **1** ***v*** To hit; =CLOBBER, SOCK **2** ***n*** A party, esp a good, exciting one: *Her little soiree turned into a real bash* **3** ***n*** An attempt; =CRACK, WHACK: *Let's have a bash at moving this thing*

-basher ***combining word*** A person who harasses or beats the person or item indicated: *car-basher/ fag-basher*

-bashing ***combining word*** Hating and attacking what or who is indicated: *author-bashing/ faggot-bashing/ gringo-bashing/ Paki-bashing*

basket **1** ***n*** The pit of the stomach; =BREADBASKET: *a blow flush in the basket*—Joseph Auslander **2** ***n*** *homosexuals* The male genitals, esp when prominently displayed in tight pants: *Steep enthusiastic eyes, Flicker after tits and baskets*—WH Auden

basket case **1** ***n phr*** A helpless, hopeless, distraught person: *If I worried after a decision... I'd be a basket case*—Time **2** ***n phr*** Anything ruined and hopeless: *Those are only the best-known corporate basket cases*—Toronto Life

◁ **bassackward** or **bassackwards**▷ **1** ***adj*** Backwards; reverse; =ASS BACKWARDS: *sort of bass-ackward hydraulic gimcrackery*—Car and Driver **2** ***adv:*** *He got it all bassackwards*

◁ **bastard**▷ **1** ***n*** A man one dislikes or disapproves of, esp a mean, dishonest, self-serving man; =PRICK, SON OF A BITCH **2** ***n*** Anything unpleasant or arduous; =BITCH: *Ain't it a bastard the way it keeps raining*

bat **1** ***n*** *fr early 1600s* A prostitute **2** ***n*** =OLD BAT **3** ***n*** *fr middle 1800s* A spree; carousal; =BINGE **4** ***n*** *horse-racing* A jockey's whip
See GO TO BAT FOR, LIKE A BAT OUT OF HELL, RIGHT OFF THE BAT

not **bat an eye** ***See*** NOT BAT AN EYE

bat around **1** ***v phr*** To do nothing in particular; go about in idle pursuit of pleasure: *I want the kids home instead o' battin' around the street*—Elmer Rice **2** ***v phr*** To discuss the pros and cons of an idea, project, etc: *We batted around the notion of a sick-out*

batch ***See*** BACH IT, LAY A BATCH

batch out ***v phr*** *hot rodders* To start and accelerate a car from a standstill

bat one's **gums** ***v phr*** (Variations: **beat** or **hump** or **flap** may replace **bat**; **chops** or **jaw** or **jowls** or **lip** may replace **gums**) To talk, esp idly or frivolously: *He didn't mean it, he was just batting his gums/ Well, you weren't just flapping your lip that time*—Peter De Vries

bath ***See*** TAKE A BATH

bathtub ***See*** WIN THE PORCELAIN HAIRNET

bathtub gin ***n phr*** *esp 1920s* Gin made at home by mixing alcohol with flavoring, often literally in a bathtub

bat out ***v phr*** To write more quickly than one ought; =WHOMP UP: *He kept batting out scenes*—Budd Schulberg/ *Bat me out a memo, please*

bats or **batty** ***adj*** Crazy; =NUTS: *He was grinning like he was bats/ funnier than you'd expect, fairly batty*—Village Voice

battery acid ***n phr*** *WW2 armed forces* Coffee

bat the breeze ***v phr*** To chat; converse, esp easily and idly; =RAP, SHOOT THE BREEZE: *a couple of cops batting the breeze*

Battle of the Bulge ***n phr*** The constant struggle to keep slim [fr the name of the Ardennes campaign of late 1944 in World War 2]

battlewagon **1** ***n*** *Navy* A battleship **2** ***n*** *hoboes & railroad* An iron railroad coal-car **3** ***n*** *1920s underworld* A police patrol wagon

batty ***See*** BATS

bawl baby ***n phr*** =CRYBABY

bawl someone **out** ***v phr*** To reprimand severely; rebuke; =CHEW someone OUT

bay window ***n phr*** A protuberant stomach; paunch; =POTBELLY: *He's lean and mean, no bay window and no patience*

◁ **bazongas** or **bazoongies**▷ (bə ZAHN gəz, bə Z͞OON geez) ***n*** A woman's breasts; =BAZOOM, JUGS

bazoo (bə Z͞OO) ***n*** *fr middle 1800s* The mouth, esp regarded as a speech organ: *if you would close that big bazoo*—Walt Kelly [fr Dutch *bazuin* "trumpet"]
See SHOOT OFF one's MOUTH

◁ **bazoom**▷ (bə Z͞OOM) ***n*** A woman's breast or breasts: *Whatever Julie Andrews wants to do with her bazooms is OK with me*—Susan

Rausch [fr comic mispronunciation of *bosom*, and association with the excitement of *zoom*]

B-bag *See* BLOW IT OUT

beach blanket bingo *n phr* Sexual activity on the beach

beach bum *n phr* A man who frequents beaches, esp one who is a surfer, who conspicuously shows his muscles, etc

beach bunny *n phr* A girl who, whether or not a surfer, spends time with surfers; =GREMLIN

bead *See* DROP BEADS, GET A BEAD ON something or someone

beady eye *See* GIVE someone THE FISH-EYE

beagle *n outdated underworld* A lawyer or judge

See LEGAL EAGLE

beak[1] **1** *n* A mayor, magistrate, or trial judge • Outdated in US use, though still current in British slang **2** *n* A lawyer [fr Celtic *beachd* "judgment, judge"]

beak[2] *n* The nose: *The beak-buster in the opening round was the first punch Moore had thrown*—Associated Press

the **beam** *See* OFF THE BEAM, ON THE BEAM

bean **1** *n outdated underworld* A five-dollar gold piece **2** *n* A dollar: *without a coat on his back or a bean in his pocket*—J Lilienthal **3** *n gambling* A poker chip **4** *n* The head, esp the human head and brain: *Whistling at a crook is not near as effective as to crack him on the bean with a hickory stick*—Will Rogers **5** *v* To strike someone on the head, esp to hit a baseball batter on the head with a pitch: *The Landmark itself can make a reader feel beaned*—Time ◀**6**▶ *n* (also **beaner**) A person of Spanish-American background, esp a Chicano

See FULL OF BEANS, LOOSE IN THE BEAN, SPILL THE BEANS, USE one's HEAD

beanball *n* A baseball pitch that hits or nearly hits the batter's head and is sometimes used to intimidate the batter: *Mr Bender places much reliance on the bean ball*—C Dryden

bean counter *n phr* A statistician or arithmetical clerk in government or business; =GNOME, NUMBER CRUNCHER: *Even in Britain, the bean counters couldn't tolerate a negative cash flow forever*—Car and Driver

bean-counting *modifier* Having to do with bureaucratic statistics and calculations: *We have our bean-counting ways, they, Russians, Cubans, etc, have their bean-counting ways*—National Public Radio/ *This bean-counting approach is an easy way to score debating points*—New York Times

bean-eater **1** *n* A resident of Boston ◀**2**▶ *n* A person of Spanish-American background, esp a Chicano; =BEAN

◀ **beaner**▶ *See* BEAN

beanery **1** *n* A restaurant or diner, esp a cheap one: *a beanery in Hell's Kitchen*—John McCarten **2** *n underworld* A jail

beanie *n* A skull cap, esp one worn by schoolboys and college freshmen

beanpole *n* A tall, thin person *She was tall, but no beanpole*—Raymond Chandler

beans **1** *n fr middle 1800s* Nothing; a minimal amount; =DIDDLY • Semantically very similar to **bubkes**: *She would get all of her famous friends to appear and pay them beans*—Time **2** *interj* An exclamation of disbelief or contempt

See FULL OF BEANS, a HILL OF BEANS, KNOW one's ONIONS

Bean Town *n phr* Boston, Massachusetts

bear **1** *n narcotics* A capsule containing a narcotic **2** *n students* A difficult school or college course **3** *n* Anything arduous or disagreeable; =BITCH **4** *n* A large, gruff man

See DOES A BEAR SHIT IN THE WOODS

Bear *See* SMOKEY BEAR

beard **1** *n 1950s beat & cool talk* An up-to-the-minute, alert person; =HIPSTER **2** *n fr gambling* A person used as an agent, to conceal the principal's identity: *Use him as a beard, is what Donny thought he'd do*—Dan Jenkins **3** *n* A bearded man, esp someone of apparent dignity and authority: *I can't believe the sainted beards would bang me with a manufactured case*—Paul Sann **4** *n* The pubic hair; =BUSH

See GRAYBEARD

◁ **bearded clam**▷ *n phr* The vulva

a **bear in the air** *n phr* A police officer in a helicopter [fr *Smokey Bear*]

bear trap *n phr citizens band* A police radar trap for speeders [related to *Smokey Bear* "policeman"]

◁ **be** someone's **ass**▷ ***See*** IT WILL BE someone's ASS

beast **1** *n* A cheap prostitute **2** *n* (also **beastie, beasty**) An especially unattractive woman **3** *n* Any woman whatever, but esp a young attractive one

beat **1** *n fr middle 1800s* A loafer; drifter; =DEADBEAT, MOOCHER **2** *v hoboes* To avoid paying train fares and other bills **3** *v fr underworld* To avoid a fine or conviction: *to beat a burglary rap* **4** *n news media* News printed or broadcast first, before one's competitors; =SCOOP: *The News scored an important beat* **5** *n fr police & news media* The area or subject matter which one is assigned to handle: *cop on his beat/ a reporter on the courthouse beat* **6** *adj* Looking as if battered; disheveled; damaged; =BEAT UP **7** *adj* Very tired; =ALL IN, POOPED **8** *n* The basic meter of a piece of music, esp the insistent percussive rhythm of some jazz styles and rock and roll **9** *adj 1950s beat talk* Alienated from the general society, and expressing this by a wandering life, the avoidance of work, the advocacy of sexual freedom, the use of narcotics, a distinctive style of dress and grooming, and the adoption of certain aspects of Far Eastern religions: *the beat generation/ beat poets* **10** *n* =BEATNIK **11** *v* To be robbed or shortchanged, esp in an illegal exchange: *I sure got beat when I bought marijuana in the park*

See DOWNBEAT, OFFBEAT, UPBEAT

beat a dead horse *v phr* To continue arguing, discussing, or broaching a matter which is settled or proved unavailing

beat around *v phr* To loaf or idle; =GOOF AROUND

beat around (or **about**) **the bush** *v phr* To avoid speaking directly and precisely; evade; tergiversate

beat one's **brains out** **1** *v phr* To labor strenuously with the mind, often with a sense of having failed: *I beat my brains out getting ready for it, but flunked anyway* **2** *v phr* To threaten with bodily harm: *If you don't come through, I'll beat your brains out*

beaten-up ***See*** BEAT-UP

beater *n* A car, esp an old and used one: *when he's stolen the beater off the streets*—Ann Rule

beat one's **gums** ***See*** BAT one's GUMS

beating ***See*** GUM-BEATING, TAKE A BEATING

beat it *v phr* To go away; depart; =SCRAM • Often a command: *When the cop told us to beat it we didn't waste any time*

◁ **beat** one's **meat**▷ *v phr* (Variations: **flog** or **pound** may replace **beat**; **dummy** or **log** may replace **meat**) To masturbate

beatnik *n fr 1950s* A person who is beat in the sense of alienation from society, etc [See *beat* and *-nik*; coined by San Francisco newspaper columnist Herb Caen in 1958]

◁ **beat off**▷ *v* To masturbate

beat someone **out** *v phr* To surpass or best, esp by a narrow margin: *She just beat me out for the job, probably because she had more schooling*

beats me **1** *interj* An exclamation or acknowledgment of ignorance; =SEARCH ME **2** *sentence* I don't know; I don't understand: *Why was he hired? Beats me*

be at square one ***See*** GO BACK TO SQUARE ONE

beat the bushes *v phr* To search diligently; seek ardently: *They're beating the bushes for a new president*

beat the rap *v phr underworld* To go unpunished; be acquitted: *Every time they arrest him he beats the rap*

◁ **beat the shit out of** someone or something▷ *v phr* (Variations: **bejesus** or **daylights** or **hell** or **kishkes** or **living daylights** or **living shit** or **stuffing** or **tar** may replace **shit**; **kick** or **knock** or another term denoting assault or punishment may replace **beat**) To defeat or thrash thoroughly; trounce; =CLOBBER: *The two joggers caught up with him and beat the shit out of him/ He told us that the cops kicked the bejesus out of his old man/ If he tries that again I'd knock the living shit out of him/ "I'll sue the shit out of her," vowed Professor Gold* —Joseph Heller

beat the socks off someone *v phr* To defeat decisively; trounce; =CLOB-

BER: *In a surprising upset, Hart beat the socks off Mondale*

beat someone's **time** *v phr* To win out over a rival, esp to take someone's girlfriend or boyfriend away

beat someone **to the draw** (or **to the punch**) *v phr* To act sooner or quicker than someone else; forestall: *The President beat Congress to the punch with that recommendation*

beat-up *adj* Battered and damaged, esp by age and use: *He drove a beat-up Volvo/ an old beat-up dog*

beat up on *v phr* To attack and damage; criticize harshly; trounce; =CLOBBER: *a message to people who beat up on the public programs*—New York Times

beaut (BYōōT) *n* A person or thing that is remarkable or extraordinary; =HUMDINGER, LOLLAPALOOZA: *While the President doesn't go off on these tangents often, when he does, they are beauts*—Drew Pearson

the **beautiful people** *n phr* People who are fashionable, wealthy, admired for style and opulence, etc; =the JET SET

beauty *adj Canadian* Excellent; superior; =GREAT: *I thought the guy was beauty*

beauty contest *n phr* A canvass or occasion that reveals preference, without the force of an election: *the mini-convention billed as a beauty contest for those seeking the presidential nomination*—Village Voice

beaver **1** *n* A full beard **2** *n* A bearded man ◁**3**▷ *n* The female genitals, esp with a display of pubic hair ◁**4**▷ *n* Pornography: *The editor... lovingly runs his beaver one column over from his furious tirade*—New York Times ◁**5**▷ *n* A pornographic film; =SKIN FLICK ◁**6**▷ *n citizens band* A woman

See SPLIT BEAVER

◁ **beaver loop**▷ *n phr* A pornographic film strip in a coin-operated viewing machine

◁ **beaver-shooter**▷ *n* A man obsessed with peering at female genitals: *A beaver shooter is, at bottom, a Peeping Tom*—Jim Bouton

◁ **beaver shot**▷ *n phr* A photograph showing the female genitals prominently, esp one focusing on the vulva

bebop *See* BOP

not **be caught dead** *See* NOT BE CAUGHT DEAD

bed *See* GO TO BED WITH someone, HOTBED, MUSICAL BEDS

bee *See* PUT THE BITE ON someone or something

beef **1** *n fr middle 1900s underworld* A complaint; grievance: *Her mother called up to register a beef*—Billy Rose **2** *v: The hospital beefed when the city announced plans*—Philadelphia Bulletin **3** *n* A quarrel; argument: *I've got no beef with you, buddy* **4** *n* A customer's bill or check; =BAD NEWS **5** *n* Muscle; strength; huskiness ◁**6**▷ *n* The penis

beefcake *n* A photograph or photographs of a muscular male body with little or no clothing: *The actor has no objections to male cheesecake, or beefcake as it is called in Hollywood*—Bob Thomas

beef trust *n phr* Any group of stout or fat people, esp a chorus line of hefty women [fr the muckraker term for those who controlled the meat business]

beef up *v phr* To strengthen; reinforce: *The Patriots beefed up their defense by adding an all-star lineman*

bee in one's **bonnet** *n phr* A particular idea or notion, esp a fantastic or eccentric one; obsession: *He's got a bee in his bonnet about wheat germ curing all the world's ills*

beely bopper *See* DEELY BOPPER

beep **1** *v* To sound the horn of a car **2** *n: The car gave a few hearty beeps* **3** *v* A usu high-pitched short burst of sound used as a signal in an electronic device, on the telephone, etc: *Please give your message when you hear the beep*

beeper *n* A tiny radio receiver that gives a coded signal to a person being notified of a telephone call or other summons: *Beepers proliferate, tolling for many besides the doctor*—Wall Street Journal

beer *See* CRY IN one's BEER, SMALL POTATOES

beer belly **1** *n* A protuberant paunch **2** *n* A man with a prominent paunch

beer bust (or **blast**) *n phr chiefly college students* A party where beer is the featured drink; =BREW OUT: *It was* *supposed to be a party, a beerbust* —James Jones

beerslinger *n fr late 1800s* A bartender

Beertown *n* Milwaukee, Wisconsin: *tiny minimum-security prisons right in the midst of Beertown* Milwaukee Journal

beeswax *n* Business; concern: *What I do at home is none of his beeswax*

beezer **1** *n fr hoboes and prizefight* The nose **2** *n* The face

beggar's velvet *n phr* =HOUSE MOSS

be good *interj* A parting salutation

behind *n* The buttocks; rump; =ASS: *her broad, plain Slavic face, absence of waistline, and enormously broad behind*—Vogue

behind the ears *See* NOT DRY BEHIND THE EARS

behind the eight ball *adv phr* In a losing or endangered position: *He was sick and broke, right behind the eight ball* [fr the position of a pool player *behind the black eight ball*, which he must not hit]

behind the stick *See* WORK BEHIND THE STICK

beige **1** *n black* A black person with a light complexion **2** *adj high school students* Boring; insipid; =HO-HUM

be-in *n esp 1960s counterculture* A large, peaceable gathering of young people, esp of hippies, where they don't do anything in particular: *a San Francisco "Be-in" attracted more than 100,000 persons*—New York Times/ *with buttons and beards and Be-Ins*—WH Auden [modeled on *sit-in*]

the **bejesus** *See* BEAT THE SHIT OUT OF someone or something

believe *See* YOU BETTER BELIEVE something

bell *See* DUMBBELL, MA BELL, RING A BELL, RING someone's BELL, RING THE BELL, SAVED BY THE BELL, WITH BELLS ON

bell-ringer **1** *n* A door-to-door salesman or canvasser **2** *n* A local politician **3** *n* A fact or event that causes one to recall something

bells *See* WITH BELLS ON

bells and whistles **1** *n phr* Unessential elements, esp when impressive and decorative; frills: *the latest "bells and whistles," as high-tech frills are called*—Time/ *you strip away the technological bells and whistles and...*—New York Times **2** *n phr* Accessories and accoutrements esp of the flashier sort; refinements; adornments; finishing touches: *Maserati... with all the bells and whistles*—Wall Street Journal **3** ***modifier:*** *If you are a bells and whistles guy, you will probably find these cars to be of more value*—New York Times

belly **1** *n* The stomach; abdomen; paunch; =GUT: *That's not my belly, my chest just sagged a little south* **2** *n* =BELLY LAUGH

See BEER BELLY, JELLY-BELLY, MELON-BELLY, POTBELLY, SOURBALL, YELLOW-BELLY

bellyache **1** *v fr early 1900s* To complain, esp to do so habitually; =BITCH: *always bellyaching about me* —James T Farrell **2** *n* A complaint; =BEEF

belly-buster *See* BELLY-WHOPPER

belly button *n phr* The navel

belly flop *n phr* A dive in which one strikes the water stomach first; =BELLY-WHOPPER

belly-flopper *See* BELLY-WHOPPER

bellyful *n* The limit of what one can stand; an overplus; surfeit: *I've had a bellyful of your bellyaching*

belly laugh *n phr* An especially loud, vigorous, and appreciative laugh; =BELLY, BOFFOLA

belly-smacker *See* BELLY-WHOPPER

belly telly *n phr* A small television set, such as might be perched on one's stomach for viewing as one lies flat

belly up **1** *v phr fr cowboys* To die; be down and out; collapse; =GO BELLY UP: *were the schools to belly up tomorrow*—Philadelphia **2** ***adj phr:*** *The whole project's belly up*

See GO BELLY UP

belly up to *v phr fr cowboys* To push or come up close to, esp to a bar for a drink: *Sammy Davis, Jr bellied up to the bar*—People Weekly/ *Meat Loaf bellies up to Billy Joel at a softball showdown*—Rolling Stone

belly-whopper (Variations: **-buster** or **-flopper** or **-smacker** may replace **-whopper**) **1** *n* A sled ride begun by running with the sled held at one's side, then leaping onto it stomach down **2** *n* =BELLY FLOP

belt **1** *v* To hit; strike; =SOCK: *Ed belts him in the kisser/ He belted the* *ball a mile* **2** *n* A blow; stroke; =WHACK: *She gave it a good belt* **3** *n* A thrill; transport of pleasure; =KICK: *You'll get a belt out of this one* **4** *n narcotics* A marijuana cigarette; =JOINT **5** *v* To drink, esp vigorously and often: *He's belting down the booze again* **6** *n* A drink; swig; swallow: *He handed me the bottle and I took a belt at it*—H Allen Smith

See BORSCHT BELT, TIGHTEN one's BELT

belt out *v phr* To sing in a loud and vigorous style

be my guest *sentence* Do as you please • Often an ironical acquiescence to something ill-advised: *You want to tell the cop he's wrong? Be my guest*

bench warmer *n phr* A person not among the most active and important members of an enterprise; esp, a substitute athlete who seldom plays

bend *See* AROUND THE BEND

bend someone's **ear** *v phr* To talk to someone insistently and at length: *He was bending my ear about his new car*

bender **1** *n fr middle 1800s* A spree, esp a drinking spree; =BAT, BINGE: *That three-day bender left Jim hurting all over/ a carrot-juice bender* **2** *n underworld* A stolen car [first sense fr *hell-bender* "alligator," of obscure origin, which came to mean "anything spectacular and superior" and was applied to a great spree in the mid-19th century]

See EAR-BENDER, ELBOW-BENDER, FENDER-BENDER, MIND-BLOWER

bending *See* ELBOW-BENDING

bend someone's **mind** *v phr* To have a very strong and usu disturbing mental effect; impress powerfully: *This one really bends her mind; she starts philosophizing*—Washington Post

bend over backwards *v phr* To make every effort; strive mightily: *I bent over backwards trying to be fair*

bend the (or one's) **elbow** (Variations: **crook** or **tip** may replace **bend**; **his** or **her** or **an** may replace **the**) *fr early 1800s* **1** *v phr* To drink frequently and heavily, esp whiskey: *They cautioned him that maybe he was bending the elbow a little too often* **2** *v phr* To have a drink: *We'll tip the elbow over at my place*

benny or **bennie** **1** *n narcotics* Any amphetamine pill, esp Benzedrine (a trade name) **2** *modifier: The kid was a benny addict*

bent **1** *adj* Intoxicated, either from alcohol or narcotics **2** *adj* Having very little money: *I'm not quite broke, but quite bent* **3** *adj* Homosexual **4** *adj* Sexually aberrant; =KINKY: *Charley got bent bad over women... he was kinky when it came to ladies* —Harry Crews **5** *adj* Dishonest; shady; =CROOKED: *look a little bent... look like you were up for a little whoremongering and black-marketing and smuggling*—Richard Merkin **6** *adj underworld fr early 1900s* Stolen, said esp of car **7** *adj fr Air Force* Angry; upset

bent-eight *See* FORKED-EIGHT

bent out of shape **1** *adj phr* Intoxicated; drunk; =STONED **2** *adj fr Air Force* Very angry; extremely upset: *He is so far bent out of shape by the press reaction*—Washington Post/ *Why are you bent out of shape?*—Armistead Maupin

the **berries** *n phr esp 1920s & 1930s* The best; =the MOST [fr early-20th-century college slang *berry* "something easy and pleasant, a good thing"]

berry *n fr early 1900s* A dollar [perhaps fr the notion of a small unit of something good, and alliterating with *buck*; see the *berries*]

Bertha *See* BIG BERTHA

best *See* someone's LEVEL BEST

best bib and tucker *n phr fr early 1800s* One's best clothes; =GLAD RAGS

best fellow *n phr* =MAIN MAN

best girl *n phr* =MAIN SQUEEZE

best shot *See* GIVE something one's BEST SHOT

the **best** (or **greatest**) **thing since sliced bread** *n phr* A person or thing that is superlative; a paragon; =WINNER: *I thought she was the best thing since sliced bread*—Washington Post

bet one's **bottom dollar** *v phr* To be absolutely sure of something; be totally convinced; =BET THE FARM: *I'll bet my bottom dollar she'll be back*

betsy or **Betsy** or **Betsey** *n* A firearm of any sort: *I got a lot of votes in ol' Betsey here*—Walt Kelly

better *See* NO BETTER THAN SHE OUGHT TO BE, YOU BETTER BELIEVE something

bet the farm (or **the rent** or **the ranch**) *v phr* Bet everything one has; =GO FOR BROKE, BET one's BOTTOM DOLLAR: *I wouldn't have bet the farm ... but I'd sure bet the back forty*—Washingtonian/ *I wouldn't bet the ranch that he'll be reappointed*—National Public Radio/ *You can bet the rent the Jacksons will go where the big money is*—Washington Post

between a (or **the**) **rock and a** (or **the**) **hard place** *adv phr fr cowboys* In a dilemma: *So a writer is caught between the rock and the hard place*—New York Times/ *informants, caught between the rock of prison and the hard place of the snitch*—Washington Post

bet your boots *v phr* (Variations: **ass** or **sweet ass** or **bibby** or **bippy** or **bottom dollar** or **life** or **shirt** or **whiskers** may replace **boots**) To be absolutely assured; count on it: *You can bet your boots I'll be there/ You bet your sweet ass it was easier at the museum*—Leslie Hollander

B-girl *n fr 1940s* A promiscuous girl or woman, esp one who works in a bar as a sort of hostess to stimulate the sale of drinks; =BAR-GIRL

bi (BĪ) **1** *adj* Bisexual; =AC-DC **2** *n: I think maybe Vi is a bi*

bibby *See* BIPPY

Bible *See* SWEAR ON A STACK OF BIBLES

Bible-banger or **Bible-thumper** *n* A strict religionist, esp a Protestant fundamentalist: *to ensure it doesn't offend some Bible-banger in Mississippi*—Playboy

◁ **bicho** ▷ (BEE choh) *n* The penis [fr Spanish]

bicoastal *adj* Active on both the Atlantic and Pacific coasts: *bicoastal type A males*—Time

biddy **1** *n* A woman, esp an old shrewish woman • Nearly always with "old": *Charley had met an old biddy named Zoe Winthrop*—W Fuller **2** *n* =CHICK [diminutive of the name *Bridget*] =BIFFER

◁ **biffer** ▷ *n black* A homely woman who compensates by being promiscuous

biffy *n chiefly Canadian* A toilet; bathroom

big **1** *adj* Important; powerful: *the big names in this business/ the big guy* **2** *adj* Popular; successful: *If I do say so, we were very big*—Bing Crosby/ *The book's big in Chicago* **3** *adv* Successfully; outstandingly well: *to hit it big*

See BIG WITH someone, GO OVER BIG, MAKE IT BIG, TAKE IT HARD, TALK BIG

Big *adj* Good, decent; admirable • Used as an epithet for an admired person: *Hey, what's up, Big Eddy?*

See MISTER BIG

the **Big Apple** or the **Apple** **1** *n phr* New York City: *New York is the Big Apple*—Stephen Longstreet/ *young musicians storming into the Apple*—Village Voice **2** *n phr* A jitterbug dance of the late 1930s [fr jazz musicians' term *apple* for a city, esp a city in the North]

◁ **bigass** ▷ **1** *adj* Pretentiously large: *Abraham opened the door of his bigass Cadillac*—Hugh Selby, Jr **2** *adj* Pretentious; self-important: *Don't act bigass with me*

Big Bertha **1** *n phr* A large or fat woman **2** *n phr fr WW1* Any very large cannon [the artillery sense is said to be fr *Frau Bertha Krupp*, a member of the German armaments-making family]

big boy **1** *n phr* You there; man; =MAC • A term of address variously used with the intention to challenge, flatter, attract, etc: *Want a little fun, big boy?* **2** *n phr* An important man; =BIGGIE, BIG SHOT: *He tried to shake down one of the big boys*—Raymond Chandler

Big Brother or **big brother** **1** *n phr* The faceless and ruthless power of the totalitarian or bureaucratic state personified **2** *n phr airline* The tracking radar used by ground controllers [fr its use by George Orwell in his novel *1984*]

big brown eyes *n phr* A woman's breasts

big bucks *n phr* A large amount of money; great sums of money; =MEGABUCKS: *That car would cost you big bucks today*

big butter-and-egg man *See* BUTTER-AND-EGG MAN

big buzz *n phr* Loudest current rumor: *the big buzz around Broadway is the announcement*—Aquarian

Big C *n phr* Cancer

big cheese **1** ***n phr*** =BIG SHOT **2** ***n phr*** A stupid or rude man; lout [for first sense, see the *cheese*]

big D ***n phr*** LSD

Big D **1** ***n phr*** Detroit, Michigan **2** ***n phr*** Dallas, Texas

Big Daddy or **big daddy** **1** ***n phr*** You there; man; =BIG BOY, MAC • Term of address used to any man, usu with a view to flattering him **2** ***n phr*** =DADDY **3** ***n phr*** =DADDY-O

big deal **1** ***n phr*** Anything very important; consequential event or circumstance • Often used ironically to deflate someone or something, esp in the retort "Big deal" after someone has made an earnest reference: *Getting good grades is a big deal around here/ So you just bought an Audi. Big deal* **2** ***n phr*** An important person; =BIG SHOT

See MAKE A BIG PRODUCTION, NO BIG DEAL

bigdome ***n*** An important person, esp a manager or business executive; =BIG SHOT: *if the NBA bigdomes are concerned about their image and popular appeal*—New York Daily News

big doolie ***n phr*** An important person, esp a winning athlete; =BIG SHOT: *I got a gold today, so I'm a big doolie*—New York Times [perhaps related to the earlier term *dooly* "dynamite"]

big drink of water *See* LONG DRINK OF WATER

big enchilada ***n phr*** The chief; the head person; =BOSS: *The Big Enchilada is tied up with the Chief Honcho at the moment, but the Little Enchilada can see you now*—New Yorker cartoon

big fat ***adj phr*** Embarrassingly obvious; blatant and humiliating: *I couldn't keep my big fat mouth shut/ His big fat trademark heart greets you in this show*—Village Voice

big fish (or **frog**) ***n phr*** An important person; =BIG SHOT

big foot ***n phr newspaper office*** A senior editor, important editorialist or columnist, etc: *but many an editor or pundit, a "big foot" in the parlance of the bus*—Time [fr *bigfoot*, one of the designations of Sasquatch, a large hairy humanoid creature thought by some to inhabit the forests of the Pacific Northwest, and probably applied to senior newspaper persons because of metaphorical size and menace]

bigger (or **other**) **fish to fry** ***n phr*** Other and more pressing matters to attend to; more important things in prospect: *Tell him to relax, we've got bigger fish to fry*—Ed McBain

biggie **1** ***n*** A prominent or stellar person; =BIG SHOT: *Sullivan continues putting the bee on other Government biggies*—Variety **2** ***n*** Something important and successful; =BIG DEAL: *a tubular biggie, not only in LA and NY, but in Chicago, Detroit, and Atlanta*—Time **3** ***n*** Anything large and important: *a real biggie, like Brazil, went to the wall*—Playboy

See NO BIGGIE

big gun ***n phr*** =BIG SHOT

big guns *See* HEAVY ARTILLERY

big H ***n phr narcotics*** Heroin

Big Harry ***n phr narcotics*** Heroin

bighead ***n*** A self-important, conceited person

bigheaded ***adj*** Conceited

big hole ***n phr truckers*** The low gear of a truck

the **big house** or the **Big House** ***n phr underworld fr middle 1800s*** A state or federal penitentiary: *to go to the big house for the rest of his life*—Morris Bishop

the **big idea** *See* WHAT'S THE BIG IDEA

the **big joint** ***n phr*** =the BIG HOUSE

big-league ***adj*** Serious; important; professional: *No more fooling around, now it's big-league stuff*

the **big leagues** **1** ***n phr*** In baseball, the major leagues **2** ***n phr*** The higher, more serious and arduous reaches of a profession, business, government, sport, etc; =the BIG TIME, HARDBALL

the **big lie** ***n phr*** A major political untruth, usu of a demagogic sort, uttered frequently by leaders as a means of duping and controlling the constituency [fr a notion of Adolf Hitler in *Mein Kampf*]

big man on campus ***n phr college students*** A male college student leader; =BMOC

big money *See* HEAVY MONEY

bigmouth **1** ***n*** A person who talks constantly and loudly **2** ***n*** A person who freely announces personal opinions and judgments; =KNOW-IT-

ALL, SMART-ASS **3** ***n*** A person who can't keep a secret

See HAVE A BIG MOUTH

big name **1** ***n phr*** A celebrated person, personality or entity, esp a star entertainer: *Hollywood figures only the big names are bankable* **2** ***n phr*** A prominent reputation; fame: *The group has a big name in the Boston area* **3** ***modifier:*** *a big-name star/ They get a big-name fee*

big nickel ***n phr*** *gambling* A $5000 bet

big noise **1** ***n phr*** Important news: *Big Noise from Moscow*—New York Daily News **2** ***n phr*** An important person; most influential person: *Who's the big noise around here?*

big one ***n phr*** *fr gambling* A thousand dollars, esp as a bet: *The highjackers are handed 50 cents a gallon, which is 15 big ones and OK for a couple hours' work*—Time/ *The next time you want me to do the Today show, it's going to cost you ten big ones* —Art Buchwald

the **big one** ***n phr*** The most important or crucial item: *Having a winning season is fine, but now we've got to win the big one*

the **big picture** ***n phr*** The large strategic situation as distinct from little details; inclusive of the surrounding circumstances

the **Big Pretzel** ***n phr*** Philadelphia

Big Pretzelite ***n phr*** A Philadelphian: *several reasons for Big Pretzelites to swing into the Franklin Plaza*—Philadelphia

big production ***See*** MAKE A BIG PRODUCTION

the **bigs** ***n phr*** The major leagues, in baseball or other areas; =the BIG TIME: *When Backman was in the bigs, he wasn't your regular Mr. Sunshine* —Village Voice

the **big score** ***n phr*** Success; spectacular achievement: *Jobs' entrepreneurial flair and his instinct for the big score*—Time

big shot or **bigshot** **1** ***n phr*** or ***n*** *fr early 1900s* A very important person; influential person; leader; =BIG CHEESE, BIGGIE: *eight big shots of various farmers', manufacturers', or veterans' organizations*—HL Mencken/ *"Hey, bigshot," his father would bellow on the telephone*—Joseph Heller **2** ***modifier*** • Often used sarcastically: *a big-shot chest surgeon/ big-shot notions*

big stick ***n phr*** *firefighters* An aerial ladder

big stiff ***n phr*** A large, rough man, esp one who is somewhat stupid as well • Sometimes used as a term of affection by a woman

big stink **1** ***n phr*** A loud and prolonged complaint; an extensive fuss; =MAKE A FEDERAL CASE OUT OF something: *He made a big stink about my using his screwdriver* **2** ***n phr*** A scandal: *There'll be a big stink about these tapes*

big talk **1** ***n phr*** Boastful and extravagant talk; esp, promises or claims beyond one's capacity: *His promises were just big talk* **2** ***v:*** *Don't big-talk a big-talker, man*

big (or **high**) **ticket** *salespersons* **1** ***adj phr*** Expensive; high-priced: *very low for the promotion of a big-ticket item*—Fortune/ *More and more complete-text services are becoming available, especially in high-ticket fields like law*—Philadelphia **2** ***n phr*** The sale of an expensive item: *He wrote up a couple of big tickets yesterday*

big time ***adv phr*** *Army* Very much; extremely: *He's gonna complain big time*

the **big time** **1** ***n phr*** The upper reaches of a profession, business, government, sport, etc; =the BIG LEAGUES **2** ***modifier:*** *a big-time outfit/ big-time crime* [fr the outdated theater use designating certain important vaudeville circuits or houses]

big-time operator ***n phr*** A person conspicuously active in affairs where trade-offs, special favors, private understandings, etc, are crucial; machinator; =BTO, MACHER, WHEELER-DEALER

big-time spender ***n phr*** A person who is generous and extravagant, esp for lavish entertainment; =HIGH ROLLER

big wheel **1** ***n phr*** An important person; =BIG SHOT: *Up to that juncture I was boss man of the family and big wheel*—SJ Perelman **2** ***modifier:*** *a big-wheel attitude*

big with someone ***prep phr*** Popular with; preferred by; relished by: *That's* *big with her*—Armistead Maupin/ *Baggy sweaters are real big with the kids this year*

bike 1 *n* A bicycle or motorcycle **2** *n* A motorcycle police officer
See DIRT BIKE, TOWN PUMP

biker *n* A motorcycle rider and enthusiast: *Bikers in black leather roared through the town*

bilge 1 *n* Nonsense; worthless and vain matter; =TRIPE, BLAH **2** *v* (also **bilge out**) *Annapolis fr 1920s* To fail or expel a student **3** *v* To use the toilet

bill 1 *n* The nose **2** *n outdated black* A knife, esp a small one easily concealed **3** *n* A hundred dollars: *I laid out four bills for that shearling* **4** *n* A single dollar: *Can I borrow a couple of bills until tomorrow?*
See PHONY AS A THREE-DOLLAR BILL

Billyball *n* The style of baseball played under the management of Billy Martin

billy club or **billy** *n phr* or *n fr middle 1800s* A police officer's nightstick

billy-goat *n armed forces* Mutton

bim *n esp 1920s* A girl or woman, esp one's girlfriend [fr *bimbo*]

bimbette *n* A frivolous or stupid young woman; a man's plaything • Regarded by some women as offensive: *itching to play something more demanding than bimbettes and stand-by wives*—Times

bimbo 1 *n fr early 1900s* A man, esp a mean and menacing one; =BABY, BOZO: *The bimbos once helped pluck a bank*—Dashiell Hammett **2** *n fr early 1900s* An insignificant person; =NEBBISH: *Nobody listened to the poor bimbo* **3** *n 1920s* A baby ◁**4**▷ *n fr 1920s* A woman, esp a young woman: *What kind of a bimbo did he think I am?*—Hal Boyle **5** *n fr 1920s* A prostitute; =HOOKER: *Some escort services are just fronts for prostitution... men call up and the service just sends out some bimbo in blue jeans from Brooklyn*—New York [fr Italian, "baby, bambino"; the final sense is probably related to the common use of *Bimbo* as the name of a monkey or a monkey doll, in turn probably related to the monkey that accompanied street organ-grinders, typically Italians]

Bimmer *n* A BMW car: *Bum out a Bimmer driver. Unleash a Chevette*—Car and Driver

the **bin** *n phr* =LOONY BIN

bind *n* A very tight and awkward situation; cleft stick; =BOX, JAM: *This is a nasty sort of bind*
See IN A BIND

binders *n police, hot rodders & students* The brakes of a car

bindlestiff *fr early 1900s* *n* A migrant harvest worker, esp a hobo with his bindle: *I was a bindlestiff. That's the class that will do some work once in a while*—JR Kennedy [fr *bindle* "blanket-roll, bundle" and *stiff* "worker, migratory worker"]

binge *n* A spree, esp a drunken spree; =BAT, BENDER: *with the studios on an economy binge*—Variety/ *one last banana binge*—Philadelphia Bulletin

binged (BINGD) *adj armed forces fr WW1* Vaccinated

bingle 1 *n baseball* A base hit, esp a single **2** *n gambling* A poker chip, usu worth 25 cents **3** *n narcotics* A large supply or cache of narcotics

bingo *interj* An exclamation in reaction to something sudden and unexpected, or expressing sudden success: *Have your contracts and debts declared void and, bingo, you're back in business*—Newsweek
See BEACH BLANKET BINGO

bio *n* A biography, esp a brief one in a yearbook, theater program, etc: *By now Jenny had read my bio in the program*—Erich Segal

bioflick or **biopic** *n* A movie or television show based on some person's life story: *star in a bioflick on... Charlie Parker*—People Weekly

bippy or **bibby** *n* The buttocks; =ASS
See BET YOUR BOOTS

bird 1 *n* A person of either sex, usu a man and often elderly: *I'm a literary bird myself*—F Scott Fitzgerald **2** *n* A young woman; =CHICK • Much commoner in British usage; regarded by some women as offensive **3** *n fr late 1800s* An odd or unusual person; an eccentric; =FLAKE, WEIRDO: *He was a funny bird in many ways*—Armistead Maupin ◁**4**▷ *n fr late 1800s* A male homosexual; =GAY **5** ***modifier:*** *a gaggle of the guys in a Third Avenue bird bar*—Judith Crist **6** *n armed forces fr WW1* The eagle as an insignia of rank **7** *modifier: a bird colonel* **8** *n* Any aircraft, esp a helicopter **9** *n astronautics* A rocket or guided missile **10** *n aerospace* A communications satellite: *A VTR operator in Vancouver is editing a local piece for The National. "Gotta make the bird," the guy says*—Toronto Life

See EARLY BIRD, FOR THE BIRDS, HAVE A BIRD, JAILBIRD, OFF one's NUT, RAILBIRD, WHIRLYBIRD, YARDBIRD

the **bird** **1** *n phr* A rude flatulatory noise made with the tongue and lips to express disapproval, derision, or contempt; =BRONX CHEER, RASPBERRY: *Give him the boid, the raspberry* —Eugene O'Neill **2** *n phr* =the FINGER [first sense fr the mid-19th-century expression *give the big bird* "hiss someone like a goose"]

birdbrain *n* A person of meager intelligence; idiot: *whatever bird-brain is rendering one of the ditties of the day* —Robert Ruark

birdbrained *adj* Stupid: *Nancy Fox, an abducted bride, is unquestionably birdbrained*—Village Voice

bird colonel *n phr* =CHICKEN COLONEL

bird course *n phr Canadian students* An easy college course; =GUT COURSE

bird dog **1** *n phr* A person, like a detective, talent scout, etc, whose job is to find something or someone **2** *n phr students* A chaperon at a dance **3** *n phr service academy* A tactical office, enforcing order and discipline **4** *n phr WW2 Army Air Force* A fighter or interceptor aircraft **5** *n phr airline* The automatic direction-finding instrument of an aircraft **6** *n phr gambling* A minor gambler who seeks the company and instruction of professionals

birdfarm *n Vietnam War Navy* An aircraft carrier: *The days are gone when a carrier was called a flattop. The craft is now a "birdfarm"*—New York Times

birdie or **birdy** *adj teenagers* Eccentric; weird; =FLAKY

birdies *n* =BIRD LEGS

bird legs *n phr* Thin bony legs

birds *See* FOR THE BIRDS

◁ **birdseye maple**▷ *n phr black fr 1920s* A light-skinned black girl, esp if sexually attractive

◁ **birdshit**▷ *n* =CHICKEN SHIT

◁ **birdturd**▷ *n* A despicable person; =PRICK, SHIT: *Suppose those birdturds come back here today*—Bernard Malamud

birdyback *n* The transport of loaded containers or semitrailers by airplane

birthday suit *n phr fr middle 1800s* What one is wearing when completely nude

bissel (BISS əl) *n* A bit; a little: *I'd hold onto your God's little acre a bissel longer*—Village Voice [fr Yiddish]

bit **1** *n underworld* A prison sentence: *Ferrati, whose "bit" was three to seven years*—PL Quinlan **2** *n* (also **bit part**) *theater* A small part in a play or other show **3** *n fr theater* A display of pretended feeling, or an outright imitation; =ACT, SHTICK: *So he does his hurt-puppy-dog bit/ You should see my Jimmy Cagney bit* **4** *n fr 1950s beat & cool talk* A person's particular set of attitudes, reactions, behavior patterns, etc; style; life style; =THING: *Zen never was my real bit*

See FOUR-BIT, TWO-BIT

bit banger *n phr computer* A programmer who works out details of a computer program, rather than a subordinate or assistant programmer

bitch ◁**1**▷ *n* A woman one dislikes or disapproves of, esp a malicious, devious, or heartless woman • The equivalent of the masculine **bastard** as a general term of opprobrium: *a cold-hearted bitch*—Budd Schulberg ◁**2**▷ *n homosexuals* A waspish or insolent male homosexual **3** *n* The queen of any suit in playing cards **4** *v* To complain; gripe; =BEEF, BELLYACHE: *College students always bitch about the food* **5** *n: What's your bitch today?* **6** *n* Anything arduous or very disagreeable: *That last mile was a bitch/ I had a bitch of a toothache* **7** *n* Anything pleasant or admirable; =BEAUT, HUMDINGER: *I just read his new book, and it's a bitch* **8** *v* To cheat; =CHISEL: *You never tried to bitch me out of anything*—Budd Schulberg

See BULL BITCH, IT'S A BITCH, SON OF A BITCH

bitch box *n phr armed forces fr WW2* A public-address system; =SQUAWK BOX

bitchen or **bitchin'** or **bitching** **1** *adj teenager* Good; excellent; superior: *A bitchen new single from Southern California has been riding the airwaves to the max this summer*—Newsweek/ *Because of your bitchin' body, I'm going to put you on hold for a couple of days*—Easyriders **2** ***adv*** Very; extremely: *That was a bitching good party*

bitch kitty ◁**1**▷ ***n phr*** An especially disliked or disagreeable woman **2** ***n phr*** An especially unpleasant or difficult task: *Taking the rusty muffler off the car was a bitch kitty* **3** ***n phr*** Anything especially pleasant or admirable; =HUMDINGER: *a real bitch kitty of a performance*
See IT'S A BITCH

a **bitch of a** or **one bitch of a** ***adj phr*** Very remarkable, awful, admirable, distressing, etc; =a HELL OF A: *Getting the thing together was a bitch of a job/one sweet bitch of a dress*

bitch up ***v phr*** To ruin; spoil; =LOUSE UP: *His goof bitched up the whole project*

bitchy ◁**1**▷ ***adj*** Having the traits of a bitch; mean; nasty; vindictive **2** ***adj*** *1930s* Good-looking; chic; =CLASSY **3** ***adj*** Sexually provocative: *two bitchy strip queens*—Time

bite **1** ***v*** To accept a deception as truth: *She said she was rich, and he bit* **2** ***v*** To borrow money from; ask a loan from: *He bit me for six bills and left town* **3** ***n*** One's share of, or the amount of, a sum owed or demanded: *We owe ten thousand, so what's my bite?* **4** ***v*** *teenagers* =SUCK

the **bite** ***n*** Expense; charge; cost: *It's a good place, but the bite is fierce*
See PUT THE BITE ON someone or something

bite someone's **head off** ***v phr*** To react angrily; =JUMP DOWN someone's THROAT: *Don't mention the survey or she'll bite your head off*

◁**bite my ass**▷ ***v phr*** =KISS MY ASS

bite the bullet ***v phr*** To accept the cost of a course of action; do something painful but necessary: *Will he bite the bullet and become the... leader that Philadelphia's black community wants and needs?*—Philadelphia [fr the early surgical practice of having the patient bite hard on a bullet to divert the mind from pain and prevent screaming]

bite the dust **1** ***v phr*** *fr middle 1800s* To die or be killed **2** ***v phr*** To fail; be destroyed: *The ledgers showed too much red ink, and the company bit the dust*

bite your tongue ***sentence*** Retract or be ashamed of what you just said

bit-grinding ***n*** *computer* The processing of data into a computer

bit part ***See*** BIT

biz ***n*** *fr middle 1800s* Business
See SHOW BIZ, THAT'S SHOW BUSINESS

blab **1** ***v*** (also **blab off**) To talk on and on, without necessarily making sense **2** ***n:*** *That's stupid, just blab* **3** ***v*** (also **blab off**) To say more than one ought; esp, to incriminate oneself or others; =SING, SQUEAL: *We better leave town: the little rat blabbed*

blabbermouth ***n*** A person who talks too much, esp one who reveals personal or secret matters indiscreetly; =BIGMOUTH

black bag job ***n phr*** A burglary or robbery done by government agents: *In the FBI... he'd never had anything to do with the famous black bag jobs*—New York Review of Books

blackball or **blacklist** ***v*** To punish by denial of work, boycotting of products, etc: *Some members of the* Twilight Zone *movie crew say they are being blackballed*—Washington Post

black book ***See*** LITTLE BLACK BOOK

black diamonds ***See*** DIAMONDS

black eye **1** ***n phr*** An eye surrounded with darkened areas of contusion; =MOUSE, SHINER **2** ***n phr*** A bad reputation; an adverse and damaging public image: *That story gave me a black eye*

black hat **1** ***n phr*** A villain; =HEAVY: *The only way I can do that is to make you the black hat*—Philadelphia Journal/ *This time, perhaps, there are black hats on both sides*—New York Times **2** ***v:*** *They do not try to penetrate security systems or conduct clandestine tests... "There is no black-hatting"*—Associated Press **3** ***modifier:*** *the black-hat rustler in the horse opera* **4** ***n phr*** The badge or symbol of a villain: *Companies have this black hat on when they go to court*—New York Times [fr the Hollywood tradition that villains in Western movies always wore *black hats*]

blacklist ***See*** BLACKBALL

Black Maria (mə RĪ ə) **1** ***n phr*** *fr middle 1800s* A patrol wagon used to carry police prisoners **2** ***n phr*** A hearse

black money (or **cash**) **1** ***n phr*** Money obtained illegally, esp by politicians and organized crime operations, that must be "laundered" before it can be used: *Money that derives from an illegal transaction... is considered "dirty" or "black" cash* —Philadelphia **2** ***n phr*** Income not reported for tax purposes; =SKIM

black operator ***n phr*** A secret agent: *At the Central Intelligence Agency, he was a "black operator" who never quite made it*—New York Times

black out **1** ***v phr*** To faint; lose consciousness **2** ***v phr*** To lose one's memory of something: *He totally blacked out that evening* **3** ***v phr*** To exclude an area from television coverage, esp of a sports event: *The whole region was blacked out for the final game*

blackshoe ***n*** *Navy* A nonflying member of an aircraft carrier's complement

black stuff **1** ***n phr*** *narcotics* Opium **◀2▶** ***n phr*** A black woman or women as sex partner(s), esp for a white man

blade **1** ***n*** A knife considered as a weapon; =SWITCHBLADE **2** ***n*** *hospital* A surgeon
See SWITCHBLADE

blah (also **blah-blah** or **blah-blah-blah**) **1** ***n*** Idle and meaningless talk; falsehoods and vanities; =BALONEY, BUNK: *a lot of romantic blah*—Wolcott Gibbs **2** ***adj*** Unstimulating; bland; featureless; dull: *He seems stupefyingly blah* **3** ***adj*** Tired; mildly depressed; enervated: *fever, chills, sore throat... and an allover "blah" feeling*—A Fishbein

the **blahs** ***n phr*** A condition of dullness, fatigue, malaise, etc: *The radicals are suffering from a case of the blahs*—Life

blank **1** ***n*** *narcotics* A weakened or diluted narcotic, or a non-narcotic substance sold as a narcotic; =FLEA POWDER **2** ***v*** *sports* To hold an opponent scoreless; =SHUT OUT, SKUNK: *The hapless Tigers were blanked twice last week*
See SHOOT BLANKS

blank check ***See*** GIVE someone A BLANK CHECK

blanket ***See*** BEACH BLANKET BINGO, SECURITY BLANKET, WET BLANKET

blankety-blank ***adj*** or ***n*** or ***v*** A generalized euphemism substituted for a taboo or vulgar term; =BLEEP, BLEEPING: *You blankety-blank idiot!/ Stick it up your blankety-blank*

blap **1** ***n*** Stroke; bit: *little blaps of revelation and no affect*—Philadelphia **2** ***v*** To strike; =SOCK: *continually blapped about the head and shoulders with pig bladders* —Philadelphia Bulletin

blast **1** ***n*** A blow; =SOCK: *a blast in the kisser* **2** ***v:*** *She blasted him in the gut* **3** ***v*** To shoot: *They blasted him with a sawed-off shotgun* **4** ***n*** In baseball, a long or strong hit, esp a home run **5** ***v:*** *So the Babe blasts it right out of there* **6** ***v*** To attack, esp with strong verbal condemnation: *He blasted the Secretary for saying that* **7** ***n:*** *He figures the opposition's blast won't hurt him* **8** ***v*** To defeat utterly; trounce; =CLOBBER **9** ***v*** To speed or speed up in a vehicle; =BARREL: *He got in the Porsche and blasted out of there* **10** ***v*** *narcotics* To take narcotics; use: *to start blasting opium from a water pipe*—H Braddy **11** ***n*** *narcotics* A single dose or portion of a narcotic or other stimulant; =BELT, FIX: *Maybe it's a little early in the day for that first blast*—D Harris **12** ***n*** A thrill; a transport of pleasure; =CHARGE, KICK: *Meeting her was a blast* **13** ***n*** A noisy and jolly party or other especially exciting occasion; =BALL **14** ***n*** Anything good or admirable; =GASSER **15** ***n*** A dismal failure; =BOMB, FLOP **16** ***interj*** An exclamation of dismay, irritation, frustration, etc • Chiefly British use **17** ***v*** =DYNAMITE
See BEER BUST, FULL BLAST

blaster ***See*** GHETTO BOX

blastissimo ***adj and adv*** *musicians* Very, very loud; fortississimo: *You ought not to sing the berceuse blastissimo* [modeled on *fortissimo*]

blat **1** ***v*** =BLAB **2** ***n*** A newspaper

blaxploitation **1** ***n*** The commercial exploitation of putative black experience, esp in films with blacks in sensational heroic roles of police officers, criminals, gamblers, etc **2** ***modifier:*** *the blaxploitation films...have been shoddy ripoffs*—Village Voice

blaze ***See*** LET'S BOOGIE

blazes ***See*** BLUE BLAZES

as **blazes** or **as hell** or ◁**as shit**▷ ***adv phr*** To a very great degree; =TO THE MAX: *the life now...hard as blazes* —Village Voice/ *cold as hell/ tough as shit*

blech (BLEKH or BLECH) ***interj*** An exclamation of disgust, revulsion, etc: *The House Democratic Caucus launched its response to Reaganomics: "BLECH!"*—National Review

bleed **1** ***v*** To take someone's money by overcharging or extortion: *His creditors bled him to death* **2** ***n*** *black* A black person; =BLOOD

bleeding heart **1** ***n phr*** A person regarded as unduly softhearted, esp towards idlers who do not merit sympathy • Very commonly used by the politically conservative to condemn the politically liberal **2** ***modifier:*** *a bleeding-heart wimpy liberal* [fr religious art showing the *bleeding heart* of Jesus]

bleep or **bleeping** or **blipping** ***adj*** or ***n*** or ***v*** A generalized euphemism substituted for a taboo or vulgar term; =BLANKETY-BLANK: *He bleeped right in my face so I told him to bleep off/ I was going to be a bleeping star* —Inside Sports/ *That 270 you recommended ain't no blipping good* —Sports Afield [fr the practice of erasing objectionable material on a tape or in a sound track with a high-pitched sound called echoically a *bleep*]

bletcherous ***adj*** *computer* Disgusting; nasty; ugly: *The whole design is bletcherous* [fr *bletch* or *blecch*, a comic-book expression of disgust similar to *yuck*]

blind **1** ***n*** *post office* A letter with an incomplete or illegible address **2** ***adv*** *esp students fr early 1900s* Completely; =COLD: *He had his story blind/ Goddam car was eating me blind*—George V Higgins **3** ***adj*** *homosexuals* Uncircumcised

See COLOR-BLIND, STEAL someone BLIND

blind date (or **drag**) *esp students fr 1920s* **1** ***n phr*** An arranged appointment for a show, dance, etc, where one's partner is a previously unknown person, usu the friend of a friend **2** ***n phr*** One's partner on such an occasion

blind drunk or **blinded** ***adj phr*** or ***adj*** Very drunk

blind pig (or **tiger**) ***n phr*** *fr early 1900s* An unlicensed or illegal saloon; =SPEAKEASY

blind-side **1** ***v*** (also **blind-pop**) *football* To tackle or block from an unseen quarter: *have to worry about gettin' blind-popped from a corner blitz*—Dan Jenkins **2** ***v*** To be burdened or attacked unexpectedly: *Business men began to be blind-sided by enormous legal bills*—Newsweek

blind tiger ***See*** BLIND PIG

Blind Tom ***n phr*** *baseball* An umpire

blinger (BLING ər) ***n*** Something remarkable, wonderful, superior, etc; =HUMDINGER

blink ***See*** ON THE BLINK

blinkers ***n*** The eyes

blip **1** ***adj*** *jive talk* Excellent; very good **2** ***adj*** =HIP **3** ***n*** A luminous signal on a radar screen: *Birds can cause blips on radar screens*—P Wagner **4** ***n*** A rapid increase and decrease; quick peaking: *It's not a form of communication, it's a temporary blip*—New York/ *despite temporary blips up and down*—Time **5** ***v*** To encroach upon, as one aircraft's image on a radar screen might enter the territory of another aircraft: *Cartridge-makers blip into Atari's airspace, attracted by the enormous profit potential*—New York **6** ***v*** To censor a taped word or passage by erasing it electronically from the tape and substituting a "bleep": *Occasionally Mr Carson's lines are "blipped"* —New York Times

blip (or **ping**) **jockey** ***n phr*** *armed forces* A person who monitors electronic detection devices

blipping ***See*** BLEEP

bliss out ***v phr*** To become ecstatic; go into a mystic daze, esp under the influence of a guru: *Don't get high, don't space out, don't get blissed out* —National Review

blitz¹ ***v*** *students around 1900* To absent oneself from a class or examination; =CUT, SHINE

blitz² ***v*** *armed forces* To polish one's brass buttons, etc; prepare for inspection [fr *Blitz Cloth*, trade name for a brand of metal-polishing cloth]

blitz[3] **1** *v* To defeat decisively; =CLOBBER: *They blitzed the Mariners 12-zip* **2** *v football* To rush the quarterback in force, hoping to prevent him from completing a pass **3** *n* Any heavy onslaught or attack: *His best strategy was a blitz of TV spots just before the election* **4** *v: We blitzed her with questions* [fr German *Blitzkrieg* "lightning war," an overwhelmingly heavy and rapid attack]

blitzed *college students* **1** *adj* Drunk: *really blitzed. Six beers on an empty stomach*—Cameron Crowe **2** *adj* Completely exhausted; =WIPED OUT

blitzed out *adj phr* Intoxicated; =STONED: *We were pretty blitzed out by the time Lee walked in*—Richard Merkin [probably fr *blitz*[3], perhaps influenced by *bliss out*]

blivit *n* Anything superfluous or annoying • The word, when one is asked in puzzlement to define it, is said to mean "ten pounds of shit in a five-pound bag": *This is about as useful as a blivit*

blob **1** *n students early 1900s* A mistake **2** *v: He blobbed the second question* **3** *n* A mass of viscous matter; an amorphous portion; =GOB

block *n* The head

See GAPER'S BLOCK, KNOCK someone's BLOCK OFF, NEW KID ON THE BLOCK

blockbust *v* To persuade white property owners to sell their houses quickly by arousing a fear that blacks are moving into the neighborhood

blockbuster[1] *n* A great success; a lavish and popular film, show, etc: *A gangster movie can be a box-office blockbuster*—Saturday Review [fr the large high-explosive aerial bombs of World War 2 called *blockbusters*]

blockbuster[2] *n* A real estate dealer who blockbusts

blockhead *n* A stupid person; =KLUTZ

blocks ***See*** PUT THE BLOCKS TO someone

bloke[1] *n fr early 1800s* A man; fellow; =GUY • More common in British usage

bloke[2] *n narcotics* Cocaine

blood *n black* A fellow black; =BLOOD BROTHER: *and these cats...well, we was all bloods*—D Evans

See SMELL BLOOD, TIRED BLOOD, TOO RICH FOR someone's BLOOD

blood brother *n phr black fr about 1960* A fellow black; =BLEED, BLOOD

bloody (or **blue**) **murder** **1** *n phr* A shattering defeat; total destruction: *After the second quarter it was bloody murder* **2** *adv phr* As if announcing general slaughter and universal destruction: *yelling bloody murder/ screaming blue murder on the arms of their seats*—Village Voice

blooey ***See*** GO BLOOEY

bloomer *n* A blunder; =BONER, GOOF: *a "bloomer" by Truman and Marshall about a grave that was not there*—United Press/ *This dictionary, I'm afraid, is scarcely free of bloomers*

bloop **1** *n* An unwanted sound in a phonograph record, resulting from a poor splice between two pieces of magnetic tape **2** *n* =BLOOPER **3** *v* To hit a ball relatively weakly and slowly: *He blooped a lob over her head* **4** *v* To launch and land a long, curving blow: *Turner blooped a bolo to the heart*—New York Daily News

blooper **1** *n* A blow with the fist, esp a long, looping punch: *So I could hang a blooper on your kisser*—John O'Hara **2** *n baseball* A high, looping pitch, throw, or hit: *I poked an easy blooper over third* **3** *n* A blunder; =BONER, BOO-BOO: *He may have felt he pulled a blooper*—J Marlow

blotter **1** *n police* The daily record of arrests at a police station **2** *n* A drunkard **3** *n college students* LSD **4** *n* (also **blotter acid**) *college students* A sheet of absorbent paper to which liquid LSD has been applied and then allowed to dry

blotto *adj fr early 1900s* Drunk: *the drivers who are blotto*—Philadelphia

blow **1** *v jazz musicians fr early 1900s* To play a musical instrument, esp in jazz style and not necessarily a wind instrument: *There will be three kids blowing guitar, banjo, and washboard*—Ed McBain **2** *n esp 1950s beat & cool talk* To do or perform something, esp to do it well: *He blows great conversation*—E Horne ◁**3**▷ *v* To do fellatio or cunnilingus: SUCK OFF ◁**4**▷ ***v*** To be disgusting, nasty, worthless, etc; =SUCK: *This blows and you do too*—National Lampoon **5** ***v*** To treat someone to something; buy something expensive or unusual for someone: *I blew myself to a new pair of shoes* **6** ***v*** (also **blow** something **in**) *fr middle 1800s* To spend money, esp foolishly and all at once: *And blow it in on smokes*—Joseph Auslander **7** ***v*** *narcotics* To take a narcotic, esp but not necessarily by inhalation: *Jimi blew every kind of dope invented*—New York Times/ *You been blowing a little LSD?*—New York Times **8** ***v*** *narcotics* To smoke marijuana; =BLOW SMOKE: *He enjoys sex; he does not blow grass*—Commonweal **9** ***v*** *fr middle 1800s* To spend or lose money: *The state blew my money buying votes for Roosevelt*—Westbrook Pegler **10** ***v*** *fr middle 1800s* To leave; depart; =SPLIT: *I'm blowing, I got a job in Detroit*—Dorothy Parker **11** ***v*** *fr middle 1800s* To lose or ruin by mistake, inattention, incompetence, etc; =BLOW IT: *I blew the best chance I ever had* **12** ***v*** *theater* To forget or botch one's part in a show **13** ***v*** To eliminate or cancel part of an agreement or business: *Let's just blow this next paragraph, OK?* **14** ***v*** *outdated underworld* To inform against someone; =SING **15** ***v*** To expose or publicize something secret, esp something scandalous: *Treat me right or I'll blow it about the love nest* **16** ***v*** To explode; blow up **17** ***v*** To lose one's temper; =BLOW one's TOP **18** ***v*** To brag; =TOOT one's OWN HORN **19** ***v*** *baseball* To pitch a ball so hard and fast that the batter cannot hit it: *He blew a fast ball right by the slugger*

See BLOW someone AWAY, BLOW one's COOL, BLOW someone's or something's COVER, BLOW someone's HAIR, BLOW something HIGH AS A KITE, BLOW someone's MIND, BLOW OFF one's MOUTH, BLOW someone or something OUT OF THE WATER, BLOW SMOKE, BLOW THE LID OFF, BLOW THE WHISTLE, BLOW one's TOP, BLOW UP, BLOW UP A STORM, BLOW something WIDE OPEN, CIRCUIT BLOW, LET OFF STEAM, LOW BLOW, ONE-TWO, TOOT one's OWN HORN

Blow ***See*** JOE BLOW

blow a gasket (or **a fuse**) ***v phr*** To lose one's temper; =BLOW one's TOP: *The higher-ups blew a gasket when they heard*—Bing Crosby

blow away ***v phr*** To depart; =TAKE OFF

blow someone **away** **1** ***v phr*** To kill; assassinate; get rid of; =OFF: *and boom, Jack Blumenfeld gets blown away*—Philadelphia **2** ***v phr*** To defeat utterly; trounce; =CLOBBER **3** ***v phr*** To overcome, often with admiration: *I read the book and it blew me away*—Philadelphia Bulletin

blow one's **cool** ***v phr*** *1960s counterculture* To lose one's composure; become flustered, excited, or angry: *I always blow my cool when they honk at me*

blow one's **cork** ***See*** BLOW one's TOP

blow someone's or something's **cover** **1** ***v phr*** *espionage & police* To ruin or nullify one's disguise or assumed role; reveal one's true identity: *The undercover cop had to blow his cover by pulling his gun when he thought they might have spotted him* **2** ***v phr*** To reveal, esp inadvertently or mischievously: *I'm not blowing the movie's cover story by giving you this information*—Philadelphia

blower ***See*** MIND-BLOWER

blow grits ***v phr*** *college students* To vomit

blow someone's **hair** ***v phr*** To frighten; be scary: *When I think... things... could have happened, it blows my hair*—Playboy

blowhard *fr middle 1800s* **1** ***n*** A braggart; self-aggrandizer **2** ***n*** An insistent and aggressive talker

blow something **high as a kite** ***v phr*** To spoil or ruin utterly by revealing it: *That discovery blew the scheme high as a kite*

blow hot and cold ***v phr*** To be indecisive; dither

blow something **in** ***See*** BLOW

blowing ***n*** *jazz musicians* The playing of jazz music: *This music is the culmination of all my writing and blowing*—Duke Ellington

blow it ***v phr*** To fail; make a botch; ruin one's chances: *We are winning. If we don't blow it*—Village Voice/ *I think I blew it. I talked too much and said too little*—Erma Bombeck

blow it out ***interj*** (Variations: **your asshole** or **your B-bag** or **your bar-**

racks bag or **your ear** or **your tailpipe** may be added) *fr WW2 armed forces* A generalized exclamation of contempt, anger, incredulity, etc • Most often uttered in challenge or rebuke

◁ **blow job**▷ *n phr* An act of fellatio or of cunnilingus

blow someone's **mind** **1** *v phr fr narcotics & 1960s counterculture* To evoke deep feelings of awe, admiration, strangeness, etc; stir one profoundly: *The simplicity of the thing blew my mind* **2** *v phr* =BLOW one's COOL

blowoff **1** *n* A climax; a final provocation: *She said I was late, and that was the blowoff* **2** *n* A quarrel: *She and Hobart have had a big blowoff*—J Kelly **3** *n teenagers* Something very easy; =PIECE OF CAKE

blow off *v phr* To avoid or shirk; not attend to: *He guessed he could blow off work that day and get away with it*

blow off one's **mouth** or **blow** one's **mouth off** *v phr* (Variations: **trap** or **yap** may replace **mouth**) =SHOOT OFF one's MOUTH

blow off steam *See* LET OFF STEAM

blow someone **out** *v phr fr cowboys* To kill or destroy; =BLOW someone AWAY: *The Redskins got blown out*—CBS Sports

blow someone or something **out of the water** *v phr* To defeat utterly; =SHOOT someone DOWN IN FLAMES: *Are you afraid of being blown out of the water?*—Playboy

blow one's **own horn** *See* TOOT one's OWN HORN

blow smoke **1** *v phr* To boast; brag; exaggerate: *four cops sitting around drinking, blowing smoke, and kidding*—Lawrence Sanders **2** *v phr* (also **blow smoke up** someone's **ass**) To mislead; confuse; deceive: *Anybody who tells you different's just blowing smoke up your ass*—George V Higgins **3** *v phr* To smoke marijuana or hashish: *Everybody blew smoke there. You could buy hash*—New Yorker [fr the presumed effects of smoking opium]

blow someone's **socks off** *See* KNOCK someone's SOCKS OFF

blow the lid off *v phr* To expose a scandal, esp political or governmental corruption

blow the whistle **1** *v phr underworld* To inform; =SING: *She hadn't been Dutch Schultz's wife for four years not to know the penalty for blowing the whistle*—NY Confidential **2** *v phr* To expose or begin to resist wrongdoing: *The detective who blew the whistle was also transferred*—Village Voice [fr the *whistle* signal of a sports official that an infraction, foul, etc, has been committed]

blow one's **top** (Variations: **cork** or **topper** or **stack** or **wig** may replace **top**) **1** *v* To go insane; become violently mad **2** *v* To become wildly excited or enthusiastic: *Here's an idea'll make you blow your cork* **3** *v* To become violently excited by narcotics; =FLIP, FREAK OUT **4** *v* To become violently and suddenly angry; have a tantrum [perhaps fr the violence of an oil well that *blows* as a gusher]

blowup **1** *n* A fit of anger **2** *n* A quarrel; violent rift between persons **3** *n* A photographic or other enlargement: *He already has a blowup of your proverb... on a wall of his breakfast room*—Joseph Heller

blow up **1** *v phr* To enlarge a photograph **2** *v phr* To assign too much importance to; exaggerate; =MAKE A FEDERAL CASE OUT OF something, PUMP UP **3** *v phr* =BLOW one's TOP **4** *v phr* =BLOW one's COOL **5** *v phr theater* To forget or garble one's lines on stage; =BALLOON: *Barrymore "blew up" in his lines*—Gene Fowler

blow up a storm **1** *v phr jazz musicians* To play, esp jazz trumpet, cornet, clarinet, etc, with great skill and verve: *I first heard Buddy Bolden play.... He was blowing up a storm*—Louis Armstrong **2** *v phr* =PISS UP A STORM

blow something **wide open** *v phr* To expose a scandal, esp political or governmental corruption; =BLOW THE LID OFF: *That'll be the perfect time to blow this thing wide open*—Washington Post

BLT (pronounced as separate letters) *n* A bacon, lettuce, and tomato sandwich

blue **1** *adj fr early 1800s* Drunk: *When you were blue you got the howling horrors*—Dorothy Parker **2** *adj fr middle 1800s* Lewd; rude;

suggestive; =DIRTY • The term covers the range from obscene to slightly risqué: *a blue movie/ blue gags* **3** ***adj*** Melancholy; depressed; woeful: *I feel a little blue and blah this morning* **◀4▶** ***n*** A very dark-skinned black person **5** ***n*** A police officer: *By the time the first blues got there, there's like maybe ten people milling about*—Lawrence Sanders

blue around the gills ***See*** GREEN AROUND THE GILLS

◁ **blue balls**▷ **1** ***n phr*** A turgid and painful condition of the testicles due to sexual excitement and frustration: *Sex will relieve testicular congestion, or blue balls*—Playboy **2** ***n phr*** Any of various venereal diseases, esp gonorrhea or lymphogranuloma inguinale

blue blazes **1** ***n phr*** *fr early 1800s* An extreme situation, pace, pitch, etc **2** ***n phr*** Something extreme; the utmost: *It hurt like blue blazes* **3** ***adv phr*** To an extravagant degree: *lying blue blazes*—Ken Kesey [fr the *blue blazes* of Hell, an extreme environment]

blue cheer ***n phr*** *narcotics* LSD

blue-chip ***adj*** Of the best sort; first rate: *a blue-chip stock* [fr the color of the highest denomination of gambling chip]

blue chipper ***n phr*** Persons or things of the highest quality, ability, etc: *But the crop does not contain many blue chippers*—Inside Sports

bluecoat ***n*** *fr middle 1800s* A police officer: *He told the damn bluecoat... he'd punch him all over the corner*—James T Farrell

blued ***See*** SCREWED, BLUED, AND TATTOOED

blue-devil ***See*** BLUE HEAVEN

blue-eyed **1** ***adj*** Innocent; unsophisticated **2** ***adj*** *black* White; Caucasian

blue-eyed boy ***See*** FAIRHAIRED BOY

blue-eyed devil ***n phr*** *black* A white person; a Caucasian

blue-eyed soul ***n phr*** *musicians* Black music with its style and mannerisms, as performed by white musicians: *Boz came on like an inspired amateur of blue-eyed soul*—Village Voice

blue flags ***n phr*** *narcotics* LSD

blue flick ***See*** BLUE MOVIE

blue flu ***n phr*** A mythical disease epidemic during a police job action when numbers of officers telephone to say that they are ill

blue funk ***n phr*** A profoundly melancholy state • More common in British use: *Losing his girl put him into a blue funk for weeks*

bluegrass **1** ***n*** Music based on the songs and dances of the Southern Appalachians and played usu at a fast tempo by a string group **2** ***modifier:*** *the bluegrass sound* [fr the nickname of Kentucky, the *bluegrass* state]

blue heaven or **blue-devil** ***n phr*** or ***n*** A capsule of Amytal (a trade name), a type of barbiturate

blue hell ***n phr*** An extremely nasty and trying situation: *It was more than tough, it was blue hell*

blue in the face ***See*** TILL ONE IS BLUE IN THE FACE

blue meany ***n phr*** A very, very cruel and nasty person; =BASTARD: *It's not that all landlords are blue meanies*—Washington Post [fr cartoon characters in the film *The Yellow Submarine* of the English rock group The Beatles]

blue movie (or **flick**) ***n phr*** A pornographic movie; erotic film; =SKIN FLICK

blue murder ***See*** BLOODY MURDER

bluenose ***n*** *fr early 1800s* A prude; prig: *The moral bluenoses were sniffing around*—Stephen Longstreet

the **blues** **1** ***n phr*** A state of melancholy; depression **2** ***n phr*** A usu slow style of singing, guitar-playing, and jazz originally reflecting in its melancholy and resignation the special plight of black people and the general vicissitudes of life and love; esp, songs having in each stanza a repeated opening statement and single closing statement **3** ***n phr*** *New York City narcotics* The police [first sense ultimately fr *the blue devils* "a fit of melancholy"]

blue-sky ***adj*** *fr early 1900s* Having no sound factual or value basis; recklessly imaginative: *a budget figure, as it turned out, and a blue-sky one at that*—Time

a **blue streak** *fr middle 1800s* **1** ***adv phr*** (also **like a blue streak**) In a very rapid or excessive manner; extravagantly: *She talked a blue* *streak/ She split out like a blue streak* **2** ***n phr*** An extreme amount, speed, etc: *He yelled a blue streak/ We ran a blue streak* [fr the *blue streak* of a lightning bolt]

◁ **blue veiner** ▷ ***n phr*** A very stiff penile erection: *Even the Dragon Lady couldn't have given you a blue veiner* —Joseph Wambaugh

bluff ***See*** CALL someone's BLUFF

blurb ***n*** A statement in praise of something or somebody; esp an encomious passage from a book or theater review, used as advertising [coined by Gelett Burgess, early-20th-century US humorist]

BMOC (pronounced as separate letters) ***n phr*** A college-student leader or idol [fr *big man on campus*]

B movie ***n phr*** A usu low-budget movie intended for the broad middle ground of taste and meant to be primarily entertaining and narrative rather than serious, artistic, etc

bo[1] or **'bo** ***n*** *hoboes* A hobo: *From some bo on the drag I managed to learn what time a certain freight pulled out*—Jack London

bo[2] **1** ***n*** *prison* A boy or young man, esp a prisoner's catamite; =PUNK **2** ***n*** A man; fellow • Now outdated, but once used in direct address, like "mac" or "dad"

BO (pronounced as separate letters) **1** ***n*** Body odor, esp from underarm perspiration **2** ***n*** *show business* Box office, the gauge of how well a show is doing by its receipts **3** ***adj*** *show business* Theatrical appeal: *The show is really big BO*

board ***n*** *show business* A ticket to a show or game

See ACROSS THE BOARD, IDIOT CARD, JINKY-BOARD, PUNCHBOARD, TOTE[3]

boards ***n*** *gambling* Playing cards

boat ***See*** GRAVY TRAIN, MISS THE BOAT, ON THE GRAVY TRAIN, RIDE THE GRAVY TRAIN, ROCK THE BOAT

boat people ***n phr*** Political refugees who escape by small boat

bob ***See*** BOOB JOB, DITTYBOP, FLY COP, NOSE JOB

bobber ***See*** DEELY BOPPER

bobble **1** ***v*** To blunder, esp in baseball, to mishandle or drop the ball: *The shortstop bobbled an easy out* **2** ***n:*** *The President's denial was a bad bobble*

bobby socks ***n phr*** White cotton socks worn below the knee, and esp worn folded over shoes [origin unknown; perhaps related to *bobbed* "short, cut short," influenced by the diminutive name *Bobby*]

bobby-soxer ***n*** *esp 1940s* An adolescent girl [fr the 1930s and 40s fashion of wearing *bobby socks* folded down over saddle shoes]

bobtail **1** ***n*** *armed forces fr WW1* A dishonorable discharge • So called because the phrase "service honorable and faithful" was deleted from the discharge form **2** ***n*** *truckers* A truck tractor without a semitrailer **3** ***v:*** *Returning with just the tractor (bobtailing) represented a loss* —Smithsonian

bod **1** ***n*** A person • Chiefly British use **2** ***n*** The body; physique

See WARM BODY

bodacious (boh DAY shəs) ***adj*** *chiefly Southern fr middle 1800s* Extreme; audacious; blatant: *as complicated as "Gaucho"'s bodacious cowboy Custerdome business*—Village Voice [fr early-19th-century *bodyaciously* "bodily, totally"]

bodice-ripper or **bodice-buster** ***n*** *publishing* A romantic-erotic novel, esp one with a historical plot; =HEAVY BREATHER: *the offensive term bodice-ripper*—Publishers Weekly/ *literary set that swoons over such bodice-busters as "Rapture's Slave," "Love's Sweet Agony"*—Philadelphia Journal

body ***See*** KNOW WHERE THE BODIES ARE BURIED, WARM BODY

body-shake ***See*** SKIN-SEARCH

boff **1** ***n*** A blow with the fist or open hand **2** ***v:*** *LaGuardia bade his cops to muss them up and boff them around on sight*—Westbrook Pegler **3** ***v*** To do the sex act: *professors boffing coeds in their offices*—New York/ *I was trying for the world boffing championship* —John D MacDonald **4** ***n*** A sex act; coupling: *a quick bathroom boff* —Playgirl **5** ***v*** To vomit; =BARF **6** ***n*** *show business* A laugh, esp one following a comedian's joke; =BOFFOLA **7** ***n*** *show business* A joke or witty remark **8** ***n*** *show business* A show that pleases the audience

See THROW A FUCK INTO someone

boffer *n* A man who does the sex act; =COCKSMAN: *The All-American boffer* —John D MacDonald

boffin *n* An expert, esp in a scientific or technical field: *Computer boffins... play a game called hunt the wumpus* —Time [fr World War 2 British RAF slang, possibly fr a humorous comparison between the laboratories and shops of experts and the enormous trash heaps of Mr and Mrs Boffin in Dickens's *Our Mutual Friend*]

boffo **1** *n* A dollar: *That's worth a million boffos*—Joel Sayre **2** *n underworld* A year, esp a one-year prison sentence **3** *n show business* A laugh, esp a loud laugh in response to a comedian; =BOFFOLA **4** *n show business* A joke or a witty remark; =BOFF **5** *adj: Hey, that's a very boffo line* **6** *adj* Loud and appreciative: *The zany Brewsters... still get laughs, boffo laughs*—Philadelphia Evening Standard **7** *n show business* A successful entertainment; =BOFF, HIT: *her string of box-office boffos*—Bob Thomas **8** *adj: Red-blooded boffo entertainment for both sexes*—SJ Perelman [fr a 19th-century carnival term based on the idea of a good *box office*]

boffola or **buffola** *show business* **1** *n* A loud appreciative laugh; =BELLY LAUGH, BOFF: *This ability brought out the old boffola from coast to coast* —B Herndon **2** *n* A joke or remark that provokes such laughter: *All I need is a funny hat and a buffola* —Fred Allen

bogart or **Bogart** or **bogard** *fr black* **1** *v* To behave truculently; get by intimidation: *some hotshot from Brooklyn trying to Bogart a game from the regulars*—Village Voice **2** *v* (also **bogart a joint**) To take more than one's share, esp of a marijuana cigarette; =HOG [fr the tough roles played in films by Humphrey *Bogart*]

bogue[1] **1** *adj narcotics* In need of narcotics; suffering from deprivation: *I'm bogue....I'm trying to kick*—Clarence Cooper **2** *adj* False; fake; =BOGUS, PHONY [origin unknown]

bogue[2] *adj teenagers* Disgusting; unattractive; =GROSS [fr *bogus*]

bogue[3] *high school students* **1** *n* A cigarette **2** *v* To smoke a cigarette [fr Humphrey *Bogart*, who smoked so often in his films]

bogue out *v phr computer* To become bogus, that is, false, misleading, useless, etc

bogus **1** *adj fr early 1800s* False; fake; counterfeit; =PHONY **2** *adj teenagers* Ignorant; not up-to-date; unattractive; =LAME, SQUARE: *"Bogus" is a different shading of "lame"* —Time [origin unknown; perhaps from *bagasse*, perhaps fr *Borghese*, the name of a forger of the 1830s]

◀ **bohunk** ▶ *fr loggers* **1** *n* An immigrant from central or eastern Europe, usu a Czech, Slovak, Hungarian, or Pole; =HUNKY **2** *n* A stupid, clumsy person

boiled *See* HARD-BOILED, HARD-BOILED EGG

boilermaker **1** *n* (also **boilermaker and his helper**) A drink of whiskey with or in a glass of beer

boiler room *See* BUCKET SHOP

boing or **boing-boing** *interj WW2 armed forces* An exclamation of appreciative delight and intentness at the sight of an attractive woman: *dropped what they were doing and their eyes went "Boing, boing"*—Pete Martin [fr the sound a plucked spring makes, suggesting tenseness and quivering response, with a hint perhaps of penile erection]

bojie *See* BOOJIE

boke or **boko** *n underworld* The nose

bollixed (or **bolaxed** or **bolexed**) **up** *adj phr* In a thoroughly confused and futile condition; =BALLED UP, FUCKED UP: *You're getting your cues all bollixed up*—Jerome Weidman [ultimately fr old English *bealluc* "testicle"; see *balled up*]

boll weevil *n phr esp 1980s* A conservative Southern Democrat who votes with Republicans in Congress [fr the insidious reputation of the *boll weevil*, an insect that eats cotton bolls]

bolo **1** *n armed forces fr 1920s* A very inaccurate rifleman **2** *n prizefight* A long, looping punch: *Turner blooped a bolo to the heart of Jim Jennings*—New York Daily Mirror [probably fr *bolo*, the long, heavy knife of the Philippines, as suggesting a looping stroke]

boloney *See* BALONEY

bolts ***See*** BUCKET OF BOLTS, NUTS AND BOLTS

bomb **1** ***n*** =BOMBSHELL **2** ***n*** *football* A very long forward pass intended to score a quick touchdown **3** ***n*** A conspicuous and total failure; =BLAST, FLOP **4** ***v:*** *The show bombed everywhere on the road/ I took the test, and bombed* **5** ***v*** To do very well at or on: *I really bombed the math test, aced it* **6** ***n*** *hot rodders* A car, esp a hot rod [in the sense of failure, perhaps fr the outdated expression *make a baum of it* "fail"]

See STINK BOMB

bombed ***adj*** Drunk

bombed out ***adj phr*** *narcotics* Very much intoxicated by narcotics; very dozy or exhilarated; =SPACED-OUT, STONED

bomb out ***v phr*** To fail; =BOMB: *Stephanie Moody ... "bombed out" last year: failed to complete her opening lifts*—New York

bombshell **1** ***n*** A startling, striking event; something that makes one gape: *Her entrance astride the crocodile was a bombshell* **2** ***n*** A sexually stimulating woman

bond ***See*** JUNK BOND

bone[1] **1** ***n*** *teenagers* Money; cash **2** ***n*** A dollar, esp a silver dollar **◁3▷** ***n*** The erect penis

See HAVE A BONE ON, HAVE A BONE TO PICK WITH someone, JAWBONE, PRAYER BONES

bone[2] *college students fr late 1800s* **1** ***n*** A diligent student **2** ***v*** (also **bone up**) To study, esp to study intensely for an examination [fr the student's use of *bohns* "translations, ponies," named after *Bohn's* Classical Library]

bone-breaker **1** ***n*** A physician **2** ***n*** A very difficult task; =BALL-BUSTER **3** ***n*** A wrestler

bonehead **1** ***n*** A stupid person: *four sons, all bone-heads*—F Scott Fitzgerald **2** ***modifier:*** *a bonehead idea/ bonehead play* **3** ***n*** A stubborn person

See PULL A BONER

boneheaded ***adj*** Stupid

bonehead play ***n phr*** *sports* An error, esp one caused by bad judgment: *Merkel's throw was the most renowned bonehead play in history*

◁ **bone-on**▷ ***n*** An erect penis: *Sometimes he could still get a pretty respectable bone-on*—Stephen King

bone-orchard ***n*** A cemetery

boner **1** ***n*** *fr early 1900s baseball* A blunder; error; =BLOOPER, HOWLER **2** ***n*** *college students* A diligent student; =BONE **◁3▷** ***n*** An erect penis; =HARD-ON: *the time you coveted your neighbor's wife. You had a big boner*—Stanley Elkin

See PULL A BONER

bones **1** ***n*** Dice **2** ***n*** Any thin person **3** ***n*** Two sticks held between the fingers and used to make a clacking rhythm **4** ***n*** Dollars; money

See MAKE NO BONES ABOUT, PRAYER BONES, SAWBONES

Bones ***n*** *merchant marine* A ship's doctor

bone up ***See*** BONE[2]

boneyard ***n*** A cemetery: *lie on a blanket out on the boneyard*—Tennessee Williams

bong **1** ***n*** *narcotics* A water pipe for smoking narcotics: *the array of glass and plastic water pipes or bongs*—New York Times **2** ***v*** *teenagers* To smoke marijuana using a water pipe **3** ***v*** *teenagers* To drink beer from a keg through a hose

bonged-out ***adj*** Intoxicated by a narcotic, esp one smoked through a bong: *You feel like a bonged-out Cubist painting*—Penthouse

bonkers ***adj*** *fr British use* Crazy; insane; =NUTS: *Folks are going slightly bonkers these days over anything that glitters*—Newsweek [probably fr *bonk* "to hit on the head" + the British slang suffix *-ers*]

bonnet ***See*** BEE IN one's BONNET

bonzo ***adj*** Crazy; =NUTS: *almost drove me bonzo*—Philadelphia Bulletin

boo **1** ***adj*** *esp early 1950s* Excellent; remarkable: *Something that used to be known as the cat's whiskers is now called... "deadly boo"*—Hal Boyle **2** ***n*** *narcotics* Marijuana or another narcotic: *I got over there and she lays this dynamite boo on me*—Richard Price [second sense said to be fr black English *jabooby* "marijuana, so called because it induces a state of fear or anxiety," of unknown origin]

See TICKETY-BOO

boob **1** *n fr the late 1800s* A stupid person; =DIMWIT: *There are still boobs, alack, who'd like the old-time gin-mill back*—Sinclair Lewis **2** *n* A person who is too innocent and trusting; =SUCKER: *The poor boob fell for his line and gave him the money* ◁**3**▷ *n* A woman's breast; =BUB, KNOCKER **4** *n* A blunder; error; =BOO-BOO **5** *n underworld* A jail [sense 3 perhaps fr German dialect *bubbi* "a woman's breast"]

boobie[1] or **bubbie** (Bo͞o bee) *n* Friend; buddy; =SWEETIE ● A term of affection with general application [fr Yiddish *bubele*, an endearing epithet]

◁ **boobie**[2] or **bubbie**▷ (Bo͞o bee) *n* A woman's breast [fr *boob*]

◁ **boob job** (or **bob**)▷ *n phr* A mastectomy: *saying that Julie had had a boob job*—Playboy

boo-boo **1** *n fr early 1900s* A dollar **2** *n* Any error or misstep, esp one with embarrassing consequences; faux pas: *The original boo-boo that started all this public confusion*—HR King

the **boob tube** *n phr* Television or a television set; =the TUBE

booby hatch *n phr* An insane asylum; mental hospital: *King Bolden cut hair in the booby-hatch*—Stephen Longstreet

booby trap **1** *n phr esp WW2 Army fr middle 1800s British* A hidden explosive charge designed to be set off by some ordinary act **2** *v: They booby-trapped his car and six people died* **3** *n phr* The seemingly harmless appearance that conceals vexations arranged for an unsuspecting opponent: *Don't debate him, it's a booby trap*

boodle **1** *n* An entire lot; a large number or amount; =CABOODLE **2** *n underworld fr middle 1800s* Counterfeit money **3** *n fr late 1800s* Bribe money or other money obtained by graft and corruption **4** *n fr late 1800s* Money in general **5** *n prison & students* Sweets; treats; delicacies **6** *v 1940s students* To hug, kiss, etc; =NECK [fr Dutch *boedel* "estate, lot"]

boog *v 1930s* To dance: *to go booging*—Life [fr *boogie-woogie*]

boogaloo or **bugaloo** (Bo͞oG a lo͞o, Bo͞oG-) **1** *n* A shuffling, shoulder-swinging dance: *feet doing a fast boogaloo in the grass*—Stephen King **2** *v: They boogalooed down the street* **3** *modifier: That's really voodoo music, man, boogaloo music*—Rolling Stone **4** *v* To carry on jocularly; play; tease; =FOOL AROUND **5** *modifier: go out and have a bugaloo good time*—Village Voice

booger *See* BUGGER

boogie or **boogey** (Bo͞o gee, Bo͞o-) **1** *n fr early 1900s black* Syphilis, esp advanced syphilis ◀**2**▶ *n* A black person ◁**3**▷ *modifier: a boogie hair-style/ boogie music* **4** *n* =BOOGIE-WOOGIE **5** *v* To move, shake, and wriggle the body in time to rock-and-roll music; do a sort of boogaloo: *Amanda boogies and bangs a tambourine while her 39 sisters sit on steps and force shattered smiles*—G Mitchell **6** *v* =BREAK **7** *v* To carry on jocularly; play; tease; =FOOL AROUND: *back from a long weekend and ready to boogie*—Philadelphia Journal **8** *v* To do the sex act: *a lot of heavy boogieing going on at Iowa State*—Playboy ◁**9**▷ *n* The buttocks; behind; =ASS: *a high boogey and thin legs* ◁**10**▷ *v* To do anal intercourse; =BUGGER: *Would Ronnie be averse to being boogied by Kiss during his acceptance speech*—National Lampoon **11** *n WW2 Army Air Force* An enemy aircraft, esp a fighter plane **12** *n* A piece of solid mucus from the nose

See LET'S BOOGIE

boogie board *n phr* A skateboard

boogie box *See* GHETTO BOX

boogie-woogie (Bo͞o gee Wo͞o gee, Bo͞o-, Wo͞o-) **1** *n fr early 1900s black* Syphilis, esp advanced syphilis **2** *n jazz musicians* A fast jazz piano style with a heavy rolling bass played eight beats to the measure, often used as a song accompaniment **3** *modifier: Jimmy Yancey... created the boogie woogie blues*—Stephen Longstreet **4** *n* Any jazz, swing, or jive music **5** *v black* To enjoy oneself thoroughly

boojie (Bo͞o zhee, Bo͞o-) (Variations: **bojie** or **boochie** or **booj** or **boojy** or **bourgie** or **buzhie**) *black* **1** *n* A middle-class black person; also, such persons collectively: *the black bourgeoisie... better known to most of us as the bourgie*—Washington

Post **2** *n* Any middle-class person **3** *modifier: a bourgie couple mourning their 20-year-old daughter's comatose state*—Village Voice/ *exaggerating the slumminess of the tenements and playing down the boojy trappings of our apartment* —Richard Price

book **1** *n underworld* A one-year prison sentence **2** *n gambling* =BOOKIE **3** *n gambling* A bookie's function and place of business: *Joey keeps a book* **4** *v* To be certain of; bet on: *It'll happen, you can book on it* **5** *n police* The daily logbook of a police station **6** *v police fr middle 1800s* To charge with a crime or misdemeanor at a police station: *They took the bum in and booked him for vagrancy* **7** *v* To engage in advance; reserve: *Please book me a table for 7 at 8* **8** *v* To arrange in advance, esp a performer, show, lecture, etc: *They booked eight readings in three days for the visiting poet* **9** *v students* To study hard **10** *v fr students* To run or depart, esp rapidly: *and the couple booked off into the sunset for their honeymoon* —Easyriders

See BY THE BOOK, IN someone's BAD BOOKS, KEEP BOOK, LITTLE BLACK BOOK, ONE FOR THE BOOK, POUND THE BOOKS, READ someone LIKE A BOOK, STROKE BOOK, TAKE A PAGE FROM someone's BOOK, THROW THE BOOK AT someone, WRITE THE BOOK

the **book** **1** *n phr underworld* The maximum sentence allowed by law, esp a life sentence to prison **2** *n phr* Instructions or conventional wisdom about someone's performance; =FORM: *The "book" on this player... was to leave him alone*—Lou Cannon *See* THROW THE BOOK AT someone

bookie *n gambling* A person who accepts and handles bets on horseraces; bookmaker

book it **1** *v phr students* To depart quickly **2** *v phr* To be confident of; count on: *I'll be back. Book it* —Albuquerque Tribune

boom *See* LOWER THE BOOM

◁ **boom-boom** ▷ *n* Sexual activity; copulation; =ASS: *dragging girls into the woods "for a little boom-boom"* —Time

boomer *n esp 1930s* A womanizer; ladies' man

boom sticks *n phr cool musicians & rock and roll* Drumsticks

◁ **boon coon** ▷ *See* ACE BOON COON

boondagger *n* A tough woman or aggressive lesbian; =BULLDYKE: *the boondaggers, you know, like bulls that come offa the street*—L Berry

boondocker *n fr WW2 Navy and Marine Corps* A person who lives or works in a remote region, esp by preference

boondockers or **boon dockers** *n* or *n phr fr 1930s Marine Corps* Shoes suitable for rough outdoor use, esp heavy duty military shoes or boots

the **boondocks** or **the boonies** *n fr Marine Corps* Remote places; rural regions: *The people out there in the boonies may not know you're past it* —Washingtonian [fr Tagalog *bundok* "mountain"]

boondoggle *esp 1930s* **1** *v* To spend public funds on futile activity or outlandishly **2** *n: The public's got the idea that this is a boondoggle, a Rube Goldberg*—Time

booshwa or **booshwah** *See* BUSHWAH

boost **1** *v* To steal, esp by shoplifting: *slept on park benches and boosted from the A&P*—Herbert Gold **2** *v* To praise highly: *to boost one's home town* **3** *n: I'll give you a good boost*

booster **1** *n* A shoplifter; pilferer: *Got a booster for you. The chunky girl in blue at the lace counter* —Dashiell Hammett **2** *n* A person who praises extravagantly; =FAN

boot **1** *v* To kick: *Let's boot a football around* **2** *n: Give him a boot in the ass* **3** *v* To discharge; =FIRE, SACK **4** *v* To dispraise; disrecommend **5** *n: I needed a boost but got a boot* **6** *v* To lose or waste by incompetence, inattention, etc; botch; bungle; =BLOW: *I booted three good chances* **7** *v baseball* To commit an error, esp in handling a ground ball **8** *n: Dark atoned for his boot by making a good play on Kiner's slow roller*—J McCulley **9** *n* A thrill; surge of pleasure; =BANG, KICK: *I get a boot from boats* **10** *v* (also **back-track**) *narcotics* To inject a narcotic gradually by pulling back and reinjecting blood again and again to increase the drug's effect: *The technique, known as*

"booting," is believed to prolong the drug's initial effect—J Mills **11** *n Navy & Marine Corps* A recruit **12** *adj fr Navy & Marine Corps* Newly recruited; fresh on the job **◀13▶** *n black* A black person **14** *v computers* =BOOT UP **15** *n* (also **Denver boot**) A metal locking device put on the wheels of a scofflaw's car to prevent driving
See RUBBER BOOTS, TO BOOT

the **boot** *n phr* Dismissal, discharge
See GET THE BOOT, GIVE someone THE BOOT

boot camp *n phr Navy & Marine Corps* A basic training center

bootleg 1 *v esp 1920s* To make or sell illegal whiskey **2** *n esp 1920s* Whiskey illegally made or sold **3** *modifier: a bottle of bootleg hooch* **4** *v football* To carry the ball deceptively by holding it against the leg, esp after pretending to hand it off to another player [fr the idea of concealment in the upper part of one's boots; the phrase *on the boot-leg plan* to describe illegal whiskey sales is attested from the mid-19th century]

bootlegger or **booter** or **bootie** *n esp 1920s* A person who bootlegs: *5,000 booters on Manhattan Island alone*—HL Mencken

boots *n* A shoeshine boy
See BET YOUR BOOTS, JESUS BOOTS, RUBBER BOOTS

boot up or **boot** *v phr* or *v computers* To start up or input a computer's operating system: *The typical first step in working with a computer, then, is to load the DOS programs (this is called "booting up")*—Computers at Home/ *showed me how to log in and boot the operating system* —New York Times [fr earlier *bootstrap,* because after a simple action like pressing one key, the computer loads the operating system itself, as if it were *raising itself by its own bootstraps*]

booze 1 *n* Any alcoholic drink, esp whiskey and other spirits **2** *v* To drink alcoholic beverages, esp to drink whiskey heavily [fr *bowse* "drink, carouse," reinforced by the name of a 19th-century Philadelphia distiller, EG Booze]
See HIT THE BOTTLE

boozed or **boozed up** *adj* or *adj phr* Drunk

booze up *v phr* To drink a great deal of liquor

booze-up *n* A drinking spree; =BINGE: *the morning booze-up which was still fouling his blood*—Robert Stone

boozy *adj* Drunk

bop 1 *v* To strike, esp with the fist: *Nina reached out and bopped her on the head*—Hal Boyle **2** *n: a bop on the beezer* **3** *v* To defeat: *The home team got bopped again* **4** *n street gang* A fight among gangs; =RUMBLE **5** *v: You gotta go on bopping and hanging around street corners all your life?*—Life **6** *n* The sex act; =a SCREW **7** *v: He bopped her in the nearest room* **8** *n* (also **bebop**) A style of modern jazz characterized by complex harmonics, sudden changes in register, the use of fast and nearly unintelligible lyrics, etc: *Bop is "cool" jazz* —American Speech **9** *modifier: a bop musician* **10** *v* To walk or go, esp in a slow and relaxed mood: *They bopped over to the bar* [echoic]
See DITTYBOP, HARD BOP, TEENYBOPPER, THROW A FUCK INTO someone

bop cap *n phr* =APPLEJACK CAP

bopper *See* DEELY BOPPER, TEENYBOPPER

bopping 1 *n* The act of a person who bops **2** *n Philadelphia cabdrivers* Tampering with taxicab meters to register illegally high charges: *The United Cab Association here has expelled about 40 cab drivers in the last two years for "bopping"*—Philadelphia Inquirer **3** *modifier: "bopping" cabbies expelled*—Philadelphia Inquirer

bored stiff *adj phr* Very bored [fr the notion of being *bored to death*]

born loser *See* LOSER

borscht belt *n phr* The region in and near the Catskill Mountains north of New York City where many predominantly Jewish resort hotels are found [fr Russian *borshch* "beet soup," which was frequently on the menu of such hotels, in its Yiddish spelling]

borscht circuit *n phr* The resort hotels of the borscht belt, regarded as a circuit for entertainers, lecturers, etc

bosh *n* Nonsense; poppycock; =BULLSHIT

boss 1 *n* The chief; the person in charge **2** *n* A person or thing regarded as the best: *Of all the poets, Moss is the boss* **3** ***modifier:*** *Geoff's the boss drummer* **4** ***adj*** *teenagers fr black and jazz musicians* Excellent; wonderful; =COOL: *Aw, this is boss*—Rolling Stone/ *Japan has leaped into the implements-for-bosser-living gap*—San Francisco [fr Dutch *baas* "master"]

boss trick ***See*** CHAMPAGNE TRICK

bossy[1] ***adj*** Domineering; autocratic: *She's very bossy, a take-charge gal*

bossy[2] **1** ***n*** A cow **2** ***n*** *lunch counter* Beef [fr Latin *bos* "cow"]

bot ***n*** A bottle

BOT (pronounced as separate letters) ***n*** *prison* The balance of time remaining to be served in prison

both hands **1** ***n phr*** Ten: *How many? Both hands* **2** ***n phr*** *underworld* A ten-year prison sentence

both sides of the street ***See*** WORK BOTH SIDES OF THE STREET

both ways ***See*** HAVE IT BOTH WAYS, SWING BOTH WAYS, WORK BOTH WAYS

bottle **1** ***n*** A bottle of liquor; =JUG: *He had a bottle on him* **2** ***n*** *line repairers* A glass insulator for electric or communications line **3** ***n*** *radio operators* A vacuum tube
See FIGHT A BOTTLE

the **bottle** **1** ***n phr*** Liquor; =BOOZE **2** ***n phr*** Prostitution, esp male prostitution [sense 2 perhaps fr cockney rhyming slang *bottle and glass* "ass"]
See HIT THE BOTTLE

bottom ***n*** The buttocks; =ASS

Bottom ***See*** FOGGY BOTTOM

bottom dollar ***See*** BET one's BOTTOM DOLLAR, BET YOUR BOOTS

bottom-end ***n*** *hot rodders* The crankshaft, main bearing, and connecting rod bearings of an automobile engine

the **bottom line** **1** ***n phr*** The bookkeeping figure showing profit or loss **2** ***n phr*** The result of any computation or estimate, esp one showing total costs: *I'll go half if the bottom line's OK* **3** ***n phr*** Any final decision or judgment: *Let me tell you the bottom line* **4** ***n phr*** A fundamental or crucial point of fact; the essence; =the NITTY GRITTY: *The bottom line is I am paid to win games* —Inside Sports **5** ***modifier:*** *a bottom-line matter*

bottom man on the totem pole ***See*** LOW MAN ON THE TOTEM POLE

bottom of the barrel ***See*** SCRAPE THE BOTTOM OF THE BARREL

bottom out ***v phr*** To get as low or bad as possible; reach nadir: *If [Watergate] ever bottoms out, we might be all right*—Time

bottoms ***n*** *jazz musicians* Shoes; a pair of shoes

◁ **bottoms up** ▷ ***adv phr*** =DOG FASHION

bounce **1** ***v*** To expel; throw out: *When he started swearing they bounced him* **2** ***v*** To discharge or dismiss; =FIRE **3** ***n*** Energy; vitality; =PISS AND VINEGAR, PIZZAZZ: *more bounce to the ounce* **4** ***v*** To be rejected for lack of funds in the bank: *His checks never bounce*

the **bounce** **1** ***n phr*** Forcible ejection, esp by a person hired to remove unwanted customers; =the BUM'S RUSH **2** ***n phr*** A dismissal, polite or otherwise; =KISS-OFF: *After a brief dialogue with my boss I got the bounce*

bounce something **around** ***v phr*** To think about and discuss an idea, project, etc: *Let's bounce it around a little before we decide*

bounce for ***v phr*** To pay for; treat; =PICK UP THE TAB: *somewhere that doesn't bounce for bluecoats* —Joseph Wambaugh

bounce off the walls **1** ***v phr*** *Army* Be in a nervous and confused condition; =be HYPER **2** ***v phr*** *hospital* To be in a very agitated condition; be psychotically frantic and disturbed

bouncer **1** ***n*** *fr late 1800s* A person employed to eject unwanted customers from a saloon, restaurant, dance hall, etc **2** ***n*** A check that is returned for lack of funds; =RUBBER CHECK **3** ***n*** *underworld* A forged check **4** ***n*** *railroad* A caboose

◁ **bouncy-bouncy** ▷ ***n*** The sex act
See PLAY BOUNCY-BOUNCY

bouquets ***See*** THROW BOUQUETS AT someone or something

bourgie ***See*** BOOJIE

bow-and-arrow squad ***n phr*** A police assignment involving unarmed duty: *They pull an officer's weapon and send him off to a desk-bound bow-and-arrow squad*—Newsweek

bowels ***See*** NOT GET one's BALLS IN AN UPROAR

bowl ***See*** FISH TANK, GOLDFISH BOWL, RUST BOWL

bowzed *adj* =BOOZED

box **1** *n* A coffin: *Keep that up and you'll go home in a box* **2** *v hospital* To die: *Oh, she boxed last night*—New York Times **3** *n underworld* A safe; vault; bank vault ◁**4**▷ *n* The vulva; vagina ◁**5**▷ *n homosexuals* The male genitals, esp as displayed by tight pants; =BASKET **6** *n jive & cool talk* Any stringed instrument, esp a guitar **7** *n* An accordion **8** *n* A camera, esp one with a simple shutter and lens at the front of a small box **9** *n* An icebox or refrigerator **10** *n* A phonograph **11** *n* =GHETTO BOX: *Hey, man, don't mess with my box*—Wall Street Journal **12** *n police* A police telephone operator **13** *n* A very tight and awkward situation; cleft stick; =BIND: *Those guidelines put me in a hell of a box* **14** *adj hospital* Dead

See BITCH BOX, FIRST CRACK OUT OF THE BOX, IDIOT BOX, IN A BIND, NUT HOUSE, SQUAWK BOX, STUFF THE BALLOT BOX

the **box** *n phr* Television or a television set

boxcar **1** *n WW2 Army Air Force* A large cargo aircraft or bomber **2** *adj gambling* In high numbers: *boxcar odds* [second sense from the high numbers seen on the sides of railroad boxcars]

boxcar numbers (or **figures**) *n phr* Very high numbers: *bringing in the kind of boxcar numbers that advertisers like*—Village Voice

boxcars *n crapshooting* A throw of two sixes

boxed *adj* Drunk

box someone **in** *v phr* To put in a tight and awkward situation; incapacitate

◁**box lunch**▷ *n phr* Cunnilingus

box man **1** *n phr underworld* A criminal specializing in opening safes **2** *n phr gambling* A professional blackjack or twenty-one dealer **3** *n phr gambling* A cashier or croupier at a gambling table: *the box men, who are the cashiers of the tables*—J Cannon

box office *n phr fr show business* A popular and financial success, esp in the entertainment field: *just because you're no longer box office*—Roddy McDowall

boy ◀**1**▶ *n* A black man: *Don't call me "boy"... I'm as old as you are if not older*—Langston Hughes ◁**2**▷ *n* Any male, regardless of age, working as a porter, elevator operator, etc **3** *n homosexuals* A male who takes the subservient role in a homosexual relationship **4** *n narcotics fr 1920s* Heroin: *But now he had the boy; he could lie around*—C Cooper

See BIG BOY, FAIRHAIRED BOY, FLY-BOY, GOOD OLD BOY, JEWBOY, OLD BOY NETWORK, ONE OF THE BOYS, PADDY, PERCY, PRETTY-BOY, THAT'S MY BOY

the **boys** ***See*** ONE OF THE BOYS

the **boys in the backroom** *n phr* Any group of men, esp politicians and their aides, who are privy to and control the inner workings of an enterprise or place: *the salad boys in the back room, oiling up the cabbage*—WT Tyler

the **boys uptown** **1** *n phr* The political bosses of a city, and their staffs; =CITY HALL **2** *n phr* Any group of influential and unnamed criminals: *The tricksters... were "the boys uptown," not yet identified*—New York Daily News

bozo *n fr early 1900s* A fellow; a man, esp a muscular type with a meager brain: *This bozo right here next to me [Rep. Thomas P. O'Neill incognito] could probably be a better Congressman than those guys in Congress*—Cheers (TV program) [fr Spanish *boso*, a version of *vosotros* "you" plural]

bra (BRAH) *n* A brassiere

bra-burner (BRAH bər nər) *n* A derogatory term for a very militant feminist: *The media decided henceforth to label feminists as "bra-burners"*—Esquire [fr the putative symbolic burning of brassieres as a protest against the restriction of women's freedom]

brace **1** *v* To stop or approach a person and beg for money: *This panhandler came up to me and braced me*—John O'Hara **2** *v* To confront someone with an accusation: *When I braced the guy he proved that Decker had paid him back*—Mickey Spillane

See SPLICE THE MAIN BRACE

brack-brain *n* A stupid, silly person: *this particular brack-brain*—Village

Voice [fr Brit dialect *brack* "crack, flaw" + *brain*]

brack-brained *adj* Stupid and silly: *April Fool's Day...makes some characters go completely brack-brained* —Village Voice

bracket creep *n phr* The raising of wage-earners into higher income-tax brackets, esp because of wage-raises triggered by inflation: *Tax payments will mount next year from "bracket creep"*—Wall Street Journal

brag-rags *n* =FRUIT SALAD

brain **1** *n* An intelligent person; intellectual; good scholar: *The publicity of being a brain did not further her movie career as a glamor girl*—Bob Thomas **2** *v* To injure with a hard blow to the head: *The left hook really brained him*

See BIRDBRAIN, BUBBLE BRAIN, HAVE something ON THE BRAIN, LAMEBRAIN, NOT HAVE BRAIN ONE, PICK someone's BRAIN, RATTLEBRAIN, SCATTERBRAIN

brain bucket *n phr Army* A steel helmet

brain drain *n phr fr British* The loss of useful educated persons, esp professionals, from a place because they can find better conditions elsewhere: *Stalled Economy Speeds Puerto Rico's Brain Drain*—New York Times

brained *See* AIRHEADED, BIRDBRAINED, CRACKBRAINED, DICK-BRAINED, LAMEBRAINED

brain-fade *n* Stuporous boredom; tedium: *She and her colleagues fight brain-fade by sizing up customers* —Time

brain one *n phr* The most elementary intelligence; a minimum of sagacity: *Our leader doesn't exhibit brain one*

See NOT HAVE BRAIN ONE

brain-picker *n* A person who exploits the creative notions of others: *nothing but scorn for brain-pickers and imitators*—A Lomax

brains **1** *n* Intelligence; mind; =SAVVY, SMARTS **2** *n* The person who does the thinking and planning; guiding mind: *The brains of this outfit is the secretary* **3** *n merchant marine* A ship's officer; the official in authority

See BEAT one's BRAINS OUT, FUCK someone's BRAINS OUT, HAVE SHIT FOR BRAINS, NOT HAVE BRAINS ENOUGH TO COME IN OUT OF THE RAIN, SHIT-FOR-BRAINS

one's **brains out** *adv phr* To one's utmost; extremely much; spectacularly; =one's HEAD OFF: *Everyone across this great nation shortly would be "partying" their brains out*—Village Voice

brainstorm **1** *n* A sudden idea, esp one that is apt and useful; a happy insight **2** *v* To examine and work on a problem by having a group sit around and utter whatever relevant thoughts they have: *We'll brainstorm the drop in enrollment*

brainwash **1** *v* To cause profound attitudinal changes, usu in a prisoner, by psychological conditioning, supplemented by drugs and physical abuse **2** *v* To change or influence opinions or attitude by methods less stringent than those used on prisoners: *They were brainwashed into joining that crazy cult* **3** *n: Your line is persuasive, virtually a brainwash* [fr Chinese *hsi nao* "wash brain," which came into US use during and after the Korean War, apparently because of its use by North Koreans and their Chinese allies as custodians of US prisoners of war]

brain wave *n phr* A sudden useful idea; =BRAINSTORM: *Lou had a brain wave. He offered the boy a C note to let him drive*—Raymond Chandler

brand X **1** *n phr Army* The infantry insignia, crossed rifles **2** *n phr narcotics* Marijuana [fr the phrase used in television advertising for unnamed and inferior products]

brannigan or **branigan** *fr early 1900s* **1** *n* A spree: *a prolonged crossword puzzle brannigan*—Benjamin de Casseres **2** *n* A brawl or fracas; =DONNYBROOK: *Republicans and Democrats alike are guilty of this brannigan*—P Edson

brass **1** *n fr 1500s* Impudence; effrontery; =CHUTZPA **2** *n outdated fr 1700s* Money • More common in British usage **3** *n* High officials or managers in general; =the BRASS: *There's lots of vice presidents here but they're not really brass*

See DOUBLE AS, FREEZE THE BALLS OFF A BRASS MONKEY

the **brass** *n phr armed forces fr WW2* The upper ranks of the military or other uniformed services: *Many a GI hated the brass and the enemy [equally]*—JB Douds

See the TOP BRASS

◁ **brass balls**▷ ***n phr*** Courage; audacity; =GUTS: *But I had the brass balls to hold out for a piece of the action* —Rolling Stone

brass hat **1** ***n phr*** *armed forces fr WW2* A high-ranking officer in the military or other uniformed services **2** ***n phr*** Any high-ranking official; manager; chief; =BOSS

brass monkey ***See*** FREEZE THE BALLS OFF A BRASS MONKEY

brass tacks ***See*** DOWN TO BRASS TACKS

bread ***n*** *cool talk & 1960s counterculture* Money; =DOUGH [perhaps related to earlier *gingerbread* "money"]

See the BEST THING SINCE SLICED BREAD, SMALL POTATOES

breadbasket ***n*** The stomach; abdomen

bready ***See*** WHITE BREADY

break **1** ***n*** A prison escape **2** ***n*** A brief period of rest or relaxation: *Take a five-minute break* **3** ***v:*** *Let's break while I think about it all* **4** ***v*** To interrupt or abandon some regular practice: *to break training/ break an old routine* **5** ***n*** A stroke of luck, good or bad: *I got a break and made it on time/ Football's a game of breaks to some extent* **6** ***n*** A stroke of mercy or favor: *Give me one break and I'll never flunk again* **7** ***v*** To happen; occur; fall out: *If things break right I'll be OK* **8** ***v*** To tame a wild horse; subdue someone's spirit **9** ***v*** To bankrupt a company or person **10** ***v*** To ruin; destroy someone's chances and standing: *If you cross me on this I'll break you* **11** ***v*** *esp armed forces* To demote; reduce in rank: *They broke him back to buck private* **12** ***v*** To separate, esp from a clinch: *The boxers broke and came at each other again* **13** ***n*** *jazz musicians* An improvised passage; solo; =LICK **14** ***v*** *esp 1980s black teenagers* (also **breakdance** or **boogie**) To do a kind of dancing that evolved in the inner-city ghettos, and characterized esp by intricate writhings and shows of balance and strength close to the floor: *You can go running. You can swim. Or you can break*—New York Times **15** ***n*** *horse-racing* The start of a horse-race or other race

See TAKE A BREAK

break a leg *sentence fr theater* Best wishes; good luck; I hope you do very well [perhaps fr German *Hals und Bein brechen* "break your neck and leg," a similar good-luck formula]

◁ **break** one's **ass**▷ (or ◁**balls**▷ or **buns** or **butt** or **cork** or **hump** or **nut** or ◁**sweet ass**▷) ***See*** BUST one's ASS

breakaway **1** ***modifier*** *theater* Made to break or collapse easily: *bashed with a breakaway chair* **2** ***adj*** Unconventional; schismatic; rebellious: *a breakaway rock group/ breakaway mind set*

break (or **bust**) **chops** ***v phr*** To injure; punish; literally, to break someone's face or mouth: *Whoever did this hoax on NYPD was someone who wanted to break chops* —New York Times

break (or **bust**) someone's **chops** **1** ***v phr*** To verbally assault; harass: *His old man was starting to break his chops about the union*—Richard Price **2** ***v phr*** =BUST one's ASS

breakdance ***See*** BREAK

break something **down** ***v phr*** *fr black* To explain; present in detail: *Break it down for me, Baby*—Eldridge Cleaver

breaker ***See*** BACK-BREAKER, BONE-BREAKER, JAWBREAKER

breakfast ***See*** FROM HELL TO BREAKFAST, MEXICAN BREAKFAST, SHOOT one's COOKIES

break someone or something **in** ***v phr*** To put through an initial period of easy use or training before requiring full function

break it up ***v phr*** To stop fighting, quarreling, chatting, etc • Usu a stern command

breakout ***n*** An escape

break out **1** ***v phr*** To escape from prison or some other confining situation **2** ***v phr*** To show symptoms of disease or discomfort: *He broke out in a purple rash* **3** ***v phr*** To bring out; produce for use: *When I came he broke out the Scotch*

◁ **break out into assholes**▷ ***v phr*** To become very frightened [an allusion to the loose bowels associated with fear]

the **breaks** **1** ***n phr*** Good luck; special favors: *If I get the breaks I'll prevail* **2** ***n phr*** Bad luck: *Them's the breaks*

break the back *v phr* To achieve the hardest part of a job, journey, etc: *We got the back broken, the rest is a piece of cake*

break the ice *v phr* To dissipate the sense of strain among people who do not know each other: *I broke the ice by saying she looked like Charlemagne's mother*

breakthrough *n* An abrupt solution or surge of progress: *Understanding the reaction was a breakthrough*

break up *v phr* To laugh or cause to laugh uncontrollably: *His doctor's shtick broke them up*

break-up *n* A separation or dissolution

◁ **breastworks**▷ *n* The female breasts; =BAZOOM

breather *n* A person who makes obscene telephone calls and merely breathes, rather than talking, into the mouthpiece
See HEAVY BREATHER, MOUTH-BREATHER

breathing *See* MOUTH-BREATHING

breeder *n homosexuals* A heterosexual person; =STRAIGHT: *They are ridiculous things, and they are meant for breeders*—Armistead Maupin

breeze 1 *n* An easy task; anything easy; =CINCH, CAKEWALK **2** *v* To go or move rapidly and easily: *to breeze through work/ I breezed out*

the **breeze** *See* BAT THE BREEZE, BURN THE BREEZE

breeze off *v phr* To leave; depart; =BOOK

breezy *adj* Very easy-going and jovial; cheery: *a breezy "Good morning"*

brekkie *n* Breakfast: *It was brekkie with Ed Meese*—Washington Post

a **brew** (or **brewskie**) *n phr esp college students* A glass, bottle, or can of beer; a beer: *She treated me to a brew*

brew out *n phr college students* A beer party; =BEER BUST

brick *n narcotics* A kilogram (2.2 pounds) of tightly compacted marijuana
See DROP A BRICK, HIT someone LIKE A TON OF BRICKS, HIT THE BRICKS, THREE BRICKS SHY OF A LOAD

brick agent *n phr* An FBI agent of the lowest rank: *brick agent, the Federal infantry who... knock on doors*—Philadelphia

the **bricks 1** *n phr* The streets and sidewalks of a city: *I had to get out on the bricks and hustle* **2** *n phr prison* The world outside prison
See HIT THE BRICKS

◁ **brick shithouse**▷ *See* BUILT LIKE A BRICK SHITHOUSE

bricktop *n* A redheaded person

the **Brickyard** *n phr* The motor speedway at Indianapolis, Indiana, site of the annual 500-mile race [fr the *brick* construction of the track]

bright *n black* A light-skinned black person

bright-eyed and bushy-tailed *adj phr* Eager and energetic; in splendid fettle
See STREET-SMART

bringdown *esp 1950s beat & cool talk* **1** *n* A cutting rebuke or comment; a deflation: *Polite applause is a bit of a bringdown* **2** *n* A disappointing or depressing performance **3** *modifier: a bringdown scene* **4** *n* A morose person: *A "bringdown" is a depressing character*—Stephen Longstreet **5** *modifier: that bringdown face*

bring down the house *v phr fr theater* To score a resounding theatrical success: *Old Man Dillinger strode onto the stage and brought down the house*—A Hynd

bring home the bacon (or **the groceries**) **1** *v phr* To achieve a tangible goal or task: *Their new tailback brought home the bacon* **2** *v phr* To earn enough to support oneself and one's family

bring it *v phr baseball* To throw a baseball fast

bring (or **keep**) someone **up to speed** *v phr* To give necessary information; brief; =FILL someone IN, PUT someone IN THE PICTURE: *Well, look, I appreciate your keeping me up to speed*—Washingtonian [fr the need to increase gradually the speed of a machine or phonograph turntable, video recorder, etc, to the proper rate]

the **briny** *n phr fr early 1900s* The ocean; the sea

Brit 1 *adj* British: *the Brit rock scene* **2** *n: two Brits and a Yank*

bro' or **bro 1** *n* Brother **2** *n black* A black person: *the slick-speaking bro who scores points off the ofay*—Time **3** *n motorcyclists* A motorcyclist; =BIKER: *the pack of twenty-seven bros jamming along the freeway*—Easyriders

◁**broad**▷ *fr early 1900s* **1** *n* A woman • Used almost entirely by men, and considered offensive by many women: *Sorry lady, no broads allowed in here/ So here was this suburban broad*—Saul Bellow **2** *n* A promiscuous woman; prostitute [probably from the notion "*broad* in the beam"]

brodie or **Brodie** **1** *n* A total failure; fiasco; =FLOP, TURKEY **2** *v* To commit suicide, esp by jumping from a high place [fr Steve *Brodie*, who claimed to have leaped off the Brooklyn Bridge in 1886, but failed to have the act witnessed]

broke *adj fr late 1800s* Entirely out of money; destitute

See ALL HELL BROKE LOOSE, DEAD BROKE, FLAT BROKE, GO BROKE, GO FOR BROKE, STONY COLD BROKE

broken record *n phr* Something or someone repetitive, tedious, and importunate: *He kept asking for a raise, like a broken record*

bronco **1** *n cowboys* A horse not tamed for riding **2** *n homosexuals* A young male not accustomed to nor complaisant in homosexual relations [fr Spanish *broncho* "rough, rude"]

bronco buster *n phr* (Variations: **peeler** or **snapper** or **twister** may replace **buster**) *cowboys* A cowboy who tames broncos to riding; also, a rodeo performer who rides unruly horses in competition

Bronx cheer **1** *n phr* A loud, rude, flatulating noise made with the tongue and lips; =the BIRD, RASPBERRY: *The Duchess was startled but serene when the crowd greeted her with a fortissimo Bronx cheer* **2** *n phr* Any outright and precise expression of derision: *That book will get Bronx cheers from every critic*

broom *See* HAVE A BROOM UP one's ASS

broomstick *n* =BEANPOLE

brother **1** *n* A man; fellow; =GUY • Used in addressing strangers: *I don't know you, brother, but you said a mouthful* **2** *n black* A black person; =BLOOD: *All you brothers here, and you white people too, got to take care of business*

See SOUL BROTHER

Brother *See* BIG BROTHER

brow *See* HIGHBROW, LOWBROW

◁**brown** or **brown-hole**▷ *v* or *v phr* To do anal intercourse; =BUGGER, BUNGHOLE

brown-bag or **brown-bag it** *v* or *v phr* To take one's lunch to the office, or one's liquor to a club or restaurant, in a paper bag: *for brown-bagging booze at places that allow this practice*--Esquire/ *to reduce the dangers of brown-bagging it for lunch* —Wall Street Journal

brown bagger **1** *n* A person who brown-bags **2** *n* A very ugly person; =DOUBLE-BAGGER [second sense fr the notion that such a person should wear a bag over the head to hide the face]

brown eyes *See* BIG BROWN EYES

Brownie points *n phr* A fancied unit of credit and approval: *I'll get Brownie points for helping him/ a place where you get big shiny brownie points, cash, sex, and adulation*—Village Voice [fr merit points awarded to *Brownies* toward promotion to Junior Girl Scouts]

brown-nose **1** *v* To flatter and pamper in order to gain approval and advantage; curry favor; =APPLE-POLISH: *He's just like any other person who's in a position to screw you. You gotta brown nose*—John R Powers **2** *n: He got there by being a pious and effective brown-nose*

brown-noser *n* A person who brown-noses

brown off *v phr jazz musicians* To make a mistake; blunder; =GOOF

brud *n* Brother

bruh *n* Brother: *The man had me and I know what it's like, bruh*—Rolling Stone

bruiser *n fr middle 1800s* A big, strong man

the **brush** **1** *n phr* The backwoods; jungle; =the BOONDOCKS **2** *n phr* A snub; quick dismissal; =BRUSH-OFF

See GIVE someone THE BRUSH

brushback **1** *modifier baseball* Pitched very close to the batter, as if to hit him: *knocked me over like a good brushback pitch*—New Yorker **2** *n: Throw another brushback and you're out of the game*

brusher *See* SAGEBRUSHER

brush someone **off** *v phr* To pointedly snub or dismiss; =GIVE someone THE BRUSH

brush-off *n* =the BRUSH

brush up **1** *v phr* To clean; make neat and clean **2** *v phr* (also **brush up on**) To improve, review, or perfect one's mastery: *Brush up your Shakespeare. Start quoting him now*—Cole Porter

BS or **bs** (pronounced as separate letters) *n* = BULLSHIT

B-side *n* The second or other side of a phonograph record; = FLIP SIDE

BTO or **bto** (pronounced as separate letters) *n* = BIG-TIME OPERATOR

bub *n* A man; fellow; brother; = GUY • Used in direct address, with a slightly insulting intent: *Okay, bub, get the hell outa my way* [fr *bubba* fr *brother*]

bubba *n* Brother • Not uncommon as a nickname: *Here comes big Bubba Jones*

bubbie *See* BOOBIE

bubble brain *n phr* A stupid and vapid person; = AIRHEAD: *Did I want to establish that, bubble brain though I seemed to him, there were sound reasons?*—Saul Bellow

bubblegummer *n* A young teenager; = TEENYBOPPER

bubble-gum music or **bubble gum** **1** *n phr* Rock-and-roll music that appeals to young teenagers: *young adult audience dissatisfied with "bubble-gum music"*—New York Times/ *so fundamental that one might refer to it as "heavy bubble gum"*—Aquarian **2** *modifier: The rap itself is sheer bubble-gum monotony*—Variety

bubblehead *n* A stupid person, esp one who is frivolous and flighty; = AIRHEAD: *Linda was, a polite word for dumb cunt, a bubblehead*—Richard Merkin

bubbly *n* Champagne; sparkling wine

bubkes (BŏŏB kəs, BŏŏP-) **1** *n* Something trivial; nothing; = BEANS: *We've gone from bubkes to big deals in a year*—People Weekly **2** *adv* Absurdly little: *That it sold bubkes... may say just as much for his laziness and his hubris*—Village Voice [fr Yiddish fr Russian, "beans"]

◁ **bubs** ▷ (BŏŏBZ, BōōBZ) *n* A woman's breasts; = BOOBS

buck **1** *n fr middle 1800s* A dollar **2** *n gambling* A hundred dollars, esp as a bet **3** *n* = BUCK PRIVATE **4** *n hoboes* A Roman Catholic priest **5** *n* A young male Indian; Native American brave **6** *n* A young black man **7** *n* Any young man, esp a strong and spirited one **8** *v* To resist; defy; go up against • Usu in the negative: *You can't buck the system* **9** *v fr WW2 armed forces* To work for personal advancement; aspire eagerly; covet: *I'm bucking for that dealership* **10** *v fr WW2 armed forces* To pass along a letter, memorandum, problem, etc, usu without taking action; = PASS THE BUCK: *Let's buck this one to the Committee on Hot Potatoes*

See BANG FOR THE BUCK, BIG BUCKS, the BUCK STOPS HERE, FAST BUCK, HALF-BUCK, PASS THE BUCK, SAWBUCK

bucket **1** *n* A car, esp a big, old car **2** *n merchant marine & Navy* A ship, esp an old and slow ship **3** *n Navy* A destroyer; = CAN **4** *n* The buttocks; rump: *Knocked him on his bucket* **5** *v* To speed; = BARREL: *They bucketed right through the light* **6** *n basketball* The basketball net **7** *n basketball* A basketball goal: *He'll make ten buckets a game* **8** *n baseball* The rearmost part of the batter's box: *Emily steps into the bucket when going for a pitch*—New York Times

See BRAIN BUCKET, someone CAN'T CARRY A TUNE IN A BUCKET, FOR CRYING OUT LOUD, GO TO HELL IN A HANDBASKET, GUTBUCKET, KICK THE BUCKET, LARD-BUCKET, SLEAZE-BUCKET, SLIMEBAG

the **bucket** *n phr* Jail; = the COOLER

bucket of bolts *n phr* An old car, airplane, etc

bucket of warm spit *See* WORTH A BUCKET OF WARM SPIT

bucket shop or **boiler room** **1** *n phr from late 1800s* A place where very dubious stocks, real estate, etc, are sold, often by telephone solicitation **2** *modifier: what law enforcement officials call a "boiler room" operation*—Time [fr comparison with cheap saloons]

buck general *n phr Army* A brigadier general

buckle down *v phr* To set seriously to work; put slothful ease behind one

buck naked *n phr* Entirely nude; = BARE ASS: *My God, Sal, them women is buck naked in them magazines*

buck private *n phr Army fr late 1800s* An Army private; soldier of the lowest rank

bucks *See* BIG BUCKS, IN THE BUCKS, LIKE A MILLION BUCKS

buck sergeant *n phr Army fr WW1* An Army sergeant, wearing three stripes [fr *buck* "dollar" as the symbolic relative value of the most junior type of sergeant]

the **buck stops here** *sentence* This is the place where responsibility must be accepted; a decision must be made here • Attributed usually to President Harry S Truman

buck up *v phr* To cheer up; brace: *Buck up, old chap, it may be good news*

bud[1] **1** *n* Friend; fellow; =GUY • Used only in direct address, often with hostile intent: *Okay, bud, that'll do* **2** *n* A very close friend; =PAL: *Just be glad I'm your bud*—Cameron Crowe [fr *brother*]

bud[2] *n teenagers* Marijuana

◀ **buddahead** or **buddhahead** ▶ *n black & police* An Asian person

buddy *fr middle 1800s* **1** *n* =BUD[1] **2** *n* A man's closest male friend; =PAL • During World War 1 this term took on a particularly strong sentimental value **3** *n* A male's partner in work or sport [fr earlier *butty* "partner, chum," said to be fr Romany; probably influenced by *brother*]

See ACE BOON COON, ASSHOLE BUDDY, GOOD BUDDY, OLD BUDDY

buddy-buddy *fr WW2 armed forces* **1** *n* A close friend; =BUDDY **2** *n* A person who is too friendly; an importunate acquaintance **3** *v: Look at that guy buddy-buddying Joe* **4** *adj: It's just one of his buddy-buddy moves* **5** *adj* Very friendly; amenable to companionship: *He is not buddy-buddy... although he... insisted that the photographer take their pictures together*—Irwin Shaw

buddy up to *v phr* To become close and comradely with; ingratiate oneself with: *Lawrence smarmily buddies up to these women*—Washington Post

buff[1] *n* A devotee or enthusiast; hobbyist; =FAN, NUT: *I like to think I'm a people buff* [originally *fire buff*, because 19th-century New York City volunteer firefighters wore *buff*-colored coats; transferred to persons who like to watch fires, then to enthusiasts in general]

buff[2] *adj* Naked [probably fr the pale yellowish color of the leather called *buff*, likened to skin]

See IN THE BUFF

buff[3] or **buff up** *v* or *v phr hospital* To make a patient's chart look good, esp in preparing him or her for discharge [fr *buff* "to polish"]

buffalo **1** *v fr middle 1800s* To confuse purposely, esp in order to cheat or dupe **2** *v fr early 1900s* To intimidate; cow; =BULLDOZE **3** *n* A heavy or fat woman; =COW

buffalo butt *n phr students* A person with large buttocks; =FAT-ASS

buffaloed *adj* Baffled; puzzled

bug **1** *n* Any insect whatever **2** *n* Any bacterium, microbe, virus, etc: *Syph is caused by a bug* **3** *n* Any upper-respiratory or flulike complaint, esp one that is somewhat prevalent: *There's a bug going around* **4** *n* Any fault or defect in a machine, plan, system, etc: *You've got to get the bugs out of the program before trying to run it on the computer* **5** *n circus & carnival* Any small, cheap item sold by a vendor or huckster **6** *n poker* A joker or a wild card **7** *n outdated teenagers* A girl: *Boys prowl for "bugs"*—Time **8** *n radio operators* A semiautomatic or automatic radiotelegraph key used for fast sending **9** *n print shop* Any small symbol or label, such as a copyright or trademark symbol **10** *n print shop* An asterisk **11** *n horse-racing* An asterisk printed beside the weight a horse is to carry, showing that a five-pound decrease has been granted because the jockey is an apprentice **12** *n horse-racing* An apprentice jockey who has ridden his or her maiden race during the current year or has not yet won his or her fortieth race **13** *n horse-racing* A horse that has never won a race; =MAIDEN **14** *n hot rodders* A hot rod **15** *n* A Volkswagen beetle, or any small foreign car **16** *n astronautics* A small two-person lunar excursion vehicle **17** *n fr middle 1800s* An enthusiast; devotee; hobbyist; =FAN, NUT: *Momma's a football bug* **18** *n* A compelling idea or interest: *His bug is surf-casting* **19**

n A current fashion; epidemic preference or interest: *I never gave in to the hula-hoop bug* **20** *n* An insane person; =NUT: *Only a bug is strong enough for that*—Eugene O'Neill **21** *n prison fr 1930s* An irrational, touchy mood; bad mood **22** *n prison* A psychiatrist **23** *v prison* To do a psychiatric evaluation; pronounce one insane **24** *v 1960s counterculture fr black* To irritate or anger; pester or harry: *I suspected something was bugging her* —Louis Armstrong **25** *n underworld* A confidential message or signal; confidential information **26** *n underworld* A burglar alarm **27** *v: They've got that safe bugged eight ways* **28** *v police & espionage* To prepare a room or other place for electronic surveillance by installing hidden microphones; equip for electronic eavesdropping: *to bug a room/ Bug the Secretary's telephone* **29** *n: The team planted bugs in about six flowerpots* **30** *n* A large industrial crucible [the sense "irritate, pester" may be a shortening of black English *humbug*, attested in such uses as "Him wife de humbug him too much"; *humbug* itself, attested in English fr the mid-18th century, is apparently found in and may derive fr Pacific Pidgin English and West African Pidgin English]

See HAVE A BUG UP one's ASS, JITTERBUG, LITTERBUG, PUT A BUG IN someone's EAR, SHUTTERBUG

-bug ***combining word*** A devotee or energetic practitioner of what is indicated: *firebug/ money-bug*

bugaboo *n* Something that frightens or defeats one

bugaloo *See* BOOGALOO

bugeyed **1** *adj* Having protruding eyeballs; exophthalmic **2** *adj* Startled; astonished: *He looked all bugeyed* [fr humorous or dialectal pronunciation of *bulge*]

bugged *adj* Fitted with a concealed microphone or otherwise equipped for electronic surveillance: *do-it-yourself sex manuals, bugged phones* —WH Auden

bugged up *adj phr* Confused; flustered; upset

bugger[1] (BUH gər) *n* A person who bugs, esp one who installs electronic surveillance devices

bugger[2] (BUH gər, Bo͝o-, Bo͞o-) **1** *n* Fellow; man; child; thing • Used affectionately: *What have been up to, you old bugger?/ Ain't he a cute little bugger?* **2** *n* An object, esp something admired, wondered at or scorned; =FUCKER, SUCKER: *Give that bugger a push, will you?* ◁**3**▷ *n* A male with a taste for anal intercourse; sodomite ◁**4**▷ *v* To do anal intercourse or sodomy; sodomize; =BUNGHOLE: *who immediately announced that the Reverend Mr. Alger had been "buggering" him*—Village Voice **5** *v* (also **bugger up**) *fr cowboys* To spoil; ruin; confuse; abuse; impair; =BOLLIX UP: *Between them they buggered up the mimeo machine/ The practice of how you bugger these numbers of US-Soviet armaments*—Village Voice

bugger[3] or **booger** or **boogie** (BUH gər, Bo͝o-, Bo͞o-) *n* A piece of solid mucus from the nose

buggy[1] **1** *n railroad* A caboose **2** *n* A car, esp an old and rickety one; =HEAP, JALOPY: *I wouldn't exactly call my Maserati a buggy*

See BUZZ-BUGGY, HORSE-AND-BUGGY, IRISH BUGGY

buggy[2] *adj* Crazy; =BUGHOUSE, NUTS

buggy whip **1** *n phr* A long radio antenna on a car **2** *modifier: a buggy-whip antenna* **3** *adj* Old-fashioned; outmoded; antique; =OLD-TIMEY: *still manages to epitomize buggy-whip thinking in an increasingly sophisticated high-tech communications world*—Village Voice

bughouse *fr late 1800s* **1** *n* An insane asylum: *Who cares whether you're free or locked in a bughouse?* —Calder Willingham **2** *adj* Crazy; =NUTS: *He's a bughouse pimp*—William Kennedy/ *The local constabulary haul the bughouse blighter off to prison*—Washington Post

See GO BUGHOUSE

bug off *v phr* To leave; depart • Often an irritated command: *I'm done with you, so bug off* [perhaps fr late-19th-century British slang *bugger off*, of the same meaning; perhaps fr early-19th-century US *bulge* "to rush, dash"]

bugout *fr Korean War Army* **1** *n* A person who usually withdraws and evades; a slacker **2** *n* A military retreat **3** *modifier:* *a bugout plan*

bug out[1] *v phr fr middle 1800s* To bulge; protrude: *His eyes bugged out like a frog's*

bug out[2] **1** *v phr* *fr Korean War Army* To retreat; turn one's back and run **2** *v phr* *esp teenagers & hot rodders fr 1950s* To leave rapidly, esp to drive away in a hurry [Probably related to *bug off*]

bugs or **bugsy** *adj* Crazy; =NUTS: *The idea is so bugs it might work/ Don't act bugsy*

See STIR-CRAZY

build **1** *n* One's physique, esp one's figure or shape: *a husky build/ sexy build* **2** *n* *theater* A show whose earnings continue to increase: *The revue was a build once word-of-mouth took hold* **3** *v* *underworld* To prepare someone for swindling, extortion, etc; =SET someone UP **4** *n:* *It's been a long build, but we can make our move now*

build a collar *v phr police* To gather evidence for an arrest

buildup **1** *n* Publicity and other provisions for introducing a new product, entertainer, etc: *the buildup for a concert* **2** *n* The careful preparation of a potential customer or victim

build up *v phr* To increase, esp someone's self-esteem: *He's shy, needs building up*

built *adj* Physically well developed, esp in a sexually attractive way; =HUNKY, STACKED: *She wasn't especially smart, but she was built*

◁ **built like a brick shithouse** ▷ *adj phr* Very solidly and well constructed; =BUILT • Said usually of a woman

bulb *n* =DIM BULB

bulge *See* BATTLE OF THE BULGE

bull **1** *n* *fr 1700s* A peace officer of any kind, esp a uniformed police officer **2** *n* *lumberjacks* An ox **3** *n* *circus* An elephant, of either sex **4** *n* *poker* An ace **5** *n* Bull Durham, a very popular brand of tobacco for rolling cigarettes **6** *n* *railroad* A locomotive **7** *n* *lumberjacks & cowboys* The chief; head man; =BOSS **8** *n* *stock market* A dealer who favors higher prices and quicker selling **9** *modifier:* *a bull market* **10** *n* =BOONDAGGER, BULLDAGGER **11** *n* =BULLSHIT **12** *v:* *We were sitting around bulling/ He was bulling about his enormous talent*

See BULL SESSION, BULLWORK, COCK-AND-BULL STORY, FULL OF SHIT, SHOOT THE BULL, SLING IT, THROW THE BULL

◁ **bull bitch** ▷ *n phr* A woman with masculine traits; virago

bulldagger *n black* A lesbian, esp a tough and aggressive one; =BOONDAGGER, BULLDYKE: *That's a bull-dagger, baby*—Claude Brown

bulldoze *v fr late 1800s* To intimidate; overcome by force: *to bulldoze employees* [fr *bulldose* "to beat," perhaps fr the notion of the *dose* of force needed to cow a *bull*]

bulldozer *fr late 1800s* **1** *n* A person who bulldozes **2** *n* A revolver

bulldyke *n fr black* A lesbian, esp an aggressive one; =BOONDAGGER, BULLDAGGER, DYKE

bullet **1** *n* *poker* An ace **2** *n* *WW2 aircraft workers* A rivet **3** *n* Anything thrown very fast, esp a baseball: *He's throwing bullets out there* **4** *n* *recording industry* A record rising very fast on the popularity charts **5** *v:* *currently bulleting up the charts*—Rolling Stone

See BITE THE BULLET

bullfest *n* =BULL SESSION

bull fiddle *n phr* The double bass; bass fiddle

bullfrog *n truckers* A male hitchhiker

bullheaded *adj* Obstinate

bullhorn *n fr Navy* An electronic megaphone; loud hailer

bullish **1** *adj* *stock market* Favoring and exhibiting high prices and relatively quick turnover: *a bullish market/ bullish advice* **2** *adj* Showing a positive and hopeful attitude; encouraging • Often used with "on" or "about": *She tends to be bullish about our prospects/ He's quite bullish on the new restaurant* **3** *adj* Strong; stubborn; bull-like

bullpen **1** *n* *prison* A cell or secure area where prisoners are kept temporarily: *We're in the bullpen waiting to go to court* **2** *n* *baseball fr late 1800s* A usu enclosed area where pitchers practice and warm up: *The bullpen's getting active now* **3** *n* *baseball* The relief pitching staff of a baseball team: *They've got starters but no bullpen* **4** *n* *lumberjacks* A bunkhouse [baseball sense perhaps fr the fact that some baseball clubs would admit latecomers very cheaply and herd them like *bulls* into foul territory beyond first and third bases, where some bullpens are still located]

bull session *n phr* A discussion, esp one among good companions passing time idly but investigating important topics

bullseye ***See*** HIT THE NAIL ON THE HEAD

◁ **bullshit** ▷ **1** ***n*** Nonsense; pretentious talk; bold and deceitful absurdities; =BALONEY: *I'm afraid your theory is chiefly bullshit* **2** ***v:*** *He tried to bullshit his way out of it* **3** ***interj*** An exclamation of disbelief, derision, and contempt in retort to some proposition

◁ **bullshit artist** ▷ ***n phr*** A person who habitually and effectively exaggerates, cajoles, seduces verbally, etc: *A good college president must be something of a bullshit artist*

bullwork **1** ***n*** *lumberjacks, miners, cowboys & merchant marine* Hard work needing a bull's strength **2** ***n*** Tedious work requiring little thought or skill; =DONKEYWORK, SCUT: *sees computers taking over only the bullwork of secretaries*—Westworld

bullyrag ***v*** To harass; pester; =RAG [fr *ballyrag*, of unknown origin; influenced by *bully* "ruffian, blustering tyrant"]

bully up ***v phr*** To press one's way forward; =BELLY UP: *Sharkey... was bullying up to the bar*—George Warren

bum¹ **1** ***n*** *fr middle 1800s* A person who seldom works, seldom stays in one place, and survives by begging and petty theft; drifter; vagrant; hobo **2** ***v*** To live as a tramp, drifter, etc: *It wasn't easy bumming that winter/ He bummed for a couple of years, then got a job* **3** ***v*** To beg or borrow; cadge: *That's the third drink you've bummed in an hour* **4** ***v*** To hitchhike: *They bummed a ride to Nashville* **5** ***n*** A promiscuous woman, esp a cheap prostitute: *picking up bums in public dance halls*—James T Farrell **6** ***n*** Any male who is disliked by the speaker, esp for lack of energy, direction, or talent • Often used of inept or despised athletes: *The bum strikes out three times in a row* **7** ***n*** A person who lives or tries to live by his or her sports talent and charm, without being genuinely professional: *ski bum/ tennis bum* **8** ***n*** An inferior animal, breed, racehorse, etc **9** ***n*** Anything inferior or ineffectual: *Money is a bum, a no-good bum*—Hal Boyle **10** ***adj:*** *a bum record/ bum heart* **11** ***adj*** False; invalid: *I told a bum story first*—James M Cain/ *bum rap* **12** ***v*** *computer* To improve, esp by exploiting its full potential or rearranging its parts: *I bummed the whole program to show up all possible mistakes* [probably fr German *Bummler* "loafer"]

See BEACH BUM, CRUMB-BUN, ON THE BUM, STEWBUM, STUMBLEBUM

bum² ***n*** The buttocks or anus; =ASS • More common in British usage: *after getting a shot of something in her bum*—Philadelphia [fr Middle English *bom* "anus"]

bum around ***v phr*** To go about idly; loaf: *I just bummed around last summer*

bumble-bee ***See*** KNEE-HIGH TO A GRASSHOPPER

◀ **bumfuck** ▶ ***v*** =ASSFUCK

bummed or **bummed out** ***adj*** or ***adj phr*** In a bad mood; dejected; depressed: *I'm heavily bummed... if I've realigned anybody's karma*—Playboy/ *the most bummed-out generation*—Chicago [fr narcotics and teenager senses of *bummer*]

bummer **1** ***n*** *fr middle 1800s* A bum: *an old bummer named Rumson*—AJ Lerner **2** ***n*** *narcotics* An unpleasant or depressing experience with a narcotic, esp with LSD; =BAD TRIP **3** ***n*** *teenagers fr 1960s counterculture* Any bad experience or occasion; bad situation or place: *May 17: Trip was a bummer*—Erma Bombeck/ *This school's a bummer*

bum out ***v phr*** To depress; discourage; irritate: *At a fraternity... the things you observe totally bum you out*—Esquire

bump **1** ***v*** To discharge; dismiss; =FIRE: *They bumped him for insubordination* **2** ***v*** *fr middle 1800s* To take away one person's status in order to accommodate someone of greater importance or seniority: *A person is bumped by someone with a larger number of retention points*—Jane Eads **3** ***v*** To cancel a reserved seat on an airline, bus, etc because the vehicle has been oversold: *To be bumped...means to be put off a flight because too many seats have been sold*—Wall Street Journal **4** *v* To displace a sports opponent by defeat: *The Indians bumped the Tigers out of third place* **5** *v* To kill; =BUMP OFF **6** *n: They blew him away, gave him the bump* **7** *v* To make pregnant; =KNOCK someone UP: *She had to blame someone for bumping her*—Len Yinberg **8** *v* To promote: *He got bumped to assistant manager* **9** *n: I see old Pipkin has got the bump to full professor*—Morris Bishop **10** *v poker* To raise a bet **11** *v show business* In dancing, esp in striptease, to thrust the pelvis forward and up • Nearly always in combination with **grind** **12** *n: She unreeled about fifty bumps in dazzling staccato* **13** *n* A drink; =SLUG: *They go out...and have a bump of whiskey*—Garrison Keillor

bump along *v phr* To progress haltingly: *The interest rate has been bumping along*—New York Times

bump one's **gums** *See* BAT one's GUMS

bumpoff *n fr early 1900s underworld* A killing; murder; assassination

bump someone **off** *v phr fr early 1900s underworld* To kill, esp to murder

bumps *See* DUCK BUMPS, GOOSE BUMPS

bumpy *See* GOOSE-BUMPY

bum rap **1** *n phr underworld* An erroneous conviction or sentence **2** *v: he had been bum-rapped*—Stephen King **3** *n phr* Any unjustified condemnation: *Reagan said, "Nancy's taken a bit of a bum rap on that buying White House china"*—Newsweek **4** *v: the Philadelphia Navy Yard has been bum-rapped*—Philadelphia

the **bum's rush** *fr early 1900s* **1** *n phr* The ejection of a person by force, esp from a public place: *Dey gimme de bum's rush*—Eugene O'Neill **2** *n phr* Any discourteous or summary dismissal: *with Stanfill telling the press that she had given her husband "the bum's rush"*—Washington Post

bum steer *n phr fr early 1900s underworld* Erroneous guidance or advice

bum trip *See* BAD TRIP

bun **1** *n fr early 1900s* A state of drunkenness; alcoholic exhilaration: *A bun is a light jag*—R Connell **2** *n* The buttocks; =BUM **3** *n* A single buttock; =CHEEK: *a boil on my left bun*

See CRUMB-BUN, HAVE A BUN IN THE OVEN, HAVE A BUN ON

bun-buster *n* A very hard task or job; =BALL-BUSTER: *This job is a bun-buster*—People Weekly

bunch of fives *n phr* A fist

bunco or **bunko** **1** *v esp late 1800s* To swindle; defraud; =FLIM-FLAM: *He was buncoed out of his seat in the House*—Greenough and Kittredge **2** *n* A swindle; =CON GAME, SCAM **3** *modifier: a bunco scheme/ instead of bunko artists*—Herbert Kastle [said to be fr *Banko* fr Cuban Spanish *banco* "banker of a gambling game," first used for a cheating dice game]

bunco (or **bunko**) **artist** *n phr* A professional swindler; =CON MAN: *The other fellow is, in most instances, a bunko artist*—Time

buncombe *See* BUNK

bundle **1** *n fr early 1900s* A large amount of money: *I hear you made a bundle in real estate/ Can the Pentagon Save a Bundle?*—New York Times/ *He's dropped a bundle that way*—WT Tyler **2** *n* A large, quick profit; =KILLING: *I made a bundle yesterday on the market* **3** *n* An attractive woman: *I saw Charley yesterday with this cute bundle* **4** *n narcotics* Twenty-five $5 packets of a narcotic, esp marijuana or cocaine

See DROP A BUNDLE

bung or **bung up** *v* or *v phr* To dent; hurt by hitting; =BANG: *He bunged up the left fender pretty good*

◁ **bung fodder** ▷ *n phr* Toilet paper

◁ **bunghole** ▷ **1** *n* The anus **2** *v* To do anal intercourse; =BUGGER

bunk *fr late 1900s* **1** *n* Nonsense; pretentious talk; =BALONEY, BULLSHIT **2** *v* To cheat; defraud; =BUNCO: *couldn't possibly have done a better job of bunking the American people*—Chicago Tribune [fr the explanation by a 19th-century politician that his extraordinary statements were meant only for his constituents in *Buncombe* County, North Carolina]

Bunker *See* ARCHIE BUNKER

bunko *See* BUNCO

bunkum or **buncombe** *n* =BUNK

bunny **1** *n early 1900s students* Welsh rabbit **2** *n* A habitually puzzled or victimized person: *She is always criticizing some poor bunny* —Sinclair Lewis ◁**3**▷ *n* Any young woman, esp a pert and attractive one **4** *n* A young woman who associates with the men in some exciting, daring, or otherwise glamorous activity, sometimes as a participant; =GROUPIE: *snow bunny/ surf bunny/ to eliminate any chance that newsroom chauvinists could tag her as an electronic bunny*—Time **5** *n homosexuals* A prostitute who serves his or her own sex **6** *n basketball* A layup shot

See BEACH BUNNY, DUMB BUNNY, DUST KITTY, FUCK LIKE A BUNNY, GUNBUNNY, JUNGLE-BUNNY, SEX KITTEN, SKI BUNNY

bunny (or **rabbit**) **food** *n phr* Lettuce, salad, green vegetables, etc

◀ **bunny fuck** ▶ **1** *n phr* A very quick sex act; =QUICKIE **2** *v: They pulled beside the road and bunny-fucked* **3** *v* To stall; waste time: *Quit bunny-fucking and let's move*

buns *n* The buttocks, esp male buttocks: *I'll grab Ron's or Alan's buns sometimes and they're firm and hard* —Playboy

See one's ASS OFF, BUST one's ASS, WORK one's ASS OFF

one's **buns off** *adv phr* Very energetically; with maximum effort; =TO THE MAX: *You'll be playing your buns off with your left hand*—Toronto Life

burg *n fr middle 1800s* A city; town; village ● Usu expresses contempt: *stuck two days in this ghastly burg*

-burger *combining word* A sandwich made with cooked portions of what is indicated: *beefburger/ cheeseburger/ snakeburger* ● The definition does not apply to **hamburger**, the source of the term

burgle *v fr middle 1800s* To break into a place for robbery; burglarize

burleycue or **burlecue** or **burlicue** **1** *n* A burlesque show; the burlesque stage or circuit **2** *modifier: burleycue top banana/ burlicue stripper*

burly *n* Burlesque: *even when Buttons was in burly*—Gilbert Milstein

burn **1** *v* To cook or heat food **2** *v* To put or be put to death in the electric chair; =FRY **3** *v* To kill; assassinate **4** *v* To become angry: *He began making cracks....I burned but went on singing*—John O'Hara **5** *n: He didn't blow up, just did a slow burn* **6** *v* To anger; infuriate; =PISS-OFF: *You must have done something to burn him*—Elizabeth Morgan **7** *v fr middle 1800s* To cheat; swindle; victimize; rob; =RIP OFF: *If you go along with that guy you'll get burned* **8** *n: It was a burn, but it didn't start out to be* —Rolling Stone Interviews **9** *v street gang* To assault or fight a rival gang or gang member **10** *v* To harass a person relentlessly; hound: *I'll burn you right off the force*—Ira Wolfert **11** *v teenagers & students* To insult; =PUT DOWN: *I burned this chick...."Whereja get those jeans, like Sears or something?"* —The Valley Girls' Guide to Life **12** *n: I didn't mean it as a burn* **13** *v* To infect or become infected with a venereal disease **14** *v* To pass; spend; waste: *I'll start a conversation just to burn time*—Washington Post/ *if it burns tomorrow afternoon* —George V Higgins **15** *v* To move very rapidly; speed; =BARREL: *He wasn't just running, he was burning* **16** *v black fr jazz musicians* To perform, esp to improvise, superbly; excel; =be HOT: *The cat was getting down and burning* **17** *v* To borrow; beg **18** *v* To throw something, esp a baseball, very fast: *He burned the fastball right down the middle* **19** *v* To outdo; outshine in competition: *in the direction of the Spanish kids, who are already looking humiliated. Tony has burned the guy*—Village Voice

See BURNOUT, DO A SLOW BURN

burn someone's **ass** *v phr* To anger; irritate extremely: *Still, it burns my ass to be so close and miss it*—Lawrence Sanders

burn someone **down** **1** *v phr* To shoot someone **2** *v phr* To deflate; humiliate: *He's so cocky someone has to burn him down*

burned *adj* Very angry: *Everyone is sitting there really pissed, really burned*—WT Tyler

burned out **1** *adj phr* Tired; exhausted; =POOPED **2** *adj phr* At the end of one's vigor and productivity: *an old burned-out teacher* **3**

adj phr *narcotics* Depressed and exhausted after the effects of a narcotic have worn off **4** *adj phr* Bored

burner **1** *n* The electric chair **2** *n* *black* A superlative performer; =the TOPS **3** *n* *football* A pass receiver whose speed is excellent for the first few yards run, but then is not notable
See COOK WITH GAS, FAST BURNER, ON THE BACK BURNER

burn one in (or **over**) *v phr* In baseball, to throw a fastball

burnout **1** *n* Total and incapacitating exhaustion; inability to go on: *Many report lawyer burnout after two or three years in practice/ high rate of teacher burnout* **2** *n* Boredom; satiation; end of tolerance ● The currency of this and the previous sense are due to the various narcotics-users' meanings of **burn out**: *I feared polka burnout, but it never happened...I became a polkaholic* —Village Voice **3** *n* (also **burn**) *teenagers* A user or abuser of drugs, liquor, etc: *There are two groups in my school, the jocks and burn-outs. The burn-outs smoke and take pills and drink*—New York Times/ *except for the long hairs (or "burns," shorty for "burnouts") who hang out on the steps and smoke*—Washington Post **4** *n* *hot rodders* A very high-speed hot rod race

burn rubber *v phr* To leave; depart, esp very precipitately: *When I got back to the flat, you had burned rubber out the back*—Village Voice [fr the scorching of tires in the fast acceleration of a car]

burn the breeze *v phr* To run or drive at very high speed

burn someone **up** **1** *v phr* (also **burn** someone **off**) To anger: *His egocentricity burns me up* **2** *v phr* To put to death in the electric chair **3** *v* *circus* To cheat; swindle; victimize

burp *fr early 1900s* **1** *n* A belch, esp a gentle one **2** *v: She burped thrice and smiled* **3** *v* To cause a baby to belch, esp by holding it over the shoulder and patting its back

burp gun **1** *n phr* *WW2 Army* A German Schmeisser machine pistol, with a very high rate of fire **2** *n phr* Any submachine gun; =TOMMY GUN

◀ **burrhead** ▶ *n* A black person

bus **1** *n* A car: *Whose old bus is in the drive?* **2** *n* An aircraft **3** *v* To clear dirty dishes and tableware from the tables in a restaurant or cafeteria [the restaurant sense probably fr the four-wheeled cart often used to carry dishes]
See JITNEY

bush **1** *n* A beard; whiskers ◁**2**▷ *n* The pubic hair, esp of a female; =BEAVER ◁**3**▷ ***modifier:*** *Bush shot. You could see the pubic hair, but not the sex parts*—John Irving **4** *adj* Rural; provincial; =BUSH LEAGUE: *a bush town* **5** *adj* Mediocre; second-rate; amateur: *seemed pretty bush for...pros*—John D MacDonald **6** *v* To fatigue; exhaust; sap; =POOP: *The climb bushed him/ Our dialogues always bush me*
See BEAT AROUND THE BUSH, BEAT THE BUSHES

bushed *adj fr loggers* Tired out; exhausted; =POOPED [perhaps fr mid-19th-century meaning "lost in the woods"]

busher or **bush leaguer** **1** *n* or *n phr* A baseball player in a minor league **2** *n* or *n phr* Any mediocre or second-rate performer; amateur: *He's a busher at the piano*

the **bushes** *n phr* Rural regions; small towns and villages: *When I was... working 12-hour tricks as a newspaper cub in the bushes*—Westbrook Pegler

bush league **1** *n phr* A baseball minor league of professional or semiprofessional players **2** *n phr* Any subordinate, apprentice, or amateur enterprise: *The road companies are sometimes bush leagues for aspirants to Broadway* **3** *adj phr* Mediocre; second- or third-rate; =BUSH, SMALL-TIME: *Your ideas are invariably bush league*

the **bush leagues** *n phr* The mediocre and inferior reaches of business, entertainment, sports, etc; =the SMALL TIME: *For years he made a perilous living as a singer in the bush leagues*

bushwah (BŏŏSH wah, BŏŏSH-) (Variations: **booshwah** or **bushwa** or **booshwa**) *n fr around 1920* Nonsense; pretentious talk; bold and deceitful absurdities; =BALONEY, BULLSHIT: *But the President's own managers concede this is so much bushwah*

—Washingtonian [a euphemism for *bullshit* fr a cowboy corruption of French *bois-de-vache* "dried cow dung"]

bushy-tailed ***See*** BRIGHT-EYED AND BUSHY-TAILED

business ***n*** Excrement, esp that of a house pet
See IN BUSINESS, KNOW one's ONIONS, MONKEY BUSINESS, TAKE CARE OF BUSINESS, THAT'S SHOW BUSINESS

the **business** ***n phr narcotics*** The equipment used for giving oneself a narcotic injection
See GET THE BUSINESS, GIVE someone THE BUSINESS

the **business end** ***n phr fr middle 1800s*** The dangerous or crucial part, esp the muzzle of a gun

bussy ***n*** A bus driver: *Where the blazes was that bussy?*—Sports Illustrated

bust **1** ***v fr late 1800s*** To break: *I busted my nose* **2** ***v Army fr late 1800s*** To reduce in rank; demote: *He got busted from buck sergeant to buck private* **3** ***v cowboys fr late 1800s*** To tame a wild horse for riding: *Two rides will usually bust a bronco so that the average cowpuncher can use him*—Harper's Magazine **4** ***v underworld*** To break open a safe, vault, etc; also, burglarize a place **5** ***n street gang*** To disperse or chase a rival street gang **6** ***n*** A police raid: *One whiff (of marijuana) and we get a bust*—Meyer Berger **7** ***n*** An arrest; = COLLAR: *Beating a Bust: Two Views*—Rolling Stone **8** ***v:*** *I've been busted, bring bail* **9** ***v teenagers fr 1950s*** To catch in an illegal or immoral act **10** ***v*** To hit: *She busted me in the kishkes* **11** ***n:*** *That one bust decked me* **12** ***n fr middle 1800s*** A failure; fiasco: *My try for her sweet favors was a total bust* **13** ***n*** A person who fails; = NONSTARTER, LOSER: *At baseball I was a risible bust* **14** ***v college students*** To fail an examination or course; = FLUNK: *I miserably busted the econ final* **15** ***n fr middle 1800s*** A spree; drinking bout: *took his paycheck and went on a bust* **16** ***adj*** Out of funds; destitute; = BROKE
See BEER BUST, GO BROKE

bust a gut ***v phr*** = BUST one's ASS

◁ **bust** one's **ass**▷ ***v phr*** (Variations: **break** may replace **bust**; ◁**balls**▷ or **buns** or **butt** or **chops** or **conk** or **hump** or **nuts** or ◁**sweet ass**▷ may replace **ass**) To work or perform to one's utmost; exert oneself mightily: *If They Break Their Asses They Might Get into College Program*—John R Powers/ *I'm finished busting my hump on that kind of work*—Rolling Stone

◁ **bust balls**▷ ***v phr*** To discipline harshly; punish: *They gonna be bustin' balls, man*—David Rabe

bust chops ***See*** BREAK CHOPS

bust someone's **chops** ***See*** BREAK someone's CHOPS

buster **1** ***n fr middle 1800s*** A big person, esp a boy: *He was a buster... nigh as big as his Mammy*—Robert Penn Warren **2** ***n*** (also **Buster**) Man; fellow; = GUY, BROTHER • Used in direct address with a somewhat hostile tone: *That'll just about do, buster* **3** ***combining word*** Someone or something that destroys, thwarts, or otherwise defeats what or who is indicated • Popularized by an early 1980s film comedy called *Ghostbusters*: *troll buster/ gridlock buster/ fuzz buster/ virus buster*
See BALL-BUSTER, BELLY-WHOPPER, BRONCO BUSTER, BUN-BUSTER

bust hump ***v phr*** To work extremely hard; = BUST one's ASS: *Nobody's ever accused you of being unwilling to bust hump*—Hannibal Boris

bust out **1** ***v phr*** To be dismissed from a school for academic failure **2** ***v phr*** To lose all one's money gambling, esp at craps; = TAP OUT **3** ***v phr*** = BREAK OUT

busy bee ***n phr narcotics*** The powdered form of phencyclidine, a tranquilizer used in veterinary medicine, which as a narcotic is either sniffed or smoked in a tightly rolled cigarette; = ANGEL DUST: *angel dust, also known as busy bee*—New York Times [fr the fact that a low dosage produces a *buzz*]

but ***adv*** Really; definitely: *He noticed it and began making cracks but loud*—John O'Hara [probably fr a Yiddish speech pattern]

butch **1** ***n*** A rough, strong man; = TOUGH • Often used as a nickname **2** ***n homosexuals*** An aggressive lesbian; = BULLDYKE, DYKE **3** ***adj:*** *short round blonde of butch* *self-sufficiency*—Saul Bellow [fr *butcher*]

bute *n* Butazolidin (a trade name), a drug sometimes used to stimulate race horses

but good *adv phr* Very well; extremely; really: *They hate us but good/ Your brother fucked you but good*—Saul Bellow

butt 1 *n* The buttocks; rump; =ASS: *So drunk he couldn't find his butt with both hands*—H Allen Smith **2** *n* The remainder of a smoked cigarette or cigar **3** *n* A cigarette: *a pack of butts* **4** *n armed forces & prison* The final year of a prison sentence or a term of military enlistment
See BUST one's ASS, DUCK-BUTT, DUSTY BUTT, GET OFF one's ASS, GOOFY-BUTT, GRIPE one's ASS, NO SKIN OFF MY ASS, SCUTTLEBUTT

butter *n* Flattery; cajolery; =SOFT SOAP
See LIKE SHIT THROUGH A TIN HORN

butter-and-egg man *esp 1920s* **1** *n phr* A wealthy business executive or farmer from the provinces: *The visiting Butter and Egg Men [making] Whoopee in New York*—C Bragdon **2** *n phr* A person who finances a theatrical production; =ANGEL

butterball *n* Any plump person

butter bar *n phr Army* A second lieutenant

butterfingers *n fr cricket fr middle 1800s* A clumsy, unhandy person, esp one who regularly drops things: *Brunhilde is a regular butterfingers*

butterflies *n* Dull spasms in one's stomach, caused by anxiety and nervousness; flutters: *I sure got butterflies thinking about it*

butterfly ball (or **pitch**) *n phr baseball* A slow and erratic pitch; =KNUCKLEBALL: *All this exertion took the butter off his butterfly ball*—New York Daily News

butterfly kiss *n phr* A caress made by winking an eye so that the lashes brush one's partner: *She worked her eyelashes and made butterfly kisses on my cheeks*—Raymond Chandler

butter up *v phr* To flatter, esp in view of some special advantage; cajole: *You butter up the boss, you get the raise*

◀ **buttfuck** ▶ *v and n* =ASSFUCK, BUMFUCK

◀ **buttfuck buddy** ▶ *See* ASSHOLE BUDDY

◁ **butthole** ▷ *n* The anus; =ASSHOLE: *Did those butt-holes score again?*—Dan Jenkins
See ASSHOLE

butt in *v phr* To intrude oneself; proffer unwanted counsel; =BARGE IN: *The Wagner Act forbade any employer to butt in on such matters*—Westbrook Pegler/ *"Greenspan, don't butt in," said Gold*—Joseph Heller

buttinsky *n* (Variations: **butterinsky** or **buttinski** or **butt-in**) *fr early 1900s* A person who rudely intrudes himself, esp one who does so habitually [fr *butt in* + the Slavic or Yiddish suffix *-sky*, added for humorous effect]

button 1 *n* The chin; point of the chin: *I got clipped square on the button* **2** *n* The clitoris; =CLIT **3** *n narcotics* A small quantity of a narcotic: *There exists some traffic, however, in "buttons," or small amounts*—H Braddy **4** *n narcotics* The rounded top of the peyote plant **5** *n* A police officer's badge
See BELLY BUTTON, CHICKEN SWITCH, HIT THE PANIC BUTTON, ON THE BUTTON, PUSH one's BUTTON

buttondown or **buttoned-down** *adj* Conventional; of unmistakable respectability; conservative; =SQUARE: *The button-down, dispassionate, country club racism of the nouveau riche*—Paul Good/ *One of the most squeaky-clean and buttoned-down of US corporations is a partner*—Wall Street Journal [fr the wearing of *buttondown* collars by business executives and other conservatives]

button down 1 *v phr* To classify; =PEG, PIGEONHOLE: *I buttoned him down from the start as a probable bore* **2** *v phr* To make precise; discard all but one alternative: *First we decide to buy, then we button down the price* **3** *v phr* To prepare for action; get ready: *He was all buttoned down and ready to go* [third sense fr a military term for closing all ports and hatches for action]

buttoned-up *adj* Neat; trim; prim: *Betty Crocker's very serious, buttoned-up, orderly*—Wall Street Journal

button one's **lip** *v phr* To stop talking; not tell what one knows: *Tell that gasbag to button his lip*

button man (or **player** or **soldier**) *n phr underworld* A low-ranking member of the Mafia; =SOLDIER [probably fr the fact that such humble associates would be paid in *buttons* rather than valid coin]

buttons *See* HAVE ALL one's BUTTONS, HAVE SOME BUTTONS MISSING

button up **1** *v phr* To keep quiet; =BUTTON one's LIP, CLAM UP: *If you don't button up they'll shut you up* **2** *v phr* To finish, esp tidily and handsomely: *We buttoned it up in a couple days* **3** *v phr* To lock up, close up, or make secure: *I told John Sanderson to button up the generator* —JC Clark

butt out **1** *v phr* To stop intruding; reverse one's butting in • Usu an exasperated command: *Look, I'm busy, so butt out* **2** *v phr* To depart, esp abruptly; =BUG OUT: *I butted right out of there when it went off*

butts or **butts on** *interj* The declaration that one has or wants first rights to something; =DIBS: *The kids hollered "Butts on the drumstick!"* [fr the claiming of a cigarette *butt* seen in the street]

buy **1** *v* To believe; accept as true: *These guys bought the myth and now it's costing them dearly*—Toronto Life **2** *v* To agree to; acquiesce in: *If that's the plan I'll buy it* **3** *v* To do; effectuate: *She pointed her gun at me. I said, "What are you trying to buy with that?"*—J Evans **4** *v* To hire; engage: *He bought him a lawyer and filed suit* **5** *v* To bribe: *He tried to buy a couple of jury members*

buy a pig in a poke *v phr* To accept or agree to without careful examination; risk the unknown: *It is unfair for anyone running for President "to ask people to buy a pig in the poke"* —Associated Press [fr dialect *poke* "bag, sack"]

See CAN'T BUY

buy into *v phr* To accept; acquiesce in • Thought of and perhaps coined as the opposite of **sell out**, which has a more contemptuous suggestion of betrayal: *lots of guilt and I bought into that*—San Francisco/ *I bought into the whole materialistic trip*—San Francisco

buy it *See* COP IT

buy off on *v phr Army* To agree to; =BUY: *Will you buy off on letting us go back to garrison?*

buy the farm (or **the ranch**) *v phr fr armed forces* To be killed; die: *the cat that bought the farm when Harvey hit him on his bike*—Cyra McFadden/ *Luna crash confirmed. They bought the ranch*—Playboy [fr earlier Air Force term *buy a farm* "to crash"; probably from the expressed desire of wartime pilots to stop flying, buy a farm, and live peacefully]

buy time *v phr* To be dilatory or evasive in order to gain time; temporize; =STALL

buzhie *See* BOOJIE

buzz **1** *v* To call on the telephone; =RING: *Why not buzz Eddy for the brawl?*—HT Webster **2** *n: I think I'll give the Guided Child a buzz*—K Brush **3** *v* To talk; converse: *The crowd was buzzing about some pretty raunchy divorces* **4** *n* Subject of talk; gossip; rumor: *What's the dirtiest buzz?* **5** *n* A feeling or surge of pleasure, esp a pleasant sense of intoxication; =HIGH: *After two Scotches he got a nice buzz* **6** *v: I was pleasantly buzzed by a belt of Bourbon* **7** *n teenagers fr 1950s* A police squad car **8** *n* A kiss, esp a quick kiss on the cheek **9** *v* To flatter; court **10** *v* To inform someone in confidence, esp by whispering: *You'll buzz me later*—Mickey Spillane **11** *v* To fly an aircraft alarmingly close to something, esp to the ground **12** *v WW2 armed forces* To roister drunkenly at: *They were all buzzing the bar*

buzz along *See* BUZZ OFF

buzzard colonel *n phr armed forces* =CHICKEN COLONEL

buzz book *n phr* A best-selling book; a book everyone is talking about: *The nation's latest buzz book is not a fast summer read*—Time

buzz-buggy or **buzz-wagon** *n* A car

buzz-buzz *n esp early 1900s* Unintelligible or tedious noise, esp continuous vociferation: *All the buzz-buzz from without may be said to go in one ear and out the other*—Atlantic Monthly

buzzed *adj* Intoxicated, esp mildly so: *Getting a little buzzed on a second Bloody Mary*—Peter de Vries

buzz in *v phr* To arrive: *Old JK buzzed in from Syracuse*

buzz off (or **along**) *v phr* To depart; =TODDLE OFF

buzzword or **buzzphrase** *n* A modish technical or arcane term used to make one appear sophisticated: *The rhetoric has sputtered with buzzwords like "anticolonialist" and "progressive"*—Time

by **1** *prep* With; as far as concerns: *Five skins is jake by me*—American Mercury **2** *prep* At; to; at the place of: *I'll buy you a drink by Antek*—Nelson Algren [fr direct transcription of Yiddish prepositional use into English]

See GET AWAY WITH something, GET BY

not **by a long shot** (or **a jugful**) *See* NOT BY A LONG SHOT

by a nose *adv phr* By a narrow margin; barely: *win by a nose*

bye *See* TAKE A BYE

by ear *See* PLAY IT BY EAR

-by God- *infix* Used for emphasis: *I was born in West-by God-Virginia*

by guess and by God *adv phr* By approximation and instinct; not by precise or infallible means: *She didn't know exactly how to make a quiche, so had to do it by guess and by God*

BYOB (pronounced as separate letters) **1** *v phr* Bring your own bottle, or your own booze **2** *modifier: a BYOB party*

◁**by the balls**▷ *See* HAVE someone BY THE BALLS

by the bell *See* SAVED BY THE BELL

by the book *adv phr* According to correct procedures; as one should under regulations, law, contract, etc: *He said there would be no more corner cutting, we'd do everything strictly by the book*

by the numbers *adv phr fr WW1 armed forces* In a prescribed way; mechanically: *He even makes love by the numbers* [fr the military training device of analyzing a complex action by breaking it into a numbered series of simpler actions, performed as the *numbers* are called out]

by the seat of one's **pants** *See* FLY BY THE SEAT OF one's PANTS

C

C ***n*** Cocaine

See BIG C, C-NOTE, GENTLEMAN'S C, H AND C

cabbage ***n*** Money; =LETTUCE: *the salad boys in the back room, oiling up the cabbage. And it's big cabbage, too*—WT Tyler

See FOLDING MONEY, HAPPY-CABBAGE

cabin fever ***n phr*** Restlessness, impatience, and other signs of having been restrained too long

caboodle ***n fr middle 1800s*** A totality; discrete unit; =BOODLE: *Keep the whole caboodle* [perhaps fr *boodle*; see *boodle*]

See KIT AND CABOODLE

caboose ***n*** A jail [prob fr *calaboose* "jail"]

ca-ca or **caca** or **kaka** **1** ***n*** Excrement; =SHIT: *not worth ca-ca* **2** ***n*** *narcotics* Heroin; =HORSE, SHIT [fr late-19th-century *cack* "to defecate," perhaps fr Latin *cacavi* "to defecate," used as a euphemism in the presence of children; ultimately fr the Indo-European root *kakka* or *kaka*, designating defecation]

Cad or **Caddy** or **Caddie** ***n*** A Cadillac car

cadet ***See*** SPACE CADET

cadge (CAJ, CAYJ) ***v fr early 1800s*** To borrow; beg; =BUM, MOOCH

Cadillac ***n narcotics*** An ounce of heroin

cage **1** ***n*** ***fr 1600s*** A prison **2** ***v:*** *The punk concealed a genuine terror of being caged*—Nelson Algren **3** ***n*** *motorcyclists* A car or van: *The cage behind me bleated its horn*—Easyriders **4** ***v*** =CADGE **5** ***n*** *sports fr early 1900s* A basketball basket or net **6** ***n*** *sports fr early 1900s* Basketball **7** ***modifier:*** *a big cage star/ the cage standing*

See RATTLE someone's CAGE, RATTLE CAGES

cage rattler ***n phr*** A person not content with the humdrum or conventional: *The governor wants "cage rattlers"... thinkers, dreamers, and gadflies*—Newsweek

cagey or **cagy** ***adj fr late 1800s*** Shrewd; wary; pawky: *a quiet, cagy observer*

cahoots ***See*** IN CAHOOTS

Cain ***See*** RAISE CAIN

cake ◁**1**▷ ***n black*** The female genitals **2** ***n*** *black* A sexually attractive woman; =FOX **3** ***n*** *esp 1920s* A ladies' man; =DUDE: *his brown hat, fixed square-shaped the way the cakes were wearing them*—James T Farrell **4** ***n*** *college students* =PIECE OF CAKE

See BABYCAKES, FRUITCAKE, HEAVY-CAKE, ICE THE CAKE, NUTBALL, PIECE OF CAKE, TAKE THE CAKE

cakewalk ***n*** Something very easy; =BREEZE, CINCH, PIECE OF CAKE: *Our players thought this season was going to be a cakewalk*—Sports Illustrated [fr the name of a 19th-century dance contest, influenced by *piece of cake*]

calaboose ***n fr 1700s*** A jail or prison; cell [fr Spanish *calabozo*]

calk off ***See*** CAULK OFF

call **1** ***n*** *hoboes* A stew **2** ***n*** =NATURE'S CALL

See CATTLE CALL, CLOSE SHAVE

call someone's **bluff** ***v phr*** To force someone to justify or validate a pretense; require the truth: *When she called his bluff, he had to admit he was lying*

call someone **down** *v phr* To reprimand; rebuke

call girl *n phr* A prostitute, esp one who may be engaged by telephone

call it quits *v phr* To stop or terminate something; declare one has had enough: *After four years they called it quits*

call someone **on the carpet** *v phr* To reprimand or summon for a reprimand; =CHEW someone OUT [probably fr early-19th-century British *walk the carpet*, having the same sense and based upon a servant's being called into the parlor to be reprimanded]

call one's **shots** *v phr* To explain or predict what one will do: *She'll never try to trick you, she always calls her shots* [fr the announcement of a target-shooter where the next *shot* will hit]

call the shots *v phr* To be in charge: *Who's calling the shots around here?*

calm as a Christian with aces wired *See* COOL AS A CHRISTIAN WITH ACES WIRED

◀ **camel-jammer** ▶ *n* An Arab or Iranian

camp **1** *n homosexuals fr 1940s* A male homosexual **2** *adj: a camp bar/ the camp scene* **3** *n homosexuals fr 1930s* Effeminate behavior, such as mincing gait, fluttering gestures, or pronounced lisp **4** *v* (also **camp it up**): *Malcolm was camping perilously in the blue-collar bar* **5** *n fr 1960s* Something, esp in art, decoration, theater, etc, so naively stylized, artificial, affected, old-fashioned, and inadequate to good modern taste as to be highly amusing and inviting to parody: *television's inexhaustible supply of crash courses in camp*—Washington Post **6** *adj: a camp advertisement/ camp clothing* **7** *v* (also **camp it up**) To behave in a humorously affected, exaggerated way, esp imitating the acting and oratorical styles of the 1800s: *She started camping, vamping me like Theda Bara*

See BOOT CAMP, HIGH CAMP, LOW CAMP

campaign *See* WHISPERING CAMPAIGN

campy **1** *adj homosexuals* Effeminate; overtly homosexual **2** *adj* Displaying naive, affected, and old-fashioned style: *a campy evocation of World War 1 patriotism*

can **1** *n* A toilet; =JOHN **2** *n* The buttocks; rump; =ASS **3** *v fr early 1900s* To discharge an employee; =FIRE: *He is not the first commentator to be canned by an editor*—Heywood Broun **4** *v fr early 1900s* To stop; cease, esp some objectionable behavior • Usu a stern command: *Let's can the noise* **5** *n* A jail or prison; cell **6** *v: They caught him and canned him for two weeks* **7** *n Navy* A destroyer **8** *n hot rodders* A hot rod **9** *n narcotics* An ounce of marijuana

See IN THE CAN, SHITCAN

canary[1] **1** *n fr late 1800s* A girl or woman; =CHICK **2** *n* A woman singer, esp of popular music **3** *v: She used to canary with Stan Kenton* **4** *n underworld* An informer; =STOOL PIGEON

canary[2] *n* A compliment; critical approval [fr Yiddish *kayn aynhoreh* "(may you have) no bad luck or no evil eye," a formula used to ward off bad luck]

can be *See* EASY AS PIE

can do **1** *sentence fr late 1800s armed forces* I can do it; I'm the one you want: *We asked them to design a whole new bridge in a week, and they said "Can do"* **2** *adj: The CIA was a can-do outfit*—New Republic

See NO CAN DO

candy *See* NEEDLE CANDY, NOSE CANDY

candy ass *n phr* A timid person; weakling; =WIMP

candy-assed or **candyass** *adj* Timid; feeble; cowardly; =WIMPY: *not that candy-assed dreck played by legions of Spandexed clones*—Worcester Magazine/ *Some candyass Barry Manilow type might be at ease in this setting*—New York Times

candy man *n phr narcotics* A narcotics supplier; =CONNECTION, PUSHER

canned **1** *adj* Drunk: *They was already pretty canned*—James M Cain **2** *adj* Recorded; played from a phonograph record or magnetic tape: *canned music* **3** *adj* Not fresh for the occasion; kept for easy and general use: *The candidate uttered one or two canned one-liners, to small effect* **4** *adj movie studio* Filmed; completed: *That scene is already canned*

canned cow *n phr fr cowboys* Canned milk; condensed milk

cannibal *n* =SIXTY-NINE

cannon¹ *n* A pistol; firearm; =PIECE: *He holstered his own cannon*—Raymond Chandler

See LOOSE CANNON

cannon² **1** *n* *underworld fr early 1900s* A professional thief, esp a pickpocket: *grand larceny, when a cannon lifts a wallet from a pocket* —New York Times **2** *v: You're too small to cannon the street-cars* —Nelson Algren [an extension of *gun* "thief," fr Yiddish *gonif*]

can (or **tall can**) **of corn** *n phr baseball* A high, easy fly ball

can (or **bag**) **of worms** *n phr* A complex and troublesome matter; a Pandora's box: *The Social Security problem is a can of worms/ the current bag of worms*—Armistead Maupin

See OPEN UP A CAN OF WORMS

one **can really** (or one **sure knows how to**) **pick 'em** *sentence* One is very selective, accurate, and successful in choices • Nearly always used ironically: *Is this turkey your idea of a good show? You can really pick 'em*

cans ◁**1**▷ *n* A woman's breasts; =TITS: *that chanteuse with the huge cans* **2** *n* Earphones worn over the ears

See KNOCK someone or something FOR A LOOP

can't buy *v phr* To have no possibility of; be totally denied: *From then on, I couldn't buy a good review*—Saturday Review/ *You couldn't find a job. You couldn't buy a job*—Newsweek

someone **can't carry a tune in a bucket** *sentence* Someone is tone-deaf; someone sings very badly: *Ashley can't carry a tune in a bucket* —New York Times

can't fight (or **punch**) one's **way out of a paper bag** *v phr fr prizefight* To be a very weak or ineffective puncher; put up a poor showing

you **can't get there from here** *See* YOU CAN'T GET THERE FROM HERE

someone **can't hit the side of a barn** (or **a barn door**) *sentence* Someone is unable to throw accurately enough to hit anything at all

you **can't make an omelet without breaking eggs** *See* YOU CAN'T MAKE AN OMELET WITHOUT BREAKING EGGS

canto *n sports* A round, inning, period, or other division of a contest: *Lefty got decked in the third canto* [fr Italian, "song," with reference to the 100 poetic divisions of Dante's *Commedia*]

someone **can't win for losing** *sentence* Someone seems entirely unable to make any sort of success; someone is persistently and distressingly bested: *We busted our humps, but we just couldn't win for losing*

Canuck **1** *n* A Canadian, esp a French-Canadian **2** *modifier: Canuck booze/ my Canuck pal* • Regarded as offensive by some, but apparently becoming more acceptable

can you read lips *See* READ MY LIPS

cap¹ **1** *n* Captain **2** *n* Mister; sir • Used in direct address to a man one wishes to flatter

cap² *narcotics* **1** *n* A capsule of narcotics: *I didn't have the money to buy a cap with*—D Hulburd **2** *v* To buy narcotics; =COP: *I capped me some more pot*—H Braddy **3** *v* To open or use a capsule of narcotics

cap³ *v* To best or outdo, esp with a funnier joke, stranger story, etc; =TOP: *She told a lie that capped mine*

See APPLEJACK CAP, GIMME HAT

◁ **cap⁴** ▷ *n* Fellatio; =HEAD: *Give Jerry some cap*—Donald Goines

capeesh *See* COPPISH

caper **1** *n* A drunken spree **2** *n* Any spree; =BINGE **3** *n fr middle 1800s* A prank; stunt **4** *n fr underworld fr 1920s* A crime, esp a robbery

capo (KA poh, KAH-) *n* The head of a local unit of the Mafia; Mafia captain [fr Italian, "head, chief"]

car *See* PROWL CAR

carbo *n* A carbohydrate food: *She knew she shouldn't be munching out on carbos like this*—Cyra McFadden

carborundum *See* ILLEGITIMATI NON CARBORUNDUM

card **1** *n fr middle 1800s* A remarkable person, esp an eccentric or amusing one **2** *n narcotics* A portion of a narcotic; =DECK **3** *n sports* A schedule; program of events: *six fights on the card* **4** *v* To require someone to show identification, esp at a bar

See FACE CARD, IN THE CARDS, MEAT CARD, PAINT CARDS, STACK THE DECK, WILD CARD

card-carrying *adj* Authentic; genuine and longstanding: *These women tend* *not to be card-carrying feminists* —New York Daily News/ *a service for all us card-carrying optimists* —James Michener [fr the *carrying* of a membership *card* in an organization]

card sharp (or **shark**) *n phr fr late 1800s* A very clever cardplayer, esp an unscrupulous poker or bridge player

care *See* TAKE CARE, TAKE CARE OF BUSINESS

carhop *fr 1920s* **1** *n* A waitress or waiter who serves food to patrons in parked cars at a drive-in restaurant; =CURBIE **2** *v: She carhopped at Beef Babylon* [formed on the model of *bellhop*]

carny or **carney** or **carnie** *carnival* **1** *n* A carnival **2** *n* A carnival worker or member of such a worker's family: *outdoor show people, the "carnies," who travel from town to town with carnivals*—AJ Liebling **3** ***modifier:*** *carny talk/ a carney family* **4** *n* The occupational idiom or jargon of carnival people: *I thought you talked carney by now*—F Brown

carpet *See* CALL someone ON THE CARPET, ON THE CARPET, RED CARPET, ROLL OUT THE RED CARPET

carpet-rat *See* RUG APE

carrier *See* JEEP CARRIER

carrot-top *n* A redhead

carry **1** *n police* A person who needs to be carried on a stretcher **2** *v underworld* To be armed

carry a tune in a bucket *See* someone CAN'T CARRY A TUNE IN A BUCKET

carrying *See* CARD-CARRYING

carry the load (or the **ball**) *v phr* To do or be responsible for the major part of a job: *His wife carried the load in that family*

carry (or **haul**) **the mail** **1** *v phr* =CARRY THE LOAD **2** *v phr* To go very fast; =BARREL

carry the torch *v phr fr 1930s* To love in a suffering way, esp because the desired one does not reciprocate: *She was carrying the torch for WC Fields*—E Johnson [origin unknown; said to have been coined by a Broadway nightclub singer named Tommy Lyman, but the semantic links are not apparent; Venus, of course, carried a torch regularly]

cart *v* To transport; take: *I carted him over to the drug store/ Why did you cart all that crap in here?*

not **carved in stone** *See* NOT CARVED IN STONE

Casanova or **casanova** *n* A ladies' man and seducer; =LOVER-BOY: *Do ravish me, you bold casanova you* [fr the name of Giacomo Girolamo *Casanova*, legendary debaucher]

case **1** *n fr middle 1800s* An odd, eccentric person; =CARD, CHARACTER **2** *v underworld* To inspect, scrutinize, esp a place with a view to robbery or burglary **3** ***n:*** *Lefty gave the bank a case*

See DROP CASE, GET OFF someone's CASE, GET ON someone's CASE, HAVE A CASE ON someone, HEADCASE, MAKE A FEDERAL CASE OUT OF something, NUTBALL, OFF someone's CASE, ON someone's CASE, SHOWCASE, WORST-CASE SCENARIO

case ace *n phr cardplayers* The fourth ace after three have been dealt, esp in stud poker [fr the dealing box or *case* used in the game of faro]

case someone or something **out** *v phr* To examine or inspect; find out the facts: *I'll case the situation out and let you know*

cash *See* COLD CASH

cash cow *n phr* A source of money, esp a generous one: *But all this leaves The New Republic Inc without a cash cow*—New Republic

cash in one's **chips** **1** *v phr* (also **cash it in**) *fr middle 1800s* To die; =KICK THE BUCKET **2** *v phr* To withdraw from some arrangement, esp a business deal

cast a kitten *See* HAVE KITTENS

casting couch *n phr* The fancied lounge in a theatrical or film decision-maker's office upon which he appraises the talent of young women seeking roles: *only slightly detoured by a refusal to join Darryl F Zanuck on the casting couch*—New York Times

cast-iron balls *See* HAVE BRASS BALLS

cast-iron overshoes *See* WIN THE PORCELAIN HAIRNET

cat[1] **1** *n outdated hoboes* A hobo or a migrant worker **2** *n fr 1500s* A prostitute ◁**3**▷ *n* (also **catty-cat**) *black* The vulva **4** *v* (also **cat around**) To spend time with women for amatory purposes; chase and stalk women; =TOMCAT **5** ***n*** A woman who, often subtly, attacks and denigrates other women; spiteful and malicious woman: *Dorothy Parker was a super cat* **6** ***n*** *black* A man who dresses flashily, and ostentatiously pursues worldly pleasure; =DUDE, SPORT: *I was a sharp cat* —Louis Armstrong/ *The cool chick down on Calumet has got herself a brand new cat*—Gwendolyn Brooks **7** ***v*** *black* To move stealthily: *began to cat toward the door*—Donald Goines **8** ***v*** *street gang* To loaf and idle; spend one's time on street corners admiring young women **9** ***n*** *jazz musicians* A jazz musician: *It was all right to the early cats*—Stephen Longstreet **10** ***n*** =HEPCAT **11** ***n*** =HIPSTER **12** ***n*** *fr jive and cool talk* Any man; fellow; =GUY: *Who's that cat sitting next to the Pope?* **13** ***n*** A sailboat with one fore-and-aft sail; a catboat: *He sails a little cat* [black sense, "dude," may be influenced by a Wolof term; see *hepcat*]

See ALLEY CAT, FAT CAT, FRAIDY CAT, HELLCAT, HEPCAT, HIP CAT, HOLY CATS, LET THE CAT OUT OF THE BAG, LOOK LIKE SOMETHING THE CAT DRAGGED IN

cat² or **Cat** ***n*** A bulldozer or Caterpillar tractor [fr *Caterpillar*, trade name for a kind of continuous-track tractor]

cat³ ***n*** A catamaran boat

Cat ***n*** *black* A Cadillac: *Tia Juana pulled up in his long green Cat*—CB Himes

catbird seat ***See*** SIT IN THE CATBIRD SEAT

catch **1** ***v*** To see or attend a particular entertainment: *I caught Mickey Rooney on TV* **2** ***n*** A highly desirable acquisition or engagement: *Getting Von Karajan for our benefit would be a catch* **3** ***n*** *fr middle 1800s* A hidden cost, qualification, defect, etc; something to make one think twice: *It looks like all gravy, but there's a catch to it* **4** ***v*** *police* To do desk duty, answering the telephone and receiving complaints: *Thompson was catching in the squad room at Manhattan South*—Richard Lockridge **5** ***v*** *homosexual* To be penetrated in an anal sex act

See SHOESTRING CATCH

catch hell (Variations: **holy hell** or **it** or **merry hell** may replace **hell**) **1** ***v phr*** To be severely rebuked or punished **2** ***v phr*** To be severely damaged or injured: *The dock caught holy hell in that last approach*

catch it (or **get it**) **in the neck** ***v phr*** To be very severely rebuked or punished: *One more time and you catch it right in the neck*

catch on **1** ***v phr*** To see and understand, esp with insightful suddenness; grasp: *As long as they don't catch on, we can cheat them forever* **2** ***v phr*** To be accepted and approved; succeed with the public: *Lots of artists catch on only after they're dead*

catch someone **redhanded** ***v phr*** To find or seize someone in the act of doing something criminal or reprehensible; catch in flagrante delicto

catch-22 or **Catch-22** **1** ***n*** A condition or requirement very hard to fulfill, esp one which flatly contradicts others: *It's a catch-22; I need experience to get a job, and I need a job to get experience* **2** ***modifier:*** *puts me in a Catch-22 fix*—William Appel [fr the title of a satirical novel by Joseph Heller]

catch-up ***See*** PLAY CATCH-UP

catch someone **with** someone's **hand in the till** ***See*** WITH one's HAND IN THE TILL

catch someone **with** someone's **pants down** ***v phr*** To find someone in the wrong with no possibility of evasion; catch in flagrante delicto: *Every time someone catches us with our pants down, catches us in an outright lie, up pops Ron to admit it*—Earl Thompson

catch Zs ***See*** COP ZS

cat fight ***n phr*** A particularly noisy and vicious struggle or squabble: *to judge from the cat fight that erupted among members of the advisory council*—Washington Post

Catholic ***See*** IS THE POPE POLISH

cathouse **1** ***n*** *early 1900s hoboes* A cheap lodging house; =FLOPHOUSE **2** ***n*** *fr early 1900s* A brothel: *New Orleans was proud and ashamed of its cathouses*—Stephen Longstreet **3** ***n*** *outdated jazz musicians* An insinuating style of jazz music [second sense fr earlier *cat* "prostitute, vulva"]

cats and dogs *n phr stock market* Low-priced stocks, such as those returning no dividends at all
See RAIN CATS AND DOGS

the **cat's meow** *n phr* (Variations: **balls** or **eyebrows** or **nuts** or **pajamas** or **whiskers** may replace **meow**; the phrase may be shortened to **the cat's**) *fr 1920s* Something or someone that is superlative: *He thinks he's the cat's pajamas*

cattle call **1** *n phr show business* An audition announcement, esp for a number of extras; also the crowd resulting from such an announcement: *Mr Allen is having what is known in show business as a cattle call*—Wall Street Journal **2** *modifier: Nonprofessionals may vie for spaces... in "cattle-call" auditions* —Washington Post

cattle show *n phr* A convention or other occasion where political candidates display their notions, charisma, etc: *raise money for themselves by holding "cattle shows"*—Washingtonian

catty-cat *See* CAT[1]

be **caught dead** *See* NOT BE CAUGHT DEAD

cauliflower ear *n phr fr early 1900s* A boxer's or wrestler's ear deformed by injuries and accumulated scar tissue

caulk (or **calk** or **cork**) **off** *Navy fr middle 1800s British* **1** *v phr* To sleep; go to sleep **2** *v* To rest from work; =TAKE A BREAK

caveman **1** *n* A strong, crude man, esp one who is sexually rough and masterful; =MACHO **2** *n prizefight* A strong hitter or slugger [fr the conventional image of the brutal, fur-draped troglodyte dragging a woman by the hair]

Cecil or **Cee** *n narcotics* Cocaine

ceiling *n* An upper limit: *The Gov put a two-billion-dollar ceiling on office expenses*
See HIT THE CEILING

celeb (sə LEB) *n fr early 1900s* A celebrity: *each a certified celeb from the realms of cafe, style, or theatrical society*—New York Daily News/ *surrounded by giggling celebs*—New York

the **cellar** *n phr* The lowest standing in a sports league, esp in a baseball league: *struggling not to finish in the cellar*

cellar-dwellers *n* The team in last place

cement overcoat (or **kimono**) *n phr* A casing of cement containing a corpse for disposal in deep water

cent *See* a RED CENT

centerfold *n* A sexually desirable person: *a woman with a centerfold's chest going for her*—Dan Jenkins [fr the photographs of such persons decorating the *centerfolds* of erotic magazines]

cents *See* PUT one's TWO CENTS IN

Cessna repellent *n phr airline* The landing lights of an airliner when switched on in a busy area to warn other aircraft of its presence [fr *Cessna*, trade name for a line of relatively small airplanes, and *repellent* fr the model *insect repellent*]

chain *See* BALL-AND-CHAIN, PULL someone's CHAIN

chain-smoke *v fr early 1900s* To smoke cigarette after cigarette, lighting the next one from the previous one

chair *See* BARBER CHAIR

the **chair** **1** *n* The electric chair; =the HOT SEAT **2** *n* Death by legal electrocution: *They convicted him, and he got the chair*

chair-warmer *n* An idle and dispensable person; =WARM BODY

Chamber of Commerce *n phr* A toilet [fr *chamber pot*]

chamber pot *See* WIN THE PORCELAIN HAIRNET

champagne (or **boss**) **trick** *n phr prostitutes* A rich or high-paying client: *I take only champagne tricks, $100 an hour*—Gail Sheehy

chance *See* CHINAMAN'S CHANCE, OUTSIDE CHANCE, a SNOWBALL'S CHANCE IN HELL

change *n* Money: *a sizable chunk of change*—Bob Thomas
See LOOSE CHANGE, PIECE OF CHANGE, SMALL POTATOES

change-up **1** *n baseball* A slow pitch delivered after a motion that might precede a fast pitch; a change of pace **2** *v: Holy cow! He changed him up for a strike!* **3** *n* Any change, esp a pronounced one: *McDowell exhibits a first-rate change-up*—Richard Schickel

channel **1** *n* *narcotics* A vein, usu in the crook of the elbow or the instep, favored for the injection of narcotics; =MAIN LINE **2** *v* *esp 1950s hot rodders* To lower the body of a car by opening channels around parts of the frame: *Johnny Slash, the punk in wraparound shades, lusts for a chopped and channeled '49 Merc* —Village Voice

chapped *adj* Angry; =PISSED OFF

chappie or **chappy** *n* A man; fellow • More common in British use: *which may amuse the chappies around Labuses*—John O'Hara

chaps *See* CHOPS

character **1** *n* *fr 1700s* A person who behaves oddly and often amusingly; an eccentric: *My uncle's quite a character* **2** *n* A person; =JOKER: *You know a character name of Robert Ready?*

charge **1** *n* *narcotics* An injection of a narcotic **2** *n* *fr 1930s jazz musicians* An acute thrill of pleasure; =BLAST, RUSH: *What kind of ol' creep'd get a charge out of this stuff?* —SJ Perelman **3** *n* *narcotics* Marijuana ◁**4**▷ *n* The semen produced by an orgasm; =LOAD ◁**5**▷ *n* A penile erection

See GET A BANG OUT OF someone or something

charged up **1** *adj phr* *narcotics* Intoxicated by a narcotic; =HIGH **2** *adj phr* Agitated and upset: *He got all charged up about my silly mistake* **3** *adj phr* In a state of excited preparedness and heightened keenness; =PUMPED UP: *They lost, the coach declared, because they were not charged up*

charger *n* *hot rodders* A driver, esp of a hot rod

chariot *n* A car

charity *See* COLD AS HELL

charity girl *n phr* *esp 1940s* A sexually promiscuous young woman

Charley *See* GOOD-TIME CHARLIE

Charley coke or **Charlie** *narcotics* **1** *n phr* or *n* Cocaine **2** *n phr* or *n* A cocaine addict

Charlie *n* *Vietnam War armed forces* The Vietcong or a Vietcong soldier [fr Victor *Charlie*, military voice alphabet designation for VC]

Charlies *n* *Army* Army C-rations, packages of tinned and dried food

charm the pants off someone *v phr* To ingratiate oneself decisively

the **charts** *n phr* The listings which show the popularity of a song, a record, etc: *Stevie's latest single is way, way up on the charts*

See OFF THE CHARTS

chase *See* PAPER CHASE

chaser **1** *n* A drink, usu of water, taken immediately after a measure of whiskey **2** *n* A man in amatory pursuit of women; =SKIRT-CHASER: *Mark always was a lady-killer, a chaser*—AR Hilliard **3** *n* *truckers* An employee assigned to hurry others in their work **4** *n* *show business* An exit march; music played as the audience is leaving

See AMBULANCE CHASER, MONKEY-CHASER, SKIRT-CHASER, WOMAN-CHASER

chassis *n* The human physique, esp the body of a well-built woman; =BUILD

See CLASSY CHASSIS

chat up *v phr* To charm and seduce with talk • More common in British use, fr 1930s: *You hear Elvis laughing, chatting up the crowd*—Rolling Stone/ *while Dartmouth seniors, a little tight, chatted up Smithies*—Time

chauvinist pig *See* MALE CHAUVINIST PIG

chazeray or **chazerei** *See* KHAZERAY

cheap **1** *adj* Stingy; overly frugal; =CHINTZY: *Cheap old bastard won't give you the time of day* **2** *adj* Reputedly easy of sexual conquest: *a cheap tramp with a heart of gold* **3** *adj* Squalid; repulsive; =CRUMMY: *Sheesh, what a cheap joint you've got here*

See ON THE CHEAP

cheapie or **cheapo** **1** *n* Any cheaply made or cheaply sold item: *No ticket in town is a cheapie these days/ the problem with retreads, ethnic shoes, and Woolworth cheapos is* —Village Voice **2** *modifier:* *cheapie ripoffs of* The Godfather—T Meehan/ *Our Tenth Annual Cheapo Guide*—Toronto Life

See EL CHEAPO

◁**cheapshit**▷ *adj* Inexpensive and inferior: *ten million pair of cheapshit jeans without any labels on them* —National Lampoon

cheap shot **1** *n phr* A malicious insult or action; something crude, underhanded, and damaging: *Well,* *the race for governor isn't a festival of cheap shots*—New York **2** *v phr: If a person's going to cheapshot me, it just shows how low he is*—Playboy **3** *modifier: some dirtymouth comedian who made cheap-shot race jokes*—Village Voice

cheat *v* To be sexually unfaithful; =GET A LITTLE ON THE SIDE

cheaters *fr early 1900s underworld* **1** *n* Spectacles **2** *n* Marked playing cards

check **1** *interj* An expression of understanding, approval, etc: *I'll say check to that!/ It's time to leave? Check!* **2** *v* (also **check that**) *esp broadcasting* To cancel; introduce a correction: *He made eight yards; check that, six yards* **3** *v* To look at; pay attention to; =CHECK OUT: *Check the guy at the end of the counter* **4** *n narcotics* A small quantity of a drug

See GIVE someone A BLANK CHECK, PICK UP THE TAB, RAIN CHECK, RUBBER CHECK, TAKE A RAIN CHECK

check out **1** *v phr* To look closely at, esp for evaluation; scrutinize; =GIVE someone or something THE ONCE-OVER: *Check out the guy at the counter. Do you know him?/ Before you buy anything, check out our low, low prices/ If you're in doubt, check it out* **2** *v phr* To prove valid; be accurate: *Your story checks out* **3** *v phr* To examine and approve one's competence: *I'm checked out on that machine* **4** *v phr* To add up purchases and collect money at a supermarket or similar store: *I'll check you out over here* **5** *modifier: a check-out counter/ check-out man* **6** *n: express check-out/ slow sloppy check-out* **7** *v phr* To pay for one's purchases at a supermarket or similar store: *It took me an hour to check out of that place* **8** *v phr* To pay one's bill and leave a hotel or motel: *When did Almendorfer check out of this fleabag?* **9** *v phr* To leave; depart; =BOOK: *Let's check out of this joint and find a livelier one* **10** *v phr* To die: *She checked out before they reached the hospital*

check the plumbing *v phr* To go to the toilet

cheeba *n narcotics* Marijuana

cheek **1** *n fr late 1800s* Impudence; audacity; =BRASS, CHUTZPA: *She had the infernal cheek to stick out her tongue at me* **2** *n* A buttock; =BUN: *I took the injection in the left cheek*

cheeky *adj* Impudent; impertinent; rude • More common in British use, fr middle 1800s

cheer *See* BRONX CHEER

cheese **1** *n* Nonsense; lies; exaggerations; =BALONEY: *What a line of cheese*—Richard Bissell **2** *n baseball* A fastball **3** *v* =CHEESE IT **4** *v* (also **cut the cheese**) To flatulate; =FART **5** *v* To vomit; =BARF **6** *n: There was cheese all over the floor in the subway station*

See BIG CHEESE, GET one's CHEESE, HARD CHEESE, MAKE THE CHEESE MORE BINDING

the **cheese** *n phr esp 1920s fr early 1800s British* An important person; something or someone genuine: *She's the real cheese*—A Lewis [perhaps fr Anglo-Indian slang *chiz* fr Hindi fr Persian, "the thing"]

cheesecake **1** *n fr early 1900s* Photographs and photography of women in clothing and poses that emphasize their sexuality: *a magazine full of cheesecake* **2** *modifier: unless one perceives in cheesecake photographs illicit and limitless pleasures*—Toronto Life **3** *n* A woman's legs, breasts, hips, etc: *standing on the corner scoping out the cheesecake* [apparently fr the appreciative comments of one or another early-20th-century New York City newspaper photographer at the ocean-liner docks who posed women so that their legs were featured, and pronounced the pictures to be "better than *cheesecake*"]

cheese it *fr early 1800s underworld* **1** *interj* An exclamation of alarm and warning uttered when properly constituted authorities are approaching: *Cheese it, Muggsy, the cops!* **2** *v phr* To leave; depart; =SCRAM

cheesy **1** *adj* Lacking in taste; vulgarly unesthetic: *an altogether hideous room, expensive but cheesy*—JD Salinger **2** *adj* Of inferior workmanship; shoddy: *Where'd you get this cheesy pair of pliers?* **3** *adj* Shabby; ugly: *Why stay in this cheesy neighborhood?*

chemistry *n* Feelings between persons; attractions and repulsions: *He* *also struck up what one aide calls "instant chemistry" with US Secretary of State George Shultz*—New York Times

cherry ◁**1**▷ *n* A virgin, of either sex ◁**2**▷ *n* Virginity: *Does he still have his cherry?* ◁**3**▷ *adj* Virgin; sexually uninitiated: *She confessed she was cherry* ◁**4**▷ *n* The hymen **5** *adj* In an unproved or maiden state of any sort: *He hasn't published anything yet; still cherry* **6** *n Army* An inexperienced soldier sent to the front lines as a replacement: *A Cherry who survived long enough earned the right to harass the next rookie*—New York Times Magazine **7** *n* The red light atop a police car [sexual senses fr the fancied resemblance between the hymen and a *cherry*]

See COP A CHERRY, HAVE one's CHERRY, POP someone's CHERRY

cherry-picker ◁**1**▷ *n* A man who especially prizes the sex act with young girls **2** *n* An articulated crane with a bucketlike platform: *a guy in a cherry-picker fixing the phone lines*

cherry-top *n teenagers* A police car; =PROWL CAR

chest *See* PLAY CLOSE TO THE CHEST

chestnut *n fr late 1800s* A trite old story, joke, song, etc; =OLD TURKEY

chev *See* SHIV

chevy *See* CHIVVY

Chevy (SHEH vee) *n* A Chevrolet car

◁ **chew** someone's **ass** (or **ass out**)▷ *v phr* =CHEW someone OUT

chew someone's **ear off** *v phr* To talk overlong and tediously to: *I just wanted the time, not to get my ear chewed off*

chewed *adj 1940s black* Tired; defeated; =BEAT: *I know you feel chewed*—Zora Neale Hurston

chew gum at the same time *See* NOT HAVE BRAINS ENOUGH TO COME IN OUT OF THE RAIN

chew someone **out** (or **up**) *v phr fr WW2 armed forces* To reprimand severely; rebuke harshly; =EAT someone OUT, REAM: *In the boss's office he got chewed out good*

chew something **over** *v phr* To discuss thoroughly: *Let's chew over the budget*

chew the fat (or **the rag**) *v phr fr late 1800s* To converse, esp in a relaxed and reminiscent way

chew up the scenery *v phr show business* To overact; =HAM: *Beery... and Lionel Barrymore chew up all the scenery that isn't nailed down*—Village Voice [originally fr a 1930 theater review by Dorothy Parker: "more glutton than artist...he commences to *chew up the scenery*"]

chewy *adj* Substantial and desirable; rich: *Hepburn... may have a less chewy part than has Fonda*—Richard Schickel

chib *See* SHIV

chiba shop *See* SMOKE SHOP

chichi (SHEE SHEE, CHEE CHEE) **1** *n* Something frilly, fancy, precious, and overdecorated: *Another bit of chichi that has come to our notice lately is Eleanor Roosevelt's letterhead*—New Yorker/ *So much chichi. The pretty glass people*—New York **2** *adj: a chichi concern for his poses/ chichi little chapeau* [fr French]

chick **1** *n underworld* Prison food **2** *n esp beat, cool & 1960s counterculture* A woman, esp a young woman

See HIP CHICK

chicken **1** *n fr early 1900s* A young woman, esp an attractive one; =CHICK **2** *n homosexuals* An adolescent boy regarded as a sexual object for an adult homosexual **3** *modifier: had I written extensively about the mechanics of chicken sex*—Village Voice **4** *n* A coward; an overly timid person; =SISSY: *Don't be a chicken; dive right in* **5** *adj: He seems like a chicken guy* **6** *n esp hot rodders* A trial of valor in which two persons drive cars at each other down the middle of a road, the first to swerve aside being designated "chicken" **7** *n Army fr 1920s* The eagle worn as insignia of rank by an Army colonel **8** *n* =CHICKEN SHIT **9** *adj* =CHICKEN-SHIT **10** *n underworld* The victim of a robbery or swindle; =MARK, SUCKER **11** *n* A person, esp a durable one: *John's a tough old chicken* [homosexual senses perhaps fr late-19th-century sailor term for a boy who takes a sailor's fancy and whom he calls his *chicken*]

See RUBBER-CHICKEN

chicken colonel ***n phr*** *Army* A full colonel; =BIRD COLONEL

chicken coop ***See*** RAIN CATS AND DOGS

chicken feed (or **money**) ***n phr*** A small amount of money; =PEANUTS, SMALL POTATOES: *Two million? That's chicken feed in this milieu*

chickenhearted **1** ***adj*** Cowardly; =SISSIFIED: *Here's a potbellied, chickenhearted slob*—J & W Hawkins **2** ***adj*** Squeamish; overly fastidious

chicken-livered ***adj*** Cowardly; =CHICKENHEARTED

chicken out ***v phr*** To cancel or withdraw from an action because of fear; =HAVE COLD FEET: *You'll think of something to chicken out*—Erma Bombeck

◁ **chicken shit** ▷ *fr WW2 armed forces* **1** ***n phr*** The rules, restrictions, rigors, and meanness of a minor and pretentious tyrant, or of a bureaucracy: *The new regulations are so many parcels of chicken shit* **2** ***n phr*** An excessive display of authority; a hectoring insistence **3** ***adj:*** *a chicken-shit requirement/ chicken-shit new task force*

chicken (or **egads**) **switch** (or **button**) **1** ***n phr*** A control used to destroy a malfunctioning rocket in flight; a destruct switch **2** ***n phr*** A control used to eject an astronaut or pilot from a damaged vehicle [*chicken* fr the sense "coward"; *egads* an acronym for *electronic ground automatic destruct sequencer* and coincides with an archaic interjection of dismay]

chicken tracks ***See*** HEN TRACKS

chickie **1** ***n*** A young girl; =CHICK: *But I do not really envy the guys my age who... are making out with the young chickies*—San Francisco **2** ***interj*** *esp New York City teenagers* An exclamation of alarm and warning, uttered when properly constituted authorities are approaching; =CHEESE IT, JIGGERS

chicklet or **chiclet** ***n*** A young girl; =CHICK: *Teenies and chicklets came into fashion*—Gail Sheehy [normal diminutive form, reinforced by *Chiclet*, trade name of a brand of chewing gum sold in small sugared bits]

child ***See*** FLOWER CHILD

children ***See*** FLOWER CHILDREN

◀ **chili** ▶ ***adj*** Mexican

chill **1** ***v*** To resolve or relax a perilous situation: *They agreed to talk, and that chilled the riot* **2** ***v*** To frighten: *a sight that chilled him* **3** ***v*** *underworld* To render unconscious; =KNOCK someone OUT: *She chilled him with a kick on the chin* **4** ***v*** *fr 1940s black* To kill; murder: *Remember the night Stein got chilled out front?*—Raymond Chandler **5** ***v*** To quench enthusiasm and amiability abruptly: *He chilled me with a glance* **6** ***v*** =CHILL OUT **7** ***v*** *esp black teenagers* To do a move in dancing intended to show one's ease and nonchalance **8** ***n*** *students* A glass or can of beer **9** ***adj*** *teenagers* Wonderful; excellent; =COOL, NEAT: *A "chill" outfit for a girl is tight Sergio Valente or Tale Lord jeans*—New York Times

See PUT THE CHILL ON someone

chiller ***n*** *fr 1950s* A film, play, etc, intended to evoke delicious shudders of fear; horror show or story

chiller-diller ***n*** *fr 1950s* A chiller, esp a very effective one

chill out ***v phr*** *teenagers fr black* To relax; calm oneself; =COOL OUT: *offers her a lit joint. "Chill out," he says*—New York

chime in **1** ***v phr*** To interrupt and intrude one's counsel; =BUTT IN, KIBITZ **2** ***v phr*** To offer comment: *Chime in whenever you want*

chin **1** ***v*** *fr late 1800s* To talk; converse: *happily chinning in the corner* **2** ***n*** *fr early 1900s* A talk; a chat **3** ***v*** To talk to: *The cop was chinning... a nurse*—James M Cain

See TAKE IT ON THE CHIN

china **1** ***n*** The teeth **2** ***n*** *esp jazz musicians* Money **3** ***n*** *lunch counter* A cup of tea

china chin ***See*** GLASS JAW

◀ **Chinaman** ▶ **1** ***n*** *merchant marine* A sailor who works in a ship's laundry **2** ***n*** *police* A police officer's patron and influential political friend; =RABBI: *police officer... needed a Chinaman, or sponsor*—Chicago Magazine

◀ a **Chinaman's chance** ▶ ***n phr*** *fr middle 1800s* No chance at all • Nearly always in the negative: *He hasn't got a Chinaman's chance of landing that job* [fr the unfortunate situation of Chinese prospectors in the California gold rush, who were forced to work exhausted or unpromising claims]

chinchy *adj esp black fr 1930s* Parsimonious; stingy; mean; =CHINTZY [perhaps related to *chinch* "bedbug" and associated notions of squalor]

◀ **Chinese ace**▶ *n phr aviators fr WW1 armed forces* A pilot who lands an airplane with one wing low [fr the possible *Chinese* name Wun Wing Low or the purportedly humorous invention Wun Hung Low referring to the low wing]

◀ **Chinese fire drill**▶ *n phr* Something incredibly confused and confusing: *an eight-page letter with a Chinese fire drill of your life*—Chicago Tribune/ *did their Chinese fire drill of calling the fix-it man*—Richard Merkin [perhaps fr the World War 2 Marine Corps expression "fucked up like *Chinese fire call*"]

◀ **Chinese landing**▶ *n phr aviators* A landing made with one wing low [see *Chinese ace*]

◀ **Chinese opera**▶ *n phr Army* An extremely elaborate event, parade, briefing, etc

Chinese pagodas *See* KNOCK someone or something FOR A LOOP

◀ **Chinese three-point landing**▶ *n phr aviators* An airplane crash, esp one due to pilot error

chinfest *n* A session of talk and gossip; =BULL SESSION, GABFEST

◀ **Chink** or **chink**▶ **1** *n* A Chinese person **2** *adj: Chink food/ a chink chick*

chintzy[1] *fr 1950s* *adj* Parsimonious; stingy; =CHEAP [perhaps fr *chinch* "bedbug," hence the semantic equivalent of "lousy"; the sense is either derived fr or is a partial source of *chintzy*[2]]

chintzy[2] **1** *adj* Cheap and ill-made, but showy: *the window filled with chintzy plastic couches* **2** *adj* Lacking chic and style; unfashionable: *White shoes with a dark dress is considered very definitely... "chintzy"* —Syracuse Post-Standard [fr the printed cotton fabric *chintz*, regarded as cheap, gaudy, and unstylish]

chin-wag *n* A conversation, esp a long and intimate chat: *You haven't had a good chin-wag with your sister-in-law since she got the joystick for her Apple*—Washington Post

chip **1** *n* A flat piece of dung **2** *v golf* To hit a short, usu high shot onto the green **3** *v narcotics* To use a drug or drugs clandestinely while abstaining from using the drug for which one is being treated or is undergoing psychotherapy: *The men and women of the group... also look at the man who is chipping*—Washington Post

See BARGAINING CHIP, BLUE-CHIP, HAVE A CHIP ON one's SHOULDER

chiphead *n* A computer enthusiast: *I'm not a chiphead, but if you don't keep up with the new developments ... you're not going to have the competitive edge*—Time [fr silicon *chip* + *head* "addict"]

chip in **1** *v phr fr middle 1800s* To contribute, esp a share of some expense: *We each chipped in twenty bucks and got him a new suit* **2** *v phr* To interject a comment; contribute to a colloquy: *She chipped in some honeyed reminiscences* [fr the adding of poker *chips* to the pot]

a **chip off the old block** *n phr* A child that resembles one or both parents, esp a boy that resembles his father

chippy or **chippie** **1** *n fr late 1800s* A woman presumed to be of easy virtue; woman who frequents bars, public dance halls, etc: *the same as in Storyville except that the chippies were cheaper*—Louis Armstrong **2** *v* To be sexually unfaithful to one's wife; =CHEAT, GET A LITTLE ON THE SIDE **3** *v narcotics* To take narcotics only occasionally [origin unknown; senses relating to women possibly from the chirping sound of a sparrow, squirrel, or other small creature, suggesting the gay frivolity of such women]

chippy (or **chippie**) **joint** *n phr* A brothel

chips *See* CASH IN one's CHIPS, IN THE CHIPS

Chips *n merchant marine* A ship's carpenter • Used as a nickname, as Sparks is for a radio officer and Bones for a ship's doctor

the **chips are down** *sentence* The time of final decision and hard confrontation has come; resolution is at hand: *When the chips are down he goes to pieces* [fr the final bets of a poker hand]

chip shot **1** *n phr* *golf* A shot, usu a high shot made onto the green **2** *n phr* *football* An easy field goal or field goal opportunity [perhaps fr hitting under the ball as if to chop a *chip* from it]

chirpy *adj* Bright and energetic; vivacious: *a nice, wholesome, chirpy, reasonably intelligent woman*—Philadelphia Magazine

chisel **1** *v* *fr early 1800s* To cheat or defraud, esp in a petty way; deal unfairly: *Every time I buy a part he chisels a buck or two* **2** *v* To get without intending to repay or return: *Can I chisel a cigarette from you, pal?*

chisel in *v phr* *underworld fr 1920s* To intrude oneself; =MUSCLE IN

chitchat *n* Talk, esp relaxed and idle conversation *The members were enjoying a bit of chitchat when the gavel sounded*

chiv or **chive** *See* SHIV

chivvy or **chivey** or **chevy** (CHIH vee, CHEH vee) *v* To harry and annoy; badger; =BUG

chockablock *adj* *fr early 1800s nautical* Crammed; crowded full: *The plays and stories... are chockablock with figures*—Washington Post [fr a nautical rhyming phrase used to mean that the two *blocks* of a block and tackle are touching after the device has been tightened to its limit]

choke a horse *v phr* To be very large: *That bankroll would choke a horse*

See ENOUGH TO CHOKE A HORSE

choke up **1** *v phr* *esp sports* To become tense and ineffective under pressure; =SWALLOW THE APPLE, TAKE THE PIPE: *He choked up, lost his concentration, and got clobbered in the third* **2** *v phr* To cause one to be speechless with pleasure: *Your new book doesn't exactly choke me up*

chompers *n* Teeth, whether genuine or false

choo-choo *See* PULL A TRAIN

the **chop** *See* GIVE something THE CHOP

chopped **1** *adj* *hot rodders* Of a car, having the chassis lowered or the fenders removed or both **2** *adj* *motorcyclists* Of a motorcycle, having the front brake and fender removed, the wheel fork extended forward, and the handlebars raised

chopped liver **1** *n phr* A beaten and scarred person; one who has undergone a humiliating defeat: *That mugger made chopped liver of him* **2** *n phr* An insignificant person or thing • Often in the negative: *Even if he didn't win, being the first black nominee wasn't chopped liver/ She may be great, but her sister's not exactly chopped liver*

See THAT AIN'T HAY

chopped top *n phr* *hot rodders* A car with the windshield, windows, upper body, etc, removed

chopper **1** *n* *esp 1920s* A submachine gun, esp a Thompson; =TOMMY GUN **2** *n* A gangster who uses a submachine gun: *Johnny Head had met the "chopper"*—John Gunther **3** *n* A helicopter: *the traffic reporter from the chopper* **4** *n* *hot rodders & motorcyclists* A chopped car or motorcycle

choppers *n* Teeth, esp false teeth

chops **1** *n* (also **chaps**) The jaws; the mouth; the cheeks beside the mouth; jowls: *old turkey with pendulous chops/ Open your chops and sing* **2** *n* *jazz musicians fr 1920s* Musical technique or ability: *With electronically amplified music you lose your chops, your right hand, you lose your dexterity*—Philadelphia Journal **3** *n* Talent or skill in general: *We'll see what kind of chops they got*—Jimmy Breslin [senses related to skill fr notion of a jazz musician's lips, *chops*, the essential for technique in "blowing" the instrument; see *ax*]

See BAT one's GUMS, BREAK CHOPS, BREAK someone's CHOPS, BUST one's ASS, KLOP IN THE CHOPS, LICK one's CHOPS

chop shop **1** *n phr* A place where stolen cars are dismantled to be sold as parts: *I started off takin' 'em to a chop shop for $100*—Philadelphia **2** *modifier:* *mixed up with chop shop operators in the Midwest*—Saul Bellow

chop one's **teeth** *v phr* =BAT one's GUMS

chow **1** *n* *fr middle 1800s* Food; meals; fare: *How's the chow at Maxim's these days?* **2** *v:* *OK gang, let's chow* [fr Pidgin English *chow-chow* "a mixture (of foods)"]

chowderhead *n* *fr early 1800s* A stupid person

chow down *v phr fr Navy* To eat; have a meal: *They should bundle up, chow down, and stay home*—Fran Lebowitz

Christian with aces wired *See* COOL AS A CHRISTIAN WITH ACES WIRED

Christmas goose *See* AS FULL OF SHIT AS A CHRISTMAS GOOSE

Christmas tree *See* LIT UP

chub *n fr middle 1800s* A Texan [origin unknown]

chubbette *n* A chubby woman, esp a small one: *The poor thing was petrified that Graig would find out what a chubbette she'd become*—Armistead Maupin/ *a chubbette with "railroad tracks" across her teeth*—New York

chuck 1 *n fr middle 1800s fr British* Food; a meal; =CHOW: *She invited us in for some chuck* **2** *v* To throw, esp to throw or pitch a ball: *chuck a mean slider* **3** *v* To discard; throw away: *Is it possible she has chucked her aloofness*—Sinclair Lewis **4** *v* To vomit; =UPCHUCK [relation of the food sense to the others is obscure and uncertain]

chuck-a-lug *See* CHUG-A-LUG

chucklehead *n fr early 1900s* A stupid person

chuck you, Farley *interj* (Variation: **and your whole famn damily** may be added) May you and yours be reviled, abused, humiliated, rejected, etc; =FUCK YOU, UP YOURS • This amusing variant of the damning formula goes beyond the brevity of an interjection but retains the force [based on earlier *fuck you, Charley* and the euphemism *whole famn damily*]

chug *v* To move along, esp slowly and laboriously and in the water: *The USS Saratoga came chugging up the Delaware*—Philadelphia [echoic of a steam engine operating]

chug-a-lug or **chug** or **chuck-a-lug** *v* To drink the whole of what is in a glass or bottle without pausing: *He chugged a liter of vodka and dropped dead*

chum 1 *n fr 1700s* A very close friend; =BUDDY, PAL **2** *v* (also **chum around**): *He chums with Georgie Ogle* **3** *n* Man; fellow; =GUY • Used in direct address esp to strangers, usu with mildly hostile overtones: *Knock it off now, chum*

chum-buddy *n* A particularly close friend: *Yesterday's villains are tomorrow's chum-buddies*—Robert Ruark

chummy 1 *adj* Very friendly; =BUDDY-BUDDY, PALSY-WALSY **2** *n:* *Hey, chummy, how about a drink?*

chump *n fr late 1800s fr British* A stupid person, esp a dupe; =SUCKER: *If he wasn't such a chump he wouldn't be tempted/ I look like a chump these days*—William Kennedy [origin unknown; perhaps a blend of *chunk* and *lump*, both referring to blockheadedness]

◀ **chungo bunny** ▶ *n phr* A black person: *looked like he hadda be the biggest chungo bunny innu world*—George V Higgins [fr *jungle bunny*]

churn *v* To increase the level of activity in a law firm or other enterprise in order to seem busy and productive

chutzpa (HŏŏTS pə, KHŏŏTS-) *n* (Variations: **chuzpa** or **hutzpa** or **hutzpah**) Extreme and offensive brashness; arrogant presumption; hubris: *Chutzpa is that quality enshrined in a man who, having killed his mother and father, throws himself on the mercy of the court because he is an orphan*—Leo Rosten/ *The hutzpah of using Studio 54...was much commented on*—Pulpsmith

ciao (CHOW) *interj* A salutation either on meeting or parting [fr Italian]

cinch *fr late 1800s fr cowboys* **1** *n* A certainty; something sure to happen; =SURE THING: *It's a cinch they'll win* **2** *n* Something easily done; =BREEZE, PIECE OF CAKE: *Going up is a bother, coming down's a cinch* **3** *v* To make something certain; =CLINCH, NAIL something DOWN: *We cinched it with a last-second field goal* [fr Spanish *cincha* "saddle girth," which, when tight, fosters certainty] *See* HAVE something CINCHED, LEAD-PIPE CINCH

cinched *See* HAVE something CINCHED

cinchers *n esp 1930s truckers & bus drivers* The brakes of a truck, car, or bus

◁ **circle jerk** ▷ **1** *n phr esp teenagers* A sex party of mutual masturbation **2** *n phr* Any futile occasion, meeting, session, etc

circuit *See* BORSCHT CIRCUIT, CLOUT FOR THE CIRCUIT, STRAW-HAT CIRCUIT

circuit blow (or **clout** or **wallop**) *n phr baseball* A home run

circuit slugger *n phr baseball* A talented home-run hitter: *Gil Hodges ... became the greatest circuit slugger ever to wear Dodger flannels*—New York Daily News

circular file *n phr* A wastebasket

citizen *n esp black & counterculture* A person of a more conservative, established, and prosaic caste than oneself; =SQUARE

Citizen *See* JOHN Q CITIZEN

city **1** *combining word* The place or milieu of what is indicated: *hamburger city* **2** *combining word* A prevalence or instance of the thing indicated: *trouble city/ dumb city* [coined on the model of the **-sville** suffix]

See FAT CITY, SOUL CITY, TAP CITY, WRINKLE CITY, YUCKO CITY

city hall *n phr* The political powers and their haunts; those who control purse strings and patronage: *See how city hall reacts*

city slicker *n phr fr early 1900s* A shrewd and modish urban person, esp as distinct from the honest and gullible provincial

clam **1** *n fr early 1900s* A silent, secretive person, esp one who can be trusted with a confidence **2** *v* =CLAM UP **3** *n* A dollar: *That'll be eight clams for the oil* **4** *n broadcasting* A verbal mistake; =HOWLER **5** *n jazz musicians* A wrong or sour note; =CLINKER

See BEARDED CLAM, HAPPY AS A CLAM

clamp down *v phr fr 1940s* To increase the severity of measures against persons who break rules and laws; punish rather than tolerate: *The whole country's clamping down now on drunk drivers*

clam up *v phr fr early 1900s* To stay or become silent; stand mute; =BUTTON UP: *When I ask for details he just clams up*—HL Wilson

clank or **clank up** *v* or *v phr students fr Air Force* To panic; be paralyzed by fear; =FREEZE UP

the **clanks** *n phr* Delirium tremens; =the SHAKES: *He had the clanks from Purple Passions*—Hal Boyle/ *The old rum-bum was sick with the clanks*

◁ the **clap**▷ *n fr late 1500s* Gonorrhea [fr early French *clapoir* "bubo, swelling"]

clapped-out *adj fr British fr 1940s Air Force* Worn-out; ready for the junk heap; =BEAT-UP: *The civilian jumped into his clapped-out Mercury*—Car and Driver

◁ **clapped-up**▷ *adj* Infected with gonorrhea: *In reality she's a gotch-eyed ... clapped-up ... hooker*—Dan Jenkins

class **1** *n fr late 1800s* High quality; admirable style; cachet: *quiet dignity under fire, real class* **2** *modifier: a real class joint*

See HIGH-CLASS, WORLD-CLASS

a **class act** *n phr fr show business* A person or thing of admirable style, quality, competence, etc: *48 HRS. clicks anyway. It's a class act*—Playboy

classy **1** *adj* Of high quality; first-rate; superior: *That's a very classy speech you just made* **2** *adj* Having or showing prestige; aristocratic; =POSH: *a classy school/ classy manners*

classy chassis *n phr* A good figure; trim body: *sassy lassie with a classy chassis*

Claus *See* SANTA CLAUS

claw **1** *n* A police officer **2** *v* To arrest

clean **1** *adj* Not carrying anything forbidden, esp a firearm: *Cops gave him a body-shake and he came out clean* **2** *adj* Innocent; unincriminated **3** *adj* Not producing radioactive contamination: *a clean bomb* **4** *adj* Lacking money; =BROKE, CLEANED OUT **5** *adj* Not lewd or obscene; morally unexceptionable: *a couple of clean jokes/ a clean old man* **6** *adj* Trim; neat; elegant: *Mies's clean lines and crisp angles* **7** *adv: I was crazy about Lester. He played so clean and beautiful*—Charlie Parker **8** *adj narcotics* Free of drug addiction

See COME CLEAN, KEEP one's NOSE CLEAN, SQUEAKY-CLEAN

Clean *See* MISTER CLEAN

clean someone's **clock** **1** *v phr* To attack and punish: *Carlson suddenly really wanted to clean Ron Connelly's clock*—Earl Thompson **2** *v phr* To defeat; trounce; =CLOBBER: *The DA ... had his clock cleaned for him*—George V Higgins [probably fr *clock* "face," and the notion that chastisement is a sort of cleaning, as in *clean up on* someone]

cleaned out *adj phr* Lacking money, esp having lost it gambling or speculating; =BROKE, TAPPED OUT: *Georgie was cleaned out after the third race*

the **cleaners** *See* GO TO THE CLEANERS, TAKE someone TO THE CLEANERS

cleaning *See* HOUSE-CLEANING

clean someone **out** **1** *v phr* To win all of someone's money at gambling, esp in a crap game **2** *v phr* To require or use up all of someone's money: *Buying the condo just about cleaned them out*

cleanup **1** *n* An intensive effort or campaign against crime, filth, etc, of the sort periodically undertaken by the authorities: *The Mayor vowed a definitive cleanup of the Times Square area* **2** *modifier: another cleanup campaign*

clean up *v phr fr early 1800s* To make a large profit; get an impressive return for one's money; =MAKE A KILLING: *The West today knows many a ghost town where men of too much enterprise cleaned up and cleared out*—Sierra Club Bulletin

clean up one's **act** (or ◁one's **shit**▷) *v phr* To correct one's behavior; act properly and decently; =STRAIGHTEN UP AND FLY RIGHT: *I told the kid to clean up his act or leave*

clean up on someone *v phr fr late 1900s* To defeat decisively; trounce; thrash; =CLEAN someone's CLOCK: *We really cleaned up on them in the second half*

the **cleanup spot** (or **slot**) *n phr baseball* The fourth position in the batting order: *The manager didn't have a very reliable hitter for the cleanup spot* [fr the fact that the batter in this position may, or ought to, get a hit and *clean* the runners off the bases by driving them in to score]

clean up the floor with someone *See* WIPE UP THE FLOOR WITH someone

clear *See* READ someone LOUD AND CLEAR

clear out *v phr fr late 1800s* To depart; =HIT THE ROAD

clear up **1** *v phr* To make understandable: *Can you clear this matter up for me?* **2** *v phr* To become more orderly and comprehensible: *when the Persian Gulf situation clears up* **3** *v phr* To become cloudless and fair: *The weather cleared up in the afternoon* **4** *v phr* To heal: *The rash cleared up by itself* **5** *v phr narcotics* To stop using narcotics; get help in withdrawing from drug addiction

clerks and jerks *n phr Army* Soldiers in other than front-line units; rear-echelon troops

click **1** *v early 1900s* To succeed; please an audience or constituency: *If I can click with a wholesalers I should be ready to open up in about 3 weeks*—George Orwell **2** *v* To evoke or precede a flash of insight: *Something clicked and I knew what I had to do next* **3** *n* An insight, esp a sudden one; flash of comprehension: *She gifts us with this click: most men want their wives to have a jobette*—Gloria Steinem/ *a turbulent period of feminist clicks*—Ms **4** *v fr early 1900s* To fit together precisely; go well together: *Those two really click, like a well-oiled machine* **5** *n fr 1920s* A clique **6** *n* (also **klick**, **klik**) *armed forces* A kilometer: *a hundred and sixty clicks north of Saigon*—George Warren

cliffdweller *n* A resident of a tall apartment house; high-rise dweller

cliffhanger *n fr early 1900s* A very suspenseful story, film, book, situation, etc: *The election was a cliffhanger, right through the recount* [fr the fact that the actress Pearl White actually ended some episodes of her early serial movies *hanging* from the Palisades above the Hudson River]

climb on the bandwagon *See* GET ON THE BANDWAGON

climb (or **go up**) **the wall** *v phr* To become frantic, esp from frustration or anxiety; =GO OUT OF one's SKULL: *By the time the cops came I was about to climb the wall*

clinch **1** *n fr early 1800s* A close contact of two boxers, where they hold each others' arms to stifle blows **2** *v: Two palookas clinched through six rounds* **3** *n fr 1930s* An embrace; passionate hug **4** *v* To determine conclusively; finish definitively and positively; =NAIL something DOWN: *They claim new evidence that'll clinch their case* [fr the bending over, *clinching*, of the point of a nail to ensure it does not pull out; ultimately fr *clench*]

clincher *n fr early 1800s* The deciding or conclusive element; =BOTTOM LINE:

One smudged fingerprint was the clincher

the **clink** ***n phr*** A jail or prison; =the SLAMMER [fr the old prison on *Clink* Street in the Southwark district of London]

clinker 1 ***n*** *fr late 1800s* A biscuit **2** ***n*** =the CLINK **3** ***n*** *telephone workers* An unwanted noise on a long-distance telephone line **4** ***n*** *musicians* A squeak or unintended reed sound made on the clarinet, saxophone, or oboe **5** ***n*** *musicians* An obvious wrong or sour note: *One of the louder sopranos hit an excruciating clinker* **6** ***n*** An error; =BONER **7** ***n*** Anything inferior in workmanship, esp a play, movie, or other show; =LEMON, TURKEY **8** ***n*** Something damaging, esp when unseen or unforeseen; a hidden flaw: *There was a clinker in the works apart from his writing, a sort of catch* —Earl Thompson **9** ***n*** An incompetent person; a failure; =LOSER: *There have been some ultraconservative judges, but there has been an absence of real clinkers*—Time [fr *clinker* "unburnable cinder"]

clip 1 ***v*** To hit; strike sharply and neatly: *He clipped and decked the local goon* **2** ***n:*** *You hit him a good clip*—P Starnes **3** ***v*** To steal; =SWIPE: *Where'd you clip the new car?* **4** ***n*** *underworld* A thief **5** ***v*** To cheat someone, esp by overcharging: *That joint'll clip you every time* **6** ***v*** To arrest **7** ***v*** To kill, esp by shooting **◀8▶** ***n*** =CLIPPED DICK **9** ***n*** Pace; rate: *She took off at a real good clip* **10** ***n*** Each one; each occasion; =POP: *two treatments at $100 a clip/ Every clip cost him half a day's pay* **11** ***n*** A clipping from a newspaper, magazine, etc: *Thanks for sending the clips about the kid's wedding* **12** ***n*** A portion of a movie or television tape: *television clips from the period of the accident* —New York Times **13** ***n*** A brief news item on televison: *Now for a couple of clips to end the show* [senses denoting fraud and theft are probably fr the practice of *clipping* bits of metal off coins and passing them at face value]

See ROACH CLIP

clip joint ***n phr*** A business establishment that regularly overcharges, or where one is likely to be robbed or swindled: *One man's gourmet noshery is another man's clip joint*

◀ clipped dick▶ ***n phr*** A Jewish male

◁ **clit**▷ ***n*** The clitoris; =BUTTON

◁ **clit-licker**▷ ***n*** A person who does cunnilingus

clobber 1 ***v*** *fr British fr early 1900s* To hit or attack very hard; =BASH **2** ***v*** To defeat decisively; trounce; =MURDER, WIPE OUT: *Rommel got clobbered at El Alamein*

clock ***See*** CLEAN someone's CLOCK

clock in (or **out**) ***v phr*** To come or go at a certain recorded time, esp to or from a job where a time clock is used; =PUNCH IN (OF OUT)

clock-watcher ***n phr*** A person who vouchsafes more attention to the time of quitting than to work: *a hard worker, no clockwatcher*—Ira Wolfert

clod ***n*** A stupid person [fr *clodpate* or *clodpole*, fr 17th century]

clodhopper 1 ***n*** *fr late 1600s* A farmer; rustic **2** ***n*** A strong, heavy shoe, esp a workshoe; =BOONDOCKER **3** ***n*** An old vehicle, suitable for only short passages

clone ***n*** An imitation, esp a person who imitates or emulates another; a mindless copy: *Not a clone in sight. No one has the same color hair*—Village Voice [fr *clone* "the asexually produced offspring of an organism," ultimately fr Greek *klon* "twig, branch"]

clong ***n*** *politics* The impact of a powerfully inept speech, line, phrase, etc: *Clong is speechwriter talk for "the rush of s--- to the heart when a line drops dead in the hall"*—Globe and Mail/ *His call is a grand clong* —Washington Post [probably echoic of something falling with a loud, dull clang, like *clonk* and *clunk*]

clonish ***adj*** Inclined to copy; unoriginal and duplicative: *The crowd was decidedly clonish*—Armistead Maupin

clonk ***v*** =CLUNK

close but no cigar ***adv phr*** Very nearly correct; not quite the thing: *If you answered George Lucas's Star Wars you're close, but no cigar* —Washingtonian [fr carnival feats where one gets a *cigar* as a prize]

close shave (or **call**) ***n phr*** *fr late 1800s* A very narrow avoidance or evasion of some danger; =SQUEAKER

closet ***modifier*** Secret; unsuspected: *Puddin' calls me his closet red neck*—Dan Jenkins/ *fellow who was known around the White House as a "closet liberal"*—New York Times

the **closet** ***n phr*** The condition of concealment in which a homosexual or other nonconforming person lives: *If you're out of the closet, you're out of the armed service*—Ms
See COME OUT OF THE CLOSET

close to the chest *See* PLAY CLOSE TO THE CHEST

closet queen (or **queer**) ***n phr*** A secret homosexual

clothes *See* SUNDAY CLOTHES

clothesline **1** ***n*** *baseball* A very flat, fast line drive **2** ***v*** *football* To block or tackle by holding out one's arm in the path of a running player: *He clotheslined him*—Esquire

cloud *See* ON CLOUD NINE, UP IN THE CLOUDS

cloud nine (or **seven**) *See* ON CLOUD NINE

clout **1** ***v*** To hit; strike; =BASH: *My old man would have clouted the hell out of me*—Calder Willingham **2** ***n:*** *She gave him a clout on the snoot* **3** ***v*** To steal, esp to shoplift or steal a car **4** ***n*** Force; power; impact; =PUNCH: *This wimpish paragraph lacks clout* **5** ***n*** Influence or power, esp of a political sort: *He has lots of friends in high places, but no clout*
See CIRCUIT BLOW

clout (or **hit**) **for the circuit** ***v phr*** To hit a home run in baseball

clover *See* IN CLOVER, LIKE PIGS IN CLOVER

clover-kicker ***n*** =SHITKICKER

clown **1** ***n*** A person for whom the speaker feels mild contempt, esp one whose behavior merits derision: *So these clowns start in about karma or something* **2** ***v*** (also **clown around**) To behave frivolously; persist in inappropriate levity

club *See* DEUCE OF CLUBS, FIVE OF CLUBS, MILE-HIGH CLUB, RAP CLUB, WAR CLUB, WELCOME TO THE CLUB

clubhouse lawyer ***n phr*** *baseball* A baseball player who is a prominent self-appointed authority on the game and its regulations, and who generously instructs his associates

cluck or **cluckhead** or **kluck** **1** ***n*** A stupid person; idiot **2** ***n*** *black* A very dark black person
See DUMB CLUCK

clue ***v*** or ***v phr*** (also **clue in**) To inform someone of pertinent facts; =PUT someone IN THE PICTURE: *Neil Sheehan and I were terribly clued-in. We had a lock on that story*—David Halberstam
See GET A CLUE, HAVE A CLUE, NOT HAVE A CLUE

clunk **1** ***v*** (also **clonk**) To hit; strike; =CLOCK: *She clunked him in the teeth* **2** ***n:*** *He hit me a good clunk* **3** ***n*** A stupid person; =CLUCK: *scheming maids who have been working on the poor clunks all spring*—Robert Ruark **4** ***n*** An old and worn-out machine, esp a car; =CLUNKER: *Look at that fuckin' broad in the clunk next to us*—Rolling Stone

clunk down *See* PLANK DOWN

clunker **1** ***n*** Anything inferior; =LEMON, TURKEY: *His last clunker was Lolly Madonna*—New York **2** ***n*** An old, worn-out machine, esp a car; =CLUNK, JALOPY: *let in someone in an old clunker with a broken muffler and a fuming exhaust*—New York Times **3** ***n*** A clumsy person, esp an unskillful athlete; =DUFFER, HACKER: *Tell one of those clunkers what a great stroke he has*—G Edson

clunkily ***adv*** Ungracefully; stolidly: *Her clunkily earnest lyrics are very big on concepts like the Necessity of Being Your Own Person*—Ms

clunky or **clunkish** ***adj*** Blockish and ungraceful; stolidly unsophisticated: *I don't like clunky shoes or heavy soles*—Village Voice/ *a clunkish magazine called Pick-Up Times*—Village Voice

clutch **1** ***n*** An embrace; =CLINCH **2** ***n*** A group; bunch: *a clutch of drunken sailors* **3** ***n*** *restaurant* A customer who does not tip, or tips too little **4** ***v*** (also **clutch up**) To panic; be seized with anxiety

the **clutch** **1** ***n phr*** A moment when heroic performance under pressure is needed: *You could always depend on Gladys when the clutch came* **2** ***modifier:*** *a clutch hitter/ clutch play*

clutcher *See* DOUBLE-CLUTCHER

clutching *See* DOUBLE-CLUTCHING

clutz *See* KLUTZ

clyde ***n fr rock and roll & cool talk*** A person who does not appreciate rock-and-roll music, culture, etc; =SQUARE

C-note *n* A hundred-dollar bill

coal ***See*** HAUL someone OVER THE COALS, POUR ON THE COAL

the **coast** (or **Coast**) *n phr* The Pacific coast, esp California, or the Atlantic coast

See LEFT COAST

coattail ***modifier*** Based on another person's achievement or quality; derivative: *not likely to remain contented with coattail power for long* —Newsweek

See ON someone's COATTAILS

cob ***See*** ON THE COB, ROUGH AS A COB

cock ◁**1**▷ *n* The penis; =PRICK **2** *n* A friend; =PAL • Chiefly British: *How goes it, old cock?*

See DROP YOUR COCKS AND GRAB YOUR SOCKS, HORSE COCK, POPPYCOCK

cockamamie or **cockamamey** or **cockamamy** (kahk ə MAY mee) ***adj*** Crazy; confused: *The picture ends with a cockamamie implication that love will conquer all*—Time [fr New York City dialect, perhaps fr British; somehow connected with *decalcomania*; perhaps because decalcomanias as given in candy boxes and chewing-gum packets were used by children for antic self-decoration]

cock-and-bull story *n phr* An improbable account, usu an alibi; a mendacious farrago: *He gives me this cock-and-bull story about six flat tires* [said to be fr the stories that would be told in the barrooms at the *Cock* Hotel and the *Bull* Hotel, on the high street of Stony Stratford in England]

cocked ***adj*** Drunk

See HALF COCKED

cocked hat ***See*** KNOCK something INTO A COCKED HAT

cocker ***See*** ALTER KOCKER, OLD COCKER

cockeye *n baseball* A lefthanded pitcher; =SOUTHPAW

cockeyed **1** *adj* Crosseyed; walleyed; strabismic **2** *adj* Crazy; weird; all wrong; =SCREWY: *Anybody who thinks I'm kidding is cockeyed* —Heywood Broun/ *This plan appears to be completely "cockeyed"* —AH Marckwardt & FG Cassidy **3** *adj* Drunk **4** *adj* Unconscious: *Izzy knocks him cockeyed* **5** *adv* Askew; crooked: *He put his hat on cockeyed and got a polite chuckle* **6** *adv* Very; extremely: *That is cockeyed silly*

◁**cocksman**▷ **1** *n* A man regarded and evaluated as sex partner **2** *n* An ardent womanizer and copulator; =STUD

◀**cocksucker**▶ **1** *n* A person who does fellatio, esp a male homosexual **2** *n* A man held by the speaker in extreme contempt; =BASTARD, PRICK: *Oh, Sid, you fucking cocksucker.... You nailed me again*—Joseph Heller

◀**cocksucking**▶ **1** *adj* Despicable; contemptible: *So I told the cocksucking little pimp to get lost* **2** *adj* Wretched; =DAMNED • A very general intensive use, often for euphony: *Here, take your cocksucking money* **3** *adv: Don't talk so cocksucking silly*

cocktail ***See*** MOLOTOV COCKTAIL

◁**cock-teaser** or **prick-teaser**▷ *n* A woman or a male homosexual who arouses a man sexually by granting certain favors, then denies him the sex act

coco *n* The head

coffee grinder **1** *n phr* A strip teaser or other performer who features slow pelvic gyration **2** *n phr* A prostitute **3** *n phr movie studio* A cinematographer **4** *n phr WW2 Army Air Force* An aircraft engine

coffin nail (or **tack**) *n phr fr late 1800s* A cigarette; =BUTT

coin *n fr early 1900s* Money; =BREAD, LOOT

cojones (coh HOH neez) *n* Courage; audacity; =BALLS: *requiring cojones the size of the award-winning cabbages at the state fair*—Car and Driver [fr Spanish "testicles"]

coke *fr early 1900s* **1** *n* Cocaine **2** ***modifier:*** *coke peddlers/ coke sniffer* **3** *n* =COKE

Coke *n* Coca-Cola, a trade name

See CHARLEY COKE

coke-bottle glasses *n phr* Very thick eyeglass lenses: *He had thinning hair, Coke-bottle glasses, a big nose*—New York Review [fr their resemblance to the thickness of the bottom of a soft-drink bottle]

coked or **coked-up** or **coked-out** ***adj*** Intoxicated with cocaine; =HIGH: *the new generation of "coked"... gunmen*—E Lavine/ *the pair of strippers, a coked-out Pakistani princess* *and a coked-up Fire Island queen* —Village Voice

cokehead **1** *n narcotics* A cocaine addict **2** *n* Any dull, stupid person

cokie or **cokey** *narcotics* **1** *n* A narcotics addict, esp a cocaine addict: *the horde of Hollywood cokies* **2** *modifier: a cokey friend/ cokie chat*

cold **1** *adj* Unconscious; =OUT: *The snowball knocked him cold* **2** *adj* Having or displaying no emotional warmth: *He's a cold sort of fish* **3** *adj* Undergoing a spell of bad luck: *I got out of that game because I was cold and Pop was hot* **4** *adj* Without rehearsal, practice, or warmup: *When the star got sick, this woman had to take over the part cold* **5** *adj* Perfectly; in every detail; =BLIND: *She knew the subject cold* **6** *adv* With no possibility of evasion; definitively; =DEAD TO RIGHTS: *After that slip they had him cold*
See BLOW HOT AND COLD, HOT AND COLD, STONY COLD BROKE

cold as (or **colder than**) **hell** (Variations: **charity** or **Kelsey's ass** or **a welldigger's ass** or **a witch's tit** may replace **hell**) *adj phr* Very cold: *In Chicago, that December 1955, it was cold as a well-digger's ass in the Klondike*—Earl Thompson

cold cash *n phr* Unmistakably valid money, as distinct from checks, promises, etc; =HARD CASH: *The place wants payment in cold cash, nothing less* [fr the notion that definite and inalterable things are *cold* and hard]

coldcock **1** *v* To knock unconscious; =KNOCK someone OUT: *He told me to step aside and I wouldn't, so he cold cocked me*—Village Voice **2** *n* The act of knocking unconscious quickly before the victim can resist [perhaps fr the hammering of *caulking* into a boat's or ship's seams; perhaps related to Canadian lumberjacks' *put the caulks to* someone "stamp in someone's face with spiked boots"]

cold day in hell *n phr* An impossible time; never: *It'll be a cold day in hell when you catch me taking dope*

cold feet *See* HAVE COLD FEET

cold haul **1** *v phr* To take advantage of; dupe **2** *v phr* To do in a slipshod way, and esp to miss a good opportunity **3** *v phr* (also **cold haul it**) *black* To leave; depart; =HAUL ASS: *He cold hauled it!*—Zora Neale Hurston

cold in hand *adj phr black* Lacking money; =BROKE

cold shoulder **1** *n phr fr early 1800s fr British* A deliberate snub; display of chilly contempt **2** *v: I cold-shouldered him and he looked puzzled*

cold sober *adj phr* Completely sober
See STONE COLD SOBER

cold storage *See* IN COLD STORAGE

cold turkey **1** *adv phr* Without warning, rehearsal, overture, etc: *simply walk in cold turkey and talk things over*—DH Beetle **2** *n phr narcotics* Total and abrupt deprivation of narcotics, as distinct from gradual withdrawal **3** *adv phr: He kicked his habit cold turkey* **4** *adj narcotics* Requiring abrupt and complete deprivation: *They tried the cold-turkey cure* **5** *v phr auctioneers* To stop auction bidding and sell at a previously set price **6** *adj fr early 1900s* Basic; unadorned; =HARD-CORE: *Stalin didn't like certain cold-turkey facts Kennan reported*—New York Daily News [perhaps fr the contrast between the unadorned *cold turkey* and the warm, prepared, tasty bird served at the feast]

collar **1** *n* A police officer **2** *n police* An arrest: *The bull makes a collar on me*—American Mercury **3** *v: He collared the muggers in the next block* **4** *v* To comprehend; grasp: *I don't collar your meaning, Sam*
See DOG COLLAR, HOT UNDER THE COLLAR

college *See* COW COLLEGE, NUT HOUSE

College *See* JOE COLLEGE

college try *See* the OLD COLLEGE TRY

colly *v black* To understand; =DIG

colonel *See* CHICKEN COLONEL

color-blind **1** *adj* Unable to distinguish one's own money from someone else's, hence likely to cheat or steal **2** *adj* Making no prejudicial distinctions among races: *The law is, in design, perfectly color-blind*

colors *See* WITH FLYING COLORS

combo **1** *n fr 1940s musicians* A musical group or band: *a combo like Led Zeppelin* **2** *n* The combination of a safe, lock, vault, etc **3** *n* Any combination: *gin and tomato juice combo*

◁ **come** ▷ **1** *v* To have an orgasm; ejaculate semen **2** *n* (also **cum**) Semen, or any fluid secreted at orgasm **3** *n* An orgasm **4** *n* (also **cum**) Any viscid food or other substance resembling semen

See HOW COME, WHAT GOES AROUND COMES AROUND

come across **1** *v phr* To give something, esp to do so somewhat reluctantly: *When will you come across with the rent, you bum?* **2** *v phr* To accede to the sex act; bestow oneself sexually: *She came across without more fuss* **3** *v phr* To impress one; appear to be: *Walter doesn't come across as a crusader, or muckraker*—Esquire

come again *v phr* To repeat something; =RUN something BY AGAIN • Nearly always a request, or an expression of disbelief at what one has heard: *Come again? Did I hear what I hope I didn't?*

come apart at the seams *v phr* To lose one's normal poise and competence: *It was rather a long kiss. Silas felt himself coming apart at the seams*—S McNeil

comeback **1** *n* A regaining of success, fame, health, etc: *He's trying another comeback at 38* **2** *n* A quick and witty retort; a withering riposte: *Dorothy Parker was famous for devastating comebacks* **3** *n salespersons* A customer who returns merchandise; also, the returning itself **4** *n citizens band* A response to a call: *Thanks for your comeback, Dead Duck*

come back *v phr* To regain success, renown, health, etc: *It's hard to come back after a fiasco like that*

come clean *v phr* To tell the truth, esp the whole truth; make a plenary confession

comedian *See* STAND-UP COMIC

comedown **1** *n* A reduction of one's status; loss of prestige: *Riding the bus was a comedown for her* **2** *n* =LETDOWN **3** *n narcotics* The ending of a drug experience: *I cooled it with Quaalude... the comedown wasn't too bad*—Saturday Review

come down **1** *v phr narcotics* To experience the ending of a drug intoxication: *as if he had just come down off methedrine*—J Bradshaw **2** *v phr narcotics* To become firmly established: *when a chick's habit came down on her*—Claude Brown **3** *v phr fr black* To happen: *Something weird had to be coming down*—Cyra McFadden

come down hard *v phr* To punish or suppress severely; =CLAMP DOWN: *He always comes down real hard on two-time losers*

come down the pike *v phr* To appear; come on the scene: *every dumbass little news story that comes down the pike*—Armistead Maupin

come hell or high water *adv phr* No matter what happens; in any event: *I'll find out come hell or high water*

come-hither *adj* Inviting; seductive: *Courage and come-hither eyes Have a genius for taking pains*—WH Auden

come in out of the rain *See* NOT HAVE BRAINS ENOUGH TO COME IN OUT OF THE RAIN

come-lately *See* JOHNNY-COME-LATELY

come off ◁**1**▷ *v phr* To have an orgasm; ejaculate semen **2** *v phr* To succeed: *To everybody's astonishment, the scheme came off*

come off something *v phr* To stop doing or saying something immediately • Usu a stern command: *Come off that crap. Keep your jaw shut*—Calder Willingham

come on **1** *v phr* To show as; present oneself as; act: *Your friend comes on real dumb* **2** *interj* An exclamation of disbelief, disapproval, request, etc: *Come on, Arnold, don't give me that shit* **3** *v phr horse-racing* To gain: *Aching Axel is coming on real fast in the home stretch*

come-on **1** *n* Anything designed to attract or seduce; an enticement: *I gave her a big grin, but she knew it was a come-on* **2** *modifier: football bowls baited with $100,000 or so of come-on money*—Arthur Daley

come on like gangbusters *v phr* To begin or proceed in a vigorous fashion: *The campaign's coming on like gangbusters* [fr the radio program *Gangbusters* of the 1930s and 40s, which was introduced by a noisy miscellany of sirens, shots, screeches, music, etc]

come on strong **1** *v phr horse-racing* To gain steadily and rapidly in a race **2** *v phr* To be vehement and positive: *He always comes on a little too strong about taxes*

come out **1** *v phr fr homosexuals* To become an acknowledged homosexual; =COME OUT OF THE CLOSET: *Their eldest son had "come out"* —Shana Alexander **2** *v phr* To end; eventuate: *How'd that whole deal come out?* **3** *v phr* To declare oneself; take a position: *Did she come out for the Equal Rights Amendment?*

come out of the closet **1** *v phr fr homosexuals* To become an acknowledged homosexual; =COME OUT: *He came out of the closet last year and his parents damn near died* **2** *v phr* To reveal or acknowledge some personal conviction, political position, etc: *In 1978 Timmy came out of the closet and showed a genuine interest in the club*—Sports Illustrated

come out of the woodwork *See* CRAWL OUT OF THE WOODWORK

◁ **come-queen** ▷ *n* A person who prefers and practices fellatio: *a nutty come-queen named Linda Lovelace* —Deep Throat Papers

comer *n* A person doing very well and promising to do better in a certain field: *She's a comer, a potential champ*

comes around *See* WHAT GOES AROUND COMES AROUND

come through **1** *v phr* To succeed as expected and desired: *Jim Thorpe always came through to win*—Bill Stern **2** *v phr* To cope successfully with perils and troubles; weather adversity: *All seems bleak, but we'll come through unscathed* **3** *v phr* =COME ACROSS

come to a screeching halt *v phr* To finish abruptly and immediately: *All this damn foolishness must come to a screeching halt*

come unglued (or **unstuck** or **unwrapped**) *v phr* To go out of control; deteriorate to chaos: *Mr Foster ... succeeded in keeping the proceedings from coming unglued*—New York Times/ *She was bound to come unwrapped*—John Farris

comeuppance or **come-uppings** *n fr middle 1800s* A deserved chastening, esp some event that checks a wrongdoer; just deserts

come up smelling like a rose (or **with the five-dollar gold piece**) *v phr* To have extraordinarily good luck; emerge from peril with profit [fr the traditional image of the happy person who "falls in the shitpile and *comes up smelling like a rose*"]

come up to the wire *v phr* To approach the finish; come near the end: *The crucial project is coming up to the wire and we're a bit nervous* [fr the *wire* that marks the finish line of a race]

come within an ace *v phr fr late 1600s* To come very near to doing something, winning something, etc: *She came within an ace of getting the world title* [probably a version of the 13th-century term *within ambs ace* "very close to," *ambs ace* being the lowest point in dice, two ones or snake-eyes, fr Old French fr Latin *ambas as* "both ace"]

come with the territory *See* GO WITH THE TERRITORY

comic *See* STAND-UP COMIC

the **comics** *See* the FUNNIES

coming from *See* WHERE someone IS COMING FROM

coming out of someone's **ears** *See* STEAM WAS COMING OUT OF someone's EARS

Commerce *See* CHAMBER OF COMMERCE

commo¹ *n prison* Treats, cigarettes, etc, from the prison commissary

commo² *n* Commotion: *What's the commo about?*

commo³ **1** *n Army* Communications: *Commo okay?* **2** *modifier fr Army: a commo platoon/ went over the commo signals for the fiftieth time*—Richard Merkin

communist *n Army* Any despised person; =BASTARD: *Some communist swiped my typewriter*

comp **1** *n* A complimentary ticket; =ANNIE OAKLEY **2** *n* A nonpaying guest at a restaurant, casino, club, etc **3** *n* Something given free to a privileged guest or customer: *The first was the comps he got in the casino for dropping his $2000*—Philadelphia Journal **4** *v: Now, because I'm a high roller, everything is comped. I don't pay for anything*—Philadelphia

the **Company** *n phr espionage* The US Central Intelligence Agency

compleat *See* REET

compo *n* A cheap dress shoe that is pasted or nailed together rather than sewn [fr *composition*]

con¹ *n* A convict or former convict; prison inmate

con² **1** *n* A swindle; confidence game; =SCAM: *It's a clever con and you're a greedy rat* **2** *v: We conned the old fart out of three big ones* **3** *n* A dishonest sort of persuasion; =PUT-ON: *a slick young man with a line of deferential con*—Pete Hamill/ *His pretense of concern was all con* **4** *v: He conned her into thinking he'd marry her*

con artist *See* CON MAN

conchy or **conchie** *n fr WW2 British* A conscientious objector to military service

condo *n* A condominium apartment, house, etc

cone *See* GIVE CONE

conehead *teenagers* **1** *n* An intellectual; =POINTED HEAD: *These coneheads are retards*—Village Voice **2** *n* A stupid person

confab (KAHN fab) **1** *n fr early 1900s* A talk; discussion **2** *v: Let's confab a bit about that idea* [fr *confabulation*]

con game (or **job**) **1** *n phr* A confidence game; swindle; =SCAM **2** *n phr* An easy job; sinecure

conk¹ **1** *n* The head **2** *v* To hit on the head: *I got conked by the bat* **3** *v* To defeat utterly; =CLOBBER [probably fr *conch*]
See BUST one's ASS

conk² or **gonk** *black* **1** *v* To apply a mixture sometimes containing lye to the head in order to straighten kinky hair **2** *n: I couldn't get over marveling at how their hair was straight and shiny like white men's hair; Ella told me this was called "conk"*—Malcolm X [probably fr *Congolene*, trade name of a preparation used to straighten hair, influenced by *conk¹*]

conk off **1** *v phr* To stop work; rest when one should work; =GOOF OFF **2** *v phr* To go to sleep; sleep: *You been conking off for eight hours*—Mickey Spillane

conkout *n* An act or instance of conking out: *I did a swift conkout when I got to bed*

conk out *fr WW1 British RAF* **1** *v phr* To stop running or operating: *The engine conked right out* **2** *v phr* To lose energy and spirits suddenly; become abruptly exhausted **3** *v phr* To go to sleep; =CONK OFF **4** *v phr* To die: *So she's conked out, eh?*—Agatha Christie/ *John Le Mesurier wishes it to be known that he conked out on Nov. 15.* —Time [probably echoic]

con man (or **artist**) **1** *n phr* A confidence man **2** *n phr* One adept at persuasion, esp at dishonest or self-serving persuasion **3** *n phr* One who manages to lead an easy and indolent life

connect **1** *v* To hit very hard: *He connected with a rude one to the jaw* **2** *v narcotics* To buy narcotics or other contraband **3** *v* To get along with; establish rapport with: *She's never been able to connect with her tenant*

connection *n narcotics* A seller of narcotics; a person who can get drugs; =PUSHER

constant *See* FINAGLE FACTOR

contact high *n phr narcotics* A seeming intoxication induced by being with persons who are intoxicated with narcotics: *that sympathetic vibration known as the "contact high"*—Tom Wolfe

contract **1** *n* An arrangement to have someone murdered by a professional killer: *The word is there's a contract out for Taffy Taylor* **2** *n police* Any illegal or unethical arrangement: *contract, any favor one policeman says he'll do for another*—GY Wells

cooch **1** *n* Any sexually suggestive or imitative dance; =HOOTCHIE-COOTCHIE **2** ***modifier:*** *a slow hot cooch dance* ◁**3**▷ *n* The female crotch; vulva

coo-coo *See* CUCKOO

cook **1** *v* To be put to death in the electric chair; =FRY **2** *v* To suffer and quake while awaiting some outcome **3** *v fr jive talk* To happen; occur: *Is anything cooking on the new tax rule?* **4** *v fr jive talk* To do very well; excel: *if the performers begin cooking together and most of the director's intuitions and skills pay off*—Washington Post **5** *v* To falsify; tamper with • Chiefly British use: *The British government cooked press stories shamelessly in order to* *deceive the Argentine enemy*—Newsweek

cooked-up *adj* Specially contrived; expedient and dishonest: *It's insane why we give ourselves cooked up reasons for not moving the issue*—Westworld

cooker *See* PRESSURE COOKER

cook someone's **goose** *v phr fr middle 1800s* To ruin or destroy • Very often in the passive form, "our goose is cooked": *If he doesn't like it our goose is cooked*

cookie or **cookey** **1** *n* (also **cookee**) *merchant marine, lumberjacks & cowboys fr middle 1800s* A cook or cook's helper **2** *n narcotics* A person who prepares opium for smoking; opium addict **3** *n* An attractive young woman **4** *n* A person; =GUY: *real tough cookie/ shrewd cookie* ◁**5**▷ *n* (also **cookies**) *black* The female genitals; vulva **6** *n baseball* A base hit: *knowing I was going to get at least one cookie every game*—Sports Illustrated
See GRIPE one's ASS, THAT'S THE WAY THE BALL BOUNCES, TOUGH COOKIE

cookie-cutter or **cooky-cutter** **1** *n circus* A police officer's badge **2** *n* A weak and unenterprising person; =WIMP **3** *n* An inadequate weapon, esp a knife **4** *modifier* (also **cookie-cut**) Identical and unoriginal; standardized; stereotyped: *Friedman has created a cookie-cutter version of one of the most complex personalities*—New York/ *Each store is a cookie-cutter copy, laid out according to plans devised at the corporate headquarters*—New York Times/ *I'd never want to read that kind of cookie-cut magazine*—Philadelphia

cookie jar *See* WITH one's HAND IN THE TILL

cookies *See* COOKIE, SHOOT one's COOKIES

cooks *See* WHAT'S COOKING

cook the books *v phr* To tamper with and falsify records, esp financial accounts: *The managers had cooked the books to the tune of $34 million*—Newsweek

cook up *v phr* To devise; fabricate; =HOKE UP: *We'll cook up a story to explain your swollen lip*

cook with gas (or **on the front burner**) *v phr fr 1930s jive talk* To perform very commendably; =GROOVE

cool **1** *v* To postpone; await developments in: *Let's cool this whole business for a week or so* **2** *v fr 1930s* To kill **3** *adj* In control of one's feelings; stoic: *Learn to be cool under fire* **4** *n: He lost his cool and bolted like a rabbit* **5** *adj beat & cool talk* Aloof and uninvolved; disengaged, as an expression of alienation; =BEAT, HIP: *He's cool, don't give a shit for nothing* **6** *n: My guru drifted me to a total spiritual cool* **7** *n 1940s cool musicians* Jazz marked by soft tones, improvisation based on advanced chord extensions, and revision of certain classical jazz idioms **8** *adj: cool jazz/ a real cool passage* **9** *adj beat & cool talk & counterculture* Excellent; good: *a cool shirt/ cool sermon* **10** *adj* Pleasant; desirable; =COPACETIC
See BLOW one's COOL, LOSE one's COOL, PLAY IT COOL

cool (or **calm**) **as a Christian with aces wired** *adj phr* Serenely assured; tranquilly confident: *"We will take care of that," he says, cool as a Christian with aces wired*—Edward Abbey

the **cooler** *fr middle 1800s* **1** *n* A jail; =the SLAMMER **2** *n prison* A cell or cellblock for solitary confinement

cool one's **heels** *v phr* To wait, esp to be kept waiting: *I cooled my heels for two hours before the great one would see me*

cool it *beat & cool talk* **1** *v phr* To relax; stop being excited or angry **2** *v phr* To slow one's pace; stop being strenuous **3** *v phr* To stop what one is doing, esp what is annoying the speaker • In all three senses often an exhortation or irritated command

cool out **1** *v phr horse-racing* To walk a horse after a race to calm and moderate it gradually **2** *v phr beat & black* To do the sex act **3** *v phr* To relax; become calm; =COOL IT: *I told him to cool out and stop complaining*

cool-out *n* A device or strategy intended to relax someone, esp to calm justified apprehensions: *cooperating in an Uncle Tom cool-out this late in the game*—Eldridge Cleaver

cool someone **out** *fr beat & cool talk* **1** *v phr* To mollify and appease; calm apprehensions or anger: *He is the one who has to cool people out and pay off State officials*—New York **2** *v phr* To relax; become calm: *We've got to cool Bobby out before the teacher gets pissed off* **3** *v phr* To kill someone

coolville or **Coolville** *n* (also **coolsville** or **Coolsville**) Excellent; splendid: *Your little scheme's coolville*

◀ **coon** ▶ *n fr middle 1800s* A black person

See ACE BOON COON

◀ **coon box** ▶ *See* GHETTO BOX

coop **1** *n* Any small and wretched building; hovel **2** *v police* To sleep while on duty; nap on the job, esp in a police car: *the cops cooping in a police car at the corner*—Earl Thompson **3** *n* A coupe car: *It's a Plymouth convertible coop*—John O'Hara

See FLY THE COOP, IN THE COOP, RAIN CATS AND DOGS

co-op or **coop** (KOH ahp) **1** *n* A cooperative apartment house, store, etc **2** *modifier: co-op prices/ coop apartment complex* **3** *v* To convert an apartment or building from a rental to a cooperative unit: *The old Sussex Arms got co-oped last year*

coot *n fr late 1700s* A stupid or silly person, usu an aged one: *a harmless old coot*

See CRAZY AS A LOON

cootchie *See* HOOTCHIE-COOTCHIE

cootie *n esp WW1 Army fr British* A body louse [fr Malay, "dog tick"]

◁ **cooz** ▷ (Variations: **cooze** or **cou** or **couz** or **couzie** or **couzy** or **cuzzy**) **1** *n* A woman: *killed two quarts of tequila last night in Olvera Street, this Mexican cooz and I*—SJ Perelman/ *He runs. He screams like a cooze*—Robert Stone **2** *n* The female genitals; vulva **3** *n* A person, esp a woman, viewed solely as a sex object: *a piece of beautiful, dumb eighteen-year-old cooze*—Jackie Collins

cop **1** *n fr middle 1800s* A police officer **2** *v* To steal: *He copped six PCs from the shop* **3** *v* To win; be awarded: *to cop second place* **4** *v* To comprehend; grasp: *I don't quite cop your sense, pal* **5** *v narcotics* To buy or get narcotics: *The pusher has appeared, ... they will make their roundabout way to him to "cop"*—J Mills [origin uncertain; perhaps ultimately fr Latin *capere* "seize," by way of French]

See GOOD COP BAD COP

copacetic (KOH pə SET ik) *adj* (Variations: **copesetic** or **kopasetic** or **kopesetic** or **kopasetee** or **kopesetee**) *fr 1920s* As it should be; quite satisfactory; = COOL, OK [origin unknown]

◁ **cop a** (or someone's) **cherry** ▷ *v phr* To deprive of virginity; deflower

cop a feel *v phr* To feel or caress someone's body, esp the sex organs, usu in a sly or seemingly inadvertent way: *I thought he wanted to help me into the car, but I think he just wanted to cop a feel*

cop an attitude *See* HAVE AN ATTITUDE

cop a plea *v phr police & underworld* To plead guilty to a lesser charge than one might otherwise be tried for; escape a worse punishment by accepting a lesser one

copilot *n truckers* An amphetamine taken in order to stay awake

cop (or **buy**) **it** *v phr fr WW1* To die, esp to be killed in battle or otherwise: *He had a feeling he wouldn't cop it that day/ The guy who buys it ... does it off camera*—Washington Post

cop-killer *n* A bullet capable of penetrating bullet-proof vests: *the apple-green bullets they call cop-killers*—Chicago Tribune

cop out **1** *v phr underworld* To be arrested **2** *v phr* = COP A PLEA **3** *v phr esp 1960s counterculture* To avoid trouble and responsibility; evade an issue or problem; disengage oneself: *When his friends really needed help he copped out*

cop-out *n* An evasion; an excuse for inaction: *Arguing about standards is a "cop-out"*—P Sourain

copper[1] **1** *n fr middle 1800s* A police officer **2** *v: My old man coppered for thirty years* **3** *n underworld* An informer; = STOOL PIGEON

copper[2] *v gambling fr middle 1800s* To bet against a card, roll of the dice, person, etc [fr the use of a special metal chip by a gambler to indicate a "lose" bet in faro]

coppish or **capeesh** (kə PEESH) **1** ***question*** Do you understand?: *All right, class, that's all there is to it. Coppish?* **2** ***affirmation*** I understand: *Ten tonight? Capeesh* [fr Italian informal or dialect fr *capito* "I understand"]

cop shop ***n phr*** A police station

copycat **1** ***n*** *fr late 1800s* An imitator; mimic **2** ***modifier:*** *a copycat inventor/ copycat crime*

copycat crime ***n phr*** A crime committed in imitation of another crime, esp one which is sensational and highly publicized: *Copy-Cat Crimes of the Heart*—Time

cop Zs (or **some Zs**) ***v phr*** (Variations: **bag** or **catch** or **cut** or **get** or **pile up** or **stack** may replace **cop**) *fr black* To take a nap; sleep; =SNOOZE: *got to peck a little, and cop me some Z's*—Malcolm X/ *sits around all day cutting Zs*—Motorcross Action Magazine [see some *Zs*]

core ***See*** HARD-CORE, SOFT-CORE

core dump **1** ***v phr*** *computers* To empty out the central memory of a computer **2** ***v phr*** *fr computers* To explain oneself fully; say one's piece, esp in the mode of complaint: *She told a friend that she had "core dumped" on the boss*—New York Times

Corine ***n*** *narcotics* Cocaine

cork ***See*** BLOW one's TOP, POP one's CORK

corker ***n*** *fr early 1800s* A person or thing that is remarkable, wonderful, superior, etc; =HUMDINGER, PISS-CUTTER [perhaps fr nautical slang *caulk* "do the sex act," whence the notion of something special or prodigious]

corking *fr late 1800s* **1** ***adv*** Extremely; very: *to have a corking good time* **2** ***adj*** Excellent; wonderful: *a corking party*

cork off ***See*** CAULK OFF

corksacking ***adj*** Disgusting; depraved; =COCKSUCKING • Euphemistic form of **cocksucking**: *you effing corksacking limey effer*—Anthony Burgess

corn **1** ***n*** Corn whiskey; moonshine **2** ***n*** *fr jive talk* Music, poetry, sentiment, etc, that is maudlin and naively affirmative of old-fashioned values; banal and emotionally overwrought material; =SCHMALTZ: *His ethical sincerity verges on corn* [second sense probably from the notion of *cornfed* as indicating rural simplicity and naivete]

See CAN OF CORN

cornball *fr jive talk* **1** ***n*** A person who admires or produces markedly sentimental material and utters relatively simpleminded moral convictions: *Eisenhower on no account can be called a cornball*—Robert Ruark **2** ***adj:*** *Where did you get those cornball notions?*

corned ***adj*** *fr late 1700s* Drunk

See HALF-CORNED

corner ***See*** HOT CORNER

corn-fed **1** ***adj*** Plump and sturdy; rural or as if rural: *a corn-fed beauty* **2** ***adj*** Naive and sentimental; =CORNY

◀**cornhole**▶ ***v*** *fr early 1900s* To do anal intercourse; =BUGGER, BUNGHOLE: *so the Germans would get castrated when they cornholed him*—Trevanian

corny ***adj*** *fr jive talk* Overly sentimental; banal; devoted to or expressing old-fashioned moral convictions; =CORNBALL: *He uses a corny ethos to get himself elected*

corral (kə RAL) ***v*** To find; gather: *to corral votes*

cosh **1** ***n*** *chiefly British fr late 1800s* A bludgeon; blackjack **2** ***v*** To hit with a blackjack: *as these samurai cosh, ignite, bludgeon and blow away a host of contemptible nincompoops*—Washington Post

cotics ***n*** *narcotics* Narcotics

cotton ***See*** IN TALL COTTON, SHIT IN HIGH COTTON

cotton-picking or **cotton-pickin'** ***adj*** Despicable; wretched; =DAMNED: *Take your cotton-pickin' hands off me/ none of your cotton-picking business/ They're out of their cotton-picking minds*—Washington Post [fr the inferior status of the field hand or poor farmer in Southern US society]

cotton to ***v phr*** *fr late 1700s British* Approve of; like; appreciate; fancy: *We just didn't cotton to one another/ I don't cotton to your ogling my little sister* [perhaps fr Welsh *cytuno* "agree, consent"]

◁**cou**▷ ***See*** COOZ

couch ***See*** CASTING COUCH

couch potato ***n phr*** A habitual lounger, esp a person who spends much time watching television: *They're not couch potatoes. They're* *mobile, they go out*—Washington Post

cough up *v phr fr late 1800s* To pay money or produce goods, esp with some reluctance: *When'll you cough up the rent?/ I saw you taking those pens. Cough them up*

could be *See* EASY AS PIE

could not (or **could**) **care less** *v phr* One simply does not care; one is sublimely indifferent • In a curious development, the original British negative form has been changed to affirmative by many US speakers, without change of meaning: *I couldn't care less if you like me or not/ I could care less about his comfort, the old bastard*

count *See* DOWN FOR THE COUNT, NO-COUNT

be **counted** *See* STAND UP AND BE COUNTED

not **count for spit** *See* NOT COUNT FOR SPIT

country *adj* Very competent; reliable: *He's a country ball player; gets his pitches over the plate*

See ANOTHER COUNTRY HEARD FROM

a **country mile** *n phr* A very long distance: *She chased him a country mile*

county mounty *n phr citizens band* A county sheriff or deputy sheriff [second element fr *Mounty* or *Mountie* "member of the Royal Canadian Mounted Police"]

coupe *See* DEUCE

courage *See* DUTCH COURAGE

course *See* BIRD COURSE, CRIB COURSE, GUT COURSE, PAR FOR THE COURSE, SNAP COURSE

court *See* the BALL IS IN someone's COURT, FULL COURT PRESS, HOME-COURT ADVANTAGE, KANGAROO COURT

cousin **1** *n* Friend; person • An amiable form of address: *How you doin', cousin?* **2** *n* A dupe; = MARK, PIGEON

See KISSING COUSIN

◁ **couz** or **couzie** or **couzy** ▷ *See* COOZ

cover **1** *v* (also **cover up**) To protect someone with one's testimony: *I'll cover for you if you're caught* **2** *v* To substitute for someone; replace someone temporarily and protectively: *I'll cover if you want to take a day off* **3** *v* To attend to, esp temporarily: *Will you cover the switchboard while I'm at the dentist?* **4** *v* To travel: *I covered two miles in one minute* **5** *v* To complete an account; provide pertinent information: *That about covers what happened* **6** *v* To aim at with a firearm: *Freeze, I got you covered* **7** *n* A popular song recorded by artists other than those who made it famous: *third album, like the first two, contains many covers of recent chart-busters*—Rolling Stone **8** *v: They did best covering Springsteen and Stones hits* **9** *n espionage* An identity, usu an elaborate falsification, assumed by a secret agent for concealment: *To improve his cover he "resigned" from the agency*—C McCrystal

See BLOW someone's or something's COVER

◁ **cover** one's **ass** ▷ (or **tail**) (also **CYA**) **1** *v phr* To provide or arrange for exculpation; devise excuses and alibis: *Some call it "risk management," others "covering your ass"*—Toronto Life/ *The one aspect I don't like up here is the covering-your-tail cautiousness*—Washington Post/ *CYA, you know, that old French expression*—Washington Post **2** *modifier: writing long cover-your-ass memos*—Village Voice

cover story **1** *n phr espionage* The biography and plausible account devised for a secret agent for concealment **2** *n phr* An alibi; a false narrative explanation: *We agree on the cover story, that you haven't seen me for three weeks*

cover the waterfront *v phr* To be a complete account of something; be the whole story: *Lake covers premarital agreements, no-fault divorce... even a... will. That covers the waterfront*—Playboy [fr the title of a 1932 book by Max Miller, a journalist, exposing crime and corruption on the *waterfront*]

cover-up *n* Anything designed to conceal or obfuscate the truth by replacement: *Sending the Navy south instead of north was an obvious cover-up*

cow *See* CANNED COW, CASH COW, HOLY CATS

cowboy **1** *n* A reckless person, esp a driver or pilot: *Here comes that cowboy in his Porsche/ City Subway Mishaps Attributed To Speeding "Cowboy" Motormen*—New York

Times **2** ***n*** The king of a suit of playing cards **3** ***v*** *underworld* To murder recklessly and openly: *even if we had to cowboy them (which) means that we were to kill them any place we found them* —CA Wyer

cowboy job ***n phr*** *underworld* A robbery done recklessly and clumsily

cow college (or **tech**) ***n phr*** *college students* A college rurally located and of humble distinction, esp an agricultural college: *Every instructor in every cow college is trying to get to be an assistant professor*—Philadelphia

cowflop or **cowflap** or **cowplop** **1** ***n*** Cattle dung: *He is dumb as cowflop and hopeless at foot shufflin' and finger snappin', but he tries hard* —John Skow **2** ***n*** Nonsense; pretentious talk; =BULLSHIT: *I don't believe that cowflap*—Paul Theroux/ *Urban Cowplop*—Rolling Stone

cowhide ***n*** A baseball

◁ **cow pilot**▷ ***n phr*** *airline* An airline stewardess; woman cabin attendant

crab **1** ***v*** *fr early 1800s* To complain, esp to do so regularly; nag; =BITCH: *Crab, crab, crab, that was all she ever did*—Dorothy Parker **2** ***n:*** *He's an awful crab, never gives her a moment's peace* **3** ***n*** A resident of Annapolis, Maryland **4** ***v*** To spoil; ruin: *He's trying to crab the deal*

crabs ***n*** An infestation of crab lice in the pubic area: *Her friends slobbered, ripped off girls' dresses at parties, had crabs*—Philip Wylie

crack **1** ***v*** To enter or leave a place by force, esp to enter a place for robbery **2** ***v*** To open a safe or vault by force **3** ***n*** A try; attempt; =SHOT: *It looks impossible, but I'll take a crack at it* **4** ***v*** To go uninvited to a party; =CRASH **5** ***v*** To gain admittance to some desired category or milieu: *He finally cracked the best-seller list* **6** ***v*** To solve; reveal the secret of: *If they ever crack the problem of nuclear fusion* **7** ***v*** *circus & carnival* To reveal; disclose **8** ***v*** To change a banknote; =BREAK: *Can you crack a fifty?* **9** ***v*** (also **crack up**) To suffer an emotional or mental collapse; go into hysteria, depression, etc: *After six months of that it's a wonder she didn't crack* **10** ***v*** To give information, or to confess, after intense interrogation: *Buggsy cracked and spilled everything* **11** ***v*** To speak; talk; make remarks: *Listen, Ben, quit cracking dumb*—James M Cain **12** ***n*** A brief, funny, pungent, and often malicious remark; =WISECRACK: *One more crack like that and I'm going to sock you*—K Brush **13** ***n*** A great pleasure; a notable treat or regalement; kick: *That really gives me a crack!* **14** ***v*** *card players* In bridge, to double ◁**15**▷ ***n*** The vulva; =CUNT ◁**16**▷ ***n*** The deep crease between the buttocks **17** ***n*** *narcotics* Very pure cocaine intended for smoking rather than inhalation: *Crack's low price and quick payoff make it especially alluring to teenagers*—Time

See FALL BETWEEN THE CRACKS, GIVE something A SHOT, HAVE A CRACK AT something, WISECRACK

crack a deal ***See*** CUT A DEAL

crack a smile ***v phr*** To start to smile: *I wiggled my ears but she wouldn't crack a smile*

crackbrained ***adj*** *fr 1600s* Crazy; eccentric; wild; =CRACKPOT

crackdown ***n*** A particular instance or severity of punishment, law enforcement, etc: *The Mayor again vowed a crackdown on the porn shops*

crack down *fr 1920s* **1** ***v phr*** To enforce the law more vigorously; =CLAMP DOWN: *Cops will crack down on drunk drivers* **2** ***v phr*** To exercise a prerogative of severity not ordinarily used: *If there's any more tardiness I'll crack down*

cracked **1** ***adj*** Crazy; eccentric: *You're cracked if you think I'll stay now* **2** ***adj*** Stupid; foolish

See GET one's NUTS

cracked up ***part phr*** Said; praised • Most often in the negative: *The beer ain't what it's cracked up to be* [fr earlier sense of *crack*, "boast, brag"]

cracker ***n*** *late 1700s* A Southern rustic or poor white; =REDNECK [probably from their use of whips with a piece of buckskin at the end for *cracking*]

See JAWBREAKER

cracker-barrel **1** ***adj*** Unsophisticated; basic: *a cracker-barrel philosophy* **2** ***adj*** Intimate; gossipy: *a cracker-barrel discussion of family* [fr the archetypical image of rural discussants sitting on or around the *cracker barrel* in the general store]

crackerjack or **crackajack** **1** *n fr late 1800s* A person or thing that is remarkable, wonderful, superior, etc: *Signorelli is a crackerjack* **2** ***modifier:*** *Orne... estimates that a crackerjack examiner working under optimum conditions would find 10 to 15 percent of his cases to be inconclusive*—Washingtonian/ *I'm a crackerjack story teller*—Pulpsmith [apparently a reduplication of *cracker* in the mid-19th-century British sense "something approaching perfection," which is also reflected in terms like *crack shot*, *crack troops*, etc, and based on an echoic expression of speed; hence also *cracking*; the term is reinforced in the US by late-19th-century trade name *Cracker Jack* for a popcorn and peanut confection]

crackers *adj* Crazy; =CRACKED • Chiefly British use: *Also he was plain crackers*—Saul Bellow [formed with the British suffix *-ers*, like *bonkers*, *preggers*, etc]

cracking *See* GET CRACKING

crack one's **jaw** *v phr* To brag

crackpot **1** *n* A crazy idiot; an addled fool; eccentric: *He's a crackpot about flying saucers* **2** *adj: my colleague's crackpot notions*

cracks *See* FALL BETWEEN THE CRACKS

crackup **1** *n* A collision, crash, etc: *a bad car crackup/ airline crackup* **2** *n* A mental or emotional breakdown: *Have you read Fitzgerald's* The Crackup? **3** *n* A very funny person or thing: *His Cagney sketch is a crackup*

crack up **1** *v phr* To collide; crash: *The trucks cracked up head-on* **2** *v phr* (also **crack**) To suffer an emotional or mental breakdown; go into hysteria, depression, etc: *Jimmy felt that he was cracking up*—Calder Willingham **3** *v phr* To have a fit of uncontrollable laughter: *He cracked up when he heard Richard Pryor*

crack wise *v phr* To make quick, pungent, witty, and often malicious remarks: *All you do is crack wise*—Raymond Chandler

cradle *See* ROB THE CRADLE

cradle-robber or **cradle-snatcher** **1** *n* A person who prefers relatively younger sex or courtship partners **2** *n* A recruiter or sports scout who solicits very young persons

See ROB THE CRADLE

cram it *See* STICK IT

cramp someone's **style** *v phr fr 1920s* To be a hindrance or distraction: *Your blank stare cramps my style*

crank **1** *n fr late 1800s* An eccentric person, esp one who is irritable or maliciously mischievous: *That crank wants a yogurt shampoo/ All kinds of cranks took credit for the murder* **2** ***modifier:*** *crank letters/ crank phone calls* **3** *n narcotics* Methamphetamine, a stimulant; =SPEED [fr earlier English, "twisted, bent"; hence the bent lever for turning or starting machines with associated senses of producing, commencing, speeding, etc]

crank something **out** *v phr* To produce or make, esp with mechanical precision and regularity: *with the kind of junk the studios are cranking out* —J Bell

crank someone or something **up** **1** *v phr* To get someone started; instigate action: *The people around Reagan... talk about "We'll crank him up on this"*—Washington Post **2** *v phr* To make excited, eager, keenly ready for action, etc: *You better crank the quarterback up if you want this team to score* **3** *v phr* To get started; put in operation: *Let's crank up the dog project tomorrow*

cranky *adj* Very irritable; touchy: *The baby was cranky all day*

◁**crap**▷ **1** *n fr middle 1800s British* Feces; excrement; =SHIT **2** *v: Where's the bathroom, I have to crap* **3** *interj* An exclamation of disbelief, disgust, disappointment, rejection, etc: *Oh, crap, I broke it again* **4** *n fr early 1900s* Nonsense; pretentious talk; bold and deceitful absurdities; =BULLSHIT: *I'm not interested in stories about the past or any crap of that kind*—Arthur Miller **5** *v* To lie, exaggerate; try to deceive: *You can't crap an old crapper* **6** *n* Offensive and contemptuous treatment; overt disrespect: *but I don't take crap from anybody*—Us **7** *n* Anything of shoddy quality; pretentious and meretricious trash: *Her new show is pious crap* [by extension fr

Middle English *crap* "chaff, siftings of grain, residue"]

See FULL OF SHIT, SHOOT THE BULL

crape-hanger **1** *n* A habitually morose person; pessimist; =KILLJOY **2** *n* An undertaker

◁**crap list**▷ *See* SHIT LIST

◁**crapoid**▷ *adj* Disgusting; nasty; wretched; =CRAPPY: *Clover said they were crapoid for thinking that*—Paul Theroux

◁**crapola**▷ **1** *n* Lies and exaggeration; =BULLSHIT: *grinding out the old heart-felt crapola*—Peter De Vries **2** ***modifier:*** *the latest trends in crapola entertainment*

◁**crapper**▷ **1** *n* A toilet: *that damned thing in the crapper*—Earl Thompson **2** *n* A person who regularly lies and exaggerates; a boaster and self-advertiser: *I call your great guru a mean little crapper* **3** *n* Something disgusting, nasty, or shoddy: *Oh, Mondays are a crapper* —Westworld [fr *crap*]

◁**crappy**▷ **1** *adj* Of inferior quality; shoddy: *the crappiest shoes I ever had* **2** *adj* Very unpleasant; nasty: *a crappy thing to say*

crash **1** *v* To break into a building; enter by force: *Hoover's men crashed Doc's apartment*—A Hynd **2** *v* To rob a place, esp by breaking in; =CRACK **3** *v* To gain admittance to some desired category or milieu: *In LA she tried to crash TV* **4** *v* (also **crash the gate**) To go to a party or other event uninvited or without tickets **5** *v* *beat talk & counterculture* To sleep or live at a place for a day or so, usu without invitation: *I heard about this place and hoped I could crash here for a day or two*—P Curtis **6** *v* To go to sleep **7** *v* *narcotics* To lose consciousness from narcotics or alcohol **8** *n* *narcotics* The empty feeling, depression, etc, felt when a euphoric intoxication ends; =LETDOWN: *The "crash" from coke... is grim*—Time **9** *v* *computer* To fail suddenly: *The spacecraft's No 1 computer... "crashed" or shut down*—Time

crash and burn *Army* **1** *v phr* To fail entirely; =BLOW IT **2** *v* To collapse from exhaustion; =POOP OUT: *I was just about to crash and burn* —Armistead Maupin

crash pad *n phr beat talk & counterculture* A place to sleep or live for a day or so, esp for young people traveling about aimlessly and with little money

crash program (or **project**) *n phr* An intense and extraordinary effort to a specific end: *Getting the refugees housed needed a crash program*

crate **1** *n* A car, bus, airplane, etc, esp an old rickety one **2** *n* *hoboes* A jail

crawl **1** *v* To go or move very slowly: *Traffic was crawling that day* ◁**2**▷ *v* To do the sex act with; mount: *He crawled her once or twice* **3** *v* *WW1 Army* To reprimand severely; =CHEW OUT **4** *n* *1930s college students* A dance; =HOP

crawl someone's **hump** *v phr cowboys* To assault; =CLOBBER

crawling with *adj phr* Well provided with; =LOUSY WITH: *He's crawling with guilt*

crawl (or **come**) **out of the woodwork** *v phr* To appear, materialize, interfere, etc, as or like something very loathsome: *weirdos who just crawled out of the woodwork*—WI Tyler [fr the notion that worms, spiders, maggoty creatures, rats, etc, dwell in hidden places]

crazy **1** *adj* *esp 1940s bop talk* Excellent; splendid; =COOL **2** *n* An inmate of a mental hospital; psychiatric patient **3** *n* A destructive and irrational person; =LOONY: *We're going to prevent the right-wing crazies from bombing and destroying* —Playgirl

See LIKE CRAZY, STIR-CRAZY

-crazy ***combining word*** Inordinately devoted to or manic over what is indicated: *boy-crazy/ kill-crazy/ speed-crazy*

crazy about (or **over** or **for**) *adj phr* Very enthusiastic about; infatuated with; =NUTS ABOUT: *I'm crazy about Ronnie*

crazy as a loon (or **a coot** or **a bedbug**) *adj phr fr middle 1800s* Insane; =NUTTY: *If you think that, you're crazy as a loon* [fr the *loon's* or *coot's* cry, like an insane laugh, and the *bedbug's* frantic rushing about when exposed]

crazy-house *n* A mental hospital; insane asylum

cream **1** *v* *esp 1920s* To cheat or deprive someone of something, esp by silky glibness: *I got creamed out of the hotel spot in Ohio*—John O'Hara/ *a smoothie who wolfed on a friend and creamed his lady*—World's Work **2** *v* *esp students* To do very well against; overcome; =CLOBBER: *The basketball team got creamed* ◁**3**▷ *v* To be sexually aroused, esp so as to secrete sexual fluids, either semen or lubricants: *It made me cream in my panties, isn't that fun?* —Interview

See ICE CREAM, ICE CREAM HABIT

◁ **cream** one's **jeans** (or **silkies**)▷ *v phr* To become sexually excited; exude sexual fluids: *any idea how them ladies cream their silkies watching a muscular and handsome guy* —Tom Aldibrandi

cream puff **1** *n phr* A weakling; =SISSY, WIMP: *Opponents might get the idea... Lemonick is a cream puff* —D Cresan **2** *n phr* *salespersons* Something for sale, esp a used car in splendid condition and a tremendous bargain: *before you believe, much less see, any of the "creampuffs" in the... classifieds*—Philadelphia

creative accounting *n phr* Fraudulent or dubious bookkeeping; falsification of financial records: *secret takeover deals, creative accounting just this side of Internal Revenue Service rules*—New York Times

creek *See* UP SHIT CREEK

creep *n fr 1930s students* A disgusting and obnoxious person; =CRUD, JERK, NERD: *poets loyal to Blake and Whitman, the "holy creeps"*—Saul Bellow [fr the notion of making one's flesh *creep*]

Creepers *n* & *interj* Christ • A euphemistic form: *Creepers, but that was a nasty moment*

See JEEPERS CREEPERS

creeping *adj* Slow and gradual: *creeping idiocy*

the **creeps** **1** *n phr* *fr middle 1800s* Sensations of fear and loathing, such that one's flesh seems to formicate; revulsion: *His smarm gives me the creeps* **2** *n phr* Delirium tremens: *He was not in with the creeps but with a broken leg*—John McNulty

creepy **1** *adj* Frightening; scary; =HAIRY: *a creepy show about necrophiles* **2** *adj* Loathsome; disgusting: *a creepy little chap with an enormous bow tie*

creepy-crawly **1** *adj* Loathsome; repellent; =CREEPY: *The trio plunges into the creepy-crawly high life of Acapulco*—Richard Grenier **2** *n* A nasty creature, esp the caterpillar, snake, or centipede sort: *the lair, maybe, Of creepy-crawlies or a ghost* —WH Auden

cretinoid *college students* **1** *n* A cretin; idiot; =SPASTIC **2** *modifier: El Presidente, and others too cretinoid to mention*—Drew Acorn

cretinous *adj computer* Wrong; inoperative; wretchedly designed; =BLETCHEROUS

crib **1** *n* *students fr early 1800s* A set of answers used to cheat on an examination **2** *v: He cribbed on the econ exam and got caught* **3** *n hoboes & underworld fr 1920s* A place where thieves and hoodlums congregate; cheap saloon: *a sleazy crib on Second Ave* **4** *v* *fr 1700s* To steal **5** *n* *fr Australian fr early 1900s* A brothel **6** *n* A nightclub; =DIVE: *I am singing for coffee and cakes at a crib on Cottage Grove Avenue*—John O'Hara

crib course *n phr college students* An easy college course; =GUT COURSE: *The student in desperate need of a crib course can be sure to find one* —Washington Post [fr student senses of *crib*]

not **cricket** *See* NOT CRICKET

crime *See* COPYCAT CRIME

Criminy or **Crimus** (KRI mə nee, KRĪ məs) *n* & *interj* Christ • A euphemistic form: *Criminy, I've been hoodwinked/ Crimus but it's cold*

Cripes or **Cripus** *n* & *interj fr 1840s* Christ • A euphemistic form: *Cripes, what a rotten deal*

Crisco *n* An obese person; =FATTY [fr *Crisco*, trade name for a kind of shortening sold in cans, hence, "fat in the can"]

Crisco disco *n phr* A nightclub or discotheque frequented by male homosexuals [fr the presumed use of *Crisco* as a lubricant for anal intercourse]

croak **1** *v* *fr early 1800s* To die: *I had the horse trained, then he up and croaked on me* **2** *v* To murder: *He croaked a screw at Dannemora* —Joel Sayre

croaker *n underworld, hoboes & circus* A physician: *Don't say "croaker," say "doctor"*—Nelson Algren

crock **1** *n* A disliked person, esp an old person: *a lot of old crocks with baggy eyes*—R Starnes **2** *n* A drunkard: *a rummy crock* **3** *n merchant marine* A bargelike cargo ship made of cement **4** *v* To hit; =CLOBBER, CLOCK: *I crocked the orderly with a bedspring*—Raymond Chandler **5** *v* To ruin; wreck; =QUEER: *Calling the pitch... lies, as you might imagine, crocked the job*—Philadelphia **6** *n* =CROCK OF SHIT **7** *n computer* Something, esp a program, that functions erratically **8** *n computer* An overly complicated and inalterable program

crocked *adj* Drunk

crockery *n baseball* A pitcher's arm that becomes lame and ineffective; =GLASS ARM

◁ **crock of shit**▷ *n phr* Nonsense; lies and exaggerations; mendacious cant; =BULLSHIT: *Asked about Burns's contention... he replied, "That's a crock of shit"*—Toronto Life

crook **1** *n fr late 1800s* A habitual or professional criminal; a consistently dishonest person: *The chief said, "I'm not a crook"* **2** *v: He crooked my socks*—E Kasser

crooked (KRŏŏ kəd) *adj* Dishonest; fraudulent; criminal

crooked arm *n phr baseball* A left-handed pitcher

crooker *See* PINKY-CROOKER

crook the elbow *See* BEND THE ELBOW

cross *v* To act contrary to someone's wishes; attempt to thwart someone; contradict: *You must not cross me on this*

See DOUBLE CROSS, NAIL someone TO THE CROSS

cross-dresser *n* A transvestite: *I'm constantly getting calls from cross-dressers who think I could use their talents*—Village Voice

crossed idiotsticks *n phr Army* The crossed rifles of the infantry insignia

cross-eyed *See* LOOK AT someone CROSS-EYED

cross someone's **palm** *See* GREASE someone's PALM

cross-up **1** *n* An error, esp one caused by misunderstanding: *nobody's fault, just a cross-up* **2** *n* =DOUBLE CROSS

cross someone **up** *v phr* To confuse or deceive: *He had to cross up the blocking backs*

crotch worker *n phr police* A shoplifter who conceals loot under her dress

crowd someone *v* To press or importune someone; encroach on someone's territory or safety: *Don't crowd me now, just let me handle it*

Crow Jim *n phr* Strong antiwhite prejudice among blacks: *the form of reverse prejudice known as Crow Jim*—Esquire

crown *v* To hit someone, esp on the head; =BEAN, CONK: *If she finds out she'll crown me*

crow tracks *n phr Army* Chevrons showing noncommissioned officers' rank; =STRIPES

crud or **crut** ◁**1**▷ *n* Dried semen **2** *n Army fr 1920s* Any venereal disease **3** *n* (also **the crud**) Any disease, esp one featuring a rash or obvious skin eruption; any unnamed disease: *I probably picked up the crud that's going around* **4** *n* A dirty and slovenly person; =DIRTBALL: *I used to be a smelly crud* **5** *n* Anything loathsome or markedly inferior: *His new show's a piece of crud* **6** *modifier: It's in your ballpark, since you love the crud detail*—Erma Bombeck [fr Middle English, "coagulated milk or other substance, curd," of unknown origin]

cruddy **1** *adj* Nasty; loathsome; repellent **2** *adj* Somewhat ill and indisposed; under par; =BLAH: *I'm not exactly sick, I just feel cruddy*

cruft **1** *n computer* A repellent substance; =CRAP, CRUD: *Clean that cruft up off the floor* **2** *n* The consequences of inferior construction: *He tried for elegance in that design, but ended up with cruft*

cruise **1** *v* To drive slowly and watchfully in the streets, walk about vigilantly in bars and parties, etc, looking for a sex partner: *He started cruising the singles bars* **2** *v* To make a subtle or casual sexual approach: *I dated girls but at the same time was still cruising guys*—Deviant Reality **3** *v Philadelphia black* To sleep **4** *v counterculture* To be smoothly going about one's business: *He was still "cruising nice and mellow" from an acid trip two*

nights before—New York/ Times were tough, but now I'm cruising along
See LET'S BOOGIE

cruising for a bruising *v phr teenagers & college students* Looking for trouble; courting violence, esp while riding about in a car

cruit (KRōōT) *n Army fr WW1* A recruit

crumb or **crum** **1** *n hoboes, cowboys & armed forces fr late 1800s* A louse or bedbug **2** *n hoboes* A blanket roll or pack **3** *n* A dirty, slovenly person; =CRUD, DIRTBALL **4** *n* A loathsome, contemptible person; =CREEP

crumb-bun or **crum-bun** *n* A contemptible person; =BUM, CRUMB: *Unlike the other critic crumb-buns, he has a soul*—Saul Bellow

crumbcrusher *n* (Variations: **crumbcruncher** or **crumbgrinder** or **crumbsnatcher**) *esp students fr 1930s black* A baby; small child: *when your own li'l crumbcrushers suffered through fatherless periods* —Douglas Turner/ *Here comes one crumbsnatcher, then two*—Joseph A Walker

crumb (or **crum**) **the deal** *v phr* To spoil a plan; =LOUSE UP

crumb (or **crum**) **up** *v phr* To spoil; confuse; =MESS UP: *He tried too hard and crumbed the whole thing up*

crummy or **crumby** **1** *adj esp hoboes, cowboys & armed forces fr middle 1800s British* Infested with body lice; lousy **2** *adj* Loathsome; disgusting; =LOUSY: *I'd be dead of the dirty monotony around this crummy neighborhood*—Nelson Algren **3** *adj* Of inferior quality; shoddy; =CHEAP: *This crumby razor doesn't work/ Where'd you get that crummy camera?* **4** *adj* Insignificant; trifling; paltry; =PISSY: *Just two days, two crummy days, an' I woulda been here myself*—WT Tyler [origin unknown; perhaps fr the resemblance of a louse to a *crumb*]

crumped out *adj phr* Drunk

crunch *fr outdated black* **1** *n* A crisis; a desperate climax: *Then came the political conventions that summer, and more crunches*—Clay Felker **2** *n* A critical situation, esp one where two seemingly contrary forces are in play; =SQUEEZE: *A "crunch" is characterized by a skyrocketing of interest rates and a choking off of the availability of credit* —L Silk **3** *n* Tension and strife between opposing interests: *The "crunch" between press and Government is inevitable in American affairs* —J Raymond **4** *v computer* To process, usu in a wearisome way

cruncher *See* NUMBER CRUNCHER

crunching *See* NUMBER-CRUNCHING, NUT-CRUNCHING

crush *See* HAVE A CRUSH ON someone

crust *n fr early 1900s* Bold audacity; gall; =CHUTZPA: *You've got a hell of a crust assuming I'll go down there* —Raymond Chandler
See the UPPER CRUST

crusty *adj* Gruff; surly; =FEISTY: *Crusty George Meany....The downturned lips, the jowls, the half-closed lids, all were dour*—Time

crut *See* CRUD

crybaby **1** *n* A person given to weeping or lamenting at the least adversity, esp from self-pity **2** *modifier: The Georgetown basketball team...has continued its crybaby act* —Milwaukee Journal

cry in one's **beer** *v phr* To indulge in a session of lamentation or weeping; feel keenly sorry for oneself

crying *See* FOR CRYING OUT LOUD

crying jag *n phr* A fit of uncontrollable weeping, often accompanying drunkenness: *Florence got regular crying jags and the men sought to cheer and comfort her*—Dorothy Parker

crying room *n phr* A fancied place where one can go to bewail a defeat, disappointment, etc

crying towel *n phr* A fancied towel offered in ironic sympathy to one who laments undeserved ill fortune, unbearable reverses, etc: *Get out the crying towel, old Frank got another parking ticket*

crystal *n narcotics* Narcotics in powdered form, esp amphetamines

◁ **ct** or **CT**▷ *n* =COCK-TEASER

CTD *adj hospital* Nearly dead [fr *circling the drain*, that is, about to go down]

cub **1** *n newspaper office* A novice reporter **2** *n* Any novice or apprentice **3** *modifier: a cub reporter/ cub professor*

cubehead *n narcotics* A frequent user of LSD [fr sugar *cube*, into which LSD can be soaked before taking]

the **cubes** *n phr* Dice; a pair of dice: *He chose to stake his hopes... on one throw of the cubes*—G Talbot

cuckoo or **coo-coo** **1** *adj fr early 1900s* Crazy; very eccentric; =NUTTY **2** *n: Stop acting like a cuckoo*

cue *v baseball* To hit a baseball hard and straight, as if with a pool cue

cueball **1** *n WW2 armed forces & students* A man or boy with a bald, shaven, or close-clipped head **2** *n* An eccentric person; =ODDBALL

cue in *v phr* To add to, or interpolate into, a script, film, etc: *Change the setting to Arizona and cue in some songs for Doris Day*—Richard Bissell

cue someone **in** *v phr* To explain: *I didn't understand until she cued me in to the procedure*

cuff *fr early 1900s* **1** *v* To borrow money from someone, usu in an urgent way **2** *v* To charge something, esp on an expense account: *No man... feels he is getting ahead until he can cuff a few tabs on the firm* —Hal Boyle [fr the notion of keeping track of debts by notations on the *cuff* of one's shirt]

See OFF THE CUFF, ON THE CUFF

◁ **cuff** one's **meat**▷ *v phr* To masturbate: *He'd still be cuffing his meat in Spain*—Tom Aldibrandi

cuffs *n* Handcuffs

culture vulture *n phr* An enthusiastic devotee of the arts and of intellectual pursuits, esp a pretentious one: *Culture vultures to the contrary, there is more integrity to the guy*—San Francisco

◁ **cum**[1] ▷ *See* COME

cum[2] (KYōōM) *college students* **1** *n* The cumulative academic average of a student **2** *v* To study hard; strive for a high grade-point average

◀ **cunt**▶ **1** *n fr 1300s* The vulva **2** *n* A woman: *Why didn't he spin off this stupid cunt*—Saul Bellow **3** *n homosexuals* A fellow male homosexual one dislikes: *and this one is from Max, the cunt*—Arthur Maling **4** *n* Sexual favors and indulgence; =ASS, FUCKING: *But some of their daughters were giving away more cunt than Dixie was selling*—Claude Brown

◀ **cuntface** or **cunthead**▶ *n* A despicable person; =BASTARD: *cunthead... you wretched fart*—John Irving

◀ **cunt-hair**▶ *n* A very small amount or distance; minute amount; =SMIDGEN, TAD: *knows when it's off center, even when it's only a cunt hair off*—William Kennedy

◀ **cunt-lapping**▶ *n* Cunnilingus: *nor induced Maurice White to advocate cunt-lapping*—Village Voice

◀ **cuntmobile**▶ *n* =RAPE WAGON

cupcake **1** *n* An eccentric person; =NUTBALL: *regarding puppeteers as kind of weird cupcakes who play with dolls*—Washington Post **2** *n* An attractive young woman; =CHICK: *Flossie was a saucy blonde cupcake then*—William Kennedy/ *In her... don't-think-I'm-just-another-cupcake suit, Geraldine A. Ferraro... gave a pep talk*—Philadelphia

one's **cup** (or **dish**) **of tea** *n phr fr British fr 1920s* One's special taste, predilection, etc; =THING: *Ugaritic paleography is not my cup of tea/ Harlem is... his forte and his dish of tea*—Carl Van Vechten

curbie *n* =CARHOP

curdle *v* To offend; disgust: *"It curdles me" [means] "I loathe it"*—Life

curl someone's **hair** *v phr* To shock or appall: *The prices here will curl your hair*

curlies *See* HAVE someone BY THE SHORT HAIRS

currency *See* HARD CURRENCY, SOFT MONEY

the **curse** *n phr* A woman's menstrual period; menstruation: *Is it any wonder that menstruation is commonly called "the curse"*—Saturday Review

curtain climber *n phr esp students* A baby or small child, esp one who is just learning to walk; =CRUMB-CRUSHER, RUG APE

curtains *n* Death; disaster; the bitter end: *It looked like curtains for Ezra then and there*—J Lilienthal [fr the final *curtain* of a show; or perhaps fr the crape *curtains* formerly hung by undertakers at the dead person's door]

cushion *See* the KEYSTONE, WHOOPEE CUSHION

cushy (KōōSH ee) *fr British fr early 1900s* **1** *adj* Easy; easeful; supplying comfort and pleasure: *I landed a cushy post, a soft sinecure at the* *foundation* **2** *adj* Fancy; luxurious; =HIGHFALUTIN, POSH: *I may not know a lot of cushy words*—Budd Schulberg [perhaps fr Hindi *khush* "pleasure" or Romany *kushto* "good," or perhaps fr a shortening of *cushiony*]

cuspy *adj computer* Neat and clean; elegant; efficiently designed [fr *commonly used system program*, a program designed for wide use and typically with a useful simplicity]

cut **1** *v* To absent oneself from without permission or legitimate excuse: *She cut choir practice twice/ to cut class* **2** *n: Anybody with more than four cuts flunks* **3** *n* A share or portion, esp of criminal or gambling profits **4** *v: They cut the million eight ways* **5** *v* To dilute something, esp whiskey or narcotics: *They cut the pure stuff before they sell it on the street* **6** *adj: cut whiskey/ heavily cut cocaine* **7** *v* To shorten a movie, book, manuscript, etc **8** *n: How much of a cut did you make?* **9** *adj: a brutally cut film/ a cut version* **10** *v* To injure someone with an insult or sarcasm: *That crack really cut me* **11** *n: What a nasty cut she gave me* **12** *v* To ignore someone pointedly, esp an acquaintance: *Next time I saw him I cut him* **13** *n: That wasn't a snub, it was a cut* **14** *v* To remove someone from a team, cast, group, etc: *I'll be happy if Coach doesn't cut me* **15** *n: I survived the cut!* **16** *v* To stop doing something; desist • Usu an irritated command: *Cut the foolishness now, and listen* **17** *v* To leave; depart: *Let's cut....We ain't no more than just time, providing we step lively*—W Henry **18** *n* A turn; time; =CRACK: *Have a cut at it yourself* **19** *v baseball* To swing at the ball **20** *n: What a thunderous cut that was!* **21** *v musicians* To outdo someone; best; surpass: *Lydia Lunch, who I feel cuts Yoko on every possible level*—Village Voice **22** *v* To make a phonograph record or tape recording; record: *He cut a couple of demos yesterday* **23** *n* A recording date or session **24** *n* A phonograph record or side, or a separate band on a record

cut someone **a break** *v phr* To give special favor: *He petitioned...Judge Michael Wallace to cut me a break*—Philadelphia Journal

cut (or **crack**) **a deal** *v phr* To make or conclude an arrangement; transact an agreement: *Doesn't it make more sense to cut a deal with the Soviets?*—Philadelphia Journal

◁ **cut a fart**▷ ***See*** LAY A FART

cut a figure *v phr fr middle 1700s* To be important; be imposing; make an impression: *I cut quite a figure in this town, but nowhere else*

cut and dried (or **dry**) *adj phr* Regular, predictable, and uninteresting; pro forma

cut and run *v phr fr middle 1800s* To leave; depart, esp hastily: *If you hear a whistle, cut and run at once* [fr the *cutting* of the anchor cable in the swift departure of a ship]

◁ **cut** someone **a new asshole**▷ *v phr* To rebuke harshly; reprimand severely; =REAM

◁ **cut ass** (or **a**)▷ *v phr* To leave; depart; =HAUL ASS

cut bait *v phr* To cease some activity; stop; discontinue: *Westway Trial: Lawyers Cut Bait*—Village Voice ***See*** FISH OR CUT BAIT

cut didoes (DĪ dohz) *v phr fr British Navy fr middle 1800s* To frivol and frolic; =HORSE AROUND [originally fr the very smart appearance of the British corvette *Dido*]

cute **1** *adj* Shrewd; sly; tricky **2** *adj* Disrespectfully frivolous; =SMART-ASS: *Don't be cute with me, you slimy pimp*

the **cutes** **1** *n phr* Arch and simpering behavior; kittenish ways: *Lina began flapping her dress to give herself air. Then she got the cutes and asked if that was allowed*—James M Cain **2** *n phr* The tendency or habit of constant joking; tasteless frivolity: *born with an incurable case of the cutes*—Time

cutesey or **cutesie** **1** *adj* Archly coy and kittenish; overtly charming: *and the children cutesy freaks*—Judith Crist/ *a cutesey fun book* **2** *n: The author oversimplifies everything and gets carried away with his own cutesies*—Playboy

cutesy-poo or **cutesy-pie** *adj* Designedly arch and simpering to a nauseating degree: *saying anything* *narsty about so cutesy-poo an endeavor*—Judith Crist/ *McWilliams writes in a cloying cutesy-pie style* —New Republic

cutie or **cutey** or **cuty** **1** ***n*** A person or thing that is charming, attractive, clever, etc: *I'm no beauty, but am counted a cutie* **2** ***n*** A person who is shrewd, deceptive, wily, and not to be trusted: *Watch out for that dumb-looking one, he's a cutey*

cutie-pie ***n*** A very attractive person, esp a woman, esp a doll-like one: *my new cutie pies*—Dan Jenkins

cut-in ***n*** The right to share something: *We've each got a cut-in on the profits* —Jerome Weidman

cut someone **in** ***v phr*** To award a share, esp of winnings, loot, etc: *They cut me in for 25 percent of the take*

cut it **1** ***v phr*** (also **cut it out**) To stop doing something; desist • Usu a stern command: *I said cut it right now, that hollering* **2** ***v phr*** *fr loggers* To achieve or finish something; succeed; =HACK IT: *They've been warned that a string group won't cut it with jazz fans*—Peter Occhiogrosso

cut it up ***v phr*** To analyze and discuss; take a close look: *Let's cut it up and see how serious the problem is*

cut one's **losses** ***v phr*** To make the best compromise in a losing situation; salvage or extricate at least something

cut no ice (or **smoke**) ***v phr*** To have no influence or effect; make no difference: *His Nobel Prize don't cut no ice with me/ but that doesn't cut any smoke with the Gov*—New York Daily News

cut oneself **off at the knees** ***v phr*** To disable oneself; =SHOOT oneself IN THE FOOT: *I don't want to cut myself off at the knees by giving figures*—Washingtonian

cut someone **off at the knees** ***v phr*** To deflate or reduce, esp surprisingly: *the nebbish with a disarming wit that could cut you off at the knees*—Philadelphia

cut (or **turn**) **off** someone's **water** ***v phr*** To subdue; deal decisively and damagingly with: *I just smiled sweetly and turned off his water*

cut out **1** ***v phr*** To leave; depart, esp hastily: *So you think you're cutting out? You're not leaving until I leave with you*—Tennessee Williams **2** ***v phr*** *fr late 1800s* To stop doing something; desist: *If you cut out the booze maybe it'll work*

cut-out ***n espionage & police*** A person, business, etc, used to conceal the identity or purpose of a secret operation; =COVER: *The firm operated as a cut-out, or front, for the FBI's purchase*—Time

cut out dolls (or **paper dolls**) ***v phr*** To be insane; behave dementedly: *She has her cutting out paper dolls* —Raymond Chandler

cut one's **own throat** ***v phr*** To ruin oneself; hoist oneself with one's own petard; =SHOOT oneself IN THE FOOT: *If you try to get him that way you'll cut your own throat*

cut someone's **papers** (or **orders**) ***v phr police & Army*** To prepare and distribute official papers such as warrants, writs, assignment orders, etc: *They're still cutting her papers*—The Gauntlet (movie) [probably fr the *cutting*, perforation by typing, of a duplicating-machine stencil]

cutter ***See*** COOKIE-CUTTER, DAISY-CUTTER, PISS-CUTTER

cut the cheese ***See*** CHEESE

cut (or **cut up**) **the melon** (or **the pie**) ***v phr*** To divide and share out receipts, profits, loot, etc

not **cut the mustard** ***See*** NOT CUT THE MUSTARD

cut the (or **a**) **rug** ***v phr esp 1930s jive talk*** To dance, esp in jitterbug style

cutthroat ***adj*** Very harsh and barbarous: *a cutthroat game/ cutthroat competition*

cut two ways ***See*** WORK BOTH WAYS

cut up **1** ***v phr*** *fr middle 1800s* To behave frivolously; frolic; =HORSE AROUND **2** ***v phr underworld*** To divide profits, loot, etc **3** ***v phr underworld*** To discuss; go over carefully **4** ***v phr*** To speak ill of; analyze maliciously: *Or they can collectively "cut up" the girls they see around*—Sexual Behavior

cut-up **1** ***n*** A prankster; practical joker; antic rogue: *Uncle is a cut-up, owner of all kinds of gimmicks* **2** ***n esp late 1800s*** An energetic and entertaining person: *a great cut-up. He could dance a bit, sing better than average, and had a sense of comedy* —HR Hoyt **3** ***adj*** Upset; hurt; distressed: *She was pretty cut up about not getting a paper*—Richard Peck

cuty ***See*** CUTIE

cut Zs ***See*** COP ZS

◁ **cuzzy** ▷ ***See*** COOZ

CYA ***See*** COVER one's ASS

the **cycle** ***See*** HIT FOR THE CYCLE

D

D *n* A dollar
See BIG D

DA (pronounced as separate letters) *n* District Attorney

daaa *See* TAH-DAH

dab *See* SMACK

dad **1** *n* An old man ● Used as a disrespectful address towards older men. The similar term **pop** is not similarly disrespectful: *Okay, dad, outa the way and you won't get hurt* **2** *n* God ● Used euphemistically as an element in various old-fashioned mild oaths like **dad-blamed**
See HO-DAD

dad-blamed or **dad-blasted** *adj* (also **dag-blamed** or **dag-blasted**) Wretched; accursed; =DARN: *Git outa my dad-blamed way*

daddy **1** *n* *fr black* A male lover, esp one who keeps a younger mistress; =SUGAR DADDY **2** *n* The most respected man in a field; cynosure; dean: *Gary Cooper, the daddy of all cowboys*
See DISNEYLAND DADDY, HO-DAD, ZOO DADDY

Daddy-o or **daddy-o** *n fr bop talk* Man; old guy; =GUY ● Used in addressing men, sometimes older men, respectfully and amiably

daffy *adj fr British fr late 1800s* Crazy; =NUTS: *He tries to convince her that she is not daffy*—SJ Perelman/ *Most of his cherished tenets are quite daffy* [fr British dialect *daff* "fool, simpleton"; *daffish* is attested fr the 15th century]
See STIR-CRAZY

daffydill *n* An insane person; =NUT

dag-blamed or **dag-blasted** *See* DAD-BLAMED

dagged *adj* Drunk

dagger *See* BULLDYKE

daggone *See* DOGGONE

dagnab *See* DOGGONE

◀ **dago** or **Dago** ▶ *fr early 1700s* **1** *n* An Italian or person of Italian descent: *Hey, Fiorello, you're a dago* —Fiorello H LaGuardia **2** *adj* Italian **3** *n* The Italian language **4** *n fr middle 1800s* A person of Hispanic birth or descent [fr *Diego* "James," used in the 17th century to mean "Spaniard"; the narrowing to "Italian" occurred in the 20th century]

◀ **dago** (or **Dago**) **red** ▶ *n phr* Cheap red table wine, esp of Italian origin or type

dagwood *n* A large thick sandwich of many ingredients [from *Dagwood* Bumstead, a comic-strip character who made tall and complex sandwiches]

dah *See* TAH-DAH

the **daisies** *n phr baseball* The outfield

daisy **1** *n fr middle 1700s* A person or thing that is remarkable, wonderful, superior, etc; =DILLY, HONEY: *My new car's a daisy* ◁**2**▷ *n* A male homosexual; =PANSY ◁**3**▷ *n* A weak, effeminate, or cowardly man; =SISSY, WIMP

daisy-cutter **1** *n baseball* A grounder or very low line drive **2** *n* A very low tennis shot **3** *n* A horse that trots with its hooves near the ground **4** *n WW2 Army* An antipersonnel bomb or mine that ejects shrapnel close to the ground

dally *See* DILLY-DALLY

damaged *adj* Drunk

dame *n* A woman; =BROAD, DOLL

damn **1** *interj* (also **damn it**) An exclamation of disappointment, irritation, frustration, etc: *Damn, it's gone!* **2** *adj* (also **damned**) Cursed; accursed; wretched: *What do I do with this damned thing?* **3** *adv: You seem damn stupid all of a sudden*
See HOT DAMN

a **damn** *See* NOT GIVE A DAMN, WORTH A DAMN

damned *See* I'LL BE DAMNED

damn-fool *adj* =DAMN, DAMNED

damn tootin' *See* YOU'RE DAMN TOOTIN'

Dan *See* DAPPER DAN

dance *n street gang* A fight between rival gangs; =RUMBLE
See GO INTO one's DANCE, RAIN DANCE, SONG AND DANCE, TAP DANCE

dancehall *prison* **1** *n* A death-house or execution chamber **2** *n* The cells or cell block adjoining an execution chamber [fr outdated underworld *dance* "die by hanging"]

dance off *v phr* To die, esp by legal execution

dance on air (or **on nothing**) *v phr* To die by hanging

dancer *See* GO-GO GIRL

D and D or **dee-dee** *adj phr* or *adj police* Drunk and disorderly

dander *See* GET one's DANDER UP

dandy **1** *n* A person or thing that is remarkable, wonderful, superior, etc: *You should get one, it's a dandy* **2** *adj: a dandy idea* **3** *adv: He does it dandy/ We get on just dandy*
See HOTSIE-TOTSIE, JIM-DANDY

◁ **dang[1]** ▷ **1** *n* The penis; =DONG **2** *adj* Sexually stimulating; =FOXY

dang[2] **1** *interj* (also **dang it**) An exclamation of disappointment, irritation, frustration, etc: *Dang, we missed the Welk show* **2** *adj* (also **danged**) Wretched; nasty; silly **3** *adv* Extremely: *You looked dang silly* [a euphemism for *damn*, which is regarded by some as taboo]

a **dang** *See* NOT GIVE A DAMN

danged *See* I'LL BE DAMNED

dapper (or **fancy**) **Dan** *n phr* An ostentatiously well-groomed man, usu one not inured to hard work: *the fancy Dans, dressed fit to kill*—A Lomax

darb *n esp 1920s* A person or thing that is remarkable, wonderful, superior, etc; =LULU [perhaps fr Ruby *Darby*, the name of an Oklahoma showgirl much admired by oil-drillers, who would praise a new gusher as a "Ruby Darby" or "a Darb"; perhaps fr *dab* "an expert"]

darbies or **derbies** *n* Handcuffs [fr a form of British usurer's bond called *Father Derby's* (or *Darby's*) bands]

dark horse **1** *n phr fr horse-racing* A person or team, esp in sports or politics, that seems very unlikely to win but might nevertheless do so **2** *modifier: a dark-horse candidate*

dark meat ◀**1**▶ *n phr* A black person, esp a woman, regarded solely as a sex partner ◀**2**▶ *n phr* A black person's body and genitals

◀ **darky** ▶ *n* A black person

darn or **dern** or **durn** *fr middle 1700s* **1** *interj* (also **darn it** or **dern it** or **durn it**) An exclamation of disappointment, irritation, frustration, etc: *Darn, I've dropped my glockenspiel!* **2** *adj* (also **darned** or **darnfool** or **derned** or **durned**) Wretched; nasty; silly: *Where does this darn lamp go?/ sentimental songs, darnfool ditties, revival hymns*—Virgil Thompson **3** *adv: She was darn excited* [euphemism for *damn*, which is regarded by some as taboo]

a **darn** or **a dern** or **a durn** *See* NOT GIVE A DAMN

darned *See* I'LL BE DAMNED

darning needles *See* RAIN CATS AND DOGS

darn tootin' *See* YOU'RE DAMN TOOTIN'

dash *n* The dashboard of a car: *I keep a gun under the dash*
See SLAPDASH

dat (DAT) *n Army* A tank-crew member [fr *dumbass tanker*]

date **1** *n* An engagement or rendezvous, esp with a member of the other sex **2** *n* A man or woman with whom one has an engagement or rendezvous: *He's her date for tonight* **3** *v: How many girls have you dated this week?*
See BLIND DATE, HEAVY DATE

date someone **up** *v phr* To schedule a social engagement or rendezvous with

Dave or **David** *n shoeshop* The shoe width D

day *See* EAGLE DAY, HAVE A FIELD DAY, MAKE MY DAY, MOTHER'S DAY, NINETY-DAY WONDER, NOT GIVE someone THE TIME OF DAY, RED-LETTER DAY

day-glo *adj* Blatantly gaudy; cheaply flashy: *smoldering pageant turns totally day-glo*—Village Voice/ *day-glo glamor*—Us [fr the trade name of a brand of paint that makes things glow under a black light and produces lurid, psychedelic color effects]

daylight *v* To work at a second job during the day: *who is daylighting in an ad agency as a producer of commercials*—Playboy
See LET DAYLIGHT INTO, PUT DAYLIGHT BETWEEN

the **daylights** or **the living daylights** *See* BEAT THE SHIT OUT OF someone or something

days *See* DOG DAYS

◁ the **day the eagle shits**▷ (or **screams**) *n phr esp armed forces* Payday [fr the *eagle* as symbol of the US government]

dazzle *See* RAZZLE-DAZZLE

dead **1** *adj* Very tired; =BEAT, POOPED **2** *adj* Not operating; not startable: *Damn battery's dead* **3** *adj* Ruined; destroyed: *As far as another chance goes, I'm dead* **4** *adj* No longer under consideration: *The ERA's dead again* **5** *adj* Dull; tedious and uninteresting: *another dead sermon* **6** *adj* Lacking brilliance and overtones; flat; dull: *The trumpets sounded dead* **7** *adj* Absolute; assured: *It's a dead certainty he'll run again* **8** *adv: I'm dead broke/ dead set against it* **9** *n post office* A letter or package that can neither be delivered nor returned [the sense "absolute, assured, certain" probably developed fr expressions like Middle English *ded oppressed* "completely overcome," 16th-century *dead drunk*, and others suggesting the inertness of death; when inertness suggested fixedness, unchangingness, certainty, etc, the term took on these present senses]
See DROP DEAD, KNOCK someone DEAD, NOT BE CAUGHT DEAD, STONE DEAD, STOP someone or something DEAD IN someone's or something's TRACKS

dead as a dodo (or **doornail**) *adj phr* Absolutely lifeless; entirely hopeless • *doornail* form fr 1300s: *The Philadelphia Bulletin is dead, dead as a doornail*—Philadelphia

◁ **deadass**▷ **1** *n* A stupid, boring person; an absolute dullard: *these deadasses in the loony bin*—Tom Wolfe **2** *adj: There are so many deadass people out there, boring each other to death*—San Francisco **3** *adv* Completely; totally: *You're deadass wrong when you say I got nothing to go on*—William Brashler
See GET OFF one's ASS

deadbeat *fr middle 1800s* **1** *n* A person who habitually begs or gets money from others, does not pay his or her debts, etc; =MOOCHER, SCHNORRER: *a chance to demand immediate payment if the clerk looks like a deadbeat*—Time **2** *n* A tramp or hobo, esp one riding on a freight train **3** *v* To sponge, loaf, etc: *Living off interest is not exactly deadbeating* [fr *dead* "complete, completely" and *beat* "sponger"]

dead broke *adj phr* Totally without money; destitute

dead duck (or **pigeon**) *n phr fr middle 1800s* A person or thing that is ruined; =a GONER: *Just one more little push and she was a dead duck*—Changes/ *Unless somebody would start this mob to the sugar bowl, I was a dead pigeon*—Max Shulman

dead from the neck up *adj phr* Stupid; dull; =KLUTZY

dead giveaway *n phr* An unmistakable and definitive clue: *His blushing was a dead giveaway*

Deadhead *n* A devotee of the rock-and-roll group the Grateful Dead

dead heat *n phr fr horse-racing fr middle 1800s* A tied race, contest, etc: *The election ended in a dead heat* [fr *dead* "absolute, total, thorough," related to the finality of death, and *heat* "a single course of a race," related either to a single firing or heating of a mass of metal, or to the heating of the body in running, or to both]

dead horse (or **letter**) *n phr* A matter no longer of concern or currency; a bygone issue: *I'm afraid free love is a dead letter these days*
See BEAT A DEAD HORSE

dead in the water *adj phr* Unable to move; stalled; defunct: *Right now, the economy is dead in the water, with 10.8 percent unemployment*—New York Times [fr the image of a disabled ship, unable to proceed]

deadly **1** *adj* Boring; extremely tedious; dull: *I came prepared for a long and deadly meeting* **2** *adj*

1940s jive talk Excellent; admirable; =COOL

dead man's hand *n phr poker fr late 1800s* A hand containing a pair of aces and a pair of eights [fr the tradition that Wild Bill Hickock held such a hand when Jack McCall shot him in 1876]

deadpan **1** *n* An expressionless face; =POKER FACE **2** *n* A person with an expressionless face: *Buster Keaton and Fred Allen were classic deadpans* **3** *v: With kids packing his audiences, he deadpanned "I promise to lower the voting age to 6"* —Newsweek **4** *adj: This is known as the deadpan system of prevarication*—AJ Liebling

dead pigeon *See* DEAD DUCK

dead ringer *n phr fr early 1900s* An exact duplicate, esp a person who is the double of another: *He was such a dead ringer for my ex-boss*—Jerome Weidman [fr *dead* "precise, exact" and *ring in* "substitute, esp fraudulently," an early-19th-century slang term fr gambling]

dead soldier (or **marine**) *fr British Navy fr early 1800s* **1** *n phr* An empty or emptied bottle, esp a liquor bottle **2** *n phr* Food or plates of food only partially eaten: *on the way to the kitchen with the dead soldiers, or leftovers*—Louis Armstrong

deadsville *adj* Dull; boring: *the young people who always felt that cruises were deadsville*—Newsweek

dead (or **bang**) **to rights** *adv phr fr middle 1800s* With no possibility of escape or evasion; in flagrante delicto; redhanded: *was caught "dead to rights" and now languishes in the city Bastille*—San Francisco City Argus

deal **1** *v* To negotiate, esp over a purchase or sale; chaffer: *"Okay," said Mack, "let's deal"* **2** *v* To be active and aggressive in making arrangements, tradeoffs, sales, etc; =WHEEL AND DEAL: *Sophie did all the dealing there*—Nelson Algren **3** *v narcotics* To sell narcotics; be a peddler **4** *v* To pitch a baseball: *The big lefthander deals a smoker* **5** *n fr late 1800s* A usu secret arrangement between politicians, rulers, business executives, etc: *He made a deal with the Republicans... to suppress the charges*—RG Spivack **6** *n* Situation; thing in hand or at issue: *The deal is that I'm tired of this whole farce*

See BIG DEAL, CRUMB THE DEAL, GOOD DEAL, MAKE A BIG PRODUCTION, NO BIG DEAL, PLAY WITH A FULL DECK, RAW DEAL, SWEETHEART DEAL

deal someone **a poor deck** *v phr* To treat cruelly and unjustly *who's bitter and thinks she's been dealt a poor deck*—AT Fleming

dealer **1** *n gambling* A person who makes a living from gambling, whether or not an actual dealer-out of cards: *A bookmaker, who is known as a dealer in refined usage*—T Betts **2** *n* A person involved actively and aggressively in a range of negotiations, trades, purchases, etc; =WHEELER-DEALER **3** *n narcotics* A person who sells narcotics; peddler; =PUSHER: *The "dealer" (not "pusher") is the man who sells all this* —New York Times

See WHEELER-DEALER

deal someone **in** *v phr* To make someone a participant; let someone share: *He heard we were going and said deal him in*

deal with a full deck *See* PLAY WITH A FULL DECK

dearie *n* Dear person; cherished one • A somewhat vulgar term of address used chiefly by women: *If you wore it you can't return it, dearie*

Dear John **1** *n phr fr WW2 armed forces* A letter or other means of informing a fiance, spouse, boyfriend, etc, that one is breaking off the relationship **2** *modifier: Dear-John letter*

death *See* LOOK LIKE DEATH WARMED OVER, SUDDEN DEATH

death snow *n phr narcotics* Poisoned or contaminated cocaine

death warmed over *See* LOOK LIKE DEATH WARMED OVER

deb **1** *n* A debutante **2** *n street gang* A member of a girl's street gang: *organized with sub-gangs of... "debs"*—New York Times

◁ **de-ball** ▷ *See* DE-NUT

Decatur *See* EIGHTER FROM DECATUR

deceivers *See* FALSIES

deck **1** *n hoboes* The roof of a railroad car **2** *n narcotics* A package of narcotics; portion of a drug, esp three grains of heroin; =BAG: *a deck of nose candy for sale*—J Evans **3**

n A package of cigarettes **4** *v* To knock someone down, esp with the fist; =FLOOR: *Remember that guy I decked in the restaurant?*—Lawrence Sanders

See DEAL someone A POOR DECK, HIT THE DECK, ON DECK, PLAY WITH A FULL DECK

decker ***See*** JOKER

decrease the volume *v phr teenagers* To speak lower • Usu a command or request

deduck (DEE duck) *n* A deduction, esp from one's taxable income: *more deducks or we're dead ducks*

dee-dee ***See*** D AND D

deejay ***See*** DISC JOCKEY

deek *n* A detective; =DICK

deely bopper or **deely bobber** or **beely bopper** *n phr* A small hat equipped with bobbing wire antennas like those of an insect or some extraterrestrial creature: *a decor of remaindered Deely Bobbers and airsick bags*—Newsweek

deep end ***See*** GO OFF THE DEEP END, JUMP OFF THE DEEP END

deep freeze ***See*** IN COLD STORAGE

deepie or **depthie** *n esp 1950s* A three-dimensional movie: *The deepies released so far have been gimmick pictures*—Associated Press

deep pocket *n phr* Wealth; available riches and financial security: *He felt more comfortable with the deepest pocket available*—Wall Street Journal

deep pockets *n phr* Sources of much money; rich persons: *He didn't hit the really deep pockets, as divorce lawyers say, until 1964*—Washington Post

deep six *fr Navy & merchant marine* **1** *n phr* A grave **2** *v phr* To discard; jettison; throw overboard: *If any publication is deep-sixed, it will almost certainly be "The Car Book"*—Mother Jones [probably fr the combined notions of a grave as *six* feet *deep* and a fathom as *six* feet in *depth*]

See GIVE something THE DEEP SIX

deep trouble (or ◁**shit**▷) *n phr* Very serious trouble: *One slip and you're in deep trouble/ He was in deep shit with Big Lou*—Rolling Stone

defense ***See*** NICKEL DEFENSE

degree ***See*** THIRD DEGREE

deke *v fr Canadian hockey* To trick, esp by decoying; =FAKE someone OUT: *My friend, you deked me*—George V Higgins [fr *decoy*]

delay ***See*** GAPER'S BLOCK

Delhi belly *n phr* Diarrhea

deli or **delly** or **dellie** (DELL ee) **1** *n* A delicatessen: *a nice smelly deli* **2** ***modifier:*** *deli food/ treat from the deli counter*

delish (dee LISH) ***adj*** Delicious

deliver or **deliver the goods** *v* or *v phr* To perform successfully, esp after promising; =COME THROUGH: *It's a very tough assignment, but he thinks he can deliver/ He talks big, but can he deliver the goods?*

Dem or **Demo** **1** *n* A Democrat **2** *adj: the Dem boss/ Demo congressmen*

demo[1] (DEH moh) *n* A demolition worker

demo[2] (DEH moh) **1** *n* A record or tape made to demonstrate the abilities of musicians, the quality of a song, etc: *Mark's got a good demo to pitch the new song with* **2** *n* A computer disk or tape cassette made to demonstrate the abilities of a particular program: *I tried out their software demo before I bought their package* **3** ***modifier:*** *Let's try the demo disk* **4** *n* A demonstration of protest or other conviction, esp by a large crowd with banners, etc: *a no-nukes demo*

Denmark ***See*** GO TO DENMARK

den mother *n phr homosexuals* The head and sometimes provider or supporter of a group of male homosexuals, often an older man: *They had a sort of den mother. A middle-aged writer type who had given up the straight life*—Patrick Mann

◁**de-nut** or **de-ball**▷ *v* To castrate

Denver boot ***See*** BOOT

depth ***See*** OUT OF one's DEPTH

depthie ***See*** DEEPIE

derail *v* To throw off the proper course; wreck: *He managed to derail the proposal just before Christmas*—Time

derbies ***See*** DARBIES

Derbyville *n* Louisville, Kentucky

dern ***See*** DARN

a **dern** ***See*** a DARN, NOT GIVE A DAMN

derned ***See*** DARN

derriere or **derrière** (deh ree EHR) *n* The buttocks; rump: *So gangway everybody, mother's off her derriere again*—American Home [fr French]

designer **1** *n* *underworld* A counterfeiter **2** *modifier* Of high quality; bearing a famous label: *Ah, designer ennui*—Village Voice

designer drug *n phr* A synthesized narcotic, often of much higher potency than those produced from plants: *These new "designer drugs" or "super narcotics" are triply dangerous*—Good Housekeeping

desk jockey *n phr* An office worker: *Let some desk jockey in the home office envy you*—Hal Boyle

detox *v narcotics* To free someone of a narcotics addiction; detoxify: *I jumped in and out of opium habits but eventually de-toxed for good* —Saturday Review/ *We can detox a heroin addict...in three weeks*—G Hoenig

deuce **1** *n* A two of playing cards **2** *n* *poker* A pair of cards of the same value **3** *n* Two dollars **4** *n* *prison* A two-year prison sentence: *did a deuce together at Joliet*—Kansas City Confidential **5** *n* *street gang* A quitter; coward; petty thief **6** *n* (also **deuce coupe**) *hot rodders* A powerful or handsome specially prepared car, esp a 1932 Ford
See FORTY-DEUCE

the **deuce** **1** *n phr* *fr British fr 1700s* =the HELL **2** *n phr* *esp teenagers* Forty-second Street in New York City, mecca for many teenage runaways; =FORTY-DEUCE: *in the peep shows and urinals and bars of the Deuce*—Village Voice

deuce and a half *n phr Army* A two-and-a-half ton truck

deuce of clubs *n phr reformatory* Both fists

Devil *See* RED

the **devil** *See* the HELL

devil-may-care *adj fr middle 1800s* Reckless; cavalier: *a devil-may-care insouciance*

devoon (də Vo͞oN) *adj 1940s teenagers* Divine; great: *"Devoon," said Jeanie languidly*—Billy Rose

dew *See* MOUNTAIN DEW

dexie or **dexy** *n students* A tablet of Dexedrine, trade name of a brand of amphetamine: *You can take dexies, but you can get hooked on them* —Stephen Longstreet

dial something **out** *v phr* To put firmly out of one's mind; ignore designedly: *All I had to do was concentrate on driving. I had a real excuse to dial it all out*—Sports Illustrated

diamonds **1** *n* (also **black diamonds**) Coal: *throwing diamonds in the firebox*—Casey Jones **2** *n* The testicles; =FAMILY JEWELS

diarrhea of the mouth *See* VERBAL DIARRHEA

dib **1** *n* Money, esp a share of money: *I ought to collect the kid's dib, too*—Dashiell Hammett **2** *n* A dollar: *fifty sweet dibs*—Samuel Hopkins Adams [fr *divvy*]

dibs **1** *n* *fr British fr early 1800s* Money: *How did you make your dibs?* —Raymond Chandler **2** *n* (also **dibs on**) A claim; a preemptive declaration: *It's mine, I said dibs first/ Dibs on the front seat* [perhaps fr *dibstones*, a children's game played with small bones or other counters]

dice *v fr British 1950s car-racing* To jockey for position in a race: *I had no really sharp feeling about dicing with Parnelli*—Sports Afield [fr the amusing melodramatic phrase "to dice with death"]
See LOAD THE DICE, NO DICE, SLICE AND DICE FILM

dicey *adj fr British* Risky; perilous: *African investment is dicey*—Newsweek/ *Updike indulged in many dicey curlicues*—Commonweal/ *the dicey art of writing a farce*—New York Times

dick[1] or **deek** *fr early 1900s underworld* **1** *n* A detective **2** *n* Any police officer; =BULL [fr a shortening and altering of *detective*]

◁ **dick**[2] ▷ **1** *n* *fr middle 1800s British armed forces* The penis **2** *v* To do the sex act with; =SCREW: *If he went and dicked your twelve-year-old sister...he wouldn't tell you all about it*—Richard Merkin **3** *v* (also **dick around**) To potter or meddle; play; =MESS, SCREW AROUND: *That's federal merchandise you're dicking with, right, marshal?*—WT Tyler/ *still in the kitchen, dicking around with the sushi* —Armistead Maupin **4** *n* A despised person; =PRICK: *You dick!* —Cameron Crowe [perhaps fr the nickname *Dick*, an instance of the widespread use of affectionate names for the genitals; perhaps fr earlier British *derrick* "penis"; perhaps fr a dialect survival of Middle English *dighten* "do the sex act with," in a locution like "he dight her," which would be pronounced "he dicked her"]

See CLIPPED DICK, DOES A WOODEN HORSE HAVE A HICKORY DICK, DONKEY DICK, LIMP-DICK, STEP ON IT

Dick ***See*** EVERY TOM, DICK, AND HARRY

◁ **dick-brained**▷ ***adj*** Stupid; crazy; =NUTTY: *coke-snorting super freaks, dick-brained Bob Marley tribute, and jive ooh-la-la*—Village Voice

◁ **dickey**▷ ***n*** =DICK²

◁ **dickhead**▷ ***n*** A despised person; =BASTARD, PRICK: *Why would I possibly want to check out a dickhead like you?*—Richard Merkin

◁ **dick-licker** or **dickey-licker**▷ ***n*** A person who does fellatio, most often a male homosexual; =COCKSUCKER

diddle 1 ***v*** (also **diddle around**) *fr early 1800s British* To waste time; idle; loaf **2** ***v*** *fr early 1800s British* To cheat; swindle ◁**3**▷ ***v*** *fr late 1800s* To do the sex act; =SCREW ◁**4**▷ ***v*** *fr early 1900s* To insert a finger into a woman's vulva; =FINGERFUCK

diddly or **diddley** (Variations: **damn** or **poo** or **poop** or **shit** or **squat** or **squirt** or **whoop** may be added) **1** ***adj*** Trivial; insignificant: *Tennis was a diddly sport back then*—Sports Illustrated/ *If you had a choice between ...IBM or a diddly-squirt upstart*—Newsweek **2** ***n*** Nothing at all; very little; =ZILCH: *Rock critics don't mean diddley*—Rolling Stone/ *I don't know a diddly damn about theater*—Washingtonian/ *And Hannibal, he didn't do diddly-squat*—Pulpsmith

See NOT GIVE A DAMN, NOT KNOW BEANS

diddy bag ***See*** DITTY BAG

diddybop ***See*** DITTYBOP

didie ***n*** A baby's diaper

DIDO (DĪ doh) **1** ***sentence*** *fr computer* A product can be no better than its constituents; esp, the validity of a computer's output cannot surpass the validity of the input; =GIGO **2** ***modifier:*** *The DIDO principle still applies to its contents*—Village Voice [fr the abbreviation of *dreck in, dreck out* "shit in, shit out"]

didoes ***See*** CUT DIDOES

die 1 ***v*** To laugh uncontrollably: *When he puts a lampshade on his head you could die*—Max Shulman **2** ***v*** To desire very strongly: *She was dying to become Miss Pancake*

die for something ***v phr*** To have a very strong desire for something: *I'm dying for a drink/ Kids die for Sugar Glops*

die on one's **feet** ***v phr*** To become absolutely exhausted; carry on although one can hardly move

◁ **diesel dyke**▷ ***n phr*** An aggressive, masculine lesbian; =BULLDYKE: *a man fighting with a diesel-dyke over a girl they both wanted*—Maledicta

die with one's **boots on** ***v phr*** To die while still active and vital

diff or **dif** ***n*** *fr middle 1800s* Difference: *don't make no diff*

difference ***See*** the SAME DIFFERENCE

different strokes for different folks ***interj*** *fr black* A comment on the inevitable and tolerable variety of people and their ways: *Different strokes for different folks, I remarked*—Arthur Maling

dig 1 ***v*** *fr middle 1800s* To study very diligently; exert oneself: *I had to dig to master even the rudiments* **2** ***v*** To interrogate or inquire vigorously: *She won't tell you, no matter how hard you dig* **3** ***n*** A derogatory, irritating, or contemptuous comment: *It wasn't quite an insult, more a dig* **4** ***n*** An archeological excavation **5** ***v*** *cool talk & counterculture fr jive talk* To understand; comprehend: *I dig your sense, but not its pertinence* **6** ***v*** *cool talk & counterculture fr jive talk* To like; admire; prefer: *Do you dig gazpacho and macho?* **7** ***v*** =DIG UP **8** ***v*** To hear or see in performance; =CATCH: *dug a heavy sermon at Smoky Mary's last week* [the cool senses, originally black, are probably related to the early-19th-century sense, "study hard, strive to understand"]

See TAKE A DIG AT someone

dig dirt ***v phr*** *esp 1920s* To gossip

digger 1 ***n*** *fr WW1* An Australian **2** ***n*** =GOLD-DIGGER **3** ***n*** A pickpocket **4** ***n*** A person who buys tickets to be sold at prices higher than is legally permitted; =SCALPER: *They use diggers, dozens of guys who stand in lines and buy the maximum*—New York Times

diggety or **diggity** ***See*** HOT DIGGETY

digs or **diggings** *n fr early 1800s* Lodgings; quarters: *Your digs, or mine?*

dig up *v phr* To find or discover: *She dug up a shirt and we went out*

dike *See* DYKE

dikey *See* DYKEY

dildo or **dildoe** **1** *n* An artificial substitute for an erect penis **2** *n* (also **dill**) A stupid and despicable person; =JERK, PRICK

diller *See* CHILLER-DILLER, KILLER, THRILLER-DILLER

dilly or **dill** *n* A person or thing that is remarkable, wonderful, superior, etc; =BEAUT, LULU: *The last one is a dilly if you don't have an appointment*—RS Prather

dilly-dally *v* To idle; dither in an aimless or pointless fashion: *Stop dilly-dallying and get to the point*

dim *adj* Stupid; uncomprehending: *a nice man, but a trifle dim*

dim bulb *n phr* A stupid person; =DIMWIT: *a peculiar combination of dim bulb and bump-on-a-log*—Washington Post

dime **1** *n underworld* A ten-year prison sentence **2** *n gambling* A thousand dollars, esp as a bet **3** *v* (also **drop a dime**) *underworld & prison* To inform on someone; =SING, SQUEAL: *Frankie would have been okay if somebody hadn't dimed on him* [final sense from the *dime* dropped into the pay telephone for the call to the police]

See FIVE-AND-TEN, GET OFF THE DIME, NICKEL AND DIME, ON someone's DIME, ON one's OWN TIME AND OWN DIME, STOP ON A DIME, a THIN DIME

a **dime a dozen** *adj* Very common; very cheap; in surplus: *PhDs are a dime a dozen now/ Copycats are a dime a dozen*—Sports Illustrated

dime bag or **dime** *n phr* or *n narcotics* Ten dollars' worth of a narcotic

dime dropper *n phr* An informer; =FINK: *Somebody that talks, turns state's evidence on you, a dime dropper*—Village Voice

dime store *n phr* =FIVE-AND-TEN

dimwit *n* A stupid person; =BOOB

dinch *fr underworld* **1** *v* To crush out a cigar or cigarette **2** *n* A cigarette or cigar butt

din-din *n fr late 1800s British* Dinner: *kisses, candlelight, din-din, liqueurs*—Philadelphia

ding **1** *v hoboes* To go on the road as a hobo; =BUM: *When you go bumming, you go dinging*—New Yorker **2** *modifier: in the ding camp at San Jose*—New Yorker **3** *v hoboes* To beg; =BUM, PANHANDLE **4** *v college students* To vote against a candidate for membership; blackball **5** *n: She got six yeahs and five dings* **6** *n college students* A letter rejecting one's application for a job or interview: *most disappointed in the dings that come on postcards*—Wall Street Journal **7** *n* A blow; a buffet: *We get a ding a day from the Chinese*—Time **8** *v fr Army* To administer a reprimand or an adverse appraisal: *If we dinged people, very seldom did they get jobs*—Washingtonian

See RING-A-DING-DING, RING-DING

ding-a-ling **1** *n* An eccentric person; =NUT, SCREWBALL: *great for teeny-boppers and cute little ding-a-lings*—Jackie Collins **2** *adj: It's the ding-a-ling capital of the universe*—Dan Jenkins [fr the notion that such a person hears bells ringing in the head]

dingbat **1** *n fr middle 1800s* An unspecified or unspecifiable object; something one does not know the name of or does not wish to name; =DINGUS, GADGET: *I don't think any wire and glass dingbat is going to "oontz" out cheek-to-cheek dancing*—Billy Rose/ *You can take your pulse now with a little dingbat stuck on your finger* **2** *n fr early 1900s Australian* A stupid person, esp a vague and inane simpleton; =DIMWIT: *"All in the Family" was re-exported to the BBC complete with "Polack pinko meatheads," ... "dingbats," and "spades"*—D Taylor **3** *n print shop* Any of various typographic symbols used as decorations, separators, emphasizers, trademark and union-done indicators, etc [first sense fr German or Dutch *dinges* "thing"]

ding-ding *n* A stupid person; idiot; =DINGBAT: *or have that ding-ding of a driver inform the cops*—Glendon Swarthout

ding-dong **1** *n* A bell **2** *n railroad* A gas-powered or gas-electric coach **3** *adj* Vigorous and spirited; =KNOCK-DOWN-DRAG-OUT: *A ding-dong battle is in prospect*—Fortune

4 *n* An eccentric person; =DING-A-LING, NUT ◁**5**▷ *n* The penis; =DONG: *couldn't find his own ding-dong if you told him to look between his legs*—Calvin Trillin

◀ **dinge** ▶ (DINJ) **1** *n fr 1920s* A black person **2** *modifier: You say this here is a dinge joint?*—Raymond Chandler [fr *dingy* "dark," used as a term for black persons fr early 1900s]

dinger *n baseball* A base hit **1** *modifier: He was in an 11-game dinger drought*—Sports Illustrated

ding how (or **hao**) *adj phr fr WW2 armed forces* Very good; splendid: *It was a ding how operation all the way* [fr Chinese]

ding-swizzled *adj* or *adv* =DARNED, DAMNED
See I'LL BE DAMNED

dingus *n fr middle 1800s* Any unspecified or unspecifiable object; something one does not know the name of or does not wish to name; =GADGET, GIZMO: *What's that dingus in the corner?/ Hey, don't touch my dingus* [fr Dutch *dinges*, of the same meaning, essentially "thing"]

ding ward *n phr* The psychiatric ward of a hospital

dink[1] **1** *n college students* A tiny cap worn by freshmen ◁**2**▷ *n* The penis **3** *n* A despised person; =JERK, PRICK: *Nor, he insists, does he believe that any witless dink could learn to play like Ringo Starr within a week*—Rolling Stone **4** *n* Very little; nothing; =ZILCH: *He knows dink about weapons* **5** *v* To move slowly and jerkily: *after finding that the campaign was dinking along like a Toonerville trolley*—Time [fr *dinky*]

◀ **dink**[2] ▶ *n Vietnam War armed forces* A Vietnamese; =GOOK, SLOPE [related to Australian *Dink* "a Chinese," perhaps fr *dinge* or fr *Chink*]

dink[3] *n* A yacht's tender; dinghy

dink[4] *See* RINKY-DINK

dinky **1** *adj* Small; undersized: *a dinky foreign car/ dinky little town* **2** *adj* Inadequate; substandard: *What a dinky joint!*

dinner *See* SHOOT one's COOKIES

dip[1] **1** *n fr middle 1800s underworld* A pickpocket **2** *v: Frankie dipped two men on the 37 bus* [fr *dipping* one's hand into a pocket]

dip[2] **1** *n fr 1920s* A stupid person; simpleton; =DIPSHIT: *That goddamned dip's worse than the Cowboys*—WT Tyler **2** *n* An eccentric person; =NUT: *My grandmother was a woefully crazy lady... a bit of a dip*—Carol Burnett **3** *n teenagers* A slovenly, untidy person; =DIRTBAG **4** *adj* =DIPPY

dip[3] *n* Diphtheria

dip[4] *n* =DIPSO

dip[5] *v* To chew tobacco or take snuff orally

dip[6] *See* I'LL BE DAMNED, SKINNY-DIP

dipped or ◁**dipped in shit**▷ *See* I'LL BE DAMNED

dipper *n* =DIPPERMOUTH
See FANNY-DIPPER, HIPPER-DIPPER

dippermouth *n* A person with a large mouth: *Dipper, that was my nickname, short for Dippermouth*—Louis Armstrong

dippy *adj fr early 1900s British* Crazy; foolish; whimsically silly; =KOOKY: *so strange and dippy as to have come from the brain of Tolkien*—Toronto Life [origin unknown; perhaps fr *dipsomaniac*; perhaps fr Romany *divio* "mad, madman"]

◁ **dipshit**▷ or **dipstick** **1** *n* A stupid, obnoxious person; =JERK: *The other guy is the dipshit*—Village Voice/ *We're broke, dipstick*—Toronto Sun **2** *modifier: The dipshit broads*—Easyriders [*dipshit* is an emphatic form of *dip*[2], and *dipstick* is a euphemism for *dipshit*]

dipso *n fr early 1900s* A drunkard; dipsomaniac; =LUSH: *Madeline Kahn is his dipso wife, Gilda Radner his ditsy daughter*—Time

dipsy **1** *adj* Drunken; bibulous; alcoholic; =DIPSO: *Beryl Reid's appearance as a dipsy researcher*—Time **2** *adj* Foolish; silly; =DITSY: *Kelly, her dipsy counterpart at NBC*—Pulpsmith

dipsy-do or **dipsy-doo** *n baseball* A deceptive curveball that dips sharply

dipsy-doodle **1** *n* Fraud; deception; chicanery: *This dipsy-doodle allowed the Democratic candidate to preach a different sermon in every church*—Rolling Stone **2** *n* A deceiver; swindler; =CON MAN: *He's a marriage counselor, this dipsy-doodle*—New York **3** *v: That smooth chap might just have dipsy-doodled us* **4** *n* =DIPSY-DO **5** *n prizefight* A fight with predetermined outcome; a fixed fight

◁ **dip** one's **wick**▷ *v phr fr middle 1800s* To insert one's penis; do the sex act; =SCREW: *The Army forbade dipping one's wick in a WAC*

dirt **1** *n* Obscenity; pornography: *All you see in the movies these days is dirt* **2** *n* Gossip; intimate or scandalous intelligence; =SCOOP: *What's the dirt about your neighbors?* **3** *n* A despicable person; scum; filth: *He's dirt, no better*
See DIG DIRT, DISH THE DIRT, DO someone DIRT, EAT DIRT, HIT THE DIRT, PAY DIRT, TAKE SHIT

◁ **dirtbag** or **dirtball**▷ **1** *n WW2 armed forces* A garbage collector **2** *n phr* A despicable person; filthy lout; =CRUD, SCUMBAG: *He ended up being chased down the hall by a dirtball with a knife*—Your Week in Ocean City

dirt bike *n motorcyclists* =SCRAMBLER

dirty **1** *adj* Aimed at getting an unfair advantage; dishonest; shady: *a few dirty tricks/ real dirty deal* **2** *adv: They fight dirty/ play dirty* **3** *adj* Lewd; obscene; =BLUE, RAUNCHY: *This dictionary dotes on dirty words/ Eschew dirty thoughts* **4** *adv: He talks dirty* **5** *adj 1920s jazz musicians* Sexually insinuating in sound and intonation; =CATHOUSE: *dirty blues* **6** *adj* Personally malicious or snide; nasty: *a dirty crack* **7** *adj narcotics* Addicted to narcotics **8** *adj narcotics* Having narcotics in one's possession: *Cops did a body-shake and he was real dirty* **9** *adj* Well supplied with money; =FILTHY RICH: *Paddy was dirty with fifteen thousand or so*—Dashiell Hammett **10** *adj* Leaving much radioactive contamination or waste: *dirty bombs*
See DO THE DIRTY ON someone, DOWN AND DIRTY, QUICK-AND-DIRTY

the **dirty dozens** *See* PLAY THE DOZENS

dirtyleg *n* A promiscuous woman or prostitute; =FLOOZY: *flirting with a dirtyleg* —Dan Jenkins

dirty linen (or **wash**) *See* WASH one's DIRTY LINEN

dirty little secret **1** *n phr* Something shameful that must be concealed; an embarrassing fact: *Power ... has been a dirty little secret among modern economists*—New York Times **2** *n phr* Anything held secret personally or communally because it is patently shameful; a skeleton in the closet: *Everybody will know the dirty little secret of American journalism*—Time [phrase propagated by DH Lawrence, esp in his long essay "Pornography and Obscenity"]

dirty mind *n phr* A head full of sexual, malicious, and other reprehensible thoughts and fantasies

dirty old man **1** *n phr* A lecherous man, esp an elderly one; =OLD GOAT **2** *n phr homosexuals* A male homosexual whose partner is much younger than himself: *He asks Leo to be his dirty old man*—New York Times

dirty pool *n phr* Unethical and dubious practice; =DIRTY TRICKS: *triggered ugly accusations of dirty pool*—TV Guide

dirty (or **low-down dirty**) **shame** *n phr* A person or thing that is much to be lamented; a pity; a disgrace: *He did? Ain't that a dirty shame?/ Man, you're a low-down dirty shame, you're nasty*

dirty tricks **1** *n phr* Dishonest or underhanded practices, esp in politics; malicious tactics: *make into federal crimes many "dirty tricks" in presidential and congressional elections*—Time **2** *modifier: the Senate Watergate Committee's chief "dirty tricks" investigator*—Newsweek

dirty work *n phr* Dishonest, unethical, underhanded, or criminal acts: =SKULLDUGGERY

disc or **disk** *n* A phonograph record; =PLATTER

disc jockey *n phr* (Variations: **deejay** or **Dee-Jay** or **DJ** or **dj**) A radio performer who plays and comments on phonograph records; also, the person who plays records at a discotheque: *the thunder-voiced DJ* —Saturday Review

disco **1** *n* A discotheque, a kind of nightclub where patrons dance to recorded music, sometimes with synchronized psychedelic and strobe lighting: *There's not much jazzing around at the disco*—Vogue **2** *modifier: show up... for a disco party and fashion show*—Look **3** *v: We discoed the night away*
See CRISCO DISCO

discombobulate or **discomboberate** *fr early 1800s* **1** *v* To disturb;

upset; =BUG **2** *v* To perplex; puzzle: *The fancy words discombobulated me*

discombobulated *adj* Disturbed; upset; weird: *In this discombobulated society, it is far easier to get a piano shipped out to sea and lowered into the water beside the drowning man* —Washington Post

discombobulation *n* The condition of being discombobulated: *the Skinner course responsible for their emotional discombobulation*—Time

disease *See* FOOT-IN-MOUTH DISEASE

disgusto *adj* Disgusting: *disgusto special effects aside*—Village Voice

dish **1** *n* A particularly attractive woman • Regarded by some women as offensive: *I love this book and I think its 80-year-old author is a dish*—Washington Post **2** *n* A person or thing that one especially likes; what exactly meets one's taste; =CUP OF TEA: *Now, there is a book that is just my dish*—George S Kaufman **3** *n baseball* The home plate of the baseball diamond **4** *v* To say something; tell something: *What the hell is he dishing us now?* **5** *v* To gossip; have an intimate chat; =DISH THE DIRT: *She sat and dished with the girls*—H Selby **6** *v* To give; purvey: *He took everything we gave and dished it right back*—D Cresap **7** *v fr late 1700s British* To cheat; thwart: *I'm afraid that blackguard has dished us again*

See one's CUP OF TEA

dish it out *v phr* To administer punishment, injury, or abuse: *Jenny, you can dish it out, but you can't take it* —Erich Segal

one's **dish of tea** *See* one's CUP OF TEA

dish the dirt *v phr* To gossip; enjoy a cozy chat about personalities: *We sat around dishing the dirt until the gavel sounded*

dishwater *n* Weak and scarcely drinkable soup, coffee, etc

See DULL AS DISHWATER

dishy *adj* Very attractive, sexually desirable • Chiefly British use; regarded by some women as offensive: *exactly what it is to be a dishy girl bored stiff*—Penelope Gilliatt

disk *See* DISC

Disneyland daddy *n phr* A divorced or separated father who sees his children rarely; =ZOO DADDY

dissolve **1** *n movie & television studio* The gradual blending of one scene into the next; also, a device that causes this effect **2** *v: Dissolve to a closeup of the house*

ditch **1** *v fr early 1900s* To dispose of, get rid of; =CHUCK: *We'll ditch this Greek and blow*—James M Cain **2** *v* To land an aircraft on the water in an emergency

ditsy *adj* Vapid and frivolous; silly; =AIRHEADED: *Charles Ruggles's ditsy bimbo*—Village Voice/ *Is there something in the air that makes Washington wives ditsy?*—Philadelphia Journal [perhaps a blending of *dizzy* and *dotty*]

ditty (or **diddy**) **bag** *n phr fr merchant marine fr middle 1800s* A small bag for one's personal belongings, usu exclusive of clothing [origin uncertain; perhaps short for *commodity*, fr the earlier British naval term *commodity box*, which became *ditty box*]

dittybop or **dittybob** or **diddybop** *black* ◁**1**▷ *n* A stupid person, esp a crude and unsophisticated black person: *the diddybop image of JJ* —Amsterdam News **2** *v* To move, sway, etc, to music; =BOP: *A young man ...was ditty bopping in front of Saks*—New York

ditz *n* A silly and inane person; a frivolous ninny: *a brainy ditz involved with a vulnerable hunk*—Village Voice

dive **1** *n fr late 1800s* A vulgar and disreputable haunt, such as a cheap bar, nightclub, lodging house, or dancehall; =CRIB: *the girl who danced in a dive in New Orleans*—K Brush **2** *n* =SPEAKEASY **3** *n prizefight* A knockdown or knockout, esp a false prearranged knockout: *A dive is a phantom knockout*—Arthur Daley **4** *v: They fixed it so he'd dive in the fourth* [origin uncertain; perhaps fr the notion that one could *dive* into a disreputable cellar haunt and lose oneself among lowlifes and criminals; perhaps a shortening of *divan* "a smoking and gaming room," a usage popular in London in the middle and late 19th century; the places were so called because furnished with *divans* "lounges," the name ultimately fr Turkish]

See TAKE A DIVE

divot (DIV ət) *n* A toupee [fr the Scottish word, "a piece of turf or sod, esp one cut out by a golf club," of unknown origin]

divvy 1 *v* (also **divvy out** or **divvy up**) To divide; apportion: *The governor and the Paris crook divvy the swag*—Alva Johnson/ *We would pass our hats and divvy up*—Louis Armstrong **2** *n* A share of profits or spoils **3** *n* A dividend

Dixie[1] *n* New Orleans

Dixie[2] **1** *n* The Southern United States **2** *modifier: a Dixie drawl* [probably because the region is south of the Mason-*Dixon* line]
See NOT JUST WHISTLING DIXIE, WHISTLING DIXIE

Dixieland 1 *n* The Southern United States; =DIXIE **2** *n* The style of jazz played by the street bands in New Orleans, marked by a simple two-beat rhythm, ragged syncopation, improvised ensemble passages, etc **3** *adj: Dixieland trumpet*

dizzy *adj* Silly; foolish; inane; =DITSY: *some dizzy broad*—Jerome Weidman

DJ or **dj** *See* DISC JOCKEY

DMT *n narcotics* Dimethyltryptamine, a hallucinogen like LSD but with shorter effects

do 1 *v fr early 1800s British* To cheat; swindle: *He is hated by all the beggars above him, and they do him every chance they get*—J Flynt **2** *v narcotics* To use or take narcotics: *The straights do dope, ball a lot*—Saturday Review/ *I'd wonder why and do another line. But I never looked at it as if I were some big drug addict* —Playboy **3** *v* To serve a prison sentence: *He did six years up at San Quentin* **4** *n fr early 1900s British* A party or other gathering; affair; =SHINDIG: *a few of the other main do's*—Budd Schulberg/ *The Tweed do was held early last December*—Village Voice **5** *n esp black* A hairdo **6** *n* Excrement; feces: *I stepped in doggy-do* **7** *n* Something one should do or must do: *Being friendly is a do, but being possessive is a don't*
See DO someone DIRT, DO-GOODER, DO IT ALL, DO one's NUMBER, DOODAD, DO someone OUT OF, DO one's STUFF, DO one's THING, DO TIME, DO UP, DO something UP BROWN, WHOOP-DE-DO

do a job on 1 *v phr* To injure; treat roughly: *Those motherf..in' scorpions really do a job on you*—New York Times **2** *v phr* =DO A NUMBER ON **3** *v phr* To destroy: *The pup did a job on the rug*

Doakes *See* JOE BLOW

do (or **run**) **a number on 1** *v phr* To take advantage of, esp by deception; mistreat; =SCREW: *You people ran a number on us. Whenever we brought it up, you walked away*—New York Times/ *get even with Leonard for doing that... number on her*—Cyra McFadden **2** *v phr* To affect adversely, esp as to morale and self-esteem: *He really did a number on her when he told her the boss didn't like her report* **3** *v phr* To defeat decisively; trounce; =CLOBBER: *They really did a number on the poor old Sox*

do a slow burn *v phr* To become very angry gradually: *And I do a real slow burn*—Leo Rosten

doc 1 *n* A physician; doctor **2** *n* Man; fellow; =GUY • Used in address to strangers: *Hey, doc, where's the exit?/ What's up, doc?*

dock-walloper *n* A dockworker: *strolled among the dock-wallopers swinging a cane*—O McIntyre

doctor 1 *n horse-racing* A person who drugs racehorses to improve their performance **2** *v* To alter or tamper with dishonestly; =COOK: *We doctored the receipts/ He doctored the booze* **3** *v* To repair; mend: *Somebody's got to doctor this furnace*
See SPIN DOCTOR

Dr Feelgood 1 *n phr* A physician who prescribes amphetamines, vitamins, hormones, etc, to induce euphoria: *No Dr Feelgood was in the White House administering amphetamines*—William Safire **2** *n phr* Any person who soothes and pleases by hedonic ministrations: *the Dr Feelgood of American politics*—New York Times [fr the title of a 1960s song popularized by Aretha Franklin]

docu or **docudrama** (DAHK yoo) *n* A documentary film, TV program, play, etc: *one vidfilm, plus a docu on Theodore Roosevelt*—Variety

do-dad *See* DOODAD

dodge *n fr early 1800s* A person's way of making a living, esp if illegal or dubious: *We used to run gin, but we had to give up that dodge*

dodger ***See*** ROGER

do someone **dirt** ***v phr*** To cause someone trouble or embarrassment, esp by malice and slander; serve someone ill: *Don't repeat that unless you want to do him dirt*

dodo 1 ***n*** *fr late 1800s British* A stupid, inept person; =TURKEY **2** ***n*** A boring person; =FOGY: *I'm a respectable old dodo*—Philip Wylie **3** ***n*** *1940s Army Air Corps* A student pilot who has not yet made a solo flight [fr the extinct *dodo* bird, rather sluggish and flightless]

See DEAD AS A DODO

◁ **does a bear shit in the woods**▷ ***sentence*** That was a stupid question; isn't the answer very obvious?

◁ **does a wooden horse have a hickory dick**▷ ***sentence*** That was a stupid question; isn't the answer very obvious?; =DOES A BEAR SHIT IN THE WOODS

◁ **does Howdy Doody have wooden balls**▷ ***sentence*** That was a stupid question; isn't the answer very obvious?; =DOES A BEAR SHIT IN THE WOODS

do-funny ***See*** DOODAD

dog 1 ***n*** An unappealing or inferior person or thing; =DUD, LOSER: *The new show's a total dog* ◁**2**▷ ***n*** An unattractive woman: *Why'd you tell him his girl's a dog?* **3** ***n*** *esp jazz musicians* An attractive woman; =FOX **4** ***n*** A man; fellow; =GUY: *dirty dog/ handsome dog* **5** ***n*** *esp black* An untrustworthy man; seducer **6** ***n*** *black* A sexually aggressive man: *before the dogs on the ward showed their hand*—Donald Goines **7** ***n*** A foot: *His left dog pained* **8** ***n*** =HOT DOG **9** ***v*** *Army* To pester; =BUG, HASSLE

See CATS AND DOGS, DOG IT, DOG TAGS, DOG-WAGON, the HAIR OF THE DOG, HOT DIGGETY, HOT DOG, NERVOUS AS A DOG SHITTING RAZORBLADES, PUT ON THE RITZ, RAIN CATS AND DOGS, RED DOG, ROAD DOG, SEE A MAN ABOUT A DOG, SHORT DOG, TOP DOG

the **Dog** ***See*** the HOUND

dog and pony act (or **show**) ***n phr*** An elaborately prepared or staged presentation, event, etc: *Bring them in here and do a dog and pony act*—Ed McBain

See GO INTO one's DANCE

◁ **dog-ass**▷ ***adj*** Wretched; inferior; pitiable: *boning up on the dog-ass Jets*—Dan Jenkins

dog collar ***n phr*** A collar fastening at the back, like a Roman collar; also, a very high collar like the one on a Marine Corps uniform

dog days ***n phr*** The hot and humid days of late summer [fr the rising of Sirius, the *dog* star]

dog-eared 1 ***adj*** Worn, creased, and rumpled; shabby; unkempt **2** ***adj*** Old; outworn; hackneyed: *a clean reading of a dog-eared tune*—Village Voice [fr the look of a book whose pages have been repeatedly folded at the corners]

dog eye ***n phr*** A reproachful or pleading look

dogface 1 ***n*** *esp WW2 Army* A soldier, esp an infantry private: *Few wanted to be dogfaces*—Time **2** ***modifier:*** *a dogface, paddlefoot private*

◁ **dog fashion** (or **style**)▷ ***adv phr*** With one partner in a sex act entering the other from the rear; =BOTTOMS UP

◀ **dogfuck**▶ ***v*** To do a sex act with one partner entering the other from the rear: *including how to 69 and dogfuck*—Playboy

dogger ***See*** HOT DOGGER

doggie 1 ***n*** A sailor or merchant seaman **2** ***n*** =DOG **3** ***n*** =HOT DOG **4** ***n*** =DOGFACE

doggo 1 ***adj*** Inferior; unpromising; wretched; =DOG-ASS: *doggo prospects like anthropologists and landscape architects*—Washington Post **2** ***adj*** *fr late 1800s British* In hiding; quiet and unobtrusive; low-profile: *The three that got away are doggo somewhere*

doggone or **daggone** or **dagnab** *fr middle 1800s* **1** ***interj*** (also **doggone it** or **daggone it** or **dagnab it**) An exclamation of disappointment, irritation, frustration, etc; =DANG, DARN: *Doggone it, leave me be!* **2** ***adj*** (also **doggoned** or **daggoned** or **dagnabbed**) Wretched; nasty; silly: *This doggone thing's busted* **3** ***adv:*** *They left here doggone fast* [a euphemism for *God damn*]

doggy 1 ***adj*** *late 1800s college students* Stylish; well dressed and groomed **2** ***adj*** Inferior; wretched; =DOGGO: *selling off the* *doggy companies Geneen had bought*—Newsweek

doggy bag *n phr* A paper or plastic bag given a restaurant customer to take home leftovers

doghouse *See* IN THE DOGHOUSE

dogie *n cowboys* A motherless calf in a herd; =BUM

dog it **1** *v phr* =PUT ON THE RITZ **2** *v phr* To avoid or evade work; refuse to exert oneself: *The whole shop's been dogging it today* **3** *v phr* To leave hastily; flee **4** *v phr* To live as a parasite; =SPONGE: *He was dogging it, mooching his room and board*

do-good *adj* Overtly benign and altruistic: *This "do-good" laundry list draws sneers*—Saturday Review

do-gooder *n* A person whose selfless work may be more pretentiously than actually altruistic; an ostentatiously rightminded citizen: *a professional do-gooder*—Billy Rose

dogs *n* The feet
See CATS AND DOGS, GO TO THE DOGS, RAIN CATS AND DOGS

dogsbody *n* A menial; lowly pawn • Chiefly British usage

dog's breakfast *n phr* A wretched mixture; an unpalatable combination: *that dog's breakfast of fact and fancy ... docudrama*—Meg Greenfield

◁ **dogshit** ▷ *n* Despicable matter; pretentious trash; =CRAP: *None of that dogshit*—Rolling Stone

dog style *See* DOG FASHION

dog tags *n phr armed forces fr WW1* Identification tags, esp metal tags worn around the neck by members of the armed forces: *vets, if you still have your dog tags*—New York Sunday News

dog-wagon **1** *n* A modest or cheap diner, such as might occupy an old railroad car or street car, that serves hot dogs **2** *n truckers* An antiquated truck

do-hickey or **do-hinky** *See* DOODAD, DOOHICKEY

do one's **homework** *v phr* To be ready and informed, esp for a meeting, interview, report, etc: *Shana Alexander has done her homework well*—National Public Radio

do someone **in** **1** *v phr fr late 1800s British* To kill: *She did in the old woman too*—Agatha Christie **2** *v phr* To ruin; destroy: *Another flop will do us in/ why you let your brother do you in the way he did*—Saul Bellow

doing *See* NOTHING DOING

do it *v phr* To do the sex act; =FUCK • An arch euphemism very popular for a time in a series of bumper-stickers: *Divers do it deeper/Professors do it fifty minutes at a time*

do it all *v phr* To be versatile; be variously skilled: *Take that shortstop. He'll do it all for you*

do it up *v phr* To do something decisively and well: *Some of us really did it up in grand style*—Saturday Review

do-jigger *See* DOODAD

doke or **dokey** or **dokie** *See* OKEY-DOKE

dokle *See* OKEY-DOKE

doll **1** *n* (also **dolly**) A conventionally pretty and shapely young woman, esp a curly, blue-eyed blonde, whose function is to elevate the status of a male and to inspire general lust; =BIMBO: *If a blonde girl doesn't talk we call her a doll*—F Scott Fitzgerald **2** *n* Any woman, esp an attractive one; =BABE, CHICK • Considered offensive by many women **3** *n* Any notably decent, pleasant, generous person; =LIVING DOLL: *Isn't he a doll?* **4** *n* An attractive boy or young man **5** *n* (also **dolly**) *narcotics* An amphetamine or barbiturate drug in pill or capsule form
See LIVING DOLL

Doll *See* BARBIE DOLL

dollar *See* BET one's BOTTOM DOLLAR, HOT AS A THREE-DOLLAR PISTOL, PHONY AS A THREE-DOLLAR BILL

dollar-spinner *n* Commercial success; seller: *All spectator sports combined to become the No 1 dollar-spinner... in entertainment*—People Weekly

dolls *See* CUT OUT DOLLS

doll up (or **out**) *v phr fr early 1920s* To dress fancily and in one's best clothes; =GUSSY UP: *This year the girls are dolling up in calico patchworks*—New York

dolly *See* DOLL

-dom *suffix used to form nouns* The range, establishment, scope, or realm of what is indicated: *fandom/ moviedom/ klutzdom*

dome *n fr late 1800s* The head: *What's going on in that dome of hers?*

dominoes **1** ***n*** The teeth **2** ***n*** *crapshooting* Dice
See GALLOPING DOMINOES

donagher ***See*** DONNICKER

done in **1** ***adj phr*** (also **done up**) Very tired; =POOPED: *I was done up*–SJ Perelman **2** ***adj phr*** Killed **3** ***adj phr*** Ruined; wrecked: *My plans are done in but good*

◁**dong**▷ ***n*** The penis [origin unknown; possibly fr *ding-dong* fr *dingus*, a euphemism for the unnamable thing; perhaps echoic to suggest striking; compare *wang*]
See FLONG ONE'S DONG, PULL ONE'S PUD

◁**donkey dick**▷ **1** ***n phr*** *WW2 armed forces* Salami and other cold-cut sausages; =HORSE COCK **2** ***n phr*** *narcotics* A very durable penile erection, due to an effect of heroin use: *a reward known in smack circles as "donkey dick"*–High Times

donkey roast ***n phr*** A large, fancy, or noisy party: *at $100 a ticket... promises to be a real fine donkey roast*–New York Post

donkey's years ***n phr*** A very long time • Chiefly British use: *I got interested in his apprenticeship donkey's years ago*–Robert Ruark [a punning allusion to the long *ears* of a *donkey*]

donkeywork ***n*** Tedious work needing little skill or wit; =SCUT: *He uses computers to do what the "whiz kids" call their "donkey work"*–US News and World Report

donna ***See*** PRIMA DONNA

donnicker or **doniker** or **donagher** **1** ***n*** *underworld, carnival & circus fr late 1800s* A toilet **2** ***n*** *railroad* A freight-train's brake operator [fr diminutive of 18th-century British *danna* "feces," applied to a privy]

donnybrook ***n*** A riotous scene, esp a general and energetic brawl; =BRANNIGAN: *A donnybrook began when police arrested the operators*–R McCarthy [fr a fair held annually at *Donnybrook* in Ireland]

do someone **nothing** ***v phr*** To leave one unaffected, unmoved, unpleased, etc: *This book does me nothing*

don't ***n*** Something one should not or must not do =A NO-NO: *The do's and don'ts of sailing a leaky barge*

don't knock it ***sentence*** Don't be critical of it; appreciate its value: *Don't knock it. Nobody who lived in the past would want to live in the past*–A Brien/ *Don't knock it. You haven't even tried it yet*

don't take any wooden nickels ***sentence fr 1920s*** Take care of yourself; goodbye, and watch yourself • Used as an amiable parting salutation

do one's **number** ***v phr*** To behave in an expected way; play a role; =GO INTO one's ACT: *He was doing his number about how you have to alienate no one* [fr *number* "theatrical act or routine, shtick"]

doo ***See*** HOOPERDOOPER

doobie or **dubee** or **duby** **1** ***n*** *narcotics* A marijuana cigarette; =JOINT: *I smoke a doobie at lunch*–Armistead Maupin/ *and rolled myself an ample doobie*–Richard Merkin **2** ***n*** *computer* A data base

doodad **1** ***n*** (Variations: **do-dad** or **do-funny** or **doofunny** or **do-hickey** or **doohickey** or **do-hinky** or **doohinky** or **do-jigger** or **doojigger** or **doowhangam** or **do-whistle** or **doowhistle** or **do-willie** or **doowillie**) Any unspecified or unspecifiable thing; something one does not know the name of or does not wish to name; =GADGET, THINGAMAJIG: *We may have turned into what looks like a nation of doohickeys*–Time/ *Imagination and art aren't worth those little doowhangams you put under a sofa leg*–National Review **2** ***n*** Something useless or merely ornamental: *Just a flourish, a little doodad*

doodle **1** ***v*** To cheat; swindle; =DIDDLE **2** ***v*** To make drawings and patterns while sitting at a meeting, talking on the telephone, etc: *From your doodle the shrink sees what's in your noodle* **3** ***n*** Wretched material; =SHIT: *How can he write such doodle?*–Washington Post
See DIPSY-DOODLE, WHANGDOODLE, WHOOP-DE-DO

doodle-brained ***adj*** Stupid; silly: *singing a doodle-brained folk song about "travelin"*–Village Voice

◁**doodle-shit**▷ ***n*** (Variations: **doodily-shit** or **doodley-shit** or **doodly-squat** or **doodly**) Nothing; very little; =SQUAT, ZILCH: *I don't care doodily-shit about Jews and Nazis*

—Ira Levin/ *A whole lot of doodley-shit*—Richard Fariña

doodly-squat 1 *n carnival* Money **2** *n* =DOODLE-SHIT

doo-doo *n* Excrement; =DO, SHIT: *I think doo-doo is coming out of your ears*—R Grossbach

doofunny *See* DOODAD

doohickey *n* (Variations: **do-hickey** or **do-hinky** or **doohinky**) A pimple, blackhead, or other minor skin lesion; =ZIT

See DOODAD

doohinky *See* DOODAD, DOOHICKEY

doojigger *See* DOODAD

doolie *n Air Force Academy* A first-year cadet

See BIG DOOLIE

do something **on top of** (or **standing on**) one's **head** *v phr* To accomplish easily: *You can do that shit on top of your head*—Donald Goines/ *That climb? I can do that standing on my head*

doop *See* WHOOP-DE-DO

dooper *See* HOOPER DOOPER, SUPER-DUPER, WHOOPER-DOOPER

door *See* someone CAN'T HIT THE SIDE OF A BARN, KATIE BAR THE DOOR, REVOLVING-DOOR, SHOW someone THE DOOR

doorknob *See* WIN THE PORCELAIN HAIRNET

doormat 1 *n* A person who is regularly and predictably exploited by others; constant victim: *the soulful Earth Mother doormat*—New York **2** *modifier: Cornell University's doormat status on the gridiron*—People Weekly

See TREAT someone LIKE A DOORMAT, WIN THE PORCELAIN HAIRNET

do someone **out of** *v phr* To deprive by cheating, fraud, stealing, etc: *They did the poor jerk out of his pay*

doowhangam or **doowhistle** or **doowillie** *See* DOODAD

doo-wop or **do-whop 1** *n fr 1950s black musicians* A style of street jazz-singing, esp by black ensembles **2** *modifier: from the do-whop music and lovingly customized cars*—Time [echoic fr a common rhythm phrase of the songs]

doozie or **doozy** or **doosie** *n fr 1930s* A person or thing that is remarkable, wonderful, superior, etc; =BEAUT, HUMDINGER: *a little 30-page doozey called "Making Chicken Soup"*—Village Voice/ *Want a swell Naval Air Station? I got two doozies up for grabs*—Esquire [fr *Duesenberg*, the name of a very expensive and desirable car of the 1920s and 30s]

dope 1 *n fr late 1800s* Any narcotic drug: *They searched him for dope* **2** *modifier: a dope fiend/ dope stash* **3** *n* A sedative or painkilling drug, esp when prescribed or given by a physician **4** *v: The nurse doped him so he could sleep* **5** *v* To give drugs, vitamins, etc, to horses or athletes to improve their competitive prowess: *He couldn't run that fast if he wasn't doped* **6** *n* Coca-Cola (a trade name): *Jim Bob sat down and ordered a large dope* **7** *n fr middle 1800s* Any liquid, esp a viscous one, used for a special purpose: *airplane dope/ pipe dope* **8** *n fr late 1800s* =DOPER **9** *n fr early 1900s* A stupid person; idiot; =TURKEY: *Only a dope would refuse that chance* **10** *n* A cigarette **11** *n fr early 1900s* Information; data: *Get me all the dope you can on her colleagues* **12** *n* Gossip; news; =the LOWDOWN: *What's the latest dope about Ruth?* **13** *n* A prediction, esp about a race or a game, based on analysis of past performance; =FORM: *The dope says Dream Diddle in a romp* **14** *v: I dope it like this, Ali all the way* [fr Dutch *doop* "sauce for dipping"; with elaborate semantic shifts]

dope off 1 *v phr fr WW1 Navy & Marine Corps* To sleep; fall asleep: *I'll start to dope off and yawn or something*—Earl Thompson **2** *v phr WW2 armed forces* To neglect one's duty and concerns; =GOOF OFF

dope out 1 *v phr fr early 1900s* To explain or clarify; figure out: *I can't dope out how they got in* **2** *v phr* To predict a sports result from the available information

doper *narcotics* **1** *n* A narcotics addict or user: *alerting dopers of every stripe that where the penalties had been stiff, they would now be feudal*—T Ferris **2** *modifier: with all these doper cops loose*—Rolling Stone

dope sheet *n phr* Printed information or instructions, esp about the past performance of race horses; =FORM

dopey or **dopy** *fr late 1800s* **1** *adj* Stuporous, esp from narcotic intoxication: *I was dopy after they gave me the shot* **2** *adj* Stupid; idiotic: *What a dopey thing to say*

do-re-mi *n* Money: *Get the rubber band off the do re-mi*—John Kieran [fr the first three sol-fa notes, with a pun on *dough* "money"]

◁**dork**▷ **1** *n esp teenagers* The penis: *the glorious acrobatics she can perform while dangling from the end of my dork*—Philip Roth **2** *n* A despicable person; =JERK, PRICK: *a frightened, virtuous dork*—New Yorker

dorky *adj* Stupid; awkward; =KLUTZY: *a dorky kid with Dumbo ears*—Armistead Maupin

dory *See* HUNKY-DORY

dose **1** *v* To give a horse, dog, athlete, etc, a drug or other stimulant before a competition; =DOPE ◁**2**▷ *v* To infect with a venereal disease, esp gonorrhea: *What's going to happen is that you'll get dosed*—Richard Fariña

a **dose** ◁**1**▷ *n phr* A case of venereal disease, esp of gonorrhea: *Don't Give a Dose to the One You Love Most*—New York Daily News **2** *n phr* An excess; surfeit: *I got a real dose of that in freshman year and don't want any more*
See LIKE SHIT THROUGH A TIN HORN

dose of salts *See* LIKE SHIT THROUGH A TIN HORN

doss *hoboes fr late 1800s* **1** *n* Sleep: *find good barns for a doss at night* **2** *n* (also **doss house**) A cheap lodging house; =FLOPHOUSE

do (or **strut**) one's **stuff** *v phr* To display one's virtuosity; show one's skill: *Get in there and do your stuff* [ultimately fr a black expression for showing off one's sexual attraction]

the **dot** *See* ON THE DOT

do the dirty on someone *v phr* =DO someone DIRT

do the Dutch (or the **Dutch act**) *v phr* To commit suicide: *Why did the old man do the Dutch?*—Lawrence Sanders/ *She only came aboard to do the Dutch act*—John O'Hara [narrowed meaning of an earlier phrase meaning "to depart, abscond"]

do one's (or one's **own**) **thing** *v phr esp 1960s counterculture fr black* To follow one's special inclinations, esp despite disapproval; fulfill one's peculiar destiny: *Doing your own thing may be all right in prescribed doses*—AJH Brown

do time *v phr* To serve a prison sentence

do tricks *See* GO DOWN AND DO TRICKS

double **1** *n* A person or thing that strongly or exactly resembles another; duplicate; =DEAD RINGER, LOOK-ALIKE: *She's Grace Kelly's double* **2** *n* An actor or stunt person who does the dangerous things required in a part: *He never uses a double. He does his own stunts* **3** *v: We got a guy'll double for you jumping off the cliff*
See ON THE DOUBLE

double (or **double in brass**) **as** *v phr* To perform or work as, in addition to one's primary job: *He doubled in brass as a waiter when the cooking was done* [fr the skill of a circus performer who does an act and plays in the band]

double-bagger *n esp teenagers* A very ugly person; =TWO-BAGGER [fr the fact that one needs two *bags* to obscure the ugliness, one to go over the subject's head and one over one's own head]

double-clutcher *n fr black* A despicable person; =BASTARD, PRICK [a rhyming euphemism for *motherfucker*]

double-clutching *adj fr black* =MOTHERFUCKING

double cross **1** *n phr fr middle 1800s British* A betrayal or cheating of one's own colleagues; an act of treachery: *The two suspected dealers were planning a double-cross*—New York **2** *v: I would never double-cross a pal* [fr the reneging on an agreement to lose, a *cross*, by actually winning]

double-dip *v* To collect more than one income at a time, esp by drawing a military pension and holding a job

double-dipper *n* A person who double-dips: *Federal pensioners are "double-dippers" who also collect Social Security checks*—Time

double-dome **1** *n* An intellectual; scholar; =EGGHEAD: *Princeton, NJ, where the double domes congregate*—New York Post **2** *modifier: None of your double-dome pomp, please* **3** *v: legitimate double-*

doming I suppose, but totally without fact—Philadelphia

double-gaited **1** *adj* Bisexual; =AC-DC: *Duilio is not double gaited as far as I know*—John O'Hara/ *Was Danny simply double-gaited?* —Charles Beardsley **2** *adj* Strange; eccentric; =WEIRD: *These double-gaited gonzos are perpetrating a plague of best-selling takeoffs* —Newsweek [fr the various *gaits* of a horse]

double in brass as *See* DOUBLE AS

double-minus *See* X-DOUBLE-MINUS

double nickel *n phr fr citizens band* The 55-mile-per-hour speed limit

the **double-o** *n phr* A close examination; =the ONCE-OVER: *You mean give him the double-O*—John O'Hara

double sawbuck (or **saw**) *n phr* Twenty dollars; a $20 bill: *so many sheets of dollars, ten-spots and double saws*—Westbrook Pegler

double scrud *See* SCRUD

double (or **fast**) **shuffle** **1** *n phr* =DOUBLE CROSS **2** *n phr* Deception; duplicity; =RUNAROUND: *The dean gives me a quick double shuffle/ I don't want you to think I'm giving you a fast shuffle*—Lawrence Anderson **3** *v: He was fast shuffling me, but I caught him* [fr the deceptive *shuffle* of a card sharp]

double-take **1** *n* A sudden second look or a laugh or gesture over something one has at first ignored or accepted; a belated reaction: *She suddenly caught the reference and did a double-take* **2** *v: I double-took a little bit when she ordered a cigar*—Robert Ruark

double-team *v sports fr middle 1800s politics* To attack or defend against a formidable athlete with twice the usual forces: *He was gaining every play till they double-teamed him* [originally fr *doubling* the *team* of horses used for a purpose]

double-time *v* =DOUBLE-CROSS, TWO-TIME

double whammy *n phr* A two-part or two-pronged difficulty; a dual disadvantage: *the double-whammy of steep home prices and steeper interest rates*—Washingtonian

double X *n phr* =DOUBLE CROSS

douche *See* TAKE A DOUCHE

◁ **douche bag**▷ *n phr* A despicable and loathsome woman; =SCUMBAG: *dirty, filthy douchebag*—Herbert Kastle

dough **1** *n fr late 1800s* Money; =BREAD: *And to get the dough we'll put our watch and chain in hock*—HS Canby **2** *n* =DOUGHBOY

See HEAVY MONEY

doughboy *n fr middle 1800s & esp WW1* An infantry soldier; =GRUNT, PADDLEFOOT [origin unknown; perhaps fr a resemblance between the buttons of the infantry uniform and *doughboys* "suet dumplings boiled in seawater," a term fr the British merchant marine]

doughfoot *n WW1* =DOUGHBOY

doughnut *n truckers* A truck tire

See TAKE A FLYING FUCK

dough-pop *v* To defeat; hit; =CLOBBER: *dough-popped Arkansas 37 to 21* —Dan Jenkins

do up **1** *v phr* To pummel and trounce; =CLOBBER **2** *v phr narcotics* To take narcotics: *We'll do up some hash* **3** *v phr* To enhance; prepare, esp to wrap or package: *I'll do it up real nice. It's a present*

do something **up brown** *v phr fr middle 1800s* To do very thoroughly: *He didn't just finish it, he did it up brown* [fr the *brown* color of something well baked]

douse or **dowse** *v fr middle 1800s* To extinguish a light, lamp, candle, etc [specialized fr an earlier sense, "hit"]

dove (DUHV) *See* TURTLE DOVES

dovetail *v Army* To say something linked and sequential: *Let me dovetail on what you just said*

dovey *n* =LOVEY-DOVEY

dow *See* ROWDY-DOW

dowdy *See* ROWDY-DOW

do-whistle or **do-willie** *See* DOODAD

do whop *See* DOO-WOP

down **1** *v* To defeat; trounce: *She downed the bruiser* **2** *v* To knock or bring to the ground; =DECK: *They finally downed him at the three-yard line* **3** *v* To eat or drink: *I downed an enormous pizza* **4** *v* To criticize; complain of; =PUT someone or something DOWN: *My friends downed me for listening to country music* —HE Roberts **5** *v* To sell **6** *adj* Depressed; melancholy; =BLUE: *He's real down about losing that chance* **7** *adj* Lacking vitality; exhausted; =BEAT: *You look down today, old buddy* **8** *adj* Not functioning;

=ON THE BLINK: *The power plant has been down for two months/ The computer's down again today* **9** ***adv*** Behind one's opponent in score: *They were down by six at the end of the first half* **10** ***adj*** Finished; dealt with • Referring always to a series of tasks, requirements, etc: *They're well into the triathlon, with two events down and only one to go* **11** ***adj*** *lunch counter* Toasted **12** ***n*** *lunch counter* Toast **13** ***adj*** *cool talk & counterculture* Coolly cognizant; at ease in one's own skin; =COOL: *a down cat* **14** ***adj*** *cool talk & counterculture fr black* Excellent; good; profoundly satisfying: *The way she sang it was real down* **15** ***adj*** *black & teenagers* Ready; able to respond without inhibition: *They were down for it, so I got down too* **16** ***adj*** Depressing; pessimistic; dampening; =DOWNBEAT: *I don't see the point of making such a "down" picture*—Xaviera Hollander **17** ***n*** *narcotics* =DOWNER [sense "nonfunctional" probably fr a shortening of *broken down*; cool and teenager senses perhaps fr jazz musicians' terms like *low down* and *down and dirty* used to praise gutbucket and other jazz when especially well played; see *get down*]

See DOWN ON someone or something, GET DOWN, GO DOWN ON someone, HAVE something DOWN, the LOWDOWN, LOW-DOWN, MELTDOWN, PUT-DOWN, TURN THUMBS DOWN

down and dirty **1** ***adj phr*** Nasty; low; vicious and deceptive: *Mississippi: A Down And Dirty Campaign*—Newsweek/ *This is down-and-dirty time. Just witness Rizzo's angry characterization of Goode*—Philadelphia **2** ***adj phr*** *poker* With the face down, and probably nasty for someone • Uttered in stud poker as the last cards are dealt face down

down and out ***adj phr*** *fr early 1900s* Penniless and hopeless; destitute: *When you're down and out, remember what did it*—Arthur Miller [fr the condition of a fighter who is knocked out]

downbeat ***adj*** Depressing; pessimistic: *a triumph of upbeat pictures over the downbeat*—Bob Thomas

downer **1** ***n*** *narcotics* A depressant drug, esp a barbiturate; sedative; =DOWN **2** ***n*** *fr narcotics* A depressing experience; =BUMMER, DRAG: *The opening scene's a downer* **3** ***n*** =BAD TRIP

down for the count ***adj phr*** Utterly defeated; ruined; =DOWN AND OUT [fr the *count* of ten made over a *downed* boxer]

down home *esp black* **1** ***adv phr*** In the Southern US; in Dixie **2** ***n phr:*** *old buddy from down home* **3** ***modifier:*** *He was getting away from all that old down-home stuff*—Claude Brown **4** ***adv phr*** In a Southern regional or ethnic manner: *funkier than blues and playing about as down home as you can get*—Rolling Stone **5** ***adj phr*** Simple; homey: *a down-home meal*

down in flames ***See*** GO DOWN IN FLAMES

down in the kitchen ***adv phr*** *truckers* Driving in lowest gear

down on someone or something ***adj phr*** Angry with or critical: *Everybody's down on Mary since she reported Sue to the boss*

down the drain ***adv phr*** To a futile end; to waste: *All his best efforts seemed to go down the drain*

See POUR MONEY DOWN THE DRAIN

down the Goodyears (or **the rollers**) ***v phr*** *airline* To lower the landing gear • Esp the command to do so

down the hatch ***interj*** A toast, followed by the swallowing of a whole drink

down the pike ***See*** COME DOWN THE PIKE

down the river ***See*** SELL someone DOWN THE RIVER

down the tube (or **tubes** or **chute**) ***See*** GO DOWN THE TUBE

down someone's **throat** ***See*** JUMP DOWN someone's THROAT

down-thumb ***v*** To disapprove; veto; =TURN THUMBS DOWN: *We down-thumbed the shaky marriage last December*—McCall's

downtime **1** ***n*** Time during which a machine, factory, etc, is not operating **2** ***n*** Time away from work; leisure time: *He spends most of his downtime with Toby, his wife*—People Weekly

down to brass tacks ***adv phr*** *fr early 1900s* Dealing with the essentials; concerned with the practical realities:

highbrow sermons that don't come down to brass tacks—Sinclair Lewis

down to the wire *adv phr fr 1940s* Near the finish; at or to the last possible moment: *The project is getting down to the wire* [fr the imaginary line marking the end of a horserace; horses were said to pass "under the *wire*"]
See GO TO THE WIRE

down trip *See* BAD TRIP

down yonder *adv phr* =DOWN HOME

do you want an engraved invitation *question* Must you be especially asked and pleaded with?; you are being too standoffish and scrupulous

dozen *See* a DIME A DOZEN, PLAY THE DOZENS

dozer **1** *n* A powerful blow, esp with the fist; =BELT **2** *n* =DOOZIE **3** *n* A bulldozer

DPT *n* Dipropylphyptamine, a hallucinogen like LSD but having an effect lasting only an hour or two

drag **1** *n fr late 1900s* Influence; weight; =CLOUT, PULL: *We had a big drag with the waiter*—Ernest Hemingway **2** *n fr early 1900s* A street: *from some bo on the drag I managed to learn*—Jack London **3** *n* An inhalation of smoke; puff; =TOKE: *The ponies took last drags at their cigarettes and slumped into place*—F Scott Fitzgerald **4** *v: dragging on cigars and feeling grown up* **5** *n* A cigarette; =BUTT: *a drag smoking on your lip*—Stephen Longstreet **6** *n homosexuals fr late 1800s* A party or gathering, usu of homosexuals, where everyone wears clothing of the other sex; a clustering of transvestites **7** *n homosexuals* Clothing worn by someone of the sex for which the clothing was not intended; transvestite costume, esp women's clothing worn by a man **8** *modifier: a drag queen/ drag party* **9** *n esp students* A dance or dancing party; prom **10** *v esp students* To escort a partner to a dance **11** *n: I asked Jeannie to be my drag tomorrow night* **12** *adv* With a partner; escorted: *Can't come stag, have to be drag* **13** *v teenagers & hot rodders* To race down a straightaway **14** *n* =DRAG RACE **15** *n police* A roll of money, purse, etc, used to lure the victim in a confidence game **16** *n fr middle 1800s* A situation, occupation, event, etc, that is tedious and trying; =DOWNER: *Life can be such a drag one minute and a solid sender the next*—Louis Armstrong **17** *n* A dull, boring person: *Don't ask John to the party, he's such a drag*
See MAIN DRAG

◁ **drag ass**▷ **1** *v phr* To depart, esp in a hurry; =HAUL ASS **2** *v phr* To be morose, sluggish, and whiny: *Quit drag-assing and get to work*

drag one's **feet** *v phr fr loggers* To shirk; make less than a good effort, perhaps in the spirit of sabotage: *The project failed because even the managers were dragging their feet* [fr the action of an unenergetic member of a two-person sawing team, who would *drag his feet* or "ride the saw" rather than contribute the proper effort]

drag one's **freight** *See* PULL one's FREIGHT

dragged in *See* LOOK LIKE SOMETHING THE CAT DRAGGED IN

dragged out *adj phr fr middle 1800s* Exhausted; =BEAT: *I feel awful dragged out today*

dragger *See* KNUCKLE-DRAGGER

dragging *See* one's ASS IS DRAGGING

draggy *adj* Slow; monotonous; sluggish: *a draggy movie*

drag in *v phr* To arrive: *Where'd you drag in from?*

drag it *v phr* To quit; break off; =DRAG ASS

drag someone **kicking and screaming into the twentieth century** *v phr* To force to recognize or adapt to change; educate a rigid reactionary: *the group that drags the ABA kicking and screaming into the 20th century* —New York Times

Dragon Lady *n phr* A powerful, intimidating woman [fr a character in the popular comic strip "Terry and the Pirates" which originated in the 1930s]

drag-out *See* KNOCK-DOWN-DRAG-OUT

drag party *n phr homosexuals* A party where merrymakers wear the dress of the other sex; also, any party for homosexuals

drag queen *homosexuals* **1** *n phr* A male homosexual who enjoys dressing like a woman **2** *n phr* A male homosexual who affects pronounced feminine behavior; =QUEEN

drag race ***n phr*** *hot rodders & teenagers* A speed competition between or among cars, esp vehicles with very powerful engines and very elongated, skeletal bodies

dragster ***n*** *hot rodders & teenagers* A car used in drag races, esp one purposely built for such competition

drag strip ***n phr*** *hot rodders & teenagers* The straight track or portion of highway on which a drag race is held

dragsville ***adj*** Very dull; tedious; = DRAGGY, DULLSVILLE: *My much touted party proved dragsville*

drag one's **tail** (or ◁**ass**▷) ***v phr*** To work sluggishly; loaf; = DRAG ASS: *Two hours off with pay, why the hell are they draggin' their tails?*—Pietro di Donato

drain ***See*** BRAIN DRAIN, DOWN THE TUBE, POUR MONEY DOWN THE DRAIN

drama ***See*** DOCU

drape **1** ***n*** *jive talk* A suit; ensemble of suit, shirt, necktie, and hat **2** ***n*** *jive talk* A young man wearing black, narrow-cuffed slacks, a garish shirt, a loose jacket without lapels, and no necktie: *Drapes resent any comparison with zoot-suiters*—Time
See SET OF THREADS

drape ape ***n phr*** *college students* A baby or small child; = CRUMBCRUSHER

drapes ***n*** *black* Clothes; dress

draw ***See*** BEAT someone TO THE DRAW, GET A BEAD ON something or someone, the LUCK OF THE DRAW, QUICK ON THE DRAW, SLOW ON THE DRAW

draw a picture ***v phr*** To explain in very simple terms; make transparently clear: *I just don't like him. Do I have to draw a picture?*

drawer ***See*** TOP-DRAWER

dreadlock or **dredlock** **1** ***n*** A mat or clump of long ungroomed hair as worn by Rastafarians, reggae musicians, etc: *grown his hair in long dredlocks, Rasta style*—Village Voice **2** ***modifier:*** *a British skinhead playing the dreadlock music of Jamaica*—Playboy [fr the *dread* presumably aroused by the wearers]

dream ***See*** PIPE DREAM, WET DREAM

dream and cream ***v phr*** To have sexual fantasies: *the kind of man you dream and cream about*—Tom Aldibrandi

dreamboat **1** ***n*** Any very desirable vehicle: *A dreamboat for hot-rodders is a chromed roadster*—Life **2** ***n*** *fr 1940s* A very attractive person: *will star opposite James Mason, who she says is a "dreamboat"*—Associated Press

dream up ***v phr*** To invent; confect in the mind: *Julian has to start dreaming up a story*—Budd Schulberg

dreck or **drek** **1** ***n*** Wretched trash; = GARBAGE, JUNK, SHIT: *the ugliness, dreck and horror of New York City*—People Weekly/ *They may bring with them a pile of overfinished drek*—Toronto Life/ *the sad glitter of desert drek*—WH Auden **2** ***modifier:*** *no point in my keeping every drek album*—Rolling Stone/ *an opponent of the ticky-tacky world of dreck-tech architecture*—Toronto Life [fr Yiddish, "feces"]

dress ***See*** GRANNY DRESS

dressed to the teeth (or **to kill** or **to the nines**) **1** ***adj phr*** Extremely well and fancily dressed; = DOLLED UP: *She's dressed to the teeth in magenta silks*—Village Voice **2** ***modifier:*** *our dressed-to-the-teeth test car*—Car and Driver **3** ***v phr:*** *when she wrote articles about textured stockings and dressed to the nines*—Gloria Steinem [*to the teeth* implies "completely, from the bottom up"; *to the nines* is probably based on *nine* as a nearly perfect number just under ten, or on *nine* as a mystical or sacred number in numerology, the product of three times three; see the *whole nine yards*]

dried ***See*** CUT AND DRIED

drift **1** ***n*** *car-racing* A controlled sidewards skid: *Maserati or Ferrari into a corner with a four-wheel drift*—Life **2** ***n*** Meaning; intent: *Get my drift, chum?* **3** ***v*** (also **drift out**) To leave; depart: *Drift out, pal*
See GET THE DRIFT

drifter ***n*** A derelict; = BUM

drifty ***adj*** Stupidly inattentive; silly; = SPACED-OUT: *It makes Dede and me both look a little drifty*—Armistead Maupin

drill **1** ***v*** *hoboes fr middle 1800s* To walk; hike; slog: *I had to drill 20 miles*—J Flynt **2** ***v*** To speed with force, esp through obstacles: *skimmed by his head and drilled through the closed window*—New York Daily News **3** ***v*** To shoot; kill by shooting: *whirled and drilled him between the eyes* **4** ***v*** *baseball* To hit a

hard, straight grounder or line drive: *Lockman drilled a single past Hodges* —Associated Press **5** *n* The way of doing something; the plan of action • Still chiefly British use: *Now I'll show you the drill for closing the place up*
See MONKEY DRILL

drink *See* TAKE A DRINK

the **drink** *n phr fr early 1800s* Any body of water, from a rill to the ocean

drink of water *See* LONG DRINK OF WATER

drip 1 *n esp 1940s students* A tedious, unimaginative, conventional person; =SQUARE, WIMP: *the biggest drip at Miss Basehoar's, a school ostensibly abounding with fair-sized drips* —JD Salinger/ *such drips... they're just sort of dull*—Calder Willingham **2** *n hoboes* Useless and idle talk; gossip

drippy 1 *adj* Tedious; unimaginative; conventional; =WIMPY **2** *adj* Sentimental; lachrymose; =CORNY

drive 1 *n* Dynamism; insistent power: *a song with drive* **2** *v jazz & jive talk* To play music, esp jazz, with strong forward impetus and rhythms **3** *n narcotics* A thrill or transport of pleasure and energy; =KICK, RUSH **4** *n basketball* To dribble strongly and rapidly downcourt

drive someone **over the hill** *v phr* To drive to distraction; drive mad: *That kid is going to drive me over the hill. I'm at my wits' end*—Psychology Today

driver *See* BACKSEAT DRIVER, PENCIL-PUSHER, SUNDAY DRIVER, TRUCK DRIVER

driver's seat *See* IN THE DRIVER'S SEAT

drive the big bus *v phr* Vomit into the toilet, esp from drunkenness [fr the resemblance of a toilet seat to a steering wheel]

drive someone **up the wall** *v phr* To cause to become irrational or hysterical; madden: *Leave him alone and let him work. Quit driving him up the wall*—JJ Roget

drizzle or **drizzle-puss** *n* =DRIP

droid 1 *n esp teenagers* An inferior, mechanical sort of person; robot; a semi-human drone; =CLONE: *for all its ecumenical menagerie of creatures and droids*—People Weekly **2** *modifier: tends to get people in the droid positions... and pay little*—San Francisco [fr *android* "humanlike," esp as used by science-fiction writers]

drooly *1940s teenagers* **1** *adj* Very attractive; =YUMMY: *Rain can turn the sharpest dressed drooly dreamboat into a drizzly drip from the knees down*—New York Daily News **2** *n* A popular and attractive boy: *Who's the chief drooly at Cooley?*

drop 1 *v underworld* To be arrested; be caught with loot: *Just as I was climbing back out the window, I got dropped* **2** *v* To knock someone down; =DECK: *He was getting away with it until he mentioned my mother. Then I just spun around and dropped him with a quick left* **3** *v* To kill; =BUMP **4** *v underworld* To supply stolen or contraband goods to someone **5** *n: We made the drop and then waited to see if they'd keep their part of the bargain* **6** *v* To lose, esp money: *He dropped a bundle in the market yesterday* **7** *v* To collapse, esp with fatigue: *I'll drop if I don't sit down* **8** *v* To stop seeing or associating with someone: *She dropped her boyfriend* **9** *v narcotics* To take any narcotic, esp in pill or capsule form: *We want a society where you can smoke grass and drop acid*—New York Times **10** *n* (also **drop joint**) *underworld* A seemingly honest place used as a cover for illegal matters, esp as a depot for stolen goods **11** *n* A drink or drinks: *I could see by his careful walking he'd taken a drop* **12** *n black* A homeless slum boy: *accepting anywhere from 25 cents to $1 a week for taking in drops, rustles, fetches*—W Davenport **13** *n cabdrivers* A paying passenger **14** *n cabdrivers* The base fee on a taxi meter registered when the cabdriver activates the meter
See GET THE DROP ON someone, KNOCK-OUT DROPS

drop a brick *v phr* To blunder; commit a gaffe: *He rather dropped a brick when he mispronounced Lady Fuchs's name*

drop a bundle *v phr* To lose a large amount of money, esp by gambling: *He's dropped a bundle that way*—WT Tyler

drop a (or **the**) **dime 1** *v phr* To inform; give information, esp to the police; =DIME, RAT: *Chaney ques-*

tioned the man who had dropped the dime on Madison—Washingtonian/ *and then he dropped the dime (made the phone call) and turned Vinnie in* —Village Voice **2** *v phr Army* To point out the faults and failures of another; criticize [fr the *dime* put into a pay telephone] ● New York City teenagers have equated **dime** with an amount of information, and also speak of **dropping a quarter**, more information, and **dropping a dollar**, the maximum of information

drop beads *homosexuals* **1** *v phr* To use homosexual code words to elicit whether someone is homosexual **2** *v phr* To reveal oneself as homosexual inadvertently, esp during conversation

drop case (or **shot**) *n phr* A stupid person; idiot; =TURKEY: *Nobody... was a big enough drop case to bet* —Dan Jenkins/ *Mr Williams called Mr Mallard a drop shot*—New York Times [perhaps fr the notion that a stupid person had been *dropped* on his head when a baby, with some added connection with the ignominious *drop shot* in tennis]

drop one's **cookies** *See* SHOOT one's COOKIES

drop dead **1** *interj* Go to hell; screw you; =GET LOST ● Nearly always an exclamation of curt refusal or sharp disapproval: *At that rude suggestion she told him to drop dead* **2** *adj phr* Unusually striking; sensational: *A drop-dead mansion in Beverly Hills, complete with his-and-hers whirlpools*—People Weekly/ *the soulful voice and the drop-dead campiness*—Time ● So called because it is an affront to some canons of taste

drop-dead list *n phr* A usu fancied list of persons one does not wish to associate with or favor; =SHIT LIST

drop-in **1** *n* A place of temporary and often dubious resort: *drop-ins for youths wishing marijuana revels*—NY Confidential **2** *n students* A person who attends classes and other college events without being registered: *NBC did some research on college drop-ins*—D Kallman [the opposite of a *dropout*]

drop joint *See* DROP

drop someone or something **like a hot potato** *v phr* To divest or get rid of very quickly: *When she frowned I dropped the topic like a hot potato*

◁ **drop** one's **load**▷ **1** *v phr* To ejaculate semen; have an orgasm **2** *v phr* =DUMP A LOAD

drop out *v phr* To remove oneself from the conventional competitive world of politics, business, education, etc: *rush back from every excursion into Big Power and drop out with town meetings and backyard picnics* —Hugh Sidey

drops *See* KNOCKOUT DROPS

drop one's **teeth** *v phr* To be very astonished; be gapingly shocked: *I do drop my teeth at the notion that Shakespeare is busted and needs to be fixed*—Washington Post

drop the other shoe *v phr* To conclude or round out something in suspense: *The city... dropped the other shoe*—Village Voice/ *The President dropped the other budget shoe yesterday*

◁ **drop your cocks and grab your socks**▷ *sentence WW2 armed forces* Get out of bed immediately ● A jovial instruction issued by a noncommissioned officer or barracks orderly to troops quite early in the morning

drownder *See* GOOSE-DROWNDER

drowned rat *See* LOOK LIKE A DROWNED RAT

drown one's **sorrows** (or **troubles**) *v phr* To alleviate or obscure the chagrins of one's life by getting drunk

drug[1] *v* To annoy and nag at; =BUG: *His constant bitching really drugs me* *See* DESIGNER DRUG, HARD DRUG, LOVE DRUG, SOFT DRUG

drug[2] *adj* Displeased; angry; =PISSED OFF: *If other players are drug about it or feel that I'm trying to horn in... then it's not much fun*—Downbeat [past participle of *drag*, in one of its pejorative connotations]

druggie or **druggy** *n narcotics* A narcotics user or addict; =DOPER

drugola *n narcotics* Money paid by narcotics dealers for protection, esp to the police

drugstore race *n phr horse-racing* A race in which one or more of the creatures has been given drugs or alcohol: *what racketeers call "a drug store race"*—A Hynd

drum-beater *n* A person, esp a press agent, who insistently lauds someone or something: *Phil's a drum-beater for jogging now*

drummer **1** *n fr middle 1800s* A traveling salesperson **2** *n railroad* A yard conductor

drum up *v phr fr early 1800s* To stimulate; promote: *Go drum up a little enthusiasm for this turkey*

drunk *See* PUNCH-DRUNK

drunkard *n railroad* A late Saturday night train

drunk as a skunk *adj phr* Very drunk; =SNOCKERED: *They bring beer and cigarettes, are drunk as skunks* —Village Voice

drunk tank *See* TANK

druthers *n fr Southern dialect* Wishes; desires; preferred alternatives: *We know your druthers, The Marketplace*—Philadelphia [fr a dialect pronunciation of *rather* or *had rather*]

See HAVE one's DRUTHERS

not **dry behind the ears** *See* NOT DRY BEHIND THE EARS

◀**dry fuck** (or **hump**)▶ **1** *n phr* To approximate the sex act, without penetration or divestiture, and typically without orgasm: *what he would call... the dry humps*—Stephen King **2** *v: Did attack-crazy kamikazes crash into dry-humping kids on the Hell's Kitchen shore?*—Village Voice

dry out *v phr fr late 1800s* To refrain from alcohol, esp in a hospital as a part of treatment for alcohol abuse

dry run **1** *n phr* A tryout, practice version, or rehearsal of something planned: *One more dry run, then tomorrow we do it* **2** *v: so the hospital staff could "dry run" their equipment*—Associated Press **3** *n phr* =DRY FUCK

DT's *n* Delirium tremens; =the CLANKS: *When Bix got the DT's Whiteman treated Bix to a drunk cure*—Stephen Longstreet

dub¹ **1** *n* A form of reggae music marked by weird, unexpected, and discontinuous sounds: *The hypnotic weirdness of such music has helped make dub the most popular form of reggae*—Newsweek **2** *modifier: A flood of dub versions followed* —Newsweek [probably fr the electronic technique of *dubbing* sound tracks]

dub² **1** *v* To replace or augment an original sound track with another, esp to substitute a movie sound track in a language other than the original **2** *v* To add a singer, instrumental part, etc, to the tape for a recording: *They dubbed the final vocals last week* [fr *double*]

dub³ *n fr late 1800s* An awkward performer; novice; =DUFFER

See FLUBDUB, FLUB THE DUB

dubee or **duby** *See* DOOBIE

ducat or **ducket** or **duket** (DUH kət) **1** *n fr late 1800s British* A ticket or pass to a show, game, race, etc **2** *n hoboes* A union card **3** *n hoboes* A printed card begging alms for a deaf or blind person **4** *n* A dollar; money: *keep him in ducats for the rest of his life*—Ellery Queen [fr the name of an originally Italian gold coin]

duck **1** *n fr middle 1800s* A man; fellow; =GUY: *That duck isn't a critic* —H McHugh **2** *n* (also **ducks**) Dear one; precious; pet; =DUCKY: *How does that grab you, duck?/ and his wife, a darling duck of a homebody*—Village Voice **3** *n* =DUCK-EGG **4** *n* A hospital bedpan **5** *n* An amphibious vehicle, esp a World War 2 troop carrier designated DUKW 1942, whence the nickname **6** *v* To move, weave, squat, etc, so as to avoid a blow **7** *v* (also **duck out**) *fr late 1800s* To evade or escape: *He ducked over the wall/ They always felt she was trying to duck work*

See DEAD DUCK, FUCK A DUCK, HAVE one's DUCKS IN A ROW, KNEE-HIGH TO A GRASSHOPPER, LAME DUCK, SITTING DUCK

duck bumps *n phr* =GOOSE BUMPS

duck-butt *n* A person of short stature

duck-egg *n* A score or grade of zero; =GOOSE-EGG, ZIP

duck-fit *n* A noisy fit of anger: *Clarice ...would throw a duck-fit, if she knew* —Elmer Rice

ducks *See* HAVE one's DUCKS IN A ROW

duck soup *n phr* Anything easily done; =CINCH, PIECE OF CAKE: *She made it look like duck soup*

duck squeezer *n phr college students* A conservationist and environmentalist; =ECOFREAK

ducky or **duckie** **1** *adj* Excellent; splendid • Often used ironically: *What a perfectly ducky notion!* **2** *adj* Cute; too cute; =CORNY: *Pastel phials tied with ducky satin bows*

—Raymond Chandler **3** *n* Dear one; precious; =DEARIE: *Are you quite ready, duckie?*

dud **1** *n fr middle 1800s* A failure: *The show's a dud* **2** *n fr WW1* A shell or bomb that fails to explode **3** *modifier: a dud bomb*

duddy *See* FUDDY-DUDDY

dude **1** *n fr late 1800s* A dapper man, esp one who is ostentatiously dressed; dandy **2** *n fr late 1800s* A guest at a Western or Western-style ranch **3** *n esp black* A man; fellow; =CAT, GUY: *I'm sittin' in the bus stop... just me an' these other three dudes*—D Evans

dude heaver *n phr* =BOUNCER

Dudley *See* YOUR UNCLE DUDLEY

dues *See* PAY one's DUES

duff *n* The buttocks; rump; =ASS: *A bunch of lazy guys sitting around on our duffs*—Time

duffer *fr middle 1800s British* **1** *n* An elderly man; =GEEZER, JASPER • Used rather affectionately: *He's a sweet old duffer, isn't he?* **2** *n* A mediocre or downright poor performer, esp at golf; =HACKER [perhaps fr Scots *duffar* "dolt"]

dufus **1** *adj* (also ◁**dufus-assed**▷) Stupid; blundering: *many another dufus play among friends* —Richard Merkin **2** *n:* (also ◁**dufus-ass**▷) *He's a real dufus*

duke **1** *n* A hand, esp when regarded as a weapon **2** *n prizefight* The winning decision in a boxing match, signaled by the referee's holding up the victor's hand: *Even if I lose the duke I get forty per cent*—Jim Tully **3** *v* To hand something to someone: *Duke the kid a five or ten*—George V Higgins **4** *v* To fight with the fists **5** *v circus* To try to collect money from a parent for something given to a child **6** *v circus* To short-change someone by palming a coin owed him **7** *v* To shake hands; =PRESS THE FLESH [fr Romany *dook* "the hand as read in palmistry, one's fate"; but see *dukes*]

the **duke** *n phr* On a farm, the bull

duke someone **out** **1** *v phr* To beat unconscious; =KNOCK someone OUT: *What should I do, duke him or her out?*—National Review **2** *v phr* To damage or injure: *Dirk Hamilton dukes himself out, adopts a... style in which he's inferior*—Village Voice

dukes *n fr middle 1800s British* The fists or hands: *He put up his dukes to defend himself* [said to be Cockney rhyming slang fr *Duke of Yorks* "forks"]

dukes-up *adj* Combative; =FEISTY: *Her salty language and dukes-up style endeared her*—Time

duket *See* DUCAT

dull as dishwater *adj phr* Very tedious and unexciting; boring: *The sermon today was dull as dishwater, Your Eminence*

dullsville *adj* Very dull; tedious; =DRAGSVILLE: *a dullsville wimp* [see *-sville*]

dumb **1** *adj fr early 1800s* Stupid; mentally sluggish; =DIM: *You think I'm pretty dumb, don't you?*—F Scott Fitzgerald/ *a dumb trick* **2** *adv: He acts dumb sometimes* **3** *adj & adv* =DAMN, DARN [fr Pennsylvania German *dumm*]

◁**dumb-ass**▷ **1** *adj* Stupid; inane; tedious: *a dumb-ass trick/ Our private life has to take a back seat to every dumbass little news story* —Armistead Maupin **2** *n: to understand how a dumb-ass like Newton can have a following*—Playboy

dumbbell *n fr 1920s* A stupid person; idiot: *He's slow, but no dumbbell*

dumb bunny *n phr* A naive and unwary person; silly little fool: *Only a dumb bunny would fall for that crap*

dumb cluck *n phr* A stupid person; clumsy bungler; =KLUTZ: *all those dumb clucks snickering at you*—Sinclair Lewis

dumb down *v phr* To make simpler, esp to alter a textbook to make it more elementary: *what some educators have called the "dumbing down" of textbooks*—New York Times [attributed to Los Angeles Times reporter William Trombley]

dumbo (DUM boh) **1** *n* A stupid person: *an ace dumbo friend named Cleo*—Time **2** *n* A blunder; stupid mistake; =BLOOPER: *if you think you've seen dumbos pulled on the highways*—Saturday Evening Post

dumb ox *n phr* A stupid, sluggish person, esp a hulking one

dum-dum or **dumdum** or **dumb-dumb** **1** *n* A stupid or foolish person **2** *adj: his dumdum ideas/ a dum-dum crack/ The only man safe* *enough to see is this dumdum cop* —Saul Bellow

dummy **1** *n* A stupid person; idiot; =CLUCK ◁**2**▷ *n* A deaf-mute or a mute **3** *n hoboes* Bread **4** *n railroad* A train carrying railroad employees ◁**5**▷ *n* The penis **6** *n* A weakened or diluted narcotic; also, a non-narcotic substance sold as a narcotic: =BLANK **7** *n newspaper office & publishing* A pasted-up page, a blank book, or other preliminary representation of material to be published **8** *v: The designer dummied the new book* **9** *n* A model or representation **10** ***modifier:*** *a dummy machine gun/ dummy windows*

See BEAT one's MEAT

dummy up **1** *v phr* To keep silent; =CLAM UP: *You can't dummy up on a murder case*—Raymond Chandler/ *When questioned, they invariably dummy up*—SJ Perelman **2** *v phr* To make a representation or model: *The carpenter dummied up a Victorian facade/ Have layout dummy up those pages*

dump **1** *n fr late 1800s* Any place so shabby or ugly as to be comparable to a depository for trash and garbage; a repulsive venue: *What a dump my hometown is now!* **2** *n* Any building or place: *Nice little dump you got here/ fanciest dump in town* **3** *n underworld* A prison **4** *v fr middle 1800s* To sell goods, stock, etc, in order to manipulate or depress a market **5** *n gambling* A race, game, etc, that is intentionally lost, usu for gambling advantage; =FIX: *When he took a dive in the first I knew we had a dump on our hands* **6** *v: Players accepting bribes to "dump" games*—Associated Press/ *Some people would think that Goliath dumped, for that matter* **7** *v* To bunt a baseball: *Dehoney dumped one toward third* **8** *v* To kill **9** *v* To rid oneself of someone or something; =DEEP-SIX: *He dumped the whole cabinet* **10** *n* A defecation; =a SHIT: *To start the morning with a satisfactory dump is a good omen*—WH Auden

See CORE DUMP, TAKE A DUMP

◁ **dump a load**▷ *v phr* To defecate; =CRAP

dumper *n* A container for trash; dumpster: *It was determined...that disco would be in the dumper*—Playboy

dump on (or **all over**) *v phr* To criticize harshly, often unfairly; complain and carp at; =PUT DOWN: *Don't dump on the teachers we have*—New York Times/ *an acknowledgement of the fact that he had dumped on us all year*—Judith Martin

dune buggy *n phr* A small and squat open car, usu with a Volkswagen engine, equipped with very fat tires for traveling on sand

duner *n* A dune-buggy driver or rider: *Duners go out on runs, trips by a half-dozen dune buggies*—Calvin Trillin

dunk **1** *v fr 1920s* To dip something into a liquid, esp to dip food into a drink: *I dunk doughnuts in Scotch/ Scientific temperature readings cannot be taken just by dunking a thermometer on a string*—G Hill **2** *v* To go into the water: *Be right back, just want to dunk* **3** *n: Leroy had a quick dunk in the creek* **4** *n sports* A basketball field goal scored by putting the ball into the hoop from just beside or above it: *Almost all of the baskets were dunks* —Sports Illustrated/ *basketball courts ...where the dunks have been so fierce lately*—Philadelphia **5** *v: He jumped up and dunked another one* [fr Pennsylvania German *dunken* "dip"]

See SLAM DUNK

dupe *n* A duplicate copy, esp of a letter or other text

duper *See* SUPER-DUPER

durn or **durned** *See* DARN

a **durn** *See* NOT GIVE A DAMN

dust **1** *v fr middle 1800s fr 1600s British* To leave quickly; flee; fly: *Dillinger...used a Ford...when dusting from a job*—A Hynd **2** *v* To hit; swat: *dusted one of the lieutenants with an old shoe for trying to talk them back to work*—Time **3** *v* To spray insecticide from a low-flying aircraft **4** *n narcotics* Narcotics in powder form

See ANGEL DUST, EAT someone's DUST, HAPPY-DUST

the **dust** *See* BITE THE DUST

duster **1** *n baseball* A pitch purposely thrown at or close to the batter, to intimidate him or force him back from the plate; =BRUSHBACK **2** ***n*** A woman's smock or housecoat

dust kitty (or **bunny**) ***n phr*** One of the tufts of dust that accumulate under beds, tables, etc; =GHOST TURDS

dust someone **off** **1** ***v phr*** To give someone a beating; thrash **2** ***v phr*** *baseball* To pitch a ball at or close to the batter; =BRUSHBACK

dust someone's **pants** (or **trousers**) ***v phr*** To hit or kick in the rump; esp, to spank a child

dustup ***n*** A quarrel or fight; altercation; =SCRAP: *a big dustup in the office of a vice-president*—New Yorker

dusty ***See*** RUSTY-DUSTY

dusty butt ***n phr*** A person of short stature

Dutch **1** ***adj*** German: *Ann Arbor's a Dutch town* **2** ***n*** A nickname for anyone with a German surname: *Big Dutch Klangenfuss* **3** ***v*** *gambling* To place a careful series of bets such that the gambling house or owner of the game is ruined **4** ***v*** To ruin someone's business, health, reputation, etc, maliciously **5** ***adv*** With each person paying his or her own share: *This meal is Dutch, okay?*
See GO DUTCH, IN DUTCH, TO BEAT THE BAND

the **Dutch act** ***See*** DO THE DUTCH

Dutch courage ***n phr*** False or fleeting bravery resulting from liquor: *A man in liquor... is full of Dutch courage*—FK Secrist [like many other pejorative uses of *Dutch*, this comes from the 17th century, when the English and the Hollanders were chronically at war. In some uses, though, *Dutch* means "German" rather than "Netherlandish," and the cases are not easily sorted]

Dutch treat **1** ***n phr*** A meal, show, etc, where each person pays his or her own way **2** ***adv:*** *We'll eat Dutch treat tonight*
See GO DUTCH

dweeb ***n*** *teenagers* A despised person; =CREEP, NERD

◁ **dyke** or **dike**▷ **1** ***n*** A lesbian, esp one who takes an aggressive role; =BULLDYKE **2** ***modifier:*** *That woman lives with her dyke daughter and her dyke daughter-in-law*—Armistead Maupin [origin uncertain and much debated; perhaps fr a shortening of *morphodyke*, dialectal and substandard pronunciation of "hermaphrodite," perhaps influenced by *dick* "penis"]

◁ **dykey** or **dikey**▷ ***adj*** Resembling or having the nature of an aggressive lesbian: *a dykey sort of woman/ doing calisthenics with the dikey-looking brunette*—Earl Thompson

dynamite **1** ***n*** *narcotics* Heroin or cocaine of high quality: *a connection who deals in good-quality stuff, "dynamite"*—J Mills **2** ***n*** *narcotics* Marijuana, esp a marijuana cigarette **3** ***adj*** (also **dy-no-mite**) Excellent; superior; =SUPER: *a dynamite scheme* **4** ***n*** Something very disturbing or dangerous; a sensation: *Don't talk about it, it's dynamite* **5** ***n*** *gambling* A portion of bets that a bookmaker has covered elsewhere in order to minimize his risk

dynamiter ***n*** *truckers* A driver who abuses a truck by rough handling or speeding

E

eager beaver **1** ***n phr*** *esp WW2 armed forces* An energetic and willing worker; ambitious striver **2** ***modifier:*** *her eager-beaver sincerity/ eager-beaver gung-ho spirit*

the **eagers** ***n phr*** Eagerness; exaggerated willingness

eagle ***See*** the DAY THE EAGLE SHITS, LEGAL EAGLE

eagle day ***n phr*** *WW2 armed forces* Payday [fr the *eagle* depicted on US currency]

eagle freak ***n phr*** A conservationist and environmentalist; = ECOFREAK, DUCK SQUEEZER

ear **1** ***n*** The handle of a cup: *around the ear of my coffee cup* —Peter De Vries **2** ***v*** To listen; hear: *Rosen Tapes To Be Eared By The Judge*—New York Daily News ***See*** ALL EARS, BEND someone's EAR, BLOW IT OUT, CAULIFLOWER EAR, CHEW someone's EAR OFF, HAVE something COMING OUT OF one's EARS, IN A PIG'S ASS, NOT DRY BEHIND THE EARS, PIN someone's EARS BACK, PLAY IT BY EAR, POUND one's EAR, PULL IN one's EARS, PUT A BUG IN someone's EAR, PUT IT IN YOUR EAR, STAND AROUND WITH one's FINGER UP one's ASS, STEAM WAS COMING OUT OF someone's EARS, STICK IT, TALK someone's EAR OFF

ear-bender ***n*** An overly loquacious person; = WINDBAG: *James Joyce was something of an ear-bender, no?*

eared ***See*** DOG-EARED

an **earful** ***n phr*** A large or impressive quantity of talk, esp of a rambling or gossipy sort

early bird **1** ***n phr*** A person who habitually gets up early in the morning; one who greets the dawn **2** ***modifier:*** *an early-bird session/ early-bird radio program* **3** ***n phr*** A person who arrives early at a gathering, the office, etc **4** ***n phr*** The first train, bus, airplane, etc, of the day

earn one's **wings** ***v phr*** To prove oneself competent and reliable in one's work [fr the *wing*-shaped badge awarded to graduating air cadets]

ease someone **out** ***v phr*** To dismiss or remove from a post or place gradually and gently

Eastern Western ***n phr*** A Japanese or Chinese movie featuring the sort of violence and machismo typical of cowboy movies

easy ***See*** SPEAKEASY, TAKE IT EASY, TAKE THINGS EASY

easy as pie ***adj phr*** & ***adv phr*** (Variations: **can be** or **could be** or **falling off a log** or **hell** or **rolling off a log** may replace **pie**) Very easy or easily: *He did it easy as pie/ The thing's easy as can be*

easy make **1** ***n phr*** (also **easy lay**) A woman easily persuaded to engage in the sex act **2** ***n phr*** = EASY MARK

easy mark ***n phr*** A person easily victimized or cheated; = PATSY, SUCKER:

easy meat *fr 1920s British* **1** ***n phr*** Something done or acquired very easily **2** ***modifier:*** *their easy-meat score in the aerial spraying issue* —Los Angeles Times [fr the earlier sense that something or someone is vulnerable, easily hunted and caught, etc, esp in the sexual sense where *meat* means "sexual victim, conquest, object, etc"]

easy street ***See*** ON EASY STREET

eat **1** ***v*** To preoccupy or upset; engross; fret: *She asked what was eating me when I frowned so* **2** ***v***

To be forced to accept something; swallow something: *He couldn't get any redress, and just had to eat the damage* **3** *v sports* To be unable to pass the ball along: *They blitzed and the quarterback had to eat the ball* **4** *v* To accept and enjoy; =SWALLOW: *You really eat this shit, don't you?*—CDB Bryan ◁**5**▷ *v* To do fellatio or cunnilingus; =GO DOWN ON someone

eat dirt *v phr* To accept rebuke or harassment meekly; swallow one's pride; =EAT SHIT: *I ate dirt and apologized to that bastard*—Calder Willingham

eat someone's **dust** *v phr* To be behind in a race or chase: *After two laps they ate Coghlan's dust*

eater *See* FROG, GRASSEATER, HAY-EATER, MEATEATER, MOTHERFUCKER, PETER-EATER

eat one's **hat** *See* EAT one's WORDS

eat (or **live**) **high on the hog** (or **off the hog** or **on the joint**) *v phr* To live very well; thrive, prosper; =SHIT IN HIGH COTTON: *You will...eat high on the hog, as a member of the ruling mob*—Westbrook Pegler/ *The institute will eat high off the hog*—Harvey Breit

eating *See* FROG, MOTHERFUCKING

◁ **eatin' stuff** or **eating pussy** or **table grade**▷ *n phr* A woman of great sexual appeal

eat it ◁**1**▷ *v phr* To do fellatio or cunnilingus; =GO DOWN ON someone ◁**2**▷ *interj* (also **eat this**) An exclamation of contempt and defiance • A hostile invitation to fellatio: *"Gee, Les, you're such a charming guy," Frank says. "Eat it"*—Atlantic Monthly/ *When the cop questioned him he said, "Eat this, buster"* **3** *v phr* To dispose of something in an embarrassing way; swallow something: *The quarterback just had to eat the football when he found no receivers*

eat (or **have**) someone's **lunch** *v phr* To defeat decisively; =CLOBBER: *The hitters have been having his lunch*—New Yorker

eat someone **out** **1** *v phr* To reprimand severely; rebuke harshly; =CHEW someone OUT: *Out came Joe McCarthy from the Boston dugout all set to eat me out*—Gilbert Millstein ◁**2**▷ *v phr* To do cunnilingus or analingus

◁ **eat shit**▷ **1** *v phr* =EAT DIRT **2** *v phr* To be repulsive and contemptible • Usu a loud oral insult: *You eat shit, you son of a bitch!*
See TAKE SHIT

eat one **up** *v phr* To be strongly bothered or affected by: *His pontificating really eats me up*

eat someone **up** (or **up with a spoon**) *v phr* To be especially devoted to: *She's so sweet I could just eat her up*

eat one's **words** (or **hat**) *v phr* To be forced either to retract or to suffer for what one has said: *They showed him proof and he had to eat his words/ I'll eat my hat if I'm wrong*

ech (EK) *See* YUCK

ecofreak or **econut** *n* An environmentalist and conservationist; =DUCK SQUEEZER, EAGLE FREAK: *Eco-freaks will love the clean-burning engine*—National Review

ecstasy *n narcotics* A variety of amphetamine narcotic: *Ecstasy... by emergency order of the Drug Enforcement Administration, illegal*—Washington Post

edge *See* HAVE AN EDGE ON, HAVE AN EDGE ON someone

edged **1** *adj* Drunk: *When he was nicely edged he was a pretty good sort of guy*—Raymond Chandler **2** *adj teenagers* Very angry; =PISSED OFF

edge someone **out** *v phr* To defeat by a close margin; barely surpass: *We edged them out by just three votes*

edgy or **on edge** *adj* or *adj phr fr early 1900s* Tense and irritable; nervous; =UPTIGHT: *I saw he was getting a bit edgy, so I agreed to include him*

Edsel *n* Something useless; a fiasco: *We have to win out. We're not selling Edsels, you know*—Time [fr the *Edsel* car, which fell short of commercial success]

-ee *suffix used to form nouns* The object of what is indicated: *baby-sittee/ kickee/ muggee*

◁ **eff**▷ *v & n* =FUCK • This curt euphemism is also the base for equivalents of **fucked**, **fucking**, and **fucker:** *eff off back to effing Russia*—Anthony Burgess/ *otherwise effed around until... Bill Veeck was forced to*—Playboy

egads switch (or **button**) *See* CHICKEN SWITCH

egg **1** *n fr late 1800s* A person: *Evelyn's a good egg* **2** *n* Anything roughly egg-shaped, such as the head, a baseball, an aerial bomb, etc: *bopped him on the egg/ reared back and chucked the old egg* **3** *n* =EGGHEAD [first sense altered fr the mid-19th-century term *bad egg* "bad or rotten person"]
See BAD EGG, DUCK-EGG, GOOSE EGG, HARD-BOILED EGG, HAVE EGG ON one's FACE, LAY AN EGG, SUCK EGGS, YOU CAN'T MAKE AN OMELET WITHOUT BREAKING EGGS

eggery *See* HAM-AND-EGGERY

egghead **1** *n* A bald man **2** *n* An intellectual; thinker; =DOUBLE-DOME: *An egghead is "one who calls Marilyn Monroe Mrs Arthur Miller"* —P Sann [presumably fr the putative high, domed, *egg*-shaped *heads* of such persons; the term was used in a letter of Carl Sandburg about 1918]

egg in someone's **beer** *n phr* The height of luxury or pleasure; everything one could desire • Often part of an impatient question addressed to someone who asks for more than is merited or available: *So it's got no air-conditioning. You want egg in your beer?*

ego trip (or **jag**) **1** *n phr* Something done primarily to build one's self-esteem or display one's splendid qualities: *The pie-thrower... said the guru was on an ego trip*—Time/ *This isn't any ego trip, taking a job in this administration*—WT Tyler **2** *v: I was showing off, ego-tripping*

eight *See* FORKED-EIGHT

eightball *See* BEHIND THE EIGHT BALL

eighteen wheeler *n phr truckers & citizens band* A semitrailer truck; cab and trailer: *The driver of the eighteen-wheeler to my left was wearing the uniform of the West Virginia Highway Patrol*—Penthouse

eighter (or **Ada**) **from Decatur** *n phr crapshooting & poker* The card, roll, or point of eight

eight-hundred-pound gorilla *See* SIX-HUNDRED-POUND GORILLA

eighty-eight or **eighty-eights** *n* A piano

eighty-four *n WW2 Navy* A naval prison

eighty-one or **eighty-two** *n lunch counter* A glass of water

eighty-seven *n lunch counter* A signal meaning "a good-looking woman has come in; take note"

eighty-six **1** *n lunch counter* A cook's term for "none" or "nix" when asked for something not available **2** *v: We had to eighty-six the French dip*—John Sayles **3** *n bartenders* A person who is not to be served more liquor: *"eighty-six," which... means: "Don't serve him"* —Gene Fowler **4** *v* (also **eight-six**) To eject or interdict someone: *I'll have you eighty-sixed out of this bar*—John Rechy/ *I been eighty-sixed out of better situations*—George V Higgins **5** *v* To kill; destroy; annihilate: *There'd been serious pragmatic reasons for not eighty-sixing the man then and there*—Richard Merkin [probably fr the rhyme with "nix"]

eighty-two *See* EIGHTY-ONE

elbow *See* BEND THE ELBOW, NOT KNOW one's ASS FROM one's ELBOW, RUB ELBOWS

elbow-bender *n* A convivial person; drinker

elbow-bending *n* Drinking liquor: *the gentlemanly art of refined elbow-bending*—Esquire

elbow grease *n phr fr late 1700s British* Muscular exertion; physical effort

elbow someone **out** *v phr* To eliminate or replace by aggressive pressure: *He elbowed her out of the vice presidency*

elbow room *n phr fr 1700s* Barely enough space for the occupant; a minimum of space: *This office is so crowded I couldn't find elbow room for anyone else/ Don't crowd so, give me elbow room* [propagated in the US because it was a nickname for General John Burgoyne, who boasted in the 1770s that he would find *elbow room* in this country]

El Cheapo *n phr* A cheap product; a piece of shoddy merchandise: *They bought the El Cheapos and found they didn't work*—New York Times [see *el -o*, mock-Spanish combining form]

elephant *See* WHITE ELEPHANT

elephant tranquilizer *n phr* =ANGEL DUST

elevator music *n phr* Bland, pretty music, of the sort played over speakers in elevators; =MUZAK

el foldo *See* PULL AN EL FOLDO

el -o *combining form* An amusing variation of whatever is infixed: *travel el cheapo*—Time/ *flatchested el birdos in long dresses*—Stephen King/ *You still seeing El Sleazo these days?*—Cyra McFadden/ *universal emptiness ... el zilcho*—Stephen King/ *Our President ... did his famous el foldo*—Sports Illustrated/ *If it is calm, it is el snoro*—Time [fr a common pattern in Spanish]

else *See* OR ELSE

Elsewhere *See* MOUNT SAINT ELSEWHERE

embrangle *v* To involve; entangle: *The investigation threatened to embrangle ... the Duke of Argyll* —Time [a blend of *embroil* with *entangle*]

emery ball *n phr baseball* A pitch thrown with the ball partially roughened

emote 1 *v* To play a theatrical role, esp one calling for a strong display of emotion; =HAM: *all been panting to see her emote in the gangster film* —Louella Parsons **2** *v* To indulge in a display of feeling, esp a pretense: *Now she's emoting about the electric bill*

empty nester *n phr* Parent whose children have grown up and moved from home: *We are getting a lot of empty-nesters moving into a Leisure World development*—Washingtonian

enchilada *See* BIG ENCHILADA, the WHOLE ENCHILADA

end 1 *n* A share; =CUT: *Eddie would be entitled to half an end*—E DeBaun **2** *n* Particular concern or portion; sector: *Selling's his end of it* *See* GO OFF THE DEEP END, HIND END, JUMP OFF THE DEEP END, the LIVING END, REAR END, SEE THE LIGHT AT THE END OF THE TUNNEL, SHORT END OF THE STICK

the **end** *n phr beat & cool talk* The best; the greatest; =the LIVING END: *Mr Secretary General, you're the end!*

endville or **endsville** *adj esp 1950s cool talk* Superb; unsurpassed: *His last gig was endsville* [see -*sville*]

enforcer *n* A person, esp a gangster or an athlete, assigned to intimidate and punish opponents

an **engraved invitation** *See* DO YOU WANT AN ENGRAVED INVITATION

enough to choke a horse 1 *adv phr* To a very great degree; in a very large quantity: *His ego is big enough to choke a horse* **2** *n phr* A very large quantity; a plethora: *Does he have money? Enough to choke a horse*

enough to gag a maggot *adv phr* Very disgusting; repulsive: *His excuse was enough to gag a maggot*

equalizer *n* A pistol or other firearm

erase *v* To kill; =RUB OUT

-erino *suffix used to form nouns* (also **-arino** or **-orino**) A humorous version or a remarkable specimen of what is indicated: *peacherino/ bitcherino* [probably fr the Italian diminutive suffix *-ino* combined with the agentive suffix *-er*]

-eroo *suffix used to form nouns* (also **-aroo** or **-roo** or **-oo**) Emphatic, humorous, or affectionate form of what is indicated: *babyroo/ jivaroo/ screameroo/ sockeroo*

-erooney *See* -AROONEY

-ers *suffix used to form adjectives* In the condition humorously indicated • These are all British imports, coming ultimately from public school slang: *bonkers/ preggers/ starkers*

-ery 1 *suffix used to form nouns* Place or establishment where the indicated thing is used, done, sold, etc: *boozery/ eatery/ minkery* **2** *suffix used to form nouns* The collectivity or an instance of what is indicated: *claptrappery/ jerkery*

-ess *suffix used to form nouns* A woman member of the indicated group or calling • A standard suffix now used most often in slang partly because the standard use is regarded as, and sometimes meant to be, offensive: *loaferess/ muggess/ veepess*

-eteria *See* -ATERIA

Euro *adj & combining word* European: *The majority of the Euro children hit the black box first*—Psychology/ *Eurobrat/ Eurobucks/ Eurofunk/ dancing Europop strings*—Village Voice

evened out *adj phr* Restored to balance and health; rational: *"I was really emotionally fucked up." "Are you evened out now?"*—Diana Clapton

even-stephen or **even-steven 1** *adj fr middle 1800s* Fair; even; equable: *Give me the hundred and fifty and we'll call it even-steven*

—Dashiell Hammett **2** *adv: And we'll do likewise for San Francisco and Odessa, or any places we want, always even-stephen*—D Fairbairn

evergreen *n* A perennial favorite, esp a song; =GOLDEN OLDIE

every Tom, Dick, and Harry *n phr* Every and any man, esp a very ordinary one; =ORDINARY JOE: *letting every Tom, Dick, and Harry in on the election*—Max Shulman

evil **1** *adj* Excellent; splendid; =MEAN, WICKED: *Geoffrey beats an evil set of skins* **2** *adj* *homosexuals* Biting and sarcastic; catty; =BITCHY

ex[1] or **x** *n* A former wife or husband, girlfriend or boyfriend, etc: *He introduced his ex rather casually, considering they were together 27 years*

ex[2] *n circus* An exclusive concession

excuse (ek SKYōōS) *n* A version or example of: *He's a rotten excuse for a lawyer*

excuse (or **pardon**) **me all to hell** *sentence* I apologize; I am sorry • Most often said ironically, when one thinks an accusation has been undeserved or too strong

exec **1** *n Navy fr 1920s* An executive officer **2** *n* A business executive: *They'd never heard of female execs*—New York/ *I find parking space for senior execs*—New Yorker **3** *modifier: exec perks/ exec burnout*

expedition *See* GO FISHING

the **extra mile** *See* GO THE EXTRA MILE

-ey *See* -IE

eye **1** *n* A private detective; =PRIVATE EYE: *an eye named Johnny O'John*—Anthony Boucher **2** *n railroad* A signal light **3** *n* A television set or screen

See BIG BROWN EYES, BLACK EYE, DOG EYE, FISH-EGGS, FOUR-EYES, GET THE EYE, GIVE someone THE EYE, GIVE someone THE FISH-EYE, GIVE someone THE GLAD EYE, GIVE WITH THE EYES, the GLAD EYE, GOO-GOO EYES, HAVE EYES FOR, IN A PIG'S ASS, KEEP AN EYE ON someone or something, MAKE GOO-GOO EYES, MUD IN YOUR EYE, NOT BAT AN EYE, PRIVATE EYE, PULL THE WOOL OVER someone's EYES, PUT THE EYE ON someone, the RED-EYE, SHORT EYES, SHUT-EYE, SNAKE EYES, STONED TO THE EYES

the **Eye** or **the eye** *n* The Pinkerton National Detective Agency, or one of its detectives

eyeball *v teenagers fr black* To look at; look over; =SCOPE ON: *He would eyeball the idol-breaker*—Zora Neale Hurston/ *You locate trophies before they eyeball you*—Sports Afield

See GIVE someone THE FISH-EYE, UP TO one's EYEBALLS

eyeball to eyeball **1** *adv phr* Face to face; in confrontation: *We're eyeball to eyeball and I think the other fellow just blinked*—Dean Rusk **2** *adj phr: our eyeball-to-eyeball chat*

eyed *See* COCKEYED, ONE-EYED MONSTER, PIE-EYED

eye-opener **1** *n* A drink of liquor taken upon awaking: *He fumbled for the jug and slurped an eye-opener* **2** *n narcotics* An addict's first injection of the day **3** *n* Anything that informs or enlightens one: *Listening to that story was a real eye-opener*

eyepopper *n* Something that makes one's eyes bulge in astonishment: *The president added a further eyepopper*—Washington Post

eye-shut *n* =SHUT-EYE

◁ **eyes like pissholes in the snow** ▷ *n phr* Very bleary eyes; tired and dim eyes, esp those of a severe hangover: *Your eyes look like two piss holes in the snow*—Rex Burns

eyes only *adj phr* Very personal and confidential [fr the phrase "for your *eyes only*"]

eyewash **1** *n* =HOGWASH **2** *n* Flattery; cajolery: *eyewash to soften him up for the touch*

F

fab ***adj*** & ***interj*** *esp teenagers* Excellent; wonderful; fabulous: *a man who would think it a fab idea to rent a silver limo*—Village Voice

face **1** ***n*** *show business* A celebrity, esp a show-business notable **2** ***n*** *student & cool talk* A person: *bad face... a surly, mean, no-good cat*—E Horne **3** ***n*** *black* A white person; =FAY

See BAG YOUR FACE, FEED one's FACE, GET OUT OF someone's FACE, GO UPSIDE one's FACE, HAVE A RED FACE, HAVE EGG ON one's FACE, JUST ANOTHER PRETTY FACE, LAUGH ON THE OTHER SIDE OF one's FACE, LET'S FACE IT, OPEN one's FACE, POKER FACE, RED FACE, SHIT-FACED, SHOOT OFF one's MOUTH, STRAIGHT FACE, SUCK FACE, TILL one IS BLUE IN THE FACE, WHAT'S-HIS-NAME, WHITE-FACE

face card ***n phr*** An important person; star; =BIG SHOT: *Oh, don't be so modest... you're a face card yourself now*—Philadelphia Journal

faced ***See*** POKER-FACED, RED-FACED, SHIT-FACED

face hanging out ***See*** STAND THERE WITH one's BARE FACE HANGING OUT

face-off ***n*** Confrontation, esp one before action: *continuing face-off and stalemate*—Philadelphia [fr the poised situation in a hockey game, where two players prepare to drive the puck when it is dropped between them by an official]

face the music ***v phr*** *fr middle 1800s* To endure whatever punishment or rigors one has incurred; take what one has coming [perhaps fr the necessity of forcing a cavalry horse to face steadily the regimental band; perhaps fr the plight of a performer on stage]

fack ***v*** *black* To tell the truth; utter facts: *Negroes know... that facking means speaking facts*—Time [fr the normal pronunciation of *fact* in Black English]

factor ***See*** FINAGLE FACTOR

factory **1** ***n*** *narcotics* The apparatus used for injecting narcotics; =WORKS **2** ***combining word*** Place where what is indicated is done, pursued, used, etc ● A jocular appropriation of the term: *brain factory/ freak factory/ nut factory*

See GARGLE-FACTORY, JOINT FACTORY, NUT HOUSE

fade **1** ***v*** To leave; depart: *He faded to Chicago*—A Hynd **2** ***v*** *crapshooting* To take one's bet; cover one's offered bet: *When I saw I was faded, I rolled the dice* **3** ***v*** To lose power and effectiveness: *They faded in the second half/ Damned engine's fading fast* **4** ***n*** *black* A white person **5** ***n*** *black* A black person who prefers white friends, sex partners, attitudes, etc; =OREO

fag **1** ***n*** *fr late 1800s* A cigarette; =BUTT, COFFIN NAIL: *He passed them swell fags around*—Langston Hughes ◁**2**▷ ***n*** *fr 1920s* A male homosexual; =FAGGOT, QUEER: *and fags are certain to arouse the loathing of all decent fiction addicts*—Gore Vidal/ *sicker by a long shot than any fag, drag, thang, or simple gay man or woman*—Ebony ◁**3**▷ ***modifier:*** *frenetic hot-rhythm dancing, the cheap fag jokes*—Playboy/ *like a fag party*—Raymond Chandler **4** ***v*** (also **fag out**) To fatigue; exhaust: *This sort of work fags me quickly* [origin unknown; the "homosexual" sense may be connected with the British term *fag* "the boy servant, and inferentially the catamite, of a public-school upperclassman"; perhaps influenced by Yiddish *faygele* "homosexual," literally "bird, little bird"]

fag along *v phr cowboys* To ride fast

◁ **fag bag** ▷ *n phr homosexuals* A woman married to a homosexual

◁ **faggot** ▷ *n* A male homosexual: *Hot faggot queens bump up against chilly Jewish matrons*—Albert Goldman/ *an amazing job of controlling the faggots*—Tennessee Williams [origin unknown; perhaps fr *fag*]

◁ **faggotry** ▷ *n* Male homosexuality: *Faggotry was at the very least a terrible embarrassment*—RA Arthur

◁ **faggoty** ▷ *adj* Homosexual, esp in an overt way • Used only of males: *who lives with his faggoty American friend*—Playboy

◁ **fag hag** or **faggot's moll** ▷ *n phr* A heterosexual woman who seeks or prefers the company of homosexual men: *Zeffirelli seems to have created a sort of limp-wrist commune, with Clare as the fag hag*—Judith Crist/ *Michael once referred to her...as "the fag hag of the bourgeoisie"*—Armistead Maupin

fail *n stock market* A failure of a broker to deliver stocks within a customary period: *the amount of what Wall Street calls "fails"*—New Yorker

fairhaired (or **blue-eyed** or **white-haired**) **boy** **1** *n phr* A favored or favorite man or boy: *the white-haired boy of the happy family*—Budd Schulberg/ *If I could possibly pull it off, I'd be the fair-haired boy*—Lawrence Sanders **2** *n phr* A man destined for and being groomed for principal leadership or other reward; =COMER

a **fair shake** *n phr fr early 1800s* Equal treatment; the same chance as others: *He complains he didn't get a fair shake* [fr an honest *shake* of the dice]

◁ **fairy** ▷ *n fr early 1900s fr hoboes* A male homosexual, esp an effeminate one; =FAG, QUEER: *Too bad you weren't a fairy*—Philip Wylie

◁ **fairy godmother** ▷ *n phr homosexuals* A male homosexual's homosexual initiator and tutor

◁ **fairy lady** ▷ *n phr* A lesbian who takes a passive role in sex

fake *fr early 1800s British* **1** *n* A sham or deception; something spurious **2** *v* To make something spurious; imitate deceptively: *He was good at faking Old Masters* [fr earlier *feak*, *feague*, or *fig* "to spruce up, esp by deceptive artificial means"; perhaps ultimately fr German *fegen* "clean, furbish"]

fake it **1** *v phr* To make a pretense of knowledge, skill, etc; bluff **2** *v phr* (also **fake**) *jazz musicians fr early 1900s* To improvise more or less compatible chords or notes as one plays or sings something one really has not learned

fake someone **out** *v phr* To bluff or deceive; mislead: *Bailey...had faked out Keuper into using a preempt*—John D MacDonald/ *He faked the cops out by dressing like a priest*

fall **1** *v underworld fr late 1800s* To be arrested; be imprisoned; =DROP: *When you have bad luck and you fall, New York is the best place*—New York Times/ *the best thief in the city till he fell*—WR Burnett **2** *n: Another fall meant a life sentence*—D Purroy **3** *v underworld* To fail in a robbery attempt: *The whole mob may fall*—E DeBaun **4** *v* To become enamored; become a lover: *Once Abelard saw her he fell*

See PRATFALL, the ROOF FALLS IN, TAKE A FALL, TAKE THE RAP

fall apart *v phr* To lose one's usual poise and confidence; lose control; =LOSE one's COOL: *Even the seasoned troupers fall apart*—A Hirschfeld

fall (or **slip**) **between** (or **through**) **the cracks** *v phr* To be ignored, overlooked, mismanaged, or forgotten, esp because of ambiguity in definition or understanding: *a conviction that otherwise might have fallen through the cracks*—Washingtonian

fall for **1** *v phr fr early 1900s* To become enamored with; become a lover of: *He's constantly falling for long-legged brunettes* **2** *v phr* To be deceived or duped by; acquiesce to: *Americans would continue to "fall for" this*—Robert Lynd/ *Don't fall for his limp excuses*

fall guy **1** *n phr fr early 1900s* An easy victim; =EASY MARK, SUCKER **2** *n phr fr underworld* A person who willingly or not takes the blame and punishment for another's misdoings;

=PATSY: *He said he would not be the President's fall guy*

falling off a log *See* EASY AS PIE

fall off the wagon *v phr* To begin drinking liquor again after a period of abstinence; also, to breach abstinence or moderation in anything: *But like most of us, she falls off the wagon from time to time, and heads for a stadium hot dog*—Toronto Life

◁ **fall on** one's **ass**▷ **1** *v phr* (also **fall flat on** one's **ass**) To fail, esp ignominiously and spectacularly: *They want to see you fall on your ass* —Interview **2** *v phr airline* To deteriorate beneath operational limits • Said of the weather conditions at an airport

fallout 1 *n* An accompanying or resultant effect of something; an aftermath: *Talking to oneself is a fallout of watching too many primaries on TV*—Goodman Ace **2** *n* Incidental products, esp when copious and of little value: *reports, memoranda, and other printed fallout from the executive suite*—Saturday Review [fr the radioactive dust and other debris of a nuclear explosion]

fall out 1 *v phr narcotics* To go to sleep or into a stuporous condition from narcotic intoxication: *Only those who are uptight fall out*—Saturday Review/ *If you resist falling out and pass the barrier, the curve is up to a mellow stupor*—New York **2** *v phr* To become helpless with laughter or emotion; =CRACK UP: *I tried double tempo and everybody fell out laughing*—Charlie Parker

faloosie *See* FLOOZY

falsie or **falsy 1** *n* Anything false or artificial; a prosthesis: *Its tail, a falsy, fell off*—Newsweek **2** *n* A brassiere padded to give the appearance of large breasts; also, padding worn in other places to increase the generosity of a woman's body

falsies or **gay deceivers** *n* A pair of breast pads worn to give the appearance of large breasts

family *See* PLAY THE DOZENS

family jewels *n phr* The testicles; =NUTS: *A kick in the family jewels will often dampen a man's ardor*

fan[1] *n fr late 1800s* A devotee or enthusiast, esp of a sport; aficionado; =BUFF, BUG: *a tennis fan/ cathedral fan* [fr *fanatic*, or perhaps fr *the fancy* "sports followers or fanciers"]

fan[2] **1** *n WW2 Army Air Force* An aircraft propeller or engine **2** *v baseball* To strike out; =WHIFF **3** *v* To fire a revolver by working the hammer with the hand that is not holding the firearm: *Gary Cooper fanned off six shots* **4** *v underworld* To search someone; =FRISK: *The gendarmes fan them to see if they have any rods on them*—Damon Runyon **5** *n underworld* A quick brush or pat used by pickpockets to find the place of the victim's wallet **6** *v: You will be fanned by hands feeling for an impression of your wallet* —New York **7** *v* To chat; gossip; =BAT THE BREEZE: *all the other chauffeurs I'd stand around fanning with* —H Larkin **8** *v* To manipulate the coin-return lever of a pay telephone in the hope of dislodging coins: *Mary was embarrassed at being observed at her fanning activities*—New York Post

See BAT THE BREEZE, FAN someone's TAIL, IRISH BANJO, the SHIT HITS THE FAN

fancy Dan *n phr prizefight* A skillful boxer with a weak punch

See DAPPER DAN

fancy-Dan *adj* Pretentious; =HIGHFALUTIN: *It's fancy-Dan nomenclature* —National Review

fancy (or **fast**) **footwork** *n phr fr prizefight* Very adroit evasion; clever dodging and maneuver: *It will take fancy footwork to explain this one/ The American Medical Association tried a little fast footwork before Congress last week*—New York Times

fancy man *n phr* A lover, esp the adulterous sex partner of a married woman

fancy pants 1 *n phr* A dressed-up or overdressed person **2** *n phr* An effete man; =SISSY **3** *modifier: one of your fancy-pants diplomats*

fancy-schmancy *adj* Very elegant or ornate, esp pretentiously so; =HIGHFALUTIN: *mostly fancy-schmancy Roman numbers like IIs and IIIs* —Philadelphia [fr the humorous and derisive Yiddish rhyming of a first word with a second one beginning *shm-*, as in "Oedipus-shmoedipus, just so he loves his mother"]

faniggle *See* FINAGLE

fanny *n fr 1920s* The buttocks; rump; =ASS: *I can hardly sit down, my fanny is so sore*—Associated Press [fr earlier British *fanny* "vulva," perhaps fr John Cleland's 18th-century heroine *Fanny* Hill]

fannybumper **1** *n* A crowded occasion; =MOB SCENE: *The reception was a fannybumper* **2** ***modifier:*** *organized a fannybumper vernissage*—Interview

fanny-dipper *n surfers* A conventional swimmer, as distinct from a surfer

fan someone's **tail** *v phr* To spank; =TAN: *Don't let him out of your sight, or I'll fan your tail*—Ellery Queen

fan the breeze *v phr* =BAT THE BREEZE

the **fantods** *n phr fr late 1800s* Fidgety nervousness; uneasy restlessness; =the WILLIES: *You just got the fantods, that's all*—W Henry [fr British dialect, "indisposition, restlessness," perhaps fr *fanteague* "commotion, excitement" or fr *fantasy*]

fanzine **1** *n* A fan magazine: *wants to start his own fanzine*—Village Voice **2** ***modifier:*** *The fanzine set is not scared off by raunchy lyrics*—Rolling Stone

Farley ***See*** CHUCK YOU, FARLEY

farm *v Army* To be killed in action; die in the armed services; =BUY THE FARM: *Just about my whole company farmed that day* [fr *buy the farm*]
See BET THE FARM, FAT FARM, FUNNY FARM, NUT HOUSE

farmisht (far MISHT) *adj* Confused; mixed up; ambivalent and/or ambiguous: *I'm afraid she's a little farmisht* [fr Yiddish]

far out **1** *adj* Very unconventional; unorthodox and strange; =WEIRD: *Drake liked "Suzie Q." Which to us was really far out*—Rolling Stone/ *a curious combination of far-out medicine, pampering, and very shrewd doctoring*—Fortune **2** *adj* Excellent; splendid; =COOL: *The next thing I heard from her was "Far out!"*—American Scholar

◁ **fart** ▷ **1** *v fr 1300s* To expel gas through the anus; relieve flatulence by the most immediate expedient **2** *n* A man; fellow; person; =GUY: *What's that stupid fart up to?* **3** *n* The least thing; nothing; =DIDDLY, ZILCH: *I don't give a fart for that notion/ It isn't worth a fart*
See FIDDLE AROUND, LAY A FART

◁ **fart around** ▷ **1** *v phr* =HORSE AROUND **2** *v phr* =GOOF AROUND

◁ **fart sack** ▷ *n phr Army* A sleeping bag

fast *adj* Morally lax; libertine: *on Long Island with the fast younger married set*—F Scott Fitzgerald

fast (or **quick**) **buck** **1** *n phr* Money gotten quickly, esp without too fine a concern for ethics or the future: *tryin' to hustle me for a fast buck*—Arthur Kober **2** ***modifier:*** *Fast-buck speculators were getting rich*—Reader's Digest

fast burner *n phr Army* A person whose success is rapid; =BALL OF FIRE

fast food **1** *n phr* Food like hamburgers, fried chicken, etc, cooked and served very rapidly and uniformly, usu by large catering corporations **2** ***modifier:*** *a fast-food chain*

fast footwork ***See*** FANCY FOOTWORK

fast lane (or **track**) **1** *n phr* A pace and quality of life emphasizing quick success against strong competition, along with the trappings of wealth and style: *Jean Piaget... started academic life on a fast track*—Time **2** ***modifier:*** *its glittery fast-lane image*—*Time/fast-track male*—William Safire [fr the left-hand or *fast lane* of a superhighway, which slower drivers enter at their risk]

fast one *n phr* A trick or deception; clever subterfuge; =DIPSY-DOODLE: *That was sure a fast one, you wearing the false mustache* [probably fr *fast shuffle*]
See PULL A FAST ONE

fast shuffle ***See*** DOUBLE SHUFFLE

fat **1** *n* The best and most rewarding part; =CREAM: *He just took the fat; screw the long term* **2** ***adj:*** *fat profits/ fat prospects* **3** *adj fr 1920s* Wealthy; in funds, esp temporarily so; =FLUSH: *Hit him up now, he's pretty fat* **4** *n* A fat person; =FATTY: *I met the other 18 women or fellow fats*—AD Botorff
See BIG FAT, CHEW THE FAT

fat-ass **1** *n* A fat person **2** ***adj:*** *Get your fat-ass self out of here* **3** *n* A person with large buttocks; =BUFFALO BUTT

fatback *adj* Redolent of Southern black ethnic tastes; =FUNKY: *The song became progressively funkier* *with Guerin laying down a dirty fatback beat*—San Francisco [fr the particularly *fat* sort of pork that characterizes some sorts of black ethnic food]

fat cat **1** *n phr fr 1920s* Any privileged and well-treated person, esp a wealthy benefactor; tycoon: *had jousted with Nelson Rockefeller at a formal dinner for fat cats*—Joseph Heller **2** *modifier: the fat-cat cases, where big money is involved*—New York Times/ *whether fat-cat contributors* or *New Hampshire coffee-klatschers*—Meg Greenfield **3** *v: "fat-catting"... a term applied... to higher leaders who try to pad themselves with special privileges and comforts*—Hal Boyle

fat city **1** *n phr esp students fr jazz musicians* An ideal situation; splendid state of affairs: *You're in fat city while other poor slobs sweat on assembly lines*—Sports Illustrated/ *Johnny came marching home from college..., and announced he was in "fat city"*—New York Times **2** *n phr* Poor physical condition, esp because of being overweight: *Its principal characters wind up in "fat city" (argot for "out of condition")*—American Scholar

fat, dumb, and happy *adj phr* Blissfully and rather bovinely contented

fat farm *n phr* A resort or treatment center where people go to lose weight: *It'll be adventures of me, and takes place at a fat farm*—Blair Sabol

fathead *n* A stupid person

◀ **fatherfucker** ▶ *n* =MOTHERFUCKER

fat lady sings *See* the OPERA'S NEVER OVER TILL THE FAT LADY SINGS

fat-mouth **1** *v* To blab and chatter; =CHEW THE FAT **2** *v* To cajole verbally; =BULLSHIT, SWEET-TALK: *I ain't asking you to fatmouth me*—Bernard Malamud

fatso *adj* Fat, in any sense: *a fatso deal in six figures*—New York Daily News

fatter *See* HAM-FATTER

fatty *n* A fat person: *designed to keep all us fatties from committing hara-kiri*—Esquire

fave or **fave rave** **1** *n* or *n phr* A favorite song or musical number, film, person, etc: *group scats Mozart, Vivaldi, Bach and other fave raves*—Saturday Review/ *includes many of the quintet's faves*—Variety **2** *modifier: My absolute fave-rave model was printed boldly*—Village Voice

◀ **fay**[1] ▶ *n black* A white person; =HONKY, PECKERWOOD [fr *ofay*]

fay[2] *adj homosexuals* Homosexual; =GAY [fr earlier *fay* "fairy"]

feather (or **line**) one's **nest** *v phr fr 1600s* To be primarily concerned with one's own gain; take care of oneself

feature *v fr 1920s* To understand; take note of: *He shoved the picture in my face and said "Feature that!"*

Fed *n* Any federal government worker or agent, esp in law enforcement or taxation: *right up to the day the Feds dragged him into court*—Esquire

the **Fed** *n phr* The Federal Reserve System, Board, or Bank: *Now the Fed has apparently decided to let the market carry interest rates upward*—New York Times/ *The Fed was reluctant to raise its discount rate*—Wall Street Journal

Federal case *See* MAKE A FEDERAL CASE OUT OF something

fed up *adj phr fr WW1 fr British* Disgusted; tired; surfeited: *A number of people suddenly became fed up with a slang phrase like "fed up"*—J Greig

feeb **1** *n* A feeble-minded person; idiot: *Then why are you treating me like a feeb?*—Life **2** *n* =FEEB

Feeb or **Feebie** *n* An agent of the Federal Bureau of Investigation; =G-MAN: *the agents of the Federal Bureau of Investigation, whom they call "Feebs"*—FC Shapiro/ *our heroes, the feebs, however*—Village Voice/ *make sure the Feebies didn't get any credit for it*—Patrick Mann

feed *See* CHICKEN FEED

feedback *n* Response, esp information and opinion: *We'll wait for feedback before we try anything else* [fr the portion of output *fed back* to the input in an automatic control circuit or system]

the **feedbag** *n phr* A meal: *I'm ready for the feedbag*—WR Burnett [fr the *bag* of *feed* hung on the head of a horse]

See PUT ON THE FEEDBAG

feed one's **face** *v phr* To eat

◁ **feel** or **feel up** ▷ *v* or *v phr* To touch, caress, or handle the buttocks, breasts, legs, crotch, etc; =COP A FEEL

◁ a **feel**▷ ***n phr*** A caress or touch, esp of the buttocks, breasts, or crotch: *The eager amorist entreated a quick feel*
See COP A FEEL

Feelgood or **feelgood** **1** ***n*** =DR FEELGOOD **2** ***n*** A condition of contentment or euphoria: *a purveyor of religious feelgood* **3** ***modifier:*** *The President is running a feel-good campaign*—Charles MacDowell

feel good ***v phr*** To be slightly and pleasantly drunk: *Old Charley was feeling good that night*—Mickey Spillane

feel no pain ***v phr*** *fr 1940s* To be drunk: *The anticipated audience... should be feeling no pain*—GQ

feel one's **oats** ***v phr*** *fr early 1800s* To be active and high-spirited; act brashly and confidently: *The manufacturer was just feeling his oats, having accomplished his happy intention*—Village Voice [fr the vigor of a just-fed horse]

feel someone **out** ***v phr*** To examine someone's opinions, knowledge, etc, esp indirectly: *Touch bases with Riemer and feel him out on this*

feep **1** ***n*** *computer* The electronic bell- or whistlelike sound made by computer terminals **2** ***v:*** *The machine feeped inexplicably but insistently*

feet ***See*** DRAG one's FEET, GET one's FEET WET, HAVE COLD FEET, HOLD someone's FEET TO THE FIRE, VOTE WITH one's FEET

fegelah or **feygelah** (FAY gə lə) ***n*** A male homosexual; =FAG: *The guy must be a real whacko. A fegelah, you figure?*—Lawrence Sanders [fr Yiddish, "little bird"]

feh or **fehh** ***interj*** An exclamation of disgust: *Thus, soccer. Feh*—Village Voice/ *Well, fehh, Petro thinks that Dr Scholl's spray seems to work*—Village Voice [fr Yiddish]

feisty ***adj*** Truculent; irascible: *They said the President was a feisty little chap/ He was having trouble with a feisty old lady who didn't want to move* [fr Southern dialect *fice*, a small, worthless cur, esp a lapdog on which the owner's flatulence could be blamed]

fellow ***See*** BEST FELLOW, REGULAR FELLOW

◁ **femme** or **fem**▷ **1** ***n*** A woman: *He has aired the fem that got him the job*—John O'Hara **2** ***modifier:*** *whereas women with big heads of fat hair always look femme*—San Francisco **3** ***n*** *homosexuals* A lesbian who takes a passive, feminine role in sex **4** ***modifier:*** *butch-femme role players are sad relics of the uptight past*—Village Voice **5** ***n*** *homosexuals* An effeminate homosexual male: *active or passive, manly ("stud") or womanly ("fem")*—Saturday Review [fr French, "woman"]

fenagle ***See*** FINAGLE

fence **1** ***n*** *fr 1600s* A person or place that deals in stolen goods: *But even big fences like Alphonso can get stuck*—New York/ *The loot had disappeared and been handled by a fence*—Associated Press **2** ***v:*** *The clown that stole the Mona Lisa found it hard to fence* **3** ***v*** To maneuver for advantage; spar: *Their lawyers fenced for a couple hours* [all senses are shortenings of *defence*; in the case of criminal act, the notion is probably that of a secure place and trusty person, well defended; the other sense is from *fence* "fight or defend oneself with a sword"]
See GO FOR THE FENCES, ON THE FENCE, OVER THE FENCE

fender-bender ***n*** A minor car accident; trivial collision: *I've only had one fender-bender since I got it*—Don Pendleton

fer instance ***See*** FOR INSTANCE

fer sure (or **shure** or **shurr**) ***See*** FOR SURE

-fest ***combining form*** *fr late 1800s* A celebration or extensive exercise and indulgence of what is indicated: *slugfest/ gabfest/ fuckfest/ jazzfest* [fr German, "festival"]
See BULL SESSION

fever ***See*** CABIN FEVER

a **few** ***See*** WIN A FEW LOSE A FEW

feygelah ***See*** FEGELAH

fi ***See*** HI-FI, LOW-FI

the **fickle finger of fate** ***n phr*** The dire and unpredictable aspect of destiny: *It wasn't anything she specially deserved, just the fickle finger of fate at work* [regarding *finger* as both a pointer and a violator of the body]
See FUCKED BY THE FICKLE FINGER OF FATE

fiddle *fr middle 1800s US* **1** *v* To cheat; defraud • Chiefly British **2** *n: His new boat is a tax fiddle*
See BULL FIDDLE, PLAY SECOND FIDDLE, SECOND FIDDLE

fiddle around *v phr* (also ◁**fiddle fart around** or **fiddle-fart**▷) To loaf or idle about; also, tinker or tamper; =MONKEY AROUND: *He fiddled around all week/ She was fiddling around with the gearshift/ The dentist fiddle-farted for two hours while I suffered*

◀**fiddlefucking**▶ *adj* Particular and accursed; =DAMN • Used for vehement and vulgar emphasis: *Not one swingin' dick will be leavin' this fiddlefuckin' area*—Philip Roth

fiddlesticks *fr early 1800s British* *n* Nonsense; foolishness; =BULLSHIT • Often a dismissive response to a contemptible comment: *When I explained, she only said, "Fiddlesticks!"*

fiddle with *v phr* To play or tamper with; =FIDDLE AROUND: *Don't fiddle with that grenade*

field *v* To handle; receive and answer; cope with: *The secretary fielded the questions rather lamely*
See OUT IN LEFT FIELD, PLAY THE FIELD

field day *See* HAVE A FIELD DAY

fiend *combining word* A devotee or user of what is indicated: *camera fiend/ dope-fiend/ sex fiend*

fierce *See* SOMETHING FIERCE

fifth wheel *n phr* A superfluous person or thing: *I feel as though I'm a fifth wheel*—Wall Street Journal

fifty-six *n police* The time off that substitutes for the weekends of those who work Saturdays and Sundays [because the time adds up to *fifty-six* hours]

fig *See* MOLDY FIG

fight *See* CAT FIGHT

fight a bottle *v phr* To drink liquor, esp to excess: *after fighting a bottle all evening*—R Starnes

fighter *See* HOP FIEND, NIGHT PEOPLE

fightin' words *n phr* Provocative speech; words inviting combat • Often said in a broad cowboy style: *I can go along with a little ribbing, but them is fightin' words, son*

can't **fight** one's **way out of a paper bag** *See* CAN'T FIGHT one's WAY OUT OF A PAPER BAG

figure **1** *v* To make sense; be plausible and reasonable: *It figures he'd be next in line* **2** *v* To be expected; be very likely: *The pup figured to be in the room when Einstein discussed the bomb with the president*—Billy Rose
See BALLPARK FIGURE

file *See* CIRCULAR FILE

file and forget *v phr* To consign to oblivion; to refuse to take as serious and consequent

file 17 (or **13**) *n phr esp WW2 armed forces* A wastebasket; =CIRCULAR FILE

fill in *v phr* To substitute; replace temporarily: *I'll fill in for you*

fill-in **1** *n* A summary account; information meant to supply what one does not know: *A friend gives me a fill-in on how Costello is running the country*—Saturday Evening Post **2** *n* A substitute worker: *Get a fill-in, I gotta split*

fill someone **in** *v phr* To complete someone's knowledge; brief; =PUT someone IN THE PICTURE: *Fill me in so I know what's up here*

filly *n fr Brit fr 1600s* A girl; young woman [fr French *fille* "girl"]

film *See* SLICE AND DICE FILM, SNUFF FILM, SPLAT MOVIE

filthbag *n* A despicable person; =DIRTBAG, SCUMBAG: *Tony called Strumpet a filthbag*—San Francisco

filthy **1** *adj* Wealthy; rich; =LOADED: *He's filthy with dough*—Eugene O'Neill **2** *adj* Obscene; salacious; =BLUE, DIRTY: *filthy movies/ filthy minds*

the **filthy** *n phr* Money; =FILTHY LUCRE: *just trying to make a bit of the filthy*—PG Wodehouse

filthy lucre *n phr* Money [fr the Pauline epistle to Titus]

filthy rich *adj phr* Very rich; =LOADED

fin[1] **1** *n* *fr 1700s fr sailors* The hand: *Reach out your fin and grab it* **2** *n* The arm and hand

fin[2] *n fr 1920s underworld* A five-dollar bill; five dollars: *I gave my pal a fin*—John O'Hara/ *It was the fin seen round the world. Where Reagan got the five bucks is a mystery*—Time [fr Yiddish *finif* "five"]

finagle (fə NAY gəl) (Variations: **faniggle** or **fenagle** or **finigal** or **finagel** or **phenagle**) **1** *v* To manage or arrange, esp by dubious means; contrive: *He finagled it so she got the job/ He finagled the driver into doing it for him*—Hannibal and Boris **2** *v* To acquire, esp by trickery: *She finagled a couple of choice seats* [origin unknown; perhaps related to British dialect *finegue* "to evade" or *fainague* "to renege"]

finagle factor or **Fink's constant** *n phr* The putative mathematical constant by which a wrong answer is multiplied to get a right answer

a **fine how-de-do** (or **how-do-you-do**) *n phr fr early 1800s British* A situation; set of circumstances: *which is a fine how-de-do in a country that prides itself on progress*—David Dempsey

the **fine print** *See* the SMALL PRINT

the **finest** *n phr* The police force • Often in city name plus **finest** phrases like **San Francisco's finest**, **Madison's finest**

finger 1 *v underworld* To locate and point out someone, esp for a professional killer: *You're the guy that fingered Manny Tinnen*—Raymond Chandler **2** *v underworld* To tell thieves about the location, value, etc, of potential loot **3** *n underworld* A police informer; =STOOL PIGEON **4** *n underworld* A person who tells thieves about potential loot **5** *n underworld* A police officer ◁**6**▷ *v* To insert a finger into the vulva; =FINGERFUCK: *With one hand Larry was fingering me* —Xaviera Hollander **7** *n* About a half-inch of liquor in a glass: *Maybe I'd better have another finger of the hooch*—Raymond Chandler

See BUTTERFINGERS, FIVE FINGERS, FUCKED BY THE FICKLE FINGER OF FATE, GIVE someone THE FINGER, NOT LAY A GLOVE ON someone, ON THE FINGER, PLAY STINKY-PINKY, PUT one's FINGER ON something, PUT THE FINGER ON someone, STAND AROUND WITH one's FINGER UP one's ASS

the **finger 1** *n phr underworld* The act of identifying or pointing out potential loot, a hired killer's victim, a wanted criminal, etc **2** *n phr* A lewd insulting gesture made by holding up the middle finger with the others folded down, and meaning "fuck you" or "up yours"; =the BIRD *See* GIVE someone THE FINGER, PUT THE FINGER ON someone

fingered *See* LIGHT-FINGERED, STICKY-FINGERED

◀**fingerfuck**▶ *v* To insert a finger into the vulva; =FRIG, PLAY STINKY-PINKY: *She wants you to finger-fuck her shikse cunt till she faints*—Philip Roth

finger of fate *See* FUCKED BY THE FICKLE FINGER OF FATE

fingerprint *v truckers* To load or unload a truck oneself, without using paid dockside labor • Said of independent truckers: *An independent driver... may "fingerprint" the boxes on or off the trailer himself*—Smithsonian

fingers *See* BUTTERFINGERS, FIVE FINGERS

finger up one's **ass** *See* STAND AROUND WITH one's FINGER UP one's ASS

finger-wringer *n movie studio* A performer prone to overly emotional performance

finif or **finiff** or **finnif** *n fr British fr middle 1800s* A five-dollar bill; five dollars; =FIN [fr Yiddish *finif* "five"]

finigal *See* FINAGLE

finished *adj* Occupationally ruined; no longer able to function or compete; =DEAD: *After two tries he was finished/ She couldn't act any longer and was finished at thirty*

fink 1 *n fr late 1800s* A strikebreaker; =SCAB **2** *n fr late 1800s* A labor spy; worker who is primarily loyal to the employer: *unpopular with the other waiters, who thought him a fink*—New Yorker **3** *n fr late 1800s* A police officer, detective, guard, or other law enforcement agent: *This Sherlock Holmes... this fink's on the old yocky-dock*—J Cannon **4** *n underworld* An informer; =STOOL PIGEON: *Now he's looking for the fink who turned him in*—Raymond Chandler/ *The glossary runs to such pejorative nouns as fink, stoolie, rat, canary, squealer*—Time **5** *v: Dutch knew I worked for his friend... and I wouldn't fink*—George Raft **6** *n* Any contemptible person; vile wretch; =RAT FINK, SHITHEEL: *All men are brothers, and if you don't give, you're a kind of fink*—Bennett Berger **7** *n hoboes* A tramp who begs food at kitchen doors **8** *n circus & carnival* A piece of shabby small merchandise [origin unknown; perhaps fr *Pink* "a Pinkerton agent engaged in strikebreaking," or fr Ger-

man *Fink* "finch," a university students' term for a student who did not join in duelling and drinking societies]
See RAT FINK

fink out **1** *v phr esp 1960s counterculture* To withdraw from or refuse support to a project, movement, etc, esp in a seemingly cowardly and self-serving way; =BACK OUT: *or if he will "fink out," as Kauffman believed he had done so far* —Society **2** *v phr underworld* To become untrustworthy and a potential informer **3** *v phr* To fail utterly

Fink's constant *See* FINAGLE FACTOR

Finn *See* MICKEY FINN

finnagel *See* FINAGLE

finiff or **finnif** *See* FINIF

fire **1** *v fr late 1800s* To discharge from a job; dismiss, usu with prejudice; =CAN, SACK **2** *v* To throw something with great force: *The big lefthander fired a fastball down the middle* **3** *v* To ask or utter with bluntness and vehemence: *The panel fired questions at me and I soon wilted*
See BALL OF FIRE, HANG FIRE, HOLD someone's FEET TO THE FIRE, ON THE FIRE, PULL something OUT OF THE FIRE, TAKE FIRE

fire away **1** *v phr fr late 1700s* To begin; go ahead • Usu an invitation: *"Fire away!" said I when she threatened to denounce me* **2** *v phr* To attack verbally: *As soon as I walked into the room he began to fire away at me*

fireball *n* =BALL OF FIRE

fire blanks *See* SHOOT BLANKS

fireman *n baseball* A relief pitcher, esp an effective one: *a four-run blast against fireman Joe in the eighth inning*—Associated Press
See VISITING FIREMAN

fire on *v phr black* To strike; hit: *looking at this one dude Huey had fired on*—Bobby Seale

firestorm *n* An intense and often destructive spate of action or reaction: *report... has already generated a firestorm of criticism*—New York Times [fr the catastrophic and unquenchable *fires* caused by aerial bombing of cities in World War 2]

firewater *n fr early 1800s* Liquor; =BOOZE

fireworks **1** *n* Excitement; furor; noisy fuss; =HOOPLA: *speeches that... would produce the "fireworks" supporters have demanded*—J Devlin/ *low profile, please, no fireworks* **2** *n* Anger; quarrels; rancorous rhetoric **3** *n* Shooting; gunfire or cannon fire: *The riot ended when the National Guard showed up and the fireworks began*

first base *See* GET TO FIRST BASE

first crack out of the box *adv phr* Immediately; before anything else: *Get him back home and first crack out of the box he's run away again*

firstest (or **fustest**) **with the mostest** *adv phr* First with the most; soonest and best equipped [fr advice given by General Stonewall Jackson on how to win a battle]

first man (or **shirt** or **soldier**) *n phr Army* A first sergeant; =TOP-KICK

first off *adv phr* First in order; to begin with: *I said that first off I wanted an apology*

fish **1** *n prison* A new inmate: *As a "fish"... at Charlestown, I was physically miserable*—Malcolm X **2** *n street gang* A nonmember of a street gang; a person regarded as inimical and distasteful by a street gang **3** *n* A stupid person, esp one easily victimized; =PATSY, SUCKER: *Why should he be the fish for the big guys?*—Ira Wolfert **4** *n* A person, esp a criminal, thought of as being caught like a fish: *The cops catch a lot of very interesting fish*—Life **5** *n homosexuals* A heterosexual woman **6** *n students* A promiscuous woman **7** *n sports* A weak opponent: *The superteams get stronger. They can pad their schedules with the occasional fish*—Sports Illustrated **8** *n* A dollar: *The job paid only fifty fish* —Lionel Stander **9** *v* To seek information, esp by a legal or quasi-legal process having a very general aim; =GO FISHING **10** *v* To ask for something, usu a compliment, esp in an indirect and apparently modest way
See BIG FISH, BIGGER FISH TO FRY, GO FISHING, LIKE SHOOTING FISH IN A BARREL, POOR FISH, QUEER FISH

fishball *n* A contemptible person; =CREEP

fish bowl *See* FISH TANK

the fish-eye *See* GIVE someone THE FISH-EYE

fish-eyed *adj* Cold, staring, and inhuman: *have to persuade a fish-eyed insurance claims adjustor*—New York

fishhooks *n* The fingers

fishing *See* GO FISHING

fishing expedition *See* GO FISHING

fish or cut bait *sentence* Do one thing or another, but stop dithering; take action; =SHIT OR GET OFF THE POT • Usu a firm or irritated demand: *The union leader warned that the city had until Feb 1 to "fish or cut bait"*—New York Times

fishskin 1 *n* A dollar bill **2** *n* A condom

fish story (or **tale**) *n phr fr early 1800s* A series of lies or exaggerations; a false or improbable explanation: *His whole alibi is a fish story* [fr the tendency of an angler to exaggerate the size of the catch]

fishtail 1 *n hot rodders* Flaring rear fenders on a car **2** *v* To swing a car, motorcycle, etc, from side to side at the rear: *causing his rear wheels to spin or the rear end to fishtail, that is swing back and forth*—Life

fish tank (or **bowl**) *n phr underworld* The part of a jail or prison where new inmates are kept for classification, testing, etc: *I'm in the fish tank... .There are forty of us in the diagnostic center*—Ann Rule

fish to fry *See* BIGGER FISH TO FRY

fish trap *n phr* The mouth

fishwife *n homosexuals* The wife of a homosexual man

fishy *adj fr middle 1800s British* Very probably false or dishonest; very dubious: *The whole proposition is decidedly fishy* [probably fr the unpleasant odor of spoiled *fish*]

fishyback *n* The transport of loaded containers or semitrailers by ship or barge [modeled on *piggyback*]

fisted *See* HAM-HANDED

◀ **fist-fucking** or **fisting**▶ *n* Anal intercourse, usu homosexual, in which the hand is inserted into the partner's anus

fistful 1 *n* A large amount: *I've got a fistful of overdue bills* **2** *n* A large amount of money: *The digital stereo set me back a fistful* **3** *n underworld* A five-year prison sentence

fit *n narcotics* The devices used for injecting narcotics; drug paraphernalia; =WORKS [probably a shortening of *outfit*]
See DUCK-FIT, HAVE A SHIT FIT, THROW A FIT

five *See* GIVE someone FIVE, HANG FIVE, HIGH FIVE, LOW FIVE, NINE-TO-FIVE, SLIP (or GIVE) ME FIVE, TAKE FIVE

five-and-ten or **five-and-dime 1** *n* A variety store selling relatively cheap items; =DIME STORE **2** *adj* Cheap; paltry; second-rate: *Dr Ruth is strictly a five-and-dime affair*—New York

five-dollar gold piece *See* COME UP SMELLING LIKE A ROSE

five-finger discount *n phr esp teenagers* Shoplifting

five fingers *underworld* **1** *n phr* A five-year prison sentence **2** *n phr* A thief

Five-O *n teenagers* A police officer [fr the TV police-adventure series *Hawaii Five-O*]

five of clubs *n phr* A fist

five-ouncers *n prizefight* The fists [fr the minimum weight of boxing gloves]

five-pound bag *See* BLIVIT, LOOK LIKE TEN POUNDS OF SHIT IN A FIVE-POUND BAG

fiver 1 *n* A five-dollar bill; five dollars: *For a fiver, cash, you could ride*—Nelson Algren **2** *n prison* A five-year prison sentence

fives *See* BUNCH OF FIVES

five-sided puzzle palace *n phr Army* The Pentagon

five-spot 1 *n* A five-dollar bill **2** *n underworld* A five-year prison sentence **3** *n* A five of playing cards

five square (or **five**) **1** *adj phr radio operators* Of a radio signal, strong and easy to understand; loud and clear **2** *adj phr* Perfectly clear; well understood; loud and clear: *The president's message is five square* **3** *adv phr: Yes my dear, I hear you five five* [fr the military radio operator's double scale, of one to *five*, for reporting both strength and clarity of a signal]

fix 1 *v fr late 1800s* To prearrange the outcome of a prizefight, race, game, etc **2** *n* A fight, game, etc, of which the winner has been fraudulently predetermined: *The World Series that year was a blatant fix* **3** *v fr 1920s* To arrange exoneration from a charge, esp by bribery; have a charge quashed: *He had a pal could fix tickets for five bucks* **4** *n narcotics* A dose of a narcotic, esp an injection of heroin; =BLAST: *a fix to calm her jittery nerves*—San Francisco Examiner **5** *n* Anything needed to appease a habitual need or craving: *He had to have his daily fix of flattery* **6** *v* To castrate an animal, esp a cat **7** *v* To punish; injure; =FIX someone's WAGON: *Make him wash the dishes, that'll fix him* **8** *n* A difficult situation; a nasty position or dilemma: *I'm afraid her lying has gotten her in a bad fix* **9** *n* A clear idea; an accurate notion: *I can't get a fix on this guy's intentions* **10** *n police* A police officer's assignment that does not require patrolling ***See*** QUICK FIX

the **fix** **1** *n phr* Arrangements, esp illicit payments, assuring the prearranged outcome of a prizefight, game, race, etc: *It's in the bag. The fix is on*—WR and FK Simpson **2** *n phr* Arrangements assuring exoneration from a police charge: *The super hisself couldn't put the fix in any faster*—Nelson Algren

fix someone's **hash** ***See*** SETTLE someone's HASH

fixing to (or **like**) *v phr* Readying; preparing; on the verge of: *Looks like he's fixing to get drunk/ She's fixing like she's going to leave here*

Fixit ***See*** MISTER FIXIT

fix-up *n narcotics* A dose of narcotics; =FIX

fix someone **up** **1** *v phr* To provide an escort or date for **2** *v phr* To provide a sex partner for **3** *v phr* To provide anything needed: *Gas? Yeah, we can fix you up*

fix someone's **wagon** *v phr* To punish; injure; ruin; =CLEAN someone's CLOCK

fizz *n* A failure; =FIZZLE: *"It was a big fizz," the ambassador said*—Time

fizzle **1** *v fr middle 1800s* To fail; lose effect; =FLOP, PETER OUT: *The covert operation fizzled unspectacularly* **2** *n: Our monster bash was a fizzle* [fr the lackluster sibilance of a damp firecracker]

flack or **flak** **1** *n* Publicity; public relations material; =BALLYHOO, HYPE: *Mr Mogul's latest epic was preceded by wheeling galaxies of affecting flack* **2** *modifier: The flack description is also worth quoting*—Variety **3** *n* (also **flacker**) A publicity person or press agent: *something that would cause your basic, self-respecting flack to want to slit his throat*—Calvin Trillin/ *I'm a flak... a publicity man*—Irwin Shaw/ *"He's shown steady improvement," said a hospital flak*—New York Daily News **4** *v: his publishers, who flack it... into a best seller*—Atlantic Monthly/ *He's not flakking for ulterior motives*—Toronto Life [said to be fr the name of Gene *Flack*, a moving picture publicity agent, and first used in the show-business paper *Variety*; perhaps fr or influenced by *flak*]

flackery *n* Publicity; =FLACK, HYPE: *A White House insider's name, with enough flackery, can be sold like mouthwash*—Hugh Sidey

flag **1** *v underworld* To arrest; =BUST: *They flagged my reefer man yesterday*—New York **2** *n baseball* The pennant awarded annually to a league championship team **3** *n underworld* An assumed name; alias

flagpole ***See*** RUN something UP THE FLAGPOLE

flagship **1** *n* The most imposing constituent; premier specimen: *The Ritz is the flagship of my caravansery chain* **2** *modifier: and not one damn word in the nation's flagship papers*—Village Voice

flag-up *adj cabdrivers* With the taxi meter not started: *a flag-up ride*

flak **1** *n* An antiaircraft gun or guns; antiaircraft fire **2** *n* (also **flack**) Severe criticism; angry blame: *This order provoked little political flack*—Harper's/ *Little recreation clubs like ours draw a lot of flack*—John D MacDonald **3** *n* Trouble; fuss; dissension; =STATIC: *Let's not have a lot of flak about this* [fr German *Fliegerabwehrkanonen* "antiaircraft gun"]

flake **1** *n fr baseball* An eccentric person, esp a colorful individualist; =BIRD: *what is known in the trade as a flake, a kook, or a clubhouse lawyer*—Christopher Lehmann-Haupt **2** *n fr baseball* The quality of flamboyant individualism: *The Yankees have acquired... an amount of "flake"*—Leonard Koppett **3** *adj: Don't act so flake* **4** *n teenagers* A stupid, erratic person; =RETARD **5** *n* *narcotics* Cocaine **6** *v police* To arrest on false or invented charges; =FRAME **7** *v police* To plant evidence on a suspect **8** *n police* An arrest made in order to meet a quota [all except police senses ultimately fr attested phrase *snow flakes* "cocaine"]

flake off *v phr teenagers* To leave; depart • Often an irritated command: *Want to brush off such friends? Suggest that they...flake off* —J Gray [probably a euphemism for *fuck off*]

flake out **1** *v phr jazz musicians* =FLAKE OFF **2** *v phr* To fail

flaky or **flakey** **1** *adj fr baseball* Colorfully eccentric; buoyantly individualistic **2** *adj* Insane; =SCREWY, WACKY: *a flaky old professor, a snake expert*—New York **3** *adj* Disoriented; barely conscious; dizzy: *played the last 23 minutes of the game in a condition that was described as "flaky" and "fuzzy"*—New York Times

flam *See* FLIMFLAM

flamdoodle *See* FLAPDOODLE

flame **1** *n fr 1600s* A sweetheart; beloved **2** *v* (also **flame it up**) *homosexuals* To flaunt or exaggerate effeminate traits; =CAMP IT UP **3** *v esp computer* To talk long and noisily; rant; carry on, esp in a computer bulletin board or other communication network

See SHOOT someone DOWN

◁ **flamer** or **flaming asshole** or **flaming fruitbar**▷ *n or n phr* A male homosexual; =QUEEN: *It doesn't have anything to do with me being a flamer*—Richard Merkin

flames *See* GO DOWN IN FLAMES

flamethrower *n baseball* A pitcher with a very fast fastball

flaming **1** *adj* Blatantly homosexual, esp in an effeminate way; =SWISH: *in hiding the fact that Babe Ruth and Lou Gehrig were flaming homosexuals*—National Lampoon **2** *adv* Very • Used as an intensifier, usu preceded by "so": *I can't believe he'd be so flaming stupid* **3** *n computer* The use of rude, strong, obscene, etc, language on a computer bulletin board, in computer mail, etc • This sort of verbal license is said to be common and apparently to be an effect of the medium itself

◁ **flaming pisspot**▷ *n phr Army* The insignia of the Ordnance Corps, a flaming grenade bomb

flap **1** *n fr late 1800s British Navy* Disturbance; tumult; fuss: *Law was one direction open to me with the least amount of flap*—Good Housekeeping **2** *n street gang* A fight between street gangs; =RUMBLE **3** *v* To become flustered; lose one's composure: *I've seen him under hostile pressure before. He doesn't flap and he doesn't become a doormat* —DE Kneeland

flapdoodle or **flamdoodle** *n fr early 1900s British perhaps fr earlier US* Nonsense; foolishness; =BALONEY: *He then goes on to utter other flapdoodle for the nourishment of the mind*—New York Times

flap one's **gums** *See* BAT one's GUMS

flapjaw **1** *n* Talk; discourse; chat: *We caught Mannone and Moore for a moment's flapjaw before we left* —New Yorker **2** *n* A loquacious person; =MOTOR-MOUTH

flap one's **lip** *See* FLIP one's LIP

flapper **1** *n fr early 1800s* The hand **2** *n esp 1920s* A young woman of the type fashionable in the 1920s, with pronounced worldly interests, relatively few inhibitions, a distinctive style of grooming, etc **3** *modifier: the flapper era/ flat flapper chest* [origin uncertain; perhaps from the idea of an unfledged bird *flapping* its wings, as one did while dancing the Charleston]

flash **1** *n fr early 1800s* Thieves' argot **2** *n* A look; quick glance: *We slid into the cross street to take a flash at the alley*—James M Cain **3** *n* A person who excels at something; =WHIZ: *He's a flash at math* **4** *v* To vomit **5** *v narcotics* To have a hallucinatory experience from a narcotic: *He flashed he was as big as a mountain* **6** *v narcotics* To feel the sudden pleasurable effect of a narcotics injection: *As soon as the needle went in, she flashed* **7** *n: Harry shot up a couple of the goof balls and tried to think a bigger and better flash than he got*—Hubert Selby, Jr **8** *adj teenagers* Excellent; wonderful; =DYNAMITE **9** *n fr narcotics* Distinctive personal style and charm; charisma: *Flash is in the clothes, the cars, the walk, the talk*—R

Woodley **10** *v esp narcotics* To have a sudden idea, insight, or impulse **11** *n: if he should get a sudden flash to commit Cat...and wants to call her*—S Werbin **12** *n fr narcotics* Something one is currently doing; = BAG, THING: *His current "flash," as he calls it, tends toward gaucho suits*—New York Post **13** *v fr middle 1800s British* To expose one's genitals, breasts, etc • The earlier British forms were **flash it** and **flash** one's **meat**: *Judy thought she was gonna flash me. She started unbuttoning her blouse*—Dolly Parton **14** *n: He gave her a flash and she squawked* **15** *v* To display suddenly and briefly: *The cop flashed his badge/ She flashed me a big smile* **16** *n* Urination; = PISS: *and said he'd pay double in case of a "flash," which is a delicate way of describing one of nature's indelicate imperatives*—Washington Post

flashback **1** *n* A scene or passage in a novel, movie, etc, that depicts events earlier than those in the main time frame **2** *n narcotics* A hallucination or sensation originally induced by LSD or other drugs but recurring after the drug experience has ended

flasher *n* A person who exposes the genitals in public; exhibitionist

flashforward *n* A scene or passage in a novel, movie, etc, that depicts events later than those of the main time frame

flash in the pan *n phr* A person or thing that does not fulfill an apparent potential: *If he's not a flash in the pan he'll be the best poet we ever had* [fr the igniting charge in an old gun that goes off *in the pan* or holder without igniting the main charge]

flash on *v phr* To recall; realize vividly: *I flashed on all that stuff in basic about it being better dead than captured*—Rolling Stone

flash-sport *n black* A gaudily groomed man; = DUDE, SPORT: *The gals would begin to say, "My, my, who's this new flash-sport"*—A Lomax

flashy *adj* Gaudy; meretriciously showy: *flashy rings/ a flashy new car*

flat *See* GRANNY FLAT, IN NOTHING FLAT

◁ **flat-ass**▷ *adj* Totally: *Some farmers are absolutely flat-ass broke*—Time

flatbacker *n* A prostitute: *His prostitutes are well known for being unhooked flatbackers*—I Ianni

flat broke *adj phr fr middle 1800s* Entirely without funds; penniless

flatfoot *n fr early 1900s* A police officer or detective: *The flat-feet scratched their heads*—NY Confidential

flatfooted *adj fr early 1900s* Unprepared; surprised

flathead **1** *n fr late 1800s* A stupid person; = FATHEAD **2** *n* A police officer; = FLATFOOT **3** *n restaurant* A nontipping patron at a restaurant or club **4** *n hot rodders* An L-head or side-valve car engine

◁ **flat on** one's **ass**▷ **1** *adj phr* Penniless and exhausted; = DOWN AND OUT: *He blew his pay pack and he's flat on his ass* **2** *adj phr Army* Incompetent; feckless: *That platoon's a loser, flat on its ass*
See FALL ON one's ASS

flat out *fr early 1900s* *adv phr* At full speed; = ALL OUT: *The economy is running flat out and revenues are pouring in*—Wall Street Journal/ *Flat out, working on it myself, it will take a week*—John McPhee [perhaps fr the elongated shape of a horse going at top speed]

flat-out **1** *adj* Open and direct; unambiguous; plain: *Bunuel resorts to flat-out assertions in the last scene*—American Scholar **2** *adj* Total; unrestricted: *a husband who was a flat-out failure*—Time

flats *See* ST LOUIS FLATS

flat tire (or **hoop**) *n phr* A tedious person; an insipid companion

flattop *n fr WW2* An aircraft carrier

◁ **flavor**▷ *n black* A sexually attractive woman

FLB (pronounced as separate letters) *n hospital* Strange or arhythmic heartbeats [fr *funny-looking beats*]

fleabag or **fleahouse** or **fleatrap** **1** *n armed forces fr WW1* A bed; mattress; bunk or hammock **2** *n horse-racing* An inferior racehorse **3** *n* A cheap and wretched hotel or rooming house; = FLOPHOUSE: *my last French hotel of the war: a fleabag two rooms wide*—Albert Guerard/ *He has transformed the motel from the old wayside fleabag into the most popular home away from home*—Time **4** **modifier:** *will no longer* *take her dates to fleabag hotels* —New York Times **5** *n* Any cheap, dirty, or ramshackle public place: *unveiled at an owl show in a Forty-second Street flea bag*—SJ Perelman

flea powder *n phr narcotics* A weakened or diluted narcotic, or a nonnarcotic substance sold as a narcotic; =BLANK

fleece *v fr 1600s* To cheat or swindle: *get back the money he'd fleeced me out of*—J Scarne

flesh *See* IN THE FLESH, PRESS THE FLESH

flesh flick *See* SKIN FLICK

flesh-peddler **1** *n* A pimp or prostitute **2** *n* A person in charge of a show featuring unclad women **3** *n fr 1930s* An actor's or athlete's agent: *The old Hollywood flesh peddlers never stop talking money*—Raymond Chandler **4** *n* A person working at an employment agency

flesh-pressing *modifier* Handshaking, meeting and flattering voters, etc, in politics: *The flesh-pressing process remains invariable*—Toronto Life

flex one's **muscles** *v phr* To give a sample of one's power, esp in a threatening way: *I'm not sure they mean harm, probably just flexing their muscles*

flextime or **flexitime** *n* Flexible working time that varies as to hours and days worked: *flextime for working mothers and fathers in business* —Time

flic *n* A police officer: *if the flic had the slightest suspicion*—R Fish [fr French slang]

flick *fr 1920s* **1** *n* A movie: *a cheapie hard-core porno flick*—Saturday Review/ *He will play a role in the flick*—Associated Press **2** *n* A movie theater [fr the *flickering* of early movie images]
See SKIN FLICK

the **flicks** or **flickers** or **flix** *n phr fr 1920s* The movies; the cinema: *the getting-away-from-it-all surcease we seek at the flicks*—Judith Crist

flier *See* FLYER

flies *See* NO FLIES ON someone

flight *n narcotics* A hallucinogenic drug experience; =TRIP

flimflam **1** *v fr 1600s* To cheat or swindle; defraud; =BAMBOOZLE, CON: *We've been flim-flammed*—James M Cain **2** *n: Don't fall for that flimflam* **3** *modifier: a flimflam game/ flimflam man*

fling **1** *n* A period of pleasure and indulgence, often as relaxation after or before stern responsibilities: *He had a last fling before going to the monastery* **2** *n* A try; =CRACK, GO: *Ms Ready, will you have a fling at climbing that wall?* **3** *n students* A dance; party; =SHINDIG

flip **1** *adj fr early 1900s* Flippant; impudent; =CHEEKY: *Mr Lawrence... is flip and easy*—Clive Barnes/ **2** *v* To change or switch diametrically; =FLIP-FLOP: *So I flipped over to the opposite opinion* **3** *v* To respond enthusiastically; feel great excitement and pleasure: *"They flipped over it," Riveroll recalls*—Forbes/ *I flip over this record*—T Brown **4** *v* To cause one to respond with enthusiasm; give one great pleasure: *My imitation of Mr Kissinger flipped the assemblage* **5** *n* Something that causes hilarity or pleasure: *The big flip of the year is Peter Arno's book of cartoons*—Gilbert Milstein **6** *v* To become angry: *When he told me what he had done, I flipped* **7** *v fr cool talk* To go insane; behave irrationally; =FLIP OUT: *I was flipping at first... but then the marvelous vibes got to me*—Whitney Balliett

flip-flop **1** *n* A complete reversal of direction; about-face: *Commodities have been doing flip-flops on the price ladder*—K Scheibel **2** *v: So Kennedy's flip-flopped again*—Time **3** *modifier: whose flip-flop views and reluctance to confront the issues* —New Yorker

flip-flops *n* Bathing sandals, esp the kind where a strap fits between one's toes: *in a flowered housedress and Dr Scholl flip-flops*—New York Times

flip one's **lid** (or **wig** or **raspberry**) *fr bop & cool talk* **1** *v phr* To become violently angry; =BLOW one's TOP: *When she told him he flipped his lid* **2** *v phr* To go insane; behave irrationally: *flipped his lid and blew a whole list of nuclear warhead targets* —WT Tyler **3** *v phr* To show great enthusiasm and approval: *When she finished reading, the crowd flipped its raspberry*

flip (or **flap**) one's **lip** *v phr* To talk, esp idly or foolishly

flip-lipped *adj* Flippantly loquacious; =FLIP, SMART-ASS: *Pine was a flip-lipped bastard who should have had his ears pinned back long ago*—J Evans

flip out *fr bop & cool talk* **1** *v phr* To evoke an enthusiastic response: *I flipped out these guys with my crazy stories*—Xaviera Hollander **2** *v phr* To display enthusiasm; crow: *My junkie brother continues to flip out about what a cool dude I am*—Saturday Review **3** *v phr* To go insane; =FLIP, FREAK OUT: *and I flipped out and went crazy*—Rolling Stone

flip-out **1** *n fr bop & cool talk* A spell of anger, disturbance, craziness, etc: *Harriet has a minor flip-out and flees*—New Yorker **2** *n* An exciting or wondrous experience: *Her performance was a real flip-out*

flipping *adj fr 1920s British* Accursed; wretched; =DAMN, FREAKING: *Give me the flipping thing and I'll get it fixed* [a euphemism for *fucking*]

flip side **1** *n phr* The reverse surface of a phonograph record; =B-SIDE: *a golden oldie on the flip side* **2** *n phr* The other side of a question, issue, etc: *it is true that...the flip side is that*—People Weekly/ *That's the good news. The flip side is the bad news*

flip the bird *v phr students* To make a contemptuous sign with the hand, middle finger extended; =GIVE someone THE FINGER: *The six ladies flipped the bird to all their earthling viewers, lifting their minis*—National Lampoon

◁**flit**▷ *n* A male homosexual; effeminate man

◁**flitty**▷ *adj* Homosexual; effeminate; =GAY: *This isn't some weird kind of flitty pass, is it?*—Toronto Life/ *Do you know the ballet? All those flitty people up on their toes*—John Irving

flivver **1** *v fr early 1900s show business* To fail; =FLOP: *If the production flivvers, I'll need that thirty cents*—LJ Vance **2** *n* A failure **3** *n fr early 1900s* A Model-T Ford car **4** *n* Any car, airplane, or other vehicle, esp a small or cheap one [origin unknown]

the **flix** *See* the FLICKS

FLK (pronounced as separate letters) *n hospital* An abnormal, sick, or ugly child [fr *funny-looking kid*]

float **1** *v* To be so happy and contented that one feels light as air; be ecstatic **2** *v* To loaf on the job; =GOOF OFF *n students* A period in which a student has no class; a free period **3** *v* To disseminate; send out: *Reporters have been told to float their resumes*—Washingtonian

floater **1** *n fr middle 1800s* A person who habitually moves about; vagabond; =DRIFTER **2** *n hoboes* A police order to leave town within one or two days, with suspension of a jail sentence **3** *n fr early 1900s British universities* A blunder: *made an error, slip...or floater*—Sterling North **4** *n baseball fr early 1900s* A slow pitch that appears to float in the air **5** *n fr middle 1800s* A corpse taken from the water

floating on air *adj phr* Ecstatic; euphoric; =ON CLOUD NINE

floating on the clouds **1** *adj phr* Putting credence in mere hopes and dreams; deluded **2** *adj phr* =FLOATING ON AIR

a **flock** *n phr* A large number; =HEAPS: *buys him a flock of drinks afterwards, and hopes for the best*—John Crosby

flog *v fr 1930s British fr late 1800s armed forces* To sell; peddle, esp in the sense of public hawking: *I went to the...convention to flog a new book*—Art Buchwald/ *Motel and bus companies flog special charter rates*—Newsweek [fr British slang *flog the clock* "move the clockhands forward in order to deceive," applied later to the illicit selling of military stores]

◁**flog** one's **meat**▷ *See* BEAT one's MEAT

◁**flong** one's **dong**▷ *v phr* To masturbate: *If it weren't for flonging my dong, I don't know what I'd do*—Playgirl

flooey *See* GO BLOOEY

floor **1** *v fr 1700s* To knock down; =DECK **2** *v* To shock, surprise, or hurt to the point of helplessness: *His divorce floored him* **3** *v* (also **floorboard**) To drive at full speed; push the throttle pedal to the floorboard: *She floored the Porsche on the freeway and got caught*

See CLEAN UP ON someone, IN ON THE GROUND FLOOR, MOP THE FLOOR WITH someone, PUT someone ON THE FLOOR

floozy (Variations: **faloosie** or **floogy** or **floosie** or **floozie** or **flugie**) **1** *n fr late 1800s* A self-indulgent, predatory woman, esp one of easy morals; cheap and tawdry woman: *He'd learn more about their psychology by taking a floozie to Atlantic City* —WB Johnson **2** *n* A prostitute

flop **1** *v fr early 1900s hoboes* To lie down for rest or sleep; sleep; =CRASH: *"Kip," "doss," "flop," "pound your ear," all mean...to sleep*—Jack London **2** *n: I went through $30 in 20 minutes one day buying drinks and flops for everyone* —Wall Street Journal **3** *n* A place to sleep, esp a cheap and sordid hotel or shelter: *I went into the flops and the shelters and was shocked* —New York **4** *v fr late 1800s* To fail completely; =BOMB: *The show flopped, ran one night only* **5** *n: My great idea was a total flop*
See BELLY FLOP

flophouse *n* A cheap and sordid rooming house or hotel, esp one with dormitories for men; =FLEABAG: *I'm spending my nights at the flophouse*

flopper *See* BELLY-FLOPPER

flopperoo *n* A particularly spectacular failure; =FLOP: *three subdivisions: flop, flopperoo, and kerplunk*—W Holbrook

floppola *n* A failure, esp a severe one; =FLOPPEROO: *And Fortune's worst floppola seems apocalyptic: Who will care for the poor?*—Washington Post

flossy or **flossie** *adj* Fancy; frilly; =HIGHFALUTIN: *It may be highly important to know a flossy name for the boss*—F Tripp

the **flow** *See* GO WITH THE FLOW

◁ **flower¹** ▷ **1** *n* An effeminate man or boy; =SISSY **2** *n* A male homosexual

flower² *See* WALLFLOWER

flower child *n phr esp 1960s and 70s* A member of the hippie movement or counterculture, who typically advocated love, peace, and nonviolence: *a caricature of a London flower child*—New Yorker

flower children (or **people**) *n phr esp 1960s and 70s* Members of the 1960s hippie movement collectively: *Woodstock is long over, and the bloom has gone off these flower children*—Penelope Gilliatt

flub **1** *n fr early 1900s* A stupid blunderer; =LUMMOX, KLUTZ: *Pick up your feet and don't be such a flub* **2** *v* To blunder; err; commit a gaffe; =GOOF: *I flubbed as soon as I opened my big mouth* **3** *v* To ruin by blundering; spoil with mistakes: *She flubbed the introduction, but did okay afterwards* **4** *n: The flub, as generally defined, is a mistake*—Pulpsmith **5** *v* To avoid work or duty; shirk; =GOOF OFF

flubdub **1** *n fr early 1900s* Incompetence; ineptitude: *They would remove much of the amateur flubdub*—New York Daily News **2** *n* An awkward person; blunderer; =GOOF-UP, KLUTZ

flub the dub *esp WW2 armed forces* **1** *v phr* To avoid one's work or duty; shirk; =GOLDBRICK: *He learned to flub the dub, but still stay pals with his associates* **2** *v phr* To think, work, move, etc, sluggishly and haplessly **3** *v phr* To fail by blundering; ruin one's best chances: *I think I flubbed the dub again, bidding so late*

flub-up **1** *n* A blunder: *The attempt was one big flub-up* **2** *n* A blunderer; =GOOF-UP, KLUTZ: *a kooky police cadet flub-up*—People Weekly

FLUF (FLUHF) *n airline* The Boeing 737 airliner [fr *fat little ugly fucker*]

fluff ◁**1**▷ *n* A girl or young woman: *A wan little fluff steals a dress so as to look sweet in the eyes of her boyfriend*—RL Woods **2** *n* An oral error, esp one made by an actor, announcer, etc; lapsus linguae: *a hell of a fluff, talking about Montezuma's revenge to the President of Mexico* **3** *v: Show me an actor that never fluffed a line* **4** *adj* Vague, lacking in intellectual content, insubstantial: *Frankly, I found the book to be nothing but fluff*

the **fluff** *n* An easy job or task

◁ **fluffhead** ▷ *n* A frivolous or stupid young woman; =DITZ: *To judge masculinity you need a woman, and not some little fluffhead either*—Village Voice

fluff off *v phr fr WW2 armed forces* To avoid work or duty; shirk; =GOOF OFF [probably a euphemism for *fuck off*]

fluff someone **off** *v phr* To snub or cut; reject haughtily: *He thought he* *was pretty good, so he fluffed us all off*

flugie ***See*** FLOOZY

fluke *n fr middle 1800s British* A good or bad stroke of luck; an extraordinary and unpredictable event: *My winning was just a fluke/ We got onto that flight by a fluke* [origin unknown, but perhaps fr *fluke* "flatfish" by way of an early 1800s British slang sense of *flat* "easy dupe, victim," altered in billiards jargon to *fluke* to characterize the seeming chicanery of a good stroke of luck]

fluky or **flukey** *adj* Uncertain, unpredictable, and often unexpected: *It would have been a very fluky shot, even if he happened to have the camera in his hand*—Raymond Chandler

flummox *fr early 1800s* **1** *v* To spoil; upset; confound: *Fu-Manchu tries to abduct a missionary who has flummoxed his plans in China*—SJ Perelman **2** *n* A failure; disaster; =FUCK-UP: *The solemn commemoration was a total flummox* [fr British dialect, "maul, bewilder"]

flunk **1** *v fr early 1800s* To fail; make a botch of: *I tried selling, but flunked at that* **2** *v college students fr early 1800s* To fail an examination, a course, etc; =BUST: *He flunked the final but passed the course* **3** *v college students fr middle 1800s* To give a student a failing grade **4** *n: I've got three passes and two flunks* [origin unknown; perhaps a blend of *fail* with *funk*, perhaps echoic of a dull collapse]

flush **1** *adj fr late 1600s* Having plenty of money; affluent, esp temporarily; rich: *It took money, and the jazzman wasn't ever too flush*—Stephen Longstreet **2** *n* A wealthy person: *Morny took [the house] over from a busted flush*—Raymond Chandler **3** *v college students* To stay away from class; =CUT **4** *v college students* =FLUNK **5** *v* To reject or ignore someone socially [first two senses fr the notion of a full or overfull container; other senses fr the notion of *flushing* a toilet to be rid of unwanted or useless material]

See FOUR-FLUSH

flusher *n* A toilet: *right in the old flusher*—Dan Jenkins

See FOUR-FLUSHER

◁**flute** or **fluter**▷ *n fr musicians* A male homosexual [fr metaphor of *flute* as "penis," and a homosexual as one who *plays the skin flute*]

See PLAY THE SKIN FLUTE, SKIN FLUTE

fly **1** *adj fr early 1800s British* Clever; alert; shrewd **2** *adj esp black fr early 1900s* Stylish; very attractive; =SHARP, SUPERFLY: *driving a Cadillac that's fly*—R Woodley/ *They tell each other they're fly when they look sharp*—Philadelphia Inquirer **3** *v narcotics* To act in a strange or bizarre way: *The broad must be flying on something*—Philadelphia Journal **4** *v narcotics* To feel the effects of narcotic intoxication: *About a minute after the fix he was flying* **5** *v* To succeed; persuade; =GO OVER • Often in the negative: *They're experts on what will fly and what won't*—Art Buchwald/ *It's a great idea, but it won't fly/ He glanced at Keenan to see if that statement was going to fly*—Playboy **6** *n* (also **green fly**) *baseball* An annoying, importuning fan; pest **7** *v* To run or travel very fast [the sense "clever, alert, etc" is of unknown origin, though it is conjectured that it may refer to the difficulty of catching a *fly* in midair, that it may be cognate with *fledge* and hence mean "accomplished, proven, seasoned," and that it is a corruption of *fla*, a shortening of *flash*; the sense "succeed, persuade, etc" is fr a cluster of jokes and phrases having to do with the Wright Brothers' and others' efforts to get something off the ground and make it *fly*]

See BAR-FLY, FRUIT FLY, LET FLY, NO FLIES ON, ON THE FLY, STRAIGHTEN UP AND FLY RIGHT, SUPERFLY

fly a kite ***See*** GO FLY A KITE

fly-boy *n fr WW2 armed forces* An aircraft pilot, esp an intrepid one in the US Air Force: *The generals are no full-throttle "fly-boys"*—Time

fly by the seat of one's **pants** **1** *v phr fr 1930s Army Air Corps* To pilot an airplane by feel and instinct rather than by instruments: *The old-time barnstormers had to fly by the seat of their pants* **2** *v phr* To proceed or work by instinct and improvisation, without formal guides or instructive experience: *The teachers are not trained to recognize it....*

They're flying by the seat of their pants—Washington Post
See SEAT-OF-THE-PANTS

fly cop *n phr* (Variations: **ball** or **bob** or **bull** or **dick** or **mug** may replace **cop**) *fr middle 1800s British* A detective; plainclothes police officer: *an offer to make him a "fly-cop" or detective*—E Lavine [probably fr *fly* "clever, shrewd," because of the presumed intelligence of detectives]

flyer or **flier** *n circus* A trapeze performer
See TAKE A FLYER

flying *n police* Duty in places remote from one's usual post
See HAVE THE RAG ON

flying colors *See* WITH FLYING COLORS

◁ **flying frig**▷ *See* TAKE A FLYING FUCK

◀ a **flying fuck**▶ *See* NOT GIVE A DAMN, TAKE A FLYING FUCK

fly mug *See* FLY COP

fly off the handle *v phr fr early 1800s* To lose one's temper; =LOSE one's COOL

fly right *v phr* To be honest, dependable, etc: *He's my son...I want him to fly right*—J and W Hawkins
See STRAIGHTEN UP AND FLY RIGHT

fly the coop *v phr fr early 1900s* To leave, esp to escape from confinement: *He had flown the coop...via a fire-escape*—A Hynd

fly trap *n phr* The mouth

fodder *See* BUNG FODDER

fofarraw *See* FOOFOORAW

fog 1 *v* (also **fog it**) *early 1900s Western* To run; speed; hurry **2** *v* To throw with great force: *Ole Diz was in his prime then, fogging a fastball*—Hal Boyle **3** *v early 1900s Western* To attack; assault, esp with gunfire: *I takes me heat an' fogs 'em*—American Mercury [origin unknown; possibly a substitution for *smoke* in all senses]

Foggy Bottom *n phr* The US Department of State: *little affinity for the "career boys" of Foggy Bottom*—HS Villard [fr the name of a marshy region in Washington, DC, where the State Department and other federal buildings are located; also an allusion to the murkiness of some policies and pronouncements]

fog it in *v phr baseball* To pitch a fastball

fogy or **fogey 1** *n fr late 1700s* An old person; any very conservative, outdated person; =DODO: *College students today are young fogies* **2** *n armed forces fr late 1800s* A military longevity allowance, awarded for units of service: *He got his pension and eight fogies* [origin unknown]

fold 1 *v* To fail or close, esp in business or show business: *The show folded after two nights* **2** *v* To lose effect and energy; wilt; fade: *She said she was about to fold*

folding *n* Money; =FOLDING MONEY: *a handsome wallet stuffed with a liberal supply of folding*—John O'Hara
See GREEN FOLDING

folding money *n phr* (Variations: **cabbage** or **green** or **lettuce** may replace **money**) Paper money; banknotes, esp in large quantities: *They leave their folding money at home*—John O'Hara/ *lacks the folding green to pick up a nightclub tab* —Hal Boyle

follow through (or **up**) **1** *v phr* To carry on with the next useful action; finish an action completely; pursue: *Follow up these hints, and you'll find the answer* **2** *n: What's the logical follow-through to what he said?*

follow something **up 1** *v phr* To carry one's investigation further; pursue a lead **2** *v phr* (also **follow**) To do something appropriate subsequent to something else, or better than something already done: *How will she follow up her bestseller?/ I can't follow that line*

fonk *See* FUNK

fonky *See* FUNKY

food *See* BUNNY FOOD, FAST FOOD, JUNK FOOD, SEAFOOD, SOUL FOOD

foodaholic *n* A compulsive eater; glutton

fooey *See* PHOOEY

foofooraw or **fofarraw** or **foo-foo-rah** (Fo͞o fə raw) *fr middle 1800s Western* **1** *n* A loud disturbance; uproar **2** *n* Gaudy clothing and accessories, esp the latter **3** *n* Ostentation; proud show: *The refreshing thing about it is the lack of drumbeating and foo-foo-rah*—Saturday Evening Post [probably fr Spanish *fanfarrón* "braggart"]

fool *See* DAMN-FOOL, TOMFOOL

fool around 1 *v phr* To pass one's time idly; putter about; loaf **2** *v phr* To joke and tease; =KID AROUND: *Mark, stop fooling around and get to* *work* **3** *v phr* To adventure sexually, esp adulterously: *He had never fooled around or seen a prostitute until he came to us*—Xaviera Hollander **4** *v phr* To flirt or coquette with; make a faint or casual try at seduction: *She wasn't serious, just fooling around*

fool around with *v phr* To play or tamper with; =FIDDLE WITH: *I told you not to fool around with that gun; now you've shot Aunt Bessie*

◁**foop**▷ *v college students* To do homosexual sex acts [probably a backward version of British *poof* "male homosexual, effeminate male," fr early-20th-century Australian, perhaps fr the exclamation *poof* or *pooh,* regarded as effeminate]

◁**fooper**▷ *n college students* A homosexual

foot *See* BIG FOOT, DOUGHFOOT, FLATFOOT, HAVE ONE FOOT IN THE GRAVE, HEAVY-FOOT, HOTFOOT, PADDLEFOOT, PUT one's FOOT IN IT, PUT one's FOOT IN one's MOUTH, SHOOT oneself IN THE FOOT, SLEWFOOT, TENDERFOOT, WEB-FOOT

footed *See* LEAD-FOOTED

foot-in-mouth disease *n phr* The uttering of embarrassing, stupid, or indiscreet speech: *The president had another of his attacks of foot-in-mouth disease when he talked about "freedom fighters"* [blend of the veterinary term *hoof-and-mouth disease* and the idiom *put one's foot in one's mouth*]

foot it **1** *v phr* To walk: *A bus is OK during non-rush-hours if you've been footing it too long*—New York Times **2** *v phr* To escape by running; =BEAT IT: *He stopped all of a sudden and said, "Foot it, Sonny! Foot it!"*—Claude Brown

footshot *n Army* An act, choice, utterance, etc, that damages one's reputation or standing: *Saying "stuff it" out loud was a real footshot* [fr *shoot* oneself *in the foot*]

footsie (Variations: **footsy-footsy** or **footsy-wootsy** or **footy-footy**, or all these spelled with **ie** replacing the final **y**) • Nearly always in the expression **play footsie**, **footsy-footsy**, etc **1** *n* Amorous and clandestine touching and rubbing of feet between a couple; pedal dalliance: *I played footsie with her during Carmen*—Gene Fowler **2** *n* Any especially close relationship between persons or parties: *Truman is plenty burned up over the way Chiang Kai-shek...played footy-footy with the Republicans*—Drew Pearson

footwork *See* FANCY FOOTWORK

fooy *See* PHOOEY

for a loop *See* KNOCK someone or something FOR A LOOP

for crying out loud (or **in a bucket**) *interj* An exclamation of emphasis, surprise, disbelief, impatience, etc; =FOR THE LOVE OF PETE: *For crying out loud, what half-assed thing has he done now?* [a euphemism for *for Christ's sake*]

for free *adv phr* Without charge; gratis; =FREE GRATIS: *They gave him a sandwich absolutely for free*—Arthur Daley

forget it **1** *interj* An injunction to put something out of one's hopes, concern, etc, esp because it is impossible: *I can get up there most of the time, but in winter, forget it* **2** *interj* An exclamation of pardon; a token of forgiveness: *Hell no, I didn't mind. Forget it*

for one's **health** *adv phr fr early 1900s* Lightly or frivolously; for one's delightful good • Always used ironically and in the negative: *I didn't make this damn stupid trip for my health, you know*

for (or **fer**) **instance** *n phr* An example; an instance: *I'd understand the point better if you gave me a couple of concrete for instances*

◁**fork**▷ *v* To cheat; maltreat; take advantage of; =FUCK, SHAFT: *I hoped he'd take care of us, but we got forked* [a euphemism for *fuck*]

forkball *n baseball* A pitch thrown from a forklike finger grip

forked-eight or **bent-eight** *n hot rodders* A V-8 engine or a car having such an engine

for keeps *adv phr* Forever; permanently: *They put him away for keeps/ She wanted to be married for keeps* *See* PLAY FOR KEEPS

◁**forking**▷ **1** *adj* Wretched; disgusting: *I won't eat this forking stuff* **2** *adv* Very; extremely: *He sounded forking mad* [a euphemism for *fucking*]

fork over (or **up** or **out**) *v phr fr early 1800s* To pay; give; contribute: *Fork up the cash*—E Conradi/ *I imagine he* *used a picture...to make you fork over the dough*—RS Prather

forks *n fr 1940s black* Fingers: *Get your forks off that*
See RAIN CATS AND DOGS

◁ **fork you** ▷ *interj* =FUCK YOU

form *n fr horse-racing* The record of past performances by a horse, team, competitor, etc; =THE BOOK, TRACK RECORD: *What's the form on General Electric this quarter?/ The form on the little gelding is super*

form sheet *n phr fr horse-racing* A printed record of past performance; =DOPE SHEET

for openers (or **starters**) *fr poker adv phr* As a beginning; as a first move or suggestion: *So, try this for openers*—Pulpsmith/ *expensive...for starters*—Armistead Maupin [fr the set value of the hand needed to *open* the betting in a game of poker]

for real **1** *adj phr* Believably existent; as good or bad as seems; authentic: *I often wondered if the bastard was for real* **2** *adv phr* Really; truly: *I'm gonna for real do it, right now*

for serious **1** *adv phr* Seriously; with a sober intent: *The Yanks took the field for serious*—Robert Ruark **2** *adj phr: He was for serious but she wasn't*

for (or **fer**) **sure** (or **shure** or **shurr**) *teenagers* **1** *adv* Definitely; certainly: *He is for sure a nerd* **2** *affirmation* Yes: *When he asked if I'd do it I said fer sure I would*

fort *n truckers* An armored truck or car

for the birds *adj phr fr WW2 armed forces* Inferior; undesirable; of small worth; =LOUSY: *I won't buy it....It's for the birds*—John Crosby [a euphemistic shortening of *shit for the birds*, a version of *birdshit* or *chickenshit*]

for (or **just for**) **the hell of it** *adv phr* For no definite or useful reason; for fun; casually: *And just for the hell of it she told him he could come again*

for the long ball *See* GO FOR THE LONG BALL

for (or **over**) **the long haul** *adv phr* For a long and arduous effort; for a period of difficulty and strain: *He's the kind of guy you can count on for the long haul*

for the love of Pete *interj* An exclamation of emphasis, surprise, impatience, disbelief, dismay, etc; =FOR CRYING OUT LOUD: *I already did it, for the love of Pete!*

forthwith *n police* An order to report immediately

forty-deuce *n* Forty-second Street in New York City: *Forty-deuce is what its seamy inhabitants call 42d Street*—Newark Star Ledger

forty-four[1] **1** *n lunch counter* A cup of coffee **2** *n* (also **44** or **.44**) A .44-caliber pistol: *Frankie went down to the hotel, pulled out her big forty-four*

forty-four[2] *n* A prostitute [fr the rhyme with *whore*]

forty (or **six**) **ways to Sunday** *adv phr fr middle 1800s* In every possible manner, direction, etc; comprehensively: *She had him beat forty ways to Sunday* [origin unknown]

forty winks *n phr fr early 1800s British* A short sleep; nap: *He caught forty winks and perked right up*

forward in the saddle *See* LEAN FORWARD IN THE SADDLE

fossil *n* An old person; =ALTER KOCKER, FOGY: *If I got to kiss old fossils to hold this job I'm underpaid*—Hal Boyle

fouled up **1** *adj phr* Spoiled by bungling; confused; hopelessly tangled; =FUCKED UP: *never seen anything more fouled up than what happened yesterday at the White House*—J Marlow **2** *adj phr* Damaged; impaired: *The kids were fouled up...came from bad homes, went to bad schools*—New York Times [a euphemism for *fucked up*]

foulmouth *n* A person inclined to utter obscenities, profanity, etc

foul up *v phr* To ruin and confuse a project, assignments, etc; display one's ineptitude and futility; =FUCK UP, SNAFU: *I fouled up my very first chance to be a reporter* [a euphemism for *fuck up*]

foul-up **1** *n* A confused, tangled, hopeless situation; botch: *It's supposed to be a concert series, but it's a total foul-up* **2** *n* A person who consistently blunders; bungler; =FUCK-UP: *Why put that notorious foul-up in charge?*

foundry *See* NUT HOUSE

four *See* TEN FOUR

four-and-one *black* **1** *n* Friday, the fifth day of the week **2** *n* Payday

four-bagger *n baseball* A home run: *It was Bobby's 31st four-bagger and his fourth at Ebbets Field*—J Reichler

four-banger *n* A four-cylinder motor or car

four-bit *adj* Costing 50 cents; half-dollar: *to smoke four-bit cigars* —James T Farrell

four bits *n phr fr early 1800s* Half a dollar; 50 cents [originally a *bit* was a Mexican or Spanish *real*, worth 12½ cents, or a part of a more valuable coin, such that eight would make a dollar; ultimately fr 18th-century British slang *bit* "a small piece of money"]

four-by-four *n Army & truckers* A four-wheel-drive vehicle having four forward gears

four-eyes *n* A person who wears eyeglasses

four-flush *fr early 1900s* **1** *v* To live by sponging off others, or by pretense and fraud **2** *v* To cheat; swindle; victimize **3** *modifier: Four-flushing hustlers who really knew how to gamble*—Louis Armstrong [fr a poker player's attempt to bluff when he has *four* cards of one suit showing and one of another suit not showing]

four-flusher *n fr early 1900s* A bluffer or fraud; cheat; swindler

the **four hundred** *n phr* The set of socially prominent people, esp in a given place; the social elite [fr the list, attributed to Ward McAllister, of *four hundred* socially desirable people]

four-letter man **1** *n phr* A stupid man • From the four letters of **dumb** **2** *n phr* A detestable man; a contemptible wretch; =PRICK, SHIT • From the four letters of **shit** [fr the *letters*, school initials, awarded for excellence in varsity sports]

four nines *n phr* Something pure or very nearly pure: *That is four nines, or 99.99 pure gold*—Time

four on the floor *n phr* A gearshift lever emerging from the floor of a car, and controlling four speeds; hence, standard as distinct from automatic shift: *This little baby's got four on the floor and leather bucket seats*

four sheets to the wind *See* THREE SHEETS TO THE WIND

four-square *adj* Conventional; unimaginative; stolid; =SQUARE: *Undeniably the conducting is a bit four-square and heavy*—Village Voice

four-time loser *See* THREE-TIME LOSER

four-wheeler *n truckers* An automobile; =CAGE

four wide ones *n phr baseball* A base on balls; a walk, esp an intentional pass

fox **1** *v* To deceive; mislead; outwit: *He tried to fox me with that phoney accent, and did* **2** *n teenagers & black fr 1940s black* A beautiful, sexually attractive woman, or in teenage use, man

fox paw *n phr* A faux pas

foxy *adj fr 1940s black* Attractive; sexually desirable; =DANG[1]: *She was 22 years old, a real foxy little chick with auburn hair*—J Eszterhas

fracture **1** *v* To elicit loud laughter from; =LAY THEM IN THE AISLES: *We're a riot, hey. We play all kinds of funny stuff. We fracture the people*—Max Shulman **2** *v bop & cool talk* To evoke a strong reaction: *That flips me out and fractures me, man*

fractured *adj* Drunk

frag **1** *v Vietnam War armed forces* To kill or wound someone, esp a detested officer of one's own unit, typically by throwing a fragmentation grenade at him **2** *v* To kill; =ICE, WASTE: *If I hadn't've done it, he would've fragged me*—George V Higgins

fragged *adj car-racing* Ruined; blown-out: *countless fragged Ferrari engines*—Car and Driver

fraidy (or **'fraidy**) **cat** *n phr* A timorous person, esp a boy; coward

frail *n fr 1920s college students* A woman, esp a young woman: *in persuading frails to divulge what they know*—E Lavine

◁ **frail eel** ▷ *n phr black* An attractive woman; =FOX: *I can get any frail eel I wants*—Zora Neale Hurston

frame **1** *n* The human body; physique; build, esp that of a woman **2** *n homosexuals* A heterosexual man attractive to homosexuals **3** *n* A unit of a game or other contest: *Mel Queen lined a single to right field to open that frame*—R McGowen **4** *n fr early 1900s* The incrimination of an innocent person with false evidence; =FRAME-UP: *just the victim of a frame*

—J Evans **5** *v: I was framed* —Joseph Auslander

frame-up **1** *n fr early 1900s* The incrimination of an innocent person with false evidence: *I'll prove to you it's a frame-up*—W Weeks

frame someone **up** *v phr fr early 1900s* To incriminate an innocent person with false evidence: *They framed him up with a phony burglary charge* [probably fr the carpenter's term *frame up* "construct the supporting frame of a building," hence, to determine the shape of something by artifice]

frank *n* A frankfurter; =WEENIE

frantic *bop & cool talk* **1** *adj* Excellent; wonderful; =COOL **2** *adj* Conventional; bourgeois; =UNCOOL: *The man who cares is now derided for being "frantic"*—Herbert Gold

frapping *adj* Wretched; accursed; =DAMN, FUCKING: *I need a frapping medic like a hole in the head*—People Weekly [a euphemism for *fucking*]

frat *college students* **1** *n* A college fraternity **2** *n* (also **frat rat**) A fraternity member **3** *n teenagers* A male student who conforms to middle-class norms of conduct and dress: *A "frat"... is a youth who dresses neatly and conforms to the accepted patterns*—New York Times

to a **frazzle** *adv phr fr middle 1800s* Completely; totally; to a ruined condition: *After the marathon I was beat to a frazzle* [fr dialect *frazzle* "frayed end of a rope"]

frazzled **1** *adj* Exhausted; tired in nerve and flesh; =PLAYED OUT: *He was frazzled after three weeks without a break* **2** *adj* Drunk

freak **1** *n* A drink made of Coca-Cola (a trade name) and orange flavoring ◁**2**▷ *n jazz musicians* A male homosexual: *"Freak" is a homosexual*—Stephen Longstreet **3** *n* =HIPPIE **4** *v* To behave strangely and disorientedly as if intoxicated by a psychedelic drug; =FREAK OUT: *His publisher for the last two books "sort of freaked" when they got a look at this one*—New York

-freak *combining word* A devotee or enthusiast; addict; =BUG, BUFF, NUT: *plant freak/ radio freak/ porn-freak* *See* ACID FREAK, ECOFREAK, JESUS FREAKS, METH HEAD, PEEK FREAK

freaking *adj* Wretched; accursed; =DAMN, FUCKING: *who's got so much freaking talent it just turns your stomach*—Car and Driver/ *all the freaking way to the bank*—Playboy [a euphemism for *fucking*]

freak out (or **up**) *fr narcotics* **1** *v phr* To have intense and disturbing hallucinations and other reactions from psychedelic drugs **2** *v phr* To go out of touch with reality with or without narcotics; become irrational, esp frantically so; be intoxicated; =FLIP OUT: *plus the chance to freak out, speak in tongues or talk nonsense*—Herbert Gold **3** *v phr* To become very excited and exhilarated, as if intoxicated with narcotics **4** *v phr* To abandon conventional values and attitudes; =DROP OUT

freak-out *fr narcotics* **1** *n* An instance of freaking out: *a period which one feminist writer has called one of "mass freak-outs all over the place"*—Esquire/ *the same freakouts, the same strange clothes*—New Yorker **2** *n* A person who is freaked out **3** *n* A frightening or nightmarish drug experience; =BAD TRIP, BUMMER **4** *n* A congregation of hippies

freak someone **out** *v phr fr narcotics* To cause someone to show the irrationality, lethargy, excitement, withdrawal, etc, of a psychedelic experience: *The heavy metal sound freaked him out*

freaky *adj fr narcotics* Having the qualities of a freak or a freak-out; =FAR OUT: *I think it would be freaky to have an affair with my barber*—Playboy

free *See* FOR FREE, HOME FREE

freebase or **free base it** *v* or *v phr narcotics* To use cocaine by heating it and inhaling the smoke, its most powerful essence: *The addiction problem seems to be compounded by the fact that so many cokeheads are freebasing it*

freebie or **freebee** or **freeby** *n fr early 1900s black* Anything given or enjoyed free of charge: *That meal was a freebie and it didn't cost me anything*—Louis Armstrong

free gratis (GRA təs) **1** *adv phr fr late 1800s* Without charge; =FOR FREE: *The Congressmen traveled free gratis* **2** *adj phr: free-gratis tickets*

[fr combination of *free* with Latin *gratis* "free"]

freeload **1** *v* To be fed, entertained, supported, etc, without charge; live parasitically; =SPONGE: *They will successfully free load the rest of their lives*—Hal Boyle **2** *n: During the depression women free loads were rare*—J Cannon

freeloader **1** *n* A person who freeloads; =MOOCHER, SPONGER: *Congressmen are great freeloaders*—L Mortimer **2** *n* A gathering or party with free refreshments: *Somebody was tossing a free-loader over on Park Avenue*—J Bainbridge

free lunch *n phr* Something had without paying for it; an uncompensated pleasure; a perk or gratuity: *pushing the free lunch*—Wall Street Journal [fr the former custom of giving customers free food called *free lunch* in saloons]

See THERE'S NO FREE LUNCH

free-o *n* Something received without charge; =FREEBIE: *So he picks up a few free-o's here and there*—California

free ride ***See*** GET A FREE RIDE

free ticket **1** *n phr* General freedom of action, esp of forbidden action; license; carte blanche: *He thinks the uniform gives him a free ticket to be a shitheel* **2** *n phr* (also **free transportation**) *baseball* A base on balls; walk

free-vee *n* Nonpay television: *Well, pay-TV proved free-vee wrong* —Toronto Star

free-wheeling **1** *n* Independence of action and initiative; blithe and unconstrained indulgence: *No free-wheeling here, you do things strictly our way* **2** ***modifier:*** *Jonathan himself tries opium, hash, freewheeling sex, gliders*—Playboy **3** *n* Liberal spending; easy munificence: *the free-wheeling of the new rich* **4** ***modifier:*** *the free-wheeling out-of-towner*—Hal Boyle [fr the feature of certain 1930s cars permitting them to coast *freely* without being slowed by the engine]

freeze **1** *n* A stopping of change, esp in various monetary matters: *a freeze on profits/ nuclear freeze* **2** *v: The government denies it wants to freeze interest rates* **3** *v* To stay or become motionless: *The cop hollered to him to freeze right there* **4** *v* To stay where one is: *Your best bet is to freeze and wait. You can't get away*—Nelson Algren **5** *v* To treat with deliberate hauteur; snub; cut: *Next time she froze me mercilessly*

See IN COLD STORAGE

freeze someone **out** *v phr fr late 1800s* To exclude; discriminate against: *When I wanted to get into the game they froze me out*

◁**freeze the balls off a brass monkey**▷ *v phr* To be very cold: *It was the kind of clear winter day that would freeze the balls off a brass monkey*

freeze up *v phr* To become paralyzed by fear; be immobilized by panic; =CLANK

freight ***See*** PAY THE FREIGHT, PULL one's FREIGHT

◁**French**▷ **1** *n* Cunnilingus; =the FRENCH WAY **2** *v: Then the perverse chap actually Frenched her!*

See PARDON MY FRENCH

French kiss **1** *n phr fr 1920s* A kiss in which the tongue of one person explores the oral cavity of another, and vice versa **2** *v: They French-kissed and perhaps more*

French leave *n phr fr late 1700s* Departure without notice or permission, esp going AWOL from a military post

French letter *n phr fr middle 1800s* A condom

French postcard *n phr* A pornographic photograph, such as was fancied to be sold by furtive characters pulling at one's sleeve in the streets of Paris • In the form **French print**, used fr the middle 1800s

◁**French tickler**▷ *n phr* A condom with added variegated surfaces, spirals, fins, etc, to increase vaginal stimulation

French (or **Spanish**) **walk** **1** *n phr* A pained and humiliating gait used by one whose seat and neck are strongly grasped and raised to urge him along; =the BUM'S RUSH **2** *v* (also **walk Spanish**): *Mike Spanish-walked him swiftly across the little space*—WR Burnett/ *Smith... was an expert at walking 'em Spanish*—New Yorker • **walk Spanish** is attested from the early 1800s [said to be fr the custom of pirates, in the *Spanish*

Main, of forcing prisoners to *walk* while holding them by the neck so that their toes barely touched the deck]

◁ the **French way**▷ ***n phr*** Cunnilingus [fr the conviction expressed in the classic couplet: The French they are a funny race/ They fight with their feet and fuck with their face]

fresh **1** ***adj*** Impudent; disrespectful; saucy; =CHEEKY: *Don't be fresh to your Momma or I'll belt you one* **2** ***adj*** Flirtatious; sexually bold; =FAST: *I'm not that kind of girl, so don't be fresh* **3** ***adj*** Aloof and uninvolved; =COOL: *"We hang out with him because he's fresh," said Jesse MMC* —New York Daily News [first two senses perhaps related to German *frech* "impudent"]

fresh out ***adv phr*** Without; =OUT: *We're fresh out of bananas, Missus*

fribble ***n*** A trifle; a piece of inanity: *For every zap-pow fribble, there were equal servings of socially redeeming food for thought*—Newsweek

Friday ***See*** GAL FRIDAY, TGIF

fried **1** ***adj*** Drunk **2** ***adj*** *esp underworld* Electrocuted **3** ***adj*** *teenagers* Confused; muddled; exhausted; =BURNED OUT

friendly ***n*** *armed forces fr WW2* In wartime, a plane, ship, soldier, civilian, etc, of one's own side: *Friendlies ... townspeople who cooperate with the Americans*—New York Times

◁ **frig**▷ **1** ***v*** To stimulate the female genitals manually or digitally **2** ***v*** *fr middle 1800s* To masturbate **3** ***v*** *fr early 1900s* To do the sex act **4** ***v*** To cheat or trick; take advantage of; =DIDDLE, SHAFT **5** ***interj*** =FUCK [ultimately fr Latin *fricare* "rub"]
See TAKE A FLYING FUCK

◁ **frigging**▷ **1** ***adj*** Wretched; accursed; =DAMN, FUCKING: *if we could find the frigging truck*—Arthur Hailey/ *You're a walkin', friggin' combat zone*—Time **2** ***adv:*** *Ain't it frigging stupid?/ They friggin' loved it*—Washington Post

Frisco ***n*** San Francisco, California: *Ever been to Frisco?*—James M Cain • This nickname is said to be disapproved by the residents of the place

frisk *fr late 1700s British* **1** ***v*** (also **frisk down**) To search, esp for firearms or contraband, by patting or rubbing the person in places where these might be concealed: *raise your hands high, frisk him*—R Wallace/ *without getting taken-off, frisked-down or punched-out*—New York Times **2** ***n:*** *They did a quick frisk and let him go* **3** ***v*** To inspect a building, apartment, etc, for evidence or loot: *Let's go up and frisk the apartment*—Raymond Chandler

frit ***n*** A male homosexual; =FLIT

fritz ***v*** To make something inoperative; put out of working order: *Lightning hit some wires and fritzed the generator*—F Brown
See ON THE BLINK

fritzer ***n*** *underworld* Something false; =PHONY

'fro or **fro** ***n*** A frizzy style of coiffure; =AFRO: *the curly 'fro which has found particular favor among the men* —Ebony

frobnitz ***n*** *computer* An unspecified or unspecifiable object; something one does not know the name of or does not wish to name; =GADGET, GIZMO

frog **1** ***n*** =FROGSKIN ◁**2**▷ ***n*** (also **Frog** or **froggy** or **Froggy** or **frog-eater**) *esp WW1 fr middle 1800s British* A Frenchman or -woman: *My dad was in France during the last war. He knows those Frogs*—Calder Willingham **3** ***modifier:*** *frog wine/ a Frog chick* ◁**4**▷ ***n*** The French language: *He asked me in Frog* **5** ***n*** *teenagers* A dull and conventional person: *Anybody who still wears saddle shoes is ... a "frog"* —New York Times [senses referring to the French fr their eating of *frog-legs*]
See BIG FISH, KNEE-HIGH TO A GRASSHOPPER

frogging ***adj*** Wretched; accursed; =DAMN, FUCKING: *Baseball is a froggin' silly little game*—Milwaukee Journal [a euphemism for *fucking*]

frogskin *fr early 1900s* **1** ***n*** A one-dollar bill; one dollar: *I'll give you five hundred frogskins for the good will and fixtures*—SJ Perelman **2** ***n*** Any piece of paper money; =FOLDING MONEY: *He not only got his quail, but a handful of frogskins as well*—Associated Press [fr the green color]

from Adam ***See*** NOT KNOW someone FROM ADAM

from hell to breakfast ***adv phr*** Thoroughly and vehemently; violently: *Police...clubbed the Gophers from hell to breakfast*—H Asbury

from hunger 1 *adj phr fr 1930s musicians* Inferior; unpleasant; contemptible: *I started giving the three witches at the next table the eye again. That is, the blonde one. The other two were strictly from hunger* —JD Salinger **2** *adv phr: playing from hunger...in a style to please the uneducated masses*—Peabody Bulletin

from nothing *See* KNOW FROM NOTHING

from scratch 1 *adv phr* From the earliest stages; from the very beginning: *We had to do it all again, from scratch* **2** *adv phr* Using the separate basic ingredients or parts: *I never tired of watching my grandmother make the bread "from scratch"*—San Francisco **3** *adj phr: his first from-scratch musical venture*—Philadelphia [fr the mark or *scratch* indicating the starting line of a race]

from the git-go (or **get-go**) *adv phr fr black* From the very beginning: *It was his bust from the git-go*—R Woodley/ *Right from the get-go he came out smoking*—New York Times

from the hip *See* SHOOT FROM THE HIP

from (or **out of** or **straight from**) **the horse's mouth** *adv phr* From the most authentic source: *I got the tip straight from the horse's mouth*—WR Burnett [fr the fact that a *horse's* age can be determined most precisely and directly by examining its teeth]

from the shoulder *See* STRAIGHT FROM THE SHOULDER

from the top *adv phr esp musicians* From the beginning: *Let's hear it again from the top* [perhaps fr the musical instruction *da capo* "from the beginning," literally, "from the head"]

from the word go *adv phr fr middle 1800s* From the very beginning; ab ovo: *He was lying from the word go*

front 1 *n hoboes* A suit of clothes **2** *n fr 1920s* The appearance and impression one presents publicly; facade: *a real coon type. But that's just front*—Lawrence Anderson **3** *n* (also **front man**) A respectable and impressive person who represents or publicly supports persons lacking social approval: *Inability to hire a professional bondsman and "good front" results in a quick trial*—E Lavine **4** *v: If you ask them to front for you, they know you're going to do something*—Playboy **5** *n fr 1920s* An ordinary and unexceptionable business used as a cover for gambling, extortion, etc, esp as a way of decontaminating ill-gotten money: *The candy store was a front for his bookie business* **6** *v fr narcotics* To give something, esp narcotics, on promise of payment: *I'll front you some if you pay me by Thursday*
See OUT-FRONT, UP FRONT

frontal *adj* Candid; direct; open: *He's a very direct and forceful guy, a very frontal person*—Washington Post [fr *up front*, influenced by *full frontal*]
See FULL FRONTAL

front-door *adj* Legitimate; respectable: *a front-door operation*

front gee (JEE) *n phr underworld* A pickpocket's confederate [fr *gee* "guy"]

front money *n phr* An initial and impressive amount of money; cash as an earnest: *He had agreed...to help the manufacturer get the $1.2 million loan in return for 7 percent of the total, plus "green" or "front money"* —New York Times/ *in the drive for $4.5 million in "front money" by Labor Day*—New York Times

front office 1 *n phr* The chief administrative offices of a company **2** *n phr* Managers; executives: *What's the front office think?* **3** *adj phr: front-office memos* **4** *n phr underworld* A police station

front runner *n phr* The leader in a contest, election, etc: *That left as front runners Runcie and England's second-ranking churchman*—Time

frost 1 *n fr late 1800s British* A total failure; something not well received: *My idea was a dismal frost* **2** *n* Social hauteur; chill; =COLD SHOULDER: *He smiled at her and got frost* **3** *v* To anger; irritate: *That tone of voice really frosts me* [first sense fr the notion of "a killing frost"]

frosty 1 *adj* Unperturbed: *Stay frosty. Relax*—Joseph Wambaugh **2** *adj* In a reserved manner; haughty; cool: *her frosty glance*

frowsy *n* A slovenly, unkempt woman: *a few frowsies in skirts*—New Yorker

frozen rope *n phr baseball* A hard line drive: *A hard line drive is a blue* *darter, frozen rope, or an ungodly shot*—Jim Bouton

fruit **1** ***n*** An eccentric person; =FRUITCAKE, ODDBALL: *I'll bet we get a lot of fruits*—O Johnson ◁**2**▷ ***n*** *fr 1930s* A male homosexual; =FAIRY [first sense short for *fruitcake*, as in "nutty as a fruitcake"]

See HEN-FRUIT

fruitbar ***See*** FLAMER

fruitcake **1** ***n*** An insane person; =NUT: *The shrink himself is a certified fruitcake* **2** ***n*** An eccentric person; =FRUIT, ODDBALL **3** ***modifier:*** *those fruitcake sandal makers in the tractor-gear factory*—Calvin Trillin ◁**4**▷ ***n*** A male homosexual; =FRUIT **5** ***modifier:*** *his fruitcake mannerisms*

See NUTTY AS A FRUITCAKE

◁ **fruit fly**▷ ***n phr*** *homosexuals* =FAG HAG

fruit-picker ***n*** *homosexuals* A heterosexual man who occasionally seeks out homosexual partners

fruit salad **1** ***n phr*** *fr WW2 armed forces* Ribbons and other badges worn on the breast of a military jacket **2** ***n phr*** *narcotics* A mixture of tranquilizers, painkillers, and other drugs from the family medicine cabinet used secretly by adolescents ◁**3**▷ ***n phr*** (Variations: **potato patch** or **rose garden** or **vegetable garden**) *hospital* A group of stroke victims or otherwise totally disabled patients

fruity **1** ***adj*** Eccentric; odd; =NUTTY, WEIRD ◁**2**▷ ***adj*** Homosexual; =GAY **3** ***adj*** *esp British fr early 1900s* Very rich; unctuous: *a fruity upperclass accent*

fry **1** ***v*** To be executed in the electric chair, or to execute someone in the electric chair: *I built up a case against Sandmark. You probably could have fried him with it, too*—J Evans/ *Apparently everybody in Texas thinks everybody should be fried*—Washington Post **2** ***v*** *esp teenagers* To punish or injure, esp in revenge **3** ***v*** *computer* To fail; =GO DOWN **4** ***v*** *black* To remove the kinks from hair with a hot comb or curling iron

See BIGGER FISH TO FRY, SMALL FRY

fubar (Fōō bar) ***adj*** *fr WW2 armed forces* Totally botched and confused; =SNAFU [fr *fucked up beyond all recognition*]

fubb ***adj*** *fr WW2 armed forces* =FUBAR, SNAFU [fr *fucked up beyond belief*]

fubis (Fōō bis) ***sentence*** *Army fr 1950s* An irritated or defiant comment [fr *fuck you, buddy, I'm shipping*]

◀ **fuck**▶ **1** ***v*** *fr 1200s* To do the sex act with or to someone **2** ***n*** An instance of the sex act: *a quick fuck* **3** ***n*** A sex partner: *She said he's not a bad fuck* **4** ***n*** A despicable person; =BASTARD, PRICK: *Why don't you fucks find a cure for that already?*—Joseph Heller/ *Get out, you stupid fuck!* **5** ***v*** To cheat; swindle; maltreat; take advantage of; =FUCK OVER, SCREW: *I was with them twenty years, but they fucked me anyhow* **6** ***v*** To curse and vilify; revile extremely; =DAMN • Strongest of the cursing terms that include wishing the person or thing to eternal damnation; "damn," "to hell with," and mentally subjecting the person or thing to an act of sodomy: "fuck, screw," and British "bugger": *Fuck the money, I'm gone go on this ride*—Claude Brown/ *Ah, fuck that noise*—Philip Roth **7** ***interj*** An exclamation of disgust, disappointment, dismay, etc: *Oh fuck, the thing's busted!* **8** ***v*** To botch and confuse; ruin; =FUCK UP: *My God, if the doctor sent out a bill... it might fuck the whole thing*—Lawrence Sanders [origin unknown; perhaps fr or related to German *ficken* "strike, copulate with"]

See DRY FUCK, FINGERFUCK, a FLYING FUCK, GOAT FUCK, GO FUCK oneself, MIND-FUCK, NOT GIVE A DAMN, NOT GIVE A FUCK FOR NOTHING, RAT FUCK, TAKE A FLYING FUCK, THROW A FUCK INTO someone

◀ a **fuck**▶ ***See*** NOT GIVE A DAMN, NOT GIVE A FUCK FOR NOTHING

◀ the **fuck**▶ ***See*** the HELL

◀ **fuck a duck**▶ ***interj*** An exclamation of surprise and incredulity: *He did? Well fuck a duck!*

◀ **fuck-all**▶ ***n*** *esp British* Nothing; =ZILCH: *A good extra... can pull in good money to not do fuck-all*—Playboy/ *He knows fuck-all about the case*

◀ **fuck around**▶ **1** ***v phr*** To idle and loaf about; =MESS AROUND: *Although I*

do fuck around in home studios and things like that, I think that it's of no importance—Rolling Stone **2** *v phr* To tease; fool around annoyingly; =HORSE AROUND
See FUCK WITH

◀ **fuck** someone's **brains out**▶ *v phr* To do the sex act busily and for a long time: *We can spend the whole night together, fuck our brains out* —Earl Thompson/ *two people who'd just fucked each other's brains out* —Richard Grossbach

◀ **fucked by the fickle finger of fate**▶ *adj phr* Victimized by bad luck; very unfortunate

◀ **fucked out**▶ *adj phr* Exhausted; =PLAYED OUT, POOPED

◀ **fucked up**▶ **1** *adj phr* Confused; botched; ruined; =BALLED UP: *A good idea, but now it's totally fucked up* **2** *adj phr* Mentally and emotionally disturbed; neurotic: *I was so fucked up I couldn't talk sense* **3** *adj phr* Intoxicated, esp by narcotics: *I was so drunk and fucked up and shaken with tenderness*—Rolling Stone

◀ **fucker**▶ **1** *n* A detestable person; =BASTARD, PRICK: *And the fuckers are really, really twisting us up*—Rolling Stone **2** *n* Any person or thing • Often used affectionately: *The cop's really a nice old fucker/ Look at that little fucker go!*
See FATHERFUCKER, MIND-FUCKER, MOTHERFUCKER, PIG-FUCKER

◀ **fuckhead**▶ *n* A despicable person; =JERK: *some back-country fuckhead with a stethoscope*—Stephen King

◀ **fucking**▶ **1** *adj* Wretched; rotten; accursed; =DAMN: *hectic fuckin' business*—Changes/ *I hate this fucking place* **2** *adv* Extremely; very: *It's fucking difficult to get a raise these days*
See MOTHERFUCKING, A ROYAL FUCKING

◀ **-fucking-**▶ *infix* Used for emphasis: *in-fucking-credible*—Dan Jenkins/ *"Un-fucking-believable," they say in the booth*—Toronto Life

◀ **fucking a** (or **ay**)▶ *fr 1940s fr British* **1** *affirmation* Absolutely; definitely: *Fucking a, no one's gonna shoot Keith*—Playboy **2** *adv phr: Fucking ay right I did*—Patrick Mann **3** *interj* An exclamation of pleasure, triumph, joy, etc; =GREAT: *We won? Fucking a!* [fr an affirmatory phrase *your fucking arse*]

◀ **fucking well**▶ *adv phr* Nearly; precisely; just about: *not afraid of fucking well anything*—George Warren

◀ **fucking well told**▶ *adv phr* Absolutely right; definitely; =FUCKING A: *Is he stupid? You're fucking well told he is*

◀ **fuck like a bunny**▶ *v phr* To copulate readily and vigorously • Said of both sexes [fr the amatory eagerness of rabbits, also referred to in the catch-phrase "Shoot the habit to me, rabbit" as a response to "Sex is just a habit"]

◀ **fuck like a mink**▶ *v phr fr early 1900s* To copulate readily and vigorously • Said only of women

◀ **fuck off**▶ **1** *v phr* =FUCK AROUND **2** *v phr* =FUCK UP **3** *v phr fr late 1800s* To leave; depart: *Tell 'em to fuck off, I don't want anything to do with them*—Xaviera Hollander **4** *interj: Scat, Sophie! Fuck off, Jack!*

◀ **fuck-off**▶ *n fr WW2 armed forces* A habitual shirker; sluggard; =GOOF-OFF: *I mean, everybody's a fuck-off* —Rolling Stone

◀ **fuck over**▶ *v phr* To victimize and maltreat, sexually or otherwise; =FUCK: *so accustomed to being used and fucked over that they probably would do nothing*—Howard S Becker

◀ **fuck up**▶ *fr late 1800s* **1** *v phr* To fail by blundering; ruin one's prospects: *They are the prime reasons that people fuck up in bands*—Rolling Stone **2** *v phr* To confuse; botch; =BALL UP: *I had it right, but he fucked it up*

◀ **fuck-up**▶ **1** *n* A bungler, esp a chronic one: *The sergeant was a confirmed fuck-up* **2** *n* A confused situation; botch; =MESS: *The operation was a royal fuck-up* **3** *n* A blunder; =GOOF: *These things are my ideas... they've all got the same fuck-ups*—Rolling Stone

◀ **fuck** someone **up**▶ *v phr* To injure or maltreat; =FUCK OVER: *If anybody was to mess with your sister, you had to really fuck him up*—Claude Brown

◀ **fuck up, move up**▶ *sentence Army* If you blunder badly, you'll be promoted

◀ **fuck** (or **fuck around**) **with**▶ **1** *v phr* To play or toy with; meddle with: *Stop fucking around with that switch!/ Floyd was a little crazy and just liked to fuck with people by talk-*

ing a lot of nonsense—Claude Brown **2** ***v phr*** To defy or challenge; provoke; =MESS AROUND WITH: *Don't fuck with me, buster, unless you're tired of living*

◀ **fuck you**▶ ***interj*** An exclamation of very strong defiance and contempt: *Fuck you, friend, if that's your attitude*

fuddy-duddy or **fuddy-dud** **1** ***n*** An old-fashioned, esp a meticulous, person; an outdated conservative: *To this little squab, I evidently rated as a fuddy-duddy*—Billy Rose **2** ***adj:*** *There were a few fuddy-duddy requests for documentation*—Village Voice

fudge **1** ***v*** *fr middle 1800s* To cheat or misrepresent slightly; deviate somewhat: *if you're fudging on your income tax return*—Associated Press **2** ***interj*** *fr late 1700s British* A mild exclamation of surprise, disappointment, etc; =DARN **3** ***v*** To rub someone to orgasm; =FRIG [first sense recorded as used by boys playing marbles; other senses perhaps euphemisms for *fuck*]

fuie ***See*** PHOOEY

full blast **1** ***adv phr*** To the limit of capacity; with no restraint; =ALL-OUT **2** ***adj:*** *a full-blast campaign for mayor*

full court press ***n phr*** Very great or maximum pressure: *an inclination not to resume a full court press for the peace plan*—Wall Street Journal [fr an aggressive *pressing* defense in basketball, using both halves of the *court*]

full deck ***See*** PLAY WITH A FULL DECK

full frontal ***adj phr*** Total; complete; unrestricted: *a variety of forms including iambic pentameter, full frontal rhyme and ballads*—New York Times [fr the phrase "*full frontal nudity*" used to describe the ultimate grade of nakedness, as seen in art, moving pictures, television, etc]

full-mooner ***n*** An insane or very eccentric person; =LOONY, NUT: *in San Francisco, where there are full-mooners on every street corner*—Washingtonian [fr the belief that some people go crazy at the time of the *full moon*]

full of beans **1** ***adj phr*** *fr middle 1800s British* Vibrant with energy; peppy: *The old man's full of beans and bitching up a storm* **2** ***adj phr*** (also **full of hops** or **full of prunes**) Wrong; mistaken, esp chronically so; =FULL OF SHIT [first sense fr the belief that a *bean*-fed horse is particularly frisky and strong; second sense fr a connection with *beans*, hops, etc., as promoting excretion]

full of hot air ***adj phr*** Wrong; mistaken; pompously in error: *If she says that, she's full of hot air*

◁ **full of piss and vinegar**▷ ***adj phr*** Brimming with energy; very peppy and assertive: *full of the piss and vinegar her mother lacks*—Village Voice/ *full of piss and vinegar and occasionally now, a little weed*—Inside Sports

◁ **full of shit**▷ ***adj phr*** (Variations: **crap** or **bull** or **it** may replace **shit**) Wrong; mistaken; not to be credited: *Oh, he's so full of shit, that self-seeking schmuck*—Joseph Heller

◁ as **full of shit as a Christmas goose**▷ ***adj phr*** =FULL OF SHIT • An intensive use

full yard ***See*** GO THE FULL YARD

fumble-fingered ***adj*** Clumsy; =BUTTERFINGERED: *directions for the fumble-fingered*—Time

fumtu (FUHM to͞o) ***adj phr*** *WW2 armed forces* Totally confused; botched; =SNAFU [fr *fucked up more than usual*]

fun ***adj*** With which, with whom, in which, etc., one can have fun: *a fun place/ Mickey and his chums introduce each other as "a real fun guy"*—Saturday Review

See LIKE HELL, POKE FUN

fun and games ***n phr*** *fr early 1900s* Pleasure; delightful diversion • More commonly British than US, and most often ironic: *His job looks like constant fun and games/ We had some fun and games a few months ago*—Rex Burns [based on the talk and attitude used toward children by hearty people, and analogous with *show and tell*]

fund ***See*** SLUSH FUND

fun fur ***n phr*** Cheap synthetic fur for casual use

fungo **1** ***n*** *baseball fr middle 1800s* A ball hit to give practice to fielders, usu by tossing it up and swinging **2** ***v:*** *They used to fungo that ball over your head*—Philadelphia Journal **3** ***n*** A long, light bat used to hit practice balls to fielders [origin unknown;

perhaps fr dialect *fonge* "catch," fr Old English *fon* "seize, catch," or fr the German cognate *fangen* in the same sense; the *-o* ending might indicate a shouted warning, the whole meaning "Now catch!"]

funk[1] **1** *v chiefly British fr middle 1700s* To fail through panic; be frightened to immobility: *She would have won, but suddenly funked* **2** *n* Depression; moroseness; =the BLUES: *This levelheaded man of logic, however, is also a creature of moods and funks*—Playboy [perhaps fr Flemish *fonck* "perturbation"]

See BLUE FUNK, IN A FUNK

funk[2] or **fonk** **1** *n esp musicians fr 1950s* A style of urban black music that relies heavily on bass guitar and exhibits black elements like African rhythms, the blues, early rock and roll, jazz, etc: *There is no denying... the influence of Instant Funk*—Aquarian/ *the Minister of Super Heavy Funk, the legendary James Brown*—Afrika Bambaataa **2** *v* To play or move to an urban black music that features a dominant bass guitar: *I think it's all right to funk all night*—Aquarian [fr *funky*]

funkadelic *adj* Musically hard-edged and urban while also reminiscent of the effects of hallucinogenic drugs; =FUNKY: *breaks into his best funkadelic solo as the mood changes*—Village Voice [fr a blend of *funky* and *psychedelic*]

funkiness *n* The excited, hard-edged, soulful, or rhythmically compelling mood associated with funk: *Cannonball's alto sax has lost its old zesty funkiness*—Time

funky (also **fonky** or **funky-butt** or **funkyass**) **1** *adj* Repulsive; malodorous; stinking: *What a stinking, dirty, funky bitch she was*—Claude Brown/ *The Baths, though, are funky enough without booze*—Saturday Review **2** *adj fr 1950s black musicians* In the style of the blues; earthy; simple yet compelling, with a strong beat and powerful bass guitar: *He has combined a basically funky sound with experimentation*—Ebony/ *the funky-butt tune high wide an' lonesome*—George Warren **3** *adj* Excellent; effective; =GROOVY: *He wanted to get down and get funky*—Sports Illustrated/ *There's a funky-ass biker after my own heart*—George Warren **4** *adj* Musically hard-edged and urban: *the gently funky, Latin-flavored rhythms*—Variety/ *but soulful to a degree, and a little bit funky so you could kinda sway your head to it*—Rolling Stone **5** *adj* Old-fashioned; quaintly out-of-date; having a nostalgic appeal: *for those of you who are not familiar with its funky splendor*—Village Voice/ *my love for funky Forties clothes*—Playboy/ *the great old funky restaurant called Harrigan's in Southwest DC*—Washingtonian **6** *adj* Pleasantly eccentric or unconventional; =OFFBEAT **7** *adj* Deviant; =KINKY: *That guy's a little too funky for my taste* **8** *adj* Highly emotional; lacking affective restraint: *He hints that it may have its funky moments*—New Republic [fr US dialect, "musty, mouldy, old and malodorous," fr early-17th-century British *funk* "stifling tobacco smoke, strong stench," of unknown origin though perhaps fr French dialect and Old French *funkier* "smoke," perhaps fr Latin *fumicare* "smoke"]

the **funnies** (or **comics**) *n phr* Comic strips; section or page of a newspaper with comic strips

funny **1** *adj* Eccentric; odd; =WEIRD **2** *adj* Insane; =NUTS **3** *adv* In a strange way: *He looked at her real funny*

a **funny** *n* A joke; wisecrack; witty remark

See DOODAD

funny business *See* MONKEY BUSINESS

funny farm (or **house**) *n phr* A mental hospital, rest home for alcoholics, etc; =LAUGHING ACADEMY: *Who put me in your private funny house?*—Raymond Chandler/ *They must all have died in flophouses or on state funny-farms*—Saul Bellow

funny money *n phr* Worthless, counterfeit, or play money

◁ **fur** ▷ *n* The vulva; pubic hair

◁ **furburger** ▷ *college students* **1** *n* The vulva **2** *n* A very attractive woman; =EATIN' STUFF

fur-lined bathtub *See* WIN THE PORCELAIN HAIRNET

◁ **fur pie** ▷ **1** *n phr* The vulva **2** *n phr* Cunnilingus

fuse *See* BLOW A GASKET, HAVE A SHORT FUSE

fuss *See* KICK UP A FUSS

fusspot *n fr late 1800s British* A very meticulous and finicky person; fussbudget

fustest with the mostest *See* FIRSTEST WITH THE MOSTEST

◁ **futz** ▷ (FUTS) **1** *n* The vulva **2** *v* =FUCK **3** *v* (also ◁**futz with**▷) To meddle or alter wrongfully; damage; =FUCK UP: *What is clear is that this movie has been futzed with* —Newsweek **4** *n* A repulsive man, esp an old one; =ALTER KOCKER: *Inside of every American... is a scrawny, twanging old futz like me* —Kurt Vonnegut, Jr

futz around **1** *v phr* To loaf and idle; =FUCK OFF: *Stop futzing around and get to work* **2** *v phr* To experiment; try tricks; play; =MESS AROUND: *The foundation folk may get to futzing around with their computers*—Book World/ *You never really had time to sort of futz around in the sets*—Playbill **3** *v phr* To defy or challenge; provoke; =FUCK WITH: *I am nobody to futz around with* —Philip Roth

futzed up *adj phr* Confused; botched; ruined; =FUCKED UP: *I've got her all futzed up. She does everything I tell her*—Calder Willingham

fuzz *n fr 1930s black* A police officer; the police: *Cops must be annihilated. Kill the Fascist fuzz*—Newsweek [fr black slang *man with the fuzzy balls* "white man"]

See LIP FUZZ

fuzzbuster *n* A device that detects police radar signals: *Rauch discovered that I had a Fuzzbuster, designed to warn me of radar traps* —Penthouse

fuzzled *adj* Drunk

fuzzy **1** *n* (also **fuzzie**) A police officer; =FUZZ **2** *n gambling* A certainty, esp a horse sure to win; =SURE THING **3** *adj* Vague; unsure: *I'm a little fuzzy on the details* **4** *adj* Drunk

G

gabby *adj* Talkative; noisily garrulous; gossipy: *They have spoken of any gabby party*—Westbrook Pegler/ *Shaw is a gabby playwright*

gabfest *n fr late 1800s* A session of conversation; a loquacious occasion; =CHINFEST

gabs *See* GOB[1]

gadget **1** *n fr middle 1800s British merchant marine* Any unspecified or unspecifiable usu small object; something one does not know the name of or does not wish to name; =THINGAMAJIG **2** *n* An unnecessary but presumably impressive item added as decoration or inducement: *The car's full of silly gadgets* [perhaps fr French *gachette* "a small mechanical part of a rifle, lock, etc"]

gaff *See* STAND THE GAFF

gaffer **1** *n* One's father; =OLD MAN: *Studs felt that Mr O'Brien was different from his own gaffer*—James T Farrell **2** *n* An old man: *Look at that gaffer trying to stand on his head* **3** *n* A foreman or boss, such as the manager of a circus, head glassblower, chief electrician on a movie set, etc [fr British dialect, "grandfather, godfather"]
See OLD COCKER

gag **1** *n fr late 1800s fr early 1800s British* A joke; wisecrack; trick: *I'll tell you gags, I'll sing you songs*—Mel Brooks **2** *n hoboes* An old, trite alibi [first sense perhaps fr obsolete *geck* "dupe," related to German *geck* "fool"; in the late-19th century a *gag* was "a line interpolated into a play"]

gaga *adj fr 1920s British* Crazy; silly; irrational: *When prohibition comes up, the wets go gaga*—A Briggs/ *not to mention a ga-ga French gamine in Mickey Mouse ears*—Village Voice [fr French, "fool"]

gag a maggot *See* ENOUGH TO GAG A MAGGOT

gage (or **gauge**) **butt** *n phr narcotics* A marijuana cigarette; =JOINT

gag me with a spoon *sentence teenagers* I am disgusted; I am about to retch

gago *n gypsy* A non-Gypsy

gaited *See* DOUBLE-GAITED

gal (or **girl**) **Friday** *n phr* A woman assistant or secretary, esp in an office; female factotum; =GOFER [fr Daniel Defoe's novel *Robinson Crusoe* where the servant and companion was named *Friday*]

gallery *See* ROGUES' GALLERY, SHOOTING GALLERY

galley-west *adj* Confused; turbulent; =FUCKED UP: *The whole place was galley-west when we got there* [probably by folk etymology fr British dialect *collywest* or *collyweston*, of unknown origin and defined as "a term used when anything goes wrong"]
See KNOCK someone or something GALLEY WEST

galloping dominoes *n phr* Dice

galoot (gə LōōT) *n fr middle 1800s* A person, esp an awkward or boorish man ● Very often in the phrase **big galoot**: *large enough for the galoots to fit through and take over*—New York Times/ *So she told the big galoot to get lost* [fr early 1800s British, "inexperienced seaman," of unknown origin; perhaps fr the Sierra Leone Creole language Krio *galut* fr Spanish *galeoto* "galley slave"]

galumph *v* To move or cavort ungracefully; crash heavily about:

Linda Evans galumphing around the edges... like a wounded rhino—Village Voice [coined by Lewis Carroll in *Through the Looking Glass*]

gam ***n fr late 1800s fr British*** A leg, esp a woman's leg • Most often in the plural: *regarding her superb gams with affection*—V Faulkner/ *Gavilan has spindly gams, a thin neck and a wasp waist*—New York Daily News [perhaps fr Italian *gamba* or Northern French *gambe* "leg"]

gambler ***See*** TINHORN

game ***n*** One's occupation; business; =RACKET: *He's in the computer game these days*

See AHEAD OF THE GAME, BADGER GAME, BALL GAME, CON GAME, the NAME OF THE GAME, ON one's GAME, the ONLY GAME IN TOWN, PLAY GAMES, SKIN GAME, a WHOLE NEW BALL GAME, a WHOLE 'NOTHER THING

game plan ***n phr*** A strategy for winning; plan for conducting some project or affair: *That type of a game plan gave us the option to point out how badly we need a responsible press*—Tom Wicker [fr football]

gamer ***n baseball & football*** A brave and enterprising player, esp one who works with pain or against the odds: *what is known in the business as a gamer, a guy who pitches with pain... who wants the ball*—New York Daily News

gander **1** ***n fr early 1900s*** A look; close scrutiny; glance: *I'll have a gander at the prices* **2** ***v:*** *Want to gander at TV for a while?* **3** ***n underworld*** A criminal lookout [fr the stretched, gooselike neck of someone gazing intently]

ganef or **ganof** ***See*** GONIFF

◁ **gang bang**▷ (Variations: **shag** or **shay** may replace **bang**) **1** ***n phr*** An occasion when several males do the sex act serially with one woman; =TRAIN **2** ***v phr:*** *tear the place apart, leave the owner for dead, gangbang the waitress*—Joan Didion **3** ***n phr*** A group-sex orgy: *We all ended up in a big profitable gangbang*—Xaviera Hollander

gangbusters ***n*** A great and conspicuous success; =HIT: *I think it's going to be gangbusters*—Newsweek

See LIKE GANGBUSTERS

gang plank ***n phr truckers*** A toll bridge

ganja (GAHN jə) ***n narcotics*** A strong type of marijuana obtained from a cultivated strain of Indian hemp [fr Hindi]

ganze macher (GAHN sə MAH kər) **1** ***n phr*** A person busy with many affairs, esp officiously and conspiratorially; =BIG-TIME OPERATOR **2** ***n phr*** An important person; =BIG SHOT, VIP [fr Yiddish, "total busybody"]

gaper ***n jive talk*** A mirror

gaper's block or **gaper delay** ***n phr*** Traffic congestion caused by drivers slowing down to inspect an accident or other matter of interest; =RUBBERNECKING

garbage (GAR bəj, gar BAHZH) **1** ***n hoboes*** Food or meals **2** ***n*** Nonsense; pretentious talk; =BULLSHIT: *The speech was nine-tenths garbage* **3** ***n*** Anything inferior and worthless; =CRAP, JUNK: *You call that piece of garbage a sonnet?* **4** ***modifier:*** *She uses a lot of tricky garbage shots to win games and sets/ I call it a garbage movie*

garbage furniture ***See*** STREET FURNITURE

garbage habit ***n phr narcotics*** The taking of narcotics in medleys and mixes: *an increase in the garbage habit, where people mix a variety of drugs to achieve a high*—New York Times

gardener **1** ***n baseball*** An outfielder **2** ***n narcotics*** A person who plants narcotics on an airplane for smuggling

gargle **1** ***n*** A drink, esp of liquor **2** ***v truckers*** To drain and flush the radiator of a truck

gargle-factory ***n*** A saloon; bar

garlic-burner ***n motorcyclists*** A motorcycle made in Italy

garter ***See*** WIN THE PORCELAIN HAIRNET

gas **1** ***n fr late 1700s*** Empty and idle talk; mendacious and exaggerated claims; =BULLSHIT: *Most of what I say is pure gas, my friend* **2** ***n fr middle 1800s*** Talk of any sort, esp conversation: *Let's get together for a good gas* **3** ***v:*** *I haven't gassed this long for a year*—Sinclair Lewis **4** ***n fr early 1900s*** Gasoline **5** ***n hoboes*** Denatured alcohol or some other substitute for liquor **6** ***v cool talk*** To impress one's hearers very favorably; overcome with admiration: *Bird gassed them*—Metronome Yearbook/ *She gassed me, she was that good*—P Martin **7** *v* To impress an audience very unfavorably; fail with; =BOMB: *Our show appears to have gassed the critics and the public*

See COOK WITH GAS, RUN OUT OF GAS, STEP ON IT

a **gas** *n phr cool talk fr black* Something very impressive, pleasurable, effective, etc: *Therefore it's a gas for me to be the scribe of this weekly space*—Amsterdam News

gasbag **1** *n* An energetic and persevering talker; =WINDBAG **2** *v* To talk energetically and perseveringly: *plenty of gasbagging about morality*—Newsweek

gas-guzzler *n* A car, esp a large American model, that uses a great deal of gasoline

◀ **gash[1]** ▶ **1** *n fr 1700s* The vulva: *Plus ball the gash off a real foxy chick?*—Easyriders **2** *n* Women regarded as sex partners: *all that fine gash, just wasted*—Esquire **3** *n* The sex act; =ASS: *Don't you ever think of anything but gash?*—James T Farrell

gash[2] *n WW2 Army fr early 1900s British Navy* Extra or unexpected portions, bits of luck, etc; dividends; bonuses [origin unknown; perhaps fr French *gaché* "spoiled," since it occurs in *gash bucket* "garbage bin"]

gasket *See* BLOW A GASKET

gas man *n phr* A publicist; press agent; =FLACK

gassed **1** *adj* Drunk: *I begged them not to get gassed or start any fights*—Bing Crosby **2** *adj* Overcome with admiration: *After her speech the crowd was gassed*

gasser **1** *n* =GASBAG **2** *n cool talk fr 1930s black* Anything or anyone exceptionally amusing, effective, memorable, etc; =a GAS: *or examine this gasser*—Leo Rosten **3** *n* Anything or anyone exceptionally dull, mediocre, inept, etc; =CORNBALL, BOMB: *We planned a blast, and got a gasser*

gat *n fr early 1900s underworld* A pistol: *poking his gat your way*—Saturday Evening Post [probably fr *Gatling gun*]

gate **1** *n fr early 1800s* The money collected from selling tickets to a sporting or other entertainment event **2** *n jazz musicians & jive musicians* A performing engagement; =GIG **3** *n jazz talk & jive talk fr early 1920s* A musician, a musical devotee, or any man; =CAT **4** *n railroad* A switch **5** *v* =GIVE someone THE GATE [musicians' senses fr the simile *swing like a gate* "play or respond to swing music well and readily," with some influence of *'gator* and *alligator*; or perhaps fr *gatemouth*, a nickname for Louis Armstrong; first musical sense said to have been coined by Louis Armstrong]

See CRASH, GET one's TAIL IN A GATE, GIVE someone THE GATE

-gate ***combining word*** An exposed affair of corruption, venality, etc, of the sort indicated: *Allengate/ Billygate/ Koreagate/ Lancegate* [fr the *Watergate* scandals of the early 1970s]

gate-crasher *n* A person who attends a party, entertainment, etc, without invitation or ticket; uninvited guest

gatemouth *n black* A chronic and active gossip

gator or **'gator** *n black fr 1920s* =ALLIGATOR

gauge butt *See* GAGE BUTT

gawk *v fr late 1700s* To stare; gape stupidly [fr dialect *gawk, gouk* "fool, idiot," literally "cuckoo"]

gay *homosexuals fr 1930s or earlier* **1** *adj* Homosexual; homoerotic: *gay men and women/ gay attitudes* **2** *adj* Intended for or used by homosexuals: *a gay bar/ gay movies* **3** *n* A male homosexual or a lesbian: *a hideaway for live-together couples and middle-aged gays*—Albert Goldman • Widely used by heterosexuals in preference to pejorative terms [perhaps by extension fr earlier British *gay* "leading a whore's life"]

gay-bashing **1** *n* The harassment of homosexuals **2** ***modifier:*** *after his arrest in a gay-bashing case*—Village Voice

gay deceivers *See* FALSIES

gay (or **Gay**) **lib** **1** *n* The movement that advocates the rights and protection of homosexual persons: *the presence of Gay Lib and advocates for legalization of abortion*—Commentary/ *Your reporter needs to open his closet a little wider to find out how great gay lib is*—Rolling

Stone **2** ***modifier:*** *gay-lib banners/ a gay lib alliance* [modeled on *women's lib*]

gayola **1** ***n*** Bribery, blackmail, and extortion paid by homosexuals and homosexual businesses, esp to police: *for blackmail and for shakedowns by real or phony cops, a practice known as "gayola"*—Time/ *Homosexual bars... pay "gayola" to crime syndicates and to law enforcement agencies*—Saturday Review **2** ***adj*** Homosexual; =GAY: *There have to be some fulfilling alternatives to the gayola fun fair*—Village Voice [first sense modeled on *payola*]

gazer ***See*** SHADOW GAZER

gazonga ***n*** The buttocks; =ASS: *I don't get these women to sweat their gazongas off*—Village Voice

gazoo or **gazool** ***See*** KAZOO

gd or **g-d** (pronounced as separate letters) ***adj*** God-damned: *The biggest gd engine in the West*—Stephen Longstreet

gear ***adj esp 1960s teenagers fr 1950s British*** Excellent; wonderful; superb: *The opposite of "gear" is "grotty"*—Village Voice [fr the equipment and costume, the *gear*, used and preferred as a sort of uniform of the cognoscenti; see the World War 1 British Army phrase *that's the gear* "that's right"]

See IN HIGH GEAR, SHIFT INTO HIGH GEAR

gearbox or **gearhead** ***n*** A stupid person; idiot; =DIMWIT: *only gearboxes greet strangers*—Toronto Life/ *translating that into monosyllables for you gearheads*—Car and Driver

geared or **geared up** **1** ***adj*** or ***adj phr*** Drunk **2** ***adj*** or ***adj phr*** Excited; ecstatic; =HIGH: *a sexy rock star, and he got the audience so geared*—Rolling Stone [probably fr the notion of the higher, faster *gears* of a car; but *gear* "any narcotics, esp marijuana" occurs in 1940s British slang]

gear-jammer ***n truckers*** A truck or bus driver

gear up ***v phr*** To prepare; equip oneself: *seem ready to gear up realistically for the very tough political fight ahead*—New York Daily News

gee[1] (JEE) **1** ***n esp 1930s*** A fellow; man; =GUY: *He was the mayor, and he was one smart gee*—James T Farrell **2** ***n underworld*** The leader of a gang in prison; an influential inmate; =the MAN [abbreviation of *guy*]

See FRONT GEE

gee[2] (JEE) ***n hoboes*** A gallon of liquor [abbreviation of *gallon*]

gee[3] (JEE) **1** ***n*** A thousand dollars; =GRAND **2** ***n*** Money [abbreviation of *grand*]

gee[4] (JEE) ***interj*** An exclamation of surprise, pleasure, sheepishness, etc; =GEE WHIZ [a euphemism for *Jesus*]

See HOLY CATS

gee[5] ***adj teenagers*** Disgusting; rebarbative; =GROSS [abbreviation of *gross*]

gee[6] ***n underworld*** A pistol; =GAT [abbreviation of *gun* or *gat*]

◀ **geechee** or **geechie** ▶ (GEE chee) **1** ***n esp black*** A black person, esp a Southern rural black: *obsessed with hatred for the "geechees," those he feels are holding back the race*—Washington Post **2** ***n*** The dialect, culture, etc, of Southern rural or seacoast blacks **3** ***n*** A low-country South Carolinian, esp one from the Charleston area [origin uncertain or mixed; perhaps fr the *Ogeechee* River in northern Georgia or another place name and ultimately fr a Native American language; perhaps fr *geejee* "the Gullah dialect or a speaker of that dialect," and ultimately fr the name of a language and tribe in the Kissy region of Liberia]

geedus or **geetis** or **geetus** (GEE təs) ***n fr 1930s fr underworld & hawkers*** Money: *Pitchman must give the store a 40% cut on the "geedus"*—M Zolotow [see *geets*]

geek **1** ***n carnival & circus*** A sideshow freak, esp one who does revolting things like biting the heads off of live chickens **2** ***n 1920s carnival & circus*** A snake charmer **3** ***n*** A pervert or degenerate, esp one who will do disgusting things to slake deviant appetites; =CREEP, WEIRDO: *When the campus paper called the Prez a geek, he went to this dictionary, then went bananas* **4** ***n*** A drunkard; =LUSH [origin unknown; perhaps related to British dialect *geck*, *geke* "fool"]

gee string or **G-string** ***n phr*** or ***n fr middle 1800s*** A breech-cloth, or brief covering for the genitals, worn esp by striptease dancers: *Thus the G-string* *became an integral part of a stripper's apparatus*—Toronto Life [origin unknown]

geets (GEETS) *n beat & cool talk* Money; =GEEDUS [said to be a comic mispronunciation: "Money *geets* you things"]

gee whiz[1] or **gee willikers** **1** *interj* (also **Gee whiz**) An exclamation of approval, surprise, mild disapproval, emphasis, etc; =GOSH: *But gee willikers, he does arithmetic like lightning*—Washington Post **2** *adj* Enthusiastic; very much impressed; youthfully optimistic: *Finch's willed naiveté frequently leads to gee-whiz insights*—Village Voice [a euphemism for *Jesus*]

gee whiz[2] *n phr underworld* An armed pickpocket [fr *gee* "gun" and *whiz* "pickpocket"]

geez or **geeze** (GEEZ) *v narcotics* To have or give a dose of narcotics, esp an injection: *They drop acid, go up on DMT and "geeze" (mainline) meth*—Newsweek/ *I need to geez now, Bumper. Real bad*—Joseph Wambaugh

geezer[1] *n fr late 1800s* A man; fellow; =DUFFER, GUY: *It gave him all kinds of confidence just to hear the big geezer spout*—J Lilienthal/ *He is a tall geezer with chin whiskers*—H Allen Smith [fr earlier and dialect *giser* "mummer, one who puts on a guise or mask," hence, a quaint figure]

geezer[2] **1** *n* A drink of liquor; =SNORT **2** *n narcotics* A dose or injection of a narcotic

gel *v* To come to a firm and useful form; =WORK: *In this highly partisan county, it just didn't gel*—Chicago Tribune

gelt (GELT) *n fr late 1600s* Money: *To let you guys get away with the gelt?*—WE Weeks [fr German and Yiddish]

general *See* ARMCHAIR GENERAL, BUCK GENERAL

gentleman's C *n phr* A satisfactory rating, but not a high one: *The Sierra Club gives Ruckelshaus only a "gentleman's C"*—Time [fr the passing but mediocre grade traditionally given in college to well-bred but not serious students]

the **gents** *n phr* The men's toilet

george *v black* To invite to sexual activity; =PROPOSITION: *One of the girls georged him, just for kicks*—C Cooper

◁ **German goiter** ▷ *n phr* A protuberant paunch; =BEER BELLY

get **1** *v fr early 1900s* To seize mentally; grasp; understand: *Do you get me?*—Zora Neale Hurston **2** *v* To take note of; pay attention to: *Get him, acting like such a big shot* **3** *v* To have vengeance on; retaliate destructively against: *He can't say that. I'll get him* **4** *n* Offspring; progeny **5** *n show business* =GATE, TAKE **6** *n outdated underworld* The route taken by criminals in fleeing the scene of their efforts: *The get, or getaway route*—E DeBaun

get one's **1** *v phr* To get the punishment one deserves: *Don't worry, he'll get his before this is all over* **2** *v phr* To become rich; get one's large share of worldly goods: *She went into this business determined to get hers by the time she was thirty*

get a bang (or **charge**) **out of** someone or something *v phr* To enjoy especially; get a thrill out of: *The younger set is not "getting a bang" out of things anymore*—New York Times

get (or **draw**) **a bead on** something or someone *v phr* To take very careful aim at; concentrate successfully; =ZERO IN: *She has, however, got a bead on her five original characters*—Washington Post

get a broom up one's **ass** *See* HAVE A BROOM UP one's ASS

get a clue *v phr teenagers* To understand; grasp

get something **across** (or **over**) *v phr* To explain successfully; =PUT something ACROSS: *He decided to devote all his energy to getting his own platform across*—Howard Fats

get a crush on someone *See* HAVE A CRUSH ON someone

get (or **have**) **a free ride** *v phr* To enjoy something without paying; get something gratis

get a handle on something *v phr* To find a way of coping; discover how to proceed: *Sometimes I think I haven't got a handle on things anymore*—Armistead Maupin

get a hump on *v phr fr late 1800s* To speed up; hurry; =GET A MOVE ON: *Get a hump on with that assignment, OK?*

get a hustle on *See* GET A MOVE ON

get a kick out of someone or something *v phr* To enjoy immensely; take great pleasure in: *I sure get a kick...out of the way you guys kid each other along*—Joseph Heller/ *I get a kick out of you*—Cole Porter (from a song lyric)

get (or **have**) **a little on the side** *v phr* To be sexually unfaithful; =CHEAT

get a load of *v phr* To examine; attend to; =GET: *Let him get a load of the new suit of clothes*—James M Cain

get along (or **on**) **1** *v phr* To live without any great joy nor grief; pass through life more or less adequately; cope; =GET BY **2** *v phr* To be compatible; associate easily: *He didn't get along with the boss* **3** *v phr* To grow old; age

get a move on *v phr* (Variations: **hump** or **hustle** or **wiggle** may replace **move**) *fr early 1900s* To hurry; speed up; =GET GOING: *Tell him to damn well get a wiggle on* —Laurence Stallings & Maxwell Anderson

get an offer one **can't refuse** *See* MAKE AN OFFER one CAN'T REFUSE

get a rise out of someone *v phr fr early 1800s British* To get a response, esp a warm or angry one: *His limp joke got a rise and some projectiles out of the crowd* [fr the *rising* of a fish to the bait in fly-fishing]

◁ **get** (or **have**) one's **ashes hauled**▷ *v phr* To do the sex act: *that spider climbin' up that wall, goin' up there to get her ashes hauled*—Jelly Roll Morton [*ashes* may be a euphemism for *ass*]

◁ **get** one's **ass in a sling**▷ *See* HAVE one's ASS IN A SLING

◁ **get** one's **ass in gear**▷ *v phr* To get into action; stop loafing and wasting time: *If we get our ass in gear we'll win this thing*

getaway 1 *n fr early 1900s* The act of fleeing, esp from the scene of a crime: *How about a quiet getaway from this mad scene?* **2** ***modifier:*** *our getaway car/ getaway route/ getaway vacation package*
See MAKE one's GETAWAY

get away with something **1** *v phr* (also **get by with** something) To go uncaught and unpunished after doing something illegal or indiscreet: *I didn't get away with hassling the committee* **2** *v phr* To steal or run off with something: *He came for a friendly visit and got away with my stereo*

get away with murder *v phr* To go unpunished or unharmed after some risk or impudence: *bitter complaints that Reagan was getting away with murder in the press*—Washingtonian

get one's or someone's **back up** *v phr* To become angry or make someone angry, esp in a way to cause one to resist: *When they said he was lying, that got his back up*

◁ not **get** one's **balls in an uproar**▷ *See* NOT GET one's BALLS IN AN UPROAR

get one's **banana peeled** *See* HAVE one's BANANA PEELED

get behind 1 *v phr narcotics* To have a pleasurable narcotic intoxication **2** *v phr* To enjoy something: *I can't get behind this, I keep trying to tell you*—Cyra McFadden

get by 1 *v phr* To do just acceptably well; neither succeed nor fail, but survive; =MAKE OUT: *We were barely getting by on two salaries* **2** *v phr* To barely escape failure; scrape by **3** *v phr* To pass inspection; stand up to scrutiny: *His work didn't get by the manager* **4** *v phr* To pass something very closely: *I barely got by that truck*

get someone **by the short hairs** (or **curlies** or **knickers**) *See* HAVE someone BY THE SHORT HAIRS

get by with something *See* GET AWAY WITH something

get one's **cheese** *v phr* To attain one's goal; be rewarded

get cold feet *See* HAVE COLD FEET

get one's **cookies** (or **jollies** or **kicks**) *v phr* To enjoy one's keenest pleasure; indulge oneself; =GET OFF • Usually with a hint of perversion: *The owner...gets his jollies by walking around...in a Sioux war bonnet* —D Welch/ *This how you get your cookies?*—George V Higgins

get cracking (or **cutting**) *fr 1920s British RAF* **1** *v phr* To commence: *Let's get cracking with this unloading* **2** *v phr* To go or work faster: *and if we don't get cracking, get serious, and get leadership* —Washingtonian

get one's **dander** (or **Irish**) **up 1** *v phr* To cause anger; infuriate;

=PISS-OFF: *That law gets my dander up* **2** ***v phr*** To become angry; =BLOW one's TOP: *They got their dander up and decided to fight the case in court*—Washington Post

get down **1** ***v phr*** *gambling* To stake one's money or chips; bet: *All right, get down on this card*—A Lomax **2** ***v phr*** *fr black musicians* To make an effort; get serious; attend to the task: *so I get down now and then to try to block a couple of shots*—Village Voice/ *She's gonna get down. She just plans for it*—Cameron Crowe **3** ***v phr*** *fr black* To let oneself be natural and unrestrained: *to really get down and relate*—Cyra McFadden **4** ***modifier:*** *a get down player for those who enjoy that thumping sound*—Downbeat **5** ***v phr*** *teenagers* To enjoy oneself; have fun **6** ***v*** *narcotics* To use a narcotic, esp heroin [perhaps fr *get down to it* "begin to work seriously"; perhaps from an unattested *get down and dirty*; see *down*]

get someone **down** ***v phr*** To depress or annoy; =MIFF: *That constant whine gets me down*

get down on someone **1** ***v phr*** To show strong disapproval or lack of trust; rebuke; upbraid: *Mama used to get down on me about hanging out with Reno*—Claude Brown **2** ***v phr*** To nag

See GO DOWN ON someone

get down to brass tacks ***See*** DOWN TO BRASS TACKS

get (or **have**) one's **ducks in a row** ***See*** HAVE one's DUCKS IN A ROW

get one's **feet wet** ***v phr*** To initiate oneself or be initiated into something; have a first and testing experience of something: *Try one or two, just to get your feet wet* [fr the image of a person who goes into the water very carefully rather than plunging in]

get-go ***See*** FROM THE GIT-GO

get someone's **goat** (or **nanny**) ***v phr*** *fr early 1900s* To annoy: *His bitching gets my goat sometimes* [perhaps fr depriving a racehorse of its goat mascot; perhaps fr French *prendre sa chèvre* "take one's source of milk or nourishment"]

get going **1** ***v phr*** To leave; depart **2** ***v phr*** To begin a job or assignment **3** ***v phr*** To stop loafing, idling, etc; =GET CRACKING: *When the going gets tough, the tough get going*

◁ **get** one's **head out of** one's **ass**▷ ***v phr*** To start paying attention; become aware and active; =GET ON THE BALL: *Make the system work. Get your head out of your Hollywood ass*—Pulpsmith

◁ **get in** or **get it in**▷ ***v phr*** To succeed in penetrating someone sexually

get in someone's **face** ***v phr*** To be in someone's presence, esp in a provocative way: *Don't you get in my face no more... I'll kill you*—Donald Goines

get in someone's **hair** ***v phr*** To annoy; nag at: *That squeaky voice gets in my hair*

get one's **Irish up** ***See*** GET one's DANDER UP

get it in the neck ***v phr*** *fr late 1800s* To be severely punished or injured: *The poor wimp got it in the neck again* [probably an allusion to hanging]

◁ **get it off**▷ **1** ***v phr*** To have an orgasm; ejaculate semen; =COME OFF **2** ***v phr*** To do the sex act **3** ***v phr*** To masturbate

get it on ◁**1**▷ ***v phr*** To become sexually excited; get an erection ◁**2**▷ ***v phr*** To do the sex act; =GET IT OFF: *I couldn't believe that the whole time he was getting it on with Joe's wife* **3** ***v phr*** (also **get it off**) To enjoy something greatly; have a good time; =JAM: *three, five, fifteen guys in a studio just get it off*—Ringo Starr/ *And they overlay their daring with pure joy. They're getting it on*—Sports Illustrated

get it together (or **all together**) ***v phr*** (Variations: **one's act** or **one's head** or **one's shit** or **one's stuff** may replace **it**) *fr 1960s counterculture fr black* To arrange one's life or affairs properly; integrate and focus oneself: *Get your shit together, said Junior Jones*—John Irving/ *why the executive departments of government don't get their act together*—Lewis Powell

◁ **get it up**▷ ***v phr*** To achieve and retain an erection: *I couldn't get it up in the State of Israel*—Philip Roth

get one's **jollies** or **kicks** ***See*** GET one's COOKIES

get lost **1** ***v phr*** To leave; depart; =SCRAM • Usually an exasperated command: *I offered him five bucks and he told me loudly to get lost* **2** ***interj*** An exclamation of severe and abrupt rejection; =DROP DEAD

get one's **lumps** ***v phr*** To be severely beaten, punished, rebuked, etc: *Their greatest fun is to see a cop getting his lumps*—H Lee

get mileage out of something ***v phr*** To gain advantage or profit; exploit: *All of us down here can start getting mileage out of that one right away*—Joseph Heller

get nowhere fast ***v phr*** To make no progress whatever; be stuck: *He was getting nowhere fast and was more depressed*—Charles Beardsley

◁ **get** one's **nuts**▷ ***v phr*** (Variations: **cracked** or **off** may be added) To have an orgasm; ejaculate semen: *He'd get his nuts just looking at her/ When I'd gotten my nuts off about six times, we got hungry*—Claude Brown

get off **1** ***v phr*** *narcotics* To get relief and pleasure from a dose of narcotics: *How we s'posed to get off with no water to mix the stuff with?*—Philadelphia Bulletin ◁**2**▷ ***v phr*** To do the sex act; have an orgasm; =GET IT OFF: *It is led by trendy bisexual types, who love to get off amidst the chic accouterments of a big smack-and-coke party*—Albert Goldman **3** ***v phr*** *musicians* To play an improvised solo **4** ***v phr*** To avoid the consequences of; =GET AWAY WITH something: *He thinks he can get off with charging $150 for this junk*

See TELL someone WHERE TO GET OFF

get someone **off** ◁**1**▷ ***v phr*** To bring someone to sexual climax: *She was really eager and it didn't take long to get her off* **2** ***v phr*** To please greatly; move and excite: *Ron sings so fast because it gets us off*—Village Voice

get off one's **ass** ***v phr*** (Variations: **butt** or **dead ass** or **duff** may replace **ass**) To stop being lazy and inert; =GET CRACKING: *He wasn't able to get his class off their dead ass*

get off someone's **back** (or **neck**) ***v phr*** To leave alone; stop nagging or annoying: *All they need is for Government to get off their backs*—Time

get off someone's **case** ***v phr*** *fr black* To leave alone; =GET OFF someone's BACK: *Get off my case, O.K., Dad?*—New Yorker

get off one's **high horse** ***v phr*** To stop being haughty and superior; deal informally

get off on ***v phr*** To enjoy greatly; like very much: *They're getting off on wordsmithing*—Saturday Review

See TELL someone WHERE TO GET OFF

get off the dime ***v phr*** To start; stop wasting time: *How do we get off the dime we're on?*—New York Times [alteration of the expression *stop on a dime*, used to praise the brakes of a car]

get off the ground ***v phr*** To succeed, esp to do so initially: *projects misfired or didn't get off the ground at all*—Saturday Review

get something **off the ground** ***v phr*** To make a successful start: *As Wilbur said to Orville, "You'll never get it off the ground"*

get someone **off the hook** ***v phr*** To aid in evading or preventing punishment, responsibility, etc: *He falls for Ilona... and winds up trying to get her off the hook*—J Kelly

get on ***See*** GET ALONG

get on someone's **case** ***v phr*** *fr black* To meddle; pay unwanted, annoying attention to; criticize; =BUG, HASSLE: *There are times when I get on his case pretty hard*—Sports Illustrated [fr early 1900s black expression *sit on* someone's *case* "make a quasi-judicial study and judgment"]

get on one's **high horse** ***v phr*** *fr early 1700s British* To become dignified and formal; assume a haughty and arrogant mien: *As soon as I said a little slang to her she got on her high horse*

get on one's **horse** ***v phr*** To hurry; start at once: *You better get on your horse if you're going to make that plane*

get on someone's **nerves** ***v phr*** *fr late 1800s British* To be an irritant; annoy: *This word processor's humming gets on my nerves*

get on the ball ***v phr*** To pay closer attention to doing something right; improve one's performance • Often an exasperated command [fr baseball or other ball sports]

get on the bandwagon ***v phr*** (Variations: **climb** or **hop** or **leap** or **jump** may replace **get**) To join a person, party, cause, etc, esp one that is currently popular

get on the stick *v phr* To get actively to work; stop loafing; =GET one's ASS IN GEAR

get out *See* ALL GET OUT

get out from under *v phr* To extricate oneself from troubles, esp financial troubles

get out of someone's **face** *v phr* To leave alone; stop annoying; = GET OFF someone's CASE: *He turned to the cop and told her to get out of his face*

get outside of *v phr fr late 1800s* To eat or drink heartily: *as he got outside of a bowl of chili*—AJ Liebling

get over **1** *v phr* To recover or rebound from something; be restored to the previous norm: *We couldn't get over how well he managed all that/ It took me weeks to get over that head cold* **2** *v phr* To succeed; make a favorable impression: *He did everything he could think of, but still couldn't get over her* **3** *v phr* *Army* To evade duty; =FUCK OFF, GOLDBRICK [Army sense perhaps fr *get over* someone]

◁ **get over** someone▷ *v phr* To do the sex act with someone

get something **over with** *v phr* To finish or end something; come to the stopping point: *It was a very tough job, but we had to get it over with*

get physical *v phr* To use the body and body contact, esp roughly or amorously: *The type who might want to get physical early in a relationship, like during the first five minutes*—New York Times

get religion *v phr* To be chastened; learn proper behavior, at last; become a convert: *It appears that Mr. Reagan has got religion on the subject of environmentalism*—National Public Radio

◁ **get** one's **rocks** (or one's **rocks off**)▷ **1** *v phr* To have an orgasm; =GET one's NUTS: *Go out, have a few drinks, and if you're lucky, maybe even get your rocks off*—Advocate/ *people who'd never be caught dead at a 42d Street skinflick to get their rocks off and feel intellectual about it*—E McCormack **2** *v phr* To enjoy very much; =GET one's COOKIES: *I think she gets her rocks off turning squid inside out*—John Irving

◁ **get** one's **shit together**▷ *v phr* To organize and manage one's affairs and life properly; =HAVE one's DUCKS IN A ROW

get smart *v phr* To become wisely aware of one's situation, the possibilities, etc: =WISE UP: *Tell him if he doesn't get smart he'll get clobbered*

get stuffed *interj* =FUCK YOU • Chiefly British

get one's **tail in a gate** ◁(or **tit in a wringer**)▷ *v phr* To get into a perilous plight; be in a painful situation: *With the whole bunch against it you got your tail in a gate/ Katie Graham's gonna get her tit caught in a big fat wringer if that's published* —John Mitchell

getter *See* GO-GETTER

get the air *v phr* (Variations: **the ax** or **the boat** or **the heave-ho** or **the old heave-ho** may replace **the air**) To be dismissed, esp to be jilted: *When she found out, he got the air/ Three more VPs got the ax this morning*

get the business *v phr* To be treated roughly; be punished or rebuked: *When they found out his record he got the business*

get the (or one's) **drift** *v phr* To understand, esp what one is hinting at • Often a question asked with or as if with a wink: *And it won't show up. Get my drift?*

get the drop on someone *v phr* To get someone in an inferior or threatened position; seize the advantage: *I got the drop on him with that question about oil*

get the eye *v phr* To be looked at in an insinuating, seductive way

get the goods on someone *v phr* To find or collect decisive evidence against: *The cops got the goods on him and he had to go to jail*

get the hang of something *v phr fr middle 1800s* To master the particular skill needed: *He couldn't get the hang of the new machines*

get the hungries *v phr* To become hungry: *I get the hungries for some breakfast*—TV ad

get the jump on someone or something *v phr* To get the lead, or an advantage, esp by alert early moves: *She got the jump on the other runners by perfect maneuvering at the* *start/ Never let the other guy get the jump on you*—Village Voice

get the lead out *v phr* (Variations: **of** one's **ass** or **of** one's **pants** or **of** one's **feet** may be added) To stop loafing; =GET one's ASS IN GEAR, HUSTLE • Often an irritated command: *Get the lead out and start writing*

get the monkey off (or **off** one's **back**) *v phr narcotics* To break a narcotics habit: *so hooked on morphine that there would be no getting the monkey off without another's help*—Nelson Algren

get the munchies *See* HAVE THE MUNCHIES

get the nod *v phr* To be approved; be chosen: *McCulloch got the nod* —Saturday Review

get the picture **1** *v phr* To understand; =COPPISH, DIG • Often a question: *Well, you won't ever be promoted here. Get the picture?* **2** *v phr* To mentally grasp something injurious or repellent to oneself; =GET WISE: *After she caught him with that whore she got the picture*

get the pink slip *v phr* To be dismissed or discharged: *When they discovered the shortage of funds he got the pink slip*

◁ **get** (or **have**) **the red ass**▷ *v phr* To become irritated and angry; be irritable: *If any of us gets the red ass about something, then we ought to talk it over*—Dan Jenkins

get there from here *See* YOU CAN'T GET THERE FROM HERE

get the shaft *v phr* To be ill-treated; be abused, esp by cruel deception: *He thought he'd get promoted, but he got the shaft instead* [a euphemism for sodomization]

get to someone **1** *v phr* To disturb or anger; =BUG, HASSLE: *I think it is starting to get to me*—Eliot Fremont-Smith **2** *v phr* To affect; make an impression: *The puppy really got to me; I couldn't send him to the shelter*

get to first base **1** *v phr* To begin well; take a successful first step • Usually in the negative: *I couldn't get to first base with the committee* **2** *v phr* To initiate sexual activity successfully, esp by hugging, caressing, kissing, etc • In the same baseball analogy, **get to third base** means touching and toying with the genitals, and **get to home plate** means to do the sex act, that is, "score"

get-together *n* A meeting or session, often social; party

get under someone's **skin** *v phr* To trouble or irritate; annoy; =BUG: *That cackle of his soon got under my skin*

get someone **up** *v phr* To inspire and energize, esp for a game, examination, or other ordeal; =PSYCH someone UP: *Steinbrenner thinks he can get the players up for games*—Inside Sports

get-up-and-go *n* Energy and initiative; pep; =PISS AND VINEGAR, PIZZAZZ: *My get-up-and-go has got up and went*

get up someone's **nose** *v phr* To irritate; provoke hostility: *Put us together and we'd get up each other's noses in a minute*—George Warren

get wise **1** *v phr fr late 1800s* To become aware, esp in matters of survival and advancement; look to one's own interest; =WISE UP • In the form **get wise with yourself** often an exhortation: *I hope you'll get wise and learn to keep your mouth shut/ If you don't get wise with yourself they'll fire you* • Often a command or bit of strong advice: *Get wise! Haven't you noticed what he's been up to* **2** *v phr* To become impudent or defiant; be saucy: *Get wise with me, punk, and you're dead*

get with it *v phr* To pay active attention to what is happening or what needs doing; =GET ON THE BALL: *We'll all have to get with it if we want this to turn out right*

get Zs *See* COP ZS

gevalt (gə VAHLT) *interj* An exclamation of woe, distress, shock, etc: *He breaks open a mezuzah, nothing inside, gevalt! but a piece of paper that says "Made in Japan"*—R Alter [fr Yiddish, "powers," hence an invocation of a higher force]

◀ **ghetto box**▶ *n phr* (Variations: **boogie box** or **box** or **coon box** or **ghetto blaster**) A large portable stereo radio and cassette player often carried and played loudly in public places: *Hey, man, don't mess with my box*—Wall Street Journal/ *that guy in the streets with his ghetto blaster* —Village Voice

ghost **1** *n fr late 1800s British* A writer paid for a book or article published under someone else's name; professional anonymous author **2** ***v:*** *I "ghosted" my wife's cookbook* —P Darrow **3** ***n*** *theater fr middle 1800s British* The treasurer of a theatrical company [Theater sense said to be fr a line in *Hamlet*: "The *ghost* walks" implying that pay is at hand; analogous with "the eagle shits" referring to the source of pay]

◁ **ghost turds**▷ ***n phr*** *Army* =HOUSE MOSS

GI (pronounced as separate letters) **1** ***adj*** *fr WW1 armed forces* Of, in, or from the US armed forces, esp the Army; government issue: *GI shoes/ His officious ways are very GI* **2** ***n*** A member of the US armed forces, esp an enlisted Army soldier serving since or during World War 2: *The GIs fought furiously to hold Taejon* —Associated Press **3** ***v*** *WW2 Army* To scrub and make trim: *They GIed the barracks every Friday night*

gidget **1** ***n*** =GADGET **2** ***n*** A lithe and pert young woman

gift ***See*** GOD'S GIFT

gift of gab (or **the gab**) ***n phr*** *fr 1700s British* The ability to talk interestingly, colorfully, and/or persuasively

gig[1] **1** ***n*** *jazz musicians* A party for jazz musicians and devotees; =JAM SESSION: *Kid Ory had some of the finest gigs, especially for the rich white folks*—Louis Armstrong **2** ***n*** *musicians fr 1930s* A playing date or engagement, esp a one-night job: *on a gig, or one night stand*—Louis Armstrong **3** ***v:*** *I forget whether we're gigging in Basin Street or Buenos Aires*—Dizzy Gillespie **4** ***n*** Any job or occupation: *it's better to take some kind of main gig for their sake* —New York **5** ***n*** A criminal act; swindle; =SCAM: *It ain't no gig, lady, and I don't really care what you think* —Sports Illustrated/ *On my first solo gig I was bagged... beaten shitless, and dumped in jail*—Bernard Malamud **6** ***n*** *armed forces* A demerit; report of deficiency or breach of rules [origin unknown; musicians' senses are extensions of earlier meanings, "spree, dance, party"]

◁ **gig**[2]▷ ***n*** *fr late 1600s British* =GIGGY [origin unknown; perhaps fr Irish or Anglo-Irish, as attested by the name *sheila-na-gig* given to carved figures of women with grotesquely enlarged vulvae found in English churches]
See UP YOURS

gig[3] ***n*** An old car [fr *gig* "one-horse carriage"]

◁ **giggy**▷ **1** ***n*** The vulva **2** ***n*** The anus
See UP YOURS

GIGO or **gigo** (GĪ goh) ***sentence*** *computer* The output is no better than the input [fr *garbage in, garbage out*]
See MEGOGIGO

GI Joe ***n phr*** *fr WW2* A US soldier, esp an enlisted soldier of and since World War 2; =DOGFACE

gilhickey ***n*** =THINGAMAJIG

gilhooley **1** ***n*** =THINGAMAJIG **2** ***n*** *car-racing* A skid in which a car ends up facing in the reverse direction

gillion ***See*** JILLION

gills ***See*** GREEN AROUND THE GILLS, SOUSED, STEWED

Gilroy's kite ***See*** HIGHER THAN A KITE

gimme or **gimmie** **1** ***n*** An acquisitive tendency: *They got da gimmies... always take, never give*—James M Cain **2** ***modifier:*** *The extent to which the "gimme" spirit has banished rationality*—New York Times

gimmick **1** ***n*** *circus, carnival & hawkers fr early 1900s* A secret device or hidden trick that causes something to work and assures that the customer will not win: *A new gimmick, infra-red contact lenses which... enabled a card player to read markings on the backs of cards*—Billy Rose **2** ***n*** *fr 1920s* Any device; =GADGET **3** ***n*** *narcotics* Apparatus used for preparing and injecting narcotics; =WORKS: *A small red cloth bag with his spike needle and "gimmicks" fell out*—New York **4** ***n*** A feature in a product, plan, presentation, etc, believed to increase appeal although it is not necessarily useful or important: *This promo isn't bad, but we sorely need a gimmick* **5** ***v:*** *Get a fairly good item, then gimmick the hell out of it* **6** ***n*** One's selfish and concealed motive; =ANGLE, PERCENTAGE: *This looks fine, Mr Mayor. What's your gimmick, anyhow?* [perhaps fr *gimcrack*]

gimmie hat (or **cap**) ***n phr*** A peaked cap like a baseball cap, bearing the trademark or name of a manufacturer and distributed as an advertising device: *a "macho" gimmie cap emblazoned with "Cat" (for Caterpillar Tractors)*—New York Times [probably fr the request "*gimme* one of those!" often heard when these were available free from dealers]

gimp *fr early 1900s hoboes & underworld* **1** *n* A limp **2** *v: The old guy was gimping across the street* ◁**3**▷ *n* A lame person: *He'd just kick a gimp in the good leg and leave him lay*—JK Winkler

◁ **ginch** ▷ *esp motorcyclists* **1** *n* A woman, esp solely as a sexual object; =CHICK: *the fifth ginch I'd had on those eerie sand barrier islands*—Easy Riders **2** *n* The vulva, and sexual activity; =ASS, CUNT: *all the free groupie ginch south of Bakersfield*—George Warren [origin uncertain; perhaps related to 1950s Australian and British sense, of surfer origin, "elegance, smartness, skill"]

ginchy *adj* Excellent; admirable; elegant; =SEXY: *Annie and I were the cat's pajamas and ginchy beyond belief*—Richard Merkin

ginder *See* CRUMBCRUSHER

◀ **ginee** ▶ *See* GUINEA

ginger *n fr middle 1800s* Energy; pep; =PIZZAZZ: *the effervescent quality that used to be called "ginger"*—LF McHugh [fr the practice of putting ginger under a horse's tail to increase its mettle and showiness]

gingerbread **1** *n fr 1600s* Money **2** *n* Fussy decoration, esp on a house; frillwork **3** *modifier: the gingerbread stacks of the old river steamers*

gink (GINK) *fr early 1900s* **1** *n* A man; fellow; =GUY: *Does a gink in Minsk suffer less from an appendectomy?*—Hal Boyle **2** *n* A tedious, mediocre person; =JERK [origin unknown; perhaps somehow fr Turkish, "catamite, punk," found in early 1800s sources both British and US]

gin mill *n phr* A saloon, barroom; tavern: *In some gin mill where they know the bartender*—New York Times

ginned or **ginned up** *adj* or *adj phr fr late 1800s* Drunk: *Hold me up, kid; I'm ginned*—P Marks

◀ **ginnee** or **ginney** ▶ *See* GUINEA

◀ **ginzo** or **guinzo** ▶ **1** *n* An Italian or person of Italian descent: *Gonna have at least eight hot ginzos looking for me*—George V Higgins **2** *adj: What ginzo broad didn't?*—Patrick Mann **3** *n* Any apparently foreign person; =HUNKY: *a Roumanian or some kinda guinzo*—Joel Sayre

gip *See* GYP

girene *See* GYRENE

girl **1** *n homosexuals* A male homosexual **2** *n narcotics* Cocaine: *They call cocaine girl because it gives 'em a sexual job when they take a shot*—C Cooper **3** *n* A queen of playing cards

See BACHELOR GIRL, BAR-GIRL, BEST GIRL, B-GIRL, CALL GIRL, CHARITY GIRL, GAL FRIDAY, GLAMOR GIRL, GO-GO GIRL, OOMPH GIRL, PLAYGIRL, SWEATER GIRL, WORKING GIRL

girl Friday *See* GAL FRIDAY

◁ **girlie** ▷ **1** *n* A girl: *this girlie and her mother*—Sinclair Lewis **2** *adj* Featuring nude or otherwise sexually provocative women: *To some extent, "girlie" magazines are information-getting*—US News & World Report

gism *See* JISM

gismo *See* GIZMO

git-go *See* FROM THE GIT-GO

give *See* SOMETHING'S GOT TO GIVE

give (or **write**) someone **a blank check** *v phr* To give someone leave to do whatever he or she wishes; give carte blanche: *The man gave me a blank check to order whatever I needed*

not **give a damn** *See* NOT GIVE A DAMN

◀ not **give a fuck** ▶ *See* NOT GIVE A DAMN

◀ not **give a fuck for nothing** ▶ *See* NOT GIVE A FUCK FOR NOTHING

give someone **a hand** **1** *v phr* To help: *Gimme a hand with this huge crate* **2** *v phr* To applaud someone by clapping the hands

give someone **a hard time** **1** *v phr* To scold or rebuke; quarrel with: *He was giving her a hard time about drinking too much* **2** *v phr* To make difficulties for, esp needless ones; =HASSLE: *I hope you won't give me a hard time this trip*

give someone or something **a miss** (or **the go-by**) *v phr* To avoid; not opt for • **the go-by** variant is attested from the mid-1600s: *Give these girls a miss*—Pan American Travel Guide/ *resolve to give it the go-by in future*—J Greig

give someone **a pain** *v phr* (Variations: **in the neck** or **in the ass** may be added) To be distasteful, repellent, tedious, etc: *one of those bragging polymath types who gave everybody a pain in the ass*—Saul Bellow

give someone **a ring** *v phr* To call on the telephone

give something **a shot** *v phr* (Variations: **crack** or **go** or **rip** or **ripple** may replace **shot**) To have a try at; make an attempt: *He gave the exam a good shot, but flunked it/ Let's give it a rip. We've nothing to lose*

give someone **a slap on the wrist** *v phr* To give a light and insufficient punishment; =RAP someone's KNUCKLES: *They caught a couple more Mafiosi and I'm sure they'll give them a real good slap on the wrist*

give someone **a tumble** *v phr fr early 1900s* To show a sign of recognition or approval; acknowledge: *Both knew me, but neither gave me a tumble* —Dashiell Hammett [probably fr the earlier *take a tumble to oneself* "examine oneself closely, esp with respect to one's faults," after which *tumble* was taken to mean "scrutiny, acknowledgment"]

giveaway 1 *n* Anything that reveals something concealed; clue: *She talked harsh, but the smile was a giveaway* **2** *n* A gift, prize, etc, esp one given to attract business; =FREEBIE **3** *modifier: a giveaway show/ giveaway offer*
See DEAD GIVEAWAY

give something one's **best shot 1** *v phr* To try one's hardest; do the best one can: *For three months, they had given it their best shot*—Toronto Star **2** *v phr* To do one's very best; make one's finest and utmost effort: *Anyway, I gave it my best shot* —Village Voice/ *A lot of people will be watching you. Give it your best shot*—Pat Conroy **3** *v phr* To make a maximum effort; =BUST one's ASS: *The whole thing is not easy... .But you must give it your best shot* —New York Times

◁ **give cone**▷ *v phr teenagers* =GIVE HEAD

give someone **five 1** *v phr* =GIVE someone A HAND **2** *v phr* (Variation: **slap** can replace **give**) *fr black* To shake hands with someone or slap someone's hand in greeting, congratulation, etc; =GIVE someone SOME SKIN: *Reno put out his hand for me to give him five*—Claude Brown

give someone **grief** *v phr* To make difficulties for; harrass; =HASSLE: *Don't let the prof give you any grief about this*

◁ **give head** (or **good head**)▷ *v phr* To do fellatio; =SUCK: *Not that Linda has anything against balling customers... but she just loves to give head* —Xaviera Hollander/ *She must give extra good head or something* —Joseph Wambaugh

give someone **heat** *v phr* To criticize; complain; =BITCH: *though she gave me heat about it not being "man's work"*—Erich Segal

give someone **hell** (or **merry hell** or **holy hell**) *v phr* To rebuke or punish severely; =CHEW OUT: *The skipper gave him merry hell for crud and drunkenness*

give (or **read**) someone **his** (or **her**) **rights** *v phr* To inform an arrested person formally of his or her legal rights, esp by reading him or her a "Miranda card" detailing them: *The judge threw it out because they hadn't given the crook his rights* [fr the requirement based on the Supreme Court decision in the Miranda case of 1966]

give someone **his** (or **her**) **walking papers** *v phr* (Variation: **running shoes** or **walking ticket** may replace **walking papers**) To dismiss or discharge; reject: *If he doesn't stop seeing other women she'll give him his walking papers/ When he objected to the new policy they gave him his running shoes*

give it the gun *v phr* To speed up an engine abruptly; accelerate to highest speed; =FLOOR

give it to someone **1** *v phr* To beat, punish, or rebuke: *He really gave it to me yesterday after I totaled his car* ◁**2**▷ *v phr* To do the sex act with or to someone: *one minute he'd be giving it to her in his cousin's Buick*—JD Salinger

give someone **leg** *v phr* To deceive; fool; =PULL someone's LEG: *Last time I saw you, you're giving me a little leg about there's nothing going on* —George V Higgins

give someone **lip** *v phr* To speak to in an impertinent and offensive way:

People get on here all day long and all they do is give me lip—Washington Post

give me five *See* SLIP ME FIVE

give out *v phr* Collapse; cease to function; die: *His old ticker gave out/ The bus gave out halfway up the hill* *See* PUT OUT

gives *See* WHAT GIVES

give some skin *v phr* To shake hands; greet; =GIVE someone FIVE: *Everybody gave some skin all around* —Richard Fariña

give someone **some skin** *v phr esp black* To shake or slap hands in salutation

not **give spit** *See* NOT GIVE SPIT

give someone **the air** *v phr* (Variations: **the ax** or **the boat** or **the heave-ho** or **the old heave-ho** may replace **the air**) To dismiss, discharge or reject: *His last girl gave him the air/ The Oval Office should give him what he really deserves: the boot* —Newsweek

give someone **the brush** *v phr* To snub; treat icily and curtly; =KISS OFF: *I got the brush in about two seconds in that fancy dump*

give someone **the business** *v phr* To treat roughly; punish; rebuke: *I really gave him the business when I caught him cheating on my exam*

give something **the chop** *v phr* To eliminate; =CUT: *A vast trade and business complex...was given the chop*—Westworld

give something **the deep six** *v phr fr Navy & merchant marine* To dispose definitively of; jettison; throw overboard: *They gave those files the deep six*

give someone **the eye** **1** *v phr* To look at in an insinuating and seductive way: *I could see he was giving you the eye* **2** *v phr* To signal with a look: *Get up when I give you the eye*

◁**give** someone **the finger**▷ **1** *v phr* To treat unfairly, dishonestly, etc; =SCREW, SHAFT: *Let me show you how to give that guy the finger*—Budd Schulberg **2** *v phr* To show contempt and defiance by holding up the extended middle finger toward someone; =FLIP THE BIRD: *When they honk at me I give them the finger/ It's a sort of collective giving of the finger to liberalism in all its forms*—Toronto Life [fr the figurative insertion of a finger punitively into the anus]

give someone **the fish-eye** (or **beady eye** or **hairy eyeball**) *v phr* To look or stare at in a cold, contemptuous, or menacing way: *A well-fed man in tails opened the door, gave them the fish eye*—G Homes/ *who gave me such hairy eyeballs that I want to slink back*—Village Voice

give someone **the gate** *v phr* To discharge, jilt, or eject: *After the last goof they gave him the gate*

give someone **the glad eye** *v phr* To look or glance at invitingly; gaze enticingly at: *A tipsy actress gives her man, Donald, the glad eye*—New York Times

give someone **the glad hand** *v phr* To greet and welcome effusively: *I gave 'em all the glad hand, but they voted for the bum anyway*

give someone or something **the go-by** *See* GIVE someone or something A MISS

give someone **the needle** *v phr* To nag at; criticize regularly and smartingly; =HASSLE, NEEDLE: *The only needle she knows is the one she gives grandpa for stopping off at the bar on his way home*—Hal Boyle

give the nod *v phr* To give approval; confer permission: *while giving the nod to the engineers*—Ebony

give someone or something **the once-over** *v phr* To examine closely; scrutinize, esp with a view to evaluation or identification; =CHECK OUT: *That guy in the corner is giving us the once-over/ I gave her papers the once-over and figured she qualified*

give someone **the pink slip** *v phr* To discharge or dismiss; =CAN, FIRE

give someone **the shaft** *v phr* To swindle, maltreat, or otherwise deal punishingly with; =FUCK, SHAFT: *He wasn't expecting much praise, but he sure didn't think they'd give him the shaft like that*

give someone **the shake** *v phr* To rid oneself of; get away from: *He gave the cops the shake a block or so away*

give someone **the shirt off** one's **back** *v phr* To be extremely generous • Usu in a conditional statement: *Open-handed? Why he'd give you the shirt off his back if you needed it* not **give** someone **the time of day** *See* NOT GIVE someone THE TIME OF DAY

give someone **the works** *v phr fr 1920s* To mistreat or beat severely; =CLOBBER, WORK someone OVER: *They took him into the adjoining room and gave him the works* [probably fr the thoroughness suggested by *the works*; see *the works*]

give someone **what for** *v phr fr middle 1800s British* To beat or punish severely; drub either physically or verbally; =CLOBBER, LET someone HAVE IT: *two or three of us would pitch on him and give him "what-for"*—Jack London

give with the eyes *v phr* To look; glance at: *gives with the big blue eyes as if to say: "Her didn't mean to"*—E DeBaun

gizmo or **gismo** or **giz** **1** *n fr Navy & Marine Corps* An unspecified or unspecifiable object; something one does not know the name of or does not wish to name; =DINGUS, GADGET: *"Why weren't you using the gismo?" "I was. It didn't work"*—New York Times/ *"What's this gizmo?" I asked. "The hand brake"*—Billy Rose/ *Guy tried to shove a Pepsi bottle in his wife's giz*—Joseph Wambaugh **2** *n gambling* =GIMMICK **3** *n* A man; fellow; =GUY: *What's this gizmo have in mind?* [origin unknown]

the **glad eye** *n phr* A welcoming and enticing look; seductive glance: *She gave me the glad eye and I wondered what she had been up to now*

glad-hand **1** *modifier:* Effusive and warm; cordial: *He gave me that glad-hand business* **2** *v: After... glad-handing the local dignitaries, he heads for the fence*—Associated Press

See GIVE someone THE GLAD HAND

glad rags *fr late 1800s* **1** *n phr* One's best and fanciest clothing; party clothes **2** *n phr* Formal evening wear

glahm *See* GLOM

glamor (or **glamour**) **girl** *n phr* A woman whose looks and life are glamorous, esp a movie star or other professional beauty: *She was a beautiful thing when she started her career as a glamor girl*—New York Daily News

glamor-puss or **glamour-puss** **1** *n* A person whose looks and life are regarded as glamorous: *Joe's a glamor-puss and a hunk* **2** *modifier: Rourke's glamorpuss girlfriend*—Washington Post

glass arm **1** *n phr baseball* A pitcher's arm that is prone to injury and inflammation; =CROCKERY **2** *n phr dock workers* An inferior worker; weakling

glasses *See* GRANNY GLASSES

glass jaw or **china chin** *n phr prizefight* A boxer's chin that cannot tolerate a hard punch: *His glass jaw gives him excruciating pain when struck/ He protects his china chin by clinching*

glaum *See* GLOM

glaze someone **over** *v phr* To make ecstatic; intoxicate: *Said one enthusiastic participant: "Doesn't this just glaze you over?"*—Washington Post

glim **1** *n fr 1600s* A light, lamp, etc: *"Douse the glim, Mugsy," said a voice from my youth* **2** *n* (also **glimmer**) *truckers* A headlight **3** *n* (also **glimmer**) *fr middle 1800s* An eye **4** *v: I glimmed her from across the room*

glitch **1** *n fr 1960s aerospace* An operating defect; malfunction; a disabling minor problem: *despite such "glitches" (a spaceman's word for irritating disturbances)*—Time/ *Most had assured themselves that the trouble signal was only a "glitch"*—Newsweek **2** *n computer* A sudden interruption of electrical supply, program function, etc: *the term "bug" to refer to a computer glitch*—Newsweek [fr German *glitschen* (or Yiddish *glitshen*) "slip"]

the **glitterati** *n* Famous and glamorous people; outstanding celebrities: *among the glitterati*—People Weekly/ *to film the glitterati at a Derby bash*—Newsweek [based on *literati*]

glitz **1** *n* High gaudy finish; flashy surface: *some optional Hollywood glitz*—Car and Driver/ *applied Vegas and hot tub glitz to the old Jack La Lanne*—Village Voice **2** *v* (also **glitz up**): *the Pirates of Penzance newly glitzed*—California

glitzy *adj* Blatantly scintillant; flashy; gaudy: *and a glitzy sister... who has backed into degeneracy*—New York Times [fr German or Yiddish *glitzern* "glitter, glisten"]

◁ **globes** ▷ *n* A woman's breasts: *I'd even seen Elena's soft globes*—HK Fink

glom or **glaum** or **glahm** *fr early 1900s underworld & hoboes* **1** *n* A hand, regarded as a grabbing tool **2** *v* To grasp; seize: *She glommed the kid and held on tight* **3** *v* =GLOM ON TO **4** *v* To steal: *"Where'd you glahm 'em?" I asked* —Jack London/ *under the pretext of glomming a diamond from the strongbox*—SJ Perelman **5** *v* To be arrested **6** *v* To look at; seize with the eyes; =GANDER, GLIM: *or walk around the corner to glom old smack heads, woozy winos and degenerates* —New York Times **7** *n: Have a glom at that leg, won't you?* [fr British dialect *glaum, glam* "hand," ultimately fr Old English *clamm* "bond, grasp," related to *clamp*]
See MITT-GLOMMER

glom (or **glaum** or **glahm**) **on to** *v phr fr underworld & hoboes* To acquire; =LATCH ON TO: *Glom on to a couple jugs and we'll have a party*

gloomy Gus *n phr* A morose, melancholic person; pessimist; =CRAPE-HANGER

glop **1** *n* Any viscous fluid or mixture; =GOO, GOOK, GUNK: *dimes that rolled into the glop*—William Kennedy/ *What's that glop on your face?* **2** *n* Sentimentality; maudlin trash; =SCHMALTZ: *That is very dull. I hate glop*—Hal Boyle

glory *n railroad* A train of empty cars

glory hole **1** *n phr homosexuals* A hole between stalls in a toilet, through which the penis may be put for oral sex **2** *modifier: A private glory-hole club makes a lot more sense*—Playboy

glossy **1** *n* A magazine printed on shiny coated paper; a high-quality magazine; =SLICK: *female editors of the powerful "glossies"*—K Fraser **2** *n* A photograph printed on shiny paper

glove *See* NOT LAY A GLOVE ON someone

glow *n* Mild intoxication; =TIDDLINESS: *After a couple of bourbons I had a nice glow*

gluepot *n* A racehorse: *pay the cost the old gluepot rates when he toes the line*—Robert Ruark [fr the conventional belief that horses go to the *glue* factory as raw material when no longer of use]

G-man *n esp 1930s* A Federal Bureau of Investigations agent; =FEEB

gnarly *adj teenagers* Excellent; wonderful; =GREAT

gnome *n* An anonymous expert, esp a statistician or an industrious observer of trends; =BEAN COUNTER ● The term is being extended from the first use, **gnomes of Zurich**, designating the faceless little men who take account of and in part determine the curiosities of the international money market: *The Gnomes of Baseball* —Time/ *small-town station managers and network gnomes*—New York Times

go **1** *n* A fight: *a ripsnorting go* —WR Burnett **2** *n* A try; =CRACK, WHACK: *She gave it a good go, and made it* **3** *v* To die **4** *v* To relieve oneself; go to the bathroom: *The dog had to go. We set him in the sink*—Nelson Algren **5** *v* To happen; transpire; =GO DOWN: *What goes here?*—WR Burnett **6** *v teenagers esp fr late 1960s* To say; utter: *So he goes "Let me breathe!"/ You wake up one morning and you go, "Wait a minute"*—Playgirl **7** *v* To weigh: *She'll go maybe 300, 400 pounds* **8** *v* To pay: *I went five bills for that* —Hy Sobol **9** *adj fr astronauts* Functioning properly; going as planned; =A-OK: *As the astronauts say... all signs are go in the National League*—Sporting News **10** *adj* Appropriate; fitting: *beatniks, whose heavy black turtle-neck sweaters had never looked particularly go with white tennis socks*—Time
See FROM THE GIT-GO, FROM THE WORD GO, GIVE something A SHOT, HAVE A CRACK AT something, HAVE something GOING FOR someone or something, LET FLY, LET oneself GO, ON THE GO, TELL someone WHERE TO GET OFF, THERE YOU GO, WAY TO GO, WHAT GOES AROUND COMES AROUND

the **go-ahead** **1** *n* Permission or a signal to proceed; consent: *She pleaded her case before state officials and got the go-ahead*—Associated Press **2** *modifier* Putting a competitor in the lead: *The Tigers got the go-ahead run in the eighth*

goal *See* KNOCK someone or something FOR A LOOP

go all the way **1** *v phr* To do the utmost; make a special effort; =GO THE EXTRA MILE: *If you decide to do it, I'll go all the way for you* **2** *v phr* =GO THE LIMIT

go along for the ride *v phr* To do something or join in something in a passive way: *I don't expect much, but I'll go along for the ride*

go along with **1** *v phr* To agree with some suggestion or statement **2** *v phr* To accept or comply with some proposal; acquiesce

go ape (or ◁**ape-shit**▷) **1** *v phr* To behave stupidly, irrationally, and violently; go wild: *When they told him, he went ape and wrecked his room* **2** *v phr* To be very enthusiastic; admire enormously: *Everyone we met, experienced native and green tourist alike, went ape for it*—Popular Science

go around the bend *v phr fr British* To become insane; go crazy; =FREAK OUT: *Jessica Lange, who goes around the bend with more style, insight, and intensity*—Washingtonian

◁ **go around the world**▷ *v phr* To kiss or lick the whole body of one's partner, esp as a prelude to fellatio or cunnilingus

goat **1** *n hot rodders & teenagers* A car, esp an old one or one with an especially powerful engine **2** *n* A person who takes the blame for failure or wrongdoing; scapegoat; =PATSY: *After the latest flop they elected me goat* **3** *n Army* The most junior officer in an Army unit *See* GET someone's GOAT, OLD GOAT

◀ **goat fuck** (or **screw** or **rope**)▶ *n phr Army* A very confused situation, operation, etc; =CHINESE FIRE DRILL

goat-smelling *adj Army* Malodorous; stinking: *Get your goat-smelling ass out of here*

gob[1] *fr British dialect fr 1500s* **1** *n* A mass of viscous matter; =BLOB: *She chucked a big gob of plaster at me* **2** *n* (also **gobs**) A quantity, esp a large quantity: *I think he's got gobs of money*

gob[2] *n* The mouth • Chiefly British use [fr Irish]

gob[3] *n fr early 1900s* A US Navy sailor [perhaps fr earlier British *gabby* "coast guard; quarterdeckman," of unknown origin]

go back to (or **be at**) **square one** *v phr* To be forced to return to one's starting point, usu after a waste of effort; make a new beginning

go bananas **1** *v phr* To become wildly irrational; =FREAK OUT, GO APE: *speculation that maybe old Strom had gone bananas at last*—John Corry **2** *v phr* To be extremely enthusiastic; admire enormously: *She went bananas over the dress* [fr the spectacle of an ape greedily gobbling *bananas*]

gobbledegook *n* Pretentious and scarcely intelligible language, esp of the sort attributed to bureaucrats, sociologists, etc [coined in 1944 by Representative Maury Maverick of Texas]

◁ **gobbler**▷ *n* A person who does fellatio or cunnilingus

go belly up *v phr* To die; collapse; cease to operate; =BELLY UP: *two major credit-card firms had gone belly up*—Wall Street Journal

go blooey *v phr* (Variations: **flooey** or **kablooey** or **kerflooey** or **kerflooie** or **kerfooey** may replace **blooey**) To end abruptly in failure or disaster; break down; collapse: *The peace talks went blooey today/ Damn telephone went kerflooey/ Will I make it... without the air conditioner in the car going kablooey*—Washington Post/ *Then, of course, the whole thing all goes flooey*—Village Voice [echoic imitation of an explosion]

go broke (or **bust**) *v phr* To become penniless; become insolvent; =GO BELLY UP, TAKE A BATH: *His newest escapade into the fashionable world of trade and manufacturing had again gone bust*—Joseph Heller

gobs *See* GOB

go bughouse *v phr* To become insane; go crazy: *Four years earlier, Travis... had gone bughouse*—Washington Post

go bust *See* GO BROKE

the **go-by** *See* GIVE someone or something A MISS

God *See* BY GUESS AND BY GOD, OLDER THAN GOD

god-awful *fr early 1900s* **1** *adv* Extremely: *Ain't it god-awful cold in here?* **2** *adj* Wretched; miserable; inferior: *"It was god-awful," Newman recalls*—New York Times/ *this god-awful legislation*—Toronto Life

God-damn or **God-damned** *adj* Accursed; wretched; nasty; =FUCKING • Often used for euphony and rhythm of emphasis: *Take your God-damn foot off my God-damn toes*

goddess *See* SEX GODDESS

godfather *n* The chief; highest authority; =BOSS: *He was Life's first publisher, the godfather of the radio and film March of Time series*—Time

godmother *See* FAIRY GODMOTHER

go down[1] *v phr esp computer* To become inoperative; stop functioning

See WHAT'S GOING DOWN

go down[2] *v phr fr black* To happen; =GO: *He wanted this scam to go down as rigged*—Lawrence Sanders

go-down *n black* A basement apartment or room

◁ **go down and do tricks**▷ *v phr* =GO DOWN ON someone

go down in flames *v phr* To be utterly ruined; be wrecked: *He became Washington bureau chief of ABC News and promptly went down in flames*—Washingtonian [fr the fate of World War 1 combat pilots, who wore no parachutes]

◁ **go down on** someone▷ *v phr* To do fellatio or cunnilingus; =EAT IT, SUCK: *Only she won't go down on me. Isn't that odd?*—Philip Roth

go down the tube (or **tubes** or **chute**) *adv phr* To wrack and ruin; to perdition; =KAPUT: *Bache was in danger of going down the chute with the price of silver*—Nicholas von Hoffman/ *speaks of a whole generation going down the tube*—New York Times

God's gift *n phr* A very special blessing; premier offering • Nearly always ironical: *He thought he was God's gift to pedagogy*

go Dutch (or **Dutch treat**) *v phr* To pay one's own way at a dinner, show, etc: *Nobody had much money, so we all went Dutch*

goes around *See* WHAT GOES AROUND COMES AROUND

gofer or **go-for** or **gopher** *n* An employee who is expected to serve and cater to others; a low-ranking subordinate: *running the robo machine and acting as a receptionist, secretary, and general go-for*—Nicholas von Hoffman/ *attractive go-fers for executive editor Frank Waldrop*—Washingtonian

go fishing (or **on a fishing expedition**) *v phr fr late 1800s* To undertake a search for facts, esp by a legal or quasi-legal process like a grand-jury investigation

go fly a kite *sentence* Go away at once; =GO TO HELL, GET LOST: *I asked for more, and he told me to go fly a kite*

go for *v phr fr early 1800s* To be in favor of; admire; be attracted to: *I really go for her*—John O'Hara

See HAVE something GOING FOR someone or something

go for broke (or **all the marbles**) *v phr* To make a maximum effort; stake everything on a big try: *We went for broke on that deal, and won/ He goes for all the marbles*—CBS News [fr a gambler's last desperate or hopeful wager]

go for it *v phr* To make a try for something, esp a valiant and risky one • Often an encouraging imperative: *Will we play it safe, or go for it?*

go for the fences *v phr baseball* To try to make long base hits; =SLUG

go for the long ball *v phr* To take a large risk for a large gain; =GO FOR BROKE: *entering the fall campaign might decide to go for the long ball*—Washingtonian [fr a *long* desperation pass thrown in a football game]

◀ **go fuck** (or **impale**) oneself▶ *sentence* May you be accursed, confounded, humiliated, rejected, etc; =GO TO HELL: *Ah, go impale yourselves, the bunch of you*—John Le Carré/ *Then they could go fuck themselves*—Village Voice

go-getter *n fr 1920s* A vigorous and effective person; =WINNER: *sometimes enviously referred to as a go-getter, a hot shot, a ball of fire*—Fact Detective Mysteries

go-go *esp 1960s* **1** *adj* Having to do with discotheques, their music, style of dancing, etc **2** *adj* Stylish; modish; =TRENDY: *She may be getting on in years but she certainly is a go-go dresser* **3** *adj* Showing vitality and drive, esp in business and commerce; urgent and energetic: *Religion is a really go-go growth industry these days*—LR Hills/ *Japan's go-go entrepreneurs*—Newsweek

See A GO-GO

go-go girl (or **dancer**) *n phr* A scantily clad or partly naked young woman employed to do solo gyrational dancing in a discotheque or club on a small stage or platform, in a cage, etc

go gunning for someone ***See*** GUN FOR someone

go halfies (or **halvies** or **halvsies**) *v phr* To award an equal share; divide in two equal parts: *I may go halvsies*—Atlantic Monthly

go haywire *fr early 1900s* **1** *v phr* To become inoperative; break down unexpectedly; =GO BLOOEY: *This radio's gone haywire*—JC Hixson **2** *v phr* To go crazy; become confused and disoriented: *Remember that I tried to talk you out of it, and don't go haywire*—S McNeil [fr the ramshackle condition of something that must be hastily repaired with *haywire*]

go (or **run**) **hog-wild** *v phr fr late 1800s* To act audaciously and unrestrainedly: *I went hog-wild and spent the whole week's pay/ I'm going to take a roundhouse wallop at the first thing I see and run hog-wild on the bases*—Everybody's Magazine

goifa ***See*** GREEFA

going ***See*** GET GOING, HAVE something GOING FOR someone or something

going down ***See*** WHAT'S GOING DOWN

going out of style ***See*** LIKE IT'S GOING OUT OF STYLE

a **going-over** **1** *n phr* A beating; trouncing: *The goons gave him a brutal going over* **2** *n phr* An examination; scrutiny: *Give these records a going-over, please*

go into one's **act** *v phr* =DO one's NUMBER

go into one's **dance** *v phr* (Variations: **dog and pony show** or **song and dance** may replace **dance**) To begin a prepared line of pleading, explanation, selling, seduction, etc: *He went into his dance, but she wasn't convinced*

go into orbit *v phr* To reach very extreme and apparently uncontrolled heights: *those whose stocks can absorb, say, $50 million or more without going into orbit*—Fortune

goiter ***See*** GERMAN GOITER, MILWAUKEE GOITER

go kerplunk *v phr* To fail; =FLOP: *If they go kerplunk, someone will have to scrape up the pieces*—Arthur Daley

gold **1** *n* Money **2** *n narcotics* A high grade of marijuana ***See*** ACAPULCO GOLD

◀ **Goldberg** ▶ *n black* A Jew, esp one who employs blacks or has a shop in a black neighborhood: *sweeping the floors for Goldberg*—Claude Brown ***See*** RUBE GOLDBERG

goldbrick **1** *n* (also **goldbricker**) *fr WW1 armed forces* A shirker; a person who avoids work or duty; =GOOF-OFF **2** *v*: *She made him promise to quit goldbricking* **3** *v esp early 1900s* To swindle; cheat; =CON [fr the convention of the confidence trickster who sells spurious *gold bricks*]

gold chamberpot ***See*** WIN THE PORCELAIN HAIRNET

gold-digger *n fr 1920s* A woman who uses her charms and favors to get money, presents, etc, from wealthy men: *Lorelei Lee... the crazy-like-a-fox gold-digger*—Billy Rose

golden-ager *n* An elderly person, usu retired

golden handcuffs *n phr* Arrangements, options, perquisites, etc, that induce one to stay in one's job: *These ties that bind have become known in industry as golden handcuffs*—Time

golden oldie or **oldie but goodie** *n phr fr 1960s* An old record, song, etc, still regarded as good, esp one that has revived or sustained popularity: *a golden oldie like "Honeysuckle Rose"*—FP Tullius/ *All the golden oldies are replayed and the untied threads neatly resolved*—Newsweek/ *oldies but goodies such as "Down by the Riverside"*—Pulpsmith [probably influenced by association with the *gold* phonograph record struck for a recording that has sold a million copies and more]

golden parachute (or **handshake**) *n phr* Very high sums, benefits, etc, offered for taking early retirement: *"Golden parachutes" or severance packages... are all becoming more common*—New York Times/ *parting golden handshake with GM included a valuable Cadillac franchise*—Time

◁ **golden shower** ▷ *n phr homosexuals & prostitutes* Urination on someone who sexually enjoys such a wetting: *what girls do through the bladder, which is otherwise known as the* *"golden shower"*—Xaviera Hollander/ *Golden showers...Not me* —Philadelphia

goldfish bowl *n phr* A place or situation where one is exposed; a venue without privacy: *Celebrities must live in a goldfish bowl*

gold piece *See* COME UP SMELLING LIKE A ROSE

go levers *n phr airline* The throttles of an aircraft

golly *interj fr middle 1800s British fr middle 1700s black* A mild exclamation of surprise, dismay, pleasure, etc; =GOSH: *Golly, Mom, did you really win it?* [a euphemism for *God*] *See* HOLLY-GOLLY

go-long *n black* A police patrol wagon; =PADDY WAGON: *Joe Brown had you all in the go-long last night* —Zora Neale Hurston

goma (GOH mah) *n narcotics* Crude opium

gomer *n hospital* A patient needing extensive care, and usu sent to a nursing home [origin unknown; perhaps related to British *gomers* "going-home clothes"]

gon or **gond** *See* GUN²

go native *v phr* To take on the behavior and standards of the place one has moved to or is visiting, esp when this means a loss of rigor, respectability, etc: *On Bleecker Street he went native and donned a black sweatshirt and sneakers*

gone **1** *adj jazz musicians* Intoxicated, esp with narcotics **2** *adj cool talk* In a trancelike condition; meditative: *a "gone" expression on his face*—Calder Willingham **3** *adj cool talk* Excellent; wonderful; =COOL: *a real gone chick*

gone goose *n phr* =DEAD DUCK [an alliterative phrase modeled on *dead duck*]

gone on (or **over**) *adj phr* In love with; enamored of: *I was so gone over her*—Louis Armstrong

a **goner** *n fr middle 1800s* Someone or something that is doomed; someone dead or about to die; =DEAD DUCK: *pray...or you're a goner*—San Diego Herald/ *for Rome will be a goner*—WH Auden

gong **1** *n* (also **gonger**) *narcotics* An opium pipe **2** *n chiefly British WW2 use* A military decoration; medal or ribbon [both senses probably fr *gong* "saucer-shaped metal bell," of Malayan origin; the sense "opium pipe" may be related to the general association of *gongs* with Chinese matters, and the military sense to the notion that a decoration is something like the ceremonial sounding of a *gong*]
See KICK THE GONG AROUND

gonged *adj narcotics* Intoxicated with narcotics; =HIGH, STONED: *She's sitting in the front row gonged to the gills with acid*—Albert Goldman

goniff (GAH nəf) **1** *n* (Variations: **gonef** or **gonif** or **gonof** or **gonoph** or **ganef** or **ganof** or **guniff**) *fr middle 1800s* A thief; a person who is in effect a thief, like an unethical salesperson: *And who is this arch-goniff?* —Dashiell Hammett/ *a gonof like Glick*—Budd Schulberg/ *all the other gonophs, consultants who peddle bullshit, builders who build badly* —Village Voice **2** *v: Are you trying to goniff me, pal?* ◁**3**▷ *n* A male homosexual [fr Yiddish, "thief," fr Hebrew *gannabh* "thief"]

gonk *See* CONK

gonsil or **gonzel** *See* GUNSEL

gonzo (GAHN zoh) **1** *adj fr early 1970s* Insane; wild; bizarre; confused: *gonzo journalism, a flamboyant if controversial style*—New York Daily News/ *the gonzo idea of a cross-country street race*—Car and Driver **2** *n: The Gonzo and the Geeks* —Vivian Gornick/ *These double-gaited gonzos are perpetrating a plague of best-selling takeoffs*—Newsweek [fr Italian, "credulous, simple, too good"]

goo **1** *n fr early 1900s* Any sticky and viscous substance; =GLOP, GUNK: *fell in the goo rounding third*—New York Daily News **2** *n* Sentimentality; maudlin rubbish; =GLOP, SCHMALTZ **3** *n* Fulsome flattery; overly affectionate greetings: *They ladle out the old goo*—Bing Crosby [perhaps sound symbolism, influenced by *glue*; perhaps fr *burgoo* "oatmeal porridge"]

goober *teenagers* **1** *n* A minor skin lesion; =ZIT: *whiteheads, blackheads, goopheads, goobers, pips* —New York Times **2** *n* A stupid and bizarre person; =WEIRDO [fr *goober* "peanut" fr Kongo *nguba* "kidney, peanut," probably because the first syllable describes the *goo* which exudes from or is squeezed from the lesion]

◁**goober-grabber**▷ ***n phr*** A Georgian [fr the general association of Georgia with its important product the peanut]

good ***See*** BE GOOD, DO-GOOD, DO-GOODER, FEEL GOOD, HAVE IT GOOD, MAKE GOOD, NO-GOOD

good buddy ***n phr*** *esp citizens band* The person one is cordially addressing

goodbye ***See*** KISS something GOODBYE

good cop bad cop or **nice cop tough cop** ***modifier*** Marked by alternations between friendliness and hostility, easiness and rigor, etc: *Successful management requires a variation of the "good cop, bad cop" routine* —New York Times/ *In short, a "nice cop" Rousseau and a "tough cop" Rousseau*—New York Review/ *I think that she's the good cop and he's the bad one, and I think it's quite deliberate*—New York [fr the interrogation technique by which one police officer pretends to sympathize with the suspect and to protect him from a pitiless and menacing fellow-officer]

good deal *fr WW2 armed forces* **1** ***n phr*** A pleasant and favorable situation, life, job, etc: *He had a good deal there at the bank, but blew it* **2** ***interj*** An exclamation of agreement, pleasure, congratulation, etc: *You made it? Good deal!*

gooder ***See*** DO-GOODER

good hair ***n phr*** *black* Straight or nearly straight and shiny hair

goodie or **goody** **1** ***n*** =GOODY-GOODY **2** ***n*** A special treat; something nice to eat: *a huge basket of goodies*—New Yorker **3** ***n*** Something nice; a pleasant feature; something very desirable: *headlight with a middle beam, the goodie you've been waiting for*—Popular Science/ *the goody he had saved for them*—New York **4** ***modifier:*** *Then I got out my goodie bag*—Xaviera Hollander **5** ***n*** Someone on the side of virtue and decency, in contrast with a villain: *It's much easier to make a girl a baddie than a goodie*—Time

See GOLDEN OLDIE

good Joe ***n phr*** A pleasant, decent, reliable man

good old (or **ole**) **boy** ***n phr*** A white Southerner who exemplifies the masculine ideals of the region: *The helpful truck driver was a good old boy from around Nashville*

goods ***n*** *narcotics* Narcotics of any sort

the **goods** **1** ***n phr*** *fr late 1800s* Something or someone of excellent quality; just what is wanted: *She's the real goods*—A Lewis **2** ***n phr*** The evidence needed to arrest and convict a criminal: *We've got the goods on him*—Erle Stanley Gardner **3** ***n phr*** Stolen property; contraband: *They caught him with the goods in his pocket*

See DELIVER THE GOODS, GET THE GOODS ON someone

good shit **1** ***interj*** =GOOD DEAL **2** ***n phr*** Anything favorable or pleasant; something one approves of: *This place is real good shit, ain't it?*

good sport ***n phr*** A person who plays fair, accepts both victory and defeat, and stays amiable: *I just want to be a good sport and get along with people* —Hal Boyle

good-time Charlie ***n phr*** A man devoted to partying and pleasure; bon vivant

good word ***See*** WHAT'S THE GOOD WORD

Goodyears ***See*** DOWN THE GOODYEARS

goody-goody ***n*** *fr late 1800s* A prim and ostentatiously virtuous person: *I'm not a mammy boy nor a goody-goody*—O Johnson

goody two-shoes **1** ***n phr*** An obviously innocent and virtuous young woman; =GOODY-GOODY • Most often used mockingly or contemptuously **2** ***modifier:*** *in spite of its Goody Two-Shoes ecological image* —Toronto Life [fr the name of the heroine of a middle-1700s child's story, probably by Oliver Goldsmith, about a little girl who exulted publicly at the acquisition of a second shoe]

gooey ***adj*** Consisting of, covered with, or resembling goo: *gooey pie/ affected and a bit gooey*—New Yorker/ *the story of Teresa Stratas, without gooey heaviness*—Toronto Life

goof **1** ***n*** *fr early 1900s* A stupid person; =BOOB, KLUTZ: *He's a goof, but harmless* **2** ***n*** An insane person; mental case **3** ***n*** *1930s prison* One's cellmate **4** ***n*** *narcotics* A narcotics addict **5** ***v:*** *He was goofing then, and had a $100 habit*

6 *n fr jive talk* A blunder; bad mistake; =BOO-BOO: *they covered their goof quite well*—Esquire **7** *v: You goofed again, it's a one-way street* **8** *v* To pass one's time idly and pleasantly; =GOOF OFF: *In Sarajevo, members of a student volunteer brigade goofed and joked as they worked* —Time **9** *v* =GOOF AROUND **10** *v* To fool; =KID: *Don't goof your grandpa*—James T Farrell [fr British dialect *goof, goff* "fool"]

goof around **1** *v phr* To pass one's time idly and pleasantly; potter about; =BEAT AROUND, FART AROUND **2** *v phr* To joke and play when one should be serious; =FUCK AROUND, HORSE AROUND: *The monarch ordered the field marshal to quit goofing around and win the goddamn war*

goof at *v phr* To examine; look at; =GAWK

goofball **1** *n* A stupid and clumsy person; =GOOF: *roles that earned him the affectionate labeling as a "goof ball"*—Washington Post **2** *n* An eccentric person; =ODDBALL, WEIRDO **3** *n narcotics* A pill or capsule of Nembutal (a trade name) **4** *n narcotics* A barbiturate, tranquilizer, etc, used as a narcotic: *took over three hundred goof balls*—A Stump **5** *n narcotics* A portion or dose of a narcotic; =BALL: *A goof ball is a narcotics preparation which is burned on a spoon and inhaled*—New York Daily News

goof-butt *See* GOOFY-BUTT

goofed *adj narcotics* Intoxicated with a narcotic, esp marijuana; =HIGH, STONED

go off ◁**1**▷ *v phr* To have an orgasm; =COME OFF **2** *v phr* To occur; succeed: *Did everything go off as planned?*

go off half-cocked *v phr* To make a premature response, esp an angry one: *She went off half-cocked before she even knew what happened* [fr the accidental firing of a gun at *half cock*]

go off the deep end **1** *v phr fr early 1900s* To go into a violent rage; =BLOW one's TOP **2** *v phr* To have a mental breakdown: *The old lady just went off the deep end after her family died in that car crash* [perhaps fr the notion of jumping into a pool at the *deep end*, hence being in *deep water*, in trouble]

See JUMP OFF THE DEEP END

goof off *v phr fr WW2 armed forces* To pass one's time idly and pleasantly; potter about; shirk duty; =GOOF AROUND: *My goofing off in the final period had knocked down a possible A average*—Life/ *Are you trying to tell me my son is goofing off?* —Erma Bombeck

goof-off *fr WW2 armed forces* **1** *n* A person who regularly or chronically avoids work; =FUCK-OFF: *getting kicked out of seminary as a goof-off* —Inside Sports **2** *n* A period of relaxation; respite: *A little goof-off will do you good*

goof up **1** *v phr* To spoil; disable; =BITCH UP, QUEER: *He goofed up the whole deal by talking too soon* **2** *v phr* To blunder; =GOOF: *that can look at a child when he goofs up and reflect, "I understand and I love you"* —Erma Bombeck

goof-up **1** *n* =FUCK-UP **2** *n* A blunder, esp a serious one; =FUCK-UP, SNAFU

goofus **1** *n* =THINGAMAJIG **2** *n early 1900s circus* A small calliope **3** *n circus & carnival* A rural person; naive spectator; =EASY MARK **4** *n show business* Tasteless and meretricious material or entertainment designed for the unsophisticated

goofy *adj* Silly; foolish; crazy • Nearly always has an affectionate and amused connotation: *a goofy grin*—HC Witwer/ *a goofy awkward kid*—Chances/ *And he looked, well, goofy*—JD Salinger

goofy about *adj phr* =CRAZY ABOUT

goofy-butt or **goof-butt** *n narcotics* A marijuana cigarette; =JOINT

goo-goo eyes *n phr fr late 1800s* Eyes expressing enticement, desire, seduction, etc [probably fr *googly*, with which it is synonymous in early uses]

See MAKE GOO-GOO EYES

gook[1] (GŏŏK) **1** *n* Dirt; grime; sediment; =GLOP: *Glim gets the gook off* —New York Daily News/ *got gook all over my shoes* **2** *n* Cheap and inferior merchandise; =SCHLOCK **3** *modifier: wearing gook jewelry*

◀ **gook**[2] ▶ (GŏŏK, GōōK) *fr late 1800s* **1** *n* An Asian or Polynesian; =SLOPE • Originally a Filipino insurrectionary, then a Nicaraguan, then any Pacific Islander during World

War 2, embraced Koreans after 1950, Vietnamese and any Asian fr 1960s: *It was there that I first heard of dinks, slopes, and gooks*—New Yorker **2** ***modifier:*** *Give it to the gook hospitals*—New York Times [fr *gugu*, a term of Filipino origin, perhaps fr Vicol *gugurang* "familiar spirit, personal demon," adopted by US armed forces during the Filipino Insurrection of 1899 as a contemptuous term for Filipinos, and spread among US troops to other places of occupation, invasion, etc; probably revived after 1950 by the Korean term *kuk* which is a suffix of nationality, as in *Chungkuk* "China," etc]

gooky (GŏŏK ee) ***adj*** Sticky; viscid; greasy: *Greaseless. Nongooky*—Cosmetics advertisement

goombah or **goombar** or **gumbah** (GŏŏM bah) **1** ***n*** A friend; companion; trusted associate; patron; =PAL: *They called him Joey Gallo's rabbi or his goombah*—Saturday Evening Post/ *trying to make these old goombars understand*—Patrick Mann/ *We want all our gumbahs to come over and get rich*—George V Higgins **2** ***n*** An organized-crime figure; Mafioso: *I'm gonna kill any greasy Guinea goombah that tries to stop me*—George Warren [fr dialect pronunciation of Italian *compare* "companion, godfather"]

goomer ***n*** *hospital* A hypochondriac [fr *get out of my emergency room*]

goon **1** ***n*** *fr early 1920s* A strong, rough, intimidating man, esp a paid ruffian **2** ***modifier:*** *goon squad/ his goon tactics* **3** ***n*** Any unattractive or unliked person; =JERK, PILL: *He had the face of a pure goon*—H Allen Smith [fr the name of Alice the Goon, a large, hairy creature in the Popeye comic strip by EC Segar; perhaps fr *gooney*]

gooney ***n*** *fr late 1800s* A stupid person; simpleton; fool [fr earlier *goney, gonus* "simpleton," as old as the late 1500s]

goonk ***See*** GUNK

goon squad ***n phr*** A group of ruffians: *A few weeks later, another "goon squad," as they have been rightly labeled*—New York Times

go on the hook for someone or something **1** ***v phr*** To go into debt: *So you'll go on the hook for one of those eighty-dollar sports-car coats*—S McNeil **2** ***v phr*** To endanger oneself for another; go out on a limb

go on track ***v phr*** *prostitutes* To patrol an area seeking prostitution customers; =HOOK: *Then I'd go on track till 4 AM, sleep two more hours, and start over*—Milwaukee Journal

goony ***adj*** Like a goon or a goon's behavior

goop[1] or **goup** ***n*** A nasty viscid substance; =GLOP, GOO: *suck up the goop and then spill it over*—John D MacDonald

goop[2] **1** ***n*** A stupid and boorish person; =CLOD, KLUTZ **2** ***n*** Stupidly sentimental material; sugary rubbish: *who can't transcend the Positive Mental Attitude goop she is forced to utter*—Village Voice [first sense fr the name of an unmannerly creature invented by the humorist Gelett Burgess in the late 1800s]

goophead ***n*** A minor skin lesion; =ZIT: *whiteheads, blackheads, goopheads, goobers, pips*—New York Times

goopy **1** ***adj*** Viscid; nastily sticky: *You certainly tend to get goopy fancy food these days*—Arizona Republic **2** ***adj*** Stupidly sentimental; maudlin; =GOOEY: *There's no way to talk about that without sounding goopy*—Tom Wolfe

goose ◁**1**▷ ***v*** To prod someone roughly and rudely in the anal region, usu as a coarse and amiable joke: *As she was bending over her lab table, a playful lab assistant goosed her*—Max Shulman ◁**2**▷ ***n:*** *He threatened a goose, and I cringed* **3** ***v*** To exhort strongly and irritably; goad harshly: *and goosed the media into hyping them*—Washington Post **4** ***n:*** *The whole bunch needed a good goose* **5** ***v*** To run an engine at full speed or with spurts of high speed; =GUN: *Vroom-vroom-vroom, he goosed the engine to full-throated life*—Earl Thompson

See COOK someone's GOOSE, AS FULL OF SHIT AS A CHRISTMAS GOOSE, GONE GOOSE

goose bumps ***n phr*** A roughness of the skin or the production of small pimples on the skin as the result of fear, cold, or excitement; gooseflesh

goose-bumpy *adj* Frightened; panicky: *goes goose-bumpy at the thought of hooking a 50-pound sailfish*—Time

goose-drownder *n fr early 1900s* A very heavy rainstorm; cloudburst

goose egg *n phr fr middle 1800s* Zero; nothing; a score of zero; =ZILCH: *My contribution appears to have been a great big goose egg*

goose something **up** *v phr* To make something more exciting, intense, impressive, etc; =JAZZ something UP: *If we tried to goose it up too much... it wouldn't help anybody*—Newsweek

goosy or **goosey** *adj* Touchy; jumpy; sensitive: *I feel a little goosy about the whole thing*—Time/ *Hennessey was goosey anyway, and he jumped* —James T Farrell

See LOOSE AS A GOOSE

go out like a light *v phr* To lose consciousness very suddenly and totally: *Something swished and I went out like a light*—Raymond Chandler

go out of one's **skull** *fr 1960s* **1** *v phr* To become very tense; get nervous: *You can go out of your skull while they're doing that*—R Musel **2** *v phr* To become very excited; be overcome with emotion; =GO APE: *They went out of their skulls when she grabbed the mike to sing* **3** *v phr* To be overcome with tedium; fret with boredom: *The silence made him go right out of his skull*

go out on a limb *v phr* To put oneself in a vulnerable position; take a risk: *OK, I'll go out on a limb and vouch for you*

go over *v phr* To succeed; be accepted: *This demonstration will never go over with the hard hats*

go over big *v phr* To succeed very well; be received with great approval: *Her proposal went over big with the biggies*

go overboard **1** *v phr* To be smitten with love or helpless admiration: *He went overboard for her right away* **2** *v phr* To commit oneself excessively or perilously; overdo: *Take a couple, but don't go overboard* **3** *v phr* =JUMP OFF THE DEEP END

go over like a lead balloon *v phr* To fail miserably; =FLOP: *My appeal to his better nature went over like a lead balloon*

go over the wall *v phr* To escape from prison

go over with a bang *v phr* To succeed splendidly; be enthusiastically approved: *My idea for a new bulletin board went over with a bang*

goozle *n* The throat

go pfft *v phr esp 1930s* To end; dissolve; break up; =FIZZLE: *Their romance went pfft after that* [used by gossip columnists; fr late 1900s British echoic phrase *go phut* "come to grief, fizzle out"]

gopher *v baseball* To pitch a gopher ball: *only about the fifth or sixth that Orosco had gophered home the eventual gamer*—Village Voice

gopher ball *n phr baseball* A pitch that is hit for a home run; a batter's favorite pitch or an easy pitch to hit [because the batter will *go for* the pitch]

go piss up a rope *sentence* Go away and do something characteristically stupid; =GET LOST, GO FLY A KITE: *He asked for a contribution and I told him to go piss up a rope*

go pittypat (or **pitterpat**) *v phr* To beat strongly and excitedly; pump with joy and anticipation: *My veteran heart went pittypat*—San Francisco

go places *v phr* To do very well in one's work; have a successful career; make good

go pound salt (or **sand**) *sentence* (Variation: **up** one's **ass** may be added) May one be accursed, confounded, humiliated, etc: *told Glazer and the feds to go pound sand in legal terms, of course*—Philadelphia

go public *v phr* To reveal onself; acknowledge openly; =COME OUT OF THE CLOSET: *how she adjusted to going public as a single-breasted woman* —Ms [fr the financial idiom *go public* "offer stock for sale in the stock market after it had previously been held in a family or otherwise privately"]

gorilla **1** *n fr middle 1800s* An extremely strong person, esp one who is not very clever **2** *n* (also **gorill**) *fr 1930s* A ruffian; =GOON: *Strong-arm men, gorillas, and tough gangsters*—E Lavine/ *Those gorills do not care anything about law*—John O'Hara **3** *n fr 1930s* A hired killer; =HIT MAN **4** *v* To steal or rob with threat and violence: *if you let somebody gorilla you out of some* *money*—Claude Brown **5** *v* To beat up; savage; =CLOBBER: *If that doesn't work, we'll gorilla a little bit*—New York Times **6** *n* Anything very powerful and unstoppable; anything very forceful and intimidating: *a "gorilla," a product with a lot of momentum*—Wall Street Journal *See* SIX-HUNDRED-POUND GORILLA

gork *hospital* **1** *n* A stuporous or imbecilic patient; patient who has lost brain function: *The gork in that room has the "O" sign, did you notice?*—Elizabeth Morgan **2** *v* To sedate a patient heavily [originally fr *God only really knows*, referring to a patient with a mysterious ailment]

go-round *n* A turn; a repetition: *That was nice, let's have another go-round*

gorp[1] *v* To eat greedily [perhaps related to *gulp*]

gorp[2] *n* A food mixture of dried fruit, nuts, and seeds, consumed esp by hikers, alpinists, etc [thought to be fr *good old raisins* and *peanuts* and probably related to *gorp[1]*]

gorp gobbler *n phr* A hiker; backpacker: *A Nature-Loving Backpacker is a Gorp Gobbler*—Nevada

gosh *interj fr middle 1700s* A mild exclamation of pleasure, disbelief, surprise, etc: *Gosh but I'm tickled, Reverend* [a euphemism for *God*]

go shank's mare *See* RIDE SHANK'S MARE

◁ **go shit in your hat** ▷ *See* SHIT IN YOUR HAT

go slumming *See* SLUM

go snooks (or **snucks**) *v phr fr middle 1800s* To share equally; go half-and-half: *We are going to go snooks on an electric golf cart*—Milwaukee Tribune [fr British dialect *go snacks*, where *snacks* is related to earlier US *snook* "a bite to eat"; hence the idiom has to do originally with sharing something to eat]

go south *v phr* To disappear; fail by or as if by vanishing: *He played unbelievably... then all of a sudden he just went south*—Sports Illustrated/ *publicly accused him of going south on me*—Philadelphia Journal [probably fr the notion of disappearing *south of the border*, in particular the Mexican border, to escape legal pursuit and responsibility; probably reinforced by the widespread Native American belief that the soul after death journeys to the south, attested in American Colonial writing fr the mid-18th century]

gospel-pusher *n* A preacher; minister

go steady *v phr* To have a constant and only boyfriend or girlfriend: *Going steady means taking out one girl until a better one comes along*—Woman's Day

go straight *v phr fr underworld* To renounce a life of crime; reform

gotcha **1** *n* A wound or injury, usu minor like a slight razor slice incurred while shaving: *Remember the gotchas you got from that worn old wrench?* **2** *n* A capture; a catch; an arrest: *"This is a gotcha," Johnson allegedly told Jaffee*—Time [fr *got you*]

go the extra mile **1** *v phr* To make an extra effort; do more than usual: *It is time to communicate that. It is time to go that extra mile*—Garrison Keillor/ *You have to go the extra mile to prove your credibility*—Nancy Landon Kassebaum **2** *v phr* To make an extraordinary effort; persevere: *When elected, my friends, I promise to go the extra mile for you all and your beloved families*

go the full yard *v phr* To do the utmost; pursue something to the limit; =GO THE WHOLE HOG [compare with *the whole nine yards*]

go the limit (or **all the way**) *v phr* To do the sex act, as distinct from heavy petting, foreplay, etc: *all-American girl must not... "go the limit"*—Frederic Morton

go the whole hog or **go whole hog** *v phr fr early 1800s* To do the utmost; not slacken; pursue to the limit; =GO THE FULL YARD: *He decided to go the whole hog and buy a real big boat* [origin uncertain; *whole hog* may be primarily an amusing alliteration with suggestions of something impressively huge]

go the whole nine yards *v phr fr armed forces* To do the utmost; =GO THE LIMIT, GO THE WHOLE HOG: *I went the whole nine yards*—St Elsewhere's (TV program) [see the *whole nine yards*]

go through changes *fr black* **1** *v phr* To work very hard; strive; =HUSTLE **2** *v phr* To pass through various emotional difficulties; be unstable and unsure: *He has* *"gone through every change, from suicidal to who gives a shit"* —Toronto Life

go (or **be**) **through the mill** *v phr fr early 1800s* To have practical experience of something; be thoroughly seasoned: *I think you can rely on her, she's been through the mill*

go to bat for *v phr* To support or defend; help: *He knew his boss would go to bat for him*

go to bed with someone *v phr* To do the sex act with someone; =SLEEP WITH someone

go to Denmark *v phr* To have a sex-change operation [fr the fact that such operations were originally done primarily in Denmark]

go toe to toe *v phr* To fight, esp to fight hard; =SLUG IT OUT: *They are going toe-to-toe with Cosmo, Glamour*—Philadelphiapatting each other on the back—Philadelphia

◁**go to hell**▷ **1** *v phr* To deteriorate; be ruined: *The whole town's gone to hell, with that new mayor/ Old Joe's gone to hell a bit lately* **2** *sentence* May you be accursed, confounded, humiliated, etc; =DROP DEAD, GO FUCK oneself: *He wanted me to lie, but I told him to go to hell*

go to hell in a handbasket (or **a bucket**) *v phr* To deteriorate badly and rapidly: *White people can go to hell in a handbasket, they can go to Burger King and not have their way* —Washington Post

go to pot *v phr* To deteriorate; worsen: *A group of men who had literally and figuratively let themselves go to pot get back into good physical condition*—Psychology Today [fr the condition of an animal no longer useful for breeding, egg-laying, etc, that will now be cooked in the *pot*]

go (or **be taken**) **to the cleaners** *v phr* To lose all one's money, esp gambling at craps; =TAKE A BATH

go to the dogs *v phr fr 1500s* =GO TO HELL, GO TO POT [fr the notion that something unfit for human food would be given to the lowly *dogs*]

go to the mat *v phr* To fight; contend mightily: *They soon stopped sparring and went to the mat* [fr the *mat* used as a wrestling site]

go to the wall **1** *v phr* To be ruined and destitute; collapse: *if a real biggie, like Brazil, say, went to the wall*—Playboy **2** *v phr* To do the utmost; =GO ALL THE WAY: *We've gone to the wall for you*—Cagney and Lacey (TV program) [first sense fr the plight of someone being executed by being shot, against a *wall*]

go to (or **down to**) **the wire** *v phr* To be in very close competition until the very end; =be NIP AND TUCK: *The 1928 pennant race between the A's and the Yanks went to the wire*—Philadelphia

go to town **1** *v phr* To do very well; succeed; perform impressively **2** *v phr* To throw off restraint; let go

got to give *See* SOMETHING'S GOT TO GIVE

goulashes or **goolashes** (GōōO lash əz) *n* Galoshes, as amusingly mispronounced

go underground *v phr* To take up a concealed life; go into hiding, typically with a false identity, esp in order to avoid arrest: *He was able to go underground until the amnesty went into effect*

goup *See* GOOP

go up **1** *v phr narcotics* To become intoxicated from narcotics **2** *v phr musicians* To make a mistake in playing; =FLUFF **3** *v phr theater* =GO UP IN one's LINES

go up against *v phr* To confront; face; challenge: *So that's the kind of piffle actors have to go up against*—H McHugh/ *He wants to go up against the champ*

go up in one's **lines** *v phr theater fr early 1900s* To forget or badly misspeak one's lines during a performance; =GO UP IN THE AIR

go up in smoke *v phr* To be ruined; be destroyed: *He just saw his careful scam go up in smoke*

go up in the air **1** *v phr theater* To miss a cue, forget one's lines, etc; =FLUFF **2** *v phr fr early 1900s* To lose one's composure; become angry; =LOSE one's COOL: *You will rouse his anger, and he may "go up in the air"*—DS Martin

go (or **hit**) **upside** one's **face** (or **head**) **1** *v phr black* To beat and pummel, esp around the head **2** *v phr* To defeat utterly; trounce; =CLOBBER

go up the wall *See* CLIMB THE WALL

gourd *n fr middle 1800s* The head; skull

See LOSE one's GOURD, OUT OF one's HEAD

gow (GOU) **1** ***n*** *outdated narcotics fr early 1900s underworld* Opium **2** ***n*** *outdated narcotics* Any narcotic **3** ***n*** *outdated narcotics* A marijuana cigarette; =JOINT **4** ***n*** Pictures of unclad or scarcely clad women: *this type of artwork, which in the newspaper field is called "cheesecake" and in the paperbooks field is "gow"*—Publishers Weekly [fr Canton Chinese, *yao-kao*, "sap, opium"]

go whole hog *See* GO THE WHOLE HOG

go with the flow ***v phr*** *fr 1960s counterculture* To consign oneself to the order and pace of things; be passive: *They pondered a while and decided to go with the flow*—Tom Wolfe

go (or **come**) **with the territory** ***v phr*** To be an integral part of some occupation or status, esp a part which is not especially delightful: *Tierney's answer was that such speculation "goes with the territory"*—New York [fr the conditions implicit in a sales representative's covering of a certain *territory*, popularized by use in the Requiem section of Arthur Miller's play, *Death of a Salesman*]

gow job ***n phr*** *hot rodders* =HOT ROD

◁ **goy**▷ **1** ***n*** A non-Jew; Gentile: *My dad reads the Talmud all the time and hates goys*—Sinclair Lewis/ *He knows no more about the Torah than a goy*—Budd Schulberg **2** ***adj:*** *The mob's strictly goy*—American Mercury [fr Hebrew]

◁ **goyische**▷ (GOI ish ə) ***adj*** Non-Jewish; Gentile: *hotsy-totsy free weekend in Atlantic City, to a fancy goyische hotel*—Philip Roth

◁ **goyische kop**▷ ***n phr*** Gentile attributes as perceived by Jews in a somewhat hostile vein, esp when found in a Jewish person: *The first Jewish mayor will be one with a "goyische kop"*—Dick Schaap [fr Yiddish, "Gentile head"]

grab **1** ***v*** *police* An arrest; =BUST, PINCH: *We will get credit for the grab, and we will also profit*—Lawrence Sanders **2** ***v*** To seize the admiration or attention of; impress: *How does that grab you?*—New Yorker/ *to reflect on a whole lot of things that had been grabbing me*—New York Times

grab a handful of air ***v phr*** *truckers* To apply the brakes of a truck or bus quickly [fr the fact that such vehicles have *hand*-operated *air* brakes]

◁ **grab-ass** or **grabarse**▷ ***n*** Sexual touching and clutching: *just a little grab-ass between them/ my merry games of grabarse*—John Cheever *See* PLAY GRAB-ASS

grab-bag ***n*** A miscellaneous mixture; random collection: *the grab-bag of memories in my head*

grabber **1** ***n*** *railroad* A passenger-train conductor **2** ***n*** Anything that seizes and rivets the attention; something that commands immediate admiration; =HOOK: *Dance within the regular format is a solid grabber*—Variety

See GOOBER-GRABBER, MOTHERFUCKER

grabby **1** ***adj*** Greedy; acquisitive; selfish: *Share that, don't be grabby* **2** ***adj*** Seizing; arresting; riveting: *spent hours working on a goddamn grabby lead*—Armistead Maupin

grabs *See* UP FOR GRABS

grab your socks *See* DROP YOUR COCKS AND GRAB YOUR SOCKS

grad **1** ***n*** *fr late 1800s* A graduate: *college grad* **2** ***modifier:*** *a grad student/ grad reunion*

grade *See* EATIN' STUFF

the **grade** *See* MAKE THE GRADE

graft **1** ***n*** *fr late 1800s British* One's occupation; =GAME, RACKET **2** ***n*** *fr early 1900s* The acquisition of money by dishonest means, esp by bribery for political favors: *the usual charges of graft at City Hall* [origin unknown]

gramps ***n*** Grandfather; any old man: *Need any help, gramps?*

grand ***n*** *fr early 1900s underworld & sports* A thousand dollars; =GEE: *A banker would scarcely call one thousand dollars "one grand"*—JC Hixson [said to have originated with Peaches Van Camp, a criminal who flashed such *grand* notes for ostentation]

the **grand bounce** ***n phr*** =the BOUNCE

Grand Central Station ***n phr*** Any place that is overcrowded and busy: *My office was like Grand Central Station this morning*

grandfather or **granddaddy** **1** ***n*** The prime example of something; the oldest, biggest, chief; dean; doyen: *That must be the grandfather of all excuses* **2** ***v*** To give someone a special status or privilege because of service prior to the time a new or definitive arrangement is made: *They gave all the newly qualified a license on examination, and grandfathered the experienced ones* [the second sense is fr the *grandfather clause* often written into new arrangements in order to be fair to older incumbents or practitioners]

grandma *n truckers* The lowest and slowest gear of a truck

grand slam **1** *n phr* The winning of all the goals, games, prizes, etc, available; total comprehensive victory: *Nobody won the tennis grand slam last year* **2** *n phr baseball* =GRAND SLAMMER **3** *modifier: grand-slam home run* [fr a bridge term for the winning of all the tricks in one hand]

grand slammer *n phr baseball* A home run hit when all the bases are occupied, and scoring four runs

grandstand **1** *v fr late 1800s* To play or perform in a brilliant and spectacular way, esp in order to get the approval of an audience; =HOT DOG, SHOW OFF: *Coach told him to stop grandstanding and take care of business* **2** *modifier: a grandstand catch*

grandstand play **1** *n phr* A play made with special brilliance and brio, esp in order to impress the spectators **2** *n phr* Any action, speech, tactic, etc, designed to appeal to spectators; a tour de force: *The President's pronouncement's just a grandstand play*

granny dress *n phr fr 1960s* A floor-length dress, usu with long sleeves and a high neckline

granny flat *n phr* A small cottage or apartment where elderly people may live near but not actually with their childrens' family

granny glasses *n phr fr 1960s* Eyeglasses with small, circular steel or gold frames

grape *n* Wine or champagne

grapefruit league *n phr baseball* The association of major league teams as they play each other in preseason training [fr the fact that most spring training camps are held in citrus-growing regions]

grapevine *adj* Coming from an unofficial source of rumor or news: *a grapevine item/ grapevine gossip*

the **grapevine** *n phr fr Civil War* The source and route of rumors and unofficial news: *I heard it through the grapevine*—Norma Whitfield and Barrett Strong

grass **1** *n* Lettuce or other salad material; =BUNNY FOOD **2** *n black* The straight hair typical of Caucasians **3** *n narcotics* Marijuana; =POT: *Scoring grass here is easier than buying a loaf of bread*—New Yorker
See one's ASS IS GRASS

grass-cutter or **grass-clipper** *n baseball* A very low and hard line drive

grasseater *n* A corrupt police officer who accepts graft money but does not demand it: *repeated the distinction between the "grass eater" and the "meat eater"*—New York Times

grasshopper *n narcotics* A person who smokes marijuana; =POTHEAD: *My wife was a little grasshopper herself*—RV Winslow

grass widow *n phr fr late 1800s* A woman who is alone because of divorce, separation, rejection, etc [because her husband is still above the *grass* rather than under it]

gratis *See* FREE GRATIS

grave *See* HAVE ONE FOOT IN THE GRAVE

gravel *See* HIT THE DIRT

graveyard shift *n phr* A working shift that begins at midnight or 2 AM

graveyard watch *n phr railroad & Army* A period of guard or watch duty from midnight to 4 AM or 8 AM

gravy *n fr early 1900s* Money or other valuables beyond what one actually earns or needs; a bonus or excess: *Once we make back our expenses, everything is gravy*

gravy train (or **boat**) *n phr fr early 1900s sports* A chance, job, business, etc, that gives a very ample return for little or no work; an obvious sinecure: *His job's a permanent gravy train*
See ON THE GRAVY TRAIN, RIDE THE GRAVY TRAIN

◀**gray**▶ **1** *n black* A white person; Caucasian; =OFAY **2** *adj: What about that gray girl in San Jose?*
—Eldridge Cleaver

graybeard *n airline* A very senior pilot

gray market *n phr* The sale of reputable products, esp cameras and electronic equipment, by persons who have not bought them from the manufacturers' authorized distributors, and hence offer lower prices because the products do not qualify for the makers' guarantees

gray matter *n phr* Intelligence; =BRAINS, SMARTS

graze *v Army, prison & students* To eat a meal

greafa or **greapha** *See* GREEFA

grease **1** *n esp 1800s* Money **2** *n underworld fr 1930s* Bribe or protection money; money given for corrupt purposes **3** *n WW2 Army* Butter **4** *n* Influence; =PULL: *You can't get a job here without plenty of grease* **5** *v police* To shoot, esp to kill by shooting: *He has a gun and might try to grease you*—Rolling Stone **6** *n: You handled the grease real good, but not good enough, you didn't kill them*—Robert Daley [police senses fr the notion of *greasegun,* whether for lubricant or for bullets]
See ELBOW GREASE, GREASE someone's PALM

greaseball ◀**1**▶ *n* A dark-skinned, dark-haired person of Mediterranean or Latin American origin; =DAGO, GREASER: *taking knives away from greaseballs in zoot suits*—Raymond Chandler **2** *n hoboes* A dirty tramp **3** *n WW2 Navy* A cook or kitchen worker

greased lightning *n phr* Something or someone extraordinarily fast; =a BLUE STREAK: *He got out of there like greased lightning*

greasegun *n phr fr WW2 armed forces* A submachine gun, esp one with a cylindrical body resembling a lubricating grease gun: *The Army's present standard model, the M-3 "greasegun"*—Associated Press

grease monkey *n phr* A worker who lubricates machines, esp automobiles: *Good grease monkeys all, they could think better with a grease rack to lean against*—J Ellison

grease (or **cross** or **oil**) someone's **palm** *v phr* To pay for a corrupt purpose; bribe; buy favors: *If you grease the commissioner's palm, you can get anything fixed*—Jim Tully/ *Officials whose palms have been crossed*—A Hynd

◀**greaser**▶ **1** *n fr early 1800s* =GREASEBALL • Used esp in referring to a Mexican or an Italian **2** *n esp 1950s teenagers* A hoodlum, petty thief, etc; =PUNK [second sense fr the *grease* used for their typical combed-back hairstyle]

grease the skids *v phr* To cause or cooperate in the rapid decline or failure of someone or something: *When your time comes, you bastard, I hope I can grease the skids*

greasy **1** *adj* Repellent in an unctuous and cunning way; =OILY **2** *adj horse-racing* Muddy and slippery: *to negotiate a "greasy" mile before an approving audience*—Morning Telegraph

greasy grind *n phr fr early 1900s* A very diligent student

greasy spoon *n phr* A small, cheap restaurant, lunchroom, or diner: *The Marx brothers ate in coffee pots and greasy spoons*—Joel Sayre

great **1** *adj* Excellent; wonderful: *Hey, that's really great* **2** *n* A famous person, esp an athlete or entertainer: *Weiss, a former football "great"*—Philadelphia Inquirer

the **greatest** *n phr fr bop & cool talk* A person or thing of superlative quality; =the MOST

the **greatest thing since sliced bread** *See* the BEST THING SINCE SLICED BREAD

great shakes *See* NO GREAT SHAKES

greedball *n* Professional baseball as administered and played by very high-paid and wealthy persons

greefa *n* (Variations: **goifa** or **greafa** or **greapha** or **greefo** or **greeta** or **grefa** or **griefo** or **griffa** or **grifo**) *narcotics* Marijuana or a marijuana cigarette [fr Mexican Spanish *griffa* "weed"]

◁ **Greek fashion** (or **style**)▷ *adv phr* Anally: *They did it Greek fashion*

◁ the **Greek way** (or **style**)▷ **1** *n phr* Anal intercourse, esp heterosexual: *Another request is for Greek style. That is, anal sex*—Xaviera Hollander **2** *adv phr* =GREEK FASHION

green *n fr 1920s underworld & sports* Money, esp ready cash; =FOLDING MONEY: *plus "green" or "front money" to pay off others*—New York Times
See FOLDING MONEY, JERSEY GREEN, LONG GREEN, MEAN GREEN, SHIT GREEN

green (or **blue**) **around the gills** *adj phr* Sick-looking; pale and miserable; nauseated: *He was looking green* *around the gills so I told him to lie down*

green fly *See* FLY

green folding *n phr* =FOLDING MONEY

greenhorn *n fr middle 1800s* An inexperienced person; newcomer; neophyte; =ROOKIE

greenie **1** *n* =GREENHORN **2** *n narcotics* A heart-shaped green stimulant pill of dextroamphetamine: *Do you take something, like greenies?* —Sports Illustrated

the **green light** *n phr* Permission, esp a superior's approval to proceed; =the GO-AHEAD: *Once she gives us the green light, we crank it up*

greenmail *n* The buying, at a premium price, of the stock holdings of someone who is threatening to take over a company, in order to induce the person to cease the attempt: *But Wall Street analysts agreed that CBS was unlikely to consider such action, since it amounts to "greenmail"* —New York Daily News [modeled on *blackmail*]

the **green stuff** *n phr* Money; ready cash; paper money; =FOLDING MONEY, LONG GREEN: *He really poured the green stuff to the bookies*—S Frank

a **green thumb** **1** *n phr* A special talent for gardening **2** *n phr* The ability to make projects succeed, like flourishing plants: *possessor of a green thumb when it comes to making musicals blossom*—H Ormsbee

greeta or **grefa** *See* GREEFA

gremlin **1** *n WW2 Army Air Force fr British perhaps fr WWI* An imaginary imp who caused malfunction in machines, problems in projects, confusion in arrangements, etc **2** *n surfers* A person, esp a girl, who frequents surfing beaches without surfing; =BEACH BUNNY: *gremlins, usually girls, those hangers-on who may never get wet*—Time [origin unknown; probably modeled on *goblin*, with the first syllable perhaps fr Irish *gruaimin* "irascible little creature"]

gremmy or **gremmie** *n* =GREMLIN

grette *See* GRIT

greyhound therapy *n phr* The practice by some municipalities or other governmental groups of ridding themselves of the homeless and other potentially burdensome persons by giving them a bus ticket to another place: *Greyhound therapy... giving the homeless a one-way bus ticket to Los Angeles*—New York Times [fr the name of the *Greyhound* bus company]

grid or **gridiron** **1** *n* A football field **2** *modifier: the grid squad/ gridiron victories*

gridlock *n* A blockage; paralysis: *Until the emotional and psychological gridlock over the Federal deficit is broken*—Newsweek [fr the traffic term designating a total blockage of traffic caused by cars stopping in intersections behind other stopped cars, and blocking traffic on the intersecting street]

grief *See* GIVE someone GRIEF

griefo or **grifo** or **griffa** *See* GREEFA

grind **1** *v fr middle 1800s* To rotate one's pelvis in the sex act or in imitation of the sex act • Nearly always in combination with **bump**: *the strippers bumping and grinding away* **2** *n: to wow the audience with her bumps and grinds*—Trans-Action **3** *v fr middle 1800s* To study diligently: *Five days to grind and two days to be social... the way it was at Yale*—Sexual Behavior **4** *n: No one except a few notorious grinds studied that night*—P Marks **5** *n* Any obnoxious or annoying person; =JERK, a PAIN IN THE NECK, PILL: *The prof's a tedious old grind* **6** *n* Any very difficult and trying task, esp one that lasts a long time and is slowly and painfully done: *Writing dictionaries is indeed a grind*

See GREASY GRIND

grinder **1** *n* A stripteaser; =STRIPPER **2** *n* A car, esp an old and ramshackle one: *bought a brand new Chev to take the place of her old grinder*—J Lilienthal **3** *n* =HERO SANDWICH **4** *n Marine Corps* A parade ground; drill field

See COFFEE GRINDER

grind-house or **grind movie** *n* or *n phr theater* A theater that runs continuously without intermissions, holidays, etc: *Four years ago, it would have been restricted to a few downtown grind-houses*—Time [probably fr *grind show*, perhaps influenced by the burlesque and sexual connotations of *grind*]

grinding *See* BIT-GRINDING

grind something **out** *v phr* To produce or make something, esp with uninspired precision or long and painful effort: *They sat down and ground the script out in two days/ They just grind them out... ten a day*

grind show *n phr outdated carnival* A show that runs continuously [probably because the show *grinds* along like a machine]

grip **1** *n theater & movie studio* A stagehand or stage carpenter: *crowded with assistant directors, character actors, movie stars, grips and electricians*—H Niemeyer **2** *n fr middle 1800s* A travelling bag; valise [second sense a shortening of *gripsack*]

gripe **1** *v fr late 1800s* To complain, esp habitually and trivially; groan; =BITCH, KVETCH, PISS: *He got good and sore and griped*—Morris Bishop **2** *n: I want to clear my desk of various matters, mostly gripes*—Bernard DeVoto **3** *v* To annoy or disgust; exasperate: *What's griping him is that he can't do anything for the kids*—James T Farrell [ultimately fr *griping of the gut* "colic, bellyache, stomach cramp"]

◁ **gripe** one's **ass**▷ *v phr* (Variations: **balls** or **butt** or **cookies** or **left nut** or **middle kidney** or **soul**, or some other organ or possession at the whim of the speaker, may replace **ass**) To disgust or annoy someone extremely: *His sycophancy gripes my ass*

the **gripes** **1** *n phr* A spell of complaining; =BITCHING **2** *n phr* The habit of frequent or trivial complaining

gripe session *n phr* A conversation or discussion consisting primarily of complaints

grit **1** *n fr late 1700s* Courage; fortitude and stamina **2** *v black* To eat **3** *n* (also **grits**) *black fr 1930s* Food **4** *n* A Southerner: *He's a hotshot down here among the grits*—Pat Conroy **5** *n* (also **Grit**) *Southern* A Northerner: *It's a God's wonder some Grit didn't kill us*—Harry Crews **6** *n* (also **grette**) A cigarette [food senses at least partially fr *hominy grits*, although *grit* was British military slang for "food" in the 1930s; Southern dialect sense probably ironically fr Civil War use of the expression *true Yankee grit* by Northern soldiers and writers]

See HIT THE DIRT

gritty *See* the NITTY GRITTY

groady or **groaty** or **groddy** *See* GROTTY

groaner *n* A singer, esp a crooner of the 1930s *See* GRUNT-AND-GROANER

groceries *See* BRING HOME THE BACON

groggy *adj fr late 1700s British* Sleepy; dazed; semiconscious

grog-mill **1** *n* A saloon; tavern **2** *modifier: no grog-mill cuties*—J Evans

◀ **groid**▶ *n esp Southern & college students* A black person: *The groids sure love to fish*—John McPhee [fr *Negroid*]

grok (GRAHK) **1** *v esp 1960s counterculture & students* To communicate sympathetically: *all rapping and grokking over the sound it made*—Tom Wolfe **2** *v esp 1960s counterculture & students* To get into exquisite sympathy with: *She met him at an acid-rock ball and she grokked him*—Playboy **3** *v esp computer* To understand: *You've come to grok that Cronenberg's narrative is merely the pretense for his imagery*—Village Voice [coined by Robert A Heinlein as a Martian word in the science-fiction novel *Stranger in a Strange Land*]

grollo *n* =GROWLER

gronk out *v phr computer* To cease functioning: *The terminal gronked out about ten minutes ago*

grooby *adj fr jive talk* Excellent; =GROOVY: *You, too, can get on the grooby side*—Time

groove **1** *n* Any habitually preferred activity; what excites and gratifies one; =BAG, KICK **2** *v* To enjoy intensely; take gratification, esp rather passively and subjectively; =GO WITH THE FLOW: *To groove means to yield yourself to the flow of activity around you*—New York Times/ *If you want to groove, go get yourself some groovy clothes*—New York **3** *v* To like and approve; =DIG: *They see the spade cat going with ofay chicks and they don't groove it*—R DeWolf **4** *v* To perform very well; be effective: *really grooving on that funny trumpet* [fr the sense that a musician is in a definite and exciting track, has hit a perfect stride, when playing well, esp a solo; perhaps influenced by the *grooves* of a phonograph record]

See IN THE GROOVE

a **groove** ***n phr*** Something excellent, desirable, exciting, etc: *Your hat is a groove*—Harper's Bazaar

groove on something or someone ***v phr*** To enjoy intensely; =GROOVE: *I can really groove on the Beatles* —New York Times/ *She walks for blocks grooving on Reality*—Gail Sheehy

groovy **1** ***adj*** *jive talk fr 1930s* Playing and enjoying music well and with concentration; =HEP, IN THE GROOVE **2** ***adj*** Excellent; wonderful; =FAR OUT: *"Hey, groovy," said Sally*—Max Shulman **3** ***adj*** *teenagers* Obsolete; out-of-date: *She was wearing groovy saddle-shoes*

grope ***v*** To touch, feel, caress, fondle, etc, with seeming or actual sexual intent

See GROUP-GROPE

grope-in ***n*** =GROUP-GROPE

gross ***adj*** *esp teenagers fr 1960s* Disgusting; rebarbative; =GROTTY: *at this moment (how gross!) blowing kisses into the phone*—Erich Segal

grossed out ***adj phr*** *esp teenagers & students fr 1960s* Disgusted; revulsed

gross-out *esp teenagers fr 1960s* **1** ***n*** Something particularly disgusting; repellent trash: *He attempts... the ultimate gross-out: "self-expression" of the kind found in Greenwich Village*—Newsweek **2** ***modifier:*** *The Animal House gross-out movies are all about groups*—New York/ *gross-out scenes of the Dalmatian mounting the smaller dog*—Toronto Life

gross someone **out** ***v phr*** *esp teenagers fr 1970s* To disgust or offend, esp with crude and obscene language and behavior: *They're grossing me out too, you know*—Cyra McFadden/ *Being a mother really grosses me out* —Erma Bombeck

grotty (GROH dee, -tee) **1** ***adj*** (Variations: **groady** or **groaty** or **groddy**; **to the max** may be added) *esp teenagers fr 1960s* Disgusting; nasty; repellent; bizarre; =GRUNGY, SCUZZY: *The magazines had covers with those grotty weirdos on them* —Philadelphia **2** ***noun:*** *the introspective hedonism and political individualism of the second group... called groddies*—Trans-Action [fr *grotesque*; popularized by the Beatles in the 1960s; perhaps fr Merseyside dialect]

ground ***See*** NOT KNOW one's ASS FROM one's ELBOW, RUN something INTO THE GROUND, STAMPING GROUND

ground someone ***v phr*** To deny privileges to, esp to keep confined at home as a punishment: *If my father got a pair of bell-bottoms, I think I'd ground him*—McCall's [fr the practice of not permitting a pilot to fly, as a punishment]

ground floor ***See*** IN ON THE GROUND FLOOR

group ***See*** IN GROUP

group-grope **1** ***n*** Mutual touching and caressing by a group of people, either plainly orgiastic or with some sort of psychotherapeutic intent; =GROPE-IN **2** ***n*** Intimate intertwining of entities: *Harvard will reestablish an independent department of sociology, ending 24 years of interdisciplinary group-grope*—John Leonard

groupie *fr 1960s rock and roll* **1** ***n*** A young woman who seeks to share the glamor of famous persons, esp rock musicians, by offering help and sexual favors; =BUNNY: *a story about "groupies"... youthful females committing sexual aggression against juvenile rock musicians/ No fool, no groupie, no teeny-bopper, she takes rock music, rightly, seriously*—Vogue **2** ***n*** An ardent devotee and votary; =FAN: *like many of Hollywood's young trendies, a political groupie* —Newsweek **3** ***modifier:*** *the "groupie" syndrome, personified by adulatory novices of science flocking around the luminaries*—Dan Greenberg

grouse ***v*** *fr late 1800s British armed forces* To complain; =BITCH: *No grousing, no foot-dragging, both signs of a solid pro*—Harper's

growl ***v*** To complain; mutter angrily

growler **1** ***n*** (also **grollo**) *esp late 1800s* A container used to carry beer home from a bar: *A can brought in filled with beer at a barroom is called a growler*—B Matthews **2** ***n*** *WW2 Navy* A public-address loudspeaker or system; =BITCH BOX, SQUAWK BOX **3** ***n*** A small iceberg

See RUSH THE GROWLER

growth ***modifier*** Becoming or likely to become more vigorous, valuable, profitable, etc: *Cancer research is a growth industry*

grub 1 *n fr late 1800s cowboys* Food: *goods one can exchange at the kitchen door for grub*—Jack London **2** *v black: Come over and grub with us*—O Johnson [fr *grub stake*, the food provided for miners or prospectors who would go out to dig (*grub*) for useful ore]

grubstake *n fr middle 1800s* The money needed for a new venture, new start, etc: *Nobody knows how much he gave away in grubstakes*—T Betts

grunge or **grunch** (GRUHNJ, GRUHNCH) *teenagers* **1** *n* A dull, tedious person; =NERD, PILL **2** *adj* Boring **3** *adj* =GRUNGY **4** *n* Slovenliness; sloppiness **5** *n* Something nasty: *Look at the grunge at the bottom of that bottle/ those globs of guitar grunge*—Village Voice

grungy (GRUHN jee) *adj teenagers fr 1960s* Shabby; squalid; dirty; =GROTTY, SCUZZY: *I put down in my grungy little notebook that Max Frisch was a wise man*—C Vetter [origin unknown; perhaps sound symbolism resembling *gross, mangy, mung, stingy*, etc]

grunt 1 *n line repairers* A line repairer's helper who works on the ground and does not climb poles **2** *n railroad* A locomotive engineer **3** *n fr Vietnam War armed forces* An infantry soldier; =PADDLEFOOT: *I was drafted... and served twelve months as a grunt in Vietnam*—Newsweek **4** *n* Any low-ranking person, neophyte, etc: *The attitude among the reporter grunts was pretty much "them against us"*—Washingtonian **5** *n* Pork or ham; pig meat **6** *n* A bill for food or drink: *I just hope Toots didn't bring along any of the grunts I must have left in that oasis*—Paul Sann **7** *n* A diligent student; =GRIND: *A grunt is a student who gives a shit about nothing except his sheepskin*—Stephen King **8** *n* A wrestler, esp an inferior one; =GRUNT-AND-GROANER **9** *n* Wrestling, as sport and entertainment **10** *modifier: the grunt scene/ grunt show on TV* **11** *v* To defecate

grunt-and-groaner *n* A wrestler

grunter *n* A wrestler

grunt work (or **labor**) *n phr* Hard and/or tedious toil; =SCUT WORK: *The machine will do the grunt work*—San Francisco

G-string *See* GEE STRING

guardhouse lawyer *n phr fr middle 1800s Army* =LATRINE LAWYER

guck (GUHK) *n* Any sticky, viscous substance; =GOO, GLOP: *Joan has white guck all over her face*—Philadelphia

guess *See* BY GUESS AND BY GOD

guff 1 *n fr late 1800s* Nonsense; pretentious talk; bold and deceitful absurdities; =BULLSHIT: *his ability to listen to all the guff, through all the tedium*—Time **2** *n* Complaints, abuse: *Don't take any guff from him*—New Yorker **3** *v* To lie; exaggerate; =BULLSHIT: *Quit your guffing and tell it right* [perhaps fr British dialect *guff* "fool," or Scots "a puff of wind"]

guide *See* TOUR GUIDE

the **guilties** *n phr* Feelings or pangs of guilt: *Sometimes... we get the guilties on this account*—Newsweek

◀ **Guinea** ▶ (GIHN ee) (also **ghinney** or **ginee** or **ginnee** or **ginney** or **guin** or **guinea** or **guinie**; any of the variants may begin with a capital letter) *fr late 1800s* **1** *n* An Italian or person of Italian descent **2** *adj: a tough Ginney bootlegger*—Damon Runyon **3** *n WW2 armed forces* A native of a Pacific island, including Japan [perhaps fr contemptuous association with the outdated term *Guinea Negro* "black slave from the Guinea coast"]

◀ **guinzo** ▶ *See* GINZO

gully *See* HOLLY-GOLLY

gully-low *adj jazz musicians* Sensuous; insinuating; =DIRTY, SEXY

gumbah *See* GOOMBAH

gumball 1 *n* The lights carried atop a police car; =PARTY HAT: *Don't believe in gumballs. I kinda like to sneak around, you know*—Car and Driver **2** *v: a dozen police cars blocking the streets, their red-and-blue lights gumballing in all directions*—Playboy

gum-beating 1 *n jive talk* A conversation; chat; =RAP **2** *n* Vain and exaggerated talk; =BALONEY, BULLSHIT

gumby *n Canadian teenagers* A dull, tedious person, esp one out of touch with current fashions; =NERD, PILL:

You can become a gumby... by wearing the wrong plaid stretch pants —The Globe and Mail [perhaps fr a repulsive character, Mr *Gumby*, in the television series "Monty Python's Flying Circus," and somehow related to a person-shaped toy rubber figure named *Gumby*]

gummy 1 *adj esp 1930s* Inferior; tedious; unpleasant: *He found himself in a very gummy situation, with both of them berating him* **2** *adj esp 1940s* Sentimental; maudlin; =CORNY: *a gummy, gooey tearjerker of a film* [first two senses, like *icky* and *sticky*, fr the unpleasant feel of glue or slime]

gums *See* BAT one's GUMS

gumshoe 1 *n* (Variations: **gum boot** or **gumfoot** or **gumheel** or **gumshoe man**) *fr early 1900s* A police officer, esp a detective or plainclothes officer **2** *v* (also **gumheel**) To work as a police officer or detective: *Still gumheeling?* —R Starnes **3** *v* To walk a police beat: *Police now ride prowl cars instead of gumshoeing around the block*—EB White **4** *v* To walk quietly and stealthily [fr *gumshoe* "rubber-soled shoe"]

gum up or **gum up the works** *v phr* To ruin; spoil; throw into confusion; =BOLLIX UP, FUCK UP

gun[1] **1** *n fr middle 1800s* An armed criminal: *They hired a gun to blast the competition* **2** *v fr late 1800s* To shoot someone: *Canales had no motive to gun Lou*—Raymond Chandler **3** *n* An important person; =BIG GUN: *He's quite a gun around there now* **4** *n fr 1920s* The throttle of a car, airplane, etc: *Get your stupid foot off the gun* **5** *v* To speed up an engine or vehicle, esp abruptly; =GOOSE: *He gunned the Rolls into the parking spot*

See BIG GUN, BURP GUN, GIVE IT THE GUN, GREASEGUN, JUMP THE GUN, SCATTERGUN, SIX-SHOOTER, SMOKING GUN, SON OF A BITCH, TOMMY GUN, ZIP GUN

gun[2] *n* (also **gon**) *fr early 1800s* A professional thief, esp a pickpocket [fr Yiddish *gonif*]

gunboats *fr late 1800s* **1** *n* A pair of shoes or galoshes, esp of large size: *He brought some of the 14EE gunboats with him from the States* —Associated Press **2** *n* A pair of large feet

gunbunny *n Army* An artillery operator

gunch 1 *n* An attempt to influence the roll of a pinball **2** *v: the body English, the nudging, gunching* —Time

gun someone **down** *v phr* To shoot so as to fell or kill: *They gunned him down in a barber chair*

gun (or **go gunning**) **for** someone *v phr* To seek out or pursue with harmful intent; aim to punish: *He gunned for her after she slapped him with a lawsuit*

gung ho *adj phr fr WW2 Marine Corps* Very zealous; totally committed; enthusiastic: *They were gung ho about the opportunity*—New Yorker [fr the name of a Chinese industrial cooperative organization, adopted as *Gung ho*! to be the battle cry of a Marine Corps raiders group in World War 2]

guniff *See* GONIFF

gunk or **goonk 1** *n* Any sticky, viscous liquid, esp hair tonic, cosmetics, lubricants, or cleaning fluids; =GLOP, GUCK **2** *n* Dirt; slime; oily grime; muck: *The anchor was clotted in noisome gunk* [fr a trade name, *Gunk*, and part of a cluster of nearly synonymous terms beginning with *g*-; perhaps a blend of *goo* and *junk*]

gun moll *n phr fr late 1800s* A female criminal or a criminal's consort [fr *gonif* rather than fr the firearm]

gunner *n* A flashy performer; =HOT DOG: *the reputation of a gunner and a hot dog, playground terms for players who showboat*—New York Times

guns *See* HEAVY ARTILLERY

gunsel[1] *n* (also **gonsil** or **gonzel** or **guncel** or **guntzel** or **gunzl**) *underworld fr early 1900s hoboes & prison* A sexually vulnerable boy or young man; catamite; =PUNK [fr Yiddish *gantzel* "gosling"]

gunsel[2] *n* (Variations: see **gunsel**[1]) An armed criminal; hoodlum: *The reformed gunzl took a quick gander* —Paul Sann/ *scores of hoodlums, gunsels, informers, shyster lawyers, and crooked shamuses*—SJ Perelman [fr a blend of *gonif*, *gunsel*[1], *gunman*, etc]

gun-slinger *n fr cowboys* An armed criminal: *The gun-slinger will spend... his life behind bars*—Associated Press

guru 1 *n fr 1960s* A leader, expert, or authority in some field, esp a charismatic or spiritual figure who attracts a devoted following: *That genial guru of the right, Barry Goldwater*—Tom Wicker **2** *n* A psychiatrist; =SHRINK **3** *n narcotics & counterculture* A person who aids and supports someone having a psychedelic drug experience [fr Sanskrit, "venerable"]

Gus ***See*** GLOOMY GUS

gussy up 1 *v phr* To dress in one's best clothes; adorn oneself; =DOLL UP **2** *v phr* To clean or make neat: *We gussied up the room before they came* **3** *v phr* To decorate or elaborate on a plain design **4** *v phr* To refurbish, renovate; polish: *They're gussying up the same old tiredness*—Village Voice **5** *v phr* To decorate; make fancy: *It resembled a gussied-up Studebaker*—Philadelphia [origin unknown; perhaps fr *gusset*, a triangular insert that might be used to prettify a dress; perhaps fr someone or some place named Augusta]

gut 1 *n* The stomach; abdomen; paunch; =BAY WINDOW, POTBELLY **2** *adj* Basic; essential; most immediate: *the gut issues in the forthcoming election*—Newsweek **3** *adj* Deep and not essentially rational; visceral; intuitive: *He has to convince me on a gut level that I can do things my mind resists*—Playboy **4** *n* =GUT COURSE **5** *adj: a "gut" humanities course where the professor is said to put on a good show*—David Riesman **6** *v beat & cool talk fr hot rodders* To remove all unessentials; =STRIPPED DOWN

See BUST A GUT, POTBELLY, PUS-GUT, ROTGUT, SPILL one's GUTS, SPLIT A GUT, TUB OF GUTS

gutbucket 1 *n jazz musicians fr early 1900s* A strongly rhythmic, emotionally evocative, uninhibited style of jazz: *puts toe-tapping tunes atop the complicated counterpoint... .I've started calling this music avant-gutbucket for its brains, historical sweep, and down-home emotion*—New York Times **2** *n* A fat, pompous person [first sense fr a New Orleans name for a low resort, where a *gutbucket*, that is, a beer bucket or a chamber pot, would be used to collect contributions for the musicians; second sense fr the notion of *a bucket of guts*]

gut course *n phr* (also **gut**) *college students* An easy course in college: *In his senior year, he needed all the gut courses he could find/ Basic religion course was considered a "gut"*—WE Chilton III

gut it out *v phr* To be strong and resistant; be sturdily stoic; persist; =TOUGH IT OUT: *Cook claimed that he was innocent of any wrongdoing and until last week insisted that he would "gut it out"*—Time

gut reaction *n phr* An immediate and instinctive response; an intuition; =HUNCH: *if the public-opinion polls and gut reaction count for anything*—Philadelphia

guts 1 *n* The insides of a person, machine, etc; viscera; =INNARDS: *He removed the cover and exposed the guts* **2** *n* The most essential material or part; essence: *The guts of the matter is that they are not here* **3** *n fr late 1800s British* Courage; nerve; =BALLS: *the guy who had guts enough to croak "Tough Tony"*—E Lavine

See HATE someone's GUTS, SPILL one's GUTS, TUB OF GUTS

gutsy 1 *adj* Brave: *a gutsy lady* **2** *adj* Energetic and tough; =ZINGY: *a gutsy car*

gutter ***See*** HAVE one's MIND IN THE GUTTER

guttersnipe or **gutterpup** *n fr middle 1800s* A vulgar person; a vile wretch

gutty 1 *adj* Forceful and assertive: *a good gutty rock number*—John Clellon Holmes **2** *adj* =GUTSY **3** *adj* =GUT **4** *adj hot rodders* Capable of high speed; having a powerful engine

guy 1 *v esp late 1800s* To mock; ridicule **2** *n fr late 1800s* A person of either sex, esp a man; fellow **3** *n* A woman's fiance, husband, lover, etc: *Just remember he's my guy* [ultimately fr the name and reputation of *Guy* Fawkes, and esp of his ugly effigies burnt in England on November 5 to commemorate the foiling of the Gunpowder Plot, his plot to blow up the houses of Parliament]

See FALL GUY, ONE OF THE BOYS, REGULAR FELLOW, RIGHT GUY, SMART GUY, TOUGH GUY, WISE GUY

guzzle **1** *v fr 1500s* To drink, esp rapidly: *He guzzled a Coke* **2** *v* To drink liquor, esp to excess: *He guzzled a lot when he got worried* **3** *n* =GOOZLE [fr French *gosier* "throat," or, perhaps like the French word, echoically based on the sound of swallowing]

gweebo *n college students* A tedious and contemptible person; =DORK, NERD

gyp or **gip** or **jip** **1** *n* A gypsy **2** *n* (also **gyp artist** or **gypster**) *fr late 1800s* A swindler; cheater; =CROOK: *denunciations of punks, tinhorns, and gyps*—Westbrook Pegler **3** *modifier: a gyp joint/ gyp terms* **4** *v fr 1920s* To cheat; swindle; =CON: *We got gypped out of it all in two days*—F Scott Fitzgerald **5** *n: the victim of any such gyp*—James M Cain **6** *n cabdrivers* A cabdriver who does not start the meter [fr *gypsy; grip* "thief" is attested fr the mid-19th century]

gyp joint *n phr* Any business place that overcharges, cheats, etc; =CLIP JOINT: *Cops tried to shut down the midtown gyp joint*

gyppy tummy *n phr* Diarrhea, esp as it afflicts travelers • Chiefly British, reflecting former Empire territory: *In the Middle East, it's gyppy tummy and Basra belly*—New York Times [fr British *gyppy* "Egyptian"]

gypsy **1** *n* =GYPSY CAB **2** *n truckers* A truck driven by its owner rather than a union driver **3** *n truckers* An owner-driver; an independent trucker **4** *v gambling* To make a risky bet or call: *You will find players consistently gypsying, flat-calling with kings up or less*—Gambling Times

gypsy cab *n phr* A taxicab operating without a taxi license or medallion, or with only a livery license that does not entitle them to pick up passengers on the street: *the advent of the latest taxi competitor: the gypsy cab*—Society

gyrene or **girene** (jī REEN) *n fr 1920s Annapolis* A US Marine; =LEATHERNECK [perhaps fr alteration of *GI Marine*]

gyve *See* JIVE

H

H *n narcotics* Heroin
See BIG H

haba-haba (HAH bə HAH bə) *interj WW2 armed forces* An exhortation or request for speed or immediate action [see *hubba-hubba*]

habit *See* GARBAGE HABIT, ICE CREAM HABIT

hack[1] **1** *n fr early 1900s* A taxicab **2** *v: I worked in an office for years ....Then I took to "hacking"*—Hal Boyle **3** *n* A taxicab driver **4** *adj: a hack license* **5** *n bus drivers* A bus **6** *n railroad* A caboose [ultimately fr *hackney* "horse", fr *Hackney*, a village incorporated into London, fr Old English "Haca's island" or "hook island"; presumably the horses were associated with the place]

hack[2] **1** *n* A persistent, often nervous, cough: *oughta see someone about that hack* **2** *v: If you quit smoking maybe you won't hack like that* **3** *n fr early 1800s* A try; attempt; =WHACK: *Let Mark take a hack at it* **4** *v* To cope with, esp successfully; manage; =HANDLE • Most often in the negative: *"I can't hack this," Sandy remarked*—New Yorker **5** *v* (also **hack at**) To attempt; do persistently but mediocrely: *Do I play tennis? Well, I hack at it* **6** *n* A mediocre performer or worker; a drudge: *they are not the hacks that Eric's scholarship would make them*—Changes **7** *v: They hacked for some of our most respected... leaders*—Washington Post **8** *n* (also **hack writer**) *fr early 1800s* A professional, usu freelance, writer who works to order • This sense belongs to **hack**[1], reflecting the notion that such a writer was for hire like a horse, but is placed here because its own derivatives blend with those of **hack**[2], esp "try, stroke, etc" **9** *n computer* A computer program, esp a good one: *A well-crafted program, a good hack, is elegant*—Rolling Stone **10** *v computer* To work with a computer or computer program, esp to do so cleverly, persistently, and enthusiastically • The term has many specialized senses in computer slang, which alter too rapidly for practical account **11** *v fr late 1800s Southern* To annoy; anger; =BURN: *That attitude really hacks me* **12** *n prison* A guard: *The guards, the hacks, as they called them*—Claude Brown **13** *n black & prison* A white person; =HONKY, OFAY [nearly all senses ultimately fr *hack* "cut, chop"; black and prison senses fr identification of prison guards with white persons in the pattern identical with that of *the man*; prison guards perhaps so called because they sometimes beat prisoners]

hack around *v phr* To do nothing in particular; idle; loaf; =BEAT AROUND: *He says he's been hacking around in some bar*—George V Higgins

hacked *adj* (also **hacked off**) *fr 1940s black* Annoyed; angered; chagrinned: *I don't know what made him so hacked about it/ How come you're so hacked off about Combs?* —WT Tyler

hacker[1] *n* (also **hackey** or **hackie**) A taxicab driver: *He enriched another hacker by an even $5,000*—Associated Press/ *He actually found a* *hackie named Louis Schweitzer* —World

hacker[2] ***n*** A persistent but generally unskillful performer or athlete; =DUFFER

hacker[3] **1** ***n*** *computer* An energetic and skillful computer programmer, often perfectionistic: *When a hacker programs, he creates worlds* —Rolling Stone **2** ***n*** *computer* Anyone who works with computers or computer programs, esp one who does so enthusiastically • The term has many senses in computer slang, which change too rapidly for practical account [said to be fr *hack*[2], computer jargon for a clever and subtle correction of a flow in a computer program]

hack hand ***n phr*** *truckers* A trucker

hack it ***v phr*** *fr loggers* To cope successfully; =CUT IT, HANDLE • Often in the negative: *John Fist can't hack it any more*—Webster Schott

hack-skinner ***n*** *bus drivers* A bus driver [fr *mule-skinner*]

be **had** (or **taken** or **took**) **1** ***v phr*** To become a partner in the sex act **2** ***v phr*** To be duped or cheated; be victimized: *You practically need a finance degree to know that you are being had*—Newsweek

had it ***See*** one HAS HAD IT

ha-ha **1** ***n*** A joke; something funny; stroke of wit: *That's a ha-ha all right* —Ira Wolfert **2** ***adj:*** *even made a ha-ha pass at him*—Psychology Today ***See*** the MERRY HA-HA

the **Haight** ***n phr*** =HASHBURY

haimish or **heimish** (HAY mish) ***adj*** Friendly and informal; unpretentious; cozy: *No one in his right mind would ever call Generals de Gaulle or MacArthur haimish*—Leo Rosten [fr Yiddish, with root of *haim* "home"]

hair ***n*** *computer* Complexity: *a system with a lot of hair*

See CURL someone's HAIR, FAIRHAIRED BOY, GET IN someone's HAIR, GOOD HAIR, HAVE A BUG UP one's ASS, HAVE someone BY THE SHORT HAIRS, IN someone's HAIR, LET one's HAIR DOWN, LONGHAIR

haired ***See*** LONGHAIR

hairnet ***See*** WIN THE PORCELAIN HAIRNET

the **hair of the dog** (or **of the dog that bit** one) ***n phr*** A drink of liquor taken as a remedy for a hangover [fr the belief that the bite of a *dog* could be healed by applying its *hair* to the wound]

◁ **hair pie**▷ **1** ***n phr*** Cunnilingus; =BOX LUNCH **2** ***n phr*** The female genitalia; the vulva; =PUSSY

hairpin ***See*** DROP BEADS

hairy **1** ***adj*** Old; hoary: *a hairy tale* **2** ***adj*** Difficult; rough; =TOUGH: *We had a hairy time getting it all organized* **3** ***adj*** *esp teenagers fr 1960s* Frighteningly dangerous; hair-raising; scary: *campus guards would comb the dorm.... "It was hairy"*—New Yorker/ *the hairy strip of 42d Street* —New York Times [last sense probably fr the *hairy* monsters of horror films, but the sense of "difficult" was used at 19th-century Oxford, and that of "dangerous" in the British armed forces of the 1930s]

hairy eyeball ***See*** GIVE someone THE FISH-EYE

half ***See*** DEUCE AND A HALF, a LAUGH, OTHER HALF

◁ **half-assed**▷ ***adj*** *fr late 1800s* Foolish; ineffectual; stupid: *You first ran into censorship problems with the words "half-assed games"*—Rolling Stone [perhaps fr a humorous mispronunciation of *haphazard*]

half-bagged ***adj*** Drunk: *They keep half-bagged all day and bore their new friends silly with stories*—Lawrence Sanders

half-baked ***adj*** *fr early 1600s* Foolish; ill-conceived; not completely thought out; =HALF-ASSED

half-buck or **half a buck** ***n*** or ***n phr*** A half-dollar; fifty cents

half cocked **1** ***adv*** Prematurely; unprepared: *not going into this half cocked*—Max Shulman **2** ***adj:*** *a half-cocked start* [see *go off half cocked*]

half-corned ***adj*** Drunk

half crocked ***adj phr*** Drunk; half-drunk: *laying around on a settee, sort of half crocked*—SJ Perelman

halfies or **halvies** or **halvsies** ***n*** *fr late 1800s* One half of what is indicated, esp as an equal share: *I claimed halvsies because I did most of the work*

See GO HALFIES

half in the bag ***adj phr*** Drunk; half-drunk: *He was half in the bag. He always is at Christmas*—Playboy

half load *n phr narcotics* Fifteen packets of a narcotic, esp of cocaine or heroin

half-pint **1** *n* A short person: *the little half-pint that she was*—John O'Hara **2** *modifier: half-pint showman*—United Press **3** *n* A boy

half-shot **1** *adj* Drunk; half-drunk: *when they were half shot with beer* —James M Cain **2** *adj* Nearly ravaged; deteriorating: *Her nerves are half shot*

half-stewed *adj* (Variations: **screwed** or **slewed** or **snaped** or **sprung** may replace **stewed**) Drunk; half-drunk

half under **1** *adj phr* Drunk; half-drunk **2** *adj phr* Semiconscious; stuporous: *He was half under when they pulled him out*

ham[1] **1** *n* An amateur, esp an amateur radio operator **2** *modifier: a ham radio operator/ ham network* [fr *amateur*]

ham[2] **1** *n fr late 1800s* An actor who overacts, dramatizes himself, emotes too broadly, etc: *had been roasted by the critics as a ham*—Russell Baker **2** *modifier: ham actor/ ham performance* **3** *v* (also **ham it up**): *The famous star was hamming all the way* **4** *n* A person who uses overtheatrical and overly expressive airs and actions: *Miss Moment was no doubt the biggest ham of a teacher*—A Lomax **5** *v* (also **ham it up**): *The prof strode into the lecture hall hamming and mugging* [fr *ham-fatter*]

hambone *n* A person who fancies himself an actor; histrionic self-advertiser; =HAM: *Every hambone from the deep sticks was constrained to make a speech* —Robert Ruark

hamburger *See* MAKE HAMBURGER OUT OF someone or something

ham-fatter *n fr late 1800s* =HAM, HAMBONE [fr a minstrel song of 1887, *The Hamfat Man*, having to do with a second-rate actor; see *ham joint*]

hamfist *n* A large fist, big as a ham: *His huge hamfist had landed me a vicious blow*—Xaviera Hollander

ham-handed or **ham-fisted** *adj* Crude and clumsy; lacking in finesse: *his hamfisted approach to a delicate matter*

ham-handedness *n* Crudeness; clumsiness; lack of polish: *In selecting the rottenest apples ... one seeks the pretension and the exploitation rather than mere ham-handedness*—Judith Crist

hammer **1** *n black* A sexually desirable woman; =FOX • Regarded by some women as offensive **2** *n truckers* The accelerator of a truck **3** *n* The penis: *How's your hammer hangin', Tiger?*—George Warren

hammer down *adv phr fr truckers* Going full speed; with throttles to the floor: *a herd of LA rednecks, all of 'em pie-eyed and hammer down* —Esquire

hammer lane *n phr truckers* The fast lane of a superhighway [fr the trucker sense *hammer* "accelerator"]

hammertails *n* A formal dress coat; swallowtail coat: *Several men in cutaway coats, called "hammertails"* —Stephen Longstreet

ham up *v phr* To make histrionic; overexpress; =HAM: *The baseball umpire was hamming up his signals* —New Yorker

hand *v* To give, esp something not desired; bestow forcefully, fraudulently, etc: *The Red Sox handed the Yankees a 12 to 3 shellacking/ What kind of con job was he trying to hand you?*
See BOTH HANDS, COLD IN HAND, DEAD MAN'S HAND, GIVE someone THE GLAD HAND, GLAD-HAND, HACK HAND, HAVE one's HANDS FULL, NOT LAY A GLOVE ON someone, SOFT HANDS, WITH one's HAND IN THE TILL

a **hand** **1** *n* A round of applause: *Well she got a big hand*—John O'Hara **2** *n* Help; aid
See GIVE someone A HAND

handbasket *See* GO TO HELL IN A HANDBASKET

handbook **1** *n horse-racing & gambling fr late 1800s* A place, other than a legal betting office, where bets are made away from the racetrack: *I was in the handbook near Loomis and Madison*—Fact Detective Mysteries **2** *n* =BOOKIE [probably fr the fact that betting records were kept in small, concealable notebooks for secrecy and portability]

H and C *n phr narcotics* A mixture of heroin and cocaine; =SPEEDBALL

handcuffs *See* GOLDEN HANDCUFFS

handed *See* HAM-HANDED, REDHANDED, RIGHT-HANDED

handful *See* GRAB A HANDFUL OF AIR

hand someone someone's **head** *v phr* To destroy; figuratively to decapitate someone and hand him his own head; =CLOBBER: *when the press is handing Francis Coppola his head* —Village Voice

hand it to someone *v phr* To compliment; praise for a success • Often said with overtones of reluctance: *I got to hand it to you*—James M Cain

◁ **hand job**▷ *n phr* An act of masturbation, usu done for one person by another: *if you were unlucky, all you got was a hand job*—Philadelphia

◁ **handkerchief-head**▷ *black* **1** *n* A black person who is obsequious towards white people; =UNCLE TOM: *A "handkerchief-head" is an old-fashioned Negro who doesn't know his rights*—Stephen Longstreet **2** *n* A black man who wears a cloth or scarf on his head to protect his processed hairdo

handle 1 *n fr early 1900s* A person's name, nickname, or alias: *He is known by that handle ever since to all his pals*—Associated Press/ *The CB freaks took handles, like Sweet Slats and Kimono Katey* **2** *n fr 1920s* The gross receipts or the profit of a sporting event, a gambling game, an illegal operation, etc: *A total handle of... between 4 and 10 billion a year in the handbooks, the numbers, and the slots*—Westbrook Pegler **3** *n gambling* The amount of money bet on a specific race or game, or in a particular day or week, etc: *The handle at Belmont dropped today on account of the blizzard* **4** *n* A way of approaching or grasping something; an initial and relevant insight: *I just can't find the handle to this problem* **5** *v* To cope with; manage; =HACK: *He can handle Tom's temper tantrums very well*

See FLY OFF THE HANDLE, GET A HANDLE ON something, PANHANDLE

handles *See* LOVE HANDLE

handout 1 *n hoboes fr late 1800s* Food, money, or other donations received or given • Nearly always with the implication that the giver is over-generous or self-interested, and the recipient undeserving: *Damn hippies lived on food stamps and other bleeding heart handouts* **2** *n* A leaflet or flyer passed out on the streets **3** *n* An official press release or communiqué: *The newspaperman's slightly derogatory slang term for the news release is "handout"*—Daniel J Boorstin

hand over fist *adv phr fr late 1800s* Very energetically, persistently, and rapidly: *It was a treat to see them go at it hand over fist*

hand-painted doormat *See* WIN THE PORCELAIN HAIRNET

hands *See* BOTH HANDS, HAVE one's HANDS FULL, SIT ON one's HANDS

hands down *adv phr* Very easily; without effort • Most often in the phrase **win hands down**: *She entered the race unheralded, and won it hands down/ We just loafed along, but beat them hands down* [probably fr the notion of winning a fight, besting someone in a confrontation, etc, without raising a *hand*]

hands-off *adj* Noninterfering; passive: *the president's hands-off policy*

handsome *See* HIGH, WIDE, AND HANDSOME

hands on 1 *adv phr* Manually, by direct control rather than automatic control: *The ship was then flown hands on* **2** *modifier: hands-on landing of the aircraft* **3** *adj* Practical and active rather than theoretical: *what we labeled a hands-on mayor*—San Francisco

hand trouble *n phr* A pronounced tendency to touch and caress; generalized tactile amorousness: *Bonnie had encountered men with hand trouble*—A Hynd

hang 1 *v* To spend time; frequent; =HANG OUT: *Who runs the coffepot where they hang?*—Scene of the Crime **2** *v horse-racing* To lack reserve speed during the last stretch **3** *v cool talk* To wait; await: *Let's hang here until Mary Beth gets off work*

See HAVE IT ALL HANGING OUT, LET IT ALL HANG OUT

hang a left (or **a right**) *v phr esp teenagers* To turn left or right, to round a corner [perhaps fr surfers' phrases *hang five, hang ten*]

hang around 1 *v phr fr late 1800s* To idle about; loiter; =HACK AROUND **2** *v phr* To stay where one is;

remain: *I decided to hang around and see what went down*

hang around with or **hang with** *v phr* To seek and prefer the company of; consort with: *Who you hanging around with these days?/ Sondra didn't hang with nobody but doctors* —Ms

◁ **hang-down** ▷ *n* The penis; =PRICK: *like the horse's hang-down that I am* —George V Higgins

hanged *See* I'LL BE DAMNED

hanger *See* CLIFFHANGER, CRAPE-HANGER, PAPERHANGER

hangers *See* APE HANGERS

hang fire *v phr* To be delayed or stalled; fail to materialize: *The whole deal's hanging fire till the jerk decides what to do next*

hang five *v phr surfers* To ride forward on the surfboard so that the toes of one foot are over the edge

hang in (or **in there**) *v phr* To endure in some difficult action or position; persist tenaciously; =HANG TOUGH: *He didn't pack it up, of course, he hung in there and saw the story through* —Playboy

hang it *v phr hospital* To administer intravenous medicine: *As soon as the nurse is free, he'll be in to hang it*

hang it easy *v phr teenagers* =TAKE IT EASY

hang it up *v phr* To retire; cease working, competing, etc: *since Joe Namath and Sonny Jurgenson hung it up*—Dan Jenkins [probably a shortened and generalized form of *hang up one's shoes* or *spikes* "retire from baseball"]

hang (or **stay**) **loose** *v phr fr 1960s counterculture* To be relaxed and nonchalant; be uninvolved; =COOL IT • Often heard as a genial exhortation: *You're healthier and happier when you hang loose*—Harper's/*Stay loose, man*—Richard Fariña

the **hang of** something *See* GET THE HANG OF something

hang on **1** *v phr* To endure; persist; =HANG IN **2** *v phr* To make an accusation; inculpate: *Let's see what felonies we can hang on this creep now that we've got him*

hang (or **tie** or **pin**) **one on** **1** *v phr* To get very drunk; go on a drinking spree **2** *v phr* To hit hard; =CLOBBER: *Will you hang one on my jaw?*—James M Cain

hang onto your hats *sentence* Get ready to hear something shocking or amazing

hangout[1] **1** *n fr late 1800s hoboes & underworld* A place for loitering, loafing, and passing time, esp with congenial companions: *a grad student hangout on Mirandola Lane/ a gay hangout* **2** *n fr 1920s* One's home; =DIGS

hangout[2] *n* Complete disclosure; total openness: *a "modified limited hang-out," meaning a response that would satisfy Watergate investigators while disclosing as little as possible* —Newsweek

hang out *v phr* To pass time; loaf pleasantly about; loiter: *just us five hangin' out*—Rolling Stone

See HAVE IT ALL HANGING OUT, LET IT ALL HANG OUT

hangover **1** *n fr early 1900s* The headache, morbid sensitivity, nausea, etc, felt upon awakening some hours after drinking too much liquor **2** *n* A remnant or survival, often an undesirable one: *The problem is a hangover from the high birthrate of the 50s*

hang ten *v phr surfers* To ride forward on a surfboard so that the toes of both feet are over the edge

hang tough *v phr* To endure in a difficult plight; show plucky and stoic persistence; =HANG ON, TOUGH IT OUT: *Mr Shannon glorifies Kennedy for his ability to "hang tough"*—Book World

hang up **1** *v phr esp 1960s* To become fixated: *Why did you hang up on Proust, anyhow?* **2** *v phr* To cease annoying or chattering; =SHUT UP • Often an irritated command [second sense fr the cessation of a telephone call]

hang-up **1** *n esp 1960s counterculture* A mental block; a psychological disturbance, fixation, or problem: *ribald anecdotes concerning his hang-up on strong women*—Changes **2** *n* Anything encumbering, frustrating, distressing, etc: *You couldn't carry around an amplifier and electric guitar and expect to survive, it was just too much of a hang-up*—Bob Dylan

hang up (or **out**) one's **shingle** *v phr* To commence professional practice; open up a law office, doctor's office, etc: *He's passed his bar exam now, so he can hang up his shingle*

hankie or **hanky** *n* A handkerchief

hankty *See* HINCTY

hanky-pank *adj fr carnival* Cheap and gaudy; trashy: *hanky-pank costume jewelry*

hanky-panky *n fr middle 1800s British* Anything dishonest, deceptive, or unethical, esp sexual infidelity; =MONKEY BUSINESS: *She seems just to be along for some hanky-panky with her pal, General Von Griem*—Ms [fr the conjurer's use of a *handkerchief* in prestidigitation]

happenings *n narcotics* Narcotics; =JUNK

happies *n* =JOLLIES

happy *adj* Drunk, esp slightly so; =TIDDLY

-happy *combining word* Somewhat insane over or excessively wrought upon by what is indicated: *bomb-happy/ car-happy/ power-happy/ trigger-happy* [probably modeled on *slap-happy*]

happy as a clam *adj phr* Very happy; euphoric: *On the boat she's happy as a clam* [fr earlier locution *happy as a clam at high tide*, that is, when it cannot be dug]

happy-cabbage *n* Money; =CABBAGE

happy-dust *narcotics* **1** *n* Cocaine **2** *n* Morphine

happy hour **1** *n phr* The hour or so of relaxation with drinks after work; cocktail hour **2** *n phr* A specified period of time, usu in early evening, in some restaurants and bars when drinks are sold at lower prices or when free food is provided

happy talk *television studio* **1** *n phr* Informal chat and chaffing among news broadcasters during the program, as an element of entertainment: *Later, happy talk evolved, to break the tension*—Washingtonian **2** *modifier: the happy-talk format that sandwiches cheerful repartee between the fire and robbery reports*—Philadelphia

hard **1** *adj* Demonstrable; verifiable; not dependent on subjective judgment, emotion, etc: *hard facts/ hard sciences* **2** *adj* =TOUGH **3** *adj jive talk* Excellent; good; =COOL ◁**4**▷ *n* =HARD-ON

See COME DOWN HARD, TAKE IT HARD

hard as nails *adj phr* Extremely durable and grim; =TOUGH

◁**hard-ass**▷ **1** *n* A severe and often pugnacious person; =HARDNOSE: *I've gotten the reputation as being a hard-ass*—Aquarian **2** *adj: He had a hard-ass way of getting what he wanted*

hardball **1** *n* Serious and consequential activity, work, etc; perilous and responsible doings: *It's hardball now, it's not games anymore*—Philadelphia Journal **2** *adj: fields hardball questions in a practice TV interview*—Time **3** *v* =PLAY HARDBALL

hard-boiled *adj* Severe and uncompromising; strict and pugnacious; =TOUGH: *The rather hard-boiled painting that hangs in Father's office*—F Scott Fitzgerald [fr *hard-boiled egg*]

hard-boiled egg *n phr* A severe and pugnacious person; =TOUGH GUY: *Our basic idea of a hero is really a "hard-boiled egg"*—P Curtiss

hard bop *n phr jazz musicians* A type of music resembling the blues that is related to, but more earthy and modal in approach than, straight bop: *swing, bop, cool jazz, hard bop, funky jazz*—BW Bell

hard (or **heavy**) **breathing** *n phr* Passionate love-making

hard cash *n phr* =COLD CASH

hard cheese *n phr* An unfortunate outcome or situation • Still chiefly British; often an interjection: *This is hard cheese indeed*—Village Voice

hard coin *n phr* Large amounts of money; =MEGABUCKS: *There's some hard coin being made by the music magnates*—Motive

hard-core **1** *adj* Essential and uncompromising; without evasion or admixture: *a hard-core Republican/ hard-core pornography* **2** *n* Pornography that openly depicts complete sex acts: *He sort of likes dirty stuff, but not real hard core*

hard currency (or **money**) *n phr* A national currency that is strong in the market and backed by considerable metal and economic power: *Sterling isn't the leading hard currency any more* [along with *hard cash* and *hard coin*, fr 17th-century terms distinguishing gold and silver from paper *currency*]

hard drug *n phr* A narcotic like heroin or morphine, that is powerfully addictive and injurious: *heroin, as* *"hard" a drug as there is*—New York Times

hard hat **1** *n phr* A derby hat: *The boys with the hard hats always ask a lot of questions about murders*—J Evans **2** *n phr* The steel or plastic helmet worn by various sorts of workers, esp construction workers **3** *modifier: Caution, this is a hard-hat zone* **4** *n phr* A worker who wears a hard hat: *The hard hats sat around whistling at the passing girls* **5** *n fr early 1970s* A very conservative right-winger; a reactionary: *He knows he can count on the hard hats to support him* **6** *n phr Vietnam War armed forces* A regular Viet Cong soldier, who wears a military helmet, as distinct from a guerilla or reservist: *some 50,000 are "hard-hats" (full-time fighters)*—Time [the political sense fr the vocal and sometimes violent opposition of many construction workers to the US peace movement during the Vietnam War, reinforced by terms like *hard line* and *hard core*]

hardhead **1** *n* An obstinate or stupid person ◀**2**▶ *n* A black person ◀**3**▶ *n black* A white person

hard line **1** *n phr* A policy or attitude based on severity and lack of compromise: *Take a hard line with them or they'll murder you* **2** *adj: the President's hard-line views on abortion*

hard liquor *n phr* Whiskey, rum, gin, brandy, as distinct from wine and beer; spirits; strong waters

hard look **1** *n phr* An intense and unblinking scrutiny; strict examination • Most often with **a**: *Take a hard look at what's going on upstairs/ We'll have a hard look at the income and expenses* **2** *n phr* A menacing or hostile stare: *She gave me a real hard look when I blurted her name*

See LONG HARD LOOK

hardnose *n* A severe, durable, and often pugnacious person; =TOUGH GUY: *The pussycat turned into a hardnose overnight*

hard-nosed **1** *adj* Stubborn; obstinate **2** *adj* Severe and pugnacious; harshly realistic; =TOUGH: *They'll take a hard-nosed look, then report*

◁ **hard-on** ▷ *n* An erection of the penis: *It was another one of those subway things. Like having a hard-on at random*—Saul Bellow

See HAVE A HARD-ON FOR someone or something

hard rock *n phr rock and roll* A form of rock and roll music with a simple, driving beat, usu played on heavily amplified guitars

hard-rock *adj* Severe; dour and pugnacious; =TOUGH: *the old hard-rock guy who would line up all the cocaine users and shoot them*—Time [probably fr the difficulty of *hard-rock* mining as distinct fr other kinds; influenced by *rock-hard*]

a **hard** (or **tough**) **row to hoe** *n phr* A difficult task; a period of trouble and travail: *With inflation and all they had a hard row to hoe*

hard sell *n phr* An act or policy of selling aggressively, forcibly, loudly, etc: *a master at hard sell*

hard-shell *adj* Strict; conservative; =HARD-CORE

hard stuff **1** *n* Whiskey and other strong liquors; spirits; =HARD LIQUOR: *The troubles the hard stuff inflicts on men with no defense against it*—John McCarten **2** *n phr* =HARD DRUG

hard time *See* GIVE someone A HARD TIME

hardtop *n esp 1950s & 60s* A car resembling a convertible, but having a metal roof

hard up **1** *adj phr fr early 1800s British* Poor; penniless: *It was no disgrace to be hard up in those times* **2** *adj phr* Sexually frustrated; needing sexual gratification; =HORNY: *He declared he was so hard up he'd fuck mud* [apparently fr a nautical expression meaning the helm is *hard up*, that is, held all the way to windward while beating and so pinched as tight as possible]

hard up for something *adj phr* Lacking; deficient in: *We're hard up for booze around here*

hardware **1** *n fr middle 1800s* Weapons and other war matériel: *military "hardware," tanks, planes, guns, rockets, weapons*—WF Arbogast **2** *n WW2 armed forces* Military insignia or medals worn on a uniform **3** *n fr 1930s* Badges and other identification jewelry **4** *n computers* Computers and computer equipment, as distinct from programs and other material used for computer operation

the **hard way** **1** ***n phr*** *crapshooting* The repetition of an even number that came up on the first roll, made by rolling two even dice that add up to it **2** ***n phr*** The most difficult and strenuous way of doing anything: *My motto is "Anything worth doing is worth doing the hard way"*

hardy-har or **hardy-har-har** or **har-har-har** **1** ***adj*** Funny; hilarious: *a mildly hardy-har gag* **2** ***adv:*** *how hardy-har funny a little quick witted humor can be*—Village Voice **3** ***n*** Joviality; laughter; jolly spirits: *Underneath the har-har-har... there was anything but fun and games*—Washingtonian

Hare Krishnas or **Hare Krishna kids** (or **people**) ***n phr*** Persons who belong to a cult called the International Society for Krishna Consciousness [fr the Sanskrit prayer or invocation *Hare Krishna* "hail Krishna"]

harness ***n*** The dress and equipment of special categories of persons, such as telephone line repairers, police officers, train conductors, motorcyclists, etc: *Wise detectives, who dread going back into "harness" or uniform* —E Lavine

See IN HARNESS

harp **◀1▶** ***n*** An Irish person or one of Irish descent **2** ***n*** A harmonica

Harry *See* BIG HARRY, EVERY TOM, DICK, AND HARRY

has-been **1** ***n*** A person who was once famous, successful, courted, etc, but is no longer so: *Some has-beens make spectacular comebacks* **2** ***n*** A person whose preferences, style, etc, are passé; =BACK NUMBER

hash **1** ***v*** To discuss, esp at length; =HASH OVER: *they had hashed and rehashed for many a frugal conversational meal*—F Scott Fitzgerald **2** ***v*** =HASH UP **3** ***n*** *narcotics* Hashish **4** ***adj*** *cool talk* Excellent; wonderful; =COOL

See MAKE HAMBURGER OUT OF someone or something, SETTLE someone's HASH, SLING HASH

one **has had it** **1** ***sentence*** (Variations: **up to here** or **up to** one's **ass** or **up to** one's **eyebrows** or some other anatomical feature may be added) One is exhausted, disgusted, unwilling to put up with any more: *All at once I've had it up to here with psychiatry*—New Yorker **2** ***sentence*** One has been given a last chance and has failed: *That's the ball game, buddy, you've had it* [fr shortening of World War 2 British Royal Air Force slang He's *had his time* "He's been killed"]

Hashbury ***n*** *esp 1960s counterculture* The Haight-Ashbury section of San Francisco, a haunt of hippies during the 1960s; =the HAIGHT

hash head ***n phr*** *narcotics* A frequent user of hashish or marijuana

hash-house ***n*** *fr middle 1800s Western* A restaurant or lunch counter, esp a cheap one: *the sort of language that one would expect to hear from a hobo in a Bowery hash-house*—Bookman

hash mark (or **stripe**) **1** ***n phr*** *armed forces* A service stripe, worn on the sleeve of a military uniform to mark each four-year period of service: *the voice of a subaltern of God, hashmarks running down his arm for a thousand miles*—Pat Conroy **2** ***n phr*** *football* An inbounds line marker used to help fix the point where the ball is put in play, and spaced one yard from the next mark [military sense fr the humorous inference that the soldier has not cleaned the uniform of accumulating food stains]

hash over *fr early 1900s* **1** ***v phr*** To discuss, esp repeatedly and lengthily: *We kept hashing over the same tired old topics* **2** ***v phr*** To rehash, review: *Asked him in to hash over a point or two*—New Yorker

hash session ***n phr*** =GABFEST

hash up ***v phr*** To ruin; spoil; =FUCK UP, MESS UP

hassle or **hassel** *fr middle 1800s* **1** ***n*** A disagreement; quarrel; fight: *The hassle over putting fluoride in drinking water*—N Boynton **2** ***v:*** *They were hassling about who would pay the bill* **3** ***v*** To harass; treat rudely and roughly: *I wanted to discuss being hassled by the police* **4** ***n*** A difficult or tedious task or concern: *Getting those tickets was a real hassle* **5** ***v*** *narcotics* To get narcotics with difficulty: *He finally hassled one bag* [origin unknown; perhaps fr French *harceler* "importune, attack constantly"; perhaps a blend: *haggle* and *tussle, haggle* and *wrestle* have been proposed; perhaps fr a Southern dialect word meaning "pant, breathe noisily"]

hat ***See*** BRASS HAT, GIMMIE HAT, HANG ONTO YOUR HATS, HARD HAT, HIGH-HAT, KNOCK something INTO A COCKED HAT, OLD HAT, PARTY HAT, PASS THE HAT, SHIT IN YOUR HAT, TALK THROUGH one's HAT, THROW one's HAT IN THE RING, UNDER one's HAT, WEAR TWO HATS, WHITE HAT

hatch ***See*** BOOBY HATCH, DOWN THE HATCH, NUT HOUSE

hatchet job **1** ***n phr*** A malicious attack; a diatribe or indictment meant to destroy: *By hatchet job is meant here... a calculated attempt to demolish the author*—Wilfred Sheed **2** ***n phr*** A discharge or dismissal; =the AX

hatchet man **1** ***n phr*** *fr 1920s* A professional killer; =HIT MAN **2** ***n phr*** A person whose task and predilection is to destroy an opponent, often by illegitimate means

hate someone's **guts** ***v phr*** To have an extreme hatred for: *I dislike him, but I don't hate his damn guts*

hat in hand ***adv phr*** Obsequiously; tamely; pleadingly: *The President stands there, hat in hand, begging the Congress for their votes*—National Public Radio

hat trick ***n phr*** *sports fr late 1800s British* The scoring of three goals in a single game by the same player • Commonly used of hockey or soccer [fr cricket, "the bowling down of three wickets with successive balls," a feat which entitled the player to the proceeds of a collection, i.e., a passing of the *hat*, or to a new *hat*]

hatty ***See*** HIGH-HAT

haul ***n*** Profits or return, esp illicit ones; loot: *The show yielded a huge haul*

See COLD HAUL, FOR THE LONG HAUL, GET one's ASHES HAULED, LONG HAUL, OVER THE LONG HAUL

haul one's **ashes** ***v phr*** To leave; depart; =HAUL ASS

haul someone's **ashes** **1** ***v phr*** To harm or injure, esp by beating ◁**2**▷ ***v phr*** To do the sex act with

See GET one's ASHES HAULED

◁**haul ass**▷ **1** ***v phr*** *fr WW1 Navy* To leave; depart; =CLEAR OUT, DRAG ASS **2** ***v phr*** To act quickly, esp in response to a command: *I want it now, so haul ass!* **3** ***v phr*** To drive or travel very fast: *They were really hauling ass when they hit that curve*

hauler ***n*** *hot rodders* A very fast car; =HOT ROD

haul someone **in** ***v phr*** To arrest; =RUN someone IN: *The police decided to haul them all in*—Life

haul it ***v phr*** *black* To run away; flee; escape [fr *haul ass*]

haul off ***v phr*** *fr middle 1800s* To launch an attack, diatribe, etc: *She hauled off and decked him* [probably fr the action of stepping back to make more room for launching the fist, and *haul* suggests a nautical origin]

haul off on someone ***v phr*** To hit or beat; launch a blow at: *counting fifty before they hauled off on a Red*—James T Farrell

haul (or **rake**) someone **over the coals** **1** ***v phr*** *fr late 1700s British* To rebuke harshly; castigate; =CHEW OUT **2** ***v phr*** To put through an ordeal [fr the old ordeal by fire]

haul the mail ***See*** CARRY THE MAIL

have ◁**1**▷ ***v*** To do the sex act with; possess sexually: *I had Mary Jane in her own bathtub ten times*—Calder Willingham **2** ***v*** To cheat; deceive; =DIDDLE: *I'm afraid it's a scam, they had us*

See be HAD

have a ball ***v phr*** To enjoy oneself particularly well and uninhibitedly: *After the dean left we had us a ball*

have a big mouth ***v phr*** To be inclined to say embarrassingly too much, esp about others' personal affairs: *Marcel Proust sure had a big mouth*

have a bird ***v phr*** To exhibit shock or anger; =HAVE KITTENS: *Charlie will have a bird when he learns she died*—William Goldman

◁**have a bone on**▷ ***v phr*** To have an erect penis [fr a hubristic anatomical misstatement]

have a bone to pick with someone ***v phr*** To have a matter to complain about or go into

◁**have a broom up** one's **ass**▷ ***v phr*** (Variations: **get** may replace **have**; **stick** may replace **broom**; **in** one's **tail** may replace **up** one's **ass**; **butt** may replace **ass**) To work diligently and eagerly; be an overachiever [fr the willing or harried worker in a joke, whose hands are full, but who would sweep the floor if one placed a *broom* in the worker's nether cavity]

◁ **have a bug** (or **hair) up** one's **ass** (or **up** one's **nose)**▷ *v phr* To be very irascible and touchy: *Cheatham had a hair up his ass, was the consensus* —Earl Thompson

have a bun in the oven *v phr* To be pregnant: *The outspoken Miss Bow, who... had a bun in the oven, replied* —Ms

have a bun on **1** *v phr fr early 1900s* To be drunk **2** *v phr* To be intoxicated with narcotics

have a case on someone *v phr* To be infatuated with or in love [*case* was specialized to mean "a case of being in love" by the mid-19th century]

have a chip on one's **shoulder** *v phr* To be very touchy and belligerent; be easily provoked

have a clue *v phr chiefly British fr 1940s armed forces* To know; be aware or apprised of: *Do you have any clue about what's going on here? See* NOT HAVE A CLUE

have a cow *See* HAVE KITTENS

have (or **take) a crack at** something *v phr* (Variations: **go** or **rip** or **ripple** or **shot** or **whack** may replace **crack**) To make an attempt at; have a try: *He said he wasn't sure he could, but he'd have a crack at it*

have a crush on someone *v phr fr late 1800s* To be infatuated or enchanted with, esp to be secretly in love with someone older and more worldly than oneself

have a few buttons missing *See* HAVE SOME BUTTONS MISSING

have a field day *v phr* To indulge oneself freely and successfully; have it entirely one's way; go all out: *When the news gets out, the press will have a field day/ I'm afraid the bunnies have had a field day with the hyacinths* [fr late-19th-century *field day,* when a school or college, a fire company, etc, would indulge in hearty outdoor sports and drills, inferentially not against the strongest competition or genuine dangers]

have a free ride *See* GET A FREE RIDE

have a hair up one's **ass** *See* HAVE A BUG UP one's ASS

◁ **have a hard-on for** someone or something▷ **1** *v phr* To be very much enamored of or attracted to: *I'm afraid the chief executive officer has a hard-on for this idea* **2** *v phr* To be very eager for; lust after: *He knows I'm a federal cop, so he's got to figure I got a hard on for Panthers* —George V Higgins **3** *v phr Army* To dislike; make problems for

have a hole in one's **head** (or **wig)** *v phr* To be very stupid; be insane; = HAVE ROCKS IN one's HEAD

have a lech for someone or something *v phr* To be especially desirous of; lust after [*lech* is a shortening of *lechery* or *lecherous*]

have a leg up on someone or something *v phr* To have a good start on some project, process, in some competition, etc; be well on the way to a goal: *They already have a leg up on it*

have a little on the side *See* GET A LITTLE ON THE SIDE

have all one's **buttons** (or **marbles)** *v phr* To be normal or mentally sound; be sane; be shrewd and aware • Most often in the negative: *When I'm sure I no longer have all my buttons I'll quit this line of work/ The old guy doesn't seem to have all his marbles, the way he mumbles to himself* [*buttons* probably refers to the neatness and completeness of a normal mind compared with the uncertainty and slovenliness of clothes lacking buttons; see *lose* one's *marbles*]

have all one's **ducks in a row** *See* HAVE one's DUCKS IN A ROW

not **have all** one's **switches on** *See* NOT HAVE ALL one's SWITCHES ON

have all the answers *See* KNOW ALL THE ANSWERS

have all the moves *v phr* To be very skillful; be expert, esp and originally in a sport or game

have a load on *v phr* To be drunk; = FEEL NO PAIN

have a lock on something *v phr* To be assured of some result; be certain of success: *Looks like the Pirates have a lock on the pennant*

have a mind like a sieve *v phr* To be very forgetful

have a monkey on one's **back** *v phr narcotics* To be addicted to narcotics

have (or **cop) an attitude** **1** *v phr Army fr black* To dislike and complain about one's plight; = BITCH, KVETCH: *If you'd put up as many bonds for nothing... as I have, you'd have a fucking* *attitude too*—Donald Goines/ *"Go ahead, cop an attitude," she says and pulls away from him*—Village Voice **2** ***v phr*** to be arrogant or haughty

have an edge on ***v phr*** To be slightly drunk

have an (or the) **edge on** someone ***v phr*** To have an advantage; enjoy a superior or winning position

have a (or one's) **nerve** ***v phr*** *fr early 1900s* To be impudently aggressive: *You sure have your nerve, telling him off that way*

not **have any** ***See*** NOT HAVE ANY

have a party ***v phr*** To do the sex act

◁ not **have a pot** (or **without a pot**) **to piss in**▷ ***See*** NOT HAVE A POT TO PISS IN

have a prayer ***v phr*** To have a chance; be able • Very often in the negative: *If everything goes right, we may just have a prayer/ The Eagles don't have a prayer, and neither will Murray*—Philadelphia

have a red face ***v phr*** To be embarrassed; have a guilty and sheepish mien; =HAVE EGG ON one's FACE: *The Chief had a red face when... he was found in possession of stolen property*—A Hynd

◁ **have a rod on**▷ ***v phr*** To have an erect penis; =HAVE A BONE ON

have a screw loose ***v phr*** To be crazy; be eccentric: *that his brains, in her opinion, were twisted, or that he had a screw loose*—Joseph Heller

have one's **ashes hauled** ***See*** GET one's ASHES HAULED

◁ **have a shit fit**▷ ***v phr*** To become very upset or furious; =SHIT A BRICK, SHIT GREEN: *Some people are going to have a shit fit when they read it*—Anne Bernays

have a short fuse ***v phr*** To have a quick temper; be irascible

◁ **have** someone's **ass**▷ ***v phr*** To punish; retaliate severely: *If you utter one word, I'll have your ass*

◁ **have** one's **ass in a sling**▷ ***v phr*** (Variations: **get** or **put** may replace **have**; the locution may be **one's ass is, was**, etc, **in a sling**) *fr 1930s* To be in serious trouble: *If she catches you changing that report you'll have your ass in a sling/ Allen has taken an introspective, but not innocent, bystander, and put his ass in a sling*—Playboy

have a thing about ***v phr*** To be especially concerned with, in love, hate, or fascination; be strongly emotional about: *She really has a thing about pyramids*

have a tiger by the tail ***v phr*** To be in a nasty situation, esp innocently or unexpectedly, that will get much worse before it gets better

have oneself **a time** ***v phr*** To enjoy oneself hugely: *Everybody had himself a time*—Billy Rose

◁ **have** (or **get**) one's **banana peeled**▷ ***v phr*** To do the sex act; copulate

not **have brain one** ***See*** NOT HAVE BRAIN ONE

◁ **have brass** (or **cast-iron**) **balls**▷ ***v phr*** To have audacity; be foolhardy: *Which one of you worthless nits had the brass balls enough to cough when I was talking*—Pat Conroy

◁ **have** someone **by the balls**▷ ***v phr*** To have in a very perilous and painful position; have a firm grip on; =HAVE someone BY THE SHORT HAIRS: *I didn't want to do it, but they had me by the balls*

◁ **have** (or **get**) someone **by the short hairs** (or **curlies** or **knickers**)▷ ***v phr*** *first form fr late 1800s* To have in a painful and helpless situation; have absolute control over; =HAVE someone BY THE BALLS: *When life gets you by the short hairs, it doesn't let go*—PlayboyYou're in no position to make deals. We got you by the curlies—Joseph Wambaugh/ *We've got him by the knickers and he's hurting*—Wall Street Journal [fr the *short hairs* growing on the scrotum]

have someone or something **by the tail** **1** ***v phr*** =HAVE someone BY THE BALLS **2** ***v phr*** To have control of: *I know all young people are sure they can have it by the tail*—Stephen Longstreet

◁ **have** one's **cherry**▷ **1** ***v phr*** To be a virgin **2** ***v phr*** To be unproved or untried in the sense indicated: *He's never been bankrupt, still got his cherry*

have something **cinched** ***v phr*** (Variations: **iced** or **knocked** or **made** or **taped** or **wired** may replace **cinched**) To be entirely sure of a favorable outcome; be sure of success, well-being, etc: *Then you see the helicopter... and you know you've got it knocked*—The Bridges at Toko-ri (movie)/ *a veteran bank shot artist who has the back boards at West 4th Street wired, does anything he pleases*—Village Voice/ *One more mile and we've got it made*/ *I thought I had it iced*—Washington Post [*have* something *cinched* is fr cowboy usage, referring to a tightly and securely *cinched* saddle; the variants *have* something *made, taped,* and *wired* fr poker terms, also fr cowboy use]

have (or **get**) **cold feet** *v phr* To be timorous or afraid; have second thoughts: *Ella was coming too, but she had cold feet*

have something **coming out of** one's **ears** *v phr* To have a surplus of: *He's got talent coming out of his ears*

have something **down** (or **down pat**) *v phr* To know or be able to do perfectly; be perfect master of: *I had my story down pat so I almost believed it myself*

have one's **druthers** *v phr* To have one's preference; have it one's way: *if George Bush had his druthers*—National Review/ *But personally, if I had my druthers, I would like nothing better than to run off to the country with some guy*—Washington Post [fr dialect pronunciation of *I'd rather* as *I'd druther*]

have (or **get**) one's **ducks in a row** *v phr* (Variations: **have** (or **get**) one's **ducks all in a row** or **have** (or **get**) **all** one's **ducks in a row**) *Army* To be fully prepared; to be organized; =DO one's HOMEWORK: *Be sure you have your ducks all in a row when the General comes around*/ *You have five years to get all your ducks in a row*—Time [perhaps fr a mother duck's marshaling of her *ducklings* in a neat flotilla behind her; perhaps fr some game]

have egg on one's **face** *v phr* To be caught in an embarrassing or guilty plight; be rueful and embarrassed: *Steve Brill, the editor... should have egg on his face this week*—Village Voice/ *He left President Reagan with egg on his face*—Washington Post

have eyes for *v phr* To desire; wish for; =HAVE A LECH FOR: *But the chick who has eyes for some cat would be uncool if she told him so directly*—S Boal

have something **going** (or **working**) **for** someone or something *v phr* To enjoy a certain advantage; have particular assets: *The best thing this mall has going for it is it's just a test*—New Yorker

have one's **hands** (or **plate**) **full** *v phr* To be occupied up to one's limit, esp in an emergency: *When the water main burst, the utility workers had their hands full*/ *They wanted me to take on another case but I had my plate full*

have one's **head pulled** *v phr* (Variation: **out of** one's **ass** may be added) *Army* To be intelligent and sensible; be aware

◁**have** one's **head up** one's **ass**▷ *v phr* To behave stupidly and blindly; be chronically wrong: *Why you gommy, stupid shit... Your head is up your ass*—William Kennedy

have hot pants *v phr* To be very lustful; crave carnally: *He has hot pants for her and she for someone else, alas*

have it *v phr* To be talented; be competent and effectual: *He tries hard, but he just doesn't have it*

See HAD IT, LET someone HAVE IT

have it all hanging out *v phr* To be concealing nothing; be entirely candid and undefensive; =LET IT ALL HANG OUT: *As the current saying goes, NCR has it all hanging out*—Forbes

have it all over someone or something *v phr* To be superior; surpass or outstrip: *In advanced technology, the North has it all over the South*

have (or **get**) **it all together** *v phr* To have one's life, feelings, energies, etc, satisfactorily arranged; be free of emotional and behavioral dysfunctions: *Dr Jung says we'll all be OK when we have it all together*

have it bad *v phr* To be very much in love; be powerfully infatuated: *He had it bad for her, though she was indifferent*

have it both ways *v phr* To hold or esp to profit from two contrary positions; =WORK BOTH SIDES OF THE STREET: *Make up your mind which one you'll support, because you can't have it both ways*

have it good *v phr* To enjoy prosperity, health, regular meals and pleasures, etc: *I had it real good up* *there, till they canned me/ We never had it so good!*

have it in for someone *v phr* To be angry with; feel vindictive towards; bear a grudge: *Hatfield had it in for McCoy*

◁ **have it off**▷ *v phr fr 1930s British* To do the sex act; copulate • Still chiefly British: *who has had it off with both of them*—Us [fr earlier use, "to achieve a crime or shady transaction, pull something off," probably transferred to sexual activity on analogy with *cheating* and *hanky panky*, and by psychological suggestions related to *pull off* and *come off*]

have kittens (or **a cow**) or **cast a kitten** *v phr* To manifest strong and sudden feeling; have a fit of laughter, fear, anger, etc: *He got so mad I thought he was going to have kittens*

have lead in one's **pants** (or ◁**in** one's **ass**▷) *v phr* To be very sluggish and lazy; move or work slowly; be unresponsive: *Frank's got lead in his ass, go jazz him up*

◁ **have lead in** one's **pencil**▷ **1** *v phr* To be sexually potent; have an erect penis **2** *v phr* To be keenly needful of sexual gratification

have someone's **lunch** *See* EAT someone's LUNCH

have something **made** *See* HAVE something CINCHED

have one's **mind in the gutter** *v phr* To be preoccupied with or devoted to crudeness and smut

have no bones about *See* MAKE NO BONES ABOUT

have someone's **nose open** *v phr black* To excite someone's sexual appetite: *What about that gray girl in San Jose who had your nose wide open?*—Eldridge Cleaver [perhaps fr the involuntary flaring of the nostrils as a symptom of strong desire, anger, etc]

have-not **1** *n* A poor person, region, etc **2** *modifier: the have-not nations of the Third World*

have someone's **number** *v phr* To know the exact truth about someone, though it be disguised; know someone completely: *She knew what I meant, and she knew I had her number*—James M Cain [perhaps fr one's telephone *number*; perhaps fr one's serial or other *number* used for identification]

have one foot in the grave *v phr* To be nearly dead; be doomed

have something **on the brain** *v phr fr middle 1800s* To be obsessed with: *She's got folk-dancing on the brain*

have papers (or **papers on**) *v phr black* To be married, or married to: *I will not be number two, I got papers on you*—Washington Post

have one's **plate full** *See* HAVE one's HANDS FULL

have problems with something *v phr* To find hard to accept; be unable to agree immediately: *Even after talking it over, she still had problems with the board's decision*

have pups *v phr* = HAVE KITTENS

have rocks in one's (or **the**) **head** *v phr* To be wrong, stupid, crazy, etc: *Kid, you got rocks in your head*—Max Shulman

See ROCKS IN one's HEAD

◁ **have shit for brains**▷ *v phr* To be very stupid: *You suffer from chronic cranial rectalitis, you have shit for brains*

have some (or **a few**) **buttons** (or **marbles**) **missing** *v phr* To be insane; be eccentric

have the edge on someone *See* HAVE AN EDGE ON someone

◁ **have the hots for** someone▷ *v phr* To desire sexually: *the stocky instructress was glaring at them. "Think she's got the hots for you"*—Earl Thompson/ *I know Grodin has the hots for you*—Village Voice

have the inside track *n phr* To have a strong advantage, esp one based on some fortuitous circumstance: *All the candidates look OK, but Hester has the inside track because she's single* [fr the advantage that a racer has by being nearest the *inside* of the *track* and having therefore the shortest distance to run]

have the jump (or **jump on**) *v phr* To enjoy a lead or advantage; be ahead of: *Who has the jump in this election?/ I got the jump on him right away, and never looked back*

have them in the aisles *See* LAY THEM IN THE AISLES

have (or **get**) **the munchies** *v phr narcotics & counterculture* To be hungry, esp for sweets and starches after using marijuana: *I just smoked the smoke and got the munchies and I got real fat*—New York Times

◁ **have the rag on** (or **Baker flying**)▷ *v phr* To menstruate [*Baker flying* is fr the red-colored B flag, called *Baker* flag in the military phonetic alphabet]

◁ **have the red ass**▷ *See* GET THE RED ASS

◁ **have the world by the balls**▷ *v phr* To be in a very profitable and dominant situation; =HAVE something CINCHED, SHIT IN HIGH COTTON: *With a good agent, you've got the world by the balls*—John Irving

have one's **ticket punched** *v phr* To be a legitimate member of something; be fully warranted in experience, qualification, etc; =PAY one's DUES: *These women have had their "tickets punched" in the corporate world*—Washington Post

hawk[1] *v* To clear one's throat; cough up and spit: *let out of their cells to wash... hawk... stretch*—Nelson Algren

hawk[2] **1** *n* A person who advocates a strong and bellicose policy or action: *Some were doves on Vietnam and hawks on Iran* **2** *n* A person who attracts and procures young men and boys for homosexuals, esp older men: *The police believe he was acting the role of a "hawk," finding "chickens" (young boys) for older men*—New York Times

the **hawk** *n phr black* The cold winter wind: *Well, looks like the hawk is getting ready to hit the scene and send temperatures down*—Ruby Dee [origin unknown; perhaps fr the strong biting quality of such a wind]

Hawkins *See* MISTER HAWKINS

hay **1** *n narcotics* Marijuana; =HERB **2** *n lunch counter* Strawberry or strawberries **3** *n* A small amount of money; =NICKELS AND DIMES, PEANUTS: *What they offered was just hay*

See HIT THE HAY, INDIAN HAY, a ROLL IN THE HAY, THAT AIN'T HAY

the **hay** **1** *n* Bed: *He is in his hotel room in the hay*—Damon Runyon **2** *n* Sleep; semiconsciousness

See HIT THE HAY, a ROLL IN THE HAY

haybag *n hoboes* A woman hobo

◀ **hay-eater**▶ *n black* A white person; =OFAY

haymaker *fr early 1900s prizefight* **1** *n* A very strong blow with the fist: *Smashes the... kid with a wild haymaker*—H Witwer **2** *n* Any powerful stroke or felling blow: *Having her arrested... would be a haymaker to your father*—J Evans **3** *n* Any supreme or definitive effort, performance, etc; =WINNER: *Her blues number was a haymaker*

hayseed **1** *n* (also **hayseeder**) *fr late 1800s* A farmer; country person: *There's still a lot of hayseed in Senator Chance*—R Starnes **2** *adj: a hayseed routine/ hayseed simplicity* **3** *adj* Rural; provincial: *The bad actors perform worse plays in hayseed theaters*—Robert Ruark

haywire **1** *adj fr early 1900s* Functioning erratically; out of order; =ON THE BLINK: *This meter's haywire* **2** *adj* Makeshift; precariously operative: *What sort of haywire gadget are you using for a pump?* **3** *adj* Crazy; confused; =COCKEYED: *He never looked inside an almanac, and was sure that anyone who did was haywire*—Stewart Holbrook

See GO HAYWIRE

head **1** *n* A headache, esp as a component of a hangover: *You won't believe the head I had next morning* **2** *n* The mouth: *Keep your head shut* **3** *n* The foam on a glass of beer **4** *n* One person as a unit in an audience, group, etc: *at twenty-five cents a head, no reserved seats* —J Lilienthal **5** *n* A person: *One head that used to claim to sell stockings called*—AJ Liebling ◁**6**▷ *n* The erect penis, esp the glans ◁**7**▷ *n* Fellatio or cunnilingus; =BLOW JOB, HAIR PIE: *Some quiff is going to give you head*—Lawrence Sanders **8** *n narcotics* A narcotics user, esp an addict: *My trip is to reach as many heads in this country as I can, and turn them around*—New York Times **9** *n narcotics* The feeling of euphoria produced by a narcotic; =HIGH, RUSH: *I take two Tuinals and get a nice head*—New York/ *much of the head, or psychic lift, that users experience*—Wall Street Journal

See ACID FREAK, ACIDHEAD, AIRHEAD, BANANAHEAD, BIGHEAD, BITE someone's HEAD OFF, BLOCKHEAD, BONEHEAD, BUBBLEHEAD, BURRHEAD, CHIPHEAD, CHOWDERHEAD, CHUCKLEHEAD, COKEHEAD, DEADHEAD, FATHEAD, FLATHEAD, GET one's HEAD OUT OF one's ASS, GIVE HEAD, HANDKERCHIEF-HEAD, HARDHEAD, HASH HEAD, HAVE A HOLE IN one's HEAD, HAVE one's HEAD PULLED, HAVE ROCKS IN one's HEAD, one's HEAD IS UP one's ASS, HEAD SHOP, HEADSHRINKER, HIT THE NAIL ON THE HEAD, HOPHEAD, HOTHEAD, IN OVER one's HEAD, JUICEHEAD, KNUCKLEHEAD, LARDHEAD, LUNKHEAD, MEATHEAD, METH HEAD, MUSCLEHEAD, MUSH-HEAD, MUTTONHEAD, NEED someone or something LIKE A HOLE IN THE HEAD, NOODLEHEAD, OFF one's NUT, OFF THE TOP OF one's HEAD, OPEN one's FACE, OUT OF one's HEAD, OVER one's HEAD, PILLHEAD, PINHEAD, POINTHEAD, POINTY-HEAD, POTHEAD, PUDDINGHEAD, PUMPKINHEAD, RAGHEAD, ROCKS IN one's HEAD, ROTORHEAD, SAPHEAD, SHITHEAD, SOFT IN THE HEAD, SOREHEAD, STAND ON one's HEAD, TALKING HEAD, TREADHEAD, USE one's HEAD, WHERE someone's HEAD IS AT, YELL one's HEAD OFF

-head *combining word* Addicted to or using the narcotic specified: *acidhead/ pothead*

the **head** *n phr fr merchant marine & Navy* The toilet; =CAN [fr the location of the crew's toilet in the bow or *head* of a ship]

headache *fr 1930s* **1** *n* Any trouble, annoyance, vexation, etc: *another headache for pro coaches* —Associated Press **2** *n* A tedious, obnoxious person; =PILL: *My learned associate is something of a headache*

headcase *n* An insane or very eccentric person; =NUT: *the wealthy headcases and professional haters*—Don Pendleton

-headed *combining word* Having a head, esp a mind, of the specified defective sort
See AIRHEADED, BALLOONHEADED, BIGHEADED, BONEHEADED, BULLHEADED, MUSH-HEADED, PIGHEADED, POINTY-HEADED, WOOLLY-HEADED

headhunter **1** *n* A person or agency that seeks out and recruits employees, esp business executives and highly paid professionals, as candidates for usu high-paying or prestigious jobs: *Headhunters head for Washington as a capital place to find executives*—Wall Street Journal **2** *n football* A very rough player, usu a defensive player

◁ one's **head is up** one's **ass**▷ *sentence* One is behaving stupidly and blindly: *Skill-wise, the FBI's head was up its ass*—Village Voice

◁ **head job**▷ *n phr* Fellatio or cunnilingus; oral sex: *receiving a listless headjob from an aging black prostitute*—Joseph Wambaugh

head kit *n phr narcotics* The set of implements used for taking narcotics; =WORKS: *Head kits are constantly being found*—LJ Berry

headlight **1** *n black* A light-skinned black person **2** *n* A large diamond, esp in a ring or clasp: *A lurid "headlight" in his tie*—Abel Green

headliner *n* The main or chief performer; main attraction: *She was headliner at the Seven Seas*

one's **head off** *adv phr* To one's utmost; extremely much; spectacularly; =one's ASS OFF, one's BRAINS OUT: *one time when Joey was vomiting his head off*—San Francisco

head someone or something **off at the pass** *v phr* To forestall or prevent by anticipation: *A single mother has to establish control fast... Before the coercive cycle... builds... you have to head it off at the pass*—New York Times [fr the stock situation in Western movies, where typically the leader of a force pursuing thieves or rustlers through rough ground declares "We'll *head them off at the pass*"]

head shop *n phr esp 1960s teenagers & counterculture* A shop selling various accessories of the drug culture and hippie culture, such as water pipes, holders for marijuana cigarettes, psychedelic posters, incense, etc

headshrinker or **headpeeper** *n* Any psychotherapist, psychiatrist, psychoanalyst, etc; =SHRINK: *with a good deal more understanding than any clergyman or headshrinker*—Sports Afield/ *you lousy smug headpeeper* —Stephen King

heads-up *adj* Clever; alert; shrewd: *They're playing real heads-up football*

heads will roll *sentence* People will be dismissed, punished, ruined, etc: *If eventually the authorities catch up with you, no heads will roll*—Punch

head trip **1** *n phr* A mental exploration; an adventure of thought, esp of a new sort; a delectable fantasy: *Private head trips seemed to be adjuncts or companions of social movements*—Andrew Kopkind **2** *modifier: The Head-Trip Dodge, verbalizing without involvement, the* *educated filibuster*—New York **3** *v phr: man seeks companion for headtripping, studying together, Scrabble, etc*—Psychology Today

heap **1** *n* A car, esp an old ramshackle one; =JALOPY **2** *n* Any old vehicle

See JUNK HEAP

a **heap** *adv phr* Very much: *Thanks a heap, old buddy*

heaps **1** *n* Very many; =a FLOCK, OODLES: *I've got heaps of scratch* **2** *adv* Very much: *She loved him heaps, but kept mum*

heart **1** *n* Courage; stamina; pluck **2** *n* Generosity; charity; kindness: *The old dame's full of heart* ◁**3**▷ *n* The erect penis, esp the glans; =HEAD **4** *n narcotics* A tablet of an amphetamine, esp Dexedrine (a trade name)

See BLEEDING HEART, PURPLE HEART

heat **1** *n underworld fr 1920s* Pursuit, prosecution, and other sorts of involvement with the law: *types of cash mark which do not involve federal heat*—E DeBaun **2** *n carnival* Mob violence, esp in resentment for being cheated **3** *n* Any sort of trouble and recrimination, esp the angry complaining of irritated persons; =FLAK, STATIC: *We better expect heat when this report gets out* **4** *n underworld fr 1920s* A firearm, usu a pistol: *I was packing about as much heat as you find in an icicle... without a gun*—J Evans

See DEAD HEAT, GIVE someone HEAT, PACK HEAT

the **heat** *n phr fr black* The police; a police officer: *Try operating an American city without the heat, the fuzz, the man*—Eldridge Cleaver

See IF YOU CAN'T STAND THE HEAT STAY OUT OF THE KITCHEN, PUT THE HEAT ON someone, TAKE HEAT, TAKE THE HEAT OFF

heater **1** *n* A firearm, esp a pistol; =HEAT **2** *n* A cigar: *those long Havana heaters*—Mike Todd

the **heat is on** *sentence* Extreme pressure and pursuit are afoot, esp by the police against criminals: *The heat is on dope. That's a big bust if they get hold of you*—New York

heave **1** *v* To vomit; =BARF **2** *n police* A shelter: *Heave. Any shelter used by a policeman to avoid the elements*—GY Wells

the (or the **old**) **heave-ho** *n phr* Forcible ejection; summary and emphatic dismissal; =the BOUNCE: *If you make any noise... you get the heave-ho*—WJ Slocum [*heave and ho*, the sailors' cry when hauling, is attested from the 16th century]

See GET THE AIR, GIVE someone THE AIR

heaven *See* BLUE HEAVEN, HOG HEAVEN, STINK TO HIGH HEAVEN, TO HELL

heavy **1** *n* A thug; hoodlum; =GOON **2** *n fr theater fr 1920s* The villain in a play, movie, situation, action, etc; =BADDIE: *It mattered not at all that his employers were the heavies of the piece*—Don Pendleton **3** *adj* Serious; intense: *heavy petting/ heavy correcting* **4** *adj cool talk & counterculture fr black* Excellent; wonderful; =COOL: *These guys were not simply cool... they were heavy, totally hip, and totally trustworthy*—San Francisco **5** *adj cool talk & counterculture fr black* Important; consequential; prominent: *You said we were meeting this heavy actress*—Paul Theroux/ *He must have been blowing some heavy politics*—Bobby Seale **6** *n* An important person; =BIG SHOT, HEAVYWEIGHT: *will continue to stitch up the local heavies*—Village Voice **7** *n surfers* A big wave: *good set of heavies*—Life

See WALK HEAVY

heavy artillery or **big guns** *n phr* The most impressive and persuasive arguments, evidence, persons, etc, available: *They're wheeling out the heavy artillery for the debate on withholding/ Against these big critics' big guns I offer Serban & Co some shelter*—Village Voice

heavy breather *n phr* =BODICE-RIPPER

heavy breathing *See* HARD BREATHING

heavy-cake *n 1920s* A ladies' man; =LOVER-BOY

heavy date **1** *n phr* A very important rendezvous, esp with someone of the other sex for sex: *A heavy date with a light lady*—K Brush **2** *n phr* One's partner on a heavy date **3** *n phr* Any important, urgent engagement: *a heavy poker date for this afternoon*—WC Burnett

heavy-foot *n police* A habitually fast driver; speeder

heavy (or **heavily**) **into** *adj phr* Much engaged in; prominent in: *his family* *very heavy into potato chips*—A Arthur

heavy leather 1 *n phr* Leather clothing and various metal accoutrements as or in imitation of motorcycle gangs, esp by extravagantly masculine homosexuals: *He's gone beyond butch, won't wear anything but heavy leather these days* **2** *modifier: A psychopathic killer cruises heavy-leather homosexual bars*—New York Times

heavy metal 1 *n phr rock and roll* A style of simple music characterized by extreme loudness, distortion, pounding drums, and played through great banks of amplifiers and speakers: *With all the sudden interest in heavy metal... Deep Purple has decided to give it a go once again* —Aquarian/ *a degree of internal intricacy that belies popular conceptions of heavy metal*—Rolling Stone **2** *modifier: As the prototypical heavy metal band, Led Zeppelin has created its fair share*—Rolling Stone

heavy money *n phr* (Variations: **big** or **important** or **real** may replace **heavy; dough** or **jack** or **sugar** may replace **money**) A large amount of money; impressive sums; =MEGABUCKS: *Why did she walk out on a movie career which was paying her heavy money?*—P Martin/ *I've been busy cleaning up some heavy dough* —Jerome Weidman

heavy sugar *n phr* A possession or condition indicating wealth: *Six Mercedeses is heavy sugar*

See HEAVY MONEY

heavyweight *n* An important person; =BIGGIE: *He's some sort of heavyweight in the rag trade*

◀ **Hebe** or **Heeb**▶ *n* A Jew

heck *interj* =HELL

the **heck** *See* the HELL

hedge 1 *v* (also **hedge off**) *gambling* To transfer part of one's bets to another bookmaker as a means of reducing possible losses if too many of one's clients were to win **2** *n* Something that offsets expected losses: *People were buying gold as a hedge against inflation*

hedgehop *v* To fly an airplane very low

the **heebie-jeebies** (Variations: the **heebies** or the **jeebies** or the **leaping heebies**) *fr early 1900s* **1** *n phr* A very uneasy and jumpy feeling; nagging frets; =the WILLIES: *His several disquisitions on the jeebies* —H Allen Smith/ *I always get the heebies there*—Harold Robbins/ *First night I had a fit of the heebie-jeebies* **2** *n phr* Delirium tremens [said to have been coined by a cartoonist named Billy De Beck]

heel 1 *n underworld fr early 1900s* A sneak-thief; petty criminal; =PUNK **2** *n carnival* A petty hawker; =SHILL **3** *n fr early 1900s* A contemptible man; blackguard; =BASTARD, PRICK, SHITHEEL: *His friend turned out to be a heel, and ran off with his wife and money* **4** *v underworld* To escape from prison **5** *n: They made a clean heel from Leavenworth* **6** *v fr late 1800s* To get a gun for oneself or another person

See COOL one's HEELS, ROUNDHEEL, SHITHEEL, TARHEEL

heeled 1 *adj fr middle 1800s* Armed; carrying a weapon: *I can talk better when I know this guy isn't heeled*—J Evans **2** *adj fr late 1800s* Wealthy; in funds; =FLUSH: *Having two bills in the kick I counted myself heeled* **3** *adj narcotics* Possessing narcotics; =DIRTY [said to be fr the spur attached to the "*heel*" of a fighting cock, hence a weapon]

See WELL-HEELED

heeler *See* WARD HEELER

heesh *n narcotics* Hashish

hefty 1 *n* A stout or obese person: *While other hefties count their calories, he counts the dollars*—Hal Boyle **2** *adj* Obese: *a hefty matron over at the corner table* **3** *adj* Large; considerable: *not only romance, but a hefty dose of fantasy these days* —New York

heimish *See* HAIMISH

a **Heinz 57 variety** *n phr* A mutt; a dog of no discernible lineage; a mongrel: *Chloe's her dog... "a Heinz 57 variety," says Ivey*—New York Daily News [fr a promotional phrase for the many kinds of food packaged and sold by the Heinz company]

heist (HĪST) **1** *v fr early 1900s underworld* To steal; stick up; rob **2** *v* To highjack **3** *n* A robbery or hold-up: *Led Zeppelin... was the victim of the heist*—New York Post [fr an early and dialectal pronunciation of *hoist*, with the sense that a thief lifts and takes his booty]

hell 1 *interj* An exclamation of disgust, regret, emphasis, etc: *Oh hell, they're back/ Hell, darling, I didn't mean it* **2** *n* Strong rebuke or punishment; =MERRY HELL: *Your old man'll give you hell/ I caught hell from the tax people* **3** *n* A bad experience: *Dinner with my in-laws is usually pure hell* **4** *v* =HELL AROUND **5** *v* To speed; =BARREL: *An ambulance, helling out the state road*—R Starnes

See ALL HELL BROKE LOOSE, BEAT THE SHIT OUT OF someone or something, AS BLAZES, BLUE HELL, CATCH HELL, COME HELL OR HIGH WATER, EASY AS PIE, EXCUSE ME ALL TO HELL, FOR THE HELL OF IT, FROM HELL TO BREAKFAST, GIVE someone HELL, GO TO HELL IN A HANDBASKET, LIKE A BAT OUT OF HELL, LIKE HELL, MERRY HELL, PLAY HELL WITH something, RAISE HELL, A SNOWBALL'S CHANCE IN HELL, TO HELL

the **hell 1** *adv phr* (also **◀the fuck▶**) Completely and immediately • A hostile intensifier: *Get the hell out of here/ Get the fuck off my back, you jerk* **2** *adv phr* (Variations: **deuce** or **devil** or **◀fuck▶** or **heck** may replace **hell**; **in God's name** or **in hell** may replace **the hell**) In fact; really • Mainly used for rhythmic fullness in a hostile question: *What the hell do you mean by that?/ How the fuck would he meet the taxes and pay so many salaries?* —Joseph Heller/ *He never told me where in God's name he was going/ Where in hell is that paper clip?* [probably derived from expressions of incredulity like "in the world," which altered to "in hell"]

hell around *v phr fr late 1800s* To lead a life of low pleasures; frequent bars, chase sex partners, etc: *I'd like to hell around a couple years, then settle down*

hell-bent-for-leather *See* HELL-FOR-LEATHER

hellcat *n* A volatile and dangerous woman

heller 1 *n* An energetic and aggressive person, esp one who is mischievous and menacing: *He was quite a heller when young* **2** *n college students* An exciting and action-packed party

hell-for-leather or **hell-bent-for-leather** *adv fr late 1800s British* Rapidly and energetically; =ALL-OUT, FLAT OUT: *You're heading hell-for-leather to a crack-up* [origin unknown; perhaps related to British dialect phrases *go hell for ladder, hell falladerly, hell faleero*, and remaining mysterious even if so, although the *leather* would then be a very probable case of folk etymology with a vague sense of the *leather* involved in horse trappings]

hellhole *n* Any unpleasant or morally degenerate place; =DUMP: *Emerson is a hellhole*—New York Times

a **hell of a** or **helluva** or **one hell of a** *adj phr* Very remarkable, awful, admirable, distressing, etc; =A BITCH OF A: *We had one hell of a good time/ They could have done a helluva lot better than cold cereal*—Armistead Maupin

a **hell of a** (or **no**) **way to run a railroad** *n phr* An incompetent, overcomplex, or disastrous way of doing something; a flawed and botched methodology: *When she saw how our department was organized she told us it was a hell of a way to run a railroad, and she suggested some improvements*

the **hell of it** *n phr* The worst part of something; what makes something very nasty: *The hell of it is that I tried all week to renew my license before they caught me*

hell on wheels *n phr* A very impressive, nasty, violent, etc, situation or event: *That party was hell on wheels/ This house is going to be hell on wheels in six months*—Lawrence Sanders [said to be fr mid-19th-century characterization of the gambling places and houses of prostitution loaded on flat-cars for railroad workers in the West]

hell or high water *See* COME HELL OR HIGH WATER

hell-raiser 1 *n* A person likely to cause trouble and disturbance, esp by an active and defiant spirit: *This town needs a few hell-raisers to liven it up* **2** *n* A person who leads a life of low pleasures; profligate; libertine; =HELLER: *He was barred from the Muskie train after lending his press pass to a drunken hell-raiser*—Saturday Review

hell to pay *n phr* A very large fuss with dangerous implications; violent repercussions: *When you come late there'll be hell to pay*

helper *See* BOILERMAKER

he-man **1** *n* A very masculine man; =HUNK, MACHO **2** *adj: a he-man pose/ a regular he-man cop*—E Lavine

hemp **1** *n* A cigar **2** *n narcotics* Marijuana [*hemp* plants produce both rope and marijuana]

See INDIAN HAY

the **hemp** **1** *n phr* Death by hanging; the noose **2** *n phr narcotics* Marijuana or a marijuana cigarette

hen-apple *n* An egg

hen-fruit *n* Eggs

hen party *n phr* A party for women only: *Men have stag parties; girls have hen parties*—JG Rothenberg

hen tracks *n phr* (Variations: **chicken** may replace **hen**; **scratches** or **scratchings** may replace **tracks**) Illegible handwriting; scrawl

hep *adj jive talk fr early 1900s jazz musicians* Aware; up-to-date; =HIP, WITH IT: *By running with the older boys I soon began to get hep*—Louis Armstrong/ *but I'm hep, man; for example, I had my vasectomy already*—Herbert Gold [origin uncertain; perhaps fr the drillmaster's *hep, hep,* with the sense "in step"; early jazz musicians often marched in parades, esp funeral parades]

hepcat *n jive talk* A man who appreciates the right sort of music, leads a life of fashionable pleasure, etc; =CAT, DUDE: *a big-timer, a young sport, a hep cat, in other words, a man-about-town*—Langston Hughes [fr *hep cat*; a possible supplementary origin fr Wolof *hipicat* "man who is aware" has been suggested]

hepster *n jive talk* A hep person; =HEPCAT

hep to *adj phr* Aware of; cognizant of: *How little we've been personally hep to what's actually going on*—New Yorker

hep to the jive *adj jive talk* Aware; informed; initiated; =WITH IT: *I commenced getting hep to the jive*—Louis Armstrong

herb or **herbs** *n narcotics* Marijuana; =POT: *So you get fines to pay and you've lost your herbs*—Wall Street Journal

herd *See* RIDE HERD ON someone or something

herder *n prison* A prison guard

here *See* UP TO HERE

here's mud in your eye *See* MUD IN YOUR EYE

herky-jerky *adj* Jerky; spasmodic; not smooth: *herky-jerky instability of Shepard's plays*—New Yorker

hero sandwich or **hero** or **Hero** *n phr* or *n* A sandwich made with a loaf of bread cut lengthwise and filled with a variety of cheeses, sausages, vegetables, etc; =GRINDER, HOAGIE, SUBMARINE, TORPEDO [perhaps because one needs to be a bit of a *hero* to eat a whole *sandwich*]

the **herring pond** *n phr fr early 1700s British* The Atlantic Ocean

Hershey bar **1** *n phr WW2 armed forces* A stripe, worn on a military uniform to indicate units of time spent on overseas service ◀**2**▶ *n phr* A black person [fr a *bar* of *Hershey* (a trade name) chocolate, the brown of the chocolate in the second sense and the yellow of the wrapper of some such bars in the first; first sense probably influenced by the name of General Lewis B *Hershey*, director of the selective service system from 1941 to 1970]

hey *interj* An exclamation used to get attention, to show surprise, delight, greeting, disapproval, etc • Increasingly used as a placative or apologetic analogue of "Listen" or "Believe me": *Hey, you can't go in there!/ Hey, how you doing?/ Hey, it's okay, I didn't mean it/ Hey, you were never better*

hi or **hiya** *interj fr early 1900s* A salutation upon meeting: *The staccato cry of "Hi!," which we... judged to be the almost universal greeting*—New Yorker

hick **1** *n fr late 1600s British* A rural person; a simple, countrified man or woman; =APPLE-KNOCKER, RUBE. *The automobile... largely nullified the outward distinctions between hick and city slicker*—DL Cohn **2** *modifier: that hick chief of police*—Erle Stanley Gardner [fr a nickname of Richard, thought of as a country name, as Reuben is the base of "rube"]

See WOODHICK

hickey or **hickie** **1** *n* *fr early 1900s* Any unspecified or unspecifiable object; something one does not know the name of or does not wish to name; =DOODAD, DOOHICKEY, GADGET: *We have little hickeys beside our seats*—Atlantic Monthly **2** *n* A blackhead, pimple, or other minor skin lesion; =ZIT **3** *n* A mark on the skin made by biting or sucking during a sex act: *line of hickeys, or love bites*—John Irving

hickeymadoodle *n* =DOODAD, HICKEY

◁ **hickory dick** ▷ *See* DOES A WOODEN HORSE HAVE A HICKORY DICK

hicksville or **Hicksville** **1** *adj* =DULLSVILLE **2** *adj* =CORNY

hick town *n phr* *fr early 1900s* A small or rural town: *any hick town in Kansas*—American Mercury

hide *n* =HORSEHIDE

See TAKE IT OUT OF someone's HIDE, TAN

hideaway **1** *n* A private retreat; personal refuge; =HIDEOUT **2** *n* A small, remote place, esp a small nightclub, restaurant, etc: *has played to punks in the hideaways*—World's Work

hideout **1** *n* *prison fr early 1900s* An inmate who hides with the intention of escaping at night **2** *n* *fr 1920s* A place of relative obscurity and safety; =HIDEAWAY: *The gang had a hideout in a ruined warehouse near Hoboken*

hides *n jazz musicians* Drums, esp a complete drum set as used by a jazz musician

hide the weenie *See* PLAY HIDE THE WEENIE

hidey hole **1** *n phr* *fr middle 1800s British* A place to hide; =HIDEAWAY **2** *modifier:* *conceal themselves in one of the hidey hole apartments of their proliferating step-parents*—Village Voice

hi-fi or **hi fi** or **high-fi** **1** *n* or *n phr* *fr late 1940s* A record player that reproduces sound without much distortion or alteration from the original **2** *modifier:* *a hi-fi amplifier/ hi fi recording* [fr *high fidelity*]

high **1** *adj* Drunk, esp slightly so: *high, slightly alcoholic, above the earth!*—Arthur Miller **2** *adj* *narcotics fr 1920s* Intoxicated by narcotics, esp in an easy and lighthearted condition induced by drugs: *An actor has less license to get high during working hours than does a musician*—Saturday Review **3** *n:* *He took a few tokes and got a pretty good high* **4** *n* A nonintoxicated feeling of exhilaration or euphoria; =LIFT: *Weddings are a high*—Saturday Review **5** *adj:* *The congregation was all high on gospel enthusiasm*

See MILE-HIGH CLUB, SHIT IN HIGH COTTON

high as a kite *adj phr* Intoxicated or exhilarated to an important degree

See BLOW something HIGH AS A KITE

highball **1** *n* *railroad fr late 1800s* A signal denoting a clear track or clearance to start or accelerate **2** *n* *railroad* A train running on schedule, or an express train **3** *v* *fr 1920s fr railroad* To speed; rush: *One New York distributor highballed 30 trucks through the Holland Tunnel*—Associated Press **4** *n* *fr late 1800s* An iced, mixed alcoholic drink taken in a high glass: *He quaffed a couple of rye highballs and left* **5** *n* *fr WW1 Army* A military salute [fr the former use of a railroad track-side signal using a two-foot globe, raised or lowered, to instruct the engineer; the military sense fr the use of a railroad conductor's raised hand or fist as a signal to the engineer to start, the term transferred from the mechanical signal; the origin of the beverage sense is uncertain, though the reference may be to the drink in a *high* glass raised *high* in a toast, and resembling the train conductor's *highball* signal]

highbrow **1** *n* *fr early 1900s* An intellectual; person of notable education and culture; =DOUBLE DOME, EGGHEAD: *One does not need to be a "highbrow" to read this book*—AG Kennedy **2** *adj* (also **high-browed**): *all them high-brow sermons*—Sinclair Lewis **3** *adj* Impractical; idealistic; unrealistic: *another silly highbrow scheme* [coined by the humorist Will Irwin around 1905]

high camp *n phr* Art work, theater performance, items of decoration, etc, that are so outrageously old-fashioned, so blatantly injurious to good contemporary taste, as to assume a sort of special value by their very egregiousness: *His way of lisping Shirley Temple lyrics is high camp*

high-class *adj* Of first quality; esp of refined and elevated culture; =CLASSY: *a high-class show/ a very high-class guy*

high cotton *See* SHIT IN HIGH COTTON

higher than a kite (or **than Gilroy's kite**) *adj phr* Very drunk or very much intoxicated by narcotics

higher-up *n* One of the persons in charge; a member of the upper echelon; =BIG SHOT • Most often in the plural: *She always fought with the movie higher-ups*—Associated Press

highfalutin or **highfalutin'** or **hi-foluting** *adj fr middle 1800s* Overblown and pretentious; bombastic; stilted: *take one with ideas less "high-falutin'"*—Scribner's/ *stilted, overstrained, and as the Americans would say, hi-foluting*—Anthony Trollope [origin unknown; originally a gerund, seemingly based on a verb *high falute*, suggesting a humorous alteration of *flute*; perhaps fr a blend of *highflown* with some other element]

high five **1** *n phr* A way of greeting by slapping raised palms together • Chiefly used by and adopted from athletes, who themselves adopted the style from black colleagues: *hand-shaking, even a few high-fives from the younger alums*—Rutland Herald **2** *n phr: Hey, Jim, high five me*

high gear *See* IN HIGH GEAR, SHIFT INTO HIGH GEAR

high-hat **1** *n* (also **high-hatter**) A person who behaves arrogantly and snobbishly; a putatively important person: *a lot of lowbrows pretending to be intellectual high-hats*—P Marks **2** *v fr 1920s: How come you're high-hatting me, old buddy?* **3** *adj* (also **high-hatty**) *fr 1920s: his high-hat posturings/ high-hatty pretentions* **4** *n fr jazz musicians* A set of two cymbals, the upper of which is crashed on the lower by operating a foot-pedal; =SOCK

high-hatter *n* =HIGH-HAT

high heaven *See* STINK TO HIGH HEAVEN, TO HELL

high horse *See* GET ON one's HIGH HORSE

highjack *See* HIJACK

high-jinks *See* HI-JINKS

high muckety-muck *n phr* (Variations: **muck-a-muck** or **muckie-muck** or **mucky-muck** or **monkey-monk** may replace **muckety-muck**) *fr middle 1800s Western* A very important person, esp a pompous one; =BIG SHOT, HIGHER-UP: *I'm gonna meet a couple of the high muckety-mucks at the university tomorrow* [fr Chinook jargon *hiu muckamuck* "plenty to eat," transferred to the important individual who has plenty to eat; the *monkey-monk* variant is a case of folk etymology]

high on someone or something **1** *adj phr* Very favorable towards; enthusiastic about: *I'm not as high on Wallace Stevens as I once was* **2** *adj phr* Intoxicated by; exhilarated with: *He says he's high on Jesus/ She gets high on wine and pot*

high on the hog *See* EAT HIGH ON THE HOG

high-rent *adj phr* Chic and expensive; =CLASSY, HIGH-CLASS: *with some kind of high-rent bitch from a women's magazine*—Dan Jenkins

high roller **1** *n phr fr late 1800s* A person who gambles for high stakes: *for the high rollers in the mysterious world of wheat and corn futures*—Time **2** *n phr* =BIG-TIME SPENDER

the **high sign** *n phr fr early 1900s fr southern Appalachian* A signal to an associate, esp one given inconspicuously by gesture: *waiting by prearrangement in the dark blue Lincoln Town Car, and George gave him the high sign*—San Francisco

hightail or **hightail it** *fr early 1900s fr cowboys* **1** *v* or *v phr* To leave quickly; =LIGHT OUT: *She took one look and hightailed for home* **2** *v* or *v phr* To speed; rush; =HIGHBALL: *We better hightail it if we want to make the first show* **3** *v* or *v phr* =TAILGATE

high tech or **hitech** **1** *n phr* or *n* Advanced technology: *From OPEC to High Tech*—Washington Post **2** *adj: takes us through three high tech happenings, a computer room, a radiology unit, an intensive care unit*—Village Voice **3** *n phr* or *n* An object or design, usu of synthetic or fabricated material, designed to look like an example of high technology: *This chair is high tech*

high ticket *See* BIG TICKET

high-toned or **high-tony** *adj* Very refined and genteel; aloof and superior; =TONY: *Look at the high-tony bum*—Toots Shor

high water ***See*** COME HELL OR HIGH WATER

high, wide, and handsome **1** *adv phr* Easily, triumphally, and masterfully; =WITH FLYING COLORS **2** *adj phr: a high-wide-and-handsome win*

◁ **high yellow** (or **yaller**)▷ *black* *n phr* A light-skinned black person, esp an attractive young woman: *I mean high-yellow girls*—Langston Hughes/ *took some little high-yaller girl in the closet one day*—Claude Brown

hijack or **highjack** **1** *v fr 1920s* To rob, esp to rob a vehicle of its load: *Hijack the truck*—E Lavine **2** *v* To commandeer a public vehicle, esp an airliner, for some extortionary or political purpose: *Two more planes were hijacked to Cuba last week* [said to be fr the command *High, Jack*, telling a robbery victim to raise his hands; an early-20th-century hobo sense, "traveling hold-up man," is attested, which suggests that the source may be railroad and hobo slang; see *ball the jack*]

hi-jinks or **high-jinks** *n fr middle 1800s* Boisterous fun; pranks and capers: *the dashing hi-jinks of the Katzenjammer Kids*—Ebony [fr the name of a dice game played for drinks]

hike **1** *v line repairers fr 1920s* To work as a line repairer, esp to climb poles and towers in such work **2** *v* To raise: *They won't hike our wages this year* **3** *n: The government got a big tax hike* [fr mid-19th-century term *hike up* "go or raise up," related to *hoick* of the same meaning, both probably fr the basic dialectal sense "go, go about"]

hill ***See*** DRIVE someone OVER THE HILL, OVER THE HILL

Hill ***See*** SAM HILL

the **Hill** **1** *n phr* Capitol Hill in Washington, DC: *They're all over the Hill, and can frighten members*—Fortune **2** *n phr* The US Congress: *Republicans or Democrats on the Hill*—Playboy

hillbilly **1** *n fr late 1800s* A southern Appalachian hill dweller **2** *adj: hillbilly music/ hillbilly crafts* **3** *n* A country bumpkin **4** *adj* Countrified; unsophisticated; =HICK: *This ain't no hillbilly joint. We got some class here*—J Cannon

a **hill of beans** ***See*** NOT GIVE A DAMN

himself ***See*** HIS NIBS

hincty (Variations: **hinkty** or **hinkty-ass** or **hankty**) *black* **1** *adj* Snobbish; aloof; =STUCK-UP: *hinkty motherfucker*—George Warren **2** *adj* Pompous; overbearing **3** *adj* =HINKY **4** *n* A white person; =OFAY [origin unknown]

hind end *n phr* The buttocks; =ASS

hinders or **hind legs** *n* or *n phr* The legs • Often in phrases connoting resistance or defiance: *He stood up on his short little hinders and got himself a lawyer/ The Packer defense rose on its hind legs again*—Milwaukee Journal

hindsight ***See*** TWENTY-TWENTY HINDSIGHT

◁ **hind tit**▷ ***See*** SUCK HIND TIT

hinge *n* A look or glance; =GANDER

hinky *adj* Suspicious; curious: *driver of the pimpmobile looks hinky*—Joseph Wambaugh [origin unknown]

See DOODAD

hip *beat & cool talk fr black* **1** *adj* =HEP **2** *adj* Being and/or emulating a hipster, hippy, beatnik, etc; =COOL, FAR OUT: *"I'm hip"... means... .Cool. In*—Herbert Gold **3** *v* To make aware; inform: *hipping black people to the need to work together*—Bobby Seale [fr *hep*]

See SHOOT FROM THE HIP

hip cat or **hipcat** *beat & cool talk* **1** *n phr* or *n* =HEPCAT **2** *n phr* or *n* =HIPSTER

hip chick *n phr beat & cool talk* An alert and up-to-date young woman, esp in matters of popular culture, music, etc

hipe ***See*** HYPE

hip-hop or **Hip Hop** **1** *n* or *n phr* =RAP SONG **2** *n* or *n phr* =BREAK DANCING **3** *adj* or *adj phr* Of or pertaining to contemporary black urban youth culture in the 1980s: *Hip-hop clubs feature rappin' DJs and bad-dressin' dudes* **4** *n* or *n phr* The activities that are emblematic of contemporary black urban youth culture: *What is "hip-hop"? That phrase includes such activities as break dancing, rap music, and graffiti art*—New York Daily News

hipped on *adj phr fr early 1900s* Enthusiastic about; obsessed with: *I ain't hipped on her, sort of hypnotized by her, any more*—Sinclair Lewis [ultimately fr *hip* or *the hip* "hypochondria," hence obsession]

hipper-dipper *esp 1940s* **1** *adj* Excellent; superb; =SUPER-DUPER: *a hipper-dipper display*—John Kieran **2** *n prizefight* A prizefight where the result is prearranged: *the last fight being a "hipper-dipper"*—Philadelphia Record [the boxing sense perhaps related to *dipper* "small swimming pool," in which one goes up to the *hips*; modeled on *take a dive* and *tank*]

hippie or **hippy** **1** *n esp 1960s counterculture* One of a group of usu young persons who reject the values of conventional society and withdraw into drifting, communes, etc, espouse peace and universal love, typically wear long hair and beards, and use marijuana or psychedelic drugs; =BEAT, BEATNIK **2** *modifier: Saigon has acquired an elaborate hippie culture*—New Yorker

hippy *adj* Having wide and prominent hips

See HIPPIE

hip shooter *n phr* A person inclined to act and respond impulsively and aggressively; =HOTHEAD

hipster **1** *n* =HEPCAT, HEPSTER, HIP CAT **2** *n* =BEATNIK, HIPPIE

hip to *adj phr beat & cool talk* Aware of; knowledgeable and informed of: *They were hip to me too and just waiting for the right moment*—Macleans

hired gun **1** *n phr* A professional killer; =HIT MAN **2** *modifier: elaborated on his "hired gun" reference in an interview*—Washingtonian **3** *n phr* An employee, esp one who does persuasional and promotional sort of work: *We're not just "hired guns" out to raise a few bucks*—Washingtonian

his nibs or **himself** *n phr* A very important person; supervisor or chief, esp one who insists on deferential treatment; =the MAN: *Take it in to his nibs yourself/ Has himself seen this?* [origin uncertain; perhaps *nibs* is related to *nob* "important person, esp a rich one"]

hit **1** *n* Anything very successful and popular, esp a show, book, etc: *He wrote two Broadway hits* **2** *v: I think this show will hit* **3** *modifier: a hit musical/ hit song* **4** *n* A win at gambling, on the stock market, etc: *a big hit on the commodities exchange* **5** *v: She hit real big at the track last week* **6** *n narcotics & underworld* A meeting between criminals, esp for the purpose of transferring loot or contraband **7** *n underworld* A premeditated murder or organized-crime execution, esp one contracted for with a professional killer: *There is no set price for a hit*—Playboy **8** *v: The mob figure got hit last night in his car* **9** *n narcotics* A dose of narcotics; =FIX: *The current price of cocaine was about $10 a "hit"*—HM Schmeck **10** *n narcotics* A puff of a marijuana cigarette; =TOKE: *He held a long hit in his mouth, then expelled it slowly*—Cameron Crowe **11** *n fr narcotics* A pleasurable sensation; =RUSH: *People jockeyed for position around the foyer to get a little hit of darshan*—Ramparts **12** *n narcotics* A cigarette into which heroin has been introduced: *the mixed tobacco-and-heroin cigarettes called "hits"*—I Peterson **13** *v* To reach; visit; attain: *He hit Frisco on the third day/ His new book... hit the best-seller list*—Philadelphia Bulletin/ *The market hit a new high today* **14** *n* Each separate occasion; each time; =SHOT: *You should be on a tour, where you can get 2000 people a hit* **15** *v students* To pass an examination, esp with a good grade; =ACE: *I really hit the eco final* **16** *v* To cause a strong reaction: *The injection hit the heart like a runaway locomotive*—Nelson Algren

See CLOUT FOR THE CIRCUIT, MAKE A HIT, PINCH HIT, SMASH

hit someone **1** *v phr* (also **hit** someone **up**) To solicit money, a favor, etc: *I'll hit Joe for ten bucks/ She hit him up for a big raise* **2** *v phr* To have a strong impact on; distress; overwhelm: *Kennedy's death hit me pretty hard* **3** *v phr* To present; reveal: *I wanna hit you with a very profitable idea* **4** *v phr poker* To deal another card **5** *v phr* To serve another drink: *He signaled the* *bartender. "Hit us again"*—JE Grove **6** *v phr narcotics* To administer a narcotic, esp by injection

hitch **1** *n* A problem or difficulty; delaying defect; =CATCH, GLITCH: *Everything went off without a hitch* **2** *n armed forces* A period of enlistment: *42 percent have "reupped" for another hitch*—New York Times **3** *n* A ride, esp one gotten by hitchhiking; =LIFT **4** *v* =HITCHHIKE **5** *v fr middle 1800s* To marry; be married

hitchhike *v* To get free rides by standing beside a road and signaling drivers; =HITCH, THUMB

hit for (or **out for**) *v phr* To start for or toward: *One time we hit for KC*—James M Cain

hit for the circuit *See* CLOUT FOR THE CIRCUIT

hit for the cycle *v phr baseball* To hit personally a single, a double, a triple, and a home run all in one game

hit it a lick *v phr* To hit very hard: *I hit it a hell of a lick, right out of the place*

hit it off **1** *v phr* To like one another: *The pair hit it off right from the start*—Billy Rose **2** *v phr* To work well together **3** *v phr* To succeed with others: *He hit it off with the whole class*

hit someone **like a ton of bricks** *v phr* To have a great sudden impact on, esp by surprise: *Then the answer hit me like a ton of bricks* [based on the mid-19th-century term *fall upon* someone *like a thousand of bricks*]

hit list *n phr* A putative or actual list of persons who are to be removed from office, punished, murdered, etc: *EPA officials maintained a "hit list" of employees*—New York Times

hit man *n phr* An assassin, esp a professional killer; =HIRED GUN: *Like every professional hit man I've ever known, I've always used a gun*—Playboy

hit on someone **1** *v phr* To ask for a favor; =HIT someone: *I hit on her to take my classes that day* **2** *v phr* To make advances to; =PROPOSITION: *Crowe/ It's amazing that a man of my own age would be hitting on me*—San Francisco **3** *v phr* To steal from someone

hit (or **head**) **out** *v phr* To start; depart; get on the way

hit pay dirt *v phr* To find what one is looking for or needs; =STRIKE OIL: *I didn't hit pay dirt until near the bottom of the second box*—J Evans

hitter *n* =HIT MAN
See SWITCH-HITTER

hit the bottle (or **the booze** or **the sauce**) *v phr* To drink liquor, esp rapidly and to excess; =BOOZE: *If he keeps hitting the bottle they'll have to dry him out*

hit the bricks **1** *v phr* To go out and start walking on a street or sidewalk **2** *v phr prison* To be released from prison: *He'll hit the bricks tomorrow, having been paroled* **3** *v phr* To go out on strike: *teachers... won't be as quick to hit the bricks*—New York Times

hit the bullseye *v phr* =HIT THE NAIL ON THE HEAD

hit the ceiling *v phr* To become violently angry; =BLOW UP: *and, according to one source, hit the ceiling with rage*—New York Times

hit the deck **1** *v phr* To be knocked down **2** *v phr* To get down on the ground quickly; duck down flat: *When I heard that airplane shoot I hit the deck* **3** *v phr fr Navy* To get out of bed; rouse oneself

hit the dirt (or **gravel**) *v phr baseball* To slide into a base

hit the fan *v phr* To cause or experience extensive trouble and chaos: *A month later it all hit the fan*—Esquire/ *Meanwhile the mailings had hit the fan*—New York
See the SHIT HITS THE FAN

hit the hay (or **the sack**) *v phr* To go to bed

hit the jackpot *v phr* To win or succeed spectacularly; get the most available: *I hit the jackpot with this new job*

hit the mat *v phr* =HIT THE DECK

hit the nail on the head *v phr* To be exactly right; say precisely the most accurate thing: *His few quiet remarks hit the nail on the head*

hit the pad *v phr* =HIT THE HAY

hit (or **push**) **the panic button** *v phr* To give way to alarm and terror; declare a general emergency: *He hit the panic button when he saw the month's figures/ a move characterized by many as pushing the panic button*—Inside Sports

hit the road **1** ***v phr*** To leave; get on one's way: *We better hit the road, it's a long way home* **2** ***interj*** An irritated request that one leave: *Hit the road, Jack, and don't you come back no more*—Percy Mayfield

hit the sauce ***See*** HIT THE BOTTLE

hit the silk ***v phr esp WW2 paratroops & Army Air Force*** To make a parachute jump

hit the skids **1** ***v phr*** To fail; =GO BELLY UP: *But if HBJ hit the skids, could the building ensure the integrity of retirees' pensions?*—Newsweek **2** ***v phr*** To show a precipitous decline; fall disastrously: *Home sales are down and sales of large cars have hit the skids*—Time

hit the spot ***v phr*** To be very satisfying, esp to some appetitive need: *That cup of coffee really hit the spot*

hit up ***v phr narcotics*** To inject a narcotic; =SHOOT UP

hit upside one's **face** (or **head**) ***See*** GO UPSIDE one's FACE

hit someone **where he lives** ***v phr fr middle 1800s*** To deliver a very painful blow, insult, insinuation, etc

hit someone **with** something ***v phr*** To present; reveal, esp a suggestion: *I want to hit you with a very intriguing proposition*

hiya ***See*** HI

hizzoner ***n*** The mayor: *Hizzoner threw them out of the meeting*

◁ **hn** ▷ (pronounced as separate letters) ***n black*** A black person who adopts or reflects white society's values; =OREO, UNCLE TOM [fr *house nigger*, a reference to the slavery-era distinction between slaves who worked in the plantation house and those who worked in the fields]

ho[1] or **hoe** ***n*** A prostitute or other disreputable woman: *like many of her sisters of the streets (she calls them "ho's")*—New York Times [fr Southern or black pronunciation of *whore*]

ho[2] ***See*** the HEAVE-HO, RIGHT-O

hoagie ***n*** =HERO SANDWICH

hobo ***n fr late 1800s*** A person who wanders from place to place, typically by riding on freight trains, and who may occasionally work but more often cadges sustenance • The hobo is sometimes distinguished from bums and tramps by the fact that he works [origin unknown; perhaps fr the call "Ho, boy," used on late-19th-century Western railroads by mail carriers, then altered and transferred to vagrants; perhaps putative *hoe-boy*, a migrant farm worker in the West, who became a *hobo* after the harvest season]

hock[1] **1** ***v fr middle 1800s*** To pawn: *I hocked my diamond ring*—John O'Hara **2** ***n*** The state of pawn: *I've got to get my typewriter out of hock* [apparently fr Dutch *hok* "prison"; the earliest US use was *in hock*, "in prison"; perhaps also fr the underworld phrase *in hock* "caught," fr the notion that one is taken "by the heels," or *hocks*]

See IN HOCK

hock[2] or **hok** ***v*** To pester; nag: *with her hokking and her kvetching*—National Lampoon [fr Yiddish *hok* in the idiom *hok a chynik* "knock a teapot," meaning "chatter constantly, talk foolishness," perhaps because such talking resembled the loud whacking of a pot]

◁ **hockey** or **hocky** ▷ **1** ***n*** Feces; excrement; =SHIT: *Great big blooping hunks of dog hockey*—William Styron **2** ***n*** Empty and pretentious nonsense; =BULLSHIT: *any of that hocky about being a white man*—Calder Willingham **3** ***n*** Semen; =CUM [origin unknown; perhaps fr a variant pronunciation of the *hokum, hokey, hocus-pocus* cluster, suggested by some spellings, and hence originally "falsehood, pretentious exaggeration, etc," whence "bullshit," whence "shit"]

hockshop ***n fr late 1800s*** A pawnshop

ho-dad (also **hodad** or **ho dad** or **ho-daddy**) ***fr surfers*** **1** ***n*** A person who claims knowledge and authority he or she does not possess; =BLOWHARD, WISE GUY: *"ho-daddy" (intruding wise guy)*—Life **2** ***n*** A nonparticipant who seeks the company of athletes and performers; hanger-on: *The true surfer is scornful of the "ho-daddies"*—Time **3** ***n esp teenagers*** An obnoxious and contemptible person; =JERK, PHONY, WIMP [perhaps fr a surfer's cry *Ho, dad!*]

hoe ***See*** A HARD ROW TO HOE

hog **1** ***n railroad & hoboes fr late 1800s*** A locomotive, originally a heavy freight engine **2** ***n motorcyclists*** A Harley Davidson (a trade name) motorcycle: *Harley, perhaps best known for its big-engine "hogs"* —Time/ *a hundred Hell's Angels on their Hogs*—Esquire **3** *n black* A large car, esp a Cadillac (a trade name): *"I got a Hog...a Cadillac"* —Clarence Cooper **4** *v* To take or eat everything available, for oneself; claim and seize all: *appeared simultaneously with* ET *and suffered as the little fungiform geek hogged the box office*—Washington Post **5** *n* (also **the hog**) *narcotics* PCP or a similar addictive drug: *threw thousands of caps of "the hog"... into the crowd*—Esquire [railroad and hobo sense fr the fact that large locomotives consumed a great deal of coal]

See EAT HIGH ON THE HOG, SEWER HOG, WHOLE HOG

hog (or **pig**) **heaven** *n phr* A place of total bliss; paradise; =FAT CITY: *For the sports junkie, this is Mecca. For the gambler, it is hog heaven*—Philadelphia Journal/ *One American woman talks gleefully of finding some Victorian pressed glass for almost nothing. "We are in pig heaven"* —Time

hog (or **hog's**) **leg** *n phr fr cowboys* A pistol, esp a large one: *his hog's leg looking like a fire plug against his ribs* —Raymond Chandler/ *a .45-caliber hogleg out of his coat pocket*—Stephen King

hogwash *n* Empty and pretentious talk; nonsense; =BALONEY, BULLSHIT: *He said most of my theory is pure hogwash*

hog-wild *See* GO HOG-WILD

ho-hum **1** *adj* Unexciting; mediocre; dull: *ho-hum sex and the dregs of countless six-packs*—RJ Battaglia **2** *v* To be bored with; be indifferent to: *On the other hand, we shouldn't ho-hum the situation*—Paul Engeler **3** *n* Boring matter; dull tripe

hoist **1** *v fr underworld fr 1700s* To rob; steal; =HEIST: *The stall... distracts the sales force while the hoister hoists*—RL Woods **2** *n: Crooks... speak of a job of hold-up as a "hoist"* —J Wilstach **3** *v* To drink some beer or liquor: *Let's stop at Harry's and hoist a few*

hoity-toity *adj fr late 1800s British* Snobbishly exclusive; haughty; uppish; =SNOOTY: *in the hoity-toitiest of Fifth Avenue shops*—S Dawson [fr earlier *highty-tighty* "peremptory, quarrelsome," perhaps related to *high* in the sense of "superior"]

hoke *n* =HOKUM

hoked-up *adj* False; dishonestly confected; =PHONY: *a zest for hoked-up violence*—Playboy

hoke up *v phr* To make something artificial or meretricious; confect; falsify: *Halaby hoked up a special ceremony*—RG Sherrill [fr *hoke* fr *hokum*]

hokey *adj* False and meretricious; very dubious; =PHONY: *hokey confections that public taste ought to repudiate*—Albert Maltz

hokey-dokey *See* OKEY-DOKE

hokey-pokey or **hoky-poky** **1** *n fr late 1800s British* Cheap ice cream and sweets made primarily to attract children **2** *modifier: candy bars on the hokey-pokey counter*—Westbrook Pegler **3** *n* A seller of such provender **4** *n* Any cheap, gaudy items **5** *n* False and meretricious material; =HOKUM: *too much of... "Hollywood hokey-pokey"*—Philadelphia Bulletin [fr an earlier sense of *hokey-pokey* "cheat, swindle," ultimately fr *hocus-pocus*]

the **hokey-pokey** *n phr* A simple, informal sort of circle dance: *people across the globe will join hands, form huge human circles.... The hokey-pokey*—Philadelphia

hokum *fr theater fr early 1900s* **1** *n* Pretentious nonsense; insane trash; =BUNK: *more hokum from the Department of State* **2** *n theater* A trick, gag, routine, etc, sure to please a gullible public: *There is some hokum in "King Penguin"* —New York Times **3** *n* =HOKEY-POKEY [perhaps fr a blend of *hocus* and *bunkum*]

hokus *n narcotics* Any narcotic

hold *narcotics* **1** *v* To have narcotics for sale **2** *v* To have narcotics in one's possession

See ON HOLD

holder *See* ROACH CLIP

hold someone's **feet to the fire** *v phr* To subject to strong and painful persuasion; use maximum pressure: *helping hold the President's feet to the fire*—New York Times

hold one's **horses** *v phr* To be patient; stop importuning; =HOLD one's WATER • Often an irritated command: *He kept on asking though she told him to hold his horses*

holdout 1 *n* A person, esp a professional athlete, who refuses to sign a contract until the salary is raised **2** *n* A person who refuses to agree to something: *coerce reluctant hold-outs into "kicking in"*—E Lavine **3** *n gambling* A playing card sneakily kept from the deck by the dealer

holds *See* NO HOLDS BARRED

hold the bag (or **the sack**) **1** *v phr fr late 1800s* To be deceived so that one takes all the losses; be duped to one's disadvantage: *Don't you let them leave you holding the bag*—Erle Stanley Gardner **2** *v phr* To be so maneuvered that one takes individual blame for a failure or a crime [fr 17th century *give the bag to hold* "victimize in a game of snipe-hunt"]

hold the phone *v phr* To wait a minute; delay • Often a request for respite and thinking space: *My body jerked back in a kind of WC Fields double take. "Hold the phone," I said*—Newsweek

holdup 1 *n fr late 1800s* A robbery, esp the armed robbery of a person, bank, store, etc; =STICKUP: *Give us no nonsense. This is a holdup*—Philadelphia Bulletin **2** ***modifier:*** *the full-fledged hold-up business*—E Lavine **3** *n* The demanding of exorbitant prices, wages, etc: *That was no sale, it was a holdup* **4** *n* A delay; stoppage; cause of delay: *a brief holdup in our magnificent progress/ What's the holdup?*

hold up 1 *v phr fr late 1800s* To rob, esp at gunpoint: *They were holding an old man up at the corner* **2** *v phr* To extort or demand higher prices, wages, etc: *That shop held me up!* **3** *v phr* To delay; cause a delay or stoppage: *The strike held up our flight for six days* **4** *v phr* To point to; single out: *Is this the one you held up as such a great example?*

hold one's **water** *v phr* To be patient; stop importuning; =HOLD one's HORSES • Often an irritated command: *Just hold your water*—Paul Sann

hole 1 *n* Any nasty or unpleasant place; =DUMP, JOINT: *The restaurant turned out to be a loathsome little hole* ◁**2**▷ *n* The vulva ◁**3**▷ *n* The anus ◁**4**▷ *n* A person regarded merely as a sex object or organ; =ASS ◁**5**▷ *n* Sexual activity; genital gratification; =ASS **6** *v* To shoot someone: *Those two cops are bound to get holed*—John Farris *See* ACE IN THE HOLE, BIG HOLE, BROWN, BUNGHOLE, CORNHOLE, IN A HOLE, IN THE HOLE, the NINETEENTH HOLE, NOT KNOW one's ASS FROM one's ELBOW

hole card *n phr poker* A card dealt face down in stud poker

hole in the ground *See* NOT KNOW one's ASS FROM one's ELBOW

a **hole in the** (or **one's**) **head** *See* HAVE A HOLE IN one's HEAD, NEED someone or something LIKE A HOLE IN THE HEAD

hole in the wall *n phr* A small and usu unpretentious dwelling, shop, etc: *Nothing fancy, just a hole in the wall on Park Lane*

hole up (or **in**) **1** *v phr* To hide; take refuge: *He might hole up for a day or two*—NY Confidential **2** *v phr* To stay for a time; lodge; =CRASH: *thinking about holing up for the night*—Sinclair Lewis

holler 1 *v* To shout **2** *v* To inform; =SING, SQUEAL: *You think he wouldn't holler if they turned the heat on him?*—WR Burnett **3** *v* To complain; =BITCH: *What's he hollering about now?* **4** *n* (also **hollersong**) A Southern black folk song with spoken or shouted words, a precursor of the blues song: *You find hollers in many of Leadbelly's recordings and songs*—Stephen Longstreet

holly-golly or **hully-gully 1** *n* Nonsense; =BALONEY, BUNK **2** *n* Disturbance; upset; racket; =FLAP: *What's this ghastly holly-golly all about?* [probably echoic symbolism for a fuss, influenced by *hullabaloo, hurly burly*, etc]

Hollywood kiss (or **kiss-off**) *n phr* =KISS-OFF

holy cats *interj* (Variations: **cow** or **gee** or **mackerel** or **Moses** or **shit** or **smoke** may replace **cats**) An exclamation of surprise, wonder, dismay, admiration, etc: *All he could manage to say upon seeing the nude blonde was "holy cow!"*—B Price/ *holy shit, the police*—Richard Fariña [euphemisms for *holy Christ*]

holy hell *n phr* Vehement rebuke; severe punishment: =HELL, MERRY

HELL: *I caught holy hell when the thing broke*

See CATCH HELL, GIVE someone HELL

Holy Joe **1** ***n phr*** *fr middle 1800s British nautical* A clergyman; chaplain: *needs twelve Holy Joes to get him past them Pearly Gates*—J Evans **2** ***n phr*** A sanctimonious, pietistic person: *In the east they're all holy Joes and teach in Sunday schools* —Stephen Longstreet **3** ***modifier:*** *these Holy Joe voices*—JD Salinger

◁ **holy shit**▷ ***interj*** An exclamation of surprise, dismay, discovery, etc: *And I think holy shit, this could be a Hitler* —Village Voice

holy terror ***n phr*** A troublesome, energetic, and aggressive person: *He's a holy terror around home*

hombre (HAHM bray, AHM bray) *See* WISE GUY

home *See* BRING HOME THE BACON, HOME BOY, MONEY FROM HOME, NOBODY HOME

home boy or **homeboy** *fr Southern, esp black* **1** ***n phr*** or ***n*** A person from one's home town **2** ***n phr*** or ***n*** (also **home**) A close friend, or someone accepted like a friend: *Home boy, them brothers is taking care of business!*—Eldridge Cleaver **3** ***n phr*** or ***n*** *chiefly college students* An easygoing, unpretentious person **4** ***n phr*** *police* A male homosexual, esp the friend or lover of another male homosexual [homosexual sense fr *homo*]

home-court advantage ***n phr*** *fr sports* The psychological and other favorable elements that come from being in familiar surroundings, with a sympathetic audience, etc: *Yojimbo is less than sympathetic here (it's clear who has the home-court advantage)* —Village Voice

home free ***adv phr*** Successfully arrived or concluded; at or assured of one's goal; out of trouble: *A couple more good days' work and I'm home free*

home plate *See* GET TO FIRST BASE

homer **1** ***n*** *baseball* A home run; =CIRCUIT BLOW **2** ***v:*** *Kaline homered in the sixth*

homework *See* DO one's HOMEWORK

homey or **homie** **1** ***n*** *black* A close friend or a fellow townsperson; =HOME BOY: *is expecting more than her homies to support her*—Amsterdam News **2** ***n*** *black* A new arrival from the South

◁ **homo**▷ **1** ***n*** A homosexual man or woman: *I knew nothing about "homos" at that time*—HK Fink **2** ***adj:*** *homo slang/ a homo bar*

honcho (HAHN choh) **1** ***n*** *fr Korean War armed forces* The person in charge; chief; =BIG ENCHILADA, BOSS: *better known as the honcho of Scientific Anglers, Inc*—Sports Afield **2** ***v:*** *He honchoed the whole deal* [fr Japanese *hancho* "squad leader"]

honey **1** ***n*** One's sweetheart, beloved, spouse, etc **2** ***n*** Any pleasant, decent person; =PUSSYCAT, SWEETIE **3** ***n*** A person or thing that is remarkable, wonderful, superior, etc; =DILLY, HUMDINGER: *Ain't this a honey of a Scotch?*

honeycakes *See* BABYCAKES

◁ **honeypot**▷ ***n*** *fr later 1700s* The vulva or vagina

honk **1** ***v*** To sound the horn of a car **2** ***v*** To make a sexual, esp a homosexual, advance by handling or pressing a man's genitals: *He's making a move to honk you, just grab his hand*—Joseph Wambaugh

◀ **honky** or **honkie**▶ **1** ***n*** *black* A white person; =GRAY, OFAY **2** ***adj:*** *No talkin' or we'll bust your honky heads*—Time [fr *hunky*[1], as often normally pronounced in black English]

honky-tonk *fr black fr late 1800s* **1** ***n*** A cheap, usu disreputable saloon and gambling place; =JOINT: *rode to my honky-tonk on a bus*—Philip Wylie **2** ***v:*** *his honky-tonking ended, naturally, at Filly's, the urban cowboy saloon*—Philadelphia Journal **3** ***n*** A cheap, small-town theater: *playin' the sticks... the honky-tonks*—Gypsy Rose Lee **4** ***n*** A brothel **5** ***modifier:*** *the honky-tonk district* [origin unknown]

hoo-boy ***interj*** *esp 1950s* An exclamation of surprise, consternation, amazement, etc [perhaps a blend of *hoo ha* with *oh boy*]

hooch[1] ***n*** *fr late 1800s* Liquor; strong drink; =BOOZE: *and the bottles of hooch, and the free food on the job* —New York Times [fr the liquor made by the *Hoochinoo* Indians of Alaska]

hooch[2] or **hootch** *fr Korean & Vietnam War armed forces* **1** ***n*** A Korean house, room, shack, etc: *gig-*

gle timidly and plead: "Come on to my hooch"—Time **2** *n* A Vietnamese village hut **3** *n* An American barracks, esp a Quonset-style barracks in Vietnam [fr Japanese *uchi* "house"]

hooch[3] ***See*** HOOTCHIE-COOTCHIE, the HOOTCHIE-COOTCHIE

hood (HŏŏD, HŏŏD) **1** *n fr early 1900s* A hoodlum: *those St Louis hoods*—American Mercury **2** ***modifier:*** *has been in the hood hierarchy for decades*—New York Post [fr *hoodlum*, origin unknown; perhaps fr Bavarian German *hodalum* "scamp"]

hooey *n esp 1920s & 30s* Nonsense; foolishness; =BALONEY: *lip-smacking imps of mawk and hooey write with us what they will*—WH Auden [perhaps based on *phooey*]

hoof **1** *n fr late 1800s* A foot: *Take your goddam hoof the hell off my fender*—J Evans **2** *v* To walk; =HOOF IT: *I better hoof over to the garage* **3** *v fr 1920s* To dance: *She's hoofing in that show about cats*

hoofer *n* A dancer, esp a professional dancer in nightclubs, musical plays, etc: *The hoofers and the chorines of a cabaret*—John Mason Brown

hoof it *fr early 1900s* **1** ***v phr*** To walk: *get off the bus... and hoof it home*—Philadelphia **2** ***v phr*** To dance: *then hoofed it a bit herself with old friend Gene Kelly*—Newsweek

hoo-ha[1] ***interj*** An exclamation of astonishment, admiration, envy, scorn, deflation, etc: *So your boy's on TV, hoo ha! Does she gossip? Hoo-ha*—Leo Rosten [fr Yiddish]

hoo-ha[2] **1** *n fr early 1900s British armed forces* Disturbance; brouhaha; uproar: *in case you're wondering what all the hoo-ha is about*—A Sainer **2** *n* A noisy celebration; a raucous fete: *But Northampton, Mass, held a weeklong hoo-ha for its favorite son*—Newsweek [perhaps influenced by *hoo-ha*[1]; first attested in early-20th-century British armed forces as "an argument; an artillery demonstration," and probably echoic-symbolic of a loud fuss, like *hoopla, to-do, brouhaha, foofaraw,* and *hooley*]

hook **1** *n merchant marine & Navy* An anchor **2** *n baseball* A curveball **3** *n narcotics* A hypodermic needle or bent pin used for injecting a narcotic **4** *n narcotics* A narcotic, esp heroin **5** *v fr 1600s* To steal, esp to shoplift: *Hooking merchandise from department stores requires no training*—Forum **6** *v* To get; find: *Since Swede had no car, he either hooked rides from the waiters who did, or walked*—New Yorker **7** *v* To arrest; stop and ticket: *My cab driver got hooked for speeding*—WR Burnett **8** *v* To entice successfully; procure more or less against one's will: *They hooked me for the main speech* **9** *v* To cheat; deceive • Most often in the passive voice: *He got hooked into paying the whole bill* **10** *n* A prostitute; =HOOKER: *Janie Ruth looked at the hook*—Dan Jenkins **11** *v* To work as a prostitute; whore: *They stress the fact that they strip and don't hook*—Trans-Action **12** *n esp musicians* Something that strongly attracts, esp something catchy in the lyrics or music of a song: *the musicians push a good hook, a high, ragged guitar line*—Rolling Stone **13** *n college students* A grade of C **14** *v* To drink, esp quickly at a gulp: *You pour a half-glass of Dewar's, hook it down and fan out the flames with a bottle of beer*—Albert Goldman

See ON one's OWN HOOK, SHITHOOK

the **hook** ***n phr*** A violent football tackle in which the head of the ball-carrier is caught and held in the crook of the tackler's arm

See GET someone OFF THE HOOK, GO ON THE HOOK FOR someone or something, LET someone OFF THE HOOK, OFF THE HOOK, ON THE HOOK, RING OFF THE HOOK

hook arm ***n phr*** *baseball* A pitcher's throwing arm

hooked **1** ***adj*** *narcotics* Addicted to a narcotic: *I was the pusher who got you hooked*—WH Auden **2** ***adj*** Captivated as if drug-addicted: *a shock to discover my wife was hooked on needlepoint*—Good Housekeeping **3** ***adj*** Married

hooker **1** *n fr middle 1800s* A prostitute: *the thirtyish ex-hooker was answering questions*—New York Post **2** ***modifier:*** *hooker district* **3** *n* A drink of liquor; =SNORT: *It took a stiff hooker of whiskey... to thaw her*—Dashiell Hammett [first sense apparently fr a resident of Corlear's *Hook* in New York City, in the 19th century the site of many brothels, esp frequented by seamen]

hook (or **rook**) someone **into** something *v phr* To obligate or involve by force or trickery: *They hooked me into paying for everybody's lunch/ She got rooked into a very boring cocktail party*

hook it *v phr fr middle 1800s* To depart hastily; run away: *Better hook it, Joan, the heat's arrived*

hooks *n* The hands
See FISHHOOKS, LUNCH-HOOKS, MEATHOOKS, POTHOOKS

hooky **1** *adj* Captivating; very attractive; catchy: *But it's hooky, the formidable Graham Parker*—Village Voice **2** *v* =PLAY HOOKY

hooligan **1** *n fr late 1800s British* A hoodlum; ruffian: *Beat me up with your hooligans*—Ira Wolfert **2** *n* =GUN **3** *n circus* The Wild West tent of a circus or show [perhaps fr a rowdy Irish family named *Hooligan* of Southwark, London, England; circus sense perhaps related to Western *hoolian* or *hooley-ann* or *hoolihan* "throw a steer by leaping on its horns, bulldog"; all senses perhaps related to Irish *hooley* "noisy party, carousal"]

hoop **1** *n* The basketball net or basket; =BUCKET **2** *n* A basketball goal; =BUCKET: *He made six hoops last night* **3** *modifier* Having to do with basketball: *a hoop team/ hoop scores*
See FLAT TIRE

hoop-a-doop or **hoop-de-doop** or **hoopty-do** *See* WHOOP-DE-DO

hooperdooper or **hooperdoo** **1** *n* A person or thing that is remarkable, wonderful, superior, etc; =HONEY, HUMDINGER: *Next Saturday's Barn Dance is going to be another hooperdoo*—National Barn Dance (radio program) **2** *modifier: we got a hooperdoo quarter hour left*—Uncle Walter's Doghouse (radio program) **3** *n* A very important person; =BIG SHOT: *The hooperdooper in front is the celebrated poet*

hoopla or **whoopla** **1** *n* A joyous and boisterous clamor; =HOO-HA: *Is this hoopla for my birthday?* **2** *n* A noisy fuss; a commotion: *His arrival started a big hoopla* **3** *n* Advertising or promotion; =BALLYHOO, FLACK: *I say this is a lot of unnecessary hoopla*—Sports Afield

hoop-man or **hoopster** *n* A basketball player

hoopty-doo *See* WHOOP-DE-DO

hoosegow (HōōS gou) *n fr early 1900s cowboys* A jail [fr Mexican Spanish *juzgao* "tribunal, court"]

Hoosier *n* A native or resident of Indiana

hoot *n* A person; =COOT: *Milo O'Shea makes a canny old hoot of the judge*—People Weekly

a **hoot** *n fr 1960s British* Something very funny and pleasant; plain fun: *Life is a hoot*—Village Voice
See NOT GIVE A DAMN

hootch *See* HOOCH

hootchie-cootchie or **hooch** *n* Sexual activity; =ASS: *He propositioned her for a little hootchie-cootchie*

the **hootchie-cootchie** (or **hootchy-kootchy** or **hooch**) *fr late 1800s* **1** *n* An erotic dance in which the woman rotates her hips, etc **2** *n* A woman who dances the hootchie-cootchie [origin unknown; *The Hootchy-Kootchy* was the name of a song associated with the dancer Little Egypt at the Chicago World's Fair of 1893, but the term is attested several years earlier in the context of the minstrel show]

hootenanny (HōōT ən annee) *n* Any unspecified or unspecifiable object; something one does not know the name of or does not wish to name; =GADGET, GIZMO: *He took a little hootenanny off the shelf and blew into it* [one of many fanciful coinages for something unspecified; probably related to *hooter* "anything trifling," attested fr the mid-19th century, and to *hewgag* "an indeterminate, unknown mythical creature," similarly attested; the syllable *hoo-*, which is prominent in such coinages, probably represents the interrogative pronoun *who*]

hooter *n students* A marijuana cigarette

◁ **hooters** ▷ *n* A woman's breasts: *Hooters (a synonym, I learn, for knockers...)*—New York

hooty *adj* Excellent; delightful; amusing: *Wasn't that a hooty rendition?*

hoover **1** *v chiefly British* To eat or drink up, esp greedily: *instead of the* *moussaka and lamb that everyone else was hoovering*—Car and Driver ◁**2**▷ *v* To do fellatio or cunnilingus with or to; =EAT: *Will you hoover me immediately, before I pay any attention to you*—National Lampoon [fr the *Hoover* (a trade name) vacuum cleaner]

hop[1] **1** *n fr middle 1700s* A dance or dancing party: *We went to a hop*—James T Farrell **2** *n* A hotel desk porter: *The hop was tall and thin*—Raymond Chandler **3** *n* A trip; stage of a journey; airplane flight: *a long hop to Singapore* **4** *v: They hopped over to Brussels* **5** *v* To board: *to hop a plane* **6** *n* A short flight, as distinct from a long one

See CARHOP, SOCK HOP

hop[2] **1** *n fr late 1800s* Opium: *So long as any smoker can obtain his hop*—The Lantern **2** *n narcotics* Any narcotic; =DOPE: *A little hop or dope was slipped to an anxious prisoner*—E Lavine **3** *modifier: a hop fiend/ hop dream* **4** *n narcotics* A drug addict; =HEAD, HOPHEAD **5** *n* Nonsense; lies; =BALONEY, BULLSHIT: *Go peddle your hop somewhere else*—J Roeburt [fr a shortening of Cantonese Chinese *nga pin*, pronounced HAH peen, "opium," literally "crow peelings," a Chinese folk etymology for English *opium*; in a subsequent US folk etymology this was changed to *hop* by assimilation with the plant used to make beer, with its suggestions of intoxication]

hop fiend (or **fighter**) *n phr* A drug addict; =HOPHEAD

hophead *n narcotics* A drug addict; =HEAD: *the bench with its bittersweet words: winos, hopheads, the omnipresent graffiti*—New York

hop on the bandwagon *See* GET ON THE BANDWAGON

hopped up **1** *adj narcotics* Intoxicated by narcotics: *The newer generation of "coked" or "hopped up" gunmen*—E Lavine **2** *adj* Excited; highly stimulated: *What are you so hopped up about?* **3** *adj* Made very exciting; deliberately intensified: *hopped-up novels*—WG Rogers **4** *adj hot rodders* =SOUPED UP

the **hopper** *n phr* The imagined place where proposed ideas, actions, etc, are placed; =PIPELINE: *Can't look at it now, put it in the hopper* [fr the *hopper* device that feeds mills, etc, so called fr its shaking]

hops **1** *n fr early 1900s* Opium; =DOPE **2** *n* Beer

See FULL OF BEANS

hop-stick *n narcotics* An opium pipe

hopup (HAHP up) *modifier hot rodders* Used to increase the power and speed of a car engine: *a pretty good selection of hopup and speed equipment*—Village Voice

hop up **1** *v phr narcotics* To administer narcotics: *He hopped himself up on heroin* **2** *v phr horse-racing* To drug a horse for speed; =DOPE: *to hop up or slow down their horses*—A Hynd **3** *v phr hot rodders* To increase the speed and power of a car; =SOUP UP: *How to Hop Up Chevrolet and GMC Engines*—Floyd Clymer Motorbook

horn **1** *n musicians* Any wind instrument **2** *n jazz musicians* The trumpet ◁**3**▷ *n* A penile erection; =HARD-ON: *I could have beat up five guys with the horn I had on*—George V Higgins

See LIKE SHIT THROUGH A TIN HORN, TINHORN, TOOT one's OWN HORN

horn in *v phr fr early 1900s cowboys* To intrude; thrust oneself in; =BUTT IN: *Some wallie tried to horn in on our gang*—Philadelphia Bulletin

hornswoggle *v fr early 1800s* To cheat; swindle; dupe; =CON

◁**horny**▷ *adj* Sexually excited and desirous; keenly amorous; lustful; =HOT • Of recent years applied to women as well as men, despite being derived fr **horn** "erect penis": *his horny teen-age daughter*—Time/ *At first it eased my head and made me less horny*—Mike Aron

horse **1** *n circus* A thousand dollars; =GRAND **2** *n narcotics* Heroin; =SHIT: *They shoot horse in the john at the local high school*—Judith Crist **3** *n narcotics* A hard-drug addict **4** *n prison* A prison guard paid by inmates to smuggle letters and other contraband in and out **5** *n truckers* A truck or a tractor **6** *n police* An honest, hard-working police officer: *We know who the horses are around here, every cop in the department knows*—Providence Journal-Bulletin **7** *v* To play and idle; =FOOL AROUND, HORSE AROUND: *He*

wasn't just horsing now—W Henry ◁**8**▷ *v* To do the sex act with or to; =SCREW: *They caught him horsing his secretary* **9** *v* To hoax; fool [the sense "heroin" may have derived fr *shit* "heroin" by way of *horseshit,* although the derivation might well have gone in the other direction; or perhaps the sense is based on the sobriquet of a Damon Runyon character *Harry the Horse* by way of the partial rhyme of *Harry* with *heroin*]
See DARK HORSE, DEAD HORSE, DOES A WOODEN HORSE HAVE A HICKORY DICK, ENOUGH TO CHOKE A HORSE, FROM THE HORSE'S MOUTH, GET ON one's HIGH HORSE, GET ON one's HORSE, ONE-HORSE, WARHORSE

horse-and-buggy *adj* Old-fashioned: *a horse-and-buggy leisureliness*

horse apple **1** *n phr* A ball of horse feces **2** *n phr* Pretentious trash; =HORSESHIT: *all that particular pile of horseapples boiled down to* —Stephen King

horse apples *interj* =HORSESHIT

horse around *v phr* To joke and caper pleasurably; indulge in horseplay; =FOOL AROUND: *He wouldn't stop horsing around, so they let him go*

horse cock *n phr fr WW2 Navy* Salami and other cold-cut sausages; =DONKEY DICK

horsehide *n* A baseball

the **horselaugh** *n phr* A loud, nasty, and dismissive laugh at someone; =the MERRY HA-HA: *When I asked for more time I just got the horselaugh*

horse opera (or **opry**) **1** *n phr fr early 1900s* A cowboy movie; Western; =OATER **2** *n phr circus* A circus

horseplayer *n* A person who bets on horse races

horserace *n* A serious contest; a hard-fought competition: *Suddenly what looked like a shoo-in for Mondale turned into a real horserace*

horses *n gambling* A pair of dishonest dice, esp of mismatched dice that can produce only specific combinations: *Karnov explained the use of "horses"*—Associated Press
See HOLD one's HORSES

◁**horse's ass**▷ *n phr* A contemptible person; a persistent and obnoxious fool; =JERK: *If, however, he wanted to present himself in Texas as a real horse's ass, none of us would dispute him*—Joseph Heller

◁**horseshit**▷ **1** *n* Nonsense; pretentious talk; bold and deceitful absurdities; =BALONEY, BULLSHIT: *You give me all that horseshit about the conditions here*—Calder Willingham **2** *modifier: Superstar! What a horseshit idiot!*—Saul Bellow **3** *v: He was horseshitting about what a great sailor he is* **4** *interj* An exclamation of disbelief, disapproval, and contempt: *Horseshit! I'll never believe that* **5** *n* Trivialities; nonessentials; =CHICKEN SHIT: *Don't bother me with that nitniny-piminy horseshit*

horse's mouth *See* FROM THE HORSE'S MOUTH

hose **1** *v* To cheat; deceive; dupe; =SCREW, SHAFT: *The IRS tried to hose me* **2** *v college students* To turn down; reject; snub: *They're afraid of getting hosed*—New York Times [origin uncertain; perhaps fr a rare but attested *hose* "penis," whereupon the term would be analogous to *diddle, fuck, screw, shaft,* etc]

hoser **1** *n* A person who cheats and deceives; =CON MAN: *Reagan is a hoser*—Drew University graffito **2** *n Canadian* A Canadian, esp a simple and durable northern type: *unavailable to us hosers, but can be bought down south*—Westworld

a **hosing** *See* TAKE A HOSING

hostess *See* BALL-BEARING HOSTESS, BANG THE HOSTESS

hot **1** *adj fr middle 1800s* Capable of high speed; moving very fast: *Hot crate, a fast plane*—A Ostrow **2** *adj* Selling very rapidly and readily, hence very much in demand: *paralleled the rise of the "hot" ticket*—New York Times **3** *adj fr late 1800s* Performing extremely well; certain to win: *When you're hot you're hot* **4** *adj fr late 1800s* Angry; furious; =PISSED OFF: *Don't get so hot about it, it was just a goof* **5** *adj* Lively; vital; vibrant: *This is a hot town* —Ernest Hemingway/ *A "hot" magazine is one that's sizzling and bubbling with activity*—New York Herald Tribune **6** *adj* Sexually excited; afire with passion; lustful; =HORNY: *Hot faggot queens bump up against chilly Jewish matrons*—Albert Goldman/ *the hottest little devil I ever met*—P Marks **7** *adj* Pornographic; salacious; =DIRTY: *a real hot movie* **8** *adj* Eager; =ANTSY: *Why so hot to get started?* **9** *adj jazz musicians* Exciting, rapid, strongly rhythmical, eliciting a visceral response: *The old jazz was mostly hot, then it was cool, and now even cool cats blow hot licks now and then* **10** *adj underworld* Stolen, esp recently stolen; contraband: *Stolen bonds are "hot paper"* —H McLellan **11** *adj underworld* Wanted by the police: *Where would a hot can of corn like Dillinger hide out* —A Hynd **12** *adj* Dangerous; menacing; potentially disastrous: *It's so hot out there, man, I'm thinking about getting into another game* —New York **13** *adj* New, esp both brand-new and interesting: *a hot tip/ the hot news from upstairs* **14** *adj* Having electrical potential; live; switched on: *Is this mike hot?/ Can I touch this wire, or is it hot?* **15** *adj* Radioactive

See BLOW HOT AND COLD, NOT SO HOT, RED HOT

hot air *fr middle 1800s* **1** *n phr* Nonsense; pretentious talk; bold and deceitful absurdities; =BALONEY, BULLSHIT: *The Jefferson family tree will never be blown down by any hot air from me*—H McHugh **2** *n phr* Pomposity and vanity; bombast: *The old fraud talks a lot of hot air*

See FULL OF HOT AIR

hot and cold *n phr narcotics* A mixture of heroin and cocaine; =SPEEDBALL

See BLOW HOT AND COLD

hot as a three-dollar pistol *adj phr* Very hot; red-hot: *The rumor is hot as a three-dollar pistol*

hotbed **1** *n black & hoboes* A bed used both day and night, by shifts of sleepers **2** *n* A place that produces or is prominently rich in specified things: *College these days is a hotbed of sobriety*

hot corner **1** *n phr baseball* Third base, esp as a fielding position **2** *n phr* Any very dangerous and crucial place: *The North African front... is a "hot corner"*—Word Study

hot damn *interj* An exclamation of pleasure, gratification, etc; =HOT DOG, HOT SHIT

hot diggety (or **diggity**) *interj* (Variations: **dog** or **doggety** or **damn** may be added; **ziggety** or **ziggity** may replace **diggety**) =HOT DOG

hot dog **1** *interj* An exclamation of delight, gratification, relish, etc; =HOT DAMN, HOT SHIT: *Did you have a good time? "Hot dog!"*—Philadelphia Bulletin **2** *n phr* A frankfurter or a frankfurter sandwich **3** *modifier: a hot-dog stand/ embattled hot-dog vendor* **4** *n phr* =HOT SHOT **5** *v phr* To perform in a brilliant, spectacular way, esp in order to seize the admiration of an audience; =GRANDSTAND, SHOW OFF: *a little careless against Bob Cousy's Royals, hot-dogging their passes and loosening their defenses*—New York Times **6** *n: Walter is one of the good guys, not a hot dog*—John Chancellor **7** *modifier: I don't appreciate that hot-dog garbage in my ball park*—Newsweek **8** *v surfers* To surf spectacularly: *Surfers may... "hot dog," do acrobatics*—National Geographic **9** *v phr* To do hot-dog skiing

hot dogger *n phr* =HOT SHOT

hot-dog skiing *n phr* Free-style skiing that features somersaults, midair turns, balletlike figures, and other feats rather than speed: *A whole new style of baroque skiing has developed. Known as "free-style," "exhibition," or "hot-dog" skiing*—Time

hotfoot **1** *v* (also **hotfoot it**) *fr early 1900s* To go fast; hurry: *Tell him to hotfoot it to the sheriff's office* —G Homes **2** *adv* At once; immediately: *I'll walk hotfoot to the doctor's office* **3** *n* A bail-jumper

hot for **1** *adj phr* Very desirous of; lusting for; wishing to possess: *She seemed hot for you*—Calder Willingham **2** *adj phr* Very eager over; enthusiastic about: *He's real hot for the new promotion policy*

hothead **1** *n* An irascible person; one quick to anger **2** *n* A fanatical, emotional person; fiery militant

hot iron *n phr* =HOT ROD

hot knife through butter *See* LIKE SHIT THROUGH A TIN HORN

hot line *n phr* An emergency telephone line or number, esp the one between the White House and the Kremlin or one modeled on it: *Clearly, hot lines are no cure for the complex, overall problem of drug abuse*—Parent/ *a community "hot* *line" to head off gang wars*—New York Times

hot number (or **item**) ***n phr*** A very sexy man or woman; =HOT PANTS

hot one ***n phr*** A very funny story, piece of news, etc

hot pants **1** ***n phr*** Strong sexual desire; lust; carnal craving: *His hot pants will get him in trouble* **2** ***n phr*** A very passionate, lustful, and potentially promiscuous person: *Catherine the Great was apparently an imperial hot pants* **3** ***n phr*** ***esp 1960s & 70s*** Very brief women's shorts

See HAVE HOT PANTS

hot potato ***n phr*** Something embarrassing and troublesome; a tricky and sticky matter: *Everyone can see how the boss looks when he handles a hot potato*—Associated Press

See DROP someone or something LIKE A HOT POTATO

hot property ***n phr*** Someone or something very valuable and marketable, esp an athlete, desirable executive, entertainer, etc: *Timmons and Co, knowing a hot property when it signs one up*—Washington Post

hot rock ***n phr*** =HOT SHOT

◁ **hot rocks** (or **nuts**)▷ ***n phr*** Male sexual craving; powerful lust: *At that time I had real hot rocks*

hot rod *hot rodders* **1** ***n phr*** A car specially modified and fitted with a powerful or rebuilt engine so as to be much faster than one of the same stock design; =A-BOMB, CAN, ROD: *Special Racing Cars and Hot Rods*—advertisement **2** ***modifier:*** *hot-rod manual/ hot-rod club* **3** ***n phr*** (also **hot rodder**) A driver or devotee of hot rods: *Right away he thinks he's a hot rod*—JA Maxwell [fr the notion of a *hot* connecting *rod* as symbolic and typical of such special engines]

the **hots** **1** ***n phr*** Strong liking; predilection: *I'd never got the deep undying hots for that rah rah collitch boy*—Hal Boyle **2** ***n phr*** Lust; =HOT PANTS: *A bare-chested photograph of this guy can give 2,300 women the hots*—Philadelphia Journal

See HAVE THE HOTS FOR someone

the **hot seat** **1** ***n phr*** The electric chair; =the HOT SQUAT **2** ***n phr*** A place where one is under uncomfortable scrutiny and pressure, esp the witness stand: *always on the cutting edge, always in the hot seat*—Washington Post

See ON THE HOT SEAT

hot shit **1** ***n phr*** & ***interj*** =HOT DOG **2** ***n phr*** Someone or something very remarkable and attractive, irresistible, etc; =HOT STUFF: *He thinks he's real hot shit/ Ain't my new boat hot shit?* **3** ***n phr*** An aggressive, self-assured person; =BIG SHOT: *like all the rest of these hot shits*—Rolling Stone

hot short ***n phr*** ***esp 1920s & 30s underworld*** A stolen car

hot shot **1** ***n phr*** An especially gifted and effective person; a notably successful person; =BALL OF FIRE, WINNER • Often used ironically: *What has been written about executives has usually dealt with the hot shots*—CW Morton **2** ***modifier:*** *In just a year I'm claiming to be a hot-shot Columbia man myself*—Dwight David Eisenhower **3** ***n phr*** *railroad* A fast train or express train **4** ***modifier:*** *a hot-shot freight* **5** ***n phr*** A news bulletin; a news flash: *When that hot-shot came in about Monahan's death*—Scene of the Crime (movie) **6** ***n phr*** *narcotics* A narcotics injection that is fatal because of an impurity or poison: *You got a hot shot! You're dead*—C Cooper

hotsie-totsie or **hotsie-dandy** ***adj*** *esp 1920s* Satisfactory; fine; =COPACETIC: *All's hotsie-totsie here, thank you so much*

hot spit ***n phr*** & ***interj*** =HOT SHIT

hot spot **1** ***n phr*** =TIGHT SPOT **2** ***n phr*** A popular night club, esp one with sexy entertainment: *became 52d Street's hot spot*—Louis Sobol

the **hot squat** ***n phr*** The electric chair: *You couldn't ever rise from the hot squat*—A Hynd

hot stuff **1** ***n phr*** *fr late 1800s* A person of exceptional merit, talents, attractions, etc; =HOT SHOT • Almost always used ironically: *I guess they think they are hot stuff*—John O'Hara/ *Don't you think I'm hot stuff*—RS Prather **2** ***n phr*** Material, entertainment, etc, that is very exciting, esp salacious: *Those magazines are real hot stuff* **3** ***n phr*** ***fr underworld*** Stolen goods; contraband **4** ***n phr*** News or information that is very important, fresh, sensational, forbidden, etc: *I peeked in your brief case, and that's hot stuff!* **5** *n phr* Food, drinks, etc, that are very hot: *Hot stuff coming through*

hot to trot *adj phr* Afire with craving, esp for sexual activity; lustful: *to ask her bluntly if she was hot to trot* —Cyra McFaddenand Driver/ *who claims her hot-to-trot boss gave her a chase around the office*—New York Post

hot under the collar *adj phr* Very angry: *the Puerto Ricans who get hot under the collar*—Village Voice

hot up **1** *v phr* To become more exciting: *Then things really hot up and January falls in love with an aging macho novelist*—Saturday Review **2** *v phr* To make something hot or hotter: *I'll just hot up some soup for lunch*

hot war *n phr* A war with combat and killing; =SHOOTING WAR

hot water *See* IN HOT WATER

hot-wire **1** *v* To start a car, truck, etc, by electrically by-passing the ignition lock: *He could hot-wire any car in about 20 seconds* **2** *v* To activate illegally; tamper with: *let the affected corporations hot-wire the regulatory process*—New York Times [fr the notion of attaching an electrically *hot* wire to the starter-motor relay; notice the earlier term *hot short*]

hound *v* To harass, pester, or annoy; =BURN

-hound *combining word* A person devoted to or addicted to what is indicated: *autograph hound/ booze-hound/ nicotine hound/ thrill-hound*

the **Hound** or **the Dog** *n phr black & students fr truckers* A Greyhound bus (a trade name)

house **1** *n* A brothel; =CATHOUSE **2** *n* The audience at a theater *See* the BIG HOUSE, BRING DOWN THE HOUSE, BUGHOUSE, CATHOUSE, CRAZY-HOUSE, DOSS, FLEABAG, FLOPHOUSE, FUNNY FARM, GRIND-HOUSE, HASH-HOUSE, JAG HOUSE, JUKE HOUSE, NUT HOUSE, ON THE HOUSE, POWERHOUSE, ROUGHHOUSE, STROKE HOUSE

house ape *n phr* A small child; an infant; =CURTAIN CLIMBER, RUG APE

house-cleaning *n* A reorganization of a business or government department, esp with dismissal of incompetent or dishonest employees; =SHAKE-UP: *Honest cops, instead of welcoming a house-cleaning... resent it*—E Lavine

house moss *n phr* The tufts and whorls of dust that accumulate under beds, tables, etc, =BEGGAR'S VELVET, GHOST TURDS

house-sit *v* To live in and care for a house free of charge while the owner is away

how *See* AND HOW, DING HOW, KNOW-HOW

how about that or **how do you like that** *interj* An exclamation of surprise, pleasure, admiration, etc: *We've only got a year to go. How about that!/ It's a first! How do you like that!*

how come *sentence fr middle 1800s* What is that?; what is the reason?

Howdy Doody *See* DOES HOWDY DOODY HAVE WOODEN BALLS

a **howl** *n teenagers* Something amusing; a funny event; =a HOOT

howler *n* A very funny mistake, esp in something written or spoken rather solemnly: *His misuse of "Rappaport" for "rapport" was the season's howler*

how's about *prep phr* What do you feel or think about: *How's about a new needle?/ How's about a drink?* —Budd Schulberg

how's tricks *sentence* How are you?; how are things going for you?

◁ **how they hanging**▷ *sentence* How are you? ● A genial greeting, usu from one man to another; an inquiry as to the condition of the testicles: *Madeline Kurnitz said, "How they hanging, kiddo"*—Lawrence Sanders

hubba-hubba *WW2 armed forces* **1** *interj* An exclamation of delight, relish, etc, esp at the sight of a woman **2** *adv* Quickly; immediately; =HABA-HABA, ON THE DOUBLE [origin unknown; perhaps a version of a Chinese greeting *how-pu-how*, apparently adopted by US airmen from Chinese pilot trainees; perhaps originally a bit of gibberish used to imitate the clamor of conversation, esp when soldiers get the command "Parade rest," after which one can talk, as distinct from the command "At ease," after which one must remain silent and contribute to no *hubbub*]

hubby *n* Husband

huckster *n fr 1950s* An advertising person or publicity agent: *so the television hucksters can peddle their shaving cream*—New York Times

huddle **1** *n* A conference; closed and intense discussion: *He went into a huddle with his aides* **2** *v: We'll have to huddle on that one* [fr the *huddle*, esp of the offensive team, before most plays in football]

huff *See* IN A HUFF

huffy *adj fr middle 1800s* Angry; petulant; irritable; =IN A HUFF: *I didn't mean to get huffy*—Sinclair Lewis

huggy-huggy *adj* Very affectionate; =BUDDY-BUDDY, PALSY-WALSY: *We are all very huggy-huggy with each other*—People Weekly

the **hully-gully** *See* HOLLY-GOLLY

humdinger *n fr early 1900s* A person or thing that is remarkable, wonderful, superior, etc; =BEAUT, LOLLAPALOOZA: *Arnold Moss gave us a humdinger of a talk*

hummer *n* A person or thing that is remarkable, wonderful, etc; =HUMDINGER: *This is Mason's first book, and it's a hummer*—Village Voice

hummy **1** *adj black* Content; happy; ignorant of danger **2** *adv: She lives real hummy*

humongous (hōō MAWN gəs) *adj esp teenagers* Very large; gigantic: *a humongous chain*—Industrial Research [perhaps a sort of echoic-symbolic blend of *huge* with *monstrous*]

hump **1** *v* (also **hump it** or **hump along**) To move or go, esp with difficulty; slog: *lack the nerve to hump it through to the end*—Partisan Review/ *put on that pack and hump for miles through the boonies*—Life ◁**2**▷ *v* To do the sex act with or to; =FUCK: *the brave pilots who hump the nubile hostesses*—Judith Crist *See* BUST one's ASS, BUST HUMP, CRAWL someone's HUMP, DRY FUCK, GET A HUMP ON, GET A MOVE ON, OVER THE HILL

◁ **humpery**▷ *n* The sex act; coupling; =FUCKING: *refused to change the X rating on "Fritz the Cat" on the ground that it depicted "anthropomorphic humpery"*—Judith Crist

◁ **humpy**▷ *adj* Sexually arousing; lubricious; sexy: *flashy, precise, and humpy*—Village Voice

hunch **1** *n fr late 1800s* An intuitive premonition; a shrewd idea or notion: *I gotta hunch she won't come back* **2** *modifier: This was too good a hunch play to let drop*—E Selby **3** *v: As I hunch it, the answer is triple*—Billy Rose [said to be fr a gamblers' belief that touching a *hunchback's* hump would bring good luck]

hung **1** *adj jazz talk* Annoyed; peeved **2** *adj* Exhausted; tired out **3** *adj* =HUNG OVER **4** *adj rock and roll* In love ◁**5**▷ *adj fr early 1800s* Having impressive male genitals; =HUNG LIKE A BULL, WELL-HUNG

hunger *See* FROM HUNGER

◁ **hung like a bull** (or **a horse**)▷ *adj phr* Possessing large genitals; =WELL-HUNG

hung over *adj phr* Suffering the ill effects of a hangover: *looking as hung over as you can get*—R Starnes

the **hungries** *See* GET THE HUNGRIES

hungry **1** *adj* Very ambitious; extremely eager to succeed: *If you don't like this job, I know a couple of hungry guys that do* **2** *adj* Impoverished; =BROKE

hung up **1** *adj phr fr beat & cool talk* Limited by conventional beliefs and attitudes; =SQUARE, UNCOOL: *Either you're way out, pops, or you're hung up*—E Klein **2** *adj phr fr beat & cool talk* Agitated or immobilized by emotional disturbance; stalled: *She suddenly got all hung up around Xmas* **3** *adj phr* Delayed; detained: *He got hung up with a phone call as he was leaving*

hung up on *adj phr fr beat & cool talk* Obsessed with; stalled or frustrated by; suffering a hangup over: *I'm hung up on fried rice*—Harper's Bazaar

hunk **1** *n* A man or woman considered primarily as a sex partner; =PIECE, PIECE OF ASS: *the hot little hunk he used to run around with*—J Evans **2** *n* A very attractive man, esp a muscular and sexually appealing one: *Wherever she goes she always manages to pick up a hunk*—Aquarian

hunker down **1** *v phr* To squat on one's haunches: *He heads for the inevitable mariachi square, hunkers down in the dark, wet and shivering*—Tom Wolfe **2** *v phr* To get into the mood and posture for hard work: *We must hunker down and get that report finished* **3** *v phr* To take a sturdy defensive attitude; become hard to move: *"We'll just have to hunker down," said Jody Powell* —Newsweek [fr Southern US fr Northern British dialect *hunker* "haunch"]

hunk of change *See* PIECE OF CHANGE

◀ **hunky**[1] ▶ (also **hunkie** or **Hunky** or **Hunkie** or **Hunk** or **hunks**) **1** *n* A foreigner, esp a Hungarian, Slavic, or Baltic laborer; =BOHUNK, GINZO **2** *modifier: hunky talk/ dumb hunkie brain* **3** *n black* A white person; =HONKY: *So I can't call everybody no Hunkie*—Ishmael Reed [fr *bohunk*]

hunky[2] *adj* =HORNY

hunky[3] *adj* Attractive, esp sexually desirable; =MACHO • Used most often of men: *hunky, bearded actor-troubadour*—Time

hunky-dory *adj fr middle 1800s* Satisfactory; fine; =COPACETIC: *That may be hunky-dory... with the jumping and jiving youngsters*—Bosley Crowther

hunter *See* HEADHUNTER, MANGO HUNTER

hurler *n baseball* A pitcher

hurtin' for certain *adj phr college students* =HURTING

hurting *adj esp armed forces & college students fr black* In great need; in distress: *If they find out about this you'll be hurting*

hush-hush **1** *adj* Very secret; classified: *a hush-hush border meeting* —Associated Press **2** *n: Why all the hush-hush about Walden?*—Raymond Chandler

husk *v* To undress; =PEEL

hustle **1** *v* To hurry: *We better hustle, the thing leaves in five minutes* **2** *n: Put a little hustle in it now* **3** *v fr late 1800s* To behave, play, perform, etc, very energetically and aggressively: *The reason they're losing is they don't hustle* **4** *v* To beg: *You'll hustle for an overcoat*—J Flynt **5** *v* To work as a prostitute; =HOOK: *whores that hustle all night long*—Louis Armstrong **6** *v* To sell; hawk **7** *v* To cheat; swindle; victimize; =CON: *It took a hell of a caddy to hustle a pro and a greenkeeper*—Saturday Evening Post **8** *n: I guess one man's "hustle" is another man's "promotion"*—Village Voice **9** *v fr early 1900s* To steal: *We must hustle us a car* **10** *n: You know I can't pay out five bills for a wash if I wasn't planning a hustle* —Lawrence Sanders [criminal senses may be related to early-19th-century *hustle* "do the sex act, fuck"]
See GET A HUSTLE ON, GET A MOVE ON

hustler **1** *n fr early 1900s* A thief or a dealer in stolen goods: *and sells to hustlers like Tommy at about one third its retail value*—New York **2** *n fr 1920s* A confidence trickster or swindler, esp one who pretends ignorance of a game where he or she is in fact an expert and sure to win; =CON MAN, SHARK **3** *n* A prostitute; =HOOKER: *I ain't nothing but a hustler* —Langston Hughes **4** *n* An energetic, aggressive performer or worker: *We need more hustlers in this department*

hutzpa or **hutzpah** *See* CHUTZPA

hype[1] **1** *n fr early 1900s* A hypodermic needle; =HYPE-STICK **2** *n fr 1920s* An injection of narcotics **3** *n* An addict who injects narcotics: *and heroin substitutes don't work with a stone hype*—Joseph Wambaugh **4** *n* A seller of narcotics; =CONNECTION: *any hype that wants to get you hooked*—D Hulburd [fr *hypodermic* referring to a needle or an injection]

hype[2] **1** *n* Advertising or promotion, esp of a blatant sort; =BALLYHOO, FLACK: *without any advance p r hype*—H Smith **2** *v: hypes no quick secondary stock offering*—New York **3** *v fr early 1900s* To trick; deceive; originally, to short-change **4** *v* =HYPE UP [origin unknown; perhaps related to *hyper* "hustle," of obscure origin, attested from the mid-19th century; recent advertising and public relations senses probably influenced by *hype*[1] as suggesting supernormal energy, excitement, etc, and by *hyper*[2]]
See MEDIA HYPE

a **hype** **1** *n phr* A high-pressure advocacy or urging; a publicity or public relations invention: *The nostalgia for the fifties is not entirely a media hype*—New York Times **2** *n phr* A person or thing promoted by hype **3** *n phr* A swindle; =CON, SCAM **4** *n phr* A lie

hyped-up **1** *adj* False; fake; =HOKED-UP, PHONY: *no hyped-up glamour*—Billy Rose **2** *adj* Excited; overstimulated; =HYPER: *The game gets him "hyped up"*—Games

hyper[1] or **hype artist** *n* or *n phr* A publicist; promoter; advertiser; =FLACK [fr *hype*[2]]

hyper[2] **1** *adj fr 1920s* Overexcited; manic; overwrought; =HYPED-UP: *It's this flaky hyper hour*—New York **2** *adj* Exceeding most; very superior; =SUPER: *with harem cushions, a hyper-hi-fi set, ha-ha candles*—Saturday Review [fr Greek *hyper* "super," and in the first sense probably fr medical terms like *hyperkinetic, hyperthyroid*, etc; in some sources this term is associated with *hipped* and *hippish*, fr *hypochondriac* "melancholic," first attested in the early 18th century] *See* THROW A FIT

hype-stick *n narcotics* A hypodermic needle

hype up **1** *v phr* To fake; manufacture; invent; =HOKE UP: *They had to hype up a convincing story* **2** *v phr* To promote or advertise by blatant, obnoxious means **3** *v phr* To give something a false impact, appeal, energy, etc: *other chemicals to hype up the produce*—Saturday Review

hypo *fr early 1900s* **1** *n* A hypodermic needle **2** *n* A hypodermic injection **3** *n narcotics* A drug addict; =HYPE **4** *v* To stimulate or strengthen; =BEEF UP: *a wilted record player hypoed by a pooped-out public address system*—John R Powers [fr *hypodermic*, referring to a needle or an injection]

I

I Can Catch *n phr truckers* The Interstate Commerce Commission

ice **1** *n* Diamonds; a diamond: *a two-carat hunk of ice* **2** *n* Gems and jewelry in general: *Gonna wear your ice?* **3** *n* Extra payment given for a desirable theater ticket: *a slight fee, say $100 worth of tickets for $120. The $20 is the "ice"*—M Zolotow **4** *v* To make something certain; =CINCH, SEW something UP: *They iced the game in the ninth* **5** *v* (also **ice** someone **out**) To ignore; snub; cut; =COLD SHOULDER: *how women were "iced" by peers during corridor conversations*—Newsweek **6** *v* To defeat utterly; trounce; =CLOBBER: *Nebraska iced Kentucky 55 to 16* **7** *v underworld* To kill; =OFF: *Ice a pig. Off a pig. That means kill a cop*—Robert Daley **8** *adj cool talk* Excellent; fine; =COOL
See BREAK THE ICE, CUT NO ICE, ON ICE

ice cream *n phr early 1900s narcotics* The crystalline form of a narcotic: *the ice cream eaters, who chewed the crystal*—H Asbury

ice cream habit *n phr narcotics* The occasional, nonaddicted, use of narcotics

iced *See* HAVE something CINCHED

ice maiden (or **queen**) *n phr* A very cool and composed woman; a chilly woman: *Margaret Thatcher, the Ice Maiden/ branded the conservative Gorsuch "the Ice Queen"*—Newsweek

iceman **1** *n* A jewel thief **2** *n* A very calm person, performer, etc: *An iceman... is a gambler who never loses his head*—J Lilienthal **3** *n* A professional killer= HIT MAN: *Maybe I hadn't seen the iceman with Bobb*—Richard Merkin

ice (or **put the icing on**) **the cake** *v phr* To put a victory beyond question; insure a favorable result: *He iced the cake with a knockdown in the seventh*

icky (Variations: **ickie** or **icky-poo** or **icky-sticky** or **ickey-wickey**) **1** *adj jive talk fr 1930s* Oversentimental; maudlin; =SCHMALTZY: *That music pleased my icky, lachrymose sensibility/ The prose gets a mite too icky-poo for comfort*—New York **2** *n* A conventional, tedious person; =SQUARE: *She turned out to be an icky* **3** *adj* Unpleasant; revolting; nasty; =GROSS, GRUNGY: *Those cool comedies and quizzes became dumb, boring, icky, weird*—Good Housekeeping/ *refuse to get involved in anything outside their own little ickey-wickey bailiwicks*—Village Voice/ *The acting is icky*—San Francisco [fr baby-talk, "sticky, nasty"; although perhaps fr Yiddish *elken* or *iklen* "nauseate, revolt"]

ID (pronounced as separate letters) **1** *n* An identity card **2** *n* Identification; evidence for one's identity: *You can't cash it here without ID* **3** *v: Who'll ID this clown?*

idea *See* WHAT'S THE BIG IDEA

idiot box *n phr* A television set; television; =the BOOB TUBE

idiot card (or **board**) *n phr television studio* A large sheet of heavy paper held up out of range of the television camera, to prompt actors or speakers; cue card: *"Idiot boards" are held out of camera range*—Saturday Evening Post/ *The scripts are gone, but* *now there are idiot cards*—Saturday Review

idiot light *n phr* A usu red light on a car's dashboard that glows to announce some sort of fact, such as the discharge of a battery, overheating, etc: *replaced by too-late-to-react idiot lights*—Car and Driver

-ie (also **-ey** or **-y** or **-sie** or **-sey** or **-sy**) **1** *suffix used to form nouns* Diminutive, affectionate, or familiar versions of what is indicated: *auntie/ cubby/ tootsie/ folksy* **2** *suffix used to form adjectives* Having the quality indicated: *comfy/ creepy/ swanky* **3** *suffix used to form nouns* Coming from the place or background indicated: *Arky/ Okie/ Yalie* **4** *suffix used to form nouns* A person of the sort indicated: *weirdie/ hippy/ sharpy*

iffy **1** *adj* Uncertain; doubtful; improbable: *His chances... were a bit iffy*—Time **2** *adj* =DICEY

-ific or **-iffic** *suffix used to form adjectives* Extremely marked by what is indicated: *horrific/ beautific* [fr *terrific*]

if you can't stand the heat stay out of the kitchen *sentence* Do not undertake a hard job if you lack the stamina and thick skin to endure sharp criticism [a favorite saying of President Harry S Truman, referring to the Presidency]

Ike *See* ALIBI IKE

◀ **Ikey** ▶ *n fr middle 1800s British* A Jew [fr a nickname for *Isaac*]

I kid you not *sentence fr 1950s* I am perfectly serious; I am not misleading nor joking with you: *It's the best thing that ever happened to me. I kid you not*

I'll be damned *sentence* (Variations: **danged** or **darned** or **ding swizzled** or **dipped** or **dipped in shit** or **fucked** or **jiggered** or **jig-swiggered** or **hanged** or **hornswoggled** or **a monkey's uncle** or **switched** may replace **damned**; **damned** may be omitted) May I be maltreated, confounded, accursed, etc; an exclamation of surprise or determination: *I'll be damned, we made it!/ I will be dipped in shit*—Larry Niven and Jerry Bournelle/ *I'll be a monkey's uncle if you put that over on me!/ Well I'll be, he made it!* [*dipped* forms fr 17th-century British *be dipped* "get into trouble"]

illegitimati non carborundum *sentence* Don't let the bastards grind you down ● Offered as a proposed motto or a pearl of wisdom [fr mock-Latin *illegitimatus* "bastard" and *Carborundum*, trade name of a brand of abrasives]

immatesticle *adj* Of no concern; not relevant; immaterial: *Whether I get called or not is immatesticle* [a play on *immaterial*]

import *n college students* An out-of-town date brought to a dance, party, etc

important money *See* HEAVY MONEY

in **1** *n* An advantage, esp through an acquaintance; entree: *He has an in at that place, since his mother owns it* **2** *adj* In fashion at the moment; now preferred: *Violence is in, sentiment is out* **3** *adj* Belonging to a select circle of the most fashionable: *one of the in people* **4** *adj* (also **in like Flynn**) Accepted; acceptable: *"Are you in or out right now?" "I'm in like Flynn. Didn't you notice the picture on my desk?"*—Art Buchwald **5** *adj police* Arrested: *Come along now, you're in* [police sense from *run* someone *in*]

See GET IN, HAVE IT IN FOR someone

-in *combining word* A communal occasion where one does what is indicated: *be-in/ lie-in/ pray-in*

in a bind (or **box**) *adj phr fr loggers* In a very tight and awkward situation; stalled by a dilemma: *I'm in a bind, damned if I do and damned if I don't* [fr the situation of a logger whose saw is caught and held tight by the weight of a tree or branch]

in a bucket *See* FOR CRYING OUT LOUD

in a funk **1** *adv phr fr British fr middle 1700s* In a depressed, nervous, or frightened state: *Jackson left San Francisco in a funk, he... looked tired and sounded like a morose, defeated candidate*—Washington Post **2** *adj phr* Depressed; melancholy: *Steve's been in a funk since he lost his dog*

in a hole *adj phr* In grave and probably insurmountable difficulties; =UP SHIT CREEK: *The death of my brother leaves me in a deep legal-financial hole*—Saul Bellow

in a huff *adj phr* Angry; petulant; grumpy

in a jam *adj phr* In trouble, esp serious trouble: *If you're in a jam, he'll fight for you*—P Jones

in a jiffy *See* A JIFFY

in a lather (or **lava**) *adj phr fr 1600s* Angry; upset; =IN A SWEAT: *The editors say they are not in a lava over the coincidence*—Time [fr the resemblance between an agitated sweat, esp the frothy sweat of horses, and frothy washing *lather* thought of as the result of vigorous agitation; the earliest attested use is in the form *in a lavour*]

◁ **in-and-out**▷ *n* The sex act; copulation; =FUCKING: *The pages of romances offered less in-and-out than a downtown parking garage*—San Francisco/ *Her refreshing answers about the old in-and-out bluntly demystified any last glitches*—Village Voice [fr the 17th-century British idiom *play at in-and-out* "do the sex act, copulate"]

in an uproar *See* NOT GET one's BALLS IN AN UPROAR

◁ **in a pig's ass**▷ (or **ear** or **eye**) *adv phr* Not at all; never; =LIKE HELL • Used for vehement denial: *In a pig's ass, I did*—Village Voice/ *Yeah, we'll get it back. In a pig's eye*—Jerome Weidman

in a pinch **1** *adv phr* If necessary; if need be: *In a pinch we could make that do* **2** *adv phr* =IN A JAM

in a poke *See* BUY A PIG IN A POKE

in a row *See* HAVE one's DUCKS IN A ROW

in a stew **1** *adj phr* Chaotic and muddled; in disarray: *The whole place is in a stew about the new appointment* **2** *adj phr* Angry and irritable; upset; =IN A SWEAT: *Well don't get in such a stew about it*

in a sweat *adj phr* Upset; irritated; tense; scared: *Don't get in a sweat, I'll return it at once*

in a tizzy *adj phr fr early 1900s* Very much upset; distractingly disturbed; in a state: *I have been in a tizzy since reading his accusations*—Saul Bellow [origin unknown]

in at the kill *adv phr* Participating in the finish of something, esp when it is very satisfying and vindictive: *Tell me when the thing'll be signed, I want to be in at the kill* [fr a fox-hunting term]

in a walk *See* WIN IN A WALK

in a zone *adj phr* Daydreaming, esp from narcotics; =SPACED-OUT [said to be fr *ozone*, implying very high up in the sky or towards outer space]

in someone's **bad books** *adv phr esp Canadian & British* Regarded as hostile; hated and menaced: *nervous about getting in the bad books of the mob guys*—Toronto Life

in business *adj phr* In operation; under way: *One more day or so of prep and we're in business/ The space shuttle is finally in business*

in cahoots *adj phr fr cowboys* In partnership; acting in a common purpose: *I told you those two were in cahoots*

in clover *adv phr* In a position of ease and affluence; =HAPPY AS A CLAM

in cold storage (or **the deep freeze**) *adv phr* Held in abeyance; reserved to be dealt with later; =ON HOLD: *The plan's in cold storage for now/ Well, let's just keep that one in the deep freeze for a few months*

Indian hay (or **hemp**) *n phr narcotics* Marijuana: *a couple of Indian hay cigarettes*—American Journal of Psychiatry

the **Indian sign** *n phr* A baleful spell or curse; =JINX: *You'd think the Indian sign was on the whole operation*

indie **1** *n movie studio* An independent, esp an independent movie producer **2** *modifier: one indie pic company*—Variety

in (or **into**) someone's **drawers** (or **pants**) *adv phr* Into the venue of venereal delight; enjoying sex with someone: *You wouldn't believe how easy it is to get into her drawers*

in Dutch *adj phr fr early 1900s* In disfavor; in trouble: *You have to promise, Pop, not to get me in Dutch with Mrs Skoglund*—Saul Bellow [origin unknown]

the **Indy** or **Indy 500** *n phr* The annual Indianapolis 500 car race

in one's **ear** *See* STAND AROUND WITH one's FINGER UP one's ASS, STICK IT

in flames *See* GO DOWN IN FLAMES

in front *See* UP FRONT

in God's name *See* the HELL

in group *n phr* An exclusive group or clique of influential persons

in someone's **hair** *adj phr fr late 1800s* Constantly annoying; nagging at: *You'll have one of these ... professors in your hair*—Mark Twain

in harness *adj phr* Working; actively employed rather than resting, retired, on holiday, etc: *He didn't know how to relax after all those years in harness*

in heck *See* the HECK

in hell *See* the HELL

in high gear *adj phr* In the most active, rapid, impressive phase; at full tempo: *The advertising campaign is in high gear*
See SHIFT INTO HIGH GEAR

in hock **1** *adj phr* Accepted for pawn; in a pawnshop **2** *adj phr* In debt; mortgaged: *We're deeply in hock to the bank*

in hot water **1** *adv phr* In trouble, esp with the law, one's superiors, etc: *He had the knack of always being in hot water with his wife* **2** *adv phr* In difficulties, esp in serious trouble; =IN THE SOUP: *He's got in hot water with the manager again*

ink *v* To write; sign, esp a contract: *He also inked the plays*—New York Daily News/ *has inked to helm two more pictures*—Variety
See PINK INK, RED INK

in like Flynn *See* IN

in line **1** *adj phr* Within appropriate bounds; acceptable; =IN THE BALLPARK: *Yes, those prices are about in line* **2** *adj phr* Behaving properly; out of trouble: *How did you keep your kids in line?*

in line for *adv phr* In position to get; about to get: *Hey, you're in line for a big bonus*

in luck *adj phr* Lucky

in mothballs *adj phr* In reserve; =ON ICE

innards *n* The viscera; =GUTS, KISHKES: *got a feeling in my innards it won't work*

inning *n prizefight fr early 1900s* A round of a prizefight

in nothing (or **no time**) **flat** *adv phr* Very quickly: *I got over there in nothing flat*

-ino *See* -ERINO

in one piece *See* ALL IN ONE PIECE

in on the ground floor *adv phr fr middle 1800s* Engaged early and profitably in a project, investment, etc: *You better act now if you want to be in on the ground floor*

in orbit *adj phr teenagers* Having a free and exhilarating experience; =HIGH, WAY OUT: *One slurp of gin and he's in orbit*

in over (or **above**) one's **head** *adv phr* In a situation one cannot cope with; helplessly committed and likely to lose: *He tried to stop, but he was in over his head*

in one's **pants** *See* ANTS

in place *adj phr* Available; ready for use; effectuated or installed; =ON LINE: *We've got a couple of new procedures in place*

in someone's **pocket** (or **hip pocket**) *adv phr* Under someone's absolute control: *He's in the hip pocket of the networks*—Washington Post

inside *See* ON THE INSIDE

inside job *n phr* A robbery, stroke of espionage, etc, done by someone or with the aid of someone within the target organization: *The cops think the hotel murder is an inside job*

insider *n* A person who has special knowledge, authority, etc, because he is within or part of some privileged group: *The insiders are saying that the President will veto it*

insides *n* =INNARDS

the **inside track** *See* HAVE THE INSIDE TRACK

in spades *adv phr* To the utmost; in the highest degree: *I detest them right back, in spades*—Saul Bellow

instant replay *n phr* Immediate repetition: *If anyone mistakes the new regimen for freedom, the full trappings of martial law remain available for instant replay*—New York Times

in sync (or **synch**) *adv phr* In order; in harmony; synchronized; without jar or clash: *perfectly in sync with Thicke's outrageous style*—Newsweek

inta *See* INTO

in tall cotton *adj phr* Very successful; enjoying excellent fortune; =FAT, DUMB, AND HAPPY: *would greet them from this office, this desk, this chair, high and dry in tall cotton*—Washington Post

intercom *n* An intercommunication system: *Marc yelled into the intercom*—Billy Rose

in the air *See* a BEAR IN THE AIR

in the altogether *adj phr* Naked

in the bag **1** *adj phr* Certain; sure; =ON ICE: *My election is in the bag/*

It's in the bag. The fix is in—WR and FK Simpson **2** ***adj phr*** Ruined; destroyed; =FINISHED, KAPUT: *If an actor is hurt or killed doing a stunt the whole film is in the bag* —Entertainment Tonight (TV program) [fr game shot and stuffed *into the game bag*; second sense fr the use of the heavy plastic body bag for the handling of military and other fatal casualties]

See HALF IN THE BAG

in the ballpark ***adj phr*** Within general appropriate limits; not exorbitant, outrageous, etc: *too high, too low, or "in the ballpark"*—Fortune

in the bucks ***adj phr*** Having money, esp a lot of it; in funds; =FLUSH, LOADED: *right after Christmas and we're not in the bucks*

in the buff ***adj phr*** Naked; =BARE-ASS, BUCK NAKED: *There we stood, in the buff and abysmally embarrassed*

in the can ***adj phr*** *fr movie studio* Successfully finished; ready for release, consumption, etc [fr the large, flat, circular tin *can* into which finished movie film is put]

in the cards ***adj phr*** Very probably; likely to or about to happen: *Another tax hike is in the cards*

in the catbird seat ***See*** SIT IN THE CATBIRD SEAT

in the chips ***adj phr*** Having money; affluent; =FLUSH, LOADED

in the chops ***See*** KLOP IN THE CHOPS

in the coop ***adj phr*** *police & underworld* Sleeping on the job; off duty for unauthorized rest: *The cruise car for that street was supposed to be in the coop*—Lawrence Sanders

in the doghouse ***adj phr*** In a position or status of obloquy; out of favor, esp temporarily: *The press secretary is in the doghouse for cussing out a reporter*

in the driver's (or **buddy**) **seat** ***adj phr*** In the position of authority; in control: *You don't make it very easy, do you? Always in the driver's seat* —WT Tyler

in the face ***See*** TILL one IS BLUE IN THE FACE

in the flesh **1** ***adv phr*** In person; in propria persona: *The great movie star appeared there in the flesh* **2** ***adj phr:*** *an in-the-flesh presentation*

in the foot ***See*** SHOOT oneself IN THE FOOT

in the groove *fr 1930s jive talk* **1** ***adj phr*** Making good sense; saying what needs saying: *Right! You're in the groove now* **2** ***adj phr*** In good form; working smoothly and well: *The professor of Classics was, as she would have put it, "in canaliculo," in the groove* **3** ***adj phr*** *jive musicians* Playing well and excitingly; =HEP

in the gutter ***See*** HAVE one's MIND IN THE GUTTER

in the hay ***adv phr*** In bed, either sleeping or cavorting: *Joe's in the hay, zonked out/ a toss in the hay with her boss*—Neal Travis

See A ROLL IN THE HAY

in the hole **1** ***adv phr*** *poker* Dealt face down, in stud poker: *What's he got in the hole?* **2** ***adv phr*** In debt: *We're in the hole to the tune of $9000*

See ACE IN THE HOLE

in the hopper ***See*** IN THE WORKS

in the hot seat ***See*** ON THE HOT SEAT

in the know ***adj phr*** Well informed, esp having current, advance, or confidential information: *My source has an inside track and is truly in the know*

in the life ***adj phr*** Occupied or engaged in some specialized and usu socially despised way of living, such as the homosexual subculture or prostitution: *By the time strippers are "in the life" they have developed an exploitative attitude to men and people in general*—Trans-Action

in the loop ***adv phr*** In the select company, esp in the circle of the powerful: *no force in the administration, observes simply, "He's not in the loop"*—Chicago Tribune [probably an alteration of the military idiom *in the net*, of the same meaning, fr the use of radio *nets* or communications nexuses that include or exclude certain headquarters]

in the money **1** ***adj phr*** Having money, esp in large amounts; =IN THE BUCKS, FLUSH: *I'm in the money at last*—H Allen Smith **2** ***adv phr*** *gambling & horse-racing* Providing winnings to bettors: *None of his horses finished in the money today at the track*

in the mud ***See*** STICK IN THE MUD

in the picture **1** ***adv phr*** In a position to understand what is happening; in an informed position • Chiefly

British: *OK, now that you're one of us, I want you in the picture* **2** ***adj phr*** Probable; distinctly conceivable: *It just isn't in the picture that they'll get married/ I'd like to travel, but it doesn't seem like it's in the picture for a year or so*
See PUT someone IN THE PICTURE

in the pipeline **1** ***adj phr*** (also **in the hopper** or **in the works**) Being prepared, processed, or worked on; =ON THE FIRE: *There could be a good raise in the pipeline for you/ We got a little gizmo in the works that'll give them a duck-fit* **2** ***adv phr*** *surfers* Riding inside the curled-over front of a wave

in the raw **1** ***adj phr*** Naked; =IN THE BUFF: *prancing around the common in the raw* **2** ***adj phr*** Without amenity or polish; relatively crude and primitive: *Up there they lived life in the raw/ His work is sculpture in the raw*

in there **1** ***adv phr*** =IN THERE PITCHING **2** ***adv phr*** *baseball* Pitched across home plate for a strike
See HANG IN

in there pitching ***adv phr*** (also **in there** or **right there** or **right in there**) Making a great effort; coping energetically and successfully; =ON TOP OF: *I'm in there pitching*—Calder Willingham/ *When they needed a strong guide, he was in there*

in the ring ***See*** THROW one's HAT IN THE RING

in the soup **1** ***adv phr*** *fr late 1800s* In trouble; under reproach: *You had better report right now, or you'll be in the soup* **2** ***adj phr*** In difficulties, esp in serious trouble; =IN HOT WATER: *Jeeves cocks an eyebrow, and Bertie knows he's in the soup*—Village Voice

in the straight lane ***adv phr*** Of a normal and respectable sort, esp not criminal nor homosexual nor drug-addicted: *another chance at life in the straight lane*—Milwaukee Journal

in the trenches ***adv phr*** In the workplace; in contact with the people or problems in a situation; unprotected by distance or illusion: *I needed to be back in the trenches where I could really relate to a community*—Philadelphia Journal

in the tub ***adj phr*** Bankrupt; ruined

in the water ***See*** DEAD IN THE WATER

in the wind ***See*** TWIST SLOWLY IN THE WIND

in the woods ***See*** DOES A BEAR SHIT IN THE WOODS

in the works ***See*** IN THE PIPELINE

in the wrong **1** ***adj phr*** Mistaken; wrong; erring: *He's usually in the wrong when he discusses music* **2** ***adv phr*** In an unfavorable light or position: *This guy is always putting me in the wrong*

into or **inta** (IN to͞o, IN tə) ***prep*** Currently interested or involved in; now practicing or absorbed in: *a former Ivy Leaguer named Crimpcut who is into Buddha*—Russell Baker

into someone **for** ***adj phr*** Indebted to; owing, esp money: *He's into Citibank for ten grand*

into the ground ***See*** RUN something INTO THE GROUND

into the twentieth century ***See*** DRAG someone KICKING AND SCREAMING INTO THE TWENTIETH CENTURY

intro **1** ***n*** An introduction or prelude of any sort: *"Listen to that intro," she says. "How awful"* —Whitney Balliett **2** ***v:*** *Who'll intro the archbishop?*

invent the wheel ***v phr*** To labor unnecessarily through the obvious and elementary stages of something: *If you guys will stop inventing the wheel we can get on with this operation*

invitation ***See*** DO YOU WANT AN ENGRAVED INVITATION

invite (IN vīt) ***n*** An invitation: *You can't go in there without an invite*

in your ear ***See*** PUT IT IN YOUR EAR

IOU (pronounced as separate letters) ***n*** A promise to pay; written acknowledgment of a debt: *had won $800,000, in cash, not IOUs*—John Scarne

Irish ***See*** GET one's DANDER UP, SHANTY IRISH

◁ **Irish buggy** (or **local**)▷ ***n phr*** A wheelbarrow

◁ **Irish pennant**▷ ***n phr*** *yachting* The end of a rope, sheet, etc, carelessly left loose or trailing off a boat

◀ the **Irish way**▶ ***n phr*** Heterosexual anal copulation [fr the notion that such a mode of intercourse was used to prevent pregnancy]

iron **1** *n motorcyclists fr 1920s* A motorcycle; motorcycles collectively: *competing on old British and American iron*—Cycle World **2** *n* A car **3** *n* A pistol; = SHOOTING IRON **4** *n* The weights used in weight-lifting *See* HAVE BRASS BALLS, HOT IRON, PUMP IRON, SHOOTING IRON

iron maiden (or **lady**) *n phr* A strict, severe, and unremittingly sober woman [in part probably fr the rigid expression and the menace of the *iron maiden*, an instrument of torture]

iron man **1** *n phr* A dollar: *two hundred iron men snatched... out of his mitt*—Charles MacArthur **2** *n phr* A very durable and tough man; tireless worker and player, esp in sports **3** *n phr musicians* A West Indian musician who plays an instrument made out of an oil drum

iron out the kinks *v phr* To solve and settle the problems; straighten things out: *Ironing out the kinks this way made them aware of just how weak their endgame was*—Games

iron pony *n phr* A motorcycle

iron-pumper *n* A weight lifter

iron up *v phr truckers* To put on tire chains

Irvine or **Irv** *n black* A police officer

Is the Pope Polish (or **Italian** or **Catholic**) *sentence* That was a stupid question; isn't the answer very obvious?; = DOES A BEAR SHIT IN THE WOODS • First variant used since the accession of John Paul II

it **1** *n fr early 1900s* A stupid person; = BOOB **2** *n fr early 1900s, esp 1920s & 30s* Sex appeal, esp female: *a girl with lots of it* **3** *modifier: Clara Bow, the original it girl* **4** *n fr 1400s* The sex act; copulation; = SCREWING • Used in numberless unmistakable but quasi-euphemistic contexts like **do it**, **go at it**, **want it**, **have it off**, **make it**, etc [first sense fr the distinction in pronoun between a person and a mere thing; sexual senses fr euphemistic and often arch uses where the indefinite pronoun takes on intense explicit meaning from the sexual referent and finally supplants the referent entirely, a process attested as early as the mid-15th century]

itch *See* SCRATCH

itchy *adj* Eager; restless; = ANTSY

it couldn't happen to a nicer guy *sentence* What punishment or damage was received was richly deserved • The sentiment is quite ironical: *Joe got canned? It couldn't happen to a nicer guy!*

item *See* HOT NUMBER

an **item** *n phr* A matter of interest and comment, esp a sexual relationship; = A NUMBER: *Book Says Ava and Adlai Were An Item*—New York

it girl *n phr esp 1920s & 30s* A young woman with sex appeal

-itis *suffix used to form nouns* An excessive and probably unhealthy involvement with or prevalence of what is indicated: *committeeitis/ symbolitis*

it's a bitch (or **bitch kitty**) *sentence* The thing referred to is very impressive, very difficult, very complicated, very sad, or in some other way extraordinary: *She shook his knee playfully. "It's a bitch, isn't it?"*—Armistead Maupin/ *The last couple of laps are a real bitch kitty*

it's at *See* KNOW WHERE IT'S AT

it's been real or **it's been** *sentence* It has been nice to meet you, it has been a nice time or party, etc • Often used ironically

it takes two to tango *sentence* This cannot happen or have happened without more than one person; cooperation or connivance is indicated: *Now, it takes two to tango, but I still think it was more her fault*—San Francisco [the name of a song popular in the 1930s]

it up *suffix used to intensify verbs* Doing energetically, vehemently, loudly, etc, what is indicated: *camping it up/ laughing it up*

◁ **it will be** (or **it's**) someone's **ass**▷ *sentence* That will be the end or ruination of someone; someone will be severely punished: *You write anything about me in an article again and it'll be your ass*—Joseph Heller [fr an elliptical way of saying *that will be the end of you* based on the notion that the *ass* equals the person]

ivories **1** *n fr late 1700s* The teeth: *as fine a display of ivories as we've seen in our time*—New Yorker **2** *n fr early 1800s* Dice; a pair of dice the **ivories** *n fr early 1900s* Piano keys; the piano

ivory-thumper *n* A piano player: *some cheap little ivory thumper* —James M Cain

ixnay *negation* No; no more; none: *Ixnay on the kabitz*—American Mercury [pig Latin for *nix*]

izzatso *interj* An exclamation of defiance or disbelief: *I'm a crud? Izzatso!*

J

J *n* (Variations: **jay** or **jay smoke** or **J smoke**) A marijuana cigarette; =JOINT [fr the *J* of *Mary Jane* "marijuana" or the *j* of *joint*]

jab a vein *v phr narcotics* To inject narcotics, esp heroin; =SHOOT UP: *smoke marijuana or opium... or jab a vein*—Stephen Longstreet

jabber 1 *n narcotics fr early 1900s* A hypodermic needle **2** *v* To talk incessantly; chatter on

See JIBBER-JABBER

jab-off *n narcotics* An injection of a narcotic

jack 1 *n* Money: *I figured it would be an easy way to make some jack* —Village Voice **2** *v Air Force fr Vietnam War* To take twisting evasive action in an airplane [first sense probably fr an 18th-century idiom *make one's jack* "succeed, get rich," perhaps fr the game of bowls; but see mid-19th-century British *jack* "a gambling counter resembling a sovereign"; second sense perhaps related to mid-19th-century British criminal slang *jack* "run away, escape," or perhaps by folk etymology fr *jank*, an echoic companion of *jink*; compare *jink-jank* with *yin-yang* and *zig-zag*]

See BALL THE JACK, HEAVY MONEY, HIGH-JACK, PIECE OF CHANGE

Jack *n* Man; friend; fellow; =MAC • Used in addressing any man, whatever his name: *Man, he's murder, Jack*—Max Shulman

jack around *fr students* **1** *v phr* To idle about; =FART AROUND, SCREW AROUND: *He and LD had been jacking around in practice and LD fell on his leg*—Peter Gent **2** *v phr* To meddle with; =FOOL AROUND: *until the lawyers started jacking around with the structure*—Toronto Life

jack someone **around** *fr students* **1** *v phr* To tease; =KID: *These guys are only trying to jack you around* —Dan Jenkins **2** *v phr* To harass; pester; victimize; =JERK someone AROUND: *Don't you think I know when people are jacking me around?* —Armistead Maupin

jackass *n fr early 1800s* A stupid person; dolt; fool

jacked up 1 *adj phr* Stimulated; exhilarated; =HIGH: *all the parents jacked up on coffee*—Cameron Crowe **2** *adj phr* Elevated, esp by artifice; =JUMPED-UP: *That he is a jacked-up cowboy and minor film star is a libel*—National Review

jacket *See* MONKEY JACKET, YELLOW JACKET

◁**jack off**▷ *v* To masturbate; =JERK OFF • Said chiefly of males [ultimately fr *jack* "penis"]

◁**jack-off** or **jagoff**▷ *n* A stupid, incompetent person; =JERK: *What's that jack-off up to now?/ those two slick-haired jagoffs*—William Brashler

jackpot *n fr late 1800s* A very large payoff in a gambling game, esp the largest win available in a slot machine [fr the *progressive jack pot* in poker, which stipulates that if no player has a pair of jacks or better to open, then on the next hand, after anteing again, someone must have queens or better, and so on; thus the *pot* could become quite large]

See HIT THE JACKPOT

◁**jack shit**▷ *n phr fr esp Southern college students* Nothing at all; =DIDDLY, ZILCH: *They had it, but jack shit was what they had*—Robert Stone

jack up **1** *v phr narcotics* To inject a narcotic; =SHOOT UP **2** *v phr* To stimulate; exhilarate: *Aren't you getting jacked up?...Ain't it great?* —Washington Post **3** *v phr* To raise; increase: *Did they jack up the price of booze again?* **4** *v phr police* =TAKE ON

jag *fr late 1800s fr 1600s British dialect* **1** *n* A drinking spree; =BENDER **2** *n* A spell or spree of a specified sort: *One had a "crying jag"* —P Marks
See CRYING JAG

jag house *n phr homosexuals* A house of male prostitution [probably fr *jack* "penis"]

jagoff *See* JACK-OFF

◁ **jail bait**▷ *n phr* A girl below the legal age of sexual consent, copulation with whom would constitute statutory rape

jailbird *n fr 1600s British* A convict or ex-convict

jailhouse lawyer *n phr* A prisoner who, authoritative or not, is disposed to lengthy discussion of his legal rights and those of other inmates; =GUARDHOUSE LAWYER: *an avid reader of good literature and a "jailhouse lawyer"*—E Ranzal

jake **1** *adj outdated fr early 1900s* Excellent; very satisfactory; =HUNKY-DORY: *She said the whole college seemed jake to her*—P Marks **2** *adv: Things could be goin' jake one minute, then presto, before you know it you're history*—Village Voice [origin unknown]

jalopy or **jaloppy** or **jalop** **1** *n fr 1920s* An old and battered car or airplane; =HEAP: *A jalopy is a model one step above a "junker"*—New York Times **2** *n* Any car; any vehicle; =BUGGY: *Let them search every jalop on the road*—Gangbusters (radio program) [origin unknown]

jam[1] **1** *n fr late 1800s British* A predicament; =BIND, TIGHT SPOT **2** *n* A tight crush of cars, people, etc **3** *n underworld* Small objects like rings and watches that are easy to steal **4** *v jazz musicians fr 1930s* To play jazz with great spontaneity, esp to improvise freely with other musicians and usu without an audience **5** *modifier: Jam bands do have styles* —C Smith **6** *n jazz musicians fr 1930s* A party or gathering where jazz musicians play for or with one another; =JAM SESSION: *Bix and the boys would blow it free and the jam was on*—Stephen Longstreet **7** *v esp students fr 1930s black* To have a good time; party joyously; =GET IT ON **8** *n: The kids were having a jam upstairs* **9** *v esp New York teenagers* To make up a rap song, esp in a competitive situation **10** *v* To make trouble for; coerce or harass, esp with physical force: *than when they're jammin' me for a penny every time I walk down the street*—Newsweek ◁**11**▷ *n fr black possibly fr late 1800s British* The vulva; a woman's genitals ◁**12**▷ *v esp college students:* To do the sex act; copulate; =SCREW: *Did what? Jammed* —Paul Theroux **13** *n narcotics* Cocaine **14** *v hawkers* To auction; act as an auctioneer **15** *v* To send an interfering signal on a broadcast channel one wishes to make unintelligible: *An attempt was made to jam* The Voice of America [all senses have some relation to the basic notion of squeezing or crushing so as to make *jam*]
See IN A JAM, JIM-JAM

jam[2] *n homosexuals* A heterosexual man [said to be fr *just a man*]

jammed up **1** *adj phr* In a glutted condition; immobilized or burdened by some sort of excess: *Traffic's jammed up for six miles on the thruway* **2** *adj phr* =IN A JAM
See CAMEL-JAMMER, GEAR-JAMMER

jamoke or **Jamoke** (jə MOHK) **1** *n fr armed forces & hoboes* Coffee **2** *n* A man; fellow; =GUY: *I don't rate your chances none too good if that jamoke's going to defend you* —George V Higgins [first sense perhaps a blend of *java* and *mocha*; second sense perhaps echoic-symbolic fr *jerk*, *joker*, and the like]

jam-packed *adj* Very tightly packed; very crowded: *those jam-packed suburban classes*—New York

the **jams** *See* the JIM-JAMS

jam session *n phr jazz musicians fr 1930s* A gathering of musicians, esp jazz musicians, playing freely and for one another, but sometimes in a public performance; =JAM: *Here's Dodo on the piano and Tiny on the bass. Looks like we'll have a fine jam session*—Slim Gaillard

jane **1** ***n*** A young woman; =CHICK, DOLL: *Ladies from Long Island, janes from New Jersey*—New York Times **2** ***n*** A man's sweetheart, fiancée, etc: *make earrings for our janes out of them studs*—Langston Hughes **3** ***n*** A women's toilet; =JOHN

Jane ***n*** An average woman
See MARY JANE

Jane Crow ***n phr*** Discrimination against women: *segregation by sex, describing it as "Jane Crow"*—Life [fr *Jim Crow*]

Jane Doe ***n phr*** Any woman; the average woman; =JANE

Jane Q Citizen (or **Public**) ***n phr*** Any woman, esp the average or typical woman: *The president seems very popular with Jane Q Citizen*

◁ **jang** ▷ ***n*** The penis
See YING-YANG

◀ **Jap** ▶ (JAP) ***n*** A Japanese or person of Japanese descent; =NIP
See JEWISH AMERICAN PRINCESS

jasper **1** ***n*** A fellow; man; =GUY: *two jaspers with a grudge*—H Birney **2** ***n*** A rustic; =HICK

java or **Java** ***n fr middle 1800s*** Coffee [fr *Java*, an Indonesian island whence coffee was exported]

jaw **1** ***v fr late 1800s*** To talk; chat; converse: *Can't stand here jawing with you all day*—SJ Perelman **2** ***n:*** *ain't had a good jaw together*—WR Burnett **3** ***v*** To exhort; lecture; strive to persuade orally; =JAWBONE: *had kept sober for several months by jawing drunks, unsuccessfully*—J Alexander
See BAT one's GUMS, CRACK one's JAW, FLAPJAW, GLASS JAW, RATCHET-MOUTH

jawbone **1** ***v fr late 1800s cowboys*** To borrow; obtain on credit: *He jawboned enough...to set up an office*—Robert Ruark **2** ***n fr late 1800s*** Credit or trust, esp financial: *Try as he might he got no jawbone from the bankers* **3** ***n fr late 1800s*** A loan **4** ***adv fr late 1800s*** On credit or trust: *He bought the machine jawbone* **5** ***v*** To discuss; talk over, esp extensively and profoundly: *a distinguished group of presidential biographers to jawbone about the situation*—Washington Post **6** ***v*** To exhort and earnestly urge in order to persuade • Used predominantly to describe high-level pressure applied on economic issues: *the Presidential promise not to "jawbone" business into not raising prices*—Commonweal **7** ***n:*** *The President launched a sustained and hot jawbone on the budget cuts* **8** ***v WW2 Army*** To fire a weapon in practice, esp for formal qualification to use it [the senses having to do with credit and trust are related to *jawbone* "talk without action," attested in the 19th century]

jawbreaker or **jawcracker** ***n*** A long word or a word difficult to pronounce: *Diphenylpentoactomaggetoneplangianoliosis is something of a jawbreaker*

jay ***n*** Marijuana or a marijuana cigarette; =J: *Let's do up a jay and truck on down to the libo*—Esquire

jay smoke *See* J

jaywalk ***v fr early 1900s*** To walk into or across a street at a forbidden place or without the right of way [fr the naive behavior of a *jay* "rustic"]

jazz ◁**1**▷ ***v*** To do the sex act with or to; =FUCK: *I jazzed her, too*—James T Farrell **2** ***v*** To increase the tempo, animation, or excitement of something; =JAZZ something UP: *Come on, jazz yourself, we're late* **3** ***n:*** *This place needs more jazz and pizzazz* **4** ***n jazz musicians fr early 1900s*** A kind of popular, often improvised, and emotive instrumental music originating among Southern black people in the late 19th century, and still evolving as an American and a world style **5** ***v*** To arrange or play in a jazz style: *They jazzed the National Anthem* **6** ***modifier:*** *a jazz trumpet/ jazz riffs* **7** ***n*** Empty talk; nonsense; lies; =BALONEY, BULLSHIT, JIVE: *You mean her most eloquent pledges were jazz?* **8** ***v:*** *Stop your jazzing and merely adduce the data* **9** ***n*** Ornamentation; embellishment, esp when merely superficial: *a clean design, without a lot of jazz* [origin unknown; *jass* was an earlier spelling]
See ALL THAT JAZZ

jazzed ***adj teenagers*** Alert and energetic; =PSYCHED UP

jazz something **up** **1** ***v phr*** To make faster, more exciting or stimulating, etc: *He tried to jazz the meeting up* **2** ***v phr*** To play in the musical style indicated

jazzy **1** *adj* Resembling or partaking of the musical style indicated: *He could turn a Beethoven sonata into a jazzy little number* **2** *adj* Exciting; stimulating: *He wore bow ties and... jazzy suits*—Truman Capote

jeans **1** *n* *fr middle 1800s* Trousers; pants: *I had the price in my jeans* —Jack London **2** *n* Blue denim work pants or trousers that are modifications of these [fr *jean fustian*, a cloth originating in *Gene* (Genoa), Italy]

jeebies *See* the HEEBIE-JEEBIES

jeep **1** *n* *fr WW2 Army* A useful and durable small open US military vehicle of World War 2, later adapted to civilian use and still evolving **2** *v:* *jeeping... through Maquis-held territory*—Time **3** *n* =JEEP CARRIER [fr the name and cry of a small versatile creature in the comic strip "Thimble Theater" by EC Segar, and the military designation *GP* "general purpose" in the designation of the little vehicle]

jeep carrier *n phr* *WW2 Navy* A US Navy escort aircraft carrier

Jeepers Creepers or **Jeepers** *interj* An exclamation of surprise, dismay, emphasis, etc: *Jeepers Creepers, another busted leg!* [a euphemism for *Jesus Christ*]

Jeez *interj* (Variations: **jeez** or **Jeeze** or **jeeze** or **Jees** or **jees** or **jeezy-peezy** or **Jeezy-peezy**) An exclamation of surprise, dismay, emphasis, etc; =JEEPERS CREEPERS [fr *Jesus*]

jelly-belly *n* A fat person

jelly-roll *black fr late 1800s* ◁**1**▷ *n* The vulva; vagina ◁**2**▷ *n* The sex act; copulation; =FUCKING **3** *n* A man obsessed with women; woman-chaser; =COCKSMAN, LOVER-BOY **4** *n* A lover or mistress; =SWEET PAPA, SWEET MAMA

jerk **1** *n* *early 1900s* A short branch railroad line: *a small "jerk" with only two locals a day*—Jack London **2** *n* *cabdrivers fr 1920s* A short ride **3** *n* *fr 1930s* A tedious and ineffectual person, esp a man; fool; ninny; =BOOB, TURKEY: *Jeez, what a jerk!* —American Scholar/ *The poor jerk just made a wrong turn* **4** *n* *fr 1930s* A contemptible and obnoxious person, esp a man; =ASSHOLE, BASTARD: *I'm not talking to that jerk since he ran out on his family* **5** *modifier:* *my jerk cousin/ a couple of jerk wops*—I, Mobster **6** *n* =SODA JERK ◁**7**▷ *v* =JERK OFF **8** *v* To draw or pull out: *He jerked a gun and that's all she wrote* [the derogatory term comes fr *jerk off* "masturbate"] *See* CIRCLE JERK, KNEE-JERK, PULL someone's CHAIN, SODA JERK

jerk around *v phr* To idle about; play casually; =FOOL AROUND: *if kids are jerking around and enter a system as a lark*—Newsweek

jerk someone **around** (or **off**) *v phr* To victimize or harass: *Salespeople feel that men who want hand holding are often jerking them around*—Philadelphia/ *I think Coyle was jerking you off*—George V Higgins

jerk (or **yank**) someone's **chain** *v phr* To victimize or harass; =JERK someone AROUND: *You came out to jerk my chain tonight*—George V Higgins/ *Are you guys yanking my chain?* —Hill Street Blues (TV program) [fr the notion of a chained man, monkey, etc, being harassed]

◁**jerk off**▷ **1** *v phr* To masturbate; =JACK OFF: *I went ahead as usual and jerked off into my sock*—Philip Roth **2** *v phr* To idle about; =FUCK OFF, GOOF OFF

◁**jerk-off**▷ **1** *modifier* Useful for masturbation: *an electric suction jerk-off device*—Village Voice **2** *adj* Stupid; =JERKY: *preparing an answer to the jerkoff question*—Easyriders **3** *n* A person who jerks off, either literally or figuratively: *I'd be tickled to death to lose the jerk-offs*—Rolling Stone

jerk (or **jerkwater**) **town** *n phr fr late 1800s* A small town; an insignificant village: *to fool around a jerk town*—J Flynt

jerky *See* HERKY-JERKY

Jersey green *n phr* *narcotics* A type of marijuana

Jersey lightning *n phr* *fr middle 1800s* Applejack brandy [fr the fact that applejack brandy was (and still is) distilled in New Jersey]

Jesus *n* =the BEJESUS

Jesus boots *n phr* *esp 1960s counterculture* Men's sandals

Jesus freaks (or **people**) *n phr esp 1960s counterculture* Members of an evangelical Christian religious movement among young people, esp ex-hippies and drug addicts: *in this light the herds of Jesus freaks*—M Rossman

the **jet set** ***n phr*** The group of wealthy, chic people who move about from one costly venue to another: *a charter member of the international jet set*—Time

◀ **Jewboy**▶ ***n*** A Jewish boy or man

◀ **Jew** (or **jew**) **down**▶ ***v phr*** *fr late 1800s* To bargain and haggle in an attempt to get a lower price: *but then the guy started jewin' me down*—Philadelphia

jewels ***See*** FAMILY JEWELS

Jewfro ***n*** *police* A hairstyle similar to the Afro: *wild curly hair that stood out from their heads like pyramids of Brillo, what police slang called a Jewfro*—Beth Gutcheon

Jewish Alps ***n phr*** The Catskill Mountains in southern New York State; =BORSCHT BELT: *I could never go back to the Jewish Alps with any woman whose name was Birdye* —Paul Sann

◀ **Jewish American Princess** or **JAP** or **Jap**▶ ***n phr*** A pampered and usu wealthy young woman who feels she deserves special treatment: *plenty of Jewish American Princesses in their wigs and false eyelashes* —Xaviera Hollander/ *the unofficial, secret JAP within me*—Village Voice

Jewish penicillin ***n phr*** Chicken soup

◀ **jibagoo**▶ ***See*** JIGABOO

jibber-jabber **1** ***v*** To talk nonsense; =JABBER: *Time for Congress to quit jibber-jabbering*—Philadelphia Bulletin **2** ***n:*** *Cut out the jibber-jabber*

a **jiffy** **1** ***n phr*** (Variations: **jif** or **jiff** or **jiffin** or **jiffing**) *fr 1700s* A short space of time; an instant: *drop off to sleep for a jiffy*—SJ Perelman/ *I'll have coffee ready in a jiff*—Lawrence Sanders **2** ***modifier:*** *a jiffy dessert/ jiffy pronouncements* [said to be fr thieves' slang *jeffey* or *jiffey* "lightning"]

jig **1** ***n*** A dancing party or public dance ◀**2**▶ ***n*** =JIGABOO

◀ **jigaboo**▶ (Variations: **jibagoo** or **jigabo** or **jig** or **zig** or **zigaboo** or **zigabo**) *fr early 1900s* **1** ***n*** A black person **2** ***modifier:*** *a jig band*

jigger **1** ***n*** *late 1800s hoboes* An artificially made sore, usu on the arm or leg, useful in begging; *whether it will pay to use his "jigger"*—J Flynt **2** ***n*** *students* An ice-cream sundae **3** ***n*** A liquor glass of one-and-a-half ounce capacity; =SHOT GLASS **4** ***v*** *hoboes* To interfere with; =QUEER: *jigger our riding on the railroad*—J Flynt **5** ***v*** To tamper with or falsify: *There is pressure from Casey... to jigger estimates*—New York Times **6** ***n*** =THINGAMAJIG [perhaps fr the agent noun of Old English *gigue* "bowed string instrument, fiddle," by way of many British slang senses including 17th-century "a shifty fellow, a trickster"]

See DOODAD, I'LL BE DAMNED

jiggered ***See*** I'LL BE DAMNED

jiggers or **jigs** ***interj*** An exclamation of alarm and warning: *Jiggers, the heat's here*

jiggery-pokery ***n*** *fr late 1800s British* Deception; trickery; =SKULLDUGGERY: *could have prevented most of the jiggery-pokery*—New Yorker [fr Scottish *joukery-paukery* fr *jouk* "trick"]

jiggle or **jiggly** **1** ***n*** The bouncing and shaking of a woman's parts, esp of the breasts • Hence the whole tone and style of blatant female sexual exploitation: *help put the jiggle back in the series "Charlie's Angels"* —People Weekly **2** ***modifier:*** *the ads for comedies in the jiggle genre* —TV Guide **3** ***v:*** *She swims, jumps rope, and practices jiggling in front of the mirror*—Philadelphia **4** ***n*** A TV program featuring the bouncing and shaking of a woman's parts: *when advertisers see wall-to-wall jigglies in prime time*—New York Times

◁ **jig-jig** or **zig-zig**▷ ***n*** The sex act; copulation; =FUCKING

jig-swiggered ***See*** I'LL BE DAMNED

jillion ***n*** (also **gillion** or **skillion** or **zillion**) A great many; an indefinitely large number; =SCADS: *a jillion jackpots*—Time/ *A zillion horny studs!* —Lawrence Sanders

Jim Crow ◀**1**▶ ***n phr*** *fr early 1800s* A black person **2** ***n phr*** Segregation and discrimination against black people, and the laws and practices that accompany them: *My first experience with Jim Crow*—Louis Armstrong/ *Jim Crow killed Bessie Smith* —Tennessee Williams **3** ***modifier:*** *Jim Crow statutes/ Jim Crow toilets* **4** ***v:*** *I would like to... say that the people who Jim Crow me have a white heart*—Langston Hughes [fr a character in a minstrel-show song]

See CROW JIM

jim-dandy **1** *n fr late 1800s* A person or thing that is remarkable, wonderful, superior, etc; =BEAUT, HUMDINGER **2** *adj: a jim-dandy speech/ Anacin is a jim-dandy remedy*—Philip Hamburger

jim-jam *v* =JAZZ, JAZZ something UP

the **jim-jams** *n phr fr middle 1800s* =the HEEBIE-JEEBIES

jimjick *n* Something one does not know the name of or does not wish to name; =GIZMO, THINGAMAJIG: *this jimjick here, the trigger*—SJ Perelman [perhaps a blend of *jim hickey* with *jigger*, both meaning "thingamajig"]

jimmies *n* Bits of candy put onto ice cream as a topping

the **jimmies** *n phr* Nervous frets; =the HEEBIE-JEEBIES: *Frankly it gives me the jimmies*—Wolcott Gibbs

jingle *n* A telephone call; a ring; =TINKLE: *We never hear from you, not even a jingle*—Any Number Can Play (movie)

jinks *See* HIGH-JINKS

jinky-board *n* A seesaw

jinny *n 1920s* A speakeasy

jinx **1** *n fr early 1900s* A cause of bad luck: *Somebody around here is a jinx* **2** *n* A curse; assured ill fortune: *Looks like the place has a jinx on it* **3** *v: Somebody jinxed him* [apparently fr *jynx* or *iynx* "wryneck woodpecker," fr the use of the bird in divination]

jip *See* GYP

jism ◀**1**▶ *n* Semen; =CUM **2** *n* (also **gism**) *fr middle 1800s* Liveliness; excitement; spunk; =ZING [origin unknown]

jitney **1** *n fr late 1800s* A nickel **2** *n* (also **jitney bus**) *fr early 1900s* A small bus used as public transportation • Formerly, jitneys were cars operating for low fare in more or less unregulated competition with taxis, buses, and street cars **3** *modifier: cracked down today on illegal jitney service*—Philadelphia Bulletin **4** *n* Any car, esp a small or cheap one **5** *n* A cheap cigar; nickel cigar **6** *adj* Cheap: *a jitney dance hall*—G Millburn [origin unknown; perhaps fr French *jeton* "token"]

jitter **1** *v* To tremble; quiver: *A line of... half-washed clothes jittered on a rusty wire*—Raymond Chandler **2** *v* To be nervous; be agitated; fret: *I jittered around the house... unable to concentrate on anything*—H Allen Smith [echoic-symbolic]

jitterbug *1930s jive talk* **1** *n* A devotee of swing music, esp one who dances to swing: *Jitterbugs are the extreme swing addicts*—Life **2** *v* To dance to swing music: *Do you feel like jitterbugging a little bit?*—JD Salinger

the **jitters** *n phr* A state of nervous agitation; acute restless apprehension: *I had the jitters*—Philip Wylie

jittery *adj* Nervous: *He felt all jittery and uptight*

jive[1] *fr black fr early 1900s* **1** *v* To banter; jest; tease; =KID: *She told him to quit jiving* **2** *v* To deceive, but not seriously; mislead, esp playfully **3** *n* Empty and pretentious talk; foolishness; =BALONEY, BULLSHIT: *Sugar Mouth Sammy with the same ol' tired jive*—D Evans **4** *n* Trifles; trash: *I bought a lot of cheap jive at the five and ten cent store*—Louis Armstrong **5** *n* Swing music of the 1930s and 40s, esp as played by the big bands and played fast and excitingly: *Man, what solid jive!*—Max Shulman **6** *modifier: jive records/ jive dancers* **7** *v* To play or dance to fast, exciting swing music **8** *n* (also **gyve**) Marijuana or a marijuana cigarette: *So Diane smoked jive, pot, and tea*—Orville Prescott [origin unknown; perhaps fr Wolof *jev* "talk disparagingly"]

See JUKING AND JIVING, SHUCK

jive[2] *v* To jibe: *The two answers do not jive*

jive and juke *v phr college students* To have a very good time

See JUKING AND JIVING

◁ **jive-ass** ▷ *fr black* **1** *n* Pretentious and deceitful talk; =BULLSHIT, JIVE: *That's like jive-ass*—Rolling Stone **2** *adj* Deceitful; undependable: *Damn his lazy, jiveass soul*—Armistead Maupin

jive stick *n phr narcotics* A marijuana cigarette

jive talk *n phr* A rapid, pattering way of talking, accompanied with finger-snapping and bodily jerks, and using the swing and jive vocabulary, affected by teenagers during the swing and jive era of the 1930s and 40s

◀ **jizz** or **jizzum** ▶ *n* Semen; =CUM, JISM: *puts a little body in his jizz, pumps a* *baby a year into the wife*—John Sayles

joanie *adj teenagers* Out-of-date; passé

job 1 *n* (also **jobbie**) A specimen or example, either of a thing or a person: *She's a tough little job*—Dashiell Hammett/ *one of those big 18-wheel jobbies* **2** *n underworld fr middle 1800s* A crime; a criminal project; =CAPER: *a big payroll job* **3** *v fr underworld* To deceive; cheat; =DOUBLE-CROSS, FRAME: *got absolutely jobbed out of the Heisman*—Sports Illustrated **4** *n* A bowel movement

See BLOW JOB, BOOB JOB, CON GAME, COWBOY JOB, DO A JOB ON, GOW JOB, HAND JOB, HATCHET JOB, INSIDE JOB, LAY DOWN ON THE JOB, MENTAL JOB, NOSE JOB, PUT-UP JOB, SHACK JOB, SNOW JOB, STRAIGHT JOB, TORCH JOB

jobbie *v* To befoul: *any ladies out there who will jobbie their pants for the camera*—Village Voice

See JOB

jock 1 *n* A jockey **2** *n* =DISC JOCKEY **3** *n fr late 1700s British* The penis; the crotch: *I'll be beating the bushes with snow to my jock*—George V Higgins **4** *n* An athletic supporter; =JOCKSTRAP: *I asked him if he wanted some sweat clothes, or a jock*—Esquire **5** *n* An athlete • Now used of both men and women, despite the phallic derivation: *The players themselves are a curious blend of woman and jock*—New York Times [the basic etymon is *jock* "penis," fr *jack*, probably the diminutive of *John*, which fr the 14th century has been applied to males, malelike things, and male organs; the sense "athlete" is fr *jockstrap*]

See VIDEO JOCK

jockey *n* The driver or pilot of any vehicle: *airplane jockey/ tank jockey*

See BLIP JOCKEY, DESK JOCKEY, DISC JOCKEY, PSYCH-JOCKEY

jockocracy *n* The athletes and former athletes who play a large role in television broadcasting: *bored with the games, utterly bored with the jockocracy*—Washington Post

jockstrap 1 *n* An athletic supporter **2** *n* An athlete; =JOCK **3** *v* To make one's living in the less glamorous and lucrative reaches of professional sports: *He spent a couple of years jockstrapping in the minor leagues*

jody *Army fr WW2 fr black* *n* A civilian who is thought to be prospering back home with a soldier's sweetheart, wife, job, etc: *Jody was the guy going in the back door while you were walking down the front walk*—Soldiers [fr the full name *Jody Grinder*, that is, fornicator, probably fr an earlier black and prison character of similar import *Oolong the Chinese Grind-boy* or *Chinese Joe the Grinder*]

Joe or **joe 1** *n* Coffee **2** *n* Man; fellow; =GUY: *Seems like a good Joe/ never seemed to share much of the problems of the ordinary joe*—Robert Ruark **3** *n fr WW2* =GI JOE **4** *n fr WW2* Any American, esp any US military man

See GI JOE, GOOD JOE, HOLY JOE, LITTLE JOE, ORDINARY JOE

Joe Blow *n phr* (Variations: **Doakes** or **Storch** or **Zilch** may replace **Blow**) *fr 1920s black jazz musicians* Any man; the average man; =JOHN DOE: *the average black "Mr Joe Blow"*—Ebony [fr the *blowing* of the musician, later probably thought of as referring to big talk]

Joe College *n phr esp 1920s & 30s* A young man whose dress and manner betoken the nonacademic aspects of college life: *a real Joe College type*—Leonard Feather

Joe Schmo (or **Schmoe**) *n phr* An undistinguished and unfortunate person

◁ **Joe Shit the Ragman** ▷ *n phr* (Variations: **Snuffy** or **Tentpeg** may replace **Shit the Ragman**) *Army* An ordinary soldier; =BUCK PRIVATE, GI

Joe Six-pack *n phr* An ordinary American male; =JOE, JOE BLOW: *Do you think that Joe Six-pack in Illinois cares?*—National Public Radio [fr the six-bottle or -can packets of beer these men typically consume]

john[1] *n fr 1930s* A toilet; =CAN: *I made a brief visit to the john*—J Evans [probably an amusing euphemism for *jack* or *jakes*, 16th-century terms for toilet]

john[2] *n fr WW2 Army* An Army lieutenant

John 1 *n* (also **john**) *fr black* Any man; an average man; =JOE: *We don't want no poor johns on here*—A Lomax **2** *n* A man regarded as an easy victim, a potential easy sale, etc: *He's pretty smart at figurin' out what* *a John'll pay*—Langston Hughes **3** *n Army* An Army recruit **4** *n* A man who keeps a girl; =DADDY, SUGAR DADDY **5** *n prostitutes fr early 1900s* (also **john**) A prostitute's customer: *even for girls turning their first tricks, pulling their first real John*—Claude Brown **6** *n homosexuals* An older homosexual male who keeps a younger one **7** *n* =JOHN LAW

See DEAR JOHN, SQUARE JOHN

John Doe or **Richard Roe** *n phr* Any man; the average man; =JOE

John dogface *n phr WW2 Army* A recruit

John Hancock (or **Henry**) *n phr* One's signature [fr the fact that *John Hancock* of Massachusetts was the first to sign the Declaration of Independence in 1776; *John Henry*, possibly by confusion with Patrick *Henry*, because of the prominence of *John Henry* as a folklore hero, and by near-rhyming resemblance]

John Law *n phr fr hoboes & circus* A police officer; the police: *gathered in by John Law*—Jack London

John L's *n phr* =LONG JOHNS

Johnny or **johnny** *n* Any man; =JOE, JOHN: *The big johnny came over to talk*

Johnny-come-lately **1** *n* A person or thing only recently arrived, esp as compared with the more seasoned: *Postwar planning... was no Johnny-come-lately*—Max Shulman **2** *modifier: a Johnny-come-lately quasi-solution* **3** *n* An upstart

Johnny-on-the-spot *n fr late 1800s* A person who is ready and effective when needed: *Ed was Johnny-on-the-spot and we got it cleaned up quick*

Johnny Trots *n phr* =the TROTS

John Q Citizen (or **Public**) *n phr* Any man, esp the average or typical man: *John Q Citizen seems to yearn for the big cars*

johns *See* LONG JOHNS

◁ **johnson** or **Johnson** or **jones**▷ *n esp black* The penis: *beat out time with their titties and their johnsons*—Village Voice/ *Enough is enough, turn my jones loose*—Donald Goines [origin unknown; such a use is recorded fr Canada in the mid-19th century, perhaps as a euphemism for the British euphemism *John Thomas* "penis"; the US black use may be related to the name of the boxer *Jack Johnson*, and hence to such penile terms as *jack* and *jock*]

John Wayne *Army* **1** *adj phr* Very tough and durable; militarily exemplary **2** *v phr* To handle a weapon, esp a machine gun, in an ostentatiously unconventional way

John Wayne it *v phr* To be very tough, taciturn, and virile: *I'm supposed to go around John Wayne-ing it all the time*—San Francisco

John Wayne's brother *n phr Army* A good soldier; ideal fighting man

John Wayne's sister (or **mother**) *n phr Army* A weak, lazy, self-indulgent person

joint **1** *n fr late 1800s* Any disgusting or disreputable place; =DIVE, DUMP: *That evening the joint buzzed with sedition*—American Scholar **2** *n fr late 1800s* Any place or venue, esp of a commercial sort: *It's a swell joint, all right*—H McHugh **3** *n* One's home; residence: *Come by my joint later and I'll give you a drink* **4** *n narcotics* A marijuana cigarette; =REEFER: *I've had to hold joints in my hand... but I never smoked even one*—New York Times **5** *n narcotics* The apparatus for injecting narcotics; =HEAD KIT, WORKS ◁**6**▷ *n* The penis [place senses fr early-19th-century Anglo-Irish *joint* "low resort," perhaps from its being a nearby, joined room rather than a main room]

See the BIG JOINT, CLIP JOINT, EAT HIGH ON THE HOG, GYP JOINT, JUKE JOINT, PULL one's PUD, PUT someone's NOSE OUT OF JOINT, RUG JOINT, SCHLOCK SHOP, SQUARE

-joint *combining word* Place where the indicated activity goes on, the indicated thing may be had, having the indicated quality, etc: *clip-joint/ hamburger joint/ gyp joint*

the **joint** *n phr* Prison: *in the joint*—Joseph Wambaugh

joint factory *n phr narcotics* =SMOKE SHOP

joke *See* SICK JOKE

joker **1** *n* (also **joker in the deck**) A hidden cost, qualification, defect, nasty result, etc; =CATCH: *It all looks very sweet, but there's a joker* **2** *n fr early 1800s* A man; fellow; =GUY, CHARACTER, CLOWN ● Often derogatory: *Ask that joker who the hell he thinks he is*

jollies *n* Pleasure and gratification; thrills, esp when somewhat disreputable; =BANGS, KICKS: *People that drive*

Buicks are getting some kind of jollies —A Sherman
See GET one's COOKIES

jollop *n* A large portion of food

jolt **1** *n narcotics* The initial impact of a narcotic injection; =RUSH **2** *n narcotics* A narcotic injection **3** *v: We didn't want to jolt*—D Hulburd **4** *n narcotics* A marijuana cigarette; =JOINT **5** *n* A drink of liquor; =SNORT: *a wee jolt of Bourbon*—F Scott Fitzgerald

Jonah *n rock and roll* =HIPSTER, CAT

Jones or **jones** *narcotics* **1** *n* A drug habit: *works at two jobs to keep up with the "Jones"*—J Lelyveld **2** *n* Any intense interest or absorption
See JOHNSON, SCAG JONES

Joneses *See* KEEP UP WITH THE JONESES

jook *See* JUKE

Jose *See* NO WAY

Josephine *See* NOT TONIGHT, JOSEPHINE

josh *fr late 1800s* **1** *v* To joke; banter; =KID **2** *n: It was just a tasteless little josh* [perhaps fr *Josh* Billings, 19th-century US humorist]

jostle *v* To pick pockets: *a junkie vocation known as "jostling"*—J Markham

jowls *See* BAT one's GUMS

◁**joy knob**▷ *n phr* The penis

joy pop *v phr narcotics* To take narcotic injections occasionally, esp intramuscularly

joy-popper *narcotics* **1** *n* A newcomer among narcotics users, esp among marijuana smokers **2** *n* A person who takes, or claims to take, only an occasional dose of narcotics: *For the "joy-poppers" had no intention of becoming addicts*—Nelson Algren

joy-powder *n narcotics* Morphine

joy ride *n phr fr early 1900s* A ride or trip taken solely for pleasure, esp a fast and merry junket that is in some way forbidden: *They stole the police car and had themselves a joy ride*

joy-stick **1** *n fr early 1900s* The control lever of an airplane **2** *n hot rodders* The steering wheel of a car, esp a hot rod **3** *n* The control lever of a computer game **4** *n narcotics* An opium pipe ◁**5**▷ *n fr late 1800s* The penis [the origin of the control-lever senses is uncertain; perhaps fr the tremulous shaking of the stick, perhaps fr the joyful sensation experienced while flying]

J smoke *See* J

jug **1** *v fr early 1800s* To put in jail; imprison: *I get jugged for parking in the wrong places?*—Lawrence Sanders **2** *n* A bottle of liquor: *Fetch me my jug* **3** *n* A relatively cheap wine, usu bought in large bottles; =JUG WINE: *Far more people drink jugs these days*—San Francisco **4** *n underworld* A vault or safe; =CRIB **5** *n police* A bank **6** *n hot rodders* A carburetor

the **jug** *n phr fr early 1800s* Jail; prison: *Refusal will result in a quick trip to the jug*—Rolling Stone

jugful *See* NOT BY A LONG SHOT

juggler *n narcotics* =PUSHER

jughandle *n* A circular portion of road shaped like the handle of a jug, used for making turns from and into a busy highway

jughead *n* A stupid person; fool; =KLUTZ

◁**jugs**▷ *n fr early 1900s Australian* A woman's breasts; =HOOTERS

jug wine *n phr* A relatively cheap domestic wine, usu bought in large bottles

juice **1** *n* Liquor; =BOOZE, the SAUCE: *liquor much stronger than the present-day juice*—Louis Armstrong **2** *n underworld* Money, esp illegally obtained and used by gamblers, loan sharks, etc **3** *modifier: a juice dealer/ juice man* **4** *n underworld* The interest paid on a usurious loan; =VIGORISH: *interest, known in the trade as vigorish, vig, or juice*—Wall Street Journal **5** *n fr late 1800s* Electricity; current and voltage: *Turn on the juice so we can see something* **6** *n* Gasoline; motor fuel: *If you have a light supply of juice you climb at about 200 mph*—New York Times **7** *n hot rodders & car-racing* A fuel additive for cars, esp hot rods; =POP **8** *n miners* Nitroglycerin **9** *n* Influence; =CLOUT, PULL: *"What's juice?" "I guess you'd call it pull. Or clout"*—John Gregory Dunne **10** *n narcotics* Methadone, often administered in fruit juice
See LIMEY

juiced or **juiced up** *adj* or *adj phr* Drunk: *Crabs was already pretty juiced up*—Easyriders

juicehead *n* A heavy drinker; =LUSH: *He had a raving juice-head for a wife* —Rolling Stone

juice up **1** *v phr* To energize; invigorate: *A thing like that can really juice* *you up*—Time **2** *v phr* To fuel: *They juiced the car up and set out*

juju *n* Any object which a person nervously plays with or manipulates; fetish; amulet [both senses probably fr Hausa, "fetish"]

juke or **jook** *fr early 1900s* **1** *n* =JUKE HOUSE **2** *n* =JUKE JOINT **3** *n* =JUKEBOX **4** *v* To tour roadside bars, drinking and dancing: *I want you to go juking with me*—Tennessee Williams **5** *v college students* To have a good time; disport oneself, esp at a party **6** *v college students* To dance **7** *v sports* To swerve and reverse evasively; trick a defender or tackler: *rather than to juke a defensive back, then duck inside*—Sports Illustrated [fr Gullah fr Wolof and/or Bambara, "unsavory"; the sports sense is probably fr the dancing sense and the echoic-symbolic force shown also in *jack*, *jank*, and *jink*]

See JIVE AND JUKE, JUKING AND JIVING

jukebox *n fr early 1900s Southern* A coin-operated record player in a restaurant, bar, etc

juke house *n phr esp early 1900s Southern* A brothel

juke joint *n phr fr early 1900s Southern* A usu cheap bar, roadside tavern, etc, with a jukebox

juking and jiving **1** *n phr* Frivolity and evasiveness; triviality and inanity **2** *modifier: Hart despises "the jukin' and jivin' phoniness of politics"* —Time

See JIVE AND JUKE

jumbo *adj* Very large; gigantic; =HUMONGOUS: *I had a jumbo portion* [fr PT Barnum's great elephant *Jumbo*, fr the word for "elephant" in various West African languages, for example Kongo *nzamba*]

jump **1** *v fr late 1800s* To attack; assault: *We jumped him as he left the place* **2** *v* To rob, esp at gunpoint; =HOLD UP **3** *v jive talk* To be furiously active; be vibrant with noise and energy: *Before long the joint was jumpin'*—H Allen Smith **4** *n jive talk* =SWING **5** *modifier: a jump tune/ jump music* **6** *n jive talk* A dance where the music is swing or jive; =HOP **7** *n street gang* A street fight between teenage gangs; =RUMBLE ◁**8**▷ *v* To do the sex act with or to; =SCREW: *She admitted she always wanted him to jump her*

See GET THE JUMP ON someone or something, HAVE THE JUMP

jump bail *v phr underworld fr middle 1800s* To default on one's bail

jump (or **jump on**) someone's **bones** **1** *v phr* To make strong sexual advances; sexually assault: *Have I tried to... jump your bones?*—The Gauntlet (movie) **2** *v phr* To do the sex act with someone

jump down someone's **throat** *v phr fr early 1800s* To make a violent and wrathful response: *When I hinted he might be mistaken he jumped down my throat*

jumped-up **1** *adj* =JACKED UP **2** *adj* Hastily organized; impromptu

jumper *See* PUDDLE-JUMPER, STUMP-JUMPER

jump (or **go**) **off the deep end** *v phr* To act precipitately; take drastic action: *He jumped off the deep end and got married again* [see *go off the deep end*]

jump on someone's **meat** *v phr* To rebuke severely; savage; =CHEW OUT: *Chickenshit lieutenant... used to jump on our meat every night at roll-call* —Joseph Wambaugh

jump on the bandwagon *See* GET ON THE BANDWAGON

the **jumps** *n phr* =the JITTERS

jump-start *v* To start a car by attaching cables to the battery from a car that runs; start anything that resists going: *Mubarak Tries to Jump Start Stalled Mideast Peace Talks*—New York Times

jump suit *n phr* A one-piece coverall modeled on those worn by paratroopers and parachute jumpers

jump the gun *v phr fr early 1900s* To act prematurely: *We planned it well, but jumped the gun and ruined it*

◁**jump through** one's **ass**▷ *v phr Army* To make a very quick response to a sudden difficult demand: *Old Man says we'll have to jump through our ass to get that done by tomorrow*

jump up *v phr* To increase the force of; =JAZZ something UP: *He decides to jump up the tune just as he jumped up "That's All Right, Mama"*—Albert Goldman

jump-up *n Army* A job that must be done at once, with little time to think and prepare

jumpy *adj* Nervous; apprehensive; =JITTERY: *One of our pals... is jumpy* *and he needs a bodyguard tonight* —George Raft

jungle **1** *n hoboes* A camp or regular stopping place near the railroad on the outskirts of a town: *always leaves the jungle like he found it* —James M Cain **2** *n* Any place of notable violence, lawlessness, etc: *The neighborhood's becoming a jungle*

◀**jungle-bunny**▶ *n* A black person

junk **1** *n fr middle 1800s* Worthless and shoddy things; useless and inept productions; trash; =DRECK, SHIT: *Why do you always buy such junk?* **2** *modifier: junk jewelry/ junk mail* **3** *n tennis* Tricky serves and lobs; soft, hard-to-reach shots: *He is a master of control and of dealing "junk"*—New York Times/ *looping junk, the players' term for soft, short shots*—Esquire **4** *n baseball* =JUNK-BALL **5** *n narcotics* Narcotics; =DOPE: *Sherlock Holmes...All he does is play a fiddle and take junk*—J Cannon **6** *modifier: one of the most dangerous junk neighborhoods in the city*—Esquire **7** *n* Unspecified heaps and objects; stuff; crap: *What's all that junk in the corner?*

junk-ball **1** *n baseball* A deceptive and unorthodox pitch; =JUNK **2** *modifier: a junk-ball artist*

junk bond *n phr* A bond having high yield but relatively little security, used as payment for one company by another in a corporate merger: *Fed adopts "Junk Bond" curbs*—New York Times

junked up *adj phr narcotics* =HOPPED UP

junker **1** *n narcotics fr 1920s* =JUNKIE **2** *n narcotics* A narcotics dealer; =JUGGLER **3** *n* A car or other machine that is worn out and ready to be discarded, or that has been discarded: *You can't litter the countryside with the kind of crap that the junkers are*—Fortune

junk food *n phr* Foods like potato chips, popcorn, sugar-coated cereals, and the like, esp popular with children and having little nutritional value

junk heap **1** *n phr* A worn and ramshackle old car; =HEAP, JALOPY **2** *n phr* Any unsightly or chaotic place: *His room was always a fetid junk heap*

junkie or **junky** **1** *n narcotics* A narcotics addict: *I didn't want to be a junkie*—Saturday Review **2** *n* A devotee or addict of any sort: *Zuckerman describes himself as a "newspaper and magazine junkie"*—Time

junque *n* Old and discarded odds and ends; rummage; =JUNK: *a wonderful collection of white elephants, trash, treasures and, as the antique dealers spell it, "junque"*—Washington Post [the pseudo-French spelling lends a certain chic and dignity to the material]

just another pretty face *n phr* Someone or something of no particular distinction; a mediocre person or thing: *He had a time convincing them he was a genuine expert, not just another pretty face* [fr the plight of a young woman, esp in popular fiction or film, who has intelligence, talent, etc, but fears she is being treated by males as only an ordinary sex object]

just for the hell of it *See* FOR THE HELL OF IT

just one of those things *n phr fr 1930s* Something that can hardly be predicted, justified, explained, or avoided, but is an intrinsic and sometimes a distressful part of living • The gestural equivalent is a shrug: *Their divorce was just one of those things*

just whistling Dixie *See* NOT JUST WHISTLING DIXIE, WHISTLING DIXIE

juve or **juvie** or **juvey** **1** *adj* Juvenile; youthful: *the next monster juve act would be*—Village Voice **2** *n* A young person; child; juvenile, esp a juvenile offender: *I'm a juve*—Hill Street Blues (TV program) **3** *n* A juvenile court or a reformatory **4** *modifier: juvey hall/ juvey books*

K

K **1** *n* A thousand dollars: *Four bastards no smarter'n you and me got ninety-seven K out of some little bank* —George V Higgins **2** *n narcotics* A kilogram, esp such a quantity of narcotics: *even occasional Ks (kilograms) of cocaine*—New York Times [fr the Greek prefix *kilo-* "one thousand"]

kablooey *See* GO BLOOEY

kaka *adj* Bad: *Overweight is kaka* —Village Voice [fr Greek]
See CA-CA

kangaroo court or **club** *fr middle 1800s* **1** *n phr prison fr hobo* A mock court: *The toughest prisoner announced that he was president of the Kangaroo Club and would hold court*—E Lavine **2** *n phr* A small-town police court where traffic fines to transients are high, and usu divided among the police **3** *n phr* Any local court that is severe with hoboes and transients **4** *n phr* Any court where procedures are arbitrary and defective [origin unknown; perhaps connected with the fact that Australia was for some time a prison colony]

kaput (kah PŎŎT) *adj fr WW2 armed forces* Inoperative; ineffective; =FINISHED: *I would be "kaput" without a folding machete*—SJ Perelman [fr echoic-symbolic German slang]

karma *n* =VIBES [fr Sanskrit "work"]

Katie bar the door *sentence* Get ready for trouble; a desperate situation is at hand: *If they were on to him, well that's all she wrote. Katie bar the door*—William Kennedy

kayo or **kay** *n prizefight* A knockout; =KO

kazoo or **gazoo** or **gazool** **1** *n* The buttocks; anus; =ASS: *an impossible, unreliable, self-destructive pain in the kazoo*—Washington Post/ *We have subcommittee staff running out the kazoo*—New York Times **2** *n* Toilet; =CAN: *I tore it up and flushed it down the kazoo*—Lawrence Sanders [origin unknown; perhaps *kazoo*, known in its standard sense fr the 1880s, suggested the anus in being tubular and emitting sounds, and *gazool* in a sort of blend with *asshole*]
See UP THE KAZOO

kee *See* KEY

keed *n* =KID

keel over *fr late 1800s* *v phr* To fall down; collapse: *He was so tired he was about to keel over* [fr nautical careening of a ship so that the *keel* is raised]

keen *adj outdated teenagers & students* Excellent; wonderful; =NEAT: *I think she's a keen kid*—Max Shulman/ *"Keen?" Blanche said. "I haven't heard that word in 20 years"* —Lawrence Sanders
See PEACHY

keep (or **maintain**) **a low profile** *v phr* To stay inconspicuous; try not to attract much attention: *Better keep a low profile until this blows over*

keep an eye on someone or something *v phr* To watch; guard over: *Will you keep an eye on my cat while I'm away?*

keep (or **make**) **book** *v phr fr gambling* To bet or be willing to cover bets; have confidence: *I wouldn't make book that he'll get the nod*

keep one's **eye on the ball** *v phr* To pay strict attention to what one is doing; be alert and undistracted

keep someone **honest** **1** *v phr* To pose a requirement or test so that someone does not go unchallenged: *We'll ask her a few questions just to keep her honest* **2** *v phr baseball* To pitch close to a batter; throw at a batter: *Keep him honest, which means, make the batter afraid of you* —Jim Bouton

keep one's **nose clean** *v phr* To avoid doing wrong or seeming to do wrong; stay above reproach: *Good boy, Billy. Keep your nose clean* —Lawrence Sanders [fr the traditional injunction of a mother to a child to wipe its *nose*, wash behind its ears, etc]

keep on trucking *v phr* To carry on; continue what one is doing, esp working, plugging away, etc

keeps *See* FOR KEEPS, PLAY FOR KEEPS

keep one's **shirt** (or **pants**) **on** *fr middle 1800s* **1** *v phr* To stay unruffled; be calm; =COOL IT: *He was beginning to holler, so I told him to keep his shirt on* **2** *v phr* To be patient; wait a bit; =HOLD one's HORSES: *Keep your pants on and the guy will be back*

keep tabs on *v phr fr late 1800s* To keep informed about; keep watch on or over: *Who's gonna keep tabs on the receipts?*

keep up with the Joneses *v phr* To strive, esp beyond one's means, to keep up socially and financially with others in the same neighborhood or in the same social circle: *Never keep up with the Joneses; drag them down to your level... it's cheaper*—Quentin Crisp [fr the title of a comic strip of the early 20th century]

kee-rect (KEE rekt) *adj* Correct

kef (KEEF, KAYF) *n* (also **keef** or **kief** or **kif**) *narcotics* Marijuana, hashish, or opium [fr Arabic, "pleasure"]

kegger *n teenagers & students* A beer party; =BEER BUST

keister (KEE stər) (also **keester** or **keyster** or **kiester** or **kister**) **1** *n* The buttocks; rump; =ASS: *I've had it up to my keister with these leaks* —Ronald Reagan **2** *n pickpockets* A rear trousers pocket **3** *n hawkers and hoboes* A suitcase that opens into a display of goods: *the typical "keister" of the street hawker*—Collier and Westrate **4** *n underworld* A safe; strongbox; =CRIB [fr British dialect *kist* or German *Kiste* "chest, box," transferred to the buttocks perhaps by the pickpocket sense or by the notion that something may be concealed in the rectum]

◁ **Kelsey's ass** ▷ *See* COLD AS HELL

◁ **Kelsey's nuts** ▷ *See* TIGHT AS KELSEY'S NUTS

Ken *n* A conformist, conventional man; a man lacking any but bland typical characteristics [fr the male counterpart of the Barbie doll]

kerflooie or **kerflooey** *See* GO BLOOEY

kerplunk *See* GO KERPLUNK

key or **kee** or **ki** *n narcotics* A kilogram (about 2.2 pounds) of a narcotic: *enough opium to produce a key (kilo) of heroin*—Time [fr *kilo*]

keyster *See* KEISTER

the **keystone** (or **keystone sack** or **keystone cushion**) *n phr baseball* Second base

khazeray or **khazerei** (KHAH zə rī) *n* Odious and worthless material; =CRAP, SHIT: *All that airtime talk, all that khazeray, wasn't worth doing* [fr Yiddish, ultimately fr Hebrew *khazer* "pig"]

ki *See* KEY

kibitz **1** *v* To give intrusive and unrequested advice while watching a game, performance, etc **2** *v* To banter, comment [fr Yiddish fr German *Kiebitz* "peewit, lapwing," a noisy little bird]

kibitzer *n* A person who gives intrusive advice: *A good kibitzer has 20-20 hindsight*—New York Post

kibosh (KĪ bahsh) *v* To eliminate; =KILL: *that was kiboshed promptly by White House spokesman*—Philadelphia Journal

the **kibosh** *n phr* The termination; sad end; sudden doom: *This latest goof is probably the kibosh* [origin unknown, and very extensively speculated upon; perhaps, eg, fr Irish *cie bais* "cap of death," referring to the black cap a judge would don when pronouncing a death sentence] *See* PUT THE KIBOSH ON someone or something

kick **1** *v fr late 1700s* To complain; protest; =BITCH: *She can just kick all she wants to*—Sinclair Lewis **2** *n: If you got any kicks, you can always quit* **3** *n fr middle 1800s* A pocket, esp a pants pocket: *I have a hundred thousand boo-boos in the kick*—H McHugh **4** ***n*** *fr jive talk* A surge or fit of pleasure; a feeling of joy and delight; =BELT, CHARGE: *He was having a real kick*—RS Prather/ *I get a kick out of you*—Cole Porter **5** ***n*** Anything that gives one a feeling of pleasure, joy, etc: *That's a kick... .Ridin' a guy down Wilshire in daylight*—Raymond Chandler **6** ***n*** *fr jive talk* A strong personal predilection; =THING: *Arthur... is on the Paris kick*—John Crosby/ *several opportunities to let her wail on a comic kick*—Bob Salmaggi **7** ***n*** Power; impact; potency: *One of those... stories with a kick*—P Marks **8** ***n*** A shoe: *Hey, nice kicks* [pocket sense fr late-17th-century *kicks* "breeches"]

See GET A KICK OUT OF someone or something, ON A ROLL, SIDEKICK, TOP-KICK

kick around **1** ***v phr*** To idle about; drift around rootlessly; =BAT AROUND: *He put in a couple years just kicking around California* **2** ***v phr*** To acquire experience; become seasoned: *sound like a band that's kicked around for a long time*—Changes **3** ***v phr*** To abuse; repeatedly maltreat: *Mr Nixon said the press wouldn't have him to kick around any more*

kick something **around** ***v phr*** To discuss or think about; consider from all angles: *Let's kick Merrill's idea around for awhile*

kick ass **1** ***v phr*** To assert power; be rough; punish: *We kicked a little ass last night*—George Bush **2** ***v phr*** To have power; have unpolished vigor: *just country that kicks ass and entertains*—Aquarian

kick-ass **1** ***adj*** (also **kick-yer-ass**) Rough; powerful; =ROUGH-ASS, TOUGH: *that kick-ass attitude*—Sports Illustrated **2** ***n*** Power; energy; virility: *He's the guy who coaxed the kick-ass back into the torque*—Car and Driver

◁ **kick ass and take names**▷ ***v phr*** To behave very roughly and angrily; =KICK ASS: *Paschal ain't gonna do nothing but kick ass and take names*—Dan Jenkins [fr the image of a rough and punitive police officer, drill sergeant, prison guard, etc]

kickback ***n*** Money given to someone illegally or unethically: *Buying another poor devil's job for $50 or a kick-back from his pay*—Westbrook Pegler

kick back **1** ***v phr*** *underworld* To return or restore, esp to give back stolen property: *Stolen goods returned to the rightful owner are "kicked back"*—H McLellan **2** ***v phr*** To give part of wages, fees, etc, illicitly to another in return for one's job or other advantage: *The cabbies had to kick back a lot to the dispatchers* **3** ***v phr*** *college students fr black* To relax: *Use the pool, kick back.... Who knows?*—Armistead Maupin

kick down ***v phr*** *truckers* To shift into a lower gear in a truck or car

kicker **1** ***n*** A small motor, esp an outboard, used for a boat **2** ***n*** Anything that gives great pleasure; =KICK: *The kicker... was the station wagon*—R Starnes **3** ***n*** A hidden cost, qualification, defect, etc; =CATCH: *The kicker to this one is simple*—Gilbert Milstein/ *It may look like a good deal, but there's a kicker* **4** ***n*** =PUNCH LINE **5** ***n*** A pocket; =KICK: *Keep it in yer kickers*—Car and Driver

kickers ***n*** *college students* Shoes, esp tennis shoes

kick in **1** ***v phr*** *fr early 1900s* To pay up money; make one's proper contribution; =FORK OVER: *to ask you guys to kick in your share of the expenses*—Jerome Weidman **2** ***v phr*** To contribute orally; =CHIME IN **3** ***v phr*** To die

kicking ass ***n phr*** *college students* A good time; =a BALL: *We went downtown and had a kicking ass*

◁ a **kick in the ass**▷ **1** ***n phr*** A surprising and dampening rebuff, misfortune, etc; a slap in the face **2** ***n phr*** A strong stimulus or impetus; =a SHOT IN THE ARM: *If this campaign doesn't get a kick in the ass we're dead*

kick it **1** ***v phr*** *narcotics* To rid oneself of narcotic addiction: *I don't think anybody knew anyone who had kicked it*—Claude Brown **2** ***v phr*** *jazz talk & jive talk* To play swing or jazz very vigorously

kick off **1** ***v phr*** To die: *after his wife kicked off*—New Yorker **2** ***v phr*** To leave; depart **3** ***v phr*** To begin something; inaugurate: *the* *chain of thought kicked off by it* —Eldridge Cleaver

kick someone **out** *v phr* To eject, expel, or dismiss; =BOUNCE

kick over *See* KNOCK OVER

kick pad *n phr narcotics* A place where one is detoxified from narcotics: *I was clean three more days, left the kick pad*—Joseph Wambaugh

kick party *n phr narcotics* A party where LSD is used

kicks 1 *n fr bop talk fr narcotics* Pleasure and gratification; =BANGS, JOLLIES: *Sock cymbal's enough to give me my kicks*—Douglass Wallop **2** *n* Shoes • Attested as an early 1900s hobo term

See GET one's COOKIES

kick the bucket *v phr fr late 1700s British* To die: *Old man Mose done kicked the bucket* [origin uncertain; perhaps fr the *bucket* a suicide might kick from under in hanging himself]

kick the gong around *v phr outdated narcotics* To smoke opium or marijuana: *He helped the world kick the gong around, Jack did*—William Kennedy

◁ **kick the shit out of** someone or something▷ *See* BEAT THE SHIT OUT OF someone or something

kick the tires *v phr* To make a quick and superficial inspection; do cursory checking: *simplistic agrarian vision bought by the war-weary nation without kicking the tires*—Michael M Thomas [fr such an examination made while appraising a car]

kick up a fuss *v phr* To make a disturbance; complain loudly and bitterly; =RAISE CAIN: *I don't want his lawyer to kick up a fuss about this*—E Lavine

kick up a storm *See* PISS UP A STORM

kick someone **upstairs** *v phr* To remove from office by promotion to a nominally superior position: *Mr Gromyko has been kicked upstairs where ... he'll no longer influence Soviet foreign policy*—New York Times

kicky 1 *adj* Very chic and modish: *a lot of kicky clothes, many of them imports*—New York Times **2** *adj* Exciting; ravishing; =FAR OUT: *a kicky way to spend a couple of years*—Mpls St Paul

kid 1 *n fr late 1500s* A child: *She's a cute little kid* **2** *n fr late 1800s* Any young or relatively young person: *the kids in college* **3** *modifier: his kid sister/ my kid cousin* **4** *v fr middle 1800s British* To joke; jest; banter; =JOSH: *a funny guy, always kidding* **5** *v* To attempt to deceive; try to fool: *Are you kidding me?* **6** *n: That's no kid, neither* —Dunning and Abbott [bantering and fooling senses perhaps fr an alteration of dialect *cod* "hoax, fool"]

See I KID YOU NOT, NEW KID ON THE BLOCK, WHIZ KID

kid around *v phr* To jest and banter; avoid seriousness; =FOOL AROUND

kiddie or **kiddy** *n* A child

kidding *See* NO KIDDING

kiddo or **Kiddo** *n fr early 1900s* A person, esp one younger than oneself • Used nearly always in direct address: *OK, kiddo, you can leave now*

kidney *See* GRIPE one's ASS

kid stuff 1 *n phr* Something too easy to challenge an adult; =CINCH, PIECE OF CAKE: *That swim to Catalina's kid stuff* **2** *n phr* Activity not appropriate for an adult; childish concerns: *Give up the kid stuff and find a real job*

kidvid 1 *n* Children's television: *a year when kidvid is being publicly scolded*—TV Guide/ *The three networks are offering the public more kidvid*—New York Times **2** *modifier: The trade journals call the children's program segment on television the "kidvid ghetto"*—American Scholar

kief or **kif** *See* KEF

kiester *See* KEISTER

kife 1 *v circus* To swindle **2** *v* To steal

◀**kike**▶ **1** *n fr early 1900s* A Jew • Sometimes used by Jews of other Jews they regard with contempt **2** *adj: kike neighborhood* [origin unknown and much speculated upon; perhaps fr Yiddish *kikel* "circle" because Jews who could not sign their names would make a circle; perhaps an alteration of *Ike* "Isaac"; perhaps because so many Jewish immigrant names ended in *-ky* or *-ki*; perhaps fr British dialect *keek* "peep," used for a spy on a rival's designs in the clothing business]

kill 1 *v* To drink or eat up: *He killed a couple beers* **2** *v* To spoil or ruin: *One bad grade killed his*

chances for med school **3** *v* To demoralize totally; make hopeless: *The third defeat killed him* **4** *v* To be extremely successful with: *The Evergreen Review kills him*—Eldridge Cleaver **5** *v* To make an audience helpless with laughter; =FRACTURE: *My McEnroe act kills 'em* **6** *v* To eliminate: *Kill half these lights/ Kill that whole paragraph*
See IN AT THE KILL, KILLER, THAT KILLS IT

to **kill** *See* DRESSED TO THE TEETH

killer 1 *n* A very attractive person: *Ain't she a killer?* **2** *n* (also **killer-diller**) A person or thing that is remarkable, wonderful, superior, etc; =BEAUT, DOOZIE: *The song's a killer!* **3** *adj* (also **killer-diller**): *not only was it a killer version*—Village Voice **4** *n narcotics* A marijuana cigarette
See LADY-KILLER

killing *n* A very large and quick profit; =BUNDLE: *It wasn't just a fair return he made, it was a killing*
See MAKE A KILLING

killjoy *n* A morose pessimist; =CRAPE-HANGER, GLOOMY GUS

kilter *See* OUT OF KILTER

kin *See* KISSING COUSIN, SHIRTTAIL KIN

the **kind** *adj phr teenagers* Excellent; superior: *He's got the kind car*

king 1 *n* (also **king pin**) The leader; chief: *king of the motorcycle jumpers* **2** *n underworld* A prison warden

king-size or **king-sized** *adj* Very large; extra large: *Your nagging gives me a king-size headache*

kink 1 *n* (also **kinko**) A person with deviant or bizarre tastes, esp sexual: *I'm not some kind of kink*—John D MacDonald **2** ***modifier:*** *a kinko diner who tries to attract Chong's attention*—Washington Post **3** *n* A deviant practice or predilection, esp sexual: *a Nazi with a kink for prepubescent girls*—A Bailey **4** *n* A defect or flaw, esp a minor one; =BUG: *We'll work the kinks out of the plan*

kinker *n circus* Any circus performer

the **kinks** *See* IRON OUT THE KINKS

kinky 1 *adj* Dishonest; illegal; =CROOKED: *"kinky" gambling paraphernalia*—WR Simpson **2** *adj underworld* Stolen: *a kinky car* **3** *adj fr middle 1800s* Eccentric **4** *adj* Bizarre; weird: *no offense so kinky that the Maximum Enchilada and his consigliores wouldn't commit it*—G Wolff **5** *adj* Deviant and abnormal, esp sexually: *a very kinky guy, likes being beat up* **6** *adj* Showing or pertaining to sexual deviation: *kinky photos/ kinky porn*

kishkes or **kishkas** *n* The entrails; innards; =GUTS: *His kishkas were gripped by the iron hand of outrage and frustration*—Philip Roth [fr Yiddish]

kiss *n* =KISS-OFF
See BUTTERFLY KISS, FRENCH KISS

KISS (KIS) ***sentence*** Keep it simple, stupid, or keep it simple and stupid

◁ **kiss ass**▷ *v phr* To flatter one's superiors; =BROWN-NOSE: *He likes to be perfect and kiss ass*—Pat Conroy

◁ **kiss-ass**▷ or **kiss-butt 1** *n* A toady; sycophant; =BROWN-NOSE, ASS-KISSER: *and not have people think, "Oh, what a kiss-butt"*—Washington Post **2** ***modifier:*** *another kiss-ass review of an extremely bad album*—Rolling Stone **3** *n* Sycophantic flattery: *using the old kiss-ass with the colonel*

◁ **kiss** someone's **ass**▷ *v phr* To flatter; curry favor with superiors: *I didn't kiss anybody's ass and I didn't expect anybody to kiss mine*—People Weekly

kisser *n fr middle 1800s* The mouth; the face: *It would be a pleasure to drop one on your kisser, I admit*—Leo Rosten
See ASS-KISSER, MOTHERFUCKER

kiss something **goodbye 1** *v phr* To abandon or renounce: *When he finally found out it was bad for him he kissed it goodbye* **2** *v phr* To accept or infer the fact that something is irrevocably gone: *You can kiss that promotion goodbye, after the way you talked to her*

kissing *See* MOTHERFUCKING

kissing cousin (or **kin**) **1** *n* A relative close enough to be kissed in salutation, hence anyone with whom a person is fairly intimate: *The two species will often prove to be kissing cousins for they'll crossbreed*—Sports Afield **2** *n* A close copy: *He had a kissing cousin of Montgomery's mustache*—JA Kugelmass

◁ **kiss my ass**▷ ***sentence*** I invite you to perform an obsequious and humiliating act; =GO FUCK oneself ● Always an insulting challenge and rejection:

"What should I say?" asked Belle. "Tell him to kiss my ass"—Joseph Heller

kiss off **1** *v phr* To dodge; evade: *had kissed off all raps*—J Evans **2** *v phr* To kill: *who kissed off Martin*—J Evans

kiss-off **1** *n* (also **California kiss-off** or **New York kiss-off**) A dismissal, esp a rude one; =the BOUNCE, BRUSH-OFF: *She's given hundreds of suitors the royal kiss-off* **2** *v black fr 1940s* To die **3** *n: How is cholesterol related to kiss-off, Doc?*

kiss someone or something **off** **1** *v phr* To dismiss rudely; =BRUSH someone OFF: *The receptionist kissed me off quite cheekily* **2** *v phr* To let go of, to attempt to forget; =KISS something GOODBYE: *You can kiss that money off*

kissy-face or **kissy-facey** or **kissy-poo** **1** *n teenagers & students* Kissing and cuddling; =MAKING OUT, NECKING: *Let's have a little kissy-face* **2** *n* A kiss: *The symbol of welcome ... is a handshake, not a kissy-poo*—Washington Post **3** *v: I've trained poodles so that they won't kissy-face everybody*—Time

See PLAY KISSIE

kister *See* KEISTER

kit *See* HEAD KIT

kit and caboodle (or **boodle**) *n phr fr middle 1800s* The totality; everything: *the whole kit and caboodle, go hang*—George Jean Nathan/ *the whole kit and boodle of 'em*—Ellery Queen [fr 18th-century British *kit* "outfit of equipment" plus early-19th-century *boodle* "lot, collection," perhaps fr Dutch *boedel* "property, effects"]

kitchen *n baseball* The space over home plate where a batter finds it easiest to hit a fair ball; a batter's preferred point of delivery: *He'd throw it in my kitchen, so I moved up a step toward the plate*—Associated Press

See DOWN IN THE KITCHEN, IF YOU CAN'T STAND THE HEAT STAY OUT OF THE KITCHEN

kite **1** *n underworld* A letter or note, esp one smuggled into prison **2** *n* An airplane **3** *v* To write a check when one does not have the funds to cover it, hoping to find them before the check is cashed: *The bill was due before payday, so I had to kite the check* **4** *v* To raise the value of a check illegally before cashing it

See BLOW something HIGH AS A KITE, GO FLY A KITE, HIGH AS A KITE, HIGHER THAN A KITE

kitsch or **Kitsch** (KITCH) *n* Literature or art having little esthetic merit but appealing powerfully to popular taste: *It stands unchallenged as a masterpiece of kitsch*—Playboy [fr German, "trash, rubbish"]

kitschy *adj* Being or resembling kitsch: *Visconti's kitschy film*—Harvey Gross/ *Its kitschy Lupe Velez ambiance*—Armistead Maupin

kitten *See* HAVE KITTENS, SEX KITTEN

kitty *n fr gambling* The pot or pool of money in a gambling game, made up of contributions from the players; a contributed fund: *Each put $25,000 in the kitty*—Philadelphia

See BITCH KITTY, DUST KITTY, IT'S A BITCH

klepto *n* A kleptomaniac: *"Bloody klepto," says Siddhartha*—New Yorker

klick or **klik** *See* CLICK

klop in the chops *n phr* A blow to the face; a severe attack: *starting with a klop in the chops from San Francisco*—Ann Landers [fr Yiddish *klop* "a blow," plus the *chop* phrase for rhyme]

kluck *See* CLUCK, DUMB CLUCK

kludge or **kloodge** or **kluge** (KLOOJ, KLUJ) *computer* **1** *n* A term of endearment for a favorite computer, esp a somewhat defective one **2** *n* A computer program that has been revised and tinkered with so much that it will never work **3** *n* A ludicrous assortment of incompatible and unworkable components: *You see this mechanical kluge (contraption), stop, think, and decide to do something*—Newsweek

klutz or **clutz** (KLUTS) **1** *n* A stupid person; idiot; =BLOCKHEAD: *Now, klutz that I am, I thought of Neal*—Esquire **2** *n* A clumsy person; a lubberly lout: *I am the world's biggest klutz...I trip over my own feet, drop things*—New York Post [fr Yiddish, "blockhead," literally "block"]

klutz around *v phr* To behave stupidly; tamper with clumsily

klutzy **1** *adj* Stupid; idiotic: *any clever kid playing a klutzy kid*—New York Times **2** *adj* Clumsy; unhandy

kneecap *v* To shoot in the kneecap or legs • Typically done by terrorists or gangsters as a disabling measure short of assassination

knee-high to a grasshopper *adj phr* (Variations: **bumble-bee** or **duck** or **frog** or **mosquito** or **spit** or **splinter** or **toad** may replace **grasshopper**) *fr early 1800s* Very short or small, esp because young: *He's been smoking since he was knee-high to a grasshopper*

knee-jerk **1** *n* A reflexlike action or response: *Being nasty to women is a knee-jerk with him* **2** *modifier: one more gesture to the knee-jerk hawks in the Congress*—W Jackson **3** *n* A person who reacts with a reflexlike response: *a seventy-year-old knee-jerk best remembered for castigating the Reverend Bill Moyers for dancing the frug in the White House*—LL King [fr the patellar reflex]

knees *See* CUT oneself OFF AT THE KNEES, CUT someone OFF AT THE KNEES

kneesies *n* Clandestine amorous friction of the knees: *We got back to the table and played kneesies while we talked*—Mickey Spillane

knee-slapper *n* Something very funny, esp a joke; =BOFFOLA: *That's a knee-slapper*—Matt Crowley/ *If she ever told a knee-slapper, I wasn't there*—Washingtonian

knickers *See* HAVE someone BY THE SHORT HAIRS

one's **knitting** *See* STICK TO one's KNITTING

knob *See* JOY KNOB

knobber *n* A male homosexual transvestite prostitute: *It is where the knobbers, or transvestites, hang out*—New York Times [perhaps fr their wearing of false *knobs* "female nipples or breasts"; perhaps because they give *knob jobs*]

knobby *See* NOBBY

◁ **knob job**▷ *n phr fr homosexuals* An act of fellatio; =BLOW JOB

◁ **knobs**▷ *n* A woman's breasts or nipples; =KNOCKERS
See WITH BELLS ON

knock **1** *v fr late 1800s* To deprecate; criticize severely; dispraise; =PUT someone or something DOWN: *Their film critic knocks every flick in sight* **2** *n: The knock on Fernandez is he can't field* **3** *v black* To borrow or lend; ask or beg **4** *v* To give: *C'mon, baby, knock me a kiss*
See BEAT THE SHIT OUT OF, DON'T KNOCK IT, HAVE something CINCHED

knock around *v phr* To idle about; loaf; =KICK AROUND

knock someone **around** *v phr* To abuse; =KICK someone AROUND

knock back *v phr* To drink in one gulp: *there to mull their downside risks and knock back free champagne*—Toronto Life

knock someone's **block off** *v phr* To hit very hard; give a severe trouncing; =CLOBBER: *One more word and I'll knock your block off*

knock someone (or **knock 'em**) **dead** *v phr* To delight or impress extremely; =KILL, KNOCK someone's SOCKS OFF, WOW: *a fantastic scenery number for my life's movie. Something that'll knock 'em dead*—Washington Post

knockdown **1** *n outdated fr late 1800s* An introduction: *You want a knockdown to something*—Jerome Weidman **2** *n* An invitation **3** *modifier* Designed to be sold unassembled, and be easy to assemble and disassemble: *a knockdown kitchen set*

knock down **1** *v phr fr middle 1800s* To pocket money taken from one's employer: *clerk who was knocking down on the till*—J Evans **2** *v phr* To earn: *Hommuch he knock down a week?*—Arthur Kober **3** *v phr* To reduce a price, salary, figure, etc: *Let's knock down the estimate a bit* **4** *v phr* To criticize; =KNOCK **5** *v phr* To drink

knock something **down** *v phr* To sell, esp at a price favorable to the buyer: *I'll knock it down to you for three bucks* [probably fr the gavel-blow given by an auctioneer to signal and conclude a sale]

knock-down-drag-out **1** *adj phr* Very violent; unrestrained; =ALL-OUT: *They were having a knock-down-drag-out argument when I got there* **2** *n: Seems the neighbors were having a knockdown-drag-out*—Washington Post

knocked *See* HAVE something CINCHED

knocked out **1** *adj phr* Drunk **2** *adj phr* Intoxicated with a narcotic; =HIGH, STONED **3** *adj phr* Overcome with delight; extremely pleased:

Everybody was knocked out to be asked—Rolling Stone **4** ***adj phr*** Very tired; exhausted; =POOPED

◁ **knocked up**▷ ***adj phr*** Pregnant

knocker¹ ***n*** A consistently negative critic; detracter: *that pack of knockers that have been howling*—The Billboard

See APPLE-KNOCKER

knocker² (KNAH kər) ***n*** A very important person; =BIG SHOT, MACHER: *Knocker means a big shot, either real or imagined, and you pronounce that first "k"*—C McHarr [fr Yiddish, literally "one who cracks or snaps a whip"]

◁ **knockers**▷ ***n*** A woman's breasts; =HOOTERS: *Dumb broads with big knockers*—A Leslie

knock someone or something **for a loop** (Variations: **throw** may replace **knock** and **goal** or **row** or **row of ashcans** or **row of milk cans** or **row of Chinese pagodas** or **row of tall red totem poles** may replace **loop**) **1** ***v phr*** *fr early 1900s* To hit very hard; =CLOBBER: *We knocked the villain for a row of ash cans*—H Witwer/ *You certainly knocked him for a row of tall red totem poles*—K Brush **2** ***v phr*** *fr early 1900s* To unsettle severely; disrupt calm and confidence; =DISCOMBOBULATE: *It must have thrown him for a loop, but he asked*—Earl Thompson **3** ***v phr*** To delight extremely; thrill and amaze; =KILL, KNOCK someone's SOCKS OFF: *if this climactic sequence doesn't knock you for a loop*—Playboy **4** ***v phr*** To cope with very well; =ACE, CREAM: *Would he hit Math 1 in the eye? He'd knock it for a loop*—P Marks

knock someone or something **galley west** (or **skywest**) ***v phr*** *fr middle 1800s* To hit very hard, esp to knock unconscious; trounce; =CLOBBER: *Jimmy likewise knocked him galley-west*—Foy and Harlow/ *something that will knock somebody around here skywest*—L Ford

knock something **into a cocked hat** ***v phr*** *fr early 1800s* To disprove, invalidate, or show the falsity of a statement, plea, etc: *This knocks our whole case into a cocked hat* [literally "flatten," since a naval officer's cocked hat could be flattened]

knock it off or **knock it** ***v phr*** *fr middle 1800s Navy* To stop doing or saying something; desist; =CUT IT OUT • Often a stern command: *I told you creeps to knock it off, now I'm gonna waste you*

knock someone's **lights out** **1** ***v phr*** To beat severely; =BEAT THE SHIT OUT OF someone, CLOBBER **2** ***v phr*** To impress enormously; =KNOCK someone's SOCKS OFF: *I have a story that would knock your lights out*—Sam Shepard

knock off **1** ***v phr*** To stop, esp to stop working; desist **2** ***v phr*** To produce, esp with seeming ease and rapidity: *He knocked off a couple of portraits at $40,000 each* **3** ***v phr*** To consume, esp to drink; =KNOCK DOWN: *after knocking off a glass of... wine*—John McCarten/ *while I knock off two or three or four drinks*—Esquire **4** ***v phr*** To delete; shorten by: *Let's knock off this last paragraph* **5** ***v phr*** To kill; murder; assassinate; =RUB OUT: *Before long the spiders knock off Michael*—Judith Crist **6** ***v phr*** To die; pass away **7** ***v phr*** To arrest, esp after a raid: *Local cops... had free authority to knock them off*—Westbrook Pegler **8** ***v phr*** To rob; =HOLD UP, KNOCK OVER: *The pair knocked off several shops*—Associated Press ◁**9**▷ ***v phr*** To do the sex act with, esp as a prostitute; satisfy a sex client: *if you're a street hooker and knock off twenty or thirty guys a day*—Xaviera Hollander **10** ***v phr*** To defeat; overcome: *The Tigers knocked off the Yankees today* **11** ***v phr*** To attain; operate at: *The old tub was knocking off 12 knots*

knockout **1** ***n*** An especially attractive person or thing; =DISH: *Saaay, you know, you're a knockout*—Jerome Weidman **2** ***modifier:*** *That was a knockout plot*—K Brush

knock oneself **out** **1** ***v phr*** To work very hard; do one's utmost: *They like "knocking themselves out" for Variety*—Abel Green **2** ***v phr*** To have a splendid and exhausting time: *They knocked themselves out drinking and dancing*

knock someone **out** **1** ***v phr*** (also **knock** someone **stiff**) To make unconscious, esp with a blow **2** ***v***

phr To delight or impress extremely; =KILL, KNOCK someone's SOCKS OFF: *I read a lot of war books and mysteries and all, but they don't knock me out too much*—JD Salinger

knock something **out** *v phr* To make or produce, esp rather quickly and crudely: *I haven't got time to knock the script out myself*—Budd Schulberg

knockout drops *n phr* Chloral hydrate or another stupefacient drug, esp when put into a drink of liquor; =MICKEY FINN

knock over 1 *v phr* (also **kick over**) *fr underworld* To rob; =HOLD UP, KNOCK OFF: *made regular sweeps by jet, knocking over airport motels* —Time **2** *v phr* To raid: *knocked over a reputed... bookmaking parlor* —J Martin

knocks *n* Extreme pleasure; gratification; =COOKIES, JOLLIES, KICKS: *They get their knocks that way*—Pete Martin

knock (or **blow**) someone's **socks off** *v phr* To delight extremely; thrill and amaze; =KILL, SEND: *We got a sound that's gonna knock your socks off* —Rolling Stone/ *a "surprise special" that we think will blow your socks off* —Playboy [these senses fr mid-19th-century sense "defeat utterly," fr the notion of hitting someone so hard that he is lifted right out of his shoes and *socks*]

knock them in the aisles *See* LAY THEM IN THE AISLES

◁ **knock the shit out of** someone or something▷ *See* BEAT THE SHIT OUT OF someone or something

knock (or **throw**) **together** *v phr* To make or produce something quickly: *what you said about knocking something together that we could eat* —James M Cain/ *In the few minutes available they threw together a cover story*

knock someone **up** ◁**1**▷ *v phr* To make pregnant **2** *v phr* To awaken; arouse by knocking

know *See* IN THE KNOW

know (or **have**) **all the answers 1** *v phr* To claim or affect special intimate knowledge: *That little creep over there always thinks he knows all the answers* **2** *v phr* To have a jaded, cynical, spiritless sort of wisdom: *She don't bother any more, knows all the answers* **3** *v phr* To know a case or subject thoroughly ● Most often in the negative: *Even your doctor doesn't have all the answers*

◁ not **know** one's **ass from** one's **elbow** (or **from a hole in the ground**)▷ *See* NOT KNOW one's ASS FROM one's ELBOW

not **know beans** *See* NOT KNOW BEANS

not **know** someone **from Adam** *See* NOT KNOW someone FROM ADAM

know (or **not know**) **from nothing** *v phr* To be ignorant; be deeply uninformed or ill-informed: *That pompous bastard knows from nothing* [fr Yiddish *fun gornisht*]

know-how *n fr middle 1800s* Skill, esp technical skill; practical competence: *Takes know-how to run that thing*

know-it-all *n* A person who pretends to virtual omniscience; =BIGMOUTH, SMART-ASS

know one's **onions** *v phr* (Variations: **beans** or **business** or **stuff** may replace **onions**) *fr early 1900s* To be very competent and authoritative in one's work: *I'm glad the tax accountant knows his onions*

◁ not **know shit from Shinola**▷ *See* NOT KNOW SHIT FROM SHINOLA

know the ropes *v phr fr middle 1800s nautical* To be seasoned and informed; know the intricacies of a job, situation, etc; =KNOW one's WAY AROUND [fr the myriad *ropes* of a sailing vessel]

know the score *v phr* To have essential and current information; understand what is important: *You look like a smart lad who knows the score*—J Evans

know one's **way around** *v phr* To be informed and experienced; be seasoned and reliable: *He's been at the job for two years but still doesn't know his way around*

know what one **can do with** something *v phr* (Variations: **where** one **can put** (or **shove** or **stick** or **stuff**) may replace **what** one **can do with**) To know that one's offer, request, possession, etc, is held in extreme contempt ● A euphemized way of saying that one can take something and **stick it up** his or her **ass**: *I saw the contract, and he knows what he* *can do with it/ I told him where he can shove that great idea of his*

know where it's at *v phr esp 1960s counterculture* To be up-to-date and cognizant; = be HIP: *the NOW generation, who, like, know what's happening and where it's at*—Trans-Action

know where the bodies are buried *v phr* To have intimate and secret knowledge, esp of something criminal, scandalous, etc: *The president reckoned he had to keep that lawyer quiet, because he knew where the bodies were buried*

knuckleball or **knuckler** **1** *n baseball fr early 1900s* A pitch thrown from the knuckles that moves slowly and erratically; = BUTTERFLY BALL: *Leonard's tantalizing knucklers*—L Effrat **2** *modifier: a knuckleball artist*

knuckle-buster *n* An end wrench

knuckled *See* WHITE-KNUCKLED

knuckle down *v phr fr middle 1800s* To work hard and seriously; stop loafing; = BUCKLE DOWN [fr the act of putting one's *knuckles down* to the taw or marble preparing for a careful shot in the game of marbles, a use dating fr the mid-18th century]

knuckle-dragger *n fr college students* A rough, somewhat stupid and crude man; = GORILLA, STRONG-ARM MAN: *the tendency of some covert agents, "the knuckledraggers" of the Special Operations Group, to revel in deception*—Washingtonian [from the image of a gorilla whose *knuckles drag* on the ground when it walks]

knucklehead *n* A stupid person; = BONEHEAD: *Movies are made by unappreciative knuckleheads*—Pete Martin

knuckler *See* KNUCKLEBALL, WHITE KNUCKLER

knuckles *See* RAP someone's KNUCKLES

knuckle sandwich *n phr* A hard blow to the mouth or face: *I feed him a knuckle sandwich*—Lawrence Sanders

knucks *n* Brass knuckles: *The "knucks" were hidden in the heel*—Associated Press

KO (pronounced as separate letters) **1** *n prizefight* A knockout; = KAYO **2** *v: He KOed six in a row* **3** *modifier: a KO punch*

kocker *See* ALTER KOCKER

kook (KŌŌK) **1** *n fr 1950s teenagers* An eccentric person; = NUT, SCREWBALL: *The bomb cannot be exploded by a single "kook"*—Nation **2** *modifier: did a kook piece with dancers*—Village Voice **3** *n surfers* A novice surfer [fr *cuckoo*]

kookie or **kooky** *adj fr 1950s teenagers* Crazy; eccentric; = DIPPY, GOOFY: *make you seem a little kookie*—David Halberstam

kootchy *See* the HOOTCHIE-COOTCHIE

kopasetic *See* COPACETIC

kosh *n* = COSH

kosher *adj* Proper; as it should be; legitimate: *Something about this arrangement ain't kosher/ It all looked kosher until Buzzy stepped on a mine* [fr Yiddish fr Hebrew *kasher* "fit, proper"]

Krishna *See* HARE KRISHNA KIDS

kvell (KVEL) *v* To display pride and satisfaction; beam: *The elderly couple... kvell also... upon making contact with a Jewish airstrip*—Philip Roth [fr Yiddish, literally "gush, flow forth"]

kvetch (kə VECH) **1** *v* To whine; complain; be consistently pessimistic: *Dealing with a controversial idea of public importance, Mobil kvetched*—Village Voice **2** *n: Your sister's a nagging kvetch/ the city hospital spirit, which is basically one of kvetch*—New York [fr Yiddish, literally "squeeze, press"]

L

labonza *n* The belly; =GUT, KISHKES: *She let him have it right in the labonza* [probably fr Italian *pancia* "paunch," with attached article and dialectal pronunciation]

labor *See* GRUNT WORK

la-de-da (Variations: **lah-de-dah** or **la-di-da** or **lah-di-dah**) *fr middle 1800s British* **1** *n* A dandyish or sissified man; super-refined and delicate person: *Some lah-de-dah with a cane*—Hecht and MacArthur **2** *adj: lunch place of the la-de-dah literary set*—New York Confidential **3** *adj* Very refined and respectable: *Nobody weren't going to make her live in a lah-di-dah place like that* —RGG Price **4** *adj* Carefree and nonchalant: *Her emotions at the dissolution of her 25-year marriage are anything but la-de-da*—Us **5** *v* To treat in a nonchalant, offhand manner: *The outfielder la-di-da'd the catch* **6** *interj* A phrase used to mean the equivalent of "It doesn't matter": *You're cancelling our date? Oh well, lah-di-dah*

ladies' (or **lady's**) **man** **1** *n phr* A man who pursues and otherwise devotes himself to women to an unusual degree; =LOVER-BOY **2** *n phr* A man who is attractive to many women: *He's so conceited... thinks he's a real ladies' man*

lady *n* Any woman; any grown-up female • Often used in quasi-polite direct address: *Lady, will you please move your car?*

See BAG LADY, FAIRY LADY, OLD LADY, the OPERA'S NEVER OVER TILL THE FAT LADY SINGS

the **lady** *n phr narcotics* Cocaine

Lady H *n phr narcotics* Heroin: *urging teens to stay away from Lady H* —Los Angeles Times

lady-killer *n* =LADIES' MAN

lagniappe (LAN yap) *n fr middle 1800s* A dividend; something extra: *I hit her with a few real hard ones for lagniappe (or good measure)*—Louis Armstrong [fr New Orleans Creole, origin unknown and much speculated; originally a little present or gratuity given to a customer by a New Orleans merchant]

laid-back *adj* Relaxed; easy-going: *a sort of laid-back, not insane Janis Joplin*—V Aletti [perhaps fr the reclining posture of highway motorcyclists]

lallygag *See* LOLLYGAG

lam *underworld fr late 1800s* **1** *v* To depart; go, esp hastily in escaping: *lammed for Cleveland*—H Witwer **2** *v* To escape from prison [ultimately fr 16th-century British sense "beat," hence the same semantically as *beat it*]

See ON THE LAM

lamb **1** *n* A person who is easily victimized; =PATSY, SUCKER **2** *n* A dear, sweet person: *Mary is such a lamb*

lambaste or **lambast** (lam BAYST, lam BAST) **1** *v fr middle 1800s* To hit very hard; =CLOBBER: *They lambasted the suspect mercilessly* **2** *v* To disparage strongly; castigate: *lambasted the idea that "mom is to blame"*—AL Blakeslee [ultimately fr British *lam* and *baste*, both "beat"]

lame **1** *n esp teenagers fr black* An old-fashioned, conventional person; =SQUARE: *and not worry about anybody naming me a lame*—Claude Brown/ *not have been as quick to* *judge him as a lame*—Rolling Stone **2** ***adj:*** *He's so lame I can't believe he was born in this century* **3** ***adj*** Inept: *their performances were sloppy, sometimes even lame*—Saturday Review

lamebrain ***n*** A stupid person; =DOPE, KNUCKLEHEAD: *Not all the lamebrains on Capitol Hill frequent the House or Senate*—Washington Post

lamebrained ***adj*** Stupid; =KLUTZY

lamed ***adj*** Stupid; dim

lame duck **1** ***n phr*** *fr middle 1800s* A public official who has lost an election or one whois not permitted by law to seek reelection for an additional term but is serving out a term **2** ***modifier:*** *lame-duck president/ lame-duck session* **3** ***n phr*** *stock market* A speculator who has taken options on stocks he or she cannot pay for

landing ***See*** CHINESE LANDING

landsman (LAHNTS mən) ***n*** A fellow countryman, townsman, etc; compatriot; =HOMEBOY, PAESAN: *You from Kalamazoo? Landsman!* [fr Yiddish]

lane ***See*** FAST LANE, HAMMER LANE, IN THE STRAIGHT LANE

lap **1** ***n*** *fr 1920s* A round of a prizefight **2** ***n*** A swallow of liquor; =SLURP

lap organ ***n phr*** An accordion

lapping ***See*** CUNT-LAPPING

lard ***See*** TUB OF GUTS

lard-bucket ***n*** A fat person; =TUB OF GUTS

lardhead ***n*** A stupid person; =FATHEAD

large ***adj*** *fr theater & jazz talk* Very popular and successful; highly favored; =BIG: *His act was quite large in Boston*

large one ***n phr*** *underworld* A year in prison: *The Tiger got fifteen large ones*—George V Higgins

larky ***adj*** *chiefly British* Playful; frolicsome; bantering: *began making larky plunges into show business*—Time

lash-up ***n*** *WW2 Army fr British* Living quarters; barracks; =DIGS

latch on to or **latch on** *fr 1930s black* **1** ***v phr*** To get; obtain; =GLOM ON TO: *Latch on to the first seat that's empty/ when you find the page, latch on* **2** ***v phr*** To comprehend; grasp; =DIG: *He finally latched onto the truth* **3** ***n phr*** To attach oneself to; be dependent on: *He latched on to me as soon as I arrived*

lately ***See*** JOHNNY-COME-LATELY

later ***interj*** *esp teenagers fr black* A parting salutation: *I dug right away what the kick was, so I said, "Later," and he split*—Eldridge Cleaver

lather ***v*** *fr late 1700s* To hit; strike: *He lathered the ball out of the park/ They caught him and lathered him* [fr the notion that frothy washing *lather* is produced by vigorous agitation or beating; see *in a lather*]

latrine (or **barracks**) **lawyer** ***n phr*** *Army* A soldier who is argumentative, esp on fine points, and tends to be a meddler, complainer, and self-server

lats ***n*** The latissimus dorsi muscles: *checking the cut of their lats in shiny windows*—San Francisco

laugh ***See*** BELLY LAUGH, the HORSELAUGH

a **laugh** or **a laugh and a half** ***n phr*** Something funny; a cause of amusement, esp of contemptuous derision: *You're gonna cook? That's a laugh*

laugher ***n*** *esp sports* A laughing matter, esp a game in which one team scores an annihilating victory: *the two games he mentioned were laughers, Oklahoma 41-7 over North Carolina*—Sports Illustrated

laughing academy ***n phr*** A mental hospital; =FUNNY FARM, NUT HOUSE

laugh on (or **out of**) **the other side of** one's **face** ***v phr*** To lament and moan; suffer a change of mood from joy to distress; undergo a defeat: *When they get through with him he'll be laughing out of the other side of his face*

launching pad ***n phr*** *narcotics* =SHOOTING GALLERY

launder ***v*** To transfer or convert funds so that illegal or dubious receipts are made to appear legitimate: *the account money that had been "laundered" by being siphoned from this country into Mexico and returned under an alias*—W Barthelmes

laundry (or **shopping**) **list** ***n phr*** A long bill of items to be obtained, discussed, done, not done: *This "do-good" laundry list draws sneers*—Maurice Moskowitz/*A shopping list is not a strategy*—New York Review

lava ***See*** IN A LATHER

lavender ***See*** LAY someone OUT

law ***See*** SUNSHINE LAW

Law ***See*** JOHN LAW

the **law** ***n phr fr underworld*** Any police officer, prison guard, etc

lawyer ***See*** CLUBHOUSE LAWYER, JAILHOUSE LAWYER, LATRINE LAWYER

lay ◁**1**▷ ***n*** A person regarded merely as a sex partner or object: *the two girls looked like swell lays* —James T Farrell/ *she's a great lay* —Saturday Review ◁**2**▷ ***n*** A sex act; =PIECE OF ASS: *anyone who is looking for an easy lay*—New York ◁**3**▷ ***v:*** *five cadets who swore they'd all laid the girl one night*—Calder Willingham **4** ***v*** To bet: *I laid her six to one he wouldn't show up* ***See*** EASY MAKE

lay a batch ***v phr hot rodders*** To leave black rubber marks on the road by accelerating a car rapidly

◁ **lay** (**cut** or **let**) **a fart**▷ ***v phr*** To flatulate; =FART: *This guy... laid this terrific fart*—JD Salinger

not **lay a glove** (or **finger** or **hand**) **on** someone ***See*** NOT LAY A GLOVE ON someone

lay an egg ***v phr*** *fr late 1800s* To fail; =BOMB, FLOP: *The plan's going to lay an egg unless we give it a shot in the arm* [fr earlier British *lay a duck's egg* "make a score of zero"]

lay back ***v phr*** *fr black* To relax; take one's ease: *not a Southern-rock band. They don't lay back*—Rolling Stone

lay down on the job ***v phr*** To loaf; dawdle and shirk

lay for someone ***v phr*** To watch for one's chance to take revenge; vigilantly stalk: *I'd lay for him in town some night*—Calder Willingham

lay it on ***v phr*** *fr middle 1800s* To exaggerate; =BULLSHIT

lay (or **put**) **it on the line** (or **on the table**) ***v phr*** To speak candidly and straightforwardly; =TELL IT LIKE IT IS: *OK, no more fancy footwork, I'll lay it on the line/ They are more likely to give it to you if you lay it on the table* —CoEvolution Quarterly

lay low ***v phr*** To stay out of sight; remain inconspicuous: *We're layin' low a couple days*—Nelson Algren

lay off **1** ***v phr*** To stop troubling or harrying someone; leave someone in peace • Often an irritated command or entreaty: *So lay off or I'll split your head, baby*—Changes **2** ***v phr*** *gambling* To place a portion of the bets one has accepted with other agents, so as to reduce one's possible losses

lay someone **off** ***v phr*** To dismiss from a job; terminate

lay something **on** someone *esp 1960s counterculture fr black* **1** ***v phr*** To present an idea, point of view, etc: *And the sisters laid the revolutionary ideology right on them*—Bobby Seale **2** ***v phr*** To tell or inform: *I have something heavy to lay on you, I'm afraid*

◁ **lay one**▷ ***v phr*** =LAY A FART

lay one on ***v phr*** To hit hard; punch; =HANG ONE ON: *She laid one on him, when he least expected it*

lay (or **put**) something **on the line** ***v phr*** To put deliberately at risk; put in peril as a wager or hostage: *If you try this, remember you are laying your ass on the line*

layout **1** ***n*** A place; house; living arrangements: *Nice little layout you got here* **2** ***n*** Place, equipment, apparatus, etc, for a particular purpose: *This layout is for writing dictionaries*

lay someone **out** (or **out in lavender**) **1** ***v phr*** *fr late 1800s* To knock down; =DECK: *If that woman gets the Republican nomination... I will lay her out in lavender*—Vivian Kellems **2** ***v phr*** To reprimand; castigate [fr the *laying out* of a dead person]

lay pipe (or **tube**) ◁**1**▷ ***v phr*** *fr black* To do the sex act; copulate; =SCREW: *If you're up all night, laying pipe, you won't be worth a shit*—Tom Aldibrandi/ *gonna lay more tube than the motherfuckin' Alaska Pipeline*—Playboy **2** ***v phr*** To specify; spell out: *You can't just infer that; you gotta lay pipe*—Don't Touch That Dial (TV program)

lay rubber ***v phr hot rodders*** To accelerate rapidly and speed in a car, so as to leave black tire marks on the road

lay them in the aisles ***v phr*** (Variations: **have** or **knock** or **put** may replace **lay**) To entertain, amuse, or impress an audience extravagantly; =WOW

lead ***n*** Bullets; gunfire
See GET THE LEAD OUT, HAVE LEAD IN one's PANTS, HAVE LEAD IN one's PENCIL

lead balloon *See* GO OVER LIKE A LEAD BALLOON

lead someone **down the garden path** *v phr* To deceive; hoodwink: *Will anyone know who led whom down the garden path?*—New Yorker

lead foot (LED fŏŏt) *n* A fast driver: *Make sure to wear your seatbelt. He's a real lead foot*

lead-footed (LED fŏŏt əd) **1** *adj* Sluggish and awkward; clumsy: *The bungling, lead-footed fellow*—R Wallace **2** *adj* Tending to drive very fast

lead-pipe cinch **1** *n phr fr 1930s* A certainty; inescapable fact: *calls ColecoVision a "lead-pipe cinch" for making a strong showing at Christmas*—Toronto Life **2** *n phr* Something very easy; =CINCH, PIECE OF CAKE: *It's a lead-pipe cinch for somebody that strong* [fr the fact that a *lead pipe* can be easily bent, in case one has bet on such a feat]

lead-poisoning *n fr cowboys* Gunshot wounds

league *See* BIG-LEAGUE, BUSH LEAGUE, GRAPEFRUIT LEAGUE, OUT OF one's LEAGUE

leaguer *See* TEXAS LEAGUER

leagues *See* the BIG LEAGUES, the BUSH LEAGUES

leak **1** *v* To give information to the press or other recipient secretly: *Then the FCC report was "leaked" to the press*—RG Spivack **2** *n* A person, channel, etc, from which secret information is reaching places it should not: *A famous leak was called Deep Throat* **3** *n* A point of weakness in a system of information security: *a leak in the department* ◁**4**▷ *n* An act of urination; =A PISS ◁**5**▷ *v* To urinate; =PISS: *He said he had to leak, his back teeth were floating*

See TAKE A LEAK

lean and mean *adj phr* Desperately and somewhat menacingly ambitious; =HUNGRY: *"Lean and mean" is the byword in publishing these days*—New York

lean forward in the saddle *v phr Army* To be eager and anxious; =be RARING TO GO

lean on someone **1** *v phr* To put pressure on, esp with violence or the threat of it: *Several restaurants and clubs... were being leaned on*—Jackie Collins **2** *v phr* To depend on for understanding, assistance, etc: *Well, we all need someone we can lean on*—Mick Jagger

the **leaping heebies** *See* the HEEBIE-JEEBIES

leap on the bandwagon *See* GET ON THE BANDWAGON

leary *See* LEERY

leather **1** *n underworld* A purse or wallet **2** *n* A football **3** *n* Boxing gloves **4** *n* The clothing and trappings of overt sado-masochism; =S AND M **5** *adj: a leather outfit/leather porn* **6** *n homosexuals* A kind of male homosexual behavior, costume, etc, based on exaggerated masculinity as symbolized esp by black-leather-clad motorcycle gangs **7** *modifier: becomes part of the leather-bar homosexual underworld*—New York Times

See HEAVY LEATHER, HELL-FOR-LEATHER

leatherneck *n fr late 1800s Navy* A US Marine; =GYRENE [fr the *leather* collars of their early uniforms]

leave *See* FRENCH LEAVE

leave a strip *v phr hot rodders* To brake or decelerate a car very rapidly, so as to leave black rubber marks on the pavement

leaves *n esp 1950s teenagers* Denim dungarees; =LEVIS [fr *Levis*]

lech or **letch** *fr early 1900s* **1** *n* Strong desire, esp sexual; lust; =the HOTS: *his lech for cam shafts and turbines*—James M Cain **2** *v: when Henry goes letching after Anne*—Vincent Canby **3** *n* A lecher: *who also appears as a good-natured lech*—Newsweek [fr *lecher, lechery*, ultimately fr the notion of licking]

See HAVE A LECH FOR someone or something

leech **1** *n* A human parasite **2** *v: insisted that MCI was not leeching off the successful campaign of its competition*—Philadelphia Journal

leery or **leary** *adj fr late 1700s British* Untrusting; suspicious; wary: *He was leery of toting so much money*—Dashiell Hammett [probably fr British dialect *lere* "learning, knowledge"]

left *See* HANG A LEFT

Left Coast *n phr* The Pacific Coast: *That's not what they're saying out on the Left Coast*—Playboy

left field *See* OUT IN LEFT FIELD

left-handed compliment *n phr* Praise that is subtle dispraise; reluctant and dubious praise: *Telling her she has the constitution of a horse is maybe a left-handed compliment*

left nut *See* GRIPE one's ASS

lefty or **leftie** **1** *n* A left-handed person, esp a left-handed pitcher or other athlete **2** *modifier: a lefty hurler/ leftie tennis ace* **3** *n* A person of liberal or socialist political beliefs; radical; liberal: *such urban lefties as Bella Abzug*—National Review

leg **1** *v* (also **leg it**) To go; travel: *I was legging down the line* **2** *n Vietnam War Army* An infantry soldier; =GRUNT **3** *n college students fr black* A woman, esp a sexually promiscuous one
See an ARM AND A LEG, BOOTLEG, DIRTYLEG, GIVE someone LEG, HAVE A LEG UP ON someone or something, HOG LEG, MIDDLE LEG, PULL someone's LEG, SHAKE A LEG, SHOW A LEG

legal eagle (or **beagle**) *n phr* A lawyer, esp a clever and aggressive one: *In 1979 Davis's legal eagles got him acquitted again*—Newsweek

leg-biter *n college students* A small child or infant; =CRUMBCRUSHER

legger **1** *n* =BOOTLEGGER **2** *n* =LEG MAN

leggy *adj fr middle 1800s* Having prominent legs, esp long and shapely ones • Nearly always used of women: *Not very chesty, but nicely leggy*

legit (lə JIHT) *fr early 1900s* **1** *adj* Legitimate; =KOSHER: *She's a legit farmer*—H Allen Smith **2** *adj* Having to do with or being of the legitimate theater: *a legit play/ specialists in legit reviewing*—Abel Green **3** *n* A legitimate theater

leg man **1** *n phr newspaper office* A newspaper reporter who goes out to gather facts, and may or may not write the story **2** *n phr* Any person who works actively and outside, rather than in, an office **3** *n phr* A man whose favorite part of the female body is the legs

leg-pull *n* The act of deceiving or fooling someone; =PUT-ON: *the wisecrack and the gag, the leg pull and the hotfoot*—James Thurber

Legree *See* SIMON LEGREE

legs *n show business* The ability of a show, song, public figure, etc, to be an enduring success; staying power: *whether a movie will have legs, the power to entice audiences week after week*—New York Times
See BIRD LEGS, HINDERS

a **leg up** **1** *n phr* An advantage: *you can go in with a leg up on other people*—Washington Post **2** *n* Aid; a boost: *He'll do OK, but he needs a financial leg up to get started*
See HAVE A LEG UP ON someone or something

lemon[1] **1** *n fr early 1900s* Anything unsatisfactory or defective, esp a car; =CLINKER: *His tale brought back memories of my first lemon*—Mother Jones/ *That show's a lemon* **2** *n black* A light-skinned and attractive black woman; =HIGH YELLOW **3** *n* A sour, disagreeable person **4** *n* (also **lemonade**) *narcotics* Weakened or diluted narcotics, or a nonnarcotic substance sold as a narcotic; =BLANK

lemon[2] *n narcotics* A Quaalude (a trade name) [*Lemmon* is the name of a pharmaceutical company that once manufactured the drug]

◁ **les** or **lez** ▷ (LEZ) *n* A lesbian: *Mary is a les and John is a fairy*—Joe E Lewis/ *I'd have figured you for a lez*—Lawrence Sanders

◁ **lesbo** ▷ (LEZ boh) *n* A lesbian: *where the Lesbos even come and watch the dress rehearsals*—John O'Hara

let a fart *See* LAY A FART

letch *See* LECH

let daylight (or **sunlight**) **into** *v phr* To bring clarity and illumination to a subject: *They called a meeting to let daylight into the sewer mess*

letdown **1** *n* A disappointment; =COMEDOWN **2** *n* A period or sensation of dullness and emptiness after activity or excitement **3** *n* The gradual descent of an airplane toward a landing

let fly (or **go**) **1** *v phr* To launch vigorously into something; begin with projective energy: *She took a deep breath and let fly* **2** *v phr* To hurl; shoot; fire: *The gunman let go with both automatics*—E Lavine

let oneself **go** *v phr* To behave in an unrestrained way; be uninhibited: *Come on, Herbert, let yourself go, have another martini*

let one's **hair down** *v phr* To be very open and candid, esp about personal matters: *A lot of men that I have been with do not let their hair down* —Sexual Behavior

let someone **have it** **1** *v phr* To hit, esp powerfully; =CLOBBER: *then let him have it, right on the chin*—James M Cain **2** *v phr* To attack verbally, esp punitively; =GIVE IT TO someone: *He allows me to count on his affection. Then he lets me have it* —Saul Bellow

let her (or **'er**) **rip** *v phr fr middle 1800s* To let something go at full speed; take off all restraints: *He decided to buckle his seat belt and let her rip*

let it all hang out *v phr esp 1960s counterculture fr black* To be entirely candid; be free and unrestrained; =LET one's HAIR DOWN: *You'll feel better if you let it all hang out*

let (or **blow**) **off steam** *v phr fr early 1800s* To talk loudly and angrily, as a method of relieving the pressure of one's feelings; express one's anger or frustration: *I've blown off steam* —Woman's Home Companion/ *They're bored, just blowing off steam* —WT Tyler

let someone **off the hook** *v phr* To relieve of responsibility or menace: *They had already given me a lot. I wanted to let them off the hook*—Philadelphia

let on *v phr fr middle 1800s* To reveal; hint

let something **ride** *v phr* To let go on as it is; decline to change or intervene: *Let the same order ride for now*

let's boogie *sentence* (Variations: **cruise** or **blaze** may replace **boogie**) *teenagers* Let us leave

let's face it *sentence* Let us freely admit it; let us accept the unhappy truth: *Let's face it, kids, we're all to blame some*

let's get the (or **this**) **show on the road** *sentence* We should get started; we should become active

let sunlight into *See* LET DAYLIGHT INTO

letter *See* DEAD HORSE, FRENCH LETTER, POISON-PEN LETTER, RED-LETTER DAY

letter man *See* FOUR-LETTER MAN

let the cat out of the bag *v phr* To reveal a secret, usu without intending to: *Her guilty smile pretty much let the cat out of the bag*

lettuce *n* Money, esp paper money; =CABBAGE: *That's a lot of lettuce* —Kenyon Review/ *the man who nipped all this lettuce from the Playboy patch*—Newsweek

See FOLDING MONEY

level **1** *v fr early 1900s* To tell the truth, be honest and candid: *Don't laugh. I'm leveling*—Joel Sayre **2** *adj* True: *There's never a place for guys like me.... That's level*—H Lee

See ON THE LEVEL

someone's **level best** *n phr* The utmost one can do; one's honest greatest effort: *I'll do my level best to keep you*

levers *See* GO LEVERS

Levis (LEE vīz) *n* Blue denim dungaree pants; denim work pants [fr *Levi* Strauss, a mid-19th-century Western company that made and makes such garments]

lez *See* LES

◁**lezzie**▷ **1** *n* A lesbian **2** *adj: It was a fantastic turn-on, watching a lezzie scene*—Herbert Kastle

lib *n* Liberation, esp as the aim of various movements: *animal lib*

See GAY LIB, MEN'S LIB

◁**libber**▷ *n* A member of one of the liberation movements, esp of the women's lib movement: *Thus... did Golda Meir vent her view of women's libbers*—Newsweek

liberate *v fr WW2 Army* To steal or appropriate, originally something in conquered enemy territory

liberty *See* AT LIBERTY

a **license to print money** *n phr* A very lucrative business: *Having a liquor store on that corner is a license to print money*

lick **1** *n fr middle 1800s* A blow; stroke: *I got in a couple good licks before he decked me* **2** *n* A try; attempt; =CRACK, SHOT: *I probably won't make it, but I'll give it a good lick* **3** *n fr 1920s jazz musicians* A short figure or solo, esp when improvised; =BREAK, RIFF: *a few solid licks on the sliphorn*—C Smith

See HIT IT A LICK

lick one's **chops** *v phr* To display hunger and anticipation, for food or for something else desired: *I licked my chops when I thought of that bonus*

licker *See* ASS-KISSER, CLIT-LICKER, DICK-LICKER

lickety-split *adj fr middle 1800s* Very fast: *They ran lickety-split to the store*

licorice stick *n phr jive talk* The clarinet

lid **1** *n* A hat **2** *n narcotics* One ounce of marijuana: *a shutdown on grass, lids were going for thirty dollars*—Saturday Review

See BLOW THE LID OFF, FLIP one's LID, SKID LID

lie *See* the BIG LIE

lieut (LōōT) *n fr 1700s* Lieutenant; =LOOT

life *See* BET YOUR BOOTS, LOW-LIFE

the **life** or **the Life** **1** *n phr* Prostitution, esp as a business: *generally understood by those in the Life*—FAJ Ianni **2** *n phr* The homosexual life, esp that of an effeminate transvestite male prostitute: *She had lived the life so long now*—Patrick Mann

See IN THE LIFE

lifer **1** *n fr late 1700s* A convict serving a life sentence **2** *n Army* A career Army officer: *"lifers" (the contemptuous GI term for career officers)*—New York Times

lift **1** *n* A surge or feeling of exhilaration; a transport of exuberance; =HIGH, KICK, RUSH: *I get a lift from watching that kid* **2** *v* To steal: *He got caught lifting a chicken from the convenience store* **3** *v* To plagiarize: *whole pages lifted from my book* **4** *n* A ride: *I need a lift to the bus terminal downtown*

light **1** *adj hoboes* Hungry; needing a meal **2** *adj* Lacking; having an insufficient amount: *I'm light about 20 bucks* **3** *adj beat & cool talk* =HEP **4** *n* The igniting of a cigarette, cigar or pipe: *Could you give me a light?* **5** *v* =LIGHT OUT **6** *adj lunch counter* With extra cream added: *light coffee*

See GO OUT LIKE A LIGHT, the GREEN LIGHT, IDIOT LIGHT, OUT LIKE A LIGHT, SEE THE LIGHT AT THE END OF THE TUNNEL

light-fingered *adj fr 1500s* Inclined to steal; thievish; =STICKY-FINGERED

lightning *See* GREASED LIGHTNING, JERSEY LIGHTNING, WHITE LIGHTNING

light out *v phr fr middle 1800s* To leave, esp hastily; =TAKE OFF, HIGHTAIL: *He lit out for the border* [fr earlier nautical *light out* "move out, or move something out," of obscure origin; perhaps "move or move something lightly, quickly, handily"]

lights out *n phr* The end; death; =CURTAINS: *otherwise lights out for me*—Dashiell Hammett

See PUNCH someone's LIGHTS OUT, SHOOT THE LIGHTS OUT

lightweight **1** *adj* Inconsequential; unserious **2** *n: He seems like a lightweight to me*

like **1** *modifier esp 1960s counterculture & bop talk* As if; really; you know; sort of • A generalized modifier used to lend a somewhat tentative and detached tone to the speaker, to give the speaker time to rally words and ideas: *Like I was like groovin' like, you know?* **2** *v* To predict as winner; bet on: *You like the Mets?/ Who do you like in the title fight?*

See MAKE LIKE

like a bandit *adv phr* Very successfully; thrivingly: *coming out of the battle with Bendix like a bandit*—New York Times [see *make out like a bandit*]

See MAKE OUT LIKE A BANDIT

like a bat out of hell *adv phr* Very rapidly; =LICKETY-SPLIT: *They were moving along like a bat out of hell*

like a blue streak *See* a BLUE STREAK

like a bunny *See* FUCK LIKE A BUNNY

like a hole in the head *See* NEED someone or something LIKE A HOLE IN THE HEAD

like a million bucks *adv phr* Very good; superb: *In that blouse she looks like a million bucks*

like crazy (or **mad**) *adv phr* Extravagantly; wildly; violently: *tearing around like crazy*—P Marks/ *Then everybody laughs like mad*—AJ Liebling

like gangbusters *adv phr* Very energetically and successfully: *The rest of the year the economy will be going like gangbusters*—Newsweek

See COME ON LIKE GANGBUSTERS

like hell **1** *adv phr* In an extravagant way; very forcefully: *Started screaming like hell*—Joyce Carol Oates **2** *adv phr* (Variations: **fun** or **shit** may replace **hell**) Never; it is impermissible that; =IN A PIG'S ASS: *Like hell you will!/ Like shit it's a good job/ When the prostitute says "Like fun you are"*—D Costello

like it is *See* TELL IT LIKE IT IS

like it or lump it *adv phr* Whether or not one wishes: *We have to go now, like it or lump it*

like it's going out of style or **like there's no tomorrow** *adv phr* Extravagantly; wildly; recklessly; with abandon: *spending money like it was going out of style/ boozing like there was no tomorrow*

like pigs in clover (or ◁**in shit**▷) *adv phr fr early 1800s* In complete happiness; blissfully: *We'll go down there and we'll live like pigs in clover/ They were giggling and euphoric like pigs in shit*

◁**like shit through a tin horn**▷ *adv phr* (Variations: **a dose of salts** or **a hot knife through butter** may replace **shit through a tin horn**) Very rapidly and easily; effortlessly: *He went through the defense like shit through a tin horn/ The pension bill went through like a dose of salts*

like shooting fish in a barrel *adj phr* Very easy; much too easy: *Beating them was like shooting fish in a barrel*

like sixty *adv phr fr middle 1800s* Very rapidly; =LIKE A BAT OUT OF HELL: *They went after him like sixty* [*sixty* is probably used as an indefinite large number, as *forty* was in similar 19th-century contexts, to express extreme briskness]

lily white **1** *adj phr* Innocent; immaculate **2** *adj phr* Having only Caucasian residents, workers, etc: *The town is lily white*

limb *See* GO OUT ON A LIMB, OUT ON A LIMB

limey or **lime-juicer** ◀**1**▶ *n fr early 1900s* An English person: *The limeys are unhappy over the weakness of the pound sterling/ The "Doctor" was a lime-juicer*—Scribner's ◀**2**▶ *adj: a limey accent* ◀**3**▶ *n* An English ship [fr the ration of *lime-juice* given to British sailors as an antiscorbutic]

the **limit** *n phr* A person, thing, etc, that exceeds or outrages what is acceptable: *Ain't he awful, ain't he just the limit?*
See GO THE LIMIT

limo (LIHM oh) *n* A limousine: *disapproves of this vast fleet (789 limos) of luxury transportation*—Saturday Review
See STRETCH LIMO

limp *adj* Drunk

◁**limp-dick**▷ **1** *n* An ineffectual man; an impotent man; =WIMP **2** *adj: I called myself every limp-dick name I could think of*—Richard Price

limp wrist **1** *n phr* A male homosexual: *I reminded her that Boke Kellum was a limp wrist*—Dan Jenkins **2** *modifier: a limp-wrist hangout*

limp-wristed *adj* Effeminate; slack and sinuous; homosexual: *the most limp-wristed "stud" in the Philadelphia metropolitan area*—Philadelphia

line **1** *n fr early 1900s* One's usual way of talking, esp when being persuasive or self-aggrandizing; =SPIEL: *of what in a later generation would have been termed her "line"*—F Scott Fitzgerald/ *You've got some line*—Ira Wolfert **2** *n* The public position of a party, faction, etc: *the Republican line* **3** *n* One's occupation, business, etc; =RACKET: *What's my line? Herring in brine* **4** *n jazz musicians & swing musicians* A musical solo or figure, esp personal and innovative: *Coasters talk of "lines," not licks, breaks, or riffs*—Artie Shaw **5** *v baseball* To hit the ball in a line drive **6** *n gambling* A bookmaker's odds on a sports event: *Baseball, basketball, and hockey lines are available on the day or night of the games*—Harper's **7** *n* A dose of cocaine, usu formed into a thin line on a mirror to be nasally ingested **8** *v: They lined twice last night, no wonder they're tired*
See someone's ASS IS ON THE LINE, the BOTTOM LINE, HARD LINE, HOT LINE, IN LINE, IN LINE FOR, LAY IT ON THE LINE, MAIN LINE, ON LINE, ON THE LINE, OUT OF LINE, PUNCH LINE, PUT one's ASS ON THE LINE, REDLINE, SHOOT someone A LINE, STAG LINE, TOE THE MARK

the **line** **1** *n phr* The chorus girls of a show **2** *n phr* An assembly line
See TOE THE MARK

linen *See* WASH one's DIRTY LINEN

line one's **nest** *See* FEATHER one's NEST

line out **1** *v phr* To sing, esp in a loud strong voice; =BELT OUT **2** *v phr baseball* To hit a line drive that is caught

liner *See* HEADLINER, ONE-LINER

lines *See* GO UP IN one's LINES

lineup **1** *n police* A number of persons displayed in line across a platform to find whether witnesses can pick a suspect from among them **2** *n sports* The roster of a team, esp for a particular game: *Just before the game started, the managers showed their lineups to the umpires*

lingo (LIN goh) *n* Language; jargon; idiom

lip **1** *n fr early 1800s* Insolent, impertinent, or presumptuous talk: *I don't want none of your lip*—W Moore **2** *n underworld* A lawyer; =MOUTHPIECE **3** *v jazz musicians* To play a musical instrument, esp in jazz; =BLOW: *he couldn't lip anything proper any more*—Stephen Longstreet

See BAT one's GUMS, BUTTON one's LIP, FLIP one's LIP, ZIP one's LIP

lip fuzz *n phr* A mustache

lip mover *n phr* A dull and stupid person; =BLOCKHEAD: *between those countless millions of lip-movers and the minuscule audience for better novels*—New York Times [fr the habit of uneducated or dull people of *moving their lips* while reading to themselves]

lippy **1** *adj* Insolent; brash and arrogant **2** *adj* Talkative

lip-sync or **lip-synch** (LIP sink) *v* To move the lips silently in synchronism with recorded singing or speaking, to give the illusion of performance: *Having taped his lines before the show, he lip-synched his pronouncements*—Time/ *staying home with her sister lip synching to Leon Russell records*—Village Voice

liquidate *v* To kill

liquor *See* HARD LIQUOR

liquored up *adj* Drunk

list *See* HIT LIST, SUCKER LIST, WISH LIST

listen up *v phr fr armed forces fr black* To listen closely; pay strict attention: *He can make you listen up with that violin of his*—Village Voice

lit[1] *n students fr late 1800s* Literature: *comp lit/ black lit*

lit[2] *adj* Drunk

litterbug *n* A person who throws trash in the streets, parks, etc [modeled on *jitterbug*]

little black book *n phr* The private notebook in which one is supposed to keep telephone numbers and details of potential and actual sex partners

Little Joe *n phr crapshooting* The point four, or four on the dice [a shortening of *Little Joe from Kokomo*; the relation to four is not patent]

little Michael (or **Mickey**) *n phr* =MICKEY FINN

little secret *See* DIRTY LITTLE SECRET

little shaver *n phr* A young boy

the **little woman** *n phr fr late 1800s* One's wife: *Tooling along with the kiddies and the little woman in his costly can*—Westbrook Pegler

lit up or **lit up like a Christmas tree** **1** *adj phr* Drunk: *I found Uncle Peter and he was also lit up*—H McHugh **2** *adj phr narcotics* Intoxicated with narcotics; =HIGH

litvak (LIT vahk) **1** *n* A Lithuanian or person of Lithuanian background ◁**2**▷ *n* A clever fellow; a sharp, tricky trader [fr Yiddish fr Polish; the second sense, derogatory in force, is used by the Galitzianer Jews of Polish or Russian background, and Lithuanians would not agree with the definition]

live (L—IV) **1** *adj* Not yet fired or exploded: *a live shell* **2** *adj* Containing bullets or shot, as distinct from blank: *live ammunition* **3** *adj* Not recorded or taped: *live music/ a live telecast* **4** *adj* Having electrical potential; =HOT: *a live circuit/ live wire* **5** *adj esp teenagers* Lively; exciting: *a very live party/ a live dude*

live high on the hog *See* EAT HIGH ON THE HOG

live-in **1** *adj* Sharing one's domicile: *Coe's former live-in girlfriend*—Newsweek **2** *n* A housekeeper who lives in one's home: *After they had their second child, they hired a live-in*

live one **1** *n phr* A lively person; up-to-date person **2** *n phr* A likely target for a confidence scheme or fast sell: *Hey, Eddie, looks like we got us a live one here*

liver *See* CHOPPED LIVER, THAT AIN'T HAY

lives *See* HIT someone WHERE HE LIVES

live wire *n phr* An energetic, vibrant person: *Jimmy's a live wire, all right*—P Marks

the **living daylights** *See* BEAT THE SHIT OUT OF someone or something

living doll *n phr* A notably decent, pleasant person: *Isn't the emcee a living doll?*

the **living end** *n phr fr beat & cool talk* A person, thing, etc, that is about as much as one can stand; =the END, the LIMIT • Usu highly complimentary

◁ the **living shit**▷ *See* BEAT THE SHIT OUT OF someone or something, SCARE THE SHIT OUT OF someone

lizard *See* LOUNGE LIZARD

load 1 *n* Enough liquor to make one drunk: *He's taking on a load again* **2** *n esp teenagers* A dose of narcotic smoked in a water pipe ◁**3**▷ *n* The semen of a single orgasm

See CARRY THE LOAD, DROP one's LOAD, FREELOAD, GET A LOAD OF, HALF LOAD, HAVE A LOAD ON, a SHITLOAD, SHOOT one's LOAD, TAKE A LOAD OFF one's FEET, THREE BRICKS SHY OF A LOAD

loaded 1 *adj fr late 1800s* Drunk: *Men act different when they get loaded*—Lantern **2** *n* Containing whiskey: *We sipped our loaded coffee*—Raymond Chandler **3** *adj narcotics* Intoxicated with narcotics, esp heroin; =HIGH: *And then you get loaded and like it*—D Hulburd **4** *adj fr early 1900s* Wealthy; =FILTHY RICH: *They're all loaded in that neighborhood* **5** *adj fr early 1900s* Having a great deal of money, if only temporarily; =FLUSH: *After the thing sold I was loaded for a few months* **6** *adj* Explosive; perilous: *The situation this fall is really loaded* **7** *adj* Carrying significance beyond the obvious or surface meaning • Often meant to embarrass or baffle: *No loaded questions if you really want information/ That was a loaded remark* **8** *adj* Prearranged; biased: *The interview was loaded in my favor*

loaded for bear *adj phr* Ready and anxious for a fight; heavily prepared for conflict, debate, etc: *I went to the board meeting loaded for bear* [fr the notion that a hunter must use particularly powerful ammunition, or *load,* to kill a *bear*]

loaded with *adj phr* Well provided with; having much of; =LOUSY WITH: *She's loaded with talent*

loader *See* FREELOADER

loadie or **loady 1** *n esp teenagers* A person who uses narcotics, drinks beer and liquor, etc: *for every high school loadie you will find a National Merit Scholar*—Time **2** *n college students* A drunkard; an alcoholic; =LUSH

a **load of VW radiators** (or **post holes** or **wind**) *n phr truckers* An empty truck; no cargo whatever [fr the fact that VW engines are air-cooled and have no *radiators*]

a **load of wind** *n phr* =WINDBAG

load the dice *v phr* To prearrange or bias some result: *helped load the dice against the dissidents*—David Halberstam

loan shark *n phr* An underworld usurer; =SHYLOCK

lob 1 *n* A softly thrown ball or a tennis ball hit very high **2** *v: He lobbed the ball back near the baseline*

local *n* A local resident; native: *The locals are suspicious of the summer types*

See IRISH BUGGY

local yokel 1 *n phr citizens band* A town or city police officer **2** *n phr* A resident of a small town or rural area

a **lock** *n phr* A certainty; =SURE THING, SHOO-IN: *this guy looks like a lock now*—New York Post/*no longer a lock to win the NFC East*—New York Daily News [fr *lock* "wrestling hold"]

See HAVE A LOCK ON something, MORTAL LOCK

lock horns *v phr* To contend with; fight: *They had locked horns with a better man*—Albert Goldman

lockup *n* A cell, esp a detention cell or holding cell; =the COOLER, TANK

loco 1 *adj fr late 1800s cowboys* Crazy; =NUTS: *He took one look and just went loco* **2** *n: She's acting like a loco* [fr the name of a weed that made cattle behave strangely, fr Spanish, "insane"]

locomotive 1 *n students* A cheer that resembles a steam locomotive starting: *we all had to stand up... and give him a locomotive*—JD Salinger **2** *n* A strong motive force; prime mover: *free trade, which has been a locomotive of prosperity since World War II*—Time

log *See* BEAT one's MEAT, EASY AS PIE

log roll *n phr hospital* A way of carefully turning a patient out of a cart onto a bed: *She said she needed my help with a log roll in Room 643*

loid **1** *v* To open a locked door by moving the catch with a strip of celluloid: *The cards...could be used to loid any door with a spring latch* —Ezra Hannon **2** *v* To burglarize an apartment, building, etc [fr *celluloid*]

lollapalooza (lah lə pə LOO zə) *n* A person or thing that is remarkable, wonderful, superior, etc; =BEAUT, HUMDINGER: *He's got a lollapalooza of a cold*

lollop *n* =JOLLOP

lollygag or **lallygag** (LAH lee gag) **1** *v fr middle 1800s* To idle about; =GOOF OFF: *the summer free for play, swimming, berry picking, and general lallygagging*—Frank Sullivan **2** *v* To kiss and caress; dally

loner **1** *n* (also **lone wolf**) A person who prefers to be alone, do things alone, etc; a solitary: *He became more of a "loner," almost a man apart from the rest of the team* —Arthur Daley **2** *n* One person or thing by itself: *Here's a loner to get you started*—Lawrence Sanders

lonesome *See* ALL BY one's LONESOME

as **long as your arm** *See* AS LONG AS YOUR ARM

the **long arm** *n phr* A police officer; =the LAW

long ball *See* GO FOR THE LONG BALL

long drink of water *n phr* A very tall, thin person

long green *n phr fr late 1800s* Money; =FOLDING MONEY: *that dear old affectionately regarded long green*—Amsterdam News [perhaps influenced by earlier sense of a kind of large-leafed tobacco]

longhair **1** *n fr early 1900s* An intellectual; =EGGHEAD **2** *adj* (also **long-haired**:) *longhair tastes in poetry* **3** *n fr 1920s jazz musicians* Classical music • Originally the term was used for musicians who play from written music, and for the music they play: *sometimes called Western music, sometimes European music, and sometimes just longhair* —Stephen Longstreet **4** *adj* (also **long-haired**): *sonatas and other longhair stuff* **5** *n fr 1960s* A young man with long hair, esp a hippie: *another longhair, a member of our commune*—J Jerome [earlier senses fr the stereotype of an intellectual or esthete as being strange and wearing *long hair*]

long hard look *n phr* A very close and careful critical scrutiny: *I advise you take a long hard look at yourself, son*

long haul *n phr* A long and arduous period: *It looks like it'll be a long haul* *See* FOR THE LONG HAUL, OVER THE LONG HAUL

longhorn *n* A Texan

long johns or **long ones** *n phr* Long winter underwear: *A generation or so ago, men, women, boys and girls put on long ones in October and wore long ones until spring*—Wall Street Journal/ *Pop, will you dig that dish out of your long johns*—Saul Bellow

long pig *n phr* A person regarded as meat for cannibals: *he offered mammoth marrow, and, perhaps, Long Pig*—WH Auden [translation of Fijian *puaka balava*]

long shot **1** *n phr fr middle 1800s British* A person, horse, project, etc, that seems not likely to win; =DARK HORSE: *The idea's a long shot, but it's worth a try* **2** *modifier: long-shot odds/ a long-shot victory* *See* NOT BY A LONG SHOT

long time no see *sentence* I haven't seen you for a long time • a quasi-Pidgin salutation

loo *n* A toilet • Chiefly British: *Everything you'd find in a powder room except the loo*—Toronto Life [origin uncertain; probably fr *Waterloo* in proportionate analogy with *water closet*]

looey or **looie** or **louie** *n WW1 Army* A lieutenant; =LOOT: *They demoted me to second looey*—Stephen Lewis

look *See* HARD LOOK, LONG HARD LOOK

look-alike *n* A person who closely resembles another; =DEAD RINGER, DOUBLE: *Barratt had an interview with his noted look-alike*—B Thomas

look at someone **cross-eyed** *v phr* To commit even a tiny fault; offend in the least way: *who would yell copper if you looked at them cross-eyed* —Raymond Chandler

looker **1** *n fr middle 1800s* A good-looking person of either sex, but esp a woman: *That waitress is a looker, a real dish* **2** *n salespersons* A person who inspects merchandise but does not buy: *A "looker" is to the* *used car lot what a browser is to a bookstore*—New York Times

looking good *interj* An exclamation of encouragement, praise, reassurance, etc; =WAY TO GO: *They hollered "Looking good!" as the leader passed*

look like a drowned rat *v phr* To have a singularly disheveled, subdued, and unsightly appearance: *When they got off the boat after a weekend they looked like drowned rats*

look like death warmed over *v phr* To look miserable; look ill and exhausted; have a wretched mien: *I don't know what the news is, but Frank looks like death warmed over*

look like something the cat dragged in *v phr* To have a dirty and bedraggled appearance; present an unkempt mien

◁**look like ten pounds of shit in a five-pound bag**▷ **1** *v phr* To be sloppily dressed, esp dressed in clothing too small, bulging, and gapped **2** *v phr* To be overstuffed, overweight, bulging, etc.

a **look-see** *n phr* A look; an inspection: *Let's have a look-see at our friend*—Ellery Queen/ *I stopped in at Jerry's for a lager and a look-see* —Billy Rose

loon *See* CRAZY AS A LOON

loony or **looney** **1** *adj fr middle 1800s* Crazy; =NUTTY: *you looney punk*—Ira Wolfert **2** *n* (also **loon** or **loonball**) *fr late 1800s: The inspired looney who hated killing* —Billy Rose/ *would have shown up in a Mel Brooks epic had that loonball thought of it first*—Toronto Life [probably fr both *lunatic* and *crazy as a loon*]

loony bin *n phr fr late 1800s* A mental hospital; =NUTHOUSE: *that fugitive from a loony-bin*—Arthur Kober

loony-tune or **loony-tunes** **1** *n* (Variations: **looney** may replace **loony**; **toon** may replace **tune**) A crazy person; =NUT: *Jesus, what a loony tune*—Richard Merkin **2** ***modifier:*** *the loony-toon acting debut of writer Stephen King*—Flare/ *It's been kind of a looney-tunes week* —William Goldman [fr *Looney Tunes*, trade name of a series of short cartoon-film comedies, a paraphrasing fr Silly Symphonies, also short cartoon-film comedies]

loop *See* IN THE LOOP, KNOCK someone or something FOR A LOOP, OUT OF THE LOOP

looped or **looping** *adj* Drunk: *The end result is a looped group*—Hal Boyle/ *Was she drunk? Looping* —Irwin Shaw

loopy *adj* Crazy; silly; =NUTTY: *visually complemented the singer's loopy Balkan bop*—Rolling Stone/ *even loopier bids for the few works in Wood's small mature oeuvre*—Time

loose **1** *adj* *cool talk* Relaxed; easy; =COOL: *You are loose in the rush, misty and safe*—New York **2** *adj* Sexually promiscuous

See ALL HELL BROKE LOOSE, HANG LOOSE, A SCREW LOOSE

loose as a goose or **loosey-goosey** *adj phr* or *adj cool talk* Very relaxed; perfectly easy; =COOL: *The pitcher's got a nice loosey-goosey motion/ He was feeling fine, loose as a goose* [probably both fr the rhyme and the perception that a *goose* has *loose* bowels]

loose cannon *n phr* A person who is quite likely to cause damage; a wildly irresponsible person: *Haig is a loose cannon on a pitching deck*—Time

loose change *n phr* Money at hand and to spare; available money: *I wanted to help, but didn't have any loose change*

loose in the bean (or **upper story**) *adj phr* Crazy; =NUTTY

loot[1] *n fr 1920s jazz musicians* Money, esp a large amount of money: *Rich planters would come and spend some awful large amounts of loot*—Louis Armstrong

loot[2] *n fr 1700s* A lieutenant; =LIEUT

lord *See* TIGHT

lose one's **cookies** *See* SHOOT one's COOKIES

lose one's **cool** *v phr fr cool talk* To become angry or flustered; lose composure: *He was unflappable, never lost his cool*

lose one's **gourd** *v phr* To become insane; go crazy; =GO APE, FREAK OUT: *Have you lost your gourd?*—Pat Conroy

lose one's **marbles** *v phr* To become foolish, irrational, forgetful, etc, as if senile [fr an earlier phrase *let his marbles go with the monkey*, fr a story about a boy whose marbles were carried off by a monkey]

loser **1** *n* (also **born loser**) A person or thing that fails, esp habitually; =BUST, DUD, LEMON **2** *v: I don't want them to think I'm losered out* —New York Times

lose the ballgame *v phr* To end disastrously: *One puff, one gust, one very small disturbance, and I'd have lost the whole ballgame right there* —John McPhee

lose one's **wig** *v phr cool talk* =BLOW one's TOP

losing *See* someone CAN'T WIN FOR LOSING

losses *See* CUT one's LOSSES

lost *See* GET LOST

lot *See* ALL OVER THE LOT, PORTABLE PARKING LOT

loud *adj fr middle 1800s* Vulgar and gaudy in taste; garish: *blatant checked suits and loud ties*

See FOR CRYING OUT LOUD, READ someone LOUD AND CLEAR

loudmouth **1** *n* A loud and constant talker, esp a braggart and self-appointed authority; =WINDBAG: *Maybe poking Loud Mouth in the kisseroo would solve everything*—D Decker **2** *v: Don't you loudmouth me!*

louie or **Louie** *See* LOOEY

lounge lizard *n phr esp 1920s* =LADIES' MAN [fr the notion that such a man *lounges*, frequents ladies' *lounges*, and is as colorful, indolent, and reptilian as a *lizard* in the sun]

louse *n* An obnoxious and despicable person, esp one who is devious and undependable; =BASTARD, CRUMB

louse up **1** *v phr* To ruin or spill; botch; =BOLLIX UP: *Boy, you certainly loused that up*—John O'Hara **2** *v phr* To fail; =SCREW UP: *He'll get promoted next month if he doesn't louse up*

lousy **1** *adj fr middle 1800s* Bad; nasty; =CRUMMY: *Crab was all she ever did. What a lousy sport*—Dorothy Parker **2** *adv: I did pretty lousy on that test*—F Brown

lousy with *adj phr fr middle 1800s* Well provided with; swarming with: *That hotel was lousy with perverts* —JD Salinger

love *See* FOR THE LOVE OF PETE

love drug *n phr esp students* A drug thought to be an aphrodisiac, such as methaqualone

love handle **1** *n phr* A bulge of fat at the side of the abdomen: *when I have strapped the metal thing to my love handles*—George V Higgins **2** *modifier: who come in rarely, and mostly for love-handle removal*—Village Voice

love-in *n esp 1960s counterculture* A gathering, esp of hippies, devoted to mutual love and understanding: *Tulsa ...recently had its first love-in*—Jack Newfield

lovely *n* An attractive woman: *flabby lovelies in polka-dot bikinis*—New York

◁ **love-muscle** ▷ *n* The penis

lover *See* MOTHERFUCKER

lover-boy **1** *n* A handsome man; matinee idol **2** *n* A womanizer; woman-chaser; =LADIES' MAN, CASANOVA, STUD

lovey-dovey **1** *adj* Affectionate; amorous: *My, aren't they lovey-dovey?* **2** *n* Affection; friendship: *a reign of peace, prosperity, and lovey-dovey*—HL Mencken **3** *n* A wife, mistress, sweetheart, etc: *their foreign lovey-doveys*—D Fairbairn

loving *See* MOTHERFUCKING

low **1** *adj fr late 1800s* Sad; melancholy: *I was so...low and depressed* —Bill Nye **2** *n narcotics* A bad reaction to a narcotic; =BUMMER

See GULLY-LOW, KEEP A LOW PROFILE, LAY LOW

low-ball *v* To lower; reduce; aim for low standards: *Had Feldstein deliberately low-balled the original numbers?* —Newsweek

low blow *n phr* An unfair and malicious stroke; =CHEAP SHOT: *It wasn't exactly unethical, but it was a pretty low blow*

lowbrow *fr early 1900s* **1** *n* A person lacking education and refinement; an ignorant lout **2** *adj: lowbrow tastes/ What are you always pulling that lowbrow stuff for?*—P Mark

low camp *n phr* Entertainment or art characterized by very broad and vulgar features: *Low camp...would mean doing it with winks and leers at the audience, in jeering collusion* —John Simon

low-down **1** *adj fr middle 1800s* Dishonest; despicable; vile: *a dirty low-down trick* **2** *adj jazz musicians* Intense and insinuating, in the blues style: *a babe with a low-down voice*—Mickey Spillane
See DIRTY SHAME

the **lowdown** *n phr* The truth; the authentic facts: *eager to get the low-down on new aircraft*—Philadelphia Bulletin

low-down dirty shame *See* DIRTY SHAME

lower the boom **1** *v phr prizefight* To deliver a knockout punch **2** *v phr* To punish; exact obedience and docility: *if we lower the boom on every nonconformist in society* —Arthur Schlesinger

low-fi or **low fi** **1** *n* or *n phr* Record- or tape-playing or other equipment that reproduces sound rather badly **2** *modifier: a room full of low-fi components* [based on *hi-fi*]

low five *n phr* A greeting or gesture of approval made by slapping hands at about waist level: *San Diego hand-slapping, high fives, low fives*—Newsweek

low-level Munchkin *n phr* A low-ranking employee, staff-member, etc; a menial: *When his calls were returned, it was by low-level Munchkins*—New Yorker [fr the name of the dwarfish helpers in L Frank Baum's *The Wizard of Oz*]

low-life **1** *n* A person of reprehensible habits; =BUM **2** *adj: fancies himself in love with the raucous, low-life Doreen*—New Yorker

low (or **bottom**) **man on the totem pole** *n phr* The person having least seniority, importance, etc

low profile **1** *n phr* Inconspicuousness; recessiveness; modesty: *He thought he'd do better with a low profile the first year or so* **2** *adj: a low-profile discreetness*
See KEEP A LOW PROFILE

low-rent *adj* Cheap; second rate; inferior: *and from that low-rent lunch at the Century Plaza*—Dan Jenkins/ *Low-Rent Himalayas*—CoEvolution Quarterly

low ride *adj phr esp southern California* Socially inferior; vulgar; =TRASHY: *low ride Mexicans down in the valley*—Time

low rider **1** *n phr esp southern California* A person who drives a car with a radically lowered suspension **2** *n phr* A car with a lowered suspension **3** *n phr* A motorcyclist, esp one who rides a customized motorcycle with the handlebars very high **4** *n phr* A rough young man from a black ghetto: *A group of low riders from Watts assembled on the basketball court*—Eldridge Cleaver [extended fr the ghetto style, among blacks and Chicanos, of the cool young man who wished, according to Calvin Trillin, "to *lower* his car to within a few inches of the ground, make it as beautiful as he knows how ... and drive it very slowly"]

lox *n astronautics* Liquid oxygen, as a rocket fuel

LP or **lp** *n* A phonograph record that plays at 33⅓ revolutions per minute [fr *long playing*]

LSD *n* Lysergic acid diethylamide, a hallucinogenic drug; =ACID: *There is no rite of passage, such as smoking pot or tripping with LSD*—Trans-Action

L7 **1** *n black* An unpopular misfit; =SQUARE **2** *adj: an uncool L7 wimp* [fr the square visual pattern made by the joining of the capital *L* and the number *7*]

LT *n college students* Living together: *the subject of living together ("LT" in college lingo)*—Washington Post

luck *See* IN LUCK, OUT OF LUCK, POT LUCK, SHIT OUT OF LUCK

luck into *v phr* To get something by luck: *Alain lucked into a goldmine* —New York Times

the **luck of the draw** *n phr* The way fortune would have it; =THAT'S THE WAY THE BALL BOUNCES

luck out • one of the slang expressions that can mean two opposite things **1** *v phr* To be lucky; get something by good luck: *that he will ... luck out after his search and create operation*—Commonweal **2** *v phr WW2 Army* To be very unlucky; be doomed

lucre *See* FILTHY LUCRE

lude *n* Quaalude (a trade name), a depressant drug; any methaqualone capsule or pill: *Only this year "ludes" (Quaaludes or "downs") were the hot sellers*—Judy Klemesrud

luded out *adj phr* Intoxicated with depressants, esp Quaalude (a trade name): *The folks who use it are usually too luded out or preoccupied* —Playboy

lug **1** *n fr 1920s* A stupid man; dull fellow; =BOZO: *Those lugs in the band would begin to kid me about it* —John O'Hara **2** *n prizefight* The face, chin, or jaw **3** *n underworld* A demand for money, esp bribe or protection money: *a captain of detectives who was collecting the lug from the gambling houses*—Westbrook Pegler **4** *v* To solicit money; borrow [origins and derivations uncertain; the first sense is probably fr *lug* "something heavy and clumsy," attested in the 16th century and retained in several English dialects where it is used derogatorily of persons]

lulu[1] *n fr middle 1800s* A person or thing that is remarkable, wonderful, superior, etc; =DARB, HUMDINGER: *He said the aquarium was a lulu*—AJ Liebling [origin unknown; earlier *looly* "beautiful girl" is attested; perhaps fr the cowboy term *loo loo* "a winning hand," explained as a hand invented by local people in order to win a game from a stranger "for the good of the *loo*," where *loo* means "party, set, community;" this sense of *loo* is related to the popular 18th-century card game of the same name, fr *lanterloo* fr French *lanterlu*, a nonsense phrase in the refrain of a song]

lulu[2] *n New York State* A legislator's perquisite of goods, services, or a stipend "in lieu" of basic legitimate compensation: *decision to abandon the "lulus" of legislators*—New York Times [fr *lieu*, influenced by *lulu*[1]]

lumber **1** *n baseball* A bat **2** *n lunch counter* Toothpicks **3** *v chiefly British* To take advantage of someone; make someone a scapegoat: *He was totally lumbered* —Washingtonian

lummox or **lummux** *n* A stupid, clumsy person; =KLUTZ [fr British dialect fr *lummock* "lump"]

lump *n* A dull, stupid person; =CLOD, KLUTZ: *What an unspeakable lump I was*—Max Shulman

lumper *n truckers* A person who loads and unloads trucks: *"Lumpers" unload the trailer for him*—Smithsonian

lump it *v phr fr late 1700s* To accept or swallow something one does not like: *It was a lousy deal, but I just had to lump it* [fr earlier sense of *lump* "dislike, reject," probably related to the sense "strike, thrash"; see *lumps*]

See LIKE IT OR LUMP IT

lumps *n* Severe treatment; punishment; a beating: *Somebody was out to give him his lumps*—J Roeburt [fr late-18th-century *lump* "beat, thrash"]

See GET one's LUMPS, TAKE one's LUMPS

lumpy *adj cool talk* Badly played

lunch or **lunchy** *students* **1** *adj* Stupid; ineffectual: *a lunch guy might as well be out to lunch for all the good he's doing*—R Scott **2** *adj* Old-fashioned; passé; out of style: *That bow tie is lunchy*

See EAT someone's LUNCH, OUT TO LUNCH, SHOOT one's COOKIES

lunch-hooks *n* The hands; =MEATHOOKS: *get a set of predatory lunch-hooks into him*—Gilbert Millstein

lunger (LUNG ər) *n* A person with tuberculosis: *at once a lunger and lifer*—J Black

◁ **lung-hammock** ▷ *n* A brassiere

◁ **lungs** ▷ *n* A woman's breasts; =KNOCKERS: *She has a great pair of lungs*—Lawrence Sanders

lunk **1** *n* A stupid person; =LUNKHEAD: *Lunks, Hunks and Arkifacts* —Time **2** ***modifier:*** *four books about a lunk hero Carlo Reinhart* —Time

lunker **1** *n* A very big fish, often the apocryphal one that got away: *In the ocean there's nothing but lunkers* —New York Times **2** *n* An old car; =CLUNKER, HEAP: *in old cars known as clunkers, lunkers, winter rats*—New York Times

lunkhead *n fr middle 1800s* A stupid person; =BOOB, DOPE: *a bulky, duck-footed lunkhead*—John Cheever

lurker *n computer* A person who enters a computer system illegally; an uninvited computer eavesdropper: *Ian had found a lurker in the system* —Toronto Life

lush **1** *n fr late 1800s* A drunkard; an alcoholic; =DIPSO: *She is still plastered, the little lush*—John O'Hara/ *The father was by no means a lush,* *but the son carried temperance to an extreme*—Joseph Mitchell **2** *v: lushing, stowing wine into our faces* —Henry Seidel Canby [origin unknown; fr early-19th-century British, "tipple, drink," perhaps fr the name of *Lushington*, a London brewer, or fr British dialect, "intoxicating drink," which is perhaps fr Romany or Shelta (tinkers' jargon)]

lush roller (or **worker**) *n phr underworld* A thief who specializes in robbing helpless drunks: *A lush roller rolls lushes*—AJ Liebling

lushwell *n* = LUSH

luxo *adj* Luxurious; = POSH: *Sapporo/Challenger luxo-coupe*—Westworld

M

M **1** ***n*** *narcotics* Morphine: *You've got to get M to get that tingle-tingle* —Nelson Algren **2** ***n*** Money

ma'am ***See*** WHAM-BAM THANK YOU MA'AM

ma-and-pa ***See*** MOM-AND-POP

Ma Bell ***n phr*** A wry nickname for the Bell Telephone system: *Ma Bell, for instance, is fair game to many* —American Scholar

mac ***See*** MACK

Mac or **Mack** ***n*** Man; fellow; =BUSTER, JACK • Used in direct address, often with a mildly hostile intent: *Take it easy, Mac*

macher (MAH kər, -khər) ***n*** An active, usu self-important person; =BIG SHOT, OPERATOR: *the Muse to numerous folk-rock machers*—New Yorker [fr Yiddish, literally "maker, doer"]

machisma (mah CHIZ mə) ***n*** The female counterpart of machismo: *Machisma, Women, and Daring* —Grace Lichtenstein

machismo (mah CHIZ moh) ***n*** Aggressive masculinity; blatant virility: *machismo, a he-man complex*—Time [fr Spanish]

macho (MAH choh) **1** ***n*** An aggressively masculine man; =HE-MAN **2** ***n*** Aggressive maleness; =MACHISMO: *It was not just a question of executive macho*—New York **3** ***adj:*** *a typical macho Mailerism* —Pauline Kael [fr Spanish]

macho it out ***v phr*** To behave with masculine courage and stamina; =TOUGH IT OUT: *I machoed it out all the way into the men's room before I threw up*—Time

mack ***n esp black fr late 1800s*** A pimp; =MACKMAN: *copped you a mack*—Donald Goines [fr 15th-century *mackerel* "pimp," fr Old French *macquerel*, perhaps related to Dutch *makelaar* " trade, traffic," hence ultimately to *make, macher*, etc]

mackerel ***See*** HOLY CATS

mackman **1** ***n*** *esp black* A pimp; =MACK: *went back to...that young mackman?*—C Cooper/ *a mere player masquerading as a mack-man* —Village Voice **2** ***modifier:*** *for all his jackass mackman shit*—Village Voice

Mack truck ***n phr*** *football* A very tough and solid player, usu a defensive one [fr the trade name of a line of heavy trucks]

mad **1** ***adj*** Angry **2** ***adj*** *bop & cool talk* Excellent; exciting; =CRAZY ***See*** LIKE CRAZY

-mad ***combining word*** Devoted to, manic over, obsessed with what is indicated: *money-mad/ computer-mad/ horse-mad*

mad as a wet hen ***adj phr*** Very angry; infuriated; =PISSED OFF

made ***n*** *black* Straightened hair; a head of straightened hair ***See*** HAVE something CINCHED

be **made** ***v phr*** =be HAD

mad money **1** ***n phr*** Money carried by a woman with which to pay her way home if her escort becomes offensive **2** ***n phr*** Money saved by a woman against the time when she wants to make an impulsive or therapeutic purchase

mafia ***n*** A group prominent in and suspected of controlling some organization, institution, etc: *Chernenko was a member of the Brezhnev mafia in the Politburo*—National Public Radio [fr Italian *mafia* or *maffia*, designating the Sicilian secret society supposed to be deeply involved in organized crime both in Italy and the US; the Italian word derives fr Old French *mafler* "to gluttonize, devour," perhaps cognate with German *muffelon* "chew"]

mag **1** *n* A magazine **2** *n* A magneto **3** *n* A car wheel made of a magnesium alloy

Magellan *n airline* An aircraft navigator

maggot *n* A cigarette butt: *snapped the maggot over the rail*—Sterling Hayden
See ENOUGH TO GAG A MAGGOT

magnum-force *adj* Very powerful: *one of Thomas Hearns's magnum-force punches* [fr the powerful *magnum* revolver]

maiden *See* IRON MAIDEN

mail *See* CARRY THE MAIL, GREENMAIL, PACK THE MAIL

main *adj black* Favorite; most admired; beloved: *This is my main nigger, my number one nigger*—Claude Brown
See MAINLINE

main brace *See* SPLICE THE MAIN BRACE

main drag (or **stem**) *n phr hoboes* The major street of a town or city: *We begged together on the "main drag"*—Jack London/ *We sifted along the main stem*—Raymond Chandler

mainline or **main** **1** *v narcotics* To inject narcotics into a blood vessel; =SHOOT UP: *after mainlining heroin the night before*—New York Post **2** *v* To take or administer stimulants or depressants of various sorts: *because the economy was mainlining bigger and bigger fixes of inflation*—Philadelphia

main line **1** *n phr* (also **Main Line**) The wealthy and fashionable elements of a place; high society and its area of residence, esp that of Philadelphia: *so young and handsome and so popular with the Main Line*—Stephen Longstreet **2** *n phr narcotics* A blood vessel, usu in the arm or leg, into which narcotics may be injected **3** *n phr prison* The mess hall [first sense fr the railroad between Philadelphia and the wealthy suburbs to the west]

main man **1** *n phr black* One's best friend: *Lou Reed, he my main man*—Aquarian **2** *n phr* A woman's lover: *He's been her main man for two years. Do you think they'll get married?*

main squeeze **1** *n phr* The most important person; =BIG ENCHILADA, BOSS: *Vance seems to be the main squeeze*—Dashiell Hammett **2** *n phr* One's sweetheart, lover, etc: *his main squeeze, a girl in his Shakespeare class*—Publishers Weekly

maintain a low profile *See* KEEP A LOW PROFILE

maisie *See* S AND M

make **1** *v underworld fr early 1800s* To rob; steal; =HEIST **2** *v underworld & police* To recognize or identify; make an identification: *He made me the minute he saw me*—John O'Hara **3** *n*: *The woman gave us a make on the guy who slugged her* **4** *v* To understand; grasp; =DIG: *I don't make you, kid. What did the boy do?*—H Witwer **5** *v* To bring fame, success, wealth, etc: *That one show made her* ◁**6**▷ *v* To do the sex act with; =LAY, SCREW: *Not only is the King in love with me, but the Queen tried to make me too*—Newsweek ◁**7**▷ *n* A person regarded merely as a sex partner; =LAY: *an easy make* **8** *v* To arrive at; =HIT: *We'll never make Padanaram before dark* **9** *v* To defecate
See EASY MAKE, ON THE MAKE, ON THE TAKE, PUT THE MAKE ON someone, RUN A MAKE

make a big production (or **big deal**) *v phr* To overdo; overreact, overplan, etc; =MAKE A FEDERAL CASE OUT OF something: *All she wanted was a simple wedding, but he had to make a big production out of it*

make a Federal case out of something *v phr* To overemphasize the importance of something; exaggerate or overreact; =BLOW UP: *So don't try to make a Federal case out of it*—S McNeil

make a hit *v phr* To succeed; be received with approval, gratitude, etc: *She made a hit with my family*

make a killing *v phr* To get a large, quick profit; win hugely

make a move on someone *See* PUT A MOVE ON someone

make (or **get**) **an offer** one **can't refuse** *v phr* To coerce or menace, esp with an ostensively plausible offer: *He's a businessman... I'll make* *him an offer he can't refuse*—Mario Puzo

make an omelet *See* YOU CAN'T MAKE AN OMELET WITHOUT BREAKING EGGS

make a pass at someone *v phr* To make a sexual advance; =PROPOSITION, PUT A MOVE ON someone: *He got high one time and made a pass at her* —Raymond Chandler [fr early 1800s in the sense of "strike at, attack"]

make a pitch *v phr* To make a persuasive case; advocate strongly: *He'll make a pitch for solar energy*

make a pit stop *v phr* To urinate

make a play for *v phr* To attempt to get or seduce, esp by applied attractiveness: *He's making a play for that cute millionaire*

make a scene (or **a stink**) *v phr* To exhibit anger, indignation, fiery temper, hysterics, etc, in a public outburst: *He thought the soup too hot, and made quite a little scene about it/ Why don't these pay cable services make a public stink about the Time Inc-Manhattan Cable monopoly?*—Village Voice

make a score **1** *v phr narcotics* To buy narcotics; =SCORE: *this Jewish cat looking to make a score*—New York Times **2** *v phr gambling* To win a bet: *But I make scores and they keep me going for a while*—New York Post

make a splash *v phr* To produce a strong and usu favorable impression; be very conspicuous: *That's the book that made such a big splash a couple of years ago*

make book *See* KEEP BOOK

make for *v phr* To encourage; promote: *This will make for renewed confidence*

make one's **getaway** *v phr* To escape; flee; fly, esp from the scene of a crime: *The thugs made their getaway in a souped-up Sherman tank*

make good *v phr* To succeed; do what one set out to do in career or life

make goo-goo eyes *v phr* To look at someone longingly, lovingly, seductively, etc: *make goo-goo eyes near a tropical lagoon*—People Weekly

make hamburger (or **hash** or **mincemeat**) **out of** someone or something *v phr* To defeat definitively; trounce; =CLOBBER: *They made hamburger out of the wilting opposition*

make it **1** *v phr* To succeed; =GO OVER: *The charts showed we had made it, and big* **2** *v phr* To survive; live: *He's so sick, I don't think he'll make it* **3** *v phr* To come through unscathed; succeed in enduring: *I don't see how she made it through that rotten day* **4** *v phr* To get to a particular goal or place: *He didn't quite make it to the john*

make it big *v phr* To succeed extraordinarily well

make it snappy *v phr* To hurry; go faster; act quickly; =GET THE LEAD OUT, SNAP TO IT

make it with someone *cool talk* ◁**1**▷ *v* To do the sex act with or to someone; =SCORE: *Man, don't think I didn't make it with her*—S Boal **2** *v phr* To succeed with someone: *Talking that way he'll never make it with the committee*

make like *v phr* To pretend to be; imitate: *A cop picked it up and made like a bookie*—New York Confidential

make mincemeat out of someone or something *See* MAKE HAMBURGER OUT OF someone or something

make one's **move** *v phr* To take a first and crucial action, esp one that will start a chain of reactions: *The cops are just waiting for the guy to make his move*

make my day *sentence* Go ahead and do what you appear to threaten, so that I can trounce you and have a successful day: *"Make my day" is much used in the New York subway system, where life is raw and tempers are short*—Mary McGrory

make nice *v phr* To pet; cosset, caress ● The syntax simulates baby talk: *Public officials... make nice to politicians they cannot stand... because they need their good will* —New York Times

make (or **have**) **no bones about** **1** *v phr fr 1500s* To be entirely candid about; to be open about; =be UPFRONT: *They make no bones about what they're going to do*—Washington Post **2** *v phr* To show or feel no doubt or hesitation about: *This spirited Labrador... had no bones about venturing out*—Milwaukee Journal [origin unknown; the earlier form *find no bones* may indicate that the reference is to bones in soup or stew, which would hinder the eating, hence hold the matter up]

make no never mind *v phr fr black* To make no difference; be insignificant: *Makes no never mind what he thinks, I'm going*

make out **1** *v phr* To succeed, esp by a slim margin; =GET BY: *Did you make out OK with that new machine?* **2** *v phr esp teenagers & students* To pet heavily; kiss and caress; =NECK: *nostalgic for duck-tail haircuts, and making out in the back seat* —New York **3** *v phr* To succeed in sexual conquest

make out like a bandit *v phr* To emerge very successfully; win everything: *You'd make out like a bandit* —George V Higgins [probably based on Yiddish *bonditt* "clever, resourceful fellow"]

maker *See* WAVE-MAKER

make something out of *v phr* To interpret as a cause for combat; regard as a challenge or insult: *So you heard what I said, huh? You want to make something out of it?*—John McNulty

make something **stick** *v phr* To cause an accusation, assertion, etc, to be believed; validate or prove: *They accused him of rape, but they'll never make it stick*

make the cheese more binding *v phr* To make things more difficult or complicated; clutter or snarl the matter: *And just to make the cheese more binding, they're also sold through mail order*—Lawrence Sanders [a humorous pun based on the fact that cheese is thought to be *binding* "constipating," and certain elements of a situation are also *binding* "constraining"]

make the grade **1** *v phr fr late 1800s* To succeed: *He made the grade as a lawyer* **2** *v phr* To meet certain standards: *His work just didn't make the grade*

make the rounds *v phr* To be passed from person to person; circulate: *A theory about the cause is making the rounds now*

make the scene *fr beat & cool talk* **1** *v phr* To arrive; appear: *When do you plan to make the scene?* **2** *v phr* To succeed; achieve something: *With this album they'll sure make the scene* **3** *v phr* To do; experience: *I think I'll make the political scene next*

make time *v phr fr railroad fr middle 1800s* To go fast; travel at a good speed: *They really made time after they let the passengers off*

make time with someone *v phr* To succeed sexually with someone, esp to make or approach a rapid conquest: *He was making time with Ezra's girl*

make up for lost time *v phr* To work, play, travel, etc, very fast to compensate for a slow start

make waves *v phr* To cause trouble; upset things: *What he said has made waves*—Milwaukee Journal [fr the joke in which a person just arrived in hell, and hearing beautiful serene singing, finds that it is being done by inmates standing in chin-high excrement and cautiously chanting "*Don't make waves*"]

make with *v phr* To use; exercise: *The poor man's Bing Crosby is still making with the throat here in Chi* —John O'Hara [fr Yiddish *machen mit* "swing or wave something about, brandish something"]

malarkey **1** *n fr 1920s* Lies and exaggerations; empty bombastic talk; =BALONEY, BULLSHIT: *Hollywood is in the business of manufacturing malarkey as well as movies*—Bob Thomas/ *That's a lot of malarkey* —Newsweek **2** *interj* =BULLSHIT [origin unknown]

male chauvinist pig **1** *n phr* A man who believes in and proclaims the superiority of men over women; =MCP: *Is it all right to call a priest a male chauvinist pig?*—New York Times **2** *modifier: male-chauvinist-pig-type man to the contrary notwithstanding*—New York

male member *See* MEMBER

mallie (MAW lee) *n* A person, esp a young person, who frequents shopping malls for sociability, excitement, etc: *"Mallies" always hang around the pay telephone*—Peanuts (comic strip)

mama **1** *n* Any woman **2** *n fr black* A sexually attractive or sexually available woman: *"Say, baby, you sportin' tonight?" "Yeah, Mama, if I could find somebody to sport with"* —Claude Brown **3** *n motorcyclists* A woman who belongs to a motorcy-

cle gang: *If a girl wants to be a mama and "pull a train,"... she'll be welcome at any Angel party*—Saturday Evening Post **4** *n homosexuals* The passive, feminine partner of a lesbian couple
See SWEET MAMA

mama-and-papa *See* MOM-AND-POP

mammyrammer *See* MOTHERFUCKER

man *n* A dollar; =IRON MAN: *You oughta grab about 300 men*—H Witwer
See ASS MAN, BOX MAN, BUTTER-AND-EGG MAN, CANDY MAN, CON MAN, DIRTY OLD MAN, FANCY MAN, FIRST MAN, G-MAN, HATCHET MAN, HE-MAN, HIT MAN, HOOP-MAN, IRON MAN, LADIES' MAN, LEG MAN, LOW MAN ON THE TOTEM POLE, PANMAN, PETERMAN, POOR MAN'S something or someone, SEE A MAN ABOUT A DOG, STRAIGHT MAN, SWEET MAN, TIT MAN, TRIGGER MAN

-man *combining word* A man preferring, doing, having, etc, the indicated thing: *bottle-man/ fifty-minute-man/ trigger man*

the **man** or **the Man** **1** *n phr* Any man in authority; =BOSS, HIS NIBS: *See the guy in front? That's the man* **2** *n phr narcotics & underworld* A police officer, detective, prison guard, etc; =the HEAT: *Careful, here's the man* **3** *n phr narcotics* A supplier of narcotics; =DEALER **4** *n phr black* A white man; the white establishment: *That's what "the man" wants you to do... to riot, so he can shoot you down*—New Yorker

a **man about a dog** *See* SEE A MAN ABOUT A DOG

manage *v* To cope satisfactorily; survive; =GET BY: *It's a lot to pay, but we'll manage*

mango hunter *n phr* A person, usu a drug addict, who sets fire to vacant buildings and steals the saleable items after firefighters have chopped up the floors, etc: *Then the "mango hunters"... move in*—Time

mangy with *adj phr* =LOUSY WITH

mano a mano *n phr* A hand-to-hand fight or duel: *Hemingway's subject... was the mano a mano between Spain's two leading matadors*—New York Times/ *a literary mano a mano with some good books as weapons*—New York Times [fr Spanish, "hand-to-hand"]

man on the street **1** *n phr fr early 1800s* The average person; the ordinary person; =JOHN Q CITIZEN **2** *modifier: and some man-on-the-street TV commercials for post-convention use*—New York

◁ **man with a paper ass** ▷ *n phr black* A person whose ideas are not important; a trivial man; =LIGHTWEIGHT

many *See* ONE TOO MANY

mao-mao (MOU MOU) *v* To coerce with rough treatment; terrorize: *The pressure ladies half-successfully mao-maoed Communications Minister Francis Fox*—Toronto Life [fr the *Mau Maus*, a terrorist group in Kenya in the 1950s]

maple *See* BIRDSEYE MAPLE

◁ **maracas** ▷ *n* A woman's breasts; =BOOBS: *gams and a pair of maracas that will haunt me in my dreams*—John O'Hara

marble orchard *n phr* A cemetery: *You'll get your names in this marble orchard soon enough*—James M Cain

marbles *See* GO FOR BROKE, HAVE ALL one's BUTTONS, HAVE SOME BUTTONS MISSING, LOSE one's MARBLES, MISSISSIPPI MARBLES

march *n circus* The circus parade

mare *See* RIDE SHANK'S MARE

Mari *See* MARY

Maria *See* BLACK MARIA

◁ **maricón** ▷ (MAH rih kahn, MA-, -KOHN) *n* A male homosexual: *"This it is, maricón," snarled the Puerto Rican*—High Times [fr Spanish]

Marines *See* TELL IT TO THE MARINES

mark **1** *n fr late 1800s underworld, circus, carnival, hawkers, & hoboes* The target or victim of a swindle, esp one who is easily duped; =PATSY, SUCKER: *not that he's more of a mark than other horse nuts*—J Lilienthal **2** *v underworld* To look for or find a likely place for robbery **3** *v teenagers* To inform; =SQUEAL: *He swore he wouldn't mark if they caught him*
See EASY MARK, HASH MARK, TOE THE MARK, UP TO SCRATCH

marker **1** *n gambling* =IOU **2** *n sports* A point or score: *eight markers in the first period*

market *See* GRAY MARKET, MEAT MARKET

marks the spot *See* X MARKS THE SPOT

marmalade *n* =MALARKEY

marriage *See* SHOTGUN WEDDING

marry *v* To join; bring together: *He tries to marry the Canadian producers with the foreign buyers*—Toronto Life

marshmallow *n black* A white person: *an Oreo fronting for a "marshmallow"*—R Levine

Mary **1** *n* A male homosexual who takes the passive, feminine role: *He passed two willowy-looking queers, Mary's who'd decided to settle for each other*—George V Higgins **2** *n* A lesbian **3** *n* (also **Mari**) *narcotics* Marijuana

Mary Ann or **Mary Jane** *n phr narcotics* Marijuana or a marijuana cigarette

Mary Warner *n phr narcotics* Marijuana

mash **1** *n esp 1920s* Love or a love affair: *just another mash*—Louis Armstrong **2** *n* A lover, of either sex: *her latest big mash* **3** *v fr middle 1800s* To make a sexual advance to; =PROPOSITION: *I wouldn't try to mash anybody like you* [apparently fr Romany, "allure, entice," and so used in mid-19th-century vaudeville by a Gypsy troupe]
See MISH-MASH

mash note *n phr* A very flattering letter, esp one proposing or offering sex: *showered him with embroidered pillows, mash notes, and cigars*—Reader's Digest

massage **1** *v* To beat; drub; =ROUGH someone UP: *caught and massaged with rubber hoses*—HF Pringle **2** *v* To handle, process, or manipulate data, esp computer data: *The results all depend on how you massage it*

massage parlor *n phr* A place that provides sexual services under the guise of legitimate body massage; =RAP CLUB

masters *See* SLAVES AND MASTERS

mat **1** *n black* A woman; one's wife **2** *n esp Navy* The floor; deck
See GO TO THE MAT, HIT THE MAT, ON THE MAT

match *See* the WHOLE SHOOTING MATCH

math *n students* Mathematics

matter *See* GRAY MATTER

mavin or **mayvin** or **maven** (MAY vən) *n* An expert; an authority; a connoisseur: *growing clientele of pizza mavins*—L Goldberg/ *A real advertising mavin must have thought that up*—Leo Rosten [fr Yiddish fr Hebrew, "understanding"]

max **1** *adv* At the most; at the highest limit: *I do three cars a week, max*—George V Higgins **2** *v college students* To win; do the very best [fr *maximum*]
See TO THE MAX

max out **1** *v phr Army* To make the best score, or one's best score **2** *v phr* To do or contribute the maximum possible amount: *go to the people with the potential of, as they say in the business, "maxing out"*—Newsweek **3** *v phr college students* To go to sleep

mazel (MAH zəl) *n* Luck: *When a man has mazel, even his ox calves*—Leo Rosten [fr Yiddish fr Hebrew]

mazuma (mə ZŌŌ mə) *n* (Variations: **mezuma** or **mazume** or **mazoomy** or **mazoo** or **mazoola** or **mazula**) *fr early 1900s* Money: *You have to leave your mazuma behind*—George Jean Nathan [fr Yiddish fr Hebrew; perhaps fr a Chaldean word meaning "the ready necessary"]

McCoy *adj* Genuine; legitimate; =KOSHER: *like every other McCoy biz*—Variety

the **McCoy** *See* the REAL MCCOY

McDucks *n college students* McDonalds (a trade name), a fast-food restaurant [reference to Disney's *Donald Duck*]

MCP or **mcp** **1** *n* =MALE CHAUVINIST PIG **2** *modifier: a sort of anarcho-Marxist MCP*—Village Voice

MDA *n narcotics* Methyl diamphetamine, a stimulant that is somewhat like LSD

meal *See* SQUARE

meal ticket **1** *n phr prizefight* A prizefighter in relation to his manager: *with his meal ticket, the Brown Bomber himself*—Arthur Daley **2** *n phr* Any person, skill, part of the body, instrument, etc, that provides one's sustenance: *His looks are his meal ticket*

mean *adj fr early 1900s black* Excellent; wonderful; =CLASSY, WICKED: *This... girl has already proved she can play a mean game of tennis*—Inside Sports
See LEAN AND MEAN

mean green *n phr fr black* Money: *Mean green won out over neighborhood purity*—Village Voice

meany or **meanie** ***n*** A cruel, unkind person; villain; =HEAVY

See BLUE MEANY

meat ◁**1**▷ ***n*** A person considered merely as a sex partner or object; =ASS ◁**2**▷ ***n*** The vulva; =CUNT ◁**3**▷ ***n*** *fr homosexuals* The penis; =PRICK ◁**4**▷ ***n*** *fr 1700s* The sex act; copulation; =FUCKING: *He says he's hard up, needs meat* **5** ***n*** *students* A stupid person; =MEATHEAD: *to see a bunch of meats play*—Sports Illustrated **6** ***n*** *car-racing* The depth of tread on a tire

See ALL THAT MEAT AND NO POTATOES, BEAT one's MEAT, DARK MEAT, EASY MEAT, JUMP ON someone's MEAT, MAKE HAMBURGER OUT OF someone or something, PIG-MEAT

one's **meat** *fr late 1800s* **1** ***n phr*** An easy and favorite opponent; a chosen opponent: *He wins every time, guess I'm his meat* **2** ***n phr*** One's preferred work, play, effort, etc: *Tennis is his meat* [probably based on the older sense of *meat* "food, sustenance"]

meat and potatoes **1** ***n phr*** The simple fundamentals; =the NITTY GRITTY **2** ***modifier:*** *It's the meat-and-potatoes appeal, the old pull at the heartstrings*—SJ Perelman

See ALL THAT MEAT AND NO POTATOES

meatball ***n*** *esp WW2 armed forces* A stupid, tedious person; an obnoxious or disgusting person; =CREEP, JERK: *"How come?" "Because he's a meatball"*—WT Tyler

meat card ***n phr*** =MEAL TICKET

meateater ***n*** A corrupt police officer who aggressively seeks illicit spoils: *Meat eaters...spend a good deal of their working hours aggressively seeking out situations they can exploit*—New York Times

meathead ***n*** A stupid person; =MEATBALL: *The copper...was a big meathead*—JB Martin

meathooks ***n*** The hands or fists

meat market ***n phr*** A place where one looks for sex partners; the milieu of the singles: *men, who are now in the meat market, just like women have always been*—New York Times

meat rack ***n phr*** *esp homosexuals* A gathering place, often public like a park bench or a shopping mall, where one seeks out sex partners: *the strip some people call "the meat rack"*—Washington Post

meat wagon **1** ***n phr*** An ambulance: *He woke up in the meatwagon*—Forum **2** ***n phr*** A hearse: *They have the meat wagon following him around*—Raymond Chandler

med **1** ***n*** A medical student **2** ***modifier*** Medical: *med school/ a med alert*

media hype ***n phr*** Concentrated favorable publicity for a person, corporation, candidate, etc: *Instead of dealing in the media hype, Coplon should have...pursued the reasons*—Village Voice

medicine ***See*** TAKE one's MEDICINE

meds ***n*** *hospital* Medications

the **meemies** ***See*** the SCREAMING MEEMIES

meet ***n*** *underworld* A meeting, esp for some illegal purpose: *She went out to make a "meet" to buy more bogus bills*—Fact Detective Mysteries

meets the road ***See*** WHERE THE RUBBER MEETS THE ROAD

mega **1** ***adj*** *esp students & teenagers* Much: *I got mega homework tonight* **2** ***adv:*** *This dude is mega gross*

mega- ***prefix*** A very large specimen, quantity, etc, of what is indicated: *megablitz/ mega-cost/ megagreed/ megahopes/ megatravel*

megabucks ***n*** Much money: *faith that moves mountains and grosses megabucks*—Village Voice

the **megillah** or **the whole megillah** (mə GILL ə) ***n phr*** Something very long and tedious told or explained exhaustively: *Let's not have the megillah*—C McHarry/ *a whole megilla (song and dance)*—New York Times [fr Yiddish fr Hebrew, "scroll, volume," esp the Book of Esther read aloud in its entirety at Purim celebrations]

MEGO (MEE goh) ***sentence*** *chiefly news media* This is a smashingly boring affair [fr *mine eyes glaze over*]

MEGOGIGO (MEE goh GĪ goh) ***sentence*** *esp teenagers* This is totally tedious [fr *mine eyes glaze over, garbage in garbage out*]

meister ***See*** PERKMEISTER

mellow **1** ***adj*** *fr early 1700s* Slightly drunk; =TIDDLY **2** ***adj*** *jive talk & cool talk* Sincere and skillful • Said of a musical performance **3** ***adj***

Relaxed; at ease; =LAID-BACK **4** *adj* Very friendly; intimate **5** *n* A close friend; =BUDDY **6** *v* =MELLOW OUT

mellow out (also **mellow**) *v phr esp musicians* To become relaxed and easy: *wondering why the family in "The Grapes of Wrath" didn't move to LA and mellow out*—Washington Post

melon ◁**1**▷ *n* A woman's breast **2** *n* The sum of profits, loot, etc, to be divided: *The stockholders have a meager melon to share this year*

melon-belly *n* A protuberant abdomen; a person with a big stomach

meltdown *n* A disaster: *They are... facing a credibility meltdown* —Toronto Life [fr the nuclear powerplant disaster in which the core of radioactive material *melts down* into the earth below]

Melvin *n teenagers* A disgusting and contemptible person; =CREEP, NERD

member **1** *n* *black* A fellow black person; =BROTHER, SISTER ◁**2**▷ *n* (also **male member**) The penis • A euphemism for the even more euphemistic **membrum virile**

the **men** *n phr truckers* The police, esp state police; =SMOKEY BEAR

mensch or **mensh** **1** *n* An admirable and substantial person; a decent and mature person: *At first I didn't like him, but then he emerged as a real mensch* **2** *n* A virile man • Can also be used of women: *mensch, a stand-up he-man*—C McHarry/ *Trigere, almost alone, is mensch enough to candidly dismiss the misogynous midi*—Stephanie Harrington [fr Yiddish, literally "person, man"]

men's lib *n phr* Men's liberation, the counterpart, and possibly reaction, to women's liberation: *Only men's lib and women's lib can alert society* —Rosemary Park

mental *adj chiefly British* Crazy; deranged; =NUTTY: *and the son, William, went absolutely mental*—New York

mental job *n phr* A neurotic or psychotic person; =NUT

meow *See* the CAT'S MEOW

merchant *combining word* A person who esp indulges or purveys in what is indicated: *heat merchant/ speed merchant*

merge *v* To marry

the **merry ha-ha** *n phr* A ridiculing and dismissive laugh; =the HORSE-LAUGH

merry hell *n phr* A severe rebuke or punishment: *He gave us merry hell for that caper*

See CATCH HELL, GIVE someone HELL

mesc *n narcotics* Mescaline, a hallucinogenic drug

meshegoss or **meshugas** *See* MISHEGOSS

meshuga (mə SHŏŏ gə, -SHIH-) *adj* (Variations: **meshigga** or **meshugah** or **meshiggah** or **mishugah** or **mishoogeh**) Crazy; =NUTTY: *Mishoogeh or mishugah... spelled either way means crazy*—C McHarry [fr Yiddish fr Hebrew; the variant pronunciations reflect major dialects of Yiddish]

meshugana or **meshiggana** or **meshiganer** (mə SHŏŏ gə nə, -SHIH-) *n* A crazy person; =NUT: *Robert, is that meshugana gone yet?* [fr Yiddish fr Hebrew]

mess **1** *n* A desperately confused situation; chaos; =FOUL-UP, FUCK-UP: *This project is turning into a mess* **2** *n* An incompetent, disorganized, and confused person: *Honey, I'm a mess* **3** *n* A disorderly or slovenly person; =SLOB: *You're always making a mess of yourself* **4** *n* Dirt, garbage, trash, etc; a dirtying: *Clean up your damn mess*

mess around *v phr* To idle about; loaf; work indolently; =GOOF OFF: *Stop messing around and get to work*

mess someone **around** (or **over**) *v phr* To victimize and exploit; maltreat; =FUCK OVER: *being messed over by Goldberg all the time*—Claude Brown/ *Here's a young black dude in a Cadillac, we'll just mess him around* —New York

mess around with or **mess with** **1** *v phr fr middle 1800s* To flirt or dally with; have a sexual involvement with: *He'd waste me if I messed around with his sister/ I don't mess with married or attached women* —New York Post **2** *v phr* To defy or challenge; provoke; =FUCK WITH: *Nobody dared to mess around with Slippers*—Louis Armstrong/ *I said don't mess with me, Buster* **3** *v phr* To consort with; frequent; play with: *They go around messing with us, because we're trying to do some-*

thing—Ishmael Reed/ *What are you messing around with that crowd for?* **4** *v phr* To play or tinker with: *I caught him messing with the heating control*

mess up **1** *v phr* To disarrange; muddle: *Who messed up these figures?* **2** *v phr* To injure; damage: *The drugs and booze messed up her mind* **3** *v phr* To get into trouble; make a botch; =FUCK UP: *If you don't mess up you get an automatic promotion*

mess someone **up** **1** *v phr* To thrash; beat up; =WORK someone OVER: *They sent a couple of goons to mess him up when he wouldn't pay* **2** *v phr* To damage or injure: *That Moony stuff messed him up pretty bad/ The wreck messed him up so much that he can't walk*

metal *fr musicians* **1** *n* =HEAVY METAL **2** *v* To play loudly amplified rock and roll music: *Nobody can metal like Blue Oyster Cult*—B Malamut

See HEAVY METAL

meter-reader *n aviators* The copilot of an airplane

meth *n narcotics* Methedrine (a trade name)

meth head (or **freak**) *n phr narcotics* A habitual user of Methedrine (a trade name)

◀ **Mex** ▶ **1** *n* A Mexican **2** *adj* Mexican: *Ensenada is all Mex*—James M Cain

◀ **Mexican breakfast** ▶ *n phr* A cigarette and a glass of water

◀ **Mexican infantry** ▶ *n phr Army* Military intelligence

◀ **Mexican promotion** (or **raise**) ▶ *n phr* Advancement in rank or status with no raise of salary

Mexican red or **Mexican** *See* PANAMA RED

Mexican standoff *n phr* A stalemate; deadlock; =STANDOFF [*Mexican* seems to be used to give a sense of peril and crudeness to the situation, as if two persons faced each other directly with raised machetes or loaded guns]

mezuma *See* MAZUMA

MF or **mf** *n* A despicable person; =MOTHERFUCKER: *He used to look right at them MFs*—Pete Hamill

Michigan roll *n phr* A bankroll having a note of large denomination on the outside and small notes or paper making up the rest

◀ **mick** or **Mick** ▶ *fr middle 1800s* **1** *n* An Irishman or person of Irish descent **2** *adj: a mick politician* **3** *n* A Roman Catholic **4** *adj: my one mick friend, although he isn't Irish*—P Marks [fr the nickname of the common Irish name *Michael*]

mickey or **Mickey** ◀**1**▶ *n* =MICK **2** *n* A potato: *We stole our first mickies together from Gordon's fruit stand*—Claude Brown **3** *n* A stupefacient drug placed in one's drink; =MICKEY FINN: *Mickeys act so drastically that one may kill a drunk with a weak heart*—AJ Liebling **4** *n Canadian* A half-bottle of liquor [potato sense probably by association with the common phrase *Irish potato*]

See SLIP someone A MICKEY

Mickey Finn or **mickey finn** **1** *n phr fr late 1800s underworld* A strong hypnotic or barbiturate dose, esp of chloral hydrate, put secretly into a drink; =KNOCKOUT DROPS: *The drug, sometimes known as "knockout drops" or "Mickey Finn," is a sedative*—New York Times **2** *n phr* A purgative similarly administered [origin unknown and richly conjectured, chiefly being fathered on various characters with names like *Mickey Finn*]

Mickey Mouse or **mickey mouse** **1** *adj phr* (also **micky-mouse**) *musicians* Sentimental and insincere: *A "micky-mouse band" is a real corny outfit*—Stephen Longstreet/ *to the dead beat of mind-smothered Mickey Mouse music*—Eldridge Cleaver **2** *adj phr* Showy; meretricious, merely cosmetic: *And I don't think Mickey Mouse changes are going to work*—Walter Mondale **3** *n: It's hard to get past the mickey mouse and see what the hell they're driving at* **4** *adj phr* Shoddy; inferior: *The carpentry work was just Mickey Mouse* **5** *adj phr college students* Simple; elementary; easy: *A "Mickey Mouse course" means a "snap course"*—M Crane **6** *adj phr college students* Petty; inconsequential: *A Mickey Mouse survey of popular culture/ A lot of the Mickey Mouse stuff has been eliminated from the program*—New York Times/ *got picked up on a Mickey Mouse thing in*

August by the State Patrol—Ann Rule **7** ***n phr:*** *That book's pure mickey mouse* **8** ***n phr*** *esp armed forces* A blunder due to confusion and stupidity; =SCREW-UP: *The only big Mickey Mouse... was a brief shortage of... jungle boots*—Time **9** ***n phr*** *black* A stupid person, esp a white person or a police officer [apparently this pejorative trend began after the wide distribution of *Mickey Mouse* wrist watches, showing the cartoon character on the face, with his arms as the watch's hands, which were regarded as shoddy, gimmicky, etc, at that time]

Mickey Mouse ears ***n phr esp students*** Lights, siren, etc, on the top of a police car; =GUMBALL [members of the TV *Mickey Mouse* Club wore large black rodent *ears* on their heads]

middle kidney ***See*** GRIPE one's ASS

◁**middle** (or **third**) **leg**▷ ***n phr*** The penis

the **middle of nowhere** ***n phr*** A very remote area; an isolated place; =BOONDOCKS: *They moved out of Manhattan way into Jersey, the middle of nowhere*

miff *v fr early 1800s* To anger; offend: *His arrogance miffed all of us*

miffed ***adj*** *fr early 1800s* Angered; offended: *miffed over failure of pleas to raise his bail*—New York Daily News

miffy ***adj*** *fr late 1600s* Angry; =MIFFED, PISSED OFF: *after a good bit of miffy correspondence*—A Logan

miggle **1** ***n*** A playing marble **2** ***n*** *narcotics* A marijuana cigarette; =JOINT

mike **1** ***n*** A microphone **2** ***v*** To amplify with a microphone: *The club was so small they decided not to mike the show* **3** ***n*** A microgram; a millionth of a gram: *I feel like I've been up on 300 mikes of acid*—Saturday Review

mile ***See*** GO THE EXTRA MILE, STICK OUT

mileage ***n*** Advantage; profit: *Do they think there's any mileage in my idea?* ***See*** GET MILEAGE OUT OF something

mile-high club ***n phr*** *airline* The putative association of persons who have done the sex act more than a mile high in the sky: *They had stayed behind to renew their membership in the mile-high club by sinking into one of the leather banquettes and making passionate love*—Newlook

military wedding ***n phr*** =SHOTGUN WEDDING

milk **1** ***v*** *fr show business* To exploit to the utmost: *She really knows how to milk the audience for laughs* **2** ***v*** To get something, esp money, unfairly or fraudulently • Originally used in the middle 1800s of manipulation in the stock market: *The agents had regularly been milking the tenants for exorbitant rents* ◁**3**▷ ***v*** To masturbate

milk cans ***See*** KNOCK someone or something FOR A LOOP

milk run **1** ***n phr*** *railroad* A train run with many stops **2** ***n phr*** A scheduled airline passage with many stops; *followed by a milk run to Charleston, Jacksonville, Daytona Beach, and Tampa*—Saturday Review **3** ***n phr*** *WW2 Air Force* An easy bombing mission: *It looked like a milk run*—C Macon [fr the stopping of a train at every rural station to pick up *milk* for delivery to the cities]

milk wagon ***n phr*** A police van; =PADDY WAGON

mill[1] ***n*** A million dollars: *That'll cost the government a cool six mill*

mill[2] **1** ***n*** *prizefight* A prizefight: *the night of the KO Kelly mill*—Joseph Auslander **2** ***n*** *armed forces fr WW1* A military prison or guardhouse **3** ***n*** An automobile or motorcycle engine: *Has it got the magnum mill?*—George V Higgins/ *They both chuckled and fired up their mills*—Easyriders **4** ***n*** *newspaper office* A typewriter

See GIN MILL, GO THROUGH THE MILL, GROG-MILL, RUMOR MILL, RUN-OF-THE-MILL, RUN someone THROUGH THE MILL

million bucks ***See*** LIKE A MILLION BUCKS

milquetoast or **milktoast** ***n*** A mild, ineffectual person; a timid person; =WIMP [fr or popularized by the comic-strip character Caspar Milquetoast in "The Timid Soul" by HT Webster]

Milwaukee goiter (or **tumor**) ***n phr*** A protuberant belly; =BEER BELLY, POTBELLY [fr the fame of the *Milwaukee* breweries]

mincemeat ***See*** MAKE HAMBURGER OUT OF someone or something

mind ***See*** BEND someone's MIND, BLOW someone's MIND, DIRTY MIND, HAVE A MIND LIKE A SIEVE, MAKE NO NEVER MIND, PIECE OF someone's MIND

mind-blower or **mind-bender** *esp 1960s counterculture & narcotics* **1** ***n*** A hallucinogenic drug **2** ***n*** Something exciting, beautiful, shocking, etc: *That little book's a mind-bender*

◀**mind-fuck**▶ **1** ***v*** To manipulate someone to think and act as one wishes; =BRAINWASH: *He was totally mind-fucked... but he seemed to know his stuff*—John Sayles **2** ***n:*** *stance and persona and pop mind-fuck*—Village Voice

◀**mind-fucker**▶ **1** ***n*** A person who manipulates others, esp for his or her own profit: *Most gurus are magnificent and filthy-rich mind-fuckers* **2** ***n*** A distressful situation; =BAD SCENE

mind one's **ps and qs** ***v phr*** *fr middle 1800s fr printers* To take care of one's affairs carefully and exclusively: *What the hell are you staring at, madam, you mind your p's and q's* —H Donohue [fr the fact that the two similar letters are particularly hard to distinguish in type, where their ordinary shapes are reversed]

mind the store ***v phr*** To attend to routine business; carry on: *Who'll mind the store while Mr Reagan is overseas?* [fr the joke about the dying man who, finding by patient inquiry that all his children are at his deathbed, inquires testily as to who is *minding the store*]

mine ***See*** RUN-OF-THE-MILL

mini *fr 1960s* **1** ***n*** A very short dress, skirt, or coat ending well above the knee **2** ***adj:*** *She looked out of place in her mini dress* **3** ***n*** The fashion or style of wearing such short garments [probably fr *miniature,* see *mini-,* although Eric Partridge derived it fr *minimum* because it insures "the minimum of decency"]

mini- ***prefix used to form nouns*** *fr 1960s & esp fr British* Small; miniature; short: *minibus/ mininuke/ minisemester/ miniskirt* [apparently greatly stimulated by the production in 1958 of a small British car called the *Mini-Minor*]

mink ***See*** FUCK LIKE A MINK, TIGHT

minus ***See*** DOUBLE-MINUS

Mirandize ***See*** GIVE someone HIS RIGHTS

mishegoss (MISH ə gahs) ***n*** (also **mishigas** or **meshegoss** or **meshugas**) Craziness; absurdities: *and free-lance mishigas*—Village Voice [fr Yiddish fr Hebrew]

mish-mash (MISH mahsh) ***n*** (also **mish-mosh**) *fr 1500s but chiefly fr late 1800s* A confused mixture; an indiscriminate miscellany: *regarded as a hopeless mishmash*—Brooks Atkinson [apparently originally fr German *mischmasch,* but probably in its modern use chiefly fr Yiddish]

mishugah or **mishoogeh** ***See*** MESHUGA

a **miss** ***See*** GIVE someone or something A MISS

missionary position ***n phr*** The sexual posture in which the male lies over the female between her spread legs: *three furtive minutes in the missionary position*—Village Voice/ *enjoying sex in that reliable missionary position*—Ruth Westheimer [fr the fancied distinction between this coital configuration of Christian *missionaries* and those of the peoples among whom they labored]

Mississippi marbles ***n phr*** Dice

Miss Right ***See*** MISTER RIGHT

miss the boat ***v phr*** To lose an opportunity; fail; =BLOW IT: *He ignored good advice, and missed the boat*

the **missus** (or **the missis**) ***n phr*** One's wife; =the LITTLE WOMAN: *He wanted the missus to get some sleep* —E Lavine

mister ***n*** Man; fellow; =GUY • Always used in direct address, usu to a stranger: *Hey, mister, where's the turn-off for Bogota?*

the **mister** ***n phr*** One's husband: *How's the mister?*

Mister Big ***n phr*** The chief or most important person; =BIG ENCHILADA: *I predict in three or four years he'll be Mister Big*

Mister Charlie ***n phr*** *black* A white man; =the MAN

Mister Clean ***n phr*** A man, esp a politician, unsullied by suspicion of corruption or bad character: *a managerial Mr Clean*—Toronto Life

Mister Fixit ***n phr*** A person who can and does repair, adjudicate, resolve, etc, difficulties: *a reputation as an ingenious Mr Fixit*—Newsweek

Mister Hawkins *n phr black & hoboes* The cold winter wind; =the HAWK

Mister Nice Guy *n phr* A decent, fair, trustworthy, amiable, etc, man • Often in a negative expression: *If I get the nomination, it'll be no more Mr Nice Guy*—Toronto Life

Mister (or **Miss** or **Ms**) **Right** *n phr* The person one would and should happily marry; one's dream mate

Mister Tom *n phr black* A black man who wishes to be or has been assimilated into the white middle-class culture; =UNCLE TOM

mitt **1** *n fr late 1800s* The hand: *snatched right out of his mitt*—Charles MacArthur **2** *n prizefight* A boxing glove: *have the big mitts on*—WR Burnett **3** *v prizefight* To clasp hands above one's head as a sign of victory and acknowledgment of applause: *sitting in his corner and mitting the crowd*—WR Burnett **4** *v* To shake hands: *Mitt me, pal, I done it* [fr *mitten*]

mitt-glommer or **mitt-glaummer** or **mitt-glahmer** *n* A handshaker

mix **1** *n* A mixture: *an auto maker's marketing mix*—New York **2** *v* To fight; =MIX IT UP: *Them last two babies mixed*—H Witwer

mixed up *adj phr fr late 1800s* Confused; chaotic: *His mind's all mixed up*

mixer **1** *n* Soda water, tonic, or any soft drink or juice to which liquor is added **2** *n fr late 1800s* A person who easily becomes acquainted and sociable with others; a gregarious person **3** *n fr 1920s* A party or other gathering intended as an occasion for people to meet and become acquainted with one another

mix it up or **mix it** **1** *v phr fr early 1900s* To fight, esp with great flailing and abandon: *The principals refused to mix it up*—F Scott Fitzgerald/ *didn't seem to want to mix it*—WR Burnett **2** *v phr* To socialize; associate with: *Richards, the traditional marketing man, mixing it up with the culture gang*—Toronto Life

mix-up **1** *n fr late 1800s* Confusion; chaos; =MESS: *There's an awful mix-up over at the plant today* **2** *n fr early 1900s* A fight, esp a free-for-all

MJ *n narcotics* Marijuana

mob **1** *n* An underworld grouping; organized-crime family: *a narcotics mob/ the Genovese mob* **2** *modifier: mob infiltration/ a mob boss* **3** *n* Any group, gathering, class, etc: *as a member of the ruling mob*—Westbrook Pegler

the **mob** *n* Organized crime; the Mafia; the syndicate: *I heard it's controlled by the mob*

mobbed up *adj phr* Controlled by or implicated with organized crime: *real hard evidence... that Schiavone or Donovan are mobbed up*—Newsweek

mobile *See* NERDMOBILE, PIMPMOBILE

mob scene *n phr* A very crowded place or occasion; =FANNYBUMPER: *The reception was a mob scene*

mobster *n* A member of a criminal grouping; a Mafioso: *nickname he got from the mobsters*—John O'Hara

moby *adj computer* Very large, complicated, and impressive [probably fr the white whale in Herman Melville's *Moby Dick*]

◀ **mockie** ▶ **1** *n* A Jew: *crashed their fists into a mockie*—James T Farrell **2** *adj: a mockie shop/ I have a mockie accent?*—Saul Bellow [origin unknown; perhaps fr *macher*; perhaps fr underworld slang "fake, phoney"; probably fr *mock*]

mod *adj esp 1960s* Modern; up-to-date, esp in the styles of the 1960s: *shows off her attributes in a mod wardrobe*—Bosley Crowther

Model-T *adj* Cheap; shabby; crude: *a real Model-T speakeasy*—Stephen Longstreet [fr the *Model T* Ford car of the early 1900s]

mohasky *narcotics* **1** *n* Marijuana **2** *adj* Intoxicated with marijuana; =STONED [fr *mohoska*]

mojo[1] *n black* A charm or amulet worn against evil; hence, power, luck, effectiveness, etc: *gets his mojo going for conventions and elections*—Washington Post [probably fr an African language]

mojo[2] *n narcotics* Any narcotic, esp morphine [perhaps fr Spanish *mojar* "celebrate by drinking"]

moldy fig *bop talk & cool talk* **1** *n phr* A prude; pedant **2** *n phr* A person who prefers traditional jazz to the more modern styles: *Moldy Figs vs Moderns*—Mark Gardner **3** *adj: my moldy-fig tastes*

moll *fr 1700s British* **1** *n* A woman **2** *n* A prostitute **3** *n* A criminal's woman companion, accomplice, girlfriend, etc; =GUN MOLL [fr *Molly*, nickname of Mary]

Molotov cocktail *n phr fr WW2* A grenade made by pouring gasoline into a bottle, adding a cloth wick and igniting [fr Vyacheslav *Molotov*, Soviet premier, used and satirically named by Finnish fighters against the Soviet invasion of 1940]

mom-and-pop or **ma-and-pa** or **mama-and-papa** *adj* Run by a couple or a family; small-scale: *still seem wedded to the "mom and pop store," small-business approach* —Albert P Blaustein/ *The constitution says nothing about a mom and pop presidency*—Ms

momism (MAHM izm) *n* Maternal domination; matriarchalism; mother worship

momma **1** *n black* =MAMA **2** *n fr black* Any specified object, esp a large, admirable, or effective one; =MOTHER, MOTHERFUCKER: *It's time to put this momma in the oven*—Cher (TV program)

mommick up (MAHM ək) *v phr* To confuse and botch; =BOLLIX UP, FUCK UP: *She's wanting to do it all by herself, then she mommicks things up* —Gail Godwin [fr British dialect, "cut awkwardly, maul," fr the disheveled and sloppy appearance of a *mommick* "scarecrow," fr *mammet* or *maumet* "doll, puppet, grotesquely dressed figure," fr earlier "idol, figure of a pagan deity," fr *Mohamet*, the name of the Muslim prophet]

momzer or **momser** (MUHM zər, MAHM-) **1** *n* A person who expects many loans and favors; =MOOCHER, SPONGER **2** *n* A contemptible person; =BASTARD, SHITHEEL: *A very cool customer, this momzer*—Ira Levin [fr Yiddish fr Hebrew, "bastard"]

Monday morning quarterback *n phr* A person who is good at predicting things that have already happened and at pointing out the errors of quarterbacks and other leaders; =ARMCHAIR GENERAL [fr the fact that *Monday* is the first weekday or business day after the weekend, when school and college football games are played]

money *See* BLACK MONEY, CHICKEN FEED, COIN MONEY, FOLDING MONEY, FRONT MONEY, FUNNY MONEY, HARD CURRENCY, HEAVY MONEY, IN THE MONEY, a LICENSE TO PRINT MONEY, MAD MONEY, ON THE MONEY, PUT one's MONEY WHERE one's MOUTH IS, RIGHT MONEY, the SMART MONEY, SOFT MONEY, THROW MONEY AT something

moneybags *n* A rich person: *some aged moneybags*—J Evans

money from home *n phr* Something very welcome and useful, esp when gratis and unexpected: *but for the TV news boys... this was money from home*—Washington Post

money talks *sentence* Wealth is power: *In New York, boy, money really talks*—JD Salinger

money tree *See* SHAKE THE MONEY TREE

monicker *n* (Variations: **moniker** or **monniker** or **monacer** or **monica** or **monaker**) *fr middle 1800s British hoboes* A person's name, nickname, alias, etc; =HANDLE: *His "monica" was Skysail Jack*—Jack London/ *Ricord picked up a new moniker among US narcotics agents*—Time [origin unknown and very broadly speculated upon; perhaps fr transference fr earlier sense, "guinea, sovereign," when used by hoboes as an identifying mark; perhaps related to the fact that early-19th-century British tramps referred to themselves as "in the monkery," that monks and nuns take a new name when they take their vows, and *monaco* means "monk" in Italian; perhaps, as many believe, an alteration of *monogram*]

monk **1** *n* A monkey **◀2▶** *n* A Chinese or Chinese-American: *known to their Occidental neighbors, the Irish especially, as monks*—RL McCardell

monkey **1** *n* A man; fellow; =GUY: *a smart monkey*—Raymond Chandler **2** *n narcotics* Narcotics addiction; a drug habit: *went from monkey to nothin' in twenty-eight days*—Nelson Algren **3** *n narcotics* A kilogram of a narcotic: *and you call and you want 100 monkeys*—Washington Post **4** *v fr late 1800s* To tinker or tamper; intrude one's action: *Look, it's*

running fine, don't monkey with it **5** *v* =MONKEY AROUND
See GET THE MONKEY OFF, GREASE MONKEY, HAVE A MONKEY ON one's BACK

monkey around **1** *v phr* To idle about; loaf; =GOOF AROUND: *I'm just monkeying around, nothing special* **2** *v phr* To tinker or tamper; attempt to use or repair: *Please stop monkeying around with that machine*

monkey (or **funny**) **business** **1** *n phr* Frivolous pranks; japes and jests, etc: *He was full of monkey business, the clown* **2** *n phr* Dubious and dishonest stratagems; trickiness: *Show these kids that you're going to stand for no monkey business*—Time

monkey-chaser ◀**1**▶ *n black fr 1920s* A West Indian **2** *n* A mixed drink based on gin: *Monkey chasers are gin and ice, with a little sugar and a trace of water*—New Yorker

monkey drill *n phr armed forces fr late 1800s* Calisthenics; physical training exercises [fr the fact that the exercisers follow the movements of the instructor, as "*monkey* see, monkey do"]

monkey jacket **1** *n phr fr early 1800s nautical* Any tight, short jacket, esp one that is part of a uniform **2** *n phr hospital* A hospital patient's gown [fr the fact that *monkey* was a nautical term for anything small, in this case a short, informal jacket as distinct from a formal frock coat; *monkey jackets* are also the traditional garb of an organ-grinder's *monkey*]

monkey-monk *See* HIGH MUCKETY-MUCK

monkeyshines *n fr early 1800s* Tricks; japes and capers; pranks

monkey suit *n phr* A fancy uniform or formal suit; tight uniform: *Neither of my two hats went well with the monkey suit*—J Evans

monkey's uncle *See* I'LL BE DAMNED

monniker *See* MONICKER

monster **1** *n narcotics* A narcotic that acts on the central nervous system **2** *modifier: users of scag and monster drugs*—American Scholar **3** *n* A best seller, esp a recording **4** *adj fr middle 1800s British* Enormous; overwhelming; =HUMONGOUS: *his monster ego/ a monster rally*
See ONE-EYED MONSTER

Montezuma's revenge *n phr* Diarrhea, esp traveler's diarrhea: *It was regarded as unfortunate that the President joked about Montezuma's revenge when he introduced the President of Mexico*

mooch **1** *v fr middle 1500s British* To beg; borrow, =CADGE, SPONGE: *He went around mooching cigarettes* **2** *n* =MOOCHER **3** *v* To steal **4** *v fr middle 1500s British* To stroll; loaf along

moocher *n* A beggar; borrower; =DEADBEAT, SPONGER: *He heard a moocher deliver the following spiel*—Billy Rose

moola or **moolah** *n fr early 1900s* Money: *So put a little moola in your portfolio and get yourself a cash cow*—Time [origin unknown]

moon **1** *n* Cheap whiskey, esp whiskey made by unlicensed distillers; =MOONSHINE: *using it to transport moon*—George V Higgins **2** *v esp teenagers & students* To exhibit one's bare buttocks as a defiant or amusing gesture, usu at a window

mooner *n police* A criminal or eccentric active during the period of the full moon
See FULL-MOONER

moonlight *v* To work at a job in addition to one's regular job: *a million guys moonlighting*—World

moonshine **1** *n fr late 1800s* Whiskey made by unlicensed distillers; corn whiskey; =MOUNTAIN DEW: *the moonshine distilled in the mountains*—Ernie Pyle **2** *n* Any cheap, inferior whiskey; =ROTGUT **3** *n* Any liquor or whiskey **4** *n* Exaggerated talk; vain chatter; =BALONEY, BULLSHIT: *His story's plain moonshine*

Moony or **Moonie** *n* A member or disciple of the Unification Church [fr the name of the leader, Sun Myung *Moon*]

moosh *See* MUSH[2]

mooter *n* (also **moota** or **mootie** or **mutah** or **mu**) *fr 1920s* A marijuana cigarette; =JOINT [fr Mexican Spanish *mota* "marijuana," of uncertain origin; since the word also means "bundle of herbs" and "sheaf of hay," it may be semantically akin to *grass, hay, bale of hay,* and *herb,* all of which are disguising names for marijuana or marijuana cigarettes]

mop *n black* The last item or act; the final result: *And the mop was he got caught* [probably from the notion of *mopping* or cleaning up, influenced by earlier jazz use "the last beat at the end of a jazz number"]

mop-squeezer *n gambling* A queen of playing cards [fr a demeaning reference to the queen with the 18th-century term meaning "housemaid, slavey"]

mop (or **mop up**) **the floor with** someone *v phr* To defeat thoroughly; trounce; =CLOBBER

morph **1** *n narcotics* Morphine **2** *n* =MORPHADITE

morphadite *n* (also **mophrodite** or **morphrodite**) *fr 1700s* A hermaphrodite: *You morphadite*—Richard Bissell [fr a probably naive rather than humorous mispronunciation of *hermaphrodite*]

mortal lock *n phr gambling* A certainty; =CINCH, SURE THING: *Brown is what bettors would call a mortal lock to win*—Time

Moses *See* HOLY CATS

mosey or **mosey along** (MOH zee) *v* or *v phr fr early 1800s* To move along, esp to walk slowly; saunter: *I think I'll mosey over and see what's going on/ A mild river that moseyed at will*— WH Auden [perhaps fr Spanish *vamos*; see *vamoose*; perhaps fr British dialect *mose about* "walk in a stupid manner"]

mosquito *See* KNEE-HIGH TO A GRASSHOPPER

moss *n fr black fr 1940s* Hair; among black people, straightened or processed hair: *Moss is hair*—Jim Bouton

See HOUSE MOSS, RIGHTEOUS MOSS

mossback *n fr middle 1800s* A very conservative person; =FOGY: *The real mossbacks will vote for the governor* [said to have been a description of a group of poor white Carolina swamp-dwellers who had lived among the cypresses until the *moss* grew on their *backs*]

the **most** *n phr beat & cool talk* The best; =the GREATEST: *New Jetliner The Most, Reds Say*—New York Daily News

the **mostest** *n phr* =the MOST [fr Southern dialect and black normal superlative of *much*]

See FIRSTEST WITH THE MOSTEST

mothball *See* IN MOTHBALLS

mother **1** *n homosexuals* An effeminate or homosexual male **2** *n homosexuals* The leader, usu the elder and mentor, of younger homosexuals **3** *n fr black* A despicable person; =MOTHERFUCKER: *I looked into the wallet of one of the mothers*—New York **4** *modifier: Every mother other one of 'em cried Foul*—H Norris **5** *n fr black* Any specified object, esp something large, admired, desirable, etc; =FUCKER, MOMMA, MOTHERFUCKER, SUCKER: *Grab these mothers. They'll really do the job*—Joseph N Sorrentino

See JOHN WAYNE'S SISTER

◀ **motherfucker** ▶ (Variations: **eater** or **grabber** or **jumper** or **kisser** or **lover** or **nudger** or **rammer** or some other two-syllable agent word may replace **fucker**; **mammy** or **mama** or **momma** may replace **mother**; other alliterating or rhyming terms like **motorscooter** may replace the whole form) *fr black* **1** *n* A detestable person; =BASTARD, SHITHEEL: *blew this motherfucker's brain out*—Bobby Seale **2** *modifier: a mammyrammer blowhard fart that has no respect*—Bernard Malamud **3** *n* An admirable or prodigious person: *We will joyfully say, "Man, he's a motherfucker"*—Bobby Seale **4** *n* Any specified object, esp something impressive, admirable, etc; =MOMMA, MOTHER, SUCKER: *We had a mother-jumper of a winter. Snow up the yin-yang*—George V Higgins

◀ **motherfucking** ▶ *adj* (Variations: see **motherfucker** for base forms from which **-ing** forms may be made) *fr black* Detestable; disgusting; nasty; accursed; =GOD-DAMN ● Often used for rhythmic and euphonious emphasis: *went down there with his motherfucking gun, knocked down the motherfucking door*—Bobby Seale/ *what he describes as "three hard mothergrabbin' years"*—Time

mothering *adj fr black* Disgusting; accursed; =MOTHERFUCKING: *till you put them motherin' dogs on me*—R Lorning

mother-nudger *See* MOTHERFUCKER

mother's day or **Mother's Day** *n phr* The day when welfare checks come: *We had picked this day* *because it was Mother's Day*—R Moore

motor-mouth **1** *n* A very talkative person; a compulsive jabberer; =FLAPJAW, WINDBAG: *What else can you do with this motor-mouth but grin and bear it?*—Village Voice **2** *adj*: *I didn't know he was motor-mouth*—George V Higgins

mountain dew *n phr* Raw and inferior whiskey, esp homemade bootleg whiskey; =MOONSHINE

mountain (or **prairie**) **oysters** *n phr* Sheep or hog testicles used as food

Mount Saint Elsewhere *n phr hospital* A place, not so prestigious, to which a patient, esp a hopelessly ill one, might be transferred

mounty *See* COUNTY MOUNTY

mouse **1** *n fr middle 1800s British* A bruise near the eye, caused by a blow; =BLACK EYE, SHINER: *One of the Kid's eyes has a little mouse under it*—H Witwer **2** *n* A young woman: *I'm pouring Dom Pérignon and black eggs into this little mouse*—Woody Allen **3** *n* One's wife, girlfriend, fiancée, etc **4** *n computer* A movable indicating device, usually handheld, controlling the cursor on a computer terminal screen: *The program employs a "mouse," a pointing device about the size of a pack of cigarettes*—Time

mousetrap **1** *n* A small, inferior theater or night club: *a mousetrap called the Blue Angel*—John Crosby **2** *v sports* To trick someone into a trap, esp by various blocking moves

mouth *See* BAD-MOUTH, BIGMOUTH, BLOW OFF one's MOUTH, DIARRHEA OF THE MOUTH, FOOT-IN-MOUTH DISEASE, FOUL-MOUTH, FROM THE HORSE'S MOUTH, LOUDMOUTH, MOTOR-MOUTH, MUSHMOUTH, POOR-MOUTH, RATCHET-MOUTH, RUN OFF AT THE MOUTH, SHOOT OFF one's MOUTH, SMARTMOUTH, TALK POOR MOUTH, WATCH one's MOUTH, ZIP one's LIP

mouth-breather *n* A stupid person; moron: *Some mouth-breather in the office told me it would be OK* [fr the noisy *breathing* of an adenoidal idiot]

mouth-breathing *adj* Stupid; moronic: *the dumb mouth-breathing bastards*—Patrick Mann

a **mouthful** *n phr* Something hard to pronounce or speak; =JAWBREAKER: *Diphosphopyridine nucleotide is a mouthful*

See someone SAID A MOUTHFUL

a **mouth full of South** *n phr* A Southern accent: *a man with a mouth full of South*—Washington Post

mouth off **1** *v phr* To talk; make comments; chat **2** *v phr* =SHOOT OFF one's MOUTH

mouth on someone *v phr* To inform on; =SQUEAL: *He got busted, and he mouthed on everybody he knew*—Claude Brown

mouthpiece **1** *n underworld fr early 1900s fr middle 1800s British* A lawyer; =LIP: *"good front," "mouthpiece" or lawyer*—E Lavine **2** *n* A spokesperson: *Each tong has an official "mouthpiece"*—E Lavine

move **1** *v* To steal; pilfer **2** *v* To sell merchandise; dispose of a stock: *We better move these monster Teddy Bears quick* **3** *v* To be desirable to customers; sell quickly: *Those pet rocks are not moving any more*

See MAKE one's MOVE, PUT A MOVE ON someone

move someone **back** *v phr* To cost someone; =SET someone BACK: *That ring'll move you back about 64 big ones*

move into high gear *See* SHIFT INTO HIGH GEAR

moves *See* HAVE ALL THE MOVES

move up *v phr* To buy a more expensive or more cherished thing: *The smoker is exhorted to "move up" to a particular brand of cigarettes, the motorist to a new car*—Russell Baker

movie *See* BLUE MOVIE, B MOVIE, GRINDHOUSE, SNUFF FILM, SPLAT MOVIE

mower *See* ARMSTRONG MOWER

moxie **1** *n fr early 1900s* Courage; =GUTS: *You're young and tough and got the moxie and can hit*—Dashiell Hammett **2** *n* Energy; assertive force; =PIZZAZZ: *We knew you had the old moxie, the old get out and get*—Max Shulman **3** *n* Skill; competence; shrewdness: *showed plenty of moxie as he scattered seven hits the rest of the way*—Associated Press [fr the advertising slogan "What this country needs is plenty of *Moxie*," used for a brand of soft drink; the name may be based on a New England Indian term found in several Maine place names]

Ms Right *See* MISTER RIGHT

mu *See* MOOTER

muck **1** *n* A viscous, slimy substance: *My boots were all covered with muck* **2** *n* An important person; =HIGH MUCKETY-MUCK • Always used with **big**, **high**, etc: *the way some of these big mucks do*—Ellery Queen

muck about *v phr* To idle about; loaf; =GOOF AROUND • Chiefly British

muck-a-muck *See* HIGH MUCKETY-MUCK

muck around *v phr* To tinker or tamper; interfere in; =FUCK AROUND: *I found myself mucking around my life as well as Jean's*—Philadelphia Journal [a euphemism for *fuck around*]

mucker *n fr late 1800s* A crude and unreliable man; lout: *cheap muckers with fine bodies*—P Marks [fr German, "sanctimonious bigot"]

mucket *n* =THINGAMAJIG

muckety-muck *See* HIGH MUCKETY-MUCK

muck up *v phr* To damage; ruin; =FUCK UP: *And let's not muck up our public spaces before we find the answers*—Philadelphia Journal [a euphemism for *fuck up*, probably influenced by mid-19th-century *mucks* "disarrange, discompose, make a muddle" fr British dialect *muxen* "make filthy"]

mucky-muck *See* HIGH MUCKETY-MUCK

mucky-muckdom *n* High circle of power: *the stratosphere of Washington mucky-muckdom*—Washington Post

mud **1** *n narcotics* Opium before it is readied for smoking **2** *n* Defamatory assertions and accusations: *Watch out, they'll throw a lot of mud at you*

See someone's NAME IS MUD, SLING MUD, STICK IN THE MUD

mudder *n horse-racing fr early 1900s* A racehorse that runs very well on a muddy track

mud (or **here's mud**) **in your eye** *interj* A toast; a health: *He raised his glass and said "Mud in your eye"*

mud-slinging *n* The use of defamation, insinuation, etc, esp in politics; =SMEAR

muff **1** *v fr middle 1800s British* To fail; botch, esp by clumsiness: *If you muff this chance you won't get another* **2** *n: dropped the ball, "the $75,000 muff," as it was called*—Arthur Daley **3** *n* A wig; a toupee: *wasn't wearing his muff*—Raymond Chandler ◁**4**▷ *n* The vulva and pubic hair; =BEAVER [first sense fr the clumsiness of someone wearing a muff on the hands]

◁**muff-dive**▷ *v* To do cunnilingus • Sometimes used as a plain insult: *You muff-diving, mother-fucking son of a bitch*—Philip Roth

mug or **mugg** **1** *n fr early 1700s British* The face: *showing so unperturbed a face... so impudent a "mug"*—Henry James **2** *n prizefight* The mouth, chin, or jaw **3** *v* To photograph a person's face, esp for police records: *When crooks are photographed they are "mugged"*—H McLellan **4** *n* A photograph of the face; =MUG SHOT: *a police mug, front and profile*—Raymond Chandler **5** *v fr middle 1800s British* To make exaggerated faces, grimaces, etc, for humorous effect: *while Danny mugs through his program*—Time **6** *n* A man; fellow, esp a tough, rude sort or a pugilist or hoodlum: *Those mugs on the corner seem menacing* **7** *v* To assault and injure someone in the course of a robbery: *mugged in the hallways of their homes*—New York Times **8** *v* To rob someone, snatch someone's purse, etc: *I've been mugged three times, but never beaten up* [probably fr drinking *mugs* made to resemble grotesque human faces; the sense of violent assault comes fr mid-19th-century British specialization of the term "rob by violent strangulation," probably fr *mug-hunter* "a thief who seeks out victims who are mugs" (easy marks); the cited sense of *mug* occurs in *mug's game*]

See FLY COP

mugger **1** *n fr late 1800s* An actor or comedian who makes exaggerated faces, grimaces, etc, for humorous effect: *where this trivial mugger is performing*—Gene Fowler **2** *n fr middle 1800s* A thief who uses extreme physical violence: *apparently the victim of muggers*—New York Times

muggles *narcotics fr early 1900s* **1** *n* Marijuana, esp dried and unshredded leaves: *Some kid was shoving muggles*—Ed McBain **2** *n* A marijuana cigarette [origin unknown]

mug's game *n phr fr early 1900s* A futile effort; a sure failure • Chiefly British: *a mug's game, a no-win proposition*—Newsweek/ *Reliving past glory is... a mug's game*—Dick Cavett [fr British sense of *mug* "dupe, fool, sucker"]

mug shot *n phr* A photograph of a person's face, esp the front and side views made for police records; =ART: *She had identified a "mug shot" from the books as the man who attacked her*—New Yorker

◁ **muh-fuh** ▷ *n esp black* A despicable person; =MOTHERFUCKER: *Them muhfuhs are superbad*—D James

mule **1** *n* A stubborn person: *He's a hardheaded mule* **2** *n* Crude raw whiskey; =MOONSHINE **3** *n narcotics* A person who carries, delivers, or smuggles narcotics or other contraband: *The danger to the mule is that a packet may rupture*—Time/ *American currency was spirited out of the country then, often by "mules"*—Philadelphia **4** *adj: otherwise law-abiding countrymen into performing muling favors*—Newsweek **5** *n narcotics* A condom stuffed with narcotics, carried in the vagina or rectum [narcotics senses perhaps originally suggested by the characteristic use of *mules* or donkeys in Mexico and other Latin-American countries]

the **mulligrubs** *n fr 1600s* =the BLUES [origin unknown]

munchies **1** *n narcotics* Snacks, esp for the hunger that follows using marijuana **2** *n* Desire for these snacks

See HAVE THE MUNCHIES

Munchkin ***See*** LOW-LEVEL MUNCHKIN

munch out (or **up**) *v phr* To eat, esp to consume hungrily: *while Nancy's sipping tea and munching out on scones*—New York Post/ *You'll get together with your friends, right, and you'll be munching up or something*—San Francisco

mung **1** *n esp teenagers* Anything nasty; filth; =GLOP, MUCK: *Fold the table down, and generations of crud and mung appear*—Scottsdale Daily Progress **2** *v computer* To make changes, often undesirable ones, in a file **3** *v computer* To destroy: *The system munged my whole day's work* [perhaps fr Latin *mungere* "blow the nose, produce nasal mucus"; perhaps fr British dialect "kneaded food for fowls"]

mung up *v phr esp teenagers* To make filthy: *I munged up my shoes walking across the field*

murder **1** *n fr jive talk* =the MOST, the GREATEST **2** *n* A very difficult or severe person or thing • Sometimes pronounced with equal stress on each syllable: *The last two hours were murder/ Man, he's murder*—Max Shulman **3** *v* To defeat decisively; trounce; =CLOBBER: *They murdered them all season*—G Talbot **4** *v* To make someone helpless with laughter; =FRACTURE, KILL: *This one'll murder you*

See BLOODY MURDER, GET AWAY WITH MURDER

Murder One *n phr* The criminal offense of murder in the first degree: *when he did get to trial, and they were going to go for Murder One*—Easyriders

muscle **1** *n* A strong-arm man; =GORILLA: *some gowed-up muscle*—J Evans **2** *n* Power; influence; =CLOUT: *DiBona will have a lot of muscle when it comes to Penn's Landing*—Philadelphia

See FLEX one's MUSCLES, LOVE-MUSCLE

musclehead **1** *n* A stupid person; =KLUTZ **2** *n* A strong-arm man; =MUSCLE: *I saw three or four muscleheads gleefully beat up on a kid*—Village Voice

muscle in *v phr underworld* To force one's way in, esp into someone's criminal operation: *attempt to muscle in on some graft*—E Lavine/ *afraid you're muscling in on his scam*—WT Tyler

muscle out *v phr* To force out: *She'll be muscled out of the movement*—F Sparks

museum piece *n phr* Something old or old-fashioned: *His hat's a museum piece*

mush[1] **1** *n* Empty and exaggerated talk; =BALONEY: *Don't hand me that mush, pal* **2** *n* Sentimentality; saccharinity; =CORN, SCHMALTZ: *all weeping over the Dickensian mush* [perhaps an alteration of *mash* "something soft and pulpy"]

mush[2] or **moosh** (often MōōSH) *n fr middle 1800s* The face, esp the mouth and jaws: *He pulled his mush* *away from the plate and sighed*—Jerome Weidman [origin unknown]

mush-head *n* A stupid person

mush-headed or **mushy-headed** *adj* Stupid: *some really mushy-headed, or at least questionable, rationalizations*—Washington Post

mushmouth *n* A person who talks indistinctly and slurringly: *Say it again so I can hear it, mushmouth*

mushy **1** *adj* Sentimental; =CORNY **2** *adj* Amorous: *The kid got mushy*—Dashiell Hammett

music *See* BUBBLE-GUM MUSIC, ELEVATOR MUSIC, RAP SONG, SOUL

musical beds *n phr* Sexual promiscuity; =SLEEPING AROUND: *The soaps were conspicuous for their preoccupation with musical beds*—Entertainment Tonight (TV program) [modeled on the game of *musical chairs*, in which players circle a set of chairs and sit in any one available when the music stops]

muss or **muss up** *v* or *v phr* To disarrange; dishevel: *He mussed his hair all up/ Who mussed the bed?*

musta *n narcotics* Marijuana [perhaps an alteration of *moota*; see *mooter*]

mustard *See* NOT CUT THE MUSTARD

mutah *See* MOOTER

mutt *fr early 1900s* **1** *n* A dog, esp a hybrid; cur **2** *n* A stupid person; =KLUTZ, MUTTONHEAD: *A mutt? Yeah, he's that all right. Not too much brains*—Lawrence Sanders

muttonhead or **mutton-top** *n fr late 1700s* A stupid person

muzak or **Muzak** *n* Sweet and bland background music; uninteresting taped music; =ELEVATOR MUSIC: *where ideas normally melt down into verbal muzak*—Toronto Life [fr the trade name of a company that provides prerecorded music to be heard in offices, elevators, etc]

muzzler **1** *n* A petty criminal **2** *n* A police officer [probably fr *muzzle* "get, take," attested from the mid-19th century]

◁ **my ass** ▷ *interj* An exclamation of strong denial, disbelief, defiance, etc; =IN A PIG'S ASS: *You're getting this job my ass/ My ass I'll pay you that much* [a dysphemism for *my eye*]

my boy *See* THAT'S MY BOY

my eye *interj fr late 1700s* =MY ASS, IN A PIG'S ASS [in the early and obsolete meaning "nonsense," perhaps fr a Joe Miller joke in which a Latin nonsense phrase *O mihi, beate Martine* ("O, to me, blessed Martin") is pronounced as *all my eye and Betty Martin*]

mystery *n restaurant fr late 1800s* Hash

mystery meat *n phr students* Meat not readily identifiable, esp as served in a student dining hall, fraternity house, etc ● Sausages were called **mysteries** in the middle 1800s

N

nab **1** ***v*** *fr late 1600s British* To catch; seize; arrest; =COLLAR: *The officers nabbed him around the corner* **2** ***n*** (also **nabs**) *street gang* A police officer or detective • The sense is recorded in British criminal slang of the early 1800s [fr dialect *nap* as in *kidnap*, perhaps related to Swedish *nappa* "catch" or Danish *nappe* "pull"; probably related to *nip*]

nabe **1** ***n*** A neighborhood: *The nabe is a honey, architecturally*—Village Voice **2** ***n*** A neighborhood movie theater: *The current films... eventually make their way to the nabes*—AD Copleman

nag ***n*** *fr 1400s* A horse, esp an old and worn-out racehorse: *to make dough on the nags*—New York Daily News

nail **1** ***v*** *fr middle 1700s* To catch; seize; =NAB: *the feared and famous Batman and Robin who'd nailed him*—New York **2** ***v*** To detect and expose: *She nailed them with her last question* **3** ***n*** *narcotics* A hypodermic needle ◁**4**▷ ***v*** To do the sex act to someone; =FUCK: *the publishing cupcake in the Florsheims who nailed you on the couch and then fired you*—Richard Grossbach

See HARD AS NAILS, HIT THE NAIL ON THE HEAD

nail something **down** **1** ***v phr*** To make securely final; =CINCH: *They nailed down the arrangement and had a drink* **2** ***v phr*** To know thoroughly: *At least I've got Columbus Circle nailed down*—New York

nail someone or something **to the cross** (or **the wall**) ***v phr*** To punish severely and publicly; make an example of; crucify: *We are going to nail them to the cross*—Time

naked ***See*** BUCK NAKED

naked as a jaybird ***adj phr*** Entirely unclothed; =BARE-ASS

name **1** ***n*** A very important person, esp in entertainment; =HEADLINER: *He's a name in the carpet business* **2** ***modifier*** Being well-known or prestigious: *a name band/ name brand*

See BIG NAME, WHAT'S-HIS-NAME, YOU NAME IT

name-calling ***n*** The assigning of malicious designations in politics, debate, etc; character assassination; vilification: *They soon sank to name-calling*

someone's **name is mud** ***sentence*** *fr early 1800s British* One is in trouble; one is doomed: *If they catch him his name is mud* [fr earlier British dialect *mud* "fool"]

the **name of the game** **1** ***n phr*** What matters most; the essence: *In business, the name of the game is the bottom line*—Philadelphia **2** ***n phr*** The inevitable; the way things are: *Lying in politics? Hell, that's just the name of the game*

nance or **nancy** or **Nancy** *fr late 1800s* **1** ***n*** A male homosexual who takes the passive role **2** ***n*** An effeminate man: *Where you need desperately a man of iron, you often get a nance*—Philip Wylie **3** ***modifier:*** *with his talk of nancy poets, his anti-intellectualism*—Esquire

nanny ***See*** GET someone's GOAT

nappy ***adj*** *black* Kinky-haired

narc or **narco** **1** ***n*** *narcotics* A narcotics agent or police officer: *another drug-scare hoax promulgated by the "narcs"*—New York Times **2** ***mod-***

ifier: down to the narco police —Esquire

nark **1** *n fr middle 1800s British* A police informer; =STOOL PIGEON **2** *v* (also **narc**): *felt the Fraynes and their youngsters had narced on them* —New York Times **3** *n* =KIBITZER, BUTTINSKY **4** *n gambling* A decoy; =SHILL: *little bookmakers, and their narks*—Fortune [fr Romany *nak* "nose"]

nash *See* NOSH

nasty **1** *n* Something unpleasant, repulsive, etc: *pathos, poverty, and other real-life nasties*—Village Voice **2** *adj black* Good; stylish; admirable

natch *fr jive talk* **1** *adv* Naturally; certainly: *The two men, natch, are soul buddies*—Judith Crist **2** *affirmation* Of course; right: *Do I like it? Natch, what else?*

native *See* GO NATIVE

natural **1** *n crapshooting* A first throw of the dice that yields seven or eleven **2** *n* Something or someone that is obviously and perfectly fitting; just the thing: *A novel which looks like a natural for Lassie*—New York Times **3** *n black fr 1960s* =AFRO

natural-born *adj black fr 1930s* Total; absolute; innate: *The man's a natural-born spazz*

nature's call *n phr* The need to use the toilet, esp when urgent: *He's only responding to nature's call*

neat **1** *adj esp teenagers fr 1920s* Excellent; wonderful **2** *adj* Without water or another mixer; =STRAIGHT-UP • Used to describe spirits: *I'll take my Scotch neat, please*

neb *n* An inconsiderable person; =NEBBISH, WIMP: *poor little nebs like Julian*—Budd Schulberg

nebbie *See* NIMBY

nebbish *n* A person without charm, interesting qualities, talent, etc; =WIMP: *Don't be a nebbish*—WT Tyler [fr Yiddish fr Czech *neboky*]

nebbishy *adj* Having the character of a nebbish: *plays a nebbishy student* —People Weekly

the **necessary** *See* the NEEDFUL

neck *v fr early 1900s* To kiss, embrace, and caress; dally amorously; =MAKE OUT, SMOOCH: *At least you'd want to neck me*—Philip Wylie/ *You "spooned," then you "petted," after that you "necked"*—E Eldridge

See CATCH IT IN THE NECK, DEAD FROM THE NECK UP, GET OFF someone's BACK, GIVE someone A PAIN, LEATHERNECK, NO-NECK, a PAIN IN THE ASS, REDNECK, ROUGHNECK, RUBBERNECK, STICK one's NECK OUT

necked *See* RED-NECKED

necking *n fr 1920s* The pleasures and procedures of those who engage in kissing, embracing, and caressing: *pupils... resort to necking*—HL Mencken

necktie party (or **social** or **sociable**) *n phr fr late 1800s* A hanging or lynching

the **needful** (or **necessary**) *n phr fr middle 1700s* Money

needle **1** *v fr late 1800s British* To nag at someone; criticize regularly and smartingly; =HASSLE: *He keeps needling the guy about his looks* **2** *n: a really nasty needle* **3** *n* A hypodermic injection; =SHOT

the **needle** **1** *n phr* Injurious and provocative remarks; nagging criticism: *He's always ready with the needle* **2** *n phr* Narcotics injections; the narcotics habit: *The needle finally killed him*

See GIVE someone THE NEEDLE, OFF THE NEEDLE

needle candy *n phr narcotics* Any narcotic taken by injection: *Holmes has need of greater stimulants than needle candy*—WF Miksch

needle park *n phr* A public place where addicts regularly gather to deal in drugs and to take injections; =SHOOTING GALLERY

needles *See* RAIN CATS AND DOGS

need someone or something **like a hole in the head** *v phr* To have emphatically no need whatsoever for: *I needed more work like a hole in the head* [fr Yiddish *loch in kop* "hole in head"]

Nellie or **Nelly** **1** *adj homosexuals fr 1940s* Homosexual; effeminate; =GAY, SWISH: *Well, his backstroke is a little Nellie*—Armistead Maupin **2** *adj* Overfastidious; finicky; schoolmarmish: *"As follow" is Nellie usage* —Red Smith

See NERVOUS NELLIE, NICE NELLY

nemmie or **nemish** *See* NIMBY

neo-con *adj* Neo-conservative: *the neo-con idol, George Orwell*—Village Voice

nerd or **nurd** *n teenagers fr hot rodders & surfers* A tedious, contemptible person; =DORK, DWEEB, JERK [perhaps fr earlier *nert* fr *nerts* fr *nuts*]

nerdmobile *n teenagers* A large ostentatious car

nerdpack *n teenagers* A plastic shield worn to keep ink off shirt pockets

nerdy *adj teenagers* Characteristic of a nerd: *Above all, stay away from anything nerdy*—Philadelphia

nerf *v hot rodders* To bump a car out of one's way

nerts or **nertz** *See* NUTS

nerty *See* NUTTY

nerve 1 *n fr middle 1800s British students* Audacity; =CHUTZPA **2** *n* Courage; =GUTS

See GET ON someone's NERVES, HAVE A NERVE

◁ **nervous as a dog shitting razorblades**▷ (or **as a cat on a hot tin roof**) *adj phr* Very nervous; =JUMPY

nervous Nellie *n phr fr late 1930s* A timid or cautious person; a worrier: *a nervous Nellie a bit like Jeanne Dixon*—Village Voice [perhaps fr *Nervous Nellie*, the nickname of Frank B Kellogg, secretary of state 1925–29, who negotiated the Kellogg-Briand differences]

nervy 1 *adj* Brave; =GUTSY **2** *adj* Brash; audacious

nest *See* FEATHER one's NEST

nester *See* EMPTY NESTER

network *v* To solicit opinion and aid from associates with common interests: *I'm networking this question*—CoEvolution Quarterly

See OLD BOY NETWORK

networking *n* The formation of an association of mutual interest: *Building friends and contacts is what everybody is referring to as networking these days*—New York Daily News

never follow a dog act *sentence fr show business* Be very careful about whom you are to be immediately compared with • Often a rueful comment after one has been outshone

never mind *See* MAKE NO NEVER MIND

new *See* WHAT ELSE IS NEW

new ball game *See* A WHOLE NEW BALL GAME

new boy *n phr* A novice; beginner: *Not a bad start for a new boy*—Time [fr the British term for a beginning school student]

Newfie *n* A Newfoundlander

new kid on the block *n phr* Any newcomer or recent arrival: *The Japanese are the new kid on the block in the personal computer field*

news *See* BAD NEWS

newsie or **newsey** *n* A newspaper seller: *Beno, a hophead newsie*—Dashiell Hammett

newy or **newey** or **newie** *n* Something new; a novelty

New York kiss-off *See* KISS-OFF

next off *adv phr* Next; at that point: *Next off, Hutch give a yell*—James M Cain

NG or **ng** (pronounced as separate letters) *adj* No good: *She is NG*—A Lomax

nibs *See* HIS NIBS, TOUGH SHIT

nice *See* MAKE NICE

nice cop tough cop *See* GOOD COP BAD COP

Nice Guy *See* MISTER NICE GUY

nice Nelly 1 *n phr* A prude; =BLUENOSE **2** *adj: My editors are ... being more rabidly nice Nelly than usual*—G Dixon

nice work if you can get it *sentence fr 1930s* That would be a very pleasant thing to do; wouldn't that be fun? • An admiring comment made when one sees something easy, pleasant, attractive, etc, used esp with sexual overtones

nicey-nice or **nicey-nicey 1** *adj* Affectedly amiable and wholesome: *You flip the book over and you see all nicey, nicey things*—Bobby Seale **2** *adj* Effeminate; overly fastidious

nick 1 *v fr early 1800s British* To rob or steal • Much more common in British than US use: *The bank is gonna be nicked*—Dashiell Hammett **2** *v* To exact something, esp by force or threat: *I think you can nick her for one fifty if you get tough*—James M Cain **3** *v* To withhold pay

nickel 1 *n underworld* A five-year prison sentence **2** *n narcotics* =NICKEL BAG

See BIG NICKEL, DON'T TAKE ANY WOODEN NICKELS, PLUGGED NICKEL

nickel and dime 1 *v phr* To drain in small increments; nibble away at:

He said the grizzly habitat was being nickeled-and-dimed out of existence —New York Times **2** *v phr* To quibble; niggle; bring up all sorts of trivia: *is being nickeled-and-dimed... nibbled to death by ducks*—Washington Post

nickel bag *n phr narcotics* A five-dollar packet of narcotics

nickel defense *n phr football* A defensive formation in which a fifth defensive back is added, to cover an almost certain pass receiver

nickels and dimes *n phr* Very small amounts of money; =PEANUTS: *We can get the improved roads for nickels and dimes*

nifty **1** *adj fr middle 1800s* Smart; stylish; =NEAT, SLICK: *a nifty way to upstage the president*—Wall Street Journal **2** *n: his six blonde nifties* —Jerome Weidman **3** *adv: You did that real nifty* [origin unknown; called by Bret Harte "Short for *magnificat*"; Eric Partridge thought it might be fr *magnificent*; perhaps fr *snifty* "proud, high-toned"]

◀ **nigger** ▶ **1** *n fr early 1800s* A black person **2** *modifier: a nice nigger lady*
See BAD NIGGER

◀ **nigger rich** ▶ *adj phr* Having much money, esp suddenly; =FLUSH: *I'm either nigger rich or stone poor* —George V Higgins

◀ **niggra** or **nigra** ▶ *n* =NIGGER

night *See* SATURDAY NIGHT SPECIAL

nightcap **1** *n* A drink taken just before going to bed or the last drink of the evening, esp an alcoholic drink: *Let's stop at Joe's for a nightcap* **2** *n baseball* The second game of a doubleheader

nightie *n* A nightgown: *Aphrodite in her nightie, Oh my God what a sightie*—Howard Moss

night people (or **fighters**) *n phr* People who work at night or prefer to be up late at night: *I happen to be "night people" and I'm always up late* —Xaviera Hollander

night person *n phr* One of the night people: *She's a night person, never gets up before the afternoon*

-nik *suffix used to form nouns* A person involved in, described by, or doing what is indicated: *beatnik/ computernik/ peacenik/ no-goodnik* [fr Yiddish fr Russian and other Slavic languages]

nimby *n* (also **nimbie** or **nebbie** or **nemmie** or **nemish**) *narcotics* Nembutal (a trade name) or any barbiturate

nine-days' wonder *n phr fr 1500s* A marvel of rather short duration; =FLASH IN THE PAN [the notion of a wonder lasting nine days appears in Chaucer's *Troilus and Criseyde* of the late 14th century]

nine-hundred-pound gorilla *See* SIX-HUNDRED-POUND GORILLA

the **nines** *See* DRESSED TO THE TEETH

nineteen *n lunch counter* A banana split

the **nineteenth hole** *n phr golf* A drink or a spell of drinking after finishing a golf game

nine-to-five **1** *adj* Occupying the time period of a regular, salaried, probably dull office job: *a nine-to-five drag of a job* **2** *v* To be regularly employed, esp in an office job: *even when he was nine-to-fiving*—R Woodley

ninety-day wonder *armed forces fr WW1* **1** *n phr* An Army or Navy officer commissioned after a three-month course at an officer candidate school **2** *n phr* Any very youthful officer **3** *n phr* A reserve officer put on active status after three months of training **4** *n phr* Any person doing a job with minimal training • Usu used sarcastically: *They sent another ninety-day wonder to run the department* [based on *nine-days' wonder*]

nine yards *See* the WHOLE NINE YARDS

◀ **Nip** ▶ **1** *n esp WW2* A Japanese or person of Japanese ancestry **2** *adj: a Nip waitress* [fr *Nippon* "Japan"]

nip and tuck *fr early 1800s* **1** *adj phr* Equally likely to win or lose; even; neck and neck: *Near the finish they're nip and tuck* **2** *adj phr* Of equal probability; equally likely: *It's nip and tuck whether I'll get there in time or not* [earlier versions included *rip and tuck*, *nip and chuck* and *nip and tack*, making the original semantics somewhat difficult to assess; the term might be from sailing or from sewing and tailoring]

nipper *n fr middle 1800s British* A small boy; lad: *warning that America's nippers are turning into* *microchip golem*—Washington Post [perhaps because he *nips* "moves quickly"]

nit *n* Nothing; =ZILCH: *If you're wondering about their homosexual records, it's nit*—Lawrence Sanders [fr Yiddish or perhaps German dialect]

nit-picking **1** *n* The act and pleasure of one who quibbles over trivia **2** *adj: a highly nit-picking attitude* [from the very slow and attentive work of a person or a simian picking tiny *nits* "insect eggs" out of hair or fur]

nitro (NĪ troh) **1** *n* Nitroglycerin; =SOUP **2** *n hot rodders* Nitromethane, a fuel additive for cars

the **nitty gritty** or **the nitty** **1** *n phr fr 1960s black* The most basic elements, esp when unwelcome or unpleasant; harsh realities: *from what they call the nitty gritty and the grass roots*—Bobby Seale **2** *adj phr: a lot of nitty-gritty campaigning as well*—Newsweek **3** *n phr* Practical details: *I'll go over the broad outlines of the program and then Leslie will fill you in on the nitty-gritties* [fr the repellent association of *nits* "the eggs of hair lice, young hair lice" and *grit* "abrasive granules"]

nitwit *n fr 1920s* A stupid person; fool; =BOOB [apparently the equivalent of *louse-brain*, fr the sense of *nits* meaning "insect eggs"]

nix *fr late 1700s British* **1** *negation* No: *I asked her for one and she said nix* **2** *n* Nothing: *wasn't taking her out here in the park for nix*—James T Farrell **3** *n* A refusal; veto: *if the Petrillo nix stands*—Variety **4** *v* To veto; reject: *had been considering marriage but have apparently nixed the idea*—Washington Post [fr German *nichts* "nothing"]

no-account or **no-count** **1** *adj fr middle 1800s* Worthless; untrustworthy; incorrigible: *I'm a lazy no-account bum* **2** *n: A no-count that never did a right thing in his life*

no bargain *n phr* A person or thing that is not especially desirable nor good: *Well, he's OK, but no bargain*

nobby or **knobby** *adj fr early 1800s British* Stylish; fashionable; smart: *In 1903 Larkin picked up a nobby one-cylinder Winton*—New Yorker

no better than she ought to be *adj phr* Sexually promiscuous; loose

no big deal *n phr* Nothing important; no problem: *What she did is no big deal/ Getting a passport's no big deal*

no biggie *n phr teenagers & narcotics* =NO BIG DEAL

a **nobody** *n* A person lacking fame, status, importance, etc; an uninteresting person; =NEBBISH

nobody home *sentence* This person is crazy, stupid, or feeble-minded; =OUT TO LUNCH

◁ **nobody loves a wise-ass** ▷ *sentence* What you just said is very offensive; you are too smart and acid for your own good: *I thought it was a pretty good pun, but she replied "Nobody loves a wise-ass, Joey"*

no bones *See* MAKE NO BONES ABOUT

no can do *sentence* I am unable or unwilling to do that • Popularized in the 1940s by a song having the phrase as a title: *On that schedule? No can do* [a phrase in pidgin English probably adopted and disseminated by seamen]

no-count *See* NO-ACCOUNT

nod *v narcotics* To be intoxicated with narcotics to a very drowsy or stuporous state: *with slews of rich kids nodding in the Scarsdale woods*—New York

a **nod** *n phr narcotics fr 1930s* A stuporous state following an injection of narcotics: *He goes on a "nod," his head drooping, eyelids heavy*—J Mills

the **nod** *n phr* The affirmative decision; the signal of choosing or preference; =THUMBS UP: *Bold Ruler gets the nod over Gallant Man*—The Morning Telegraph/ *We didn't know who'd end up with the nod*
See GET THE NOD

noddle *See* NOODLE

no dice **1** *negation* No; absolutely not; =NO SOAP, NO WAY: *Nice, but no dice*—WT Tyler **2** *adj* Worthless; =CRUMMY: *a little no-dice paper called the Rome American*—Westbrook Pegler

no flies on someone *n phr fr late 1800s* Nothing impeding one's energy, awareness, soundness, up-to-dateness, etc: *No flies on Mom, she's getting a space-age hi-tech computer* [fr the image of an active cow, horse, etc, on which *flies* cannot settle]

no-frills *adj* Restricted to the essentials; without frivolous ornamentation or flourishes: *Imagine a no-frills warehouse crossed with an abattoir* —Toronto Life

noggin *n fr early 1800s British* The head: *the psychiatrist after diagnosing his noggin*—H Allen Smith [fr *noggin* "mug," itself used for "face"; compare *mug*]

no-go *adj* Not ready to proceed; inauspicious; blocked • Probably stimulated recently by astronauts' use: *This looks like a no-go situation*

no-good **1** *n* An unreliable or deplorable person; =BUM, NO-ACCOUNT: *A high-living no-good in a derby hat*—Hal Boyle **2** *adj: His father was a no-good drunk*—Life

no great shakes *adj phr fr middle 1800s* Mediocre; not outstanding; rather ineffective: *I'm no great shakes at serve-and-volley* [origin unknown; perhaps fr the *shaking* and rolling of dice]

no holds barred **1** *adv phr* Free and uninhibited; with no limits or reservations: *They went at it no holds barred* **2** *adj phr: The commission was to produce a "no-holds-barred" study*—Washington Post

noise *n* Empty talk; meaningless verbiage; bluster: *To hell with that noise/ That press release is plain noise*
See BIG NOISE

no kidding *adv phr* Really; factually • Often a question asked when one hears something astonishing or doubtful: *No kidding? They won?/ No kidding, he's a nice guy*

no-knock *adj* Providing for or including the police right of entry without a search warrant: *The cops demanded a no-knock statute*

nonbook *n* A printed effort lacking literary value and normal publishing validity, usu one blatantly ghost-written and/or put out for reasons of sensation, meretricious chic, or brazen and high-pitched publicity

noncom (NAHN kahm) *n armed forces* A noncommissioned officer

no-neck *n* A stupid, bigoted person; a brute: *the moral and intellectual sleaziness of the media and its no-necks in residence*—Village Voice [fr the thick, *neckless* aspect of very muscular men, gorillas, etc]

nonevent **1** *n* An apparent event staged or produced for or by the media **2** *n* Something invalid; something that in effect did not happen: *The new rules are "a nonevent"* —Newsweek

no never mind *See* MAKE NO NEVER MIND

a **no-no** *n phr* Something forbidden; something very inadvisable: *The company says mustaches are a no-no* —Charlotte Observer

nonstarter *n* A failure; a total incompetent; =ALSO-RAN, LOSER: *Compromises... should be considered "non-starters"*—New Yorker

noodge *See* NUDGE

noodle[1] **1** *n fr early 1900s* The head; the mind: *Most of the fellows running television today are sick in the noodle*—Philip Hamburger **2** *v* (also **noodle around**) To think, esp in a free and discursive way; indulge in mental play: *as many drafts and as much noodling as I wanted to*—Avery Corman **3** *v musicians* To play idly at an instrument; improvise lazily: *Members of an avian orchestra are already softly noodling*—WH Auden **4** *v* To play; toy: *noodling nervously with a glass of water* —Aquarian [fr earlier *noddle* "head," probably influenced by *noodle*, the food; senses of "play" perhaps derived fr "head" to "thought" to "idle thought and idle play" influenced by *doodle*]
See OFF one's NUT

noodle[2] *n fr middle 1700s British* A stupid person; fool; simpleton • Still predominantly British when not entirely outdated: *Something that noodle at Interior might reflect on* —Washington Post [origin unknown; perhaps fr *noodle* the food, fr German *nudel*, because of its limp and wormlike connotations]

noodlehead *n* A stupid person; =NOODLE

noodlework *n* Mental work or effort; thinking; studying

noogie *See* TOUGH SHIT

◁ **nookie** or **nookey** or **nooky** ▷ (NŏŏK ee) **1** *n fr late 1800s British* Sexual activity; the sex act; =ASS, COOZ: *if you can't give her a little nooky*—People Weekly **2** *n fr 1920s* A woman regarded as a sex partner; =ASS, CUNT [origin unknown; perhaps related to 17th-century *nugging* "the sex act," and perhaps to *nudge*]

nope ***negation*** No [fr *no* plus an intrusive stop resulting from the closure of the lips rather than the glottis as is normal]

no picnic ***n phr*** A difficult or trying experience; a hard time or task: *It's no picnic, teaching people to play* —Washington Post

noplaceville **1** ***adj*** Dull and tedious; =DEADSVILLE **2** ***n*** A small, unimportant town; =JERKWATER TOWN

no potatoes ***See*** ALL THAT MEAT AND NO POTATOES

nose ***n outdated underworld*** A police informer; =STOOL PIGEON

See BY A NOSE, HARDNOSE, HAVE A BUG UP one's ASS, HAVE someone's NOSE OPEN, KEEP one's NOSE CLEAN, NO SKIN OFF MY ASS, ON THE NOSE, PAY THROUGH THE NOSE, POKE one's NOSE INTO something, the POPE'S NOSE, PUT someone's NOSE OUT OF JOINT, WET-NOSE

nose around ***v phr*** *fr late 1800s* To show strong inquisitiveness; investigate, esp closely and slyly: *I'll nose around and see if I can find out why he did that*

the **nosebag** **1** ***n*** A meal; eating; =CHOW, the FEEDBAG **2** ***n*** *hoboes* Food handed out in a paper bag **3** ***n*** A dinner pail; lunch box

See PUT ON THE FEEDBAG

nose candy ***n phr*** *narcotics* A narcotic, esp cocaine, taken by sniffing: *a deck of nose candy for sale*—J Evans

nosed ***See*** HARD-NOSED

no see ***See*** LONG TIME NO SEE

nose job (or **bob**) ***n phr*** Plastic surgery to beautify a nose

nose someone **out** ***v phr*** To defeat by a small margin; barely won over: *He nosed out the leading candidate in Iowa*

nose out of joint ***See*** PUT someone's NOSE OUT OF JOINT

nosey ***adj*** *fr late 1800s* Inquisitive, esp overly so; prying: *We shall not be nosey*—WH Auden

nosh or **nash** (NAHSH) **1** ***v*** To have a snack; nibble **2** ***n:*** *He always liked a little nosh between meals* [fr Yiddish]

◁ **no shit**▷ ***adv phr*** Really; factually; =NO KIDDING • Often a question asked when one hears something astonishing or doubtful: *Uh... now, you mean? No shit*—Armistead Maupin

no-show **1** ***n*** *fr 1930s* A person who fails to keep an appointment, use a reserved seat, etc: *The airline figures about 20 percent no-shows* **2** ***adj*** Designating a nonexistent worker or job, usu on the public payroll: *They promised to eliminate all the no-show state jobs*

◁ **no skin off my ass**▷ (or **butt** or **nose**) ***adj phr*** Of no concern, esp damaging concern, to me; immaterial: *Whether you make it or not, it's no skin off my ass/ and if you fall on your face, no skin off my nose*—WT Tyler

no slouch ***adj phr*** *fr middle 1800s* Very able or competent; skilled • Most often followed by **at** something: *She's no slouch at finding good restaurants/ That guy? He's sure no slouch!* [fr British dialect *slouch* "awkward, lazy person"]

no soap ***negation*** *fr early 1900s* No; absolutely not; =NO DICE, NO WAY: *"No soap," said the assistant warden* —New York Times [origin unknown; Eric Partridge thought it was based on rhyming *no hope*]

no sweat ***n phr*** *fr WW2 armed forces* No problem or difficulty; an easy thing: *No sweat, though!*—New York Times

not all there **1** ***adj phr*** Stupid; feeble-minded; =DIM-WITTED **2** ***adj phr*** Crazy; eccentric; =NUTS, OUT TO LUNCH

not bat an eye ***v phr*** To not show surprise or reluctance: *"I'm leaving," she said. He didn't bat an eye.*

not be caught dead ***v phr*** To be defiantly set against; be extremely reluctantly found or seen: *I wouldn't be caught dead in that dress*

not by a long shot ***adv phr*** *fr middle 1800s* Not at all; emphatically not: *It's not my best, not by a long shot*

not carved in stone ***adj phr*** Not having ultimate and permanent authority; able to be altered: *It's a good policy, but it's not carved in stone* [fr the *carved stone* tablets of the Decalogue]

notch **1** ***v*** To score; achieve: *a pacy serve that's notched a few aces in its time*—Toronto Life ◁**2**▷ ***v*** To do the sex act • Use attributed to volleyball players: *Guys don't fuck, they notch*—Playboy [first sense fr use of the term in cricket, and influenced by the cowboy tradition of filing a *notch* in the handle of one's pistol for each man killed; for second sense see *notchery*]

See TOP-NOTCH

not count for spit *v phr* To be very insignificant; be trivial: *Aptitude for speaking... amusingly doesn't count for spit*—Fran Lebowitz [*spit* is probably a euphemism for *shit*]

not cricket *adv phr* Improper; dubious; unethical; unfair: *Something not quite cricket happened*—Washington Post [fr inadmissible actions in the game of *cricket*]

not cut the mustard **1** *v phr fr early 1900s* To be unable to achieve or finish something; not succeed: *groups who have special vested interests. And that's not gonna cut the mustard*—Philadelphia **2** *v phr* To be unimportant or unimposing: *While Clifford Irving may be a celebrity throughout the United States, he cuts little mustard here on Ibiza*—G Bocca [fr *cut* "achieve," and *the mustard* in the earlier slang sense of "the genuine thing, best thing," perhaps based on the fact that *mustard* is hot, keen, and sharp, all of which mean "excellent"]

not dry behind the ears *adj phr* (also **wet behind the ears** and **still wet behind the ears**) *fr early 1900s armed forces* Not mature; inexperienced; callow: *He's not dry behind the ears yet, but he's learning* [perhaps an allusion to the wet condition of newborns]

note *See* C-NOTE, MASH NOTE

◁ **not get** one's **balls** (or one's **self**) **in an uproar**▷ *v phr* To avoid becoming excited or upset; stay calm; = COOL IT ● Often an attempt to soothe someone: *Don't get your feminist balls in an uproar*—Lawrence Sanders

not give a damn *v phr* (Variations: **a dang** or **a darn** or **a dern** or **a durn** or **diddly-damn** or **diddly-shit** or ◀**flying fuck**▶ or ◀**fuck**▶ or **hill of beans** or **hoot** or ◁**rat's ass**▷ or ◁**shit** ▷ or **squat** may replace **a damn**) To be indifferent to or contemptuous of; not care one whit: *I don't give a damn what they do to me/ Nobody gave a flying fuck who their influences were*—Aquarian/ *When do celebrities give a hoot about people who interview them?*—Philadelphia/ *We all busted up because George didn't give a rat's ass*—William Kennedy/ *Me, I don't give a shit, high road, low road, I go either way*—WT Tyler

◀ **not give a fuck for nothing**▶ *v phr* To be absolutely indifferent and unafraid

not give spit *v phr* To be indifferent; not care; = NOT GIVE A DAMN: *I wouldn't give spit for his new concept* [a euphemism for *shit*]

not give someone **the time of day** *v phr* Not do the slightest favor for; not greet or speak to; have contempt for: *Like him? I wouldn't give that bastard the time of day*

not have a clue *v phr fr 1940s British armed forces* To be uninformed or ignorant about something: *"You know who I was?" "Haven't got a clue"*—WT Tyler

not have all one's **switches on** *v phr* To be retarded or demented; be mentally subnormal ● Used as a jocular insult rather than a clinical judgment: *The movietalker... doesn't have all his switches on*—Washington Post

not have any *v phr* To refuse to accept; reject; ignore: *Home buyers weren't having any and more than a few developers went belly-up*—Apartment Life

◁ **not have a pot** (or **without a pot**) **to piss in**▷ *fr late 1800s* *v phr* To be very poor and deprived; be penniless: *My family didn't have a pot to piss in, but we were proud as devils/ entering their middle years without a pot to piss in*—Ed McBain

not have a prayer *See* HAVE A PRAYER

not have brain one *v phr* To be very stupid

not have brains enough to come in out of the rain (or **to walk and chew gum at the same time**) *v phr* To be lacking the most elementary intelligence

'nother *See* A WHOLE 'NOTHER THING

nothing *adj* Inane; lacking charm, talent, interest, etc; worthless: *a nothing guy/ That was a real nothing experience*

See DANCE ON AIR, DO someone NOTHING, KNOW FROM NOTHING

a **nothing** ***n phr*** Someone or something that lacks all talent, charm, qualities, etc; =NEBBISH: *This show's a total nothing*

nothing doing **1** ***negation*** No; absolutely not; =NIX, NO WAY: *Buy that piece of crap? Nothing doing* **2** ***n phr*** A lack of activity; stasis: *Nothing doing on the job front*

nothing flat ***See*** IN NOTHING FLAT

not just whistling Dixie ***See*** WHISTLING DIXIE

◁**not know** one's **ass from** one's **elbow** (or **from a hole in the ground**)▷ ***v phr*** *fr early 1900s* To be very ignorant; be hopelessly ill-informed; be stupid; =KNOW FROM NOTHING: *The President doesn't know his ass from his elbow when it comes to Central America/ Well, he obviously didn't know his ass from a hole in the ground*—Village Voice

not know beans ***v phr*** (Variations: **diddly** or **diddley** or **diddly-damn** or **diddly-poo** or **diddly-poop** or **diddly-shit** or **diddly-squat** or **diddly-squirt** or **diddly-whoop** or **shit** or **squat** or **zilch** or **zip** may replace **beans**) *fr late 1800s* To be very ignorant; not know even the fundamentals • In each case the positive and negative idiom have the same meaning: *You don't know beans, do you?*—Russell Baker/ *may have been England's greatest mathematical puzzle inventor, but he knew beans about spiders and flies*—Games [entry form fr earlier *know how many beans make five* fr an old joke where the answer to "How many blue beans make five white beans?" is "Five, if you peel them"]

not know someone **from Adam** ***v phr*** To be entirely unacquainted with or uncognizant of: *We're bigger than 90 percent of the companies on the Big Board, but nobody knows us from Adam*—Fortune

not know from nothing ***See*** KNOW FROM NOTHING

◁**not know shit from Shinola**▷ ***v phr*** =NOT KNOW one's ASS FROM one's ELBOW [fr *Shinola* (a trade name), a brand of shoe polish; used partly for a suggestion of brown color, mainly for alliteration]

not lay a glove (or **finger** or **hand**) **on** someone ***v phr*** To leave unscathed; fail to hurt: *They haven't laid a glove on him*—Philadelphia Inquirer

no tomorrow ***See*** LIKE IT'S GOING OUT OF STYLE

not play with a full deck ***See*** PLAY WITH A FULL DECK

not so hot ***adj phr*** Not very good; mediocre; poor: *I didn't flunk but my record isn't so hot*—P Marks

not tonight, Josephine ***sentence*** *fr late 1800s* We will not copulate tonight, my dear • Used or said to be used by men refusing sexual favors to women [attributed to Napoleon Bonaparte as addressed to the Empress Josephine]

not touch someone or something **with a ten-foot pole** ***v phr*** To be loath to have anything to do with; be suspicious or apprehensive; reject: *If I were you I wouldn't touch that proposition with a ten-foot pole* [semantically akin to the proverb advising us to use a long spoon when we eat with the devil]

not to worry ***sentence*** *fr 1950s British* There is nothing to worry about • Still chiefly British: *Not to worry, I bought plenty of food for everybody*

not worth a bucket of warm spit ***See*** WORTH A BUCKET OF WARM SPIT

not worth a plugged nickel ***adj phr*** *fr early 1900s* Valueless: *His word isn't worth a plugged nickel* [a *plugged* coin was counterfeit, or had an insertion of inferior metal]

now ***adj*** Up-to-date; very much au courant; thoroughly modern: *tripping out on now words*—Newsweek/ *the Right On, Now Generation*—Gail Sheehy

no way or **no way, Jose** **1** ***negation*** No; absolutely not; =NO DICE: *When I asked for more he said no way/ No good. No go. No way, Jose*—Village Voice/ *No way, Jose*—Washington Post **2** ***adv phr*** Never; under no circumstances: *No way will I resign, you'll have to fire me*

See THERE'S NO WAY

no way to run a railroad ***See*** a HELL OF A WAY TO RUN A RAILROAD

nowhere or **nowheresville** ***adj*** Inferior; tedious; drab: *If you're not with it, you're nowhere*—L Lipton/ *rows of folding chairs, nowheresville decor*—New York

See the MIDDLE OF NOWHERE

no-win *adj* Impossible to win; hopeless • Most often used in the phrase **no-win situation**: *Furious Volley in a No-Win Match*—Time

nudge (NōōJ, NōōD jə) (also **noodge** or **nudjh** or **nudgy** or **nudzh**) **1** *n* A chronic nagger, kibitzer, or complainer: *not as an assassin, but as a nudge and a nerd*—Time **2** *v: Usually he comes up to nudgy me while I'm writing*—Bernard Malamud/ *and oh nudjh, could he nudjh!*—Philip Roth [fr Yiddish fr Slavic "fret, dully ache"; perhaps influenced by English *nudge*]

nudge elbows *See* RUB ELBOWS

nudging *See* MOTHERFUCKING

nudnik (NōōD nihk) *n* An annoying person; pest; nuisance; =NUDGE: *remains an unreconstructed nudnik throughout*—Wilfred Sheed [fr Yiddish fr Slavic; see *nudge*]

nuke **1** *n* A nuclear device or facility; nuclear weapon; nuclear power plant **2** *v* To destroy with a nuclear weapon or weapons: *The global village has been nuked*—Time **3** *v* To destroy; =CLOBBER: *That English test really nuked me*—Time **4** *v* To cook or heat in a microwave oven

See ANTINUKE

number **1** *n fr 1920s* A person, esp one considered to be clever and resourceful or attractive; =ARTICLE, HOT NUMBER • Always preceded by an adjective or by the locution "quite a": *some dizzy broad that must have been a snappy number*—Jerome Weidman/ *bored-looking number*—J Evans/ *Dressed up he's quite a number* **2** *n* A piece of merchandise; =ARTICLE: *I found a number I liked pretty well*—James M Cain/ *This number here's going like hotcakes* **3** *n* One's profession, avocation, favorite activity, etc; =GAME: *I don't know what his number can be* **4** *n fr show business* A theatrical act or routine; =SHTICK: *He does that number with the tablecloth* **5** *n* A tactic or trick; =ACT: *When he's pulling one of his numbers, he knows what he's doing*—H Hertzberg **6** *n homosexuals* A casual homosexual partner; =TRICK **7** *n students & narcotics* A marijuana cigarette: *smoked a couple of numbers in the room*—Richard Merkin [merchandise sense fr the model *number* that most retail items have]

See BACK NUMBER, BY THE NUMBERS, DO A NUMBER ON, DO one's NUMBER, HAVE someone's NUMBER, HOT NUMBER

a **number** *n phr* Something noted, esp a sexual relationship; =an ITEM: *Hey, we're a number....We have a non-casual relationship now*—Leslie Hollander

number cruncher **1** *n phr* A computer or mechanical calculator **2** *n phr* (also **numbers cruncher**) One who regularly processes or works with figures, statistics, records, etc, esp with a computer: *promote clerks rather than bring in fancy number-crunchers from outside*—Village Voice **3** *adj* Requiring mathematics, statistics, etc: *number-cruncher course*

number-crunching **1** *n computer* Using, programming, etc, a computer **2** *n teenagers* Mathematics, statistics, computer science, etc, esp in high school courses **3** *n* Calculating; doing arithmetic; figuring: *played chartered accountant for a few sessions of number crunching*—Toronto Life

Number One or **number one** **1** *n phr fr early 1800s* One's own self, esp as competitive with others; =NUMERO UNO: *Always look out for Number One, he says* **2** *n phr* The chief, leader; =BOSS, HONCHO: *Who's Number One around here?* **3** *n phr* Urination **4** *v: The little kid had to number one real bad*

number-one boy **1** *n phr* The chief; =BOSS, HONCHO **2** *n phr* The chief lieutenant or assistant of a leader or ruler: *He's the president's number-one boy*

numbers *n sports* A player's averages, statistics, etc; =STATS: *He had 40 homers and a .325 average, the best numbers on the team*

See BY THE NUMBERS

number two **1** *n phr* Defecation **2** *v: He ran off in the woods, having to number two*

◁**numb-nuts**▷ **1** *n* A despicable person; =JERK, LIMP-DICK: *You gotta get a better job, numb-nuts*—George V Higgins **2** *modifier: not the numbnuts chatter cornballs like Bob Hope or Yellowman peddle*—Village Voice

Numero Uno or **numero uno** **1** ***n phr*** One's own self, esp as the object of one's best efforts; =NUMBER ONE **2** ***n phr*** The chief; leader; =BOSS, HONCHO: *a clear understanding between the brothers about who is Numero Uno*—Toronto Life **3** ***n phr*** The most distinguished person in a field or endeavor: *now an also-ran... but for many years Numero Uno*—Toronto Life [fr Italian or Spanish]

See TAKE CARE OF NUMERO UNO

nurd ***See*** NERD

nut **1** ***n*** *fr middle 1800s British* The head **2** ***n*** *fr late 1800s* A crazy or eccentric person; maniac; =FLAKE, SCREWBALL: *It is forbidden to call any character a nut; you have to call him a screwball*—New Yorker/ *He was acting like some kind of nut* **3** ***n*** A very devoted enthusiast; =BUG, FREAK: *He's a nut about double crostics* **4** ***n*** *fr late 1800s carnival & hawkers* The investment needed for a business; capital and fixed expenses: *Our nut is high, but our variable expenses are practically nothing*—New York **5** ***n*** *underworld* Any illegal payoff to a police officer: *what they called "the nut," payoffs to the police*—M Arnold **6** ***n*** *underworld* A share in the graft collected by police officers ◁**7**▷ ***n*** A testicle; =BALL: *He said it griped his left nut* [insanity sense probably fr late-19th-century *off* one's *nut*, that is, head; fourth and following senses based on carnival and hawkers use "rent for a stand or concession," perhaps because the rent and graft payments are a "*nut to be cracked*" before the kernel or profits are realized]

See GRIPE one's ASS, OFF one's NUT, TOUGH NUT, a TOUGH NUT TO CRACK

-nut ***combining word*** A devotee or energetic practitioner of what is indicated; =FREAK: *when one football nut writes a book*—Arthur Daley/ *But he's not just a word nut*—Playboy

nutball (Variations: **bar** or **cake** or **case** may replace **ball**) **1** ***n*** A crazy or eccentric person; =NUT: *A lot of nutballs accost you at that corner/ The Protestants in Ireland also have their share of nutcakes*—Boston Globe/ *I'm not a nut case*—Xenia Field **2** ***adj:*** *murdered by nutball moneybags Harry K Thaw*—Newsweek

nut-crunching ***n*** The sapping or destruction of masculinity; figurative castration; =BALL-BUSTING: *playing a government investigator whose best defense is nut-crunching*—Village Voice

nut house ***n*** (Variations: **academy** or **box** or **college** or **factory** or **farm** or **foundry** or **hatch** may replace **house**) A mental hospital; insane asylum: *goes away to the nut house*—Jim Tully/ *exceptional privacy and independence even in a nut hatch*—Earl Thompson

nuts or **nerts** or **nertz** **1** ***adj*** *fr early 1900s* Crazy; very eccentric; =BUGHOUSE, MESHUGA: *Heir Rejected 400G, Is He Nuts?*—New York Daily News **2** ***interj*** *fr 1920s* An exclamation of disbelief, defiance, contempt, dismay, etc • **Nerts** is a 1920s euphemization: *General McAuliffe replied "Nuts!" to the Germans at Bastogne* ◁**3**▷ ***n*** The testicles; =BALLS, FAMILY JEWELS: *They want to get their nuts out of the sand*—Eldridge Cleaver

See BUST one's ASS, the CAT'S MEOW, GET one's NUTS, HOT ROCKS, NUMB-NUTS, TIGHT AS KELSEY'S NUTS

the **nuts** or **the nerts** or **the nertz** ***n phr*** *fr 1920s* The very best; =the GREATEST: *eulogizing anything... as "the nuts"*—English Journal [probably a shortening of *the cat's nuts*; see the *cat's meow*]

nuts about (or **over** or **on**) ***adj phr*** (Variations: **nutty** may replace **nuts**) *fr early 1800s British* Very enthusiastic about; devoted to; =CRAZY ABOUT: *I think I'm nuts about you*—S McNeil/ *I'd be simply nutty about the quadrangles at Oxford*—Sinclair Lewis [fr British slang *nutty* "piquant, fascinating," fr earlier sense "rich, tasty, desirable, like the kernel of a delicious nut," altered in slang to *nuts* and originally in the phrase *nuts upon*; the US form *nuts about* may be based on all this or on the notion *crazy about*, and probably on both]

nuts and bolts **1** ***n phr*** The fundamentals; the practical basics: *dealing with the nuts and bolts of negotiations*—Fortune **2** ***modifier:*** *Berger's nuts-and-bolts discussion of film-TV music*—Village Voice

nutso or **nutsy** *adj* Crazy; =NUTTY: *the nutso names of the current batch of new bands*—Village Voice/ *drove each other nutsy*—Village Voice

nutter *n* A crazy person; =NUT, NUTBALL: *the Zodiac killer or some nutter on the loose*—Rolling Stone

nuttiness *n* Craziness; insanity: *Booth's capacity for nuttiness*—Billy Rose

nutty *adj fr late 1800s* Crazy; very eccentric; =NUTS: *I was just about nutty*—Sinclair Lewis

nutty as a fruitcake *adj phr* Crazy as can be; extremely eccentric: *The old guy's nutty as a fruitcake*

nympho *n* A nymphomaniac: *no boozing broad, no nympho, no psycho, no bitch*—Pauline Kael

O

-o **1** ***suffix used to form adjectives*** Having the indicated characteristics: *berserko/ luxo/ neato/ sicko/ wrongo* **2** ***suffix used to form nouns:*** *foldo/ freako/ klutzo/ muso* • This formation is increasingly current [fr a humorous imitation of Spanish or Italian words, more probably Spanish because of the similar *el -o* pattern of coinage]

O ***n narcotics*** Opium

See FIVE-O

oak ***See*** OK

Oakley ***See*** ANNIE OAKLEY

oar ***See*** PUT one's OAR IN, ROW WITH ONE OAR

oater or **oateater** or **oat opera** ***n*** or ***n phr movie studio*** A cowboy movie; Western; =HORSE OPERA: *horse operas, also known as sagebrushers or oaters*—Bob Thomas/ *the deputy marshall in the oateater*—Paul Sann

OBE (pronounced as separate letters) ***adj Army*** Overcome by events

Obie[1] ***n*** An award given to a meritorious off-Broadway production [fr *off Broadway*]

Obie[2] ***n narcotics*** A narcotic combining four amphetamines: *The brother makes tea and they talk about Obies*—Gail Sheehy [fr *Obetrol* (a trade name), probably a portmanteau form of *obesity control*]

the **oblate spheroid** ***n phr*** A football

OD[1] (pronounced as separate letters) ***n Army*** Olive drab; olive drab cloth

OD[2] (pronounced as separate letters) **1** ***n narcotics & hospital*** An overdose of narcotics: *I guess he'd taken a light OD*—Claude Brown **2** ***v:*** *met Jesus one day when I was ODing on speed in my room*—Village Voice **3** ***v*** To overindulge in or on anything: *Viewers may have OD'd on athletics and turned to reruns*—Time

oddball **1** ***n*** An eccentric person; a strange one; =WEIRDO: *definitely an oddball*—Saul Bellow **2** ***adj:*** *sensible drug users and the odd-ball drug users*—Saturday Review **3** ***n*** A nonconformist; outsider; odd man out: *We were generally considered to be a family of hopeless oddballs*—San Francisco **4** ***adj:*** *He had some pretty oddball ideas*

ODs (pronounced OH DEEZ) ***n Army*** The former olive drab uniform of the US Army, or the trousers of that uniform

of (əV) ***v*** Have • Used for humorous or dialect effect: *I must of gone crazy*—Joyce Carol Oates

◁ **ofay** ▷ **1** ***n black*** A white person; =FAY, GRAY: *Let the ofays have Wall Street to themselves*—B Brown/ *a white boy, an ofay*—Louis Armstrong **2** ***adj:*** *ofay business men and planters*—Louis Armstrong [probably fr pig Latin for *foe*]

off **1** ***adj*** Not working properly; =OUT OF WHACK: *The carburetor's a little off* **2** ***adj*** Spoiled; not fresh: *The wine's off at this joint/ The milk's a bit off* **3** ***adj*** Canceled; not going to happen: *The deal's off* **4** ***adj*** Not working; not on duty: *The cook is off today* **5** ***v esp 1960s fr black*** To kill or destroy; =WASTE: *We'll off any pig who attacks us*—Bobby Seale ◁**6**▷ ***v black*** To do the sex act with or to; =SCREW: *When I off a nigger bitch, I close my eyes and concentrate real hard*—Eldridge Cleaver **7** ***prep*** Not using; no longer addicted to: *She's* *off H now/ I've been off the sauce for four years*

off artist *n phr* A thief

off at the knees *See* CUT oneself OFF AT THE KNEES

off base **1** *adj phr* Not appropriate; uncalled for: *Some of his questions were way off base* **2** *adj phr* Presumptuous; impudent; =OUT OF LINE: *When I asked for her number she said I was off base* **3** *adj phr* Incorrect; inaccurate: *These stats are a mile off base*

offbeat *adj* Unusual; unconventional; strange: *its offbeat ad seeking 10 Renaissance-type men*—Wall Street Journal

off someone's **case** *adv phr fr black* Not meddling with; not nagging or pressuring: *I said I wanted her off my case, quick*

See GET OFF someone's CASE

offer *See* MAKE AN OFFER one CAN'T REFUSE

office *n aviators* The cockpit of an airplane

See BOX OFFICE, FRONT OFFICE

off one's **nut** *adj phr* (Variations: **bird** or **chump** or **head** or **noodle** or **onion** or **rocker** may replace **nut**) *fr middle 1800s* Crazy; deluded; =MESHUGA, NUTS: *I've been as near off my noodle as a... sane man can get* —K Brush/ *I suppose he was off his rocker*—New York Daily News [all variants mean "head," except *bird* and *rocker*; *off one's rocker* may suggest the erratic motion of a chair or cradle with a *rocker* broken or missing]

off one's **plate** *adv phr* No longer a matter of one's responsibility and concern: *Congress would like to get the abortion issue off its plate* —National Public Radio

off-putting *adj* Distressing; unsettling; discomfiting: *an off-putting chip on the shoulder*—Esquire

off the bat *See* RIGHT OFF THE BAT

off the beam *adv phr* Distant from truth or accuracy; in error: *That idea is way off the beam* [fr the radio *beam* that guides aircraft to an airport or runway]

off the charts *adj phr* Too great to be measured; off the scale: *His popularity, high before, is now way off the charts*

off the cuff **1** *adv phr* Extemporaneously; without rehearsal: *I don't speak well off the cuff* **2** *adj: a good off-the-cuff talker*

off the deep end *See* GO OFF THE DEEP END, JUMP OFF THE DEEP END

off the hog *See* EAT HIGH ON THE HOG

off the hook *adj phr* Free of responsibility, blame, punishment, etc; =CLEAR: *Shagan gets Harry off the hook*—Pauline Kael

See LET someone OFF THE HOOK, RING OFF THE HOOK

off the needle *adj phr narcotics* No longer injecting or using narcotics; =CLEAN

off the pace *adv phr* Behind the leader or leaders: *The red car is about two laps off the pace*

off the record *adv phr* Confidential; not for publication or attribution: *The mayor would only speak off the record, and very cryptically at that*

off the top *adv phr* Before any deductions are made; =UP FRONT: *He demanded his percentage right off the top*

off the top of one's **head** *adv phr* Without thought or calculation; impromptu: *I can't give you the figure off the top of my head*

off the wagon *adj phr* Drinking liquor, after a period of abstinence: *the fall off the wagon*—AJ Liebling

See FALL OFF THE WAGON

off the wall **1** *adj phr* Unusual; outrageous; =ODDBALL, OFFBEAT: *his off-the-wall sense of humor*—J Landau **2** *adj phr* Crazy; very eccentric; =OFF one's NUT: *They're describing him as "off the wall"*—Arizona Republic [origin uncertain; perhaps fr the erratic angles at which balls bounce *off the wall* in various games, esp squash, handball, and racquetball; perhaps related to the hospital term *bounce off the walls*, referring to the behavior of a psychotic patient; perhaps fr both of these]

See BOUNCE OFF THE WALLS, PING OFF THE WALLS

offtish *See* OOFTISH

off one's **trolley** *adj phr fr early 1900s* Crazy; demented; =NUTS: *You're off your trolley*—Max Shulman [fr the helpless condition of a streetcar of which the *trolley*, a spring-loaded shaft with a wheel at the top to engage the electric wires, has come *off* the wires]

oh yeah ***interj*** An exclamation of defiance or disbelief; =IZZATSO: *I told her I'd make her a star, and she said, "Oh yeah?"*

oid **1** ***suffix used to form nouns*** Something resembling or imitating what is indicated: *flakoid/ fusionoid/ Grouchoid/ klutzoid* **2** ***suffix used to form adjectives*** Resembling or imitating what is indicated: *blitzoid/ cheesoid/ technoid/ zomboid* ● This suffix is increasingly current, probably because of the popularity of fantasy and science fiction, esp among teenagers [fr the scientific suffix *-oid*; fr Greek *-oeides*, ultimately fr *eidos* "image, form"]

oil **1** ***n*** Flattering and unctuous talk; =BALONEY, BUNK: *marinated in good old Hollywood oil*—John McCarten **2** ***n*** Money, esp money paid for bribery and acquired by graft **3** ***v:*** *We'll have to oil the mayor to get that permit*
See BANANA OIL, PALM OIL, STRIKE OIL

oiled ***adj*** Drunk: *choose your companions, and get properly oiled as well*—New York Times

◀ **oiler** ▶ ***n*** A Mexican; =GREASER

oil someone's **palm** ***See*** GREASE someone's PALM

oily ***adj*** Cunning and ingratiating; sly and unctuous

oink ◁**1**▷ ***n esp 1960s*** A police officer; =PIG **2** ***v*** To sound and behave like a pig: *and sends masculine outrage oinking into overdrive* —Newsweek [verb sense related to *male chauvinist pig*]

OK (also **ok** or **okay** or **oka** or **okeh** or **okey** or **oak** or **oke**) **1** ***affirmation*** Yes; I agree; I accept that; I will do that **2** ***adj*** Agreeable; =COPACETIC: *He made an OK decision* **3** ***adj*** Acceptable but not excellent; satisfactory: *The play's okay, but I still prefer the book* **4** ***adj*** Good; excellent: *He's an okay guy* **5** ***affirmation*** & ***question*** Is that all right?; is that understood?; =COPPISH: *I'm going now, okay?* **6** ***adv*** Right; that's understood, let's get on: *So I told you about that, okay, so the next thing was he jumped the fence* [origin uncertain and the subject of essay after essay; Allen Walker Read is the great authority, and has shown that the locution began as a bumpkin-imitating game among New York and Boston writers in the early 19th century, who used *OK* for "oll korrect"]

okey-doke ***affirmation*** & ***adj*** & ***question*** (also **hokey-dokey** or **okie doke** or **okey-dokey** or **okie-dokie** or **okle-dokle**) Yes, satisfactory, alright, etc; =OK: *Suppose I pick you up at seven? Okie doke*—Peter De Vries

Okie **1** ***n*** A migratory worker, esp one in the 1930s who had to leave home because of dust storms; =ARKY **2** ***n*** A native or resident of Oklahoma

-ola or **-olo** ***suffix used to form nouns*** An emphatic instance or humorous version of what is indicated: *buckola/ crapola/ schnozzola*

old **1** ***adj*** Familiar and despised; tired: *the same old alibis* **2** ***adj*** Familiar and cherished; dear ● Used without regard to age or gender: *Give my best to old Fred/ Hey, you old bastard, how you doing?* **3** ***adj*** Accursed; wretched; =DAMNED: *That old ulcer'll get you yet*
See ANY OLD

the **old army game** ***See*** the ARMY GAME

◁ **old bat** ▷ ***n phr*** An old woman, esp a repulsive, gossipy old shrew; =BAG

old boy ***See*** GOOD OLD BOY

old boy network or **old boys' system** ***n phr fr 1950s British*** A reciprocally supportive, exclusive, and influential group of men, esp those who were friends at some prestigious school or college; =IN GROUP: *an "old-girl" network to rival the much-ballyhooed "old-boy" network* —Washingtonian/ *It's an old boys' system.* [fr *old boy*, the British term for public school (that is, private school) alumni]

old buddy ***n phr esp Southern*** Good friend ● Used chiefly in amiable direct address: *Right, old buddy, I'm coming right over*

◁ **old cocker** (or **fart** or **gaffer**) ▷ ***n phr*** An old man; a superannuated man; =ALTER KOCKER, POOP: *a lot of old cockers out there who wanted to hear a ball game*—New York/ *There ought to be a great advantage to prove that any old fart can do it* —Time the **old college try** ***n phr*** One's utmost effort; =GIVE something one's BEST SHOT: *You give it the old college try*—Washingtonian [fr the early and innocent legends of college football]

older than God (or **than baseball**) ***adj phr*** Very, very old: *The famous poet is older than God, and quite nasty*

◁ **old goat**▷ **1** ***n*** Any disliked elderly person, esp a man **2** ***n*** =DIRTY OLD MAN

old hat ***adj phr*** *fr 1940s British* Out of style; old-fashioned: *Isn't "old hat" pretty old hat?/ Tubular stuff is now old hat*—RM Coates

the **old heave-ho** ***See*** the HEAVE-HO

oldie or **oldy** ***n*** An old thing or person, esp an old song or story: *Our pet oldie concerns the India rubber skin man*—Walter Winchell

See GOLDEN OLDIE

oldie but goodie ***See*** GOLDEN OLDIE

old lady **1** ***n phr*** One's wife; a wife: *Losin' his old lady is what crazied him* —Nelson Algren **2** ***n phr*** A girlfriend, mistress, woman living companion, etc: *He introduced the chick as his old lady* **3** ***n phr*** One's mother; a mother: *The little kid went to ask his old lady if he could come along*

old man **1** ***n phr*** One's husband; a husband: *She can't bear to see her old man lose his money*—J Cannon **2** ***n phr*** A boyfriend or lover: *Her old man was a bass guitar player in a rock group* **3** ***n phr*** One's father; a father: *My old man wasn't mean* —Calder Willingham **4** ***n phr*** A man who supports a mistress; =JOHN, SUGAR DADDY: *"Old Man," the name we used to have for a common-law husband*—Louis Armstrong **5** ***n phr*** *prostitutes* A pimp **6** ***n phr*** Old friend; =OLD BUDDY ● Used only in direct address

See DIRTY OLD MAN

the **old one-two** ***See*** ONE-TWO

old pro ***See*** PRO

Old Smoky (or **Sparky**) ***n phr*** *prison* The electric chair: *who otherwise would have ridden "Old Sparky"* —Publishers Weekly

old thing ***n phr*** *fr early 1900s British* Old friend; =OLD BUDDY: *in conversation address you as "Old thing"* —Robert Lynd

old-timey ***adj*** Old-fashioned, esp in a pleasant and nostalgic way: *dripping with old-timey decorations*—N Winters

old turkey ***n phr*** A trite old story, joke, song, etc; =CHESTNUT

old woman ***n phr*** =OLD LADY

olive ***See*** SWALLOW THE APPLE

-olo ***See*** -OLA

omelet ***See*** YOU CAN'T MAKE AN OMELET WITHOUT BREAKING EGGS

on **1** ***adj*** Aware; informed; alerted: *I saw he was on, and quit talking* —James M Cain **2** ***adj*** Not canceled; scheduled to happen: *It's on for tomorrow night* **3** ***adj*** Accepted and confirmed as a partner, competitive bettor, etc: *You want to go up there with us? You're on* **4** ***adj*** *fr show business* Performing; presenting a talk, appeal, etc, as if one were on stage: *Better review your points, since you're on next* **5** ***adj*** Excited, acting to get attention: *She's never relaxed, she's always on* **6** ***prep*** Paid for by; with the compliments of: *This was to be on him* —James M Cain **7** ***prep*** Taking; using; addicted to: *He had her on penicillin/ He was on acid and barbiturates at the time*

on a cloud **1** ***adj phr*** Very happy; euphoric; in a blissful transport: *Oh, world, I'm on a cloud today!* **2** ***adj phr*** Intoxicated with narcotics; =HIGH

on a dime ***See*** STOP ON A DIME

on a raft ***adv phr*** *lunch counter* On toast

on a roll **1** ***adj phr*** Having great success; enjoying a winning impetus: *You're on a roll, Mr President*—Philadelphia Daily News **2** ***adj phr*** (also **on a kick**) Doing something enthusiastically and constantly: *She was on a philosophy roll*—Rolling Stone [fr a crapshooting term meaning "very, very lucky; unbeatable with the dice"]

on a shingle ***See*** SHIT ON A SHINGLE

◁ **on** one's **ass**▷ (or **ear**) ***adv phr*** In or into a sad and helpless condition; supine; =DOWN FOR THE COUNT: *He lost three jobs, and now he's on his ass/ His hat store went kerflooie, and he's on his ear now*—James T Farrell

See FALL ON one's ASS, FLAT ON one's ASS, SIT ON one's ASS

on a tear (TAIR) *adj phr* Very angry, esp punitively so; =PISSED OFF: *Ronald Reagan is on a tear over leaks* —National Review

on someone's **back** **1** *adv phr* Persistently annoying or harassing; =ON someone's CASE: *The cops were on my back after that* **2** *adj phr* Heavily dependent on: *He was always sick and always on her back*

on someone's **case** *adv phr fr black* Paying close and esp meddling or punitive attention to: *Maybe the world isn't on my case. Maybe the problem is me*—Garrison Keillor [fr the black expression *sit on* someone's *case* "discuss and judge someone's problems, behavior, etc," based on a judicial analogy]

the **once-over** *n phr fr early 1900s* A look or glance of inspection; scrutiny; =the DOUBLE-O: *The first thing we went to buy after giving all the pavilions the once-over was tomatoes* —Art Buchwald

See GIVE someone or something THE ONCE-OVER

oncer (WUN Sə) **1** *n* A woman who is faithful to one man all her life; a one-man woman **2** *n* (also **oner**) A rare and unique person; someone or something esp excellent: *a "oncer," one of a kind*—New York Times/ *That was a great joke, a oner*

on cloud nine (or **cloud seven**) *adj phr* At the very pinnacle of bliss; euphoric; =ON A CLOUD: *She came back home and he's on cloud nine*

on someone's **coattails** *adv phr* Profiting from someone else's success, esp in a decisive election: *when all these rube politicians come riding in on Reagan's coattails*—WT Tyler

on deck **1** *adv phr baseball* Waiting to be the next batter, usu in a special circle marked for the purpose **2** *adj phr: the on-deck hitter* **3** *adj phr* Present and ready; on hand and prepared: *If you need anybody else, I'm on deck*

on someone's **dime** *adv phr* At someone's expense other than the speaker's: *Yeah, we can give it a try, but it's on your dime* [fr the *dime* needed to activate a pay telephone]

one *See* BIG ONE, FAST ONE, FOUR-AND-ONE, HANG ONE ON, HOT ONE, NUMBER-ONE BOY, QUICK ONE, SQUARE ONE

One *See* MURDER ONE, NUMBER ONE, TRACK ONE

one and only *n phr* One's beloved, fiancee, sweetheart, etc: *My one and only, what am I going to do if you turn me down*—George Gershwin

on one's **ear** *See* ON one's ASS

one-arm (or **one-armed**) **bandit** *n phr fr 1930s* A slot machine

on easy street *adv phr* In a condition of solvency, ease, and tranquility

one-bagger *n baseball* A one-base hit; single

on edge *See* EDGY

one-eyed monster *n phr* A television set; television; =the BOOB TUBE

one foot in the grave *See* HAVE ONE FOOT IN THE GRAVE

one for the book (or **books**) *n phr* Something remarkable; an amazing thing, case, etc: *That storm was really one for the book*

one for the road *n phr* A last drink of the evening, party, carouse, etc

one hell of a *See* A HELL OF A

one-horse *adj fr middle 1800s* Insignificant; inferior: *It's a one-horse operation he's got there*

one-liner *n* A quick joke or quip; a funny observation; =WISECRACK: *exchanges one-liners with Lianna in the laundry room*—Toronto Life

one-man show *n phr* An enterprise, business, etc, controlled by one person: *The company had previously been run as a "one-man show"*—Fortune

one-night stand **1** *n phr* A performing engagement for one evening only: *Not a bad gig, but just a one-night stand* **2** *n phr* A casual sex act; a brief sexual encounter: *He never enjoyed one-night stands* **3** *n phr* A person who has a casual sexual encounter: *emerges as less the femme fatale than a one-night stand gone wrong*—Time

one oar *See* ROW WITH ONE OAR

one of the boys (or **the guys**) *n phr* An ordinary, amiable man; a man without side or lofty dignity; =ORDINARY JOE: *His Eminence was trying to be one of the boys*

one of those things *See* JUST ONE OF THOSE THINGS

one on one *adv phr* In immediate confrontation; person to person; =EYEBALL TO EYEBALL: *I go on the basketball court and have a 15-year-old* *guy beat me one on one*—San Francisco

one piece *See* ALL IN ONE PIECE

oner *See* ONCER

one red cent *See* a RED CENT

one-shot **1** *n* A story or article that appears once, with no sequel **2** *n* Any transaction, event, etc, that occurs only once: *He was doing poetry readings, one-shots* **3** *modifier: He put her in a one-shot whodunit*—Newsweek

one thin dime *See* a THIN DIME

one too many *n phr* Enough liquor to make one drunk, and possibly more: *Its driver had obviously had one too many*—D McFerran

one-two **1** *n* (also the **old one-two** or **one-two punch** or **one-two blow**) A combination of two blows with the fists, a short left jab plus a hard right cross, usu to the chin: *zipping "one-twos" to the jaw*—Jim Tully **2** *modifier: good potent one-two punches*—New Yorker

one-up **1** *adv phr* In a superior position; at an advantage: *I always try to be one-up* **2** *v* To get the advantage over: *I wasn't trying to one-up Arthur Schwartz*—M Williams **3** *adv phr* Ahead by one: *The Pinks were one-up on the Puces, 109 to 108*

one-upmanship *n* The technique and practice of having the advantage over one's opponent, esp keeping a psychological advantage by low cunning and subtle brilliance: *good-humored game of political one-upmanship*—Tom Wicker [coined by the late British humorist Stephen Potter]

on one's **game** *adj phr* Performing very well; =HOT: *When I was out in the water and on my game, nothing existed but the wave*—Washington Post

on one's **head** *See* STAND ON one's HEAD

on hold *adv phr* In postponement or abeyance; suspended; =IN COLD STORAGE: *All plans are on hold for a while* [fr the button on a telephone marked *hold*, used to switch temporarily from the conversation]

on ice **1** *adj phr* *fr late 1800s* Certain of being won, or of turning out well; =IN THE BAG: *The deal's on ice* **2** *adv phr* In prison, esp in solitary confinement **3** *adj phr* In reserve; ready to play a role; =IN COLD STORAGE: *If this one fails, I've got another on ice* **4** *adv phr* To the utmost; in the highest degree; =IN SPADES: *This movie stinks on ice*

See PISS ON ICE

onion *See* KNOW one's ONIONS, OFF one's NUT

on line **1** *adj phr* *computers* Computerized: *They put the whole card catalog on line* **2** *adj phr* *fr computer* Available; ready for use; installed; =IN PLACE: *The Navy's announced plans for a new destroyer class are on line* [probably fr the connecting *lines* on a flow chart used to indicate a computer and its attached apparatus]

only *See* EYES ONLY, ONE AND ONLY

the **only game in town** *n phr* The only choice available, as undesirable as it may be: *projects are the only game in town*—New York Times [a shortening of the expression *I know it's crooked, but it's the only game in town*]

on one's **own hook** *adv phr* *fr early 1800s* By one's own efforts; on one's own account: *You'll have to do it on your own hook* [origin unknown and much speculated upon; perhaps fr *fishhook*]

on one's **own time and own dime** *adv phr* Entirely at one's own expense: *She said I could go ahead, but strictly on my own time and own dime*

on sked *adv phr* On schedule: *Aside from minor setbacks... "Street Trash" has been proceeding smoothly and on sked*—New York Times

on the arm **1** *adv phr* On credit, esp when payment is not intended or expected; =ON THE CUFF **2** *adv phr* Free of charge; =FREE GRATIS: *those favors I do on the arm*—Rocky Graziano [fr *on the cuff*]

on the back burner *adv phr* Not being actively considered; in reserve; =ON HOLD: *I have some good projects on the back burner right now*

on the ball *adv phr* Skillful, alert, and effective; =WITH IT: *FBI agents were very much on the ball*—A Hynd [fr the advisability of keeping one's eyes *on the ball* when playing a ball game]

See GET ON THE BALL, KEEP one's EYE ON THE BALL, SOMETHING ON THE BALL

on the beam *adv phr* On the proper track or course; performing correctly: *It took a while, but he's on the beam now* [fr the radio *beam* used to guide aircraft]

on the blink *adj phr* (Variations: **bum** or **fritz** or **Fritz** may replace **blink**) *fr early 1900s* Not functioning properly; in poor condition: *His eyes are on the blink/ His pacemaker just went on the fritz*—WT Tyler/ *My heart's on the bum* [origin unknown; perhaps fr the notion that defective eyes or lights *blink*; *fritz* variant, fr the early 20th century, may be fr a comic strip called "The Katzenjammer Kids," in which two mischievous boys, Hans and *Fritz*, would regularly thwart and disable a character called the Captain]

on the brain *See* HAVE something ON THE BRAIN

on the bum *adj phr fr late 1800s* Leading the life of a hobo, or a similar parasitic and drifting life; =ON THE BLINK: *That year I went on the bum to California*

on the button **1** *adv phr* Precisely; exactly; =ON THE DOT, ON THE NOSE: *The meter says 35 on the button* **2** *adj phr* Perfectly placed; absolutely correct; =ON THE MONEY, ON THE NOSE: *Your estimate was right on the button*

on the carpet *adv phr* In the situation of being reprimanded: *Next time they caught him asleep he was on the carpet* [probably fr the early-19th-century British *walk the carpet* or *carpet* "reprimand, rebuke"]

on the cheap **1** *adv phr fr middle 1800s British* Very economically; as frugally as possible **2** *adj phr: the on-the-cheap set*—Toronto Life

on the cob *adj phr* =CORNY

on the cuff **1** *adv phr* On credit: *arranged for him to eat on the cuff*—New York Confidential **2** *adv phr* Free of charge; =FREE GRATIS, ON THE ARM: *He promised me lodging on the cuff* **3** *adj phr: On-the-cuff drinks are delicious* [fr the practice of noting debts on the *cuff* of the shirt, esp on a detachable *cuff*]

on the dot *adv phr* At the exact moment; punctually: *I got there on the dot*

on (or **at**) **the double** *fr Army* **1** *adv phr* At twice the rate of ordinary marching **2** *adv phr* Quickly; rapidly: *When I holler, come on the double*

on the draw *See* SLOW ON THE DRAW

on the fence *adv phr* Not taking a stand or making up one's mind; straddling

on the finger *adv phr* =ON THE CUFF

on the fire *adj phr* Pending; in preparation; =IN THE PIPELINE: *We've got a great new model on the fire for next year*

on the fly **1** *adv phr* Hastily in passing; without preparation or forethought: *We had to make up our minds on the fly* **2** *adj phr: an on-the-fly decision*

on the fritz *See* ON THE BLINK

on the go **1** *adj phr* Active; energetic; indefatigable: *I'm on the go day and night*—Calder Willingham **2** *adj phr* Always moving about; restlessly in motion: *I'm on the go all the time and don't see my family*

on the gravy train (or **boat**) *adv phr* Enjoying an effortless and prosperous life; =FLUSH: *I was a couple of years on the gravy train, then the bottom fell out of things*

on the ground floor *See* IN ON THE GROUND FLOOR

on the head *See* HIT THE NAIL ON THE HEAD

on the hog *See* EAT HIGH ON THE HOG

on the hook **1** *adv phr* In trouble; liable to blame: *You're on the hook for this mess, junior* **2** *adv phr* Trapped; ensnared: *She had the old fool on the hook right soon*

on (or **in**) **the hot seat** *adv phr* In an uncomfortable situation; =IN A JAM: *The poor jerk's on the hot seat for forgetting to shut the safe*

on the house *adj phr* Free of charge; =FREE GRATIS: *Breakfasts, luncheons, and dinner.... All "on the house"*—advertisement for Northwest Airlines

on the inside *adv phr* Having access to the most confidential information; near the focus of power and influence

on the lam **1** *adj phr underworld* In hiding from the police; wanted as a fugitive: *So I went on the lam*—D Purroy **2** *adj phr* Traveling about; vagrant; =ON THE ROAD

on the level **1** *adj phr fr early 1900s* Honest; candid: *to swear that I'm on the level*—H McHugh **2** *adv* *phr:* *and would fight on the level* —AJ Liebling

on the line *adv phr* In a risky or vulnerable position; at risk, esp deliberately; up for grabs: *The whole season's on the line this inning* [origin unknown; perhaps fr a gambling game where the bet is placed *on a line*; perhaps fr the commercial slang expression *lay* (*the price* or *payment*) *on the line* "pay, pay up"; perhaps fr the sense of *line* as separating combatants or duellists]
See someone's ASS IS ON THE LINE, LAY IT ON THE LINE, LAY something ON THE LINE, PUT one's ASS ON THE LINE

on the make **1** *adv phr* *fr middle 1800s* Aspiring and ambitious, esp in a ruthless and exploitive way; careeristic; =HUNGRY: *The rookies are very much on the make* **2** *adv phr* Offering and seeking sexual pleasure and conquest; openly amorous: *whether they are on the make, and they all are*—Sexual Behavior
See ON THE TAKE

on the mat *adv phr* =ON THE CARPET

on the money *adj phr* Absolutely perfect; precisely as desired; accurate: *She was right on the money with the advice*—Richard Merkin

on the nose **1** *adv phr* Precisely; exactly; =ON THE DOT: *It's six on the nose* **2** *adj phr* Perfectly placed; exactly as desired; =ON THE MONEY: *Your guess was right on the nose*

on the pad *adv phr police* Taking bribes and graft; =ON THE TAKE [fr the *pad* "notebook" listing the names of corrupt police officers]

on the prowl **1** *adj phr* Actively seeking; abroad and searching, esp for victims: *Be very careful for muggers on the prowl* **2** *adv phr* Seeking sexual pleasure and conquest; =ON THE MAKE

on the QT *adv phr fr middle 1800s* Secretly; quietly [fr the first and last letters of *quiet*]

◁ **on the rag**▷ *adj phr* Menstruating: *Maybe I'm on the rag*—Richard Merkin [fr *rag* used as a sanitary napkin]

on the road **1** *adv phr* Traveling from place to place with a show, musical program, etc **2** *adv phr* Drifting about; =ON THE LAM: *Lots of teenagers were on the road those years*

on the rocks **1** *adv phr* In a ruined condition; hopelessly wrecked; =KAPUT: *My little enterprise is on the rocks* **2** *adv phr* Poured over ice: *Scotch on the rocks'll be fine*

on the same (or **on** one's) **wavelength** *adj phr* In agreement; in harmony; =TUNED IN: *Her door's open, but we are not on the same wavelength*—San Francisco [fr the notion of being tuned to the same broadcast *wavelength*]

on the sauce *adj phr* Drinking liquor, esp heavily: *on the sauce in a charming school-boy way*—Stephen Longstreet

on the shelf *adv phr* Not in active use or consideration; deferred; =ON THE BACK BURNER: *We'll have to put some of those plans on the shelf for a while*

on the shikker **1** *adj phr* Drunk **2** *adj phr* =ON THE SAUCE [fr Yiddish fr Hebrew *shikor* "drunk"]

on the side *adv phr* Extra; additionally: *He moonlights as a hackie on the side*

on the skids *adj phr* On a failing or declining course; deteriorating: *After that scandal his whole career was on the skids* [ultimately fr the *skids* "long pieces of timber" on which barrels, logs, and other heavy objects were rolled or slid, sometimes on a downgrade]

on the spot **1** *adj phr* Expected to cope, explain, react, etc, at once; under sharp pressure: *She can't make it, so I guess you're on the spot* **2** *adj phr* Available and ready; keen and at hand: *When I need him he's never on the spot* **3** *adv phr* Immediately; at once and at the place in question: *I was able to fix it on the spot*
See JOHNNY-ON-THE-SPOT

on the stick *adv phr* Skillful, alert, and effective; =ON THE BALL: *She said he'd better get on the stick or she'd dump him* [perhaps related to the early-19th-century British expression *be high up the stick* "be very highly placed; be successful in one's work"]

on the take (or **the make**) *adv phr* Amenable to bribery and graft; =ON THE PAD: *everything from pigeons to cops on the make*—Time

on the town *adv phr* Enjoying the pleasures of a city, esp the night life; roistering and reveling urbanly

on the up and up *See* UP AND UP

on the uptake *See* SLOW ON THE DRAW

on the wagon (or **the water wagon**) *adj phr fr late 1800s* Abstaining from liquor; teetotal, at least temporarily: *Clifton James went on the wagon* —This Week/ *He had all the members of the Highball Association climbing on the water wagon*—H McHugh [first attested as *on the water cart* in 1902]

on tick *adv phr fr 1600s* On credit: *getting his liquor "on tick"*—Russell Janney

on top of **1** *adv phr* Actively coping with the problem; able to guide and control the matter: *It's a nasty outlook, but I think we can get on top of it* **2** *adv phr* Fully informed about something: *Get on top of this latest development right away*

on track *See* GO ON TRACK

on someone's **watch** *adv phr* During someone's tenure of responsibility; while someone is in charge, esp of protection: *Jerusalem and the West Bank were lost to Jordan and the Arab world on his watch*—New Yorker [fr the nautical setting of *watches*, the designating of officers and crew members who run the ship for a specified period]

on wheels *adj phr* To the utmost extent; of the purest sort; =IN SPADES: *We agreed she was a bitch on wheels* *See* SHIT ON WHEELS

-oo *See* -EROO, -LOO

ooch or **oonch** *See* SCRUNCH

oodles *n fr middle 1800s cowboys* A large amount; lots; =a SHITHOUSE FULL: *They have oodles of charisma* [perhaps fr *boodle, caboodle*]

oofay *See* OFAY

ooftish or **offtish** *n gamblers fr late 1800s* Money, esp money available for gambling or investment [fr Yiddish *oyf tishe* "on the table"]

oogle *v* To ogle; stare at

ooh and ah *v phr* To express wonder, amazement, etc: *How they oohed and ahhed over the new baby!*

oomph **1** *n esp 1930s & 40s* Sexual attractiveness; compelling carnality; =IT **2** *n* Energy; =CLOUT, PIZZAZZ: *substance, drive, authority, emotional power, and oomph*—Frank Sullivan [an echoic coinage suggesting the gasp of someone hit hard by a blow, a transport of desire, etc]

oomph girl *n phr esp 1930s & 40s* A young woman who is notably sexually attractive; sex goddess or queen; =DISH • A sobriquet given by press agents in 1939 to the film actress Ann Sheridan: *the oomph-girl of the Romance Language Department* —Morris Bishop

oops **1** *interj* An exclamation of surprise, dismay, apology, etc, esp when one has done something awkward: *Mr Belve, oops, I mean Webb, is ecstatic*—B Thomas/ *Oops, look at this one!* **2** *v* (also **oops up**) To vomit; =BARF: *She oopsed over the side/ This show'll make you want to oops up*

op **1** *n railroad* A telegrapher **2** *n fr 1920s underworld* A private detective: *one of your ops*—Dashiell Hammett [fr *operator* or *operative*]

OP or **op** (pronounced as separate letters) *adj* Other people's: *OP. Other people's money*—T Betts [perhaps a translation of Yiddish *yenems*; see *yenems*]

opener *See* EYE-OPENER

openers *See* FOR OPENERS

open one's **face** (or **head**) *v phr* To speak; speak out; speak up: *Don't so much as open your face*

open up a (or **that**) **can of worms** *v phr* To broach a very complicated and troublesome matter; set something messy in motion: *Merit pay? Let's not open up that can of worms* *See* CAN OF WORMS

open one's **yap** *v phr* To open one's mouth, esp to speak; speak up; say something: *He gets in trouble every time he opens his yap*

opera *See* HORSE OPERA, OATER, SOAP OPERA

the **opera's never over till the fat lady sings** *sentence* Things are never finished until they are finished; further possibilities of action exist here: *Like they say around here, "The opera's never over till the fat lady sings." What hotel are you staying at, little lady?*—WT Tyler

operate with a full deck *See* PLAY WITH A FULL DECK

operator **1** *n* A person who busily deals and manipulates, often self-importantly; =DEALER, MACHER, WHEELER-DEALER **2** *n* =LADIES' MAN

opry ***See*** HORSE OPERA

oral diarrhea ***See*** VERBAL DIARRHEA

Orange Sunshine ***n phr*** *narcotics* A kind of LSD: *"Orange Sunshine" began to appear in acid-starved New York City and in New England communes*—MJ Warth

orbit ***See*** GO INTO ORBIT, IN ORBIT

orc or **orch** ***See*** ORK

orchard ***See*** BONE-ORCHARD, MARBLE ORCHARD

order ***See*** APPLE-PIE ORDER

orders ***See*** CUT someone's PAPERS

ordinary Joe ***n phr*** An average sort of man; =JOHN Q CITIZEN

◁ **O'Reilly's balls**▷ ***See*** TIGHT AS KELSEY'S NUTS

or else ***prep phr*** Otherwise; or this unhappy thing will follow • Used at the end of a command or warning to encourage compliance: *Get that damn thing out of here or else*

◁ **Oreo**▷ ***n*** *black fr 1960s* A black person whose values, behavior, etc, are those of the white society; =AFRO-SAXON: *successful black businessmen who were regarded as "Oreos"*—AT Demaree [fr the trade name of a brand of sandwich cookies that have a white cream between round chocolate biscuits]

organ ***See*** LAP ORGAN

organized ***adj*** Drunk [perhaps fr *hoary-eyed*]

-orino ***See*** -ERINO

-orium ***See*** -ATORIUM

ork or **orc** or **orch** ***n*** An orchestra: *Pierre quit the New York ork*

ornery ***adj*** Mean and irascible; ill-tempered: *He was confident and ornery on the mound*—Inside Sports [fr a dialect pronunciation of *ordinary*]

Oscar **1** ***n*** Any of a set of annual awards, and the statuette signifying it, from the Academy of Motion Picture Arts and Sciences **2** ***n*** Any award: *You won't win any Oscars for that job, you slob* [coined about 1930 by one or more of the various people, including a woman named Margaret Herrick, to whom it is attributed; *Oscar* as a quintessentially comical name was current at the time through the influence of the comic magazine *Ballyhoo*]

ossified ***adj*** Drunk; =STONED

other fish to fry ***See*** BIGGER FISH TO FRY

other half ***n phr*** Another large sector of society, usu the rich as distinct from the poor or the poor as distinct from the rich • Nearly always in the expression "see how the other half lives": *Young people from West Berlin now spend their weekends "over there," trying to find out how the other half lives*—Joseph Wechsberg

other side of one's **face** ***See*** LAUGH ON THE OTHER SIDE OF one's FACE

ouch ***n*** An injury; a hurt: *A very serious injury is a "big" ouch*—David Dempsey [fr the pained interjection *ouch* fr German, probably Pennsylvania German, *autsch*, used fr the mid-19th century]

out **1** ***adj*** *beat & cool talk* Attractive; au courant; =HIP, WAY OUT: *Man, that Modigliani is really out* **2** ***adj*** Not modern, popular, or in accord with current taste: *Those neckties are out this year* **3** ***adj*** *homosexuals* Openly avowing homosexuality **4** ***adv*** Away from home: *The folks are out tonight* **5** ***adj*** (also **out cold**) Unconscious, esp knocked unconscious: *One more drink and he'll be out* **6** ***n*** *fr 1920s* A way of escape; a plausible alibi or evasive course: *You've got only one out, which is to lie like hell*

See FAR OUT, WAY OUT

outasight ***See*** OUT OF SIGHT

out from under ***See*** GET OUT FROM UNDER

out-front ***adj*** Honest; candid; unevasive; =UP FRONT: *intelligent, very open, out-front people*—Tom Wolfe

out in left field ***adj phr*** Very unorthodox and wrong; weirdly unconventional; crazy

out like a light ***adj phr*** Unconscious; fast asleep

out loud ***See*** FOR CRYING OUT LOUD

out of one's **depth** ***adv phr*** In a situation where one cannot cope, esp because one is inexperienced, insufficiently skillful, etc: *I felt out of my depth in that school*

out of one's **ears** ***See*** HAVE something COMING OUT OF one's EARS

out of one's **head** (or **skull** or **gourd**) **1** ***adj phr*** Insane; crazy; =NUTS: *You're out of your head if you think I'll do that* **2** ***adj phr*** Dazed; delirious; =OFF one's NUT: *He took one sniff and went right out of his gourd*

out of it **1** ***adj phr*** Unable to win or succeed: *The Hawks are out of it this season* **2** ***adj phr*** Not a part of the trend or scene; uninitiated: *He's a nice guy, but he's out of it* —New Yorker **3** ***adj phr*** Unattending, esp because of drugs or liquor: *We could accept him as being out of it*—John Irving

out of joint ***See*** PUT someone's NOSE OUT OF JOINT

out of kilter ***adj phr*** *fr early 1600s* Not in order or repair; =OUT OF WHACK [fr British dialect *kilter* or *kelter* "condition, state, frame," of obscure origin]

out of one's **league** **1** ***adj phr*** =OUT OF one's DEPTH **2** ***adj phr*** Not in one's proper province: *The matter's fortunately out of my league*

out of line **1** ***adj phr*** Not in accordance with what is appropriate or expected: *You was considered out of line if your coat and pants matched* —A Lomax/ *That remark was out of line* **2** ***adj phr*** Behaving improperly, esp presumptuously: *The little smart-ass got out of line once too often*

out of luck ***adj phr*** Having no chance of success; already too late for what one wants: *You're out of luck, pal, they've gone*

See SHIT OUT OF LUCK

out of pocket (or **the pocket**) ***adj phr*** *esp Southern and Southwestern* Absent or otherwise unavailable: *I'm out of the pocket for a bit, but I'll get back at ya*—Rolling Stone

out of shape ***adj phr*** Very upset; angry; hysterical

See BENT OUT OF SHAPE

out of sight **1** ***adj phr*** (also **outasight**) *cool talk* =WAY OUT **2** ***adj phr*** Very high-priced; exorbitantly priced: *That hat's out of sight*

out of style ***See*** LIKE IT'S GOING OUT OF STYLE

out of sync ***adj phr*** Not coinciding or compatible; arrhythmic, esp in relation to something else, a context, etc: *his presence just self-consciously regular enough to be out of sync* —Toronto Life [fr the lack of *synchronism* sometimes noted between a movie or TV image and its sound track]

out of the closet **1** ***adj phr*** Openly avowing homosexuality **2** ***adj phr*** No longer secret: *The last American taboo, that of talking about indebtedness, may be out of the closet at last*—New York Times

See COME OUT OF THE CLOSET

out of the fire ***See*** PULL something OUT OF THE FIRE

out of the loop ***adj phr*** Not one of the inner and influential group; not in the network: *George Bush was out of the loop... an ineffective second in command*—Newsweek/ *an inevitable feeling of being out of the loop* —Washington Post [probably fr the military notion of radio *nets*, conceptually like *loops*, connecting various commanders]

out of the water ***See*** BLOW OUT OF THE WATER

out of the woodwork ***See*** CRAWL OUT OF THE WOODWORK

out of this world ***adj phr*** *fr early 1900s* Excellent; wonderful; superior; =the GREATEST, WAY OUT: *She had a figure which was out of this world*—H Witwer

out of one's **tree** ***adj phr*** Insane; crazy; =APE: *She's got to be out of her tree*—Washington Post

out of turn ***See*** TALK OUT OF TURN

out of whack *fr late 1800s* **1** ***adj phr*** Not operating; out of order; =ON THE BLINK, OUT OF KILTER: *My car's out of whack so I'll take yours* **2** ***adj phr*** Not in adjustment, harmonious synchronism, etc; not in proper order: *Our priorities are out of whack* —Washingtonian **3** ***adj phr*** Strange; inexplicable; not right: *It seems out of whack to me, then, that Jakobek was the only aldermanic candidate who had a great deal of support from the young*—Toronto Life [probably fr *whack* "share, a just proportion," so called perhaps fr the blow that divides something or like the auctioneer's hammer-rap signals a fair share or deal]

out on a limb ***adv phr*** In a very vulnerable position; exposed; in peril: *The announcement put the Mayor out on a limb*

See GO OUT ON A LIMB

◁ **out on** one's **ass**▷ ***adj phr*** Discharged; rejected; superseded; =FINISHED: *She's the First Lady now, and I'm out on my ass*—Interview

outside *See* GET OUTSIDE OF

outside chance *n phr* A remote possibility; a slim likelihood: *He may have an outside chance to pass*

outtake *n* An excerpt; an extracted passage: *Is this an outtake from the $1.98 Beauty Show?*—Playboy

out to lunch *adj phr esp students* Insane; crazy; eccentric: *On critical issues of fact and analysis he is out to lunch*—Washington Post

out to pasture *adj phr* Retired; superannuated; no longer active: *My job? I've been out to pasture the last four years*

See PUT someone or something OUT TO PASTURE

over *See* the ONCE-OVER

over a barrel *adv phr* In a helpless situation: *I knew enough about him that I had him over a barrel* [perhaps fr the tying *over a barrel* of a person about to be flogged]

overboard *adj* Very enthusiastic; strongly committed, usu in favor of something: *He's overboard for the new series*

See GO OVERBOARD

over someone's **eyes** *See* PULL THE WOOL OVER someone's EYES

over one's **head** **1** *adj phr* Too difficult for one mentally; incomprehensible: *The concept's way over my head* **2** *adv phr* Better than one's usual standard; in an inspired way: *The team played over its head and by God they won*

See IN OVER one's HEAD

overkill *n* An excess, esp of needed action: *Going there twice would be overkill, don't you think?* [fr the use of the term in connection with the *killing* potential of nuclear arms and arsenals]

overshoes *See* WIN THE PORCELAIN HAIRNET

over the coals *See* HAUL someone OVER THE COALS

over the fence *adv phr airline* On approach to the runway: *His speed over the fence was much too high* [fr the *fence* or other barrier at the end of an airport runway]

over the hill **1** *adj phr* Middle-aged or past middle age: *a film for, and about, the over-the-hill gang* —Time **2** *adj phr* No longer effective; worn out **3** *adj phr* (Variation: **hump** may replace **hill**) Most of the way to success or completion: *I think that you can say that we're over the hill*—Ebony **4** *adj phr Army* Absent without leave; = AWOL [first three senses fr the notion that one is no longer going upwards towards the summit, but is descending the far side of the imagined *hill*]

See DRIVE someone OVER THE HILL

over the long haul *See* FOR THE LONG HAUL

one's **own hook** *See* ON one's OWN HOOK

one's **own horn** *See* TOOT one's OWN HORN

own time and own dime *See* ON one's OWN TIME AND OWN DIME

Owsley *See* AUGUSTUS OWSLEY

ox *See* DUMB OX

oyster *See* MOUNTAIN OYSTERS

ozone or **zone** *n college students* A psychedelic condition, usu due to drugs: *He wasn't making much sense because he was way up there in a zone* [fr the notion of being as high as the *ozone* layer of the atmosphere]

P

P or **p** or **pee** *n* Any of the various units of currency whose designations begin with "p," like the Mexican peso or the Vietnamese piastre

See PEE

pace *See* OFF THE PACE

pack *See* NERDPACK, RAT PACK

package **1** *n* An attractive woman **2** *n* A large sum of money; =BUNDLE: *That must have cost a package* **3** *n* The collective terms of a contract or agreement: *The lefthander signed for a package including 10 million in two years, three McDonald's franchises, and the state of South Dakota* **4** *n* A particular combination or set: *That rental car is part of the vacation package* **5** *n* The manner and quality of presentation, the trappings and ornamentation, etc, of something: *It's the package that impresses people* **6** *v: He never peddled his idea because he didn't know how to package it*

pack heat *v phr underworld* To carry a gun: *They knew all along that Elvis was packin' heat*—Albert Goldman

pack in (or **up**) *v phr fr 1920s British* To cease; give up; retire from: *I intended to pack up playing all together*—Rolling Stone/ *told the FBI men he is "packing in"*—Robert M Yoder

pack it in *v phr fr 1920s British perhaps fr cockney* To stop; desist; give up what one is doing: *I decided to pack it in and move to New York*—David Standish/

pack rat **1** *n phr* A person who cannot discard anything acquired; a compulsive keeper and storer **2** *n phr* A hotel porter; bellboy

pack the mail *v phr* =CARRY THE MAIL

pad **1** *n narcotics* A couch, bed, etc, on which one reclines while smoking opium **2** *n narcotics* A room, apartment, etc, where narcotics addicts and users gather to take drugs: *There were plenty of pads*—New York Post **3** *n 1960s counterculture fr musicians* A bed or place to sleep temporarily; =CRASH PAD: *Longhairs found it difficult to get work and a pad*—Time **4** *n* One's home; residence: *He and I used to live in the same pad for two years*—Douglass Wallop **5** *n prostitutes* A prostitute's working room; =CRIB **6** *n* An automobile license plate: *The job was wearing California pads*—J Evans **7** *v* To increase the amount or length of: *I padded the story with some few flourishes*

See ACID PAD, CRASH PAD, KICK PAD, LAUNCHING PAD, ON THE PAD

the **pad** *police* **1** *n phr* Graft and bribe money taken and shared by police officers **2** *n phr* The list of those police officers who share graft and bribe money

See ON THE PAD

paddle *See* UP SHIT CREEK

paddlefoot *n WW2 Army* An infantry soldier; rifleman; =DOGFACE: *Murray was a paddlefoot in Europe*—Bill Mauldin

pad down **1** *v phr* To sleep; go to bed; =SACK OUT **2** *v phr* To search; =FRISK

◀**paddy** or **Paddy**▶ **1** *n* An Irish person or person of Irish extraction **2** *n* (also **patty**) *black* A white person: *Even a drunken black shoeshine man could handle the likes of this paddy*—Joseph Wambaugh **3** *modifier: I know I can't be tight with* *this paddy boy*—Claude Brown **4** *n hoboes* A lazy, worthless person [fr the nickname of the given name *Patrick*]

paddy wagon *n phr* A police patrol wagon or van; =BLACK MARIA: *The cooperative family was being escorted into the paddy wagon*—Philadelphia Bulletin [fr *patrol wagon*]

padre (PAH dray) *n armed forces fr WW1 perhaps fr late 1800s British Navy* Any military chaplain [fr Spanish or Portuguese, "father, priest"]

paesan (pī ZAHN) *n* A fellow native of one's country or town; compatriot; =LANDSMAN [fr Italian dialect]

page *See* TAKE A PAGE FROM someone's BOOK

page turner *n phr* A book that is so absorbing that one reads it without stopping, although not necessarily for serious literary or intellectual quality: *a book that unquestionably deserves the description page turner*—New York Daily News

pain *See* FEEL NO PAIN

a **pain** **1** *n phr* Annoyance; irritation; =HEADACHE: *That clown gives me a pain/ Marvin is a real pain* **2** *n phr* =a PAIN IN THE ASS

See GIVE someone A PAIN

◁ a **pain in the ass**▷ (or **neck**) *n phr* An annoying, obnoxious person or thing: *This proved a major pain in the ass*—Village Voice

See GIVE someone A PAIN

paint *See* WAR PAINT

paint cards *n phr* Picture cards in a deck of playing cards; court cards

paint the town or **paint the town red** *v phr fr late 1800s cowboys* To go on a wild spree; carouse: *Well, sport,let's go out and paint the town a new color*—Hal Boyle

pair *n* A woman's breasts • Regarded as offensive by many women

paisano (pī ZAHN oh) *n fr middle 1800s Western* =PAESAN [fr Spanish, "countryman"]

pajamas *See* the CAT'S MEOW

pal *n fr late 1600s British* A friend, esp a very close male friend; boon companion; =BUDDY: *has many devoted friends, but he is nobody's "pal"*—New York Times [fr Romany *phral*, *phal* "brother, friend," ultimately fr Sanskrit *bhratr* "brother"]

palace *See* FIVE-SIDED PUZZLE PALACE

pal around *v phr* To be pals; consort as pals: *the people he palled around with*—Ira Wolfert

pale *n black* A white person; =GRAY

paled or **paled out** *adj* or *adj phr Canadian teenagers* Completely exhausted, esp by drugs or liquor; =WASTED

palimony **1** *n fr late 1970s* Money awarded, property shared, etc, when an unmarried couple separate **2** *modifier: a much-heralded palimony suit* [fr *pal* + *alimony*; coined for or at least popularized by a lawsuit against the film star Lee Marvin]

palm **1** *v* To conceal a playing card against the palm in order to use it in a gambling hand: *It was five cards that he palmed*—Calder Willingham **2** *v* To conceal anything from opponents or competitors

See GREASE someone's PALM

palm something **off** *v phr* To bestow something inferior as if it were of good quality; foist; fob off: *He palmed the leaky old place off like it was the Ritz*

palm oil *n phr* Money used for bribery and graft

palooka or **paluka** or **palooker** (pə LōŌ Kə) **1** *n fr 1920s* A mediocre or inferior boxer: *a paluka who leads with his right*—Dashiell Hammett **2** *n* A professional wrestler **3** *n* Any large and stupid man [origin unknown; perhaps fr Spanish *peluca* "wig," used as an insult]

palsy-walsy (PAL zee WAL zee) **1** *adj* Very friendly; =CHUMMY: *palsy-walsy with Baskerville*—Nation **2** *n: Hey, palsy-walsy, what's going down?*

pan **1** *n fr late 1700s* The face; =MUG: *too great for them to keep their pans shut*—Jerome Weidman **2** *v fr early 1900s* To criticize severely and adversely; derogate harshly; =ROAST: *The Daily Worker panned his first novel*—Leonard Lyons **3** *n: an out-and-out pan*—Billy Rose

See DEADPAN, FLASH IN THE PAN

Panama (or **Mexican**) **red** or **Mexican** *n phr* or *n narcotics* A type, esp a choice, potent grade, of marijuana

panhandle *v fr early 1900s* To beg, esp by accosting people on the street: *The boys deal drugs or panhandle*—Time [apparently because beggars held out tin *pans* in requesting alms]

panic **1** *v* To become frightened and confused, esp suddenly; =FLIP: *He panicked and dropped the ball* **2** *v* To get a strong favorable reaction, esp to get loud laughter from an audience; =FRACTURE: *Mr Todd knows how to panic the rubes*—Brooks Atkinson **3** *n* A very funny person; an effective comedian; =a STITCH

panic button *See* HIT THE PANIC BUTTON

panic rack *n phr Air Force* A pilot's ejection seat: *The jockey is in the panic rack and ready to go*—Associated Press

panky or **pank** *See* HANKY-PANKY

panman *n* A drummer in a West Indian steel band, whose players strike xylophonelike instruments made from the ends of steel containers such as oil drums

pan out *v phr fr middle 1800s* To be productive; succeed; =PAY OFF: *Ryan thought about what he'd be living with if the FBI profile panned out*—Philadelphia [fr the practice of *panning* gold in river sediments]

◁**pansy**▷ *fr 1920s* **1** *n* A male homosexual; =QUEEN: *Her friends... were pansies*—Philip Wylie **2** *n* A weak or effeminate male; =SISSY **3** ***adj:*** *Stage and screen voices in recent years have become so pansy*—HW Seaman

◁**panther piss**▷ (or **sweat**) or **panther** *n phr* or *n* Raw and inferior whiskey; =ROTGUT

pantry *n prizefight fr early 1900s* The stomach; =BREADBASKET: *another real fine left to the pantry*—R Starnes

pants *See* ANTS, CATCH someone WITH someone's PANTS DOWN, CHARM THE PANTS OFF someone, CREAM one's JEANS, DUST someone's PANTS, FANCY PANTS, FLY BY THE SEAT OF one's PANTS, GET THE LEAD OUT, HAVE LEAD IN one's PANTS, HOT PANTS, RAGGEDY-ASS, SEAT-OF-THE-PANTS, SHIT one's PANTS, SISSY PANTS, SMARTY PANTS

the **pants off** *adv phr* To the utmost; to an extreme degree: *I'm going to sue the pants off you this time, meathead*—Washington Post [probably extended fr *charm the pants off*]

pantywaist *n fr 1930s* A weak or effeminate male; =PANSY: *The hurt... pantywaist ran off a number of copies of his letter*—Bernard DeVoto [fr a child's garment with short *pants* buttoned to the *waist* of a shirt]

pap *n* Father; =PAPPY

papa *n esp black* A male lover; =DADDY

See SWEET MAN

paper **1** *n* A forged or worthless check **2** *v* To use or pass counterfeit money or worthless checks: *papered Queens and Long Island with... bum checks*—New York Daily News **3** *n theater fr late 1800s* A pass or free ticket; =ANNIE OAKLEY **4** *v police* To write traffic and parking tickets: *The sergeant complained that the patrolmen were not papering enough* **5** *n narcotics* A packet of narcotics; =BAG

See BAD PAPER, PEDDLE one's PAPERS, WALKING PAPERS, WALLPAPER

paper ass *See* MAN WITH A PAPER ASS

paper bag *See* CAN'T FIGHT one's WAY OUT OF A PAPER BAG

paper chase *n phr fr British* An intense searching and collation of files, books, documents, etc, esp for the needs of bureaucratic pomp • Popularized in the US as the title of a film and a TV series, where the **paper** was a Harvard Law School degree [fr a mid-19th-century game of hare and hounds in which the quarry would leave a trail of scraps of *paper*]

paper dolls *See* CUT OUT DOLLS

paperhanger or **paper-pusher** *n underworld* A person who passes counterfeit money or worthless checks: *The FBI's suspect was a master paperhanger, the last of a breed*—Philadelphia

paper over *v phr* To conceal or gloss over; fail to deal with: *If the tiff were nothing but a clash of personalities... it might be quickly papered over*—Newsweek

paper profits *n phr* Monetary gains recognizable by accounting but not realized in palpable money or goods

paper-pusher or **paper-shuffler** *n* An office worker or bureaucratic functionary whose work is neither very useful nor consequential, and who also cannot be held responsible: *He's fired about 10,000 paper-pushers in the Navy procurement office*

papers **1** *n black* A marriage license or certificate **2** *n narcotics* Cigarette rolling papers, used to

make marijuana cigarettes: *I've got the dope if you've got the papers*
See CUT someone's PAPERS, PEDDLE one's PAPERS, PUT one's PAPERS IN, WALKING PAPERS

paper tiger *n phr* A menacing person or thing that in fact lacks force; a blusterer: *doing battle with a paper tiger when he aims his wrath at the white liberal*—New York Times/ *suggested that the 23-year-old running back was a paper tiger*—New York Times [fr the Chinese expression *tsuh lao fu* "paper tiger" given currency by Mao Zedong]

pappy *n* Father; =PAP

parachute *See* GOLDEN PARACHUTE

parade *See* RAIN ON someone's PARADE

paralyzed *adj* Very drunk

parboiled *adj* Drunk

pard *n fr middle 1800s cowboys* Friend; partner; =PAL

pardon me all to hell *See* EXCUSE ME ALL TO HELL

pardon my French *interj* An exclamation of apology for the use of profane or taboo language: *That God-damned... pardon my French*—Tennessee Williams

par for the course *n phr* What is to be expected; normal though nasty: *He had to take a little crap from the clerk, but that's par for the course*

park *v* To put or place; locate: *Where shall I park this machine?/ Park yourself anywhere, I'll be right back*
See BALLPARK, BALLPARK FIGURE, PICKLE PARK

parking lot *See* PORTABLE PARKING LOT

park one *v phr baseball* To hit a home run: *Mantle just parked one*—New York Times

parlay **1** *v horse-racing fr late 1800s* To bet money in a series of wagers where the winnings of one are automatically placed on the next, etc **2** *n: He won a three-horse parlay* **3** *v* To build or increase something from a small initial outlay or possession: *She parlayed her dimples into movie superstardom* [fr *paralee* or *parlee*, an early-19th-century faro term fr Italian *parole* "words, promises"]

parlor *See* MASSAGE PARLOR, RAP CLUB

the **parson's nose** *See* the POPE'S NOSE

part *See* BIT

party **1** *n* A person: *the party there in the corner* **2** *n* A group of people: *We have a party of six for dinner* **3** *n* A bout of sex play or sexual activity **4** *v* To go to or give parties: *I always party a lot over the holidays* **5** *v* To enjoy oneself drinking, chatting, dancing, etc; be energetically social: *We partied all night in about eight clubs*
See DRAG PARTY, HAVE A PARTY, HEN PARTY, KICK PARTY, NECKTIE PARTY, POP PARTY, POT PARTY, STAG, TAILGATE PARTY

party hat *n phr* The array of lights on the roof of a police car or emergency vehicle; =GUMBALL

party-pooper or **party poop** **1** *n* or *n phr* The first person or couple to leave a party; a person who ends a joyous occasion **2** *n* or *n phr* A morose, pessimistic person; =KILLJOY, WET BLANKET: *No one can call Mr Bulganin and Mr Kruschchev party poopers*—Edmund Wilson/ *What a party poop you are today, Sally*—Anne Bernays

pass **1** *v* To be thought to be something one is not, esp to be thought white when one is actually black: *the oldest daughter, so fair she could pass*—A Lomax **2** *v* To suffice or be adequate, only just barely: *It's not great pasta, but it'll pass* **3** *n phr* A sexual advance; =PROPOSITION **4** *v* To decline to do something, take something, etc: *When it comes to telling him flatly, I pass*
See MAKE A PASS AT someone

passion pit *esp students* **1** *n phr* A drive-in movie theater: *taking his buxom daughter off to the local passion pit*—Stephen King **2** *n phr* A room used for seduction: *some minor-league Don Juan's passion pit*—Stephen King

pass out **1** *v phr* To lose consciousness; faint; go to sleep, esp from drinking too much liquor **2** *v phr* To die: *He left us a lot of jack when he passed out*—P Marks

pass the buck *v phr fr early 1900s* To refer a problem or responsibility to someone else, esp to a higher authority; decline to take action: *We chickened out and passed the buck to the dean* [fr poker games where one would *pass the buck*, usu a pocketknife with a *buck*horn handle, on to the next person, thereby passing the deal on]

pass the hat **1** *v phr* To ask for contributions of money; collect money from a group: *We passed the hat until we had her plane fare* **2** *v phr* To beg; solicit charity

pass something **up** *v phr fr late 1800s* To choose not to take, attend, etc; =GIVE someone or something A MISS: *I guess I'll pass up the concert tonight*

paste **1** *v fr middle 1800s British* To hit; strike very hard: *She grabbed the broom and pasted me* **2** *v* To defeat decisively; trounce; =CLOBBER: *The Jets got pasted* [origin unknown; perhaps an alteration of earlier *baste* "strike, trounce," of obscure origin and preserved in *lambaste*]

pasture *See* PUT someone or something OUT TO PASTURE

pasty or **pastie** (PAY stee) *n* A small circular bit of cloth, often sparkling, covering the nipple of a woman dancer in a burlesque show or other lewd display

◁ **pato** ▷ (PAH toh) *n* A male homosexual [fr Spanish]

patoot or **patootie** (pə TOOT) *n* The buttocks; fundament; =ASS: *tutelage in the honorable art of not making a horse's patoot of yourself*—Toronto Star [origin unknown; perhaps fr dialect *tout* "buttocks," fr Middle English, pronounced *toot*, and altered to conform with *sweet patootie* by folk etymology]

patootie or **sweet patootie** **1** *n* or *n phr* One's girlfriend or boyfriend; sweetheart: *tell their patooties how pretty they are*—New York Confidential **2** *n* or *n phr* A young woman: *a batch of pretty-panned patooties*—G Dixon [perhaps fr a play on *sweet potato* suggested by *sweetheart* and *potato* as used, like *tomato*, to mean a person]

patrol *See* YARD PATROL

patsy *fr early 1900s* **1** *n* A victim; dupe; =SUCKER: *But to retain lawyers is clear proof that you're a patsy*—Saul Bellow **2** *n* A person who takes the blame for a crime, who is put up against a superior opponent in order to lose, etc; =FALL GUY [origin unknown; perhaps fr *Pasqualino*, the Italian diminutive for *Pasquale* just as *Patsy* is the American English diminutive. *Pasqualino* is used to designate a vulnerable, weak, and small boy or man, and is probably based in this sense at least partly on the relation between *Pasqua* "Easter," the derivative names *Pasquale* and *Pasqualino*, and the notion of the Pascal sacrifice or Pascal lamb as an innocent victim]

◁ **patty** ▷ *n Hispanics* A white person; =ANGLO [probably fr black *paddy*]
See PADDY

the **pavement** *See* POUND THE PAVEMENT

paw **1** *n* A hand: *You let me get my paws on the money*—Raymond Chandler **2** *v* To touch and handle, esp in a crude sexual way
See SOUTHPAW

pay *See* HELL TO PAY

pay dirt *n phr* Profit and success: *I'll try a fast-food franchise, where there's sure to be paydirt*
See HIT PAY DIRT

pay one's **dues** *v phr* To serve and suffer such that one deserves what good comes to one; =GO THROUGH THE MILL: *I hate it when a guy who hasn't paid his dues gets it all*

payoff **1** *n underworld* Payment, esp of bribery, graft, etc: *The rogues hung around waiting for their payoff* **2** *n fr 1920s* The final outcome or bit of information, esp when it is surprising or amusing: *OK, here's the payoff, she's the Albanian consul!*

pay off **1** *v phr underworld* To give someone bribe money, blackmail money, or the like: *We'll have to pay them off handsomely to keep them quiet* **2** *v phr* To bring in profit; succeed; pay **3** *v phr* To discharge; =CAN, FIRE: *Any more of this and I'll pay off the whole bunch of you*

payola *n fr 1930s* Graft; extortion money; bribery, esp that paid by recording companies to disc jockeys for playing their records on the radio [coined probably fr *payoff* and the ending of *Pianola*, trade name of an automatic piano-playing device, or *Victrola*, trade name of a gramophone]

pay the freight *v phr* To pay for; compensate for; bear the expense of; =PICK UP THE TAB: *We may have to "pay the freight for well-meant efforts at improvement"*—New Yorker

pay through the nose *v phr* To pay exorbitantly; give too much in recompense

pay up *v phr* To pay; settle one's account: *Pay up and be done with it*

pay-wing *n baseball* A pitcher's throwing arm

pazzazza (pə ZAZ ə) *n* A piazza: *young woman is sitting on the pazzazza*—H Witwer

PC *n airline* A pilot check flight or ride, where a pilot's continued qualification to fly is periodically tested

PCP *n narcotics* Phencyclidine, an animal tranquilizer smoked as a narcotic; =ANGEL DUST

p'd *See* PISSED OFF

pdq *adv* Pretty damn quick

peabrain or **peahead** *n* A stupid person

peacenik *n esp 1960s & 70s* A member of a peace movement; pacifist; antiwar demonstrator

peach[1] *v fr 1400s British* To inform; =SQUEAL [fr *appeach* "lodge an accusation"]

peach[2] *fr middle 1800s* **1** *n* An attractive young woman: *She really was a "peach"*—SA Clark **2** *n* Any remarkable, admirable, amiable, or attractive person: *You're a peach*—Dorothy Parker **3** *n* Anything superior or admirable: *The hotel was a peach*

peacherino *n fr early 1900s* =PEACH[2]

peachy or **peachy-keen** *adj* Excellent; wonderful; =GREAT, NEAT: *this president's political health, which Wirthlin thinks is peachy*—George Will

peanut **1** *n fr early 1800s* A small or trivial person; something insignificant **2** *adj: a peanut operation/his peanut mind*

peanuts *n* A small amount of money; a trivial sum; =NICKELS AND DIMES: *They got you working for peanuts*—Budd Schulberg

See THAT AIN'T HAY

pea soup (or **souper**) *n phr* A thick fog

pec *n* A pectoral muscle: *All the male weight lifters love her a bushel and a pec*—Playboy

peck ◁**1**▷ *n black* =PECKERWOOD **2** *n railroad* A very short period for a meal **3** *v* To eat, esp to eat very little and choosily **4** *n teenagers* Food **5** *n* A perfunctory kiss: *She gave him a friendly peck and got back to work*

◁**pecker**▷ *n* The penis

◁**peckerhead**▷ *n* A despicable person; =ASSHOLE, JERK: *Do you hear me, peckerhead?*—Andrew Coburn

◁**peckerwood**▷ *black* **1** *n* A poor Southern white, esp a farmer; =CRACKER, REDNECK **2** *n* Any white Southern man: *Any white man from the South is a "Peckerwood"*—Stephen Longstreet [fr rural black use of the red-headed *woodpecker*, with dialect inversion of the word elements as a symbol for white persons in contrast with the blackbird as a symbol for themselves; the red head may be the symbolic base, suggesting *redneck*]

peckings (or **pecks**) *n fr black* Food

peckish *adj fr late 1700s British* Hungry

pedal *See* SOFT-PEDAL

peddle one's **papers** *v phr* To go about one's business • Often an irritated command that one leave the speaker alone: *I told him to go peddle his papers*—Hal Boyle

peddler *See* FLESH-PEDDLER, PILL-PUSHER

pee **1** *v* To urinate; =PISS, WHIZZ **2** *n* Urine

See P

peed off *See* PISSED OFF

peejays *n* Pajamas; =PJS

peekaboo *adj* Made of a sheer fabric; transparent; =SEE-THROUGH: *Peekaboo blouses are not the most calming of garments*

peek freak *n phr* A voyeur; Peeping Tom

peel **1** *v* To undress; strip **2** *v* =PEEL OUT

peeler *n* A striptease dancer; =STRIPPER: *grinders, peelers, and bumpers*—Louis Sobol

See BRONCO BUSTER

peel out *v phr fr hot rodders* To leave quickly; =SPLIT [probably fr the Air Force term *peel off* "break away fr a formation, esp fr one end and in a dive," fr 1920s British Royal Air Force use]

◁**peenie**▷ *n* The penis

See POUND one's PEENIE

peep *n* A word; a sound; the least utterance: *If I hear a peep out of you, you've had it*

peeper *n* A private detective; =PRIVATE EYE: *and don't bother to call your house peeper*—Raymond Chandler
See HEADSHRINKER

peepers 1 *n fr middle 1800s underworld* The eyes: *staring into the distance with those big, wet peepers* —Village Voice **2** *n* A pair of sunglasses; =SHADES: *I'd come through the employee door with one of my peepers on*—D James

peep show *n phr* A supposedly private view, usu through a hole in the wall, of some forbidden sexual activity

peeve 1 *n fr early 1900s* A cause of annoyance: *You probably have a long list of peeves* **2** *v: That crap really peeves me* **3** *n* A grudge; continued hostility: *having a peeve on a poor kid*—Budd Schulberg [by back formation fr *peeved*, which in turn derives by back formation fr *peevish*, fr Middle English *peivish*, "perverse, wayward, capricious," perhaps fr Latin *perversus*]
See PET PEEVE

pee-warmer *n* Something pleasant and agreeable: *The last issue...is a pee-warmer*—Nevada

peewee *n* A short or small person, animal, etc: *That peewee doesn't scare me*

Peewee *n* Nickname for a short or small person

peezy *See* JEEZ

peg 1 *v* To identify; classify; pick out; =BUTTON DOWN: *I could peg a joint like that from two miles away* —John O'Hara **2** *v* To taper or bind a pair of trousers at the lower end: *Pants must be pegged to fit snugly around the ankle*—Max Shulman **3** *n baseball* A throw, esp a hard one: *His peg missed and the runner scored* **4** *v: He pegged it sharply to first*

peg out *v phr fr middle 1800s* To die: *Harrison...actually pegged out in 1841*—HL Mencken [fr the ending of play in cribbage by *pegging*]

pegs *n* Legs; =PINS: *He was wobbly on his pegs*

pellet *n* The ball used in a ball game: *Berra...searched the premises for the pellet*—Asociated Press

pen *n* A prison of any sort, esp a penitentiary
See BULLPEN, POISON-PEN LETTER

pencil *See* HAVE LEAD IN one's PENCIL

pencil-pusher (or **-driver** or **-shover**) *n* An office worker, esp a clerk, bookkeeper, or the like; =DESK JOCKEY: *The number of pencil pushers and typists has increased*—S Dawson

penicillin *See* JEWISH PENICILLIN

pennant *See* IRISH PENNANT

Pennsy *n* The Pennsylvania Railroad

penny *n teenagers* A police officer [fr a play on *copper*]

penny ante 1 *n phr* A trivial transaction; a cheap offer, arrangement, etc **2** *adj: I despised his penny-ante ideas*

penny-pincher *n* A stingy person; miser; =TIGHTWAD

penny pool *n phr* A paltry game or affair; =PENNY ANTE: *I told him to shove his deal, it was penny pool*
See PLAY PENNY POOL

pen-pusher *n* =PENCIL-PUSHER

people *n* A person: *She's very nice people*
See the BEAUTIFUL PEOPLE, BOAT PEOPLE, FLOWER CHILDREN, HARE KRISHNA KIDS, JESUS FREAKS, NIGHT PEOPLE, STREET PEOPLE

the **people** *n phr narcotics* Narcotics dealers on a large or wholesale scale

Peoria *See* PLAY IN PEORIA

pep 1 *n fr early 1900s* Energy; vitality; =PISS AND VINEGAR, PIZZAZZ **2** *modifier: pep talk/ pep pill* [fr *pepper*]

pepper 1 *n fr early 1900s* Energy; vitality; =PEP: *The old moral support is what gives we players the old pepper*—Westbrook Pegler **2** *v baseball* To throw a baseball very hard; =BURN **3** *n baseball* A fast and hard session of pitch-and-catch; =BURNOUT **4** *v* To hit a baseball, golf ball, etc, hard: *She peppered it about 80 yards* **◀5▶** *n* A Mexican or person of Mexican extraction
See SALT AND PEPPER

pepper-upper *n* A thing, food, drink, person, etc, that imparts pep; stimulant: *"Say fellows," said a uniformed pepper-upper to a bunch of GI assault troops*—M Mayer

pep pill *n phr* Any amphetamine pill; =UPPER

peppy *adj* Energetic; vital; =ZINGY

pep rally *n phr* A meeting where the participants are stimulated to some activity, harder effort, etc: *a Republi-*

can pep rally in downtown Grosse Pointe

pep talk *n phr* A hortatory speech, usu given by a team coach or other leader: *had to give myself a pep talk before I went out to sing*—Peggy Lee

pep up *v phr* To stimulate; excite; energize; =JAZZ something UP

perc *See* PERK

percentage *n* Profit or advantage: *I don't see any percentage in doing it that way*

percolate **1** *v fr 1920s* To run smoothly and well: *The little engine was percolating nicely* **2** *v* To penetrate; permeate: *It was percolating through my mind that maybe I should leave* **3** *v 1930s jive talk* To saunter; stroll: *I'll percolate over and ask the cop* [all senses fr the coffee-making device; sense of "run well," for example, fr the steady cheery bubbling of the coffee-maker]

percolator *n black* A party where one sells drinks and food to friends in order to pay one's rent; =RENT PARTY: *You could always get together and charge a few coins and have a percolator*—Stephen Longstreet

Percy or **Percy boy** or **Percy-pants** *n* or *n phr* An effeminate male; =PANSY: *He never prated about his Oedipus complex like the Percy boys*—SJ Perelman

perform *v* To do the sex act; function sexually: *She didn't love him, but liked the way he performed*

perk[1] or **perc** **1** *n cowboys & hoboes* Percolated coffee **2** *v fr 1920s* To run smoothly and well; =PERCOLATE: *The project's perking now*

perk[2] or **perc** *n fr early 1800s British* Extra money, privileges, fringe benefits, etc, pertaining to a job or assignment: *Some perks belong, though, to all unwilling celibates*—WH Auden [fr *perquisite*]

perk (or **perc**) **along** **1** *v phr fr 1920s* To run smoothly and easily: *The outboard's perking along sweetly* **2** *v phr 1930s jive talk* To move at a relaxed pace; =MOSEY: *I'm not hurrying, just perking along* [fr the persistent and even sound of a coffee *percolator*]

perker-upper *n* =PEPPER-UPPER

Perkmeister *n* An official in charge of favors, jobs, patronage, etc, in a political organization: *"Perkmeister" John FW Rogers, who administers all agencies in the executive office of the president*—Washingtonian [fr *perk* + German *Meister* "master"]

perk up **1** *v phr* To stimulate; invigorate: *Gotta perk up this class* **2** *v phr fr middle 1600s* To recuperate; recover; gain energy: *He's perking up after a two-week illness/ Perk up. We're almost done* [origin uncertain; perhaps related to *perch*, and semantically to the notion of being placed high]

perky *adj fr middle 1800s* Energetic and jaunty; lively

perp *n police* A criminal engaged in a specific crime: *The perp stood up, stepped back, took out a handgun and fired at least two shots*—New York Daily News [shortened form of *perpetrator*]

persnickety or **pernickety** *adj fr early 1800s British* Overfastidious; finical; fussy [fr Scots dialect, perhaps fr *particular*]

persuader *n fr middle 1800s British* Any weapon, esp a gun; =HEAT

per usual *See* AS PER USUAL

pesky *adj fr middle 1700s* Vexatious; annoying; pesty

peso (PAY soh) *n* A dollar [fr Mexican Spanish]

pet **1** *v fr early 1900s* To kiss and caress: *torrid hugging, smooching, and petting*—Calder Willingham **2** *n* Darling; sweetheart; =DOLL: *It's you, pet! How frightfully tickety-boo!*

Pete *See* FOR THE LOVE OF PETE, PISTOL PETE, SNEAKY PETE

peter[1] *n outdated underworld* A safe; strongbox; vault [fr 17th-century British criminal slang; perhaps fr the phrase *robbing Peter to pay Paul*]

peter[2] *n narcotics* =KNOCKOUT DROPS

◁ **peter**[3] ▷ *n* The penis [fr the association with *pee* "urine"]

◁ **peter-eater** ▷ *n* A person who does fellatio, esp homosexually; =COCKSUCKER

peterman *n outdated underworld* A safe-cracker: *the petermen of half a century ago*—E DeBaun

peter out *v phr fr middle 1800s* To become exhausted; dwindle away in strength, amount, etc: *They ran well the first mile or so, then petered out* [origin unknown; fr mining jargon, and perhaps fr French *peter* "flatulate, explode weakly"; compare *fizzle*]

pet peeve *n phr esp 1920s & 30s* One's particular and most cherished dislike or annoyance: *long been one of my pet peeves*—Word Study

petting *n* The activity of those who pet: *Petting is necking with territorial concessions*—Frederick Morton

pfft (FəT) *adj* Finished; dissolved: *Their seemingly happy marriage is pfft*

pfui *See* PHOOEY

PG (pronounced as separate letters) *n narcotics* Paregoric, an opium product

phenagle *See* FINAGLE

phenom (FEE nahm) *n fr baseball fr late 1800s* A phenomenally skilled or impressive person; performing wonder, esp in sports: *Sawyer's two other 24-year-old phenoms*—F Eck

Philadelphia bankroll *n phr* A roll of $1 bills with a larger bill wrapped around it; =MICHIGAN ROLL

a **Philadelphia lawyer** *n phr* One who makes things unnecessarily complicated and obfuscates matters: *He was talking like a Philadelphia lawyer, trying to cover up* [fr a traditional reputation for the shrewdness of such attorneys, perhaps ultimately based on that of Andrew Hamilton, a *Philadelphia lawyer*, who successfully defended the New York newspaper publisher John Peter Zenger against charges of criminal libel in 1710, a defense crucial to the doctrine of the freedom of the press]

Philly or **Phillie** *n* Philadelphia

phone *See* HOLD THE PHONE

phonus bolonus (or **balonus**) **1** *n phr* Something false and meretricious: *Phonus bolonus, he said*—Irwin Shaw **2** *adj: What a phonus-balonus smile he's got on*

phony or **phoney** *fr late 1800s* **1** *adj* Not real or genuine; false; fake: *You phony little fake*—Arthur Miller **2** *n* A fake thing: *That window's a phony, it don't open* **3** *v: I ain't phoneying them woids*—Jimmy Durante **4** *n* A person who affects some identity, role, nature, etc; poseur: *some phony calling himself a writer*—James M Cain [fr late-18th-century British underworld slang *fawney* fr Irish *fáinne* "ring," referring to a swindle in which the *fawney-dropper* drops a cheap ring before the victim, then is persuaded to sell it as if it were valuable; as the sequence of spellings, *phoney* and later *phony*, indicates, the US spelling is probably based on an attested folk etymology revealing the notion that one's feelings or even identity could be readily falsified on the *telephone*]

phony as a three-dollar bill *adj phr* Very false indeed; not remotely genuine

phooey *interj* (also **phoo** or **pfui** or **fooey** or **fooy** or **fuie**) *fr 1930s* An exclamation of disbelief, rejection, contempt, etc [fr Yiddish fr German; popularized by the newspaper columnist Walter Winchell]

phreaking (FREE king) *n* The imitation of telephone touch-tone signals by whistling or by using mechanical devices, so that free calls may be readily made: *"Phreaking," the art of using the telephone for fun but no profit for the company, came into being*—Toronto Life

physical *adj* Using the body, esp roughly or intimately: *Vanderbilt is a lot better than last year and more physical*—Birmingham News

See GET PHYSICAL

piano *n black* Spareribs, esp a single section of broiled spareribs: *cornbread with a piano on a platter*—Zora Neale Hurston

pic *n* A movie; =FLICK: *Raft's next pic*—Abel Green

pick someone's **brain** **1** *v phr* To question closely for one's own profit; exploit; be an intellectual parasite **2** *v phr* To inquire of; ask for information, advice, etc

pick 'em *See* one CAN REALLY PICK 'EM

pick 'em up and lay 'em down **1** *v phr* To run, esp to run fast **2** *v phr* To dance

picker *See* BRAIN-PICKER, CHERRY-PICKER, FRUIT-PICKER

picker-upper **1** *n* A person or thing that picks up: *A hitchhiker caught a ride....The picker-upper was soon arrested*—Associated Press **2** *n* =PEPPER-UPPER, PICK-ME-UP

picking *See* COTTON-PICKING

pickings *See* SLIM PICKINGS

pickle **1** *n* (also **picklement**) A parlous situation; predicament; dilemma: *I was in a sad pickle when I lost my job* **2** *v* To ruin; wreck:

This will promptly pickle her college chances—F Sparks [first sense fr 16th-century British slang *in a pickle*, and may refer to the situation of a mouse fallen into a pickling vat; *picklement* is a handy echo of *predicament*]

pickled *adj* Drunk; =SOUSED

pickle park *n phr truckers* A roadside rest area

picklepuss *n* A frowning and pessimistic person; =SOURPUSS

pick-me-up *fr middle 1800s* **1** *n* A drink or snack that invigorates; =PEPPER-UPPER, PERKER-UPPER **2** *n* A drink of liquor taken to restore tone and morale

pickup 1 *n* A person accosted and made a companion, esp in a bar, on the street, etc, for sexual purposes: *His next girlfriend was a pickup he made at Rod's* **2** *n* An arrest **3** *n* (also **pickup truck**) A small truck having a cab, and cargo space with low sidewalls **4** *n* The ability of a car to accelerate rapidly, esp from a halt **5** *n* The act of getting or acquiring something: *He made the pickup at the post office* **6** *adj* Impromptu; unceremonious: *We'll have a pickup lunch in the kitchen* **7** *adj* For one occasion; temporary; ad hoc: *a pickup band/ a pickup corps of waiters*

pick up 1 *v phr* To resume; begin again: *We'll pick up the story where George had the nervous crisis* **2** *v phr* To increase; raise: *Let's pick up the pace a little, okay?* **3** *v phr* To get; acquire: *He picked up a few thou hustling* **4** *v phr fr middle 1800s* To make things clean and neat; tidy up: *You'd better pick up in your room, it's a godawful mess* **5** *v phr* To answer the telephone

pick someone **up 1** *v phr* To arrest: *The cops picked up six muggers and hauled their asses in* **2** *v phr* To make someone's acquaintance boldly, esp in a bar, on the street, etc, for sexual purposes: *She lets the [soldiers] pick her up*—Associated Press **3** *v phr* To stimulate or invigorate: *A book like this really picks you up*

pick something **up** *v phr* To notice; discover: *Did you pick that wink up?*

pick up on something **1** *v phr* To notice; become aware of: *I pick up on people's pain, Alexander*—New Yorker **2** *v phr* To refer to and add to; bring back to notice, esp in order to query: *Your readers can pick up on the fact*—Rolling Stone

pick someone **up on** something *v phr fr middle 1800s* To object or call special attention to; correct: *I want to pick you up on that reference*

pick up the tab (or **check**) *v phr* To pay; assume the expense; =PAY THE FREIGHT: *also somebody to pick up the tab*—Saul Bellow

picnic 1 *n* Something very easy; =CINCH, PIECE OF CAKE: *That job's a picnic* **2** *n* An enjoyable time; =a BALL, BLAST: *The last week we had a picnic*

See NO PICNIC

picture *See* DRAW A PICTURE

the **picture** *n phr* The situation; present shape of things: *After he explained he asked me if I had the picture/ I don't like the picture, it stinks*

See the BIG PICTURE, GET THE PICTURE, PUT someone IN THE PICTURE

pictures *n cardplayers* Picture cards

piddle 1 *v* To urinate; =PEE: *So you piddled on the floor. But you don't have to have your face wiped in it*—Time **2** *v* To waste; idle: *You just piddle the day away*—Washington Post [a euphemism for *piss*]

piddle around *v phr fr middle 1500s* =FART AROUND, FIDDLE AROUND

piddling *adj* Meager; trivial; paltry: *It was an effort, though a piddling one*

pie 1 *n* An easy task or job; =GRAVY: *The climb is pie for a character like Joan* ◁**2**▷ *n* The vulva: *her hot, wet pie*—Earl Thompson

See APPLE-PIE ORDER, CUTESY-POO, CUTIE-PIE, EASY AS PIE, FUR PIE, HAIR PIE, SWEETIE-PIE

piece 1 *n* A share; portion; financial interest; =a PIECE OF THE ACTION, SLICE: *a piece of the racket*—American Mercury **2** *n* A gun; pistol: *They step up to the driver's side and shove a piece in his ear*—Time ◁**3**▷ *n* =PIECE OF ASS **4** *n narcotics* An ounce of heroin or other narcotic: *He buys heroin in "pieces"*—J Mills **5** *n* A graffito on a subway car: *A train rumbles in... and we all pause to view its pieces*—M Blaine

See ALL IN ONE PIECE, COME UP SMELLING LIKE A ROSE, MOUTHPIECE, MUSEUM PIECE, TEAR OFF A PIECE, THINK-PIECE

◁ **piece of ass** (or **tail**)▷ **1** *n phr* The sex act; a completed sex act **2** *n phr* A person regarded as a sex object, organ, or partner
See TEAR OFF A PIECE

piece of cake *n phr* Anything very easy; anything easily or pleasantly done; =BREEZE, DUCK SOUP • Originally and chiefly British: *It's a piece of cake because you don't have the fear that they are going to pitch out on you*—Inside Sports

piece of change *n phr* (Variations: **hunk** may replace **piece**; **jack** may replace **change**) Money, esp a large amount: *which would come to quite a piece of change*—Village Voice

piece of meat *n phr* A person regarded as merely a physical body; unaccommodated man: *I'm just a piece of meat... but I know I'm a good piece of meat*—Sports Illustrated

piece of someone's **mind** *n phr* A strong rebuke; severe criticism and correction

◁ **piece of shit**▷ **1** *n phr* Something inferior or worthless; a wretched effort: *This show's a piece of shit* **2** *n phr* A lie; hypocrisy: *Everything she said is a big piece of shit*

◁ **piece of tail**▷ *See* PIECE OF ASS

a **piece of the action** *n phr* A share of something, esp in profits, a business, or speculation, etc: *see that everybody, regardless of party, gets a piece of the action*—Ben Wattenberg [fr *action* "gamble, gambling"]

pie-eyed **1** *adj fr early 1900s* Drunk: *the pie-eyed brothers*—P Marks **2** *adj* Astonished; wide-eyed: *Randall was pie-eyed. His mouth moved, but nothing came out of it*—Raymond Chandler

pie-faced *adj* Stupid; foolish: *a pie-faced boy from Minnesota*—Pulpsmith

pie in the sky *n phr fr early 1900s* The reward one will get for compliant behavior, later; hence, wishful thinking or utopian fantasies [fr a Wobbly expression of contempt for those who maintained that suffering and penury on earth would be compensated for by bliss and luxury in heaven; the *locus classicus* is a parody of the hymn "In the Sweet By and By," ascribed to the Wobbly martyr Joe Hill]

piffle *fr late 1800s British* **1** *n* Nonsense; =BALONEY, BUNK: *the kind of piffle actors have to go up against*—H McHugh **2** *interj* A mild exclamation of disbelief, contradiction, rejection, etc

pifflicated *adj* Drunk

pig ◁**1**▷ *n esp 1960s counterculture fr middle 1800s underworld* A police officer: *The innocent kids all hollered "Off the pigs!"* ◁**2**▷ *n* A bigot, racist, or fascist; a person who contributes to the oppression of a people ◁**3**▷ *n* Any fat, sloppy, obnoxious person ◁**4**▷ *n* A glutton **5** *v: When you eat too much, you can say "I pigged"*—Milwaukee Journal ◁**6**▷ *n* A promiscuous woman, esp one who is blowsy and unattractive: *spoke of a pig he had recently picked up*—James T Farrell **7** *n horse-racing* A racehorse, esp an inferior one: *why the hell that pig didn't win*—Fortune **8** *n railroad* A locomotive, esp a switch engine or yard engine **9** *n* (also **Pig**) A large and powerful motorcycle, esp a Harley-Davidson (a trade name)
See BLIND PIG, LIKE PIGS IN CLOVER, LONG PIG, MALE CHAUVINIST PIG, RENT-A-PIG

pigeon **1** *n underworld* An informer; =STOOL PIGEON: *I don't like pigeons*—Raymond Chandler **2** *n fr late 1500s British underworld* The victim of a swindle; dupe; =MARK, SUCKER: *I'm your pigeon now and you guys are gonna rip me off*—WT Tyler **3** *n* A young woman; =CHICK **4** *n* A former alcoholic in the care of a helpful sponsor or guardian [for first sense see *stool pigeon*; the second sense probably derives fr the expression *pluck a pigeon* and may be based on a notion that *pigeons* are easy to catch; the sense "young woman" is probably fr or related to *quail* and again suggests an easy victim]
See DEAD DUCK, STOOL PIGEON

pigeonhole **1** *v* To classify; identify; =BUTTON DOWN, PEG: *I pigeonhole this clown as a total bigmouth* **2** *v* To put away or aside; =FILE AND FORGET [fr the separate compartments of a desk or sorting system, likened to the orifices in a *pigeon* cote]

◀ **pig-fucker**▶ *n* A despicable person; =BASTARD, FUCKER, SHITHEEL

piggyback **1** *n* The transport of loaded containers or semitrailers on railroad flatcars **2** *v* To originate or prosper with the help of something else: *Aerobic dancing piggybacked on the jogging craze* [fr the term for carrying someone, esp a child, on one's back derived by folk etymology fr *pick-a-back*, of unknown origin]

pigheaded *adj* Stubborn; stupidly obstinate

pig in a poke *See* BUY A PIG IN A POKE

◁ **pig-meat**▷ **1** *n esp black* A woman, esp a sexually promiscuous one **2** *n fr prizefight* A defeated or moribund person; =LOSER

◁ **pigmobile**▷ *n esp 1960s counterculture* A police car; squad car: *that took one pigmobile off patrol*—Niven and Bournelle

pig out **1** *v phr fr teenagers* To overeat: *I pigged out on a runny Brie* **2** *v phr* To overindulge in anything: *pig out on rock and roll*—Village Voice

◁ **pig's ass** (or **ear** or **eye**)▷ *See* IN A PIG'S ASS

◁ **pig shit**▷ *See* STRONGER THAN PIG SHIT

pigskin **1** *n* A football; =the OBLATE SPHEROID **2** *modifier: the pigskin parade/ a pigskin superstar*

pike *See* COME DOWN THE PIKE

piker **1** *n fr late 1800s* A mean and stingy person; miser; =TIGHTWAD **2** *n* A shirker; loafer [originally a vagrant, esp a gambler, who wandered along the *pike*; hence a poor sport, a cheapskate]

pile **1** *n fr middle 1700s* All one's wealth, esp if it is fairly much: *He made his pile flim-flamming little old ladies* **2** *v* To dash; run; thrust oneself: *I piled after her hell to split* —James M Cain

See WOODPILE

a **pile** *n phr fr late 1800s* A large amount of money; a fortune; =a BUNDLE

pileup *n* A wreck, esp one involving a number of cars: *6-car, end-to-end pile-up*—Associated Press

pile up **1** *v phr* To wreck; =RACK UP, TOTAL: *after he piled up his car*—J Evans **2** *v phr fr late 1800s* To go aground: *We piled up at Wood's Hole*

pile up Zs *See* COP ZS

pill **1** *n fr late 1800s* A boring, disagreeable person; =a PAIN IN THE ASS: *Oh, don't be a pill, Valerie*—SJ Perelman **2** *n* A baseball or golf ball **3** *n narcotics* An opium pellet for smoking **4** *n narcotics* A Nembutal (a trade name) capsule; =NIMBY

See PEP PILL

the **pill** or **the Pill** *n phr* Any oral contraceptive for women: *now that the joint and the pill are with us* —Society

pillhead *n narcotics* A person who habitually takes tranquilizers, amphetamines, barbiturates, etc, in pill or capsule form: *Papoose and me were a bunch of pillheads*—Rolling Stone

pillow talk *n phr* Intimate talk, like that between a couple in bed

pill pad *narcotics* **1** *n phr* A place where addicts gather to smoke opium; opium den **2** *n phr* A place where narcotics users gather to take drugs of any sort; =PAD

pill-popper *n narcotics* =PILLHEAD

pill-popping *narcotics* **1** *adj* Addicted to or using narcotics in pill or capsule form: *a suicidal, pill-popping Newsweek reporter*—Saturday Review **2** *n phr* The use of narcotics in pill form: *They don't do so much pill-popping any more*

pill-pusher or **pill-roller** or **pill-peddler** **1** *n* A physician: *gynecological phenomena you pill-peddlers are always talking about*—Ellery Queen **2** *n* A pharmacist or student of pharmacy

pilot *See* COW PILOT, SKY-PILOT

pimpish *adj teenagers* Stylishly dressed

pimple *n* The head

pimpmobile **1** *n* A fancy car used by a prostitute's procurer and manager: *There's a red Cadillac pimpmobile parked outside*—New York **2** *n* Any very fancy and overlavish car **3** *modifier: The pimpmobile mantle will be donned by the 1983 Cougar*—Car and Driver

pin **1** *n* A leg **2** *v* To classify and understand someone; =PEG, PIGEONHOLE: *I got this guy pinned as a turkey* **3** *v* To look over; survey; =DIG: *just pinning the queer scene*—John Rechy **4** *v students* To declare a serious commitment to someone by giving or taking a fraternity pin

See KING, PIN someone DOWN, PIN something DOWN, PIN someone's EARS BACK, PIN ON, PINS, PIN-SHOT

pinch **1** *v fr 1600s* To steal; =SWIPE: *Who pinched the script?*—L Ford **2** *v fr middle 1800s British* To arrest; =BUST: *The stores will invite ill will if they pinch indiscriminately*—Fortune **3** *n: make a respectable number of pinches to stay off the transfer list*—Rolling Stone

See IN A PINCH

pincher ***See*** PENNY-PINCHER

pinchers *n* Shoes

pinch hit *n phr baseball fr early 1900s* A hit made by a player who bats in place of another

pinch-hit **1** *v baseball* To bat for a player who has been removed from the lineup, usu at a critical point in the game **2** *v* To substitute for someone else: *I had to pinch-hit for her when she got sick*

pinchpenny **1** *n fr middle 1600s* A miser; =TIGHTWAD **2** *adj: your pinchpenny budgets*

pin someone **down** **1** *v phr* To get a definite answer, commitment, piece of information, etc, from: *He wouldn't say just when, I couldn't pin him down* **2** *v phr* To make immobile, esp to keep soldiers in place with constant or accurate fire **3** *v phr* To identify or classify someone definitely; =PEG, PIN: *I can't pin her down, but I've seen her before*

pin something **down** *v phr* To recognize, identify, or single out definitely; make explicit: *I can't quite pin my feeling down*

pineapple *n fr WW1 Army* A hand grenade or small bomb: *Nobody tried to throw a pineapple in my lap*—Raymond Chandler [fr the resemblance of a fragmentation grenade, with its deeply segmented ovoid surface, to a *pineapple*]

pin someone's **ears back** *v phr fr 1930s* To punish, either by words or blows; chasten: *a flip-lipped bastard who should have had his ears pinned back long ago*—J Evans

ping jockey ***See*** BLIP JOCKEY

ping off the walls *v phr Army* To be very nervous; be tense and excited: *Better stop pinging off the walls and start making some plans*

ping-pong *v hospital* To refer a patient, esp a Medicaid recipient, to other doctors, in order to maximize fees: *"Medicaid mills" or clinics... reap enormous profits by such practices as "Ping Ponging"*—Time [fr Ping-Pong, trade name for a manufacturer's table tennis set and game]

pinhead *n* A stupid person

pink **1** *n black* A white person; =GRAY **2** *n* A political liberal or mild socialist radical **3** *adj: pink perspective on Palestine* **4** *n hot rodders* A legal certificate of car ownership **5** *adj* Redheaded • Often used as a nickname **6** *adj homosexuals* Homosexual

See TICKLED PINK

pink collar **1** *adj phr* Traditionally held by women of the middle class: *Mature women tended to gravitate toward pink collar jobs as secretaries, teachers, nurses, and saleswomen*—New York Times **2** *adj phr* Working in a job traditionally held by women of the middle class: *the TV character to whom real-life blue- and pink-collar working women most relate*—Time [modeled on *blue collar* and *white collar*]

pink ink *n phr* Romance novels; =BODICE-RIPPERS

pinko **1** *n* A person of liberal or mildly radical socialist political opinions; =PINK: *pinko James J Matles and pinko Julius Emspak*—Time **2** *adj: those creepy pinko hippies*—Ebony

pink puffer *n phr hospital* A thin emphysema patient

pink slip **1** *n phr fr 1920s* A discharge notice; =WALKING PAPERS: *All 1,300 employees got pink slips today*—Associated Press **2** *v: They had pink-slipped Hartz one brutal afternoon*—Washingtonian

See GET THE PINK SLIP, GIVE someone THE PINK SLIP

pinky[1] or **pinkie** **1** *n fr middle or early 1800s* The little finger: *He paused and ran his pinkie along his lower lip*—Raymond Chandler **2** ***modifier:*** *pinky ring* [fr an earlier adjective sense, "small, tiny"]

See PLAY STINKY-PINKY

pinky[2] or **pinkie** *n* A redheaded person • Often used as a nickname [fr the color]

pinky-crooker *n* A person of affectedly refined tastes and manners: *You'll find only the pinky-crookers at the concerts*—Time

pinned *adj narcotics* Contracted: *his pupils are "pinned"*—J Mills

pin on *v phr* To make an accusation; inculpate; = HANG ON: *Police indicated they had little to pin on them*—Associated Press

pin one on *See* HANG ONE ON

pins *n fr 1500s* The legs: *knocked clean off his pins*—O Johnson

pin-shot *n narcotics* A narcotics injection made with a safety pin and an eyedropper

pint *See* HALF-PINT

pin-up **1** *n esp 1940s* A picture, usu a provocative photograph, esp of a pretty young woman **2** ***modifier:*** *pin-up collections and books*—Playboy **3** *n* A young woman shown in a pin-up: *Betty Grable was the services' favorite pin-up*

pin-up girl *See* SWEATER GIRL

pip *n* A minor skin lesion, esp of teenagers: *whiteheads, blackheads, goopheads, goobers, pips, acne trenches*—New York Times

a **pip** (or **a pipperoo** or **a pippin**) **1** *n phr fr early 1900s* A person or thing that is remarkable, wonderful, superior, etc; = BEAUT, HUMDINGER: *His wildest dreams have to be pips*—Washington Post **2** ***modifier:*** *a pipperoo flick* [fr *pippin*, a prized kind of apple; the shift was probably fr *peach* as one kind of excellent fruit to *pippin* as another]

the **pip** *n phr* A severe case of being annoyed: *People gave him the pip*—P Marks [fr a disease of fowl]

pipe[1] *n fr early 1900s students* Anything easily done; = CINCH: *Getting in is a pipe* [apparently fr *pipe dream*, suggesting something as easily or magically done as in a wishful dream]

pipe[2] **1** *n* A telephone **2** *v* To speak up; say something; = PIPE UP: *But I am not suppose to know that and do not pipe*—John O'Hara **3** *v fr late 1800s* To look at; see; notice: *Did you pipe her hands?*—Eugene O'Neill **4** *n* (also **pipeline**) *surfers* The tubular inner section of a breaking wave [all senses probably derived fr *pipe* as a conduit or a musical instrument; the sense "look at" is related to criminal slang "follow, keep under surveillance," of obscure origin and difficult to relate to any sense of *pipe*]

See DOWN THE TUBE, LAY PIPE, LEAD-PIPE CINCH

pipe down *v phr fr late 1800s* To stop talking; speak more quietly: *The others got sore at him and told him to pipe down*—John O'Hara [fr naval jargon, probably related to the use of the boatswain's *pipe* for giving commands, or to its shrill noise]

pipe dream *n phr* An improbable and visionary hope, ideal, scheme, etc, such as an opium smoker might have: *He has some ambitious plans, mostly pipe dreams*

pipeline **1** *n* A channel of communication, esp a direct and special one: *You'd think he has a pipeline to Jesus* **2** *n* A channel or course for routine production, processing, etc: *We'll have fewer men in what we call the "pipeline"*—US News and World Report **3** ***modifier:*** *a pipeline review*

See IN THE PIPELINE, PIPE

pipes or **set of pipes** *n* or *n phr* The voice, esp the singing voice: *He was trying out his pipes on a new speech/ to bring that great set of pipes into your very own living room*—Changes

See BANG PIPES

pipe up *v phr* To speak up; raise one's voice; = SING OUT: *He piped up with a couple of smart-ass cracks* [perhaps fr a play on the nautical *pipe down*; perhaps fr the playing of the *pipe* or *pipes*]

◁ **piss[1]** ▷ **1** *n* Urine **2** ***v:*** *He had to piss* **3** *v* (also **piss and moan**) To complain; grumble; = BITCH, KVETCH: *whatever agency they are pissing over at the moment*—New Jersey **4** *adj* Of wretched quality; = PISS POOR: *Europe is a piss place for music*—Rolling Stone

See EYES LIKE PISSHOLES IN THE SNOW, FULL OF PISS AND VINEGAR, NOT HAVE A POT TO PISS IN, PANTHER PISS, TICKLE THE SHIT OUT OF someone

◁ **piss[2]** ▷ ***combining word*** A term placed before an adjective to intensify its meaning: *piss-awkward/ piss-elegant/ piss-ugly*

◁ **piss and vinegar** ▷ *n phr* Energy; vitality; = PEP, PIZZAZZ

See FULL OF PISS AND VINEGAR

◁ **piss and wind**▷ ***n phr*** *fr late 1800s* Pretentious but feeble show; gaudy display: *They strut with the piss and wind traditional among victors in political intrigues*—Village Voice [fr the situation of a person who can urinate and flatulate, but not achieve a substantial defecation]

◁ **pissant**▷ (PIHS ant) **1** ***n*** A despicable person; an insignificant wretch: *That sorry damn pissant*—Pat Conroy **2** ***adj*** Insignificant; paltry: *this little pissant country*—New York Times [fr *piss* and *ant*, based on earlier *pissmire* "ant" because ants were thought to have an unpleasant smell]

◁ **piss** something **away**▷ ***v phr*** To waste and dissipate something foolishly; squander: *There was a part of him that wanted to piss it away and be a loser*—Washingtonian

◁ **piss call**▷ ***n phr*** *fr Navy* Reveille, the military signal to get out of bed in the morning

◁ **piss-cutter**▷ ***n*** A person or thing that is remarkable, wonderful, superior, etc; =BEAUT, HUMDINGER, PIP: *Isn't our new colleague a piss-cutter?*

◁ **pissed off**▷ ***adj phr*** (Variations: **pissed** or **p'd** or **peed off** or **p o'd**) *fr WW2 armed forces* Angry; profoundly annoyed; indignant: *His face got all red-colored whenever he was pissed off*—Rolling Stone/ *He gets a little pissed like I'm making fun of him*—Rex Burns

◁ **piss-elegant**▷ (Variations: ◁**piss-ass** or **pissy** or **pissy-ass**▷) ***adj*** Ostentatiously elegant; affecting great refinement; =HOITY-TOITY: *a piss-elegant new wave Chinese restaurant and bar*—Rolling Stone/ *He was a jerk for needing to hang around with pissy queens*—Armistead Maupin/ *a place with a pissy-ass little fountain in the courtyard*

◁ **pisser**▷ **1** ***n*** A very difficult job or task; =BALL-BUSTER, BITCH: *That climb was a pisser* **2** ***n*** A person or thing that is remarkable, wonderful, superior, etc; =PISS-CUTTER: *You're a pisser, you are*—Lawrence Sanders **3** ***n*** A very funny person or thing: *What a pisser when he opened the wrong door by mistake* **4** ***n*** A toilet: *windowless with a pisser and no benches*—Rolling Stone [third sense fr the notion that one laughs hard enough to *piss* in one's pants]

◁ **pisshead**▷ ***n*** A despicable person; a stupid bore; =ASSHOLE: *that made such a pisshead of herself*—Stephen King

◁ **pissholes in the snow**▷ ***See*** EYES LIKE PISSHOLES IN THE SNOW

◁ **pissing contest** (or **match**)▷ ***n phr*** An argument; disagreement; confrontational debate: *warned him against getting into a pissing contest with Bittman*—Washingtonian [fr actual vying among boys as to who can project the urinary stream farthest]

◁ **piss in the wind**▷ ***v phr*** To waste one's time and effort: *If you think that'll work you're pissing in the wind*

◁ **piss-off**▷ ***n*** Anger; indignation: *There's a basic, well-justified piss-off all over the country*—Newsweek

◁ **piss** someone **off**▷ ***v phr*** To make angry; arouse indignation

◁ **piss on** someone or something▷ ***v phr*** To dismiss or treat contemptuously; defile or violate ● Often used as an angry and defiant dismissal: *I won't take it, piss on it/ As the old dog says, if you can't eat it and you can't fuck it, piss on it*

◁ **piss on ice**▷ ***v phr*** To live well; =EAT HIGH ON THE HOG, SHIT IN HIGH COTTON [fr the practice of putting cakes of *ice* in the urinals of expensive restaurants and clubs]

◁ **piss poor**▷ **1** ***adj phr*** Of wretched quality; inferior; bad: *dat a pisspoor excuse fo' a apology*—Esquire **2** ***adj phr*** *fr 1920s* Penniless; in pauperdom: *They're all born piss-poor*—Lawrence Sanders

◁ **piss-ugly**▷ ***adj*** Very ugly; nasty and menacing: *Beer-bellied brutes... peered at the world through piss-ugly eyes*—Village Voice

◁ **piss up a rope**▷ ***See*** GO PISS UP A ROPE

◁ **piss up a storm**▷ ***v phr*** (Variations: **blow** or **kick** may replace **piss**) To make a great noisy fuss about something, esp in complaint: *When I came in she was pissing up a storm because they didn't have what she wanted*

◁ **piss-warm**▷ ***adj*** As warm as fresh urine: *I can't drink piss-warm beer*

◁ **pissy** or **pissy-ass**▷ ***See*** PISS-ELEGANT

pistol **1** ***n*** A person or thing that is remarkable, wonderful, superior, etc; =BEAUT, PIP, PISS-CUTTER: *That Ruby Jean, she's a pistol*—New York Times

2 *n* *lunch counter* Hot pastrami [lunch counter sense because the eater feels as if shot in the stomach soon after eating hot pastrami]

See HOT AS A THREE-DOLLAR PISTOL

pistol Pete *n phr* A zealous and effective lover; =COCKSMAN [fr the usual jocular analogue between *pistol* and "penis," "shooting" and having an orgasm, etc, reinforced by alliteration and the fact that *Peter* means "penis"]

pit *v* To take a racing car into the pit: *He pitted for fresh rubber and thus lost a lap*—Sports Illustrated

See PASSION PIT

pitch *fr middle 1800s British* **1** *n* *hawkers* A hawker's or street vendor's place of business **2** *n* *hawkers* The sales talk or spiel of a hawker: *He recited a part of his pitch*—New Yorker **3** *n* *hawkers* A hawker **4** *v: Louie...pitches kitchen gadgets*—M Zolotow/ *He pitches household items like the Magic Towel*—New Yorker **5** *n* *fr hawkers* Any sales talk or persuasional plea: *other gifts to prospective brides, along with a pitch to honeymoon at Holiday Inns*—Time **6** *n* A sexual approach, esp a tentative one; =PASS: *I never made a pitch with Herta*—John O'Hara **7** *v: I wouldn't try to pitch to that Ice Maiden* **8** *v* *homosexuals* To penetrate the anus in anal sex [all senses are fr the notion of *pitching* or establishing a place of trade]

See BUTTERFLY BALL, IN THERE PITCHING, MAKE A PITCH, PURPOSE PITCH, THROW

the **pitch** *n phr* The situation; the matter; the point: *I think I get the pitch*

pitchforks *See* RAIN CATS AND DOGS

pitching *See* IN THERE PITCHING

pitchman **1** *n* A person who sells novelties, household items, clever toys and tricks, etc, on the streets or at a fair or carnival **2** *n* Any advocate, promoter, persuader, spokesman, etc: *chief pitchman for Big Oil*

pitchout **1** *n* *baseball* A pitch thrown wide of the plate so that the catcher can more easily throw to one of the bases to forestall an attempted steal **2** *n* *football* A lateral pass from one back to another

the **pits** *n phr* The most loathsome place or situation imaginable: *This school is the pits* [fr *armpits*]

pit stop *n phr* A stop so that people may go to the toilet: *Pit stop. Head run*—Pat Conroy [fr the *pit stops* made by racing cars for service, repair, rest, etc]

pix[1] **1** *n* Movies; the movies; =the FLICKS: *You ought to be in pix* **2** *n* Photographs, esp the artwork of a newspaper, magazine, book, etc; graphics **3** ***modifier:*** *pix credit*

pix[2] *n* A male homosexual [fr *pixie*, suggested by *fairy*]

pizzazz **1** *n* Energy; power; =PEP, PISS AND VINEGAR: *The J-57 has more pizzazz*—Time **2** *n* A feature designed mainly for a gaudy and flashy appeal; =GIMMICK: *In panoply and pizzazz, this year's Inauguration will be the most expensive*—Newsweek [origin unknown; perhaps echoically suggested by *piss*, *ass*, and *piss and vinegar*]

PJs or **pjs** *n* Pajamas; =PEEJAYS: *as though I were running around in my PJs*—Sports Afield

place *See* IN PLACE, NOPLACEVILLE

places *See* GO PLACES

plain vanilla *adj phr* Unadorned; simple; basic: *Plain Vanilla, but Very Good*—Newsweek

plain white wrapper *n phr* *citizens band* An unmarked police car

◁ **plank**[1] ▷ *v* To do the sex act with or to; =SCREW: *while his wife was out getting planked*—John Irving

plank[2] *See* WALK THE PLANK

plank down (Variations: **plunk down** or **plump down** or **clunk down** or **plank out** or **plank**) *fr early 1800s* **1** *v phr* To put down with a thud or crash; place decisively: *an overstuffed chair some admirer had planked down next to the booth*—AJ Liebling **2** *v phr* To pay money; put down or put up money; offer or bet money: *planked down a cool $8,000,000*—RH Fetridge/ *plunked down...$65,000*—Bob Thomas [fr the hard striking of the *plank* of a table]

plant **1** *v* *fr middle 1800s* To bury; hide **2** *v* To place evidence secretly so that someone will be incriminated: *Someone is planting evidence*—Erle Stanley Gardner **3** *v* To place a blow: *He planted a left* *on my poor snoot* **4** ***n*** =SHILL **5** ***n*** *hoboes* A hideout **6** ***n*** *fr early 1800s British* A cache, esp of stolen goods **7** ***n*** A false and falsely based accusation; =FRAME-UP: *They were planning to disgrace the mayor, using a plant* **8** ***n*** A spy, esp a police spy: *The new guy turned out to be a plant*

plaster **1** ***n*** A banknote, esp a one-dollar bill: *If you need a couple of plasters until Ed gets out, tell me* —Lawrence Sanders **2** ***v*** To disseminate or spread widely: *They plastered the city with leaflets* **3** ***n*** A person who surreptitiously follows another; shadow; =TAIL: *He probably knew he had a plaster*—J Evans **4** ***n*** A subpoena or summons; arrest warrant [money sense fr *shinplaster*, an early-19th-century term for "currency of little value or very small denomination"]

plastered ***adj*** Drunk

plastic **1** ***adj*** *esp 1960s counterculture* False and superficial; meretricious; =HOKED-UP, SLICK, PHONY: *in California... a plastic society*—BW Dipple **2** ***n*** A credit card; monetary credit afforded by the use of credit cards

plate **1** ***n*** =DISH **2** ***n*** =PLATTER

See GET TO FIRST BASE, HAVE one's HANDS FULL, OFF one's PLATE

platter ***n*** A phonograph record; =DISC

play **1** ***v*** To acquiesce; cooperate; =PLAY BALL: *They'd come back and get her, if I didn't play with them* —Raymond Chandler **2** ***v*** To go very well; succeed: *The O'Connor appointment's playing... you're on a roll, Mr President*—Philadelphia Daily News

See BONEHEAD PLAY, GRANDSTAND PLAY, MAKE A PLAY FOR

play along ***v phr*** =PLAY BALL

play around **1** ***v phr*** To do something, esp one's job, casually or frivolously; =HORSE AROUND: *Quit playing around and start playing hardball* **2** ***v phr*** To be sexually promiscuous; =SLEEP AROUND: *I guess I'd never given much thought to the idea of Dad playing around*—Claude Brown

play around with someone **1** ***v phr*** To flirt or dally with; have a sexual involvement with **2** ***v phr*** To treat lightly or insultingly; challenge or provoke: *I wouldn't play around with that gorilla if I were you*

play ball **1** ***v phr*** *fr middle 1800s* To begin; get started: *Let's play ball now, it's time* **2** ***v phr*** To cooperate; collaborate; acquiesce: *I might have played ball just a little*—Agnes DeMille **3** ***v phr*** To deal honestly and fairly: *He was playing ball with Artrim*—Erle Stanley Gardner [fr baseball]

◁ **play bouncy-bouncy** ▷ ***v phr*** To do the sex act, esp in the superior position; copulate: *He keeps cool... while she plays bouncy-bouncy on him* —Herbert Gold

playboy ***n*** *fr 1920s* A man devoted to glossy and luxurious self-indulgence; bon vivant; =GOOD-TIME CHARLIE

play catch-up (or **catch-up ball**) **1** ***v phr*** To play a game determinedly and desperately when one is losing: *when college wishbone teams go to the air to play catchup*—Sports Illustrated **2** ***v phr*** To work to recover from a disadvantaage, defeat, etc: *After the quarterly profits disaster we had to play catch-up/ For the last two years it's been a matter of playing catch-up ball with the budget*—Washington Post

play close to the chest (or **the vest**) ***v phr*** To be secretive and uncommunicative; keep one's counsel [fr the practice of a careful card player]

play dirty ***v phr*** To use unethical, illegal, or injurious means; be deceptive and tricky; chicane: *When he started in politics he didn't mean to play dirty*

played out **1** ***adj phr*** *fr late 1800s* Exhausted; worn out; =FRAZZLED: *I was played out, and quit at once* **2** ***adj phr*** No longer useful, viable, fashionable, etc: *I think the alienation theme is about played out*

player ***See*** BUTTON MAN, HORSEPLAYER

play footsie ***See*** FOOTSIE

play for keeps (or **rough**) ***v phr*** To be intent and serious to the point of callousness; =PLAY HARDBALL: *We're out here man for man and playin' for keeps*—Claude Brown/ *I thought, well, if they can play rough, we can too* [fr the game of marbles and other childrens' games where the tokens may be either returned or *kept* by the winner]

play games ***v phr*** To maneuver and manipulate cunningly; toy and gamble: *Don't play games with me, Linda* —National Lampoon

playgirl *n* A woman devoted to glossy and luxurious self-indulgence

◁ **play grab-ass**▷ *v phr* To indulge in sexual clutching and touching; to feel and fondle; =GROPE • Sometimes used metaphorically: *playing grabass with the counter girl*—Easyriders/ *His reluctance to play what he called grab-ass with Congress*—Newsweek

play hardball *v phr* To be intent and serious to the point of callousness; =PLAY FOR KEEPS: *Helms Plays Hardball*—Newsweek [fr the presumed distinction in difficulty, severity, and manliness between baseball, that is, *hardball*, and softball]

play hell with something *v phr* To damage or destroy: *The rain had played hell with business*—Armistead Maupin [fr *play hell and Tommy*, attested in the mid-19th century and said to be fr earlier *play Hal and Tommy*, in reference to the behavior of Henry VIII and his minister Thomas Cromwell]

◁ **play hide the weenie**▷ *v phr* To do the sex act; copulate; =SCREW

play hooky (or **hookey**) *v phr fr middle 1800s students* To stay away from work and duty, or esp from school without an excuse; be truant [probably fr *hook it*]

play in Peoria *v phr* To succeed in areas distinct from such focuses of power as Washington and New York or the Northeast in general: *When you're under a deadline, it's hard to judge what will play in Peoria*—Art Buchwald [fr the theater sense of *play*, to succeed on the stage]

play in the family *See* PLAY THE DOZENS

play it by ear *v phr* To handle a situation instinctively and extemporaneously, rather than by informed planning; improvise: *We didn't have much to go on, so we just had to play it by ear* [fr the playing of music imitatively, without training and notation]

play it cool *v phr* To behave in a calm, controlled, uncommitted way; be watchful and impassive: *We asked for a price and the agent "played it cool"*—Publishers Weekly

play it (or **play**) **safe** *v phr* To choose a cautious line of behavior; avoid much risk: *Now we're ahead, let's play it safe*

play kissie (Variations: **kissy-face** or **kissy-facey** or **kissie-kissie** or **kissy-poo** or **lickey-face** or **smacky lips** may replace **kissie**) **1** *v phr* To kiss and caress; =MAKE OUT, NECK: *busy playing lickey-face* —New York Post/ *Newlyweds play kissy-poo*—People Weekly **2** *v phr* To be friendly and flattering; =PLAY UP TO someone: *We have to play kissie with him*—New Yorker

play penny pool *v phr* To deal in paltry matters; be concerned with childish trivia: *This isn't penny pool these guys are playing*—George Warren

play rough *See* PLAY FOR KEEPS

plays *See* the WAY IT PLAYS

play second fiddle *v phr fr middle 1700s or earlier* To be in an inferior position; lack power or will to lead: *They won't play second fiddle to their spouses any more*

◁ **play stinky-pinky** (or **stink-finger**)▷ *v phr* =FINGERFUCK

play the dozens (or **the dirty dozens**) *black fr early 1900s* **1** *v phr* To play an elaborate word-game of reciprocal insult, esp against the opponent's mother: *Great God from Zion!... Y'all really playing de dozens tuhnight!*—Zora Neale Hurston **2** *v phr* To take advantage of; deceive; =DO A NUMBER ON: *He burst into tears, crying, "You all played the dozens on me"*—Joseph Wambaugh [origin unknown]

play the field *v phr* To have a number of sex or love partners, rather than settling on one: *I thought I'd play the field, until Joan came along* [fr gamblers who bet on other horses than the favorites]

◁ **play the skin flute**▷ *v phr* To do fellatio

play up to someone *v phr fr early 1800s British theater* To flatter; be compliant: *If you play up to him he'll think you're brilliant* [fr the behavior of an actor who gives featuring support to another]

play whupass (WHUHP as) *v phr* To have a rough sort of game, fight, etc: *Our Frogs are gonna play some whupass with the Rice Owls today* [fr a dialect pronunciation of *whip ass*]

◁ **play with** oneself▷ *v phr* To masturbate; =JACK OFF: *the urge to play with myself*—HK Fink

play (or **deal** or **operate**) **with a full deck** **1** *v phr* To be sane and reasonable; have normal intelligence • Usu in the negative: *Neither of the poor things was playing with a full deck*—Saul Bellow **2** *v phr* To be honest and straightforward; avoid deception: *He has bluffed you into thinking he was playing with a full deck*—Playboy

plea *See* COP A PLEA

pleat *See* REET PLEAT

plenty *adv* Very; very much; extraordinarily: *I was plenty cautious*—Erle Stanley Gardner

plonk **1** *n fr 1930s British fr Australian* Inferior wine; cheap wine: *It's a humble plonk, but you'll like it* **2** *n* A boring and obnoxious person; =PILL

plonked *adj* Drunk

plotzed *adj* Drunk: *even smashed as you were, friend, plotzed out of your wits*—John D MacDonald [probably fr Yiddish *plotzen*, German *platzen* "burst, split," reflecting the same notion of violent destruction as *smashed, bombed*, etc]

◁ **plow** or **plough**▷ *v fr time immemorial* To do the sex act with or to a woman; =SCREW

plow (or **plough**) **into** **1** *v phr* To collide with very hard; ram: *so long as they don't fry in the sun or plow into an atmosphere*—CoEvolution Quarterly **2** *v phr* To attack heartily; assault: *We ploughed into the scumbags and made quick work of them/ They plowed into the job and finished it that day*

ploy *n fr 1700s British fr dialect* A device or stratagem; a move, esp one designed to disconcert an opponent while keeping one's position; a shrewd maneuver • Popularized by the late British humorist Stephen Potter

plug[1] **1** *n fr middle 1800s* An inferior old horse; =NAG **2** *n fr early 1900s* An average or inferior prizefighter [perhaps fr Dutch *plug* "a sorry nag," related to Swiss-German *pflag* and to Danish *plag* "foal"]

plug[2] **1** *n fr late 1800s* A silver dollar **2** *n* A counterfeit coin or one tampered with by the insertion of a plug of inferior metal **3** *adj* (also **plugged**) Worthless; =PHONY • This sense may be influenced by the notion of inferiority in **plug**[1]: *and furthermore the author does not give a plug damn*—Pauline Kael **4** *v fr middle 1800s* To shoot, esp shoot to death: *The mugger got plugged by an indignant on looker* [all senses fr the notion of *plug* as hole-filler]

See PULL THE PLUG

plug[3] **1** *v* (also **plug along** or **plug away**) *fr middle 1800s British students* To work steadily and fairly hard; keep busy but not excitingly so: *I plugged away at the required subjects* **2** *v* To give a flattering appraisal, esp with a view to selling something; advocate and support; cry up: *Cosmetic manufacturers plugged products to give women ersatz tan*—R Adler/ *If you'll plug my book I'll plug yours* **3** *n: I certainly would appreciate him giving me a plug with the owners*—John O'Hara [fr Oxford University slang, apparently in imitation of heavy plodding steps, or perhaps the steps of an old and tired horse; sense of selling or advocating fr the fact that such commendation was originally constant and repetitive]

plug for *v phr* To support actively; cheer for; =ROOT FOR: *She was plugging for the coalition candidate*

plugged in (or **into**) **1** *adj phr* In direct touch with; sensitive to and aware of: *Teachers simply aren't plugged into the world*—Richard Yates/ *You have to be very careful that you stay plugged in*—Newsweek **2** *adj phr* =TURNED ON [fr the metaphor of a person as an electrical or electronic device]

plugged nickel *See* NOT WORTH A PLUGGED NICKEL

plug in (or **into**) **1** *v phr* To become a part of; participate in; gain access to: *Wilson initially plugged in to what he terms "an old-boy network of 26-year-olds"*—GQ **2** *v phr* To discover and exploit to one's advantage; tap: *Nixon... has plugged into a great national yearning*—Hugh Sidey [fr the notion of the electrical *plug* and socket]

plug-ugly *fr middle 1800s* **1** *n* A rowdy; tough; =GORILLA, HOOD **2** *n* A prizefighter; =PUG [origin unknown; perhaps fr the fact that such persons are *ugly* from being *plugged* "hit" in the face; perhaps fr competing Baltimore volunteer fire companies who became combative around *fireplugs*; a Baltimore origin is strongly suggested by the early occurrences]

plum *n fr late 1800s* Something highly prized, esp an easy job with high pay and prestige, usu given for political favors [probably influenced by Little Jack Horner's feat of reaching in his thumb and pulling out a *plum* (in fact a raisin); compare early-19th-century British *plummy* "good, desirable"]

plumb *adv fr late 1500s* Completely; entirely; =STONE: *What he said was plumb silly* [fr notions of exact extent and precision associated with the *plumb bob* or sailor's *plumb line* (for measuring depth of water), ultimately fr Latin *plumbum* "lead"]

plumber *n esp 1970s* A member of a White House group under President Richard M Nixon which exerted itself to stop various leaks of confidential information: *One of the jobs carried out by the plumbers was burglarizing the office*—New York Times

plumbing **1** *n jive musicians* A trumpet **2** *n* The digestive, excretory, and reproductive systems and organs: *Something is really wrong with my plumbing; I haven't been able to eat or make love in weeks*

plummy *adj* Rich and sonorous; orotund and fruity; unctuous; =SMARMY: *the rich, plummy voice of Edward Arnold*—K Harris

plump or **plunk** *adv* Precisely; exactly; =SMACK: *It came down plump on his head/ She stood plunk on the line* [fr *plumb*]

plump down *See* PLANK DOWN

plumpie or **plumpy** *n* An overweight person; a chubby person: *A studio of plumpies!*—Esquire

plunk down *See* PLANK DOWN

plush or **plushy** **1** *adj* Luxurious; stylish; costly: *a swank, plush, exclusive cabaret club*—Westbrook Pegler/ *singer Ella Logan at the plushy Casablanca*—Budd Schulberg **2** *n: All the plush in the world won't tidy up his vulgar soul* [fr the soft and costly fabric]

plushery *n* A plush hotel, nightclub, restaurant, etc

po *See* PISSED OFF

pocket *n* A constricted place; cul de sac: *He was afraid they had him in a pocket*
See DEEP POCKET, IN someone's POCKET, OUT OF POCKET

◁ **pocket pool** ▷ *n phr* The fondling of one's own genitals with a pocketed hand

po'd *See* PISSED OFF

pod *n narcotics* Marijuana; =POT: *Diane smoked jive, pod, and tea*—Orville Prescott [origin unknown; perhaps fr the *pod*, or seed container, the flowering and fruiting head of the female cannabis plant]

pod people *n phr* Stupid, unfeeling, machinelike people; =ZOMBIES: *Is this pure pop for pod people?*—Newsweek [fr the extraterrestrial creatures depicted in the movie *Invasion of the Body Snatchers*, who spawn in *pods* and take over the bodies of human beings]

podspeak *n* Automatic, meaningless, ritual talk, the idiom of pod people; tedious bromides: *Clerks utter such podspeak as the inescapable "Have a nice day"*—Washington Post

Podunk (POH dunk) *n fr early 1900s* The legendary small country town; =JERKWATER TOWN [originally an Algonquian place name, meaning "a neck or corner of land," used for several places in New England]

pogey or **pogie** or **pogy** (POH gee) **1** *n hoboes fr late 1800s* A poorhouse, workhouse, or old folks' home **2** *n* A jail; =POKEY **3** *n* Free food, as distributed by charity, sent to soldiers, prisoners, etc, esp candy and cake; =POGEY BAIT **4** *n* =POGUE [origin unknown; perhaps fr the common name of the trash fish menhaden, as suggesting something cheap, common, and to be caught with bait; perhaps fr the Southern pronunciation of *porgy*, another fish of a similar quality; both fish names are of obscure origin]

pogey bait *n phr* (Variations: **pogie** or **pogy** or **poggie** or **poggy** may replace **pogey**) *fr WW1 armed forces* Candy and cake, etc; sweets; nonmilitary food and delicacies carried on field exercises [so called because they could be used in the seduction of boys and young men, *pogues*, into homosexual acts]

pogue (POHG) **1** *n* A youthful homosexual male, or either willing or unwilling partner of a homosexual male; =PUNK: *The kid was a pogue* —Robert Stone **2** *n esp Vietnam War armed forces* Any despicable boy or young man; =PUNK: *I was just a pogue, humpin' connex containers at a depot in Long Binh*—Doonesbury (comic strip)/ *Yeah, that's the pogue's name*—Pat Conroy [shortened form of *pogey*]

point *See* BROWNIE POINTS

pointed head **1** *n phr* A stupid, duncelike mind; a brainless cranium: *I hope you got that idea into your pointed head, creep* **2** *n phr* An intellectual; =BIGDOME, EGGHEAD: *the guys who think we're all a bunch of pointed heads*—Washington Post

pointer *n* An item of advice or instruction: *She gave me a few pointers about how to say it*

pointhead or **pointy-head** **1** *n* A stupid person; =TURKEY **2** *n* An intellectual; =EGGHEAD: *The "pointy heads" are impractical as politicians* —Newsweek

point-shaving *n sports & gambling* The illegal practice, esp on the part of athletes, of controlling the score of a game, match, series, etc, so that professional gamblers will have to pay less to the bettors or will win for themselves

point-spread *n gambling* The difference between the handicapping points added or subtracted for various teams in football and basketball betting

pointy-headed **1** *adj* Intellectual; cultured: *uninterested in... any of the pointy-headed criticism generated in the last two decades*—Village Voice **2** *adj* Stupid; idiotic

poisoning *See* LEAD-POISONING

poison-pen letter *n phr* A malicious anonymous letter; an obscene crank letter

poke[1] **1** *v fr late 1800s cowboys* To herd cattle **2** *n fr late 1800s* A cowboy: *Each poke pays his own transportation to the Rodeo*—Ithaca Journal **3** *n* =SLOWPOKE **4** *v baseball* To hit the ball, esp to hit fairly lightly with precise aim: *He just poked it into the hole* ◁**5**▷ *v fr late 1800s* To do the sex act with or to; =SCREW

See BUY A PIG IN A POKE, SLOWPOKE

poke[2] *fr hoboes, underworld & carnival* **1** *n* A wallet, pocket, or purse: *with only about $85 in my poke* —John O'Hara **2** *n* Money; one's bankroll [fr Southern dialect, "pocket, bag," fr Middle English, ultimately fr Old Norman French]

poke fun *v phr* To tease; jape; mock

poke one's **nose into** something *v phr* To pry and meddle; examine: *and to poke your nose into all the most interesting places*—Philadelphia

poker face **1** *n phr* An expressionless face; neutral mask; =DEADPAN **2** *n phr* A person whose face is usually expressionless

poker-faced *adj* Without expression; showing a neutral mask; =DEADPAN: *She's great at poker-faced zingers*

pokery *See* JIGGERY-POKERY

pokey[1] or **poky** *n* A jail; =SLAMMER: *My thoughts centered around the prospect of the "Pokey"*—James Simon Kunen [origin unknown]

pokey[2] or **poky** **1** *adj* Slow; dawdling; sluggish: *What a pokey waiter* **2** *adj* Insignificant; paltry: *a pokey little town* [fr *poke*[1], apparently as a contrast between merely *about* and an action of more vigor]

See HOKEY-POKEY

pol (PAHL) *n* A politician: *only another pol on the take*—Newsweek

◀ **polack** ▶ (POH lahk) (also **pollack** or **Pollack** or **pollock** or **Pollock**) **1** *n* A Pole or a person of Polish extraction **2** *adj: a polack miner* • It is curious that this word is pejorative in English even though it is the Polish word for "Pole"

pole *See* BEANPOLE, NOT TOUCH someone or something WITH A TEN-FOOT POLE

police or **police up** *v* or *v phr esp armed forces fr middle 1800s* To clean up a camp, barracks, parade ground, etc; make neat and orderly

Polish *See* IS THE POPE POLISH

polish apples *v phr* =APPLE-POLISH

polisher *See* APPLE-POLISHER

polish off *fr early 1800s British* **1** *v phr* To eat; consume, esp quickly and heartily: *I had polished off a platter of beans*—Boston Post **2** *v phr* To finish; accomplish: *He polished off the week's quota in four days* **3** *v phr* To put out of action; defeat; kill: *polish him off by crowning him with a Coca-Cola bottle*—Life

politician *n* A person who succeeds through charm, diplomacy, mutual favors, etc: *If you called him an asshole to his face you're no politician*

politico (pə LI ti koh) *n* A politician, esp a spectacular or unscrupulous one: *the heavy-duty Bay State politicoes* [fr Spanish or Italian]

pollack or **pollock** or **Pollock** *See* POLACK

polluted *adj* Drunk

ponce **1** *n chiefly British fr late 1800s British* A pimp, or any man supported by a woman **2** *v: He quit work and took to poncing* [origin unknown; perhaps fr French *pensionnaire* "boarder, lodger, person living without working"]

the **pond** *n* The ocean
See the HERRING POND

pong *n fr middle 1800s British* A smell; a stink: *when I catch that pong in the air*—Robert Stone [perhaps fr Romany *pan* "stink"]

pony **1** *n students fr early 1800s* A literal translation of a foreign-language school text, used as a cheating aid **2** *n* Any cheating aid as used by a student **3** *n fr late 1800s* A small, bell-shaped liquor glass, used esp for brandy and liqueurs **4** *n* A racehorse: *Do you follow the ponies?* **5** *n* A chorus girl or burlesque dancer: *pony in a burlecue*—F Brown [in all senses fr the thing being small like a *pony*; the student senses, which have or have had *horse* and *trot* as synonyms, may also suggest something that carries one, gives one a free ride]

pony act *See* DOG AND PONY ACT

pony up *v phr fr early 1800s* To pay; =FORK OVER: *got tired of ponying up $100 for my connection*—San Francisco [fr earlier British *post the pony* "pay," fr 16th century *legem pone* "money," fr the title of the Psalm for quarter day, March 25, the first payday of the year]

poo or **pooh** **1** *interj* A mild exclamation of disbelief, dismay, disappointment, etc: *Oh poo, I dropped it* **2** *n* Excrement; =DO, POO-POO • Along with **poop**, this is a euphemism used by and to children: *Zoo Poo garden fertilizer is made from the waste of all manner of exotic creatures*—Toronto Life/ *and just about any old pooh that dribbles from McLaren's mouth*—Village Voice
See CUTESY-POO, ICKY

-poo *combining word* Little; silly little • A nonsense word used after diminutive forms to give an arch baby-talk effect: *A little kissy-poo?/ settled down for a well-bred nappy-poo*—Village Voice

pooch *n* A dog: *a card for...your pooch*—Associated Press

pooched out *adj phr* Protruding: *round shoulders, pooched out stomach*—Glamor

◁ **poof** ▷ *n* (also **poofter** or **poove** or **pouffe**) *chiefly British fr early 1900s Australian* A male homosexual; =FAGGOT, QUEER [origin unknown; perhaps echoic of a male homosexual's more or less feminine interjections *poof!* or *poo!*; perhaps fr French *pouf* "cushioned ottoman chair," with its suggestions of effete luxury; perhaps fr *puff*, attested in mid-19th-century British hobo slang as "homosexual," and semantically akin to *blow* "do fellatio"; perhaps fr *puff* in the sense of something soft and unmanly, as seen in *powderpuff* or *creampuff*]

pooh-bah *n fr late 1800s* An important person; =BIG SHOT, HONCHO, VIP: *where presidents and pooh-bahs commune*—Westworld [fr the character in Gilbert and Sullivan's *The Mikado*, the name probably coined fr two exclamations of contempt and derision]

poohed or **poohed out** *adj* or *adj phr* =POOPED

pool *See* DIRTY POOL, PENNY POOL, PLAY PENNY POOL, POCKET POOL

◀ **poon tang** or **poon** ▶ *n phr* or *n* A black woman regarded as a sex object or partner: *Eye that poon tang there*—Calder Willingham/ *watching all that young poon*—Joseph Wambaugh [probably fr French *putain* "prostitute," by way of New Orleans Creole; though perhaps fr Chinese, since variants *poong tai* and *poong kai* have been recorded, according to Eric Partridge]

poop[1] *n fr 1930s Army & students* Information; data; =SCOOP: *The girl's given us the complete poop*—G Cotler [see *poop sheet*]

poop² **1** *n fr early 1900s* Excrement; =POO • Along with **poo**, this is a euphemism for use to and by children **2** *v: The dog pooped on the rug* **3** *n* A contemptible, trifling person; =PILL • Often used ironically and affectionately, esp of an old person: *a sweet old poop who was seventy-six*—Kurt Vonnegut, Jr **4** *v* To tire; fatigue; =BUSH: *Being with him poops me exceedingly* [probably fr a merging of 14th-century *poupen* "to toot," with 15th-century *poop* "the rear part of a ship," fr Latin *puppis* of the same meaning; the fatigue sense may be related to the condition of a ship which is *pooped* "has taken a wave over the stern"]

pooped or **pooped out** *adj* or *adj phr fr late 1800s* Exhausted; deeply fatigued; =BEAT, BUSHED: *starting to get pooped out*—James T Farrell/ *deflated derrieres and pooped out pecs*—San Francisco [fr a British nautical term describing a ship that has been swept by a wave at the stern]

pooper *See* PARTY-POOPER

pooper (or **poop**) **scooper** *n phr* A shovel and container set designed for cleaning one's dog's feces off the sidewalk, and, by extension, anything so used: *bearing a paper bag and a poop-scooper*—Newsweek

poo-poo or **pooh-pooh** **1** *v* To dismiss lightly and contemptuously; airily deprecate; deride: *I don't poo-poo his talent, just his character* **2** *n* Excrement; =POO • A euphemism used to and by children: *hit in the head with a potty full of poo-poo*—High Times

poop (or **poo**) **out** *v phr* To fail; lose energy and impetus; stop striving: *They would have won, but they suddenly just pooped out*

poop sheet *n phr fr 1930s Army & students* Any set of data, instructions, official notices, etc: *Here's the poop sheet from the comptroller* [origin unknown; perhaps fr *poop* "excrement"; improbably but possibly an unaccounted shortening of *liripoop* "lore, tricks of the trade" as found in the 16th-century phrases *to know one's liripoop, to teach someone his liripoop*, perhaps related to *lerrie* "something learned or spoken by rote"]

poop someone **up** *v phr Army* To inform; brief; =FILL someone IN

poor deck *See* DEAL someone A POOR DECK

poor fish *n phr* An ordinary person, esp regarded as a victim of existential perversity: *The poor fish is damned if he does and damned if he doesn't*

poor man's something or someone *n phr fr late 1700s* A thing or person less glamorous, desirable, famous, etc, than the top grade: *the Poor Man's Palm Beach*—Ring Lardner/ *Burton, "Poor Man's Olivier"*—The Morning Telegraph

poor-mouth **1** *v* To deny one's wealth and advantages; emphasize one's deficiencies; =TALK POOR MOUTH: *Richard Nixon often poor-mouthed his chances*—J Rekkanen **2** *v* To deprecate severely; =BAD-MOUTH: *I'm not going around poor-mouthing the war*—A Shuster

◁ **poot** ▷ **1** *n fr black* Excrement; =CRAP, SHIT: *Which one of you has got the most poot stains on your underwear?*—Dan Jenkins **2** *n* A contemptible person; =PILL, POOP: *some old poots patrolling with a dog or two*—John Farris **3** *v* To flatulate; =FART **4** *n: The dog laid a loud poot* [probably a variant of *poo* or *poop*]

pootbutt *n black* A callow and ignorant person; a stupid and unfledged youth, esp one lacking the cunning of the ghetto: *show Chester that he wasn't a poot-butt*—Donald Goines

poove *See* POOF

pop¹ or **pops** **1** *n* Father: *My pop's the champ/ Your pops is an interesting guy* **2** *n* An older or elderly man • Used in informal, yet respectful, direct address: *Hey, pop, slow down a bit*

pop² **1** *n* Flavored carbonated water; soda; soda pop **2** *n* Ice cream or flavored ice on a stick; Popsicle (a trade name) **3** *n car-racing & hot rodders* Nitromethane or any other fuel additive for cars: *fuel additives... called pop*—Fort Worth Star-Telegram **4** *v narcotics* To take narcotics by injection; =SHOOT UP **5** *v narcotics* To take pills, esp barbiturates, amphetamines, etc, and esp habitually **6** *n narcotics* A quantity of narcotics; =BAG: *Each of them had a couple of pops on 'em*

—New York ◁**7**▷ *v* To do the sex act with or to; =JAZZ, SCREW: *Well, did you pop her?*—Claude Brown ◁**8**▷ *n* The sex act; sexual activity; =SCREWING **9** *v* To give birth: *She expects to pop in November* **10** *v* To hit; smack: *popped him on the snoot* **11** *v* To achieve spectacularly; hit: *I knew if I had a good day, I could really pop one*—Newsweek **12** *v* *student* To catch: *The guard popped us as we tried to sneak in the back door* [all senses related to *pop* as an echoic term for a sharp noise or a sharp blow]

pop[3] *adj* Popular; having a very broad audience: *Tom Wolfe, the pop journalist*—New York Times/ *well thought of nowadays by pop ecologists*—Sports Illustrated

a **pop** *n phr* A time; each occasion; =CRACK: *Steinem gets $3000 a pop for talking*—New York Times [fr *pop* "blow, stroke, crack," and according to Eric Partridge used by the Australians in the 1920s]

See DOUGH-POP

pop a wheelie *v phr* *motorcyclists & bicyclists* To raise the front wheel of a motorcycle or bicycle off the ground and ride on the rear wheel only

◁ **pop** someone's **cherry**▷ *v phr* To terminate someone's virginity: *I would definitely pop his cherry*—Xaviera Hollander

◁ **pop** one's **cookies**▷ *v phr* To have an orgasm; climax; =COME: *Madam Gray, who couldn't ever pop her cookies enough*—Paul Sann

pop one's **cork** *v phr* To become furious; explode angrily; =BLOW one's TOP: *I didn't expect her to pop her cork either*—Dennis Day

Pope *See* IS THE POPE POLISH

the **pope's** (or **the parson's**) **nose** *n phr* The triangular tailpiece of a cooked fowl

pop for *v phr* To pay for, esp as a treat to others; =PICK UP THE TAB: *I'll pop for the drinks*

pop off **1** *v phr* *fr middle 1700s* To die: *If he had popped off sooner, less trouble for all* **2** *v phr* To talk loudly and perhaps prematurely; =SHOOT OFF one's MOUTH: *I'm not popping off about the pennant until we get it*—Casey Stengel **3** *v phr* To leave; depart; =TODDLE OFF

pop someone **off** *v phr* *fr early 1800s* To kill, esp by shooting: *The police never found who popped the informer off*

popout *n* *surfers* A mass-produced surfboard

poppa **1** *n* One's father **2** *n* Any older man **3** *n* =DADDY, SUGAR DADDY

pop party *n phr* *narcotics* A gathering or party for the purpose of taking narcotics

popper **1** *n* *black* A pistol **2** *n* *narcotics* A pill or capsule of amyl or butyl nitrite: *use poppers and speed*—New York Times

See EYEPOPPER, JOY-POPPER, PILL-POPPER

poppycock *n* *fr middle 1800s* Nonsense; foolishness [apparently fr Dutch *pappekak* "soft dung"]

pops *See* POP

the **pops** *n phr* Popular records, songs, etc: *the best of the pops*

pop-up *n* *baseball* A high fly ball in the infield

pop wine *n phr* Any very sweet wine of low alcoholic content: *"pop" wines, low-alcohol, fruit-flavored wines specially designed for the soda- and fruit-punch palate*—New York [because they are bought by drinkers of soda *pop*]

porcelain god *See* PRAY TO THE PORCELAIN GOD

porcelain hairnet *See* WIN THE PORCELAIN HAIRNET

◁ **pork**▷ *v* To do the sex act; copulate; =SCREW: *I decided to lay some groundwork for porking her brains out*—National Lampoon

pork out *v phr* To eat over-heartily; overeat; =PIG OUT: *We were porking out on three sweet rolls*—Clark County Press

porky *adj* Obese; porcine: *a porky, middle-aged waitress*—Lawrence Sanders

porn or **porno** **1** *n* Pornography: *the merry world of pimps and porno*—Judith Crist/ *or witness the amount of porn around*—Saturday Review **2** *adj:* *The very best porn film ever made*—New York Times/ *little prospect of pay-TV turning our homes into porno palaces*—David Lachenbruch

porny *adj* Pornographic

portable parking lot *n phr* *truckers* A car-hauler truck

posh *adj fr early 1900s British* Luxurious; fancy; chic; =CUSHY, SWANKY: *The apartment... is now rather posh*—A Logan/ *have made a regular practice of roughing up the kids in the more posh Ashkenazic sections*—New Yorker [origin uncertain; perhaps fr the mid-19th-century term *posh* "money" fr Romany *pash* "a half," referring to a half-penny; perhaps fr mid-19th-century *posh* "a dandy," of unknown origin; perhaps fr early-20th-century Cambridge University slang *push* or *poosh* "stylish"; perhaps a mispronunciation of *polish*; perhaps an acronym for *port out starboard home*, said to be the formula for choosing the side of the ship with the most comfortable cabins on the steamer route from England to India or return; perhaps none of the above]

posse ***See*** PUSSY POSSE

postcard ***See*** FRENCH POSTCARD

post holes ***See*** a LOAD OF VW RADIATORS

pot[1] **1** ***n*** *gambling fr early 1800s* The total amount bet on a hand of poker or some other gambling matter; =KITTY: *The goulashes' takeout was 5 percent of the pot*—T Betts **2** ***n*** A rather obnoxious person, esp an unattractive woman; =PILL: *one of the pots that sat at the table*—Jerome Weidman **3** ***n*** *fr early 1900s* =BEER BELLY, POTBELLY **4** ***n*** *hot rodders* A carburetor **5** ***n*** *hot rodders* A car engine **6** ***n*** *railroad* A locomotive **7** ***v*** *fr middle 1800s* To shoot: *He potted a woodchuck* **8** ***v*** To hit; strike: *pots him in the puss/ He potted it right out of the park* [all senses fr cooking *pot*, as something containing a *pot*-luck mess of food, something sooty and unattractive, something fat looking, something to be filled by hitting the hunt's prey, etc, hence hitting in general]

See GO TO POT, NOT HAVE A POT TO PISS IN, RUMPOT, SEXPOT, a SHITLOAD, TINPOT

pot[2] *narcotics* **1** ***n*** Marijuana; =GRASS: *Most of the parties I had been invited to recently, pot had been passed around freely*—New York Times **2** ***modifier:*** *pot smokers/ a pot party* [origin unknown; perhaps by folk etymology fr *pod*, occurrences of which are generally earlier; perhaps fr the association between *tea* "marijuana" and *pot*]

pot[3] ***n*** A potentiometer

the **pot** ***n phr*** The toilet; =CRAPPER: *closed the stall door, and sat down on the pot*—Richard Fariña

See SHIT OR GET OFF THE POT

potato **1** ***n*** The head: *stick their potato in every office*—AJ Liebling **2** ***n*** A dollar: *You can get this wonderful coat for 497 potatoes*—Time **3** ***n*** A ball, esp a baseball

See ALL THAT MEAT AND NO POTATOES, COUCH POTATO, HOT POTATO, MEAT AND POTATOES, SMALL POTATOES

potato patch ***See*** FRUIT SALAD

potato-trap ***n*** *fr early 1800s* The mouth

potbelly or **potgut** **1** ***n*** A protuberant belly; =BEER BELLY, POT **2** ***n*** A person with a potbelly, esp a man

potboiler ***n*** A book, play, etc, written just to get money, esp something done rather badly by a writer who can do very well [fr the notion that one does such work only to keep the food *pot boiling* in the domicile]

potchkie or **potchky** or **potsky** (PAHCH kee) ***v*** (Variation: **around** may be added) To putter; tinker; =MESS: *Louie's down potchkying in the shop/ The dentist potchkied around in Stanley's mouth*—Esquire/ *how you could potsky around with such superstitions*—Billy Rose [fr Yiddish fr German *patschen* "splash, slap"]

pothead ***n*** *narcotics* A user of marijuana, esp a heavy user: *a few potheads who don't move up from marijuana*—New York Times

pothooks **1** ***n*** One's handwriting; scribble; =HEN TRACKS **2** ***n*** *cowboys* Spurs

pot luck **1** ***n phr*** A meal composed of odds and ends of leftovers, or of whatever turns up **2** ***adv phr:*** *Come on and dine pot luck* **3** ***modifier:*** *pot-luck supper*

pot out ***v phr*** *hot rodders* To stop running; fail; =CONK OUT

pot party ***n phr*** *narcotics* A gathering or party for the purpose of smoking marijuana in company

potshot ***See*** TAKE A POTSHOT AT someone

pot-slinger ***n*** A cook

potsy **1** ***n*** *police* A police badge: *Ernie goes in the lobby and flashes his potsy*—Lawrence Sanders **2** ***n*** *New York City* The game of hopscotch [perhaps a variant of the nickname *Patsy*]

potted or **potted up** **1** *adj* or *adj phr* Drunk **2** *adj* or *adj phr narcotics* Intoxicated by marijuana or another narcotic: *all potted up on something*—E Trujillo

◁ a **pot to piss in**▷ *See* NOT HAVE A POT TO PISS IN

potty **1** *n* A young child's toilet seat and chamber pot **2** *n: failure to perform potty at the proper hour* —Time **3** *n* Any toilet **4** ***modifier:*** *time out for a potty break* —Playboy **5** *adj fr early 1900s British* Slightly crazy; eccentric; =GOOFY

pot-walloper **1** *n* A pot and pan washer **2** *n lumberjacks* A cook

pouffe *See* POOF

pound one's **ear** *v phr hoboes* To sleep, esp heavily

pounder *n* A police officer, esp one who walks a beat

◁ **pound** one's **meat**▷ *See* BEAT one's MEAT

◁ **pound** one's **peenie**▷ *v phr* To masturbate; =BEAT one's MEAT: *Who is he mooning over as he pounds his peenie?*—John Farris

pound salt (or **sand**) *See* GO POUND SALT

pound the books *v phr college students* To study hard

pound the pavement (Variations: **pavements** or **the sidewalks** or **the streets** may replace **the pavement**) **1** *v phr* To walk a police beat **2** *v phr* To trudge about the streets, esp looking for work: *the liberal arts graduates... pounding the Park Avenue pavements*—New York

pour it on **1** *v phr* To make an intense effort; maximize striving: *I was pouring it on, looking for a promotion* **2** *v phr* To exert all one's charm and persuasiveness; =COME ON STRONG: *He was really pouring it on to that judge* **3** *v phr* To speed; =POUR ON THE COAL: *The driver was pouring it on to close the gap*—J Evans

pour money down the drain (or **the rathole**) *v phr* To waste money utterly; spend hugely for nothing: *The Legislature is not going to pour more money down that rathole*—Philadelphia Journal

pour on the coal *v phr fr railroad* To travel very fast; speed up; =STEP ON IT: *The pilot apparently decided to go around again and poured on the coal* —Associated Press

pout-out *n hot rodders* Engine failure in a hot rod

pow **1** *interj* An imitation of a blow, collision, explosion, etc, used for sudden emphasis or to show sudden understanding: *Suddenly bells went off and I knew that was it! Pow!*—New York Post/ *Pow, dig this*—Ramparts **2** *n* Power; influence; =CLOUT: *by government action, that is, by political "pow"*—G Tyler [second sense reinforced by *power*]

powder **1** *v underworld* To leave; depart hastily, esp in escaping: *The crooks powdered like scared rabbits* **2** *n: Bonnie murdered a constable during the powder*—A Hynd **3** *v* To hit very hard; =PULVERIZE: *after he had powdered the second pitch* —Associated Press [sense of running away probably fr similar *dust* fr the notion of raising dust as one runs; perhaps, in view of *take a powder* and *run-out powder*, the basic notion is reinforced by that of taking a medicinal *powder*, esp a laxative, so that one has to leave in a hurry, or perhaps a magical *powder* that would cause one to disappear]

See FLEA POWDER, JOY-POWDER, RUN-OUT POWDER, TAKE A POWDER

powderpuff **1** *n prizefight* A cautious, agile fighter as distinct from a slugger **2** *v: He just powderpuffed his opponent until he tired* **3** *adj* For or involving women; women's: *the pampered, powderpuff existence of the Ultra-feminine*—Eldridge Cleaver

powerhouse **1** *n* A formidable team, organization, etc: *Georgia Tech, another powerhouse*—Associated Press/ *Texas Instruments, a powerhouse in electronics* **2** *n* An energetic and effective person **3** *n* A vigorous, muscular person, esp an athlete **4** *n* Anything that constitutes winning force: *If you control six votes that's a powerhouse*

power trip *n phr* A show of personal power, esp of a blatant sort: *the classic Latin American dictator's power trip*—Toronto Life

pow-wow *n* A meeting; discussion: *The directors are having a crucial pow-wow* [ultimately fr an American Indian word for "medicine man," meaning "he dreams," extended to mean counsel and a council]

PR or **pr** (pronounced as separate letters) **1** *n* Public relations **2** *modifier: the PR department/ pr hype*

prairie oysters *See* MOUNTAIN OYSTERS

prat or **pratt** **1** *n fr late 1500s* The buttocks; =ASS: *He does not fall on his prat*—Time **2** *v underworld* To observe or menace someone from behind [origin unknown]

pratfall *fr theater* **1** *n* A fall on one's rump, esp by a clown or comedian: *a perfect pratfall*—Edmund Wilson **2** *n* A humiliating defeat; an embarrassing humiliation: *Losing the election was a resounding pratfall* **3** *n* A danger; pitfall: *the pratfalls of the rhyming racket*—Billy Rose

prayer *See* HAVE A PRAYER

prayer bones *n phr* The knees

pray to the porcelain god *v phr college students* To vomit in the toilet

preemie or **preemy** or **premie** *n fr 1920s* A premature baby: *the tiny, three-pound premie*—Good Housekeeping

preggers *adj fr 1920s British universities* Pregnant: *Meredith gets preggers by Jos*—Playboy

preggy **1** *adj* Pregnant **2** *n: Six preggies were waiting to see the doctor*

prego **1** *n* A pregnant teenager **2** *adj* Pregnant: *as if one-half the female population is... prego*—Ebony

prep **1** *n* =PREPPIE **2** *v students* To go to preparatory school: *Where'd you prep?*—F Scott Fitzgerald/ *The poorer person did not prep with your brother*—Fran Lebowitz **3** *n* Preparation; preliminary steps: *The nurses did the prep for the operation* **4** *v: a pitcher who has prepped earnestly for many years*—Arthur Daley

preppie or **preppy** **1** *n* A student or graduate of a preparatory school: *Wouldja please watch your profanity, Preppie?*—Erich Segal **2** *adj* Typical of the manners, attitudes, folkways, etc, of preppies: *The handshake is firm and preppy*—J Cameron/ *George Bush predicted with characteristic preppie self-confidence*—Time

pres (PREZ) *n* (Variations: **Pres** or **prez** or **Prez** or **prexy** or **Prexy** or **prexie** or **Prexie**) A president

press *See* FULL COURT PRESS

press the flesh (or **the skin**) **1** *v phr* To shake hands • Used chiefly of politicians and others who ingratiate themselves with the public **2** *adj: Williams conducted a press-the-flesh campaign*—Newsweek

pressure cooker **1** *n phr* A place or situation of great personal stress: *the pressure cooker on the Hudson*—Gore Vidal **2** *modifier: flung into the pressure-cooker existence of live TV*—Pauline Kael

pretty *See* be SITTING PRETTY

pretty-boy **1** *n* A man who is good-looking in an epicene way; an effeminate dandy **2** *modifier: their "pretty boy" young preacher*—Malcolm X **3** *n circus* A bouncer or professional strong man

pretty face *See* JUST ANOTHER PRETTY FACE

prevert (PREE vert) *n* A pervert

previous *See* QUICK

prexy or **Prexy** or **prexie** or **Prexie** *See* PRES

prez or **Prez** *See* PRES

pricey or **pricy** *adj fr 1940s British fr Australian* Expensive; dear: *Godiva chocolates and other pricey goodies*—Philadelphia Journal

◁**prick**▷ **1** *n fr late 1500s* The penis; =COCK **2** *n* A detestable person, esp a man; obnoxious wretch; =ASSHOLE, BASTARD: *He's an antagonistic prick*—Rolling Stone

◁**prick-teaser**▷ *See* COCK-TEASER

prima donna *n phr* A person of great and touchy self-esteem; a person who requires to be the sole focus of adulatory attention and who indulges in temperamental displays [fr Italian, literally "first lady," a title for superstar opera singers and the like]

primed *adj* Prepared; readied; =PREPPED: *The place is primed for the prima donna's visit*

prince *n* A very decent and admirable person; =ACE • Often used ironically: *He told me he thinks you're a goddam prince*—JD Salinger

Princess *See* JEWISH AMERICAN PRINCESS

print **1** *n* A fingerprint: *My prints ain't on that gun*—Erle Stanley Gardner **2** *v: They printed me*—Erle Stanley Gardner

See FINGERPRINT, the SMALL PRINT

print money ***See*** a LICENSE TO PRINT MONEY

prissy **1** *adj fr late 1800s chiefly Southern* Overfastidious; primly censorious: *He has a prissy distaste for heavy shoes* **2** *n: these do-gooding prissies*—Newsweek [origin uncertain; perhaps a blend of *prim* or *precise* with *sissy*; perhaps the nickname for *Priscilla*, thought of as conveying the priggish and effeminate essence]

private ***See*** BUCK PRIVATE

private eye *n phr* A private detective; a private investigator

pro **1** *n* A professional in any field, as distinct from an amateur, and mainly distinguished by superior and dependable performance: *hear his song played and sung by pros*—C Lowry **2** *modifier: pro golf tour/ pro ranks* **3** *n* (also **old pro** or **real pro**) A seasoned and dependable performer; expert; model of excellence **4** *n* A prostitute: *He treats all women like pros and all men like enemies*—Budd Schulberg [the last sense perhaps fr *professional* reinforced by *prostitute*, or vice versa]

problems ***See*** HAVE PROBLEMS WITH something

process *n black* =CONK

production ***See*** MAKE A BIG PRODUCTION

professor **1** *n* An orchestra leader **2** *n* The piano player in a saloon, brothel, etc: *the job of regular professor*—A Lomax

profile ***See*** KEEP A LOW PROFILE, LOW PROFILE

program *v fr computer* To train; predispose by rigorous teaching, condition: *He's programmed to be polite to old ladies and all*

See CRASH PROGRAM

project ***See*** CRASH PROGRAM

prole (PROHL) *n fr British perhaps fr 1920s Australian* A member of the lower or working class: *Chez Tom Wolfe proles, for example, wear new down coats*—Atlantic [fr *proletarian* "member of the working class," ultimately fr Latin; popularized by George Orwell's 1949 novel *1984*]

promo (PROH moh) **1** *n* Advertising and promotion: *Who's handling the promo for this show?* **2** *n* A film, tape, printed piece, etc, for promotion: *He shot some promos for his syndicated TV show*—New Yorker

promote **1** *v fr early 1900s underworld & hoboes* To get, esp by theft, hard persuasion, or begging: *He promoted a couple of new tires from the neighbors* **2** *v* To accost in an acquisitive spirit; =HIT: *begun promoting him for something to drink*—James M Cain

promotion ***See*** MEXICAN PROMOTION

◁**prong**▷ **1** *n* The penis; =PRICK **2** *v* To do the sex act to or with; =SCREW: *every guy who had ever pronged her*—Earl Thompson

pronto *adv fr middle 1800s Southwest* Immediately; quickly [fr Spanish]

property ***See*** HOT PROPERTY

proposition **1** *n* An invitation or request for sexual favors; =a PASS: *He made a rude proposition and got his ears pinned back* **2** *v: He propositioned every woman at the party*

prosty *n* (Variations: **prostie** or **pross** or **prossy** or **prossie**) A prostitute: *a retired prosty*—Playboy/ *Fighting the Prostie Problem*—New York Post/ *the dedicated pross with a meter ticking under her skirt*—New York

prowl *v* To search by running the hands over the person; =FRISK: *prowled me over carefully with his left hand*—Raymond Chandler

See ON THE PROWL

prowl car *n phr fr 1930s* A police squad car

prune **1** *n* A foolish person who is easily duped; =MARK, PATSY **2** *n* A pedantic, stiff, and prudish person; =PRISSY **3** *v hot rodders* To accelerate faster than another car in a race

prunes ***See*** FULL OF BEANS

ps and qs ***See*** MIND one's PS AND QS

psych **1** *n college students* Psychology, esp as an academic study **2** *modifier* Psychiatry; psychiatric: *makes it down from the psych ward on the 15th floor*—Maclean's **3** *v* (also **psych out**) To outsmart another person: *The bastards psyched me* **4** *v* (also **psych out**) To sense or infer the motives, behavior, etc, of others: feel out a situation: *an uncanny ability to "psych out" audiences and make them love her*—Saturday Review/ *They're very dif-*

ficult to psyche out—Sexual Behavior **5** ***interj*** *chiefly teenagers* An exclamation uttered when one has fooled or deceived another, meaning "I'm only kidding" **6** ***v*** (also **psych out**) To unnerve someone; cause someone to lose composure, will, skill, etc: *He won't psych me as he did her*—New York Post/ *He's never tried to psych us out*—New Yorker

psych oneself or **psych** oneself **up** ***v phr*** To arouse oneself emotionally, spiritually, mentally, etc, to a maximum effort; raise oneself to a state of keen readiness and capability; =PUMP oneself UP: *That's almost a whole year of psyching yourself up as high as you can go*—Esquire/ *I tried to psyche myself for this new challenge*—Anne Bernays/ *Diana Nyad would psyche herself up for grueling aquatic bouts* —New York Post

psyched or **psyched up** ***adj*** or ***adj phr*** In a state of excited preparedness and heightened keenness; =PUMPED UP: *They were all psyched up to carry the blue and white banner of Catawba College*—Charlotte Observer/ *are generally so psyched that elation becomes their bottom line*—S Shapiro

psych-jockey ***n*** The host and consultant of a radio or television call-in program on personal, emotional, sexual, and generally speaking psychological subjects [fr blend of *psychology* and *disc jockey*]

psycho **1** ***n*** A crazy person; maniac; psychopath; =NUT: *You can always tell psychos, they have dirty hands*—New York/ *no buzzing broad, no nympho, no psycho, no bitch* —Pauline Kael **2** ***adj:*** *a special psycho channel that I know nothing about*—New York [probably fr *psychotic*]

psychobabble **1** ***n*** Talk about oneself, one's feelings, motives, etc, esp in psychological jargon: *Let's call it psychobabble, this spirit which now tyrannizes conversation*—RD Rosen **2** ***v:*** *"If you want space," she tells a psychobabbling boyfriend, "go to Utah"*—Village Voice

psych up ***v phr*** To bring to a state of keen attention; excite and incite; =PUMP UP

◁ **pt** or **PT**▷ (pronounced as separate letters) ***n*** =PRICK-TEASER

pu or **PU** (pronounced as separate letters) ***interj*** An exclamation of displeasure upon smelling something fetid or encountering something disgusting or botched

pub ***n*** *fr middle 1800s British* A saloon; bar; tavern: *a round of Long Island pubs*—New York Daily News [fr British *public house*]

pub crawl ***See*** BARHOP

pubes (PYo͞o beez) ***n*** The pubic region, esp the pubic hair; crotch • Even though this is the medical, Latin anatomical term, it somehow takes on a slang aura by association in contexts: *stretching the satin front of her hot pants over her pubes* —Rolling Stone

pucker ***n*** *fr middle 1700s* Fear; state of fright: *Don't get in such a pucker*

◁ **pucker-assed**▷ ***adj*** Timid; fearful; =CHICKEN [fr *pucker*]

◁ **pud**▷ (PUHD, Po͝oD) ***n*** The penis [fr slang sense of *pudding*]
See PULL one's PUD

◁ **pudding**▷ ***n*** The penis: *You can't even come off unless you pull your own pudding*—Philip Roth

puddinghead ***n*** *fr middle 1800s* A stupid person, esp one who is also amiable: *a natural nitwit, a puddinghead, a stand-up comedian*—WT Tyler

puddle-jumper **1** ***n*** A small or rickety vehicle: *I wouldn't ride in that puddle-jumper* **2** ***n*** An aircraft that makes several stops along a cross-country route

◁ **pud-pulling**▷ **1** ***n*** Masturbation: *a frenzied bout of pud-pulling*—Village Voice **2** ***modifier:*** *a stupid pud-pulling jerk*

puff **1** ***n*** (also **puff job**) A specimen of extravagant praise, esp for commercial or political purposes; =PLUG **2** ***v:*** *There is little need for us to puff this book*—Saturday Review
See CREAM PUFF, POWDERPUFF

puffer ***See*** PINK PUFFER

puff piece ***n phr*** Something written in extravagant praise, esp for sales purposes; =HYPE

puffy ***adj*** Very favorable; adulatory; drum-beating: *extraordinarily puffy coverage of Reagan*—Time

pug **1** ***n*** *fr middle 1800s British* A prizefighter or boxer; pugilist **2** ***n*** =PLUG-UGLY [fr *pugilist*]

◁ **puke**▷ **1** ***v*** To vomit **2** ***n*** Vomit; spew **3** ***n*** Something so disgusting that it might be vomit and the cause of vomit: *Who wrote this puke?*

◁ **puker**▷ ***n*** *Pacific Northwest* A charter fishing boat

◁ **puky** or **pukey**▷ ***adj*** Nasty; inferior; disgusting: *It's a pukey sort of ballad*

pull **1** ***n*** *fr late 1800s* Influence; special power or favor; =CLOUT: *irregularities and instances of political pull* —Associated Press **2** ***n*** A sip or gulp of a drink, a puff on a cigarette, etc: *I took a big pull at my drink and looked up* **3** ***v*** To earn; receive; =PULL DOWN: *I pulled an A on the quiz* ◁**4**▷ ***v*** *prison* To masturbate

See LEG-PULL

pull a boner (or **a bonehead play**) ***v phr*** To blunder; commit an error, esp an egregious one: *I'm afraid you've pulled a boner this time, the thing sank*

pull a fast one ***v phr*** To execute or attempt a deception; achieve a clever fraud or swindle; =PULL something ON someone: *You're accusing me of trying to pull a fast one?*—Saul Bellow [probably fr *fast shuffle*]

pull an el foldo ***v phr*** To lose energy; wilt; fade; =FOLD: *The Saints chose that time to pull an el foldo* —Sports Illustrated

◁ **pull a train** (or **the train** or **the choo-choo**)▷ ***v phr*** *fr motorcyclists* Of a woman, to do the sex act with several men serially: *taking some dame in the woods and making her pull a train* —Rockford Files (TV program)

pull someone's **chain** (Variations: **jerk** or **rattle** may replace **pull**; **string** may replace **chain**) **1** ***v phr*** To deceive; fool; =PULL A FAST ONE: *too busy trying to figure out if I had been pulling his chain*—Richard Price **2** ***v phr*** To upset; anger: *She got real mad and I wondered what had pulled her chain/ I did not know you can rattle his chain with marvelous results* —Washington Post/ *He was insecure and sensitive. It was easy to pull his string*—New York Times [probably fr the image of a person who upsets a captive animal by *pulling* or *jerking* at the *chain*; perhaps influenced by the notion of *pulling* a *chain* or string to turn on an electric light]

pull down **1** ***v phr*** (also **pull in**) To earn; receive: *I pull down about 300 a week* **2** ***v phr*** To disassemble; take apart: *I am going to pull the engine down again*—Popular Science

pull (or **drag**) one's **freight** ***v phr*** *esp early 1900s* To leave; depart: *This bird's gonna pull his freight*—WR Burnett

pull in **1** ***v phr*** To arrive: *She pulled in about noon* **2** ***v phr*** =PULL DOWN

pull someone **in** ***v phr*** To arrest

pull in one's **belt** ***See*** TIGHTEN one's BELT

pull in one's **ears** **1** ***v phr*** To be cautious; watch out for oneself **2** ***v phr*** To be less aggressive; moderate oneself: *You better pull in your ears a little or you'll scare them away* [origin uncertain; perhaps in some cases an alteration of *pull in* one's *horns*]

pull in one's **horns** ***v phr*** *fr late 1500s British* To moderate or retract one's behavior; =BACK OFF: *The USFL Pulled In Its Financial Horns* —Inside Sports [fr the way an anxious snail behaves]

pull it off ***v phr*** *fr late 1800s gambling & horseracing* To accomplish something; succeed; =MAKE IT: *pull it off and keep the patients coming back for more*—San Francisco

pull someone's **leg** ***v phr*** *fr late 1800s British* To deceive in fun; fool; =KID: *I suspected that he was pulling my leg*—F Scott Fitzgerald [fr the act of playfully tripping someone]

pull off **1** ***v phr*** *fr middle 1800s* To succeed in or at; achieve: *Fegley managed to pull off a hat trick for this issue*—Playboy ◁**2**▷ ***v phr*** To masturbate: *At Smolka's signal, each begins to pull off*—Philip Roth

◁ **pull** oneself **off**▷ ***v phr*** To masturbate; =JACK OFF

◁ **pull** someone **off**▷ ***v phr*** *fr early 1900s* To cause someone to ejaculate semen by manipulating the penis

pull on ***v phr*** To take a sip of a drink, a puff of a cigarette, etc: *a 17-year-old kid pulling on a beer*—Toronto Life

pull something **on** someone ***v phr*** To deceive or cheat; take advantage of; =PULL A FAST ONE: *At first she thought I was trying to pull a slick scam on her*

pull out **1** ***v phr*** To leave; depart: *He pulled out after 45 minutes and disappeared*—Associated Press **2** ***v phr*** To withdraw; terminate one's association: *He threatened to pull out if we didn't raise the ante*

◁**pull** something **out of** one's **ass**▷ *v phr Army* To produce, esp information or an idea, unexpectedly

pull something **out of the fire** *v phr* To salvage; rescue: *We got hot and pulled the game out of the fire*

◁**pull** one's **pud**▷ (PUHD, PŏŏD) *v phr* (Variations: **dong** or **joint** or **wang** or any other word for "penis" may replace **pud**) To masturbate; =JACK OFF

pull one's **punches** *v phr fr prizefight* To soften one's blows; be lenient and moderate: *He pulled no punches because the reigning official was both a woman and a black*—Joseph Heller

pull rank *v phr fr WW1 armed forces* To overwhelm with one's authority; be officiously arrogant: *Each was frightened that the other would pull rank*—Eldridge Cleaver

pull strings (or **wires**) *v phr* To exert influence; use one's power, esp clandestinely: *If she pulls a few wires I think I might get the job* [probably fr the use of *strings* or *wires* to control marionettes]

pull teeth through the armpit *v phr armed forces* To do something in the most difficult way; do something the hard way

pull the plug **1** *v phr* To terminate something; end support or cooperation: *if the affiliates... rise up in rebellion and pull the plug*—New Yorker/ *The project's pretty shaky, but I won't pull the plug quite yet* **2** *v phr* To terminate various mechanical and electronic efforts being used to keep life in a moribund patient [fr the disconnecting of an electrical *plug*]

pull the rug from under (or **out from under**) *v phr* To undermine or disable; put opponents at a great and often sudden disadvantage: *They were intended to pull the rug out from under left-wing critics*—Nation

pull the string **1** *v phr baseball* To pitch a change-of-pace ball, a very slow ball after the motion for a fast one **2** *v phr* To rudely reveal the truth, previously kept hidden; unveil true intentions; reveal the catch: *They doubled their efforts, showering her with affection, then they pulled the string*—Playboy [perhaps fr the use of a *string* to fasten and release a concealing sheet on something about to be unveiled; perhaps fr *pull the lanyard* "to fire a cannon"]

pull the wool over someone's **eyes** *v phr fr middle 1800s* To deceive; mislead: *The whole indignant act was an attempt to pull the wool over the voters' eyes*

pull up one's **socks** *fr early 1900s British* **1** *v phr* To correct one's behavior; look to one's performance; =GET ON THE BALL: *Whittingham was terminated after having failed to pull up his socks enough during six months on probation*—Toronto Life **2** *v phr* To prepare; ready oneself: *He said we'd pull up our socks and get the damn job done*

pulp **1** *n* A magazine printed on rough paper and devoted to adventure, science fiction, cowboy stories, rude erotica, etc **2** ***modifier:*** *pulp fiction/ a pulp romance*

the **pulps** *n phr* Pulp magazines collectively: *He used to write sci-fi for the pulps*

pulverize **1** *v* To hit hard; =CLOBBER, POWDER **2** *v* To defeat thoroughly; =CLOBBER

pump ◁**1**▷ *v fr 1700s* To do the sex act; =FUCK, HUMP: *They were pumping away on the floor* **2** *v* To question someone long and closely; extract information: *The cops pumped him for three days straight* **3** *n* (also **pumper**) The heart; =TICKER: *He had a hole through his pump*—Asphalt Jungle (movie)

See TOWN PUMP

pumped up **1** *adj phr* In a state of excited preparedness and heightened keenness; =PSYCHED UP • Used most often of athletes in or before competition: *The girls were really pumped up*—Playboy **2** *adj phr* Exaggerated; artificial; =PHONY: *a pumped-up conviviality*—Barry Reed

pump iron *v phr* To lift weights

pumpkin or **pumkin** or **punkin** *n* The head

pumpkinhead or **punkinhead** *n* A stupid person

pump up **1** *v phr* To exaggerate; assign too much importance to; =BLOW UP: *His job wasn't much, but he pumped it up into a key assignment* **2** *v phr* To persuade to keen excitement; =HYPE: *Experts like*

Dr Edward Teller... have steadily "pumped up" Reagan—Newsweek

pump oneself **up** *v phr* To arouse oneself emotionally, spiritually, mentally, etc, to a maximum effort; =PSYCH oneself • Much used by sports commentators, esp by baseball announcers of pitchers: *The big left-hander's really pumped himself up for this crucial encounter*

punch *n* Power; force; impact; =CLOUT: *This article has no punch* **See** BEAT someone TO THE DRAW, CAN'T FIGHT one's WAY OUT OF A PAPER BAG, ONE-TWO, SUCKERPUNCH, SUNDAY PUNCH

punchboard *n* A very promiscuous woman; =ROUNDHEELS [fr a gambling or lottery device where one paid to *punch* a round scroll of paper out of a hole in a *board* for a possible prize; related to 18th-century *punch* "deflower"]

punch-drunk **1** *adj* Exhibiting brain damage from repeated blows to the head; slow in movement, slurring in speech, disoriented and shambling; =PUNCHY, SLAP-HAPPY **2** *adj* Dazed from overwork, excessive stress, etc: *He was punch-drunk after the annual meeting*

punched **See** HAVE one's TICKET PUNCHED

punched-up *adj* Improved; increased in energy, impressiveness, impact, etc: *no more than a punched-up form of the sentiment that the prose style of most social scientists "is Greek to me"*—New York Times

punches **See** PULL one's PUNCHES, ROLL WITH THE PUNCHES

punch in (or **out**) *v phr* To come or go at a certain time, esp to or from a job; =CLOCK IN OR OUT [fr the stamping of one's work-card at a time-clock]

punch someone's **lights out** *v phr* To beat or defeat severely; trounce; =CLOBBER: *Sugar Ray Leonard punched Thomas Hearns's lights out*—Sports Illustrated [fr the earlier *beat out someone's liver and lights,* where *lights* reflects a Middle English word for "lungs, esp of a slaughtered animal or game animal," now certainly interpreted as "eyes" and as "electric lights"]

punch line *n phr* The last line or part of a joke, which makes it funny; =KICKER, ZINGER: *I remember the jokes, but not the punch lines*

punch out **1** *v phr* To beat, esp with the fists; =BEAT UP ON, CLOBBER: *Oh...I punched out this guy*—Armistead Maupin **2** *v phr Air Force* To use the ejection seat for escape from a aircraft

punch-out *n* A fist fight; brawl; fisticuffs

punch up **1** *v phr* To improve; increase the energy, impressiveness, etc, of; =JAZZ something UP: *The TV-movie version will punch it up*—Village Voice **2** *v phr television studio & recording industry* To bring a specified part of a recording tape into view, into place at the playing head, etc **3** *v phr computers* To call up a software program

punchy **1** *adj fr 1930s* Exhibiting brain damage from repeated blows to the head; =PUNCH-DRUNK: *Sailor Bob a punchy stumble-bum*—John O'Hara **2** *adj* Feeling somewhat confused and battered, as if punch-drunk: *I feel a little punchy after that session with the committee* **3** *adj fr 1920s* Having force, impact, energy, etc; potent; =JAZZY, ZINGY: *a gift for punchy phrases*—Joseph Heller

punish **1** *v* To attack forcefully: *I had a bottle along and he punished it*—Raymond Chandler **2** *v* To have sex with; =FUCK: *Time to go home, have a brew, and punish the old lady*

punk[1] **1** *n prison, merchant marine & hoboes* A catamite; young companion of a sodomite; =GUNSEL ◁**2**▷ *v* To sodomize; do anal sex to; =BUGGER, CORNHOLE: *The guy peeled off Tate's pants and punked him*—Tom Aldibrandi **3** *n* Any young or inexperienced person; boy; =KID: *Sparky was always a fresh punk*—John O'Hara **4** *n* A petty hoodlum; meager minor tough or criminal: *to emphasize just how tough a Division Street punk could be*—Nelson Algren **5** *n* Any inferior, insignificant person, like an ineffective fighter, jockey, pool player, waiter, porter, etc [ultimately fr 16th-century British, "prostitute, harlot," of unknown origin]

punk[2] **1** *adj fr late 1800s* Inferior; poor; bad: *The idea strikes me as punk*—Westbrook Pegler **2** *n esp lunch counter fr late 1800s* Bread **3** *n hawkers* A patent medicine **4**

modifier: the punk workers who sell corn removers—M Zolotow [probably early-18th-century, "rotting wood, touchwood," of unknown origin, usu taken to be fr *spunk,* of the same meaning, fr Gaelic *spong* "tinder"]

punk[0] **1** *n* (also **punker**) An adherent to a style of dress and behavior marked by seemingly threatening, dangerous, and aggressive attributes, such as safety pins worn through ear lobes, razor blades around the neck, and torn clothes • Originally meant to be reminiscent of the hoodlums called punks in the 1950s, but soon an independent style **2** *adj: The atmosphere in north London's pubs is really punk*

punkin *See* PUMPKIN

punkoid **1** *n* =PUNK³, PUNK ROCKER **2** *adj: his punkoid slouch and sneer*

punk out **1** *v phr fr early 1900s, now esp street gang & teenagers* To quit, esp from fear; =CHICKEN OUT, FOLD: *The Soho News punked out*—Philadelphia **2** *v phr* To adopt the style of a punk rocker

punk rock *n phr* Loud and crude rock and roll music played by persons who purport, in their dress, vile behavior and language, repellent names, and ugly appearance, to be loathsome louts: *The bad equivalent of "bubble-gum," it was called punk-rock, and it was totally utilitarian music*—Changes

punk rocker **1** *n phr* A player of loud and crude rock and roll music who purports to be a loathsome lout **2** *n phr* A person who adheres to a style of dress and behavior marked by seemingly threatening, dangerous, and aggressive attributes; =PUNK

punt[1] *v fr 1700s* To gamble; bet [fr French *ponte,* Spanish *punta* "point," used for playing against the banker in faro and other games]

punt[2] **1** *v college students* To drop a course in order not to fail it **2** *v college students* To give up; withdraw; =COP OUT: *I hate to punt, but I just don't have time to finish this job* [fr the kick out of danger in football, fr middle-19th-century Rugby football, "kick the ball before it hits the ground," of unknown origin; perhaps echoic]

punter *n fr early 1700s* A gambler; a bettor: *Inside the clubhouse, the punters sit enraged on their slatted benches*—Village Voice [fr French *punter* "place a bet against the bank in a card game," of uncertain origin]

punt someone or something **off** *v phr college students* To deliberately forget; ignore and evade: *He decided to punt the whole problem off*

pup **1** *n* A young, inexperienced person; =KID, PUNK **2** *n* =HOT DOG **3** *n truckers* A small four-wheeled truck trailer

See GUTTERSNIPE

purple heart *n phr narcotics* Any barbiturate, or a mixture of a barbiturate and morphine; =NIMBY, GOOFBALL

purpose pitch *n phr baseball* A pitch thrown purposely intimidatingly close to a batter

◁ **pus bag**▷ *n phr* A despicable person; a filthy wretch; =SCUMBAG: *He hissed that I was "a goddam scum-sucking pus bag"*—Peter Gent

pus-gut or **pustle-gut** **1** *n* A protuberant belly **2** *n* A person with a pus-gut: *some pus-gut in an American Legion cap*—Time [origin unknown; perhaps from *purse,* suggesting a full, baggy gut; perhaps fr dialect *puscle* or *puskile* "pustule," suggesting a swollen gut]

push **1** *n* An intense sustained effort: *They made a big push to get the damn thing done* **2** *v esp cabdrivers* To drive a taxi, truck, etc: *pushing a hack all day*—F Dickenson **3** *v* To kill someone: *when one of our boys gets pushed*—J Evans **4** *v* To approach a specified age: *You're pushing 50*—Earl Wilson **5** *v* To advertise; publicize; promote: *They don't have to push reference books too much* **6** *v* (also **push for**) To recommend; boost; =GET BEHIND: *He decided to push my idea, and push for two new labs* **7** *v* To sell, esp in an aggressive way; hawk: *Push the specials today, okay?* **8** *v* To press or importune too often and too hard: *I'll probably do what you want, just stop pushing* **9** *v narcotics* To sell narcotics; peddle; =DEAL: *Funny cigarettes ain't all that one pushes*—Nelson Algren **10** *v underworld* To distribute and pass counterfeit money **11** *v underworld* To smuggle

push one's **button** *v phr* To annoy or provoke one; =NEEDLE: *Don't push my button. I haven't exactly been behind him, pushing and clapping* —Washington Post

push comes to shove *sentence* A touchy situation becomes actively hostile; a quarrel becomes a fight; =the CHIPS ARE DOWN: *If push comes to shove can you count on him?*

pusher **1** *n* *lumberjacks* A supervisor; =PUSH **2** *n* *narcotics* A narcotics peddler or distributor; =CANDY MAN, CONNECTION: *queen of the Broadway narcotics pushers*—Associated Press **3** *n* *underworld* A distributor or passer of counterfeit money; =PAPERHANGER

See GOSPEL-PUSHER, PAPERHANGER, PAPER-PUSHER, PENCIL-PUSHER, PEN-PUSHER, PILL-PUSHER, WOOD-PUSHER

push off **1** *v phr* To leave; =SHOVE OFF **2** *v phr* *underworld* To kill; murder; =PUSH

pushover **1** *n* *fr late 1800s* A person who is easily defeated, imposed upon, convinced, etc: *whisper to him that she thought he was sexy. After that he was a pushover*—Joseph Heller/ *I'm a pushover for flattery* **2** *modifier: He wasn't a pushover kind of cat*—Claude Brown **3** *n* =PUNCHBOARD, ROUNDHEELS **4** *n* An easy job or task; =CINCH, DUCK SOUP: *two ways to do it. One was a pushover*—Jerome Weidman [coined by Jack Conway in the late 19th century]

push the panic button *See* HIT THE PANIC BUTTON

pushy *adj* Assertive in a repellent way; aggressive: *Pushy people alarmed him*—Ira Wolfert

puss *n fr early 1900s* The face: *one sock in the puss*—American Mercury [fr Irish *pus*]

See GLAMOR-PUSS, PICKLEPUSS, SOURPUSS

pussy ◁**1**▷ *n fr late 1800s* The vulva or vagina ◁**2**▷ *n* A woman as a sex object or partner; =ASS, TAIL: *Where I come from we call that kind of stuff table pussy*—Calder Willingham **3** *n* A harmless person, either gentle or timid or both; =PUSSYCAT: *Space Invaders are pussies compared to the marketing aggression of the major producers* —Toronto Life **4** *adj* Harmless and undemanding; fit for the timid: *The bumper cars are pussy*—Cameron Crowe

See EATIN' STUFF, WOOD-PUSSY

pussycat **1** *n* A harmless, gentle, or timid person: *Iacocca is no closet pussycat masquerading as a tiger* —Washington Post **2** *n* A pleasant and amiable person; =DOLL, HONEY

pussyfoot or **pussyfoot around** *v* or *v phr fr early 1900s* To be careful and hesitant; be evasive; tergiversate; =BEAT AROUND THE BUSH: *Please stop pussyfooting and get to the point* [fr the nickname of WE Johnson, given because of his catlike stealth as a law-enforcement officer in the Indian Territory (Oklahoma); Johnson became a famous advocate of Prohibition, and the term briefly meant "prohibitionist"]

◁ **pussy posse** (or **squad**)▷ *n phr* A police morals or vice squad

◁ **pussy-whipped**▷ *adj* Dominated by one's wife or female lover; obsequiously uxorious; henpecked: *My husband would have called you pussy-whipped*—John Irving

pustle-gut *See* PUS-GUT

◁ **put**▷ *v* To proffer or do the sex act; =LAY: *With men buyers, you get them put and you can sell them the Brooklyn Bridge*—Jerome Weidman [a shortening of *put out*]

See KNOW WHAT one CAN DO WITH something, TELL someone WHAT TO DO WITH something

◁ **puta**▷ (Pōō tah) **1** *n* A prostitute: *A white puta like you got to have more money than that*—High Times **2** *n* =PUNCHBOARD [fr Spanish]

put a bug in someone's **ear** *v phr* To give someone a special and private piece of information, esp in the hope of favorable action

put something **across** (or **over**) **1** *v phr* =GET something ACROSS **2** *v phr* To succeed; =PULL IT OFF: *Ask her, she knows how to put it across*

put a move on someone *v phr* (Variations: **make** can replace **put**; **the move** or **the moves** can replace **a move**) To make a sexual advance to: *Why don't you put a move on that Tuck girl?*—John Irving/ *Remember that time down at Malibu... and this guy put the move on you?*—WT Tyler/ *when he makes a move on Diane*—Washington Post

◁ **put** one's **ass in a sling**▷ ***See*** HAVE one's ASS IN A SLING

◁ **put** one's **ass on the line**▷ ***v phr*** To assume risk and responsibility; put oneself in peril: *I agreed with him, but I wasn't going to put my ass on the line to prove the point*

put away ***v phr*** To eat or drink, esp heartily or excessively: *They were able to put away a lot of noodles, turkey hash, corn, Jell-O, bread, peanut butter, jelly, and water*—Playboy

put someone or something **away** **1** ***v phr*** To commit to an asylum or send to jail, an old age home, nursing home, etc **2** ***v phr*** To kill **3** ***v phr*** To knock unconscious: *The Champ put him away in the second round* **4** ***v phr*** To defeat an opponent, esp in sports: *The Rangers put the Devils away handily* **5** ***v phr*** To assure victory; =CLINCH: *They put it away in the first period, really, with nine goals* **6** ***v phr*** To please enormously; =KNOCK someone's SOCKS OFF: *It put me away. It destroyed me*—Washington Post **7** ***v phr*** To classify; categorize

put daylight between ***v phr*** To separate things, esp to separate oneself from someone or something disadvantageous: *The President is trying hard to put daylight between himself and the National Rifle Association*

put-down ***n*** Something disparaging, humiliating, or deflating; a reducing insult; =KNOCK: *This is a typical Reynolds self-put-down*—L Smith

put someone or something **down** ***v phr*** To criticize adversely and severely; denigrate; =DUMP ON, KNOCK: *Not that I mean to put down the Old Masters*—D Gillespie

put one's **finger on** something ***v phr*** To recall or specify a desired matter with precision; define exactly: *I remember it, but can't quite put my finger on the outcome*

put one's **foot in it** ***v phr*** To get into difficulties, esp by blundering: *Trying to be delicate, I put my foot right in it*

put one's **foot in** one's **mouth** ***v phr*** To make an embarrassing comment; say something stupid: *part of the same hysterical syndrome that caused me to put my foot in my mouth*—Saul Bellow

put someone **in the picture** ***v phr fr 1930s British armed forces*** To give necessary orienting data; brief; =BRING someone UP TO SPEED: *Nobody put me in the picture, and I was confused for weeks*

put in one's **two cents worth** ***See*** PUT one's TWO CENTS IN

put it in your ear or **take it in the ear** ***v phr*** To insert something figuratively into one's ear as a means of contemptuous disposal; =STICK IT • Mild euphemistic forms of **stick it up your ass**, used for reduced effect and among friends: *It was easy to say things like "take it in the ear" to them ... they didn't get it*—John Irving

put it on the line ***See*** LAY IT ON THE LINE

put it over on someone ***v phr fr early 1900s*** To deceive; fool: *Be careful, nobody puts it over on her*

◁ **put it to** someone▷ ***v phr*** To do the sex act with or to; =SCREW

put one's **money where** one's **mouth is** ***sentence*** Support your statements, brags, opinions, etc, with something tangible: *I won't believe he's leaving until he puts his money where his mouth is and goes away*

put someone's **nose out of joint** ***v phr*** To make envious or jealous

put one's **oar in** ***v phr*** =PUT one's TWO CENTS IN

put something **off** (or **over**) ***v phr*** To postpone; delay: *We'll put it off to next week*

put on ***v phr*** =PUT ON AIRS

put-on ***fr middle 1800s*** **1** ***n*** An act, remark, etc, intended to fool someone; a more or less amiable deception: *a master of the "put-on," a mildly cruel art*—Time **2** ***n*** (also **put-on artist**) A pretender; =PHONY: *a put-on like Andy Warhol*—Jack Newfield **3** ***adj*** Feigned; affected: *his put-on machismo*

put someone **on** ***v phr fr late 1800s*** To fool, esp by pretending; tease: *The Countess who adores the poet pities him and puts him "on"*—Wallace Stevens

put on airs **1** ***v phr*** To affect a refinement and hauteur one is not born to: *Now that I have the Rolls Royce I'll put on airs* **2** ***v phr*** To be snobbish and aloof

put on the feedbag (or **the nosebag**) ***v phr*** To eat; have a meal

put someone **on the floor** ***v phr*** To please enormously; =PUT someone

AWAY, KNOCK someone OUT: *Schaefer said the strip "put me on the floor"* —Washington Post

put something **on the line** ***See*** LAY something ON THE LINE

put on the ritz (or **the dog**) **1** ***v phr*** To make a display of wealth and luxury: *everything they could... to put on the ritz*—Car and Driver/ *put on the dog and give him the ritz like this*—Ira Wolfert **2** ***v phr*** To dress stylishly and flashily **3** ***v phr*** =PUT ON AIRS [fr the name of the Swiss César *Ritz* and the various luxurious European hotels he built; *put on the dog* fr a late-19th-century college, esp Yale, expression; see *doggy*]

put someone **on the spot** **1** ***v phr*** To require action, a solution, etc, at once: *It had to be ready tomorrow, which put our department on the spot* **2** ***v phr*** To embarrass; put in a difficult position: *I don't want her to put us on the spot again*—New Yorker

put someone **on to** someone or something ***v phr*** To introduce someone; get someone access to: *that little Andronica you put me onto*—Lawrence Sanders

◁ **put** (or **give**) **out**▷ ***v phr*** To proffer sexual favors, esp to do so readily; be promiscuous: *A guy gives a dame a string of beads... and she puts out* —Lawrence Sanders/ *A guy buys a gift for his wife because he knows she won't give out if he don't*—Lawrence Sanders

put someone **out** ***v phr*** To impose upon; cause inconvenience

put someone or something **out to pasture** ***v phr*** To retire; take out of active use, practice, etc, usu after long service: *The university put six of us out to pasture last year* [fr the farm practice of letting an old horse graze at will, and work no longer]

put over ***See*** PUT something OFF

put one's **papers in** **1** ***v phr*** *teenagers* To apply for admission, enlistment, etc **2** ***v phr*** *police* To retire or resign

put the bite (or **the bee**) **on** someone or something **1** ***v phr*** *fr early 1900s* To ask for money, esp for a loan: *I'll put the bite on my rich cousin* **2** ***v phr*** To make a request; solicit: *Sullivan continues putting the bee on other Government agencies*—Variety

◁ **put the blocks to** someone▷ ***v phr*** *fr late 1800s lumberjacks* To do the sex act with or to; =SCREW: *putting the blocks to the Winnipeg whore* —Canadian folk song [fr the logging practice of placing *blocks* on a tree that is to be felled, perhaps with the reinforcing sense that *blocks* suggests "testicles"]

put the chill on someone **1** ***v phr*** To treat coldly; snub; cut; =COLD SHOULDER **2** ***v phr*** To kill

put the eye on someone **1** ***v phr*** To look at invitingly or seductively; =GIVE someone THE EYE: *I was having the eye put on me*—Raymond Chandler **2** ***v phr*** To look at; look over; examine; =SCOPE ON

put the finger on someone *underworld* **1** ***v phr*** To locate and identify a victim; =FINGER **2** ***v phr*** To provide evidence leading to the arrest of a criminal; betray a criminal to the police: *He put the finger on my husband*—New York Daily News

put the heat on someone ***v phr*** To use coercive pressure; =LEAN ON someone: *He put the heat on me to vote that way*

put the icing on the cake ***See*** ICE THE CAKE

put the kibosh on someone or something (KĪ bahsh) ***v phr*** *fr early 1800s British* To quash or stifle; put the quietus to: *quietly put the "kibosh" on Donald Nixon, Inc*—Jack Anderson [origin unknown and richly speculated upon; many regard it as probably fr Yiddish because it sounds as if it ought to be; Padraic Colum, however, attributed it to Irish *cie bais* "cap of death," presumably the black cap donned by a judge before pronouncing the death sentence, which is a semantically appealing suggestion; the phrase was used by Dickens in his first published book, in 1836, and put into the mouth of a London urchin]

put the make on someone ***v phr*** To make sexual advances; =MAKE A PASS AT someone: *The codger was horny and put the make on the lady cop* —Playboy

put them in the aisles ***See*** LAY THEM IN THE AISLES

put the moves on someone ***v phr*** To make sexual advances; =PUT THE

MAKE ON someone: *Steve Antin put the moves on Gerri Idol*—People Weekly

put the screws to someone *v phr* To use extreme coercive pressure; harass; =PUT THE HEAT ON someone: *The only reason Fidel agreed... was to put the screws to Reagan*—Art Buchwald [fr a torturer's use of *thumbscrews*]

put the skids under someone or something *v phr* To cause to fail, be defeated, be rejected, etc: *They put the skids under him when they found out he had cheated*

put the snatch on someone or something *v phr* To take or commandeer; seize; kidnap: *The Treasury Department is going to put the snatch on virtually the entire 40 grand*—Billy Rose

put the squeeze on someone *v phr* To put under heavy pressure or exigency; =LEAN ON someone, PUT THE HEAT ON someone: *She hired me to put the squeeze on Linda for a divorce* —Raymond Chandler

put the wood to someone *v phr* To punish; coerce by threat of punishment: *Why can't Mayor Barry put the wood to school administrators and demand more caring than this?* —Washingtonian

put someone **through the mill** *See* RUN someone THROUGH THE MILL

put someone **through the wringer** *v phr* To subject to harsh treatment, esp by severe interrogation [fr the image of squeezing something out by passing it through a clothing *wringer*]

putting *See* OFF-PUTTING

put (or **add**) one's **two cents** (or **two cents worth**) **in** *v phr* To volunteer one's advice, esp when it is not solicited; =KIBITZ: *If I may put my two cents in, I think we should shut up*

put up *v phr* To contribute or pay money, esp money bet or promised

put someone **up** *v phr* To provide lodging for

put-up job *n phr fr middle 1800s underworld* A prearranged matter; a contrived affair: *The surprise award was a put-up job*

put up or shut up *sentence* =PUT one's MONEY WHERE one's MOUTH IS

put up with someone or something *v phr* To tolerate or accept: *I'll put up with it if you think I should/ How can you put up with him?*

put someone **wise** *v phr fr early 1900s* To make aware; inform, esp of something shrewd and elementary or covert: *The kindly old clerk put me wise to how things were done around there*

◁**putz**▷ **1** *n* A detestable person; obnoxious wretch; =PRICK, SCHMUCK: *Here comes the Moravian putz* —Joseph Heller **2** *n* An ineffectual person; =NEBBISH: *The poor little putz didn't realize what they were after* **3** *n* The penis [fr Yiddish, literally "ornament"]

putz around *v phr* To behave idly; putter around; =FOOL AROUND, FUTZ AROUND [fr *putz* and semantically related to *dick around, fuck around,* though less coarse than these to any but, probably, Jewish ears]

puzzle palace **1** *n phr Army* Any higher headquarters, including the Pentagon **2** *n phr* A place, like the White House, where vital decisions are made in great and pompous secrecy: *some kind of puzzle palace on the Potomac*—Ronald Reagan
See FIVE-SIDED PUZZLE PALACE

Q

the QT ***See*** ON THE QT

quail ◁**1**▷ ***n*** *fr middle 1800s college students* An attractive young woman; =CHICK: *a lovely little quail from Arkansas*—Arthur Godfrey **2** ***n*** *jazz musicians* A cornet or trumpet: *listen to that kid blow that quail* —Louis Armstrong

See SAN QUENTIN QUAIL

quarterback ***v*** To lead or direct; control; manage: *and quarterbacking the rise of Action News at Channel 6* —Philadelphia

See MONDAY MORNING QUARTERBACK

quartet ***See*** BARBERSHOP QUARTET

queen **1** ***n*** A woman, esp a wealthy and gracious one: *Wouldn't it be luck if some ritzy queen fell for him!* —James T Farrell **2** ***v*** (also **queen it**) To behave in a refined and haughty way **3** ***n*** *homosexuals* A male homosexual, esp one who ostentatiously takes a feminine role: *The queens look great strutting along the boardwalk*—Albert Goldman [homosexual sense probably a late-19th-century alteration of *quean* "harlot, prostitute," influenced by connotations of *queen* "aged, dignified, tawdry, and overadorned"]

See CLOSET QUEEN, DRAG QUEEN, TEAROOM QUEEN

queer **1** ***adj*** *fr 1500s perhaps fr Scots* Counterfeit **2** ***n*** (also **the queer**) *underworld fr early 1900s* Counterfeit money: *eagle-eyed concessionaires always on the lookout for the queer*—W & F Simpson ◁**3**▷ ***adj*** *fr 1920s* Homosexual; =CAMP, GAY: *Some girls said that I was queer*—New York Post ◁**4**▷ ***n*** (also **queerie**): *a closet queer/ a lot of queeries in the State Department* —Westbrook Pegler **5** ***v*** *fr late 1700s British* To spoil; ruin; =GOOF UP: *Food is what queered the party*—F Scott Fitzgerald

queer fish ***n phr*** A strange or weird person; =WACK, WEIRDO

quick ***adj*** *esp 1920s & 30s* Tight; snug: *That sweater seems a little quick*

quick-and-dirty ***n*** =GREASY SPOON

quick buck ***See*** FAST BUCK

quick fix ***n phr*** A hasty repair or relief job: *He called my idea a quick fix at best, but he'd do it* [fr *fix* as "repair" influenced by *fix* as "dose of narcotics"]

quickie **1** ***n*** Anything taken or done very hastily; something rushed: *a "quickie," one of those overnight film concoctions*—Picture Play **2** ***modifier:*** *the new "quickie divorce" law*—Selden Rodman **3** ***n*** The sex act done very hastily: *Do you have time for a quickie?*

quick one ***n phr*** Something taken or done hastily, esp an unleisurely drink or sex act; =QUICKIE, A SHORT ONE

quick on the draw (or **the trigger** or **the uptake**) ***adj phr*** *fr middle 1800s* Quick to respond or react; touchy; sensitive

quiff ***n*** *underworld* A prostitute or promiscuous woman; =ROUNDHEEL: *There would be a lot of loose quiff we could meet*—Philadelphia [perhaps related to late-19th-century British, "vulva," which may be fr earlier verb sense "copulate"; perhaps related to late-19th-century British armed forces slang, "a small flat curl or lock of hair on the temple or forehead," perhaps fr Italian *cuffia* "coif" or fr *coif* with sense transferred to pubic hair]

◁ **quim** ▷ *n fr 1600s* The vulva or vagina; =CUNT [origin unknown; perhaps fr Middle English *queme* "pleasure, satisfaction," cognate with Latin *convenire*, hence with *convenient*, *convenience*, etc, and perhaps influenced by Middle English *queint* "cunt"]

quits *See* CALL IT QUITS

quiz *n students fr middle 1800s* A brief examination in college

R

R ***See*** R AND R

rabbi *n politics fr police & underworld* An influential sponsor; a high-placed patron: *I see you got the gold tin, who's your rabbi?*—New York Times

rabbit **1** *n sports* The pacesetter in the early laps of a mile race **2** *v* To run away fast; escape in a hurry; =LAM: *The man who had rabbited was later identified*—Ann Rule [first sense fr the mechanical *rabbit* used to lure dogs in a race]

rabbit food ***See*** BUNNY FOOD

race ***See*** DRAG RACE, DRUGSTORE RACE, HORSERACE, RAT RACE

rack *v* (also **rack out**) *teenagers* To sleep; nap; =COP ZS: *I'll rack out for awhile on the grass till I get it together*—Perception & Persuasion

See MEAT RACK, PANIC RACK

the **rack** *n fr Navy* Bed; =SACK: *who gets some Greek broad in the rack* —WT Tyler

racked out *adj phr teenagers* Asleep; in bed

racket **1** *n fr middle 1800s British* Any illegal concern or enterprise; a criminal business; =DODGE: *the narcotics racket/ loan-shark racket* **2** *n circus & carnival* Any concession, stand, etc **3** *n* One's legitimate occupation or concern: *Lexicography's my racket* **4** *n* An easy and pleasant situation, esp a sinecure: *That's no job, it's a racket* [fr early-19th-century British underworld fr *racket* "noise, confusion," etc]

the **rackets** *n phr* Organized crime; the syndicate; the Mafia

rack up[1] *v phr* To register or post; accumulate; achieve: *with the years of hackdom racked up in his face* —New York [fr the *racking up* of pool balls in a triangular frame before a game]

rack up[2] *v phr* To wreck; ruin; damage severely; =TOTAL: *got caught raping a nine-year-old Japanese girl. He got racked up*—Lawrence Sanders/ *The fall really racked up his leg* [probably related to *rack* "junk, rubbish," as found in the mid-19th-century term *rack heap*; perhaps influenced by *wreck* and *wrack and ruin*]

raft *n fr early 1800s* A large number; =OODLES, SLEW: *I have rafts of reasons for not doing that/ She gave me a raft of excuses* [first sense fr earlier uses of *raft* to mean a dense flight of waterfowl and a mass of driftwood in a river]

See ON A RAFT

rag **1** *n* An article of clothing, esp a dress **2** *n circus* A tent **3** *n Navy* A signal flag **4** *n baseball* The pennant awarded to the annual winner of a league championship **5** *n* A newspaper or magazine, esp one that the speaker does not like: *This so-called revolutionary organ is a horrible rag*—O Chubb **6** *n cardplayers* A playing card, esp one that does not improve the hand **7** *n railroad* A switch operator **8** *n fr early 1900s* =RAGTIME **9** *n fr early 1900s* A piece of ragtime music **10** *v fr early 1900s* To play in a ragtime style: *The street bands ragged a tune by taking one note and putting two or three in its place*—Stephen Longstreet **11** *v fr early 1900s* To dance to ragtime music **12** *v fr late 1800s college students* To tease; banter disparagingly with; =NEEDLE, RIDE: *Sometimes we'd rag one another*—FG Patton

See BULLYRAG, GLAD RAGS

◁ the **rag**▷ **1** *n* A sanitary napkin; a vaginal tampon: *She told him she was wearing the rag, which cooled his ardor some* **2** *n* Menstruation; = the CURSE

See CHEW THE FAT, HAVE THE RAG ON, ON THE RAG

rag-chewing *n fr late 1800s* Talking, esp of an amiable and idle sort

ragged *See* RUN someone RAGGED

◁ **raggedy-ass**▷ or **raggedy-pants** *adj fr WW1 armed forces* Inferior; sloppy; = HALF-ASSED: *some kinda raggedy-ass agreement she thinks is a legal will*—Joseph Wambaugh/ *picked up from some raggedy-pants US trackside*—Sports Illustrated

◀ **raghead**▶ **1** *n* A Hindu or other Eastern or Middle Eastern person: *speaks Arab like a raghead*—WT Tyler **2** *n* A gypsy: *You let that raghead touch your hand*—Harry Crews

rags *n* Clothing; = THREADS: *She got into her rags*—John O'Hara

See GLAD RAGS

ragtime **1** *n fr late 1800s* A highly syncopated style of music, esp for the piano, having a heavily accented tempo and a melody consisting of many short rapid notes **2** *modifier: a ragtime classic*

ragtop or **rag-roof** **1** *n* A convertible car: *It's been a while since the ragtops rolled off the assembly line*—Aquarian/ *Return of the rag roofs*—Time **2** *modifier: I sure wouldn't sleep in that rag-top car*—Earl Thompson

the **rag trade** *n phr fr middle 1800s* The clothing and fashion industry; the garment industry; = SEVENTH AVENUE: *the enormously canny middle-aged men of the rag trade*—New Yorker

rah-rah **1** *adj fr 1920s* Naively enthusiastic and hortatory, esp in a partisan collegiate context **2** *n: I just couldn't see myself spending four years of my life with rah-rahs like them*

rail *n narcotics* A thin row of powdered narcotic to be sniffed; = LINE: *I snorted the rails that Hondo offered*—Peter Gent

railbird *n fr late 1800s* An ardent horse-racing devotee: *another three-year-old... that set the railbirds agog*—Audax Minor

railroad **1** *v fr late 1800s* To convict and imprison someone very rapidly, perhaps unjustly or illegally: *The prisoner is railroaded to jail*—E Lavine **2** *v* To force a resolution of something quickly, perhaps without due process: *if all cases were railroaded through that quick*—James M Cain

See A HELL OF A WAY TO RUN A RAILROAD

railroad tracks **1** *n phr WW2 Army* An Army captain's two silver bars, the insignia of rank **2** *n phr* Braces on teeth: *a chubbette with "railroad tracks" across her teeth*—New York

rain cats and dogs *v phr* (Variations: **chicken coops** or **darning needles** or **pitchforks** may replace **cats and dogs**) *fr middle 1700s British* To rain very hard [origin unknown, although many improbable derivations have been proposed, from classical Greek to pagan Scandinavian]

rain check *n phr* A postponement or delay, with promise of renewal, of a sports event, dinner, party, date, receipt of a sale item at a store, etc [fr the ticket stub that permits one to see another baseball game if the game one has a ticket for is not played on account of rain]

See TAKE A RAIN CHECK

rain dance *n phr* An impressive political reception or banquet

rainmaker *n* A powerful and successful representative or agent, esp for a law firm: *All such well-connected persons are "rainmakers" capable of making their employer's cause prosper*—Newsweek

rain on someone's **parade** *v phr* To spoil someone's day, performance, special occasion, etc

raise *See* MEXICAN PROMOTION

raise Cain (or **a ruckus**) *v phr fr middle 1800s* To make a disturbance; complain loudly and bitterly; = KICK UP A FUSS

raise hell **1** *v phr* = RAISE CAIN **2** *v phr* To carouse and celebrate boisterously **3** *v phr* To rebuke strongly; castigate: *He raised hell with me when he found out*

raiser *See* HELL-RAISER

raise sand *v phr* = RAISE CAIN

raise the roof **1** *v phr* To complain angrily and bitterly; issue a strong rebuke: *When the president sees this* *fuck-up she'll raise the roof* **2** *v phr* To make a boisterous noise; carouse raucously

rake-off *fr late 1800s* **1** *n* A gambling house's percentage of each pot or stake **2** *n* An illegal or unethical share or payment [fr the *rake* used by casino croupiers]

rake someone **over the coals** *See* HAUL someone OVER THE COALS

rally *See* PEP RALLY

ralph *v* (Variations: **Ralph** or **ralph up** or **rolf**) *teenagers* To vomit; =BARF: *He ralphs up the downers and the quarts of beer*—J Gallick [probably echoic]

ram-bam thank you ma'am *See* WHAM-BAM THANK YOU MA'AM

rambunctious *adj fr early 1800s* Boisterous; obstreperous; wild [perhaps fr Irish *rambunkshus*; a US contribution to a mock inkhorn series with British variants *robustious, rumbumptious*, etc]

◁ **ram it**▷ *v phr* =STICK IT

rammer *See* MOTHERFUCKER

ranch *See* BUY THE FARM

R and R *n phr* Rock and roll

randy **1** *adj fr late 1700s fr British dialect* Sexually aroused; =HORNY: *a desperately randy brain surgeon*—Time **2** *adj* Desirous; yearning: *randy for the smell of setting cement*—Washingtonian [origin unknown; various dialect senses suggest a possible derivation fr "wild movement," "boisterousness," "wantonness"]

rank **1** *v underworld* To say or do something that reveals another's guilt: *She ranked him by busting out with that new fur so soon after the robbery*—E Booth **2** *v fr 1920s* To harass; annoy; =NEEDLE ● Used by 1960s teenagers in the preferred variant **rank out**, both as a verb phrase and a noun phrase: *He will rank you for what happened*—Washingtonian

See PULL RANK

rap[1] **1** *n fr late 1700s* A rebuke; =KNOCK **2** *n fr 1920s underworld* Arrest, indictment, or arraignment for a crime: *beat about 90 percent of their "raps"*—E Lavine **3** *n* An official complaint or reprimand: *Honest cops will often take a "rap" or complaint rather than testify against a fellow cop*—E Lavine

See BEAT THE RAP

rap[2] **1** *v esp 1960s counterculture & black* To converse; chat and exchange views, esp in a very candid way: *drugs, youth cult, ecstasy questing, rapping*—New York Times **2** *n* Informal talk; candid conversation and communion **3** *v* To sympathize; be of chiming views **4** *v fr late 1970s* To chant a rap song **5** *n* =RAP SONG [origin unknown; perhaps related to *repartee*, perhaps to *rapport*, perhaps to *rapid*]

the **rap** *n phr fr middle 1800s* The blame; an accusation: *He wouldn't accept the rap for that particular screw-up*

See TAKE THE RAP

rap club (or **parlor** or **studio**) **1** *n phr* A place that offers sexual services in the guise of conversation and companionship: *"rap clubs," which have replaced massage parlors*—New York Post **2** *n phr* A nightclub, discotheque, etc, featuring rap music

rape wagon *n phr* =PIMPMOBILE

rap someone's **knuckles** *v phr* To give a light and insufficient punishment; =GIVE someone A SLAP ON THE WRIST: *Tokyo had been rapped over the knuckles*—New York Review

rapper **1** *n esp 1960s counterculture* A person who converses and chats, esp a member of a rap (discussion) group **2** *n fr late 1970s* The chanter of a rap song **3** *n fr late 1970s* A devotee of rap music and its attendant styles of dressing, dancing, etc: *as rappers pick up on a little new wave style... and make their moves*—Time **4** *modifier: rapper talk, which pulls in language from... 40s hipsters, 60s hippies, and even cockney rhyming slang*—Time

rap session **1** *n phr* A conversation; a bout of candid chat: *talk shows featuring rap sessions between hosts and listeners*—Newsweek **2** *n phr* A meeting of a discussion group: *I was asked to lead a rap session*—Betty Friedan

rap sheet *n phr* A person's record of arrests and convictions: *The last one is called a rap sheet*—Bobby Seale

rap song (or **music**) *n phr* A song that is rapidly spoken rather than actually sung, usu with an electronic rhythm accompaniment

be **raring to go** *v phr* To be very eager and keen to begin; =LEAN FOR-

WARD IN THE SADDLE [fr the image of a *rearing*, mettlesome horse]

raspberry ***n*** An instance of the raspberry, a rude labial flatulation: *You should expect an occasional heathen to utter a raspberry*—Washington Post ***See*** FLIP one's LID

the **raspberry** (or **razzberry**) (RAZ beh ree) ***n phr*** *fr late 1800s British* A rude and contemptuous expulsion of breath through vibrating lips; =the BIRD: *that staccato sputter of derision known as the Bronx cheer, or raspberry*—Newsweek [fr Cockney rhyming slang *raspberry tart* "fart"]

rat **1** ***n*** A treacherous and disgusting person: *He's acting like a prime rat on this* **2** ***n*** *fr late 1800s* An informer; =STOOL PIGEON: *In most cases they were "rats" and the best tools the keepers had*—PL Quinlan **3** ***v:*** *an inmate, rankled by Angelo's attempts to woo his daughter, ratted on them*—Time **4** ***combining word*** A frequenter and devotee of the place indicated: *arcade rat/gym rat*

See LOOK LIKE A DROWNED RAT, PACK RAT, RUG APE, SMELL A RAT

rat around ***v phr*** To idle about; loaf; =BAT AROUND: *Oh, I don't know. Ratting around*—John O'Hara

ratchet ***v*** To change by increments in one direction: *Gold... had ratcheted down to 385*—New York Times [fr the *ratchet* action of a winch or of a wrench, where an increasing pressure, torque, pull, etc, is registered by the clicking of a pawl on a gear wheel]

ratchet-mouth or **ratchet-jaw** ***n*** A person who is constantly talking; =MOTOR-MOUTH [perhaps because a *ratchet* wrench can be operated without pause, and makes a constant rapid rasping, clacking noise]

rate **1** ***v*** To merit; deserve: *He rates a big cheer, folks* **2** ***v*** To be highly esteemed: *What stunt did he ever pull that makes him rate?*—Billy Rose

rated ***See*** X-RATED

rat fink **1** ***n phr*** *esp 1960s* A treacherous and disgusting person; =BASTARD, SHITHEEL: *that rat-fink Danny's kid*—TV Guide **2** ***modifier:*** *the rat-fink Eastern press*—New Yorker [perhaps originally fr labor union use, since both terms mean "scab"]

◀ **rat fuck**▶ *college students* **1** ***adj phr*** Unacceptable to conventional moral traditions **2** ***adj phr*** =FAR OUT **3** ***v phr*** To have a good time; =JAM **4** ***v phr*** To loaf and idle about; =RAT AROUND **5** ***n phr*** A despicable person; =RAT FINK: *You lousy bastard rat-fuck*—Barry Reed

rathole ***See*** POUR MONEY DOWN THE DRAIN

rat on someone ***v phr*** To inform on; give evidence against; =SQUEAL: *No power on earth can keep her from ratting on you*—James M Cain

rat pack ***n phr*** A teenage street gang: *juvenile gangs, sometimes called rat packs*—RS Prather

rat race ***n phr*** A job, situation, milieu, etc, marked by confusion and stress; futile and enervating hyperactivity: *the rat-race of ordinary social gatherings*—E Wilder

the **rat race** ***n phr*** The everyday world of toil and struggle; the routine workaday world: *Will Heacock ever renounce the freelance life and rejoin the rat race?*

rats ***interj*** An exclamation of disgust, disappointment, dismay, etc

◁ a **rat's ass**▷ ***n phr*** Nothing; very little; =DIDDLY, ZILCH • **Not** is used to intensify rather than to negate this phrase: *That thing's not worth a rat's ass*

See NOT GIVE A DAMN

◁ **rat's asshole**▷ ***n phr*** A despicable person; =BASTARD, RAT-FINK: *You rat's asshole*—John Irving

rattlebrain ***n*** A silly or stupid person; =SCATTERBRAIN: *Mother would like to travel around but not with an old rattlebrain like you driving*—Ring Lardner

rattle someone's **cage** **1** ***v phr*** To stir into action: *Something rattling your cage?*—Easyriders **2** ***v phr*** To make a scene or disturbance; =RAISE CAIN: *I'm going into his office and rattle his cage*

rattle cages ***v phr*** To cause excitement; shake things up: *"You like to rattle cages," the saleswoman observed*—Village Voice

rattle someone's **chain** ***See*** PULL someone's CHAIN

rattler ***See*** CAGE RATTLER

rattlesnakes ***See*** UP TO one's ASS IN something

rattling **1** *adv* Very; extremely: *a rattling good story*—A Hays **2** *adj* Good; =GREAT: *a rattling party*

ratty or ◁**rat-ass**▷ *adj* Shabby; slovenly; =SCRUFFY, TACKY: *a fairly ratty bar*—T Robinson/ *the rat-ass rags he's always wearing*—National Lampoon

raunch **1** *n* Vulgarity; smut; =PORN: *the latest batch of 8mm raunch*—Playboy **2** *v* To do the sex act with or to; =SCREW: *She's raunched a few law students*—National Lampoon [back formation fr *raunchy*]

raunchy or **ronchie** **1** *adj WW2 Air Forces* Sloppy; slovenly; careless: *depending on how good or how "raunchy" we were*—R Hubler **2** *adj teenagers* Inferior; cheap; =CRUMMY, GRUNGY: *my raunchy old jeans* **3** *adj esp students* Vulgar; salacious; =DIRTY: *I'm gonna do some raunchy blues this time*—Rolling Stone/ *In the beginning there was* Playboy, *then came raunchy* Penthouse—Time **4** *adj esp students* Ill; indisposed; =BLAH, YUCKY: *I feel raunchy as hell today* **5** *adj* Drunk [origin unknown; the pronunciation and the early currency among aviation cadets in Texas suggest a possible origin in Spanish *rancio* "rank, rancid, stale"]

rave **1** *v fr late 1800s* To commend or applaud enthusiastically: *He's raving over this new book* **2** *n: The critics gave it a rave* **3** *modifier: a rave review/ rave notices*
See FAVE

rave-up **1** *n chiefly British teenagers* A wild party **2** *n* Something loud and exciting: *in "Take Me Back," a lively rave-up*—Time

raw **1** *adj* Inexperienced; unfledged; callow: *a raw young actress* **2** *adj* Harsh; inhospitable: *a raw reception* **3** *adj* Nude; naked; =IN THE RAW: *You can't go raw on this beach, ma'am* **4** *adj* Vulgar; salacious; dirty; raunchy: *He offended us all with a very raw story*
See IN THE RAW

raw deal *n phr* A case of harsh, unfair, or injurious treatment; =a ROYAL FUCKING: *heaping raw deal after raw deal on him*—Sloan Wilson

rays *n* Sunshine: *soaking up some rays*
See BAG SOME RAYS

razz *v fr early 1900s* To insult and ridicule; =NEEDLE, RIDE: *The fellows razzed the life out of me*—P Marks [fr *raspberry*]

the **razzberry** *See* the RASPBERRY

razzle-dazzle *fr late 1800s* **1** *n* Adroit deception; slick dodging and feinting; =DOUBLE SHUFFLE, RAZZMATAZZ: *suspecting some sort of razzle-dazzle*—New Yorker **2** *modifier: a razzle-dazzle quarterback/ razzle-dazzle salesmanship* **3** *n* Excitement; gaudiness; spectacular show: *put razzle-dazzle into the grocery business*—This Week **4** *adj: A great many people are reading Mr Wakeman's razzle-dazzle novel*—CV Terry [probably a reduplication of *dazzle*]

razzmatazz or **razzamatazz** **1** *n outdated jazz talk* Anything outdated, esp old and sentimental; =CORN: *"Razzmatazz" is corny jazz*—Stephen Longstreet **2** *n* Swift and adroit deception; slick jugglery; =RAZZLE-DAZZLE: *more glitter, more razzmatazz, more false human interest*—Washington Post **3** *adj* Spectacular; showy; dazzling; =RAZZLE-DAZZLE: *a razzmatazz New Year's Eve bash*—Philadelphia **4** *adj* =GEE-WHIZ, RAH-RAH

reaction *See* GUT REACTION

read **1** *v fr radio operators* To receive and interpret a radio signal; understand: *He's breaking up and I can't read him* **2** *v cool talk fr radio operators* To understand; =DIG: *I read you, baby, and I flatly agree* **3** *v* =READ someone LIKE A BOOK

reader *See* METER-READER

read someone **his rights** *See* GIVE someone HIS RIGHTS

read someone **like a book** *v phr* To know and understand someone thoroughly, including deep motives and likely actions: *She thinks she's pretty clever, but I read her like a book*

read someone **loud and clear** *v phr fr radio operators* To understand someone very well; comprehend perfectly: *Do you read me loud and clear, mister?*—Pat Conroy

read my lips or **can you read lips** **1** *sentence* I am thinking but not uttering something obscene, insulting, or otherwise not for the public ear: *Psst. Hey, parents! Read my lips*—Erma Bombeck **2** *v phr* You seem to be too stupid to understand what I'm saying, so look at me very attentively and try

read the riot act *v phr fr middle 1800s* To rebuke firmly; reprove severely, esp in the vein of a stern warning

the **ready** *n phr fr early 1700s British* Money: *Take the ready and send it along*—John Kieran [fr *ready* money]

real *adv* Really; truly
See FOR REAL, IT'S BEEN REAL

the **real cheese** *See* the CHEESE

really pick 'em *See* one CAN REALLY PICK 'EM

the **real McCoy** (or **the McCoy**) *n phr* Any genuine and worthy person or thing; the genuine article: *egg bagels, a sweeter variety of the real McCoy*—New York Times [probably fr a Scottish phrase *the real Mackay* (mə KI), of uncertain origin, attested fr the late 19th century]

real money *See* HEAVY MONEY

real pro *See* PRO

ream 1 *v* (also **rim**) To cheat; swindle, esp by unfair business practice; =SCREW: *A new technique for reaming the customers*—AJ Liebling **2** *v* (also **ream out**) To rebuke harshly; =BAWL OUT, CHEW OUT: *I've seen him just ream guys out for not getting the job done*—Time ◁**3**▷ *v* (also **rim**) *fr homosexuals* To stimulate the anus, either orally or with the penis

rear end *n phr* (also **rear**) The buttocks; =ASS: *He got a shrewd boot in the rear/ She's a pain in the rear end*—Jerome Weidman

reat *See* ALL REET, REET

rebop *n* =BOP

recap (REE kap) **1** *v* To repeat, esp in a summary form; recapitulate; =REHASH **2** *n: I gave her a quick recap of the incident*

record *See* BROKEN RECORD, OFF THE RECORD, TRACK RECORD

red *See* MEXICAN RED, PAINT THE TOWN RED, SEE RED

Red or **Red Devil** *n* or *n phr narcotics* Seconal (a trade name), a barbiturate capsule: *dropping Reds and busting heads*—Eldridge Cleaver

the **red ass** *See* GET THE RED ASS

◁**red-assed**▷ *adj* Very angry; livid; =PISSED OFF

red carpet 1 *n phr* A sumptuous welcome: *He was sort of expecting the red carpet and not the fish-eye* **2** *adj phr* Luxurious; plush; =RITZY, SWANKY: *Jewelry gives you a red carpet elegance*—Life [fr an ancient custom, at least as old as Aeschylus's *Agamemnon*, of putting down a *red carpet* over which a welcomed dignitary would walk]
See ROLL OUT THE RED CARPET

a (or **one**) **red cent** (Variation: a (or **one**) **red**) **1** *n phr* The least amount of money; =A THIN DIME: *The poor man claimed he didn't have a red cent* **2** *n phr* A cent; penny; a trivial amount; =BEANS, DIDDLY: *It didn't cost her a red cent* [fr the fact that a copper *cent* is *red*]

red dog *n phr football* A defensive assault in which the linebacker goes directly for the quarterback

the **red-eye** or **the red-eye special** *n phr* An airline flight from coast to coast, esp from west to east, that leaves one coast late at night and arrives early in the morning: *I just flew in on the red-eye*—Vincent Canby/ *boards what he calls the red-eye special for Los Angeles*—New York Times [fr the bleary sleepless look of overnight passengers]

red face *n phr* An embarrassed and guilty countenance: *You should've seen his red face when they caught him sneaking out*
See HAVE A RED FACE

red-faced *adj* Embarrassed; abashed; guilty-looking

redhanded *adv* In a situation of inescapable guilt; =DEAD TO RIGHTS: *They got me redhanded, so I confessed*
See CATCH someone REDHANDED

red hot 1 *adj phr* Very hot; sizzling • In all slang senses of **hot**: *That little lady's a red hot fox* **2** *n phr* A frankfurter; =HOT DOG

red ink 1 *n phr* Red wine, esp of an inferior sort: *A pint of red ink still sells for two bits*—NY Confidential **2** *n phr* Financial loss or losses: *a flood of red ink totaling close to $80 billion*—Fortune

red-letter day *n phr* A very important or consequential day, esp for an individual person [fr the typographical practice of printing the words of Jesus or the dates of certain holidays in *red*]

redline 1 *v Army* To cross a soldier's name off the payroll for some wrongdoing **2** *v* To designate neighborhoods, usu minority neighborhoods, as ineligible for housing loans and mortgages; discriminate in lending: *they're still redlining the city* —Neal Travis

redneck **1** *n* =CRACKER **2** *modifier: This is a redneck rural county* —Newsweek **3** *n* A bigoted and conventional person; a loutish ultraconservative: *Fred is a crude redneck, and Carol is his latest bimbo*—Time [perhaps fr the characteristic ruddy *neck* of an angry person, and influenced by the image of a bigoted rural Southern white person; perhaps fr the fact that pellagra, a deficiency disease associated with poor Southern whites, produces a dermatitis that turns the neck red]

red-necked *adj* Angry; =RED-ASSED

redshirt **1** *v sports* To extend a college student's period of athletic eligibility, usu for football **2** *n* A student whose period of athletic eligibility has been extended [fr the *red shirts* worn by such athletes in contrast with varsity players]

red tape *n phr fr early 1800s British* Delay and complication; bureaucratic routine; petty officious procedure [fr the tape used for tying up official documents]

red totem poles *See* KNOCK someone or something FOR A LOOP

reefer[1] *n hoboes, railroad, Navy & truckers* A refrigerated railroad car, truck, ship, etc; =FREEZE: *A malfunction in a refrigerated trailer, or reefer, raises the temperature*—Smithsonian [fr *refrigerated*]

reefer[2] **1** *n fr 1920s prison, black & narcotics* A marijuana cigarette; =JOINT **2** *n narcotics* A person who smokes marijuana; =POTHEAD [origin unknown; perhaps originally *rifa* fr Mexican Spanish *grifa* "marijuana," the *g-* lost because it is not aspirated or exploded in Spanish pronunciation and hence not readily heard by English speakers]

reefer weed *n phr narcotics* Marijuana; =POT

reet or **reat** *adj* (also **reet and compleat**) *jive talk* Good; proper; excellent; right: *looking extremely reet and compleat*—Stephen King

See ALL REET

reet pleat *n phr jive talk* A long, narrow pleat in a zoot suit

regs *n* Regulations; rules: *All regs say you can't*

regular **1** *adj* Real; genuine: *He thinks he's a regular Casanova* **2** *n fr lunch counter* A cup of coffee with the usual moderate amount of cream and sugar • In New York City no sugar is included **3** *adj: regular coffee*

regular fellow (or **guy**) *n phr* An honest, pleasant, convivial person, esp of the moral bourgeoisie: *A real fighter. A regular guy*—New York

rehab (REE hab) **1** *n* Rehabilitation, esp of a drug addict, alcoholic, etc: *After a few weeks' rehab they sent him back home* **2** *modifier: more work-release and rehab centers* —LJ Berry **3** *v* To rehabilitate, esp a building, factory, etc: *Williams has worked for minimum wage, rehabbing houses*—Philadelphia

rehash **1** *v* To review; discuss again; repeat; =RECAP: *the things... they had hashed and rehashed for many a frugal conversational meal*—F Scott Fitzgerald **2** *n: a rehash of stale political charges*—Associated Press

◁ **Reilly's balls**▷ *See* TIGHT AS KELSEY'S NUTS

reinvent the wheel *v phr* To go laboriously and unnecessarily through elementary stages in some process or enterprise; waste time on tediously obvious fundamentals

rejigger *v* To alter or readjust; tinker with: *Rejiggering assignments because of pregnancy is a fact of life* —Time [fr mid-19th-century *jigger* "shake or jerk rapidly," related to *jig* as a rapid movement, dance, etc, hence "rearrange or readjust by shaking," semantically similar to *shake up*]

religion *See* GET RELIGION

reno (REH noh) **1** *n* A renovated house: *Buying an off-the-rack reno is expensive and not very adventurous* —Toronto Life **2** *modifier: Today a boarded-up construction site, tomorrow a reno Parthenon* —Toronto Life

rent *See* HIGH-RENT

◁ **rent-a-pig**▷ or **rent-a-cop** *n* A uniformed security guard [coined on the model of *rent-a-car*, on which model depends also the coinage *Rent-a-Kvetch* and probably others]

rent party *n phr esp 1930s black* A party where one's friends and neighbors buy drinks, food, etc, and help one pay the rent; =PERCOLATOR, SHAKE

rep[1] *n fr late 1800s* Reputation: *gettin' the rep a not havin' a big schnozz* —Jimmy Durante

rep[2] *n* A representative: *The sales rep from Kokomo*

rep[3] **1** *n theater* Repertory: *She played in rep a couple years* **2** ***modifier:*** *a rep company*

repeat on someone *v phr* To cause eructation or belching: *I never eat that stuff because it always repeats on me*

repellent ***See*** CESSNA REPELLENT

replay ***See*** INSTANT REPLAY

repo[1] (REE poh) **1** *n* A car repossessed for nonpayment of installments **2** ***v:*** *when the best times are to repo or rip off cars*—Time

repo[2] (REE poh) *n* A type of investment: *investments known as retail repurchase agreements, or repos for short*—Newsweek

◁ **retard** ▷ (REE tard) *n* A stupid person; =AIRHEAD, SPASTIC: *the stereotype of the crazy retard*—Philadelphia [fr mentally *retarded*]

retool *v* To make improving changes, esp of one's attitudes, capabilities, etc: *if you plan for the future, and retool if necessary*—Pauline Kael

retro **1** *n* A retrospective art exhibit, movie festival, etc: *the Bleecker's current Godard retro*—Village Voice **2** ***adj*** Nostalgic; historically resurrectional: *retro fashion, American clothes from the fifties*—Philadelphia

re-up **1** *v Army fr early 1900s* To reenlist: *Are you really going to re-up and go to that chopper school?*—Earl Thompson **2** *v* To obligate or engage oneself again: *I had re-upped for two more classes with him*—Richard Price

rev or **rev up** **1** *v* or *v phr* To speed up a motor; increase the rpm's **2** *v* or *v phr* To stir up; stimulate; or enliven; =JAZZ something UP: *seems to think he has to really rev his prose every now and again*—Washington Post/ *try to rev up this deadass bunch*

revolving-door ***modifier*** Rapid and of short duration; helter-skelter: *revolving-door presidents and prime ministers, that's what's happening* —WT Tyler

rhubarb[1] *n fr late 1900s or earlier theater* A loud quarrel or squabble; a controversy of riotous potential, esp among baseball players on the field: *bean-ball throwing, rhubarbs, and umpire baiting*—J Durant [fr the theatrical practice of having people say and shout *rhubarb* repeatedly to give the effect of an angry crowd]

rhubarb[2] **1** *n fr WW2 Air Forces* A low-level aerial strafing mission **2** ***v:*** *flying for rhubarbing*—C Macon [said to be fr the resemblance between bullet-spatters and luxuriant *rhubarb* plants]

rib **1** *v fr 1920s* To tease; make fun of; =KID, RAG, RIDE: *His trick is gently ribbing the audience* **2** ***n:*** *Carson sensed that he was the victim of a rib* —Russell Baker [probably fr the tickling of the *ribs* to provoke laughter]

ribbie or **ribby** *n baseball* A run batted in; RBI: *had two other big ribbies* —Sports Illustrated

ribs *n bop & cool talk* Food; a meal [extension of barbecued spare *ribs*, semantically similar to the extension of *grits*]

rib-tickler *n* Something amusing, esp a joke

rice-burner *n motorcyclists* A motorcycle of Japanese manufacture

rich ***See*** STRIKE IT RICH, TOO RICH FOR someone's BLOOD

Richard Roe ***See*** JOHN DOE

◁ **rich bitch** ▷ **1** *n phr* A wealthy woman **2** ***adj phr:*** *his rich-bitch mother-in-law*—Newsweek

ricky-tick (Variations: **ricky-ticky** or **rinky-dink** or **rinky-tink**) *fr jazz musicians* **1** *n* Bouncy ragtime music of the 1920s **2** ***adj*** Old-fashioned; outworn; =CORNY: *a brassy, ricky-ticky big band sound* —Life **3** ***adj*** Cheap and showy; shabbily inferior: *the rickytick, ingroup details*—New York Review [probably echoic fr the clicking mechanical percussion sounds of an uninspired musical group]

ride **1** *v* To tease; make fun of; =NEEDLE, RIB: *I can remember riding Pete Rose to death from the bench* —Inside Sports ◁**2**▷ *v* To do the sex act with or to a woman; mount; =SCREW **3** ***n:*** *He asked her for a* *ride and she slapped him* **4** *n jazz musicians* An improvised passage; =BREAK, RIFF **5** *n* A race horse **6** *n narcotics* A psychedelic narcotic experience; =TRIP **7** *n black & student* A car; esp one that travels with body very close to the street or road: *The car a lowrider drives... is also called a lowrider or ride*—Calvin Trillin

See GO ALONG FOR THE RIDE, JOY RIDE, LET something RIDE, TAKE someone FOR A RIDE, THUMB

ride cymbal or **ride** *n phr* or *n musicians* A drummer's cymbal used for keeping up a constant tintinnabulation, as distinct from a crash

ride herd on someone or something *v phr fr late 1800s* To keep under control; monitor and correct; manage: *He was riding herd on a bunch of juveniles*

rider ***See*** BAREBACK RIDER, LOW RIDER

ride (or **go**) **shank's mare** *v phr* To walk

ride shotgun **1** *v phr* To act as a guard, esp on a vehicle; keep a vigilant eye peeled; insure safety: *Several wives have gotten wise and are riding shotgun on who checks in and out* —Amsterdam News **2** *v phr teenagers* To ride in the front passenger seat of a car [fr the Old West practice of having an armed guard with a *shotgun riding* beside the driver on the stage coaches]

ride the arm *v phr cabdrivers* To collect a fare without using the meter

ride the gravy train (or **gravy boat**) *v phr fr early 1900s sports* To enjoy a good and effortless life; bask in prosperous ease

rif (pronounced as separate letters or as an acronym RIF) **1** *v* To notify an employee of dismissal or layoff: *when he receives his Reduction in Force letter, and he will say, "I've been riffed"*—New York Times **2** *n* A dismissal; layoff **3** *v* To demote: *had been "rif'd" back to sergeants* —C Bryan **4** *n* A demotion [fr *reduction in force*]

riff[1] **1** *n jazz musicians* An improvised passage, esp a solo; =BREAK, LICK: *an initially funky bass riff*—Rolling Stone **2** *n* A solo passage of any sort: *showy riffs of excess energy* —Time [origin unknown; perhaps echoic; perhaps fr *refrain*; perhaps fr *riffle* or *ripple* in the sense of "try, shot, crack"]

riff[2] *n railroad* A refrigerator car; =REEFER[1]

riffle[1] *n baseball* A hard swing at the ball; =RIPPLE: *gives it a really good solid riffle*—H Lobert [probably fr *ripple* fr *rip*]

riffle[2] **1** *v* To shuffle playing cards **2** *n: Give that deck a good riffle* [probably echoic]

rig **1** *v* To prearrange or tamper with a result or process; =FIX: *Prize-fights or horse-races have been rigged*—Literary Digest **2** *n* Clothing; outfit: *How come you're wearing that rig?* **3** *n truckers* A truck; bus

right **1** *adj chiefly underworld* Reliable; safe: *He assured them his partner was a right guy* **2** *affirmation* Yes; correct: *Did you say left? Right!* **3** *question* Am I not right?; =COPPISH, OK: *He's in charge, right?*

See ALL RIGHT, ALL RIGHT ALREADY, DEAD TO RIGHTS, FLY RIGHT, HANG A LEFT

Right ***See*** MISTER RIGHT

righteous *black fr 1930s jazz musicians* **1** *adj* Excellent; genuine; =the GREATEST: *what we used to call the righteous jazz*—National Review **2** *adj* Typical of white persons or white society

righteous moss *n phr black* Hair of a Caucasian sort; nonkinky hair

right guy **1** *n phr fr underworld* A reliable and helpful person: *You was a right guy*—J Lilienthal **2** *n phr* A person who can be trusted, esp not to inform to the police

right-handed *adj* Heterosexual; =STRAIGHT: *He was about 60 percent right-handed and he ended up as a male go-go dancer*—George V Higgins

right money *n phr* =the SMART MONEY

right-o *affirmation* (Variations: **righto** or **right-ho** or **rightho**) *fr early 1900s British* Yes; correct; all right

right off the bat *adv phr* Immediately; without delay: *I normally get four cars right off the bat*—Philadelphia

right on **1** *interj fr 1960s black* An exclamation of approval, encouragement, agreement, etc: *Oh mercy, baaabeh, riiight onnnn!*—Time/ *Right on, Billie Jean!*—Sports Illustrated **2** *adj phr* Precisely right; very effective: *Michael Caine...is right on as the medic*—Judith Crist

rights *See* BANG TO RIGHTS, DEAD TO RIGHTS, GIVE someone HIS RIGHTS

right there *See* IN THERE PITCHING, THERE

right up there *adv phr* Among the leaders, the most distinguished, etc; in contention: *Two weeks to go and the Mets are still right up there*

righty *n* A righthanded person, esp a baseball pitcher

See ALL RIGHTY

◁**rim**▷ *v homosexuals* To lick or suck the anus

See REAM

rinctum *n black* The rectum

See SPIZZERINKTUM

ring *v* (also **ring up**) To call on the telephone; =GIVE someone A RING: *I rang him next day but he was out*

See GIVE someone A RING, THROW one's HAT IN THE RING

ring a bell *v phr* To remind one of something; sound familiar: *Doesn't that name ring a bell?*

ring-a-ding-ding or **ring-a-ding** **1** *n* Glamor and show; spectacular impressiveness; =RAZZLE-DAZZLE: *showbiz ring-a-ding-ding*—Albert Goldman **2** *adj: a ring-a-ding book box*—American Libraries

ring someone's **bell** *v phr* To be sexually attractive to; =TURN someone ON

ring changes *v phr* To make or try out variations, esp ingeniously: *Berle could do the same mugging bits... and ring many more changes on them*—Pauline Kael [fr *change-ringing*, the elaborate esp British ringing of sets of church bells]

ring-ding *n* A stupid person; =DING-A-LING: *that South American ring-ding*—Richard Fariña

ringer **1** *n fr late 1800s horse-racing* A person or animal substituted for another, esp a racehorse put in to run in place of an inferior beast: *"ringers," good horses masquerading as poor ones*—Fortune **2** *n fr late 1800s* A person or thing that closely resembles another; =DEAD RINGER: *Blackmer is a ringer for Teddy*—Associated Press [fr the expression *ring someone in* "announce or herald someone"]

See DEAD RINGER

ring off **1** *v phr* To end a telephone conversation; hang up **2** *v phr* To stop talking; =SHUT UP

ring off the hook *v phr* To ring constantly and often: *Says the director of the hotline: "The phones have been ringing off the hook"*—Time

ring the bell **1** *v phr* To succeed; be a winner: *That last contribution rang the bell* **2** *v phr football* To be hit so hard in play that one feels as if an enormous bell had been rung in one's head [first sense fr the carnival machine where one wins, esp a cigar, by *ringing a bell* with a hard hammer stroke]

rinktum *See* SPIZZERINKTUM

rinky-dink **1** *n carnival* Cheap and gaudy merchandise; =DRECK, JUNK **2** *n* Used merchandise; secondhand articles: *Let's go see what sort of rinky-dink the Salvation Army has this week* **3** *n* A small, cheap nightclub, cabaret, etc; =HONKY-TONK: *as she was called when she played the Rinky-dinks*—Edward Weeks **4** *adj* Inferior; cheap; =CRUMMY: *described by federal attorneys as rinky dink*—Wall Street Journal **5** *n* A deception; swindle; =RUNAROUND: *Don't give me the rinkydink*—Sherman Billingsley

See RICKY-TICK

rinky-tink *See* RICKY-TICK

a **riot** *n phr* A very amusing person or thing, joke, occasion, etc; =A HOOT, A SCREAM: *The show's a genuine laff riot!/ Carlin can be a riot*

the **riot act** *See* READ THE RIOT ACT

rip[1] *n fr late 1700s British* A debauched and dissolute person; libertine: *the proper way to treat a rip*—J Stephens [a variant of *rep* fr *reprobate*]

rip[2] **1** *n police* An official demerit or fine **2** *n esp baseball* An insult; =KNOCK: *master of the off-field rip*—Milwaukee Journal **3** *v: I was not a good enough player to rip anybody*—Milwaukee Journal **4** *n* A joy; a pleasure: *What a rip it is to know there are still people... who feel for the cars they put together*—Car and Driver **5** *n* A try; attempt; =CRACK, RIPPLE, SHOT: *I'll have a rip at that old record* [all, one way or another, fr *rip* "tear"]

See GIVE something A SHOT, HAVE A CRACK AT something

◁ **rip-ass**▷ *v* To speed; tear; =BARREL: *cars rip-assing up and down the street* —Stephen King

ripoff *fr 1960s fr black* **1** *n* A theft; an act of stealing **2** *n* A fraud; swindle; =SCAM: *The whole arms-reduction policy is a big ripoff* **3** *n* (also **ripoff artist**) A person or company that steals or swindles: *He was the biggest ripoff ever seen, even in Congress*

rip off *fr 1960s fr black* **1** *v phr* To steal: *Somebody ripped off my bike* **2** *v phr* To swindle; defraud; =GYP: *I don't know who rips us off more, business or government*

rip on someone *v phr fr black* To harass and insult: *Kids sit there and rip on you, tell you what you're doing wrong*

ripped *adj fr black* Intoxicated, either from narcotics or alcohol; =HIGH: *I'm ripped to the tits as it is*—Armistead Maupin

ripple *n* A try; an attempt; =CRACK, RIP, SHOT: *I'll never figure out how these pieces fit, so why don't you have a ripple?* [perhaps fr *rip* in the sense of a strong action or attempt; perhaps fr 19th-century *make a riffle* "succeed, make it," based on crossing or getting through dangerous rapids in a river]

See GIVE something A SHOT, HAVE A CRACK AT something

ripsnorter *n fr middle 1800s* A person or thing that is remarkable, wonderful, superior, etc; =BEAUT, HUMDINGER: *The villain is a real ripsnorter* —SJ Perelman

a **rise** *See* GET A RISE OUT OF someone

the **ritz** *n phr* Luxury; plush showiness; =SWANK: *Just a simple feed, folks, none of the ritz* [fr the name of the Swiss César *Ritz* and the various luxurious European hotels he built]

See PUT ON THE RITZ

ritzy **1** *adj fr 1920s* Elegant; luxurious; =CLASSY, POSH, SWANKY: *The ritziest dance hall was the Haymarket*—E Lavine **2** *adj* Wealthy; affluent: *a ritzy neighborhood* **3** *adj* Haughty; supercilious; =STUCK-UP

river *See* SELL someone DOWN THE RIVER, SEND UP, UP THE RIVER

rivethead *n Army* A member of a tank crew

roach **1** *n narcotics fr 1930s* The stub or butt of a marijuana cigarette: *how to roll joints, how to hold roaches*—American Scholar **2** *n students* An unattractive woman [narcotics sense perhaps fr earlier *roach mane*, a horse's mane clipped very short and tied; perhaps fr the insect]

roach clip (or **holder**) *n phr narcotics* Any tweezerlike device for holding a marijuana cigarette stub too short to be held in the fingers: *necessitating the invention of the "roach clip," which holds roaches*—New York Times

road *modifier theater* Traveling; itinerant: *a road show/ the road company*

See HIT THE ROAD, LET'S GET THE SHOW ON THE ROAD, ONE FOR THE ROAD, ON THE ROAD, SKID ROAD, WHERE THE RUBBER MEETS THE ROAD

road dog *n phr Philadelphia black* A good friend; =ACE BOON COON

road hog *n phr* A driver who takes more than his or her share of the road

roadie **1** *n* (also **roadster**) A person who travels with a musical, political, theatrical, or other group to handle booking, business arrangements, equipment, etc: *Microphones tossed by Chapman land in unlikely places, one on a roadie, another in the lap of the audience*—Changes/ *"I'm a roadie," said Bob Kholos, who has the title of deputy press secretary* —New York Times **2** *adj* Eager to travel; touched with wanderlust: *I get a little roadie on Fridays*

roast **1** *v fr early 1700s* To make fun of; ridicule; insult, often in an affectionate way: *had been roasted often by the critics as a ham*—Russell Baker **2** *n: this national love for a good "roast," this spirit of mockery* —H Spencer

robber *See* CRADLE-ROBBER

rob the cradle **1** *v phr* To marry or date someone much younger than oneself **2** *v phr* To recruit, use, or exploit young persons

rock **1** *n esp 1920s* A dollar; =BUCK: *I want to see you make twenty rocks*—R Starnes **2** *n underworld* Any precious stone, esp a diamond **3** *n* A rock and roll devotee: *teenagers called "rocks"*—Herbert Mitgang **4** *n* Rock and roll music: *punk rock/ hard rock* **5** *v* To move, dance, writhe, etc, to rock and roll music; =BOOGIE, BOP: *Soon just one couple was rocking in the middle of the floor* **6** *v* To be resonant with and physically responsive to rock and roll music; =JUMP: *Soon the whole room was rocking* **7** *n narcotics* A small cube of very pure cocaine, intended for smoking rather than inhalation: *Dealers sell pellet-size "rocks"...in small plastic vials* —Time **8** *n prison* A cellblock: *When is the wagon due back on this rock, Pops?*—Donald Goines

See ACID ROCK, HARD ROCK, HOT ROCK, PUNK ROCK

the **Rock** **1** *n phr* Alcatraz Island and its (former) federal penitentiary **2** *n fr middle 1800s* Gibraltar

rockabilly **1** *n* A blend of black rhythm and blues with white hillbilly music **2** *modifier: showing up at rockabilly dances and clubs in full '50s regalia*—Newsweek

rock and roll or **rock 'n' roll** **1** *n phr fr 1950s* A style of heavily accented music evolved from blues, folk, and country music, usu having sung lyrics, and played on very highly amplified electronic instruments **2** *modifier: a rock and roll group/ rock 'n' roll concert* **3** *n phr* Dancing done to such music

rock 'em, sock 'em *adj phr* Violent and energetic; concussive: *the rock 'em, sock 'em action that goes on inside a full-sized truck*—Car and Driver

rocker[1] **1** *n fr 1950s* A rock and roll musician, singer, radio station, etc: *general manager of rhythm-and-blues rocker WOL in Washington, DC*—National Observer **2** *n* A rock and roll song: *classic country rockers*—Playboy

See PUNK ROCKER, TEENYBOPPER

rocker[2] *See* OFF one's NUT

rocket *n fr 1930s British Army* A complaint or rebuke; =BEEF, DING: *you get a rocket from one of the parties* —Time

rocks **1** *n* Ice cubes ◁**2**▷ *n* The testicles; =FAMILY JEWELS, NUTS

See GET one's ROCKS, HAVE ROCKS IN one's HEAD, HOT ROCKS, ON THE ROCKS, TOUGH SHIT

rocks in one's (or **the**) **head** *n phr* Stupidity; foolishness; mental incapacity: *dedicated to whiny losers with rocks in their heads*—Village Voice

See HAVE ROCKS IN one's HEAD

rock the boat *v phr* To cause trouble; create inconveniences; disrupt things: *Fritz Mondale doesn't want to rock the boat*—Associated Press

rocky **1** *adj* Drunk **2** *adj* Weak and unsteady; groggy; =WOOZY: *came back to work, looking pale and rocky* —Hal Boyle

rod **1** *n underworld fr early 1900s* A pistol: *Here's a rod, blow your brains out*—Ernest Boyd **2** *n hot rodders* A car, esp a specially prepared car; =HOT ROD: *A restless youth buys a broken-down rod*—New York Times ◁**3**▷ *n* The penis; =SHAFT

See HAVE A ROD ON, WRINKLE-ROD

Roe *See* JOHN DOE

Roger or **Roge** or **Rodger-dodger** *affirmation fr WW2 armed forces* Yes; I understand; =OK: *Get your asses over there...Roge*—New York Times [fr the military phonetic alphabet word designating *R* for "received," apparently first used by the British Royal Air Force in the 1930s]

rogues' gallery **1** *n phr* A collection of photographs of criminals; =MUG SHOTS **2** *n phr* Any group or collection of unsavory persons; den of thieves: *The new building commission is a plain rogues' gallery*

rolf *See* RALPH

roll **1** *v* To rob, esp a stuporous or helpless drunkard who is literally rolled over for access to pockets: *rolling a stiff*—Jack London **2** *v* To rob any relatively helpless person **3** *v movie studio* To run or start a movie camera: *Quiet, and roll 'em* —King Vidor **4** *v* To get started; to commence; get under way: *The leader hollered "Let's roll!" and we all began the exercises/ We'd better roll now, it looks like rain* **5** *n* Money; funds; =BANKROLL **6** *n* The sex act; =a ROLL IN THE HAY **7** *v prison* To start a fight; assault someone

See JELLY-ROLL, LOG ROLL, MICHIGAN ROLL, ON A ROLL, PHILADELPHIA BANKROLL, ROCK AND ROLL

rollback *n* A reduction, esp of wages or production

roller *See* DOWN THE GOODYEARS, HIGH ROLLER, LUSH ROLLER, PILL-PUSHER, STEAMROLLER

roll in **1** ***v phr*** To arrive: *What time did you finally roll in?* **2** ***v phr*** To go to bed

rolling doughnut ***See*** TAKE A FLYING FUCK

rolling (or **swimming**) **in** ***prep phr*** Very well supplied with: *We weren't rolling in dough at the time/ We've been swimming in chicken pot pies*

rolling off a log ***See*** EASY AS PIE

a **roll in the hay** ***n phr*** The sex act, esp when regarded as casual and joyous: *A roll in the hay with Seattle Slew cost $710,000*—Philadelphia

roll out ***v phr*** To get out of bed • Often a command

roll out the red carpet ***v phr*** To give someone a very sumptuous and/or ceremonious welcome

roll over ***v phr*** To reinvest bonds, certificates of deposit, or other monetary instruments upon maturity, rather than liquidating them

roll with the punches ***v phr*** To behave so as to defend oneself against damage and surprise; absorb punishment and survive: *"You roll with the punches....My experience was, I was going to lose her....But I'm thankful for what I've gotten so far"*—Washington Post [fr the evasive action of a boxer who does not avoid a *punch* but reduces its effect by moving in the direction of the blow]

romp **1** ***n*** *street gang* A fight, esp between street gangs **2** ***v:*** *The gangs romped on Thursday*

ronchie ***See*** RAUNCHY

-roo ***See*** -EROO

roof ***See*** RAISE THE ROOF

the **roof falls** (or **caves**) **in** ***v phr*** A sudden and total catastrophe occurs; one's joy and world collapses: *long before the roof fell in on Gossage*—Village Voice/ *They were happy for about three months, then the roof caved in*

rook **1** ***v*** *fr late 1500s* To cheat; defraud; =GYP: *who would rook them for two dollars*—Abel Green **2** ***n:*** *Balcony seats for 40 bucks are a real rook* [probably fr the thieving habits of the *rook*, which it shares with other corvine birds like the crow and magpie]

rookie or **rookey** or **rooky** **1** ***n*** *fr late 1800s British armed forces* A newcomer; novice; tyro: *the rookies and substitutes*—Babe Ruth **2** *modifier: The shooting of "rookie" patrolman James A Broderick*—E Lavine [probably fr shortening of *recruit*; perhaps fr the black, *rook*-colored coat worn by some British army recruits]

room ***See*** BUCKET SHOP, CRYING ROOM, ELBOW ROOM, RUMPUS ROOM

roost ***n*** One's home; =PAD

root[1] ***v*** *fr late 1800s* To cheer; applaud; urge on: *We rooted and rooted, but they folded*

root[2] **1** ***n*** A cigarette **2** ***n*** *narcotics* A marijuana cigarette [perhaps fr *cheroot* or *cigaroot*]

◁ **root**[3] ▷ ***n*** The penis [fr something that is or can be planted]

rooter ***n*** A supporter or fan, esp of a team, fighter, school, etc

root for **1** ***v phr*** *fr late 1800s* To be a regular supporter of; be a fan of: *He rooted for the Giants* **2** ***v phr*** To urge hopefully: *I'm rooting for the tax bill* [perhaps fr British dialect *route* "roar, bellow"]

rootin'-tootin' ***adj*** Boisterous; noisy; vigorous: *a rootin'-tootin' romance*—H Birney

rootle out ***v phr*** *fr middle 1800s British* To root out: *rootle out Government fraud and waste*—Village Voice

rooty-toot ***n*** *musicians* Old-fashioned music; =CORN, RICKY-TICK

rope ***See*** FROZEN ROPE, GOAT FUCK, GO PISS UP A ROPE, KNOW THE ROPES, SUCK

rope in *fr early 1800s* ***v phr*** To swindle; cheat

rose ***n*** *hospital* A comatose and dying patient [fr the color and the perilous frailty of such a patient]

See COME UP SMELLING LIKE A ROSE, SMELL LIKE A ROSE

◁ **rosebud** ▷ ***n*** *esp homosexuals* The anus

rose garden ***See*** FRUIT SALAD

rose room ***n phr*** *hospital* A room where comatose and dying patients are treated

rot **1** ***n*** *fr middle 1800s British* Nonsense; =BALONEY, BULLSHIT **2** ***v*** *esp teenagers fr 1960s* To be deplorable, nasty, inept, or bungled, etc; =STINK, SUCK: *This idea of yours rots*

rotgut ***n*** *fr late 1500s* Inferior liquor; =PANTHER PISS: *pure Prohibition rotgut*—H Allen Smith

rotorhead ***n*** *Army* A helicopter pilot or crew member

rough **1** *adj* Lewd; salacious; =DIRTY: *Some of the jokes were pretty rough* **2** *adj* Difficult; dangerous; =TOUGH
See PLAY FOR KEEPS

rough as a cob *adj phr* Very rough [fr the rural use of *corncobs* as toilet paper]

◁ **rough-ass**▷ *adj* Harsh; crude; =KICK-ASS: *She liked his rough-ass ways for a while*

roughhouse **1** *n fr late 1800s* Boisterous and rowdy behavior; more or less harmless scuffling **2** *v fr early 1900s: The kids roughhoused half the night* **3** *n* Physical violence; mayhem **4** *adj: rough-house work for the political boss*—E Lavine **5** *v: Gun-toting bodyguards roughhoused Swedish citizens*—Associated Press

roughneck **1** *n fr early 1900s* A thug and brawler; =PLUG-UGLY, TOUGH: *The so-called roughneck is hit with everything*—E Lavine **2** *n* A worker or laborer, esp in a circus or on an oil-drilling rig

rough stuff **1** *n phr* Physical violence; mayhem: *have graduated from the "rough stuff" class*—E Lavine **2** *n phr* Obscenity; profanity; =PORN

rough trade *n phr homosexuals* A sadistic or violent sex partner, often heterosexual; ruffianly partner of a homosexual: *The gay boys call us "rough trade"*—S Silverstein

rough someone **up** **1** *v phr* To hit or pummel, esp as intimidation: *He told it like a good citizen, and got roughed up for his pains* **2** *v phr* To injure: *The wreck roughed me up some*

roulette *See* VATICAN ROULETTE

rounder *n fr middle 1800s* A debauchee; habitual carouser: *He's a rounder*—Playboy

roundheel or **roundheels** **1** *n fr 1920s* An inferior prizefighter; =PALOOKA **2** *n* A promiscuous woman; =PUNCHBOARD: *little roundheels over there*—Raymond Chandler

round the bend *adv phr* =AROUND THE BEND

round the horn *See* AROUND THE HORN

round-tripper *n baseball* A home run: *a round-tripper in the ninth*—D Parker

round up *v phr* To find and bring together, esp to a police station or lockup: *rounded up in a raid*—Louis Armstrong

roust **1** *v black* Esp of police officers, to harass someone; =CHIVVY: *always being rousted by cops*—The Gauntlet (movie) **2** *v* To arrest **3** *v* To raid: *They're rousting all the gay bars*—Lawrence Sanders **4** *n: What's the roust? You gonna close this place?*—Herbert Kastle [fr *rouster* or *rooster* "a deckhand or waterfront laborer," attested fr the mid-19th century, hence with connotations of roughness; related to *roustabout* fr British dialect *rous-about* "unwieldy," *rousing* "rough, shaggy," and *rousy* "filthy"; the semantic core seems to combine roughness with laziness, in the old heroic mold, and to be associated with the behavior of the *rooster*, who combines rough vigor with long periods on the perch]

routine *n fr show business* A passage of behavior; act; =BIT, SHTICK: *He goes into his God-save-us routine*

row *n narcotics* An elongated pile of narcotic, esp cocaine, for sniffing; =LINE: *and snorted a row of coke*—Harry Crews
See a HARD ROW TO HOE, HAVE one's DUCKS IN A ROW, a HILL OF BEANS, KNOCK someone or something FOR A LOOP, SKID ROW

rowdy-dow (Variations: **rowdy-dowdy** or **row-de-dow** or **row-de-dowdy**) *fr early 1800s* **1** *n* Boisterousness; excitement; =RUMPUS, WHOOP-DE-DO: *the old rowdy-dow of burlesque*—Brooks Atkinson **2** *adj: this rowdy-dow round-up*—Time **3** *n* A brawl; fight

row with one oar *v phr* (Variation: **in the water** may be added) To behave irrationally; be crazy or stupid: *Ellis sounds as if he is rowing with one oar*—Ann Landers

royal *adj* Thorough; definitive: *gives me a royal pain in the ass*—JD Salinger

◀ a **royal fucking**▶ *n phr* Very rough and unfair treatment; =RAW DEAL

rubber **1** *n fr late 1800s* To gaze; gape: *Don't be rubbering at McCorn*—P Dunning & G Abbott ◁**2**▷ *n* A condom: *"Rubbers," Cushie told him*—John Irving **3** *n* Automobile tires: *The thing's a wreck but has good rubber*

See BURN RUBBER, LAY RUBBER

rubber boots *n phr* Condoms: *My husband don't like rubber boots*—George V Higgins

rubber check *n phr fr 1920s* A check that cannot be cashed, because not enough money is on deposit [because it "bounces"]

rubber-chicken *modifier* Featuring the unappetizing usual sort of banquet food occupationally eaten by politicians, lecturers, etc: *one of those rubber-chicken banquets for the visiting dignitaries*

rubber duck *See* TAKE A FLYING FUCK

rubber meets the road *See* WHERE THE RUBBER MEETS THE ROAD

rubberneck **1** *n fr late 1800s fr cowboys* A person who stares and gapes; gawker **2** *v: They all slowed down and rubbernecked at the wreck*

rube or **Rube** **1** *n fr late 1800s* A rustic; farmer; =HAYSEED **2** *n* An unsophisticated person, esp a newcomer; =GREENHORN **3** *n circus* A member of the audience or public; =CITIZEN: *knows how to panic the rubes*—Brooks Atkinson **4** *adj: a rube police force*—R Starnes [short for *Reuben*]

Rube Goldberg *n phr* A much overcomplicated machine or arrangement: *The public's got the idea that this is a boondoggle, a Rube Goldberg*—Time [fr the fancifully articulated machines depicted by the cartoonist *Rube Goldberg*]

rub (or **nudge**) **elbows** *v phr* To meet and consort; spend time together; mingle: *Here we rub elbows with saints and scholars*

rub it in *v phr* To increase the pain or embarrassment of something; exacerbate: *always trying to rub it in*—WT Tyler/ *I goofed and he never let me forget it, kept rubbing it in*

rub out *v phr fr underworld* To murder; kill; =HIT: *whose husband you rubbed out*—Samuel Liebowitz

rub-out *n fr underworld* A murder; gangster-style killing: *the hombre she blamed for Paddy's rub-out*—Dashiell Hammett

rub someone **the wrong way** *v phr fr middle 1800s* To be distasteful or obnoxious to someone's sensibilities; regularly displease: *I don't quite know why, but that woman rubs me the wrong way*

ruckus *n fr late 1800s* A disturbance; uproar; brawl; =RUMPUS [perhaps fr *ruction* + *rumpus*]

rug *n fr theater* A toupee; hair piece: *I even wear a little rug up front*—John O'Hara

See CUT THE RUG, PULL THE RUG FROM UNDER

rug ape or **rug rat** or **carpet rat** *n phr* (Variations: **yard** may replace **rug** or **carpet**) An infant or small child; =CRUMBCRUSHER: *He lived with his wife and their two rug apes*

rugged *adj fr WW2 Army* Very trying; dangerous; =ROUGH: *They had a real rugged time getting away*

rug joint *n phr* An elegant club, hotel, etc: *not a rug joint (a lavishly decorated casino)*—J Scarne

rumble **1** *n underworld* Information or notification given to the police: *The cops had gotten a rumble that gangsters were holed up*—A Hynd **2** *n police* A police search or raid; =ROUST **3** *n street gang* A fight between street gangs: *Teenagers Injured in Brooklyn Rumble*—New York World-Telegram **4** *v airline* To steal; loot: *ending a run by rumbling... everything from airline glasses to grub*—Philadelphia Journal

rum-dum **1** *n* A stupid person, esp one slow-witted from habitual drunkenness: *The murmuring rum-dums were being let out to wash*—Nelson Algren **2** *adj: a sleazy rum-dum hangout*

rummy or **rummie** *n fr middle 1800s* A drunkard; =LUSH

rumor mill *n phr* The source of rumors, esp those that seem to be deliberately passed along: *There has been a rumor mill on him for years*—New York Times

rumpot *n* A heavy drinker; drunkard; =LUSH

rumpus *n fr late 1700s* A disturbance; uproar; =RUCKUS [origin unknown]

rumpus room *n phr* A family room used for games, parties, etc

run **1** *n* A route followed by a vehicle, esp regularly: *In the middle of her run, the bus driver was attacked* **2** *n* A ride **3** *n* A race, esp a car race **4** *v* To drive, or chauffeur someone, by car

See CUT AND RUN, DRY RUN, MILK RUN, TAKE A RUN AT someone

run a book *v phr* To have credit at a store

run a game on *v phr fr black* =DO A NUMBER ON [fr *running* a whole *game* of pool without yielding the cue]

run a make *v phr police & prison* To perform a checking procedure for identifying someone, that is, for "making" an identification

run-and-gun **1** *v basketball* To play in an aggressive single-handed way, for high scoring: *as a big city ball player looking to run-and-gun*—Philadelphia **2** *adj: the Lakers' run-and-gun offense*—Newsweek

run a number on *See* DO A NUMBER ON

runaround *n fr theater* Deceptive, evasive, and diversionary treatment, esp in response to a request: *I'm tired of you giving me the runaround* —WT Tyler

run something **by again** *v phr* To repeat; =COME AGAIN: *Just run that name and address by again*

rundown *n* A summary or account: *a brief rundown of what happened* —Associated Press

run something **down** **1** *v phr fr black* To tell or explain completely: *Maybe one day I'll run it down to you* —Donald Goines **2** *v phr* To denigrate; =BAD-MOUTH: *I'm not running down his sincerity, but he sounds a bit slick*

rung up *adj phr* Emotionally disturbed

run hog-wild *See* GO HOG-WILD

run-in **1** *n* A quarrel; an unpleasant confrontation: *sorry we had the run-in*—H McHugh **2** *n* An arrest

run someone **in** *v phr fr early or middle 1800s* To arrest; =PULL someone IN: *Am I going to have to run you in?* —Nathaniel Benchley

run (or **work**) something **into the ground** *v phr fr late 1800s fr cowboys* To overdo; carry too far: *You already warned us, now don't run it into the ground*

runner *See* FRONT RUNNER

running shoes *See* GIVE someone HIS WALKING PAPERS

run off at the mouth *v phr* To talk too much; =SHOOT OFF one's MOUTH

run-of-the-mill (or **-of-the-mine**) *adj* Ordinary; average

run out of gas *v phr* To lose impetus, effect, etc; fail; stall: *He ran out of gas a lot slower*—Village Voice

run-out powder *See* TAKE A POWDER

run someone **ragged** *v phr* To exhaust; wear out

the **runs** *n phr* Diarrhea

run scared *v phr* To show signs of panic and fear; try to escape: *Members... aren't exactly running scared* —New York Times

runt **1** *n* A small, short person **2** *n* A contemptible person; =JERK

run-through *n* A rehearsal; =DRY RUN: *After the first run-through, Mr Berlin casually tossed out three songs* —New York Times

run (or **put**) someone **through the mill** *v phr* To subject to an arduous experience; be rough on: *She's quite eager to try again, although they really ran her through the mill*

See GO THROUGH THE MILL

run something **up the flagpole** *v phr* (Variation: **and see if anybody salutes** may be added) *fr 1960s* To test the reaction to; to try out an idea, concept, etc • An expression attributed to the Madison Avenue advertising milieu, along with others like "Put it on a train and see if it gets off at Westport": *Television runs these vapidities up the flagpole and we salute* —Washington Post

rush **1** *v fr middle 1800s* To court a woman ardently: *He had "rushed" her, she said, for several months* —Ellery Queen **2** *n: appears to want to give her a big rush*—F Blake **3** *v college students* To entertain and cultivate a student wanted as a fraternity or sorority member **4** *n movie studio* A motion picture print made immediately after the scene is shot **5** *n narcotics* An intense flood of pleasure, with quickened heart rate, felt soon after ingestion of a narcotic: *He didn't have to wait long for the rush* **6** *n fr narcotics* A surge of pleasure; an ecstasy: *To Friend, it's a kind of a rush... the last big high*—Chicago Tribune/ *gives her a unique rush*—Time

rush (or **work**) **the growler** *fr late 1800s* **1** *v phr* To buy and take home a container of beer from a bar: *see who rushes a growler of beer* —Sinclair Lewis **2** *v phr hoboes*

To drink liquor or beer, esp in large quantities

rust bowl (or **belt**) **1** ***n phr*** The beleaguered and declining industrial areas, esp of the Middle West: *in the midwestern middle, the "rust bowl"* —Time **2** ***modifier:*** *The subjects: Wall Street, Chrysler, high-tech enterprises vs "rust bowl" basic industries* [modeled on the 1930s term *dust bowl* and the 1970s term *sun belt*]

rustle **1** ***n*** A robbery; =HEIST: *the $300,000 rustle that he got away with* —Westbrook Pegler **2** ***v*** (also **rustle up**) To find and produce; prepare: *I can rustle up some if you need it*—William Kennedy [origin unknown; perhaps fr *rush* + *hustle*]

rustle one's **bustle** ***v phr*** To get active; hurry; =GET THE LEAD OUT

rusty-dusty **1** ***n*** *esp black fr 1930s* The buttocks; rump; =ASS • Nearly always with the suggestion of torpor or laziness: *sitting around on his rusty-dusty doing nothing*—WV Shannon **2** ***n*** *theater* A property pistol [fr the notion that something not in frequent use or active motion will become *rusty* and *dusty*]

S

-s ***suffix used to form nouns*** A diminutive or affectionate version of what is indicated, used as a term of address: *babes/ ducks/ moms/ sweets*

sack[1] **1** ***v*** *fr middle 1800s British* To discharge; dismiss; =CAN, FIRE: *by refusing to sack his aide*—Philadelphia Bulletin/ *I've been sacked* —Time **2** ***n*** *fr armed forces* A bed, bunk, sleeping bag, etc; sleeping place; =RACK: *Let me stay in the sack all day*—Hal Boyle **3** ***n*** Sleep; =SACK TIME: *He needed some sack* **4** ***modifier:*** *sack duty/ sack artist* **5** ***n*** A dress that fits loosely over the shoulders, waist, and hips, and is gathered at the hem line **6** ***n*** *baseball* A base: *He slid into the sack* [first sense probably fr the notion of giving a discharged person a traveling bag or *sack*, since the earliest expression was *get the sack*]

See FART SACK, HIT THE HAY, the KEYSTONE, SAD SACK

sack[2] ***v*** *football* To tackle the quarterback behind the line of scrimmage [fr *sack* "assault and pillage"]

the **sack** ***n phr*** *fr middle 1800s* Discharge from a job; dismissal; =the BOOT: *He was late once too often and got the sack* [apparently fr an old practice of giving someone a *sack* when sending him away; corresponding expressions are found in French: *donner son sac à quelqu'un*]

sacker ***See*** SECOND SACKER

sack out (or **in** or **up**) ***v phr*** *WW2 armed forces* To go to bed; sleep; =HIT THE SACK: *Well, it's time to sack out*—Hal Boyle

sack time *fr WW2 armed forces* ***n phr*** Bedtime; time to retire

sad apple **1** ***n phr*** An obnoxious individual; a contemptible person; =DRIP, JERK, A PAIN IN THE ASS **2** ***n phr*** A gloomy or pessimistic individual

saddle ***See*** LEAN FORWARD IN THE SADDLE

saddle shoes ***n phr*** Low-cut, laced white shoes with a brown or black instep

sadie-maisie ***See*** S AND M

sad sack ***n phr*** *students fr 1920s & esp WW2 armed forces* An awkward, unfortunate, harried, and maladjusted person; =SCHLEMAZEL: *an inexplicable sad sack of a leading man* —Washington Post [fr the unflattering image of a human being as primarily a container for feces]

safety or **safe** ***n*** A condom; =RUBBER

sagebrusher ***n*** =HORSE OPERA

someone **said a mouthful** ***sentence*** Someone spoke accurately and cogently; someone said something very important • Often an expression of vehement agreement: *Daisy sure said a mouthful*

said it ***See*** YOU SAID IT

sail into ***v phr*** To attack; criticize severely; =LAMBASTE: *He quickly sails into anyone that complains*

Saint Elsewhere ***See*** MOUNT SAINT ELSEWHERE

salad ***See*** FRUIT SALAD

salt **1** ***n*** *fr early 1800s* A sailor, esp an old and seasoned one **2** ***n*** *narcotics* Heroin in powder form

See GO POUND SALT

salt and pepper **1** ***n phr*** *narcotics* Impure or low-grade marijuana **2** ***adj phr*** Interracial: *a salt and pepper neighborhood in Detroit* the **salt mines** *See* BACK TO THE SALT MINES

salts *See* LIKE SHIT THROUGH A TIN HORN

salty **1** *adj* *Navy fr early 1900s* Audacious; daring; aggressive **2** *adj* *teenagers fr jive talk* Terrible; nasty; unpalatable **3** *adj* *esp black* Angry; hostile **4** *adj* Crude; uncouth; earthy: *His language is often quite salty*

salute *See* RUN something UP THE FLAGPOLE

Sam or **sam** *n narcotics* A federal narcotics agent; =NARC

the **same difference** *n phr fr early 1900s* The same thing; something exactly equal: *So they fire him or he quits, it's the same difference*

the **same wavelength** *See* ON THE SAME WAVELENGTH

Sam Hill *n phr fr early 1800s* Hell: *Where in Sam Hill do you think you're going?/ What the Sam Hill's that?* [an echoic euphemism]

sand *See* GO POUND SALT

sandbag **1** *v* To attack someone viciously, esp with a blackjack or similar bludgeon: *I was sandbagged from behind*—Life **2** *v* To intimidate; cow; =BULLDOZE: *Persuasion didn't work, so they tried to sandbag her* **3** *v* *gambling* To check and then to raise the bet **4** *v* *fr gambling* To pretend weakness or ineptitude; mislead an opponent by apparent inferiority: *He charged that the Aussies were "sand bagging" (deliberately losing) to take the limelight off their disputed keel*—Time **5** *v* *hot rodders* To drive a hot rod very fast

sandlot **1** *n* A rough or improvised baseball field **2** *modifier: sandlot ball*

S and M or **S/M** or **sadie-maisie** **1** *n phr* or *n* Sado-masochism; perverse sexual practices featuring whips, chains, etc **2** *n phr* or *n* The dominant person in a sado-masochistic sexual relation; slave master

sandwich *See* HERO SANDWICH

San Quentin quail *n phr* A girl below the legal age of sexual consent; =JAIL BAIT [fr the name of a California state penitentiary]

Santa Claus **1** *n phr* *airline* A check pilot who is very lenient and agreeable on a pilot check flight **2** *n phr* A male donor or benefactor; a very generous man: *What the orphanage needed was a Santa Claus to pay the debts*

sap *n fr early 1900s fr early 1800s British* A stupid person; fool, esp a gullible one: *Quit acting like a sap* [fr British dialect, short for *sapskull* "person with a head full of soft material"; probably influenced by early-19th-century British schoolboy slang, "compulsive studier, grind," which is probably fr *sap* as an ironic abbreviation of Latin *sapiens* "wise," and is hence semantically akin to *sophomore*]

saphead *n fr late 1700s* A stupid person; =BLOCKHEAD, SAP: *one young woman who just seems to be a saphead*—Wolcott Gibbs

◁ **sapphire**▷ *n black* An unattractive, unpopular black woman [fr the name of a character on the Amos 'n' Andy radio program popular fr the late 1920s until the 1950s; *Sapphire* was the shrewish wife of a character called "The Kingfish"]

sappy **1** *adj* Stupid; foolish; =GOOFY: *lay off them sappy songs*—WR Burnett **2** *adj* Sentimental; mawkish; =SCHMALTZY

sarge *n fr middle 1800s armed forces* A sergeant

sashay *v fr early 1800s* To go; walk; flounce: *after a great deal of extravagantly publicized sashaying about*—Washington Post [fr the square-dance gait, fr French *chasser* "chase"]

sass **1** *n* *fr middle 1800s* Impudence; impertinent backtalk: *if this reporter was going to give her any sass*—Washington Post **2** *v: He kept sassing his mama till she decked him* [fr *sauce* "rude and impudent language or action"]

satchel **1** *n* The buttocks; rump; =KEISTER: *a chance to rest my satchel*—G Moore **2** *n* *jazz musicians* A jazz musician who plays a horn **3** *v* To prearrange the outcome of a fight, race, etc; =FIX, RIG: *It was satcheled against him*—D Egan [verb sense fr *in the bag*]

Saturday night special **1** *n phr* A cheap, small-caliber revolver quite easy to obtain: *Detroit lawmen began to refer to the weapons as "Saturday night specials"*—B Kaiser **2** *n phr* *hospital* A person, often an alcoholic, who comes to a hospital on weekends seeking a bed and board

sauce *See* APPLESAUCE

the **sauce** *n* Liquor; whiskey; =BOOZE: *It made him sad and he almost began hitting the sauce*—John O'Hara
See HIT THE BOTTLE, ON THE SAUCE

savage *n police* A young police officer eager to make arrests

saved by the bell *adj phr fr prizefight* Rescued, relieved, or preserved at the last minute [fr the plight of a boxer who is being severely punished when the *bell* rings to end the round]

savvy or **savvey** *fr early 1800s* **1** *v* To understand; know; grasp: *I'm the honcho here, savvy?* **2** *n* Comprehension; intelligence; =BRAINS, SMARTS: *He's a guy with much savvy* **3** *adj: a very savvy lady* [fr West Indian pidgin fr Spanish *sabe usted* "do you know?"]

saw *See* DOUBLE SAWBUCK

sawbones *n fr early 1800s British* A surgeon; a physician: *without being able to rouse a sawbones*—R Ruark

sawbuck *n fr middle 1800s* A ten-dollar bill; ten dollars [fr the resemblance of the Roman numeral X to the ends of a *sawhorse*]
See DOUBLE SAWBUCK

sawed-off *adj fr late 1800s* Short of stature: *sawed-off fight manager from Newark*—J Cuddy

saw wood **1** *v phr fr early 1900s* To sleep, esp very soundly **2** *v phr* To snore [fr the sound of snoring]

sax **1** *n* A saxophone **2** *modifier: a sax virtuoso*

say a mouthful *See* someone SAID A MOUTHFUL

say-so *n fr late 1700s* One's word, report, recommendation, etc: *No jury'll convict Manny on your say-so alone*—Raymond Chandler

says which *interrogation* What did you say?: *Says which? I don't believe what I heard*

says you or **says who** *interj* (Variations: **sez** or **sezz** may replace **says**) *fr early 1900s & esp fr WW1 armed forces* An exclamation of defiance, disbelief, mere pugnacity, etc; =IZZATSO: *I'm in the wrong seat? Says who?*

say uncle *v phr* To surrender; give up: *Despite your exquisite Byzantine torture, I will never say uncle*

say what *interj esp teenagers fr black* A request for more information; excuse me?

scab *n labor union fr early 1800s* A nonunion worker, esp one who attempts to break a strike; =FINK

scads **1** *n fr middle 1800s* A large quantity of money **2** *n* A large quantity of anything; =BAGS, OODLES: *I have scads of study*—Philadelphia Bulletin [origin unknown; perhaps fr British dialect, "shed," and hence semantically akin to *a shithouse full*]

scag *See* SKAG

scag jones *n phr narcotics* A heroin addiction: *sell them to janitors for a quarter to support their "scag jones"*—Claude Brown

scairdy cat *See* SCAREDY CAT

scalper **1** *n fr middle 1800s* A person who scalps tickets **2** *n gambling* A person who places bets and backs bets in such a way that he will win whether the horse wins or loses

scam **1** *n fr carnival* A swindle; confidence game; fraud; =CON: *It was a full scam*—Time/ *when I made the bust on the scam*—Joseph Wambaugh **2** *v* (also **scam on**): *You guys are scamming me/ good place to scam on the rich tourists*—Joseph Wambaugh **3** *n* The information; =the LOWDOWN, the SCOOP: *Here's the scam.... We're holing in for the night*—Patrick Mann [origin unknown; perhaps related to early-19th-century British *scamp* "cheater, swindler"]
See WHAT'S THE SCAM

scandal sheet *n phr* A sensationalistic and vulgar newspaper, magazine, etc; cheap tabloid; =RAG
See SWINDLE SHEET

◁**scank**▷ *n black teenagers* An unattractive girl

scankie *adj black teenagers* Disheveled; sloppy

scare badge *n phr Army* A badge given in recognition of paratroop or other rigorous and prestigious training

◁**scared shitless**▷ *adj phr* Very frightened; terrified: *And the producer is scared shitless of the sponsor*—Sterling Hayden [based on the expression *scare the shit out of* someone]

scared spitless (or **witless**) *adj phr* Very frightened; terrified; =SCARED SHITLESS: *They were scared spitless at the prospect of appearing in a play*

—Richard Wright [two plausible euphemisms for *scared shitless*]

scared stiff *adj phr* Very frightened; paralyzed by terror [fr the notion of being *scared to death*]

scaredy (or **scairdy**) **cat** *n phr* =FRAIDY CAT

scarehead *n newspaper office* A very large and conspicuous headline

◁ **scare** someone **shitless**▷ (or **spitless** or **witless**) *v phr* To frighten very much; terrify: *It scared me shitless, but that didn't stop me*—Edward Koch

◁ **scare the shit** (or **living shit**) **out of** someone▷ *v phr* To frighten very much; terrify: *It scares the living shit out of them*—National Lampoon

scare up *v phr fr middle 1800s* To find and produce; =RUSTLE: *was among the goodies scared up at a flea market*—Casper Star-Tribune [fr the rising of birds frightened by hunters]

scarf *esp teenagers fr black* **1** *n* Food; a meal; =CHOW, SCOFF **2** *v* (also **scarf up**) To eat or drink; consume: *scarfing up a beer*—Easyriders **3** *v* (also **scarf up**) *esp students* To pilfer; =SWIPE: *People scarf up food after truck overturns*—Casper Star-Tribune **4** *v students* To throw away; discard; =DEEP-SIX [see *scoff*]

scarf out *v phr* To eat very heartily; overeat; =PIG OUT: *I took the band there and we scarfed out*—Vegetarian Times

scat[1] **1** *n jazz musicians* Pattering staccato gibberish sung to songs, esp jazz songs: *using scat for novelty back in 1906*—Alan Lomax **2** *modifier: precise "scat" singing*—F Grunfeld **3** *v: Scatting has almost always been used by jazz singers as an interlude*—San Francisco [attributed to Louis Armstrong, fr the 1920s, echoic of the nonsense sounds he used when he forgot song lyrics or was imitating instruments in an interlude]

scat[2] *v* To drive or otherwise move very fast [fr early-19th-century *s'cat*, a hissing address designed to drive away a cat; the earliest occurrence is in the expression *quicker than s'cat*]

scatback *n football* A very fast and agile backfield runner

scatterbrain *n fr middle 1800s* A silly or stupid person, esp one who cannot attend properly to a subject or get simple things done; =DITZ, RATTLEBRAIN

scattergun **1** *n fr cowboys* A shotgun **2** *n WW2 Army* A machine gun, submachine gun, or machine pistol; =BURP GUN **3** *modifier* Broadly and imprecisely directed; crudely comprehensive: *the scattergun memo*—New York Daily News

scatty *adj fr British* Irrational; crazy; =GOOFY, SCATTERBRAINED: *the ferociously ambitious, slightly scatty Louise Bryant*—Vincent Canby

scenario *n* A reasoned or imagined pattern of events in the future; a possible plan: *According to one scenario we only kill 80 percent of them*
See WORST-CASE SCENARIO

scene *esp 1960s counterculture fr black* **1** *n* The setting or milieu of a specific activity or group; specialized venue: *It is really quite difficult... to understand their scene*—Trans-Action **2** *n* One's particular preference, activity, etc; =BAG, THING: *I mean that's not my own scene or anything*—Changes
See ALL-ORIGINALS SCENE, BAD SCENE, MAKE A SCENE, MAKE THE SCENE, MOB SCENE, SPLIT THE SCENE

scenery *See* CHEW UP THE SCENERY

schizo (SKITSO, SKIH zoh) **1** *n* (also **schiz**) A schizophrenic: *Docs find he's a schizo*—New York Daily News **2** *adj: a schizo drug addict* **3** *adj* (also **schizy** or **schizzy** or **schizie** or **schizoid**) Crazy; demented, esp in a self-contradictory way; psychotic; =NUTTY: *People in democracies... are a little schizzy about authority*—Newsweek/ *with dramatically schizoid effect*—Rolling Stone/ *this same schizy little brain*—Esquire/ *I was in fact extremely schizie*—Ms

schiz out *v phr* To go crazy; become schizophrenic; =FLIP: *She thought he'd schizzed out completely*—Cyra McFadden

schlang *See* SCHLONG

schlemazel or **schlemasel** or **shlemozzle** (shlə MAH zəl) *n* An awkward, unfortunate, maladjusted person; =SAD SACK [fr Yiddish *shlimazel* fr *shlim mazel* "rotten luck"]

schlemiel or **schlemihl** or **shlemiel** (shlə MEEL) ***n*** A stupid person; fool; oaf; esp, a naive person often victimized: *Don't talk like a schlemiel, you schlemiel*—Budd Schulberg [fr Yiddish *shlemiel*, probably fr the name of the main character in A von Chamisso's German fable *The Wonderful History of Peter Schlemihl*, 1813]

schlep or **schlepp** or **shlep** **1** ***v*** To carry; drag along: *go through a contortionist's routine to schlepp your packages*—Village Voice **2** ***v*** To move or advance with difficulty; drag: *then I'd have to schlep around to the Quarter Note*—Nashville **3** ***n:*** *even with the four-flight schlep to the editorial office*—New York **4** ***n*** A stupid person; oaf; =KLUTZ: *a real drudging, seat-of-pants schlepp*—Earl Thompson **5** ***n*** =SCHLEPPER [fr Yiddish *shleppen*]

schleppy or **shleppy** ***adj*** Awkward; stupid; =KLUTZY

schlock **1** ***n*** (also **schlack** or **schlag** or **shlock**) Inferior merchandise; an inferior product; =CRAP, JUNK: *that "Macbird" is a piece of schlock*—Russell Baker **2** ***adj:*** *unlike all those schlock films*—CL Westerbeck, Jr [fr Yiddish *shlak* "a curse"]

schlockmeister ***n*** A successful maker or seller of schlock: *Hollywood's premier schlockmeisters*—Newsweek [fr *schlock* + German *Meister* "master"]

schlock shop (or **joint**) ***n phr*** A store that sells inferior merchandise, esp a junk shop, thrift store, etc

◁**schlong**▷ ***n*** (Variations: **schlang** or **shlang** or **shlong**) The penis; =PRICK: *Don's big schlong was staring at me*—Xaviera Hollander [fr Yiddish *shlang* "snake"]

◁**schlontz** or **shlontz**▷ ***n*** The penis [perhaps a blend of Yiddish *shlong* and *shwants*]

schloomp (SHLŏŏMP) (Variations: **schlump** or **shloomp** or **shlump**) **1** ***n*** A stupid person; =KLUTZ: *calling George Shultz a dumb shlump*—Washingtonian **2** ***v*** (also **shalump** or **schloomp around**) To loaf; idle about; =GOOF OFF: *She shalumps around the Ritz in her loose clothes and sneakers*—Washington Post [fr Yiddish *shlump*, related to German *Schlumpe* "a slovenly woman"]

schlub ***See*** ZHLUB

schmaltz or **shmaltz** (SHMAWLTS) **1** ***n*** *fr 1930s swing musicians* Blatant sentimentality, esp musical or theatrical material of a cloyingly sweet and maudlin sort; =CORN: *happy combination of good theater and good pathos known as schmaltz*—New Yorker **2** ***n*** A viscid substance; =GLOP, GOO [fr Yiddish *shmalts*, literally "rendered fat"]

schmaltzy or **schmalzy** or **shmaltzy** ***adj*** Sentimental; sweetly melancholy; =CORNY, ICKY: *It is not always the schmalzy moment that dissolves me*—New Yorker

schmancy ***See*** FANCY-SCHMANCY

schmatte (SHMAH tə) ***n*** (Variations: **schmattah** or **schmatteh** or **shmatte** or **shmotte**) A shabby or unstylish garment: *a tired old schmattah*—Xaviera Hollander [fr Yiddish *shmatte*, literally "rag"]

schmear[1] or **shmear** or **shmeer** **1** ***v*** To bribe; =GREASE someone's PALM **2** ***n:*** *The prime minister took a big schmear from the airplane company* **3** ***v*** To flatter and cajole; =BUTTER UP, SOFT SOAP **4** ***v*** To spread a large dab of something such as butter or cream cheese: *Just schmear it on real thick* **5** ***n:*** *I'll have a bagel with a schmear* [fr Yiddish *shmeer*, literally "grease"]

schmear[2] **1** ***v*** To treat very roughly; =CLOBBER, CREAM, SMEAR **2** ***n*** An accusation or innuendo meant to harm someone's reputation; a slander [fr a humorous mispronunciation of *smear*]

the **schmear** ***n phr*** =the WHOLE SCHMEAR [fr Yiddish *shmeer*]

schmeck or **shmeck** **1** ***n*** A taste; a bite: *How about a little schmeck?*—Esquire **2** ***n*** *narcotics* Heroin; =SMACK: *She's hustling right now, schmeck, tail, abortion, the whole bit*—Lawrence Sanders [fr Yiddish *shmek* "a smell, sniff," related to German *schmecken*]

schmegeggy or **shmegeggy** or **schmegegge** (shmə GEG gee) **1** ***n*** A stupid person; oaf; =SCHLEMIEL: *the shmegeggy she lives with*—Philip Roth/ *a new story...about some gringo schmegegge*—Village Voice **2** ***n*** Nonsense; foolishness;

=BALONEY [fr Yiddish *shmegegi* of unknown origin, perhaps coined in American Yiddish]

schmendrick or **shmendrick** *n* A stupid person, esp an awkward and inept nonentity; =SCHLEMIEL: *a schmendrick with a noodle for a brain* —A Hirschfield [fr Yiddish *shmendrik*, fr the name of a character in an operetta by A Goldfaden]

schmo (Variations: **schmoe** or **shmo** or **shmoe**) **1** *n* A naive and hapless person; fool; =GOOF: *I've been standing here like a schmoe for 20 minutes*—Fred Allen **2** *n* A person; man; =GUY: *Them big-time schmoes was stockholders*—Saturday Evening Post [perhaps a euphemistic alteration of Yiddish *shmok* "penis"; perhaps a quasi-Yiddish coinage for amusing effect; the term has been adopted into American Yiddish] *See* JOE SCHMO

schmooz (Variations: **schmoo** or **schmooze** or **schmoos** or **schmoose** or **schmoozl** or **schmoozle** or **schmoosl** or **schmoosle** or any of these spelled with **sh**-) **1** *v* To converse, esp lengthily and cozily: *lawyers schmoozing in the halls*—Village Voice/ *It's very hard for me to just sit around and shmoo*—Washington Post **2** *n: Two buddies enjoying a quiet schmooz* [fr Yiddish fr Hebrew *schmuos* "things heard"]

schmuck or **shmuck** *n* A detestable person; an obnoxious man; =BASTARD, PRICK: *You must be a real schmuck*—Nora Ephron [fr Yiddish *shmok* "penis," literally "ornament"]

schnockered *See* SNOCKERED

schnook or **shnook** (SHNŏŏK) *n* An ineffectual person; a naive person often victimized; =PATSY • A more affectionate and compassionate way of designating a **schlemiel**: *Don't be such an apologetic schnook*—Jack Benny [fr American-Yiddish *shnook*, said to be fr German *Schnucke* "small sheep"; probably related to the pet names *snooks, snookums*, etc]

schnorrer or **shnorrer** **1** *n* A beggar, esp one who counts parasitically on a family or community; =MOOCHER, SPONGER: *The room has generally been ignored by serious schnorrers*—Toronto Life **2** *n* A person who habitually haggles; niggard [fr Yiddish *shnorrer*]

schnozz *n* (Variations: **schnoz** or **schnozzle** or **schnozzola** or any of these spelled with **sh**- or **snozzle**) The nose, esp a large one: *the rep of not havin' a big schnozz*—Jimmy Durante/ *Five players broke their schnozzolas*—Associated Press [fr Yiddish *shnoz* fr *shnoitsl* fr German *Schnauze* "snout"]

schpritz *See* SHPRITZ

schtarker *See* SHTARKER

schtick *See* SHTICK

schtoonk (SHTŏŏNK) *n* (Variations: **schtunk** or **shtoonk** or **shtunk**) A person one detests or despises; =JERK, STINKER [fr Yiddish *shtunk*]

schtup *See* SHTUP

schvantz or **schvontz** *See* SHVANTZ

◀ **schvartze** ▶ (SHVAHR tsə) *n* (Variations: **shvartzeh** or **shvartze** or **schwartze** or **schvartzer** or **shvartzer** or **schwartzer**) A black person: *irons even better than the schvartze*—Philip Roth [fr Yiddish fr *shvartz* "black"]

sci-fi (SĪ FĪ) **1** *n* Science fiction **2** *adj: sci-fi fans... secretly crave*—Rolling Stone

scillion *See* SKILLION

scoff **1** *v fr hoboes & merchant marine fr middle 1800s British merchant marine* To eat or drink; =SCARF: *I'll take you over... so you can scoff*—Jim Tully **2** *n* Food: *Beef heart is their favorite scoff* **3** *v teenagers* To steal; pilfer; =SWIPE: *Who scoffed my butts?* [origin uncertain; perhaps fr Afrikaans *schoft*, defined in a 17th-century dictionary as "eating time for labourers or workmen foure times a day"; perhaps fr British dialect *scaff*; South African use in current senses is attested in late 18th century]

scooch *See* SCRUNCH

scoop **1** *v newspaper office fr late 1800s* To publish or file a news story before another newspaper or another reporter: *I was afraid of being scooped because I knew a lot of reporters were on the same story* —New York Post **2** *n: The paper scored a major scoop with that revelation* **3** *v fr early 1900s* In singing, to attain a desired note by beginning lower and sliding up to pitch

the **scoop** *n phr fr 1940s students & armed forces* News or data, esp when anxiously awaited, heretofore secret, etc; =POOP: *We all gathered around when he said he had the scoop*

scooper *See* POOPER SCOOPER

scoot **1** *v fr middle 1700s* To move rapidly, esp in fleeing or escaping: *When they saw the cops they scooted right out of there* **2** *v fr middle 1800s* To slide, esp suddenly as on a slippery surface: *Let's scoot this thing into the corner* **3** *n* A dollar: *Greg could have the sixty scoots, the guns, everything*—Joseph Wambaugh [origin unknown; perhaps ultimately fr a Scandinavian cognate of *shoot*, by way of Scottish dialect; the third sense may have an entirely different derivation than the first two]

scope a vic *See* VIC[3]

scope on (or **out**) *v phr esp teenagers fr black* To look at; examine; =CHECK OUT, DIG: *scoping on the foxy sisters*—New York Times/ *I'd scoped him out pretty well*—Richard Merkin

scorch **1** *v esp early 1900s* To travel very fast; =BARREL: *I proceed to scorch to make up for lost time*—Jack London **2** *v baseball* To throw the ball very fast and hard; =BURN

score **1** *n fr underworld* A success or coup in theft, swindling, gambling, etc: *He was always hoping for a big score* **2** *n fr underworld* The loot or proceeds from a robbery, swindle, gamble, etc; also, the amount of such loot; =HAUL **3** *n fr 1930s underworld* A share of loot; =CUT **4** *v* To succeed, esp to please an audience, interviewer, or others who judge; =RATE: *The show didn't score with the TV critics* **5** *v* To do the sex act with or to someone; =MAKE IT WITH someone **6** *n: He was always looking for an easy score* **7** *v prostitutes* To find a client for prostitution **8** *n: The little hooker got only five scores all evening* **9** *n underworld* A planned murder; =HIT **10** *v narcotics* To buy or get narcotics: *Want to score, Blackie?*—New Yorker **11** *n: He's out looking for a score* **12** *v students* To get: *Most of them score their clothes as gifts from parents*—Time

See MAKE A SCORE

the **score** *n fr 1940s students* The main point; crux; =BOTTOM LINE: *I heard the facts, now what's the score?*

See KNOW THE SCORE

scosh *See* SKOSH

scow *n truckers* A large truck

scrag **1** *v* To kill; murder: *overshoot or undershoot and scrag some scared civilian*—Robert Ruark **2** *v* To destroy or severely damage; ruin: *The beet sugar people... try to scrag the cane sugar people*—R Starnes ◁**3**▷ *v* To do the sex act with or to; =SCREW, SCROG: *the middle-American hobby of scragging the random housewife at any opportunity*—John D McDonald [fr earlier slang, "hang by the neck"]

scraggy *adj* Disheveled; unkempt-looking; gaunt and wasted: *snapshot of a scraggy Sindona as an apparent captive*—Time

scram **1** *v fr early 1900s underworld & circus* To leave quickly; flee; =BEAT IT: *Customers scrammed screaming when the trailer went on*—Village Voice/ *Scram, you kids* **2** *n: I got ready for a sudden scram*

scrambled eggs *armed forces* **1** *n* Gold braid, embroidery, etc, on the uniform of a senior officer, esp on the bill of a cap **2** *n* Senior officers; =BRASS, the TOP BRASS

scrambler *n motorcyclists* A motorcycle used for mountain or hill riding

scrap **1** *n fr late 1800s British* A fight; quarrel; =DUSTUP **2** *v: They scrapped for days over the appointment* [origin uncertain; perhaps fr *scrape*]

scrape along (or **by**) *v phr* To survive; carry on; =GET BY: *I'm not flourishing, but I'm scraping along, barely*

scrape the bottom of the barrel *v phr* To use one's last and worst resources; be forced to desperate measures: *He scraped the bottom of the barrel when he proposed that topic for his paper*

scrape (or **scratch**) **up** *v phr* To get, esp laboriously and bit by bit: *Where'll I scrape up some support?/ even if you can't scratch up all of that cash now*—Sports Afield

scratch **1** *n fr early 1900s* Money; =BREAD, DOUGH: *If the mayor doesn't come up with the scratch*—Saturday Review **2** *n* A loan; an act of borrowing money: *They gave him a scratch for the tuition* **3** *v horse-*

racing To cancel a horse from a race **4** *n: two scratches in the third race* **5** *v* To cancel a plan, an entrant, someone on a list, etc; =SCRUB: *Looks like our tête-à-tête will have to be scratched* **6** *v* (also **itch**): *pool fr late 1800s* To put the cue ball into a pocket inadvertently **7** *n* (also **itch**): *He made a scratch at a crucial juncture/ And when the cue ball goes into the pocket, you call that an itch* —Max Shulman **8** ***modifier*** *sports fr middle 1800s* Competing without an assigned handicap: *a scratch boat in the race/ a scratch golfer* **9** *adj* Hastily arranged; impromptu; spur of the moment; =PICKUP: *a scratch jazz ensemble/ scratch ball team*

See FROM SCRATCH, START FROM SCRATCH, UP TO SCRATCH, YOU SCRATCH MY BACK, I SCRATCH YOURS

scratch someone's **back** *v phr* To please someone, esp by flattery; be very accommodating to someone

scratcher *n underworld fr middle 1800s* A forger

scratch (or **scratch around**) **for** something *v phr* To search for something, esp something hard to find or get: *I was scratching around for whatever work I could get* [fr the food-seeking action of chickens]

scratch hit *n phr baseball* A lucky base hit that is nearly an out: *scratch single/ scratch double*

a **scream** *n phr fr early 1900s* Someone or something that is hilariously funny; =a HOOT, a RIOT: *Isn't this decor a scream?*

screaming ***See*** DRAG someone KICKING AND SCREAMING INTO THE TWENTIETH CENTURY

the **screaming meemies** or **the meemies** *n phr fr WW1 Army* A state of nervous hysteria; =the HEEBIE-JEEBIES: *a town that would give the ordinary thrill-seeker the screaming meemies*—GS Perry/ *Knowing (a chimpanzee) was on the loose gave him the meemies*—F Brown [apparently fr the soldier's echoic name for a very loud and terrifying German artillery shell, and then the battle fatigue caused by exposure to such materiel; the name may reflect a soldier's pattern of giving feminine names, here the French *Mimi*, to projectiles and weapons, such as *Betsy, Big Bertha, Moaning Minnie*, etc]

◁**screw**[1]▷ **1** *v fr 1700s* To do the sex act with or to someone; =FUCK • Felt by many to be excusable when **fuck** is the term really intended, and used as an attenuated form in nearly the whole range of **fuck** senses and compounds: *At last people are screwing like minks*—Saturday Review **2** *n: She loves a good screw* **3** *n* A person regarded merely as a sex object: *She's only a medium screw* **4** *v* To take advantage of; swindle; maltreat; =FUCK • Rapidly losing all offensive impact: *The city's taxpayers get screwed*—Village Voice

See GOAT FUCK, PUT THE SCREWS TO someone, THROW A FUCK INTO someone

screw[2] **1** *n underworld fr 1700s* A prison guard or warden; turnkey: *a hard-boiled screw*—E Lavine **2** *n underworld* Any law officer; =COP [fr 18th-century underworld, "a skeleton key," then turnkey, the bearer of such a key]

screw[3] *v* To leave hastily; flee; =SCRAM: *Now go on. Screw*—Nathaniel Benchley [perhaps imitative of *scram*; perhaps semantically derived fr *fuck off* "leave, depart," by way of less taboo *screw off*]

screw around **1** *v phr* To pass one's time idly and pleasantly; potter about; =GOOF AROUND **2** *v phr* To joke and play when one should be serious; =FUCK AROUND: *Quit screwing around and take this call* **3** *v phr* To flirt or dally, esp promiscuously; =be a SWINGER: *After he met Janet, he stopped screwing around*

screw around with someone **1** *v phr* To flirt or dally with; have a sexual involvement with; =PLAY AROUND WITH someone: *Anyhow he never screwed around with anybody's wife* **2** *v phr* To treat lightly or insultingly; provoke; =MESS AROUND WITH someone: *I wouldn't screw around with her, she's got a terrible temper*

screw around with something *v phr* To play or tinker with; =MESS WITH: *I told her to stop screwing around with the TV dial*

screwball[1] **1** *n fr 1930s* An eccentric person; =FREAK, ODDBALL: *It is forbidden to call any character a nut; you have to call him a screwball* —New Yorker **2** *adj: screwball* *antics*—Time/ *my screwball consciousness* **3** *n 1930s jazz musicians* Inferior, commercial jazz played for indifferent faddists [fr *screwy* and probably based on *screwball*[2]; the *-ball* of this term is the source of the very productive combining word that yields *oddball, nutball*, etc]

screwball[2] *n baseball fr 1930s* A pitched ball that moves to the right from a righthanded pitcher and the left from a lefthanded pitcher, unlike a curve ball [said to have been coined by the pitcher Carl Hubbell around 1930]

screwed *adj chiefly British* Drunk *See* HALF-STEWED

screwed, blued, and tattooed *adj phr* Thoroughly cheated; victimized; maltreated [*blued* is probably fr earlier *blewed* "robbed"; *tattooed* has the standard sense "struck rapidly and repeatedly"]

screwed up **1** *adj phr esp WW2 armed forces* Confused; tangled; spoiled, esp by bungling; =BALLED UP, FUCKED UP: *He screwed up the punch line/ Our plans got all screwed up* **2** *adj phr* Mentally and emotionally disturbed; neurotic; =FUCKED UP: *Hamlet was a sad, screwed-up type guy*—JD Salinger/ *screwed-up Washington wives*—Playboy/ *We weren't as screwed up with sexist attitudes*—Esquire

screw-loose *n* An eccentric person; =NUT, SCREWBALL

a **screw loose** *n phr fr late 1800s* A mental disorder; extreme eccentricity; craziness: *Or was he a man with a screw loose*—WR Burnett

screw-off *n esp WW2 Army* A person who evades work; idler; loafer; =FUCK-OFF

screw someone **over** *v phr* To take advantage of; swindle and victimize; =FUCK OVER: *don't trust the Government. They feel it screwed them over*—Time

screws *See* PUT THE SCREWS TO SOMEONE

screw up **1** *v phr fr WW2 Army* To fail by blundering; ruin one's prospects, life, etc; =FUCK UP: *I screwed up and got canned* **2** *v phr* To confuse; tangle; spoil by bungling; =BALL UP, FUCK UP: *It really screws up my sex life*—JD Salinger

screw-up **1** *n fr WW2 Army* A chronic bungler; a consistently inept person; =FUCK-UP **2** *n* A confused situation; a botch; =FUCK-UP: *The program's a total screw-up*

screwy **1** *adj outdated fr early 1800s British* Drunk **2** *adj fr 1920s* Very eccentric; crazy; =NUTTY, SCREWBALL: *Newspaper guys are mostly screwy* [semantically the gait of a drunk person suggested by the twistiness of a *screw* thread, whence the various senses of deviation; influenced by the notion of having a *screw loose* in one's head]

◁ **screw you**▷ *interj* An exclamation of strong defiance and contempt; =FUCK YOU: *Screw you all*—New York

◁ **scrog**▷ **1** *v* To do the sex act with or to; =SCRAG, SCREW: *You guys gotta scrog the sociable cervix*—Samuel Shem **2** *modifier: All that scroggin' material out there*—Calvin Trillin [probably fr *scrag*]

scrooch or **scrooge** or **scrouge** (SKRōōCH, SKRōōJ) *See* SCRUNCH

scrooge up *v phr* To tense and narrow one's eyelids: *scrooging up my eyes*—Sports Afield

scroogie or **scroogy** (SKRōō jee) *n baseball* An unconventional pitch, esp a screwball thrown with a change of pace: *It was some sort of a scroogie ... a changeup screwball*—Associated Press [said to have been coined by Mickey Mantle, probably fr *screwball* and *screwy*]

scrounge or **scrounge up** **1** *v* (also **scrounge up**) *fr WW1 British Army* To acquire by such dubious ways as habitual borrowing, begging, foraging, scavenging, pilfering, etc; =CADGE, MOOCH: *eating what little he could scrounge*—Louis Armstrong **2** *v* (also **scrounge up**) To seek and collect: *Let's see what we can scrounge up for supper* **3** *n* (also **scrounger**) A person who acquires by begging, borrowing, or pilfering; =CADGER, MOOCHER, SCHNORRER [probably fr British dialect *scrunge* "squeeze," hence "steal," semantically parallel with *pinch*]

scroungy or **scrounging** or **scrungy** *adj* Inferior; wretched; =CRUMMY, GRUNGY: *I'd tell my own children to wear something scroungy*—Time/ *could have bundled all this scrungy stuff into my car*—John D McDonald

[probably fr the notion of inferior things *scavenged* and *scrounged*, with the form now influenced by *grungy*]

scrub[1] *v* To cancel or eliminate: *They were forced to scrub the whole plan* [ultimately fr the British naval practice of writing signals or orders on a slate, and *scrubbing* or *washing* them *out* if they were cancelled]

scrub[2] *n fr late 1800s* An athlete who is not on the first or varsity team; a lowly substitute [ultimately fr 16th-century British slang, "a contemptible person, shabby fellow," related to another sense, "an inferior or mongrel animal," the basic notion being stuntedness]

scrud or **double scrud** *fr 1930s Army* **1** *n* or *n phr* Any disease, esp something quite serious and painful; =CRUD **2** *n* or *n phr* Any venereal disease; =CRUD

scruff *adj teenagers* =SCRUFFY [fr *scruffy*]

scruffy *adj* Dirty and unkempt; shabby; slovenly: *The scruffy little city, Knoxville, did it*—Wall Street Journal [fr obsolete British *scruff* "valueless, contemptible," probably an alteration of *scurf* "scabbiness of the skin," hence related to *scurvy*]

scrumptious *adj fr early 1800s* Excellent; superior; luxurious [perhaps a humorous alteration of *sumptuous*]

scrunch (Variations: **ooch** or **oonch** or **scooch** or **scrooch** or **scrooge** or **scrouge**) **1** *v* To squeeze oneself into a tighter space: *I scrunched into the corner and covered my ears/ She scrooged over and patted the sofa beside her/ Ooch over*—WR Burnett **2** *v* To squeeze, esp so as to make small changes: *If what chiefly interests him is literary stunts... the writer can oonch... just a little*—John Gardner/ *He kept tuning the engine to ooch every bit of speed from the boat* [ultimately fr late-16th-century *scruze* "squeeze," perhaps a blend of *screw* and *squeeze*]

◁ **scum** ▷ *n* Semen; =COME

◁ **scumbag** ▷ **1** *n fr 1920s* A condom; =RUBBER **2** *n* A despicable person; =ASSHOLE, BASTARD: *calls... Charlton Heston a scumbag*—National Review **3** *modifier: accused us of practicing scumbag journalism*—Village Voice [fr *scum* "semen"]

a **scunner** *n fr late 1800s* Extreme dislike; hostility: *had taken a scunner against the main competitor*—Atlantic Monthly [fr Scots dialect]

scurve *n* A despicable person; =CRUMB, SCUMBAG, DIRTBAG: *a beer-bottle-in-pocket, fast-talking scurve*—Village Voice [fr *scurvy*; see *scruffy*]

scut **1** *n* A detestable or contemptible person; =CRUMB, LOUSE: *You bloody scut!*—Lawrence Sanders **2** *n* A novice; recruit; neophyte: *The fraternity was famous for treating scuts very roughly* **3** *n* (also **scud** or **scut work**) Menial work such as would be given to a novice: *a detention company doing scut work around the fort*—Newsweek **4** *n* (also **scut work**) *hospital* Routine and tedious medical procedures usually relegated to the least senior members of the staff **5** *n hospital* A patient held in very low regard [the 16th-century slang use, "vulva, cunt," and the standard use "tail of a hare or deer," suggest a core sense "tail, buttocks, ass," reinforced by British dialect *skut* "crouch down," and perhaps related to Old Norse *skutr* "stern of a ship"]

scuttlebutt *n Navy fr 1930s* Rumors; gossip; presumed confidential information: *worry about a slump, according to business scuttlebutt*—Associated Press [fr the chit-chat around the *scuttlebutt* "drinking fountain, water cask," on naval vessels]

scuzz *teenagers* **1** *n* (also **scuzzo**) Dirt; filth; a nasty substance; =GRUNGE, MUNG: *He has scuzz all over his pants and in his mind* ◁**2**▷ *n* An unattractive young woman; =SCANK, SKAG

scuzzbag or **scuzzo** *n* A despicable person; =CRUMB, SCURVE, SLEAZEBAG: *He calls a minister a "scuzzbag"*—Time

scuzz-food *n* Food like potato chips, popcorn, sugar-coated cereal, etc; =JUNK FOOD: *I will take a back seat to no one as a scuzz-food fanatic*—Car and Driver

scuzz someone **out** *v phr esp teenagers* To disgust mightily; nauseate; =GROSS someone OUT: *With-it slanguists are scuzzed out at the* *squared-out weirdos who still use grossed out*—William Safire

scuzzy or **scuz** *adj teenagers* Dirty; filthy; repellent; =GRUNGY: *a bunch of scuzzy Moroccan A-rabs*—Village Voice [perhaps fr *disgusting*; perhaps a blend of or influenced by *scum* and *fuzz*]

seafood 1 *n esp 1920s underworld* Whiskey **2** *n homosexuals* A sailor regarded as a homosexual sex partner **3** *n* Cunnilingus; =HAIR PIE: *Want some seafood, mama*—Hold Tight (song) **4** *n* A woman regarded as a sex organ for cunnilingus; =EATIN' STUFF [fr various aspects of seafaring, trade, and the taste of *seafood*; the last two senses perhaps a pun, *c food* "cuntfood"]

seams *See* COME APART AT THE SEAMS

search me *interj* An exclamation or acknowledgment of ignorance; =BEATS ME: *Who said it? Search me, I couldn't say*

season *See* SILLY SEASON

seat *See* DRIVER'S SEAT, the HOT SEAT, SMOKY SEAT, TAKE A BACK SEAT

seat-of-the-pants *adj* Inclined to work by instinct, feel, impulse, etc, rather than by precise rules; practical: *The news had seat-of-the-pants editors who knew their audience*—Washingtonian [see *fly by the seat of* one's *pants*]

sec[1] *n* A second of time: *Come here a sec, Billy*—Sinclair Lewis

sec[2] *n* A secretary: *His femme secs open the mail*—Variety

second fiddle 1 *n* A person or thing that is not the most favored, the best, the leader, etc: *definitely second fiddle before the Convention started*—Pete Martin **2** *adj: a sort of second-fiddle appointment*

See PLAY SECOND FIDDLE

second off *adv phr* Second in order; secondly: *and, second off, readers and authors both*—New York Times

second sacker *n phr baseball* A second baseman

secret *See* DIRTY LITTLE SECRET

security blanket *n phr* A thing or person that provides someone with a sense of safety and emotional comfort: *Zeigler instead is...Mr Nixon's "security blanket"*—Newsweek [fr the *blanket* or token fragment of blanket that some small children carry about as a source of comforting familiarity; Charles M Schulz, creator of the comic strip "Peanuts," has claimed coinage of the term]

see 1 *n police* Recognition; complimentary notice by a superior: *He was a good cop ten years, but never got a see* **2** *n police* A visit of inspection: *numerous "sees" or visits from the sergeant*—E Lavine **3** *v underworld* To pay protection money or graft: *doing business without "seeing the cops"*—E Lavine **4** *v poker* To equal a bet or a raise rather than dropping out of the game [first sense perhaps an abbreviation of *commendation*]

See LONG TIME NO SEE

see a man about a dog *v phr fr late 1800s* To take one's leave for some urgent purpose, esp to go to the bathroom or in earlier times to go have a drink or to meet one's bootlegger • Usu a smiling apology for one's departure; a bland euphemism to conceal one's true purpose

seed *n narcotics* =ROACH

See HAYSEED, SWALLOW A WATERMELON SEED

see red *v phr* To become very angry: *Politics make him see red*

see the light at the end of the tunnel *v phr esp Vietnam War period* To see at last the beginning of the end of a difficult struggle, period, etc: *The Flower People of Saigon...invite you to see the light at the end of the tunnel*—New York Times

see-through *adj* Transparent; made of a very sheer fabric; =PEEKABOO: *a see-through blouse*

see you *interj* A casual farewell; =SO LONG: *the careless "see you's" that people say*—Life

segue or **seg** (SEHG way or SEHG) **1** *v musicians* To go from one piece of music, record, etc, to the next without an obvious break; make a smooth transition **2** *v* To go smoothly from one thing to another: *His features seg rapidly from fascination to fear*—Playgirl/ *So we'll segue from wooing them to screwing them, somehow* **3** *n college students* A sequel; something that follows or follows up [fr Italian, "now follows," an instruction on musical scores]

sell 1 *v outdated fr early 1600s* To cheat; swindle; hoax **2** *n fr middle 1800s:* A hoax or swindle; a decep-

tion: *The Cardiff Giant was a "sell"* —AT Vance **3** *v* To convince someone of the value of something; =SELL someone ON something: *After his spiel I was sold*
See HARD SELL, SOFT SELL, be SOLD ON

sell someone **down the river** *v phr* To betray; take victimizing advantage of [perhaps fr slavery days, when a black person or escaped slave *sold down the river* was sent to or returned to the South]

sell someone **on** something *v phr fr early 1900s* To convince someone of the value of something; successfully extol: *She sold me on the new wage policy*

sell out *v phr fr middle 1800s* To become a traitor, esp to prostitute one's ideals, talents, etc, for money or other comforts: *are often labeled Toms and mammies who sold out* —Saturday Review

sell-out **1** *n* An act or instance of selling out, in either sense: *He disappointed us, but he was honest enough and it was no sell-out/ The new bathing suits should be a quick sell-out* **2** *n* A person who sells out, in the sense of betrayal or pecuniary self-serving: *In spite of his early protestations of loyalty, he was a contemptible sell-out*

sell someone or something **out** *v phr* To betray; sacrifice or desert for one's own advantage: *accuse them of selling out Chiang Kai-shek*—David Halberstam

send *v esp 1940s jive talk fr jazz talk* To arouse keen admiration, esp as an ecstatic response; excite; =TURN someone ON: *Bessie Smith really sent him*—Stephen Longstreet

send someone **to the showers** **1** *v phr baseball* To remove or eject a player from a game **2** *v phr* To dismiss or reject

send up **1** *v phr* (also **send up the river**) *fr middle 1800s* To send to prison: *He got sent up for grand theft* **2** *v phr fr 1930s British* To ridicule, esp by parody; mock; lampoon; =SPOOF: *cracking jokes, sending up everyone and everything in sight* —Rolling Stone [first sense fr or influenced by the course from New York City *up* the Hudson *River* to Sing Sing Prison at Ossining; second sense fr British public school *sending* of a delinquent boy *up* to the headmaster for punishment]

send-up *n fr British* A mocking, teasing parody; lampoon; =SPOOF: *just another stupid soap send-up*—People Weekly

sensaysh (sen SAYSH) *adj* Sensational: *I had a sensaysh time*—Max Shulman

sergeant *See* BUCK SERGEANT

serious **1** *adj black fr 1940s bop talk* Very commendable; excellent; superb **2** *adj* Intended to make a good and sober impression; overtly conformistic; =SINCERE: *in a serious suit and striped tie*—Dan Jenkins
See FOR SERIOUS

session **1** *n esp 1930s teenagers* A dance or party; =HOP **2** *n narcotics* The period of intoxication from a dose of narcotics, esp of LSD; =TRIP **3** *n musicians* An occasion at which a recording is made in a studio; a studio rehearsal or performance: *They never let anybody in for their sessions* **4** **modifier:** *He used to do a lot of session playing but hardly ever worked for an audience*
See BULL SESSION, GRIPE SESSION, HASH SESSION, JAM SESSION, RAP SESSION, SKULL SESSION

set **1** *n musicians* The group of pieces musicians perform during about a 45-minute period at a club, show, etc: *clarinetist Scott opened his set*—Metronome **2** *n jazz musicians* An improvisatory musical interchange of about half an hour **3** *n black & jazz talk* A small party or friendly conversational gathering; =SCENE: *Don't stop belly rubbing just because we showed on the set*—Donald Goines **4** *n chiefly black* A discussion; =RAP: *He never said get those Panthers out... all through the whole set*—Bobby Seale **5** *n narcotics* A narcotic dose of two Seconals (a trade name) and one amphetamine
See the JET SET

set someone **back** *v phr fr late 1800s* To cost: *set us back what was then an astonishing $18 a person*—San Francisco

set of pipes *See* PIPES

set of threads (or **drapes**) *n phr jazz & bop talk fr 1940s* A suit of clothing, esp a new and stylish one: *the smart set of threads*—Stephen Longstreet

set of wheels *n phr* A car: *If you're feverish for a great set of wheels* —Playboy

settle (or **fix**) someone's **hash** *fr late 1700s* **1** *v phr* To injure or ruin definitively; =COOK someone's GOOSE: *I'll check you out after I settle his hash*—Pulpsmith **2** *v phr* To deflate; humiliate; defeat; =FIX someone's WAGON [origin unknown; semantically related to such similar and ironic expressions as *clean* someone's *clock, cook* someone's *goose*, and *fix* someone's *wagon*]

setup 1 *n* A person who is easily duped, tricked, etc; =PATSY, SUCKER: *a set-up, a tout's dream come true*—J Lilienthal **2** *n 1920s underworld* A one-day jail sentence **3** *n fr 1920s* A glass, ice, soda, etc, to be mixed with liquor: *They supplied the set-ups*—NY Confidential **4** *n* Arrangement; organization; situation; mode of operation: *except its size and its co-op set-up*—New York Times **5** *n* A house, office, apartment, etc: *He has a very comfy setup in a rehabbed brownstone* [most senses apparently fr the *setting up* of billiard or pool balls to insure a special or a trick shot]

set up *adj* Gratified; elated; braced: *He looks real set up now that they've published his book*

set someone **up 1** *v phr* To prepare and maneuver someone for swindling, tricking, etc; =BUILD **2** *v phr* To gratify and encourage; brace: *Finishing first for a change really set me up* **3** *v phr fr middle 1800s* To treat someone; provide food or drink

seventeen *See* FILE 17

Seventh Avenue *n phr* The garment and fashion industry; =the RAG TRADE [fr the fact that New York City's *Seventh Avenue* is the traditional center of the garment industry]

sewer *n narcotics* A vein or artery: *put it right in the sewer instead of skin popping*—RV Winslow

sewer hog *n phr construction workers* A ditch digger

sew something **up 1** *v phr* To finish; put the finishing touches on: *They sewed up the contract today* **2** *v phr* To insure a victory; make a conclusive score, stroke, etc; =CLINCH, ICE: *The last-period goal sewed it up for the Drew Rangers*

sex goddess *n phr* A woman, usu a movie star, who is a provocative and famous sexual object

sex kitten (or **bunny**) *n phr* A young woman who is highly attractive, provocative, and seemingly available sexually

sexploitation 1 *n* Commercial exploitation of sex: *Female chauvinist sexploitation will reach a new level* —Time **2** *modifier: a camp sexploitation horror musical*—Esquire

sexpot *n* A person, esp a woman, who is especially attractive and provocative sexually: *who cannot command the smile of a sexpot*—Frederic Morton

sex wagon *n phr* =PIMPMOBILE

sexy *adj* Very appealing; exciting; desirable; stimulating: *Acid rain is politically sexy but it hasn't half the allure of jobs*—Toronto Life

-sey *See* -IE

sez (or **sezz**) **you** *See* SAYS YOU

shack 1 *n* =SHACK JOB **2** *v* =SHACK UP [fr late-19th-century *shack* "hut, shanty," probably fr earlier *shackle* fr American Spanish *jacal* fr Aztec *xacalli*]

◁ **shack job** ▷ *n phr esp WW2 Army* A woman one lives with adulterously; common-law wife; mistress: *This was an early shack-job, not the girl mentioned above*—New Yorker

shack up 1 *v phr esp WW2 Army fr 1920s truckers & traveling salespersons* To live with, do the sex act with, and support a woman who is not one's wife; keep a mistress: *The medicine man had shacked up with a halfbreed cook*—Time **2** *v phr* To do the sex act; esp, to lead a promiscuous sex life; =SLEEP AROUND: *If you drink and shack up with strangers you get old at thirty*—Tennessee Williams **3** *v phr* To live; reside, esp in a nonpermanent place: *got rid of his home and shacked up in a hotel* —Westbrook Pegler

shade *v sports* To defeat by a narrow margin: *Michigan shaded Iowa. The final score was 98 to 96*

shades *n fr 1940s bop musicians* Sunglasses

shadow 1 *v fr late 1800s* To follow a person secretly; do physical surveillance; =TAIL **2** *n: They put a shadow on the suspect*

shadow gazer *n phr hospital* A radiologist

◁ **shaft**▷ *v* To treat unfairly or cruelly; victimize: *When do you shaft a pal, when do you hand him the poison cup?*—Saul Bellow [fr the notion of sodomizing a victim]

◁ the **shaft** or **a shafting**▷ *n phr* Unfair or cruel treatment: *learned from past experience to expect the shaft from foreign journalists*—Newsweek/ *He was hoping for a raise and got a shafting*

See GET THE SHAFT, GIVE someone THE SHAFT

shag 1 *v fr middle 1800s* To depart; leave, esp quickly; =SHAG ASS: *You'd best shag now*—W Henry **2** *v fr late 1800s* To chase: *I was allowed to "shag" foul balls*—CH Claudy **3** *v 1930s teenagers* To tease and harass; =HASSLE, HOUND **4** *n teenagers fr 1930s* A party or session where boys and girls experiment sexually: *The kids were fondling each other, having a shag* **5** *adj esp 1950s teenagers* Excellent; wonderful [all senses probably ultimately fr *shake* by way of *shack*; the sexual senses are attested in late-18th-century British slang]

See GANG BANG

◁ **shag ass**▷ *v phr* To depart; leave, esp hurriedly; =HAUL ASS, SCRAM

shake 1 *n fr middle 1800s* A dance: *charge a few coins and have a shake* —Louis Armstrong **2** *n* A moment; =SEC: *Be ready in two shakes* **3** *n fr 1920s* Blackmail or extortion; =SHAKEDOWN: *This isn't any kind of a shake*—Raymond Chandler **4** *v: tried to shake one of the big boys*—Raymond Chandler **5** *v* To search a person or place thoroughly; =SHAKE DOWN **6** *n: We'd better give the entire house a shake; I know it's here somewhere* **7** *v* =GIVE someone THE SHAKE

See a FAIR SHAKE, SKIN-SEARCH, TWO SHAKES

shake a leg *v phr fr late 1800s* To hurry; speed up

shakedown 1 *n fr early 1700s* A night's lodging; an impromptu bed **2** *n* Sleep: *I'll get a shakedown on the couch*—The Thirty-Nine Steps (movie) **3** *n fr underworld* An instance of or a demand for blackmail, extortion, etc; victimization by the protection racket: *Listen, I know this is a shakedown*—New York **4** *n* A thorough search of a person or place; =SHAKE: *We gave the room a first-class shakedown*—R Starnes **5** *n* A trying-out or first tentative use, esp of a machine, ship, process, etc: *Let's give this new idea a shakedown and see if it works* [final sense fr *shakedown cruise*]

shake down 1 *v phr* To blackmail or extort; demand protection money: *The cat who was shaking you down heard some change jingling*—Claude Brown **2** *v phr* To search a person or place thoroughly; =SHAKE: *a couple of policemen to shake down the neighborhood*—R Starnes

shake it or **shake it up** *v phr* To hurry; =SHAKE A LEG: *We've got to shake it*—Dashiell Hammett

the **shakes** *n phr* An attack of trembling, esp one due to alcoholism or drug abuse; =the CLANKS

shake the money tree *v phr* To produce profit, esp in great amounts: *It took two to shake the money tree* —Village Voice

shake-up *n fr late 1800s* The reorganization of a working group, its methods, etc, usu including some dismissals: *The remedy is a shake-up in the Bureau of the Budget*—Ithaca Journal

shaking *See* WHAT'S SHAKING

shalump *See* SCHLOOMP

shame *See* DIRTY SHAME

shamus (SHAH məs, SHAY-) (also **shammus** or **shamos** or **shommus**) **1** *n* A police officer, private detective, security guard, etc; =COP: *a British-accented burlesque of the tough American shamus*—New York Times **2** *n* A police informer; =STOOL PIGEON [fr Yiddish, "sexton of a synagogue," fr Hebrew *shamash* "servant"; probably influenced by the Celtic name *Seamus* "James," as a typical name of an Irish police officer]

shank 1 *n prison & street gang fr 1950s* A stilettolike weapon: *looks like a large screwdriver and is known in prison parlance as a shank*—Philadelphia Journal **2** *v: that dude the dicks want for shanking his old lady* —Joseph Wambaugh **3** *v sports* To kick: *is shanking punts all over the* [illegible] Philadelphia **4** *n fr early 1800s* The end or last part of a period of time, esp of the evening • Also interpreted as the early or chief part of a period of time: *Leaving already? It's only the shank of the evening* [all senses reflect the basic notion of something long and thin]

shank's mare *See* RIDE SHANK'S MARE

shanty **1** *n fr early 1800s* A rickety hut, a hovel; a shack **2** *n railroad* A caboose [probably fr Irish *sean-tig*; perhaps fr Canadian French *chantier*, although this is more probably a borrowing of *shanty*]

◁ **shanty Irish** ▷ *n phr* Poor or disreputable Irish people: *oh, not shanty Irish* —Stephen Longstreet

shape *See* BENT OUT OF SHAPE

shape up **1** *v phr* (also **shape up or ship out**) *esp WW2 armed forces fr cowboys* To correct one's behavior; conform and perform • Often a firm command or admonition: *From this day on you're going to shape up or ship out. Is that understood?*—Art Buchwald **2** *v phr* To progress; go along: *How are your plans shaping up?*

shark **1** *n fr 1500s* A confidence man or swindler; =HUSTLER, SHARP **2** *n early 1900s college students* A very able student, esp one who does not seem to work hard **3** *n esp 1920s & 30s* An expert, esp a somewhat exploitive or unscrupulous one • Usually preceded by a modifier showing the field of skill: *the gunshark's report*—Raymond Chandler [all senses fr the predaceous fish, except that the oldest sense may originally have been fr German *schurke* "rascal"]

See CARD SHARP, LOAN SHARK

sharp **1** *n fr middle 1800s* An expert, esp at card games; =PRO: *Hurstwood's a regular sharp*—Theodore Dreiser **2** *n* (also **sharper**) *fr late 1700s* A confidence trickster; a swindler, esp a dishonest card player; =CARD SHARP **3** *adj fr jive talk* Stylish; of the latest and most sophisticated sort: *He wore bow ties and sharp suits*—Truman Capote **4** *adj fr jive talk* Good; excellent; admirable; =COOL: *I sound like everything was sharp*—John O'Hara

See CARD SHARP

sharpie **1** *n jive talk* A devotee of swing music, esp one who dances well to swing **2** *n fr jive talk* A stylish dresser in the flashy modes: *and not just among the sharpies*—Associated Press **3** *modifier: an incredible sharpie opulence of leather pockets and hand-wrought belt loops* New York **4** *n* A shrewd person watchful of his or her profit: *an open invitation for a sharpie to have the free use of a new car for 30 days* —Time **5** *n* A confidence trickster; a swindler; =SHARP, SHARK: *been beset by hustlers, sharpies, hangers-on, bad-advice artists*—Playboy

◁ **shat on** ▷ *v phr* Maltreated; victimized; =SHAFTED: *Because women have been shat on for centuries*—Off Our Backs [fr the humorous past tense form of *shit*]

shave points or **shave** *v phr* or *v sports & gambling* To get a gambling or money advantage by failing to score as much as one could; fraudulently lose a game

shaver *See* LITTLE SHAVER

shaving *See* POINT-SHAVING

shay *See* GANG BANG

shazam (shə ZAM) *interj* An exclamation of triumphant and delighted announcement, emphasis, etc: *Go ahead and say it, Shazam!, juice it up* —Tom Wolfe [fr the operative or command word of a magician, similar to *presto change-o*]

the **shebang** (shə BANG, shee-) *n* Everything; =the WHOLE SHEBANG: *You can have the shebang* [fr a mid-19th-century sense, "shanty, hut," of obscure origin; perhaps fr an approximate pronunciation of French *char-à-banc,* "buslike wagon with many seats," in which case the semantics of *the whole shebang* would depend upon the hiring of the whole vehicle rather than one or two seats]

shed *See* WOODSHED

◁ **shee-it** ▷ (SHEE ət) *interj* =SHIT [a humorous imitation of a drawled Southern pronunciation]

◀ **sheeny** or **sheenie** ▶ **1** *n fr early 1800s British* A Jew **2** *adj: one of those Sheeny employment bureaus* —Sinclair Lewis **3** *n* A pawnbroker, tailor, junkman, or member of another traditionally Jewish occupation [origin unknown]

sheepskin *n fr 1700s* A college or university diploma [fr the fact that diplomas used to be made of *sheepskin*]

sheesh[1] *interj* An exclamation of disgust, frustration, etc: *Pronounce this ... sheesh! and it gives you some idea of what you'll say living with a cheap bastard*—Village Voice [a euphemism for *shit*]

sheesh[2] *n narcotics* Hashish

sheet **1** *n* A newspaper: *Both morning sheets have written it up*—J Evans **2** *n police* =RAP SHEET

See DOPE SHEET, POOP SHEET, RAP SHEET, SWINDLE SHEET, THREE SHEETS TO THE WIND

sheive *See* SHIV

shekels (SHEK əls) *n fr middle 1800s* Money; wealth [fr the Hebrew name of a unit of weight and money]

shelf *See* ON THE SHELF

shell *See* HARD-SHELL

shellac *v sports* To defeat decisively; trounce; =CLOBBER: *The Giants got shellacked again Monday* [perhaps fr the use of *shellac* as a finish]

shellacking **1** *n* A beating: *"Shellacking" ... and numerous other phrases are employed by the police as euphemisms*—E Lavine **2** *n sports* A decisive defeat; a drubbing; an utter rout: *Should Black take a shellacking, the National Leaguers are in bad trouble*—Associated Press

shell out *v phr fr early 1800s* To pay; put out; contribute; =FORK OVER: *Several companies shelled out upwards of $150,000 for the weekend's fun and games*—Rolling Stone

shemale **1** *n* A female **2** *n* A male transvestite

shemozzle (also **shimozzle** or **shlamozzle** or **shlemozzle**) *chiefly British & Canadian fr late 1800s* **1** *n* A difficult and confused situation; an uproar; melee; =MESS, RHUBARB: *It became clear that the whole shlamozzle, introns and exons, are transcribed into RNA*—Gordon Rattray Taylor **2** *v* To depart; =POWDER, SCRAM [ultimately probably fr Yiddish *shlim mazel* "rotten luck," hence "a difficulty or misfortune," and related to *shlemazel*]

shenanigan or **shenanigans** *n fr middle 1800s Western* A trick or bit of foolery; a mild cheat or deception [origin unknown; perhaps fr Irish *sionnachuighim* "play tricks, be foxy"]

Sherpa or **sherpa** *n* A high-ranking assistant of a head of state, esp one who makes the arrangements for a summit meeting: *high-level civil servants known in the diplomatic community as Sherpas*—New York Times [fr the Himalayan tribe that specializes in guiding and assisting mountain climbers to summits]

shift *See* GRAVEYARD SHIFT

shift (or **move**) **into high gear** *v phr* To begin to work at top speed; become serious: *although the Senate hearings are just shifting into high gear*—George Will

shikker or **shicker** *adj* Drunk: *We'll eat good, then we'll get shikker*—AJ Liebling [fr Yiddish fr Hebrew *shikkur*]

See ON THE SHIKKER

shikkered *adj esp Australian* Drunk

◁ **shikse** or **shiksa** or **shikseh** ▷ (SHIK sə) *n* A non-Jewish woman, esp a young woman • Usually at least somewhat derogatory: *That Alice was so blatantly a shikse*—Philip Roth [fr Yiddish fr Hebrew *sheques*, literally "blemish"]

shill **1** *n* (also **shillaber**) *fr circus* An associate of an auctioneer, gambler, hawker, etc, who pretends to be a member of the audience and stimulates it to desired action: *The shill is innocuous-looking*—New York Times **2** *v: That summer he shilled for a sidewalk hawker* **3** *n fr 1940s* A barker, hawker, advertising or public relations person, or anyone else whose job is to stimulate business; =FLACK [origin unknown; perhaps, since it is a shortening of *shillaber*, ultimately fr *Shillibeer*, the name of an early-19th-century British owner of a large bus company, the reference being to persons hired as decoys to sit in buses and attract passengers]

shimmy[1] **1** *n* A very energetic vibrational dance and dancing style **2** *v: I wish that I could shimmy like my sister Kate* **3** *n* A flick or flirting of the buttocks: *She calls to the owner, with a little shimmy*—New York **4** *n* (also **shimmy pudding**) *lunch counter* Gelatin desserts and other foods that shake when moved

shimmy[2] *n gambling* Chemin de fer: *a "shimmy" (chemin de fer) table*—J Scarne

shimozzle *See* SHEMOZZLE

shindig *n fr middle 1800s* A party, reception, festival, etc, esp a noisy dancing party [probably fr *shin dig* "a blow on the shin incurred while dancing"; perhaps by folk etymology fr the older *shindy*]

shindy *n fr early 1800s British nautical* An uproar; a confused struggle; =DONNYBROOK [origin unknown; perhaps fr Irish *sinteag* "skip, caper"; perhaps fr *shinny*, the name of a rough hockeylike schoolboy game; perhaps fr Romany *chindi* "a cut, a cutting up"]

shine ◀**1**▶ *n fr early 1900s* A black person ◀**2**▶ *modifier: another shine killing*—Raymond Chandler **3** *n* Bootleg whiskey; =MOONSHINE: *non-blinding shine sold in fruit jars*—Robert Ruark **4** *v teenagers fr black* To ignore; disregard; avoid; =SKIP **5** *v students* To abandon; fail; =PUNT [the racial sense may have originated among blacks, may refer to the glossiness of a very black skin, and hence may reflect the caste system based upon color; among white speakers, this sense was surely influenced by the fact that most *shoeshine* persons were black; the teenager sense has a black parallel, *shine on*, and the origin may be the poetic notion that when one turns one's back on something one is letting his "moon (that is, buttocks) *shine on*" it]

See MONKEYSHINES, STICK IT, TAKE A SHINE TO someone or something, WHERE THE SUN DOESN'T SHINE

shiner **1** *n fr early 1900s* A bruise near the eye; =BLACK EYE, MOUSE: *a pip of a shiner*—John McNulty **2** *n gambling* A shiny table top or other mirrorlike surface a dealer can use to see the faces of the cards he deals

shingle *n fr middle 1800s* A signboard, esp one designating professional services: *He got him a shingle and started practice last year*

See HANG UP one's SHINGLE, SHIT ON A SHINGLE

Shinola *See* NOT KNOW SHIT FROM SHINOLA

ship *See* SHAPE UP

shirt *See* BET YOUR BOOTS, GIVE someone THE SHIRT OFF one's BACK, KEEP one's SHIRT ON, SKIVVY, STUFFED SHIRT

shirttail kin *n phr Southern & Midwestern* Distant relations; third and fourth cousins, etc

shirty *adj fr middle 1800s British* Angry; very upset; =HUFFY, PISSED OFF: *He was a little ashamed of himself for getting shirty with Ivar*—Lawrence Sanders [said to be fr the dishevelment resulting when one is actively angry, since a mid-19th-century verb variant was *get someone's shirt out*]

◁ **shit** ▷ **1** *n fr 800s or earlier* Feces; excrement; =CRAP, POO **2** *v: They diurnally shit, shave, and shower* **3** *interj* An exclamation of disbelief, disgust, disappointment, emphasis, etc: *Oh, shit, I missed the bus!/ Shit, I never had it so good!* **4** *n* Nonsense; pretentious talk; bold and deceitful absurdities; =BULLSHIT: *The judge was talking a lot of shit* **5** *v* To lie; exaggerate; try to deceive: *"Don't shit me," said Dina*—Joseph Heller/ *The sky's the limit, Wilson, I shit you not*—WR Tyler **6** *n* Offensive and contemptuous treatment; disrespect; insults: *I took a lot of shit from her before I left* **7** *n* Anything of shoddy and inferior quality; pretentious and meretricious trash; =CRAP, DRECK: *a costly flop, gilded shit/ What kind of shit are they selling here?* **8** *modifier: as well as shit loans to companies like Massey-Ferguson and Turbo Resources*—Toronto Life **9** *n* One's possessions; one's personal effects: *Get your shit, both of you are moving*—Donald Goines **10** *n* An obnoxious, disgusting, or contemptible person; a despicable wretch; =PRICK, SHITHEEL **11** *v* To respond powerfully, esp with alarm, anger, or panic: *He'll shit when we tell him about this* **12** *n narcotics* Heroin; =HORSE: *insisted on retaining the word "shit" as junkie slang for heroin*—Dwight MacDonald **13** *n* Nothing; the least quantity; =DIDDLY: *of whom I hadn't seen shit*—R Grossbach

See ACT LIKE one's SHIT DOESN'T STINK, BAD SHIT, BEAT THE SHIT OUT OF someone or something, as BLAZES, BULLSHIT, CHICKEN SHIT, CLEAN UP one's ACT, CROCK, the DAY THE EAGLE SHITS, DEEP

TROUBLE, DIDDLY, DOES A BEAR SHIT IN THE WOODS, DOODLE-SHIT, EAT SHIT, FULL OF SHIT, GOOD SHIT, HAVE SHIT FOR BRAINS, HOLY SHIT, HORSESHIT, HOT SHIT, I'LL BE DAMNED, LIKE HELL, LIKE PIGS IN CLOVER, LIKE SHIT THROUGH A TIN HORN, LOOK LIKE TEN POUNDS OF SHIT IN A FIVE-POUND BAG, NO SHIT, NOT GIVE A DAMN, NOT KNOW BEANS, NOT KNOW SHIT FROM SHINOLA, PIECE OF SHIT, SCARE THE SHIT OUT OF someone, SHOOT THE BULL, SHOVEL SHIT, STRONGER THAN PIG SHIT, SURE AS SHIT, TAKE A DUMP, TAKE SHIT, THINK one's SHIT DOESN'T STINK, TICKLE THE SHIT OUT OF someone, TOUGH SHIT, TREAT someone LIKE A DOORMAT, WORTH A DAMN

◁ **shit a brick** (or **bricks**)▷ *v phr* To be very upset and angry; have an emotional crisis; =SWEAT BULLETS: *Swarthmore College would shit a brick*—Off Our Backs/ *I had a few scenes where I was really shittin' bricks*—Rolling Stone

◁ **shit-all**▷ *adj* Not any; none at all: *Monica, we have shit-all evidence of what the killer looks like*—Lawrence Sanders [related to and perhaps derived fr British *bugger-all* and *fuck-all* in the same sense, used as intensives and based on *not at all*; Dylan Thomas's mythical Welsh village *Llareggub* has a pseudo-Welsh name which is *bugger-all* spelled backwards]

◁ **shit-ass**▷ **1** *n* An insignificant, contemptible person; =JERK **2** *n* =SHITHEEL **3** *v* To behave like a despicable or contemptible person, esp by betrayal of a duty or promise: *I don't want anybody shitassing out of it*—Jackie Collins

◁ **shit bullets**▷ *See* SWEAT BULLETS

◁ **shitcan**▷ *v* To discard; throw away; abandon: *If it rained before he entered the tunnel, he would have to shitcan his plans*—Easyriders [fr *shitcan* "refuse can"]

shit creek *See* UP SHIT CREEK

◁ one's **shit doesn't stink**▷ *See* THINK one's SHIT DOESN'T STINK

◁ **shit-eating grin**▷ *n phr* An expression of satisfaction; a gloating look: *Go ahead, sit there with that shit-eating grin on your face*—Earl Thompson

◁ **shit-faced**▷ *adj esp students* Drunk

◁ **shit fit**▷ *See* HAVE A SHIT FIT

◁ **shit-for-brains**▷ *n* A very stupid person: *What's old Shit-for-brains trying to say?*

See HAVE SHIT FOR BRAINS

◁ **shit for the birds**▷ *n phr esp WW2 armed forces* Nonsense; lies and exaggerations; =BULLSHIT [probably an alteration of *birdshit* akin to *chickenshit*]

See FOR THE BIRDS

◁ **shit green**▷ *v phr* To be alarmed, shocked, or enraged; =SHIT A BRICK: *The second the going gets jumpy, you shit green*—Patrick Mann

◁ **shithead** or **shitface**▷ **1** *n* A stupid, confused, and blundering person; =FUCK-UP: *and this shithead comes sneaking around, asking questions*—WT Tyler **2** *n* =SHITHEEL

◁ **shitheel**▷ *n* A despicable person; a scoundrel and blackguard; =BASTARD, PRICK [probably an intensive form of *heel*]

◁ the **shit hits the fan**▷ *sentence fr 1930s* Trouble breaks out; a fearful crisis ensues; things turn nasty ● Often part of a time clause beginning with **when** or **then**: *The shit didn't hit the fan till this guy, Eddie Jaffe, takes the pad*—Rocky Graziano [apparently fr and certainly related to the classical joke about the man who, finding no toilet, defecated into a hole in the floor; back downstairs, finding the barroom emptied of its celebrants, he inquired why, and was asked, "Where were you when the shit hit the fan?"]

◁ **shithook**▷ *n* =SHITHEEL

◁ **shithouse**▷ **1** *n* A toilet: *This ain't no shithouse, man*—John R Powers **2** *n* A filthy, sloppy place; a shambles: *How can you live in this shithouse?*

See BUILT LIKE A BRICK SHITHOUSE

◁ a **shithouse full**▷ *n phr* A very large number or amount; =OODLES: *He had to wade through a shithouse full of people to get here*

◁ **shit in high cotton**▷ *v phr* To live well and opulently; enjoy prosperity, esp newly; =EAT HIGH ON THE HOG, PISS ON ICE [fr the notion that well-grown *cotton* means wealth]

◁ **shit** (or **go shit**) **in your hat**▷ *sentence* =GO TO HELL, GO FUCK oneself: *It's unfair, but say so and people tell you to go shit in your hat*—Village Voice

◁ **shitkicker**▷ **1** *n* A farmer or other rural person; =HICK, RUBE: *nothing but a Midwest shitkicker*—Washingtonian **2** *adj* Rural; country; country and western: *the old shitkicker country guitarist*—George Warren **3** *n* A cowboy movie; =HORSE OPERA

◁ **shitkickers** or **shit stompers**▷ *n* or *n phr* Heavy boots such as farm, cowboy, or hiking boots: *I never see you in anything but those old shitkickers*—Stephen King

◁ **shit-kicking**▷ *adj* Rough and rural; crude: *It's down-home, shit-kickin', ball-scratchin' country*—Aquarian

◁ **shitless**▷ ***See*** SCARED SHITLESS, SCARE someone SHITLESS

◁ **shit** (or **crap**) **list**▷ *n phr* One's fancied or real list of persons who are hated, not trusted, to be avoided, etc: *I wondered how I got on her shit list*

◁ a **shitload** (or **shitpot**)▷ *n* A very large number or amount; =a SHITHOUSE FULL: *They sure sell a shitload of them*—San Francisco/ *a whole shitpot of that stuff*—George Warren

◁ **shit on** someone or something▷ *interj* An exclamation of powerful disgust, contempt, rejection, etc: *Shit on his suggestions!*

◁ **shit on a shingle**▷ *n phr WW2 Army* Creamed chipped beef on toast, or some similar delicacy

◁ **shit on wheels**▷ *n phr* =HOT SHIT

◁ **shit or get off the pot**▷ **1** *sentence* (Variation: **piss** may replace **shit**) =FISH OR CUT BAIT **2** *modifier: It's shit-or-get-off-the-pot time*—Armistead Maupin

◁ the **shit out of** someone▷ ***See*** BEAT THE SHIT OUT OF someone or something

◁ **shit out of luck**▷ *adv phr fr early 1900s* Having no chance of success; already too late for what one wants; very ill-starred; =OUT OF LUCK: *I guess I'm shit out of luck on this one*

◁ **shit** one's **pants** (or **in** one's **pants**)▷ *v phr* (Variations: **drawers** may replace **pants**) To become frightened; be scared; panic: *Michael was shitting in his drawers*—Richard Merkin

◁ the **shits**▷ *n phr* Diarrhea; =the TROTS

◁ **shitstick**▷ *n* A contemptible, stupid person; =SHIT-ASS

◁ **shitstorm**▷ *n* A very confused situation or affair; a crazy jumble: *an artist trying to turn the shitstorm of his life into music*—Village Voice

◁ **shitsure**▷ *adv* Very certainly; definitely: *Shitsure it's gonna be a rough winter*—Village Voice

◁ **shitter**▷ *n* A toilet: *Know where the movie of the week went? Right in the old shitter*—Dan Jenkins

◁ **shit through a tin horn**▷ ***See*** LIKE SHIT THROUGH A TIN HORN

◁ **shitty**▷ **1** *adj* Mean; malicious; nasty: *accepted what he characterized as his "shitty offer"*—Inside Sports **2** *adj* Tedious and unpleasant; futile; wearing: *a real shitty day* **3** *adj* Unwell; ill: *Ralph, I feel shitty tonight*—Joseph Heller

◁ the **shitty** (or **shit**) **end of the stick**▷ ***See*** SHORT END OF THE STICK

◁ **shitwork**▷ **1** *n* Menial and tedious work; degrading routine work; =SCUT WORK: *the boredom, the shitwork, the perpetual deadlines*—Armistead Maupin **2** *modifier: something better than shitwork jobs*—Ms

shiv (Variations: **chev** or **chib** or **chiv** or **chive** or **sheive** or **shive**) **1** *n fr 1600s British* A knife, esp a claspknife or similar weapon: *She gets this anonymous letter sticking the shiv in my back*—John O'Hara/ *The big knife called the chib*—Louis Armstrong **2** *v fr 1700s British: being shivved by Johnny Mizzoo*—Damon Runyon [fr Romany *chiv* "blade," by way of British underworld slang]

shlamozzle ***See*** SHEMOZZLE

shlang or **shlong** ***See*** SCHLONG

shlemiel ***See*** SCHLEMIEL

shlemozzle ***See*** SCHLEMAZEL, SHEMOZZLE

shlep ***See*** SCHLEP

shleppy ***See*** SCHLEPPY

shlock ***See*** SCHLOCK

shlontz ***See*** SCHLONTZ

shloomp or **shlump** ***See*** SCHLOOMP

shlub or **shlubbo** ***See*** ZHLUB

shlunk *v* To cover in a viscid and repellent way: *He dumped the bucket of slime and let it shlunk all over me*—Time [apparently a quasi-Yiddish echoism]

shmaltz ***See*** SCHMALTZ

shmaltzy ***See*** SCHMALTZY

shmatte ***See*** SCHMATTE

shmear or **shmeer** ***See*** SCHMEAR[1], the WHOLE SCHMEAR

shmeck or **shmack** ***See*** SCHMECK, SMACK

shmee *n narcotics* Heroin [perhaps a shortening of *shmeck*]
shmegeggy ***See*** SCHMEGEGGY
shmendrick ***See*** SCHMENDRICK
shmo or **shmoe** ***See*** SCHMO
shmooz ***See*** SCHMOOZ
shmotte ***See*** SCHMATTE
shmuck ***See*** SCHMUCK
shnook ***See*** SCHNOOK
shnorrer ***See*** SCHNORRER
shnozz ***See*** SCHNOZZ
shoe **1** *n esp underworld* A plainclothes police officer; =GUMSHOE **2** *n underworld & espionage* A forged passport **3** *n car-racing* An automobile tire **4** *n gambling* A box from which cards are dealt in casinos: *The state requires dealing from a box called a "shoe"*—New York Times **5** *n 1950s bop musicians* A person who is well dressed, esp in the latest fashion **6** *n* =WHITE SHOE
See GUMSHOE, SADDLE SHOES
shoehorn *v* To insinuate by effort; force or fit in: *Cannon manages to shoehorn all that into its new ad campaign*—Wall Street Journal
shoestring catch ***n phr*** *baseball* A catch made near the ground, usu by an outfielder while running, stooping, and lunging
shommus ***See*** SHAMUS
shoo-in or **shoe-in** **1** *n horse-racing* A horse who wins a race by prearrangement **2** *n* A person, team, candidate, etc, who will or did win easily: *Harvey Fierstein and Kate Nelligan are shoo-ins*—Village Voice **3** ***modifier:*** *to be a shoe-in candidate* —Ms • This spelling may simply be a misspelling, but it is probably based on a misunderstanding of the origin of the term; it is a sort of folk etymology
shook up (Variations: **shook** or **all shook** or **all shook up**) **1** ***adj phr*** or ***adj*** *fr late 1800s but esp teenagers fr 1950s* In a state of high excitement or extreme disturbance; very much upset: *So Woody kept his voice down, but he was all shook up* —Saul Bellow **2** ***adj phr*** or ***adj*** *teenagers & rock and roll fr 1950s* Very happy; exhilarated; =HIGH: *I expected years in prison ... they let me go free, boy was I shook up*—New York Post
shoot **1** *v fr early 1900s* To photograph, esp to make a movie: *They were shooting over in Jersey* **2** *n* a photographic or movie-making session: *That one shoot took six hours* **3** ***interj*** *fr 1920s* An invitation to speak, explain, etc: *He asked if I wanted to know, and I said shoot* **4** ***interj*** *fr late 1800s* A mild exclamation of disgust, disappointment, distress, etc • A euphemism for **shit**: *Shoot, the guy forgot to pay me* **5** *n* =SHOOT THE BREEZE **6** *v narcotics* =SHOOT UP ◁**7**▷ *v* (also **shoot off**) To ejaculate semen; =COME **8** *v* To play certain games: *watch the flamingos, shoot a little golf, grow a little garden*—WT Tyler
See TURKEY-SHOOT
shoot someone **a line** ***v phr*** To flatter and cajole; overwhelm with glib plausibility
◁**shoot** (or **fire**) **blanks**▷ ***v phr*** To do the sex act without causing pregnancy
shoot one's **cookies** ***v phr*** (Variations: **breakfast** or **dinner** or **lunch** or **supper** may replace **cookies**; **toss** or **lose** may replace **shoot**) To vomit; =BARF, RALPH: *If I'm any judge of color, you're going to shoot your cookies*—Raymond Chandler/ *smelled like someone just tossed his cookies*—JD Salinger
shoot someone **down** (or **down in flames**) ***v phr*** ***esp students*** To defeat; thwart or ruin somone's efforts; =BLOW someone OUT OF THE WATER: *Woody, who had been flying along, level and smooth, was shot down in flames*—Saul Bellow
shoot-'em-up **1** *n* A movie or TV program with much gunplay and violence: *gambled for cigarettes, slurped Tang or watched shoot-'em-ups on TV*—New York Times **2** ***modifier:*** *an exaggerated reaction to the male-oriented "shoot-'em-up games"* —Washington Post
shooter ***See*** BEAVER-SHOOTER, HIP SHOOTER, SIX-SHOOTER, SQUARE SHOOTER
shoot from the hip ***v phr*** To act or respond impulsively and aggressively; be recklessly impetuous
shooting gallery *narcotics* **1** ***n phr*** A place where a narcotics user can get a dose or injection **2** ***n phr*** A party or gathering where narcotics users take injections: *in a fellow musician's hotel room during a "shooting gallery" (dope party)*—New York Daily News

shooting iron *n phr fr late 1700s* A pistol

shooting match *See* the WHOLE SHOOTING MATCH

shooting war *n phr* =HOT WAR

shoot oneself **in the foot** *v phr* To wound or injure oneself by ineptness; attack wildly and hurt oneself: *Ted Turner has taken to shooting himself in the foot*—Village Voice

◁ **shoot** one's **load**▷ *v phr* To ejaculate semen; have an orgasm; =COME

shoot off one's **mouth** *v phr* (Variations: **bazoo** or **face** or **gab** or **yap** may replace **mouth**) *fr middle 1800s* To talk irresponsibly and inappropriately, esp to bluster and brag; =TALK BIG: *You come busting in here and shoot off your bazoo at me*—J Evans

shoot-out **1** *n* (also **shoot-up**) *fr early 1900s* A gunfight: *the justly famous shoot-out between the Earps and the Clantons*—New York Times/ *The shoot-up may have been a skirmish between Mafia factions*—New York Times **2** *n* Any fight or violent confrontation; a hotly contested game or issue: *another sociological shoot-out, with men as the heroes this time*—New Yorker **3** *n soccer* A form of tie-breaker used in the North American Soccer League, in which five players from each team have five seconds each to attempt goals one-on-one against the goalkeeper

shoot the breeze (or **the fat**) *v phr* To chat amiably and casually; =CHEW THE FAT: *making transatlantic calls just to shoot the breeze*—Village Voice/ *sit down on a bench and shoot the fat*—Village Voice

◁ **shoot the bull** (or **crap** or **shit**)▷ **1** *v phr* To lie and exaggerate; talk grandly but emptily; =BULLSHIT: *And they weren't just shooting the crap*—JD Salinger **2** *v phr* To chat amiably; =SHOOT THE BREEZE: *stand on a corner, shoot the bull*—Langston Hughes

shoot the lights out *v phr esp sports* To excel; perform superbly: *These kids will jump right up and shoot the lights out on you*—Sports Illustrated [perhaps fr the accuracy of marksmanship implied if one is to hit a small target like a *lightbulb*; certainly influenced by the notion of knocking the *daylights*, or earlier the *liver and lights*, "liver and lungs, innards," out of someone or something]

shoot the works *v phr* To act, give, spend, etc, without limit; =GO FOR BROKE: *In whatever pertains to comfort, shoot the works*—James M Cain [fr the *shooting* of dice in craps, with its extended sense of betting or gambling all one has]

shoot up *v phr narcotics* To take an injection of narcotics; =JAB A VEIN, MAINLINE

shoot-up *n narcotics* A narcotics injection

See SHOOT-OUT

shoot one's **wad** *fr 1920s* **1** *v phr* To commit or bet everything one has; =GO FOR BROKE, SHOOT THE WORKS **2** *v phr* To say everything one can on a subject; have one's say **3** *v phr* To exhaust one's resources; be unable to persist ◁**4**▷ *v phr* =SHOOT one's LOAD

shop *See* BUCKET SHOP, CHOP SHOP, HEAD SHOP, HOCKSHOP, SCHLOCK SHOP, SMOKE SHOP

-shop *combining word* Place where the indicated thing is carried on, used, etc; =FACTORY: *brain shop/ love-shop/ talk shop*

shopping-bag lady *See* BAG LADY

shopping list *See* LAUNDRY LIST

short **1** *n 1920s prison & underworld* A prisoner near the end of his term **2** *n hot rodders & black fr 1920s underworld* A car; =WHEELS **3** *v narcotics* To inhale a narcotic in crystal or powder form; =SNORT [origin of automobile sense unknown; perhaps a back formation fr *hot short* with its reference to electrically *shorting* the ignition to bypass the key, an operation later called *hot-wiring*]

See HOT SHORT

short dog *n phr* A derelict's bottle of wine or liquor: *staggering down Broadway sucking on a short dog*—Joseph Wambaugh

◁ **short** (or **shitty** or **shit**) **end of the stick**▷ *n phr fr late 1930s* The worst of a transaction, encounter, etc; very bad treatment; =the SHAFT: *Pastorini got the shit end of the stick, as usual*—Rolling Stone

short eyes *n phr prison* A sexual molester of children: *end up in the punk tank with the free-world queers and the short eyes*—Ezra Hannon

short fuse *See* HAVE A SHORT FUSE

short hairs *See* HAVE someone BY THE SHORT HAIRS

a **short one** *n phr* A single shot of whiskey, often drunk quickly; a small drink

the **shorts** *n phr* Lack of money; a shortage of funds: *I told him I had the shorts*—Lionel Stander

short-sheet *v* To play a nasty trick; maltreat: *headed for big things until the Reagan crowd short-sheeted you* —WT Tyler [fr a student and barracks practical joke in which a *bedsheet* is folded in half and made to appear as an upper and lower sheet, so that when the victim gets into bed the stretching legs and toes are painfully arrested]

shortstop **1** *v* To take food being passed to someone else at table **2** *n: I avoided that table where the shortstop always sat* **3** *v salespersons* To wait on another salesperson's customer

shot **1** *n* A drink of straight liquor **2** *n esp Southern & Western lunch counter* A glass or other serving of Coca-Cola (a trade name) **3** *n narcotics fr late 1920s* An injection of narcotics; =FIX ◁**4**▷ *n* An ejaculation of semen; a male orgasm **5** *n* An atomic explosion, a rocket or missile launching, or some other complex sort of military and technological blasting **6** *n* =BIG SHOT **7** *n fr 1960s* A person's particular preference, style, etc; =BAG, THING: *That's our shot. That's who we are*—Rolling Stone **8** *n* A try; an attempt, esp at something rather difficult: *He didn't make it, but he gave it a hell of a shot* **9** *adj fr middle 1800s* Drunk **10** *adj fr late 1920s* Worn out or out of repair: *This old machine is shot* **11** *adj fr 1930s* Exhausted; ill; in bad shape: *Say, am I shot?*—James T Farrell [the drinking senses are shortenings of an early-19th-century expression *shot in the neck* meaning both "a drink" and "drunk"]

See BEAVER SHOT, CALL THE SHOTS, CHEAP SHOT, DROP CASE, GIVE something A SHOT, GIVE something one's BEST SHOT, HALF-SHOT, HAVE A CRACK AT something, HOT SHOT, LONG SHOT, MUG SHOT, NOT BY A LONG SHOT, ONE-SHOT, UNGODLY SHOT

shot glass *n phr* =JIGGER

shotgun **1** *n football* An offensive formation in which the quarterback lines up well behind instead of immediately behind the center **2** *adj* Very diffuse and general; indiscriminate: *I hate it when the administrators make shotgun accusations*

See RIDE SHOTGUN, SIT SHOTGUN

shotgun wedding (or **marriage**) *n phr fr 1920s* A wedding under duress, esp when the bride is pregnant; a forced marriage; =MILITARY WEDDING

a **shot in the arm** *n phr fr 1900s* Something that stimulates and enlivens; an invigorating influence or event: *has given his campaign for the Democratic presidential nomination a shot in the arm*—Washington Post

◁a **shot in the ass**▷ **1** *n phr* =a SHOT IN THE ARM **2** *n phr* =a KICK IN THE ASS

shoulder *See* COLD SHOULDER, STRAIGHT FROM THE SHOULDER

shove *See* KNOW WHAT one CAN DO WITH something, PUSH COMES TO SHOVE, TELL someone WHAT TO DO WITH something

shove it *See* STICK IT

◁**shovel shit** (or **the shit**)▷ *v phr fr 1930s* To lie and exaggerate; =BULLSHIT, SHOOT THE BULL: *no varsity letters for shoveling shit*—John Irving

shove off **1** *v phr fr late 1800s* To leave; depart; =SCRAM: *when we shoved off*—James M Cain **2** *v phr underworld* To kill; murder: *People got shoved off for their money*—Agatha Christie [fr the boating term]

shover *See* PENCIL-PUSHER

show *v fr early 1800s* To arrive; appear: *You suppose he'll show?* —WR Burnett

See CATTLE SHOW, GRIND SHOW, LET'S GET THE SHOW ON THE ROAD, NO-SHOW, ONE-MAN SHOW, PEEP SHOW

show a leg *v phr* =SHAKE A LEG

show-and-tell *n* An elaborate display, usu for selling or other persuasion; =DOG AND PONY ACT: *No one seems to have been impressed by the show-and-tell*—New Yorker [fr the name of an elementary-school teaching technique where pupils exhibit and explain things]

show biz *n phr* The entertainment industry; show business

showboat **1** *v* To behave in a showy, flamboyant way; =GRAND-

STAND, HOT DOG: *I don't believe in showboating or playing the martyr*—Arizona Republic **2** *n* (also **showboater**): *Jesse is a showboater, privately*—Amsterdam News **3** *v* =PULL RANK

show business *See* THAT'S SHOW BUSINESS

showcase **1** *n theater* A theater, performance, etc, where a major aim is to exhibit relatively unknown performers and work **2** *v* To feature or exhibit a relatively unknown player, performer, work, etc: *You don't showcase a guy by sending him smack into the middle of the line*—Sports Illustrated

showdown **1** *n poker* A hand where the cards are dealt face up and the best hand wins at once **2** *n fr late 1800s* A confrontation, esp a last one **3** *modifier: the opening game of the showdown Yankee-Red Sox series*—Associated Press

shower *See* GOLDEN SHOWER, SEND someone TO THE SHOWERS

show off *v phr* To behave in an ostentatiously skilled and assured way in order to impress others; =GRANDSTAND, HOT DOG: *He ran a quick eight miles, just showing off*

show-off *n* A person who habitually shows off; =HOT DOG, SHOWBOAT

show someone **the door** *v phr* To dismiss summarily; eject

show someone or something **up** *v phr* To reveal; expose: *That slip showed him up for a fraud*

shpos (SHPAHS) *n hospital* An obnoxious patient [fr *subhuman piece of shit*]

shpritz *n* A bit or touch; a dose: *each a free-associational shpritz of surreal hi-de-ho*—Village Voice [fr Yiddish, literally, "a squirt"]

shrimp *n* A very short or small person; =PEANUT

shrink *n fr 1960s* A psychiatrist, psychoanalyst, or other psychotherapist; =HEADSHRINKER
See HEADSHRINKER

shtarker or **schtarker** or **starker** (SHTAHR kə, -kər or STAHR kər) *n* A strong person; =TOUGH GUY: *I went from dealing with shtarkers to intellectual bullies*—Playboy [fr Yiddish]

shtick or **schtick** or **shtik** *fr show business* **1** *n* A small theatrical role or part of a role; a piece of theatrical "business"; =BIT: *It turned out to be a nice little "shtick"*—New York Post **2** *n* A characteristic trait of performance or behavior; a typical personal feature: *To each his own schtick. Chapman performs his with gusto*—Changes **3** *n* A clever device; =GADGET, GIMMICK: *The "shtick" is that the taped remarks of a number of political figures are tacked onto questions dreamed up by writers*—Playboy [fr Yiddish, literally, "piece, bit"]

shtoonk or **shtunk** *See* SCHTOONK

◁ **shtup** or **schtup** or **stup** ▷ (SHTŏŏP) **1** *v* To do the sex act with or to; =FUCK: *Why of course he was shtupping her*—Philip Roth **2** *modifier: take a big video plunge, coming closer than any outfit yet to breaking the shtup barrier*—Village Voice **3** *n* A person regarded merely as a sex partner; =ASS **4** *n* The sex act; copulation [fr Yiddish, literally, "push, shove"]

shuck **1** *v fr middle 1800s* To undress; strip oneself **2** *v* (also **shuck and jive**) *esp black* To joke; tease; =FOOL AROUND: *22 percent of each trash-truck crew's workday is spent shucking and jiving and shadowboxing*—Philadelphia/ *We ain't got no time for shuckin'*—Joseph Wambaugh **3** *v* (also **shuck and jive**) *black & student fr black* To swindle; cheat; deceive; esp to bluff verbally and counterfeit total sincerity **4** *v cool musicians fr black* To improvise chords, esp to a piece of music one does not know; =FAKE IT, VAMP **5** *n esp black* A theft or fraud; =RIP OFF: *Linear thinking was a total shuck*—Cyra McFadden **6** *v black* To lie; exaggerate; =BULLSHIT [black senses probably fr the fact that black slaves sang and shouted gleefully during *corn-shucking* season, and this behavior, along with lying and teasing, became a part of the protective and evasive behavior normally adopted towards white people in "traditional" race relations; the sense of "swindle" is perhaps related to the mid-19th-century term *to be shucked out* "be defeated, be denied victory," which suggests that the notion of stripping someone as an ear of corn is stripped may be basic in the semantics]

shucks *See* AW SHUCKS

shuffle **1** *v* *street gang* To have a gang fight; =RUMBLE **2** *v* *black* To behave in the stereotypical obsequious way of a black person in "traditional" race relations; =TOM: *Are we just going to shuffle and jive?*—Ebony *See* DOUBLE SHUFFLE

shuffler *See* PAPER-PUSHER

shunt *n car-racing* An accident; a collision

shure or **shurr** *See* FOR SURE

shush *v* To tell someone to be quiet and stop talking • Very often a command: *He kept shushing his wife/ "Shush!" he shouted, uselessly, to the large noisy hound*

shut *See* EYE-SHUT

shut-eye *n fr early 1900s* Sleep; =some ZS: *I've got to get some shut-eye before the exam*

shut one's **face** *v phr fr early 1900s* To stop talking; =SHUT UP • Often an irritated command

shutout *n sports* A game in which one side is held scoreless

shut out *v phr sports fr late 1800s* To hold an opponent scoreless; =BLANK, SKUNK: *The Lakers shut them out 95 zip*

shutterbug *n* A photographer, esp an enthusiastic amateur: *two of the more prominent Senate-shutterbugs*—Washington Post

shut one's **trap** *v phr fr 1600s* =SHUT one's FACE

shut up *v phr* To be quiet; stop talking • Very often a stern or angry command

◁**shvantz**▷ (SHVAHNTS) *n* (Variations: **schvantz** or **schvanz** or **schwantz** or **schwanz** or **schvontz** or **shvonce** or **shvuntz**) The penis; =SCHLONG [fr Yiddish, literally, "tail"; hence semantically analogous with *penis*, literally, "tail"]
See STEP ON IT

◀**shvartze** or **shvartzer**▶ *See* SCHVARTZE

shylock or **Shylock** **1** *n* A usurer; =LOAN SHARK: *In Toronto and Hamilton both, loan sharks ("shylocks") appeared in the gambling clubs*—Maclean's **2** *v: the shylocking that went with it as hot dogs go with baseball*—Mario Puzo [fr the character in Shakespeare's *The Merchant of Venice*]

shy of a load *See* THREE BRICKS SHY OF A LOAD

shyster **1** *n fr middle 1800s* A dishonest and contemptible lawyer or politician: *You lousy little shyster bastard*—Ira Wolfert **2** *n* Any lawyer [origin unknown and hotly disputed; perhaps fr the name of a Mr Sheuster, a New York City lawyer of the early 1800s; perhaps fr German *Scheisse* "shit" or *Scheisser* "shitter" by way of anglicized forms *shice* and *shicer* attested fr the mid-19th century; perhaps because prisoners were said and advised to *fight shy of* "avoid," lawyers who frequented jails, esp the Tombs in New York City; perhaps fr earlier sense of *shy* "disreputable, not quite honest"]

sick **1** *adj* (also **sicko** or **sicksicksick**) *fr 1950s* Mentally twisted; psychopathic, esp in a sadistic vein: *some sick vandal/ a rapist or a sicko father who abuses his teenage daughters*—Philadelphia Journal **2** *adj* (also **sicko** or **sicksicksick**) *fr 1950s* Gruesome; morbid; mentally and spiritually unhealthy: *a sick sense of humor/ Label it S for Sicko*—Philadelphia/ *He is even better at establishing a sicksicksick atmosphere*—New York Times **3** *adj narcotics* Needing a dose of narcotics **4** *n narcotics* The craving and misery of an addict in need of a narcotic dose

sickie or **sicky** *n* A mentally unhealthy person; a psychopath: *Only sickies get involved with married women*—New York

sick joke *n phr fr 1950s* A joke with a grimly morbid tone or point; a nasty sort of jape

side **1** *n* *theater fr 1920s* A line of dialogue for one performer; also, a sheet containing the lines and cues for one performer **2** *n fr black fr 1930s* A phonograph record **3** *n* The music on one side of a phonograph record, one band of a long-playing record, one segment of a cassette or other tape, etc • Usu used in the plural: *He had never heard these classic sides until recently*—San Francisco

See ON THE SIDE, STATESIDE, TOPSIDE, the WRONG SIDE OF THE TRACKS

sidebar **1** *n news media* A news or feature story serving as a supplement or background to a main story: *Sidebar after sidebar flashed in front of our eyes*—New York Times **2** *adj* Auxiliary; supplementary: *Now he has a side-bar job, hustling beer or sports equipment*—Robert Ruark [perhaps fr the late 19th century use of *sidebar buggy* or *wagon* for a vehicle having longitudinal reinforcements along the *sides*; perhaps fr *side-bar* "an auxiliary toll-gate on a road leading into a main toll-road"]

sidekick *n fr early 1900s* A close friend, partner, associate, etc: *Wayne and his side-kick James Arness*—New York Herald-Tribune [fr earlier *sidekicker*, perhaps fr the cardplaying sense of *kicker* as a reserve of dependable strength, perhaps fr the notion that a companion can *kick* to the *side* while the principal kicks to the front in fighting]

the **side of a barn** *See* someone CAN'T HIT THE SIDE OF A BARN

side of one's **face** *See* LAUGH ON THE OTHER SIDE OF one's FACE

sides of the street *See* WORK BOTH SIDES OF THE STREET

sidewalks *See* POUND THE PAVEMENT

sidewalk superintendent **1** *n phr* A person who watches excavation or other construction work, usu through a hole in the surrounding fence **2** *n phr* Any amateur critic or observer

sidewinder **1** *n* A dangerous and pugnacious man **2** *n underworld* A gangster's bodyguard; =GORILLA: *Eddy Prue, Morny's sidewinder* [fr the dangerous *sidewinder* rattlesnake, so called fr its lateral locomotion, and presumed to be treacherous]

-sie *See* -IE

sieve *n* A leaky boat or ship
See HAVE A MIND LIKE A SIEVE

◁ **siff** or **the siff**▷ *See* SYPH

sight gag *n phr* A joke or comic turn that depends entirely on what is seen

sign *See* the HIGH SIGN, the INDIAN SIGN

signify *black* **1** *v* To boast; =SHOW OFF **2** *v* To insult and derogate someone, esp in a formal and gamelike way; =PLAY THE DOZENS: *signifying back and forth between themselves*—Donald Goines

sign off on something *v phr* To agree to or approve of a proposal, a legislative bill, etc, esp without actual formal endorsement: *When enough Senators had signed off on the treaty, the President announced it*

sign up *v phr* To join; enroll; enlist: *They signed up for a course in hands-on interpersonal relations*

Silicon Valley *n phr* The Santa Clara Valley south of San Francisco in California: *smack in the middle of Silicon Valley*—San Francisco [fr the concentration of manufacturers of *silicon* chips for computers, watches, etc in the Santa Clara *Valley*]

silk *See* HIT THE SILK

silk-stocking *adj fr late 1700s* Wealthy; affluent: *a silk-stocking neighborhood*

silly season *n phr fr middle 1800s British* Any period when people do silly things, esp when these are reported in the news media [fr a term designating the months of August and September, when Parliament was not sitting and valid and useful news was scarce, and the newspapers resorted to reporting frivol and trivialities]

simmer down *v phr* To become calm and quiet, esp after anger; =COOL IT • Often a command or a bit of advice

simoleon (sih MOH lee ən) *n fr late 1800s* A dollar [origin unknown; perhaps fr an earlier slang term *Simon* "dollar," influenced by the French *napoleon* "twenty-franc coin"]

Simon Legree *n phr* A cruel, unsympathetic person, esp a tyrannical superior; a slave-driver [fr the character in *Uncle Tom's Cabin*, somewhat unfairly]

simp *n fr early 1900s* A simpleton; a stupid person; =KLUTZ: *Simps with mustaches are a menace to society*—Playboy

simpatico *adj* Nice; pleasant; sympathetic and congenial [fr Italian or Spanish]

simple *See* STIR-CRAZY

sincere *adj* Intended to make a good and sober impression; overtly conformistic; =SERIOUS: *packaged in a sincere apothecary-type bottle*—New York Times

sing *v underworld* To inform; incriminate oneself and others; =SQUEAL: *Vice Prisoners Ready To Sing*—New York Daily News [perhaps related to the expression *a little bird told me*]

See the OPERA'S NEVER OVER TILL THE FAT LADY SINGS

singer *n underworld* =CANARY, STOOL PIGEON

single *n* An unmarried person: *The place tried to attract singles*

See SWINGING SINGLE

singles *modifier* For unmarried persons: *a singles bar/ a singles party*

sing out **1** *v phr* To speak up; make oneself known and heard; =PIPE UP: *If anybody doesn't like it, just sing out* **2** *v phr fr early 1800s* To inform; =SQUEAL: *and get him to sing out*—J Roeburt

sinker[1] *n fr late 1800s* A biscuit or doughnut [fr the lead weight used by fishermen to *sink* line and bait, probably an ironic reference to the weight of the biscuit or doughnut]

sinker[2] *baseball* **1** *n* A pitch that dips downward as it nears home plate **2** *n* A line drive or other batted ball that sinks suddenly toward the ground

sis **1** *n* A sister: *That's his sis with him* **2** *n* Woman; girl • Used in direct address: *What's up, sis?* **3** *n late 1800s* A weak, effeminate boy; =SISSY **4** *n cool talk* A young woman or girl; =CHICK [a shortening of *sister*]

sissified *adj* Timorous; weak and effeminate; =CHICKENHEARTED

sissy *fr late 1800s* **1** *n* A timorous, weak, and effeminate male; =DAISY, PANSY **2** *adj: his sissy ways/ wearing sissy clothes* **3** *n* A male homosexual; =PANSY [fr *sis* fr *sister*]

sissy bar *n phr* A high metal projection at the back of a bicycle to prevent it from rolling over backwards [fr the fact that someone adopting such a device is timorous]

sissy pants *n phr* =SISSY

sister **1** *n* Woman; girl • Used in direct address: *Hey, sister, you'd better leave* **2** *n black* A fellow black woman **3** *n* A fellow feminist

See JOHN WAYNE'S SISTER, WEAK SISTER

sister act *n phr homosexuals* Sexual relations between a homosexual man and a heterosexual woman

sit *v* To take care of; attend and watch over: *Who'll sit your house while you're gone?*

See BABY-SIT, HOUSE-SIT

sitcom *n* A situation comedy series on television: *the new family of sitcoms*—Newsweek

sit in **1** *v phr musicians* To join and play with other musicians, esp on one occasion or temporarily: *had the very good fortune of sitting in with him*—Metronome **2** *v phr fr 1960s* To occupy a place as a participant in a sit-in

sit-in *n fr 1960s* An illegal occupation of a place, in order to make a political or philosophical statement • The term was popularized during the movement for black civil rights and has many offspring: **be-in**, **love-in**, **puke-in**, etc

sit in the catbird seat *v phr* To be in the position of advantage; =be SITTING PRETTY: *willing to give us a hundred seventy million in preferred notes. We're sitting in the catbird seat*—Art Buchwald [fr a term used by a poker opponent of the superb sportscaster Red Barber to explain his situation with an ace in the hole at stud poker; Mr Barber adopted the term, which was afterwards used by James Thurber in a story called "The Catbird Seat" with attribution to Red Barber; probably a Southern dialect term based on a folk notion of the cleverness and masterfulness of *catbirds* and/or their high and superior perch]

sit on one's **ass** *v phr* To remain inactive; esp, to fail to cope or deal with a responsibility: *The congressman sat on his ass while the neighborhood hospital deteriorated*

sit on one's **hands** **1** *v phr* To refrain from applauding; be an unresponsive or adverse audience: *They sat on their hands until he started waving the flag* **2** *v phr* To do nothing; be passive; =SIT ON one's ASS: *Even when the thing fell down they just sat on their hands*

sit shotgun *v phr* To sit in the passenger seat of a car; =RIDE SHOTGUN: *I sat shotgun in my pop's flower truck*—Philadelphia

sit still for something *v phr* To accept or condone; tolerate something provocative: *The nation will simply not sit still for... the years of slow growth*—Time

◁ **sit there with** one's **finger** (or **thumb**) **up** one's **ass**▷ *v phr* To be passive and unresponsive; fail to cope; be useless: *just sitting around every day with my thumb up my ass* —Village Voice

sit tight **1** *v phr* To keep one's present position, stance, convictions, etc; refuse to be moved; =STAND PAT **2** *v phr* To wait patiently: *Just sit tight, she'll be here in a minute*

sitting duck *n phr* An easy target; a totally defenseless person

be **sitting pretty** *v phr fr early 1900s* To be in a superior and very pleasant position: *He's just the same genial idiot whether he is out of luck or sitting pretty*—WW Rose

situash (sit yoo AYSH) *n* Situation

situation *See* ON TOP OF

six *See* DEEP SIX, EIGHTY-SIX, FIFTY-SIX

six bits *n phr fr middle 1800s* Seventy-five cents

six-by *n truckers* A truck, esp a large one [fr *six-by-six*, the designation of a truck with six wheels and a six-speed transmission]

six-hundred-pound gorilla *n phr* (also **eight-hundred-pound gorilla** or **nine-hundred-pound gorilla**) A powerful force; a virtually irresistible influence: *She is a 600-pound gorilla ....She can intimidate anybody* —Time/ *likens Spielberg to an "800-pound gorilla," which can be defined as a high-priced Hollywood species that makes its own decisions*—Los Angeles Times [fr a joke in which the question "Where does a *six-hundred-pound gorilla* sleep?" is answered "Anywhere it wants"]

six-pack *See* JOE SIX-PACK

six-shooter or **six-gun** **1** *n fr middle 1800s cowboys* A revolver with a cylinder holding six cartridges **2** *n* Any revolver

sixty *See* LIKE SIXTY

◁ **sixty-nine** or **69**▷ *n* Simultaneous oral sex between two persons, whose reciprocally inverse positions suggest the numeral 69

six ways to Sunday *See* FORTY WAYS TO SUNDAY

size *See* KING-SIZE

size up *v phr fr middle 1800s* To estimate or assess: *How do you size up his chances?*

sizzling *adj* Hot, in any sense: *sell some of the sizzling green at a discount*—Abel Green

ska (SKAH) *n* An early form of reggae music: *various musical trends, punk, New Wave, power-pop, ska* —Aquarian [origin unknown]

skag or **scag** **1** *n armed forces fr early 1900s* A cigarette or cigarette butt **2** *n 1960s teenagers fr black* A despicable person or thing, =JERK **3** *adj: a very skaggy guy* **4** *n black fr 1920s* An unattractive woman; =BAT, SKANK **5** *n narcotics* Cheap, low-quality heroin

skank **1** *n black* An unattractive woman; a malodorous woman; =SKAG **2** *n* A prostitute; =HOOKER: *How long would it take for them to find them f— skanks [the hookers] again?*—New York Times **3** *v* To move rhythmically in place like a rock and roll performer: *They move in sympathetic response to the music, skankin' from side to side* —Village Voice **4** *n: then back to that gentle skank*—Village Voice

skanky *adj teenagers fr black* Nasty; repellent; =GROTTY, SCUZZY: *The girls were somewhat skanky, with lank hair and rotten posture*—Richard Price

sked *See* ON SKED

skedaddle *v fr middle 1800s* To run away; flee; fly; depart hastily [origin unknown; perhaps fr an attested Scots dialect sense, "spill," which could suggest "scatter, disperse"]

skeeter *n fr middle 1800s* A mosquito

ski (or **snow**) **bunny** *n phr* A young woman who frequents skiing resorts and skiers, and who may or may not ski herself

skid lid *n phr motorcyclists* A motorcyclist's helmet: *suffered severe brain damage while wearing one of the company's skid lids*—Easyriders

skidoo or **skiddoo** *v* To depart hastily; =SCRAM • Often a command or a bit of advice: *Skidoo, skidoo, and quit me*—H McHugh [coined in 1906 by Billy Van, a musical comedy star, fr *skedaddle*]

skidoodle *v* =SKEDADDLE

skid road or **skidroad** **1** *n phr* or *n fr lumberjacks fr late 1800s* A forest track over which logs are dragged **2** *n phr* or *n* (also **Skid Road** or **Skidroad**) *fr lumberjacks, hoboes & underworld* A street or district of cheap shops and resorts; a relatively disreputable district: *I headed towards the Skidroad and its cheap* *eating joints*—Atlantic Monthly/ *no skid road for the professor* —Westworld **3** ***modifier:*** *a tightwad with latent skid-road tendencies*—Washington Post [fr the log-paved path on which the Seattle lumberman Henry Yesler skidded logs to his sawmill]

skid row or **Skid Row** *n fr 1920s* A street or district frequented by derelicts, hoboes, drifters, etc, such as the Bowery in New York City [fr *skid road*]

the **skids** ***See*** GREASE THE SKIDS, HIT THE SKIDS, ON THE SKIDS, PUT THE SKIDS UNDER someone or something

skillion or **scillion** ***n*** An indefinite very large number: *I have a scillion things to say*—Philadelphia Bulletin

See JILLION

skim 1 ***n*** *gambling* Income not reported for tax purposes, esp from the gross earnings of a gambling casino or other such enterprise; =BLACK MONEY: *"skim," untaxed gambling profits*—New York Times **2** ***v:*** *"appropriate, conceal, and skim" part of the winnings*—New York Times

skin 1 ***n*** *esp black* The hand as used in handshaking or hand-slapping as a salutation • Nearly always in the expression **some skin**: *My man!... Gimme some skin!*—Malcolm X **2** ***n*** *fr earlier armed forces and rural* An inferior racehorse: *They take the first bunch of skins out to gallop* —Ernest Hemingway **3** ***n*** *fr 1920s fr early 1800s British* A pocketbook, wallet, etc **4** ***n*** One dollar; a dollar bill: *One laid out 190 skins*—New Yorker ◁**5**▷ ***n*** A condom; =RUBBER **6** ***modifier*** Featuring nudity; indecently exposing; =GIRLIE: *a skin flick/ skin mag* **7** ***n*** *fr jazz musicians* A drum **8** ***n*** Life and health: *If he doesn't like you your skin isn't worth shit* **9** ***v*** To defeat decisively; trounce; =SKUNK: *They skinned the Wolverines 20 zip* **10** ***v*** To cheat or swindle; victimize: *You got skinned in that deal*—C Kuhn **11** ***v*** To slip through; squeeze hurriedly out: *and then skin out the window* —Harold Robbins

See FROGSKIN, GET UNDER someone's SKIN, GIVE SOME SKIN, NO SKIN OFF MY ASS, PIGSKIN, PRESS THE FLESH, SHEEPSKIN

skin (or **flesh**) **flick** ***n phr*** A movie featuring nudity and more or less patent sexual activity; =BLUE MOVIE

◁ **skin flute**▷ ***n phr*** The penis

See PLAY THE SKIN FLUTE

a **skinful** ***n phr*** One's intoxicating fill of liquor; =a SNOOT FULL: *Dey bot' got a skinful*—Eugene O'Neill

skin game ***n phr*** *fr late 1800s* A confidence game; =SCAM

skinhead 1 ***n*** A bald person or person with a shaved head **2** ***n*** *Marine Corps* A Marine recruit

skinner ***See*** HACK-SKINNER

skinny ***n phr*** Information; facts: *claims to be the true, accurate, inside skinny on the David Begelman scandal*—GQ [probably fr *skinny* "naked, bare" as in *skinny dipping*]

the **skinny** ***n phr*** *fr WW2 armed forces* The truth; =the LOWDOWN, the SCOOP: *Are you giving me the straight skinny?*—Rex Burn/ *Here's the skinny: the show's an old-fashioned formula musical*—Village Voice [origin unknown; perhaps an alteration of *the naked truth*]

See the STRAIGHT SKINNY

skinny-dip ***v phr*** To swim naked: *Andrew went skinny-dipping in rocky pools*—Newsweek

skinny something **down** ***v phr*** To reduce something, esp to a minimum: *We were told to skinny the budget down still more*

skin pop ***v phr*** *narcotics* To inject narcotics into the skin or muscles, rather than into the circulatory system: *I'll have to skin pop*—H Braddy

skins 1 ***n*** *jazz musicians* A set of drums **2** ***n*** *fr hot rodders & truckers* Automotive tires: *Protect your present skins*—Playboy

skin-search or **body-shake** *police* **1** ***n*** A thorough scrutiny of a naked person, esp for hypodermic needle marks, concealed narcotics, etc **2** ***v:*** *They skin-searched both couples*

skip 1 ***v*** *esp students* To fail to attend; absent oneself; =SHINE: *if I let you skip school this afternoon*—JD Salinger **2** ***v*** (also **skip out**) *fr middle 1800s* To depart hastily, escape, abscond, esp to avoid paying a bill, being arrested, etc: *They skipped out of the motel at 2 AM* **3** ***n*** A person who absconds, esp to avoid paying a bill: *The skip took off ... with a girl friend*—John D McDonald **4** *n esp armed forces* =SKIPPER

skipper **1** *n nautical* The captain of a ship or boat **2** *n Army* Any commanding officer

skirt *n fr late 1800s* A woman, esp a young woman; =BROAD, CHICK • Regarded by some women as offensive: *a real skirt*—Eugene O'Neill

skirt-chaser *n* A ladies' man; =LOVER-BOY

skiv *n* =SHIV

skivvy *fr Navy* **1** *n* (also **skivvy shirt**) A man's undershirt, esp a T-shirt: *pants, sneakers, some skivvy shirts*—Harper's **2** *n* A pair of mens' underpants, esp of the boxer type

skosh or **scosh** (SKOHSH) *n fr Korean War armed forces* A little bit; =SMIDGEN: *You need a skosh more room here for your desk* [fr Japanese *sukoshi*]

skull *See* GO OUT OF one's SKULL, OUT OF one's HEAD

skullduggery or **skulduggery** *n fr middle 1800s* Shady behavior; =DIRTY WORK, HANKY-PANKY [a US alteration of Scots *sculduddery* "bawdry, obscenity," which is attested from the early 18th century]

skull session *n phr* An intensive learning and teaching period, esp a briefing session: *two separate "skull sessions" with six members of the US negotiating team*—Newsweek

skunk *v fr middle 1800s* To defeat utterly, esp to hold the opponent scoreless in sports; trounce; =CLOBBER: *They're saying I'm going to get skunked in the black community*—Time [perhaps fr the definitive way in which a spraying *skunk* routs all present]

See DRUNK AS A SKUNK

sky *v sports* To hit or kick or throw a ball very high: *Winfield skied one into the bleachers* *See* PIE IN THE SKY

skycap *n* A porter at an air terminal [modeled on *red cap* "a railroad terminal porter"]

skyjack **1** *v* To take control of an aircraft illegally, usu by claiming to have a weapon or a bomb; commit air piracy **2** *n: the week's third skyjack to Cuba*

sky-pilot *n fr late 1800s nautical* A member of the clergy

skyscraper *n baseball* A very high fly ball

skywest *See* KNOCK someone or something GALLEY WEST

slab **1** *n baseball* Home plate **2** *n truckers* A highway

slag *v* To denigrate; =BAD-MOUTH, PUT DOWN: *Everybody was getting slagged*—Rolling Stone [origin unknown; perhaps fr German *schlagen* "beat, whip"]

slag someone **off** *v phr apparently fr rock & roll* To denigrate severely; =SLAG: *This time I can't give it to you, can't totally slag you off*—Village Voice

slam **1** *n fr late 1800s* An uncomplimentary comment; a jibe; =KNOCK: *took a slam at the male stars who dress like "ranch hands"*—Associated Press **2** *v: Stop slamming the place and maybe they'll like you better* **3** *v* (also **slam-dance**) To do a physically colliding and athletic sort of rock-and-roll dancing, esp in the vein of punk rock: *The music is hardcore, the dance is slamming*—Village Voice

See GRAND SLAM

the **slam** *n phr* =the SLAMMER

slam-bang **1** *n prizefight fr 1920s* A wild and vicious fight **2** *adv* Violently: *They went at it slam-bang* **3** *adj* Raucous, violent, vigorous, etc: *in climaxes as slam-bang as a four-horse stretch drive*—Heywood Hale Broun

See SLAP

slam dunk *v phr basketball* To score a field goal by leaping up and thrusting the ball violently down through the hoop: *the first to slam-dunk a football over the crossbar after a touchdown*—Philadelphia Journal

slammer *n basketball* =SLAM DUNK

See GRAND SLAMMER

the **slammer** **1** *n phr fr 1930s jive talk* A door: *twister to the slammer*—Variety **2** *n phr* (also the **slams**) *fr black* A jail, prison, etc: *Drunk drivers go to the slammer in this town*

slang *n fr middle 1700s British* A style or register of language consisting of terms that can be substituted for standard terms of the same conceptual meaning but having stronger emotive impact than the standard terms, in order to express an attitude of self-assertion towards conventional order and moral authority and often an affinity with or membership in occupational, ethnic, or other social groups, and ranging in acceptability from sexual and scatological crudity to audacious wittiness (see Preface) [origin unknown; probably related to *sling*, which has cognates in Norwegian that suggest the abusive nature of slang; the British dialect original term *slang* meant both "a kind of projectile-hurling weapon," and "the language of thieves and vagabonds," reinforcing the connection with "sling"]

slant **1** *n* A look; an ocular inspection: *Take a slant at dat*—Eugene O'Neill **2** *n* One's opinion or point of view; =ANGLE: *something about his tone or his "slant" that irritated*—Joseph Wood Krutch

◀ **slant-eye** ▶ *n* An Asian person or person of Asian descent

slap or **slap-bang** or **slam-bang** *adv* Precisely; directly: *Streets that ended slap in a courtyard*—Sinclair Lewis/ *The storm was pointed slam-bang at Tampa*—Associated Press

slapdash *adj* Hasty and careless; heedless of the fine details; =SLOPPY

slap someone **five** *See* GIVE someone FIVE

slap-happy **1** *adj* Disoriented and stuporous, esp from being hit too often about the head: *a slap-happy bum*—Jim Tully **2** *adj* Vertiginous; off balance: *designed to knock philologists slap-happy*—Newsweek **3** *adj* Euphoric; intoxicated; =HIGH: *He was slap-happy a whole week after the baby came*

a **slap on the wrist** *See* GIVE someone A SLAP ON THE WRIST

slapper *See* KNEE-SLAPPER

slap someone's **wrist** *v phr* To punish very lightly • Usu said when the punishment is felt to be unjustly lenient

slat *n* A ski

slaves and masters *n phr* Sadists and masochists, in sexual taste: *referred to by the cognoscenti as "S and M," or "slaves and masters,"... the most prevalent of the freak syndrome*—Xaviera Hollander

slay *v fr 1930s* To impress someone powerfully, esp to provoke violent and often derisive laughter: *Pardon me, this will slay you*—Heywood Broun

sleaze **1** *n* Anything shabby and disgusting; particularly revolting trash; =CRAP, SCHLOCK, SHIT: *a paragon of Dorothy Malone low-fashion sleaze*—Village Voice **2** *n esp teenagers & students* =SLEAZEBAG **3** *v esp teenagers & students* To be sexually promiscuous and disreputable **4** *v students* To scrounge; =MOOCH [a back-formation from *sleazy*]

sleazebag or **sleazeball** *n* A despicable person; =DIRTBAG, SCUZZBAG: *Tartikoff calls the character "a total sleazebag"*—Time/ *If you're a sleazeball, you deserve a recall*—Newsweek

sleaze-bucket *adj* Nasty; degradingly repellent: *sleaze-bucket movies*

sleazemonger *n* A producer or seller of nasty entertainment: *one of Hollywood's lowlier sleazemongers*—Washington Post

sleazy or **sleazo** or **sleazoid** *adj* Disgusting; filthy; nasty; =GRUNGY, SCUZZY: *dirty buildings in sleazy sections*—New York Daily News/ *a tremendous evocation of the sleazoid speed-freak scene*—Rolling Stone/ *who makes sleazo blood films*—Pauline Kael [fr late-17th-century British *sleasie* "thin, flimsy, threadbare," of uncertain origin, whence it came to mean "of inferior workmanship, shoddy"; perhaps fr *Sleasie* "Silesian," used of linen cloth from that part of Germany]

sleep around *v phr* To be sexually promiscuous; =PLAY AROUND

sleeper *fr 1930s* **1** *n* Anything, esp a low-budget movie, a show, or a book, which achieves or probably will achieve success after a time of obscurity: *the first "sleeper" to come to Philadelphia in months*—Philadelphia Bulletin **2** *modifier: a sleeper play* **3** *n football* A player who unexpectedly and cunningly gets the ball and runs **4** *n narcotics* A sleeping pill or a sedative [the first sense may be fr the mid-19th-century gambling term *sleeper* meaning both "an unexpected winning card," and "a pot whose owner has ignored it, and hence is free to anyone who takes it"]

sleep with someone *v phr* To do the sex act with someone; =GO TO BED WITH someone • Perhaps not so much slang as merely a much-needed euphemism: *No girl could love a man unless she had slept with the man over a period of time*—Calder Willingham

sleeve *See* ACE UP one's SLEEVE

slew *n fr middle 1800s* A large quantity; =OODLES: *a slew of cops*—G Homes [origin uncertain; perhaps fr Irish *sluagh*]

slewfoot **1** *n fr late 1800s* A clumsy, stumbling person; a person who moves awkwardly **2** *v* (also **sloughfoot**) To walk with the feet turned away from the straight direction: *The Airedale slough-footed away*—Richard Starnes **3** *n* A police officer or detective [fr the awkwardness of a person whose feet *slew* outwards overmuch or are otherwise ill-controlled]

slice *n fr 1920s* A portion or share; =PIECE: *Five grand wouldn't get you a slice of her*—Fredric Brown

slice and dice film *n phr* A horror movie, esp one featuring bloody mutilation: *Mr De Palma's movies are distinguished from "slice and dice films"*—New York Times

sliced bread *See* the BEST (or GREATEST) THING SINCE SLICED BREAD

slick **1** *adj fr early 1600s* Smooth and clever; smart: *She's a very slick talker* **2** *adj* Cunning; crafty: *more than a match for any slick city lawyer*—Erle Stanley Gardner **3** *adj fr early 1800s* Excellent; =NIFTY: *The soup was "simply slick"*—Sinclair Lewis **4** *adj fr 1940s* Glib and superficial; without real substance: *They turn out people with slick plastic personalities* **5** *n* A magazine printed on glossy paper and usu having some artistic or intellectual pretensions: *magazines...from top slicks to minor pulps*—New York Times **6** *n hot rodders* An automobile tire with a very smooth tread [earlier 19th-century uses were in comparative phrases like *slick as bear's grease* and *slick as molasses*]

slicker **1** *n fr early 1900s* A clever and crafty person, esp a confidence trickster, a dishonest business executive, a shrewd and predatory lawyer, etc; =CROOK: *I don't admire slickers who peddle get-rich-quick bubbles*—Major Hoople (comic strip) **2** *n esp 1920s* A socially smooth and superficially attractive person; =SMOOTHIE: *The slicker was good-looking and clean-looking*—F Scott Fitzgerald **3** *v* To cheat; =CON, SCAM: *outsmarted and slickered by Moscow*—CV Jackson

See CITY SLICKER

the slicks *n phr* Glossy, expensive, and high- or middle-brow magazines, as distinguished from pulp magazines: *She finally sold a story to the slicks*

slick someone or something **up** *v phr* To make neat and more attractive; furbish; =GUSSY UP: *What are they all slicked up for?*

slimebag or **slimeball** or **slimebucket** *n* A despicable person; a repugnant wretch; =GEEK, SCUMBAG, SLEAZEBAG: *I'm a disgusting slime bag, but I don't grovel*—Washington Post/ *I remember when the slime-balls used to be packed in there so solid*—Joseph Wambaugh

slim pickings *n phr* Very little to be had or earned; extremely unprofitable returns: *You'll find slim pickings if you're looking for a fast buck*

sling *See* HAVE one's ASS IN A SLING

slinger *See* GUN-SLINGER, POT-SLINGER

sling hash *v phr fr middle 1800s* To work as a waiter or waitress: *I used to sling their hash*—Joseph Auslander/ *She slung hash for a couple of weeks*—Life

slinging *See* MUD-SLINGING

sling ink *v phr fr middle 1800s* To write, esp as a newspaper reporter or otherwise professionally

sling it or **sling the bull** *v phr* To exaggerate and lie; talk smoothly and persuasively; =BULLSHIT, SHOOT THE BULL: *The chief reason for the conversational effectiveness of many individuals is their inherent ability to sling it*—AH Marckwardt and FG Cassidy

sling mud *v phr* To defame; malign one's character: *They've got no real case, so all they can do is sling mud at her*

slinky *adj* Sinuous and sexy: *one of those slinky glittering females*—Raymond Chandler

slip **1** *v fr 1930s* To give; hand, esp surreptitiously: *So I slip him a double Z*—Lawrence Sanders **2** *v fr 1920s* To lose one's competence or touch; decline: *Only six pages today? I must be slipping*

See PINK SLIP

slip someone **a mickey** (or **a Mickey**) *v phr* To give knockout drops, esp chloral hydrate, secretly in a drink: *He passed out as if someone had slipped him a Mickey*

slip between the cracks *See* FALL BETWEEN THE CRACKS

slip (or **give**) **me five** *sentence fr early 1900s* Shake hands with me: *Slip me five so I know you're alive*

slippy *adj* Quick; fast

slipstick *n students fr 1920s* A slide rule

slip one's **trolley** *v phr* To lose one's rational composure; =FLIP OUT, FREAK OUT: *She was going around babbling as if she had slipped her trolley*

slip-up *n fr middle 1800s* A miscalculation; an accident; =GLITCH: *There must have been a hell of a slip-up somewhere along the line*

◁ **slit** ▷ *n* The vulva; =CUNT

slob **1** *n fr late 1800s British* A pudgy, generally unattractive, and untidy person: *You great, fat slob!* —Owen Johnson **2** *n* A slovenly and disorderly person; a sloppy and disheveled person: *What a slob! You'd think his room was the town dump* **3** *n* A mediocre person, esp one who is likely to fail or be victimized: *just another poor slob* —Jerome Weidman [fr Anglo-Irish, used affectionately of a quiet, fat, slow child]

slo-mo *adv* Slowly; in slow-motion: *A man named Ahmed skated slo-mo* —Village Voice

slope[1] **1** *v* (also **slope out**) *fr early 1800s* To run away; depart; =LAM **2** *v underworld & hoboes* To escape from jail [perhaps fr Dutch *sloop* "sneaked away"]

◀ **slope**[2] ▶ *n Vietnam War armed forces* An Asian; =DINK, GOOK [fr the apparent slanting of eyes caused by the typical epicanthic fold of Asian peoples]

sloppy **1** *adj fr 1920s* Slovenly; disorderly **2** *adj* Careless; =SLAPDASH

sloshed *adj* Drunk: *a youngish man in a bar, a little sloshed and pouring out his troubles to the bartender* —New Yorker

slot *n* A slot machine; =ONE-ARM BANDIT: *The slots are going day and night* —Richard Bissell

slouch *See* NO SLOUCH

sloughfoot *See* SLEWFOOT

slow burn *See* DO A SLOW BURN

slowly in the wind *See* TWIST SLOWLY IN THE WIND

slow on the draw (or **the uptake**) *adj phr* Dull and dilatory; mentally sluggish [fr the action of drawing one's pistol, in the classical cowboy context]

slowpoke *n fr late 1800s Australian* A slow, sluggish, slothful person: *an old slowpoke*—Philip Wylie [fr *slow* used for vowel rhyme with the early-19th-century *poke* "behave dilatorily, potter, saunter," perhaps influenced by 16th-century *slowback* "sluggard"]

sludgeball *n* A slovenly person; =DIRTBALL, SLOB: *I saw her drink beer out of a paper cup....I thought she was a sludgeball*—Washington Post [probably based in part on the increased currency of *sludge* as the product of sewer treatment plants]

sluff *v* To avoid work and responsibility; shirk: *No one accused Bo of sluffing*—People Weekly [fr *slough off*]

slug[1] **1** *n fr middle 1800s* A bullet: *Doctors said they're still unable to remove the slug*—New York Post **2** *n fr late 1800s hoboes & circus* A dollar: *do the job at 125 slugs a week* —Associated Press **3** *n* A drink of liquid, esp of whiskey; =SNORT: *ordering a slug of old stepmother*—Westbrook Pegler **4** *v* (also **slug down**:) *We were happily slugging our martinis/ in between slugging down at least ten Dr Peppers a day and puffing on as many fat cigars* —Time [origin uncertain; perhaps fr the resemblance of a lump of metal to the snail-like creature the *slug*; the earliest attested US senses are "gold nugget, lump of crude metal"; the drink and drinking senses appear to be derived fr phrases like *fire a slug* and *cast a slug* "take a drink of liquor," found as metaphors in late-18th-century British sources]

slug[2] **1** *v fr middle 1800s* To hit hard, esp with the fist; =CLOBBER: *He tried to make peace, but he got slugged* **2** *v baseball* To make or try for long base hits, esp regularly; =GO FOR THE FENCES [fr British dialect *slog*, probably ultimately fr Old English *slagan*, cognate with German *schlagen*]

slugfest **1** *n* *fr early 1900s* A hard and vicious fight, esp a prizefight more marked by powerful blows than by skillful boxing **2** *n* *fr 1930s* A baseball game in which many base hits are made

slugger **1** *n* *baseball fr late 1800s* A consistent long-ball hitter: *He's no slugger, he likes to place his hits* **2** *n* A boxer more notable for hard hitting than for artistic finesse
See CIRCUIT SLUGGER

slug it out *v phr* To fight with powerful blows; try to smash one another; =GO TOE TO TOE: *The principals were slugging it out in the alley*

slum or **go slumming** *v* or *v phr fr middle 1800s* To visit places or consort with persons below one's place or dignity; mix with one's inferiors: *So we went slumming over in Philadelphia* [fr *slum* "wretched poor area," origin unknown]

slurb *n* A suburb of cheap mass-produced houses, ugly business places, etc: *The towns all merged in one faceless, undifferentiated slurb* —George Warren [probably a blend of *slum* and *suburb*]

slurp or **slup** **1** *v* *fr 1920s* To eat or drink with noisy sucking sounds: *slurping porridge from a wooden spoon*—Ogden Nash/ *The cat slupped up the milk in no time* —Christian Science Monitor **2** *n:* *Take a slurp of this soup, it's great!* **3** *n* *jazz musicians* A glissando passage [echoic]

slush *n fr late 1800s* Blatant sentimentality; =GOO, SCHMALTZ: *I sort of wept and uttered a lot of slush*

slush fund *n phr fr late 1800s* In politics, money used for shady enterprises like buying votes, bribing officials, etc: *the use of slush funds to defeat selected victims*—Westbrook Pegler [fr the armed forces and especially nautical practice of selling grease and other garbage to accumulate a *fund* to buy little luxuries for the troops or crew]

smack[1] **1** *n* A blow; a slap: *He gave her a smack on the kisser* **2** *v:* *She smacked him hard* **3** *n* A kiss; =SMACKER **4** *v:* *She smacked him square on the lips* **5** *n* A try; =CRACK: *Let's have a smack at it, shall we?* **6** *adv* (also **smack dab**) *fr late 1800s* Exactly; precisely: *What he said was smack on the mark* [probably ultimately echoic]

smack[2] or **shmack** or **shmeck** *n narcotics* Heroin; =HORSE: *The cocaine pulled from the front while the smack pushed from the back. It was an incredibly intense high*—High Times [fr Yiddish *shmek* "a smell, sniff"; an earlier sense was "a small packet of drugs," hence merely a sniff or whiff]

smacker **1** *n* *fr early 1900s* A dollar; =BUCK: *having to cough up a thousand smackers*—Lowell Thomas/ *That car's not worth a smacker* **2** *n* A kiss; =SMACK: *Slip me a smacker, sister*—Jimmy Durante [the money sense, attested also of pesos and pounds sterling, may echo the slapping down of a bill on a counter, gambling table, etc, and hence be semantically related to *plank* and *plunk* for coins]
See BELLY-SMACKER

smacky lips *See* PLAY KISSIE

small-bore *adj fr late 1800s* Trivial; insignificant; petty: *No more of your small-bore notions, please* [fr the *bore* or caliber of a gun, which indicates its size and importance]

small fry **1** *n phr* Children or a child • Often used as a term of address, either affectionate or derogatory **2** *n phr* An insignificant person or persons; nonentities: *conveniences not enjoyed by the small fry overhead*—Theodore Dreiser **3** *adj:* *small-fry writers like me*—Budd Schulberg [fr *fry* "small or immature fish"]

small potatoes (Variations: **beer** or **bread** or **change** may replace **potatoes**) *fr middle 1800s* **1** *n phr* A trivial amount of money; =CHICKEN FEED, PEANUTS: *I received $120,000, which is no small potatoes*—Danny Thomas **2** *n phr* An insignificant person, enterprise, etc: *His highest ambition is pretty small potatoes/ Those plans look like small beer to me*

the **small** (or **fine**) **print** *n phr* Unsuspected and injurious conditions or requirements, esp when part of a contract, an insurance policy, etc: *Does the mayor read the fine print?* —Philadelphia

the **small time** *n phr fr show business fr early 1900s* Mediocre or inferior businesses, enterprises, entertainment or sports circuits, etc; =the BUSH LEAGUES: *After six years in the small time she finally had a big hit and went to Broadway*

small-time *adj fr show business fr early 1900s* Characteristic of the small time; inferior; petty; second-rate; =BUSH LEAGUE: *I was a small-time gun-runner/ a small-time political power*—E Lavine

smarmy **1** *adj fr early 1900s British* Smooth and flattering; unctuously ingratiating; fulsome: *a rather smarmy doctor and a highly officious nurse*—Time **2** *adj* Rich and sonorous; orotund and fruity; =PLUMMY: *an announcer with a smarmy voice* **3** *adj* Smug and self-righteous: *Uncle Sam's Smarmy Look Into Employee Sex Lives*—Nashville [origin unknown; since the earliest attested uses have to do with hair oil, it may be a vague blend of *smooth, smear, palm oil, cream,* etc]

smart *See* GET WISE, STREET-SMART

◁ **smart-ass** or **wise-ass**▷ **1** *n* A person who is quick to offer often abrasive opinion or comment from a posture of superior intelligence and learning; smart aleck; =BIGMOUTH, KNOW-IT-ALL, WISE GUY: *Only a real smart-ass would try to tell the general what to do/ You're a real wiseass sometimes, Mary Anne*—Pat Conroy **2** *adj: a smart-ass tone of voice*—Mother Jones

smart guy *n* A smart aleck; =SMART-ASS: *Well, I've got news for you, smart guy*—Joseph Heller

the **smart money** *n phr* The predictions, expectations, and bets of those who know best: *The smart money says you better stock lots of prunes*

smartmouth *n* An annoyingly impudent, assertive, and critical person; =SMART-ASS: *He's a smartmouth at school*—Philadelphia

smarts *n* Intelligence; =BRAINS, SAVVY: *If they had any smarts, they would have put a silencer on a gun and pumped a bullet in his head*—Playboy [probably on analogy with *brains* and *wits*]

See STREET SMARTS

smarty *n fr middle 1800s* A smart aleck; =SMART-ASS • Most often used in address: *I will bid seven on hearts, smarty*—Sinclair Lewis

smarty-pants *n* A smart aleck; =SMART-ASS, SMARTY: *That smarty-pants always gives a flip answer*

smash **1** *n fr middle 1800s* A total failure; a disaster **2** *n* (also **smash hit**) *fr show business fr 1920s* A great success; =HIT: *"Key Largo" is an unqualified smash*—Variety **3** *n black* Wine

smashed *adj* Drunk

smasher *See* BAGGAGE SMASHER

smashing *adj fr late 1800s British* Excellent; wonderful • Still chiefly British: *I told her she looked smashing*

smear[1] **1** *v prizefight fr 1920s* To knock unconscious; =KAYO **2** *v* To defeat decisively; trounce; =CLOBBER, SKUNK: *The Rangers got smeared 12 zilch* **3** *v* To attack someone's reputation, esp with false or vague charges of the ad hominem sort; defame: *His technique was always to smear his opponent* **4** *n: His whole campaign was a vile smear of the other party's man* **5** *modifier: They never stoop to smear tactics*

smear[2] *v* To bribe or otherwise make an illegal payment to someone; =SCHMEAR

smell **1** *v* To be nasty and contemptible; =STINK, SUCK: *The whole damn situation smells* **2** *v* To take narcotics by inhaling; =SNIFF: *You must be smelling the stuff*—John Roeburt

smell a rat *v phr* To be suspicious: *impossible for Schwartz not to have smelled a rat if he had day-to-day contact*—Village Voice

smell blood *v phr* To be aroused and exhilarated by the imminent destruction of one's prey or opponent: *The Democrats "smelled blood" over the trade issue*—New York Times [fr the behavior of predators who attack prey, esp wounded prey]

smelling *See* GOAT-SMELLING

smell like a rose *v phr* To be pure and innocent; be in good odor: *Some of the President's associates don't quite smell like a rose*

See COME UP SMELLING LIKE A ROSE

smidgen *n fr middle 1800s* A little bit; =CUNT-HAIR, SKOSH: *The deck may be* *stacked a smidgen against Lianna's husband*—Playboy

smile ***See*** CRACK A SMILE

-smith ***combining word*** A person who makes or skillfully uses what is indicated; =ARTIST: *tunesmith/ wordsmith/ wafflesmith*

smoke 1 ***n*** A cigarette: *I mooched a couple of smokes* **2** ***n*** *narcotics* Marijuana; =POT: *something called smoke or snow*—Carson McCullers **3** ***n*** Artful lies; talk meant to deceive; =BULLSHIT: *Those sections of the article are pure smoke*—New York Times **◀4▶** ***n*** A black person **5** ***v*** *underworld fr 1940s* To shoot someone; =PLUG **6** ***v*** *police & underworld* To be executed in a gas chamber: *still faced death and might one day be smoked*—Joseph Wambaugh **7** ***n*** *baseball* A very fast fastball: *Has Joe lost his smoke?* —Newsweek/ *the Yankees' smoke-throwing reliever*—Aquarian **8** ***v:*** *pitchers are supposed to be cranked up and smoking*—Sports Illustrated **9** ***v*** To be very angry; =BURN: *He was smoking for about an hour after she called him that* **10** ***n*** *college students* A dollar: *He paid six smokes for that shirt*
See BLOW SMOKE, GO UP IN SMOKE, HOLY CATS, J

a **smoke** ***n*** Tobacco and a smoking of tobacco

the **smoke** ***n phr*** *narcotics* Opium: *He went for the smoke himself*—Stephen Longstreet

smoke and joke ***v phr*** *Army* To relax; idle and be casual

smokeball ***n*** *baseball* A very fast fastball

smoke-eater ***n*** *fr 1930s* A firefighter

smoke someone **out 1** ***v phr*** To get information from: *He isn't saying now, but she'll smoke him out* **2** ***v phr*** To cause someone to emerge, esp from hiding: *The offer of clemency smoked out the whole gang*

smoke (or **chiba**) **shop** ***n phr*** *narcotics* A place where one may buy marijuana, esp a shop where it is sold rather openly: *Smoke shops are taking over our streets*—New York Times

Smokey Bear or **Smokey the Bear** or **Smoky** ***n phr*** or ***n*** *citizens band & truckers* A police officer, esp a state highway patrol officer: *Keep Don advised for the location of "Smokies"*—Rolling Stone [fr the fact that many state highway patrol police wear a broad-brimmed ranger's hat like that worn by the US Forest Service's ursine symbol]

smoking gun ***n phr*** *esp fr early 1970s* Incontestable evidence; =the GOODS: *They had discovered the "smoking gun" that would destroy the general's case*—New York Times [fr the image of a murderer caught with the fatal firearm still in hand, smoking]

Smoky ***See*** OLD SMOKY

smoky seat ***n phr*** The electric chair; =OLD SMOKY

smooch or **smooge** or **smouge 1** ***v*** To steal; pilfer; =MOOCH: *Then she went over to the cash box and smooched four $20 bills*—James M Cain **2** ***v*** *fr late 1500s fr British dialect* To kiss and caress; =NECK, PET • Even though quite old, the term was reestablished in US use in the 1930s: *College kids are still smooching*—Max Shulman **3** ***n:*** *I'd rather have hooch, and a bit of a smooch* —Hal Boyle [the pilfering sense probably derives from the kissing sense by way of *mooch*; the kissing sense is perhaps echoic, imitating a noisy smacking osculation]

smooth ***adj*** *fr late 1800s* Excellent; pleasing; attractive: *Boy, she was smooth*—Jerome Weidman

smoothie or **smooth article** or **smooth operator** ***n*** or ***n phr*** A person who is attractive, pleasant, and full of finesse • **Smoothie** is like **slicker**, but today lacks the connotations of dishonesty and trickiness: *thought of Dr Hugo Barker as a smooth article*—AR Hilliard/ *You think you're such a smoothie*—Sinclair Lewis

snafu (SNA Fo͞o) *fr WW2 armed forces* **1** ***n*** A very confused situation; =FUCK-UP, MESS: *The snafu occurred at Markwood Road*—New York Daily News **2** ***adj:*** *It's a very snafu setup here* **3** ***n*** A blunder; an egregious mistake; =BLOOPER: *My attempt to set things right was a total snafu* **4** ***v:*** *He gave it a good shot, but snafued horribly* [fr *situation normal, all fucked up*]

snake-bitten ***adj*** Helplessly incapacitated; ineffective: *O'Neal seems par-*

ticularly snake-bitten these days —Playboy

snake eyes *n phr crapshooting* The point or the roll of two

snake-hips or **swivel-hips** *n* A person whose hips move smoothly and effectively, such as a clever runner in football, a hula dancer, etc

snap **1** *n fr middle 1800s* Energy; vim; dash; =PIZZAZZ **2** *n fr late 1800s* A photograph; snapshot **3** *v: The photographer snapped him making a rude gesture* **4** *v esp college students* To go crazy; =FREAK OUT: *that Richard Herrin should have snapped*—Ms [the last sense is fr the cliché "something *snapped* in his mind"]

a **snap** *n phr fr late 1800s* Something easily done; =BREEZE, CINCH: *Winning next time will be a snap* [fr mid-19th-century *a soft snap* "something *snapped* up easily, a bargain"]

snap course *n phr college students fr late 1800s* An easy course: *His heavily attended snap course is good for a laugh*—Atlantic Monthly

snap it up *v phr* To hurry; act faster; =SNAP TO IT: *Drop over to the main drag and snap it up*—Raymond Chandler

snap out of it *v phr fr early 1900s* To recover, esp from gloom or sluggardness; become energetic

snapper *n* The point or risible climax of a story or joke; =PUNCH LINE, ZINGER: *Neil Simon's vaudeville snappers*—Pauline Kael

See BRONCO BUSTER

snappers *n* Teeth

snappy **1** *adj* Quick; energetic: *Be snappy about it* **2** *adj fr late 1800s British* Trim and attractive; fashionable; smart: *wearing a snappy light gray suit*—Associated Press

See MAKE IT SNAPPY

snap to *v phr* To become sharply attentive and responsive: *His soldiers snapped to and did what they were told*—New York Times [fr the quick way a military person *snaps to attention* on command]

snap to (or **into**) **it** *v phr fr early 1900s* To hurry; go faster; =MAKE IT SNAPPY: *Get that floor clean and snap to it*

snarky *adj fr early 1900s* Irritable; touchy: *She's just in a snarky mood, that's all*—Noel B Gerson [fr British dialect *snark* "find fault, complain," fr the basic sense "snort, snore"; of echoic origin, with cognates in many Germanic languages]

snatch **1** *v fr 1920s* To kidnap: *The kid was snatched as he left school* **2** *n: a $50,000 ransom to get him back from a snatch*—Westbrook Pegler **3** *v* To steal, esp by shoplifting **4** *n: A piece of paper covering the slit was rolled aside in the course of a snatch*—Forum ◁**5**▷ *n* The vulva; =CUNT

See PUT THE SNATCH ON someone or something

snatcher *n* A kidnapper

See CRADLE-ROBBER

snazz something **up** *v phr* To make something smarter and more elegant; enhance; =GUSSY UP: *and snazzes them up with appliqués*—Philadelphia

snazzy **1** *adj* Elegant; smart and fashionable; clever and desirable; =NIFTY, RITZY: *mounted on snazzy mag-type wheels*—New Yorker **2** *adj* Gaudy and meretricious; =HOKEY, JAZZY: *TVs wittiest, toughest, least snazzy news strip*—Time [perhaps a blend of *snappy* and *jazzy*]

sneaky pete (or **Pete**) **1** *n phr* Inferior liquor, often homemade or bootleg; =PANTHER PISS: *discussing the effects of "sneaky-pete"*—Collier's **2** *n phr hoboes* A cheap fortified wine sold in pint bottles called "jugs": *full of that cheap wine they call "sneaky pete"*—A Lomax **3** *n phr* Any cheap and inferior wine **4** *n phr* Marijuana mixed in wine [perhaps all senses fr Navy use "medicinal or other ship's alcohol drunk as liquor," *sneaky* because it had to be taken by stealth and because its effects were sudden and powerful, it would *sneak up on* the drinker; *Pete* simply gives a vowel rhyme]

snide *adj fr late 1800s* Contemptible; mean; nasty, esp in an insinuating way • Now used nearly exclusively in reference to remarks and persons who make them: *A woman gets nothing but snide remarks about her driving skills*—Associated Press [origin unknown]

sniff *v narcotics* To inhale a narcotic powder; =SNORT

sniffer *n narcotics* A cocaine user or addict: *The Baron was "a sniffer" himself*—American Mercury

snifter **1** *n fr middle 1800s* A drink of liquor; dram; =SLUG, SNORT: *plastered on a couple of snifters*—New Yorker **2** *n fr 1930s* A large, bulbous, stemmed glass used for drinking brandy **3** *n narcotics* =SNIFFER [origin uncertain; perhaps fr the common upper-respiratory reaction to taking a strong swallow of liquor, also noted in the earlier term *sneezer* and in *snorter*; *snifter*, *sneezer*, and *snorter* were all three used to mean "a strong breeze, gale," and all three came to mean "something large and impressive, something very strong," apparently after the drinking senses were established; before the drinking senses, the terms applied to snuff-taking, with its even more pronounced nasal spasms]

snipe **1** *n fr late 1800s hoboes* A cigarette or cigar butt **2** *n Navy fr early 1900s* An engine-room hand, aircraft mechanic, or other below-decks crew member: *"Snipes" ... service and maintain their flying crews' birds*—New York Times [origin obscure, although apparently these, along with several other slang uses, both British and US, all refer somehow to the long-billed bird and its habits]

snit *n* A fit of angry agitation: *He has a reputation for throwing considerable snits*—Car and Driver

snitch **1** *v early 1800s* To inform; =SING, SQUEAL **2** *n* An informer; =RAT, STOOL PIGEON: *Maybe some of my old snitches have run across something new*—Rex Burns **3** *v fr 1920s* To steal; pilfer; =SWIPE: *He snitched a couple of cookies* [first senses probably fr underworld slang *snitch* "nose"]

snockered or **schnockered** *adj* Drunk: *while all the male guests get snockered*—Philadelphia/ *He looks snockered. Are you snockered, Ed?*—WT Tyler [perhaps fr British dialect *snock* "a blow"]

snooker (SNŏŏ kər, SNōō-) *v fr early 1900s* To cheat; swindle; =SCAM: *The Chinese clearly believe that they snookered Nixon*—National Review [fr the pool game called *snooker*, apparently because a novice at the game can easily be tricked and cheated by an expert; compare *euchre*]

snookums *n* Precious one; sweet and dear one • Used to address small dogs, babies, etc: *Yes, you are. You're my little snookums*—New Yorker

snoop *n* A detective: *Private snoop, hunh?*—J Evans [ultimately fr Dutch *snoepen* "pry"]

snoot **1** *n fr late 1800s* The nose; snout; =SCHNOZZ: *Pokin' him one in the snoot*—Arthur Kober **2** *v* To behave haughtily toward; disdain: *people who snoot goat milk*—R Starnes

a **snoot full** **1** *n phr* One's intoxicating fill of liquor; =a SKINFUL: *You've had a snoot full*—Robert Ready **2** *n phr* More than enough of something; a great quantity: *By that time I'd had a snoot full of good advice*

snooty *adj fr 1930s* Snobbish; haughty and disdainful; supercilious; =HOITY-TOITY: *a generally vain and snooty class of men*—HL Mencken [fr the mien of a person who smells something nasty and holds the nose high]

snooze **1** *v fr late 1700s* To sleep; =COP ZS, SACK OUT **2** *n: not comfortable enough to suit me for a snooze*—Jack London **3** *n* Something that induces sleep; a soporific event, person, etc: *The concert was a snooze*—William Goldman [origin unknown; perhaps echoic of a snore]

snort **1** *n fr early 1900s* A drink of liquor, esp of plain whiskey; =HOOKER: *Who's ready for another short snort?*—K Brush **2** *v narcotics* To inhale narcotics, esp cocaine; =SNIFF: *since ma was a viper, and daddy would snort*—H Braddy [drinking sense fr earlier *snorter* of same purport; see *snifter*]

snorter *See* RIPSNORTER

◁**snot**▷ **1** *n fr 1400s* Nasal mucus **2** *n* A despicable person, esp a self-important nonentity: *Tell that little snot to get lost* **3** *v* To treat disdainfully; be haughty: *I should not be "snotted" by an owner, maitre d', or waiter*—Time [ultimately fr a common Germanic term for "nose," also represented by *schnozzle*, *snout*, *snoot*, etc; the last two senses probably influenced by *snooty*]

◁ **snotnose** or **snottynose**▷ **1** *n* An importunate upstart; a neophyte, esp a knowing one: *I won't be instructed by any snotnose* **2** *modifier: He's just a snotnose kid/ some snot-nose in New York*—Washington Post

◁ **snotty**▷ *adj* Disagreeable; nasty, esp in the sense of supercilious and disdainful: *I won't give that snotty bastard the time of day* [fr *snot* and influenced by *snooty*]

snow **1** *n narcotics fr early 1900s* Cocaine: *And he was also snorting snow* **2** *v* To persuade in a dubious cause, esp by exaggeration, appeals to common sentiment, etc; =BLOW SMOKE: *The electorate will not be snowed into supporting that silly measure* **3** *n: I thought his rationale was pure snow* [second sense fr the idea of *snowing* someone *under* with articulate reasons]

See DEATH SNOW, EYES LIKE PISSHOLES IN THE SNOW

a **snowball's chance in hell** *n phr* No possibility whatever; =A CHINAMAN'S CHANCE: *He doesn't have a snowball's chance in hell of getting that degree in time*

snowbird **1** *n fr early 1900s hoboes* A person, esp a migratory worker or a hobo, who goes south in the winter to escape the cold **2** *n narcotics* A cocaine user or addict; =COKEHEAD: *Nelly's eyes had a glassy, faraway look. Snowbird, he thought to himself*—William Weeks **3** *n narcotics* Any narcotics addict

snow bunny *See* SKI BUNNY

snow job **1** *n phr esp fr WW2 armed forces* Strong and persistent persuasion, esp in a dubious cause; an overwhelming advocacy: *Don't let Slattery give you a snow job and get you into trouble*—Halls of Montezuma (movie) **2** *v: I was snowjobbed into giving the maximum* [fr the idea of *snowing under* with insistent reasons; now probably reinforced by the narcotics sense of *snow*]

snow someone or something **under** *v phr fr late 1800s* To burden or assail with excessive demands, work, etc; overwhelm: *until a frailer man than he would have been snowed under*—F Scott Fitzgerald

snozzle *See* SCHNOZZ

snuff **1** *v* To kill: *more chillingly, STRESS snuffed at least 20 civilians*—Ramparts/ *Garlic never snuffed me*—Cyra McFadden **2** *modifier* Showing or doing murder, esp the killing of women in sadistic shows or orgies: *the snuff murder of an abused and homeless teenaged girl*—Penthouse [latterly fr black English, ultimately fr the idea of *snuffing out* a flame]

See UP TO SNUFF

snuff film (or **movie**) *n phr* A movie in which the actual killing of a person is shown: Year Zero *has the shock value of a snuff film*—Village Voice

snuffing *n* A killing, esp a murder: *too eager to put together two unconnected snuffings*—Lawrence Sanders

snuffy *adj* Drunk

snuggy *n* A sexually interesting and interested woman: *It's a snuggy. No, too young, a snugette. Fourteen years old and hot to trot*—Flare

so *See* SAY-SO

soak **1** *v fr late 1800s* To hit; =SOCK: *Why don't you soak him?*—Sinclair Lewis **2** *v fr late 1800s* To overcharge; make someone pay exorbitantly: *a good case of how soak-the-rich corporation taxes wind up right in the pocketbooks of all of us*—Associated Press **3** *n fr late 1800s* A drunkard; =LUSH, SOUSE

so-and-so *n* A despicable person; =BASTARD, JERK: *I think I'll sue the so-and-so*—Heywood Broun

See SON OF A BITCH

soap **1** *v* To flatter and cajole; =SWEET-TALK: *one of those Republicans who soaped Vivien*—Westbrook Pegler **2** *n* =SOFT SOAP **3** *n* =SOAP OPERA

See NO SOAP, SOFT SOAP

soaper or **soper** or **sopor** *n narcotics* A sedative drug, methaqualone; Quaalude (a trade name): *an apparently insatiable market for the "sopers"*—Newsweek [fr *Sopor* the trade name of a brand of the drug, fr the Latin root for "sleep"]

soap opera **1** *n phr* A radio or television daily dramatic series typically showing the painful, passionate, and riveting amours and disasters of more or less ordinary people: *a new soap opera which threatens to out-misery all the others*—John Crosby **2**

modifier: *The average man and woman in this country live a soap-opera existence*—Robert Ruark **3** ***n phr*** A life or incidents in life which resembles such shows: *You want to hear the latest in my never-ending soap opera?* [fr the fact that in radio days such shows were typically sponsored by *soap* manufacturers]

the **soaps** ***n phr*** Radio or television daily dramatic series collectively

◁ **sob** or **SOB** ▷ (pronounced as separate letters) ***n*** =SON OF A BITCH

sober ***See*** COLD SOBER, STONE COLD SOBER

sob story ***n phr*** A very affecting tale, esp an account of one's disabling troubles; a story that disingenuously appeals to one's charitable nature

sob stuff ***n phr*** Affecting stories collectively, or the material of which they are made: *Eppingham had prepared to lay on the sob stuff*—William Weeks

soch or **soc** or **sosh** (SOHSH) **1** ***n*** *teenagers* A social climber; a person who does the things required to be socially acceptable ● **Sosh** form attested fr early 1900s: *the true sign of a high school social climber known as the "sosh"*—Cameron Crowe **2** ***adj:*** *The entire sosh face detonated into a grin*—Cameron Crowe

sock **1** ***v*** *fr late 1600s British* To strike; hit hard; =CLOBBER, PASTE: *bein' socked to dreamland*—H Witwer **2** ***n:*** *To land another sock on Mr Renault's nose*—Ben Hecht **3** ***n*** *baseball* A base hit **4** ***n*** *musicians* A set of mounted cymbals sounded by tramping on a foot-pedal; =HIGH-HAT [probably echoic]

sock away ***v phr*** To save or horde; put away as savings: *Last year that group socked away $128 billion in savings bonds*—Time [perhaps fr the notion of concealing money in a *sock*; but *sock* "sew up and conceal" is attested fr the alteration of 19th-century *sock* or *sock down* "pay, dispose of money"]

sockdollager or **socdollager** **1** ***n*** *fr early 1800s* A decisive blow **2** ***n*** *fr early 1800s* A person or thing that is remarkable, wonderful, superior, etc; =HUMDINGER: *This book is a genuine sockdollager!/ his Dauntless Quest to lay his Sockdollager of a Product at the feet of the Public*—Washington Post [fr a metathesis of *doxology* "the finish or finishing part of a religious service," as suggesting something that terminates, like a heavy blow; influenced by *sock*]

socked in ***adj phr*** Plagued by adverse weather, esp by fog, heavy rain or snow, etc: *You may find yourself partly socked in if you're coming down the Jersey Turnpike this morning/ The captain told us the Boston field was socked in and we would have to land at Bridgeport* [probably fr the adverse weather indications given by the *wind sock* at early or small airports; perhaps influenced by the notion of being closed up in a *sock* as money is when it is *socked away*]

sock 'em ***See*** ROCK 'EM, SOCK 'EM

socker ***See*** BOBBY-SOXER

sockeroo **1** ***n*** A great success; something with extraordinary power and impact; esp, a lavish and popular film, show, etc; =BLOCKBUSTER: *an old-fashioned Hippodrome sockeroo*—Time **2** ***modifier:*** *putting some sockeroo catches in the president's plan*—Drew Pearson

sock hop **1** ***n phr*** *esp 1950s teenagers* An easy and intimate party where young people typically dance in their stockinged feet: *I feel like a kid at a sock hop, sneaking in here*—Philadelphia Journal **2** ***modifier:*** *a kind of sock-hop benefit for Approaching Middle Age*—Time

sock it to someone ***v phr*** *fr late 1800s* To attack vigorously and effectively; =LET someone HAVE IT: *Some congressional liberals would like to sock it to business by taking away the tax reductions*—Fortune

socko **1** ***n*** *prizefight fr 1920s* A hard punch **2** ***interj*** An exclamation imitating the impact of a hard blow, and expressing abrupt force: *Socko!... he punches the villain in the jaw*—Waverly Root **3** ***adj*** *fr show business* Very powerful; explosively impressive; terrific: *Okay, now a socko surprise*—Xaviera Hollander **4** ***adv:*** *find they do socko in their native heath*—Variety

socks ***See*** BOBBY SOCKS, DROP YOUR COCKS AND GRAB YOUR SOCKS, KNOCK someone's SOCKS OFF

the **socks off** ***adv phr*** Very thoroughly ● Always used, like the semantically similar **the brains out** and **the pants off**, to intensify a verb: *undressed her and screwed the socks off her*—George V Higgins/ *absolutely bored the socks off me* —Washington Post

See BEAT THE SOCKS OFF someone

soda jerk (or **jerker**) ***n phr*** *fr early 1900s* A person who makes ice cream sodas and other treats at a soda fountain: *She worked for a while as a soda jerk*—Life/ *the champion soda jerker of the United States* —Ernie Pyle [fr earlier *beer jerk* "tapster," perhaps fr the action of drawing back on the vertical handle that controlled the flow of beer; perhaps also related to *jerkwater*]

soft *See* WALK SOFT

◁ **soft-ass** ▷ ***adj*** Slack and feeble; ineffectual; =WIMPY: *basic economic psychology, not the soft-ass welfarism of Down East*—Toronto Life

softball ***adj*** Trivial and contemptible; nonserious; =PISS-ELEGANT: *a softball question if ever there was one*—New York [based on *hardball*]

soft-core **1** ***adj*** Somewhat less than extreme; moderated; slightly ameliorated: *He's a soft-core radical, really* **2** ***n*** Something that is not extreme, esp a sexually arousing but not carnally explicit movie, magazine, etc: *She doesn't care for X-rated, but enjoys a little soft-core now and then* [based on *hard-core*]

soft drug ***n phr*** A narcotic like marijuana and some hallucinogens, thought of as nonaddictive and only slightly damaging to health [based on *hard drug*]

soft hands ***n phr*** *baseball* The particular ability to field ground balls, esp those hit very hard: *He has "soft hands," baseball slang for an uncanny ability to field ground balls* —Washingtonian

softie or **softy** ***n*** A person who is amiably and quickly compliant; someone easy to cajole and victimize: *You are a patsy, a quick push, a big softie* —WR Burnett

soft in the head ***adj phr*** Stupid; dimwitted; =LAMEBRAINED

soft money (or **currency**) **1** ***n phr*** *fr middle 1800s* Currency that is highly inflated or likely to become less and less valuable **2** ***n phr*** *politics* Campaign donations that are not regulated by the Federal Election Commission: *raising millions of dollars of what is known in election-financing language as "soft money"* —Washington Post National Weekly Edition [based on *hard money*]

soft-pedal ***v*** To make less prominent; de-emphasize: *Even my friends advised me to soft-pedal my criticisms* —New York Daily News [fr the *pedal* on a piano that *softens* the notes played]

soft sell ***n phr*** Selling or advertising in a nonstrident, noninsistent tone [based on *hard sell*]

soft soap **1** ***n phr*** *fr early 1800s* Flattery; cajolement; =SWEET-TALK: *I won her over finally with a lot of soft soap* **2** ***v:*** *We had to soft-soap the electorate pretty shabbily*

soft touch **1** ***n phr*** A person from whom it is easy to borrow or wheedle something: *You get the reputation of being a soft touch*—John O'Hara **2** ***n phr*** =SOFTIE **3** ***n phr*** An easy job; a sinecure: *He spent his life seeking the ultimate soft touch*

SoHo ***n*** The area in New York City that is located south of Houston Street

so hot *See* NOT SO HOT

soldier ***n*** *underworld* A low-ranking member of the Mafia; an ordinary thug or gangster; =BUTTON MAN

See FIRST MAN

soldier on ***v phr*** To persist doggedly: *The odds were against us, but we decided to soldier on*

be **sold on** ***v phr*** To be convinced of the value of something or someone; strongly favor or accept: *It took me a half hour to get sold on the job* —James M Cain

solid ***adj*** *jive talk fr 1930s* Wonderful; remarkable; =GREAT, GROOVY: *Man, what solid jive*—Max Shulman/ *That's solid, Willie, let's get together and blow*—Slim Gaillard

solid gold chamber pot *See* WIN THE PORCELAIN HAIRNET

so long ***interj*** *fr middle 1800s* A parting salutation [origin unknown; perhaps fr German *adieu so lange*; perhaps fr Hebrew *shalom* and related Arabic *salaam*, both greetings meaning "peace"; perhaps fr Irish *slan* "health," used as a toast and a salutation]

somebody *n* A consequential person: *Leroy was a somebody*—New York Post/ *I could have been somebody, Charley. I could have been a contender*—On the Waterfront (movie)

some skin *See* GIVE SOME SKIN, SKIN

something *n fr late 1500s* A remarkable person or thing: *Did you see his shirt? It's something!*
See MAKE SOMETHING OUT OF

something else *n phr jive talk* =SOMETHING [an intensive of *something*]

something fierce (or **awful**) *adv phr* In a harsh and pronounced way; severely • Slang or dialect relics of the adverbial use of **something** attested from the early 1500s: *He cusses her out something fierce*—Sinclair Lewis/ *She came at me something awful*

something on the ball *n phr fr early 1900s* Talent; skill; ability: *a guy with something on the ball*—Budd Schulberg [fr the curve, speed, etc, that a baseball pitcher puts *on the ball*]

something's got to give *sentence* A resolution is necessary and imminent now; the situation is tense and perilous: *The negotiators are deadlocked and something's got to give*

some Zs *See* COP ZS, SOME ZS

song *See* RAP SONG, TORCH SONG

song and dance or **song** *n phr* or *n* A prepared account or speech aimed at persuasion, apology, advocacy, wheedling, etc: *I got this song and dance about how his car wouldn't start/ Some bum will brace you with a long song of utter inconsequence*—Robert Ruark
See GO INTO one's DANCE

◁ **son of a bitch** or **sumbitch**▷ (also **son of a b** or **son of a gun** or **son of a so-and-so**, all euphemistic) **1** *n phr* or *n* A despicable person; =BASTARD, SHITHEEL: *I told the son of a bitch what I thought of him* **2** *n phr* or *n* Something very difficult or vexatious, esp a hard task: *Getting that thing fitted was a son of a bitch/ What a sumbitch of a job it was!* **3** *n phr* or *n* A person or thing that is remarkable, wonderful, superior, etc; =BITCH: *Their new album is a son of a bitch, I tell you* **4** *interj* An exclamation of anger, annoyance, amazement, disappointment, etc: *Son of a bitch! The thing's busted again!* [the *son of a gun* variant is said to refer to a time when women could accompany men to sea, and when children could be born and cradled under a gun or gun carriage, hence have no proper legitimate parentage]

◁ **son-of-a-bitching** or **sumbitching**▷ *adj* Wretched; accursed; =DAMNED: *Get that son-of-a-bitching thing out of here right now*

SOP or **sop** (pronounced as separate letters) *n fr WW2 armed forces* The way things are properly and usually done: *The SOP here is that you ask the chairman first* [fr *standard operating procedure*]

soper or **sopor** *See* SOAPER

soppy *adj* Sentimental; maudlin; =MUSHY, SCHMALTZY: *the soppy story of a rich-boy drop-out*—Judith Crist

sore *adj fr late 1800s* Angry; irritated; =PISSED OFF: *I was sore*—Eugene O'Neill

sorehead *n fr middle 1800s* An irritable person; a constant complainer; a grouch

sore thumb *See* STICK OUT

sorrow *See* DROWN one's SORROWS

sorry about that *sentence* I am sorry; please forgive me • Most often an ironic understatement, as when one has been responsible for making a big mistake; popularized in the 1960s TV program Get Smart

◁ **sorry-ass**▷ *adj* Wretched; sorry; inferior; =HALF-ASSED: *The reputation of the Barclay...has been one of sorry-ass service*—Philadelphia

SOS[1] (pronounced as separate letters) *n fr WW2 armed forces* The usual tedious exaggerations, pieties, wretched food, etc [fr *same old shit*]

SOS[2] (pronounced as separate letters) *n esp WW2 armed forces* Chipped beef on toast or some similar food; =SHIT ON A SHINGLE: *It was commonly referred to in the service as SOS*—Prison [fr *shit on a shingle*]

sosh *See* SOCH

so-so *adj* Average; ordinary: *It's a so-so movie*

soul *fr black, esp fr musicians* **1** *n* An instinctive, sensitive, humorous, and sympathetic quality felt by black persons to be inherent and to constitute their essential and valuable attribute: *He's got soul when he dances! I mean SUPER SOUL!*—New York

Post **2** *adj: program content on soul radio stations*—Black Week/ *That's what the Soul scene taught everybody*—Albert Goldman **3** *n* (also **soul music**) This quality in music, and music having this quality: *When Aretha Franklin pours forth a thousand cups of soul*—S Leaks **4** *adj: a soul ballad*—Playboy/ *See* BLUE-EYED SOUL, GRIPE one's ASS

soul brother *n phr esp black* A male black person; =BLOOD, BROTHER

Soul City or **Soulville** *n phr black* Harlem

soul food *n phr black* Food characteristic of and preferred by black persons, esp of Southern culture

soul sister *n phr esp black* A female black person; =SISTER

sound **1** *v street gang fr 1950s* To taunt or provoke; goad; =RAZZ **2** *v black* =SIGNIFY

sound off **1** *v phr fr WW1 Army* To talk, esp to complain, loud and long; bluster: *Its leaders have sounded off on various issues*—Philadelphia Bulletin **2** *v phr fr WW2 Army* To boast; brag: *always sounding off about what a big shot he is*

soup *See* DUCK SOUP, IN THE SOUP, PEA SOUP

soup-and-fish *n fr early 1900s* A man's formal evening dress: *getting into the soup-and-fish*—Sinclair Lewis [fr the formality of a dinner that commences with the *soup* and then the *fish* course]

soupbone *n baseball fr early 1900s* A pitcher's pitching arm [probably fr the notion that *soup* represents one's sustenance]

souped up **1** *adj phr* Producing a higher power or acceleration than the normal: *a Ford with a souped-up motor*—A Hynd **2** *adj phr* Increased or heightened in value, attraction, production, etc: *the souped-up Premium Bonds are also designed to this end*—N Ridley [fr *supercharged*, referring to a pump that forces additional air into the cylinders of an engine to increase its power; perhaps reinforced by *soup* "fuel for a powerful engine," and "material injected into a horse with a view to changing its speed or temperament," the latter attested fr 1911 and earlier]

souper *n baseball* =SOUPBONE

soup job *n phr teenagers* A car that has been altered mechanically for increased power and speed

soup up *v phr* To increase power and speed above the normal: *He souped up the motors*—A Hynd

soupy *adj* =SOPPY

sourball or **sourbelly** *n* =SOREHEAD

sourpuss or **sourpan** *n* A morose person; a chronic complainer and moaner; =PICKLEPUSS: *the regular assortment of first-night sourpusses and professional runners down*—Philadelphia Bulletin/ *He'd change into a sour-pan*—American Mercury

souse **1** *n fr early 1900s* A drunkard; =LUSH: *A wonderful thyroid substance... sobered up the souse in 30 minutes*—New York Post **2** *n* Drunkenness; intoxication: *Economic and religious saviors give a new kind of emotional souse*—American Mercury [fr an extension of *souse* "pickle brine, something pickled," hence semantically akin to *soak* "drunkard" and *pickled* "drunk"]

soused *adj* (Variation: **to the gills** may be added) *fr early 1900s* Drunk [probably fr the image of a pickled herring or other pickled fish]

South *See* a MOUTH FULL OF SOUTH

southpaw **1** *n baseball fr late 1800s* A lefthanded player, esp a pitcher: *Southpaw Warren Spahn pitched his 17th victory*—Associated Press **2** *n* Any lefthanded person: *Many brilliant persons are southpaws, although perhaps only coincidentally* **3** *modifier: switched to a southpaw stance for his 11th round*—Associated Press [apparently coined by the humorist Finley Peter Dunne in 1887 when he was a Chicago sports journalist and baseball diamonds were regularly oriented with home plate to the west]

so what **1** *interj* An exclamation of specified indifference; =BIG DEAL: *When she heard the president was outside, she said, "So what?"* **2** *interj* An exclamation of defiance, reciprocal challenge, etc: *He told me I had screwed the affair up, and I said, "So what?"*

so what else is new or **what else is new** *sentence* Do you have any other startling information? ● Always used with heavy irony: *The*

Mayor's a crook? So what else is new?

soxer *See* BOBBY-SOXER

sozzled *adj fr late 1800s* Drunk

space or **space out** *v* or *v phr teenagers* To daydream; wool-gather; not attend to what one is doing: *He didn't get much work done because he kept spacing*

space cadet or **space-out** *n phr* or *n* A mad or eccentric person, esp one who seems stuporous or out of touch with reality as if intoxicated by narcotics; =NUT, SPACED-OUT: *Alda presents her as such a space cadet that the agony of divorce is tempered*—Kings Courier/ *meant to convince the jury that he is an unreliable space-out, that perhaps he was hallucinating*—Washington Post [probably fr the 1950s TV program Tom Corbett, Space Cadet which followed the adventures of a group of teenage cadets at a 24th-century space academy, thought of humorously as being *far out, way out*, etc]

spaced-out **1** *adj* (also **spaced** or **spacey** or **spacy**) Stuporous from narcotic intoxication; in a daze; =BOMBED OUT, HIGH, STONED: *queerly bashful, shy, respectful, or spaced-out*—New York/ *with very spaced-out movements, examines the parts of her body*—New York Times/ *You get into a trance, spaced, makin' plans*—Esquire **2** *adj* Crazy or eccentric; =NUTTY: *the teacher, a spacey and sweetly strange spinster*—Richard Peck/ *He is not spaced-out, a point he makes clear in his new book*—TG Harris [probably fr black *space* or *space out* "go, depart," reinforced by the notion of distance and remoteness in *outer space* and by the notion of blanks, gaps, and *spaces* in an otherwise sane and reasonable train of thought, speech, etc]

◀ **spade**▶ *n fr early 1900s* A black person: *The spades inhabited Harlem and let the ofays have Wall Street to themselves*—American Mercury [fr the color of the playing-card symbol and fr the phrase *black as the ace of spades*]

spades *See* IN SPADES

spaghetti Western *n phr fr early 1970s* A cowboy movie usu made by Italian directors and producers, often in Europe: *The best turkeys, he went on, were spaghetti Westerns, because they earned a lot of bread*—Russell Baker

spang **1** *adv fr middle 1800s* Precisely; exactly; =SMACK: *Abilene was spang on a new westering railroad line*—advertisement for Time-Life books **2** *adv* Entirely; totally: *I had got spang through the job before they interrupted me* [fr British dialect, "spring, leap," and so semantically similar to an expression like *jump on the hour he got there*, because of the sharp precipitousness of a leap]

Spanish walk *See* FRENCH WALK

spare tire **1** *n phr fr 1920s* Flab about the waist; a certain embonpoint; =BULGE: *At forty, many men have a definite spare tire and must undertake the Battle of the Bulge* **2** *n phr fr 1940s* A superfluous and unwelcome person: *I didn't come because I knew I'd be a spare tire in that crowd* **3** *n phr* A tedious person; a bore

Sparky *See* OLD SMOKY

spas-out (SPAZ-) *n* A showing or experiencing of strong emotional spasms, esp by children: *Every time we mentioned homework the kid would have a spas-out* [fr *spastic*]

◁ **spastic** (also **spas** or **spaz**)▷ **1** *n esp teenagers fr 1960s* A strange and stupid person; =WEIRDO: *Her brother's a spastic/ The man's a spaz, a total spaz*—Joseph Wambaugh **2** *adj: only the spastic twits in competition*—Village Voice **3** *n students* A nonathletic person, esp an awkward one [cruelly, fr the plight of cerebral palsy patients exhibiting constant body *spasms*]

◁ **spazzy** or **spassy**▷ *adj esp teenagers fr 1960s* Stupid; =WEIRD: *You gotta be spassy if you think that*—Philadelphia Inquirer [fr *spastic*]

speakeasy or **speak** or **speako** *n fr late 1800s* A cheap saloon, esp an illegal or after-hours place: *It had been a speakeasy once*—L Ford/ *All they give you in these speaks is smoke*—James M Cain/ *one thing that puts a speako over*—Joel Sayre [Samuel Hudson, a journalist, says in a 1909 book that he used the term in Philadelphia in 1889 after having heard it used in Pittsburgh by an old Irish woman who sold liquor clandestinely to her neighbors and enjoined them to "spake asy"; hence related to early-19th-century Irish and British dialect *spake-aisy* or *speak softly* shop "smugglers' den"]

special ***See*** the RED-EYE, SATURDAY NIGHT SPECIAL

specs[1] *n fr late 1800s* Spectacles: *Oh Lord, I broke my new specs*

specs[2] *n fr WW2* The specifications of a blueprint, architectural plan, printing order, etc

speed **1** ***n*** A usu affectionate nickname or term of address for a man: *Hi, Speed, what's up?* **2** ***n*** *narcotics* An amphetamine, esp Methedrine (a trade name)

See BRING someone UP TO SPEED

speedball ***n*** *narcotics* A dose of a stimulant and a depressant mixed, esp of heroin and cocaine: *smack, coke, reefers, acid, speedballs (snorting cocaine and heroin together)* —New York

speed merchant **1** ***n phr*** A very fast runner: *The little guy could really scoot, a speed merchant* **2** ***n phr*** A very good fastball pitcher: *He certainly was no speed merchant*—Ithaca Journal

spell out **1** ***v phr*** To explain very patiently in great detail: *Are you a schoolboy I have to spell out everything for you?*—Ira Wolfert **2** ***v phr*** To explain; define: *to spell out the difference between right and wrong* —Associated Press

spender ***See*** BIG-TIME SPENDER

sphere ***n*** A baseball, golfball, etc

spheroid ***n*** A baseball: *Hitting the ball is just as important as slugging the spheroid*—Associated Press

See the OBLATE SPHEROID

◀ **spick** or **spic** ▶ ***n*** A Latino or person of such descent: *female spick, short fat*—Ira Wolfert [fr the presumed protestation "*No spick English*"]

spiel *fr late 1800s circus* **1** ***n*** A barker's or hawker's persuasive talk **2** ***n*** A speech meant to persuade by force and eloquence; a sales patter; =LINE: *I'll give his honor a spiel* —Jack London **3** ***n*** *fr 1940s* An advertising monologue on radio or television [fr German *spielen* "play"]

spieler ***n*** A person who makes a persuasively eloquent speech: *a real accomplished spieler*—Outlook

spiffed out ***adj phr*** Fancily and formally dressed; =DOLLED UP

spiff someone or something **up** ***v phr*** To spruce up; smarten; groom handsomely and neatly; =GUSSY UP: *You are really attractive when you spiff yourself up* [fr British dialect *spiff* "dandified, bedizened"]

spiffy **1** ***adj*** *fr middle 1800s British* Elegant; smart and fashionable; =SNAZZY: *They wear spiffy red-and-gold scarves*—Time/ *New Model Buggy for Amish Is Spiffy*—Cleveland Plain Dealer **2** ***adv*** Well: *They don't translate so spiffy*—Arthur Baer

spike **1** ***v*** *fr early 1900s* To strengthen a drink by adding alcohol or liquor: *He spiked his coffee with brandy* **2** ***adj:*** *This drink is spiked!* **3** ***n*** *narcotics* A hypodermic needle **4** ***v*** To rise to a high level, esp rapidly: *He also...spikes into the upper registers*—Down Beat/ *push fluids when the patient has spiked a temp* —American Speech **5** ***v*** To reject; quash: *confident the man's disbelieving New York editors will spike the story*—People Weekly **6** ***v*** *volleyball* To punch a volleyball powerfully and unreturnably down **7** ***v*** *football* To slam the ball down, usu done by a player who has just scored a touchdown [all senses fr *spike* "large nail," hence "sharp point"; the sense "to reject" may be fr the earlier phrase *spike a gun* "render a cannon useless by driving a spike into the touchhole," or fr the notion of dealing with a paper, bill, manuscript, etc, by impaling it on a spindle or spindle file]

spike up ***v phr*** *narcotics* To inject narcotics; =SHOOT UP: *if he came home and found her spiking up* —Richard Merkin

spill one's **guts** ***v phr*** *fr hoboes* To tell everything one knows; be totally and lengthily candid: *"Can I be perfectly frank with you?" "Good. Spill your guts"*—Armistead Maupin

spill the beans ***v phr*** *fr early 1900s* To tell something inadvertently; blurt out a secret

spinach **1** ***n*** *fr late 1800s* A beard **2** ***n*** *esp 1930s* Nonsense; worthless matter; =JUNK: *You could put up with this spinach*—Richard Bissell/ *"I say it's* spinach *and I say to hell with it"*—a Carl Rose New Yorker cartoon

spin doctor ***n phr*** An advisor or agent, esp of a politician, who imparts a partisan analysis or slant to a story for the news media: *Just after the debate, Johnson took his place with the other "spin doctors"*—Washington Post [fr the notion of *spin* on a baseball or pool ball, which gives a deviant rather than a straight track; semantically related to throwing someone a curve]

spinner *n truckers* A truck driver

spin off **1** *v phr* To produce as an entity separated from the whole: *The conglomerate spun off five new companies* **2** *n: This store is a spin-off from the big one downtown* **3** *v phr* To dispose of; rid oneself of; =DITCH: *Why didn't he spin off this stupid cunt?*—Saul Bellow

spin one's **wheels** *v phr* To waste time; work fruitlessly: *Nobody spun his wheels. I'm proud of them*—Washington Post/ *Stop spinning your wheels, get yourself in gear*—WT Tyler

spit *See* HOT SPIT, NOT COUNT FOR SPIT, NOT GIVE SPIT, WORTH A BUCKET OF WARM SPIT

spitball **1** *v* To make harmless jibes or attacks; make weak accusations: *Well, I'm just spit-balling*—Paul Theroux **2** *n* A nasty but feeble attack: *despite the spitballs he keeps getting*—Philadelphia Journal [fr the mischievous schoolboy's vice of throwing bits of paper soaked in saliva]

spitless *See* SCARED SPITLESS, SCARE someone SHITLESS

spizzerinktum or **spizzerrinctum** *n outdated fr middle 1800s* Vigor; pep; =PIZZAZZ: *the fellow who put foresight, science, and spizzerinktum into their business*—American Mercury [origin unknown; since the earliest meaning is "money," perhaps a coinage fr Latin *species rectum* "the right sort"]

splash *See* MAKE A SPLASH

splat movie or **splatter film** *n phr* A movie that features a major catastrophe or other event where things and people are severely damaged [fr echoic *splat*, indicating a smashing and jellying blow]

splice *v fr middle 1700s* To marry • Most often in the passive: *crying to be spliced*—Joseph Auslander

splice the main brace *v phr nautical* To have a drink of liquor

splinter *See* KNEE-HIGH TO A GRASSHOPPER

split *v fr 1950s black musicians* To leave; depart; =CUT OUT: *This party is dullsville, let's split*

See LICKETY-SPLIT

split a gut *v phr* To try very, very hard; make a maximum effort; =BUST one's ASS: *We may not make it, but we'll split a gut trying*

◁ **split beaver** ▷ *n phr* A photograph or view of a woman's vulva between spread legs; =SPREAD BEAVER: *I can toss off phrases like "split beaver" with almost devil-may-care abandon*—Esquire

split the scene *v phr fr 1950s black musicians* To leave; depart; =CUT OUT, SPLIT: *just as I was about to split the scene*—Tennessee Williams

spoil *v* To kill; =WASTE: *You wanted to hate his guts so it would be easier to spoil him?*—Lawrence Sanders

spondulics or **spondulix** (spahn DOO liks) *n fr middle 1800s* Money [origin unknown]

sponge **1** *n* (also **sponger**) *fr 1500s* A parasite; =FREELOADER, MOOCHER, SCHNORRER: *You avoided college boys, sponges*—F Scott Fitzgerald **2** *v: We were able to sponge lots of meals off his parents* **3** *n* A drunkard; =SOAK

See THROW IN THE SPONGE

spoof **1** *v fr late 1800s British* To fool; hoax; tease: *He was just spoofing*—Sinclair Lewis **2** *n: Don't take it seriously, it was just a spoof* **3** *n* A parody or pastiche; =SEND-UP, TAKEOFF: *The show was a spoof of a TV sit-com* [coined by the British comedian Arthur Roberts as the name of a nonsense game that he invented]

spook ◀**1**▶ *n* A black person: *Some are just spooks by the door, used to give the organization a little color*—Amsterdam News **2** *n espionage* A spy; secret agent: *Mr Wolfson isn't a spook for the CIA*—Wall Street Journal **3** *v fr middle 1800s* To put on edge; make apprehensive; frighten: *"It's the first time in my life I've ever been spooked," says a Byrd staffer*—Washington Post

spoon *v outdated fr late 1800s* =NECK, PET

See EAT someone UP, GREASY SPOON

sport **1** *n* A stylish and rakish man • Often used as a term of address, sometimes with an ironical tinge: *What did she tell you, sport?* **2** *n* =GOOD SPORT

spot **1** *v* *sports & gambling* To give odds or a handicap: *They spotted Pittsburgh five runs before getting down to serious business*—New York Times/ *I spotted him a rook and two pawns* **2** *v* To give, but with the suggestion of a loan: *I spotted her a couple drinks* **3** *v* *fr early 1700s British* To recognize or identify: *I spotted her as a phony long ago* **4** *n* A short commercial or paid political announcement on radio or television: *How do you like the spots, Senator?*—New York **5** *n* A night club, restaurant, or other such venue of pleasure: *They were seen in a fashionable spot uptown*
See FIVE-SPOT, HIT THE SPOT, HOT SPOT, JOHNNY-ON-THE-SPOT, ON THE SPOT, PUT someone ON THE SPOT, SWEET SPOT, TWO-SPOT, X MARKS THE SPOT

spotlight *v* To single out prominently; focus on for emphasis: *He was trying to spotlight the danger of high deficits*

spout *See* UP THE SPOUT

spread oneself *v phr fr middle 1800s* To make a great effort; do one's utmost: *You may be sure the staff will spread itself to accommodate you*

◁ **spread beaver** ▷ *n phr* =SPLIT BEAVER

◁ **spread for** someone ▷ *v phr* For a woman, to do or offer to do the sex act with someone

spread it thick *v phr fr middle 1800s* To exaggerate; overstate; =BULLSHIT • Very often used with **on**: *To say it was for the good of humanity is spreading it a bit thick/ She spread it on very thick with those compliments*

spring **1** *v* *underworld fr early 1900s* To get out of or be released or escape from prison: *When's he springing?*—Lawrence Sanders **2** *v* To reveal or do something as a surprise • Very often used with **on**: *John L Lewis is preparing to spring a dramatic move*—Lowell Thomas/ *If we spring it on them suddenly they won't know how to react*

spring for something *v phr* To pay for, esp a treat of food or drink; =POP: *always more than glad to guzzle the pitchers of Michelob you sprung for on payday*—Philadelphia

spritz **1** *v* To spray or sprinkle: *the fixative with which he spritzed it so it would not smear*—Earl Thompson **2** *n* A serving of carbonated water, esp an addition of carbonated water to a glass of wine: *She asked for white wine with a spritz* **3** *n* A slight rain or shower: *We may get just a wee spritz this afternoon* [fr Yiddish, "spray"]

spritzer *n* A glass of wine mixed with carbonated water

spritzy *adj* Light and volatile; airy; frothy: *She now does a string of spritzy little jetés that barely get her off the ground*—New Yorker/ *the hair-trigger switch between Nathan's spritzy charm and the scary violence of his anger*—Newsweek

sproutsy *adj* Unconventional, unorthodox in habits and opinions: *I joined a sorority, now I'm seen as a sister, not as a sproutsy type*—MS [fr the eating of *bean-sprouts* as symbolizing radical or nonconformist behavior]

sprout wings **1** *v phr fr late 1800s* To become very chaste and upright: *Noticed how he's sprouted wings since he got married?* **2** *v phr* To die [fr the *winged* nature of angels]

spunk **1** *n fr late 1700s* Energetic courage; mettle; =BALLS, GUTS: *little girl's got a lot of spunk* ◁**2**▷ *n fr late 1800s* Semen: *rushing with their hot spunk in their hands to the microscope*—John Irving ◁**3**▷ *v* To ejaculate semen; =COME: *the filthy pigs spunking into women*—Herbert Kastle [apparently fr Celtic *spong* "tinder, touchwood, punk" fr Latin *spongia* "sponge"; apparently semantically fr a resemblance between semen and a spongy excrescence found on trees, in which sense the word is found in British dialect]

spurs *See* WIN one's SPURS

squab *n fr 1920s* A young woman; =CHICK • Considered offensive by some women

squad *See* GOON SQUAD, PUSSY POSSE

square **1** *n* (also **square meal**) *fr late 1800s* A copious meal: *I've had my three squares every day*—J Flynt **2** *n fr black jazz musicians* A conventional person, esp one with musical tastes not extending to jazz, swing, bop, etc; =CLYDE, UNCOOL: *I do a little vocal number for the squares*

—Mary Lou Williams **3** ***adj:*** *You do not try to convert the square world* —Eugene Burdick **4** ***n*** (also **square joint**) *narcotics* A tobacco cigarette; =STRAIGHT **5** ***adj*** Fair; even-handed; just: *I'll be square with you* **6** ***v*** *fr late 1800s* To make things right, just, proper, etc: *He could never square himself with the police after that/ I know I was wrong, and now I'll square it* [the sense "conventional person, etc," is said to come fr a jazz musician's and standard conductor's hand gesture that beats out regular and unsyncopated four-beat rhythm, the hand doing so describing a *square* figure in the air]

square John (or **john**) ***n phr*** *fr underworld fr 1920s* An ordinary honest person; a good citizen; a noncriminal person who can be victimized by, and is contemptuously regarded by, criminals

square off ***v phr*** *fr early 1800s* To put oneself in a fighting posture: *The two biggest companies are squaring off over the microchip market*

square one ***n phr*** The place where some process begins or has begun; the original configuration: *So after all this fuss we are at square one* [fr board games where a token is moved off the *first square* after the shake of a die, drawing of a card, etc]

See GO BACK TO SQUARE ONE

squares ***See*** THREE SQUARES

square shooter ***n phr*** *fr early 1900s* An honest and candid person; =STRAIGHT ARROW • Now used nearly always with the conscious irony of archaic sincerity

Squaresville or **squaresville** **1** ***n*** *fr 1960s bop talk* A putative city inhabited entirely by dull, conventional people: *The Innocent Nihilists Adrift in Squaresville*—The Reporter/ *intimidated by being in the squaresville which is also the power center of the free world*—Hugh Sidey **2** ***adj:*** *on campus, where it once was squaresville to flip for the rock scene*—Time

squat **1** ***v*** To sit: *Hey, squat there a minute and I'll be right with you* ◁**2**▷ ***v*** To defecate; =SHIT, TAKE A DUMP ◁**3**▷ ***n:*** *Don't step in the squat* **4** ***n*** Nothing; zero; =DIDDLY, ZILCH, ZIP: *I didn't hear squat*—WT Tyler

See the HOT SQUAT, NOT GIVE A DAMN, NOT KNOW BEANS, TAKE A DUMP

◁**squaw**▷ ***n*** A woman, esp one's wife

squawk **1** ***v*** *fr late 1800s* To complain; =BEEF, BITCH: *Will you stop squawking about the food, please?* **2** ***n:*** *Okay, what's your squawk this morning?* **3** ***v*** *underworld* To inform; =SQUEAL: *Joe squawked* —WR Burnett [echoic of an unpleasant sound, esp the grating screech of a bird]

squawk box ***n phr*** *esp WW2 Navy* A military public address system; =BITCH BOX

squeak by (or **through**) ***v phr*** To pass, succeed, achieve a goal, etc, by the narrowest of margins: *He just barely squeaked through his medical boards*

squeaker **1** ***n*** A very closely contested and uncertain game, contest, etc: *They met in a squeaker that year, 23 to 24* **2** ***n*** Something poised on the edge of one result or another, esp a success versus a disaster: *"It'll be a squeaker," Bartow said. "This is a nervous time for us"*—Washington Post

squeaky-clean ***adj phr*** Perfectly clean; white, sanitary, and untarnished • Sometimes used ironically to emphasize conventionality and unimaginativeness: *this English band, made up of six squeaky-clean men in their early twenties*—Westworld [fr the *squeaky* sound produced by rubbing a finger across chinaware free of grease or dirt]

squeal **1** ***v*** *fr late 1800s underworld fr British dialect* To inform; =RAT, SING, SQUAWK **2** ***n*** *fr early 1800s* An informer; =RAT, SNITCH, STOOL PIGEON: *He was working on a case with a squeal*—New York Post **3** ***n*** (also **squeak**) A complaint to the police: *cop at stationhouse took the squeal* —Ed McBain

squealer ***n*** *fr middle 1800s* An informer; =RAT, SNITCH

squeeze ***n*** A situation of great pressure or peril; =CRUNCH: *I'm afraid we're in something of a squeeze just now*

See MAIN SQUEEZE, PUT THE SQUEEZE ON someone

squeeze-box ***n*** An accordion

squeezer ***See*** DUCK SQUEEZER, MOP-SQUEEZER

squib *n* A brief, sometimes witty piece of material in a newspaper or magazine, usu a space-filler: *He writes those witty "squibs"*—Westbrook Pegler [fr *squib* "a small firecracker," of unknown origin]

squiffed or **squiffy** or **squiffy-eyed** *adj fr late 1800s British* Drunk: *so-and-so's getting "squiffy" at a dance* —Robert Lynd/ *one of Frenise's squiffy-eyed nieces*—Paul Theroux

squiggle *n computer* The tilde, a sinuous diacritical mark

squirrel **1** *v* (also **squirrel away**) To hoard or cache something; hide and save something for later **2** *n* A crazy or eccentric person; =NUT, WEIRDO: *I seen some squirrels in my life, but you got 'em all beat*—H Allen Smith **3** *n hot rodders* A hesitant or confused hot rod driver **4** *v hot rodders* To weave about the road while driving, esp a hot rod **5** *n* An internal combustion cylinder; =BANG: *That car boasts six mighty squirrels* ◁**6**▷ *n college students* The vulva; =PUSSY

squirrely *adj* Crazy; eccentric; =NUTTY: *working out alone can make you squirrely*—Erma Bombeck

squirt **1** *n fr middle 1800s British* A short or small person, esp an insignificant, contemptible little male; =PEANUT: *Ah, what a little squirt is there* —WH Auden **2** *n* (also **young squirt**) *fr late 1800s students* A young man, esp a presumptuous or foppish youth

squishy *adj* Sentimental; =SCHMALTZY, SOPPY: *The sentiment may sound squishy*—Washington Post [fr late-19th-century *squshy* "soft and yielding," fr earlier echoic *sqush*]

squooshy (SKWōō shee) *adj* Soft; yielding and insubstantial: *Support for Reagan is "all very squooshy"* —Newsweek

SRO (pronounced as separate letters) **1** *n theater* Standing room only, usu indicating a full house and a successful production **2** *n* Single room occupancy residence hotel: *They're planning to demolish the SROs on this street*

stab *n* A try; =CRACK, SHOT, WHACK: *Well, I'll have a stab at it*

stable *n* The group of people performing similar work, managed by one person: *She's part of his stable of writers*

stache *See* STASH

stack *n* A car's tail pipe or exhaust pipe: *It was a twin-stack Bugatti* *See* BLOW one's TOP

stacked *adj* Very well-built in the sexual sense; having an attractive body: *She's well-stacked and sort of young* —Lionel Stander

stack of Bibles *See* SWEAR ON A STACK OF BIBLES

stack the deck (or **the cards**) *v phr* To prearrange something dishonestly; assure one's advantage fraudulently: *I should have had the job, but they stacked the deck against me/ He'll win if he stacks the cards*

stack up **1** *v phr fr late 1800s* To transpire; go along; succeed: *How are things stacking up for you?* **2** *v phr* To compare; measure against: *to begin stacking up Native Son with some of Frank Norris's stuff*—American Scholar **3** *v 1950s teenagers* To wreck a car; =RACK UP **4** *n* A multiple car wreck [first two senses fr the *stacking up* of one's poker chips to show winnings or for comparison]

stack Zs *See* COP ZS

stag **1** *n fr early 1900s* A man who goes to a party alone, without a woman partner **2** *adj* For men only; without women: *a stag function* **3** *adv: Several of the brothers were going to the dance stag*—P Marks **4** *n* (also **stag party**) A party for men only: *as broad as the jokes at a Legion stag*—J Evans

stage *See* UPSTAGE

stagflation *n* A simultaneous stagnation and inflation in the economy

the **staggers** *n phr fr late 1800s* A faltering and unsteady physical state, esp from liquor or narcotics intoxication: *The next day you've got the staggers and your fine coordination is destroyed for 72 hours*—Albert Goldman

stag line *n phr esp 1920s* The group of unescorting males at a dance, thought of as a line beside the floor, studying the women as possible dance partners

stairs *See* UPSTAIRS

stake *See* GRUBSTAKE

stake out *v phr police* To put someone or something under constant police surveillance: *He's been staked* *out often enough*—Mickey Spillane [fr earlier senses, as old as the 17th century, where *stake out* meant "mark off a territory, a line, a track, etc, with stakes"]

stake-out ***n*** *police* A police surveillance: *The stake-outs continued* —Dragnet (radio program)

stake someone **to** something ***v phr*** *fr late 1800s* To give or provide something to someone, inferentially as a loan: *Could you stake me to a new suit so I can get a job?* [fr the earlier senses where *stake* meant someone's basic provisions for farming, prospecting, etc]

stall 1 ***v*** *fr late 1800s* To delay; temporize; consume time and delay action; =BUY TIME: *I told him to quit stalling and give us a decision* **2** ***v*** To be halted or delayed; stagnate; bog down • Usually in the passive: *The negotiations are hopelessly stalled* **3** ***v*** (also **stall off**) To subject someone to delay; make excuses for inaction: *You stall her while I try to find her original letter/ He kept stalling the women off with one excuse or another*—A Hynd **4** ***n*** A pretext or excuse for delaying; a reason for inaction: *His claim of illness is only a stall* **5** ***n*** *fr middle 1800s* A pretense or false indication, esp as part of a criminal alibi: *I think that was just a stall*—Erle Stanley Gardner [fr Old English *steall* "standing, state, place, animal stall," whence the notion of stubbornly holding one's place]

stallion 1 ***n*** =STUD **2** ***n*** *black* A sexually attractive and/or active woman; =FOX

stamping ground (or **grounds**) ***n phr*** One's particular domain or territory; one's native heath: *Ann Arbor used to be my stamping ground* [fr 18th-century sense, "a place frequented by animals"]

stand 1 ***v*** *fr early 1800s* To give or pay for as a treat: *She stood him tea and muffins*—Sinclair Lewis **2** ***v*** To cost; =SET someone BACK: *The suit I got on stood me ten cents*—AJ Liebling **3** ***n*** A shop or store; a place of business: *You can get it at the Brooks Brothers stand on Fifth Avenue*

See ONE-NIGHT STAND

◁ **stand around with** one's **finger up** one's **ass**▷ (or **in** one's **ear**) ***v phr*** To be idle and helpless; fail to cope; be useless: *If you're just standing around with your finger up your ass you might as well lend a hand here*

stand (or **stand still**) **for** something ***v phr*** *fr late 1800s* To tolerate or abide something; swallow something • Usu in the negative: *He said he wouldn't stand for being replaced*

stand-in 1 ***n*** *show business fr early 1900s* A performer who takes the place of another, and is often hired to be prepared to do so at any time **2** ***n*** A substitute or proxy; a deputy: *Naive Stingo, as stand-in for us*—Philadelphia [perhaps fr the use of a substitute to replace a performer during such tedious procedures as adjusting lights, arranging the stage or set, etc; perhaps also fr the earlier notion of a deputy or place-holder, literally a lieutenant, in French "place-holder"]

standing on one's **head** ***See*** DO something ON TOP OF one's HEAD

standoff ***n*** *fr middle 1800s* A balanced and static conflict; a stalemate; a deadlock: *The union and the company are locked in a standoff*

See MEXICAN STANDOFF

standoffish ***adj*** Haughty; aloof; reserved and snobbish: *He gave us all a standoffish look* [fr late-19th-century *stand-off* "aloof, proud"]

stand on one's **head** ***v phr*** To make a very great effort; =BUST one's ASS: *I may not make it, but I'll sure stand on my head trying*

stand-out ***n*** A person or thing that is extraordinary, usu uncommonly good or talented; an outstanding person or thing: *Her performance of Amanda is the stand-out of the season*

stand pat 1 ***v phr*** *poker fr late 1800s* To keep one's original five cards in draw poker, without drawing new ones **2** ***v phr*** *fr late 1800s* To retain one's position; refuse to shift; carry on as one is; =SIT TIGHT: *The President stood pat on his decision to cut taxes* [fr the adverb *pat* "exactly, precisely to the purpose," and ultimately perhaps fr the echoic noun *pat*, analogously with expressions like *smack on the mark* and *smack-dab*, where precision and aptness are equated with a sharp blow or sound]

stand tall *v phr fr Army* To be proud and ready; have an imposing and confident stance

stand the gaff *v phr* To persist and endure against rigors; =TAKE IT: *I've learned to stand the gaff*—New York Times [fr *gaff*, the steel spur attached to the leg of a fighting cock]

stand the heat *See* IF YOU CAN'T STAND THE HEAT STAY OUT OF THE KITCHEN

stand there with one's **bare face hanging out** *v phr* To speak openly and brazenly; behave without shame or reticence: *Do you mean to stand there with your bare face hanging out and tell me such a weird story?/ My boss, his bare face hanging out, suggested it would be a nice idea*—Modern Maturity

stand-up *adj* Courageous and personally accountable; =GUTSY • Most often in the expression **stand-up guy**: *He handled the humiliating defeat like a stand-up guy*—Philadelphia [probably fr *stand up and be counted*]

stand someone **up** *v phr fr late 1800s* To fail to keep an appointment with, esp a date: *You won't stand me up, now will you?*—Jerome Weidman [perhaps related to *stand up* in the sense of "go through a wedding ceremony," the image being the forsaken bride or groom left standing alone at the altar]

stand up and be counted *v phr fr early 1900s* To announce and be accountable for one's convictions, opinions, etc; not be afraid to speak up: *Maybe a lot agree with you, but they won't stand up and be counted*

stand-up comic (or **comedian**) *n phr* A performer who typically stands alone before the audience in a nightclub, telling jokes, engaging in patter, etc: *We saw Woody Allen way back when he was a rather obscure stand-up comic*

stand up for someone *v phr* To defend and support; =GO TO BAT FOR someone: *Nobody stood up for her so she had to back off*

◀ **starfucker** ▶ **1** *n* A person, esp a young woman, who spends time with star performers and relishes the sex act with them; =GROUPIE **2** *modifier: Mellencamp appears to revel in the starfucker mentality he pokes fun at*—Village Voice

starker *See* SHTARKER

starkers *adj fr early 1900s British students* Naked; stark naked; =BARE-ASS: *You jog about, absolutely starkers*—Vogue [fr *stark* + the British slang suffix *-ers*]

starter *See* ARMSTRONG STARTER

starters *See* FOR OPENERS

start from scratch **1** *v phr* To begin on an even footing, with no advantage or handicap: *We're gonna have a good life together starting from scratch*—Inside Sports **2** *v phr* To begin with the very first and simplest steps; build from the ground: *Starting from scratch she got it finished in just two years* [fr the *scratch-line*, the starting line for races, often scratched in the earth]

stash or **stache** **1** *v* (also **stash away**) *fr early 1900s* To hide; hoard; save up: *I'd stash that jug*—James T Farrell **2** *v* To put or place; deposit; dispose of: *Just stash your coat on the chair* **3** *n* A hoard or cache: *She had a little stash of money in her bureau drawer* **4** *n* A hiding place: *if he wasn't home or in his stash, people would say*—Claude Brown **5** *n narcotics* A supply of narcotics, esp one's personal supply: *samples of their "special stash"*—New York Times **6** *n narcotics* A place where narcotics and associated paraphernalia are hidden, esp by a dealer [origin unknown; perhaps a blend of *stow* or *store* with *cache*]

stash bag *n phr fr narcotics* A small bag for carrying personal possessions, esp one used for marijuana

state of the art *adj phr fr 1970s* The latest; the very newest and most advanced: *Many of the escort services are so state-of-the-art that they make Toner's look primitive*—Philadelphia [the phrase has specialized fr the 1960s sense, "the present condition of knowledge, technique, etc, in a given field"]

Stateside or **stateside** **1** *n esp fr WW2 armed forces* The United States itself as distinct from foreign places, overseas possessions, etc **2** *adj: a genuine Stateside flavor to the celebration*—Yank

static *n* Complaints, backtalk, trivial objections, etc: *Here's the policy, and let's not have any static*

stats *n* Figures or statistics, esp relating to sports; =NUMBERS: *They are the kind of stats that a college powerhouse...might covet*—Time

◁ **stay** ▷ *v* To maintain a penile erection

stay loose *See* HANG LOOSE

stay out of the kitchen *See* IF YOU CAN'T STAND THE HEAT STAY OUT OF THE KITCHEN

steady *n fr late 1800s* One's constant and only boyfriend or girlfriend
See GO STEADY

steak *See* TUBE STEAK

steal *n* A great bargain: *I got that for half price, a real steal*

steal someone **blind** *v phr* To rob absolutely thoroughly; strip [fr the notion that the person being robbed must or might as well be *blind*]

steam **1** *v* To anger; make furious: *I steam easily*—Richard Starnes **2** *v* To make someone hotly amorous: *Be thrilled by...chilled by...and steamed by Gilbert and Garbo*—San Francisco
See LET OFF STEAM

steamed *adj* Angry; =PISSED OFF: *I'm too steamed to sleep, Lacey*—Doonesbury (comic strip)

steamed up **1** *adj phr* Angry; =PISSED OFF: *The first thing she does is get all steamed up about it*—Hal Boyle **2** *adj phr* Eager; excited: *He's really steamed up about the new initiative*

steamroller *n* To dominate and crush; achieve by sheer force: *The governor tried to steamroller the bill through*

steam someone **up** *v phr* To excite and stimulate; incite enthusiasm

steam was (or **is**) **coming out of** someone's **ears** *sentence* He or she was or is very angry: *Houk...was red-faced with anger....Steam was coming out of his ears*—Inside Sports

steamy *adj* Excitingly carnal; sexually arousing; =HOT, SEXY: *Hollywood's steamiest starlet*—Esquire

steer **1** *v underworld* To take or inveigle someone to a place or person where gamblers or confidence men might victimize him: *I been steerin' for Schwiefka all day*—Nelson Algren **2** *n* (also **steerer**) A person who steers patrons and victims: *He is nothing but a steer for a bust-out joint*—Damon Runyon **3** *n* Advice or information; a bit of useful data
See BUM STEER

stem **1** *n esp hoboes* A street, often the main street of a town or city **2** *v hoboes* To beg; =PANHANDLE **3** *n narcotics* An opium pipe
See MAIN DRAG

stems *n* The legs, esp the attractive legs of a woman

stephen *See* EVEN-STEVEN

step on it **1** *v phr* (also **step on the gas**) *fr 1920s* To accelerate; hurry; speed up: *We better step on it, there's only five minutes left* **2** *v phr* (Variations: one's **dick** or one's **shvantz** may replace **it**) *Army* To blunder; make a serious mistake

step out **1** *v phr fr late 1800s* To go out socially, esp to a dance or a party: *I haven't stepped out much lately, too busy* **2** *v phr* To escort someone socially; =DATE: *Who is she stepping out with these days?*

-ster *suffix used to form nouns* A person involved with, doing, or described by what is indicated: *clubster/ gridster/ mobster/ oldster*

steven *See* EVEN-STEVEN

stew[1] **1** *n* A drunkard **2** *n* A drunken carouse; =BINGE **3** *n* Confusion; chaos; =MESS
See IN A STEW

stew[2] or **stewie** *n* An airline cabin attendant, esp a female one: *Aeroflot personnel, beefy pilots and no-nonsense stewies*—Village Voice

stewbum *n* A drunken derelict: *Get up and go home, you stewbum*—William Kennedy

stewed or **stewed to the gills** *adj* or *adj phr fr 1700s* Drunk: *He knew where the colonel lived from the time he'd taken him home stewed*—Peter De Vries/ *He came in stewed to the gills*—Nelson Algren
See HALF-STEWED

stick **1** *n fr late 1800s* A baseball bat **2** *n* A baton, esp a conductor's baton **3** *n fr early 1900s* A golf club: *The golf dudes had their bag of sticks*—Sinclair Lewis **4** *n* A billiard cue: *I lived off the stick three months*—Nelson Algren **5** *n* The mast of a ship or boat: *The gale blew the sticks right out of her* **6** *n* A control lever or handle; =JOY-STICK **7** *n* (also **stick shift**) A manual gearshift lever, esp one mounted on the floor **8** *n* A slide rule; =SLIPSTICK **9** *n* A ski pole **10** *n* A clarinet; =LICORICE STICK **11** *n hawkers* A fountain pen **12** *n narcotics* A marijuana cigarette; =JOINT: *Marijuana was easy to get, 25 cents a "stick"*—New York Post **13** *n* A tall, thin person; =BEANPOLE **14** *n* A stiff, awkward person; an over-formal person **15** *n* A dull person; =STICK IN THE MUD **16** *v fr late 1600s* To cheat; swindle; esp, to overcharge: *runs the Bowie garage, routinely sticking what customers come his way*—Washington Post

See BIG STICK, DIPSHIT, GET ON THE STICK, HAVE A BROOM UP one's ASS, HOP-STICK, JIVE STICK, JOY-STICK, KNOW WHAT one CAN DO WITH something, LICORICE STICK, MAKE something STICK, ON THE STICK, SHITSTICK, SHORT END OF THE STICK, SLIP-STICK, SWIZZLE-STICK, TELL someone WHAT TO DO WITH something, WORK BEHIND THE STICK

stick around *v phr* To stay at or near a place; =HANG AROUND: *I asked the cops to stick around for a few minutes*

stick in the mud *n phr fr early 1700s* A dull, conservative person; =FOGY: *Be cautious, but don't be a stick in the mud*

stick it ◁**1**▷ *v phr* (Variations: **cram** or **ram** or **shove** or **stuff** may replace **stick**; **up** one's **ass** or **in** one's **ear** or **where the sun doesn't shine** may be added) To dispose of or deal with something one vehemently rejects; take back something offered and scorned • Very often used as a rude interjection conveying both rejection and insult: *Take that token raise and stick it/ Take the job and shove it*—Pietro di Donato/ *Cram it, will you?*—John Irving/ *He told them to take the money and ram it*—Interview/ *You can send them to President Carter or stick them in your ear*—Atlantic **2** *v phr* (also **stick it out**) To endure; =HANG IN: *It's rough as hell, but I'll stick it*

stick it to someone or something *v phr* To assault violently and definitively; =SOCK IT TO someone or something: *If he finds out he'll really stick it to you*

stick one's **neck out** *v phr fr 1930s* To put oneself at risk; invite trouble: *Don't stick your neck out too far*—Budd Schulberg

stick something **on** someone *v phr* To subject someone to something; force something on someone: *He's nervous and he sticks shtick à la Don Rickles on everyone*—Village Voice

stick out *v phr* (Variations: **like a sore thumb** or **a mile** may be added) To be very conspicuous; stand out starkly: *She really sticks out in that bunch/ Low profile? He sticks out like a sore thumb/ His humility doesn't exactly stick out a mile*

sticks *n fr middle 1800s* Legs; =GAMS: *a shapely pair of sticks*

See BOOM STICKS

the **sticks** *n phr fr early 1900s fr lumberjacks* Rural or suburban places; the provinces; =the BOONDOCKS: *a revue being tried out in the sticks*—HI Phillips [fr *sticks* "trees," representing the backwoods]

stick shift ***See*** STICK

stick to one's **knitting** *v phr* To attend strictly to one's own affairs; not interfere with others; be single-minded: *I'm not a personal confidant. I stick to my knitting*—Washington Post

stickum **1** *n* Glue; paste; cement **2** *n* Any viscous fluid; =GLOP, GUNK

stickup **1** *n* An armed robbery; =HOLDUP: *a robbery or a "stick-up"* —John Gunther **2** *n* An armed robber: *Mallory looked at the dark stick-up*—Raymond Chandler

stick up *v phr fr early 1900s* To rob, esp at gunpoint; =HOLD UP: *being "stuck up" by highwaymen*—Nation [apparently fr the command *stick 'em up* "hold up your hands"]

stick up for someone or something *v phr* To defend and support: *If his own family won't, who will stick up for him?*

sticky **1** *adj fr early 1900s British* Difficult; tricky; nasty: *We all had a very sticky half hour until the firefighters came along* **2** *adj* Sentimental; =SCHMALTZY, SOPPY: *a sticky little song about a crippled puppy* [first sense apparently fr the notion of a *stick* as being unbending and unyielding, represented in *stick* "a stiff, awkward person," perhaps reinforced by the notion of something that is hard to move or disengage because it is *stuck* or more or less glued; the second sense fr the viscousness of a *sticky* substance]

See ICKY

sticky-fingered *adj fr middle 1800s* Prone to steal or pilfer; larcenous; =LIGHT-FINGERED: *What are you, sticky-fingered?*—James Thurber

sticky wicket *n phr fr 1940s British* A very difficult or awkward situation; a nasty affair: *It's the original sticky wicket*—Car and Driver [fr the British phrase *bat on* (or *at*) *a sticky wicket* "contend with great difficulties," fr the game of cricket; *sticky* probably means simply "tricky, nasty," rather than having to do with the case where the bails or small horizontal pieces of wood are not readily dislodged from the three vertical ones of the wicket; in any event, cricket is a rather mysterious game]

stiff **1** *adj fr middle 1700s* Drunk: *when the regular piano player got stiff and fell from the stool* —Westbook Pegler **2** *n* A drunken person: *Robbing a drunken man they call "rolling a stiff"*—Jack London **3** *n fr middle 1800s* A corpse: *They found a couple of stiffs in the millpond* **4** *n hoboes fr late 1800s* A hobo; tramp; vagabond: *He bore none of the earmarks of the professional "stiff"*—Jack London **5** *n fr early 1900s* A migratory worker; =OKIE **6** *n fr early 1900s* A working man or woman; a nonclerical and nonprofessional employee; =WORKING STIFF: *Coolidge always seemed unreal to the ordinary stiff*—Robert Ruark **7** *n underworld fr late 1800s* A clandestine letter, esp one passed around among prisoners **8** *n underworld fr late 1800s* A forged check, banknote, etc **9** *adj underworld* Forged; =PHONY: *"I put over a couple of stiff ones," is the way a paperhanger describes an operation* —Saturday Evening Post **10** *n fr late 1800s British horse-racing* A team, fighter, contestant, etc, that is bound to lose; esp, a race horse that will not, cannot, or is not permitted to win: *There is also a rumor that Fol low You is a stiff in the race*—Damon Runyon **11** *n* Any failure; =FLOP, TURKEY: *gets a million dollars worth of hype, and I hear it's a stiff*—Aquarian **12** *v fr horse-racing* To cause a horse to lose a race: *He admitted that he himself had stiffed horses for a fee*—Sports Illustrated **13** *v* To fail to tip a waiter or other employee: *who not only stiffs waiters and cab drivers, but golf caddies as well*—Art Buchwald **14** *v* To cheat, esp out of money, fair wages, etc: *which creditors he could stiff, which he could stall, which had to be paid at once* —Lawrence Sanders **15** *v* To swindle; defraud; =SCAM: *In other words, New York City got stiffed*—Village Voice **16** *v* To maltreat; mislead and trick: *I was stiffed*—Ronald Reagan **17** *v* (also **stiff-arm**) To treat unfairly and harshly; snub or push aside brutally: *He had stiffed a Philadelphia charity golf tournament without explanation*—Sports Illustrated/ *understandable for President Reagan to stiff-arm the issue as "much ado about nothing"*—New York Times [the underworld senses having to do with forged and clandestine papers, cheating, etc, are derived fr an early-19th-century British sense, "paper, a document," probably based on the *stiffness* of official documents and document paper; the senses having to do with failure, etc, are related to the *stiffness* of a corpse; the sense of harsh snubbing, etc, is fr the *stiff-arm* in football, where a player, usu a runner, straightens out his arm and pushes it directly into the face or body of an intending tackler]

See BIG STIFF, BINDLESTIFF, BORED STIFF, KNOCK someone OUT, SCARED STIFF, WORKING STIFF

still wet behind the ears ***See*** NOT DRY BEHIND THE EARS

sting **1** *v fr early 1800s* To cheat; swindle; defraud; =SCAM **2** *v* To overcharge; =STICK: *He got stung in the corner hockshop* **3** *n esp fr early 1970s* A tricking or entrapment, either in a confidence scheme or as part of a law enforcement operation: *have used sting to describe undercover operations that use a bogus business operation as a front*—New York Times

stink **1** *v* (also **stink on ice**) To be deplorable, nasty, totally inept or bungling, disgusting, etc; =ROT: *The whole idea stinks, if you ask me/ The group and its main man stunk on ice* —Rolling Stone **2** *n* A complaint;

a noisy fuss or row: *He decided to make a stink about it*

See ACT LIKE one's SHIT DOESN'T STINK, BIG STINK, THINK one's SHIT DOESN'T STINK

stink bomb ***n phr*** Something disgusting, inept, deplorable, etc: *the stink bomb of a film,* Flashdance—Village Voice

stinker **1** ***n*** A despicable person; =BASTARD: *Stop acting like a stinker* **2** ***n*** (also **stinkeroo**) Something disgusting, nasty, badly done, etc: *Few of Hitchcock's films were genuine stinkers/ If it proves to be a "stinkeroo" leave the theater quietly or suffer in silence*—Coronet

◁ **stink-finger** ▷ *See* PLAY STINKY-PINKY

stinking **1** ***adj*** Despicable; wretched; =LOUSY: *Ain't it a stinking shame?/ It was a stinking way to treat her* **2** ***adj*** (also **stinking rich**) Very wealthy; =FILTHY RICH, LOADED: *The family, in those years, was stinking* **3** ***adj*** (also **stinko**) Drunk: *and he got pretty stinking*—Max Shulman

stinkpot ***n*** *sailors* A motorboat, esp a cabin cruiser

stink to high heaven ***v phr*** To be very disgusting, inept, nasty, etc: *filler items that definitely stunk to high heaven*—Village Voice

stink with ***v phr*** To have much of; be oversupplied with: *He stinks with confidence, certainly*

stinky ***adj*** Despicable; nasty

stinky-pinky *See* PLAY STINKY-PINKY

stir **1** ***n*** *fr middle 1800s British underworld* A jail or prison: *John went to stir*—E DeBaun **2** ***modifier:*** *with the stir haircuts*—Damon Runyon [perhaps fr Romany *steriben*; the mid-19th-century *sturbin* "state prison" may represent a transitional sense]

stir-crazy ***adj*** (Variations: **bugs** or **daffy** or **simple** may replace **crazy**) *prison* Insane, stuporous, hysterical, or otherwise affected mentally by imprisonment: *Any number of others were what we call "stir-crazy," going about their routine like punch-drunk boxers*—American Mercury

a **stitch** ***n phr*** An amusing or hilarious person or thing; =a HOOT: *The Gossages were a stitch, playing it very loose*—Sports Illustrated [fr the expression *in stitches* "laughing uncontrollably," perhaps fr the notion of laughing so much that it gives one *stitches* "sudden sharp pains"]

stocking *See* SILK-STOCKING

stoked ***adj*** *esp teenagers* Enthusiastic; happily surprised: *Everyone's stoked that he's here and... would he do a couple of tunes*—Playboy

stoked on ***adj phr*** Enthusiastic over; very much pleased with: *I was really stoked on that chick, man*—Dan Jenkins [fr the notion of being fueled and hot like a furnace]

stomp **1** ***n*** *fr early 1900s* A jazz number with a heavy rhythmic accent **2** ***v*** To assault viciously; savage; =CLOBBER: *These chaps went about stomping everyone they thought might be homosexual* **3** ***n*** *teenagers* A person who habitually wears cowboy boots [fr a dialect pronunciation of *stamp*]

◁ **stomp-ass** ▷ ***adj*** Violent and pugilistic; rough and vicious: *There's gonna be some sort of stompass scene*—Easyriders

stompers ***n*** *students* Boots, esp cowboy boots

See SHITKICKERS, WAFFLE-STOMPERS

stone **1** ***adj*** *fr black* Thorough; perfect; total: *Reba's a stone psycho, I tell you*—Joseph Wambaugh **2** ***adv*** Totally; genuinely: *He is a stone crazy dude* [fr earlier adverbial sense "like or as a stone," in phrases like *stone* blind or *stone* deaf]

See NOT CARVED IN STONE

stone cold sober ***adj phr*** Totally unintoxicated; =COLD SOBER

stoned or **stoned-out** ***adj*** *fr 1940s cool talk* Intoxicated with narcotics or liquor; =BOMBED OUT, ZONKED: *They get themselves stoned on beer*—Dorothy Parker/ *The old man was stoned mad*—Robert Stone/ *giggling in that mutually exclusive stoned-out way*—San Francisco

stone dead ***adj phr*** As dead as can be

stoned to the eyes ***adj phr*** Completely intoxicated; =HIGH: *Under that tree, stoned to the eyes, I wolf down Daybreak, Joan Baez's autobiography*—Village Voice

stonewall **1** ***v*** *fr British fr late 1800s Australian* To delay and obstruct, esp by stubbornly keeping silent • The term became prominent during the early 1970s Watergate scandal: *I want you all to stonewall it*—Richard M Nixon **2** *n: A sustained stonewall, no one's been willing to answer questions for a week*—Village Voice [fr a cricket term used of a determined batsman who blocked everything as if he were a *stone wall*; in the US probably influenced by the stolid reputation of the Confederate general Thomas J "*Stonewall*" Jackson]

stonies *n phr* Urgent sexual desire: *They passed a local law prohibiting a dude with stonies from soliciting a woman-of-the-night for a piece of ass*—Easyriders [semantically similar to *hard up*, with its suggestion of penile erection; probably transferred because of the hardness of *stone* and the sense of *stones* as "testicles"]

stony cold broke *adj phr fr late 1800s* Absolutely penniless; pauperized; destitute

stooge 1 *n fr late 1800s show business* A servile assistant; a mere flunky or tool: *Whenever Gulliver is not acting as a stooge there is a sort of continuity in his character*—George Orwell **2** *v: We're glad to stooge for him*—Raymond Chandler [origin unknown; perhaps an alteration of *student*, humorously mispronounced as STōō jənt, in the sense of an apprentice, especially one unskilled at or learning a theatrical turn of some sort while serving as the underling of a master]

stool 1 *n underworld* A police informer; =STOOL PIGEON: *He's nothing but a cop's stool*—James M Cain **2** *v: to make me stool on a friend*—J Evans [back formation fr *stool pigeon*]

stoolie *n underworld* A police informer; =STOOL PIGEON: *There was stoolies and wire tappers working all over town* [back formation fr *stool pigeon*]

stool pigeon *n phr underworld fr early 1800s* A police informer; =SNITCH, SQUEALER: *In New York he is also called a stool pigeon*—J Flynt [fr earlier sense "decoy," fr the early-19th-century practice of fastening *pigeons* and other birds to *stools* or stands as decoys; this term was applied to the decoy or "hustler" for a faro bank]

stoop *See* STUPE

stop *See* PIT STOP, WHISTLE STOP

stop someone or something **dead in** someone's or something's **tracks** *v phr* To stop very definitely and abruptly: *The economy could be stopped dead in its tracks*—Art Buchwald [fr the image of a person or animal dropping straight down on being struck]

stop on a dime *v phr* To stop quickly and neatly: *The car corners smoothly and stops on a dime*

storage *See* IN COLD STORAGE

Storch *See* JOE BLOW[1]

store *n circus & carnival* A concession *See* MIND THE STORE

storm *v hot rodders fr 1950s* To speed; drive very fast
See BARNSTORM, BLOW UP A STORM, BRAINSTORM, SHITSTORM, UP A STORM

story *See* FISH STORY, LOOSE IN THE BEAN, SOB STORY

stow it *Navy* **1** *v* To stop doing something • Often an irritated command **2** *v* =STICK IT

STP (pronounced as separate letters) *n narcotics* A powerful hallucinogen: *a strictly contemporary folk drug, called STP by its Haight-Ashbury discoverers*—Scientific American [fr *Serenity Tranquility Peace*, named in imitation of the oil additive STP (a trade name)]

strack *adj Army* Very strict in one's military appearance and grooming [fr *STRAC*, acronym for *Strategic Army Corps*, chosen units in constant combat readiness, hence elite troops]

straddle the fence *v phr* To avoid taking a public position on one or another side of an issue; remain neutral or ambiguous: *The candidate kept straddling the fence about abortion*

straight 1 *adj fr middle 1800s* Unmixed; undiluted: *He takes his liquor straight* **2** *adj narcotics fr 1960s* Not using narcotics; not addicted **3** *adj narcotics since 1960s* Having had a narcotics dose, esp the first one of the day: *Once the addict has had his shot and is "straight" he may become... industrious*—Reader's Digest **4** *n esp musicians & students* A tobacco cigarette; =SQUARE **5** *adj fr homosexuals* Heterosexual; not sexually deviant **6** *adj* True; honest and direct:

from straight-poop tough to moral—Village Voice/ *straight talk/ straight goods/ just a straight kind of guy* **7** *adv* Truthfully and directly: *I'll tell it to you straight*
See GO STRAIGHT

straight-ahead *adj* Unflinching; undeviating: *Bill was a straight-ahead guy*—Philadelphia

straight arrow **1** *n phr* A person who observes the social norms of decency, honesty, legality, heterosexuality, etc; a nondeviant: *This is a supervisory job that ordinarily is won by the group Straight Arrow, the Eagle Scout type*—Harper's **2** *adj: For marches you have to be straight arrow because what if they interview us for TV?*—Ms [fr an archetypical upright Native American brave named *Straight Arrow*, mythically associated with a similar Caucasian who is a *straight shooter*]

straighten up and fly right *v phr* =CLEAN UP one's ACT

straight face *n phr* A face revealing no ironic amusement or disbelief: *He couldn't tell me that story with a straight face*

straight from the horse's mouth *See* FROM THE HORSE'S MOUTH

straight from the shoulder *adv phr* Honestly and directly; unflinchingly; =STRAIGHT: *He gave it to us straight from the shoulder* [perhaps from the notion of an honest blow delivered *straight from the shoulder* rather than deviously, from the side, etc]

straight job *n phr truckers* An ordinary truck as distinct from a semi-trailer

straight lane *See* IN THE STRAIGHT LANE

straight man *n show business* A comedian's interlocutor and companion, who acts as the foil

the **straight skinny** *n phr* The truth: *lame enough to have told me the straight skinny about that*—Richard Merkin [see *the skinny*]

straight talk *n phr* Direct and honest discourse

straight-up **1** *adj* Honest; upright; =STRAIGHT ARROW: *They were straight-up, nice people*—Claude Brown **2** *adj* Of cocktails, served without ice cubes; =NEAT

strap *n esp students* A student interested primarily in sports; =JOCK [fr *jock strap* "athletic supporter"]

strapped *adj fr middle 1800s* Short of money; penniless; =BROKE: *He happens to be strapped financially*—Ellery Queen [origin unknown; perhaps related to the idea of tightening one's belt when it becomes necessary, perhaps related to British dialect *strap* "credit," so that a *strapped* person would be one forced to buy on credit]

strategist *See* ARMCHAIR GENERAL

straw-hat circuit *n phr show business* Summer theaters collectively

streak **1** *v esp early 1970s* To run naked in public **2** *n: The students did a streak across the square*
See a BLUE STREAK

streaker *n* A person who streaks: *She complained that several streakers marred her view of the campus*

street *modifier* Having to do with the streets and the street life of a city, esp of a ghetto: *Curtis Sliwa, founder of the street-tough Guardian Angels*—Philadelphia Journal
See EASY STREET, TWO-WAY STREET

the **street** *See* WORK BOTH SIDES OF THE STREET

street (or **garbage**) **furniture** *n phr* Furniture put in the street for the trash collectors, and sometimes taken for use

street people *fr 1960s* **1** *n phr* Ghetto dwellers **2** *n phr* Homeless people like transient hippies, bag ladies, and the like; drifters

the **streets** *See* POUND THE PAVEMENT

street-smart or **street-bright** or **street-wise** *adj* Cunning and clever in various practical ways, esp in the street culture of the urban ghetto: *a place for very sophisticated, street-bright people*—Toronto Life/ *supplanting preppie glamour with what's euphemistically called a "streetwise" look. Supertramp is more like it*—Us

street smarts *n phr* Cunning and cleverness of a very practical sort, esp that useful in the urban ghetto: *that raging philosophical conflict between street smarts and pinstripes*—Philadelphia

stretch limo *n phr* A limousine that has been lengthened to provide more seating and more luxurious surrounds: *certified designer fashions, eye-popping jewelry, stretch limos*—Philadelphia [probably modeled on the earlier term *stretch* or *stretched* applied to a jetliner with a lengthened fuselage providing more seating]

stretch out *v phr jazz musicians* To play uninhibitedly: *When a cat stretches out, he can make the moon* —E Horne

strictly *adv* Totally; entirely: *Everything about it is strictly from yuck* —Washington Post

stride **1** *n jazz musicians* A jazz piano style of alternating bass with treble notes in particular patterns **2** *modifier: stride piano, Harlem's version of ragtime*—Albert Goldman/ *stride bass*

strike it rich *v phr fr middle 1800s* To have a sudden financial success

strike oil *v phr fr middle 1800s* To succeed: *I worked at the problem eight days before I struck oil*

string *v fr middle 1800s* To deceive; fool; hoax: *Who are you trying to string, anyhow?*—Elmer Rice
See PULL someone's CHAIN, PULL THE STRING

string along *v phr* To agree; follow; join in: *As long as you string along with me, your cafeteria days are over* —Jerome Weidman

string someone **along** *v phr fr late 1800s* To deceive; fool, esp into a continuing adherence, cooperation, etc; =STRING: *I'm afraid that he's just stringing me along, trying to encourage me*—P Marks [probably fr early-19th-century British *string on*, in the same sense]

stringbean *n* A tall, thin person; =BEANPOLE

string someone **out** **1** *v phr* To intoxicate: *I couldn't figure what she had done in there to string him out so bad*—Harry Crews **2** *v phr* To disturb; upset: *The one thing that strings me out...is punks who travel in packs* —Noel Gerson

strings *See* PULL STRINGS

string someone **up** *v phr* To hang

strip *See* DRAG STRIP, LEAVE A STRIP

Strip *See* SUNSET STRIP

the **Strip** *n phr* Any of various main streets in US cities, esp the street in Las Vegas where most of the gambling casinos are found

stripe *See* HASH MARK

stripes **1** *n circus* A tiger **2** *n Army* Chevrons worn as insignias of noncommissioned rank; =CROW TRACKS

stripped down **1** *adj phr* Of a car, divested of ornaments and other unnecessary parts **2** *adj phr* Reduced to the essentials; disencumbered: *a stripped-down version of the Oedipus myth*

stripper *n* A striptease dancer: *Norma Vincent Peel, the noted stripper*

strip-search *n* =SKIN-SEARCH

stroke **1** *v fr black* To praise and please; caress the ego of; flatter; cosset: *and ads in Rolling Stone were more for the purpose of stroking recording artists*—Wall Street Journal **2** *n: Everybody needs a stroke or two every once in a while* ◁**3**▷ *v* To masturbate [*stroker* "flatterer" is attested in the early 17th century]

stroke book *n phr* A lewd or suggestive publication; a pornographic book or magazine: *It took a stroke book for me to break the ice*—Richard Price [fr *stroke* "masturbate"]

stroke house *n phr* A pornographic movie theater [fr *stroke* "masturbate"]

strong *See* COME ON STRONG

strong-arm *fr late 1800s* **1** *modifier* Using threats of violence; physically brutal: *strong-arm work around election time*—E Lavine **2** *v* To use force and intimidation: *We can't strong-arm them into voting our way*

strong-arm man *n phr* A man who uses physical force, usu as a hired agent; a thug; =ENFORCER, GOON

◁**stronger than pig shit**▷ *adj phr* Very strong: *beautiful and a genius... stronger than pig shit*—Dan Jenkins

struggle **1** *n outdated college students & Army* A party or dance; =FIGHT **2** *v sports* To have difficulty winning or holding the pace; be in athletic travail: *Lendl Struggles to Win*—New York Times

strung out **1** *adj phr narcotics fr 1950s* Using or addicted to narcotics; intoxicated with narcotics: *The entire college population is "strung out" thrice weekly*—New York Post/ *got fairly well strung out, fairly well addicted*—Esquire **2** *adj phr narcotics & students fr 1960s* Emotionally disturbed; psychologically tense, brittle, and vulnerable; =UPTIGHT: *She got herself strung way out...just one more little push and she was a dead duck*—Changes **3** *adj black* Infatuated; in love: *He's strung out on her* [apparently by extension fr the black term *on a tight leash* "in love; addicted," stressing the tethered helplessness of each condition]

strut one's **stuff** *See* DO one's STUFF

stuck on someone or something *part phr fr late 1800s* In love with; infatuated: *That feller was stuck on yuh, Bess*—H Witwer

stuck-up *adj fr early 1800s* Haughty and conceited; snobbish; =HINCTY: *We didn't like her at first because we thought she acted stuck-up*

stuck with *past part phr* Burdened with; endowed with: *Imagine being stuck with a moniker like that all your life*—Leslie Ford

stud 1 *n fr 1930s jive talk* A man, esp one who is stylish, au courant, etc; =DUDE **2** *n* A sexually prodigious man; =COCKSMAN **3** *n* An attractive man: *Her boyfriend's such a stud!* [fr early-19th-century US *stud* or *studhorse* "stallion, esp one kept for breeding"]

studio *See* RAP CLUB

stuff 1 *n 1920s prohibition era* Liquor, esp bootleg liquor: *The stuff is here and it's mellow* **2** *n narcotics* Any narcotic: *He came out and seemed to be off the stuff*—New York Post ◁**3**▷ *n* A woman regarded as a sex object; =ASS, COOZ, PUSSY: *classiest stuff this side of Denver*—Stephen Longstreet ◁**4**▷ *v* To do the sex act; =FUCK • Chiefly British and most often heard in the passive imperative form **get stuffed**, a rude insult; used in any sense of **fuck**: *No women, no children, no fun. Stuff this*—John Leonard

See BLACK STUFF, EATIN' STUFF, the GREEN STUFF, HARD STUFF, HOT STUFF, KID STUFF, KNOW one's ONIONS, KNOW WHAT one CAN DO WITH something, ROUGH STUFF, SOB STUFF, TELL someone WHAT TO DO WITH something, WHITE STUFF

stuffed *See* GET STUFFED

stuffed shirt *n phr fr early 1900s* A pompous person; a stiff, self-important bore

the **stuffing** *See* BEAT THE SHIT OUT OF

stuff it *See* STICK IT

stuff the ballot box *v phr fr middle 1800s* To cast or record fraudulent votes in an election

stuffy 1 *adj fr early 1800s* Angry; sulky; obstinate **2** *adj fr 1920s* Tediously conventional; pompous and self-righteous: *He was inclined to be a bit stuffy in sexual matters* [later sense fr *stuffy* "stale, lacking freshness," influenced by *stuffed shirt*]

stumble *v underworld* To be arrested; =FALL

stumblebum *n* An alcoholic derelict; a drunken drifter: *paint the candidates as a wrangling collection of stumblebums*—Washington Post

stump for someone or something *v phr* To advocate or support, esp very actively [fr the notion of giving speeches from *stumps*]

◁**stump-jumper**▷ *n* A rural person; farmer; =SHITKICKER

stunt *n* Act; bit of behavior; thing to do: *That was a stupid stunt, my dear*

◁**stup**▷ *See* SHTUP

stupe or **stoop** *n fr middle 1700s* A stupid person: *"Don't call me stupe," Humphrey said*—G Homes

style 1 *v fr black* To act or play in a showy, flamboyant way; =HOT DOG, SHOWBOAT **2** *pres part: The proper reward for a styling player is a fast ball in the ribs*—Philadelphia Journal

See CRAMP someone's STYLE, DOG FASHION, LIKE IT'S GOING OUT OF STYLE

stymie *v fr early 1900s fr golf* To block or thwart; frustrate: *We have to figure a way to stymie that guy* [fr British dialect *stimey* "dim-sighted person," fr *stime* "ray or bit of light"; adopted in golf for situations where the player or, as it were, the ball, cannot "see" a clear path ahead]

suave or **swave** (SWAYV) *n teenagers* Smooth skill; polished adroitness: *He has plenty of suave when it comes to girls*

sub[1] **1** *n* A substitute of any sort, esp an athlete who replaces another or an athlete not on the first team **2** *v: Who'll sub for me when I go on leave?*

sub[2] **1** *n* A submarine: *Saw sub, sank same* **2** *n* =HERO SANDWICH

◁**suck**▷ **1** *v* To do fellatio; =EAT **2** *v* (also **suck rope**) To be disgusting or extremely reprehensible; be of wretched quality; =ROT, STINK: *a failure as an album. It sucks*—Rolling Stone/ *Your decision sucks rope*—Bob Newhart (TV program) **3** *v* =SUCK ASS **4** *n* =SUCTION

suck air *v phr* To be afraid, so as to pant: *Were you afraid? I was sucking air a couple of times*—Bernard Arkules

suck around *v phr* To loiter about; frequent a place, esp with a view to currying favor: *What's the kid sucking around the clubhouse for?*

◁ **suck ass**▷ *v phr* To curry favor; flatter and cajole; =BROWN-NOSE, POLISH APPLES: *He sucks ass with everybody in the front office*

suck eggs **1** *v phr* *esp Southern* To be mean and irritable: *We've sucked on these eggs long enough*—Peter Gent **2** *v phr* To be disgusting or reprehensible; be of wretched quality; =SUCK • A euphemism for the same sense of **suck**: *his own pet phrase, "That sucks eggs," for expressing disdain*—Washington Post **3** *v phr* To do something very nasty, esp when invited to; =GO FUCK oneself • A euphemism: *Tell your husband to suck huge eggs*—Village Voice

sucker **1** *n* *fr early 1800s* An easy victim; dupe; =MARK, PATSY: *I'm no sucker*—Theodore Dreiser **2** *v* To victimize or dupe someone: *if I can sucker him into drawing first*—Mickey Spillane **3** *n* Any specified object, esp one that is prodigious, troublesome, effective, etc; =MOMMA, MOTHERFUCKER • A euphemism for **cocksucker**: *It took me 90 days to get that sucker straightened out*—New York/ *Careful, that sucker's heavy* [origin uncertain; perhaps fr the *sucker*, a fish supposed to be easily caught; perhaps fr the notion of an unweaned and relatively helpless creature, as suggested by an earlier sense, "greenhorn, simpleton"]
See COCKSUCKER

sucker list *n phr* A list of prospective customers, victims, etc: *The directory is not intended to be a sucker list*—Philadelphia Bulletin

suckerpunch **1** *n* A blow that fools and surprises the recipient, who ought to have dodged or parried it **2** *v*: *He suckerpunched me*—Peter Gent

suck face *v phr* To kiss and caress; =NECK, PET: *You know, kiss. Suck face, kiss*—Ernest Thompson

suck hind tit *v phr* To be in a disadvantageous situation; get the worst and least of things: *They all collected a fortune and I was left sucking hind tit again* [fr the presumed disadvantage of a *suckling* at the *nethermost teat*]

suck someone **in** *v phr* *fr middle 1800s* To deceive; befool or dupe, esp with false promises [said to be fr the action of quicksand]

sucking *See* COCKSUCKING

◁ **suck off**▷ *v phr* To do fellatio or cunnilingus; =BLOW, GO DOWN ON someone

◁ **suck-off**▷ **1** *n* A despicable person, esp a flatterer; =BROWN-NOSE **2** *adj* Despicable; nasty; =SCUZZY: *We did a suck-off thing*—Stephen King

suck up *v phr* To defeat in a speed race; pass in a drag race: *I have also sucked up plenty of cherry red Vettes*—Car and Driver [fr the notion of drawing the passed car along in one's turbulence behind]

suck up to someone *v phr* *fr middle 1800s British* To flatter and cajole; curry favor with; =BROWN-NOSE, SUCK ASS: *He gets ahead by sucking up to the mayor*

suction *n* Influence; =DRAG, PULL

sudden death **1** *n phr* *sports* Any of several arrangements for breaking a tie by playing an extra period during which the first team to score wins the game: *They were tied, so went into sudden death* **2** *modifier:* *It's like playing a sudden death inning at the beginning of a game*—Walter Mondale

suds *n* *fr early 1900s* Beer

sudser *n* A soap opera; =SOAP: *Harvey Fierstein's savvy sudser about a not-so-gay drag queen*—Time

sugar **1** *n* *fr middle 1800s* Money; =BREAD: *I'd take a trip if I had the requisite sugar* **2** *n* Dear one; sweetheart • Most often a term of address: *I hear you, sugar* **3** *n* *narcotics* LSD; =ACID [narcotics sense fr the taking of LSD soaked in a *sugar* cube]
See HEAVY MONEY

Sugar *See* UNCLE SUGAR

sugar-coat something *v phr* To make something more acceptable or palatable: *He did not have to sugar-coat the facts for us*

sugar daddy *n phr* A man who provides money, esp one who supports a clandestine sweetheart or a gold-digger: *Mrs Shawsky must have had a sugar daddy on the side*—Fact Detective Mysteries

See DADDY

◁ **sugar tit**▷ ***n phr*** Something that gives comfort and security; =SECURITY BLANKET [fr the use of a cloth soaked in *sugar* water to appease a suckling infant]

suit ***n*** A serious business or professional person: *They thought it was time he got out of jeans and became a suit* [fr the wearing of a *suit*, shirt, tie, etc, at work]

See BIRTHDAY SUIT, JUMP SUIT, MONKEY SUIT, ZOOT SUIT

suit up ***v phr*** *fr astronautics* To get into the appropriate clothing; prepare for action by donning proper gear or uniform

◁ **sumbitch**▷ *See* SON OF A BITCH

◁ **sumbitching**▷ *See* SON-OF-A-BITCHING

sun *See* STICK IT

Sunday 1 ***modifier*** The best; one's best: *Sunday punch/ Sunday clothes* **2** ***modifier*** Amateur; occasional: *For a Sunday painter he's not bad*

See FORTY WAYS TO SUNDAY

Sunday clothes ***n phr*** One's best clothes; =BEST BIB AND TUCKER [fr the earlier *Sunday-go-to-meeting clothes*]

Sunday driver ***n phr*** A slow and careless driver, like one out for a leisurely Sunday drive

Sunday punch 1 ***n phr*** *prizefight* A very hard and effective blow or assault, with the fist or otherwise: *and lay his Sunday punch on your snoot* —Damon Runyon **2** ***modifier:*** *rockets, the "Sunday punch" weapon of the war*—Associated Press **3** ***n phr*** *baseball* A strong and effective pitch, esp an overpowering fastball

sunlight *See* LET DAYLIGHT INTO

Sunset Strip ***n phr*** A section of Los Angeles, along Sunset Boulevard, frequented by alienated teenagers, drug users, derelicts, and other sub- and counterculture persons

sunshades ***n*** Sunglasses; =SHADES

sunshine ***n*** *narcotics* LSD, esp taken as an orange tablet; =ACID, ORANGE SUNSHINE: *powerful as a tab of "sunshine" dropped before you step in the cab*—Albert Goldman [fr the yellow-orange color]

See YELLOW SUNSHINE

Sunshine *See* ORANGE SUNSHINE

sunshine law ***n phr*** A law requiring that meetings of legislative bodies be opened to the public: *After the sunshine law the city council had to open its doors*

super[1] ***n*** A superintendent, esp one who is custodian of an apartment building

super[2] ***adj*** *esp teenagers fr 1940s* Wonderful; excellent; very superior • Also British fr 1920s and still very common in Great Britain among a larger group than teenagers: *America's Teenage Girls Speak Language of Their Own That Is Too Divinely Super*—Life [perhaps fr *superior* or *superfine*]

super- 1 ***prefix used to form nouns*** A superbly qualified and prodigious specimen of what is indicated: *superjerk/ superjock/ superchick/ Supermom* **2** ***prefix used to form adjectives*** Having the indicated quality to an extraordinary degree: *superhappy/ superwonky*

super-duper or **sooper-dooper** ***adj*** *esp 1940s* Excellent; wonderful; splendid; superb: *this new MGM sooper-dooper musical smash*—New York Times/ *Bloomingdale's sells a super-duper pooper-scooper* [rhyming]

superfly ***adj*** *black* Superior; wonderful; =SUPER: *He really thinks he's superfly when he gets into his thing* —Richard Woolley

superintendent *See* SIDEWALK SUPERINTENDENT

Superwoman ***n*** A woman who successfully undertakes marriage, motherhood, and a full working life all at the same time

supper *See* SHOOT one's COOKIES

sure ***affirmation*** *fr early 1700s British* Yes; certainly: *Sure, I'll support you*

See SHITSURE

◁ **sure as shit**▷ (or **as shooting**) **1** ***affirmation*** Yes; certainly **2** ***adj phr*** Certain; definite: *It's sure as shit that she doesn't want to go* **3** ***adv phr:*** *Thousands of them are sent by civic leaders... and, sure as shooting, by other federal judges*—Saul Bellow [alliterating, perhaps fr *shitsure*]

one **sure knows how to pick 'em**

See one CAN REALLY PICK 'EM

sure thing ***affirmation*** *fr middle 1800s* Yes; certainly; willingly: *Sure thing I'll go with you*

sure thing *n phr fr early 1800s* A certainty, esp a bet which one cannot lose: *His election is a sure thing, right?*

surf bunny *n phr* =BEACH BUNNY

suss out *v phr* To discover by intuition or inquiry; find out; learn: *I sussed out Whoosh was the chief my first time... here*—Richard Price/ *I've got to start sussing out nonscuzzy places to pee all along our most-traveled routes*—Village Voice [fr *suspect* or *suspicion*, attested as *sus* in British sources fr about 1925; perhaps popularized and brought to the US by British rock-and-roll groups]

-sville or **-ville** **1** *suffix used to form adjectives* Characterized by what is indicated: *dragsville/ squaresville* **2** *suffix used to form nouns* Place characterized by what is indicated: *Derbyville/ Motorsville*

swacked *adj* Drunk: *Besides, you're swacked all the time*—Saul Bellow

swak or **SWAK** (pronounced as separate letters) *sentence* Sealed with a kiss

swallow something *v* To affirm or endure reluctantly; stomach: *What I can't swallow is that he was then promoted*

swallow a watermelon seed *v phr* To become pregnant: *Did you hear that Pamela Wall swallowed a watermelon seed?*—Pat Conroy

swallow the apple (or **the olive**) *v phr sports* To become tense and ineffective; =CHOKE UP: *I flat-out swallowed the apple and blew it*—Philadelphia Journal

swamper *n truckers fr late 1800s teamsters* A trucker's helper or loader: *The cops want to know if any of the wives knew which swampers their husbands were using*—George Warren

swank **1** *adj* (also **swanky**) *fr early 1900s* Elegant; stylish; =RITZY: *Carroll's swank office*—Associated Press **2** *n: the... swank of his riding clothes*—F Scott Fitzgerald **3** *v: I saw her swanking up the avenue in furs* [origin unknown; perhaps fr Middle English *swanken* "to sway," cognate with German *schwenken* "to flourish"; perhaps fr Efik *swanga buckra* "well-dressed white man"]

swat *v fr early 1900s* To strike; hit: *He spoke up and got swatted for it*

swat (or **SWAT**) **team** *n phr fr 1960s* A police unit wearing militarylike uniforms and using military assault weapons on assignments requiring extraordinary coordination and force: *When the terrorists took over the whole building, the commissioner sent in the swat team* [fr *special weapons and tactics* used as a modifier]

swave *See* SUAVE

swear (or **swear to**) **on a stack of Bibles** *v phr* To affirm with absolute confidence and considerable vehemence: *Don called all those short-term signals for Joe. I'd swear to that on a stack of Bibles*—New York

sweat **1** *v* To suffer; stew; =COOK: *Let 'em sweat for a while before you tell them* **2** *v* To work very hard and meticulously: *I do the main job and let my partner sweat the details* *See* IN A SWEAT, NO SWEAT, PANTHER PISS

sweat bullets **1** *v phr* To be very worried; be apprehensive; =SHIT A BRICK: *They've been sweating bullets since they heard he was looking for them* **2** *v phr* To work very hard: *Their father has to sweat bullets to make a living*—People Weekly

sweater (or **pin-up**) **girl** *n phr esp 1940s* A young woman, esp a movie actress or a model, with a notably attractive body which she features by wearing tight and short clothing

◁ **sweat hog**▷ **1** *n phr college students* A heavy and unattractive woman **2** *n phr* A sexually promiscuous woman

sweat it *v phr fr rock and roll fr 1950s* To be apprehensive; =be UPTIGHT • Most often used in the negative: *Well, don't sweat it. Look, is a buck and a quarter okay?*—New York

sweat out *v phr* To endure or suffer, esp with nervous anticipation: *a young writer sweating out the creation of his first short stories*—Village Voice

sweat something **out of** someone *v phr* To discover by intimidation or harsh questioning: *The cops finally sweated his name out of Duke*

sweep **1** *n sports* The winning of a tournament, series, etc, without losing a single game: *He took the match in a sweep, straight sets* **2** *v: The*

Giants swept the World Series that year

sweet ass *See* BUST one's ASS

sweeten someone **up** **1** *v phr* To bribe or otherwise recompense someone in exchange for something: *He had to sweeten the cops up even after he had the license* **2** *v phr* To flatter and cajole; =SUCK UP TO someone: *He sweetened up the audience a little by praising the town*

sweetheart **1** *n* Something excellent; a cherished and valuable object; =HONEY: *See that sweetheart of a car?* **2** *n* A pleasant person; =DOLL: *Wait'll you meet her father, he's a sweetheart*

sweetheart deal *n phr* A mutually profitable and either unethical or illegal arrangement, usu involving a public agency: *what the cable companies now term a "sweetheart deal." The Port Authority just turned over the whole thing to Merrill Lynch*—Village Voice

sweetie *n* A sweetheart, in all senses • Often a term of endearment in address: *And Tom's the first sweetie she ever had*—F Scott Fitzgerald/ *Are you calling me, sweetie?/ Ain't my new computer a sweetie?*

sweetie-pie *n* A sweetheart, in all senses: *His sweetie pie came home in the early hours*—Associated Press/ *He showed us a sweetie-pie of a little boat*

sweet mama *n phr esp black* A female lover

sweet man (or **papa**) *n phr esp black* A male lover

sweet on someone *adj phr fr 1700s* Enamored of; in love with: *He was never really sweet on Miss Carlisle*—Agatha Christie

sweet patootie *See* PATOOTIE

sweets *n* =SWEETHEART, SWEETIE • A term of endearment: *I'll get it for you, sweets*

sweet spot *n phr* The best area on a tennis racket, hockey stick, or baseball bat for contact with the ball or puck

sweet-talk **1** *v phr* To seek to persuade or soften someone, esp by flattery and endearments; =FAT-MOUTH **2** *n: He listened to her sweet-talk very receptively*

swell **1** *n fr early 1800s British* A stylish and well-groomed person; =DUDE **2** *n fr early 1800s British* A wealthy, elegant person; a socialite: *up on the hill where the swells live* **3** *adj fr middle 1800s* Excellent; wonderful; superb: *The hotels are swell*—Theodore Dreiser/ *He was a hell of a swell fellow*—Charles MacArthur **4** *adv: The new owners have treated me swell*—Associated Press [perhaps fr the late-18th-century phrase *cut a swell* "swagger," describing the behavior of a person who *swells* with arrogance]

swellhead **1** *n* A conceited person; a person whose head is swollen with pride: *She acted like a swellhead after she got the prize* **2** *n* Conceit: *I was afraid you'd get the swellhead*—WR Burnett

swimming in *See* ROLLING IN

swindle (or **scandal**) **sheet** *n phr* An expense account: *Only one goes on the swindle sheet*—AR Hilliard

swing **1** *n* A style of white jazz music of the 1930s and 40s, developed from hot jazz and usu played by big bands: *That pastime was called Swing, and its king, Benny Goodman, and most of its greatest exponents and exploiters were quartered here in New York*—Albert Goldman **2** *v musicians* To have a strong but easy and pleasant impetus: *Chaucer and Jazz are quite similar; they both swing, they both have the same punch, vitality, and guts*—Jazz World **3** *v* To perform very well, as a good jazz musician does: *It is appropriate that gifted, gravel-voiced Herschel Bernardi should swing eight times a week in this particular hit*—Walter Wager **4** *v black fr musicians* To have a good time; enjoy oneself hugely, as at a good party **5** *v fr late 1960s* To do the sex act, esp promiscuously with various partners either seriatim or at once: *The sexual revolution is not new, people have been swinging as long as they are on this earth*—Rona Jaffe **6** *v fr 1960s* To be stylish, au courant, sophisticated, etc; =be HIP: *"Songs for Swingin' Lovers"*—Frank Sinatra album title **7** *v street gang* To be a member of a teenage street gang **8** *n* An interval between work periods: *with two hours' swing in the afternoon for lunch*—Ira Wolfert

swing both ways *v phr fr late 1960s* To be bisexual; =be AC-DC

swinger *n* A person who swings, esp in the mode of sexual promiscuity: *Kissinger, who enjoyed a reputation as a swinger, was asked to explain his oft-quoted remark*—Joseph Heller

swinging single *n phr* A merry and celebratory unmarried person, esp one who is sexually promiscuous as well as au courant: *making jokes about the "swinging singles" all around them*—Albert Goldman

swipe **1** *v fr middle 1800s* To steal, esp something small or trivial; pilfer: *nix on swiping anything*—EB White **2** *n fr late 1800s* A stroke or blow, esp a strong one • Most often in the phrase **take a swipe at**: *Let somebody...take a swipe at him*—Bennett Cerf **3** *n fr early 1900s* A stable groom who rubs down horses [all senses perhaps fr alterations of *sweep* or *swoop* and the actions of sweeping or swooping up, or of hitting a sweeping blow; second sense perhaps fr dialect preservation of Old English *swippan* "beat, scourge"; final sense may in addition be a blend with *wipe*]

See TAKE A SWIPE AT someone or something

swish[1] **1** *adj fr homosexuals fr 1930s* Showing the traits of an effeminate male homosexual; mincing; limp-wristed; =NELLIE: *His walk was quite swish* **2** *n fr homosexuals* An effeminate male homosexual; =QUEEN: *that fat swish*—Budd Schulberg **3** *v fr homosexuals* To move, walk, speak, etc, in the manner or presumed manner of effeminate male homosexuals [fr the swinging movements of the hips in a mincing walk, and perhaps the *swishing* sound of a gown]

swish[2] *adj fr late 1800s British* Elegant; fancy; =POSH, RITZY, SWANKY: *You can get a very swish version... or a very basic version*—New York Times [fr British dialect, an apparent variant of *swash* "a swaggerer," hence semantically related to *swank*]

switch **1** *v underworld* To inform; =SNITCH **2** *n* A knife; =SHIV

See ASLEEP AT THE SWITCH, CHICKEN SWITCH, NOT HAVE ALL one's SWITCHES ON

switchblade *n fr 1940s* A knife with a blade that springs out when a switch is pressed

switched ***See*** I'LL BE DAMNED

switched-off *adj* Not in the current fashion; unconventional; =OUT OF SYNC: *responding...to his unconventional (at that time), bohemian, "switched-off" quality*—Garry O'Conor

switched on **1** *adj phr fr 1960s British* Fashionable and admirable; au courant; up-to-date; =GEAR: *A larger number of the women were in short, switched-on dresses*—New Yorker **2** *adj phr* Exhilarated; stimulated; =HIGH, PLUGGED IN, TURNED ON: *In his moments of happiness the person with machine envy will declare himself "plugged in" or "switched on"*—Russell Baker

switcheroo *n* A switch or shift; a reversal: *For people in search of titillating diversion from their daily lives, switcheroos may seem exciting*—American Scholar

switch-hitter **1** *n baseball* A player who bats both righthanded and lefthanded **2** *n* A versatile person **3** *n* A bisexual person

switch on **1** *v phr fr 1960s British* To join the current trends, tastes, etc; become up-to-date **2** *v phr* To excite and exhilarate; arouse sexually; =TURN ON: *He didn't see any girls that switched him on much* **3** *v phr* To become intoxicated with narcotics; =TURN ON

swivel-hips ***See*** SNAKE-HIPS

swizzle-stick *n fr late 1800s* A stick for stirring a mixed drink [fr earlier *swizzle* "stir a drink," fr *swizzle* "a drink, to drink," perhaps related to *switchel* "drink of molasses and water, often mixed with rum"]

swoopy ***See*** ULTRASWOOPY

-sy ***See*** -IE

sync **1** *v* To synchronize: *Let's sync our plans, okay?* **2** *n* Synchronism; synchronization

See IN SYNC, LIP-SYNC, OUT OF SYNC

◁ **syph** or **the syff** ▷ *n* or *n phr* (Variations: **siff** or **the siff**) *fr early 1900s* Syphilis: *syphilis, not siff*—Calder Willingham

sysop (SISS ahp) *n computer* The computer operator who manages a computer bulletin board, a computer display where those with access may get or convey information: *People look up to the sysop*—New York Times [fr *system operator*]

system *See* OLD BOY NETWORK

T

T *narcotics* **1** *n* Marijuana **2** *n* A gram of methamphetamine

◁**TA** or **T and A**▷ (TA pronounced as separate letters) **1** *n phr fr show business* A display of female bosoms and bottoms; a show featuring such display; =CHEESECAKE: *the realm of feminine esthetics or, as it is known in the profession, TA*—Playboy/ *to enliven their product they call for T and A*—Toronto Life **2** *adj phr: They turned it into a T and A show*—Philadelphia Journal [fr *tits* + *ass*]

tab[1] **1** *n phr fr late 1800s* The bill or check for something, esp for food or drink: *three- or four-hundred-dollar tabs for unpaid liquor*—Stephen Longstreet **2** *n* A written acknowledgment of debt; =IOU: *They're liable to go out and stick up a bank if they owe you a tab*—Jimmy Cannon [origin unknown; perhaps a shortening of *tabulation*]
See PICK UP THE TAB

tab[2] *v fr early 1900s* To identify or designate; label: *I tabbed him immediately as a crook* [fr *tab* "a tied-on baggage label," of unknown origin; perhaps an alteration of *tag*]

tab[3] *narcotics* **1** *n* A tablet **2** *n* A dose of LSD; =HIT

table *See* UNDER THE TABLE

table grade *See* EATIN' STUFF

tabs *See* KEEP TABS ON

tach *n* A tachometer

tacks *See* BRASS TACKS

tacky *adj fr late 1800s Southern* Inferior; shabby; vulgar; =ICKY, RATTY: *a bit countrified, if not slightly tacky*—Calder Willingham/ *That would be tacky... I'm not here promoting myself*—Washington Post [apparently fr *tacky* "small, useless horse," and later "hillbilly, cracker"]
See TICKY-TACKY

◀**taco**▶ *n* A Mexican or person of Mexican descent

◁**Taco**▷ *See* TIO TACO

tad **1** *n fr late 1800s* A small boy; a child: *I've liked reading since I was just a tad* **2** *n* A small amount; =CUNT-HAIR, SKOSH, SMIDGEN: *may be taking his new series... just a tad too seriously*—People Weekly [origin uncertain; perhaps a shortening of *tadpole*; perhaps fr British dialect *tadde* "toad"]

tag **1** *n* A person's name **2** *n underworld* An arrest warrant: *Is there a tag out for me?*—Raymond Chandler **3** *n* An automobile license plate: *The Seminoles get special tags*—Associated Press
See DOG TAGS

tah-dah or **ta-daaa** **1** *interjection* A vocal imitation of a stage or circus fanfare, used to call attention to one's entrance, to something dramatically revealed, etc: *and tah-dah, a whole section of the model flipped over to show the change*—Philadelphia **2** *adj: a big tah-dah promotion*

tail **1** *n fr 1300s* The buttocks; =ASS: *I hadn't tossed him out on his tail*—Jerome Weidman ◁**2**▷ *n* A person regarded solely as a sex partner, object, or organ; =ASS: *a nice piece of tail* ◁**3**▷ *n* Sexual activity or gratification; =ASS, FUCKING: *It was said that the freshmen up at Yale got no tail* **4** *n* A person who follows another for surveillance; =SHADOW: *The security officer was even going to put a tail on the children*—John

McCarten **5** *v*: *tailing a jewelry salesman*—American Mercury

See one's ASS OFF, DRAG one's TAIL, GET one's TAIL IN A GATE, HAVE A BROOM UP one's ASS, HAVE A TIGER BY THE TAIL, HAVE someone or something BY THE TAIL, PIECE OF ASS, WORK one's ASS OFF

tailgate **1** *v* To follow another car, truck, etc, dangerously closely; =HIGHTAIL: *drove her car behind him, tailgating him between red walls of dead brick*—Saul Bellow **2** *v* *college students* To watch girls go by **3** *v* *Army* To join what one says closely to what has just been said; =DOVETAIL

tailgate party **1** *n phr* An outdoor party or picnic, typically in the parking lot of a sports stadium, and served on the tailgates of station wagons **2** *n phr* *jazz musicians* A style of jazz said to resemble the early New Orleans sort [final sense fr the fact that the *tailgate* of the band's wagon was left down to give slide-room for the trombone]

tailpipe *See* BLOW IT OUT

take **1** *n* The money taken in for a sporting event, at a gambling casino, etc; =GROSS: *Nevada's take has been hit by a recession*—New York Post **2** *v* *fr early 1900s* To cheat or defraud; swindle; =SCAM: *The old couple got taken for their life savings* **3** *v* (also **take** someone **into camp** or **take** someone **downtown**) *fr middle 1800s* To defeat someone utterly; trounce; =CLOBBER: *UCLA took Illinois in the Rose Bowl/ Last year Tanner took Borg downtown in the same round*—Sports Illustrated **4** *n* An acceptable portion of movie or TV recording, musical recording, taping, etc: *The director said okay, it was a take* **5** *n* A portion; extract; bit; =OUTTAKE: *fast takes from the latest research*—Working Woman

See DOUBLE-TAKE, ON THE TAKE

take a back seat *v phr fr middle 1800s* To assume or accept a subordinate position; demote or degrade oneself: *He said he wouldn't take a back seat to anybody but the president himself*

take a bath *v phr* To suffer a financial loss; esp, to go into bankruptcy; =GO TO THE CLEANERS, TAKE A BEATING: *Is it possible to take a bath on items previously thought to be incapable of depreciation?*—Toronto Life [fr Yiddish, where *er haut mikh gefirt in bod arayn*, literally "he led me to the bath," means "he tricked me"; the sense is derived fr the deception of persons reluctant to take a steam bath and have their clothing decontaminated, who hence had to be tricked; probably reinforced by *cleaned out* and *taken to the cleaners* as terms for loss of money in gambling or business]

take a beating **1** *v phr* =TAKE A BATH **2** *v phr* To be bested in a transaction; pay too much: *You really took a beating if you paid $2 a pound*

take a break *v phr* To rest or cease temporarily from working; =CAULK OFF, KNOCK OFF: *Why don't you guys take a break while I figure this out?*

take a bye *v phr fr sports* To decline; choose not to take; =PASS something UP: *The kid took a bye on breakfast* —Tom Aldibrandi [fr the term *bye* used when a participant in a tournament passes to the next level without playing, since he or she has drawn no opponent]

take a crack at something *See* HAVE A CRACK AT something

take a dig at someone *v phr* To make an irritating or contemptuous comment; =BAD-MOUTH: *When he took a dig at his mother his brother decked him*

take a dive *v phr fr sports* To fall in a feigned knockdown or knockout; lose a fight, game, etc, dishonestly; =TANK: *He refused to take a dive, so they took him out*

take a douche *v phr teenagers* To leave hurriedly; =BEAT IT, GET LOST • Usually an irritated command

take a drink *v phr baseball* To strike out [fr the fact that the player can then go to the *drinking fountain* in the dugout]

◁**take a dump**▷ *v phr* (Variations: **crap** or **shit** or **squat** may replace **dump**) To defecate; =SHIT: *two dogs taking a dump in a restaurant* —Village Voice

take a fall *v phr underworld* To be arrested; =FALL: *He took a fall, Duke* —Lawrence Sanders

take a flyer (or **flier**) *v phr fr late 1800s* To take an ambitious gamble; take a risky chance or chancy risk, esp financially: *I don't believe you, but what the hell, I'll take a flyer* [fr *flyer* "jump, leap"]

◀ **take a flying fuck**▶ *v phr* (Variations: **frig** may replace **fuck**; **at a rubber duck** or **at a rolling doughnut** may be added) May you be accursed, confounded, humiliated, rejected, etc; = GO FUCK oneself, GO TO HELL: *about four guys who could really tell me to go take a flying frig and make it stick*—Larry Niven & Jerry Bournelle/ *They told me as gently as possible to take a flying fuck*

take a hosing *v phr* To be cheated or duped; be unfairly used: *The average worker and his family think they're taking a hosing*—Walter Mondale

◁ **take a leak**▷ *v phr* To urinate; = PISS, WHIZ: *fella has to take a leak* —Tom Wolfe

take a load off one's **feet** *v phr* To sit down; rest; relax

take a page from someone's **book** *v phr* To imitate or emulate someone: *I think I'll take a page from Castro's book and grow a beard and cigar*

take a potshot at someone *v phr fr middle 1800s* To criticize harshly; assault critically: *I don't want to take potshots at Frank*—Changes [fr the notion of a *shot* taken merely to put game in the cooking *pot*, hence not sportsmanlike or punctilious but crudely practical]

take a powder (or **a run-out powder**) *v phr* To leave; depart hastily, esp to avoid arrest or detection; = POWDER: *and take a powder out of here that day*—John O'Hara

take a rain check *v phr fr sports* To arrange postponement or delay of some occasion which one cannot attend at the invited time: *Thanks awfully, Syl, but we're booked that night and will have to take a rain check* [see *rain check*]

take a run at someone *v phr* To approach or assault with a view to capture or seduction: *such a close associate that nobody was going to take a run at him*—Toronto Life

take a shine to someone or something *v phr fr early 1800s* To incur a liking for; like: *May Venus... take such a shine to you both*—WH Auden

◁ **take a shit** (or **a squat**)▷ *See* TAKE A DUMP

take a swipe at someone or something *v phr* To strike or aim a blow at; esp, to criticize very harshly: *The Council couldn't adjourn before taking a swipe at the Mayor*

take a walk *v phr fr middle 1800s* To leave; absent oneself, esp fr labor negotiations, etc; go out on strike: *If they don't at least look at our terms we'll have to take a walk*

take care *v phr* To be wary; pay attention ● Nearly always a parting salutation

take care of business *v phr black fr 1950s* To perform stylishly and effectively; deal well with what one needs to: *I got up and took care of business* —Time

take care of Numero Uno *v phr* To devote oneself to one's own profit and well-being; see to oneself; = FEATHER one's NEST: *The Lord helps them that take care of Numero Uno* [see *Numero Uno*]

take someone **downtown** *See* TAKE

take fire *v phr* To have a sudden spurt of enthusiasm, activity, success, etc; become meteoric; = TAKE OFF: *When the show takes fire we'll all get rich*

take five *v phr* To take a short respite from work; = TAKE A BREAK

take someone **for a ride** **1** *v phr esp 1920s & 30s* To murder by kidnapping and disposing of the body in a remote place, in gangster fashion **2** *v phr* To cheat or swindle

take heat *v phr* To endure punishment, complaints, etc: *I took a lot of heat and I stayed in the kitchen*—New York Post [fr *if you can't stand the heat stay out of the kitchen*]

take someone **into camp** *See* TAKE

take it *v phr fr prizefight* To endure pain, violent attack, the buffets of fate, etc; = HANG TOUGH, TOUGH IT OUT: *Valley Forge proved the Continentals could take it*

take it easy **1** *v phr* To keep one's anger and excitement under check; be calm: *Take it easy, Mac, nobody's hurt* **2** *v phr* To work slowly and smoothly: *Hurry and you're dead, take it easy and you survive* **3** *v phr* To stop working; relax; loaf: *I got to take it easy for a few minutes* ● **Take it easy** is most often used as a parting salutation or a bit of advice for living, in each case intending all senses at once

take it hard (or **big**) ***v phr*** To react very strongly to something: *I thought she'd ignore it, but she took it big/ We were surprised he took the news so hard*

take it in the ear ***See*** PUT IT IN YOUR EAR

take it on the chin **1** ***v phr*** =TAKE IT **2** ***v phr*** To be soundly defeated; be trounced: *They took it on the chin badly in the last period*

take it out of someone's **hide** ***v phr*** To exact the harshest kind of compensation, even physical punishment, usu in place of a gentler or a monetary one: *He'll pay up, by God, or I'll take it out of his hide!*

take it out on someone or something ***v phr*** To punish or mistreat an innocent subject for wrongs one has suffered: *Whenever his boss yells at him, he takes it out on his secretary* [perhaps fr *take it out of* someone's *hide*]

take one's **lumps** ***v phr*** To accept and endure severe treatment; =TAKE IT: *The boys were taking their lumps trying to stay on wild Brahma bulls* —New York Daily News/ *Taking your lumps is living*

take one's **medicine** ***v phr*** To accept and endure what one has deserved; =FACE THE MUSIC

be **taken** ***See*** be HAD

take names ***See*** KICK ASS AND TAKE NAMES

take no shit ***See*** TAKE SHIT

be **taken to the cleaners** ***See*** GO TO THE CLEANERS

takeoff **1** ***n*** An imitation, esp of a famous person, actor, etc; an impression: *You should hear her takeoff of Liz Taylor* **2** ***n*** A robbery, esp an armed street robbery or mugging: *He always uses the mugger's jargon for a street robbery: "take-off"*—New York Post **3** ***modifier:*** *and if it comes to a takeoff thing in the street*—New York

take off **1** ***v phr*** *esp fr WW2 armed forces* To leave; depart; =SPLIT: *He had to take off early* **2** ***v phr*** To have a sudden success, spurt of activity, etc; =TAKE FIRE: *but nonsense that doesn't take off can be a trial*—Edith Oliver **3** ***v phr*** *police & underworld* To rob; commit burglary; =HOLD UP, RIP OFF: *We took off a bar*—Clarence Cooper **4** ***v phr*** *black* To kill; =WASTE, ZAP **5** ***v phr*** *narcotics* To give oneself a narcotic injection; =SHOOT UP **6** ***v phr*** To leave work for a time: *I'm going to take off without pay for a week or so* **7** ***v phr*** *fr middle 1700s* To imitate; mimic; parody: *She takes off a drunk hilariously* [first sense based on the rising and departure of an airplane]

takeoff artist ***See*** RIPOFF

take on **1** ***v phr*** To behave angrily; make a fuss: *How you do take on!* **2** ***v phr*** *police* To stop and search someone, demand identification, question harshly, etc; =JACK UP, ROUST: *We were also taught that good cops take on a lot of people*—Rolling Stone

take someone or something **on** **1** ***v phr*** To accept an assignment, job, role, etc: *I'm a bit diffident about my qualifications, but I'll take the chairmanship on* **2** ***v phr*** To accept combat or confrontation with someone or something: *The Knights took over the Philadelphia Inquirer... and later took on the Morning Journal head-to-head*—San Francisco

take someone or something **out** ***v phr*** To kill; destroy; totally disable: *asked Col Beckwith what he intended to do with the Iranian guards. "Take them out," said Col Beckwith*—Wall Street Journal/ *The Brits were just seeking to reassure themselves that we were not planning to take out a country*—Time [probably fr the football term *take out* "block an opponent decisively"]

takeover ***n*** The buying of the control of one company by another, usu by the wooing and rewarding of stockholders and often against the wishes of the acquired company's management: *a popular means of conducting corporate takeovers*—New York Times

taker ***n*** A person who accepts a bet, challenge, offer, etc: *I dared them all but got no takers*

◁**take** (or **eat**) **shit**▷ ***v phr*** To accept or endure humiliation, victimization, bullying, etc; =EAT DIRT ● Often in the negative: *She told us she took no shit from nobody/ They thought I would eat shit, so I just quit*

it **takes two to tango** ***See*** IT TAKES TWO TO TANGO

take the cake **1** *v phr fr late 1800s* To win or deserve the highest award and admiration: *His new sonnets quite take the cake* **2** *v phr* To be improbable; be incredible: *That excuse really takes the cake* [fr the prize awarded in a *cakewalk* dancing contest]

take the heat off *v phr* To reduce or remove harassing pressure; =COOL IT: *She won't say yes or no till you take the heat off*

take the pipe *v phr esp sports* To become ineffective under pressure; =CHOKE UP, SWALLOW THE APPLE: *He could have taken the pipe after that horrendous first half, but he didn't* —Sports Illustrated

take the rap (or **the fall**) *v phr fr underworld* To accept or suffer the punishment for something, esp for something one did not do: *If she gets caught, I'll take the rap for her/ He has to take the fall right along with Beck*—Hannibal & Boris

take things easy *v phr* To cease being upset or excited over things; relax; =COOL IT: *I'm gonna buy a boat and take things easy*

take someone **to the cleaners** *v phr* To win or otherwise acquire all or very much of someone's money, esp at gambling, in a lawsuit or business deal, etc; =CLEAN someone OUT: *Smarten up, Chrystie, take him to the cleaners*—People Weekly

tale *See* FISH STORY

talk **1** *v somewhat outdated underworld* To inform; confess and implicate others; =SQUEAL: *Socks would never never talk* **2** *v* To mean something; have something particular in mind • Always in the progressive tenses: *Okay, we're talking three or four million, right?/ Are you talking a strike?*

See BACK TALK, BIG TALK, HAPPY TALK, PEP TALK, PILLOW TALK, STRAIGHT TALK, SWEET-TALK

talk big *v phr* To boast and exaggerate; be self-aggrandizing; =SHOOT OFF one's MOUTH: *He was talking pretty big about how they treated him*

talk someone's **ear off** *v phr* To talk incessantly; prate; =GAS: *Donna talked his ear off*—New York Daily News

talking head (or **hairdo**) *n phr television studio* A person, esp a news reporter, an interviewer, an expert, etc, who appears on television in a close-up, hence essentially as a bodiless head: *using the medium as something more than a static platform for talking heads*—John J O'Connor/ *one of those plays for which talking hairdos go to the videotape*—Sports Illustrated

talk out of turn *v phr* To speak too candidly; be too bold verbally; =SHOOT OFF one's MOUTH: *I may be talking out of turn, but I think you ought to make the decision right now, and live with it*

talk poor mouth *v phr* To deny one's wealth, advantages, etc; depreciate one's assets; =POOR-MOUTH: *And it is hard to talk poor mouth just after the papers have written of your daughter's coming-out party for 2,000 guests*—New York Times

talk through one's **hat** *v phr fr late 1800s* To lie and exaggerate; talk nonsense; =BULLSHIT [said to be fr the deceptive demeanor of men who hold their *hats* over their faces on entering church, and are supposed to be praying]

talk turkey *v phr fr early 1800s* To speak candidly and cogently; =LAY IT ON THE LINE, LEVEL: *Do you want to talk turkey, or just bullshit?* [fr a story attested in 1830, of the white man who said to the Native American, Wampum, that in dividing the game he would give him the choice: "You take the crow and I'll take the turkey, or I'll take the turkey and you take the crow," whereupon Wampum declared that the white man was not *talking turkey* to him]

talk up a storm *v phr* To talk loud, long, impressively, incessantly, etc; =CHEW someone's EAR OFF: *City Teen-Agers Talking Up a "Say What?" Storm*—New York Times

tall *See* STAND TALL, WALK TALL

tall can of corn *See* CAN OF CORN

tall cotton *See* IN TALL COTTON

tall red totem poles *See* KNOCK someone or something FOR A LOOP

tan or **tan** someone's **hide** *v* or *v phr fr middle 1800s* To beat severely; thrash [fr the making of a hide into leather by *tanning*]

◁ **T and A** ▷ *See* TA

tang *See* POON TANG

tangle *v* To fight; =MIX IT UP

◁ **tangle assholes** ▷ *v phr* To come into conflict; disagree; quarrel; fight

tango ***See*** IT TAKES TWO TO TANGO

tank **1** *n* A detention cell; a jail cell: *A police reporter had to pick him out of the collection in the drunk tank*—AR Bosworth **2** *v* (also **tank up**) *fr late 1800s* To drink liquor, esp heavily: *I think he'd tanked up a good deal at luncheon*—F Scott Fitzgerald **3** *v sports* To lose a game, match, etc, deliberately; =THROW: *He lost so implausibly they were sure he had tanked* **4** ***pres part:*** *the "tanking" of unlucrative doubles matches merely to catch a plane*—Time [for sports senses, see *go in the tank*]

See DRUNK TANK, FISH TANK, THINK TANK

tanked or **tanked up** *adj* or *adj phr fr late 1800s* Drunk

tap **1** *v* To attack; =MUG: *Only chicks this guy taps?*—Ed McBain **2** *adj* Lacking money; =BROKE, TAPPED OUT

Tap City *adj* Lacking money; penniless; =BROKE, TAP: *You're Tap City? No problem*—Philadelphia Journal

tap dance *v phr Army* To improvise, tergiversate, etc, in order to hide one's ignorance: *I didn't read the poop sheet, so I had to tap dance when the question came*

tape ***See*** RED TAPE

taped *adv* For certain; under control; =IN THE BAG: *By the third round he had the fight taped*

See HAVE something CINCHED

tap someone **for** something *v phr* To solicit money from; beg or borrow from; =HIT someone, TOUCH: *I tapped my brother for another two hundred*

tap out *v phr gambling* To lose all one's money, esp in a gambling game; =be CLEANED OUT: *"It's tapping me out," he says*—Philadelphia Journal [perhaps fr the gesture of *tapping* the table when one cannot or does not wish to bet in his turn; perhaps fr having *tapped* everyone available for a loan and found none]

tapped out **1** *adj phr* Penniless; =BROKE, TAP CITY: *Tapped out, a... bank goes under*—Time/ *the tapped-out underdog he is supposed to be*—Sports Illustrated **2** *adj phr* Exhausted; =FRAZZLED, POOPED: *thought he looked terrible, haggard, pale, tapped out*—Time

tar ***See*** BEAT THE SHIT OUT OF someone or something

◁ **tard** ▷ *n* =RETARD

tarfu (TAR FōōJ) *adj WW2 armed forces* Totally botched and confused; =SNAFU [fr *things are really fucked up*]

Tarheel *n fr middle 1800s* A native or resident of North Carolina [origin uncertain; perhaps fr the gummy resins of the pine barrens, which would cling to their feet; perhaps because a North Carolina unit which lost a hilltop position in the Civil War were jestingly told they had not *tarred their heels* to make them stick]

tart *n fr late 1800s* A promiscuous woman, esp a prostitute; harlot; =HOOKER: *nothing cheap for us like the grimy tarts on Mercury Street*—Stephen Longstreet [fr *tart* the pastry confection, esp the English *jam-tart*; in original early-19th-century use it meant any pleasant or attractive woman, and only specialized at the end of the century]

tart up *v phr fr 1920s British* To decorate; prettify; bedizen; =GUSSY UP: *American directors feel obliged to tart up Shakespeare*—San Francisco

taste **1** *n theater* A share or percentage of profits; =a PIECE OF THE ACTION **2** *n narcotics* A dose of a narcotic; =HIT **3** *n black* Liquor in general; a drink of liquor

tater *baseball* **1** *n* A base hit: *the man who hit all those taters in the American League*—Sports Illustrated **2** *n* A home run [fr a dialect term for *potato*, and perhaps related to the admiring term *some potatoes* that would describe a base hit or home run]

tattooed ***See*** SCREWED, BLUED, AND TATTOOED

taxi ***See*** TIJUANA TAXI

TCB (pronounced as separate letters) *v black* To perform very well what one needs to do: *where he is always to be found TCBing*—New Times [fr *take care of business*]

tchotchke (CHAHCH kə, TSAHTS kə) (Variations: **tchatchka** or **tchotzke** or **tsatske**) **1** *n* Something trivial, esp a gew-gaw or decorative trifle; bagatelle; plaything: *little rainbows and neon tchatchkas found in California neon boutiques*—New Times/ *you know, the tchotzkes, the jewelry*

—Boston Globe/ *Kafka Tchotchke* —Village Voice **2** *n* A precious or adorable person, usu a child: *The baby is a tchotchke* **3** *n* A woman considered as a plaything: *She's Harry's tsatske* [fr Yiddish *tsatske* fr Slavic *shaleh* "play pranks"]

t'd off *See* TEE'D OFF

tea *See* one's CUP OF TEA

teacups *See* ASS OVER TINCUPS

tea'd up *adj narcotics* Intoxicated with marijuana; =HIGH

teakettle *See* ASS OVER TINCUPS

team *See* SWAT TEAM

tea party **1** *n phr outdated narcotics* A gathering where marijuana is smoked: *Marijuana "tea parties" are little things*—Eugene Burdick **2** *n phr* An easy, pleasant, safe occasion • Most often used in the negative: *It wasn't exactly a brawl, but the meeting was no tea party either*

tear (TAIR) *n fr middle 1800s* A drinking spree; =BENDER, BINGE: *Fred wanted to go on a little tear in the big town*—Fact Detective Mysteries
See ON A TEAR

tear-jerker **1** *n* A sentimental story, movie, song, etc: *see the old tear-jerker*—HR Hoyt **2** *n* A person who appeals to sentimentality; a fomenter of pathos: *a magniloquent tear-jerker named Delmas*—American Mercury

tear off *v phr* To play or perform: *The musicians began to tear off a La Conga*—Richard Starnes

◁ **tear off a piece** (or **a piece of ass**) ▷ *v phr* To do the sex act; =FUCK

tearoom queen *n phr homosexuals* A male homosexual who frequents public toilets seeking sexual encounters

tears *See* THAT KILLS IT

teaser **1** *n* A woman who invites or offers sexual activity but refuses to do the sex act; =COCK-TEASER: *Maybe Bella was right in calling his "uptown lady" a "teaser"*—Stephen Longstreet **2** *n* Anything offered as a sample and intended to increase appetite or desire: *He showed them one chapter as a teaser*
See COCK-TEASER

tea (or **tearoom**) **trade** *homosexuals* **1** *n phr* Male homosexuals who seek encounters in public toilets **2** *n phr* Sexual encounters in public toilets

tec or **teck** **1** *n fr late 1800s British* A detective; =DICK **2** *n* A detective story [a shortening of *detective*]

tech[1] *n* An engineering or technology college [fr *technology*]
See HIGH TECH

tech[2] *n* A technician, esp an electronics or wire-tapping expert: *I got a guy to do it, a tech named Ernie Mann* —Lawrence Sanders

techie *n* A computer enthusiast, expert, etc: *You don't have to be a "techie" or a "computer nut" to join*

techno- *prefix used to form nouns* Having the indicated knowledge of, involvement with, or attitude towards technology, esp advanced and computer technology: *technofreak/ technopeasant*

tee'd (or **teed** or **t'd**) **off** *adj phr* Angry; =PISSED OFF: *When people get teed off they want to march*—Time [perhaps fr *ticked off*; perhaps a euphemism for *pee'd off* "pissed off"]

teen **1** *n* (also **teener** or **teenie** or **teeny**) A teenage person; teenager: *a really interesting biz for a teen who loves being busy*—Deseret News/ *a robust health that would be remarkable on a teener*—Robert Ruark/ *"You only pass this way once," he tells a teenie in persuading her to come along for a ride*—Terry Southern **2** *modifier: teen flicks/ the teen scene*

teensy-weensy *adj* Very small; tiny: *the teensy-weensy kind that small-town dailies like*—Philadelphia

teenybopper *n* (also **teenie bopper** or **teenybop** or **teeny-rocker**) *fr 1960s counterculture & rock and roll* A teenager or preteenager, esp one who undertakes the hippie or rock-and-roll culture and way of life: *Teenyboppers opt for zodiac signs* —Village Voice

teenzine *n* A magazine for teenagers: *this teen-zine cover boy*—Rolling Stone

tee off *v phr* To hit someone or something very hard: *He hit a homer, really teed off* [fr the opening shot of each hole in golf, off the *tee*]

tee someone **off** *v phr* To make angry; =PISS someone OFF: *and this moping is teeing me off*—Hannibal and Boris [probably a euphemism for pee or *piss* someone *off*, influenced by *tee off on* someone, fr golf]

tee off on someone or something **1** *v phr* To verbally assault, esp to reprimand: *The critic really teed off on my book, alas* **2** *v phr baseball* To make many hits against a particular pitcher: *They teed off on Gossage in the twelfth* **3** *v phr baseball* To hit the ball very hard: *He teed off on it and it went right over the wall*

teeth *See* DRESSED TO THE TEETH, DROP one's TEETH, PULL TEETH THROUGH THE ARMPIT

telegraph *v* To signal one's intentions, often inadvertently: *The tone of her voice telegraphed it*—J Evans

tell *See* SHOW-AND-TELL

tell it like it is *v phr esp 1960s fr black* To be candid and cogent; tell the truth, even though it be unpleasant; =GIVE IT TO someone: *by Negro psychiatrists William H Grier and Price M Cobbs, who tell it like it is* —McCall's [perhaps fr an exhortation used in black church services]

tell it to the Marines *sentence fr early 1800s British Navy* I do not believe what you have just told me; what you say is false and futile [the usage reflects the contempt in which *marines* were held by naval seamen, leading to the assertion that they would believe nonsense that sailors would never believe]

tell someone **off** *v phr fr early 1900s British armed forces* To reprimand; =CHEW someone OUT: *The man had just been told off, and told off plenty* —G Homes

tell someone **what to do with** something *v phr* (Variations: **where to put** (or **shove** or **stick** or **stuff**) may replace **what to do with**) To reject something vehemently and defiantly • A euphemism for **stick it up your ass**: *She told me rudely what to do with my proffered assistance/ The first thing I did when I got home was to tell my old boss where to stick my old job*—Max Shulman

tell someone **where to get off** (or **to go**) *v phr* To rebuke, rebuff, or deflate firmly; =LET someone HAVE IT • A euphemism for **go to hell**: *I advised Alice to tell him where to get off when he tries that big-shot stuff*

telly *See* BELLY TELLY

ten *See* FIVE-AND-TEN, HANG TEN

a **ten** *n phr* A young woman who is maximally sexually attractive; a perfect female specimen [perhaps fr *ten-carat*; perhaps fr the conventional question "Where would you put her (him, it) on a scale of one to *ten*?"]

tenderfoot *n fr middle 1800s Western* A newcomer; neophyte; callow person

ten-foot pole *See* NOT TOUCH someone or something WITH A TEN-FOOT POLE

ten four **1** *n phr citizens band* The signal that a message has been received, the equivalent of the earlier and military "roger" **2** *affirmation fr citizens band* That is correct: *That's a ten four, you have it just right* [fr a code of conventional procedure signals used esp by the police, where *ten* was a sort of prefix, and the numeral following bore the message; *ten seven*, for example, meant "transmissions finished"]

tenner **1** *n fr late 1800s* A ten-dollar bill: *spent the tenner on Jersey applejack*—Billy Rose **2** *n prison* A ten-year prison sentence

ten pounds of shit in a five-pound bag *See* BLIVIT

ten-spot **1** *n fr late 1800s* A ten-dollar bill; ten dollars: *A ten-spot can't get you past two counters in a grocery store without limping*—Hal Boyle **2** *n prison* A ten-year prison sentence: *after having served a ten-spot*—D Purroy

-teria *See* -ATERIA

terps *n narcotics* Elixir of terpin hydrate with codeine, a cough syrup prized as a narcotic

terrific *fr early 1900s* **1** *adj* Excellent; wonderful; =GREAT: *The script is apt to be terrific*—Time **2** *adj* Prodigious; extreme; amazing: *Times Square hotel biz is on the terrific fritz* —Variety

territory *See* GO WITH THE TERRITORY

terror *See* HOLY TERROR

tetchy *adj* Crazy; eccentric; wild: *the days when tetchy film crews invaded the center of soporific conferences* —Washington Post [fr dialect *tetched* "crazy, touched in the head"]

Texas leaguer *n phr baseball fr late 1800s* A hit that falls out of reach between the infielders and the outfielders [fr the fact that such hits were used in minor-league baseball's *Texas League* as trick plays]

Tex-Mex 1 *adj* Texan-Mexican **2** *n* A native of the Texas-Mexico border region: *Fender... who calls himself a Tex-Mex, was born in the south Texas valley border town of San Benito*—Washington Post **3** *n* A style of cooking characteristic of the Texas-Mexico border region: *exemplars of Tex-Mex, the mongrel cuisine that has grown up along America's southern border*—Newsweek

TGIF (pronounced as separate letters) *sentence* Thank God it's Friday

thank you ma'am *See* WHAM-BAM THANK YOU MA'AM

that ain't (or **isn't**) **hay** *sentence* (Variations: **peanuts** or **chopped liver** may replace **hay**) That is a large sum; that is not insignificant: *And what they pay me in addition ain't hay*—John O'Hara/ *We have spent $25 million to adapt. And that isn't chopped liver*—New York Times/ *He asked for a million, which ain't peanuts*

that kills (or **does** or **tears**) **it** *sentence* That ruins things; that's the last straw

that's all someone **needs** *sentence fr 1930s or earlier* That is precisely what someone does not need; that is excessive, fatal, very ill-timed, etc: *Another tax increase is all I need right now/ A speeding ticket? Brother, that's all you needed* [perhaps fr a translation of the ironical Yiddish lament *Dos felt mir nokh* "I still lack that"]

that's all she wrote *sentence* That is the sum and end of it; that is the bitter end: *Tell him that's it, brother, that's all she wrote*—Hannibal & Boris [fr the sad case of someone, esp a World War 2 soldier, who got a Dear John letter from his sweetheart, ending the affair]

that's my boy (or **girl**) *sentence* You have done very well; I'm proud of you; =WAY TO GO

that's show business (or **show biz**) *sentence* Such is the unpredictable or grim nature of things; =THAT'S THE WAY THE BALL BOUNCES: *We didn't get invited, but that's show business*

that's the ball game *sentence* That's the end of the affair ● Usu spoken by the loser

that's the way the ball bounces (or **the cookie crumbles**) *sentence fr 1950s* Such is life; such are the buffetings of fate; c'est la vie: *guess that's the way the ball bounces*—Sidney Skolsky

therapy *See* GREYHOUND THERAPY

there or **right there** *adj* or *adj phr fr 1920s* Very competent; very well informed; =WITH IT: *When it comes to piano-playing he's right there/ She's there, if you want to know about feminist criticism*

there's no (or **no such thing as a**) **free lunch** *sentence* The world is a hard place and one must work for what one gets (and even then one may not get it) [fr the memory of old-time saloons, where one could eat from a copious *free lunch* on the bar with even a minimal liquor purchase]

there's no way *adv phr* Under no conceivable circumstances: *There's no way I'll ever see it your way*

there you go or **there you are 1** *sentence* That is, unfortunately, the way things happen; =THAT'S THE WAY THE BALL BOUNCES: *She ran out on him? Well, there you go* **2** *sentence* Things happen as expected; results follow actions: *You push this one, see? There you go, it turned on* **3** *sentence* You have done something wrong again, of your habitual sort: *There you go, meddling again*

thick 1 *adj* Stupid; dull-witted **2** *adj* (also **thick as thieves**) Intimate; very well acquainted: *The two of them are very thick*

See SPREAD IT THICK

thicko *n* A stupid person; =DIMWIT: *Charlie doesn't know anything. He's a thicko*—Paul Theroux

thighs *See* THUNDER THIGHS

a (or **one**) **thin dime 1** *n phr fr 1920s* The least amount of money; =A RED CENT: *He was stony broke, not a thin dime could he produce* **2** *n phr* A dime; ten cents: *which sells old-fashioned ice cream sundaes for one thin dime*—Associated Press [fr the fact that the *dime* is the *thinnest* and smallest of US coins]

thing *n esp 1960s counterculture* One's particular predilection, skill, way of living or perceiving, etc: *He ignored the world and stuck to his thing*

See the BEST (or GREATEST) THING SINCE SLICED BREAD, DO one's THING, HAVE A THING ABOUT, JUST ONE OF THOSE THINGS, OLD THING, SURE THING, a SURE THING, a WHOLE 'NOTHER THING

thingamajig *n most forms fr middle 1700s British* (also **thingumabob** or **thingumadoodle** or **thingummy** or **thingamadoger** or **thingamadudgeon** or **thingumbob** or **thingamananny**) An unspecified or unspecifiable object; something one does not know the name of or does not wish to name; =DINGUS, DOODAD, GADGET: *When you want to go down you push this thingamajig up as high as it will go/ a thingummy so addicted to lethal violence*—WH Auden

thingy *n* A thing; =GIZMO, THINGAMAJIG: *one of those thingies on the roofs of churches that the water spouts through*—Patrick Mann

thin in the upper crust *adj phr* Stupid; =DIM-WITTED

think-piece *n* A newspaper or magazine article of intellectual virtue or pretension; a thoughtful essay: *a think-piece on the nature of romantics and the state of the nation*—Partisan Review

◁ **think** one's **shit doesn't stink**▷ *v phr fr middle 1800s British* To be very conceited; be stuck up and self-impressed: *The way she looks down her nose you know she thinks her shit doesn't stink*

think tank *n phr* An institute or institution that specializes in the custody of interpretive intellectuals, esp in the social sciences, and usu caters to and is financed by a government in return for studies, prognostications, etc: *part graduate school, part think tank* —George F Will

third base *See* GET TO FIRST BASE

third degree or **third** *n phr* or *n fr late 1800s* Long and harsh, even brutal, questioning, esp by the police: *The Third Degree, A Detailed and Appalling Exposé of Police Brutality* —A Lavine/ *He's giving me a third about some gun he says I had*—Raymond Chandler

third leg *See* MIDDLE LEG

third wheel *n phr* An unwanted or superfluous person; =EXCESS BAGGAGE: *I'm afraid I was a sort of third wheel there, they wanted to be alone*

thirteen *See* FILE 17

thirty or **30** *sentence fr newspaper office, telegraphers & broadcasting* That's all; that's the end of the story or message [fr the use by early telegraphers of the symbol XXX to designate the end of a story filed by a newspaper correspondent]

this is it *sentence* The final crisis is here; the unavoidable has come; prepare for the worst: *He held her hand fast and said, "This is it, kid"*—Saul Bellow

thou (THOU) *n fr middle 1800s* A thousand, esp a thousand dollars; =GRAND: *A hundred and fifty thou is business*—Dashiell Hammett

threads *n fr 1930s jive talk* Clothes, esp a suit of clothes

See SET OF THREADS

three-bagger *n baseball* A three-base hit; a triple

three bricks shy of a load *adj phr* Stupid; =NOT ALL THERE

three-dollar bill *See* PHONY AS A THREE-DOLLAR BILL

three-dollar pistol *See* HOT AS A THREE-DOLLAR PISTOL

three-point landing *See* CHINESE THREE-POINT LANDING

three (or **four**) **sheets to the wind** *adj phr fr early 1800s British* Drunk [fr the fact that a drunken person is as helpless and disorganized as a sailboat with its *sheets,* that is, with its sails flying, and hence its course and movement entirely out of control]

three squares *n phr* Enough to eat; an acceptable standard of living: *He isn't rich, but he gets his three squares every day*

three- (or **four-**) **time loser** *n phr* A criminal who has been convicted several times, and is in jeopardy of an automatic life sentence if convicted again; hence, a hardened and perhaps dangerous criminal

thriller *n* An exciting movie, play, etc, esp a horror show; =CHILLER

thriller-diller *n* A very effective thriller; =CHILLER-DILLER

throat *See* CUT one's OWN THROAT, JUMP DOWN someone's THROAT

through a tin horn *See* LIKE SHIT THROUGH A TIN HORN

through one's **hat** *See* TALK THROUGH one's HAT

through the mill *See* GO THROUGH THE MILL, RUN someone THROUGH THE MILL

throw **1** *v* *esp sports & gambling fr middle 1800s* To lose a game, race, etc, deliberately; =TANK: *Basketball players confess that they have accepted bribes to "throw" games* —Arthur Daley **2** *v* (also **pitch** or **toss**) *fr early 1900s* To be host or hostess at; arrange for: *The president has to throw him a luncheon*—P Edson/ *One of his assistants actually pitched a party for me*—Robert Ruark/ *Kendall tossed a cocktail party for a group of us visiting writers* —New York Daily News

a **throw** *adv phr fr early 1900s* For each; apiece: *The meetings were a dollar "a throw"*—P Marks [probably fr carnival games where the customer pays so much for several *throws* of a ball, a ring, etc, trying to win a prize]

throw someone **a curve** *v phr* To do something quite unexpected; deceive by the unpredicted: *But Spicoli threw him a curve*—Cameron Crowe

throw a fit (or **a hyper**) *v phr fr late 1800s* To behave or react very angrily; =HAVE KITTENS: *She just about threw a fit when I told her we weren't going/ My teacher threw a hyper at that dumb remark*

◀ **throw a fuck into** someone ▶ *v phr* (Variations: **bop** or **boff** or **screw** may replace **fuck**) To do the sex act with someone; =FUCK: *It's inevitable that someone is going to want to throw a bop into someone else's wife* —Esquire

throw something **at** something *v phr* To cover or pelt a problem with some usu futile remedy: *Experience with throwing bureaucrats at such problems does not presage success* —New York Times

throwaway **1** *n fr show business* A line, joke, etc, deliberately spoken unemphatically, thus increasing its effect **2** *modifier: He had a sort of throwaway casualness about him* **3** *modifier* Designed to be thrown away; disposable: *It came in throwaway bottles* **4** *modifier* Useless; superfluous: *a three-times convicted killer, a throwaway man now*—Ann Rule

throw away *v phr show business* To deliver a throwaway line, joke, etc: *I love the way he threw away that misquotation from Plato*

throw bouquets at someone or something *v phr* To praise; give kudos to: *I don't make a practice of throwing bouquets at any politician*

throw down **1** *v phr* To threaten or challenge; start trouble: *irate macho mesomorphs about to throw down*—Village Voice **2** *v phr esp teenagers* To challenge a rival break dancer by performing a particularly difficult feat or gyration [perhaps fr late-19th-century *throw down on* "aim one's pistol at"; perhaps fr *throw down the gauntlet* "issue a challenge"]

throw someone or something **for a loop** *See* KNOCK someone or something FOR A LOOP

throw one's **hat in the ring** *v phr fr early 1800s* To issue a challenge, esp to announce one's candidacy in an election, for an appointment, etc

throw in the sponge (or **the towel**) *v phr fr middle 1800s British* To concede defeat; give up; =FOLD [fr the signal of surrender given by a defeated boxer's manager or associate when he tosses a *sponge* or a *towel* in the air or into the ring]

throw money at something *v phr* To spend extravagant amounts of money, in the hope of solving some problem: *The answer to the quality of schools is not just to throw money at the problem*

◁ **throw** someone **out on** someone's **ass** ▷ (or **ear**) *v phr* To eject someone, esp violently: *I just raised a little question and they threw me out on my ass*

throw the book at someone *v phr* To give a severe punishment, esp to assign a maximum sentence to a criminal; treat mercilessly [fr the image of a judge *throwing the* whole *lawbook* full of punishment indiscriminately at the convicted person]

throw the bull *v phr* =SHOOT THE BULL

throw together *See* KNOCK TOGETHER

throw one's **weight around** *v phr* To use one's influence, esp in a crude way; exploit one's authority: *You'll never get picked if you start throwing your weight around*

thrush *n* A female singer; =CANARY

thumb **1** *v* (also **thumb a ride**) To solicit rides along a highway by pointing with one's thumb in the direction

one wishes to travel; =HITCHHIKE **2** ***n*** *narcotics* A marijuana cigarette; =JOINT [narcotics sense fr the fact that one sucks the cigarette as a baby does its *thumb*]
See DOWN-THUMB, a GREEN THUMB, STICK OUT

thumbs ***See*** ALL THUMBS, TWIDDLE one's THUMBS

thumbs down ***n phr*** A negative response; a negation: *It's thumbs down on his promotion this year* [fr the *pollice verso* gesture of the audience at a Roman gladiatorial show, indicating that a defeated gladiator was to be killed rather than spared]
See TURN THUMBS DOWN

thumbs up ***n phr*** *fr early 1900s* A positive response; an affirmation; =the NOD: *We go, the answer is thumbs up* [the opposite of *thumbs down*; see *thumbs down*]

thumper ***See*** IVORY-THUMPER

thunder thighs ***n phr*** Heavy thighs, esp when regarded as ugly and undesirable: *the sinewy thunder thighs of marathoner Gayle Olinekova*—Time

tick[1] ***n*** *fr 1600s* Credit: *plenty of canned goods and plenty of tick at the store*—Westbrook Pegler [fr *ticket*]
See ON TICK

tick[2] **1** ***n*** A degree, esp of upward motion or increase; a discrete amount: *if the price would have stayed where it was or skipped up a few more ticks*—Nicholas von Hoffman **2** ***n*** A second; =a JIFFY: *I'll be there in a couple of ticks*
See RICKY-TICK, UPTICK, WHAT MAKES someone TICK

tick[3] ***See*** TIGHT

ticked off or **ticked** ***adj phr*** or ***adj*** Angry; =PISSED OFF, TEE'D OFF: *Steve Kemp is ticked off*—Village Voice/ *a ticked future cop*—Car and Driver

ticker ***n*** *fr late 1800s* The heart: *tapped the left side of his chest. "Ticker," he said*—JD Salinger

ticket ***See*** BIG TICKET, HAVE one's TICKET PUNCHED, MEAL TICKET, WALKING PAPERS

the **ticket** ***n phr*** *fr middle 1800s British* Exactly what is wanted: *That's the ticket, my dear, exactly what we needed* [perhaps fr *the winning ticket* in a lottery, a race, etc]

tickety-boo **1** ***adv*** *fr WW2 British armed forces fr 1920s British Navy* Very well; splendidly: *Weitz's report just after liftoff that "everything's going tickety-boo so far"*—Newsweek **2** ***adj:*** *The sergeant reported that all was tickety-boo* [origin uncertain; perhaps fr *the ticket*; more likely fr the slightly earlier Royal Air Force *tiggerty boo* in the same sense, fr Hindi *teega* plus unexplained but euphonious *boo*]

tickled pink ***adj phr*** Very much pleased; happy as can be: *I am tickled pink to have been asked*

tickler ***See*** FRENCH TICKLER, RIB-TICKLER

◁ **tickle the shit** (or **piss**) **out of** someone▷ ***v phr*** To please someone very much; overjoy someone

tick someone **off** ***v phr*** To anger; =PISS someone OFF: *Her tone of voice ticked him off/ Just the slightest thing could tick off Harold*—Philadelphia

tick over ***v phr*** To idle; barely run; operate very slowly *The motor was just ticking over*

ticky-tacky **1** ***n*** Shabby materials; insubstantial and inferior goods: *little houses made of ticky-tacky* **2** ***adj*** (also **ticky-tack**) Inferior; shabbily made or done; =TACKY: *oil rigs and ticky-tack motels*—Advertisement for Time-Life Books/ *ticky-tacky direction by Allan Arkush*—Newsweek/ *draw their energy from the ticky-tacky-taco style of curio shops*—Newsweek [coined by Malvina Reynolds and used in "Little Boxes,"a 1960s satirical song about California housing tracts where the houses are described as little boxes made of *ticky-tacky*]

tiddly ***adj*** *late 1800s British* Drunk, esp slightly drunk: *a little tiddly, which is to say, shot or blind*—Philip Wylie [probably related to the mid-19th-century British term *tiddlywink* "an unlicensed saloon or tavern," and to the early-20th-century British *tiddlywink*, rhyming slang for "drink"]

◁ **tiddy**▷ ***See*** TOUGH SHIT

tied up **1** ***adj phr*** Very busy; totally occupied **2** ***adj phr*** Snarled; blocked; knotted: *Traffic was tied up for miles this side of the tunnel*

tie into ***v phr*** *fr early 1900s* To assault; attack or deal with vigorously: *She put her head back and tied into her drink*—J Evans

tie it up ***v phr*** =WRAP something UP

tie one on ***See*** HANG ONE ON

tie up *v phr narcotics* To inject narcotics into a vein, or put a rubber tubing around one's arm in order to find a vein; =SHOOT UP: *pop a handful of bennies, then tie up, smoking a joint at the same time*—Harper's

tiger *n* A strong, virile man; a dangerous man: *He's switched from being a pussycat to being a regular tiger*
See BLIND PIG, HAVE A TIGER BY THE TAIL

tight 1 *adj fr early 1800s* Parsimonious; tight-fisted; stingy: *He is tight in his dealings*—A Lavine **2** *adj* (Variations: **as a drum** (or **a lord** or **a mink**) may be added) *fr middle 1800s* Drunk: *Little tight, honey?* —Dorothy Parker **3** *adj* Close, sympathetic: *John and Mary are very tight*
See SIT TIGHT, WRAPPED TIGHT

◁ **tight as Kelsey's nuts** (or **Reilly's balls** or **O'Reilly's balls**)▷ *adj phr* Very parsimonious; stingy; close; =TIGHT

◁ **tight-ass**▷ **1** *n* A tense and morally rigid person: *I know that one...a real tight-ass*—Erich Segal **2** *adj: a very tightass sort of guy*

tightassed 1 *adj* Tense; overly formal: *tightassed British film critic* —Changes **2** *adj fr late 1800s* Not disposed to sexual promiscuity; chaste: *Washington, I saw, was full of tight-assed women*—Irwin Shaw

tighten (or **pull in**) one's **belt** *v phr* To prepare for an end of ease and plenty; become austere and earnest: *The economic predictors say we have to tighten our belts*

tight spot *n phr fr middle 1800s* A difficult situation; =JAM: *I'm in a tight spot and would appreciate your help*

tightwad 1 *n fr late 1800s* A parsimonious person; a stingy person; a miser: *the "tightwads" who have saved money*—New Republic **2** *adj: Don't be so tightwad with that hootch*—Sinclair Lewis

Tijuana taxi *n phr citizens band* A police car [probably because of the relatively colorful decoration of such cars]

till *See* WITH one's HAND IN THE TILL

till (or **until**) one **is blue in the face** *adv phr* Until one is able to do no more; to the point of helpless exhaustion: *Hail and beware the dead who will talk life until you are blue in the face*—Charles Olson [fr the *facial blueness* or darkening symptomatic of choking]

till the fat lady sings *See* the OPERA'S NEVER OVER TILL THE FAT LADY SINGS

time *See* BEAT someone's TIME, the BIG TIME, DOUBLE-TIME, GIVE someone A HARD TIME, HAVE oneself A TIME, MAKE TIME, MAKE TIME WITH someone, ON one's OWN TIME AND OWN DIME, SACK TIME, the SMALL TIME

the **time of day** *See* NOT GIVE someone THE TIME OF DAY

time warp *n phr* A blank, an inordinate rapidity or slowness, a seeming anachronism, or some other anomaly of time: *The case of five people indicted more than four years ago... has been "lost in a time warp" of delays, state prosecutors say*—Arizona Republic [fr science fiction notions of instantaneous eons and the like, devised to legitimize travel over enormous distances within conceivable and dramatically useful periods of time, and based on Albert Einstein's concept of "curved space"]

timey *See* OLD-TIMEY

tin 1 *n police* A police officer's badge; =POTSY: *Boone had to flash his tin*—Lawrence Sanders **2** *n narcotics* A few grains of cocaine **3** *n* A trifling amount of money; =SMALL POTATOES

tin ear *n phr* Unselective and unmusical hearing; auditory tastelessness: *He sometimes has a tin ear for dialogue*—Village Voice

tinfoil doorknob *See* WIN THE PORCELAIN HAIRNET

tinhorn or **tinhorn gambler** *n* or *n phr fr late 1800s* A petty but flashy gambler, or any person with those characteristics: *denunciations of punks, tin-horns, and gyps*—Westbrook Pegler [fr the *horn*-shaped metal can used by chuck-a-luck operators for shaking the dice; the notion of inferiority comes fr the presumed superiority of other, more sophisticated, kinds of gambling, and fr the generalized inferiority of *tin* to other metals]

tin horn *See* LIKE SHIT THROUGH A TIN HORN

tinkle 1 *n fr early 1900s British* A telephone call • Chiefly in the expression **give** someone **a tinkle** **2** *v fr early 1900s* To urinate;

=PEE • Child's and humorous euphemistic use

Tin Pan Alley *n phr fr early 1900s* The site where popular music was composed, arranged, published, recorded, etc, designating the neighborhood on Seventh Avenue between 48th and 52d Streets in New York City; also, the realm of popular music composition, publishing, etc [fr the late-19th-century musicians' term *tin pan* "cheap, tinny piano"]

tinpot *adj fr late 1800s* Inferior; petty; =TINHORN: *individual liberty from coercive tin-pot bigots*—Toronto Life [apparently in part fr the image of a ludicrous military figure wearing a grandiose *tin* helmet, a sort of *tin* soldier]

Tinseltown 1 *n* Hollywood; the Los Angeles-Hollywood movie and TV area and culture: *if he couldn't nab a ride to Tinsel Town in an hour's time*—George Warren **2** ***modifier:*** *With familiar Tinseltown inventiveness, the new film has been entitled Grease 2*—Time [fr *tinsel* "gaudy, glittering decoration" + *town*]

◁**Tio Taco**▷ *n phr* A Chicano who emulates or truckles to the values of the non-Hispanic majority [fr Spanish, literally "Uncle Taco," using the name of the Mexican fried tortilla; modeled on *Uncle Tom*]

tip 1 *v* (also **tip off**) *fr middle 1700s British* To give useful information or advice, esp advance information that gives an advantage of some sort: *The room clerk tipped him*—Scene of the Crime (movie)/ *Who tipped Larkin off?*—Erle Stanley Gardner **2** ***n:*** *our tip to Doc Jansen would be*—New York Daily News/ *Any hot tips on the election?* [origin uncertain; perhaps fr the notion of *tipping*, that is, tilting something in someone's direction]

tip-off *n fr early 1900s* A revealing, esp a warning; a particularly useful clue: *the tip-off on what's ahead*—Associated Press

tip over *v phr underworld* To rob; =HEIST, KNOCK OVER

tipster *n fr late 1800s* A person who gives tips, esp on horse races

tip the elbow ***See*** BEND THE ELBOW

tip-top *adj* Excellent; first-rate: *He assured me his health was tip-top*

tire ***See*** FLAT TIRE, SPARE TIRE

◁**tired-ass**▷ *adj* Tedious; overused; tired: *thinking in tired-ass racial cliches*—Philadelphia Journal

tired blood *n phr fr 1950s* A condition and presumed cause of listlessness, enervation, etc: *a battle against tired blood by shuffling the lineup*—New York Times [fr an advertising slogan used by a nonprescription brand of tonic]

◁**tit**▷ *n fr 1600s* A woman's breast: *She couldn't make it out there....No tits*—Calder Willingham [a respelling of *teat*]

See COLD AS HELL, GET one's TAIL IN A GATE, SUCK HIND TIT, SUGAR TIT

◁**tit art**▷ *n phr newspaper office* Appealing photographs of young women; =CHEESECAKE

◁**tit man**▷ *n phr* A man whose favorite part of the female body is the breasts

◁**tits**▷ **1** *adj* Excellent; wonderful; =GREAT, NEAT: *What a tits car she's got!* **2** *adj college students* Easy; simple: *a real tits quiz*

See WITH BELLS ON

◁**tits and ass**▷ **1** *n phr* A display of female bosoms and bottoms; also, a show, dance, etc, featuring such a display; =CHEESECAKE, TA: *Tits and ass, that's what the attraction is*—Lenny Bruce **2** ***modifier:*** *The magazine had a tits-and-ass section purporting to be a review of bathing-suit styles*

◁**tits-and-zits**▷ ***modifier*** Dealing with teenage love and sex: *yet another entry in the lamentable tits-and-zits genre of teenage sex comedies*—Time [modeled on *tits-and-ass*]

◁**titty**▷ *n* A woman's breast; =TIT: *His dipping titties touched the floor before his chin did*—Saul Bellow

See TOUGH SHIT

tizzy ***See*** IN A TIZZY

TL *n* A person who curries favor; toady; sycophant; =ASS-KISSER [fr *tokus licker* fr Yiddish *toches lecher* "ass-licker"; see *trade-last*]

TO (toh) *n* Toronto, Ontario: *What makes you so sure Holden Caulfield is in TO?*—Toronto Life

toad ***See*** KNEE-HIGH TO A GRASSHOPPER

toast 1 *v musicians* A kind of talking or chanting done in the reggae music mode: *not exactly toasting, it was a kind of primitive rapping, consisting mainly of new slang words and* *an occasional joke*—Village Voice **2** ***adj*** *teenagers fr black* Excellent; wonderful; =COOL, TITS, TUBULAR: *She told me my clothes were real toast*

to beat the band (or **the Dutch**) ***adv phr*** *fr late 1900s* In an unrestrained way; to the highest pitch; very much; =ALL OUT: *I hollered to beat the band/ We ran to beat the Dutch* [fr the notion that such extreme effort could even drown out *the band*; or, in the mid-18th-century version *this beats the Dutch*, could convince even a stolid, phlegmatic *Dutch*man]

to boot ***adv phr*** *fr 1000s* In addition; in extra measure: *She has lots of talent and more to boot* [fr Old English, "as profit"]

to'd (TEE OHD) ***adj*** =TEE'D OFF

toddle off ***v phr*** To leave; =BUZZ OFF, POP OFF

toe ***See*** GO TOE TO TOE

toe the mark (or **the line**) ***v phr*** To behave properly; =KEEP one's NOSE CLEAN: *If he doesn't toe the mark, fire him* [fr the *mark* or *line* indicating the starting point of a race]

toe to toe ***See*** GO TOE TO TOE

together **1** ***adj*** *fr 1960s counterculture fr black* Composed and effective; free of tension and anxiety: *Now they're together, unless they're strung out*—William Zinsser **2** ***adj*** *black* Stylish and au courant; socially adept

See GET IT TOGETHER, HAVE IT ALL TOGETHER

to hell **1** ***adv phr*** (also **to hell and gone**) Thoroughly; irretrievably: *This thing's busted to hell/ The plan's wrecked to hell and gone* **2** ***adv phr*** (also **to heaven** or **to high heaven**) Very strongly; fervently; sincerely: *He swore to hell he'd never do it again/ I wish to heaven she'd leave*

toity ***See*** HOITY-TOITY

toke[1] **1** ***n*** A puff or drag at a cigarette, cigar, etc, esp a marijuana cigarette: *He still took a toke of marijuana from time to time*—Norman Mailer **2** ***v:*** *to toke vigorously on an oversize cigar*—Rocky Mountain Magazine **3** ***n*** A cigarette, esp a marijuana cigarette: *Elaborately, I lit a toke*—Easyriders [probably fr Spanish *tocar* in its sense "touch," or "tap, hit," or "get a shave or part," or a combination of these]

toke[2] **1** ***n*** *gambling* A gambling chip or token, esp one given to a dealer as a tip **2** ***n*** A gratuity given by a gambling casino, brothel, or other business to cab drivers for bringing in clients: *Cab drivers have long been paid "tokes"...when they deliver customers to a long list of varied business establishments* —Toronto Globe and Mail

tokus (TOH kəs, TŎŎ kəs) ***n*** (also **tokis** or **tuchis** or **tuckus** or **tush** or **tushie** or **tushy**) The buttocks; =ASS, BOTTOM ● A frequent euphemism for **ass**: *knocked him right square on his tokus/ He shakes his tushie with elegant languor*—New York Post/ *bumps her tush gently along*—Village Voice [fr Yiddish; *tush* forms are affectionate, used esp with children]

told ***See*** FUCKING WELL TOLD

◁ **Tom** or **tom** ▷ **1** ***n*** *black* A black person who emulates or truckles to the white majority taste and culture; =OREO, UNCLE TOM **2** ***v:*** *sleeping, resisting, tomming, killing the enemy* —Amiri Baraka/ *You too young to be Tomming*—John Godey

See AUNT TOM, BLIND TOM, MISTER TOM, UNCLE TOM

Tomahawk ***See*** UNCLE TOMAHAWK

tomato ***n*** *fr early 1900s* An attractive young woman; =CHICK: *the idea that such a luscious tomato might be mixed up in murder*—RS Prather [fr the connotations of lusciousness, tautness, full color, etc]

tomcat **1** ***v*** To pursue male sexual activity avidly **2** ***n:*** *In his younger days he was a notorious tomcat*

Tom, Dick, and Harry ***See*** EVERY TOM, DICK, AND HARRY

tomfool ***adj*** Stupid; foolish; =NUTTY: *some tomfool scientist*—Newsweek

Tommy ***n*** *fr late 1800s* A private in the British army; =TOMMY ATKINS: *He met three Tommys in a bar*

Tommy Atkins ***n phr*** *fr late 1800s* A private in the British army; =TOMMY [fr the name *Mr Thomas Atkins* used on sample forms of the British army]

Tommy (or **tommy**) **gun** ***n phr*** *fr underworld* A handheld automatic repeating firearm; a submachine gun; =BURP GUN, CHOPPER [fr the name of the .45-caliber *Thompson* submachine gun, the earliest well-known weapon of this sort, and a favorite arm of the gangster era]

tommyrot *n fr late 1800s British* Nonsense; balderdash; =BALONEY, BULLSHIT [origin unknown; perhaps fr British *tommy* "goods, esp food, supplied to workers in lieu of wages"]

toned *See* HIGH-TONED

tonk *n* =HONKY-TONK

ton of bricks *See* HIT someone LIKE A TON OF BRICKS

tony or **toney** **1** *adj fr late 1800s* Stylish; very elegant; =SWANKY **2** *n: St Michael's alley, still inhabited by the tony*—HL Mencken [probably fr French *bon ton* "high fashion, chic"] *See* HIGH-TONED

toodle-oo *interj fr early 1900s British* A parting salutation • Thought of as a humorous affectation, like **cheerio** [perhaps an alteration of French *à tout à l'heure* "see you soon, so long"]

took *See* be HAD

tool ◁**1**▷ *n fr middle 1500s* The penis **2** *n underworld fr early 1900s* A pickpocket **3** *n* A stupid and gullible person; =PATSY, SUCKER **4** *n college students* A diligent student; =GREASY GRIND **5** *v* (also **tool along**) To speed: *They were tooling down the freeway/ Look at them tool along* **6** *v* To drive a car very fast; tear; =BARREL: *I climbed into the Buick and tooled it down the ramp*—Raymond Chandler [underworld sense perhaps fr the practice of using a small boy as a sort of *tool* in pickpocketing, or perhaps fr Romany *tool* "handle, take"; driving senses fr early-19th-century British *tool* "drive," apparently fr the notion of handling a coach and team as skillfully as one handled a *tool*]

toolie *n college students* An engineering student: *My friends are engineers, or, as they call themselves, toolies* —New York Times

too many *See* ONE TOO MANY

too much **1** *adj phr jazz musicians* Wonderful; superb; =the MOST: *The way she blows that horn is too much* **2** *adj phr fr 1930s jive talk* Excessively good, bad, wonderful, incredible, etc; prodigious; overwhelming: *You ate 23 hot dogs in one sitting? Man, you're too much* **3** *n* =FAR OUT

toon *See* LOONY-TUNE

too rich for someone's **blood** *adj phr fr middle 1800s* Exceeding someone's capabilities, purse, desires, etc; too much: *I don't go out with them anymore, it's too rich for my blood*

toot **1** *n fr middle 1800s* A spree, esp of drinking; =BENDER, BINGE, KICK: *It gave me an excuse to go off on a four-day toot*—Humphrey Bogart **2** *n narcotics* Cocaine: *Am I witnessing mere incompetence or too much toot?*—Playboy **3** *n narcotics* A whiff of cocaine into the nose; =SNORT **4** *v: He was himself tooting cocaine on a daily basis*—New York [the drinking sense is probably fr the image of someone *tooting* on a drinking horn, that is, holding a glass up as if it were a horn one were blowing; *toot* or *tout* "drink deeply, quaff" are attested fr the 17th century; narcotics sense probably related to *honker* "horn, nose" as something to be *tooted*]

tootin' *See* ROOTIN'-TOOTIN', YOU'RE DAMN TOOTIN'

toot (or **blow**) one's **own horn** *v phr* To praise and flatter oneself; advertise one's virtues; boast: *I am not ashamed of the text, but of being thought to "toot my own horn"* —Washington Post

toots (TŏŏTS) **1** *n* (also **tootsie** or **tootsy** or **tootsie-wootsie** or **tootsy-wootsy**) A woman; =DOLL • Often used in address, often disparagingly, and as a nickname: *Not any more, toots, not any more, my precious darling angel*—Raymond Chandler/ *How about one of those tootsie-wootsies?*—Saturday Evening Post/ *He was also paying for a penthouse apartment on Park Avenue for his tootsie*—Art Buchwald **2** *n fr middle 1800s* A foot, esp a child's or baby's foot [the second and earlier sense is a childish pronunciation of *foot*; the woman-designating sense perhaps developed from the fact that one plays affectionately with a baby's foot, eg, "This little piggie went to market," and that this cozy toying led by semantic association to notions of *tootsie* or *toots* as a baby, a doll, a cherished woman, etc; perhaps fr Yiddish *zees tushele* "sweet bottom," used affectionately of babies and euphemized to *toots* and *tootsie*, under the influence of English *tootsie*, for older children, adults, women, etc; see *tushie*]

tootsies *n fr middle 1800s* The feet: *Pull up a chair and warm your tootsies*

top 1 *v fr 1700s* To hang someone: *A colleague sent to the gallows has been topped*—HL Mencken **2** *v underworld* To kill; =BUMP OFF, HIT **3** *v* To surpass; better; =CAP: *I'll top that story with one of my own* **4** *n fr WW1 Army* =TOP SERGEANT **5** *n circus & carnival* A tent: *The cook tent is the cookhouse. All others are called tops*—American Mercury **6** *adj* Best; most superior: *He got the top recommendation*
See BLOW one's TOP, CHOPPED TOP, FROM THE TOP, MUTTONHEAD, OFF THE TOP, ON TOP OF, RAGTOP, TIP-TOP

top banana 1 *n phr show business* The leading or featured comedian in a burlesque show; the chief comic **2** *n phr* The leader, president, manager, etc; =BOSS, BIG ENCHILADA: *refuses its members... opportunity to become top banana*—Fran Lebowitz [said to have originated fr a burlesque routine having to do with a bunch of *bananas*]

the **top brass 1** *n phr fr 1930s* The highest of military officers: *They went to the top brass at the Pentagon* **2** *n phr* The highest of executives, managers, etc: *The top brass at Xerox liked the idea*

top dog 1 *n phr* The most important person; the chief; =BOSS: *Who's top dog around this place?* **2** *adj phr* Most important; most superior; =TOPS: *The small strong bands were not top dog anymore*—Stephen Longstreet

top-drawer *adj fr early 1900s British* Of the highest quality; most superior; =TOPS: *The drinks they serve are absolutely top-drawer* [fr a British expression *out of the top drawer* "upper-class, well-bred"]

top-kick *n fr WW1 Army* A first sergeant; =FIRST MAN: *The Top Kick was caught shorthanded*—American Legion Magazine

topless 1 *modifier* Not wearing anything on the upper body; with breasts exposed: *walking about the square topless/ a topless dancer* **2** *modifier* Having to do with entertainment, bars and clubs, etc, featuring women bare from the waist up: *only at bars and only if they were topless*—Rolling Stone

top-notch *adj phr fr early 1800s* Superior; of the highest quality; =TOP-DRAWER: *She's a top-notch racquetball player* [fr *notch* as representing position, rank, etc]

top of one's **head** *See* OFF THE TOP OF one's HEAD

topper *See* BLOW one's TOP

tops *adj fr 1930s* Best; most superior; absolutely first rate; =the TOPS: *I wish you could print Mencken every month, he's tops*—American Mercury/ *Sanitation Service Is Tops*—New York Times

the **tops** *n phr* The best; the acme: *The English department is the tops here*

top sergeant 1 *n phr Army fr late 1800s* A first sergeant; =TOP-KICK **2** *n phr homosexuals* A lesbian who takes the dominant, masculine role; =BUTCH, DYKE

topside *adv nautical* Upstairs; above

torch 1 *v* To set a fire deliberately; burn a building: *The lumberyard at 12th and C was torched, for the insurance*—Village Voice **2** *n* An arsonist; an incendiary: *If your suspicions are right, the torch will be close by*—L Turner
See CARRY THE TORCH

torch job *n phr* An instance of arson: *mob-linked torch jobs for a 10 percent cut of insurance proceeds*—New York Times

torch song *n phr* A popular song bemoaning one's unrequited love: *If it is unrequited, the song is a torch song*—Haskin News Service [see *carry the torch*]

-torium *See* -ATORIUM

torpedo 1 *n fr underworld* A gunman, esp a hired killer; =HIT MAN: *the torpedoes who worked for Ciro Terranova*—Time **2** *n* =HERO SANDWICH

torqued *adj Air Force* Angry; upset; =PISSED OFF [probably somehow fr the sense "twisted," and so semantically akin to *bent out of shape*]

toss *v underworld* To search, esp a person for weapons, drugs, etc; =SHAKE DOWN: *The cops regularly toss anybody they stop on the street*

[fr the sometimes violent way such searches are made]
See THROW

toss one's **cookies** (or **lunch**) *See* SHOOT one's COOKIES

toss in the sponge *v phr* =THROW IN THE SPONGE

toss it in *v phr* To surrender; stop fighting; quit

toss off 1 *v phr* To do something easily and casually: *They sat down and tossed off a couple of limericks* **2** *v phr* To drink, esp at one gulp; =KNOCK BACK: *She tossed off three double Scotches*

a **toss-up** *n fr early 1800s* An even matter; a case of even probabilities, values, etc: *It's a toss-up between those two candidates/ I don't know which way to bet, it's a toss-up* [fr the fact that the choice might as well be made by *tossing up* a coin]

total 1 *v* To destroy; totally wreck, esp a car: *It didn't look like much of a wreck, but his car was totaled/ The paratroopers got mad and totaled the place* **2** *v* To maim or kill; grievously injure; =WASTE: *I'm gonna total that bastard*—Erich Segal [fr the phrase *a total loss*, having to do with something insured]

totaled 1 *adj* Destroyed; wrecked completely: *The totaled car made you wonder how they survived the wreck* **2** *adj* Stuporous from narcotics, liquor, etc; =STONED, WASTED

a **total loss** *n phr* A person or thing that is hopelessly futile; =LOSER: *Don't tell me about that guy, he's been a total loss since he got divorced*

tote[1] *v* Total; add up to: *How much does it tote?*—James M Cain

tote[2] *n* (also **tote board**) A totalizator, a machine that displays odds at a race track

totem poles *See* KNOCK someone or something FOR A LOOP

to the eyes *See* STONED TO THE EYES

to the gills *See* SOUSED, STEWED

to the mark *See* UP TO SCRATCH

to the max *adv phr teenagers & Army* To the highest degree; utterly; totally: *Many of these were obscure to the max*—Philadelphia [fr a shortening of *to the maximum*]
See GROTTY

to the nines *See* DRESSED TO THE TEETH

to the salt mines *See* BACK TO THE SALT MINES

to the teeth *See* DRESSED TO THE TEETH

to the tune of *adv phr* In the amount of; to the extent of: *It'll cost him a bundle, to the tune of sixty grand or so*

to the wall *See* BALLS TO THE WALL

totsie *See* HOTSIE-TOTSIE

touch 1 *v* (also **touch up**) *fr middle 1700s* To solicit money, a loan, etc; =HIT: *He touched his sister for a couple of bucks/ Who better to touch up than the richest guys in town?* —Philadelphia **2** *n: a quick ten- or twenty-dollar touch*—E Lavine [*touch up* variant may be influenced by British *touch up* "caress in order to excite"]
See SOFT TOUCH

touch all bases 1 *v phr* To be thorough; leave nothing undone, esp in matters of consultation, communication, etc: *The plan flopped because you didn't touch all bases on the way* **2** *v phr* To be very versatile; be apt for various experiences: *Humphrey is a man to touch all bases*—Toronto Life [fr the necessity of *touching all bases* in baseball when one makes a home run]

touch base with someone *v phr* To consult with or inform as to an impending matter: *Before you sign it you'd better touch base with your lawyer* [fr *touch all bases*]

not **touch** someone or something **with a ten-foot pole** *See* NOT TOUCH someone or something WITH A TEN-FOOT POLE

tough 1 *adj fr early 1900s* Physically menacing; vicious: *Don't act tough with me, you little jerk* **2** *n fr early 1900s* A hard and menacing person **3** *adj cool talk & students fr 1960s* Excellent; superb; =the MOST • Sometimes spelled **tuff**: *That's a really tough set of wheels*
See TOUGH IT OUT

tough cookie *n phr* A durable person; a survivor • Usually said in admiration: *You gotta respect the old guy, he's a real tough cookie*

tough cop *See* GOOD COP BAD COP

tough guy *n phr* A menacing man; a hoodlum; =BIMBO, ROUGHNECK, TOUGHIE: *Bogart used to play tough guys a lot*

toughie or **toughy** **1** *n* A menacing person, esp a man; =TOUGH, TOUGH GUY: *getting the toughies off the streets*—New Republic/ *That servant will talk her out of it. She's a toughie* —Saul Bellow **2** *n* Something difficult; a severe test: *This is a toughie* —Max Shulman/ *has 3 toughies barring its way to a perfect season* —Associated Press

tough it out *v phr fr early 1800s* To endure something doggedly and bravely; persist and survive against rigors; =HANG TOUGH: *He's never really had to tough it out in this world of ours*—J Bell

tough nut *n phr* An obstinate, difficult person [fr the phrase *a tough nut to crack*]

a **tough nut to crack** *n phr* A difficult problem; =BITCH, TOUGHIE: *Getting them all here on time will be a tough nut to crack*

a **tough row to hoe** *See* a HARD ROW TO HOE

◁ **tough shit**▷ *sentence* (Variations: **nibs** or **noogies** or **rocks** or **tiddy** or **titty** may replace **shit**) That's too bad; that's a terrible shame • Always ironical and mocking: *"Tough tiddy," the Boss said* —Robert Penn Warren/ *Well, my friend, that's just tough shit about your lost plane ticket/ to which one has to say, with whatever empathy... tough nibs*—Village Voice/ *That's tough shit, man, my heart really bleeds*—WT Tyler/ *Well... tough titty* —Armistead Maupin [most forms probably fr black or Southern; the mammary forms seem based on a black folk-saying, "It's tough titty, but the milk is good"]

tour *n* A period of duty; an enlistment period; a working shift

tour guide *n phr narcotics* A person who aids and supports someone having a psychedelic drug experience or "trip"; =GURU

tourist trap **1** *n phr* A museum, pageant, shop, etc, of minimal significance established to attract transient visitors **2** *n phr* A restaurant, nightclub, etc, in a tourist resort, that charges exorbitant prices for often inferior goods or services: *We had to eat in a shabby tourist trap, and it cost far too much money*

tout **1** *n fr middle 1800s* A person who sells betting advice at a race track; =TIPSTER **2** *n: He makes a slender living with his touting at Belmont* **3** *v* To advocate aggressively; publicize; =BALLYHOO, FLACK: *He's now touting acupuncture* [ultimately fr Middle English *tuten* "look around, peer," by way of *tout* "be on the lookout"]

towel *See* CRYING TOWEL, THROW IN THE SPONGE

town *See* GO TO TOWN, HICK TOWN, the ONLY GAME IN TOWN, ON THE TOWN, PAINT THE TOWN, TINSELTOWN

Town *See* BEAN TOWN

town pump (or **bike**) *n phr* A very promiscuous woman; =PUNCHBOARD: *whose reputation as a town pump makes Stony doubt her worth as a human being*—Richard Price [a pun on the commonness and availability of the *town pump* and the coital sense of *pump*; *bike* variant based on the phrase *common carrier*]

track **1** *v Army* To agree with other information; chime: *What you say doesn't track with what I know* **2** *v* To make sense; be plausible; =FIGURE: *It does not necessarily track that because Son of Sam sells papers in New York he will sell books in Seattle* —California Magazine/ *She's practically out of her mind. Like, she isn't even tracking*—Cyra McFadden [probably fr *track* "the groove of a phonograph record, a continuous line or passage of a tape recording," influenced by earlier *track* "follow, come closely and directly behind"]

See FAST LANE, GO ON TRACK, HAVE THE INSIDE TRACK

the **track** *See* the TURF

Track One *n phr Canadian police* The brothel district of a city; the red-light district

track record *n phr* Any record of performance, esp of success; =FORM: *I have a lot of relevant experience and a good track record*—New York Times [fr the *record* of performance of a racehorse on the race*track*]

tracks **1** *n WW2 Army* =RAILROAD TRACKS **2** *n narcotics* The scars or puncture-marks caused by narcotics injections: *wear long sleeves (to cover their "tracks," needle marks)* —Reader's Digest

See CROW TRACKS, HEN TRACKS, RAILROAD TRACKS, STOP someone or something DEAD IN someone's or something's TRACKS, the WRONG SIDE OF THE TRACKS

Track Two *n phr Canadian police* The homosexual quarter of a city; the gay ghetto

trade **1** *n prostitutes & homosexuals* A person regarded merely as a sex partner; =ASS, PIECE OF ASS **2** *n homosexuals* A man, usu heterosexual, who takes gratification from homosexuals without reciprocation, identification, etc; a man of masculine build attractive to homosexuals: *decidedly sexy trade in a Czardas with six girls*—Village Voice **3** *v homosexuals* To look for sexual encounters; =CRUISE

See the RAG TRADE, ROUGH TRADE, TEA TRADE

trade up *v phr* To achieve higher status, esp by expenditure; climb socially: *If you're trading up you'll avoid this unchic resort* [fr an advertising term of the car industry, advising one to *trade up* "trade in one's present car for a more expensive one laden with prestige"]

train **1** *v underworld* To do the sex act on a woman serially, man after man, in a gang; =GANG-BANG: *announced that they were going to train her*—Philadelphia Journal **2** *n: popularly known as gang bangs or trains*—Ms [related to *pull a train*; perhaps influenced by earlier *train* "romp, carry on wildly"]

See GRAVY TRAIN, ON THE GRAVY TRAIN, PULL A TRAIN, RIDE THE GRAVY TRAIN

tramp *n* A promiscuous woman; a harlot; =PUNCHBOARD, TOWN PUMP

trank *n* A tranquilizer; a tranquilizer tablet or capsule

tranquilizer *See* ELEPHANT TRANQUILIZER

trans *n black teenager* A car; =TRANSPORTATION

transportation *n* An old or decrepit car; an unappealing car: *It ain't pretty, but it's transportation*

trap **1** *n fr late 1700s* The mouth; =YAP: *When she opens her trap she has an accent that is British*—John O'Hara **2** *n* A nightclub: *a pretty good East Side trap*—Gilbert Milstein **3** *n* (also **trap money**) *black* An amount of money earned by a prostitute, and usu given to her pimp: *Her trap was fat*—Donald Goines **4** *modifier: to figure out why my trap money was shitty*—Donald Goines

See BEAR TRAP, BLOW OFF one's MOUTH, BOOBY TRAP, FISH TRAP, FLEABAG, FLY TRAP, POTATO-TRAP, SHUT one's TRAP, TOURIST TRAP

trash **1** *n* A despicable, ill-bred person or group: *Don't mind them, they're just trash* **2** *v fr late 1960s* To vandalize; mutilate or destroy, sometimes as an act of political protest; =WASTE: *They have also made it a practice to "trash" (wreck) restaurants, publishing houses, and other businesses that discriminate against the third world of sex*—Saturday Review/ *One year we were trashed three times*—Time **3** *v fr late 1960s* To vilify; excoriate; =DUMP ON: *Much given to the rave-pan approach to her craft, she can trash in a flash*—Toronto Life **4** *v* To hit repeatedly; trounce; =CLOBBER **5** *v* To scavenge discarded furniture and other items that have been thrown away [first sense fr *white trash*, a black term of opprobrium]

See WHITE TRASH

trashy *adj* Despicable; inferior; ill-bred; =LOW-RENT, LOW-RIDE

treadhead *n Army* A member of a tank crew

treat someone **like a doormat** (or ◁**like shit**▷) *v phr* To deal with in a humiliating, haughty, or oppressive manner: *We treated poor old Uncle Bob like a doormat/ and is also a fucking nitwit imbecile who treats me like shit and makes me talk about vultures*—Joseph Heller

tree *See* LIT UP, OUT OF one's TREE, SHAKE THE MONEY TREE, UP A TREE

Trekkie or **Trekker** *n* A devotee of the television science-fiction series "Star Trek": Star Trek II. The Wrath of Khan. *Come, all ye Trekkers*—Playboy

trenches *See* IN THE TRENCHES

trendy **1** *adj fr 1960s British* Following new trends in fashion, art, literature, etc; anxiously au courant: *Fetch a tumbril for these fellows, or at least a trendy tailor*—Saturday Review **2** *n: That will undoubtedly have great appeal to all you trendies out there*—East Side Express

trey *n narcotics* A three-dollar packet of a narcotic, esp of cocaine

trial balloon *n phr* Something done or said in order to test the reaction: *Those provocative comments were a sort of trial balloon*

Tribeca or **TriBeCa** (trī BEK ə) *n early 1980s New York City* An area in Manhattan being developed as an artists' and residential neighborhood: *They've traipsed all over Lower Manhattan, from Greenwich Village to Tribeca*—Playboy [fr *triangle below Canal* Street]

trick **1** *n fr early 1900s prostitutes* A prostitute's client or sexual transaction: *woman walking the streets for tricks to take to her room*—Louis Armstrong **2** *v prostitutes* To serve a customer: *She had tricked a john from Macon*—Playboy **3** *n homosexuals* A casual homosexual partner; =NUMBER **4** *v* (also **trick out**) To do the sex act, either hetero- or homosexually; =FUCK: *They can go "tricking out" with other gay people*—Deviant Reality **5** *v underworld* To inform; =RAT, SQUEAL: *I wasn't going to trick on him* **6** *n fr nautical fr late 1900s* A shift: *She doesn't require any breaks at her eight-hour trick*—New York Daily News

See CHAMPAGNE TRICK, HAT TRICK, TURN A TRICK

trickledown **1** *n* The stimulation of a whole economic system by the enrichment and encouragement of those in the upper reaches **2** *modifier: The planners counted on a trickledown effect when they relieved the rich of all taxation*

tricks ***See*** DIRTY TRICKS, GO DOWN AND DO TRICKS, HOW'S TRICKS

trigger **1** *n underworld fr 1930s* A gunman; =HIT MAN, TRIGGER MAN: *He's a trigger*—Scene of the Crime (movie) **2** *v* To commit a robbery: *Sims has triggered dozens of holdups*—Associated Press **3** *v* To initiate something; provoke something: *What triggered the feud in the first place?*

See QUICK ON THE DRAW

trigger man *n phr underworld fr 1920s* A gunman; =HIT MAN, TRIGGER

trikini *n* A woman's bathing suit with two top parts [fr *bikini,* based on the amusing assumption that *bi-* is Greek for "two," to be replaced with *tri-* "three"]

trim **1** *v* To defeat utterly; trounce; =CLOBBER: *They got trimmed 8 zip* ◁**2**▷ *n fr black* The vulva; =CUNT ◁**3**▷ *n fr black* The sex act with a woman; =ASS, CUNT, GASH: *you looking for some trim*—Ed McBain

trip[1] *n underworld fr 1930s* An arrest; a prison sentence; =FALL [fr *trip* "stumble, fall"]

trip[2] **1** *n narcotics & students fr 1960s* A psychedelic narcotics experience: *users like beat poet Allen Ginsberg (30 trips)*—New York Post **2** *v* (also **trip out**): *Are you still tripping on LSD?/ They were stoned, as if they were tripping out* **3** *n* Any experience comparable with a psychedelic experience: *The park is an ikon. A nostalgia trip back into a youth*—Boston Magazine/ *His lecture was a pure trip* [fr *trip* "journey"]

See BAD TRIP, EGO TRIP, HEAD TRIP, POWER TRIP

tripe **1** *n fr late 1800s* Nonsense; exaggerations; =BULLSHIT: *Stop peddling that tripe* **2** *n fr late 1800s* Contemptible material; worthless stuff; =CRAP, JUNK: *What the hell do they have to give us that tripe for?*—P Marks [fr *tripe* "animal stomach used as food," because it is held in low regard]

tripes *n fr middle 1400s* The intestines; =GUTS, INNARDS, KISHKES: *He doesn't put their tripes in an uproar*—Westbrook Pegler

triple whammy *n phr* A three-part attack, difficulty, threat, etc: *Triple Whammy on the Farm*—Newsweek

tripped out *adj phr* Having or symptomatic of a psychedelic narcotics experience: *a tripped-out laughing jag*—Crawdaddy

tripper **1** *n fr late 1800s* An excursionist; a tourist: *the tripper class*—Sinclair Lewis **2** *n narcotics & students fr 1960s* A person who takes psychedelic narcotics

See ROUND-TRIPPER

trippy *teenagers* **1** *adj* Intoxicated with narcotics; dazed; =SPACED-OUT, STONED **2** *adj* Bizarre; phantasmal; surreal: *a trippy fantasy, the Harvard University Press version*—Village Voice

troll[1] *n Army* A stupid person; a dullard [probably fr the dwarf or demon of Norse mythology]

troll[2] *v* To go about looking for sexual encounters; =CRUISE: *Women who are out trolling bars do not deserve the protection of the law*—Ms [fr the action of fishing by *trolling*]

trolley *See* OFF one's TROLLEY, SLIP one's TROLLEY

the **trots** *n phr fr early 1900s* Diarrhea; =the SHITS

trouble *See* DROWN one's SORROWS, HAND TROUBLE

trouser *See* DUST someone's PANTS

truck **1** *v* To carry; haul; lug: *Why are you trucking all that weight around?* **2** *v* *1930s jive talk fr early 1900s black* To leave; go along **3** *v* *1930s jive talk* To dance the jitterbug; esp, to do a jitterbug dance called "Truckin'"

See MACK TRUCK

truck driver **1** *n phr* *narcotics* An amphetamine capsule or pill **2** *n phr* *homosexuals* A very masculine homosexual [narcotics sense fr the fact that *truck drivers* use stimulants to stay awake while driving]

trucking *See* KEEP ON TRUCKING

trust *See* BEEF TRUST

try *See* the OLD COLLEGE TRY

try-out *n fr early 1900s* A trial, esp of someone's skill, acting or singing ability, etc

TS *n* =TOUGH SHIT

tsatske *See* TCHOTCHKE

tsuris or **tsoris** or **tzuris** (TSŏŏR əs, TSAWR əs) *n* Troubles; tribulations; anxieties; sufferings: *if Samuels, with all his tsuris, wins the Democratic nomination*—New York/ *There is a tsoris, which is a kind of trouble spot*—New York Times [fr Yiddish fr Hebrew *tsarah* "trouble"]

tub *See* IN THE TUB

tubby *n* A fat person ● Used as a nickname, and nearly always affectionately and sympathetically: *the ex-tubbies trying to live on lettuce leaves* —Hal Boyle

the **tube** *n phr* Television, as an industry, a medium, a television set, etc: *making a name for herself as a singer on the tube*—New York Sunday News [shortening of *cathode ray tube* or *picture tube*]

See the BOOB TUBE, DOWN THE TUBE

tube it *v phr students* To fail an examination, course, etc

tube steak *n phr* A frankfurter; =HOT DOG

tub of guts (or **of lard**) *n phr* A fat person, esp a repulsive one: *that tub-o'-guts*—G Holmes

tubular *adj teenagers* Wonderful; excellent; =AWESOME, GREAT [fr surfing term describing a wave with a *tube*, that is, a cylindrical space around which the crest is curling as the wave breaks, and inside which the surfer happily rides]

tuchis or **tuckus** *See* TOKUS

tuck *See* NIP AND TUCK

tucker *See* BEST BIB AND TUCKER

tude *n teenagers fr black* Attitude; view of things; typical reaction ● Usually negative, sour, or surly [fr *attitude*]

tuff *See* TOUGH

tumble *v underworld* To be arrested; =FALL, TRIP

See GIVE someone A TUMBLE

tumble to something *v phr fr middle 1800s* To discover; suddenly understand: *I tumbled to what she was really up to*—James M Cain [fr the notion of falling upon something, perhaps by stumbling over it]

tumor *See* MILWAUKEE GOITER

◁ **tuna** or **tuna fish** ▷ *fr black* **1** *n* or *n phr* The vulva; =CUNT **2** *n* or *n phr* A woman; a female [fr the similarity, recognized esp in black slang, between the odor of the vulva and that of fish or other seafood; see *seafood*; perhaps somehow influenced by *Tiny Tuna*, homosexual slang for a sailor as a sex object]

tuna wagon *n phr* An old, decrepit car; =HEAP, JUNKER: *the title of an article...in Vermont Life, "Junkers, Beaters, and Tuna Wagons"*—New York Times

tune *See* LOONY-TUNE, TO THE TUNE OF

tune in *v phr esp 1960s counterculture* To become aware, au courant, involved, etc: *Tune in, turn on, drop out*—Timothy Leary

tune out *v phr esp 1960s counterculture* To cease being aware, au courant, etc; the opposite of "tune in"

tune someone or something **out** *v phr* To ignore deliberately; withdraw attention: *If he annoys you, just tune him out*

tunnel ***See*** SEE THE LIGHT AT THE END OF THE TUNNEL

tunnel vision ***n phr*** Very narrow and restricted vision or perception; the inability to see anything except what is directly in front: *He's an idiot afflicted with tunnel vision*

◁ **turd** ▷ **1** ***n*** *fr 1000s* A piece of excrement **2** ***n*** A despicable person; = PRICK, SHIT
See GHOST TURDS

turd in the punchbowl ***See*** GO OVER LIKE A LEAD BALLOON

turf 1 ***n*** *1930s jive talk* The sidewalk; the street **2** ***n*** *street gang* The territory claimed or controlled by a street gang: *I tried to imagine my Deacons pacing the turf or talking about me*—Life **3** ***n*** *fr street gang* A particular specialized concern; = THING: *Counterterrorism is not their exclusive turf*—Newsweek **4** ***v*** *hospital* To transfer a patient to another ward or service in order to evade responsibility, decisions, irritations, etc

the **turf** (or **track**) ***n phr*** The work and venue of a prostitute; the street: *During early years "on the turf," as the saying went, she was... thrifty and ambitious*—H Asbury/ *I didn't want to lose her, now that she was ready for the track*—Donald Goines [fr an analogy between the prostitute's work and that of a racehorse]

turista ***n*** Diarrhea; = AZTEC TWO-STEP, MONTEZUMA'S REVENGE [fr Spanish, "tourist"]

turk ***n*** = TURKEY

Turk ***n*** *football* An employee of a professional football team, generally not a highly placed one, who tells players they are to be dismissed [fr the image of a *Turk* with a scimitar sword, who "cuts" the player]
See YOUNG TURK

turkey 1 ***n*** *show business fr 1920s* An inferior show, esp a failure; = BOMB, FLOP: *Management prudently kept the turkey out of town*—Gene Fowler/ *Stars generally attract an audience no matter what picture they are in (unless it's a turkey)*—Bob Thomas **2** ***n*** Anything inferior, stupid, or futile; = LEMON, LOSER: *For all ordinary purposes it was simply a turkey*—James M Cain **3** ***n*** A stupid, ineffectual person; = JERK: *You'd be stuck with that turkey practically until he died*—D Larsen **4** ***n*** *underworld & teenagers* The victim of a mugging or street robbery: *On an average night, they... attacked eight victims or "turkeys," taking a total of about $300*—Time [fr the common and perhaps accurate perception of the *turkey* as a stupid creature, an avian loser]
See COLD TURKEY, FULL OF SHIT, OLD TURKEY, TALK TURKEY

turkey-shoot ***n phr*** Something very easy; = CINCH, PIECE OF CAKE: *Getting a job is no turkey-shoot any more* [fr the marksmanship contests where *turkeys* are tied behind a log with their heads showing]

turn ***See*** TALK OUT OF TURN

turn someone **around** ***v phr*** To change someone's attitude, behavior, etc: *You fuck it up, that's turning me around*—Robert Stone

turn a trick ***v phr*** To do the sex act for profit; do one piece of work as a prostitute; = TRICK: *Many of the prostitutes were students, models, or would-be actresses who turned tricks part-time*—Washington Post

turned off 1 ***adj phr*** *narcotics* No longer using narcotics; = CLEAN **2** ***adj phr*** Indifferent; bored **3** ***adj phr*** Tired; = FED UP

turned on 1 ***adj phr*** *esp narcotics fr late 1950s* Intoxicated, esp from narcotics; = HIGH: *I'm really turned on, man.... I'm higher than a giraffe's toupee*—Stephen Longstreet **2** ***adj phr*** Stimulated; aroused; excited; switched on: *You are so sexualized, and so turned on*—Sexual Behavior **3** ***adj phr*** Aware and up-to-date; au courant; = HIP, PLUGGED IN: *an outlaw lobbyist, a turned-on Nader*—New York Times

turner ***See*** PAGE TURNER

turn off ***v phr*** To become indifferent; lose concern: *When he found he couldn't hack it, he just turned off*

turn-off ***n*** Something that damps one's spirits; a sexual or emotional depressant; = WET BLANKET: *The film is in fact a sexual turnoff*—Saturday Review

turn someone **off** ***v phr*** *fr 1950s beat talk* To depress; be a deterrent to someone's spirits: *It seems like everybody turns you off*—New York Times

turn off someone's **water** ***See*** CUT OFF someone's WATER

turn on *fr 1960s counterculture & narcotics* **1** *v phr* To use narcotics, esp to begin to do so: *Tune in, turn on, drop out*—Timothy Leary **2** *v phr* To take or inject narcotics: *Do you turn on with any of the local heads?*—Trans-Action

turn-on 1 *n* Something that arouses and excites; a sexual or emotional stimulant: *which physical attributes of men are a turn-on for women* —Saturday Review **2** *n* Excitement; ecstasy; elation: *He'd never felt a turn-on like that*

turn someone **on 1** *v phr fr musicians & 1950s beat talk* To excite or stimulate; arouse: *The professor was trying to find out what turns women on* **2** *v phr fr beat talk* To introduce someone to something; pique someone's curiosity: *He turned me on to Zen*—Lawrence Lipton

turn on the heat *v phr* To increase effort, pressure, activity, etc; =COME ON STRONG

turn on the waterworks *v phr fr middle 1800s* To weep; begin to cry: *I turned on the waterworks*—Paul Theroux

turnout 1 *n* An audience, the participants at a meeting, etc: *We always get a good turnout for the council sessions* **2** *n* Clothing; dress

turn someone **out** *v phr esp black* To introduce someone to something; initiate someone, esp to narcotics, sex, prostitution, etc

turn thumbs down *v phr* To refuse, reject, or negate; =NIX: *The voters turned thumbs down to the change in zoning*

turn turtle *v phr* To turn upside down; capsize: *The big truck turned turtle right on the highway* [fr an equivocation on *turn*, with the sense of "rotate" and the sense of "become" both present; the thing that capsizes becomes like an unhappy *turtle* on its back]

turtle *See* TURN TURTLE

turtle doves *n phr* A pair of sweethearts

tush or **tushie** or **tushy** *See* TOKUS

tux *n* A tuxedo

TV *n* A transvestite: *TVs are not as feminine as they themselves think they are*—The Realist

◁ **twat** ▷ (TWAHT) **1** *n fr middle 1600s* The vulva; =CUNT **2** *n* A woman considered merely as a sex object or organ; =ASS, PIECE OF ASS

tweak *v computer* To adjust a computer program slightly; refine

twee *adj fr late 1800s British* Tiny; dainty; miniature; cute ● Chiefly British; the term is used especially to describe villages, thatched cottages, and other aspects of ye olde England as preserved: *no tiny, twee money to dole out*—Village Voice [fr *tweet*, a childish pronunciation of *sweet*]

twenty-twenty (or **20-20**) **hindsight** *n phr* Perfect foresight of what has already been seen: *observers empowered with 20-20 hindsight wanted to know*—New York Times

twerp or **twirp** *n esp 1930s & 40s teenagers* A contemptible person; =JERK, NERD: *ill-mannered, foul-mouthed little twirp*—Westbrook Pegler/ *Wrangel may have been a pretentious twerp*—Saul Bellow

twiddle 1 *v computer* To change something in a small way; =TWEAK **2** *n* The tilde, a diacritical mark

twiddle one's **thumbs** *v phr* To waste time; be forced to sit idly: *I was anxious to help, but all I could do was twiddle my thumbs while they debated*

twink or **twinkie** or **twinky 1** *n esp teenagers & homosexuals* A young, sexually attractive person; a tempting teenager: *You know, the twink who used to be Fielding's lover* —Armistead Maupin/ *The Weemawee twinkies troop out to the kick-off line*—New York **2** *modifier: I found this gorgeous twink carpenter in the Mission*—Armistead Maupin **3** *n* A weird or deviant person, esp a homosexual; a social outcast: *They think "twinky" or sissy or something like that*—Washington Post **4** *adj: Quentin Crisp... croaks in a nasal monotone like a twinkie Mr Magoo* —Village Voice [origin, and indeed semantics, uncertain; perhaps related to *Twinkies* (a trade name), a sort of cupcake with a soft center, a favorite confection esp of young persons; the trade name may in turn be related to the rather nubile *Tinkerbelle* of *Peter Pan*, and to the *twinkling* of little stars; perhaps all senses are fr *twinkle-toes*, an arch name for a dainty, mincing person or ironically for an awkward dancer]

twin pots *hot rodders* **1** *n phr* Dual carburetors **2** *n phr* A car with dual carburetors

twist *n fr underworld* A young woman: *sexy little twist... but a kook* —Joseph Wambaugh/ *a tough, smart twist who got away with murder* —Lawrence Sanders [fr rhyming slang, US and not British, *twist and twirl* "girl," attested in a poem of EF Cummings]

the **twist** *n phr fr 1950s* A social or ballroom dance in which the pelvis and upper body are vigorously counterrotated

twist someone's **arm** *v phr* To induce or persuade very strongly; importune powerfully, as if by physical force: *You grab this opportunity to twist my arm*—Saul Bellow

twisted *adj narcotics* Very much intoxicated with narcotics; =HIGH: *twisted... that's when he's so high he doesn't know where the hell he is* —Clarence L Cooper

twister *See* BRONCO BUSTER

twist slowly (or **twist**) **in the wind** *v phr* To suffer protracted humiliation, obloquy, regret, etc: *The second mistake was to let Sherrill twist slowly in the wind*—Washington Post [fr the gruesome image of a hanging body]

twisty *adj* Attractively feminine; =SEXY: *Most female doctors aren't as, uh... young. No, ah, say twisty might be more like it*—William Brashler

twit *n fr 1920s British* A contemptible and insignificant person; a trivial idiot • Being very rapidly adopted, perhaps because of the popularity of the British comedy series "Monty Python's Flying Circus," on which the term is often employed: *I've got the authorization, you fucking twit*—Stephen King [origin unknown; perhaps a blend of *twat* with *twirp*; perhaps a shortening of *nitwit*]

two *See* NUMBER TWO, ONE-TWO

Two *See* TRACK TWO

two-bagger **1** *n baseball* A two-base hit; a double **2** *n* A very ugly person; =DOUBLE-BAGGER: *two-bagger, a girl who needs exactly that to cover her ugliness*—Time

two-bit *adj fr middle 1800s* Cheap; tawdry; trivial; =TACKY: *the two-bit bureaucrats*—Billy Rose/ *Congressmen were panic-stricken, running around like two-bit whores*—Washingtonian [literally, worth only *two bits*]

two bits *n phr fr early 1700s* A quarter; twenty-five cents [fr the quarter part of a Mexican *real*, which had eight *bits*]

two cents *See* PUT one's TWO CENTS IN

two cents' worth *n phr* A little; a trivial amount: *I'll give you two cents' worth of advice about that*

twofer (Tōō fər) **1** *n* A cheap cigar **2** *n* A theater ticket sold at half the normal price [fr the phrase *two for*, in these cases *two for a nickel* and *two for the price of one*]

two hats *See* WEAR TWO HATS

two shakes or **two shakes of a lamb's tail** *n phr* A moment; a wink; =a JIFFY: *Hold it, I'll just be two shakes*

two-spot *n* A two-dollar bill

two-step *See* AZTEC TWO-STEP

two-time *v* To deceive and betray; esp, to betray one's proper sweetheart by consorting with someone else: *Two-Timing Boy Wrecks Girl's Dream*—New York Daily News [perhaps fr *two at a time*; perhaps fr *making time with two at once*]

two-time loser **1** *n phr underworld* A person who has been convicted twice, and therefore risks a higher sentence another time **2** *n phr* A person who has been divorced twice: *It does sound odd coming from a two-time loser*—Bob Thomas

two to tango *See* IT TAKES TWO TO TANGO

two ways *See* WORK BOTH WAYS

two-way street *n phr* A situation that cannot or should not be handled by only one person: *After all, Sam, keeping a marriage happy is a two-way street*

tzuris *See* TSURIS

U

ugly *See* PLUG-UGLY

ultraswoopy *adj* Very spectacular; glamorously styled: *a down-sized, hitech, ultraswoopy model next year* —Car and Driver

umpteen *modifier fr WW1* Of any large unspecified number: *exhausted all the encomia in your vocabulary on umpteen reviews*—Anthony Boucher [said to have been first used by British military signalers during World War I to disguise the number designations of units]

umpty *modifier fr WW1* Of an unspecified number of the decimal order: *the umpty-fifth regiment*—Bill Mauldin

umpty-umpth *modifier fr WW1* Of a large and unspecified ordinal number: *the umpty-umpth revision* —Bennett Cerf

unc *n* Uncle

uncle **1** *n fr 1700s British* A pawnbroker **2** *n underworld* A receiver of stolen goods; =FENCE **3** *n underworld & narcotics* A federal narcotics agent; =NARC

See SAY UNCLE

Uncle Dudley *See* YOUR UNCLE DUDLEY

Uncle Sam **1** *n phr fr early 1800s* The US Government; the US as a nation **2** *n phr underworld* A federal agent or agency [said to have originated during the War of 1812 when Samuel Wilson of Troy, New York, locally known as *Uncle Sam*, stamped US on supplies he provided for the Government, and this was jocularly taken to be his own initials]

Uncle Sugar *n phr WW2 armed forces* The United States government; =UNCLE SAM [fr the military phonetic alphabet words for *U* and *S*]

Uncle Tom *n phr fr black* A black man who emulates or adopts the behavior of the white majority; a servile black man; =AFRO-SAXON, OREO [fr the title character of Harriet Beecher Stowe's novel *Uncle Tom's Cabin*, who was stigmatized as a dishonorably submissive black]

Uncle Tomahawk *n phr Native American* A Native American who emulates or adopts the behavior of the majority culture; a servile Native American

uncool *adj fr cool talk* Not cool; wrong, excited, rude, etc

under *See* GET OUT FROM UNDER, HALF UNDER

under one's **belt** *adj phr* Successfully achieved or survived: *Get a couple more months' experience under your belt and we'll talk about a promotion*

underground **1** *adj fr 1960s counterculture* Apart from and opposed to conventional society; esp, advocating and representing the hippie and narcotics subculture: *The Voice started as a sort of underground newspaper* **2** *adj* In hiding; concealing one's identity and whereabouts, esp to escape arrest: *He escaped, and had to live underground for the next ten years*

See GO UNDERGROUND

the **underground** *n phr esp WW2 & 1960s counterculture* Political or cultural dissenters collectively who lead a partly or wholly clandestine life and resist the dominant regime; also, their arena of life and operations • This term first applied to the various resistance movements against German occupation in World War 2, and then was adopted by the 1960s counterculture, which saw the US government and culture as analogous with the Hitlerian: *Marc Bloch fought in the underground for several years, then was betrayed to the Gestapo/ Her daughter dropped out of college in 1964 and joined the Haight-Ashbury underground*

under one's **hat** *adj phr fr early 1900s* Secret; in confidence: *Here it is, but it's strictly under the hat, see?* —Joel Sayre

under the collar *See* HOT UNDER THE COLLAR

under the table **1** *adj phr* Very drunk: *After six vodka martinis I was under the table* **2** *adv phr* Illegal; secret and illicit; unethical: *He would never make any deals under the table* **3** *adj phr: What was the best under-the-table offer you got?*—Playboy

under the weather **1** *adj phr fr middle 1800s nautical* Not feeling well; ill **2** *adj phr* Drunk: *I'm a little under the weather*—Gene Fowler [probably fr the seasickness or lesser malaise felt at sea when the *weather* roughens]

underwhelm *v* To impress very little; be quite insignificant; be less than overwhelming: *Her performance rather underwhelmed the audience*

under wraps *adv phr* In secrecy; in obscurity: *We had better keep this under wraps for a while*

undies *n fr early 1900s* Underwear, esp women's panties: *a glimpse of her undies*—Morris Bishop

unflappable *adj fr WW2 Army Air Force* Calm; imperturbable; cool: *They admired Mrs Thatcher's unflappable quality*

unglued *See* COME UNGLUED

ungodly shot *n phr baseball* A hard line drive: *A hard line drive is a blue darter, frozen rope, or an ungodly shot*—Jim Bouton

unmentionables *n fr early 1900s* Underwear; undergarments: *required to don upper and lower unmentionables*—Owen Johnson

uno *See* NUMERO UNO, TAKE CARE OF NUMERO UNO

un poco (o͞oN POH KOH) *n phr* or *adv phr* A little; a small amount [fr Spanish or Italian]

unreal *adj fr beat talk & cool talk* Excellent; wonderful; =GREAT: *Like great. She's real unreal*—Harper's Bazaar

unstuck *See* COME UNGLUED

until one **is blue in the face** *See* TILL ONE IS BLUE IN THE FACE

untogether *fr black* **1** *adj* Ineffectual; confused; =SCREWED UP: *leading us to think you are so untogether that you want other blacks to go through the same thing*—Ebony **2** *adj* Not fashionable or stylish **3** *adj* Not smooth and effective socially

up **1** *adj* Exhilarated; happy; hopeful: *I was feeling up. I thought it had been a very successful evening*—Lawrence Sanders **2** *adj* Encouraging; hopeful; =UPBEAT: *I don't like down movies, I like up movies*—New Yorker **3** *n* A source of excitement; a pleasurable thrill; =LIFT: *Her words gave me a huge up* **4** *v* To raise; increase: *My confidence has upped itself*—New York Post **5** *adj* Ready and effective; keyed up; in one's best form: *Obviously, Kennedy wanted to be "up" for the meeting* —Village Voice **6** *adj narcotics* Intoxicated by narcotics, esp amphetamines; =HIGH: *as it does when you're up on bennie*—Hubert Selby, Jr **7** *n narcotics* An amphetamine dose, capsule, etc; =UPPER: *Let's do some ups tonight* **8** *n* A blunder; =GOOF, FUCK-UP: *Joining that company was the biggest up of my life*

up against the wall *sentence esp 1960s counterculture fr black* Prepare to be humiliated, attacked, robbed, despised, etc; =GO FUCK oneself: *our commune motto, "Up against the wall, motherfuckers"* —James Simon Kunen/ *Up against the wall, IBM and General Electric and Xerox and Procter & Gamble and American Express*—Wall Street Journal [fr a line in a poem by Leroi Jones (Amiri Baraka), "Up against the wall, motherfuckers," fr the command of a holdup man to his victim, or of the police to a person being arrested, forcing him to immobilize himself by leaning forward arched with hands against a wall; probably influenced by the fact that people are executed by being shot against a wall]

up and up or **on the up and up** *adj phr fr middle 1800s* Honest; reliable; =STRAIGHT-UP: *It's an up and up place* —WR Burnett/ *I almost wonder if the* *whole bunch of 'em are on the up and up*—Sinclair Lewis

up a rope *See* GO PISS UP A ROPE

◁ **up** one's **ass**▷ *See* SIT THERE WITH one's FINGER UP one's ASS, STICK IT

up a storm *adv phr* Very intensively; very diligently; very competently: *and they're really dancing up a storm* —Washingtonian/ *She spent the morning writing up a storm*

up a tree *adj phr fr early 1800s* In a predicament; faced with a dilemma; helpless

upbeat *adj* Optimistic; encouraging; positive: *They use catchy, upbeat phrases*—Saturday Review/ *A triumph of upbeat pictures over the downbeat*—Associated Press [apparently fr the musical term *upbeat* "a beat on which a conductor raises his baton," but since such beats have no emotional connotations, the coiner must have seized on the general positive notion of *up* and taken *beat* to mean "stroke, movement"]

upchuck *v fr 1920s* To vomit; throw up; =BARF, RALPH [fr *up* + *chuck* "throw"]

update **1** *v* To give, add, record, etc, the latest information: *He updated me on a couple of gimmicks* —John Crosby **2** *n: I'll give you a quick update* **3** *modifier: Is this the update material?*

up for grabs *fr black* **1** *adj phr* Available, esp newly available: *I got two doozies up for grabs*—Esquire **2** *adj phr* Problematical or undecided, esp newly so: *The whole question of one-man-one-vote is up for grabs again*

up front **1** *adv phr* (also **in front**) In advance; before any deductions: *Don't pay your money up front* —Consumers Digest **2** *adj phr* In the beginning; first; at once: *we knew right up front that if I did the film* —Rolling Stone **3** *adj phr* Honest; open; truthful: *very up-front about who she is and what she thinks* —J Nolan **4** *adj phr* In the forefront; on the firing line

up in the air *adj phr* Unsettled; undecided; uncertain: *When he left, the whole project was up in the air for a while*

up in the clouds *adj phr* Not alert and attentive; preoccupied with idealism, romance, etc: *can't keep his mind on business, always up in the clouds somewhere*

upmanship *See* ONE-UPMANSHIP

upmarket *adj* Appealing to or created for people to whom price is not important: *upmarket book/ upmarket store*

upper **1** *n narcotics* An amphetamine; a stimulant narcotic; =UP: *the effect of mixing "uppers" and "downers"*—New Republic **2** *n* A source of excitement; a pleasurable thrill; =UP: *It may not be the same kind of thrill as winning a hand of poker at a casino, but it's definitely an upper* —Games

See PEPPER-UPPER, PICKER-UPPER

upper crust *See* THIN IN THE UPPER CRUST

the **upper crust** *n phr fr early 1800s* The social aristocracy; the elite

upper story *See* LOOSE IN THE BEAN

uppity *adj fr late 1800s black* Conceited; arrogant; snobbish; =HINCTY ● Once used almost exclusively of black people felt to be too self-assertive by the white speaker: *to estimate if this reporter was going to give her any sass or put on any uppity airs* —Washington Post

See GET one's BALLS IN AN UPROAR

upscale *adj* Having to do with upper social and economic reaches; wealthy; aristocratic; =RITZY: *The killing... by Jean Harris was... an upscale crime*—Time

◁ **up shit** (or **shit's**) **creek**▷ or **up the creek** *adj phr* (Variation: **without a paddle** may be added) In serious difficulty; very unfortunate; ruined: *If the cops see you you'll be up shit creek for sure/ Then you guys'll be up the creek for good*—Jerome Weidman [perhaps related to the early-19th-century term *up Salt River*, of much the same meaning, and which may refer to the Salt River in Kentucky, a legendary abode of violent and brutal people; but the term is attested in British armed forces use without US attribution fr the early 20th century]

upside or **upside of** *prep esp black* On the side of; in: *He got whacked upside the head with a board*—William Brashler

upside one's **face** *See* GO UPSIDE one's FACE

up one's **sleeve** *See* ACE UP one's SLEEVE

upstage **1** *v theater* To attract attention to oneself and away from other performers, esp by standing upstage so that they must look at you and turn their backs to the audience **2** *v* To demand and receive inordinate attention at the cost of others: *The secretary was trying to upstage the president on this, so he had to act at once* **3** *adj* Haughty; aloof; snobbish: *"Upstage" has taken on the additional meaning of "ritzy," that is, arrogantly proud and vain*—B Sobel

upstairs *adv* In the brain; mentally: *became a little balmy upstairs*—Hal Boyle

See KICK someone UPSTAIRS

uptake *See* QUICK ON THE DRAW, SLOW ON THE DRAW

up the ante *v phr* To raise the price, offer, sum in question, etc; increase; make a higher demand: *I think I may up the ante to a cool fifty*—Pat Conroy

up the flagpole *See* RUN something UP THE FLAGPOLE

up the kazoo (or **gazoo** or **gazool**) *adv phr* To a very great extent; in excess; =UP TO HERE: *I've got lawsuits up the gazool, which is one thing that disillusions me about writing*—Billy Joel/ *We're up the kazoo in leaflets here*

See KAZOO

up the river *adv phr underworld fr 1930s* In prison [fr the fact that Ossining Correctional Facility, formerly called Sing Sing, is *up the Hudson River* from New York City]

See SEND UP

up the spout *adv phr* To waste; fruitlessly gone; =DOWN THE TUBE: *Fifty dollars tuition, all our plans... just gone up the spout*—Tennessee Williams/ *I'm afraid the project's up the spout*

up the wall *adj phr fr 1930s or earlier* Crazy; wild; =NUTTY: *It doesn't drive us crazy. At least, I don't know anybody who is up the wall about it*—Washingtonian [fr the image of insane persons, frantic and deprived drug addicts, wild animals, etc, trying to climb a wall, to escape]

See DRIVE someone UP THE WALL

uptick **1** *n* A rise, esp in stock prices; an increase of value: *the strongest and broadest uptick in the history of the company*—Time **2** *n* Improvement; raising: *His apparent uptick in spirit was contagious*—Newsweek [fr the use, on boards above stock-market stations, of a plus sign (compare British *tick* "check mark") beside a stock of which the last sale represented a rise in price; a minus sign represents a *down tick*; probably influenced by the *tick*, like *click*, or *notch*, representing one degree of change; compare *ratchet up*]

uptight *adj fr 1960s counterculture fr black* Tense; anxious: *He was all uptight about student plagiarism*

up to one's **ass** *See* one HAS HAD IT

◁**up to** one's **ass in** something▷ *adj phr* (Variations: **in alligators** or **in rattlesnakes** may be added for emphasis; **asshole deep** may replace **up to** one's **ass**) Deeply involved; overwhelmed: *Every time I turn around we're up to our asses in something*—Leslie Hollander/ *Coldiron was up to his ass in cotton*—Tom Aldibrandi/ *Suddenly we were asshole deep in candidates for the deanship/ Call me later, I'm up to my ass in alligators here now*

up to one's **eyeballs** (or **eyebrows**) *adv phr* To a very great extent; totally; =UP TO HERE: *one smaller outfit... which is in farm equipment smack up to its corporate eyeballs*—Barron's

up to one's **eyebrows** *See* one HAS HAD IT

up to here **1** *adv phr* To the utmost; excessively • Most often in the expression "I've had it up to here": *Look, my friend, I've had it up to here with your bitching* **2** *adj phr* Surfeited; disgusted; =FED UP: *I'm so up-to-here with the primaries and the TV news interviews*—Washington Post [fr the notion of being fed to excess, fed up, and with the implicit gesture of indicating one's throat as the place up to which one has had it]

See one HAS HAD IT

up to scratch (or **the mark**) *adj phr fr prizefight* Satisfactory; acceptable; qualified: *I'm afraid this story isn't quite up to scratch* [fr the early custom of drawing a line across a boxing ring and requiring that the able and willing fighter stand with his toe touching the *mark* or *scratch-line*]

up to snuff **1** *adj phr fr early 1800s British* Satisfactory; acceptable; =UP TO SCRATCH: *His work doesn't come anywhere near up to snuff* **2** *adj phr* In good health; feeling well: *I don't feel quite up to snuff this morning* [origin uncertain; the original British sense was "shrewd, not gullible," apparently referring to the fact that one could be blinded with *snuff* in the eyes, and victimized; the early-19th-century US phrases *in high* (or *great*) *snuff* "in good form, high fettle, etc," perhaps having to do with *snuff* as an aristocratic commodity and symbol, may also be related]

up to speed ***See*** BRING someone UP TO SPEED

up to the wire ***See*** COME UP TO THE WIRE

uptown ***See*** the BOYS UPTOWN

◁ **up yours**▷ *interj* (Variations: **you** or **your ass** or **your butt** or **your gig** or **your giggy** or any other synonym of **ass** may replace **yours**) *fr late 1800s* An exclamation of strong defiance, contempt, rejection, etc: *Up yours, sister, he thought tardily as the barbs quivered home*—WT Tyler ● A shortening of **stick it up your ass**

use *v narcotics* To use narcotics; take a dose or injection of a narcotic: *I used this morning and I'm still nice*—Clarence Cooper

use one's **head** (or one's **bean**) *v phr* To think; reason out one's actions: *teaches a man to use his head and to do the best he can*—Hal Boyle/ *You certainly used the old bean*—P Marks

user *n narcotics* A person who uses narcotics, esp an addict

usual ***See*** AS PER USUAL

V

vamoose or **vamose** (va MOOS) *v fr middle 1800s Southwestern* To leave; depart, esp hastily; =LAM, SCRAM, SPLIT: *We better vamoose, Moose* [fr Spanish *vamos* "let us depart"]

vamp[1] *v musicians fr middle 1800s* To improvise, esp an accompaniment; play casually and extemporaneously; =FAKE, SHUCK [probably fr 16th-century *vamp* "provide with a new (shoe) vamp, renovate," ultimately fr conjectured Anglo-French *vampé* fr Old French *avant-pié* "foot-sock"; a refooted sock or a *revamped* shoe were felt to be in a way false, or improvised, hence the sense of "fake"]

vamp[2] **1** *n fr early 1900s* A seductive, sexually aggressive woman; a temptress: *The flirt had become the "baby vamp"*—F Scott Fitzgerald **2** *v: She's vamping you, Harold*—P Marks [fr *vampire,* and esp fr the 1914 movie *A Fool There Was,* in which Theda Bara played a seductive woman, the title and concept coming fr Rudyard Kipling's poem "The Vampire"]

vamp[3] or **vamp on** **1** *v* or *v phr esp black* To assault; trounce; =BEAT UP, CLOBBER: *They knew that he'd vamp on them if they got wrong* —Bobby Seale *the Pigs are vampin'* —New York Times **2** *v* or *v phr fr black* To arrest; =BUST [perhaps related to black English *vamp* someone "come at someone suddenly and aggressively"; probably fr *vamp*[2] reinforced by the murderous aggression of Count Dracula, a genuine and popular *vampire* in Bram Stoker's novel and the movies made from it]

vanilla **1** *n black* A white person, esp a white woman **2** *n* A person of ordinary and normal sexual preferences; a usual heterosexual; =STRAIGHT: *They called women who did not proclaim joy at being chained to the bedposts or chaining someone else "vanilla"*—Village Voice **3** *adj: As a self-confessed vanilla-sexual*—Village Voice [fr the white color and the perhaps unimaginative choice of *vanilla* ice cream]

See PLAIN VANILLA

varnish remover *n phr* Raw and inferior whiskey; =PANTHER PISS

varoom ***See*** VROOM

Vatican roulette *n phr* The rhythm method of birth control

va-voom or **va-va-voom** **1** *interj* An exclamation of delight, esp of excited sexual interest **2** *adj* (also **voomy**): *fressing the tits of this va-va-voom sophomore and shtupping her pussy*—National Lampoon/ *Under that icky mask, I think you're the voomiest*—Spiderman (comic strip) [probably fr *vroom* and *varoom*]

veeno ***See*** VINO

veg[1] (VEJ) **1** *n fr late 1800s British* A vegetable **2** *n* =VEGETABLE

veg[2] (VEJ) *v* (also **vedge** or **veg out**) *college students* To relax luxuriously and do nothing; vegetate; =GOOF OFF, MELLOW OUT [fr *vegetate*]

vegetable *n* A person lacking normal senses, responses, intelligence, etc; =BASKET CASE, RETARD: *He was fine the first couple of years of marriage, but then he turned into a vegetable*

vegetable patch ***See*** FRUIT SALAD

veggies or **vegies** *n* Vegetables

veggy **1** *n* A vegetarian **2** *adj: a veggy pal of ours*

vein *See* JAB A VEIN

velvet *See* BEGGAR'S VELVET

verbal (or **oral**) **diarrhea** *n phr* (also **diarrhea of the mouth**) Logorrhea; uncontrollable loquaciousness: *You've got verbal diarrhea*—Calder Willingham

vest *See* PLAY CLOSE TO THE CHEST

vet[1] **1** *n* A veteran, esp a former member of the armed forces: *I'm a combat vet*—Nelson Algren **2** *modifier: the vet producer of scouting plays*—Esquire

vet[2] **1** *n* A veterinarian **2** *modifier* Veterinary: *the vet school* **3** *v fr early 1900s British* To examine closely; scrutinize critically: *The hosts are a carefully vetted collection of bubble brains*—Time [third sense fr the close examination of an animal by a *veterinarian*]

vibes[1] *n jazz musicians* A vibraphone or vibraharp

vibes[2] or **vibrations** *n esp 1960s counterculture* What emanates from or inheres in a person, situation, place, etc, and is sensed; = CHEMISTRY, KARMA: *The vibes were good that morning for our reunion*—Saturday Review

vic **1** *n New York City teenagers* A victim; = MARK, PATSY **2** *v* (also **scope a vic**) To look for someone to rob, mug, etc

vicious *adj teenager* Excellent; superb; wonderfully attractive

vidaholic *n* An addict of television: *a lifelong vidaholic, the 33-year-old Simmons*—Newsweek [fr *video* + *-aholic*]

video jock or **VJ** *n phr* A television performer who plays and comments on music videos

Vietnik **1** *n 1960s & 70s* A person who actively protested US military involvement in Vietnam **2** *modifier: the latest Vietnik demonstration*—Time

vig or **vigorish** or **viggerish** *n fr gambling* Profits of a bookmaker, a usurer, a criminal conspirator, a casino, etc: *I'm not nailing you no vig for last week*—George V Higgins/ *About 180 percent a year in interest, known in the trade as vigorish, vig, or juice*—Wall Street Journal/ *The Vig? Seventy-five percent plus my fourteen-year-old sister*—Richard Price [probably fr Yiddish fr Russian *vyigrysh* "profit, winnings"]

-ville *See* -SVILLE

vinegar *See* FULL OF PISS AND VINEGAR

vino or **veeno** (VEE noh) *n* Wine, esp red jug wine [fr Italian, "wine"]

vinyl **1** *n* Phonograph records; recording: *Now this disco graffiti has found its way to vinyl and created quite a bit of excitement*—Variety **2** *modifier: woman who rides the vinyl grooves*—New York Daily News **3** *modifier* Having to do with discotheques, the dancing done there, etc: *The only vinyl junkies were the nattily-suited variety*—Circus [fr the chemical material used for phonograph records, semantically analogous with earlier *wax*]

VIP (pronounced as separate letters) *n fr WW2* A very important person; = BIG SHOT

vision *See* TUNNEL VISION

visiting fireman *n phr* An out-of-town visitor, esp a dignitary: *He meets a good many distinguished visiting firemen*—New Yorker [fr the earlier sense *fireman* or *fire maker* "a Native American ceremonial dignitary who was responsible for lighting the fires"]

VJ *See* VIDEO JOCK

volume[1] *n* A dose or capsule of Valium (a trade name), a tranquilizer: *I'd take maybe five volumes in the morning*—New York Times

volume[2] *See* DECREASE THE VOLUME

vomity or **vomitrocious** *adj* So nasty as to cause one to vomit: *Gross and even grossening are out. Vomitrocious is in*—George F Will [longer form fr *vomit* + (a)*trocious*]

voomy *See* VA-VOOM

vote with one's **feet** *v phr* To escape; become a refugee or emigrant: *Nearly three million people voted with their feet*—New York Times

vroom or **varoom** **1** *n* The noise of a powerful car **2** *modifier* (also **vroom-vroom**): *if you drive a sporty, vroom-vroom model*—Washingtonian **3** *v* To speed, esp in a roaring car: *as we vroomed up and down the Watchung Mountains*—Esquire/ *He would presumably be vrooming a Porsche through the streets of Bel-Air*—Richard Schickel

VW radiators *See* A LOAD OF VW RADIATORS

W

wack or **whack** *n fr 1940s* A crazy or eccentric person; =NUT, SCREWBALL, WEIRDO: *two wacks if I ever saw one* —John O'Hara/ *a father who was so abrasive and married now to such a wack*—Joseph Heller [see *wacky*]

wack off *See* WHACK OFF

wacky or **whacky** *adj* (also **wacked-out** or **wacko**) Crazy; eccentric; =NUTTY, WEIRD: *You think I'm going wacky?*—John O'Hara/ *annually collects whacky accidents*—NEA Service/ *the most wacked-out cop game anybody had ever seen any cops play* —Tom Wolfe [fr British dialect *whacky* "fool," attested fr the early 20th century; *whacky* "a person who fools around," is attested in British tailors' talk fr the late 19th century; perhaps fr being *whacked* over the head too often; perhaps influenced by *whack off* "masturbate," and semantically akin to *jerk*]

-wacky *combining word* =CRAZY, NUTTY: *car-wacky/ chick-wacky*

wad *n fr early 1800s* A roll of money: *My grandmother'd just sent me this wad about a week before*—JD Salinger
See SHOOT one's LOAD, SHOOT one's WAD

waffle **1** *v fr British fr late 1800s* To speak or behave evasively; tergiversate; equivocate: *When asked for specifics, I demur, I waffle*—New York **2** *n: I was tired of all the candidates' waffle* [fr northern British dialect, "fluctuate," probably by way of late-19th-century British printers' talk, "incessant and copious chat"; perhaps influenced by US *whiffling* "using shifts and evasions, wavering," attested from 1865]

waffle-stompers *n* Heavy hiking boots; =SHITKICKERS [fr the pattern of the soles, which make a *wafflelike* print]

wag *See* CHIN-WAG

wagon *See* BUZZ-BUGGY, DOG-WAGON, FALL OFF THE WAGON, FIX someone's WAGON, MEAT WAGON, MILK WAGON, OFF THE WAGON, ON THE WAGON, PADDY WAGON, RAPE WAGON, SEX WAGON, TUNA WAGON

wailing or **whaling** *adj esp black students* Excellent; wonderful; =GREAT

waist *See* PANTYWAIST

wait up *v phr* To pause, when well ahead, for someone to overtake one • Often a panting request

walk *See* FRENCH WALK, TAKE A WALK, WIN IN A WALK

walk and chew gum at the same time *See* NOT HAVE BRAINS ENOUGH TO COME IN OUT OF THE RAIN

walkaway *See* WALKOVER

walk heavy *v phr fr black* To be important and influential; =have CLOUT

walking papers (or **ticket**) *n phr fr early 1800s* A dismissal or discharge; esp, a rejection; =PINK SLIP: *Two baseball veterans got their walking papers today*—Associated Press
See GIVE someone HIS WALKING PAPERS

walking wounded *n phr* Persons who are injured, esp in a psychological or spiritual way, but still functional; depressed people [fr a military medical term for a *wounded* person who is ambulatory]

walk-on *n fr theater* A very minor, usu nonspeaking, role; an insignificant or minimal sort of participation

walk out on someone or something *v phr* To abandon; =TAKE A WALK: *She was fed up, and just walked out on the whole deal*

was fed up, and just walked out on the whole deal

walkover or **walkaway** *n* An easy victory; =CINCH, PUSHOVER: *It looked like a walkover for Clarence*—H McHugh/ *The odds were on the Redskins in a walkaway*

walk soft *v phr black* To behave quietly and peacefully; be modest: *I told him he was acting like an ass, and he walks a lot softer now*—Eugene E Landy

walk Spanish *See* FRENCH WALK

walk tall *v phr* To be brave and honest; be upright and proud: *Take the 89G. Run....Walk tall, turn it in*—New York Daily News

walk the plank *v phr* To be dismissed: *Rostow's Deputy Walks the Plank; Rostow Hangs In*—New York Times [fr the pirate practice of forcing unwanted persons to *walk* out on a *plank* and plunge into the sea]

wall *See* BALLS TO THE WALL, BOUNCE OFF THE WALLS, CLIMB THE WALL, DRIVE someone UP THE WALL, GO TO THE WALL, HOLE IN THE WALL, NAIL someone or something TO THE CROSS, OFF THE WALL, PING OFF THE WALLS, UP AGAINST THE WALL, UP THE WALL

wall banger *n phr teenagers & narcotics* A dose or capsule of Quaalude (a trade name) or methaqualone; =LUDE: *called wall bangers by the kids*—Albert Goldman

wallflower *n fr early 1900s* A person, esp a woman, who is peripheral and uncourted at a dance, party, etc: *the homely and ugly girls who were called wall-flowers*—James T Farrell

wallop **1** *n* A hard blow; a severe and resounding stroke: *She gave him a wallop on the chin* **2** *v: He walloped the ball right over the wall* **3** *n fr early 1800s British* Power; =CLOUT, MOXIE: *She'd be good if she had a little more wallop* [fr British dialect, "beat, thrash," apparently fr *gallop*]

See CIRCUIT BLOW

walloper *See* DOCK-WALLOPER, POT-WALLOPER

wallpaper *n* Worthless monetary paper such as counterfeit bills, invalid securities, and the like

wall-to-wall *adj* Total; all-encompassing: *a wall-to-wall nightmare in which society dissolves*—S Kanfer [fr the phrase *wall-to-wall carpeting*]

walrus *n fr 1920s* A short, fat person

walsy *See* PALSY-WALSY

waltz **1** *n prizefight* A single round of a fight; =CANTO **2** *v prizefight* To box and spar lightly and unseriously **3** *n* Something easily accomplished; =CINCH, PIECE OF CAKE

walyo or **Wally-O** (WAHL yoh) **1** *n* A young man; =GUY ● Like **goombah**, used in affectionate address, often by an older man to a younger: *how the walyo had kept his muscles so finely tuned on health food*—Paul Sann **2** *n* An Italian or a male of Italian descent: *Did you hear how the Wally-Os stole a ballot box in the Fifth Ward?*—William Kennedy [fr Italian dialect *uaglio* or *uaiu* pronounced wah YŌŌ, meaning something like "young squirt," but nearly always used affectionately]

wampum *n* Money; cash; =BREAD [short for Algonquin *wampumpeag* "beads made from quahog shells and used as money"]

◁ **wang** or **whang** or **whanger** ▷ *n fr early 1900s* The penis; =COCK, PRICK: *I can see your whang. Your dong is visible*—William Goldman/ *a trigger that was bigger than an elephant's proboscis or the whanger of a whale*—John Steinbeck [origin uncertain; perhaps fr late-19th-century British *whanger* "something extraordinarily large and admirable," fr dialect *whang* "beat, hit," in the same semantic pattern as terms like *whacking, socko* and others where the power to hit is equated with impressive merit; the penis as the sexual instrument is of course thought of as *banging* a woman, or *socking it to her*]

See PULL one's PUD

wangdoodle *See* WHANGDOODLE

wangle **1** *v fr late 1800s British* To get or arrange by shrewd maneuvering; contrive cunningly: *President Truman has given Ching a free hand in trying to wangle agreements*—Associated Press **2** *n: made a precise science out of the wangle*—H Allen Smith [origin unknown; perhaps a form of *waggle* "overcome, get the better of"]

wanker *n chiefly British fr late 1800s* A masturbator, either literally or figuratively; =JERK-OFF: *all manner of artsy bubbleheads and academic* *wankers*—Village Voice [perhaps fr British dialect *wank* "a violent blow," and semantically analogous with *beat one's meat, whack off*, etc]

wank off *v phr chiefly British fr late 1800s* To masturbate

want list *See* WISH LIST

war *See* HOT WAR, SHOOTING WAR

war club *n phr* A baseball bat

ward heeler *n phr fr late 1800s* A low-ranking associate or flunky of a political boss; a menial crony [fr *heeler* "one who follows obediently at the heels of another"]

warhorse *n fr late 1800s* A seasoned and reliable veteran; a grizzled doyen

warm body *n phr* A person regarded as merely such, without individual qualities, virtues, vices, etc; an animate person who occupies space; =CHAIR-WARMER: *Why come to these lectures if you're only going to be a warm body?/ We need a warm body to sit at this desk*

warmed over *adj phr fr late 1800s* Derivative and only slightly changed; revived unimaginatively: *The president, he wrote, had "offered the poor the Protestant Ethic warmed over"* —Daniel Patrick Moynihan/ *out of the mouths of bunnies and gulls, some warmed-over Gibran*—Irving Kolodin

See LOOK LIKE DEATH WARMED OVER

warmer *See* BENCH WARMER, CHAIR-WARMER

warm fuzzy *n phr* A compliment; a word of praise; also, such praise collectively; =STROKE: *You need some warm fuzzy*—Time [probably fr the notion of a snuggling small animal, like Charles Schulz's *warm puppy*]

warm spit *See* WORTH A BUCKET OF WARM SPIT

warm up *v phr* To do exercises and preparatory maneuvers before some activity, esp some sports effort

warm someone **up** *v phr* To induce a receptive and approving attitude, esp by joking and cajoling: *The second banana warmed the audience up before the star appeared*

Warner *See* MARY WARNER

warp *See* TIME WARP

war paint *n phr fr middle 1800s* Cosmetics

warp factor *n phr* A very large factor of multiplication; a high exponent: *We feel it won't increase by warp factor five, either*—Toronto Life [fr the notion of *warp speed*, a velocity greater than the speed of light, popularized in science fiction and especially by the TV series "Star Trek"; it is necessary to imagine such enormous speeds in order to keep fictional cosmic travel more or less in the realm of the humanly compassable; see *time warp*]

warp out *v phr* To move, esp to leave, very rapidly; =CUT OUT

wart *n* A flaw; an imperfection: *The new format has some warts, but no integrity warts*—Philadelphia Journal

See WORRY WART

warts and all *n phr* The accurate totality of someone or something, including the imperfections: *Your friends see Doherty, warts and all* —George V Higgins [fr the putative remark of Oliver Cromwell to his portraitist Peter Lely: "Remark all these roughnesses, pimples, warts, and everything as you see me"]

wash 1 *n* A drink to follow another, to wash it down; =CHASER: *what for a wash?*—Richard Bissell **2** *v fr middle 1800s British* To prove valid; bear testing • Usually in the negative: *Well, it just won't wash*—Atlantic/ *That washes. I'll buy it*—Lawrence Sanders **3** *n* An elaborate justification; =WHITEWASH: *It looked like a wash to me*—George V Higgins **4** *n* A balance between opposing values, cases, effects, etc; a moot situation; =STANDOFF, a TOSS-UP: *The net effect of the medical testimony was a wash*—Legal Times [final sense perhaps fr the notion that equal opposing elements *wash* each other out or away, or *scrub the slate clean*]

See WHITEWASH

wash (or **air**) one's **dirty linen** *v phr* (Variation: **in public** may be added) To talk or argue about intimate matters in public

washed up or **all washed up** *adj phr* No longer valid or active as a performer, competitor, worker, etc; =FINISHED: *I'm all washed up*—Ben Hecht & Charles MacArthur [fr the notion of *washing up* one's hands at the finish of a job or a day's work]

washout 1 *n fr early 1900s British* A failure; a total fiasco; =FLOP: *I'm afraid our big birthday bash was a washout* **2** *n aviators* A crash landing **3** *n* *fr WW1* A student pilot or aviation cadet who fails to complete the course and become a qualified pilot: *the major cause for the large number of "washouts"* —New York Times [origin unknown; perhaps fr the damage done by strong erosion; perhaps fr the 19th-century British military practice of indicating a marksman's hits on iron targets with a paint or *wash*, so that a *wash out* would be nowhere near the bullseye; perhaps fr the notion of a party or picnic ruined, *washed out*, by a storm]

WASP or **wasp** **1** *n* *fr black* A person of nonminority or nonethnic background, ancestry, etc, as conceived in the United States; a White Anglo-Saxon Protestant: *The Republican Party is run largely by "wasps"* —Stewart Alsop **2** *adj: Westchester and Darien and places like that, WASP country*—New York Herald Tribune [said to have been coined by the Philadelphia author E Digby Baltzell]

waste **1** *v* *teenagers fr 1950s street gang* To defeat utterly; trounce; =CLOBBER **2** *v* *fr 1960s counterculture* To wreck; destroy; mutilate; =TRASH **3** *v* *fr black* To kill; =BLOW someone AWAY, TAKE someone or something OUT

wasted **1** *adj* *fr 1950s cool talk* Penniless; =BROKE **2** *adj* *narcotics & cool talk* Intoxicated by narcotics; =STRUNG OUT: *Everybody was getting kind of high on acid, wasted, in fact*—Tom Wolfe **3** *adj* Wrecked; ruined; destroyed: *Like, I'm wasted... I can't lose no more*—Claude Brown

watch *See* GRAVEYARD WATCH, ON someone's WATCH

watcher *See* CLOCK-WATCHER

watch one's **mouth** *v phr* To be careful of what one says, esp to stop being provocative, obscene, presumptuous, etc • Often an irritated command: *Just watch your mouth, Buster*

watch my lips **1** *sentence* *Army* Listen very carefully to me **2** *sentence* Do you read lips? • Second sense is a euphemism for a silently spoken obscenity or insult

water *See* BLOW someone or something OUT OF THE WATER, COME HELL OR HIGH WATER, CUT OFF someone's WATER, DEAD IN THE WATER, FIREWATER, HOLD one's WATER, IN HOT WATER, JERKWATER, LONG DRINK OF WATER, ON THE WAGON

waterfront *See* COVER THE WATERFRONT

Watergate **1** *n* A scandal usu involving corruption **2** *v* To find and publicize, or at least to publicize, instances of corruption: *The news media have been Watergating the Department pretty good*—CBS Television [fr the name of the Washington building complex where Democratic headquarters were burglarized in 1972, an act that led finally to the resignation of Richard M. Nixon as President of the US]

waterhole or **watering hole** *n* or *n phr* A bar; a saloon; a drinking place: *That place is the waterhole of choice for aspiring actors/ a posh watering hole on Madison Avenue*

watermelon seed *See* SWALLOW A WATERMELON SEED

water wagon *See* ON THE WAGON

waterworks *See* TURN ON THE WATERWORKS

wavelength *See* ON THE SAME WAVELENGTH

wave-maker *n* A person who raises questions, imposes difficulties and objections, etc: *said that he is a wave-maker whose troubles arose from his insistence on injecting moral values* —Philadelphia Journal

wax *See* the WHOLE BALL OF WAX

waxed *adj* Drunk

way *See* the FRENCH WAY, GO THE LIMIT, the GREEK WAY, the HARD WAY, the IRISH WAY, KNOW one's WAY AROUND, NO WAY, RUB someone THE WRONG WAY, THERE'S NO WAY

the **way it plays** **1** *adv phr* According to the usual pattern: *The way it plays in there, you can't plead the Fifth*—Paul Sann **2** *n phr* The usual pattern; what is to be expected: *Well, I guess that's the way it plays when you get old*

way out **1** *adj phr* *1930s jazz musicians* Imaginative; original and bold, esp successfully and admirably so **2** *adj phr* *fr 1950s cool talk fr jazz musicians* Excellent; wonderful; =FAR OUT, GREAT, OUT OF SIGHT **3** *adj phr* *narcotics* Intoxicated with narcotics; =HIGH, OUT OF IT

ways *See* FORTY WAYS TO SUNDAY, HAVE IT BOTH WAYS, SWING BOTH WAYS, WORK BOTH WAYS

way the ball bounces (or **the cookie crumbles**) *See* THAT'S THE WAY THE BALL BOUNCES

way to go *sentence* You are doing extremely well; that is splendid • An exclamation of praise and encouragement: *Ron, stick that old hand out... .Way to go, Prez*—Washingtonian [a shortening of *that's the way to go*]

wazoo *n* The buttocks; anus; =ASS [perhaps a variant of *kazoo*]

weak sister *n phr fr middle 1800s* An unreliable and timid man

wear two hats *v phr* To have two separate jobs or functions • The phrase may specify more than two hats: *Rockefeller to Wear Two Hats* —New York Post/ *Busy women may complain that they wear three hats, wife, mother, worker*

weasel **1** *v fr late 1800s* To evade and equivocate; use deceptive language; =WAFFLE: *They told the candidate to stop weaseling and get to the substance* **2** *v underworld fr 1920s* To inform; =SING, SQUEAL **3** *n: Little Joe turned weasel* [the first sense is said to be based on the *weasel's* habit of sucking the meat or substance from an egg, leaving only the shell; the other senses reflect the more general nasty reputation of the *weasel*]

weasel out *v phr* To withdraw from or evade, esp a promise or obligation, in a sneaky, underhanded way: *We made an open agreement, and you cannot weasel out of it*

weasel words *n phr* Language designed to deceive; empty talk; self-serving verbiage

weather *See* UNDER THE WEATHER

web *n radio studio* A broadcast network

web-foot *modifier* Devoted to and advocating preservation of the environment: *Anyone favoring the bottle bill must be web-foot conservationist* —Boston Globe [presumably fr the notion that lovers of wild life are thus adapted to walking about in swamps; similar to *web-foot* "a native of the wet state of Oregon," and British "a dweller in the fens of East Anglia"]

wedding *See* MILITARY WEDDING, SHOTGUN WEDDING

weed **1** *n* (also **the weed**) *fr 1500s* Tobacco **2** *n fr middle 1800s* A cigar, esp an inferior one: *Throw that weed away and have a good one* —Earl Wilson **3** *n fr early 1900s* A cigarette; =BUTT, COFFIN NAIL **4** *n* (also **the weed**) *narcotics fr 1920s* A marijuana cigarette; =JOINT

See REEFER WEED

weejuns *n teenagers* Mocassins; loafers [fr *Weejuns*, trade name of a brand of such shoes]

weekend warrior *See* SUNDAY SOLDIER

weenchy *adj fr late 1800s* Very small; tiny: *just a weenchy... little dash of perfume*—Ira Wolfert [fr *wee*]

weenie (also **weeny** or **weeney** or **weinie** or **wienie**) **1** *n* (also **wiener** or **weener**) A frankfurter; =HOT DOG: *this wienie and kraut combination*—New York Daily News ◁**2**▷ *n* (also **wiener** or **weener**) The penis; esp, the relaxed penis **3** *n* An ineffectual, despised person; =JERK: *She plans to be a weenie, is a weenie, asks to be loved anyway, and is loved anyway*—Village Voice **4** *n* (also **ween**) *college students* A very serious student; =GREASY GRIND: *premeds... known to their less pressurized campus colleagues as throats and weenies*—Newsweek/ *Weens are strange creatures with pallid faces, glassy eyes, and calculators strapped to their belts*—Dirk Johnson [fr German *Wienerwurst* "Vienna sausage," with pejorative senses developing fr its penile shape]

See PLAY HIDE THE WEENIE

weensy *See* TEENSY-WEENSY

the **weeps** *n phr* Weeping; crying

weevil *See* BOLL WEEVIL

wee-wee **1** *v* To urinate **2** *n: specimen of wee-wee*—Carson McCullers [perhaps a euphemism for the euphemism *pee-pee* for *piss*]

weigh in *v phr* To make a contribution to something, esp to a debate, quarrel, etc: *John weighed in with the suggestion that we adjourn* [fr the formal *weighing* or *weighing in* of a prizefighter before a match]

weight *n narcotics* The amount of narcotics an addict needs for a week: *I'm going up there to give her her weight for the week, you know* —Claude Brown

See THROW one's WEIGHT AROUND

weird *adj 1940s bop talk & cool talk* Excellent; wonderful; =COOL • Also attested as 1920s British upper-class use

weirdo or **weirdie** or **weirdy** *n fr 1940s* A very strange, eccentric, repellent person; =BIRD, CREEP, GEEK: *He's a weirdy, all right*—WR Burnett

weird out *v phr* To become intoxicated by narcotics; suffer hallucinations, loss of sense of reality, etc: *Talk to me. I'm weirding out*—Armistead Maupin

welcome to the club *sentence* Now you have joined me in adversity; now you see how badly things turn out: *So you've been fired? Welcome to the club, old buddy*

◁ **welldigger's ass**▷ *See* COLD AS HELL

well-heeled **1** *adj fr late 1800s* Having much money; rich: *the average, fairly well-heeled, middle-aged American male*—New Yorker **2** *adj fr middle 1800s* Well armed: *He's always well-heeled*—Gangbusters (radio program)

◁ **well-hung**▷ *adj fr early 1800s British* Having large genitals: *Death takes the innocent young. And those who are very well hung*—WH Auden/ *A guy with 640K of RAM is the electronic equivalent of well-hung*—New Republic

well told *See* FUCKING WELL TOLD

welsh or **welch** **1** *v fr middle 1800s British gambling* To default on or evade an obligation, esp paying a gambling debt: *Some American officials feel that the Syrians welshed on their promise*—New York Times **2** *n: Link can't take a welsh so he looks around for a way to get his dough*—Mickey Spillane [apparently fr the same bigoted stereotype of the *Welsh* reflected in the English nursery rhyme "Taffy was a Welshman, Taffy was a thief," although perhaps a borrowing of German *Welsch* "foreigner"]

west *See* GALLEY-WEST

western or **Western** *n* A book, movie, etc, about the Old West

See EASTERN WESTERN, SPAGHETTI WESTERN

wet **1** *adj fr late 1800s* Permitting or advocating the sale of liquor: *This is a wet county* **2** *adj fr early 1900s* Inferior; stupid and unappealing • Nearly obsolete in the US but still in occasional British use: *A man is "wet" if he isn't a regular guy*—P Marks

See ALL WET, GET one's FEET WET

◁ **wetback**▷ *n fr 1940s* A Mexican who enters the US illegally, esp as a migratory worker • The term may be generalizing to include all illegal immigrants: *a wetback, who is a Mexican that we don't know how he got here*—James M Cain [fr the fact that they get their *backs wet* in wading across the Rio Grande; the terms *wet pony, wet cow*, etc, were used earlier for animals brought illegally across the border]

wet behind the ears *See* NOT DRY BEHIND THE EARS

wet blanket *n phr* A person who dampens and smothers all enthusiasm; a person who prevents fun; a pessimist; =KILLJOY

◁ **wet dream**▷ *n phr* A male's erotic dream during which he has an orgasm

wet hen *See* MAD AS A WET HEN

wet-nose *n* =SNOTNOSE

wet one's **whistle** *v phr* To have a drink, esp of liquor

whack **1** *v fr early 1700s* To strike; hit **2** *n: He took a whack at the ball and missed* **3** *v* To cut; chop: *He whacked off a big slice for me* **4** *n fr late 1800s* A try; =BASH, CRACK, SHOT: *He was given a whack at drama reviewing*—Bennett Cerf **5** *v narcotics* To dilute a narcotic; cut a narcotic **6** *n* =WACK [probably echoic]

See HAVE A CRACK AT something, OUT OF WHACK, WACK

◁ **whack** (or **wack**) **off**▷ *v phr* To masturbate; =JERK OFF

whacky *See* WACKY

whale[1] *n fr late 1800s* A large or fat person; =WALRUS

whale[2] *v fr early 1800s* To hit; thrash; trounce: *They whaled us six zip* [fr British dialect spelling of *wale* "strike, beat," perhaps related to Old English *wæl* "slaughter, carnage, death"]

whale away *v phr* To attack or do something vigorously and joyfully: *He's best when he's whaling away at the other candidates*

whale into someone or something *v phr* To attack vigorously: *He'd barely met me when he whaled into me for not answering his letter* a **whale of a** someone or something *n phr fr early 1900s* An excellent or large example; a very superior specimen: *That woman is a whale of a politician* [fr the prodigious size of the *whale*]

whaling *See* WAILING

wham **1** *v* To hit; strike; =SOCK: *And the whamming continues*—E Lavine **2** *interj* (also **whammo**) An exclamation signalling the suddenness, violence, surprise, etc, of a quick, sharp blow: *And then when I was off guard, whammo!*—Fibber McGee and Molly (radio program)/ *I turned my back and, wham, they were gone* [echoic, and related in sound symbolism to *whip, whale, whack* and other *wh-* words denoting blows]

wham-bam (or **ram-bam**) **thank you ma'am** *n phr esp WW2 armed forces fr Southwestern US* A very quick sex act, esp a casual coupling: *a regular "wham, bam, thank you, Ma'am"*—CoEvolution Quarterly

whammy *See* DOUBLE WHAMMY, TRIPLE WHAMMY

the **whammy** *n phr* The evil eye; a crippling curse; =the INDIAN SIGN: *When threatened with the whammy they quickly agreed/ That pitcher tried to put the whammy on me, but I hit a home run anyway* [fr and perhaps coined in the comic strip "Li'l Abner" by Al Capp, where one character can paralyze with a stare]

whams *See* the WHIM-WHAMS

whang *v* To hit; =WHAM: *She whanged him a shrewd one*
See WANG

whangdoodle or **wangdoodle** or **wingdoodle** *n fr early 1900s* An unspecified or unspecifiable object; something one does not know the name of or does not wish to name; =GIZMO, THINGAMAJIG: *Push in this dingus, step on this wingdoodle*—Billy Rose [fr mid-19th-century sense, "a mythical beast of strange but indefinite traits"]

whanger *See* WANG

what *See* SAY WHAT

whatchamacallit or **what-you-may-call-it** (WHUT chə mə CAWL it) *n fr middle 1800s* An unspecified or unspecifiable object; something one does not know the name of or does not wish to name; =GIZMO, THINGAMAJIG: *Bring me that whatchamacallit over there, it's leaking*

what else is new *See* SO WHAT ELSE IS NEW

what for *n phr fr late 1800s* A drubbing, either physical or verbal; a thrashing; severe punishment: *a sadistic desire to watch the big shots get what for*—John Crosby [fr the startled question *what for? why?* asked by someone being assaulted]
See GIVE someone WHAT FOR

what gives **1** *sentence* What is going on?; =WHAT'S UP: *What gives, I asked her*—John O'Hara **2** *sentence* How are you?; how have things been with you? **3** *sentence* What is wrong?; I do not understand: *"What gives?" he croaked in an annoyed tone*—Raymond Chandler [a translation of Yiddish or German *was gibt* "what's going on"]

what goes around comes around *sentence esp black* Things will happen as they will; what will be will be, and fate has its ironies: *"What goes around comes around," Young said*—Philadelphia

what it takes *n phr* The desirable strength, character, appeal, etc: *I wonder if he has what it takes to get this job done*

what makes someone **tick** *n phr* Someone's motives, inner psychology, system of principles, etc: *It's the gambling instinct that makes me tick*—Esquire [fr the analogy of human motivation with the mechanism of a clock]

what's been shaking *See* WHAT'S SHAKING

what's cooking or **what cooks** **1** *sentence fr 1930s jive talk* What is happening?: *What cooks, Jimmy?*—Lionel Stander **2** *sentence* How have you been?

what's going down *sentence fr black* What is happening?; =WHAT'S COOKING

what she wrote *See* THAT'S ALL SHE WROTE

what's-his- (or **-her-** or **-its-**) **name** (or **-face** or ◁**-ass**▷) *n* An unspecified or unspecifiable person or thing; someone or something one does not know or remember the name of or does not wish to name; =WHOOZIS: *What did old what's-his-face have to tell you?*

what's-it or **whatsis** or **whatzis** (WHUT sit, -səs) ***n*** An unspecified or unspecifiable object; something one does not know the name of or does not wish to name; =DINGUS, THINGAMAJIG: *the world's tallest free-standing what's-it*—Toronto Life/ *What's that whatsis he's playing with?*

what's shaking or **what's been shaking** ***sentence*** What is happening?; =WHAT'S GOING DOWN: *Hello, what's shakin'?*—Buffalo Bill (TV program)

what's the big idea ***sentence*** Why are you being so presumptuous, aggressive, etc?; account for your behavior at once

what's the good word ***sentence*** How are things going with you?; what have you to tell me about yourself? • A cordial greeting

what's the scam ***sentence*** What is happening?; =WHAT'S GOING DOWN, WHAT'S UP

what's up ***sentence*** What is happening?; what is the matter, question, problem, etc?; =WHAT'S THE SCAM

what's with someone or something **1** ***sentence*** What is the problem, difficulty, etc?: *What's with this guy? All I did was say hello* **2** ***sentence*** What is the explanation?; why is this?: *What's with the free food? Explain*—John O'Hara [fr Yiddish *vos iz mit* "what is with"]

what the hell **1** ***interj*** An exclamation of surprise, puzzlement, resentment, etc: *What the hell! Who does this clown think he is, anyhow?* **2** ***interj*** An exclamation of resignation, acceptance, etc: *What the hell, it isn't the greatest, but it'll do*

what the Sam Hill ***interj fr early 1800s*** =WHAT THE HELL • A euphemistic form

what-you-may-call-it ***See*** WHATCHAMACALLIT

what you see is what you get ***sentence*** The situation, thing, person, etc, is precisely as it appears to be; no trickery, decoration, glowing promises, etc, are involved here [probably fr the supposed statement of a salesperson both assuring and warning a customer about the wares]

whatzis ***See*** WHAT'S-IT

whee ***n*** Urine; =PISS, WHIZZ: *that will scare the whee out of you*—Car and Driver [probably fr *wee-wee*]

wheel ***See*** BIG WHEEL, INVENT THE WHEEL, REINVENT THE WHEEL, THIRD WHEEL

wheel and deal ***v phr*** To make many and frequent arrangements and agreements, esp in business and aggressively

wheeler ***See*** EIGHTEEN WHEELER, FOUR-WHEELER

wheeler-dealer ***n*** A person who wheels and deals; =BIG-TIME OPERATOR, GANZE MACHER

wheelie ***n motorcyclists & bicyclists*** A riding on the rear wheel only, with the front wheel raised off the ground
See POP A WHEELIE

wheeling ***See*** FREE-WHEELING

wheels **1** ***n*** The legs: *even the veiny old wheels*—Joseph Wambaugh **2** ***n fr 1950s hot rodders*** A car
See SET OF WHEELS, SHIT ON WHEELS

wheeze ***n fr middle 1800s British*** An old joke; =CHESTNUT: *this tired little wheeze*—Billy Rose [origin unknown; perhaps fr a *wheezing* delivery used by clowns in telling jokes; the earliest attested use refers to a circus clown's joke]

where someone's **head is at** ***adv phr*** One's mental condition; one's attitudes, thoughts, aberrations, etc: *They have the maturity to understand where a freak's head is at*—Xaviera Hollander

where he lives ***See*** HIT someone WHERE HE LIVES

where someone **is at** ***n phr fr black*** Someone's essential nature, current value system, attitudes, etc: *might make sense in evaluating where you are all at*—New York Times

where someone **is coming from** **1** ***n phr fr black*** What someone means; what someone is saying: *Where I'm coming from, what I'm getting at*—New York Times/ *He doesn't know where this guy is coming from*—WT Tyler **2** ***n phr*** =WHERE someone IS AT

where it's at **1** ***n phr*** The essential locus of the truth; the core of things: *A lot of cats are finding out where it's at in the joint*—Claude Brown **2** ***adv phr:*** *Why should only book writers write books?... They're not where it's at*—James Simon Kunen **3** ***adv phr*** At the site of stimulating and modish events, trends, etc; =WHERE THE ACTION IS: *Where the*

important stuff is going on. This is where it's at—New York Times
See KNOW WHERE IT'S AT

where someone **lives** *adv phr* In one's most essential nature, feelings, etc; profoundly: *zap you where you live*—Playgirl/ *Her appeal hit me where I live*

where the action is **1** *n phr* The site of stimulating and modish events, trends, etc; a place of excitement; =WHERE IT'S AT: *Don't come here if you're looking for where the action is* **2** *adv phr: Do you want to live where the action is?*

where the bodies are buried *See* KNOW WHERE THE BODIES ARE BURIED

where the rubber meets the road *n phr Army* The lower echelons; those in the trenches

where the sun doesn't shine **1** *n phr* One's anus; =ASS, ASSHOLE **2** *adv phr: Put it and all his other contributions where the sun doesn't shine*—Car and Driver/ *Give you a hickey where the sun doesn't shine*—National Lampoon
See STICK IT

where to get off (or **to go**) *See* TELL someone WHERE TO GET OFF

where to put (or **shove** or **stick** or **stuff**) something *See* KNOW WHAT one CAN DO WITH something, TELL someone WHAT TO DO WITH something

the **wherewithal** *n phr fr early 1800s* Money; =the NEEDFUL

which *See* SAYS WHICH

whiff **1** *v sports* To strike at a ball and miss **2** *v baseball* To strike out: *surpassed Sandy Koufax's single-season strikeout record, whiffing 383 batters*—Inside Sports **3** *n narcotics* Cocaine; =SNOW: *Hey, man, know where I can score some whiff?*—Dan Jenkins **4** *v narcotics* To inhale cocaine into the nose; =SNORT, TOOT

whimp *See* WIMP

the **whim-whams** (or **wim-wams**) *n phr* Nervousness; =the JIM-JAMS, the JITTERS: *gives Pavarotti the whim-whams before every performance*—Time/ *Kittenish dames give us the wim-wams*—Time

whingding *See* WINGDING

whip *See* BUGGY WHIP

whip out *v phr* To shake hands or give some other gesture of greeting

whip-out *n* Money, esp a first payment, investment, etc: *a whole lot of what you call your up-front whip-out*—Dan Jenkins

whipped *See* PUSSY-WHIPPED

whipsaw **1** *v* To attack or operate by letting rival parties attack one another, to the benefit of the more or less passive manipulator: *pit one plant against another, using inter-plant rivalries to spur production, a tactic called "whipsawing"*—Time **2** *v* To assault; =CLOBBER: *I'm not trying to sandbag anybody, and I'm not trying to whipsaw anybody*—George V Higgins [first sense perhaps fr the reciprocal action of the *whipsaw*, a pit saw operated by one person above and one in the pit below; in an earlier slang use *whipsaw* meant "to take bribes from two political sources at once"; second sense probably fr the cutting efficiency of this two-person saw]

whip up *v phr* To make hurriedly: *Let's whip up a new policy on this/ Just relax while I whip up dinner*

whirlybird *n* A helicopter; =CHOPPER

whiskers *n* An old man: *I had those whiskers by the short hairs*—Paul Sann
See BET YOUR BOOTS, the CAT'S MEOW

whispering campaign *n phr* An effort at discrediting someone or something, esp by starting false rumors: *start a whispering campaign against your product*—SJ Perelman

whistle *See* BELLS AND WHISTLES, BLOW THE WHISTLE, DOODAD, NOT JUST WHISTLING DIXIE, WET one's WHISTLE, WHISTLING DIXIE

whistle-blower **1** *n underworld* =STOOL PIGEON **2** *n* A person who makes an accusation of wrongdoing, illegality, etc: *trading inside information with whistle-blowers and publicity seekers*—Washingtonian

whistle stop *n phr fr railroad* A small town [perhaps fr the fact that the train does not regularly stop at such a town, or stops only when signalled to stop, and announces itself by blowing the *whistle* when it does *stop*]

whistling Dixie **1** *v phr* To say something of no consequence for the purpose of making a positive impression **2** *v phr* To engage in wishful thinking

white *n narcotics fr 1940s* Cocaine

See LILY WHITE

white bready or **white-bread** *adj phr* or *adj* Conventional; bourgeois; =PLASTIC, SQUARE: *Some of the sequences are Middle American. Evans calls them white bready* —Time/ *He taught them to give up the safe, white-bread types*—Playboy

white buck *See* WHITE SHOE

white elephant *n phr* Something putatively valuable, often a gift, that one does not want; an embarrassing piece of bric-a-brac: *a wonderful collection of white elephants, trash, treasures*—Washington Post [fr a consideration of the *white elephant* of Thailand which, although it is sacred and royal, is also a clumsy sort of possession for one's house]

white-face *n circus* A clown

white-haired boy *See* FAIRHAIRED BOY

white hat **1** *n phr* A law-abiding, morally upright, and heroic person, as distinct from the villainous black hat **2** *modifier: I told them they were the white-hat guys*—Larry Hagman

white-knuckle *adj* Marked by tension, suspense, fear, etc: *Invocations of a Soviet threat have become so common....He calls it "the white-knuckle show"*—Washingtonian

white-knuckled *adj phr* Tense; anxious; frightened: *Metro's countless thousands of white-knuckled motorists*—Toronto Life [fr the *whiteness* of *knuckles* when the hands are clenched in anxiety and suspense]

white knuckler **1** *n phr* An airplane flight, esp an anxious one: *You take a white-knuckler. Smilin' Jack at the controls*—Paul Theroux **2** *n phr* A tense and anxious person; someone or something frightened: *A list of companies in trouble: The white knucklers*—New Jersey Monthly

white lightning **1** *n phr* Inferior whiskey; =PANTHER PISS, ROTGUT: *He had a pint of bootleg white lightning* —Carson McCullers **2** *n phr narcotics* LSD; =ACID

the **whites** *n phr* Gonorrhea; =the CLAP [fr the color of the characteristic genital discharge]

white shoe (or **buck**) **1** *n phr college students fr early 1900s* A typical Ivy League student **2** *adj phr* Having the attitudes, appearance, etc, of the Ivy League [fr the *white buckskin shoes* that were part of that student's dress]

white stuff **1** *n phr fr 1920s* Grain alcohol used for making bootleg liquor **2** *n phr narcotics* Cocaine or morphine; =SNOW

◁ **white trash** ▷ *n phr fr middle 1800s black* =PECKERWOOD, REDNECK

whitewash **1** *v fr middle 1800s* To win decisively, esp not permitting the opponent to score; =SKUNK **2** *v* To make something unsavory, damaging, etc, seem to be legitimate and acceptable, usu by falsification or concealment; decontaminate someone's actions or reputation **3** *n: The report was a "whitewash" of McCarthy's charges*—Associated Press

white wrapper *See* PLAIN WHITE WRAPPER

Whitey or **whitey** *n black* A white person; =MISTER CHARLIE, OFAY

whiz[1] *n fr early 1900s* A very successful performer; an outstanding expert; =HUMDINGER: *the town's most promising high school football whiz*—Associated Press [shortened form of *wizard*]

whiz[2] or **whizz** **1** *v* To urinate; =PISS: *exactly twenty-five minutes after whizzing in his pants for the last time*—Stephen King **2** *n: I just came down for a whizz*—Paul Theroux [perhaps echoic; perhaps related to late-19th-century British *hold your whiz* "be quiet, shut up," similar to *hold your water*]

whiz[3] *v underworld fr early 1900s* To pick pockets [apparently fr the *whizzing* speed with which an expert pickpocket works]

whiz[4] *See* GEE WHIZ[2]

whizbang **1** *n* A person or thing that is remarkable, wonderful, superior, etc; =BEAUT, HUMDINGER: *It's a whiz-bang of an idea* **2** *modifier: definitely has been a whiz-bang franchise-winning tool*—Village Voice **3** *n* A very successful performer; an outstanding expert; =WHIZ: *In time we'll all be varsity whizbangs*—Arthur Daley/ *The TV whizbangs were sweating through their pancake makeup*—Washington Post **4** *n narcotics fr 1920s* A mixture of cocaine and morphine; an injection of this mixture [fr an intensification of *whiz* either due to or influenced by the echoic use of *whizbang* to designate an artillery shell in World War 1]

whiz kid **1** *n phr fr 1960s* A very clever young person; a youthful prodigy: *the physics whiz kid*—WT Tyler **2** *modifier: Then the whiz-kid lawyers collided with a tougher adversary* —Village Voice [fr *whiz*[1] blended with *quiz kid* "very bright child or young person," used of participants in a 1930s radio quiz program]

whizzer *n underworld* A pickpocket; =WHIZ

who *See* SAYS YOU

whodunit *n fr 1930s* A mystery or detective story, play, movie, etc, esp a novel: *a conventional whodunit* —Anthony Boucher [fr *who done it,* "who committed the crime?"; claimed as a coinage by and of various persons]

the **whole ball of wax** *n phr fr 1950s* The totality; everything; the whole thing; =the WHOLE SHEBANG: *For that price you get the whole ball of wax* [origin unknown; perhaps fr a manner of distributing the land of an estate to heirs, described in the early 17th century, in which the amount of each portion is concealed in a *ball of wax* which is drawn out of a hat in a sort of lottery]

the **whole enchilada** *n phr* The totality; everything; the whole thing

whole hog *adv phr* Utterly; without reservation: *He believed me whole hog* [fr the early-19th-century *go the whole hog* "act, give, etc, without reservation"; perhaps fr the fact that Muslims were said to have been denied the eating of pork because one unspecified part of the swine was unclean, and, as the poet William Cowper wrote in 1779, "thought it hard from the *whole hog* to be debarred"]

the **whole megillah** *See* the MEGILLAH

a **whole new ball game** *n phr* A totally new situation; something completely different from what has been the case; =a WHOLE 'NOTHER THING: *Since the government got into it this has been a whole new ball game*

the **whole nine yards** *n phr fr Army & Air Force* The totality; everything; the whole thing; =the WHOLE SHEBANG: *went with the odd-looking ship, built a press platform in front of it, had power brought in for press lights, "the whole nine yards"*—Washingtonian [origin unknown; perhaps fr or related to the mid-19th-century British term *to the nines* or *up to the nines* "perfectly, thoroughly," still heard in *dressed to the nines* and apparently based on *nine* as a perfect number in numerology; perhaps based on the load of a concrete mixing and hauling truck, which normally comes in a *nine-yard* and a ten-yard size; perhaps based on *yard* "one hundred dollars," rather than on the linear or cubic measure]

a **whole 'nother thing** *n phr* A completely different or new affair, process, question, etc: *Now whether you get to go along, that's a whole 'nother thing*

the **whole schmear** *n phr* (Variations: **schmier** or **schmeer** or **shmear** or **shmeer** or **shmier** may replace **schmear**) The totality; everything; the whole thing; =the WHOLE SHEBANG: *names, ages, business they're in, daily schedules, the whole schmear*—Lawrence Sanders/ *the whole fucking schmeer*—George Warren [fr Yiddish *shmeer* fr *shmeeren* "spread"; probably immediately fr the spreading out of the hand in a pinochle or rummy game]

the **whole shebang** *n phr* The totality; everything; the whole thing; =the WHOLE SCHMEAR: *We could move the whole shebang*—Washington Post/ *The whole shebang is festive, pleasantly show-offy and communal*—Village Voice [fr earlier *shebang* "hut, hovel," perhaps fr Irish *shebeen* "cheap saloon," hence, "the house and everything in it"]

the **whole shooting match** *n phr fr late 1800s* The totality; everything; the whole thing; =the WHOLE SCHMEAR [probably fr the crowd that would gather at a frontier *shooting match,* hence, "the whole crowd"; perhaps influenced by earlier British *the whole shoot* of the same meaning, fr *the whole shot* "the whole cost or price"]

the **whole works** *See* the WORKS

whomp or **whump** **1** *v* To defeat utterly; =CLOBBER: *The Tigers got badly whomped* **2** *v* To hit; =BASH: *sturdily whumped at the New Deal's "insane deficit policy"*—Life [fr dialect *whup* "whip"]

whomp up *v phr* To make; devise or build: *I whomped me up one heck of a nightmare*—Billy Rose/ *I better whomp up an explanation for this black eye*

whoop-de-do (HOOP dee doo) (Variations: **hoopty-doo** or **hoopty-do** or **hoop-de-doo** or **hoop-a-doop** or **hoop-de-doop** or **whoop-de-doo** or **whoop-de-doodle**) **1** *n* Raucous confusion; noisy celebration; jolly fuss: *a gay sense of flossy whoop-de-doo*—Esquire/ *but, in spite of this whoop-de-doo*—Time/ *Cowboys and soldiers created a deafening hoop-a-doop*—New York Times **2** *adj: The racketeering, gossiping, whoop-de-doodle thing, it is a piece of stinking fish*—Thomas Wolfe [echoic]

whoopee (WHOO pee) **1** *n fr middle 1800s* Exuberant merriment; wild celebration; =WHOOP-DE-DO **2** *interj* An exclamation of joy and approval; hurrah

whoopee (or **whoopie**) **cushion** *n phr* A bladder that makes a loud flatulating sound when sat upon: *It's Grandma's whoopie cushion. I thought you'd like that, you little fart*—National Lampoon

whooper-dooper *n fr 1920s* A carouse; a wild party: *He finds himself off on a rousing whooper-dooper*—Saturday Evening Post

whoop it up *v phr fr late 1800s* To celebrate; carouse; have raucous fun: *It's natural the Boys should whoop it up for so huge a phallic triumph*—WH Auden

whoopla *See* HOOPLA

whoops (HOOPS) *v* To vomit; =OOPS: *A man...had whoopsed into his National Observer*—Stephen King

whoozis or **whozis** (HOO zəs) *n* An unspecified or unspecifiable object; something one does not know the name of or does not wish to name; =THINGAMAJIG: *Is impotence in the whoozis?*—San Francisco/ *There should be a whozis over the first* n—AH Holt/ *What do you call this whoozis on top here?*

whoozit (HOO zət) *n* A person whose name one does not know; =WHAT'S-HIS-NAME: *Hello to Fred and Whoozit*—Village Voice

whop **1** *v fr 1700s* To hit; =WHACK **2** *n: Give a good whop this time* **3** *n* A try or chance; =CRACK, SHOT: *politicians, judges, people from out of town, $50 to $100 a whop*—Milwaukee Journal [echoic]

whopper **1** *n fr 1700s British* Something huge: *the Mauritius tortoise must have been a whopper*—J Williams **2** *n* A very bold lie: *He told a whopper and got away with it* [fr *whop*]
See BELLY-WHOPPER

whopping *adj* Huge; very impressive: *It was a whopping idea she had*

whump *See* WHOMP

whupass *See* PLAY WHUPASS

Wichita *n prison* A betrayal; =DOUBLE CROSS

wicked **1** *adj fr early 1900s* Impressive; prodigious; =MEAN: *He can shake a wicked spatula*—AL Bass/ *Look at the wicked bat he swings!* **2** *adj teenagers* Excellent; wonderful; =BAD, GREAT

wicket *See* STICKY WICKET

wickey *See* ICKY

wide *See* HIGH, WIDE, AND HANDSOME

wide ones *See* FOUR WIDE ONES

widget or **widgit** **1** *n fr early 1920s* A mechanical, electrical, or electronic device; =GADGET, GIZMO: *It's three floors of sights, sounds, illusions, movements, gadgets, widgets, and gizmos*—Westworld/ *not an activity I would recommend to anyone daunted by a widgit more complicated than a stapler*—Village Voice **2** *modifier: as though it were read aloud from the press release of a widget manufacturer*—Time [an alteration of *gadget*, perhaps based on hypothetical *which it* on the model of *whatzit*]

widow *See* GRASS WIDOW

wiener *See* WEENIE

wife **1** *n prostitutes* A member of a pimp's group of prostitutes: *She is his favorite "wife" at the moment*—New York Times **2** *n homosexuals* The more passive of a homosexual couple

wiff or **wif** (WIF) **1** *n* A wife **2** *n* =WHIFF

wig **1** *n fr 1930s jive talk* One's head; one's mind **2** *v fr 1930s jive talk* To talk, esp casually and freely; =RAP: *We stood around wigging* **3** *v fr 1930s jive talk* To annoy someone; =BUG: *She ordered me to stop wigging her* **4** *n fr 1950s jazz* musicians A cool jazz musician **5** *v fr 1950s jazz musicians* To play cool or progressive jazz **6** *v fr cool talk* To behave more or less hysterically; =FLIP, FREAK OUT, WIG OUT: *I realized my goddamn father wasn't there, again, and I wigged*—Richard Price **7** *v fr cool talk* To be happy and in harmony; =DIG **8** *adj esp 1960s teenagers* Excellent; wonderful; =GREAT, NEAT: *a real wig rock trio*

See BLOW one's TOP, FLIP one's LID, a HOLE IN THE HEAD

wiggle *See* GET A MOVE ON

wiggy **1** *adj fr cool talk* Exciting and up-to-date; =COOL, FAR OUT: *But I have some really wiggy experiences*—Dayton Daily News **2** *adj* Intoxicated on or using narcotics; =OUT OF IT, SPACED-OUT: *one of whom is so wiggy that she got fired from her job*—Newsweek **3** *adj* Crazy; weird; strange: *Things were wiggy*—Robert Stone

wig out *1950s cool talk fr jazz musicians* **1** *v phr* To become ecstatic; =FLIP, FREAK OUT, WIG: *The first time I read The Collected Stories I wigged out*—Saturday Review **2** *n phr* To become mentally unbalanced; lose one's sanity: *whose guiding genius, Brian Wilson, spent years wigging out in a sandbox*—Rolling Stone

wild *adj fr cool talk* Excellent; exciting; wonderful; =COOL

wild about (or **over**) **1** *adj phr fr early 1900s* Enthusiastically approbatory of; =CRAZY ABOUT: *the new lemon flavored cough drop everyone's wild about*—New York Post **2** *adj phr* In love with

wild and woolly *adj phr fr late 1800s* Crude and raucous; untamed; uncouth: *a couple of good old country boys having a wild and woolly time* [fr an alliterating phrase *wild and woolly West*, the *woolly* perhaps referring to range steers, to range horses, or to the unkempt heads of cowboys and frontiersmen]

◁ **wild-ass** or **wild-assed**▷ *adj* Madly exuberant; untamed; =CRAZY: *Shepard tops himself as a wild-ass country boy*—Playboy/ *and for goddamned sure a wild-assed warrior*—Don Pendleton/ *Ijah was a kind of wild-ass type*—Saul Bellow

wild card **1** *n phr* Something outside of the normal rules, category, etc; an unpredictable thing, event, etc: *Being from Princeton wasn't like being from Jersey, it was a wild card*—Philadelphia **2** *n phr sports* A team picked for a playoff by some more or less arbitrary method, not having won its championship during the season: *We can always hope the Lions will be the wild card* **3** *modifier: the wild-card slot/ last year's wild-card team* [fr poker, where in some games one or more *wild cards*, having any value the player desires, may be designated]

willie *See* DOODAD

the **willies** *n phr fr late 1800s* Acute nervousness; a spell of uneasiness; =the JITTERS: *all soft and womanish from the willies*—Ira Wolfert/ *For years her friends' shoptalk gave him the willies*—Geoffrey T Hellman [origin unknown]

willikers *See* GEE[2]

wimp or **whimp** *n* An ineffectual person; a soft, silly person; a weakling; =DRIP, NEBBISH: *unmacho. Short hair, glasses, awkward, uncertain. WIMP*—New York Sunday News/ *his unfortunate and unfounded charge that Thompson portrayed him as a "wimp"*—Newsweek/ *Apparently whimps complained it was too hot*—Nashville [origin unknown; perhaps fr J Wellington *Wimpy*, a relatively unaggressive character in the comic strip "Popeye"; perhaps fr the early-20th-century Cambridge University *wimp* "young woman," perhaps fr *whimper*]

wimpy or **wimpo** or **wimpoid** *adj* Having the traits of a wimp; soft; weak: *less wimpy version of the husband she leaves*—Ms/ *seats that go wimpo during cornering*—Car and Driver/ *a wimpoid MOR ballad with the refrain "the doggone girl is mine"*—Rolling Stone

win a few lose a few *sentence* One cannot always be victorious or successful; =YOU CAN'T WIN 'EM ALL

wind *See* BAG OF WIND, a LOAD OF VW RADIATORS, PISS AND WIND, TWIST SLOWLY IN THE WIND

windbag *n* A person who talks too much, esp a pompous prater; =BAG OF WIND, GASBAG: *a windbag who shoots the gab*—JR Williams

wind down **1** *v phr* To come or bring to a gradual halt or conclusion:

The campaign has begun to wind down/ Shall we wind down our collection drive? **2** ***v phr*** To relax gradually: *Let me sit here for a few minutes, to wind down* [modeled on the *winding down* of a clock or other machine]

winder ***See*** SIDEWINDER

window ***n fr astronautics*** A time period when something may be accomplished; a critical period: *We now have a window of opportunity to try for peace in Lebanon again/ They're worried about a window of vulnerability* [originally fr the exact time and directional limits governing the launching of a rocket to achieve a certain orbit or destination, which were pictured as a *window* through which the rocket must be shot]
See BAY WINDOW

windows ***n*** Eyeglasses; =SPECS

wind up ***v phr*** To have as an end result; finish with: *We wind up learning less*—Philadelphia Journal/ *How much did he wind up with, after taxes?*

wind something **up** ***v phr*** To finish; bring to a conclusion: *I suggest we wind this discussion up and go home*

windy ***adj*** Given to talking too much; overly garrulous, esp pompously so: *It's another one of his windy orations*

wine ***See*** JUG WINE, POP WINE

win for losing ***See*** someone CAN'T WIN FOR LOSING

wing **1** ***n fr early 1800s*** An arm, esp a baseball pitcher's throwing arm **2** ***v fr middle 1800s*** To shoot, esp to wound with a shot, not necessarily in the arm: *You were winged by something big, 45 maybe*—R Starnes **3** ***v*** =WING IT **4** ***n teenagers*** A raucous party; =WINGDING
See PAY-WING

wingding or **whingding** **1** ***n hoboes, prison & narcotics fr early 1900s*** A drug-induced or epileptic fit; also, such a fit counterfeited in order to attract sympathy **2** ***n fr 1930s*** A fit of anger; a violent outburst of feeling: *going to throw a wingding they'll hear in Detroit*—J Evans **3** ***n*** (also **wingdinger**) ***fr 1940s*** An energetic celebration or commotion; a noisy party; =RUCKUS: *Then they did their wingding out in front of the West Wing*—Washington Post

wingdoodle ***See*** WHANGDOODLE

wing it or **wing** ***v phr*** or ***v*** To extemporize; improvise; =FAKE IT: *Winging It, Coping Without Controllers*—Time

wings ***See*** EARN one's WINGS, SPROUT WINGS

wingy ***adj*** Intoxicated with narcotics; =HIGH: *I've never been wingy or suffered a psychotic episode*—New York Daily News

◁ **Wingy** ▷ ***n*** Nickname for a one-armed man

win in a walk ***v phr fr late 1800s*** To win easily; be a confident victor

winks ***See*** FORTY WINKS

winner ***n*** A very promising and successful person or thing; =HOT SHOT: *Your new poem is a winner*

wino **1** ***n fr early 1900s hoboes*** A habitual drunkard, esp a derelict who drinks cheap wine; =STUMBLEBUM: *a couple of "winos" who had been drinking cheap sherry in the bar*—G Homes **2** ***n*** A person who drinks wine in preference to liquor; a wine drinker

win out ***v phr fr late 1800s*** To win; prevail: *De Bird of Time will win out in a walk*—L Coley

win one's **spurs** ***v phr fr cowboys*** To be fully accepted as competent: *After a few months on the job he had won his spurs*

win the porcelain hairnet ***v phr*** (Variations: **barbwire garter** or **cast-iron overcoat** or **fur-lined bathtub** or **hand-painted doormat** or **solid gold chamber pot** may replace **porcelain hairnet**) To deserve a spectacularly useless reward; merit nothing more than something absurd • Said ironically either about something stupid and ineffective or something guardedly admirable

wipe ***n*** A killing; a murder: *I don't know a goddam thing about this goddam Covino wipe*—Rex Burns

wiped out **1** ***adj phr*** Drunk: *Everybody had been too wiped out to watch*—Washington Post **2** ***adj phr*** Tired; exhausted: *At the end of that hearing she felt wiped out*

be **wiped out** ***v phr*** To be wrecked, ruined, finished; =GET IT IN THE NECK, SHOOT someone DOWN

wipe out **1** ***v phr surfers*** To lose control of the surfboard during a ride and be thrown off into the water:

About six of them wiped out on one big wave **2** *n phr* A failure; =LOSER: *The guy's a total wipe out* —Washington Post **3** *v phr: The strike wiped out after only two days*

wipe someone **out** **1** *v phr fr 1920s* To kill; =ICE, OFF: *In the St Valentine's Day massacre, Capone wiped out his whole opposition* **2** *v phr* To defeat utterly; trounce; =CLOBBER, CREAM: *Unexpectedly, Baylor wiped Syracuse out that year*

wipe (or **clean** or **mop**) **up the floor with** someone *v phr* To defeat utterly and abjectly; trounce easily; =CLOBBER: *That bum? The Champ'll wipe up the floor with him*

wire **1** *n underworld fr early 1900s* A pickpocket, esp the one of a team that actually steals the loot: *the wire who abstracts the objective from the victim's kick*—American Mercury **2** *v fr middle 1800s* To send a telegram: *Wire me when you get there* **3** *n: Send me a wire if you get the job* **4** *n* Information; news; a message: *He had heard the wire through the grapevine that the man was a paid informer*—Donald Goines **5** *v* To place eavesdropping devices in a room, office, etc; =BUG: *She quietly checked to see if her bedroom was wired* **6** *n* An overstimulated person; an anxious, excitable person: *You know I'm a natural wire.... What I need is a drink to calm me down* —Harry Crews [the first sense derives fr the use of *wire* as a lifting line; the second, third, fourth, and fifth senses from *wire* as the conductor of electric messages; the sixth sense fr *wire* as the conductor of stimulating impulses]

See COME UP TO THE WIRE, DOWN TO THE WIRE, GO TO THE WIRE, HAYWIRE, HOT-WIRE

wired **1** *adj* (also **wired up**) *narcotics* Intoxicated by narcotics; =HIGH, SPACED-OUT: *"If you're wired, you're fired," is how Willie Nelson warns band members about cocaine usage*—Chicago Tribune/ *That night Elvis was wired for speed*—Albert Goldman **2** *adj* (also **wired up**) Eagerly excited; overstimulated; =HIGH, JACKED UP: *Keeping the people wired with a mix of sixties vines and eighties technology*—Rolling Stone/ *Yes, I was definitely wired... I was so wired I couldn't concentrate*—Richard Price/ *They have him wired up tight with the slogans of TV and the World Series*—Eldridge Cleaver **3** *adj* Anxious; nervous; =UPTIGHT: *I got wired when Myrt was sneaking a break and Jerry showed up*—Ms **4** *adj* Securely in the proper circles, esp those of political or business power; =IN THE LOOP: *Bob Gray was wired. There wasn't a political celebrity there who wouldn't return his phone calls*—Washingtonian **5** *adj* (also **wired up**) Certain and secure; totally under control; assured; =TAPED: *Mention of all those other top contenders is just a smokescreen and Brown's got it wired*—Washington Post/ *This deal has already been, er, wired*—Village Voice/ *Then I get this wired up and I think, well* —George V Higgins [the first three senses derive fr *wire* as the conductor of stimulating electricity; the fourth sense probably fr *wire* as a conductor of messages and as a connector; the fifth sense fr *wire* as used for tying and binding; *wired up* is recorded as a US term for "irritated, provoked" in the late 19th century, and may be related to the sense "anxious, nervous"]

See COOL AS A CHRISTIAN WITH ACES WIRED, HAVE something CINCHED

wired into *adj* Intimately involved in; closely and sympathetically connected with; =INTO: *for the first time, I really felt wired into that poem* —Adrienne Rich

wires ***See*** PULL STRINGS

wise **1** *adj fr late 1800s* Aware; cunningly knowing; =HEP: *Get wise, son!*—Sinclair Lewis **2** *v* To make aware; inform, esp in shrewd particulars; =WISE someone UP: *She wised me about how to get promoted*

See CRACK WISE, GET WISE, PUT someone WISE, STREET-SMART

◁ **wise-ass** ▷ ***See*** NOBODY LOVES A WISE-ASS, SMART-ASS

wisecrack *n fr early 1900s* a witty remark, esp one with a knowing, sarcastic edge; a joke; =GAG, ONE-LINER: *makers of wars and wise-cracks, a rum creature*—WH Auden [said to have been coined by the early-20th-century American humorist Chic Sale; probably related to *crack* "brag, boast" attested fr the mid-15th century and basically echoic]

wise guy **1** *n phr* (also **wise apple**) *fr early 1900s* A person who is ostentatiously and smugly knowing; a smart aleck; =SMART-ASS: *My little brother is an irrepressible wise guy* **2** *n phr* (also **wise hombre**) *fr early 1900s* A shrewd and knowing person; a person who is "wised up": *The wise guys said Frank didn't stand a chance*—Philadelphia Bulletin

wise up *v phr* To become shrewdly aware; =GET SMART • Often an exhortation: *Wise up or you'll lose this opportunity*

wise someone **up** *v phr* To give useful and usu covert particulars; =PUT someone WISE: *My adviser was a good scout and wised me up*—P Marks

wish (or **want**) **list** *n phr* A presumed list of things one wants: *intent on buying every weapon the generals and admirals put on their wish lists*—Time

wishy-washy *adj fr 1700s* Marked by imprecision and vacillation; inconstant; uncertain: *It's not overpowering like Opium and not wishy-washy*—Washington Post [fr a rhythmic reduplication of *washy* "weak, diluted, watered-down," probably influenced by *wishy* as suggesting vacillating desires]

wit *See* NITWIT

witch's tit *See* COLD AS HELL

with a bang *adv phr* Very impressively; very successfully: *The thing succeeded with a bang*

See GO OVER WITH A BANG

with a full deck *See* PLAY WITH A FULL DECK

with a ten-foot pole *See* NOT TOUCH someone or something WITH A TEN-FOOT POLE

with bells on *adv phr* (Variations: **on** may be dropped; **knobs** or **tits** may replace **bells**) *fr 1930s* Very definitely; without any doubt; emphatically • Used especially in affirming that one will be present at a certain time and place: *Don't worry, I'll be there with bells on/ I'll be here Thursday. With bells*—James M Cain [perhaps the suggestion is that one will be very conspicuous, like a train or a fire engine *with bells*]

with one's **feet** *See* VOTE WITH one's FEET

◁ **with** one's **finger up** one's **ass**▷ *See* SIT THERE WITH one's FINGER UP one's ASS

with flying colors *adv phr* In a bold and assured way; grandly; =HIGH, WIDE, AND HANDSOME: *She won nicely, in fact with flying colors* [probably fr the image of a naval vessel with the national flag bravely *flying*]

with one's **hand in the till** (or **the cookie jar**) *adv phr* With no possibility of escape or evasion; in flagrante delicto; =DEAD TO RIGHTS: *Sure enough, there he was with his hand in the till* [fr the situation of a thief caught *with his hand in the money-box* or *cash register*]

within an ace *See* COME WITHIN AN ACE

with it **1** *adj phr fr 1950s beat talk & cool talk fr black* Coolly cognizant; absolutely in touch; stylish and au courant; =HEP: *Shadows of course there are, Porn-Ads, with-it clergy*—WH Auden **2** *adj phr carnival & circus fr 1920s* Working in a carnival as a full-time professional: *had previous short experiences traveling with carnivals ... before becoming fully "with it" (as carnival workers describe the fully-initiated member)*—Society

See GET WITH IT

◁ **without a pot to piss in**▷ *See* NOT HAVE A POT TO PISS IN

with one's **pants down** *See* CATCH someone WITH someone's PANTS DOWN

with the punches *See* ROLL WITH THE PUNCHES

with the territory *See* GO WITH THE TERRITORY

witless *See* SCARED SPITLESS, SCARE someone SHITLESS

wobble *n narcotics* =ANGEL DUST

◀ **wog** or **Wog**▶ *n WW2 armed forces fr British* A native of India, esp a laborer [the British usage, "any native of an Eastern country," is said to derive fr an arch acronym for *Worthy Oriental Gentleman* or *Westernized Oriental Gentleman*; some think it is more likely to be a shortening of *golliwog* "a black doll with wild frizzy hair and staring eyes," fr the name of such a doll in late-19th-century childrens' stories by Bertha Upton, and a popular toy in British nurseries]

wolf **1** *n fr early 1900s prison & hoboes* An aggressive male homosexual; a homosexual rapist: *the sodomist, the degenerate, the homosexual "wolf"*—New Republic **2** *n fr 1930s* A sexually aggressive man;

an ardent womanizer; =COCKSMAN: *Mary considered him quite a wolf* **3** *v: I give with the vocals and wolf around in a nite club*—John O'Hara
See LONER

woman *See* BAG LADY, the LITTLE WOMAN, OLD WOMAN

woman-chaser *n* A womanizer; =LADIES' MAN, SKIRT-CHASER, WOLF

wonder *See* NINE-DAYS' WONDER, NINETY-DAY WONDER

wonk *n esp college students* An overstudious student; an intellectual; =GREASY GRIND: *Along come these wonks with slide rules sewn into their sports jackets*—John Leonard [perhaps fr *wanker* "masturbator"]

wonky[1] *adj esp Canadian fr middle 1800s British printers* Badly done or made; ineffective; weird; =COCKEYED: *Only the steering feels wonky to me*—Car and Driver [fr British dialect *wanky* or *wankle* "weak, unsteady"]

wonky[2] *adj esp Harvard students* Tedious and serious, esp anxious and overstudious in an academic situation: *a class which I have long dismissed as hopelessly wonky*—Illinois Times [fr *wonk*]

◁ **wood** ▷ *n black* A white person; =PECKERWOOD, REDNECK: *just because they find some cum in that wood's ass*—Donald Goines [fr a shortening of *peckerwood*]
See SAW WOOD

wooden nickels *See* DON'T TAKE ANY WOODEN NICKELS

woodhick *n* A rural person; =HAYSEED, HICK, SHITKICKER

woodpecker *n* =PECKERWOOD

woodpile *n jazz musicians* A xylophone

wood-pusher *n* A chess player, esp an unskilled one: *enough to make any parlor wood-pusher loosen his collar and roll up his sleeves*—Time

wood-pussy *n* A skunk; a polecat

the **woods are full of** someones or somethings *sentence* The named things or persons are in plentiful supply; these things are cheap and available: *Look, the woods are full of computer programmers, I want one that's a real whiz*

woodshed **1** *v fr jazz musicians fr 1930s* To rehearse; practice one's part, role, etc, esp to do so alone and rigorously: *Bix did plenty of woodshedding, playing alone*—Stephen Longstreet **2** *v* To work out the harmonies of a barbershop quartet number, esp by ear [fr the *woodshed* as the traditional place where one could be alone to work, think, smoke, etc]

woodwork *See* CRAWL OUT OF THE WOODWORK

woody *n surfers* A station wagon with wooden outside trim: *Get your woody working*—Rocky Mountain Magazine

woof **1** *v fr 1930s jive talk* To talk idly; chatter; =BAT one's GUMS: *I ain't woofin'. I'm not fooling*—Life **2** *v esp black* To boast, esp menacingly; bluff: *The extreme of arguing is "woofing," like Ali and Frazier*—Washington Post [echoic fr the idle or menacing barking of a dog]

woofer **1** *n* A person who woofs **2** *n fr 1950s* A loudspeaker designed to reproduce bass notes faithfully

◁ **wool** ▷ *n* A woman: *She's deep down a pretty good wool*—Dan Jenkins [perhaps like *pussy*, a metonymic reference to pubic hair, in this case stressing its curliness]
See PULL THE WOOL OVER someone's EYES

woolly *See* WILD AND WOOLLY

woolly-headed *adj* Inclined to idealism and hopeful fantasy; impractical: *She dismissed it as another woolly-headed scheme of mine*

wootsie or **wootsy** *See* TOOTS

woozy **1** *adj fr late 1800s* Not fully alert and conscious; half-asleep; befuddled: *You'll just get woozy if you stay up any longer*—P Marks/ *some woozy tourist*—Gene Fowler **2** *adj* Dizzy; faint; unwell [origin unknown; perhaps fr *oozy*, suggesting the insolidity and limpness of mud]

◀ **wop** or **Wop** ▶ **1** *n fr early 1900s* An Italian or a person of Italian extraction; =DAGO **2** *adj: big wop tenor*—James M Cain [apparently fr southern Italian dialect *guappo* "dandy, dude, stud," used as a greeting by male Neapolitans]

word *See* EAT one's WORDS, FIGHTIN' WORDS, FROM THE WORD GO, WEASEL WORDS, WHAT'S THE GOOD WORD

work *v* To exert one's charm, power, persuasiveness, etc, esp on an audience: *We watched in admiration as the candidate skillfully worked the huge crowd*

See BULLWORK, DIRTY WORK, DONKEY-WORK, GRUNT WORK, NICE WORK IF YOU CAN GET IT, NOODLEWORK, RUSH THE GROWLER, SCUT

workaholic **1** *n* A person whose primary and obsessive interest is work; a compulsive worker: *This type of person is a work freak, a workaholic*—National Observer **2** ***modifier:*** *I made a hardy attempt to suppress my workaholic tendency*

◁ **work** one's **ass**▷ (or **buns** or **tail**) **off** *v phr* To work very hard; =BUST one's ASS: *I worked my sweet ass off trying to convince her/ The dead acoustics of the room force the quartet's ensemble students to work their tails off*—Esquire/ *Complains one Apple staffer: "People are working their buns off"*—Time

work behind the stick *v phr* To be an active police officer, esp a patrolling officer: *I used to work behind the stick in the afternoons*—Lawrence Sanders [fr the patrolling officer's *nightstick*]

work both sides of the street *v phr* To take two contrary positions at once; =HAVE IT BOTH WAYS: *Most politicians have a good instinct for working both sides of the street* [probably fr the notion of a hoboes' or beggars' agreement to parcel out the territory]

work both ways or **cut two ways** *v phr* To suggest or entail a necessary contrary; have double and opposite application: *Most often the claim of mental cruelty works both ways in a marriage/ I see your point, but don't you see it cuts two ways?*

worker *See* GLIM WORKER, LUSH ROLLER

working *See* HAVE something GOING FOR someone or something

working girl *n phr prostitutes* A prostitute; =HOOKER: *an old white pimp named Tony Roland who was known to handle the best-looking "working" girls in New York*—Xaviera Hollander

working stiff *n phr fr early 1900s* A common working man: *The author has been a novelist... he has also been a movie and TV working stiff*—Time

work it into the ground *See* RUN something INTO THE GROUND

work out **1** *v phr* To do strenuous exercises; have a hard session of physical conditioning: *The president works out every day in the palace gym* **2** *v phr* To amend, finish, repair, etc, by careful effort: *They agreed to work out the flaws and snags before trying the idea on the public* **3** *v phr* To turn out right; sort itself out: *I hope it works out for you*

work something **out** *v phr* To achieve an agreement, esp by compromise: *We'll just stay at it until we work something out*

work someone **over** *v phr* To beat, esp cruelly and systematically; =MESS someone UP: *The secret police worked him over brutally until he confessed*

works *n narcotics* The devices used for injecting narcotics; drug paraphernalia; =FIT: *When he awakes in the morning he reaches instantly for his "works," eyedropper, needle,... and bottle top*—Reader's Digest

the **works** or **the whole works** *n phr fr early 1900s* Everything; the totality of resources; =the WHOLE SCHMEAR, the WHOLE NINE YARDS: *I want it all, the whole works/ the works, shave, haircut, massage, and tonic*—Hal Boyle [perhaps like *kit and caboodle* in referring to an entire outfit of equipment, conceived as a *works* "factory, workplace and equipment"; perhaps referring to the entirety of a mechanism like that in *gum up the works*]

See GIVE someone THE WORKS, GUM UP, IN THE PIPELINE, SHOOT THE WORKS

work the growler *See* RUSH THE GROWLER

work up *v phr* To devise; =WHOMP UP: *We'll have to work up a good story to explain this one*

world *See* OUT OF THIS WORLD

the **world** *n phr Army* The territorial US

See GO AROUND THE WORLD, HAVE THE WORLD BY THE BALLS

world-class *adj* Very superior; outstanding; superexcellent: *This guy's a world-class bullshit artist* [fr the superiority of an athlete who competes successfully in the Olympic Games or other worldwide events]

worm *n* A despicable person; =BASTARD, JERK: *Cut that out, you little worm*

See CAN OF WORMS

worm out of something *v phr* To evade or avoid an unpleasant situation, esp by ignominious means: *This* *time we have him dead to rights, and he won't worm out of it*

worry *See* NOT TO WORRY

worry wart *n phr fr 1930s* A person who worries excessively; a constantly apprehensive person [fr the designation of such a person in the comic strip "Out Our Way" by JR Williams]

worst-case scenario *n phr fr armed forces fr 1960s* A speculation or prediction as to what would happen if everything turned out as badly as possible: *our worst-case scenario in Western Europe*—Time

worth *See* TWO CENTS' WORTH

worth a bucket of warm spit *adj phr* Of very little value; worthless • Often used in the negative: *The new telephones are not worth a bucket of warm spit/ a cable TV contract for the Bronx, Brooklyn, Queens, and Staten Island that's worth about as much as a bucket of warm spit*—Village Voice

worth a damn (or **a shit**) **1** *adv phr* At all; in the least degree • Most often in the negative: *This guy doesn't sing worth a damn/ She doesn't like me worth a shit* **2** *adj phr: Those promises aren't worth a damn*

not **worth a plugged nickel** *See* NOT WORTH A PLUGGED NICKEL

wounded *See* WALKING WOUNDED

wow 1 *interj* An exclamation of pleasure, wonder, admiration, etc • This interjection, which probably dates to the early 1900s, had a new popularity and currency during the 1960s and later: *Wow, what a nice voice you have!/ Oh, wow, far out!* **2** *n fr early 1900s* Something very exciting and successful; a sensation: *a wow of a line!*—Katharine Brush **3** *v fr 1920s* To impress someone powerfully and favorably; =KNOCK someone DEAD, LAY THEM IN THE AISLES: *all self-proclaimed poets who, to wow an audience, utter some resonant lie*—WH Auden [origin unknown; perhaps echoic of a bark or howl of approval; perhaps fr *pow-wow* by sound alone, the associations of *pow* "sound of a blow, power of impact," carrying to *wow*]

See POW-WOW

wowser[1] *n* Something very successful and impressive; a sensation; =WOW[1]: *The four-beat peroration is a wowser*—National Review [fr *wow*, perhaps influenced by *rouser*]

wowser[2] *n esp 1920s fr British fr early 1900s Australian* A stiff and puritanical person; a prude and prig • Probably imported by HL Mencken: *men of letters, who would swoon at the sight of a split infinitive, such wowsers they are in regard to pure English*—Robert Lynd [origin unknown; perhaps echoic of a bark of disapproval; perhaps related to British dialect *wowsy* "an exclamation of surprise"; said to be, surely ex post facto, an acronym for the name of a reform organization *We Only Want Social Evils Righted*]

wrap 1 *v esp show business* To complete; finish; =WRAP UP: *Filming, based on Bob Randall's 1977 thriller, wrapped last summer*—People Weekly **2** *n: Well, it's a wrap on the squash*—Dan Jenkins

wrapped tight *adj phr* Sane; of sound mind • Often used in the negative: *I told him he wasn't wrapped too tight himself* [fr the image of something *wrapped* neatly without loose ends, spillage, etc]

wrapper *See* PLAIN WHITE WRAPPER

wraps *See* UNDER WRAPS

wrap up *v phr* To complete; finish: *Let's wrap up the negotiations and get to the next stage*

wrap-up *n* A completion; a final treatment, summary, etc: *This is the 11:30 pm wrap-up of the news*

wrap something **up 1** *v phr* To complete, esp successfully; be the final touch, act, event, etc: *Well, folks, that about wraps it up for this time/ They wrapped the job up ahead of schedule* **2** *v phr* To be the winning or conclusive score, stroke, element, etc; =ICE: *They wrapped the game up in the third period with a power-play goal*

wreck 1 *n* An old car or other vehicle; =HEAP, JALOPY **2** *n fr 1920s* An exhausted or dissipated person; a human ruin: *He's pretty smart, but physically a wreck*

wringer *See* FINGER-WRINGER, GET one's TAIL IN A GATE, PUT someone THROUGH THE WRINGER

wrinkle 1 *n fr middle 1500s* An idea, device, trick, notion, style, etc, esp a new one: *Wearing the thing sideways is a nice wrinkle* **2** *n* A defect or problem, esp a minor one; = BUG: *The plan's still got a few wrinkles, nothing we can't handle* [origin of first sense unknown; perhaps fr the same semantic impulse as *twist* in a similar sense, referring to a quick shift in course; perhaps a reference to a lack of plain simplicity in dress or decoration, and the prevalence of stylish pleats, folds, etc, since the earliest form is *without all wrinkles*; second sense fr the notion of *ironing the wrinkles out* of something; see *iron out the kinks*]

Wrinkle City **1** *n phr* Wrinkled or lined skin, as a sign of age: *Women live with an unspoken fear of Wrinkle City*—Time **2** *n phr* A place inhabited or frequented by old people

wrinkle-rod *n esp hot rodders* A car's crankshaft

wrist ***See*** GIVE someone A SLAP ON THE WRIST, LIMP WRIST, SLAP someone's WRIST

write someone **a blank check** ***See*** GIVE someone A BLANK CHECK

write the book *v phr* To be very authoritative or seasoned; be an expert ● Usu in the past tense: *Can she sing? Hell, she wrote the book*

write-up *n fr late 1800s* A written article, news story, etc: *I figure you have seen the write-ups*—John O'Hara

wrong *adj* Dubious and suspect; illegal; criminal: *You're guilty the second that spotlight hits you 'cause you're a wrong guy*—Nelson Algren ***See*** IN THE WRONG

wrongo **1** *n* A wicked or criminal person; a villain **2** *n* An undesirable person; a person of the wrong sort: *a "closet for wrongos" on the second floor that "looks like an attic decorated by a cross-eyed paper hanger in a hurry"*—Playboy **3** *n* Something wrong or improper; an error, lie, misstatement, etc: *They haven't hit me with a wrongo yet, although they did miss a whopper this morning*—Paul Sann **4** *adj* Prone to error; inept: *an almost endearingly wrong-o, sloppily managed outfit*—Washington Post

the **wrong side of the tracks** *adv phr* A socially and economically inferior neighborhood; the slums: *He did very well for a boy from the wrong side of the tracks/ I was born on the wrong side of the tracks* [fr the fact that poor and industrial areas were often located on one side of the railroad *tracks*, partly because prevailing wind patterns would carry smoke into them and away from the better-off neighborhoods]

the **wrong way** ***See*** RUB someone THE WRONG WAY

wrote ***See*** THAT'S ALL SHE WROTE

wussy or **wuss** (WŏŏSEE) *n teenagers* A weak person; =PUSSYCAT, WIMP: *"Wussy" was a particularly expressive word... the handy combination of wimp and pussy*—Cameron Crowe [perhaps a shortening of hypothetical *pussy-wussy*]

X

X *n* A person's signature: *Just put your X on this and we're in business* [fr the custom of an illiterate person to make an X in place of a written signature]

X-double-minus *adj* Very much inferior; wretched

X marks the spot *sentence* This is the place; here is the exact location: *I pointed to the map and told her "X marks the spot"* [fr the graphic convention of designating a precise location on a picture, map, etc, with an X]

x out **1** *v phr* To delete something from a written text, esp by covering it with xs **2** *v phr* To annul or cancel something

X-rated *adj* Lewd; obscene; pornographic; =BLUE, DIRTY: *He uttered a few well-chosen X-rated words* [fr the system of rating movies according to the amount of sex, verbal obscenity, violence, etc, they contain, X being the most censorious rating]

XX (duh bəl EKS) *n* A betrayal; =DOUBLE CROSS: *I know you gave me the XX*—John O'Hara

Y

-y ***See*** -IE

yak (Variations: **yack** or **yack-yack** or **yack-yack-yack** or **yackety-yack** or **yackety-yak** or **yak-yak** or **yak-yak-yak** or **yakitty-yack** or **yak-kity-yak** or **yock** or **yock-yock** or **yock-yock-yock** or **yok** or **yok-yok** or **yok-yok-yok** or **yuck** or **yuck-yuck** or **yuck-yuck-yuck** or **yuk** or **yuk-yuk** or **yuk-yuk-yuk**) **1** ***n*** Talk, esp idle or empty chatter; mere babbling: *All they can talk about... yack-yack-yack is their own specialty*—Associated Press/ *I don't care how owlish you look, how convincing you sound, this is just yak yak yak until you do it*—John McPhee/ *in the midst of all the political yuk-yuk that dins around us*—New York Times/ *if the State Department would stop its incessant yakitty-yak*—Associated Press **2** ***v*** (Variations: **yack it up** or **yak it up** or **yock it up** or **yuk it up**): *Everybody is yakking out an opinion on whether he should now reconsider his candidacy*—Life/ *sparing the rod and yak-yakking and explaining all the time*—Associated Press/ *The students were seated on the floor, still yocking away*—Max Shulman/ *I'll be 75 and hanging around bars yocking it up*—Newsweek **3** ***n*** A laugh; a guffaw: *"Take off your clothes." Pause for audience yuks*—Judith Crist/ *It makes me furious when I have a corny line and it gets a yock*—New York Times **4** ***v*** (Variations: **yack it up** or **yak it up** or **yock it up** or **yuk it up**): *Ken Gaul is yukking, tugging at his pointy satyr's beard*—Changes/ *There'd be Don, yockin' it up like crazy... he's so hysterical with laughter*—Arthur Kober/ *former senator George McGovern, yukking it up with... Paul Volcker*—Washington Post [echoic]

yang ***n*** The penis; =JANG, WANG: *A macho... machine... a celebration of the yang, bang... whang*—Penthouse

See YING-YANG

yank ***v*** To victimize or harass; dupe; mislead: *The detective uses expressions like "You gotta be yankin' me"*—Washington Post [an alteration and shortening of *yank* someone's *chain* or *jerk* someone *around* or *jack* someone *around*]

Yank **1** ***n*** *fr middle 1800s* A US citizen; an American: *inquiring after the "Yank" and swearing to have his life*—Life **2** ***n*** *fr WW1 British* A US soldier: *Some Tommies resented the Yanks for being overpaid* [a shortening fr *Yankee* for both senses]

yank someone's **chain** ***See*** JERK someone's CHAIN

yap **1** ***n*** *fr late 1800s* The mouth; =BAZOO: *every time you open your yap to say something*—Jerome Weidman **2** ***v*** To talk, esp idly or naggingly: *You've been yapping away*—Jerome Weidman/ *come home with a little jag on, yapping in a phony cheerful way*—Harper's [probably echoic, and similar to the sense "yelp," esp as a small dog does]

See BLOW OFF one's MOUTH, OPEN one's YAP

YAP (pronounced as separate letters) ***n*** A young person in one of the learned and well-paid professions [fr *Young American Professional*]

yard ***n*** *fr early 1900s hawkers* A hundred dollars; a $100 bill: *"Mac, what you payin' for this?" Stony looked* *around the room. "A yard and a half"*—Richard Price [fr the unit of measure]

See GO THE FULL YARD

yard ape ***See*** RUG APE

yardbird **1** *n* A convict **2** *n armed forces* A recruit; a basic trainee **3** *n armed forces* A soldier who because of ineptitude or misdemeanor is confined to a certain area, and often ordered to keep it clean and neat [fr the fact that convicts exercise in the *yard* of the prison, and that neophyte soldiers are confined to the grounds of the training post during their first weeks; the basic metaphor is probably based on the behavior of urban pigeons]

yard patrol *prison* **1** *n phr* The convicts in a prison or jail **2** *n phr* The guards at a prison or jail

yards ***See*** the WHOLE NINE YARDS

yatata (YA tə tə) **1** *n* Talk, esp idle talk and chatter; =YAK **2** *v: mustn't yatata yatata yatata in the public library*—William Saroyan [echoic]

yatter *n* Talk, esp loud talk; chatter; =YAK: *the yatter against a military man in the White House*—Time [echoic, and perhaps also a blend of *yak* and *chatter*]

yea (YAY) **1** *adv fr 1950s & esp black* To this extent; this; so • A sort of demonstrative adverb used with adjectives of size, height, extent, etc, and often accompanied by a hand gesture indicating size: *Dorsey almost did him in yea years ago*—WT Tyler/ *The thing was about yea big and sort of green/ I'd say the fence is about yea high* **2** *interj* An expression of support, accolade, triumph, encouragement, etc; harrah: *Yea for our side!/ Yea, hurray, we made it!* [first sense perhaps fr *yea* "yes," specialized fr an earlier sense "even, truly, verily" to something like "even so, truly so, verily so"; second sense probably a vehement affirmation, conveniently rhyming with *hurray!*]

yeah (YE, YE ə) *affirmation* Yes; certainly; right: *Don't say "yeah." It's common*—Raymond Chandler

See OH YEAH

year *n fr underworld* One dollar; a dollar bill

yecch or **yech** ***See*** YUCK

yegg *n fr underworld fr late 1800s hoboes* A thief or burglar, esp an itinerant thief or safecracker [origin unknown; said to be fr the name of John *Yegg*, an early hobo safecracker; perhaps fr German *Jäger* "huntsman," applied to a safecracker's advance scouts, but originally *yeggman*]

yell one's **head off** *v phr* To complain loudly and persistently; express oneself forcefully

yellow **1** *adj fr middle 1800s* Cowardly; fainthearted; =CHICKEN: *Don't get into this race if you're yellow* **2** *n* Cowardice; poltroonery; excessive timidity • Most often in the expression "yellow streak" or "streak of yellow": *I'm afraid he has a streak of yellow in him* **◀3▶** *adj fr early 1800s* Having light skin for a black person: *You know that baker we hired. The yellow boy*—Calder Willingham [the origin of the coward sense is unknown; perhaps it is derived fr the traditional symbolic meanings of *yellow*, among which were "deceitfulness, treachery, degradation, the light of hell"]

See HIGH YELLOW

yellow-belly *n* A coward; a poltroon: *He is a contemptible yellow-belly, scared of his own shadow* [probably a rhyming expansion of yellow; influenced by the early-19th-century sense, "a Mexican, esp a Mexican soldier," perhaps fr the color of their uniforms]

yellow jacket *n phr narcotics* A capsule of Nembutal (a trade name), a barbiturate narcotic

yellow sunshine *n phr narcotics* LSD; =ACID

yelper *n* The screaming and wavering warning signal used on police cars, ambulances, and other emergency vehicles: *two police cars going north ... with yelpers wide open*—John Farris

yen **1** *n fr early 1900s West Coast & hoboes* A strong craving; a keen desire; a passion: *He's got a yen for faro*—WR Burnett/ *a yen to put on paper what I was saying in class*—AAUP Bulletin **2** *v: I yenned to own a Rolls Royce*—Billy Rose [fr a Peking dialect Chinese word, "smoke," hence opium, perhaps reinforced by *yearn*]

yenems (YE nəmz) Someone else's property, cigarettes, liquor, etc: *What's my favorite smoke? Yenems* [fr Yiddish, "those, that one's, hence, not my own"]

yenta (YEN tə) *n* A garrulous and gossipy person, usu a woman; =BLABBERMOUTH: *The people in Washington think we're a bunch of screaming yentas here*—New York [fr a Jewish woman's given name perhaps derived fr Italian *Gentile* or French *Gentille*, degraded by its association with a humorous character *Yente* Telebende in a regular column of the New York Yiddish newspaper the *Jewish Daily Forward*]

yep *affirmation fr early 1800s* Yes; certainly; sure; =YEAH [the *p* is produced by closing the mouth to finish the pronunciation of *yeah*, and thereby producing the voiceless bilabial stop; see *nope*]

yes-man *n fr early 1900s* An obsequious and flattering subordinate; =ASS-KISSER: *This president doesn't want yes-men*—Joseph Heller [said to have appeared first in a 1913 drawing by the sports cartoonist TA Dorgan, showing a group of newspaper assistants, each labeled *yes-man*, all firmly agreeing with their chief]

◀ **Yid** or **yid** ▶ (YID) *n* A Jew • Not felt to be offensive if pronounced (YEED) by Jews themselves: *Some boy was not admitted to a secret society... because he was a "Yid"*—Stephen Longstreet [fr Yiddish, ultimately fr Hebrew *Yehuda* "Judea"]

ying-yang or **yin-yang** **1** *n* The anus; =ASS, ASSHOLE, WHERE THE SUN DOESN'T SHINE: *A mother-jumper of a winter. Snow up the yin-yang*—George V Higgins **2** *n* The penis; =PRICK: *a peek at one of my troopers with tubes up his ying-yang*—Richard Merkin **3** *n Army* A stupid or foolish person [perhaps coined because of the increasing currency of the Chinese term *yin and yang* "the female and male principles in nature," influenced by *wang* "penis"]

yipe or **yipes** or **yikes** *interj esp teenagers* An exclamation of dismay, alarm, emphatic response, etc: *Yipes, it's a rattlesnake!/ Yipe, that hurt!* [probably fr the spontaneous interjection *yi*, a cry of pain or dismay, with the *p* or *k* stop intruding after lip closure, as it does in *nope* and *yep*]

yippee (yip EE) *interj* An exclamation of pleasure, approval, triumph, etc: *Yippee, all my candidates won!*

yippie *n esp late 1960s* A member of the Youth International Party, a left-wing group espousing values of the counterculture movement of the 1960s and early 70s [fr the acronym of the name of the group, reinforced by the rhyme with *hippie*]

yock *See* YAK

yok *See* YAK

yokel *n fr British dialect* A rural person; a bumpkin; =HAYSEED, HICK [perhaps fr a dialect name for a woodpecker, hence semantically similar to British dialect *gowk* "cuckoo, simpleton"]

See LOCAL YOKEL

yonder *See* DOWN YONDER

you *See* SAYS YOU

you bet (or **betcha**) *affirmation fr middle 1800s Southwest* Yes; certainly; surely; =BET YOUR BOOTS: *You bet I'll be there!/ Am I happy? You betcha!* [*betcha* form fr *you bet you* or *you bet your life*]

you (or **you'd**) **better believe** something *sentence fr middle 1800s* Something is absolutely certain; something is assured; you are absolutely right: *Am I ready to fight? You better believe it!/ You'd better believe she's the best*

you can't get there from here **1** *sentence* The place referred to is very remote and the route hard to describe **2** *sentence* The problem described is insoluble

you can't make an omelet without breaking eggs *sentence* One must sometimes do evil or cause damage and inconvenience to accomplish good; the end justifies the means [attributed to VI Lenin, the Russian Bolshevik leader]

you can't win 'em all *sentence* One cannot always be successful; =WIN A FEW LOSE A FEW • Often said ruefully after one has failed, or comfortingly to someone else who has failed

you go *See* THERE YOU GO

you-know-what *n* Something one does not wish to name, usu because it is both obvious and indelicate or taboo; =WHATSIS: *They were knocked on their you-know-what*

you name it *sentence* You cannot designate anything not included here; =the WHOLE SCHMEAR: *She got looks, talent, ontological authenticity, you name it* [fr the retailing locution *you name it, we got it*]

young squirt *See* SQUIRT

Young Turk *n phr* A person, usu a young one, who threatens to overthrow an established system or order; an active rebel or reformer: *He scrutinizes the new staff very carefully, and is dreadfully fearful of potential Young Turks* [originally, a member of *Young Turkey*, a revolutionary party of late-19th-century Turkey which finally established constitutional government in 1908]

your ear *See* PUT IT IN YOUR EAR

you're damn (or **darn**) **tootin'** *affirmation* That is emphatically true; you are absolutely right: *Did I run? You're damn tootin' I did*

yours truly *pron phr fr middle 1800s* I; me; myself; =YOUR UNCLE DUDLEY: *If nobody else wants that, just ask yours truly* [fr the conventional parting salutation of a letter]

your Uncle Dudley *n phr* Oneself; I or me; =YOURS TRULY: *If you want to know about that, just ask your uncle Dudley*

you said it *affirmation* You are absolutely right; that is correct

you scratch my back, I scratch yours *sentence* Let us cooperate; let us be reciprocally and mutually helpful: *how a labor union's supposed to run! You scratch my back, I'll scratch yours!*—Hannibal & Boris

yo-yo 1 *n* A vacillating person; one who has no firm convictions: *makes the president look like a yo-yo* —Newsweek **2** *n fr teenagers* A stupid and obnoxious person; =JERK, NERD: *Some yo-yo yells "What happened, you bum..."*—Inside Sports

yuck (also **ech** or **yecch** or **yech**) **1** *interj* An exclamation of disgust: *"Those women on the PBS specials seem to love it." "Yuck," Connie mugged*—Armistead Maupin/ *Then there is this little item entitled YECH* —Village Voice **2** *n* A disgusting substance, person, or thing; someone or something nasty: *precipitation in the form of rain, snow, and assorted other atmospheric yuck*—Washington Post/ *clean all the yecch out of her system*—Cyra McFadden [perhaps echoic of gagging or vomiting] *See* YAK

Yucko City *adj phr* Disgusting; nasty; =YUCKY: *Have you ever tried any popular American beer warm?... Yucko City*—Illinois Times

yucky or **yecchy** *adj* Disgusting, esp in a filthy and viscous way; thoroughly nasty: *Some of it is awful yucky*—Philadelphia Daily News/ *What's that yucky blob on your collar?/ He looked at me like I was something yecchy*

yuk *See* YAK

yummy *adj* Pleasant, esp sensually; delicious; delightful: *What a yummy cake!/ a yummy prospect*

Yumpie *n* =YUPPIE: *the highly desirable "Yumpies," young, upwardly mobile professionals*—Washingtonian [fr *young upwardly mobile professional*]

yum-yum 1 *interj fr late 1800s* An exclamation of pleasure, esp of sensual delight **2** *n* Something sweet or pleasant, esp to eat [perhaps fr a locution used with children, hence contextually as well as phonetically related to *tummy* or *tum-tum*]

yup *affirmation fr early 1900s* =YEP

Yuppie *n* (also **Yup**) An affluent, usu city-dwelling, professional in his or her 20s and 30s; a prosperous and ambitious young professional: *Yuppies are dedicated to the twin goals of making piles of money and achieving perfection through physical fitness and therapy*—Time/ *The Yups discover that the locals have been putting up with this...for years*—Philadelphia [fr *young urban professional*, and modeled on *yippie*; perhaps coined for a 1983 book called *The Yuppie Handbook*, which was modeled on the earlier book *The Official Preppy Handbook*]

Z

Z[1] or **Zee** **1** *v teenagers* To sleep; snooze; =COP ZS: *Gotta Z a little while* **2** *n* Some sleep; a nap: *If he wants a few zees we can go on automatic* —Robert Stone [fr the conventional sibilant or buzzing sound attributed to a sleeping person]

Z[2] *n narcotics* An ounce of a narcotic: *trips to the rundown neighborhood to purchase Zs (ounces) and even Ks (kilograms) of cocaine*—New York Times [fr the conventional abbreviation of *ounces* "oz"]

za (ZAH) *n teenagers* Pizza [a shortening of *pizza*]

zaftig *See* ZOFTIG

zap **1** *v fr underworld, street gang & Vietnam War armed forces* To kill or disable; strike violently; =CLOBBER, WASTE: *Sitcom Zaps Boardroom Bozos*—Time **2** *v hospital* To administer electroshock therapy **3** *interj* An exclamation imitating sudden impact; =WHAM: *It's a gradual thing. It ain't zap, you're healed* —Philadelphia Journal **4** *n* Vitality; force; =PIZZAZZ, ZIP [fr the echoic word used to convey the sound of a ray gun in the comic strip "Buck Rogers in the Twenty-Fifth Century"]

zazz something **up** *v phr* To make more decorative and impressive; =GUSSY UP, JAZZ UP: *relied heavily on somewhat musty shadings, zazzing them up, however, with bursts of dusty mauve*—Cosmopolitan [perhaps fr *jazz* something *up*, influenced by *pizzazz*]

zebra **1** *n sports* A referee or other sports official, who wears a striped shirt on the playing field: *Pro football zebras point immediately toward the offending team*—New York Daily News/ *a crooked Zebra (also known as an umpire)*—Washington Post **2** *n hospital* An unlikely, arcane, or obscure diagnosis [the medical sense is fr the saying "If you hear horse's hoofbeats going by outside, don't look for *zebras*"]

zero in *v phr* To aim at or concentrate on a specific person, thing, etc; single out: *We're trying to zero in on the problem* [fr the *zeroing* of the sights of a rifle, that is, adjusting the sights so that the round hits the exact point aimed at and the shooter needs to make no, or *zero*, estimated correction in aiming]

zetz *n* A blow; a punch: *I'd love to give that guy such a zetz*—National Lampoon [fr Yiddish, related to German *Zurücksetzung* "a setting back"]

zhlub *n* (also **schlub** or **shlub** or **shlubbo** or **zhlob** or **zshlub**) A coarse person; a boorish man; =JERK, SLOB: *the presence of fine wines and the absence of shlubs* —Philadelphia/ *replied Angela as she glided off to cut the poor schlub out of her will*—Newsweek/ *Lieberman was the worst. Lieberman was a real zshlub*—Joseph Heller [fr Yiddish fr Slavic, "coarse fellow"]

◀ **zig** or **zigabo** or **zigaboo** ▶ *See* JIGABOO

ziggety *See* HOT DIGGETY

zig-zig *See* JIG-JIG

zilch **1** *n fr late 1960s* Nothing; zero; =ZIP: *The city... has turned its smaller islands into zilch*—New York/ *got the jeep for practically zilch* —George V Higgins **2** *modifier: York has close to zilch industry* —Toronto Life **3** *n teenagers* A minor skin lesion; =ZIT [probably fr

zero, and like *zip*[1], primarily a variant coined from a familiar word beginning with *z*; notice, in this regard, how *zilch* has become a variant of *zit*; in British use, but not US, *zilch* might be reinforced by *nil* "zero"; all senses may derive fr the early-20th-century US college use *Joe Zilsch* "any insignificant person," popularized during the 1930s by ubiquitous use in the humor magazine *Ballyhoo* with the spelling *Zilch*, an actual German surname of Slavic origin; see *Joe Blow*[1]; Eric Partridge's suggestion that *zilch* is a three-element blend of *zero* with *nil* and Yiddish *nich* is extremely unlikely and unnecessary]
See JOE BLOW, NOT KNOW BEANS

zillion ***See*** JILLION

zillionaire ***n*** An enormously rich person; a super-tycoon: *and Larry Dunlap will become an instant zillionaire*—Village Voice

-zine (ZEEN) ***suffix used to form nouns*** Magazine: *teenzine/ fanzine*

zing **1** ***n*** *fr early 1900s* Energetic vitality; power; vigor; =OOMPH, PEP, PIZZAZZ, ZIP: *Rock... adds zing*—Toronto Star/ *with plenty of zing in both the... V-8 engine and the powerful Six*—Philadelphia Bulletin **2** ***v*** *also* **zing along** To move rapidly and strongly; =ZIP: *The movie zings right along*—Playboy **3** ***v*** To throw; inject, esp rapidly and strongly: *like the Beatles every once in a while can zing it in there*—Rolling Stone **4** ***v*** To insult; assault verbally, esp with bitter humor: *King Caen, who zings everyone, gets a taste of his own medicine*—California [probably echoic of the whishing sound of rapid movement, like *zip* and *zoom*]

zinger **1** ***n*** A quip, esp one that is somewhat cruel and aggressive; a funny crack or punch line: *The plump little actor is polished and funny; his zingers stay zung*—Washington Post **2** ***n*** A quick and sharp response; a sturdy retort: *get right in there with Williams, stand eyeball to eyeball, and plant the zinger on him, bang, or else you would be dismissed*—Harper's

zingy ***adj*** Full of energy and vigor; =PEPPY: *written by no less than the zingy Nora Ephron*—Philadelphia/ *Zingy Zeroes, Wall Street's hot bonds*—Time

zip[1] or **zippo** **1** ***n*** *students fr late 1800s* A mark or grade of zero **2** ***n*** Zero; nothing; a score of zero; =ZILCH: *The Tigers won 12-zip/ People aren't exactly beating down the doors to buy California port. "The market... is zip, zero, and not too much"*—San Francisco/ *dipped into your moneybag and found zippo*—Washington Post [like *zilch*, probably coined from a familiar word beginning with *z*; see *zilch*]
See NOT GIVE A DAMN, NOT KNOW BEANS

zip[2] or **zippo** ***n*** *fr early 1900s* Energy; vitality; vim; =PIZZAZZ, ZING: *There is a zip and a zing here*—NY Confidential/ *bounced back with the real zippo*—Joseph Wambaugh [echoic of the sound of something swishing rapidly through the air, giving an impression of force, and also of the tearing of cloth; such a use is attested fr 1875]

◀ **zip**[3] ▶ ***n*** *Vietnam War* A Vietnamese; =DINK [said to be fr *zero intelligence*]

zip gun ***n phr*** *esp 1950s street gang* A homemade pistol: *a zip gun, the kind kids make themselves*—Pageant

zip one's **lip** (or one's **mouth**) ***v phr*** To stop talking, esp abruptly and completely; =SHUT UP: *She ordered me to zip my lip/ I just had to zip my mouth and do what I could*—Toronto Life [fr the notion that one has a *zipper* fastener *on one's mouth*]

zippo ***v*** *Army* To set something on fire; ignite something [fr *Zippo*, trade name of a cigarette lighter, probably fr the sound made as one turns the sparking wheel, and the speed with which the lighter ignites]

zit *esp teenagers* **1** ***n*** A minor skin lesion; a pimple; a blackhead: *First Arnie's zits mysteriously clear up*—Newsweek **2** ***n*** A mark left by a love-bite, a strong kiss, etc; =HICKEY: *She tried to conceal the big zit on her neck* [origin unknown; perhaps echoic of the squishy pop made when the pus is squeezed from a blackhead]

zits ***See*** TITS-AND-ZITS

zizz **1** ***v*** *fr 1920s British armed forces* To sleep; snooze; nap; =COP ZS: **2** ***n:*** *She stretched out for a short zizz* [echoic of the sibilance or buzzing of one who sleeps, hence semantically akin to the notion of *sawing wood*]

zod 1 *n teenagers* An eccentric and obnoxious person; =CREEP, NERD **2** *adj: Yuck, what a weird and zod idea* [origin unknown; perhaps related to the alligator represented on *Izod* (a trade name) apparel]

zoftig or **zaftig** (ZAWF tik,ZAHF-) *adj* Sexually appealing or arousing to males, esp in a plump and well-rounded way; curvaceous; =BUILT LIKE A BRICK SHITHOUSE: *zoftig... pleasantly plump and pretty*—New York Daily News/ *Parton's film debut... was clearly just a warm-up for this zaftig after-hours diversion*—People Weekly [fr Yiddish, literally "juicy"]

zoid *n* A nonconforming person; a misfit: *Andie doesn't "fit in," she's an outsider, a "zoid"*—Washington Post

zombie (ZAHM bee) **1** *n fr 1930s students* A very strange person, esp one with a vacant corpselike manner; =WEIRDO **2** *n* An unresponsive person; a mentally numb or dead person: *My students are all zombies this term* [origin uncertain; perhaps fr an African word akin to *nzambi* "god"; perhaps fr Louisiana Creole, "phantom, ghost," fr Spanish *sombra* "shade, ghost"; popularized by horror stories and movies featuring the walking dead persons of voodoo belief]

zone[1] *See* IN A ZONE, OZONE

zone[2] or **zoner** *n narcotics* A person intoxicated with narcotics, esp habitually so; =SPACE CADET [fr *ozone* "a very high level of the atmosphere"]

zoned or **zoned out** *adj* or *adj phr* Intoxicated with narcotics; =HIGH [fr *zone*; influenced by *spaced out*]

zone something **out** or **zone out** *v phr* To omit from consciousness; shut out of the mind: *I can just zone everything out and keep going*—New York Sunday News/ *If she'd just zone out for a while, we could plan her surprise party*

zonk or **zonk out 1** *v* or *v phr* To lose consciousness, esp from alcohol or narcotics; fall asleep; become stuporous: *He suddenly zonked and went rigid* **2** *v* or *v phr* To strike a stupefying blow; =CLOBBER: *"We've been zonked," said Jim Robbins*—Washington Post [fr *zonked*]

zonked or **zonked out** or **zonkers 1** *adj* or *adj phr students & narcotics* Intoxicated by narcotics or alcohol; =HIGH, STONED: *zonked, one step past being stoned*—E Horne/ *I guess you weren't as zonked as I thought*—Easy-riders **2** *adj* or *adj phr* Very enthusiastic; excited; =HIGH: *Rene Carpenter remembers Gilruth as "a kindly, wonderful man who was zonked on this project"*—Washingtonian [probably echoic, like *bonk*, of a dull and stupefying blow; the variant *zonkers* is like the phonetically and semantically similar *bonkers*, from which it probably derives; see *bonkers*]

zoo *n railroad* The caboose of a freight train

zoo daddy *n phr* A divorced or separated father who sees his children rarely; =DISNEYLAND DADDY

zoom someone **out** *v phr black* To impress strongly; overwhelm; =BLOW someone's MIND

zoomy *adj* Fast and stylish; high-flying; showy and flaunting: *and it isn't just a matter of zoomy looks, either*—Car and Driver/ *zoomy people*—George V Higgins [fr *zoom* "fly up spectacularly"]

zoot suit *n phr esp 1930s & 40s* A man's suit with a jacket having very wide lapels, heavily padded shoulders, and many-buttoned sleeves, with very high-waisted trousers full in the leg and tapering to narrow cuffs • Such garments were worn as symbols of status and defiance, esp by urban black hipsters and Los Angeles Chicanos: *Some were garbed in short sleeve shirts, others in zoot suits*—Associated Press/ *Jelly got into his zoot suit with the reet pleats*—Zora Neale Hurston [origin unknown; probably in essence a rhyming phrase of the sort common in black English and slang; perhaps related to other jive and cool talk terms like *vootie*]

zot or **zotz** *n esp students* Nothing; zero; =ZILCH, ZIP: *Zero. Nothing. Absolutely zotz*—Psychology Today [like *zip* and *zilch* based mainly on the initial *z* suggesting *zero*; perhaps influenced by *squat* in the same sense]

zowie 1 *interj* An exclamation imitating sudden impact; =POW, WHAM: *I ducked, but zowie, it caught me on the nose* **2** *n* Energy; vitality; vim; =ZING, ZIP: *full of zing, full of zest, full of zowie*—Mad Wednesday (movie)

some Zs ***n phr*** Sleep; =SHUT-EYE: *He was bleary and needed some Zs* [fr the traditional likening of snoring with sawing wood, and its representation in comic strips by a series of *Zs*]

See COP ZS

zshlub ***See*** ZHLUB